.NET WINDOWS FORMS

IN A NUTSHELL

Ian Griffiths and Matthew Adams

O'REILLY®

Beijing • Cambridge • Farnham • Köln • Paris • Sebastopol • Taipei • Tokyo

.NET Windows Forms in a Nutshell
by Ian Griffiths and Matthew Adams

Published by O'Reilly & Associates, Inc., 1005 Gravenstein Highway North, Sebastopol, CA 95472.

O'Reilly & Associates books may be purchased for educational, business, or sales promotional use. Online editions are also available for most titles (*safari.oreilly.com*). For more information, contact our corporate/institutional sales department: 800-998-9938 or *corporate@oreilly.com*.

Editor: Ron Petrusha
Production Editor: Linley Dolby
Cover Designer: Ellie Volckhausen
Interior Designer: David Futato

Printing History:
March 2003: First Edition.

ISBN: 0-596-00338-2
[M]

Table of Contents

Part II. API Quick Reference

Part III. Appendixes

Preface

This book is a desktop reference and tutorial for Windows Forms, the new API for writing GUI applications for Windows. Windows Forms is a part of the .NET Framework, the first version of which shipped in February 2002.

.NET Windows Forms in a Nutshell is divided into two parts. The first half is a tutorial, which introduces the most important concepts and classes in Windows Forms and describes how to use these to build interactive applications. It also describes GDI+, the drawing API that most Windows Forms applications will use.

The second half is a quick reference to the Windows Forms and GDI+ namespaces. It provides namespace maps, type descriptions, member signatures, and useful cross-references and annotations.

Who This Book Is For

This book is intended for C# and Visual Basic .NET developers who are writing Windows Forms applications. If you are moving from previous Windows GUI technologies such as Visual Basic 6.0 or MFC, or from those of other platforms such as Swing, or even if you are new to writing Windows applications, the tutorial section provides a complete introduction to the most important aspects of the Windows Forms API.

Part I of this book, which offers a Windows Forms tutorial, presents code examples in both C# and VB.NET. Part II, which documents the namespaces used in Windows Forms development, uses C# syntax. However, for VB programmers, a chapter is devoted to converting C# syntax to that of Visual Basic.

Regardless of your level of experience with Windows Forms, the reference section provides a great deal of useful information and insights into the namespaces that make up the Windows Forms and GDI+ APIs.

How This Book Is Structured

Part I of this book is a tutorial describing the fundamental concepts and classes in the Windows Forms API. It consists of the following 10 chapters:

Chapter 1, *.NET and Windows Forms Overview*
: This chapter provides an overview of the .NET Framework (focusing on the parts that are relevant to Windows Forms developers) and the Windows Forms API.

Chapter 2, *Controls*
: The Control class is at the heart of every Windows Forms application. Its role and usage are examined in detail in this chapter.

Chapter 3, *Forms, Containers, and Applications*
: Forms are top-level windows, and almost all Windows Forms applications use Forms (hence the name). We examine Forms in their role as containers for controls. The chapter also discusses how form-based applications are constructed.

Chapter 4, *Menus and Toolbars*
: Most nontrivial applications use menus and toolbars to present their functionality in a structured way. This chapter shows the relationship between menus, forms, and controls. It also describes the techniques for dynamically modifying menus in MDI applications.

Chapter 5, *Building Controls*
: This chapter shows the techniques for building your own reusable user interface components. It describes both user controls (collections of other controls grouped into a reusable element) and custom controls, which give developers complete control over all aspects of the control's appearance and behavior.

Chapter 6, *Inheritance and Reuse*
: The .NET type system's support for inheritance is fundamental to the way in which controls work. Chapter 6 describes the role of inheritance in Windows Forms applications. It also highlights the many pitfalls of misuse of inheritance.

Chapter 7, *Redrawing and GDI+*
: Although GDI+ is not strictly a part of Windows Forms, this powerful drawing API gives you the ability to control the appearance of your programs. Chapter 7 describes how to use GDI+ in your Windows Forms applications.

Chapter 8, *Property Grids*
: The Property Grid control is important for two reasons. First, it is a very useful control for presenting and editing information. Second, it is a central part of Visual Studio .NET, and understanding its use is crucial to integrating your controls with the development environment. This chapter offers thorough coverage of the Property Grid control.

Chapter 9, *Controls and the IDE*
: This chapter describes how to build controls that integrate into the Visual Studio .NET Forms Designer. It shows how to build custom control designers and extender property providers.

Chapter 10, *Data Binding*

Windows Forms has a data-binding architecture that allows any data source to be bound to any property of a control. Chapter 10 describes how to configure these bindings and how to use the specialized data source class, the `DataSet`.

Throughout Part I, code examples are given in both C# and Visual Basic .NET.

Part II of this book is the quick reference. It covers the basic Windows Forms namespace, `System.Windows.Forms`, and the GDI+ namespaces, `System.Drawing`, `System.Drawing.Drawing2D`, `System.Drawing.Imaging`, and `System.Drawing.Printing`. It also describes the design-time namespaces, `System.ComponentModel` and `System.Windows.Forms.Design`. Throughout Part II, C# syntax is used to document types and their members. In addition to the core namespace documentation, Chapter 11 discusses how to use the quick reference, while Chapter 12 shows VB.NET programmers how to convert the reference section's C# syntax to VB.NET syntax.

Assumptions This Book Makes

To program with the Windows Forms API, you must have installed one of the many editions of Visual Studio .NET on your system (Standard, Professional, Enterprise, or Architect). Although you can write Windows Forms applications using the .NET Framework SDK alone, the Forms Designer is only available with Visual Studio .NET, and it is very hard work to write forms-based applications without the Forms Designer.

What's on the CD

The CD that accompanies this book contains a copy of *.NET Windows Forms in a Nutshell for Microsoft Visual Studio .NET*. This software plugs directly into Microsoft Visual Studio .NET and makes the contents of Part II, *API Quick Reference*, available to you as a fully integrated member of Visual Studio .NET Dynamic Help.

By making *.NET Windows Forms in a Nutshell* a part of your Visual Studio .NET development environment, you gain the following benefits:

- Continuous access to the contents of the .NET Windows Forms Quick Reference as you work in the online Visual Studio .NET development environment
- Ability to browse the contents of the book in the Visual Studio .NET Help Contents window
- Constantly updated Dynamic Help links to relevant Quick Reference entries as you write C# or VB.NET code (these links appear in a separate Dynamic Help window link group named O'Reilly Help)
- Links to both Quick Reference topics and Microsoft documentation topics when you use either the Help Search facility or interactive Index
- Access to the O'Reilly web site, *http://www.oreilly.com*, for additional books and articles on Visual Basic .NET, C#, and the .NET Framework
- Cross-links from Quick Reference topics to related topics in the MSDN documentation

For more information on *.NET Windows Forms in a Nutshell for Microsoft Visual Studio .NET*, please read the release notes on the CD.

To use *.NET Windows Forms in a Nutshell for Microsoft Visual Studio .NET*, you must be running a version of Visual Basic .NET or Visual Studio .NET on your computer or laptop. To install *.NET Windows Forms in a Nutshell for Microsoft Visual Studio .NET*:

1. Shut down all anti-virus software and be sure that Visual Studio .NET is not currently running.
2. Place the CD in the CD player.
3. If you are running Visual Studio .NET 2003, double-click on the installation file named *WinFormsinaNutshell2003.msi*. If you are still running Visual Studio . NET 2002, double click on the file named *WinFormsinaNutshell2002.msi*.
4. Follow the instructions contained in the install program windows. Be sure to read and to accept the terms of the software license before proceeding.

To uninstall *.NET Windows Forms in a Nutshell for Microsoft Visual Studio .NET*, repeat the above procedure, but click on the Remove button when the program prompts you to select an install option.

Conventions Used in This Book

Throughout this book, we've used the following typographic conventions:

`Constant width`
: Constant width in body text indicates a language construct, such as a C# or VB.NET statement (like `for` or `Do While`), an enumeration, a .NET type or type member, a user-defined type or type member, an operator, a declaration, a directive, or an expression (like `dblElapTime = Timer – dblStartTime`). Code fragments and code examples appear exclusively in constant-width text. In syntax statements and prototypes, text set in constant width indicates such language elements as the function or procedure name and any invariable elements required by the syntax.

`Constant width italic`
: Constant width italic in body text indicates parameter names. In syntax statements or prototypes, constant width italic indicates replaceable parameters.

Italic
: System elements, such as paths and filenames, are italicized. In addition, URLs and email address are italicized. Finally, italics are used the first time a term is used.

This icon indicates a tip, suggestion, or general note.

This icon indicates a warning or caution.

How to Contact Us

Making the *.NET Windows Forms in a Nutshell* Quick Reference available as a Visual Studio .NET plug-in is is a new venture for O'Reilly & Associates and Microsoft. We want very much to hear your comments and ideas. Please address comments and questions concerning this book and CD to the publisher:

O'Reilly & Associates, Inc.
1005 Gravenstein Highway North
Sebastopol, CA 95472
(800) 998-9938 (in the United States or Canada)
(707) 829-0515 (international/local)
(707) 829-0104 (fax)

There is a web page for this book, which lists errata, examples, or any additional information. You can access this page at:

http://www.oreilly.com/catalog/netwinformian

To comment or ask technical questions about this book, send email to:

bookquestions@oreilly.com

For more information about books, conferences, Resource Centers, and the O'Reilly Network, see the following O'Reilly web sites:

http://www.oreilly.com
http://dotnet.oreilly.com

Acknowledgments

The authors would like to thank all those who have helped them to create this book. Many thanks to Ron Petrusha, John Osborn, Claire Cloutier, Daniel Creeron, and Brian Jepson at O'Reilly. We also thank all those who generously gave up their free time to review the manuscript, especially Glyn Griffiths, Reuben Harris, David Minter, Chris Sells, Bob Beauchemin, Craig Andera, Mark Boulter, Daniel Strawson, Tim Richard, and Daniel Creeron. We would also like to thank Abigail Sawyer and Una McCormack, who not only helped review the manuscript, but also put up with us during the writing process.

The *.NET Windows Forms in a Nutshell for Visual Studio .NET* CD is the work of many individuals. Mike Sierra of O'Reilly converted the `System.Windows.Forms` namespace references to Microsoft Help 2.0 format and added the XML tags needed to integrate their content with the Visual Studio .NET Dynamic Help system. He was assisted by Lenny Muellner and Erik Ray. Greg Dickerson and the O'Reilly Tech Support group tested each prerelease build of the software. Kipper York and Shane McRoberts of the Microsoft Help team provided invaluable technical assistance at critical moments, and Eric Promislow of Active State built the install package that makes our Help files an integral part of the Visual Studio .NET developer environment. Frank Gocinski of the Visual Studio .NET third-party integration program was instrumental in making us full VSIP partners. A special tip of the hat as well to Rob Howard who understood our original vision and helped us make the right connections to get this project off the ground.

I

Introduction to Windows Forms

Part I consists of a very fast-paced tutorial on developing Windows applications using the .NET Windows Forms package. It consists of the following chapters:

1

.NET and Windows Forms Overview

In early 2002, Microsoft shipped .NET, a suite of new technologies for Windows first announced in the summer of 2000. The attendant media frenzy concentrated on its support for web services, but .NET has far greater scope than that—it could change the way all Windows programs are written. .NET offers greatly improved productivity to developers by replacing swathes of the Win32 API with new, much higher level object-oriented APIs, allowing you to focus on the task at hand without being distracted by myriad petty details.

This book is about the technology behind Windows applications that run on this new .NET platform. In particular, it focuses on *rich client* applications—i.e., traditional interactive programs with a graphical user interface (GUI) that run locally on your computer. Although web applications have become very popular in recent years, experience with these *thin clients* has taught us that there is still very much a place for the more traditional style of Windows application. If you've ever had to switch from Outlook to a web mail service when working away from the office, you know just how much web applications leave to be desired.

The new programming interface for writing Windows applications with GUIs is called Windows Forms. This replaces all the old programming models, and not just the C++ favorites, such as MFC or raw Win32, but also the Forms package used in Visual Basic 6.0 and earlier. Windows Forms combines the best features from all these models, and it is the long term future of Windows development.

Windows Development and .NET

It is important to understand why Microsoft decided to make such sweeping changes to Windows software development. Deprecating all the APIs used by the vast majority of programs seems like a wildly irresponsible move calculated to alienate anyone who ever wrote a Windows application. And yet, the majority of developers who look at .NET in any detail soon become big fans, especially those from a C++ background.

.NET raises the level of abstraction that developers work with—almost every service provided by the platform is now exposed through a higher-level programming interface than before. In Win32, the API was procedural in that all services were accessed through C function calls, using opaque handles to represent entities that outlived single function calls (e.g., windows or files). Developers had to expend a lot of effort dealing with low-level details such as memory management, which as the lucrative market in memory leak detection tools illustrates, was a source of much grief. By contrast, .NET provides all its services through a class library, and many low-level programming details are now dealt with by the platform (for example, the .NET runtime manages memory with a garbage collection scheme).

Veteran MFC or WTL developers might well point out that they have always used object-oriented abstractions for constructs such as windows and files. And Visual Basic developers can equally remind us that they have never had to deal with low-level minutiae. However, all these programming systems suffer from being wrappers on top of the "real" API, Win32. This is problematic because none of them provides a watertight abstraction—the underlying API is forever making its presence felt. This is particularly intrusive with the C++ class libraries: it's just not possible to write a nontrivial C++ Windows application without having to deal with some Win32 construct sooner or later.

Visual Basic does slightly better—it has enabled many people to become productive developers without ever understanding how Windows really works at the lowest levels. But Visual Basic runs into trouble as soon as you need to do something that it wasn't designed to support. It relies on ActiveX controls or COM components to exploit certain platform services, which is fine when such a component exists, but it means that support for the latest features of the OS can be somewhat late in arriving. While C++ developers can use new features as soon as they appear, Visual Basic developers must wait for a C++ developer to write them an ActiveX control. Visual Basic also suffers from a slightly more insidious problem. The high-level model it presents is a simplification of the Win32 model, and as such it differs in certain respects. If you write nothing but data entry forms this will almost certainly never cause you any problems, but if you need to exercise fine control over an application's behavior, Visual Basic's supposedly helpful model can sometimes be extremely frustrating.

So why is .NET any better? The crucial difference is that with .NET, all languages use the same API: Windows Forms. Of course, to provide its services, the current .NET Framework still relies on Win32 (or, in the case of the .NET Compact Framework, either Pocket PC or Windows CE.NET), but developers are strongly discouraged from bypassing the class libraries to call the underlying platform. Windows Forms has been designed to be a comprehensive abstraction rather than a thin wrapper, and it is entirely possible to write nontrivial GUI applications without ever needing to resort to calling into Win32 directly. This is very unlike MFC, which was effectively impossible to use without being exposed to Win32. Furthermore, because all languages use the same API, any new features added to the .NET Framework are instantly available to everyone—Visual Basic developers are no longer beholden to third parties to write them wrappers for new functionality.

There are two elements of .NET that allow this to work where the previous technologies, such as MFC and Visual Basic 6.0, have had only partial success. One is the new runtime—all languages share a single runtime, the Common Language Runtime (CLR), which means that all languages have the same type system and runtime semantics. This crucial development enables the platform's services to be exposed through a single API that is accessible to all languages. And this API itself is the second element—the platform's services are exposed through an object-oriented programming interface called the .NET Framework Class Library. We will spend the rest of this chapter looking at these two new features.

The Common Language Runtime

The Common Language Runtime (CLR) is the environment in which all programs run in .NET, so it affects everything we do as developers. It is therefore important to understand what it does and what that means to our programs, so we will now look at the most important features of the CLR.

All high-level programming languages have a runtime. This is because an OS process provides a fairly low-level set of features, typically just memory, pointers, threads, machine code, and system calls. The job of any language's runtime is to bridge the gap between these OS facilities and the constructs defined by the programming language. In C++, the runtime provides such features as exception handling, runtime type information, and the standard C++ library. The Visual Basic runtime includes intrinsic handling for COM and automatic memory management. Traditionally, each language has provided its own runtime, such as *MSVCRT.DLL* for C++, *MSVBVM60.DLL* for Visual Basic, and the Java Virtual Machine (*MSJAVA.DLL*, if you're using Microsoft's VM) for Java.

In .NET, there is just one runtime, which is used by all languages, the CLR. The fact that all languages use this one runtime is important for a number of reasons. It means components can easily be written in and used from any language because all languages represent types and objects in the same way. (Anyone familiar with COM in C++ will be amazed at how simple it is to write and use .NET components.) Moreover, it means that all languages can use the same API to access the platform's services.

Managed Code

C++ developers are used to writing low-level code. All the abstractions with which Win32 assembly language developers work (virtual memory, threads of execution, numbers, and pointers) are also exposed directly in C++. (Yes, there are still a few diehards who insist on writing Win32 applications in assembly language.) The C++ compiler supplies a useful veneer on top of these, providing facilities such as object-oriented programming and optional type safety, but the fact remains that all the platform's lowest level details are visible. For many developers, this is the appeal of C++—it hides nothing, imbuing the developer with a feeling of ultimate power.

But this power has its price. First, there is the amount of effort required to wield this power. Java and Visual Basic developers often marvel at how much time C++

developers seem to spend writing code to deal with things that simply aren't an issue in higher-level languages. Second, the power of C++ is often its Achilles' heel—C++ offers opportunities to crash and burn that are simply not available elsewhere. Very often, these costs are not outweighed by the benefits because, in practice, the full power of C++ is rarely required.

Software development has been using more and more abstraction throughout its history. A few years ago, it would have been considered essential for performance-critical parts of an application to be written in assembly language, but this practice has all but disappeared, because computers are now fast enough that it is rarely worth the extra development costs. Likewise, less than a decade ago, PC applications ran without the crash protection offered by modern operating systems and had absolute power over the whole machine. These days, we all benefit from the improved robustness achieved by abandoning that level of control and running most applications in secure sandboxed processes. If an application crashes, it no longer takes all the other applications on the machine with it—only the operating system and its device drivers need to live in the dangerous world of the kernel, where one false move can bring the entire machine to its knees. Most people welcome the resultant improvement in productivity and consider it to be worth the slight loss of control.

.NET takes a step forward that is very similar to the transition from assembly language to high-level languages, or the move from DOS-style operating systems to more reliable and secure modern operating systems. Once again it involves a slight loss of control in exchange for higher productivity, so we will inevitably hear the same kind of lamentation as we did when these older technologies were marginalized. But most developers don't find the loss of control to be a big deal in practice.

The name given to this advance is *managed code* or *managed execution*. Managed code is code that does not use the abstractions of assembly language—it deals with higher-level constructs. The most important difference is that the environment in which managed code runs has an intrinsic type system. With unmanaged code, Win32 simply gives us raw virtual memory and lets our programs use the processor to do whatever we like with that memory. Nothing stops code from storing a floating-point number in some memory location and then trying to read it as though it were a pointer—the code would be allowed to proceed, despite the fact that the binary value of the floating-point number will make no sense as a pointer and the code will almost certainly either crash or malfunction. But in .NET, this is not allowed to happen, because all information is strongly typed in the CLR. It knows whether a particular piece of memory represents, say, an integer or a floating-point number or an object reference, and actively prevents us from misinterpreting that data. The .NET managed runtime prevents such code from running in the first place—all code must pass type-safety verification before it is allowed to execute.

The runtime also has an intrinsic understanding of concepts such as objects, strings, heaps, and components. This means that compiled programs look very different under .NET—as we will now see, the very nature of the binaries generated by compilers has changed.

Compilation in .NET

To examine the new features of the runtime and to get a feel for how they change the world our programs live in, here's a simple program that runs under .NET. We will of course start with the canonical first program in C#:

```
class Hello
{
    static void Main()
    {
        System.Console.WriteLine("Hello, World");
    }
}
```

.NET and the Command Line

For a simple example such as this, it is easiest to compile the program from the command line. Visual Studio .NET provides a command prompt (under Visual Studio Tools from the Start Menu) with the path and environment set up suitably. The C# compiler is called CSC, and is pretty similar to the C++ compiler to use from the command line. If you put the source code in this example in a file called *Hello.cs*, just type `csc Hello.cs` at the command line. ILDASM can also be launched from this prompt.

Alternatively, a Visual Studio .NET C# console project would work just as well, but Visual Studio provides no way of launching ILDASM, so you will still need the command prompt.

If you compile this and examine the output of the compiler with a disassembler (such as the ILDASM tool that ships with the .NET Framework SDK) you will find that it is very different from the output of the old C++ compiler, as Figure 1-1 shows. The most immediately obvious difference is that the compiled code contains type information—the first thing ILDASM presents is a tree view of the types defined inside the component. We will look into the nature of this type information shortly, but first we will look at some compiled code.

If you expand the tree in ILDASM and double-click on any method, it will show the disassembled code of that method in a new window. Here is the compiled code for the `Main` method defined above:

```
ldstr       "Hello, world!"
call        void [mscorlib]System.Console::WriteLine(string)
ret
```

This shows the second most striking difference between the output from a traditional compiler and the code that a .NET compiler generates. This is not assembly language for an Intel processor—instead of strings, type names, and method signatures, the operands in disassembled Pentium code would just be so many hexadecimal digits. In fact, no processor is capable of running this code directly. Code in .NET binaries is stored in a so-called Intermediate Language (IL or CIL,

Hello.exe - IL DASM
File View Help
Hello.exe
MANIFEST
Hello
.assembly Hello

Figure 1-1. A simple program in ILDASM

as it is sometimes abbreviated), which the runtime will translate into the processor's native machine code to execute it. All languages compile into IL, so the equivalent Visual Basic program would look very similar in ILDASM.

All managed code is compiled into IL. It is similar in nature to Java's bytecode in that it is a processor-independent machine language that supports type-safe object-oriented programming. As a quick glance at this example has already shown, it is very different from Pentium code. Looking at the first line, it is clear that strings are supported as an intrinsic data type. The second line contains evidence that type information permeates .NET code even at the lowest level—in unmanaged (i.e., pre-.NET) code, a call instruction would simply contain the address of the function it was calling; here, it contains the name of the method (`WriteLine`), and also the name of the class the method belongs to (`System.Console`), and the component in which that class is defined (*mscorlib*; more on components shortly). Furthermore, the signature of the method is present—this call instruction is clearly expecting to call a method that takes a single parameter of type `string` and has a `void` return type.

Type information is embedded this deeply throughout all managed code. This is what enables the CLR to verify that code does not break any of the type safety rules—all managed code is required to be explicit about the types it is using at all times.

Of course the problem with this code is that there is no CPU in the world that can execute it. So one of the services the runtime must provide is a way of bridging the gap between this strongly typed code and the world of raw, untyped memory in which the processor lives. It does this by compiling the IL into native code on demand. This is done one method at a time—code will only be compiled when it is needed (i.e., the first time a method is called). This compilation process is therefore known as just-in-time compilation (JIT).

The type safety verification tests are applied before JIT happens, which means the JIT compiler doesn't need to generate code that wastes a lot of time enforcing the CLR type system's rules; it checks the code just once, up front. And the JIT compiler has a lot in common with the code generator used by the standard unmanaged C++ compiler, so the performance of code in the CLR turns out to be almost as good as that of code compiled in the traditional way. The main cost is that methods are much slower the very first time you run them, because they need to be compiled before they can run; also, the JIT-compiled code is discarded when the program exits, so this compilation cost is paid every time the program runs. Fortunately, this happens quickly (typically within a few milliseconds), so it's not slow enough to cause a perceptible slow down. And remember that this price is only paid the first time the method is called—for every subsequent call, the compiled code is used. So for long-running applications, the proportion of time spent in the JIT compiler is negligibly small.

For some applications, the slower startup that can be caused by JIT compilation may be a problem. For such programs, .NET provides a facility that allows components to be precompiled at installation time, so no JIT compilation needs to occur at runtime. This facility is called NGEN (short for native code generation), and certain critical system libraries (including Windows Forms) use it. However, this causes programs to take up considerably more disk space, and under some circumstances it can increase memory usage, so you should not use this feature unless you have identified startup time as a problem and your tests show that NGEN actually improves matters. Note that NGEN is not a viable way of making reverse engineering harder—an NGENed binary still contains all the IL and type information from the original. It is not possible to remove this.

In fact, there are performance benefits to JIT compilation. Only the code that needs to run is compiled, which can reduce a process's working set. Furthermore, applications always get the benefit of the latest compiler technology, whereas a traditional application is stuck with whatever the state of the art was when it was compiled.

Furthermore, as 64-bit systems become more widespread, managed code will be ready for them, as the CLR will just generate native 64-bit code from the IL instead of 32-bit code. This should make the transition from 32-bit to 64-bit systems considerably less painful than the decade-long transition from 16-bit to 32-bit systems. This also makes it possible for components to work both on normal PCs and on mobile systems that support the Compact .NET Framework, even though these typically use an entirely different processor architecture.

But the single most important aspect of IL is that it is permeated with type information, and the type system is arguably the most significant feature of the .NET runtime.

The Role of the Type System

With the classic C++ compilation model, the type system was for the most part something that only existed during compilation. The compiler typically did its best to remove as much evidence of the types used in the source code as possible. There would inevitably be some residue; for example if Runtime Type Information (RTTI) was enabled, objects would be annotated with type information, but it was somewhat minimal. For example, given a reference to an object, you couldn't find out at runtime what fields and methods it contained, or what their types and signatures were. The vast majority of the type information present in the source would be gone by runtime.

As we have already seen, this is not the case with .NET. The ILDASM tool presents us with a tree view showing every single type defined in the component, and provides full information on the contents of these types. This even includes members marked as private. And as we have seen, compiled code also contains full information about the types it is trying to use.

Reverse Engineering

The ubiquity of type information worries some people, because it can make it easier to reverse engineer software. However, third-party tools exist that will obfuscate the names. Although these tools still have to leave the fundamental structure of the type information in place, they will make reverse engineering hard enough to put most people off. The only way to deter the truly determined is to make sure they never get hold of your code in any form, compiled or not—it is not in fact particularly hard to reverse engineer a traditionally compiled component, and the presence of type information makes much less of a difference than, say, the symbol names, so obfuscation of symbols will make it almost as hard to decompile a .NET component as it is to reverse engineer classically compiled code.

The situation is exactly the same for Java, and there was a similar amount of hysteria about reverse engineering in Java's early days. A market for obfuscation tools emerged, but most people seem to have decided that it isn't actually a big deal, because little code contains truly sensitive information. And as the DeCSS debacle shows, any code that does contain interesting and sensitive information will be reverse engineered regardless of how hard you try to make it.

This ubiquitous nature of type information is fundamental to many of the services .NET provides. Because absolutely everything is fully annotated with type information (and this information is accessible at runtime through the reflection API), it is possible for the runtime to automate many facilities in a way that was not previously possible. For example, the runtime can automatically serialize objects by examining the type information to find out what fields are present and what their types are. The remoting services examine method definitions at runtime to determine how to make them work over the network. Service descriptions for web services are generated by the system automatically by analyzing the classes that provide those services.

To make use of this type system, we will of course need a programming language. A wide range of common languages is available for .NET, but we will now look at two .NET-specific languages, C# and Visual Basic .NET.

.NET Programming Languages

.NET has been designed to support multiple languages. Microsoft anticipates that most Visual Basic developers will want to carry on using the syntax they are familiar with, and will therefore stick with Visual Basic .NET. But developers with a C++

background are encouraged to change to a new language called C#. The problem with C++ is it is designed to support a very low-level style of programming—it fully supports all the classic C idioms, and C has often been described as a machine-independent assembly language. The low-level nature of C++ does not sit well with the new high-level nature of the CLR and the class libraries. (Visual Basic does not have this problem because it has always been a relatively high-level language.)

Although C++ is supported in .NET, it is not being pushed as the language of choice for erstwhile C++ developers. Instead, Microsoft has created a new language called C#. Designed by Anders Hejlsberg (creator of Delphi), C# is a language with syntax based on C++, but that works natively with exactly the same set of abstractions as the CLR provides. Just as C++ was the natural choice for developers who wanted to write code that was at home in the Win32 world, C# is a great choice for .NET programming, because it was designed to be a perfect match for the CLR. Its syntactic origins mean that anyone familiar with C or C++ (or Java) can learn C# very quickly.

For the most part, C# is like C++ without the low-level grunge. In fact, it is possible to use C-style features like pointers even in C#, although you need to turn off the relevant safety catches on the compiler before it will let you do this. However, this is mostly to make sure that C++ developers don't feel emasculated by moving to C#. While it is comforting for C++ veterans to know that pointers are still there if required, in practice, it is extremely rare to need to use these features in C#.

All example code in this book is presented in both C# and Visual Basic .NET, because the majority of Windows applications will be written in one or the other of these languages in the future.

Components

Whatever language we build our software in, we end up creating executable files that are loaded and run by the operating system. In days gone by, software was monolithic in nature—all the code and data required for an application was compiled and linked into a single executable lump of code. While there may be a certain elegant simplicity to this approach, it did little to encourage code reuse.* It also tended to encourage a programming style sometimes referred to as the "big ball of mud," where any individual part of the code is messily intermingled with lots of other parts, and there is no overall structure to the code. This was not especially conducive to code quality or developer productivity, and in extreme cases, a software project could become so entangled and intractable that fixing one bug could easily introduce several more bugs due to the unforeseen side effects of the change. The object-oriented (OO) features of C++ were not a sure-fire solution to this problem, because unless developers were scrupulous about encapsulating their code and keeping classes independent of each other, all the same problems could emerge in an OO program.

* Actually, there was one style of reuse popular in such code, often known as *Clipboard Inheritance*. This refers to the widespread practice of copying useful working code onto the clipboard, pasting it into some other part of the project, and then modifying it to suit its new environment.

Component-based software development was one of the most significant advances in software engineering to be adopted over the last decade. Componentized applications are not monolithic—they are broken down into discrete chunks (or *components*) with clear roles and well-defined boundaries. A key feature is that software components are binaries (i.e., compiled executables rather than collections of source code). This has the effect of preventing unrelated parts of the system from gradually merging just because of expediency—it means there are always clear divisions between parts of the system. This is particularly true if the individual components are developed by different groups: if there are any structural problems with the code, these must be dealt with by fixing the problems rather than resorting to hacks to work around them.

Of course, it is possible to write bad code in any programming system, and .NET doesn't change that. As always, there is no silver bullet. But with component-based systems like .NET, developers have to go out of their way to make one component depend on internal features of another component, so at least it encourages better practice, even if it can't enforce it.

For a component system to be workable, it must define two things: what constitutes a component and how components communicate with one another. Prior to .NET, the Component Object Model (COM) provided both definitions. Components were DLLs (or occasionally EXEs) with certain standard entry points, and that normally had type information attached. They communicated with each other by adhering to COM's programming model. .NET replaces these definitions with assemblies and the CLR, respectively.

An assembly is usually a DLL or EXE file, and it contains type definitions, along with any code and data for those types. In .NET, type definitions (and therefore all associated code) always live inside an assembly. Assemblies define the physical representation of a component in .NET. As with COM, they still rely on the same PE file format used by all executables in Windows, but they extend it to provide much more type information than was previously available. COM's type information provided no way of determining which other types a particular component depended upon, making it hard to be certain which components needed to be deployed to form a complete working system. In .NET, this is no longer a problem, because all assemblies list not only the types that they define but also all of the externally defined types that they use and the components in which those types are defined.

The .NET Type System

So what does a type look like in .NET? In many respects, types are very similar to C++ classes: just like a C++ class, a .NET type is a collection of members, which may be fields (i.e., they hold data of some type), methods (i.e., they contain code), or nested type definitions, and all members have some level of protection (e.g., public, private, protected). However there are a number of differences between the C++ and the .NET type systems. The following sections describe the main features of types in .NET.

Overview

Members of Types

Any type will need to define some members to be of any use. Members are either associated with data or behavior. In C++ this means fields and methods, respectively. In addition to these, which the CLR supports, the CLR adds some new member types. All these member types are described here.

Methods

Methods are where we define code. In most .NET languages, all code must be defined in a method of some type. (Because properties also can contain code, they would appear to be an exception, but they are actually implemented by .NET language compilers as method calls.) As with C++, the method must have a signature (consisting of its name and the types of parameters it takes), and that signature must be different from any other methods defined in the same class. Overloading is allowed, i.e., the names of two methods can be the same if their signatures are different. Methods must also have a return type (even if the method returns `void` or `Nothing`); overloading based on return type alone is not allowed. (C++ doesn't allow this either.) Note that methods that return `void` or `Nothing` in VB are declared using the `Sub` statement rather than the `Function` statement.

Methods can either be instance methods or static methods. (Instance methods are the default, but you can use the `static` keyword in C# or the `Shared` keyword in Visual Basic to specify a static method.) Instance methods are invoked with respect to a particular object or value, and they have access to that object through the `this` keyword in C# and the `Me` operator in VB. They can also refer to members simply by their names—if they are instance members, the `this` or `Me` reference will be used implicitly. Static methods do not need an object in order to be invoked, but they will only have access to other static members of the class. Visual Basic is not trying to maintain any look-and-feel compatibility with C++, so it uses the rather more sensible `Shared` keyword for members that are shared across all instances of a class.

Here is an example C# method declaration in a class:

```
public class MyFirstClass
{
    public int MyMethod (string s)
    {
        return int.Parse(s);
    }
}
```

The equivalent VB code is:

```
Public Class MyFirstClass
    Public Function MyMethod(s As String) As Integer
        Return Integer.Parse(s)
    End Function
End Class
```

The method takes a string as a single parameter and returns an integer. The code for the method attempts to convert the string to an integer by using the C# `int` type's or VB `Integer` type's static `Parse` method. (Both `int` and `Integer` are identical to the .NET Framework's `System.Int32` type.) `MyMethod` is an instance method—users of `MyFirstClass` will need an instance of `MyFirstClass` to call this method.

The `public` keyword in both languages indicates that any code is allowed to call this method. We will talk more about such protection keywords towards the end of this section.

Fields

Fields hold data. As with methods, fields can be either instance or static. If a field is declared as static, it is singular—all instances of the class or value will share the same piece of data, and that data will be accessible to instance and static methods alike. But instance fields (the default) are stored as part of each instance of the type, so every instance has its own set.

A field must have a name and a type. Here is an example instance field, along with a method that uses the field:

```
public class MySecondClass
{
    private int x;

    public int IncrementTotal(int val)
    {
        x = x + val;
        return x;
    }
}
```

The equivalent VB code is:

```
Public Class MySecondClass
    Private x As Integer

    Public Function IncrementTotal(val As Integer) As Integer
       x = x + val
       return x
    End Function
End Class
```

This class defines a private instance field called `x`, which can store an integer. The method `IncrementTotal` adjusts this field and returns its value. The code does not use the `this` or `Me` reference; it just refers to `x` by name. The compiler will detect that the code refers to the instance field `x` and presume that the author meant `this.x` or `Me.x`.

Properties

It is considered good practice never to expose a data field as a public member of an object, because that would cause client code to become too tightly coupled with that type's implementation. Exposing properties through *get* and *set* methods is a popular technique for allowing components' implementations the flexibility to evolve while still providing public members that feel like fields.

Just as COM did, .NET specifies a standard way of exposing properties through methods. And as with COM, some languages (including Visual Basic .NET and C#) provide special syntax to support this, allowing field-like syntax to be used when reading or writing properties, even though they are implemented in terms of methods. So in C#, we can provide properties like this:

```
public class ClassWithProperties
{
    public int MyProp
    {
        get
        {
            return 42;
        }
        set
        {
            Console.WriteLine("MyProp set to {0}. That's nice",
                value);
        }
    }
}
```

And in VB, we can do it like this:

```
Public Class ClassWithProperties
    Public Property MyProp( ) As Integer
        Get
           Return 42
        End Get
        Set
            Console.WriteLine("MyProp set to {0}. That's nice", _
                Value)
        End Set
    End Property
End Class
```

This defines an `int` or `Integer` property called `MyProp`. Note that `value` is a keyword in C# and VB, and it is used in property *set* functions. It is the value that the caller is trying to give the property. (In this case, we are just writing that value to the console.)

> The use of `{0}` in the string passed to `Console.WriteLine` indicates that the parameter following the string should be inserted into the output at this point. It has a similar role to placeholders such as `%d` in the format string for `printf` in C.

The syntax for using properties in C# is exactly the same as for accessing fields:

```
MyClass obj = new ClassWithProperties( );
int val = obj.MyProp;
obj.MyProp += 99;
```

The same is true of VB:

```
Dim obj As New ClassWithProperties()
Dim val As Integer = obj.MyProp
objMyProp += 99
```

In this particular example, there is no field. (Feel free to implement your own properties using private fields internally.) This will just run the *get* and *set* methods defined for the property. In this case, reading the property will always get the value 42, and writing it will just cause a message to be printed. Most properties behave more usefully, of course, but the point is the client code is not dependent on how the property works—it could rely on a normal field, derive the value from those in other fields, or retrieve the value from a database. The client just accesses the property, and the object can handle that however it sees fit.

Event handling

Components often need to notify client code when something interesting has happened. This is particularly common in user interface code—applications need to know when buttons are clicked, when windows are resized, when text is typed in, and so on. .NET defines a standard way in which objects can deliver event notifications to their clients. Visual Basic and C# both have special syntax for declaring and consuming such events. These two syntaxes are quite different—C# presents the CLR's event handling mechanisms directly, while VB uses a style that is much more like the event handling in previous versions of VB. However, both languages are based on the same fundamental mechanisms, so they have much in common.

A class that wishes to be able to raise events (most Windows Forms controls do this) must declare the fact by adding a special member for each type of event it can raise. In C#, we use the following syntax:

```
public class EventSource
{
    public event MouseEventHandler MouseDown;
    . . .
}
```

In Visual Basic, the equivalent event declaration looks like this:

```
Public Class EventSource
    Public Event MouseDown As MouseEventHandler
    . . .
End Class
```

Both examples declare an event whose name is `MouseDown` and whose type is `MouseEventHandler`. (The `MouseEventHandler` type is defined in the `System.Windows.Forms` namespace, and we will see its definition later.) As it happens, all Windows Forms controls support this event—it is raised whenever a mouse button is pressed while the cursor is over the control.

When an event occurs, the event source notifies the client by calling the relevant handler function. The way we determine which particular function it calls is different in VB and C#. In VB, the class that wishes to receive the event simply uses the `WithEvents` keyword to indicate that it is interested in events from the event source object. It then identifies a particular method as being the handler for a given event using the Handles keyword. The signature of the handler method must match the type of the event. In this case, the event is of type MouseEventHandler. (We will look at this type's definition shortly.) So our code looks like this:

```
Public Class EventReceiver
    Private WithEvents src As EventSource
    . . .
    Private Sub src_OnMouseDown( _
        sender As Object, e As MouseEventArgs) _
        Handles src.MouseDown
        Console.WriteLine("src object raised MouseDown event")
End Class
```

This style is similar to how previous versions of Visual Basic handled events. However, it hides the details of how events really work. C# does not provide such a level of abstraction—it exposes the CLR's underlying mechanisms directly. Consequently, we need to do slightly more work in C# to handle events. Moreover, we must understand the mechanism on which events are based.

The CLR provides a special kind of object that is used to connect an event source to its corresponding event handler method. These special objects are called *delegates*. Delegates are .NET's nearest equivalent to function pointers—they hold typed references to functions. As with a C++ function pointer, a delegate's type (MouseEventHandler, in this case) determines the signature that the client's handler function must have. MouseEventHandler is defined (in System.Windows.Forms) thus:

```
public delegate void MouseEventHandler(
    object sender, MouseEventArgs e);
```

The equivalent Visual Basic definition is:

```
Public Delegate Sub MouseEventHandler( _
    sender As Object, e As MouseEventArgs
```

So if we wish to receive MouseDown event notifications from some control, we must provide a function with a matching signature:

```
private void OnMouseDown (object sender, MouseEventArgs e)
{
    ... handle the MouseDown event ...
}
```

Of course, we must also tell the control that we are interested in the MouseDown event and would like notifications to be delivered to our OnMouseDown method. In Visual Basic, we did this by using the Handles keyword, but in C#, we must create a MouseEventHandler delegate initialized with a reference to our method, and then attach it to the relevant event on the control, using the following rather strange syntax:

```
src.MouseDown += new MouseEventHandler(OnMouseDown);
```

This is roughly equivalent to passing the address of a callback function as a function pointer in C++; the delegate acts as a typed reference to a function that can be passed as a parameter or stored in a field so that the function can be called back later. But we can't use function pointers as we would in C++, and not just for the ideological reason that it doesn't enter into the spirit of the brave new pointerless world of the CLR. There is a rather more prosaic reason not to use raw function pointers: JIT compilation means that functions don't necessarily remain in the same place for the life of a program. In fact, when the code above is run, there is every chance that the `OnMouseDown` method has not been JIT compiled at all yet, so it might not even have an address. So instead, we rely on delegates to provide us with behavior equivalent to function pointers, while shielding us from the complexities of using pointers in the world of movable code.

Delegates can hold an object reference as well as a function reference. (In C++ terms, this would mean that a delegate is really two pointers—a function pointer and a pointer to an object.) In the example above, `OnMouseDown` is not a static function, so it can only be invoked in conjunction with an object reference. (The value for the implicit `this` reference has to come from somewhere.) If a function requires an object reference, a suitable one must be supplied when a delegate to that function is created. This can be done explicitly, for example:

```
myDelegate = new MyDelegateType(myObj.MyMethod);
```

creates a new delegate whose type is `MyDelegateType` and attaches it to the `MyMethod` method on the object to which `myObj` refers. (Delegates store their own copy of the reference, so if the `myObj` variable is later modified to refer to a different object, the delegate will still refer to the original one.) Or the object reference can be inferred—if the delegate is created in the scope of a non-static method, the `this` reference will be used if no explicit reference is supplied. The `MouseEventHandler` example above illustrates this, and is typical of code inside a form's initialization function: because an object reference has not been supplied explicitly, the C# compiler automatically supplies a reference to whichever form is being initialized. That code is shorthand for the following:

```
src.MouseDown += new MouseEventHandler(this.OnMouseDown);
```

This use of the `+=` syntax, peculiar to C#, is simply shorthand for a method call. For each event that a class defines, the C# compiler will actually define two methods, one for adding a handler and one for removing it. C# hides this detail with the `+=` syntax (and the corresponding `-=` syntax used for disconnecting an event handler), and it also shields us from the details of declaring events if we wish to raise them ourselves. If we add an event declaration such as the one shown above to our own class, the C# compiler will automatically generate the functions to add and remove event handlers for us; the code it generates is able to cope with multiple event handlers being attached simultaneously, as all events should.

Note that the `-=` syntax used for detaching an event handler is smart enough to work out which method a delegate refers to. It doesn't require the same delegate object that was used in the `+=` to be passed back in. So looking at the code above, you might have thought that we would need to store the delegate being created with the `new` operator to pass it back when we wish to detach. In fact, it works just fine if we create a new delegate at detachment time:

```
src.MouseDown -= new MouseEventHandler(this.OnMouseDown);
```

Overview

In Visual Basic, all these details of creating delegates and attaching them are hidden—using the WithEvents and Handles keywords causes all this code to be generated automatically. However, VB also supports the explicit style that C# requires. The syntax is different, but the meaning is the same. We can create a delegate object using VB's AddressOf keyword. And VB's equivalents to the += and -= event operators are the AddHandler and RemoveHandler keywords. So we can add a handler explicitly, just as we are required to in C#, with the following VB code:

```
AddHandler src.MouseDown, AddressOf Me.OnMouseDown
```

And the corresponding code to remove a handler is:

```
RemoveHandler src.MouseDown, AddressOf Me.OnMouseDown
```

Most of the time, you would not need to use this explicit style in Visual Basic. However, it can be useful for attaching handlers dynamically at runtime. In addition, if you want a single event handler to handle an event from every object in a collection, you will need to use this explicit style.

All the event handler delegates defined in the .NET Framework follow a common pattern. They define function signatures that take two parameters. The first parameter is always of type object, and is a reference to the object that raised the event. (So when a control raises the MouseDown event, it passes a reference to itself to the event handler. This can be useful it you want to have events from multiple controls on a form all handled by a single function—this parameter lets it know which control a particular event came from.) The second parameter contains information about the event. The various delegates defined in .NET all specify different types for this second parameter. For example, the drag-and-drop events use a delegate type called DragEventHandler, which defines the second parameter to be a DragEventArgs, while MouseEventHandler (see above) defines it to be a MouseEventArgs. Some events provide no special information—for example, the Click event raised by a button simply indicates that a particular button has been clicked, so there is no use for a final parameter. .NET defines a generic delegate for such methods:

```
public delegate void EventHandler(object sender, EventArgs e);
```

The second parameter is usually a special value, EventArgs.Empty. This may seem pointless—if the same value is passed every time, why not just leave off the second parameter? It is left there just in case peculiar circumstances arise in which it would be useful to be able to pass some information. For example, if you were to define a custom derivative of the standard Button class, you might wish to pass some information in your Click event. If you define a class that derives from EventArgs, you can pass it as the second parameter. If EventHandler didn't provide this second argument, you would not be able to do this.

Note that you are not required to use this style of event handling for your own components. You can define classes whose events use a delegate of your own devising, which may have any signature you like. Of course, if you stick to the framework's style, your code will look more consistent, so it is recommended that you do this. But there is nothing magic about delegates whose first parameter is an object and whose second parameter is some type deriving from EventArgs.

Protection levels

Encapsulation (making the implementation details of a class inaccessible to keep a clear division between a class's public interface and its internal workings) is crucial in all object-oriented systems. Without proper encapsulation, client code can become dependent on arbitrary implementation details of an object, meaning that changes to the object that don't change its external programming interface (e.g., bug fixes) still can end up breaking client code. This could happen in C++ because compiled code was implicitly dependent on features of a class that were not strictly part of its public interface, e.g., the number of bytes required to store an instance of the class, and the offsets of public fields. These values can change when private implementation details are modified. This feature of C++ reflects its origins in the world of monolithic software, where all client code can be rebuilt whenever a class's implementation changes (assuming your build process detects such changes properly). In a dynamically linked world, this is simply not good enough.

Encapsulation is fundamentally important in component-oriented software because individual components tend to evolve independently both of each other, and of the code that uses them. To maintain the freedom to evolve, components must be able to draw a clear line between their internal workings and their public programming interface.

To enable this, .NET supports the protection levels familiar to C++ developers. Members of a type can be defined as `public`, indicating that they are available to all; `private`, indicating that they are for the type's internal use only; and `protected`, indicating that they can be accessed by the type and by any types that derive from it. (We will talk about inheritance in the next section.) However, because .NET has a formal definition for a component, it is able to provide protection facilities at a wider scope than this. Unlike standard C++, .NET supports component-level encapsulation as well as class-level encapsulation.

It is common to want to write a class designed to be used inside a component, but that is not intended to be used by external clients of the component. One solution available in C++ (and supported in .NET) is to define a `private` nested class—a class defined inside another class that is only accessible to code within that class. The problem is this does not allow a class to be accessible to other classes within the component; in C++, it is an all or nothing choice—a class is either entirely private or is available to all classes. However, .NET offers another level of protection: `internal` (in C#) or `Friend` (in VB).

Types and their members can be marked as `internal` (in C#) or `Friend` (in VB), indicating that they are available only to code that is in the same assembly. So it is possible to define types or members that exist entirely for the benefit of the component in which they are defined, and that will not be accessible to clients of the component.

> The assembly-level protection provided by `internal` or `Friend` is superficially similar to package-level protection in Java. However, although it serves the same purpose, it works rather differently. In Java, package-level protection is based on the naming of classes. In .NET, internal protection is based entirely on component membership—even if two classes belong to different namespaces, they can still access each other's internal members if they belong to the same assembly.

Inheritance and Interfaces

The .NET type system supports inheritance, although unlike standard C++, it does not support multiple inheritance. However, one of the most common uses of multiple inheritance in C++ was to support an interface-based programming style. Fortunately, .NET supports interfaces directly, so the absence of multiple inheritance is not a problem.

This section describes the inheritance and interface-based features of the CLR.

Inheritance

The CLR supports single implementation inheritance—a type can have a single base type. In fact, use of inheritance is effectively mandatory in .NET—a user-defined type has to inherit from something. This is because .NET provides a unified type system in which every type is compatible with a single base type called `System.Object`. (`System.Object` is the only type not to have a base type—every other type in .NET, including intrinsic types, inherits either directly or indirectly from `System.Object`.)

> ### Intrinsic Types
>
> Intrinsic types are those built in to the programming system, such as integers and floating-point numbers. Most languages have keywords for the intrinsic types they support (e.g., `int` and `double` in C++, `Integer` and `Double` in Visual Basic.) Before .NET, all languages defined their own set of intrinsic types, although they were usually much the same as each other, because they are mostly types supported directly by the processor architecture. But now the CLR defines the set of intrinsic types, and these are the types supported directly in CIL, the Intermediate Language.
>
> The intrinsic types are all the numeric types, `System.Boolean`, `System.String`, and object reference. `System.String` is a special case—it is an intrinsic type that is not a value type. You might think that object references would be an exception too, but they are not. Objects are reference types, but an object reference is in fact a value type. This is similar to pointers in C++. A pointer is just a value, even though its purpose is to refer to something; the current implementation of the CLR represents an object reference as a pointer, and these pointers are passed by value.

By default, any user-defined type can act as a base class (unless it is a value type—see later), but this can be inhibited if necessary. A type may prevent further derivation by marking itself as `sealed` (in C#) or `NonInheritable` (in VB). Conversely, a type may mark itself with the `abstract` keyword (in C#) or the `MustInherit` keyword (in VB), indicating that it cannot itself be instantiated, and can only be used as a base class from which other classes are derived.

Unlike standard C++, inheritance in .NET can not only cross component boundaries, it can also span language boundaries—a C# class can derive from a Visual Basic class, for example.

Interface-based programming

As seasoned COM developers will be aware, it is possible to use an interface-based style of programming in C++ by defining pure abstract base classes. But in .NET, interfaces are directly supported by the runtime. Interfaces are not fully fledged types; they are wholly abstract. This means that although .NET only supports single inheritance, it is possible for a type to implement multiple interfaces, because interfaces are not really types. (So unlike C++, implementing an interface on a .NET type doesn't involve inheritance at all.)

.NET languages typically have special syntax for dealing with interfaces, but in all other respects, .NET interface-based programming is very similar to using an interface idiom in C++. Example 1-1 defines an interface with two methods, followed by a class that implements the interface.

Example 1-1. Implementing an interface in C#

```
public interface IMyItf
{
    void MyMethod1(string s);
    int MyMethod2(string s, int x);
}
public class MyImplementation : IMyItf
{
    // Must implement the methods defined in IMyItf,
    // or the compiler will complain that we're not
    // honoring our claim to implement the interface
    // and refuse to compile the code
    public void MyMethod1(string s)
    {
        System.Console.WriteLine(s);
    }
    public int MyMethod2(string s, int x)
    {
        return int.Parse(s) + x;
    }
}
```

Example 1-2 shows the equivalent interface definition and implementation in Visual Basic.

Example 1-2. Implementing an interface in VB

```
Public interface IMyItf
    Sub MyMethod1(s As String)
    Function MyMethod2(s As String, x As Integer) As Integer
End Interface

Public Class MyImplementation
    Implements IMyItf

    Public Sub MyMethod1(s As String) Implements IMyItf.MyMethod1
        System.Console.WriteLine(s)
    End Sub
    Public Function MyMethod2(s As String, x As Integer) As Integer _
            Implements IMyItf.MyMethod2
        return Integer.Parse(s) + x
    End Function
End Class
```

The Different Types of Type

Types in .NET fall into two categories: value types and reference types. Instances of these are referred to as values and objects, respectively. The principal difference between value types and reference types is that variables of value types contain the bytes of data that make up the instance, while variables of reference type just contain the address of the instance. With reference types, the instance itself lives on the garbage-collected heap.

We will now look at the differences in behavior between reference types and value types.

Reference types

Reference types are defined in C# with the `class` keyword and in VB with the `Class` keyword. Each instance of any reference type has a distinct identity and lives on the heap. If you declare a variable of a reference type, it will refer to an object of that type on the heap. (Or the variable may be `null` in C# or `Nothing` in VB, a special value meaning that the variable isn't referring to any object right now.)

The CLR uses garbage collection to determine when a particular object no longer has any variables referring to it. There is no equivalent of the C++ `delete` operator in .NET-based languages. You can simply lose track of objects you no longer care about, and the runtime will eventually notice that such objects have fallen out of use and reclaim the memory they occupied.

Objects are always annotated with type information. If you have a variable of type `System.Object` (or `object`, as it is usually abbreviated in C# and VB), it could refer to any kind of object at all, but you can always find out by calling the object's `GetType` method. This relies on there being some information at the start of the object describing its type. In fact, lots of different services supplied by the runtime, including all the polymorphic features such as virtual functions and interfaces, rely on this type information.

Value types

In C++, intrinsic types (e.g., `int`, `float`, etc.) are fundamentally different from and unrelated to class types, whereas in .NET, everything belongs to a single type hierarchy: everything, including the intrinsic types, derives from `System.Object`. However, .NET does make a distinction between value-like types and object-like types—there is a special type called `System.ValueType`, and all types deriving from it have value-like behavior. The built-in types (`System.Int32`, `System.Single`, etc.) all derive from `System.ValueType`.

Value types don't have any meaningful identity—because they are usually passed by value, they frequently get copied. This means that they don't have to live in a distinct space on the heap. Value types usually live either on the stack or as fields inside some other type.

This distinction between values and objects is necessary for performance reasons—if every single integer in a program had to be allocated its own space on the heap, this would be disastrous for the program's memory and CPU consumption. This becomes particularly important if large arrays are used. An array of reference types is roughly equivalent to an array of pointers in C++, and requires a heap block to be allocated for each element in the array if it is to be of any use. But for value types, a single heap block is allocated for the entire array, and the values are stored contiguously inside this block, just like in a C++ array.

The tradeoff is that value types are slightly less flexible, the principal limitation being that they cannot be derived from. This makes it possible for the runtime to know exactly how much memory will be required for a value type. If inheritance were allowed, how could the runtime be sure that 32 bits would be enough to hold an `Int32`? A derived type might require more room. Also, because the inheritance-based polymorphic features available to reference types will never be used, value types don't need to carry the associated overhead of type information and virtual method tables. This means that a value type is only as large as it needs to be to hold its fields and no larger.

> Despite the requirement for a value type to have a fixed size, it can still contain fields of reference type. This is fine because although those fields may refer to objects of indeterminate size, the value type will only contain the references, not the objects. A reference is always the same size (32 bits, in the current implementation), regardless of how large the object it refers to may be.
>
> For example, it is allowed for a value type to contain a string—a string could be any length, but this doesn't matter, because the value will just contain a reference to that string.

The set of value types is not restricted to the built-in types. It is possible to create user-defined value types. The C# language uses the `struct` keyword to define custom value types, while VB.NET uses the `Structure...End Structure` construct. This means that it is not just the intrinsic types that can benefit from the performance advantages that value types can offer in certain circumstances—user-defined types for things such as complex numbers and 3D coordinates can use exactly the same memory allocation strategies that are used for intrinsic types.

Values and boxing

Value types are not always more efficient than reference types. Although they don't carry the normal overheads of reference types (heap blocks, type information, virtual method tables, etc.), there can be situations where they are nevertheless less efficient. One reason is they are passed by value—a value type will always be copied when passed as a method parameter. If it is large, this can get expensive. The other reason is that the runtime needs to perform a trick to cast a value type down to a base type. Remember that all types in .NET are compatible with `System.Object`, including all the value types. This sounds as though it should be impossible, because `System.Object` supports reference-like behavior—for example it defines the `GetType` method mentioned earlier.

The CLR performs a trick to make this work. When you cast, say, an integer to a `System.Object`, the runtime creates an object-like wrapper on the heap, and copies the value of the integer inside this wrapper. This operation is called *boxing*. (There is a corresponding *unboxing* operation when casting back to the original type to extract the wrapped value.) Boxing is also used to enable a value type to support interfaces. Interfaces are polymorphic by nature—the exact method that is called when you invoke a method on an interface is not determined by the type of variable you call it through, it is determined by the type of object that variable refers to—so they rely on the object type header being present. This means that if your value type implements any interfaces, it will be boxed every time you cast it to a reference of some interface type.

Boxing a value type has its costs—an object must be allocated on the heap. (The cost is similar to that of instantiating a reference type in the first place. The problem is that you pay this price every time boxing occurs, rather than just once when you create the object.) Any type that is often cast to `System.Object` is likely to be better off as a reference type to avoid the boxing overhead. For example, all the standard collection classes in the .NET Framework store references of type `System.Object`, so if you plan to store your objects in one of these containers, you should make them reference types, not value types (i.e., classes, not structs).

This caveat does not apply if you are simply using normal arrays. Although, say, a `System.Collections.ArrayList` of `int`s will box every item it contains, a simple `int` array (`int[]` or `Integer()`) will not use boxing.

The .NET Framework Class Library

All platform services are exposed through the .NET Framework Class Library. So whether you want to make a window appear, read a file, open a network connection, parse an XML document, or use any of the other myriad features of the platform, you will do so by using one or more classes in the class library.

The class library is divided up into *namespaces*. For each area of the API, there is an appropriate namespace, e.g., XML services are provided by the `System.Xml` namespace, GUI services are provided by the `System.Windows.Forms` namespace, and graphical services are provided by the `System.Drawing` namespace. Namespaces are hierarchical, and large namespaces are frequently subdivided into several smaller namespaces, e.g., the design-time parts of the Windows Forms API appear in the `System.Windows.Forms.Design` namespace.

Because the Class Library replaces large amounts of the Win32 API, and also adds new functionality not previously available, it is large and contains many namespaces. This book concentrates on the Windows Forms namespace, and the related `System.Drawing` namespace, although we will discuss other relevant classes as necessary.

Windows Forms and GDI+

Windows Forms is the name given to the parts of the .NET Framework Class Libraries used for building *rich client* applications, i.e., traditional GUI applications such as those built using the MFC before .NET. Central to Windows Forms is the `Control` class, the foundation of all UI applications and the subject of the next chapter. In fact, almost everything that happens in a .NET UI application revolves around controls, so most of the rest of the book is about controls.

GDI and GDI+

There are actually two versions of GDI+, one for unmanaged (non-.NET) code and one for managed code. The unmanaged GDI+ came first—it shipped with Windows XP, and a redistributable for other versions of Windows was released at the same time. Managed GDI+ shipped a few months later with the release of .NET, and is described in the documentation as "a set of wrappers." This turns out to be a somewhat misleading description, because it is not in fact a wrapper for unmanaged GDI+. The two APIs are nearly identical, both are object oriented and provide a set of objects for two-dimensional drawing and image manipulation. The object models look exactly the same, except one is a classic C++ object model, while the other is a .NET object model. However, neither is a wrapper for the other—both turn out to be wrappers for the same undocumented API. They may look the same, but they are in fact two parallel implementations of the same thing, one in managed code, the other in unmanaged code.

GDI+ is the successor to Win32's GDI—it is the API used for drawing. If a Windows Forms application wants to customize its own appearance, it must use GDI+, so this API (which lives in the `System.Drawing` namespace) is a fundamental part of most .NET GUI development. It provides a wide range of drawing facilities, including support for text, bitmaps, metafiles, line drawing, Bezier curves, and filled paths. It also provides advanced high-quality rendering features, such as antialiasing support for all graphical output (as opposed to just on text), and interpolation for bitmap resizing (both bilinear and bicubic).

The rest of this book is devoted to describing how to use the classes in these Windows Forms and GDI+ namespaces.

2 Controls

The `System.Windows.Forms` namespace defines a class called `Control`. This class is at the heart of all Windows Forms applications. Any visual element of an application—whether it is a window, a button, a toolbar, or a custom user-defined control—is represented by an object of some class deriving from `Control`.

This chapter describes the role played by the `Control` class within the Windows Forms framework, and examines the basic behavior that all controls inherit from `Control`. It also introduces the classes that represent the traditional Windows controls.

Windows Forms and the Control Class

Each different type of user interface element is represented by a specialized class deriving from `Control`. For example, top-level windows are represented by the `Form` class; each of the standard Windows control types has a corresponding class (such as `Button` and `TreeView`); you can also define custom controls by creating your own classes. All these inherit (either directly or indirectly) from the `Control` class.

Because all visual elements derive from `Control`, they share a single implementation of the features common to all controls. This ensures a certain minimum level of functionality and guarantees consistent behavior across all control types. The `Control` class defines standard properties, events, and methods for all the common features of user interface components. These include size and position, input handling, and appearance.

The `Control` class also defines the nature of the relationships controls on a form have with one another. As with classic Windows programming, a parent-child relationship is supported—a control may contain several child controls, and most controls (except top-level windows) have a parent control. The containment relationship is detailed in the next chapter, but it affects all controls for certain operations, such as moving and resizing windows. It also has some slightly more subtle implications for features such as focus management and control validation.

The Windows Forms framework defines a class hierarchy for the various kinds of controls. The Control class sits at the root of this hierarchy, but there are specializations for various types of controls, as Figure 2-1 shows. All the built-in controls (buttons, labels, tree views, etc.) inherit directly from the Control class. As you will see in Chapter 5, you can write your own controls that do the same.

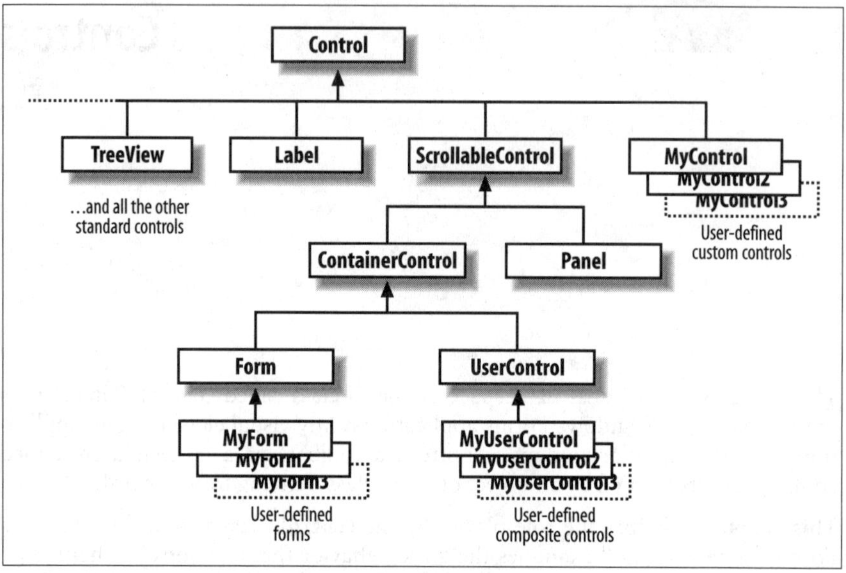

Control
TreeView
Label
ScrollableControl
MyControl
MyControl2
MyControl3
...and all the other standard controls
User-defined custom controls
ContainerControl
Panel
Form
UserControl
MyForm
MyForm2
MyForm3
MyUserControl
MyUserControl2
MyUserControl3
User-defined forms
User-defined composite controls

Figure 2-1. The Control class hierarchy

In practice, most user-defined controls only inherit indirectly from the Control class. The single most common type of custom user interface element you will define will be top-level windows deriving from the Form class. The Form class is discussed in detail in the next chapter, as are its base classes, ScrollableControl and ContainerControl. The closely related UserControl class will be discussed in Chapter 5. For now, the main thing to be aware of is that a typical simple Windows Forms application will define a class derived from Form for each type of window it displays, and this class will be implemented using several of the built-in control types. We will now see how to use the facilities provided by Control that are common to all control types.

Using Standard Control Features

The Control class provides uniform management of all the standard facets of a control, including visual features such as color, caption, and typeface, dynamic features such as event handling and accessibility, and other standard behaviors such as layout management. There are two ways of using most of these features: at design time in the Windows Forms designer and at runtime from code.

The Windows Forms designer allows most of the features of a control to be configured visually at design time using the Properties tab. (Also, certain common operations can be performed directly with the mouse; for example, the position of a control can be adjusted by dragging it.) However, this visual editing simply causes the designer to generate code. It just writes a class that creates control objects and manipulates their properties. Unlike earlier Windows development environments, .NET doesn't have dialog template resources—everything is done in code. (The strings used in a form can be stored as resources, though, to support localization.) For example, dropping a button onto a form in the designer causes the following code to be added to the form's class definition for projects written in C#:


```
private System.Windows.Forms.Button button1;
...
private void InitializeComponent()
{
    ...
    this.button1 = new System.Windows.Forms.Button( );
    ...
    this.button1.Location = new System.Drawing.Point(8, 8);
    this.button1.Name = "button1";
    this.button1.TabIndex = 0;
    this.button1.Text = "button1";
    ...
}
```

The corresponding code for projects written in VB is:

```
Private WithEvents Button1 As System.Windows.Forms.Button

Private Sub InitializeComponent( )

   Me.Button1 = New System.Windows.Forms.Button( )
   Me.SuspendLayout( )
   '
   'Button1
   '
   Me.Button1.Location = New System.Drawing.Point(8, 8)
   Me.Button1.Name = "Button1"
   Me.Button1.TabIndex = 0
   Me.Button1.Text = "Button1"
   ...
End Sub
```

So using the designer is functionally equivalent to writing the code by hand, although it is rather more convenient. The mechanisms through which we use controls are the methods, properties, and events that they expose (just as with any other component in .NET). The Windows Forms designer is effectively just a code generation mechanism. Because the programming model provided by the `Control` class is fundamentally important whether you use the forms designer or not, the following sections concentrate on this model.

The following sections deal with the various aspects of a control that can be managed through the standard properties on the `Control` class. We will start by looking at how to set a control's size and position. Next, we will see how to control its appearance. Finally, we will see how to make our controls respond to input from the user.

Location, Location, Location

Visual components must occupy some space on the screen if they are to be visible. The Control class allows us to have complete control over the location and size of our UI elements, but it is also possible to get the Windows Forms framework to do some of the work for us. So first we will look at how to set the size and position of a visual component manually, and then we will see how to exploit automatic layout.

Position and size

Position and size are fundamental features of all controls. We turn out to be spoiled for choice here, because `Control` provides several different representations of this information. For example, there is a `Location` property that allows the position of the top-left corner of the control to be set in screen coordinates as a `Point` (a value type containing a two-dimensional coordinate). The designer uses `Location` to position controls, as shown above. But we can also set the dimensions individually—the following code is equivalent to what the Forms designer produced in the previous example:

```
this.button1.Left = 8;
this.button1.Top = 8;
```

`Control` also provides `Right` and `Bottom` properties, although these are read-only because it is ambiguous whether changing these should leave the `Left` and `Top` properties as they are, thus changing the size, or whether they should move the control. Note that these properties define the control's position relative to its container. For example, when a form is moved, all the controls inside that form move with it, but the value of their `Location` (and associated properties) does not change.

The size can also be set in various ways. The control will choose a default size for itself in its constructor, and it is best to use the constructor if possible, because resizing the control after creation is slightly slower. This is why the designer doesn't generate any code to set the button's size. But if we wish to set the size ourselves (maybe the default size is inappropriate), we can either set the `Width` and `Height` properties individually, or we can set the `Size` property:

```
this.button1.Size = new Size(100, 50);
```

The `Size` type is a value type similar to the `Point` type, but it is always used to denote something's size. We can also use the following code, which is functionally equivalent to the previous example:

```
this.button1.Width = 100;
this.button1.Height = 50;
```

If we want to set both the position and the size, we can do so in one go with the `SetBounds` method:

```
this.button1.SetBounds(8, 8, 100, 50);
```

(The four parameters are equivalent to the `Left`, `Top`, `Width`, and `Height` properties.) It doesn't matter which of the various techniques you use to change a control's size and position—they are all equivalent, so you can use whichever is most convenient. (As it happens, they all end up calling the same internal method in the current implementation of the .NET Framework.) Alternatively, you may decide to let the automatic layout facilities of Windows Forms set some of these properties.

Automatic layout

A control's size and position does not necessarily need to be set manually. It is possible for these properties to be controlled (or influenced) by automatic layout, using the `Dock` and `Anchor` properties.

The `Dock` property allows a control's position and size to be managed by its containing window. This property is set to one of the six values in the `DockStyle` enumeration. The default value is `None`, which disables docking, but if any of the `Top`, `Bottom`, `Left`, or `Right` values is used, the control will attach itself to the relevant edge of the window, much like a docking toolbar. Setting it to `Fill` causes the control to fill the containing window completely. The effect of each option is illustrated in Figure 2-2. With docking enabled, the control's `Location` property does not need to be set, because it will always be at the edge of the window, wherever that may be.

Form
Docked Left
Form
Docked Right
Form
Docked Top
Form
Docked Bottom
Form
Not Docked
(None)
Form
Docked Fill

Figure 2-2. DockStyles in action

For the `Left` and `Right` docking styles, the `Height` property is managed automatically (it will be the same as the containing window). Likewise for the `Top` and `Bottom` docking styles, the `Width` property is determined by the containing window. If `Fill` is specified, the `Width` and the `Height` properties are both set by the containing window, so none of the position or size properties need to be set.

(This is the only layout mode for which all aspects of the control's size and position are managed automatically.)

Docking is not the only way of automatically arranging the contents of a window. A control may instead use its `Anchor` property to cause its size, position, or both to be updated when its containing window is resized. (Note that the `Anchor` property is used only if the `Dock` property is set to `None`.) This property is set with any combination of the flags in the `AnchorStyles` enumeration, which are `Top`, `Bottom`, `Left`, and `Right`. When the containing window is resized, the edges of the control specified in the `Anchor` property are kept a constant distance from the same edge of the window. The default is `Top, Left`, which means controls stay put as the window is resized, but changing its value to `Top, Right` causes the control to move with the righthand side of the window during resizing. If `Top, Left, Right` were specified, both the left and right edges of the control would follow the window edges, causing the control to be resized with the window. `AnchorStyles` also defines a `None` value to indicate none of the above. In this case, the control remains the same size, but as its container is resized, the control moves half of the distance that it is resized by. This allows controls to remain centered as the container resizes.

Anchoring makes it very easy to produce dialogs that can be usefully resized. (This was very tedious with classic Windows programming—its dialog handling was not designed to perform dynamic layout.) Dialogs that have some central feature containing potentially large amounts of information (like the file list in the standard Open and Save File dialogs) can make this item resize as the window is resized, while any controls around the edge of the feature simply move with the window edges to accommodate it. This style of resizing can improve the usability of certain kinds of dialog considerably. It is easy to achieve with the `Anchor` property.

Note that anchoring doesn't manage our position and size for us completely. We must still specify the initial position and size of each control; it will simply move and resize them for us thereafter.

Appearance

Having gotten our control where we want it, next we want to make sure it looks how it should. We can determine the color of our UI elements. We can set the text and fonts they use. Some controls can have an image associated with them, and all controls can modify the appearance of the mouse pointer while it is over them.

Color

Color is managed by the `ForeColor` and `BackColor` properties. These are both of type `Color`, a value type defined in the `System.Drawing` namespace that allows the color to be specified in various ways. You can use known system colors, e.g., `System.Drawing.SystemColors.ActiveCaption`; if the user has customized her system colors, these color values will reflect those customizations. Alternatively you can specify standard web colors such as `Color.LemonChiffon` or `Color.GoldenRod`. Or you can just define custom colors from their RGB values, e.g., `Color.FromArgb(255, 192, 192)`. (The "A" stands for Alpha—a color's alpha value specifies transparency, but most controls don't honor transparent colors properly, so here we just use the default, i.e., a non-transparent color.)

Text

The `Control` class defines two properties relating to text: `Text` and `Font`. The `Text` property is a string containing basic text associated with a control. Most controls have a sensible use for this property (e.g., the contents of an edit box, the text in a label, or the caption on a button), but because not all controls display text, the property is simply ignored where it is not appropriate.

The text's font is controlled by the `Font` property, which is a `System.Drawing.Font` object. The `Font` class has properties that allow all the normal font characteristics to be set, e.g., the typeface name (`Name`), emphasis (`Bold`, `Italic`, and `Underline`), and size (`Size` or `SizeInPoints`; both of these properties represent the size, but they do so in different units. `Size` is in *design units*, the units in which control positions and dimensions are specified. `SizeInPoints` is in points, a unit of measurement commonly used for defining font sizes.)

> Setting the window's `Font` property is the easiest way to use the same font for all the controls in a given window—all the controls will automatically pick this font up unless their `Font` is explicitly set to something different.

Note that all the properties of a font object are read-only. This means that you cannot change a control's font to be bold in the obvious way. For example, the statement:

```
ctl.Font.Bold = true;
```

will not compile. If you want to change the font, you must create a new font object, even if you want it to be almost identical to the existing font. (While inconvenient, this does reflect the underlying reality that changing to a different font is a fairly expensive operation, even if the new font is similar to the original.) If you are only changing one or more of the emphasis properties, there is a `Font` constructor that takes a prototype font and a `FontStyle` value. The `FontStyle` enumeration lets you specify any combination of `Bold`, `Italic`, `Strikeout`, and `Underline`, or just `Regular` if you want none of these. If you want to change anything else, you must use the more long-winded approach of reading all the existing font's properties, and then using these (modified appropriately) to create a new font.

Images

The `BackgroundImage` property allows an object of type `Image` (a bitmap or a metafile) to be set as the background of a control. If the image is too small to fill the control, it will be tiled to fill the space available. The `Control` class does not provide a property for a foreground image. However, there are several controls that support foreground images (`Button`, `CheckBox`, `RadioButton`, `Label`, and `PictureBox`), and these all allow the foreground image to be set with a property called `Image`, also of type `Image`.

Several bitmap formats are supported. As well as standard Windows BMP and ICO files, the GIF, TIFF, JPEG, and PNG formats are also supported. Even animated bitmaps (for the formats that support animation) can be used.

Mouse cursors

If the Cursor property is set, it causes the mouse cursor's appearance to change while it is over the control. The property is of type System.Windows.Forms.Cursor, and the easiest way to obtain an instance of this class is to choose one of the standard cursor types defined by the Cursors class. The Cursors class exposes all the standard cursor types, e.g., Cursors.WaitCursor or Cursors.AppStarting.

You can also define a custom cursor. The Cursor class provides various constructors, one of which just takes the name of a CUR file. However, you will usually want to compile a cursor resource into the executable and use that rather than shipping separate cursor files with your program. The following C# code will obtain a cursor from a resource compiled into the executable:

```
myCtl.Cursor = new Cursor(typeof(MyForm), "MyCursor.cur");
```

or in VB:

```
myCtl.Cursor = New Cursor(GetType(MyForm), "MyCursor.cur")
```

The first parameter must be a Type object for a type defined in the assembly that contains the cursor resource. In this case, we are using a type called MyForm, but it doesn't matter which class is used so long as it is in the same assembly as the resource. (It is just used by Cursor to determine which file the resource is stored in.) The second parameter must match the name of the cursor file that is being compiled into the component. If you are using Visual Studio .NET, a cursor file can be built into the assembly as a resource by adding it as an item to the project, and then setting that item's Build Type to Embedded Resource on the Properties tab. If you are not using Visual Studio. NET, you can simply tell the C# or VB compiler to embed the file as a resource by adding a /res:MyCursor.cur command-line switch.

Handling Input

We have seen how to arrange our components on the screen as we see fit, and to make their appearance meet our needs. But this would be a pointless exercise if our programs were unable to respond to the user, so next we will examine the three sources of user input: mouse input, keyboard input, and interaction through accessibility aids. We will also look at Windows Forms' validation features, which provide a way of checking that the input supplied by the user actually makes sense to the application.

Mouse Input

Mouse input is dealt with at two different levels: we can either be notified of the low-level events such as movement and button state changes, or we can be notified of higher-level concepts such as a click. (There is also special support for drag and drop, but we will deal with this later.)

Two of the high-level mouse events are Click and DoubleClick. These are simple events that pass no special information, so they use the standard EventHandler delegate type in C#. As with all events raised by the Control class, the first parameter is the control object that raised the event, and for these particular events, the second parameter is always EventArgs.Empty (i.e., it is in effect unused). Handling these events is therefore straightforward. Example 2-1 shows the kind of C# code that the Visual Studio .NET Forms designer would generate to handle a Click event, while Example 2-2 shows the VB code generated by the Visual Studio .NET Forms designer.

Example 2-1. Handling the Click event in C#

```
private System.Windows.Forms.Button myButton;
...
private void InitializeComponent( )
{
   ... myButton created and initialized in usual fashion ...

   // Attach Click handler
   myButton.Click += new EventHandler(myButton_Click);

   ... further initialization as usual ...
}

private void myButton_Click(object sender, System.EventArgs e)
{
   System.Windows.Forms.MessageBox.Show(
        "Please do not click this button again");
}
```

Example 2-2. Handling the Click event in VB

```
Friend WithEvents myButton As System.Windows.Forms.Button

Private Sub InitializeComponent( )
   Me.myButton = New System.Windows.Forms.Button( )
'   ...further initialization as usual ...

End Sub

Private Sub myButton_Click(ByVal sender As Object, _
      ByVal e As System.EventArgs) Handles myButton.Click
   MsgBox("Please do not click this button again.")
End Sub
```

The DoubleClick event works in exactly the same way. Note that there is no significance to the name of the handler function in either C# or VB. There is a convention (used by the Forms Designer in Visual Studio .NET) that these names are of the form *controlName_EventName*, but this is not a requirement—the function name can be anything, it merely has to have the correct signature. The control simply calls whichever function we choose to initialize the delegate with in C#, or whatever method with the correct signature that has been designated as an event handler using the Handles keyword.

The other high-level mouse events are MouseEnter, MouseLeave, and MouseHover. The first two are raised when the mouse pointer enters or leaves the area of the screen occupied by the control, and the last is raised if the pointer remains stationary over the control for more than about half a second. Note that between every MouseEnter/MouseLeave pair, you will never get more than one MouseHover event. Even if the mouse enters the control, hovers for a bit, moves a bit, and hovers again for a bit, the control remembers that it has already given you the hover event and won't give you a second one. As with the `Click` event, these all use the standard simple `EventHandler`, and supply no information other than the reference to the control raising the event (the *sender* parameter).

Sometimes you will need to monitor mouse activity in more detail than this, so the `Control` class also provides a set of more low-level events. The `MouseMove` event is raised whenever the cursor is over the control and is moving. Button presses are handled by the `MouseDown` and `MouseUp` events, mouse movement is reported through the `MouseMove` event, and wheel rotation is indicated with the `MouseWheel` event. These events all share a special event handler type called `MouseEventHandler`, which is similar to the standard `EventHandler`, except the final parameter is a `MouseEventArgs`.

The `MouseEventArgs` class provides properties that describe what the user just did with the mouse. These properties are predictable, if a little inconsistent. For example, there is a `Button` property that indicates which button's state just changed for the `MouseDown` and `MouseUp` events, but for the `MouseMove` event, it indicates what combination of buttons is currently pressed, while for the `MouseWheel` event it is always `MouseButtons.None`, regardless of what buttons may be pressed at the time. There is a `Clicks` property, which is either 1 or 2 to indicate a single- or double-click in the `MouseDown` event, and is otherwise always 0. The `X` and `Y` properties are always used to indicate the current position of the mouse, relative to the top-left corner of the control.

There is also a property that is used only during the `MouseWheel` event. The `Delta` property indicates in which direction and how far the wheel was moved. At the time this book went to press, its value was always either 120 or -120, but it is possible that future wheel devices will provide more detailed input, so the values could be smaller. You should bear this in mind if you handle these events, or else your application will not behave correctly with such an input device. One strategy is to scale the effect of your response—so if you are scrolling a window, smaller `Delta` values should scroll the window less far. An alternative approach is to keep a cumulative total and only respond to these events once the total is larger than 120. Note that most of the built-in controls deal with this event for you, including any forms with the `AutoScroll` property enabled, so you only need to handle it if you need to do something unusual with the mouse wheel.

> Microsoft is not entirely consistent here. Almost all the documentation recommends these techniques, apart from one of the help pages, which suggests that you just look at `Delta`'s sign and ignore its magnitude. However, that is at odds with the Windows documentation, so your application's behavior would be out of step with non-.NET applications. It also contradicts the other .NET documentation, so this suggested simple handling is presumably an error and should be ignored.

Note that the `MouseWheel` event is delivered to whichever control has the focus, even if the mouse is not over the control, whereas the other events are only delivered either when the pointer is over the control or was dragged out of the control.

If a button is pressed while the cursor is over the control, the cursor is automatically captured until the button is released. This means that MouseMove events will be delivered while the button is held down even if the cursor leaves the control. It also guarantees that for every MouseDown event, a matching MouseUp event will be received, even if the mouse is moved away from the control before the button is released. (If you were used to working in the Win32 world, where this had to be done by hand, you are entitled to give a small cheer at this stage.)

The .NET platform also makes certain guarantees about the order in which mouse events occur. Figure 2-3 shows the states that a control can be in with respect to mouse input, and which events it can raise in any given state.

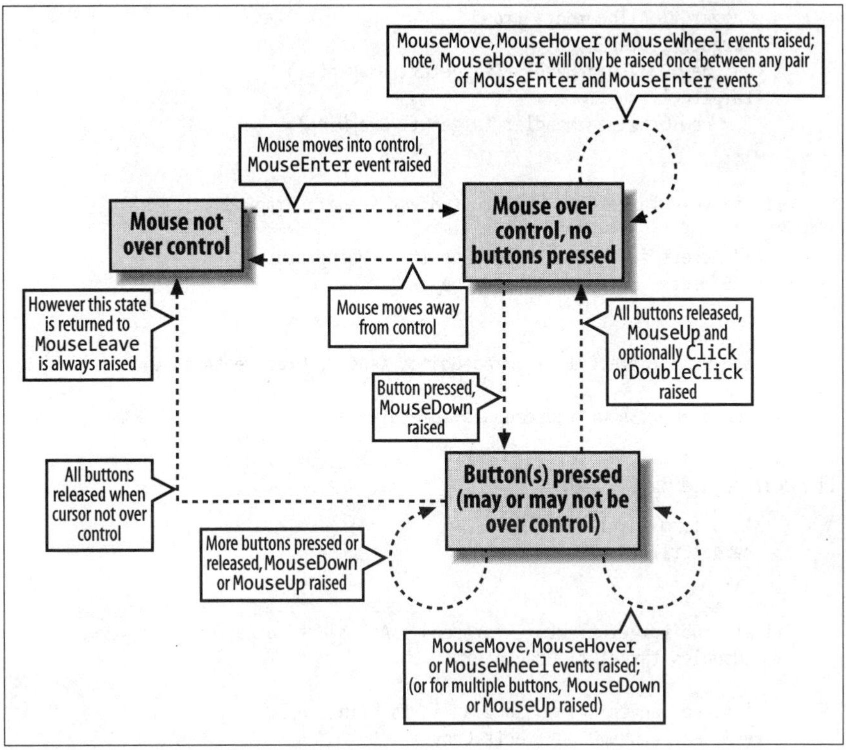
MouseMove, MouseHover or MouseWheel events raised; note, MouseHover will only be raised once between any pair of MouseEnter and MouseEnter events
Mouse moves into control, MouseEnter event raised
Mouse not over control
Mouse over control, no buttons pressed
However this state is returned to MouseLeave is always raised
Mouse moves away from control
All buttons released, MouseUp and optionally Click or DoubleClick raised
Button pressed, MouseDown raised
All buttons released when cursor not over control
Button(s) pressed (may or may not be over control)
More buttons pressed or released, MouseDown or MouseUp raised
MouseMove, MouseHover or MouseWheel events raised; (or for multiple buttons, MouseDown or MouseUp raised)

Figure 2-3. Mouse events state diagram

Drag and drop

The Control class supports participating in Windows drag-and-drop operations, both as a source and as a target.

To act as a drop target, a control's AllowDrop property must be set to true. By default, this property is false, so if the user attempts to drag an item onto the control, the "no entry" cursor will be displayed, and no drag-and-drop events will be raised. But if this flag is set, the control will raise certain events whenever an item is dragged over it. The handlers for these events can then decide whether the mouse cursor should indicate that the control is a valid drop target.

When the mouse first moves over the control during a drag operation (e.g., if a file is dragged from a Windows Explorer window), the control will raise the DragEnter event. This event, whose type is DragEventHandler, supplies a DragEventArgs object, which can be used to examine the item being dragged, and to determine whether the control would accept it if it were dropped. This is achieved by setting the Effect property on the DragEventArgs, which determines the kinds of drop the control is prepared to accept, (e.g., Copy, Link, or Move). By default, the Effect property is set to DragDropEffects.None, so unless your DragEnter handler changes it, the control will not behave as a potential drop target even if AllowDrop is true. The following C# code sets up a control to accept a copy of any kind of object:

```
    // In form initialization...
    targetCtl.AllowDrop = true;
    targetCtl.DragEnter +=
        new DragEventHandler(targetCtl_DragEnter);
    targetCtl.DragDrop +=
        new DragEventHandler(targetCtl_DragDrop);
    ...

private void targetCtl_DragEnter(object sender, DragEventArgs e)
{
    // Accept anything, so long as it is being copied
    e.Effect = DragDropEffects.Copy;
}

private void targetCtl_DragDrop(object sender, DragEventArgs e)
{
    MessageBox.Show("You dropped something");
}
```

The corresponding VB code is:

```
    ' In form initialization...
    targetCtl.AllowDrop = True
    ...

Private Sub targetCtl_DragEnter(sender As Object, e As DragEventArgs) _
     Handles targetCtl.DragEnter

    ' Accept anything, so long as it is being copied
    e.Effect = DragDropEffects.Copy
End Sub

Private Sub targetCtl_DragDrop(sender As Object, e As DragEventArgs) _
     Handles targetCtl.DragDrop

    MsgBox("You dropped something")
End Sub
```

The DragEnter event handler has indicated that it is happy to be the target for a copy operation. This means that if the user drops an object on the control, the control will raise its DragDrop event. This event will only ever be raised if the control has explicitly changed the DragEventArgs.Effect property to something other than None during either the DragEnter or the DragMove event. And these events will only be raised if the AllowDrop property is true.

Most applications are slightly pickier about what they accept than this code, because they want to know if they can actually do anything with the object before deciding to receive it. You can find out about the nature of the object being dragged from the `DragEventArgs.Data` property. This property is an `IDataObject` interface that allows us to find out which formats the object can present itself in. Most drag-and-drop objects are able to present themselves in several different ways—for example, selected text dragged from an Internet Explorer window can be accessed through `IDataObject` as (among other things) plain text, RTF, and HTML. The following variation on the previous C# code makes the control receptive only to drop objects in one of these three formats. If a suitable object is dropped, it will be displayed in whichever of these three formats the object supports:


```
private void targetCtl_DragEnter(object sender, DragEventArgs e)
{
    // Only accept the object if we can access it
    // in a format we understand
    if (e.Data.GetDataPresent(DataFormats.Text) ||
        e.Data.GetDataPresent(DataFormats.Rtf) ||
        e.Data.GetDataPresent(DataFormats.Html))
    {
        e.Effect = DragDropEffects.Copy;
    }
}

private void targetCtl_DragDrop(object sender, DragEventArgs e)
{
    if (e.Data.GetDataPresent(DataFormats.Text))
    {
        string text = (string) e.Data.GetData(DataFormats.Text);
        MessageBox.Show(text, "As Text");
    }
    if (e.Data.GetDataPresent(DataFormats.Rtf))
    {
        string text = (string) e.Data.GetData(DataFormats.Rtf);
        MessageBox.Show(text, "As RTF");
    }
    if (e.Data.GetDataPresent(DataFormats.Html))
    {
        string text = (string) e.Data.GetData(DataFormats.Html);
        MessageBox.Show(text, "As HTML");
    }
}
```

The corresponding VB code is:

```
Private Sub targetCtl_DragEnter(sender As Object, e As DragEventArgs) _
    Handles targetCtl.DragEnter

    ' Only accept the object if we can access it
    ' in a format we understand
    If e.Data.GetDataPresent(DataFormats.Text) Or _
       e.Data.GetDataPresent(DataFormats.Rtf) Or _
       e.Data.GetDataPresent(DataFormats.Html) Then
        e.Effect = DragDropEffects.Copy
```

```
        End If
    End Sub

    Private Sub targetCtl_DragDrop(sender As Object, e As DragEventArgs) _
         Handles targetCtl.DragDrop
        If e.Data.GetDataPresent(DataFormats.Text) Then
            Dim text As String = CStr(e.Data.GetData(DataFormats.Text))
            MessageBox.Show(text, "As Text")
        End If
        If e.Data.GetDataPresent(DataFormats.Rtf) Then
            Dim text As String = CStr(e.Data.GetData(DataFormats.Rtf))
            MessageBox.Show(text, "As RTF")
        End If
        If e.Data.GetDataPresent(DataFormats.Html) Then
            Dim text As String = CStr(e.Data.GetData(DataFormats.Html))
            MessageBox.Show(text, "As HTML")
        End If
    End Sub
```

If you add these event handlers to a control in a project of your own, you will find that if you attempt to drag a file onto the control from Windows Explorer, the control will refuse to accept it. This is because Windows Explorer does not present its files in any of the three formats this code happens to accept. But if you drag in selected text from IE or Word, it will appear in all three formats, while text dragged from Visual Studio .NET will appear as just plain text and RTF.

This code illustrates the use of standard formats defined in the `DataFormats` type. This type contains static fields for each of the predefined formats recognized by the framework. These fields are strings containing the names of the formats; e.g., `DataFormats.Html` is simply the string constant "HTML Format". But you can pass other strings to `IDataObject.GetDataPresent`; a nonstandard string will be interpreted as the name of a custom format. This nonstandard string might be a custom format defined by some other application you wish to interact with. Or it could be your own custom format that you have designed to associate the information you choose with your data. Custom formats local to your application can be useful if you are acting as both a source and a target, because they let you associate any data you want with a drag-and-drop operation. (See below for using the `DoDragDrop` method to initiate a drag-and-drop operation).

Sometimes you may want to change whether your target accepts a particular object continuously as the mouse moves, rather than just when it first moves over your control. For example, you might want only certain areas of the control to be a target. (This is particularly common for user-drawn controls.) If this is the case, the `DragOver` event is useful, because it is raised repeatedly while the cursor is dragging an object over your control. You can modify the `Effect` property each time this event is raised to indicate whether your object will accept a drop right now. The `DragEventArgs` object provides `X` and `Y` properties to indicate the position of the mouse, and a `KeyState` property indicating the current state of modifier keys (Shift, Ctrl, and Alt), which may be useful in determining whether the control should accept an object at any particular instant.

Sometimes it is useful to know when a control has stopped being considered a potential drop target—maybe the user cancelled the drag by hitting Escape, or has simply moved the mouse cursor away from the control. This is useful if your control changes its appearance while it is a potential drop target (e.g., Windows Explorer highlights EXE files when you drag other files over them). You'd want such a control to set its appearance back to normal when it ceases to be a target. The Control class provides a DragLeave event that is raised when this happens. This event uses the standard simple EventHandler delegate type, rather than the DragEventHandler used by all the other drag-and-drop events. This is because the event is raised to inform you that you are no longer involved in this drag-and-drop operation, so providing you with a DragEventArgs object would be pointless.

The Control class also provides the DoDragDrop method, which allows a control to act as the source of a drag-and-drop operation. The simplest way to use this method is to pass the information to be dragged either as a String, a Bitmap, or a Metafile (these are all classes provided by the .NET Framework), along with a set of DragDropEffect flags indicating what kinds of drag operations are permitted. (The flags passed here will be reflected in the DragEventArgs.Effects property seen by drop targets.) The following C# code (the VB code would be almost identical, except for slight syntactic differences) will allow a string to be dragged into any application that allows text to be dropped into it (e.g., Microsoft Word):

```
// MouseDown event handler for some control
private control_MouseDown(object sender, MouseEventArgs e)
{
    control.DoDragDrop("Hello, world!", DragDropEffects.Copy);
}
```

When you use String, Bitmap, or Metafile objects like this in a drag-and-drop operation, the framework automatically presents them using the appropriate data formats (such as DataFormats.Text and DataFormats.UnicodeText for String, or DataFormats.MetafilePict and DataFormats.EnhancedMetafile for Metafile). This is convenient, but not very flexible. A more powerful approach is to use the DataObject class, which lets you start drag-and-drop operations with objects that can present themselves in as many different data formats as you like, including custom formats. It is used as follows:

```
DataObject obj = new DataObject( );
MyType t = new MyType("Hello!");
obj.SetData("My custom format", t);
obj.SetData("Hello!");
obj.SetData(bmpMyBitmap);
myControl.DoDragDrop(obj, DragDropEffects.Copy);
```

The corresponding VB code is:

```
Dim obj As New DataObject( )
Dim t As New MyType("Hello!")
obj.SetData("My custom format", t)
obj.SetData("Hello!")
obj.SetData(bmpMyBitmap)
myControl.DoDragDrop(obj, DragDropEffects.Copy)
```

Any number of data formats, standard or custom, can be attached to a single DataObject. Here, we are passing some data in a custom format—an instance of some class MyType—as well as providing some standard formats by passing a String and a Bitmap.

The control on which DoDragDrop was called can raise events to notify us of the progress of the drag operation. The GiveFeedback event is raised repeatedly during the operation, and it uses the GiveFeedbackEventHandler delegate type. The GiveFeedbackEventHandler delegate passes a GiveFeedbackEventArgs object, which allows the Effect property to be changed (e.g., this might change between DragDropEvent.Copy and DragDropEvent.Move according to which modifier keys are pressed). It also allows the mouse cursors to be changed. By default, the standard system drag-and-drop cursors are used, but setting the GiveFeedbackEventArgs.UseDefaultCursors property to false disables this, allowing the source control to set the cursor itself. It can do this by modifying the Cursor.Current static property.

The source control also repeatedly raises the QueryContinueDrag event to allow the operation to be cancelled if necessary. The QueryContinueDrag event uses the QueryContinueDragEventHandler delegate, which supplies a QueryContinueDragEventArgs object. QueryContinueDragEventArgs allows the drag to be cancelled or completed by setting its Action property to either DragAction.Cancel, or DragAction.Drop. For convenience, it also provides the current state of the modifier keys through its KeyState property, and an EscapePressed flag indicating whether the user has attempted to cancel the drag by pressing escape.

Keyboard input

Of course, not all input comes from the mouse. As you would expect, Windows Forms also provides extensive support for handling keyboard input.

There are three events associated with keyboard input. Two of these, KeyDown and KeyUp, provide information for each individual key that is pressed. The third, KeyPress, deals with character-level input from the keyboard. For example, if the user holds down the Shift key and presses the A key, there will be a KeyDown and a KeyUp event for each key. But because this combination of keys corresponds to only a single character, a capital A, there will be just one KeyPress event. If the user presses and releases only the Shift key, there will be no KeyPress event at all, just a KeyDown and a KeyUp.

Keyboard autorepeat is reflected through these messages. Each time a character is repeated, an extra KeyDown and (unless the current keys held down don't generate characters, e.g., just the Shift key is pressed) an extra KeyPress are raised. However, a KeyUp event is raised only when the key really is released.

The KeyUp and KeyDown events both use the KeyEventHandler delegate. As always, the first parameter of the event handler function is the control raising the event, but the second parameter is a KeyEventArgs object. The KeyEventArgs class describes the key being pressed, using an entry from the Keys enumeration, which defines a value for every key on the keyboard. KeyEventArgs presents this information in a variety of ways: the KeyCode property is the Keys value for the key being pressed, and the KeyData property is the same value but with any modifier keys added. (So for Shift-A, for example, KeyCode would be Keys.A, but KeyData would be Keys.A|Keys.Shift or Keys.A Or Keys.Shift). The modifier keys themselves are presented individually through the Alt, Control, and Shift properties, or combined through the Modifiers property. For example, consider the following C# code:

```
// for debug output
using System.Diagnostics;
...
private void InitializeComponent( )
{
    ...
    myControl.KeyDown += new KeyEventHandler
                                (myControl_OnKeyDown);
...
}
...
private void myControl_OnKeyDown(object sender, KeyEventArgs e)
{
    string dbg = string.Format("KeyCode: {0}, KeyData {1}",
                                e.KeyCode, e.KeyData);
    Debug.WriteLine(dbg);
}
```

or the following VB code:

```
' for debug output
Imports System.Diagnostics
...
Private Sub myControl_OnKeyDown(sender As Object, e As KeyEventArgs) _
     Handles myControl.KeyDown

    Dim dbg As String = String.Format("KeyCode: {0}, KeyData {1}", _
                                e.KeyCode, e.KeyData)
    Debug.WriteLine(dbg)
End Sub
```

As an aside, this code illustrates a couple of interesting features of the .NET Framework Class Library. The Debug class, which is defined in the System.Diagnostics namespace, lets us send output to the debugger. In Visual Studio .NET, anything we print with Debug.WriteLine will appear in the Output window. (And in non-debug builds, the compiler is smart enough to omit these calls.) To build the debug output string we are using the System.String (in C# this corresponds to the string and in VB to the String data types) class's Format method to build a string in a style similar to the C printf function. The numbers in braces refer to parameters following the string. Because all data in the CLR has type information associated with it, the Format method can discover that it has been passed parameters whose types are both of type Keys. So rather than displaying numbers, the debug output will actually show the enumeration members by name. For example, for a Shift-A key press, we would see the following debug output:

```
KeyCode: ShiftKey. KeyData: ShiftKey, Shift
KeyCode: A. KeyData: A, Shift
```

The first line is for the Shift key. Notice that the KeyCode property just contains the key that was pressed. The KeyData property is a little surprising. As mentioned above, it contains both the key code and any modifier keys. The surprising thing is that there are two values in the Keys enumeration to represent the Shift key—one as a modifier (Keys.Shift) and one as a key press (Keys.ShiftKey). The second line is for the second event, raised when the A key is pressed. Again, the KeyCode property describes the single key for which this event was raised, but the KeyData member shows it in conjunction with the modifiers.

The KeyPress event's type is KeyPressHandler, which supplies a KeyPressEventArgs object. This supplies a KeyChar property (of type char), which is the character value of the key press.

Both KeyPressArgs and KeyPressEventArgs have a bool or Boolean member called Handled. Setting this to true when handling the KeyPress event prevents the default handling of the key press; e.g., this blocks input to a text box. It appears to have no effect for the KeyDown or KeyUp events.

It is possible to read the state of the Shift, Ctrl, and Alt keys without handling these messages. This is particularly useful for handling certain mouse events, because their behavior is often changed by the use of these modifier keys. For example, when selecting items from a list, any previous selection is usually cleared each time the user clicks, unless he is holding down the Shift key. The Control class provides a static property called ModifierKeys that allows the current state of these keys to be read at any time. (It returns a value of type Keys, but this only contains some combination of Keys.Shift, Keys.Control, and Keys.Alt.) This means it is not necessary to handle keyboard events just to read the state of the modifier keys.

Accessibility

Windows has a technology called Active Accessibility that supports accessibility aids (programs designed to enable people with disabilities to use computers more effectively). It provides programs such as screen readers and speech interpreters with a programming interface that lets them find and interact with user interface elements. All the standard Windows controls provide accessibility information automatically, as do their .NET counterparts, so if a user interface consists entirely of standard controls, these will already expose information to accessibility aids, such as their screen location and any text they contain, as well as provide programmatic ways to perform the operations they support (e.g., clicking on a button).

For some applications, this built-in accessibility is not sufficient—accessibility aids cannot automatically pick up certain visual cues such as the juxtaposition of controls or the contents of bitmaps. Such user interfaces may need to be annotated with extra textual hints if they are to be usable through accessibility aids, so the Control class has features that enable the standard basic support to be extended. This is important for nonstandard user interface elements such as custom controls. It may also be necessary to extend the basic support to make complex forms usable, even if all the individual controls on those forms are standard.

The name and role can be specified by setting the control's AccessibleName and AccessibleRole properties. AccessibleName is just a string, whereas the AccessibleRole property uses an enumeration type, also called AccessibleRole, that defines values for all the standard roles listed by the Active Accessibility API. Sometimes the name and role are not sufficient to describe the purpose of a control (e.g., there is a further visual cue, such as a bitmap that would normally be used to infer the button's purpose, or its position relative to other controls). Consider a simple application whose user interface is show in Figure 2-4. This program is an example of a Chi Squared test being used in some hypothetical study to determine whether there is any correlation between where programmers place the { character in their source code and whether they use spaces or tabs for indentation. (The Chi Squared test is a very common kind of statistical tool—it determines the likelihood that two properties are connected. A discussion of the details is beyond the scope of this book, but suffice it to say that you simply plug in figures for how your sample population breaks down, and it returns the probability that such figures could have emerged by chance without there being some underlying connection.)

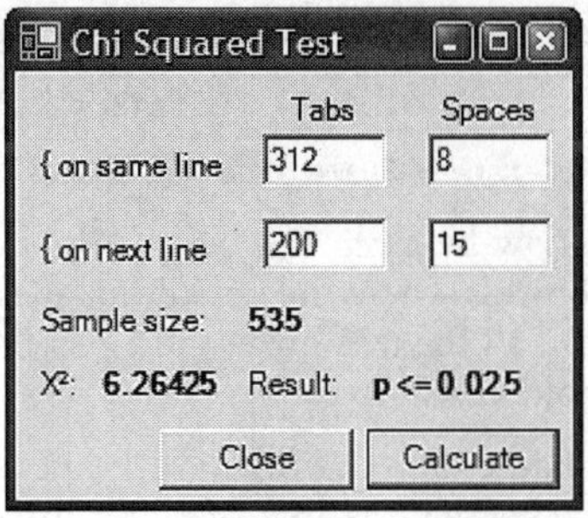
Chi Squared Test
Tabs
Spaces
{ on same line
312
8
{ on next line
200
15
Sample size:
535
X²:
6.26425
Result:
p<=0.025
Close
Calculate

Figure 2-4. Application with potential accessibility problems

Anyone who is familiar with simple Chi Squared tests will instantly recognize the layout and know what information is expected. And it will not take long for someone unfamiliar with them to realize that the first text box should contain the number of people surveyed who put their { on the same line as their function declarations and also use tabs to indent code, while the next box should contain the number of people who put the { on the same line as the declaration, but who use spaces to indent their code, and so on.

The problem with this example is it relies on the user being able to see the layout in order to work out what each textbox is for. This is unfortunate because it is difficult for accessibility aids to deduce the role of a text box from its position, so it might be hard for a visually impaired user to use this program. Fortunately, we can control the information available to an accessibility aid, so we can adapt this program to be useful without relying on the information implicit in the visual layout of the form.

To understand how we can make such programs accessible, it is important to understand exactly what information is available to accessibility aids. Controls present certain properties to accessibility clients. (*Accessibility clients* are any programs that read accessibility information. This includes all accessibility aids, the accessibility explorer supplied in the Accessibility SDK, and may even include automated test software.) The most important of these are the name, role, and optional values, because they supply the same information that visual cues provide. For example, the two buttons on the form in Figure 2-4 would have the names `Close` and `Calculate`, respectively, and both would have the role `AccessibleRole.PushButton`. (Buttons don't have values.)

For a text box control, the role is `AccessibleRole.Text` and the value is simply the text in the field, but it is less obvious where its name comes from. By default, a text box takes its name from the nearest label control in the tab order. For many applications, this is perfect: a text box usually has a label indicating its purpose, and it is usually just before it in the tab order to make sure that any accelerator key assigned to the label ends up moving the focus to the text box. But for this application, this default behavior is not good enough. Multiple text boxes end up picking up the same name (for instance, there are two named "{ on next line"), and in any case, these names are not particularly informative. So this application should name these controls explicitly. This can be done by setting the `AccessibleName` property; doing so in the designer adds the following code in C#:

```
this.textBoxAY.AccessibleName = "Same line and Spaces";
```

or this code in VB:

```
Me.textBoxAY.AccessibleName = "Same line and Spaces"
```

Accessibility clients will now be given this text as the name of the control. This should be done for all controls where the default name is not appropriate. In this example, that would mean all the text boxes, and also the label controls showing the output (the ones in bold in Figure 2-4).

In addition to having a name, all controls have a role, which can be set by the `AccessibleRole` property. Its value is one of those listed in the `AccessibleRole` enumeration type, which defines values for all the standard roles listed by the Active Accessibility API. For the standard controls, the default value of the role is usually appropriate, but sometimes it might need to be modified—for example, a button might bring up a menu when clicked, so its role should be `AccessibleRole.ButtonMenu`, not the default `AccessibleRole.PushButton`.

Sometimes the name and role are not sufficient to describe the purpose of a control. In this case, the control can also supply a textual description, which is set by the `AccessibleDescription` property. You would normally try to keep the control's name short because it would typically be read out by default by a screen reader. So the description is the appropriate place for a more verbose description.

Controls also indicate their default action, i.e., what would happen if the control were to be clicked right now. For example, the standard checkbox control sets this property according to its current state: if it is unchecked, a click on the control checks the box, so its default action is `Check`, whereas if it is currently checked, its default action is `Uncheck`. Buttons set this value to `Press`, and some controls (e.g., text boxes) have no default action. You can supply your own string by setting the `AccessibleDefaultActionDescription` property.

To control any of the other accessibility features (e.g., the value property or the screen area the control claims to occupy) there is a more powerful but slightly more cumbersome mechanism. Each control has an `AccessibleObject` property, providing access to an object of type `AccessibleObject`. This object is the liaison between the control and the Active Accessibility API—it is through this object that all accessibility properties are presented. You will not normally use `AccessibleObject` on a standard control, but for custom controls it may be necessary, particularly if it can supply meaningful values for the `Value` property. (`Value` is a text string representing the control's value; for a text box this property is the text in the control, for example.)

It is even possible to supply your own AccessibleObject. The object is created on demand, using the control's CreateAccessibilityInstance method; custom controls can override this and supply their own objects, which must derive from AccessibleObject. For example, if you wish to perform your own hit testing for accessibility, you must supply your own AccessibleObject. It is also necessary to do this if you wish to supply your own setting for the State property. (State contains some combination of the flags in the AccessibleStates enumeration, which defines values such as Checked and Pressed. It is a read-only property, so you must provide your own AccessibleObject implementation to modify it.)

The Control class also supports a property called IsAccessible. According to the documentation, if this is false, the control will not be visible to accessibility clients. However, this property is ignored. It is a relic from an older version of the Windows Forms framework that, for some reason, was not removed before the first public release. All controls are visible to accessibility clients, regardless of their IsAccessible setting.

As well as allowing accessibility clients to navigate through the controls in a window, the Active Accessibility API also provides a notification framework, so that accessibility clients can know when certain events happen, such as when the focus changes, or when the appearance of a control changes. Again, most of the work here is done automatically—all the built-in control types raise the appropriate events on your behalf. However, you can raise these events manually, by calling the protected AccessibleNotifyClients method on the Control class. This requires you to derive from Control, but because you would normally only need to raise accessibility events manually from a custom control, this is not normally a problem. Alternatively, you can retrieve the control's AccessibleObject and cast it to Control.ControlAccessibleObject—the accessibility object is of this type unless you supply your own. This provides a NotifyClients method that does the same thing as AccessibleNotifyClients.

Validation

We have now seen the various ways of getting input from the user. But the Windows Forms framework can go further than this—it can help us verify that the input we are given is correct, and if it is not, to alert the user.

It is common for an application to want to apply constraints to fields on a form. This might be as simple as requiring that a particular field is not blank, or it might be a little more sophisticated, such as checking that a field's contents match some pattern, or do not exceed certain limits. Windows Forms has support for such validation, and it also supplies a mechanism for providing visual notification of errors.

These two mechanisms can be used independently of each other. This is useful because the validation architecture can be a little too simple for some applications. In particular, once an error has been detected, it can impose unreasonable restrictions on what the user can do until the problem is fixed. (It effectively enforces modal behavior for offending data—you must fix the input before you are allowed to do anything else.) The error-reporting mechanism is rather more flexible than this.

There are two events directly connected with validation. The Validating event is raised when a control is asked to validate its contents, and the Validated event is raised after its contents have been successfully validated. If the contents are not acceptable, the handler for the Validating event can indicate this, causing the validation process to fail. The handler is of type CancelEventHandler, and this passes a CancelEventArgs object. Setting the Cancel flag to true on this object causes the validation process to fail, and the Validated event will not be raised. Note that the control may have its own internal rules for validation, which apply in addition to any rules you write in your Validating event handler. So even if you don't cause the Validation event to fail, the Validated event might not be raised.

So what causes a control to be validated in the first place? Validation is always managed by the ContainerControl in which the control lives, which is typically (but not always) the Form. We can ask a container to validate the control with the input focus by calling its Validate method. However, this is usually done automatically as a result of a focus change event—whenever a new control is given the focus, its parent container checks to see if its CausesValidation property is true (which is the default). If this property is true, the container automatically checks to see if there is some other control on the form that requires validation and, if so, validates it. (This only ever validates a single control; nothing will ever cause all the fields to be validated at once.).

In fact, the CausesValidation property performs two functions. Not only is it used when a control acquires the focus to decide whether validation needs to occur, it is also used to determine whether the control that just lost the focus should be validated. The Validating and Validated events are raised only on controls whose CausesValidation property is true, *and* when the focus moves to a control that also has its CausesValidation property set to true. This raises an interesting scenario: what happens if the focus is on a control that requires validation (CausesValidation is true, and it has a handler attached to the Validating event) and the focus is then moved to a control for which CausesValidation is false? The newly selected control will not cause validation to occur, so is the original control simply forgotten about? Fortunately not, because in this case, the ContainerControl remembers that there is a control that has not yet been validated, and will deal with it next time validation occurs (i.e., when something calls Validate on the container, or when the focus moves to a control whose CausesValidation property is true).

This dual-purpose nature of CausesValidation means that the ContainerControl will only ever validate a single child control during a validation operation. There will never be a list of controls pending validation. To be validated, a control's CausesValidation flag must be true, which also ensures that any pending validation is performed before it acquires the focus, so there can never be more than one control waiting for validation at any time. If the Validate method is called when there is no control pending validation, the active control will be validated instead, unless its CausesValidation flag is false, in which case nothing will happen.

If nested containers are in use (e.g., you are using a user control—see Chapter 5 for details), validation is slightly more complex. Once the control has been validated, its containing parent is also validated, and if there is further nesting, validation continues up the chain, stopping when the container that initiated validation is reached. (A container that starts a validation operation will never validate itself, it will only validate one of its child controls.)

So, what happens if our control is not valid, and we fail the Validating event by setting the Cancel property to true in the CancelEventArgs object? When the relevant control is validated (e.g., the Validate method is called explicitly, or the focus is moved away from the control), validation will now fail. This will cause the focus to remain with the control, indicating to the user that something is wrong. The user will not be able to move away from the control without modifying it so that it validates correctly. If the user is unable to work out what is wrong with the control's contents, she will never be able to move the focus away from the control! (There is an emergency escape route—the user can still access any controls whose CausesValidation property is set to false.)

This simple approach to validation may be sufficient—if the nature of the error in the user input is sufficiently obvious, simply keeping the focus on the offending item will be enough to prompt the user into fixing it. However, this will not always be the case, so the framework provides a class to be used in this situation. The ErrorProvider class provides feedback to the user that something is wrong with her input. Here is a slightly more useful version of the validation code written in C#:

```
private ErrorProvider errorProvider =
    new ErrorProvider( );
...
private void textbox_Validating(object sender, CancelEventArgs e)
{
    string errText = "";
    if (textbox.Text.Length == 0)
    {
        e.Cancel = true;
        errText = "This field must not be empty";
    }
    errorProvider.SetError(textbox, errText);
}
```

Here is the corresponding Visual Basic code:

```
Private errProvider As New ErrorProvider( )

Private Sub textbox_Validating(sender As Object, e As CancelEventargs) _
            Handles textbox.Validating
    Dim errText As String = ""
    If textbox.Text.Length = 0 Then
       e.Cancel = True
       errText = "This field must not be empty"
    End If
    errProvider.SetError(textbox, errText)
End Sub
```

If the user tries to leave this field with its contents empty, it will fail validation, and the focus will remain with the field. But in addition, the field will now have an indicator next to it. (By default, this is an exclamation mark inside a small red circle, but you can supply your own icon if you wish.) If the user moves the mouse over this or clicks it, the error text will appear in a tool tip.

Once some error text has been set on an error provider, it stays there until it is explicitly removed, so once your control has been validated successfully, you must clear any errors you set by passing an empty string to `ErrorProvider.SetError`. In this example, we deal with this by always calling `SetError` in the `Validating` event handler, passing an empty string if validation succeeds. Another approach is to handle the `Validated` event and clear the error text there.

Remember that validation will only be applied to controls that have had the focus at some point. If you initialize your form with invalid data (e.g., you leave fields blank, and those fields must be filled in), automatic validation will not detect this unless the user happens to move the focus into the invalid fields. If you need to make sure that the user fills in several initially blank fields, you will need to add code to check this yourself. And more generally, any form-wide constraints must be checked manually; for example, if there are integrity constraints that require two or more fields to be consistent with each other, the automatic validation architecture cannot help here. The `ErrorProvider` class can still be used to provide feedback though. It is able to provide error indicators on several controls simultaneously, which is useful in these situations.

It is important to make sure your form cannot enter a state in which it can never be validated. For example, opening a modal dialog that requires a field to correspond to information in a database is dangerous if the relevant table might ever be empty. The user might not be able to close the dialog to populate the table.* Even if the table is not empty, the user might want to use some other part of your UI to find out what he should type, but won't be able to. Once a control has the focus, if it fails the `Validating` event, any attempt to click anywhere else will fail by default, because the focus will not leave the invalid field. As mentioned above, you can work around this by setting the `CausesValidation` property to `false` on any buttons that you want to be accessible while a field is failing validation. (Note that by default this property is `true`.) For example, if your control has a Cancel button, it should almost certainly have this flag set to `false`; otherwise, the user will not be able to dismiss a form she cannot fill in. Also, if the user might need to use certain parts of the UI to get the information she needs to fill in the form correctly, it is vital that the `CausesValidation` properties are set to `false`, because otherwise they will be inaccessible when the user needs them most.

Built-in Controls

Windows provides several kinds of widely used controls, such as buttons and text boxes, which act as the fundamental building blocks in most user interfaces. All these standard control types have .NET equivalents. This section shows which controls are available and what their Win32 equivalents are. It also describes some of the issues common to all the standard controls. More detailed technical descriptions of each control can be found in the reference section.

* If the form is modal, the user will be able to click on the close icon, but by default he will not be able to click on the Cancel button. Note that if the form is not modal, even the close icon doesn't work if the control with the focus fails validation! This is less serious, because with a non-modal form, you are more likely to be able to move away from the window to resolve the problem if necessary.

Available Controls

Table 2-1 shows the list of available controls and the nearest equivalent window class in Win32. (Some Win32 classes, such as `Button`, have several different modes, each of which is represented by a different class in Windows Forms. In this case, a Win32 window style is also specified to indicate which particular flavor of this class the relevant .NET type represents.)

Table 2-1. .NET controls and their equivalent Win32 control classes

Control class	Equivalent Win32 window class (and style)	Purpose
Buttons		
`Button`	`Button (BS_PUSHBUTTON)`	Normal button for actions (e.g., OK or Cancel)
`CheckBox`	`Button (BS_CHECKBOX)`	Yes/no selection button
`RadioButton`	`Button (BS_RADIOBUTTON)`	Single selection from a range of choices
Labels and pictures		
`GroupBox`	`Button (BS_GROUPBOX)`	Visual grouping for sets of related controls
`Label`	`Static (SS_LEFT, SS_CENTER, SS_RIGHT)`	Text label, usually providing a name or description for some other control (e.g., a text box)
`PictureBox`	`Static (SS_BITMAP, SS_ICON or SS_ENHMETAFILE)`	A picture: supports various bitmap formats (BMP, ICO, JPEG, TIFF, and PNG) and Windows metafiles
`LinkLabel`	`SysLink`	Hyperlink, e.g., a URL; this effectively combines label-like and button-like behavior
Text editing		
`TextBox`	`Edit`	An editable text field (plain text only)
`RichTextBox`	`RichEdit20W/ RichEdit20A`	An editable text fields supporting text with formatting (based on RTF—the Rich Text Format)
`NumericUpDown`	`msctls_updown32`	A text box containing a number, and an associated pair of up/down buttons (often known as a spin control)
`DomainUpDown`		Similar to a `NumericUpDown`, only the text box can contain any string; the up and down buttons move through a list of strings
Time and date		
`DateTimePicker`	`SysDateTimePick32`	UI for specifying a date or time
`MonthCalendar`	`SysMonthCal32`	UI showing a single calendar month
Lists and data		
`ListBox`	`ListBox`	A vertical list of selectable text items (items may also have images)
`ComboBox`	`ComboBox`	An editable text field with an associated drop-down list of selectable items
`ListView`	`SysListView32`	A list of selectable items similar to the contents of a Windows Explorer window; supports Large Icon, Small Icon, List and Details views
`TreeView`	`SysTreeView`	A hierarchical display, similar to that used in the Folders pane of Windows Explorer

Table 2-1. .NET controls and their equivalent Win32 control classes (continued)

Control class	Equivalent Win32 window class (and style)	Purpose
PropertyGrid		A UI for editing properties on some object; very similar to the Properties panels in Visual Studio .NET
DataGrid		A grid control showing the contents of a DataSet
Position and progress bars		
HScrollBar	ScrollBar	A horizontal Windows scrollbar
VScrollBar	ScrollBar	A vertical Windows scrollbar
TrackBar	msctls_trackbar32	A UI for selecting from a linear range of values (useful for continuous ranges such as percentages)
ProgressBar	msctls_progress32	A bar indicating what proportion of a long-running task has completed
Layout		
TabControl	SysTabControl32	Allows multiple similarly sized dialogs to share a single window, with card index style tabs selecting between them—similar to those used on Properties pages in Windows Explorer
Splitter		A bar dividing two parts of a window either vertically or horizontally, allowing the proportion of space given to the two parts to be modified—similar to the divider between the Folders pane and the main pane of a Windows Explorer window
StatusBar	msctls_statusbar32	A bar along the bottom of the window providing textual information appropriate to the application, and a window resizing grip (most Windows applications have these)
ToolBar	ToolbarWindow32	A bar containing shortcut buttons to frequently used UI operations (most Windows applications have these)

Note that some controls don't have an equivalent Win32 window class—the Windows Forms class library adds some new features. There are also some Win32 controls that appear to be absent, but in most cases, this is because their roles can be filled by one of the other controls. For example, Windows Forms does not provide a direct replacement for the `Animation` control, but this is because the `PictureBox` control supports animated bitmaps. There is also no `ToolTip` control, but `ToolTips` are dealt with through a different mechanism, called an *extender property*.

The Win32 `DragList`, `Header`, and `Pager` control types don't have any equivalent in Windows Forms.

Using the Built-in Controls

Not all the features supported by the `Control` class make sense for certain controls. For example, the `GroupBox` control does not respond to mouse events—its only purpose is to provide a visual grouping for controls. Fortunately, if you use Visual Studio .NET it will only present the features supported by the controls you use. (Chapter 5 explains how to determine which features are enabled for any custom controls you write, and Chapter 8 shows how to control the way in which Visual Studio. NET presents these features.)

Some controls (group boxes, labels, and all three button types) support a property called `FlatStyle`. This property modifies the way controls are drawn. By default, it is set to `Flat.Standard`, which means the control is drawn by the Windows Forms class library and not by the underlying OS. While this means that extra nonstandard functionality is available (e.g., the ability to set background colors or images), it has the disadvantage that your application will not be able to take advantage of themed controls. So in Windows XP, buttons will come out looking like normal Windows 2000 buttons regardless of what theme the user may be running with. If you would like to have themed controls (and don't mind losing support for background color and bitmaps), you must set the `FlatStyle` property to `FlatStyle.System`.* Although this means that Windows Forms will now let the operating system draw the controls, this in itself is not enough to get themed controls—as with any theme-aware application, you must also supply a manifest file. (Application manifests in .NET are used in exactly the same way as they are for non-.NET programs. They also have nothing to do with .NET assembly manifests. Consult the Win32 SDK documentation for details on how to create and use such manifests.)

Summary

The `Control` class is central to any Windows Forms application. Every visible element of the user interface is a control of some kind. This means there is a rich standard set of features that all controls support. All the standard Windows controls have counterparts in Windows Forms.

In the next chapter we will look in more detail at how controls work together on a form to provide a cohesive user interface.

* To complicate matters further, some controls, e.g., `TextBox`, use system drawing in any case. These controls don't support background bitmaps and colors, so they never need to draw themselves.

3
Forms, Containers, and Applications

Any interactive application must have at least one window through which to present its user interface. In the Windows Forms framework, all such top-level application windows are represented by objects whose types derive from the `Form` class. As with any user interface element, the `Form` class inherits from the `Control` class, but it adds windowing features, such as management of the window border and interaction with the Windows taskbar. All Windows Forms applications have at least one class derived from `Form`.

In this chapter we will examine the structure of a typical Windows Forms application and the way its constituent forms are created. We will look at the programming model for forms, and the way that the Visual Studio .NET Forms Designer uses this model. We will look in detail at the relationship between a form and the controls it contains, and also at the relationships that can exist between forms. The mechanisms underpinning the automatic layout features described in the previous chapter will be examined, and we will see how to use these to add our own custom layout facilities.

Application Structure

All Windows Forms applications have something in common, regardless of whether they are created with Visual Studio .NET or written from scratch:

- They all have at least one form, the main application window.
- They all need to display that form at start up.
- They must shut down correctly at the appropriate time.

This section describes the basic structure that all applications have and the way that their lifetime is managed by the .NET Framework.

Startup and Shutdown

All programs have to start executing somewhere, and .NET applications have a special method that is called when the application is run. This method is responsible for creating whatever windows the application requires and performing any other necessary initialization.

In C# and Visual Basic, this entry point is always a static method called `Main`. It doesn't matter which class this is defined in, although Visual Studio always makes it a member of the main form that it puts in any new project. It generates code like the C# code shown in Example 3-1.

Example 3-1. A typical application entry point

```
[STAThread]
static void Main()
{
    Application.Run(new Form1());
}
```

Although Visual Studio makes `Main` visible if you're developing with C#, it hides it if you're developing with Visual Basic. In Visual Basic projects, the code for `Main` is not displayed in the form's code window, nor is it listed in Class View or in the Object Browser. However, examining a compiled Windows Forms application using ILDASM, the .NET disassembler, indicates that a hidden public method named `Main` is present in the application's main form, as Figure 3-1 shows. Its source code corresponds to that shown in Example 3-2.

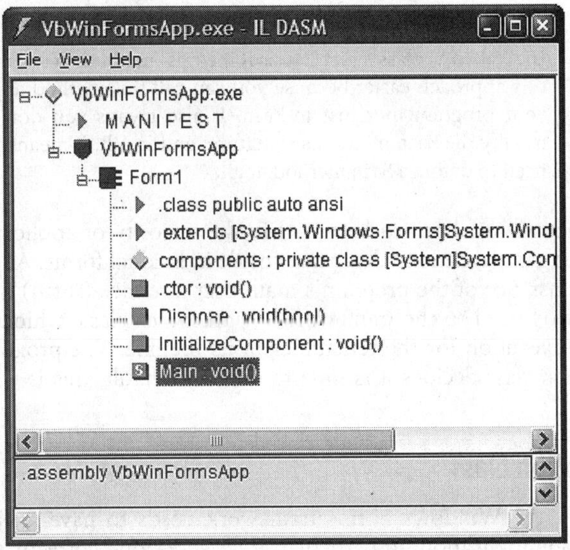
VbWinFormsApp.exe - IL DASM
File View Help
VbWinFormsApp.exe
MANIFEST
VbWinFormsApp
Form1
.class public auto ansi
extends [System.Windows.Forms]System.Wind
components : private class [System]System.Co
.ctor : void()
Dispose : void(bool)
InitializeComponent : void()
Main : void()
.assembly VbWinFormsApp

Figure 3-1. The hidden VB entry point revealed in ILDASM

Example 3-2. An application entry point in VB

```
<STAThread> Public Shared Sub Main( )
   Application.Run(new Form1( ))
End Sub
```

If your application needs to read the command-line parameters, you can modify `Main` (or, if you're coding in Visual Basic, you can add it yourself, rather than have the compiler add it) so that it takes a parameter of type `string[]` or `String( )`. You will then be passed an array of strings, one for each argument. You can also change the return type to `int` if you wish to return an exit code. Examples 3-3 and 3-4 illustrate these techniques. The `STAThread` custom attribute is a backward-compatibility feature that will be discussed shortly.

Example 3-3. C# application entry point with parameters

```
[STAThread]
static int Main(string[] args)
{
    Application.Run(new Form1( ));
}
```

Example 3-4. VB application entry point with parameters

```
<STAThread> _
Public Shared Function Main(args As String( )) As Integer
   Application.Run(New Form1( ))
End Sub
```

> It is also possible to retrieve the command-line arguments using the `Environment` class's `GetCommandLineArgs` method. You might find this approach easier because you can call this method anywhere in your program, not just in `Main`. It also means you don't need to modify the `Main` method's signature, and in VB, it means you don't need to define a `Main` method at all.

The `Main` function turns out to be trivial in the majority of applications because most interesting initialization takes place inside individual forms. All that happens in `Main` is an instance of the program's main user interface (`Form1`) is created, and control is then passed to the framework's `Application` class, which manages the application's execution for the remainder of its lifetime. The program runs until the `Application` class decides it is time to exit. By default, this is when the main form is closed.

The Application Class

To do its job, the Windows Forms framework needs to have a high degree of control over our application. In particular, it must respond correctly to the kind of input that all Windows applications are required to handle, such as mouse clicks and redraw requests. This means the framework needs to be in charge of our application's main thread most of the time; otherwise, it cannot deal with these events.*

Although our application's execution is stage-managed by the framework, we can still influence its behavior by using the `Application` class. For example, we can tell the framework to shut down our program by calling the `Application.Exit` method. In fact, interacting with the `Application` class is the first thing most programs do. They typically start like Example 3-1, calling `Application.Run` to surrender control to Windows Forms. This causes the framework to display the `Form` object that it is given, after which it sits and waits for events. From then on, our code will only be run as a result of some activity, such as a mouse click, causing the framework to call one of our event handlers.

This event-driven style of execution is an important feature of Windows Forms. The framework is able to deal with events only because we leave it in charge. Of course, while one of our event handlers is running (e.g., the code in a `Click` handler is executing), we are temporarily back in charge, which means the framework will be unable to process any other events until our event handler returns. Most of the time, this is a good thing, because life would become unbearably complex if we could be asked to start handling a new event before we had finished dealing with the previous one; reentrant code is notoriously hard to get right, so it is a good thing that it is not usually required.

The only problem is that if our event handlers take a long time to execute, the user interface will become unresponsive. Until our code returns control to the framework, the user will not be able to click on or type into our program, or to move the windows around. (Strictly speaking the input won't be lost—such events are stored in a queue, just as they are with normal Windows programs. But there will be no response to this input until the handler returns.) We can't even give the user a way to abort the operation if it takes too long because the inability to process user input makes it difficult to support any kind of Cancel button.

While the obvious solution is to avoid writing event handlers that take too long to execute, this is not always possible. Fortunately, long-running event handlers can choose to give the framework a chance to deal with any events that may be queued up and awaiting processing. The `Application` class provides a method called `DoEvents`. This handles any pending input and then returns. Of course, any code that calls this method needs to be careful, because it is inviting reentrant behavior, so whenever you call this method, you must consider the implications of another of your event handlers being run before `DoEvents` returns. But it does mean that slow code has a way of making sure the application does not appear to lock up completely.

The `DoEvents` method is not the only way of reentering the framework's event handling code. Whenever you display a modal dialog (e.g., by using the `MessageBox` class, or by displaying a form with the `ShowDialog` method, as described later), Windows Forms is once again in charge of your thread and will process events for you for as long as the window is displayed.

* This is similar to the way that classic Win32 applications must service the message queue.

Because the Application class effectively owns our thread, we must get its help when we wish to shut down our program. By default, it monitors the form that we passed to its Run method (usually the program's main form), and it exits when that form closes. However, we can also force a shutdown by calling its Exit method; this closes all windows and then exits. (In other words, when Exit is called, the Run method returns. This will usually cause the program to exit, because the only thing the Main function usually does is call the Run method, as shown in Example 3-1. When the Main method finishes, the program exits.)

The Application class also provides a few miscellaneous utility features. For example, you can modify the way exceptions are handled. If any of your event handlers should throw an exception, the default behavior is for the application to terminate. But the Application class has a static (or shared) event called ThreadException that is raised whenever such an exception occurs; handling this event prevents the unhandled exception dialog from appearing, and the application will not exit unless you explicitly terminate it in your handler. The Application class also exposes an Idle event that is fired whenever some input has just been handled and the application is about to become idle. You could use this to perform background processing tasks.

Forms and Threads

With all this talk of the Application object owning our thread, and of keeping the user interface responsive in the face of long-running operations, you may well be wondering about the use of threads in Windows Forms applications. Although it is possible to write multithreaded Windows Forms applications, there are some serious restrictions. A full discussion of multithreaded programming is well beyond the scope of this book, but it is important to know what the restrictions are.

There is one fundamental rule for threads in Windows Forms applications: you can only use a control's methods or properties from the thread on which it was created. In other words, you must *never* call any methods on a control from a worker thread,* nor can you read or write its properties. The only exceptions to this rule are calls to the Invoke, BeginInvoke, and EndInvoke methods and to the InvokeRequired property, which can all be used from any thread.

This may seem a surprisingly draconian restriction, but it is not as bad as it sounds. It is possible to use the Control class's Invoke method to run code on the right thread for the control—you just pass a delegate to the Invoke method, and it calls that delegate for you on the correct thread. The call will not occur until the next time the Windows Forms framework processes messages on the control's thread. (This is to avoid reentrancy.) Invoke waits for the method to complete, so if an event is being handled by the user interface thread currently, Invoke will wait for that handler to finish. Beware of the potential for deadlock here; BeginInvoke is sometimes a better choice because it doesn't wait for the invoked method to finish running—it just adds the request to run the method to the framework's internal event queue and then returns immediately. (It is possible that your user interface thread was waiting for your worker thread to do something, so if you

* A worker thread is any thread other than the UI thread.

also make your worker thread wait for the user interface thread to do something, both threads will deadlock, causing your application to freeze.)

The `InvokeRequired` property is a `bool` or `Boolean` that tells you whether you are on the right thread for the control (`InvokeRequired` returns `False`) or not (`InvokeRequired` returns `True`). This can be used in conjunction with the `BeginInvoke` method to force a particular method to run on the correct thread, as shown in the following C# code fragment:

```
private void MustRunOnUIThread( )
{
    if (InvokeRequired)
    {
        BeginInvoke(new MethodInvoker(MustRunOnUIThread));
        return;
    }
    ... invoke not required, must be on right thread already
}
```

This method checks to see if it is on the right thread, and if not, it uses `BeginInvoke` to direct the call to the control's own thread.* `MethodInvoker` is a delegate type defined by Windows Forms that represents methods with no parameters and no return value (or, in Visual Basic, a `Sub` with no parameters). In fact, you can use any delegate type you like, and there is an overloaded version of `Control.BeginInvoke` that takes a parameter list (as an `object` array) as its second parameter, allowing you to use a delegate that requires parameters to be passed.

You may also be wondering why Visual Studio .NET places an `STAThread` attribute on your application's `Main` function, as shown in Example 3-1. This is required for ActiveX controls to work. If you want to use ActiveX controls, the COM runtime must be initialized in a particular way on the user interface thread. In .NET, COM is always initialized by the CLR, so we use this attribute to tell the CLR how we would like it to configure COM on this thread. A full discussion of COM interop and COM's threading model is beyond the scope of this book, although if you are familiar with COM, you might find it helpful to know that this attribute ensures that the main thread will belong to an STA.

So the `Application` class is responsible for managing our application's lifetime, main thread, and event processing. But all the interesting activity surrounds the forms that make up our applications, so let's now look in more detail at the `Form` class.

The Form Class

All windows in a Windows Forms application are represented by objects of some type deriving from the `Form` class. Of course, `Form` derives from `Control`, as do all classes that represent visual elements, so we have already seen much of what it can do in the previous chapter. But we will now look at the features that the `Form` class adds.

* This particular example shows a member function of some class that derives from `Control`—this is why it is able to use the `InvokeRequired` and `BeginInvoke` members directly. This is not a requirement—the methods are public, so you can call them on any control.

You will rarely use the Form class directly—any forms you define in your application will be represented by a class that inherits from Form. Adding a new form in Visual Studio .NET simply adds an appropriate class definition to your project. We will examine how it structures these classes when generating new forms, and we will look at how it cleans up any resource used by the form when it is destroyed. Then, we will consider the different types of forms. Finally, we will look at extender properties. These provide a powerful way of extending the behavior of all controls on a form to augment the basic Control functionality.

The Forms Designer

Most forms are designed using the Forms Designer in Visual Studio .NET. This is not an essential requirement—the designer just generates code that you could write manually instead. It is simply much easier to arrange the contents of a form visually than it is to write code to do this.

When you add a new form to a project, a new class definition is created. The Designer always uses the same structure for the source code of these classes. They begin with private fields in C# and Friend fields in VB to hold the contents of the form. (The Designer inserts new fields here as you add controls to the form.) Next is the constructor, followed by the Dispose and InitializeComponent methods; these are all described below. If this is the main form in your application, the program's entry point (the Main method described above) will follow in C# programs; in VB programs, it will be added by the compiler at compile time, but will not be displayed with the form's source code. Finally, any event handlers for controls on your form will be added at the end of the class.

The Designer does not make it obvious where you are expected to add any code of your own, such as fields or methods other than event handlers. This is because it doesn't matter—Visual Studio .NET is pretty robust about working around you. It is even happy for you to move most of the code that it generates if you don't like the way it arranges things, with the exception of the code inside the InitializeComponent method, which you should avoid modifying by hand. (The editor hides this code by default to discourage you from changing it.)

Initialization

Any freshly created form will contain a constructor and an InitializeComponent method. The job of these methods is to make sure a form is correctly initialized before it is displayed.

The generated constructor is very simple—it just calls the InitializeComponent method. The intent here is that the Forms Designer places all its initialization code in InitializeComponent, and you will write any initialization that you require in the constructor. The designer effectively owns InitializeComponent, and it is recommended that you avoid modifying its contents, because this is liable to confuse the Designer. So when you look at the source code for a form class, Visual Studio .NET conceals the InitializeComponent method by default—it is lurking behind a line that appears as "Windows Form Designer generated code."* You can see this code by clicking on the + symbol at the left of this line in the editor.

> You must not make any modifications to the overall structure of the `InitializeComponent` method. It is usually acceptable to make small changes to existing lines, or to remove them entirely, but more substantial changes will almost certainly confuse Visual Studio .NET, and you could find that you can no longer edit your form visually in the designer. Most changes can be made using the Forms designer or by modifying values in its Properties window, which causes Visual Studio to update the `InitializeComponent` method automatically.

Although the theory is that you will never need to modify anything inside this generated code, you may occasionally have to make edits. If you do make such changes by hand, you must be very careful not to change the overall structure of the method, as this could confuse the Designer, so it is useful to know roughly how the method is arranged. It begins by creating the objects that make up the UI: each control on the form will have a corresponding line calling the `new` operator, and store the result in the relevant field. In C#, for example, such code appears as follows:

```
this.button1 = new System.Windows.Forms.Button( );
this.label1 = new System.Windows.Forms.Label( );
this.textBox1 = new System.Windows.Forms.TextBox( );
```

and in VB, it appears as follows:

```
Me.Button1 = New System.Windows.Forms.Button( )
Me.Label1 = New System.Windows.Forms.Label( )
Me.TextBox1 = New System.Windows.Forms.TextBox( )
```

Next, there will be a call to the `SuspendLayout` method, which is inherited from the `Control` class. Layout is discussed in detail later on, but the purpose of this call is to prevent the form from attempting to rearrange itself every time a control is set up. Then each control is configured in turn—any necessary properties are set (position, name, and tab order, at a minimum), and event handlers (in C# only) are added. In C#, this looks like the following:

```
this.textBox1.Location = new System.Drawing.Point(112, 136);
this.textBox1.Name = "textBox1";
this.textBox1.TabIndex = 2;
this.textBox1.Text = "textBox1";
this.textBox1.TextChanged += new
    System.EventHandler(this.textBox1_TextChanged);
```

The corresponding VB code appears as follows:

```
Me.TextBox1.Location = New System.Drawing.Point(112, 136)
Me.TextBox1.Name = "TextBox1"
Me.TextBox1.TabIndex = 2
Me.TextBox1.Text = "TextBox1"
```

* It is hidden with a pair of `#region` and `#endregion` directives. These are ignored by the compiler, but used by the editor in Visual Studio .NET to hide parts of the file automatically behind single summary lines. You can also use these directives yourself if you want to make blocks of code collapsible.

After this, the form's size is set and then all the controls are added to its `Controls` collection. (Simply creating controls and storing them in private fields is not enough to make them appear on screen—they must be explicitly added to the form on which they are to appear; this process will be discussed in detail later.) Finally, the `ResumeLayout` method, which is inherited from the `Control` class, is called. This is the counterpart of the earlier call to `SuspendLayout`, and it indicates to the form that the various additions and modifications are complete, and that it won't be wasting CPU cycles when it manages its layout. This call will also cause an initial layout to be performed, causing any docked controls to be positioned appropriately.

Disposal

The other method created on all new forms is the `Dispose` method. This runs when the form is destroyed and frees any resources that were allocated for the form. In fact, all controls have two `Dispose` methods: one public, supplied by the framework, and one protected, which you usually write yourself. To understand why, we must first look at the way resources are normally released in .NET.

The CLR has a garbage collector, which means that when objects fall out of use, the memory used by those objects will eventually be freed automatically. Classes can have special functions called finalizers, which are run just before the garbage collector frees an object. Classes in the .NET Framework that represent expensive resources such as window handles usually have finalizers that release these resources. So in the long run, there will be no resource leaks—everything will eventually be freed either by the garbage collector or by the finalizers that the garbage collector calls. Unfortunately, the garbage collector only really cares about memory usage, and only bothers to free objects when it is low on memory. This means that a very long time (minutes or even hours) can pass between an object falling out of use and the garbage collector noticing and running its finalizer. This is unacceptable for many types of resources, especially the kinds used by GUI applications. (Although current versions of Windows are much more forgiving than the versions of old, hogging graphical resources has never been a good idea and is best avoided even today.)

So the .NET Framework defines a standard idiom for making sure such resources are freed more quickly, and the C# language has special support for this idiom. Objects that own expensive resources should implement the `IDisposable` interface, which defines a single method, `Dispose`. If code is using such an object, as soon as it has finished with the object it should call its `Dispose` method, allowing it to free the resources it is using. (Such objects usually also have finalizers, so if the client code forgets to call `Dispose`, the resources will be freed eventually, if somewhat late. But this is not an excuse for not calling the method.)

The `Control` class (and therefore any class deriving from it) implements `IDisposable`, as do most of the classes in GDI+, so almost everything you use in Windows Forms programming relies on this idiom. Fortunately, the C# language has special support for it. The `using` keyword can automatically free disposable resources for us at the end of a scope:

```
using(Brush b = new SolidBrush(this.ForeColor))
{
    ... do some painting with the brush ...
}
```

When the code exits the block that follows the `using` statement, the `Brush` object's `Dispose` method will be called. (The `Brush` class is part of GDI+, and it implements `IDisposable`; this example is typical of redraw code in a custom control.) The most important feature of this construct is that it will call `Dispose` regardless of how we leave the block. Even if the code returns from the middle of the block or throws an exception, `Dispose` will still be called, because the compiler puts this code in a `finally` block for us.*

> Unfortunately, Visual Basic does not have any equivalent to `using` blocks in C#. You must remember to call `Dispose` yourself.

Forms typically have a lot of resources associated with them, so it is not surprising that they are always required to support this idiom. In fact, all user elements are—the `Control` class enforces this because it implements `IDisposable`. The good news is that most of the work is done for us by the `Control` class, as is so often the case. It provides an implementation that calls `Dispose` on all the controls contained by the form and frees all resources that the Windows Forms framework obtained on your behalf for the form. But it also provides us with the opportunity to free any resources that we may have acquired that it might not know about. (For example, if you obtain a connection to a database for use on your form, it is your responsibility to close it when the form is disposed.)

The picture is complicated slightly by the fact that there are two times at which resource disposal might occur. Not only must all resources be freed when `Dispose` is called, they must also be freed if the client has failed to call `Dispose` by the time the finalizer runs. The model used by the `Control` class† enables you to use the same code for both situations: any code to free resources allocated by your form lives in an overload of the `Dispose` method, distinguished by its signature: `void Dispose(bool)` (in C#) or `Sub Dispose(Boolean)` (in VB). This method will be called in both scenarios—either when the user calls `IDispose.Dispose` or when the finalizer runs.

It is important to distinguish between timely disposal and finalization when cleaning up resources. In a finalizer, it is never possible to be sure whether any references you hold to other objects are still valid: if the runtime has determined that your object is to be garbage collected, it is highly likely that it will also have decided that the objects you are using must be collected too. Because the CLR makes no guarantees of the order in which finalizers are run, it is entirely possible

* A `finally` block is a block of code that the CLR guarantees to run, regardless of how the flow of execution leaves the preceding block. It allows a single piece of cleanup code to be used in the face of normal exit, premature returns, and exceptions.

† Strictly speaking it inherits this model from its base class, the `Component` class in the `System.ComponentModel` namespace.

that any objects to which you hold references have already had their finalizers run. In this case, calling Dispose on them could be dangerous—most objects will not expect to have their methods called once they have been finalized. So most of the time, your Dispose method will only want to do anything when the object was explicitly disposed of by the user. The only resources you would free during finalization would be those external to the CLR, such as any temporary files created by your object or any handles obtained through interop.

The Dispose method that you are intended to override is protected, so it cannot be called by external code. It will be called by the Control class if the user calls the public Dispose method (IDispose.Dispose). In this case, the parameter passed to the *protected* Dispose method will be true. It will also be called when the finalizer runs, in which case the parameter will be false. (Note that this method will only be called once—if IDispose.Dispose is called, the Control class disables the object's finalizer.) So the parameter indicates whether resources are being freed promptly or in a finalizer, allowing you to choose the appropriate behavior. Consider the code generated by the Designer, as shown in Examples 3-5 and 3-6.

Example 3-5. The default protected Dispose method in C#

```
protected override void Dispose( bool disposing )
{
    if( disposing )
    {
        if (components != null)
        {
            components.Dispose( );
        }
    }
    base.Dispose( disposing );
}
```

Example 3-6. The default protected Dispose method in VB

```
Protected Overloads Overrides Sub Dispose(ByVal disposing As Boolean)
   If disposing Then
      If Not (components Is Nothing) Then
         components.Dispose( )
      End If
   End If
   MyBase.Dispose(disposing)
End Sub
```

This checks to see if the *public* Dispose method was called, and if it was, it disposes of the components object, if present. (The components object is a collection of any non-Control components in use on the form, e.g., data sources.) But if finalization is in progress (i.e., the *disposing* parameter is false), it doesn't bother, for the reasons detailed above. If you add any code to this Dispose method, it too will normally live inside the if(disposing) { ... } block.

Components added to a form using the Forms Designer in Visual Studio .NET will not necessarily be added to the form's `components` collection. Only those components with a constructor that takes a single parameter of type `IContainer` will be added. (All the components in the framework that require disposal have such a constructor.) If you are writing your own component that has code in its `Dispose` method, you must supply an appropriate constructor. This constructor must call `Add` on the supplied container to add itself to the `components` collection.

There are two very important rules you must stick to if you need to modify this resource disposal code in your form. First, you must always call the base class's `Dispose` method in your `Dispose` method, because otherwise the `Control` class will not release its resources correctly. Second, you should never define your own finalizer in a form—doing so could interact badly with the `Control` class's own finalizer; the correct place to put code to release resources in a form (or any other UI element) is in the overridden protected `Dispose` method. This is precisely what the code generated by the forms designer does, as shown in Examples 3-5 and 3-6.

You may be wondering what the `components` member is for, and why it needs to be disposed of. It is a collection of components, and its job is to dispose of those components—if you add a component such as a `Timer` to a form, the Forms Designer will automatically generate code to add that component to the `components` collection. In fact, it does this by passing `components` as a construction parameter to the component, e.g.:

```
this.timer1 = new System.Windows.Forms.Timer(this.components);
```

The component will then add itself to the `components` collection. As you can see from Examples 3-5 and 3-6, the default `Dispose` method supplied by the Designer will call `Dispose` on the `components` collection. This in turn will cause that collection to call `Dispose` on each component it contains. So if you are using a component that implements `IDispose`, the easiest way to make sure it is freed correctly is simply to add it to the `components` collection. The Forms Designer does this automatically for any components that require disposal. (It determines which require disposal by examining their constructors—if a component supplies a constructor that takes an `IContainer` as a parameter, it will use that constructor, passing `components` as the container.) You can also add any objects of your own to the collection:

```
components.Add(myDisposableObject);
```

or:

```
components.Add(myDisposableObject)
```

Showing Modal and Non-Modal Forms

All forms created by Visual Studio .NET will conform to the structure just described. But as with dialogs in classic Windows applications, there are two ways in which they can be shown: forms can exhibit either modal or non-modal behavior.

A *modal form* is one that demands the user's immediate attention, and blocks input to any other windows the application may have open. (The application enters a *mode* where it will only allow the user to access that form, hence the name.) Forms should be displayed modally only if the application cannot proceed until the form is satisfied. Typical examples would be error messages that must not go unnoticed or dialogs that collect data from the user that must be supplied before an operation can be completed (e.g., the File Open dialog—an application needs to know which file it is supposed to load before it can open it).

You select between modal and non-modal behavior when you display the form. The `Form` class provides two methods for displaying a form: `ShowDialog`, which displays the form modally, and `Show`, which displays it non-modally.

The `Show` method returns immediately, leaving the form on screen. (The event handling mechanism discussed earlier can deliver events to any number of windows.) A non-modal form has a life of its own once it has been displayed; it may even outlive the form that created it.

By contrast, the `ShowDialog` method does not return until the dialog has been dismissed by the user. Of course, this means that the thread will not return to the `Application` class's main event-handling loop until the dialog goes away, but this is not a problem because the framework will process events inside the `ShowDialog` method. However, events are handled differently when a modal dialog is open—any attempts to click on a form other than the one being displayed modally are rejected. Other forms will still be redrawn correctly, but will simply beep if the user tries to provide them with any input. This forces the user to deal with the modal dialog before progressing.

There is a more minor (and somewhat curious) difference between modal and non-modal use of forms: resizable forms have a subtly different appearance. When displayed modally, a form will always have a resize grip at the bottom righthand corner. Non-modal forms only have a resize grip if they have a status bar.

Be careful with your use of modal dialogs, because they can prove somewhat annoying for the user: dialogs that render the rest of the application inaccessible for no good reason are just frustrating. For example, older versions of Internet Explorer would prevent you from scrolling the main window if you had a search dialog open. If you wanted to look at the text just below the match, you had to cancel the search to do so. Fortunately this obstructive and needless use of a modal dialog has been fixed—Internet Explorer's search dialog is now non-modal. To avoid making this kind of design error in your own applications, you should follow this guideline: do not make your dialogs modal unless they really have to be.

Closing forms

Having displayed a form, either modally or non-modally, we will want to close it at some point. There are several ways in which a form can be closed. From a programmer's point of view, the most direct approach is to call its `Close` method, as follows:

```
this.Close();                // C#

Me.Close()                   ' VB
```

A form may also be closed automatically by the Windows Forms framework in response to user input; for example, if the user clicks on a form's close icon, the window will close. However, if you want to prevent this (as you might if, for example, the window represents an unsaved file), you can do so by handling the Form class's Closing event. The framework raises this event just before closing the window, regardless of whether the window is being closed automatically or by an explicit call to the Close method. The event's type is CancelEventHandler; its Boolean Cancel property enables us to prevent the window from closing if necessary. Examples 3-7 and 3-8 illustrate the use of this property when handling the Closing event.

Forms, Apps, Containers

Example 3-7. Handling the Closing event in C#

```
private void MyForm_Closing(object sender,
    System.ComponentModel.CancelEventArgs e)
{
    if (!IsWorkSaved())
    {
        DialogResult rc = MessageBox.Show(
            "Save work before exiting?",
            "Exit application",
            MessageBoxButtons.YesNoCancel);

        if (rc == DialogResult.Cancel)
        {
            e.Cancel = true;
        }
        else if (rc == DialogResult.Yes)
        {
            SaveWork();
        }
    }
}
```

Example 3-8. Handling the Closing event in VB

```
Private Sub MyForm_Closing(sender As Object, _
        e As System.ComponentModel.CancelEventArgs)
    If Not IsWorkSaved() Then
        Dim rc As DialogResult = MessageBox.Show( _
            "Save work before exiting?", _
            "Exit application", _
            MessageBoxButtons.YesNoCancel)

        If rc = DialogResult.Cancel Then
            e.Cancel = True
        Else If rc = DialogResult.Yes Then
            SaveWork()
        End If
    End If
End Sub
```

The form in Examples 3-7 and 3-8 checks to see if there is unsaved work. (IsWorkSaved is just a fictional method for illustrating this example—it is not part of the framework.) If there is, it displays a message box giving the user a chance to save this work, abandon it, or cancel, which keeps the window open. In the latter case, this code informs the framework that the window should not be closed after all by setting the Cancel property of the CancelEventArgs argument to true.

If you write an MDI application (i.e., an application that can display multiple documents as children of a single main frame), the framework treats an attempt to close the main window specially. Not only does the main window get a Closing and Closed event, so does each child window. The child windows are asked first, so if each child represents a different document, each child can prompt the user if there is unsaved work. But none of the children are closed until all of the windows (the children and the main window) have fired the Closing event. This means the close can be vetoed by any of the windows. The close will only happen if all the child windows and the main window are happy.

If nothing cancels the Closing event, the window will be closed, and the Closed event will be raised. If the form is shown non-modally, the framework then calls the form's Dispose method to make sure that all the form's resources are freed. This means once a non-modal form has been closed, you cannot reuse the object to display the form a second time. If you call Show on a form that has already been closed, an exception will be thrown. For modal dialogs, however, it is common to want to use the form object after the window has closed. For example, if the dialog was displayed to retrieve information from the user, you will want to get that information out of the object once the window closes. Modal dialogs are therefore not disposed of when they are closed, and you must call Dispose yourself, as shown in Examples 3-9 and 3-10. You should make sure that you use any properties or methods that you need before calling Dispose (i.e., inside the using block).

Example 3-9. Disposing of a modal dialog in C#

```
using (LoginForm lf = new LoginForm( ))
{
    lf.ShowDialog( );
    userID = lf.UserID;
    password = lf.Password;
}
```

Example 3-10. Disposing of a modal dialog in VB

```
Try
   Dim lf As New LoginForm( )
   lf.ShowDialog( )
   userID = lf.UserID
   password = lf.Password
Finally
   If.Dispose()
End Try
```

Although the framework will automatically try to close a window when its close icon is pressed, it is common to want to close a form as the result of a button click. It turns out that if the button does nothing more than close the form, you do not need to write a click handler to make this happen. The Windows Forms framework will automatically close the form when any button with a DialogResult is clicked. So we will now look at dialog results.

Automatic button click handling

A dialog might be closed for several different reasons. Instead of clicking the OK button, the user might attempt to cancel the dialog by clicking on its close icon or Cancel button, or by pressing the Escape key. Most applications will distinguish between such cancellation and normal completion, and some may make a finer distinction still, such as a message box with Yes, No, and Cancel buttons. Windows Forms provides support for automatically managing the various ways of closing a window without having to write click handlers. It also makes it easy for users of a form to find out which way a form was closed. Both of these facilities revolve around dialog results.

The Form class's ShowDialog method returns a value indicating how the dialog was dismissed. The returned value corresponds to the DialogResult property of the button with which the user closed the window. The following code shows an excerpt from the initialization of a form containing two buttons, buttonOK and buttonCancel (the Forms Designer will generate such code if you set a button's DialogResult property in the Properties window):

```
buttonOK.DialogResult = DialogResult.OK;
buttonCancel.DialogResult = DialogResult.Cancel;
```

Any code that shows this dialog will be able to determine which button was clicked from ShowDialog's return code. The returned value can also be retrieved later from the DialogResult property of the Form object.

The type of the ShowDialog method's return value and of the DialogResult property of both the Form object and of individual Button controls is also DialogResult, which is an enumeration type containing values for the most widely used dialog buttons: OK, Cancel, Yes, No, Abort, Retry, and Ignore.

To handle button clicks without an event handler, you must set a button's DialogResult property to any value other than the default (DialogResult.None). Then clicking that button will cause the framework to close the form and return that value. If you want, you can still supply a Click event handler for the button, which will be run before the window is closed. But the window will be closed whether you supply one or not (unless there is a Closing handler for the form that cancels the close, as described earlier).

It is also possible to return a dialog result without using a Button control. If you wish to close the form in response to some event that did not originate from a button, you can also set the Form class's DialogResult property before calling Close.

But what about when the form is cancelled by pressing the Escape key? We normally want the form to behave in the same way regardless of how it is dismissed. Specifically, we would like to run the same event handler and return the same DialogResult in all three cases. This turns out to be simple because the Windows Forms framework can fake a click on the Cancel button when the Escape key is pressed. All we need to do is tell the form which is our Cancel button (which could be any button—it doesn't have to be labeled Cancel)—with the Form class's CancelButton property:

```
this.CancelButton = buttonCancel;            // C#

Me.CancelButton = buttonCancel               ' VB
```

If buttonCancel has a handler registered for its Click event, that handler will be called either when the button is clicked, or when the Escape key is pressed. In both cases, the same two things to happen: first, the Click handler (if there is one) is called, then the window is closed. The Click handler for the button indicated by the CancelButton property does not need to take any special steps to close the window.

> The CancelButton property is ignored if the user simply closes the window. In this case, the button's click handler will not be called, and its specified DialogResult will not be returned from ShowDialog. So you will need to override the OnClosed method in your form to handle all the possible ways of closing the dialog.

As with all buttons, if you specify a DialogResult other than None for the Cancel button, that value will be used as the dialog result. However, the button referred to by the CancelButton property is unusual in that if this property is set to None, it behaves as though it were set to Cancel: the form will be closed, and the dialog result will be Cancel. (Also, when you choose a CancelButton in the Forms Designer, it sets the button's DialogResult property to Cancel automatically. This seems to be overkill, because it would return Cancel in any case.)

As well as supporting a CancelButton, a form can also have an AcceptButton. If set, this will have a Click event faked every time the user presses the Enter key while on the form. However, this turns out to be less useful than the CancelButton because this behavior is disabled if the control that currently has the focus does something with the Enter key. For example, although Button controls behave as though clicked when Enter is pressed, if some button other than the AcceptButton has the focus, that button will get a Click event, not the AcceptButton. If a multiline TextBox control has the focus, it will process the Enter key instead. So if your form consists of nothing but buttons and multiline text boxes, there is no point in setting the AcceptButton property.

Note that unlike the CancelButton, if you do assign an AcceptButton, the form will only be closed automatically when this button is clicked if you explicitly set the accept button's DialogResult property to something other than None.

We have now seen how to create, display, and dismiss forms. But of course, a form's main role is to act as a container of other controls—empty windows are rarely useful. So we will now look in more detail at the nature of control containment in the Windows Forms framework.

Containment

All useful forms contain some controls. There is more to this containment relationship than meets the eye, and if you are familiar with the old Win32 parent/child relationship, you will find that things do not work in quite the same way. We will look at the control nesting facilities supplied by both the `Control` class and the `ContainerControl` class, paying particular attention to the implications of containment for focus and validation events.

Parents and Owners

Controls rarely exist in complete isolation—top-level windows usually contain some controls, and all non–top-level controls are associated with a window. In fact, Windows Forms defines two kinds of relationships between controls. There is the parent/child relationship, which manages containment of controls within a single window. There is also a looser association that can exist between top-level windows, which is represented by the owner/owned relationship.

Forms, Apps, Containers

Parent and child

A *child window* is one that is completely contained by its parent. For example, any controls that you place on a form are children of that form. A child's position is specified relative to its parent, and the child is clipped to the parent's bounds—i.e., only those parts of the child completely inside the parent are visible. Forms can be children too: document windows in an MDI application are children of the main MDI frame.

A control's parent is accessible through its `Parent` property (of type `Control`). If you examine this property on a control on a form, you will typically find that it refers to that form. However, many controls can behave as both a parent and a child—if you place a button inside a group box on a form, the button's parent will be the group box, and the group box's parent will be the form.

We can also find out if a control has any children—they are available through its `Controls` property, of type `Control.ControlCollection`. Examples 3-11 and 3-12 show this property being used to attach a `Click` event handler to all controls on a form. (Note that this only attaches itself to direct children of the form. It will not handle clicks from controls nested inside other controls, e.g., a button inside a panel. This could be fixed by writing a recursive version of the method.)

Example 3-11. Iterating through child controls with C#

```
private void AddClickHandlers( )
{
    foreach(Control c in Controls)
    {
        c.Click += new EventHandler(AnyClick);
    }
}
```

Example 3-11. Iterating through child controls with C# (continued)

```
private void AnyClick(object sender, System.EventArgs e)
{
    Control clicked = (Control) sender;
    Debug.WriteLine(string.Format("{0} clicked", clicked.Name));
}
```

Example 3-12. Iterating through child controls with VB

```
Private Sub AddClickHandlers( )
   Dim c As Control
   For Each c in Controls
      AddHandler c.Click, AddressOf AnyClick
   Next
End Sub

Private Sub AnyClick(sender As Object, e As EventArgs)
    Dim clicked As Control = DirectCast(sender, Control)
    Console.WriteLine(String.Format("{0} clicked", clicked.Name))
End Sub
```

The parent/child relationship can be established through either the `Parent` property or the `Controls` property. A child control's `Parent` property can be set to refer to a parent. Alternatively, you can use the `Controls` property on the parent—this is a collection that has `Add` and `AddRange` methods to add children. The Forms Designer uses the latter. If you examine the `InitializeComponent` method generated by the Designer for a form with some controls on it, you will see something like this towards the end of the function in a C# project:

```
this.Controls.AddRange(new System.Windows.Forms.Control[] {
                              this.checkBox1,
                              this.btnCancel,
                              this.btnOK});
```

In a VB project, the code appears as follows:

```
Me.Controls.AddRange(New System.Windows.Forms.Control( ) _
                     {Me.checkBox1, Me.btnCancel, Me.btnOK})
```

(`checkBox1`, `btnCancel` and `btnOK` are controls that would have been initialized earlier in the method.) This code would have worked equally well if the Designer had set the `Parent` property to `this` in C# or to `Me` in VB on each of these controls, but using `Controls.AddRange` is slightly more efficient, because it allows all the controls to be attached to the form in one operation.

When nesting is in use, you will see a similar call to the `AddRange` method. For example, if you create a panel with some controls in it, those controls will be added with a call to `Controls.AddRange` on the panel. This panel itself would then be added to the form's `Controls` collection.

A control might not have a parent—its `Parent` property could be `null` (in C#) or `Nothing` (in VB). Such controls are called top-level windows. Top-level windows are contained directly by the desktop, and usually have an entry in the taskbar. For normal Windows Forms applications, a top-level window is a form of some kind.*

Ownership

Ownership defines a rather less direct association between windows than parenting. It allows a group of windows, such as an application window and its associated tool windows, to behave as a single entity for certain operations such as minimizing and activation.

Ownership is used to group related forms. It is often used for toolbox windows—when an application is minimized, any associated tool windows it displays should also be minimized. Likewise, when the application is activated (i.e., brought to the front by a mouse click or Alt-Tab), the tool windows should also be activated. You can automate this behavior by setting up an ownership association between the tool windows and the main windows. Unlike parenting, ownership only exists between top-level windows, because an owned form is never contained by its owner. (For example, undocked toolbars can usually be moved completely outside the main window, which would not be possible if they were children of that window.)

Although an owned form may live outside or overlap its owner, it will always appear directly in front of it in the Z-order.† Bringing the owner to the foreground will cause all the forms it owns to appear in front of it. (This is not the same thing as a top-most form, which is described below.) Bringing an owned form to the front will have the same effect as bringing its owner to the front. Minimizing an owner causes all its owned windows to be minimized too, although an owned window can be minimized without minimizing the owner.

Owned windows typically don't need their own representation on the Windows taskbar because they are subordinate to their owners. Because activating an owned window implicitly activates the owner and vice versa, it would merely clutter up the taskbar to have entries for both. So owned forms normally have their `ShowInTaskBar` properties set to `false`.

The following code fragments (in VB and C#) show a new form being created, owned, and displayed:

```
// defining an owner form in C#
MyForm ownedForm = new MyForm( );
ownedForm.ShowInTaskbar = false;
AddOwnedForm(ownedForm);
ownedForm.Show( );
```

* Strictly speaking, the framework allows for top-level controls that are not forms, so you should not presume that a top-level control can necessarily be cast to `Form`. You can determine whether a control is top-level from its `TopLevel` property.

† Windows defines a *Z-order* for all windows on the screen. It determines which windows are on top of which other windows; i.e., if two windows were to overlap, the one that is highest in the Z-order will obscure the one underneath. *Z* is used because it effectively determines the position of the window in third dimension: X and Y are screen position, so Z must define the stacking order.

```
' defining an owner form in VB
Dim ownedForm As New [MyForm]
ownedForm.ShowInTaskbar = False
AddOwnedForm(ownedForm)
ownedForm.Show( )
```

(This fragment would be inside some method on the owner form, such as its constructor.) `AddOwnedForm` is a method of the `Form` class that adds a form to the list of owned forms. (Using `ownedForm.Owner = this;` or `ownedForm.Owner = Me` would have exactly the same effect; as with parenting, the ownership association can be set up from either side.) Note the use of the `ShowInTaskBar` property to prevent this window from getting its own entry in the taskbar.

All owned forms are closed when their owning form is closed. Because they are considered wholly subordinate to the owner, they don't receive the `Closed` or `Closing` events when the main form closes (although they do if they are closed in isolation.) So if you need to handle these events, you must do so in the owning form.

Top-most forms

It is important not to confuse owned forms with top-most forms. (These in turn should not be confused with top-level forms, as defined earlier.) Superficially, they may seem similar: a top-most form is one that always appears on top of any non–top-most forms. Viewed in isolation, owned forms may look like they are doing the same thing—an owned form always appears on top of its owner. However, top-most forms are really quite different—they will appear on top of *all* other windows, even those from other applications.

If you need a form to sit above all other windows, set its `TopMost` property to `true`. Certain kinds of popup might need to set this property to `true`—your application might need to display some visual alert that should be visible regardless of what windows are currently open, much like Windows Messenger does. But exercise good taste—making all windows top-most is pointless because ultimately only one window can really be at the very top (the top-most window with the highest Z-order), and it can be very annoying for the user to be unable to hide a top-most window. If you decide to make a window top-most, unless it is a short-lived pop-up window, you should provide a way of disabling this behavior, as the Windows Task Manager does with its Always on Top menu option.

Owned forms and top-most forms are useful when we need to control the ordering of forms either with respect to all other windows on the desktop or just between specific groups of forms. But arguably the most important relationship is the one between parent and child controls—this association is fundamental to the way controls are contained within a window. Although the parent/child relationship is managed by the `Control` class, there can be complications with focus management for nested controls. This issue is dealt with by the `ContainerControl` class, which we will look at now.

Control and ContainerControl

As we have seen, the ability to act as a container of controls (i.e., to be a parent) is a feature supplied by the `Control` class. Its `Controls` property manages the collection of children. Only certain control types elect to present this container-like behavior in the Designer (e.g., the `Form`, `Panel`, and `GroupBox` controls), but more bizarre nesting can be arranged if you write the code by hand—it is possible to nest a button inside another button, for example. This is not useful, but it is possible as a side effect of the fact that containment is a feature provided by the base `Control` class.

But if you examine the `Form` class closely, you will see that it inherits from a class called `ContainerControl`. You might be wondering why we need a special container control class when all controls can support containment. The answer is that `ContainerControl` has a slightly misleading name. `ContainerControl` only really adds one feature to the basic `Control`.* The main purpose of a `ContainerControl` is to provide focus management.

Sometimes you will build groups of controls that act together as a single entity. The most obvious example is a form, which is both a group of controls and also a distinct entity in the UI. But as we will see in Chapter 5, it is possible to build non–top-level controls composed from multiple other controls (so-called user controls).

Such groups typically need to remember which of their constituent controls last had the focus. For example, if a form has lost the focus, it is important that when the form is reactivated, the focus returns to the same control as before. Imagine how annoying it would be if an application forgot which field you were in every time you tabbed away from it. And we also expect individual controls on a form to remember where they were—when the focus moves to a list control, we expect it to remember which list item was selected previously, and we expect tree controls to remember which tree item last had the focus.

Users expect UI elements to remember such state in between losing the focus and reacquiring it. (Most users probably wouldn't be conscious of the fact that they expect this, but they would soon complain if you were to provide them with an application that forgot where it was every time it lost the focus.) So the Windows Forms framework helpfully provides us with this functionality in the `ContainerControl` class.

Most of the time, you don't really need to think about `ContainerControl`. It should be used whenever you build a single UI element that consists of several controls, but because the `Form` class and the `UserControl` class (see Chapter 5) both inherit from `ContainerControl`, you are forced into doing the right thing.

Note that the `Panel` and `GroupBox` classes do not derive from `ContainerControl`, even though they usually contain other controls. This is because they do not aim to modify focus management in any way—they are essentially cosmetic. Focus for

* Strictly speaking, it adds two, but one is a feature it acquires by deriving from `ScrollableControl`: the ability to add scrollbars to a control automatically.

controls nested inside these controls is managed in exactly the same as it would have been if they were parented directly by the form, because a `ContainerControl` assumes ownership not just for its children, but for all its descendants. (Of course, if it has any `ContainerControl` descendants, it will let those manage their own children; each `ContainerControl` acts as a boundary for focus management.)

Focus and validation

As discussed in the previous chapter, focus management is closely related to validation. A control whose `CausesValidation` property is `true` will only normally be validated when two conditions are met: first, it must have had the focus; and second, some other control whose `CausesValidation` property is also `true` must subsequently receive the focus. (Any number of controls whose `CausesValidation` property is `false` may receive the focus in between these two events.)

Because `ContainerControl` groups a set of controls together and manages the focus within that group, it has an impact on how validation is performed. When the focus moves between controls within a `ContainerControl`, the validation logic works exactly as described above. But when the focus moves out of a `ContainerControl` that is nested within another `ContainerControl` (e.g., a `UserControl` on a `Form`), things are a little more complex.

Figure 3-2 shows a form (which is a `ContainerControl`) and a `UserControl`. We will discuss the `UserControl` class in Chapter 5, but for now, the important things to know are that it derives from `ContainerControl` and that it is treated as a single entity by the containing form (the form will not be able to see the individual text boxes and labels inside the control). All the text boxes have `Validating` event handlers, and all the controls have their `CausesValidation` properties set to `true`. Currently, the focus is in the `Foo` text box.

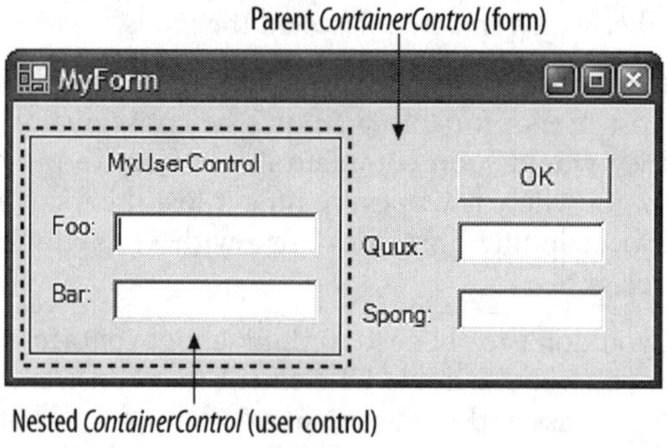

Parent *ContainerControl* (form)
MyForm
MyUserControl
OK
Foo:
Quux:
Bar:
Spong:
Nested *ContainerControl* (user control)

Figure 3-2. Validation and ContainerControl nesting

When the focus moves to `Bar`, the rules of validation say that `Foo` must be validated. This is not a problem—both controls are inside the same `ContainerControl` (`MyUserControl`). It is responsible for their focus management, so it will ensure that `Foo` is validated. But what would happen if instead the focus moved to `Quux`? `Quux` is not inside the user control—its focus is managed by another `ContainerControl`, the form.

The form knows nothing of the Foo and Bar fields—these are just encapsulated implementation details of the user control. But it will correctly determine that MyUserControl should be validated because both MyUserControl and Quux have their CausesValidation property set to true. Fortunately, when any ContainerControl (such as a UserControl) is validated, it remembers which of its member controls last had the focus, and validates that. So in this case, when the focus moves from Foo to Bar, the form validates MyUserControl, which in turn validates Foo.

Ambient Properties

Regardless of whether your controls are all children of the form, nested inside group boxes and panels, or nested within a ContainerControl for focus management, you will want your application to look consistent. When you modify certain properties of a form's appearance, all the controls on the form should pick up the same properties. For example, if you change the background color of your form, you will probably want any controls on the form to use the same background color. It would be tedious if you had to set such properties manually on every single control on the form. Fortunately you don't have to—by default, the main visual properties will propagate automatically.

The properties that behave like this are known as ambient properties. The ambient properties on the Control class are Cursor, Font, ForeColor, and BackColor. It is useful to understand exactly how ambient properties work—the Forms Designer in Visual Studio .NET doesn't show you everything that is going on, and the results can therefore sometimes be a little surprising.

Using the Designer, you could be forgiven for assuming that if you don't set a visual property of a control, it will just have a default value. For example, the background color of a button will seem to be SystemColors.Control. However, a control distinguishes between a property that has had its value set and a property that hasn't. So when you don't set the BackColor of a control, it's not that the BackColor has a default value; it actually has no value at all.

This is obfuscated somewhat by the fact that when you retrieve a control's BackColor, you will always get a nonempty value back. What is not obvious is that this value didn't necessarily come from the control in question. If you ask a control for its background color when the background color has not been set on that control, it starts looking elsewhere to find out what its color should be.

If a control doesn't know what value a particular property should have, the first place it looks is its parent. So if you put a button on a form, then read that button's BackColor without having set it, you are implicitly reading the form's BackColor.

But what if there is no parent to ask? A Form might have no parent, so what does it do when asked for its BackColor if none has been specified? At this point it attempts to see if it is being hosted in an environment that supplies it with an AmbientProperties object. To find this out, it uses the Control class's Site property, and if this is non-null, it will call its GetService method to determine whether the environment can supply an AmbientProperties object. Usually there will be no site, in which case, it finally falls back to returning its default value. (This will be the case if the form is just being run as a standalone application; you usually only get a site when being hosted in something like Internet Explorer.)

So what impact do these ambient properties have on your application's behavior? Their effect is that unless you explicitly specify visual properties for your controls, they will automatically pick up appropriate values from their surroundings. If a control is being hosted in some environment that supplies values for these ambient properties, such as Internet Explorer, it will use those. Otherwise, the system-wide defaults will be used.

Some controls deliberately ignore certain ambient properties, either because they have no use for them or because they positively want to use something else. For example, the `TextBox` class overrides the `BackColor` property so that its background is always the `SystemColors.Window` color (typically white) by default, regardless of what the ambient background color is.

Remember that whenever you read an ambient property on a control, you will get back something, but unless that property was set explicitly on that control, the value you get back will have been retrieved from elsewhere. Visual Studio .NET makes it clear when you have modified a property on a control by showing the value of that property in bold type. This is useful, but it does not tell you how the property obtains its value when it has not been set explicitly—the Properties window always shows the effective value, without telling you where that value came from. In some cases, you may need to examine the source code to see exactly what it has done: if the property has not been set explicitly in the `InitializeComponent` method, the value shown will be the ambient one.

MDI Applications

Many Windows applications use the Multiple Document Interface (MDI). This defines a user interface structure for programs that can display multiple files. The application has a main window, and each document being edited is displayed inside a child window. Windows Forms provides special support for this.

We could just create our document windows as children of the main application window. However, this still leaves us with a certain amount of work to do to manage menus correctly—MDI applications usually present their menus in the main application window, but modify which items are present according to whether a document window is active. Windows Forms is able to manage MDI menus correctly for us, including automatically merging a child window's menu into the main application window. The details of menu merging are discussed in Chapter 4, but to make this happen automatically, we must tell Windows Forms that we are building an MDI-style application. First of all, we must set the parent window's `IsMdiContainer` property to `true`. Second, when we display a child window, we must let Windows Forms know that is should behave as an MDI child, as in the following C# code fragment:

```
ChildForm cf = new ChildForm( );
cf.MdiParent = this;
cf.Show( );
```

or in its equivalent VB code fragment:

```
Dim cf As New ChildForm( )
cf.MdiParent = Me
cf.Show( )
```

By establishing the parent/child relationship with the MdiParent property instead of the normal Parent property, we enable automatic menu merging.

Layout

As we saw in the previous chapter, the framework can modify a control's position and size automatically. We looked at the docking and anchoring facilities, but Windows Forms provides support for other styles of layout. The simplest of these is a fixed layout in a scrollable window. Splitter support is also built in. In this section, we will look at all these styles of layout, and then examine the mechanism in the framework that underpins them all. It is possible to extend the layout facilities to provide your own automatic layout strategies. We will look at the standard events that support this, and then see a simple example custom layout engine.

Scrolling

Windows Forms provides a facility for enabling the contents of a control to exceed the control's size on screen, and for scrollbars to be added automatically to enable the user to access all of it. This functionality is provided by the `ScrollableControl` class. This is the base class of `ContainerControl` and of `Panel`, which means that this behavior is available to all forms, panels, and user controls.

To enable automatic scrolling management, simply set the `AutoScroll` property to `true`. If the window is smaller than its contents, scrollbars will be added automatically. Of course, the class will need some way of knowing how large the window's contents are. By default, it will deduce this from its child controls—it will assume that the window's size should be exactly large enough to hold all the controls.

Because automatic scrolling will make the scrollable area exactly large enough to hold the controls and no larger, the controls will be right up against the edge of the window when it is scrolled as far down or across as it can go. However, you can add some padding by setting the `AutoScrollMargin` property. This property's type is `Size`, which enables you to specify the vertical padding and the horizontal padding separately. So specifying a margin of `new Size(10, 20)` would leave 10 units of blank space to the right of the right-most control and 20 units of blank space beneath the lowest control.

Alternatively, you can set the scroll size explicitly with the `AutoScrollMinSize` property, which is also of type `Size`. The space occupied by the controls will still be calculated as described above, but if the `AutoScrollMinSize` property is larger, its value will be used instead. (In fact, each dimension is used individually—the effective window size will be wide enough for the controls and any padding specified with `AutoScrollMargin`, and at least as wide as `AutoScrollMinSize.Width`, and it will be tall enough for the controls and any padding, and at least as tall as `AutoScrollMinSize.Height`.)

You should not use both docking (discussed in the following section) and scrolling in a single control. If you wish to have controls docked to the edge of a scrolling window, you should add a child `Panel` control and make that do the scrolling, setting the panel's `Dock` property to `Fill` so that it will use all the remaining space not used by other controls docked to the edges of the form. This is because the automatic scrolling logic does not interact well with the automatic layout logic used when docking. Figure 3-3 shows such a form—it has a TextBox docked to the left and a Panel docked to fill the remaining area. The Form itself is not scrollable. The scrollbar is present because Panel's AutoScroll property has been set to true.

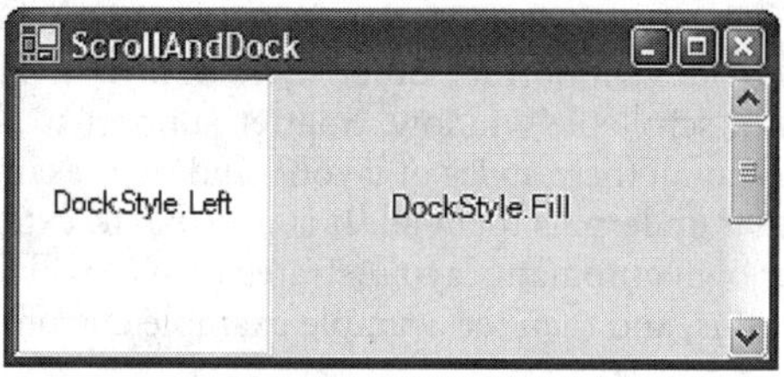

ScrollAndDock
DockStyle.Left
DockStyle.Fill

Figure 3-3. Combining scrolling and docking

In fact, there is a little more to docking than was discussed in Chapter 2, so it is time to revisit the topic.

Docking

We saw in Chapter 2 how to get a control to attach itself to the edge of a form by using the Dock property. What we didn't look at was what happens when more than one control in a given window uses docking. Not only can you have multiple controls docked in a single window, you can even have more than one docked to the same edge, but it is important to understand exactly what the Windows Forms layout logic does under these circumstances.

When two controls are docked on the same edge of a window, the behavior is straightforward. The control that is docked first will be up against the edge of the window, and the next one will be up against the first control, and so on. Every time a control is docked, it effectively defines that edge of the window for docking as far as other controls are concerned. (And any control that specifies Dock.Fill gets all the space left over.)

This rule applies to multiple controls docked to different edges too—the first one to be docked always gets the entire edge, and each subsequent control gets whatever is left over. Figure 3-4 shows the effect of this for a pair of controls, one of which is docked to the top of the form, the other to the side.

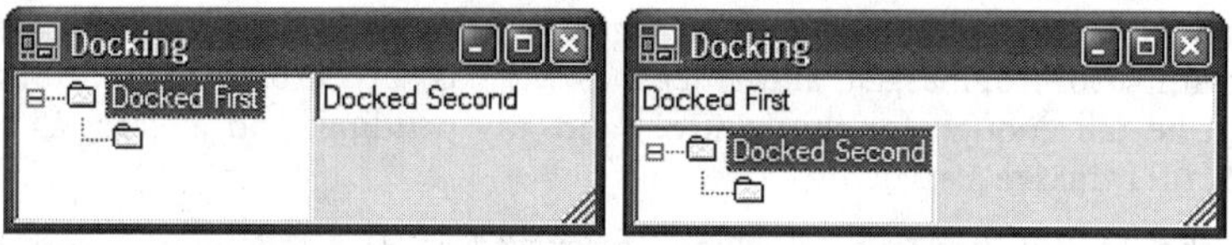

Docking
Docked First
Docked Second
Docking
Docked First
Docked Second

Figure 3-4. The impact of docking order

But what determines the order in which docking occurs? If I have three controls all docked to the left edge of a window, the order in which they will appear is determined by the fact that the children of a control are held in an ordered collection. (The `Controls` property remembers the order in which you added the controls.) The later a control was added to the collection, the earlier it will be considered for docking.

You can modify this order with the Forms Designer. If you bring a control to the front, it is moved to the top of the list of controls passed to `AddRange`, because when controls overlap, the ones at the front of this list appear on top. For docking, this will cause it to be docked last, so it will appear innermost. So if you have multiple controls docked to the same edge of a form, sending one of those controls to the back in the editor will move it to the edge of the form, and bringing it to the front will move it inwards.

Splitters

The purpose of a splitter is to divide a window into two resizable portions. For example, the bar that divides the folders pane from the contents pane in a Windows Explorer window is a splitter. The user can drag the splitter around to change the way the space is shared between the two panes. The Windows Forms framework supplies a `Splitter` control that provides this functionality.

The `Splitter` control never actually moves anything—it relies on the framework's docking mechanism to do the work for it. The usual way of using a splitter is to have one between two other controls. The first control and the splitter are docked to the same edge of the window, usually the left or the top. The splitter should be docked towards the inside of the window (i.e., it should be ahead of the other control in the list passed to `AddRange`, which means putting it to the back in the Designer). The remaining control is then set to `Dock.Fill` so that it uses the remaining space. Figure 3-5 shows a typical layout for a vertical splitter.

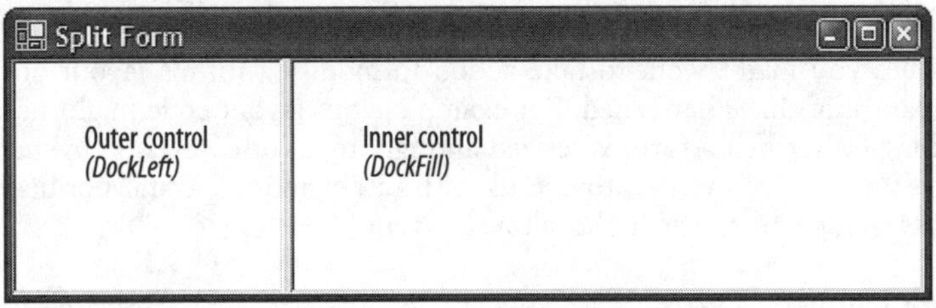
Split Form
Outer control
(DockLeft)
Inner control
(DockFill)

Figure 3-5. Use of docking for splitters

When the user drags a splitter, the splitter control only resizes the outermost control. This causes the window to perform a layout operation, recalculating the position of all docked controls. As a side effect of resizing the outermost control, when the splitter's position is calculated, it will automatically be moved to the edge of that panel. The splitter doesn't have to move itself—resizing the control it is docked up against is enough, because Windows Forms' automatic layout moves the splitter automatically. This in turn changes the amount of space available for the other control, and because that is set to `Dock.Fill`, the other control will fill the space available, shrinking or expanding as required.

For the splitter to work, all three controls must be docked and in the correct order. It is fairly common practice for one or both of the controls to be `Panel` objects—this allows you to place multiple controls inside the areas that the splitter resizes. This is useful if you want to use multiple controls in conjunction with a splitter, because a splitter can only cause the two controls on either side of it to be resized.

Layout Events

The splitter relies on the automatic layout features of the `Control` class. Moreover, it relies on the control class automatically recalculating the layout as a result of one of its child controls being resized. This works because the Windows Forms framework is designed to support automatic re-layout in response to certain events. It also allows us to influence the way in which layout is performed.

Any time a control is added to or removed from another control, or something is moved or resized, it is presumed that this will have an impact on how the form's contents should be arranged. So whenever this happens, the framework calls the parent control's `PerformLayout` method. This will perform the automatic docking and anchor layout, but before doing that it raises the `Layout` event. This gives our code a chance to execute custom layout logic.

So during normal operation, layout will be performed every time a window changes size, or any of its contents are moved or resized. Most of the time, this is fine, but what about when we are creating the window? Everything we do during initialization would cause it to perform another layout. This would be a waste of time, because only the very last layout it does would stick. So during initialization, we call the form's `SuspendLayout` method at the start, and then the form's `ResumeLayout` method when we have finished arranging the contents of the form. (Visual Studio .NET puts these calls in for us.) This means we just get the one layout performed at the end of the initialization process, which is what we require.

Sometimes you might want to take action to modify a form's layout only when particular things have happened. For example, your layout code might need to do something only when a form is resized and ignore all other events. In such cases, the `Move` and `Resize` events provide us with rather more specific notifications of what has changed than the firehose `Layout` event.

Custom Layout

So why would we ever care about the `Layout` event? Unfortunately the `Dock` and `Anchor` properties don't cover every possible automatic layout eventuality. For example, a common requirement is to have several controls fill the width of a form (or maybe a panel in a form), sharing the space evenly between all the controls. (So if there are three controls across, each will take exactly a third of the space available.)

This cannot be done with the standard docking and anchoring layout, so some custom logic must be used. The `Layout` event simply notifies us when it is time to apply that logic.

Example 3-13 shows a simple custom layout handler that can be attached to a control's Layout event like so:

```
myPanel.Layout += new LayoutEventHandler(HorizontalLayout);
```

Example 3-14 shows the corresponding custom layout handler in VB. (The Panel control must also be declared programmatically using the WithEvents keyword.)

Example 3-13. Example custom layout in C#

```
private void HorizontalLayout(object sender,
    System.Windows.Forms.LayoutEventArgs e)
{
    Control parent = (Control) sender;
    for (int i = 0; i < parent.Controls.Count; ++i)
    {
        Control child = parent.Controls[i];
        int pos = i * parent.Width;
        pos /= parent.Controls.Count;
        child.Left = pos;
        child.Width = parent.Width/parent.Controls.Count;
    }
}
```

Example 3-14. Example custom layout in VB

```
Private Sub HorizontalLayout(sender As Object, _
                              e As LayoutEventArgs) _
                              Handles myPanel.Layout
   Dim parent As Control = DirectCast(sender, Control)
   Dim child As Control
   Dim I, pos As Integer
   For i = 0 to parent.Controls.Count - 1
      child = parent.Controls(i)
      pos = i * parent.Width
      pos /= parent.Controls.Count
      child.Left = pos
      child.Width = parent.Width/parent.Controls.Count
   Next
End Sub
```

It will automatically adjust the width and horizontal position of each child control, so that they fill their parent control and are each of the same width. Note that you must attach this to the Layout event of the parent control whose children you wish to arrange, not the children themselves.

Localization

The software market is a global one, and many programs will ship in regions where the users' first language will be different from the application developers' native tongue. While many software products get away with making the highly parochial assumption that everybody speaks English, .NET lets us do better than that. It provides support for building applications that support multiple languages.

The .NET Framework supplies facilities for localization of resources such as strings and bitmaps, and the Forms Designer can create forms that make use of this. To understand how to create localizable user interfaces, it is first necessary to understand the underlying localization mechanism that it is based on, so we will first look at global resource management, and then we will see how it is applied in a Windows Forms application.

Resource Managers

The programming model for localizable applications is based on a simple premise: whenever you require information that might be affected by the current language, you must not hardcode this information into your application. All such information should be retrieved through a culture-sensitive mechanism. (In .NET, the word *culture* is used to describe a locality; it implies all the relevant information, such as location, language, date formats, sorting conventions, etc.) The mechanism we use for this is the `ResourceManager` class, which is defined in the `System.Resources` namespace.

The `ResourceManager` class allows named pieces of data to be retrieved. (We'll see where this data is stored in just a moment.) For example, rather than hardcoding an error message directly into the source, we can do the following in C#:

```
ResourceManager resources = new ResourceManager(typeof(MyForm));
string errorWindowTitle = resources.GetString("errorTitle");
string errorText = resources.GetString("errorFileNotFound");
MessageBox.Show(errorText, errorWindowTitle);
```

The equivalent code in VB is:

```
Dim resources As New ResourceManager(GetType([MyForm]))
Dim errorWindowTitle As String = resources.GetString("errorTitle")
Dim errorText As String = resources.GetString("errorFileNotFound")
MessageBox.Show(errorText, errorWindowTitle)
```

This creates a `ResourceManager` object and asks it for two named resources: `errorTitle` and `errorFileNotFound`. It uses the strings returned by the `ResourceManager` as the error text and window title of a message box.

So where will the `ResourceManager` find this information? It will look for a resource file—a file that contains nothing but named bits of data, and it will expect to find it embedded as a named resource in an assembly. (Any .NET assembly can have arbitrary named files embedded in them. Any kind of file can be attached in this way—e.g., text files, bitmaps, binary files. But the `ResourceManager` will be looking for an embedded file in its special resource format.) It needs to know two things to locate the embedded resource file: the name of the resource file and the assembly in which it is embedded.

The name of the resource file is typically based on a class name. So in the previous code fragments, the `ResourceManager` will be looking for a file named after the `MyForm` class. It will always use the full name of the class, including its namespace, so if `MyForm` is defined in the `MyLocalizableApp` namespace, the `ResourceManager` will look for an embedded resource called `MyLocalizableApp.MyForm.resources`. (We will see shortly how to get Visual Studio .NET to add an appropriately named resource file to your project.)

But the ResourceManager also needs to know which assembly the resource file will be contained in. The assembly it will load is determined by the culture in which the code is running (i.e., what country and with which language).

A culture is identified by a two-part name. The first part indicates the spoken language, and the second part indicates the geographical location. For example, en-US represents the English-speaking U.S. locality, while fr-BE indicates the French-speaking Belgian culture. We need both the spoken language and the region to define a culture, because either on its own is not enough to determine how all information should be presented. For example, many localities have English as a first language, but can differ in other details. For example, although the en-US and en-GB cultures (American and British, respectively) both use the same language, dates are displayed differently—in the United Kingdom, the usual format is day/month/year, while in the U.S., the month is usually specified first. In this particular case, the country name alone would be sufficient, but that is often ambiguous, because many countries have more than one official language (e.g., Canada and Belgium).

The culture that is in force is determined by the Regional and Language Options Control Panel applet in Windows. The ResourceManager will use the two-part culture string to locate the assembly. It will always look for an assembly called *AppName.resources.dll*, where *AppName* is your application executable's name. The current culture merely determines the directories it will look in. If the culture is, say, fr-BE, it will first look for a subdirectory called *fr-BE*. (It will look for this directory beneath whatever directory your program happens to be running in.) If it doesn't find it there, it will then fall back to looking for generic French-language resources in an *fr* directory. Finally, if it finds neither of these, it will look in the application executable itself. This means that if there are no resources for the appropriate culture, it will revert to using whatever resources are built into the program itself. (These are referred to as the culture-neutral resources, but they are usually written for whatever culture the application developer calls home.)

Figure 3-6 shows the directory structure of a typical localized application. The executable file itself would live in the *Localizable* directory shown here. (There is no significance to that name—you can call the root directory anything.) This particular application has several culture-specific subdirectories, each of which contains an assembly called *AppName.resources.dll* (where *AppName* is whatever the main executable file is called). Both French and Dutch are supported. The resource DLLs in the *fr* and *nl* directories would contain resources appropriate to the French or Dutch languages respectively, which are independent of any particular French- or Dutch-speaking region. There are also location-specific resources supplied. For example, if there are any phrases that require slightly different idiomatic translations for French as spoken in France and French as spoken in Wallonia, these will be in the resource files in the *fr-FR* and *fr-BE* subdirectories, respectively. Note that this application should be able to function correctly in locales such as fr-CA and nl-NL—even though there are no subdirectories specific to these cultures, they will fall back to the *fr* and *nl* directories.

These resource assemblies in the culture-specific subdirectories are often referred to as *satellite assemblies*. This is intended to conjure up a picture of the main application assembly being surrounded by a collection of small but associated assemblies. (Satellite assemblies are typically smaller than the main application because they just

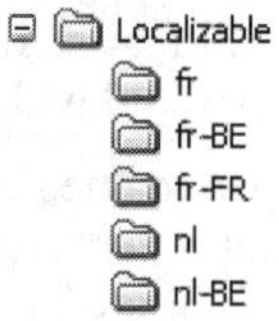
Localizable
fr
fr-BE
fr-FR
nl
nl-BE

Figure 3-6. A localized directory structure

contain resources; the main application assembly tends to be at least as large as the satellites because it usually contains both code and default resources.)

Resources and Visual Studio .NET

Visual Studio .NET can automatically build satellite resource assemblies for your application, and the Forms Designer can generate code that uses a `ResourceManager` for all localizable aspects of a form.

This raises an interesting question: what should be localizable? Text strings obviously need to be localizable, because they will normally need to be translated, but there are less obvious candidates too. Some languages are more verbose than others, and once the text of a label or button has been translated, the control may not be large enough to display it. This means that for localization of strings to be of any use, a control's size must also be localizable. And if controls need to be resized for localization purposes, this will almost certainly mean that other controls on the same form will need to be moved. So on a localizable form, the Forms Designer also retrieves the size and position of controls from the `ResourceManager`, rather than hardcoding them in. In fact, it retrieves almost all the properties that affect a control's appearance from the `ResourceManager`, just in case they need to be modified for a particular culture.

To get the Forms Designer to generate this localizable code, simply set the form's `Localizable` property (in the `Misc` category) to `true`. This will cause it to regenerate the entire `InitializeComponent` method so that all relevant properties are read from a `ResourceManager`. It also adds a new file to the project named after your form: if your form's class is `MyForm`, it will add a *MyForm.resx* file. By default, this file will be hidden, but if you go to the Solution Explorer window and enable the Show All Files button on its toolbar, your *MyForm.cs* or *MyForm.vb* file will grow a + symbol. If you click this, you will see the *MyForm.resx* file. This file contains all the culture-neutral values for your form's properties. It is hidden by default because you do not normally need to edit it directly; we will examine its contents shortly. (You may remember that the `ResourceManager` class will actually be looking for a *.resource* file, not a *.resx* file. Visual Studio .NET stores all resources in *.resx* files, but it compiles these into *.resource* files when it builds your component.)

Having made your form localizable, any properties that you edit will simply be changed in the resource file. So how do we exploit this to make a localized version of the form for some other culture? Alongside the `Localizable` property, you will see a `Language` property. This is usually `(Default)`, to indicate that you are editing the default resource file. But you can change this to another culture. If you set it to German, you will see that another resource file is added to your application—*MyForm.de.resx*. Visual Studio .NET will compile this file into a satellite assembly in the *de* subdirectory.* If you do any further editing to the form, new property values will be stored in this file, meaning that those values will be used when running in a German culture. You can also specify a more specific culture—if you select German (Austria), Visual Studio will add a *MyForm.de-AT.resx* file. This will be built into a satellite assembly in the *de-AT* subdirectory, allowing you to supply properties that will be used specifically in the German-speaking Austrian culture.

So your form will now have multiple faces. Whenever you change the `Language` property, you will be shown how the form will look when displayed in the selected culture. Any edits you make will only apply to the selected culture. Visual Studio .NET takes care of the build process, creating whatever satellite assemblies are required in the appropriate directories. If you want to see the effects of this without modifying your computer's regional settings, you can modify the culture for your application with the following change to your `Main` method in C#:

Forms, Apps, Containers

```
[STAThread]
static void Main()
{
    System.Threading.Thread.CurrentThread.CurrentUICulture =
        new System.Globalization.CultureInfo("fr-FR");
    Application.Run(new PropForm());
}
```

The corresponding VB code is:

```
<STAThread> Public Shared Sub Main()
   System.Threading.Thread.CurrentThread.CurrentUICulture = _
       New System.Globalization.CultureInfo("fr-FR")
   Application.Run(New PropForm())
End Sub
```

This sets the main thread's culture to `fr-FR`. This will cause the `ResourceManager` class to try to locate satellite assemblies containing French resources.

Resource Files

Visual Studio .NET will create and maintain the necessary resource files as you edit your forms for the cultures you choose to support. However, it is often useful to edit these files directly—for example, if you wish to support localization for any error messages you display in a message box, you will need to add your own entries to these files.

You can edit the *.resx* files that Visual Studio .NET creates—it provides a special user interface just for this purpose. If you double click on a *.resx* file for a form (having first made sure that the Solution Explorer is in Show All Files mode), you will see a grid representing the contents of the file, as shown in Figure 3-7.

* Each *.resx* file in a project will end up as a single embedded resource in some assembly. All the resource files for a given culture will be in the same assembly, so you will end up with one satellite assembly for each culture you support. The name of the embedded resource will be determined by the name of the *.resx* file. Visual Studio .NET always prepends the project's default namespace to the resource name, so *MyForm.de.resx* will end up being the *MyNamespace.MyForm.resources* resource in the satellite assembly in the *de* directory. Any *.resx* file whose name does not contain a culture code will end up in the main assembly, so *MyForm.resx* will become the *MyNamespace.MyForm.resources* resource in the main executable assembly.

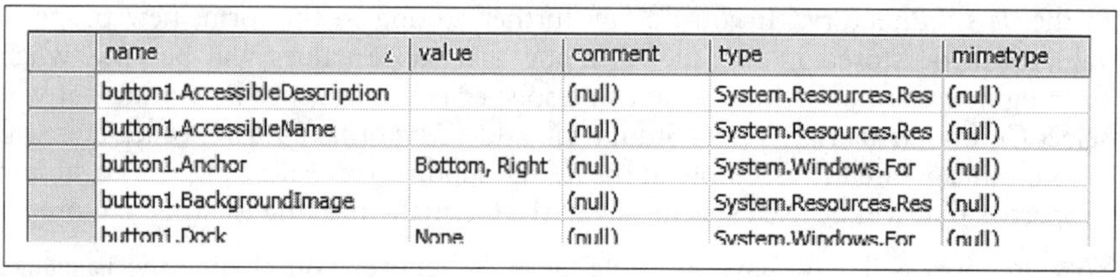

name	value	comment	type	mimetype
button1.AccessibleDescription		(null)	System.Resources.Res	(null)
button1.AccessibleName		(null)	System.Resources.Res	(null)
button1.Anchor	Bottom, Right	(null)	System.Windows.For	(null)
button1.BackgroundImage		(null)	System.Resources.Res	(null)
button1.Dock	None	(null)	System.Windows.For	(null)

Figure 3-7. Editing a .resx file

The Forms Designer uses a naming convention for resource entries. Properties of a control are always named as `control.PropertyName`, where `control` is the name of the control on the form and `PropertyName` is the property whose value is being stored. The value column indicates the value that the property is being set to; an empty value indicates that the property is not to be set. The property's type is also stored in this file—the `ResourceManager` needs to know the data type (e.g., a `string`, a `Color`, a `Size`, etc.) of each property to return the correct kind of object at runtime.* The default type is `string`, so for string lookups you don't need to supply anything other than the name and value. To add your own resource entries (e.g., error text), just type new entries at the bottom of the list. You may use whatever name you like, so long as it is unique within the resource file.

You can also add new *.resx* files to a project. This allows you to add a resource file that is not attached to any particular form. (This is useful for custom control libraries, which will not necessarily contain any forms at all.) Visual Studio .NET uses the same naming convention here as it does for the *.resx* files it creates: if there is a culture name in the filename, it determines which satellite assembly the resource will be held in. And as before, the name of the embedded resource is determined by putting the project default namespace in front of the filename. So *MyStuff.fr-BE.resx* would create an embedded resource called *MyAppNamespace.MyStuff.resources* in the satellite assembly in the *fr-BE* subdirectory.

The easiest way to use such a custom resource file is to name it after some class in your code, and pass the type of that class to the `ResourceManager` when you construct it like so:

```
ResourceManager rm = new ResourceManager(typeof(MyClass));
```

or:

```
Dim rm As New ResourceManager(GetType([MyClass]))
```

This would create a `ResourceManager` that would look for a *MyAppNamespace.MyClass.resources* embedded resource, using the current culture to determine where to find the assembly.

Extender Providers

Although the `Control` class provides a very rich set of features, inevitably it cannot be all things to all people. UI innovations continue to emerge, so even if the

* Values are stored and retrieved using .NET's serialization facility. A type needs to support serialization to be used in a resource file.

Control class were to represent the state of the art today, in time, it would inevitably end up looking short on features.

However, Windows Forms provides a very useful way of extending the abilities of the basic Control class. It is possible to place a component on a form that adds a feature to every single control on that form. Such a component is referred to as an *extender provider*. We will see how to write extender providers in Chapter 9, but no discussion of forms would be complete without looking at how to use them.

The Forms Designer supports extender providers. An extender provider can add new properties to all controls on a form. An example of this in the Windows Forms framework is the ToolTip class. As mentioned in Chapter 2, the Control class does not provide ToolTip support. But this doesn't matter—the framework has a ToolTip class that is able to augment any control with ToolTip support. If you drop the ToolTip component onto a form, it will appear in the component tray at the bottom of the designer. (All non-UI components appear here; the only kind of component that has any business appearing on the form at design time is a control, so everything else appears in the component tray. And the ToolTip isn't strictly a UI component; it is a component that modifies the behavior of other controls.) Once you have done this, if you look at the Properties tab for any of the controls on your form, you will see that each has acquired a ToolTip property in the Misc category. If you set some text for this property for a particular control, that text will appear as a ToolTip whenever the mouse hovers over that control at runtime.

Of course, the classes representing each control haven't really grown a new property—.NET doesn't allow class definitions to change at runtime. The extra property is an illusion presented by the Designer. If you set the ToolTip property on one of your controls in the designer, you will see that what really happens is that code like this is added to the C# InitializeComponent method:

```
this.toolTip1.SetToolTip(this.button1, "This is a button!");
```

or code like this is added to the VB InitializeComponent method:

```
Me.toolTip1.SetToolTip(Me.button1, "This is a button!")
```

Because we cannot really add a new property to somebody else's class, it is the responsibility of the extender provider to remember which controls have had their extender properties set to what. So the ToolTip class maintains a list of which controls have ToolTips and what the text is. It must also provide a method for setting the property. The name of that method is just the property name with Set in front of it. It takes a reference to the control whose property is being set and the property's value. (We will see in Chapter 9 how an extender provider tells the designer what extender properties it adds to the controls on a form.)

Whenever you use an extender provider, it will look like the previous code fragments. You will call a Set*Xxx* method on the provider itself, passing in a reference to the control you would like to set the property on, and the value for the property. It is up to the provider to decide what to do with that value—for example, the ToolTip class attaches its own event handlers to the control and uses these to make the ToolTip appear when the mouse hovers over it.

Summary

All Windows Forms applications have at least one window in them, and each window is represented by an object whose class derives from the `Form` class. These classes are typically generated by the Visual Studio .NET forms designer, which uses a standard structure for handling initialization and shutdown. An application could have just one form or it might have several, but in any case, its lifetime is managed by the `Application` class. The controls in a form can have their layout managed automatically, and while there are several built-in styles of automatic layout, the underlying mechanisms are also exposed, allowing custom automatic layout systems to be written. Another useful feature of forms is the ability to use an extender provider—these are components which add pseudo properties (so-called *extender properties*) to some or all the controls on a form, allowing the basic functionality of the `Control` class to be augmented.

Of course, a great many Windows applications adorn their forms with menus, so in the next chapter we'll look at how to add menus to your applications.

4

Menus and Toolbars

Menus are often the only practical way to present a rich array of functionality without cluttering up the user interface. Whether appearing at the top of the window, or as a context menu accessed through the righthand mouse button, menus allow an application to show concisely which operations are available. An application's usability can be further enhanced by making the most important operations available through toolbar buttons as well as menus.

The Windows Forms framework provides support for both menus and toolbars. Despite the fact that these two technologies serve similar roles—toolbar buttons often correspond directly to menu items—they are presented through two largely unrelated parts of the class library. However, as we will see later, it is possible to unify the way you handle events from them in your application.

In this chapter, we will first examine the support for menus. Then we will see how to create toolbars. Finally, we will see how events from both can be dealt with by a single set of event handlers.

Menus

The Windows Forms framework provides support for adding menus to your applications. It uses a single programming model both for normal window menus and for context menus. The model allows menus to be modified dynamically, or even combined, providing flexibility at runtime, and supports the ability to reuse and extend menu definitions.

We will start by examining the object model used for constructing menus. Then we will see how to attach them to a form. Next, we will look at how to add context menus. Finally, we will see how to reuse and extend your menu definitions by merging items from one menu into another, both in the context of MDI applications, and also when reusing forms through inheritance.

The Object Model

For your application to use menus, you must provide Windows Forms with a description of their structure and contents. You do this by building hierarchies of objects that represent menus and the items they contain. Although you will typically get Visual Studio .NET to do this for you, a sound understanding of the object model it uses is important to use menus effectively in your applications.

This object model revolves around the `Menu` class, which is arguably misnamed, because it represents a more abstract concept than its title suggests. It can correspond to any element of a menu structure, and it is the base class of all the other types in the menu object model. So while a `Menu` object might represent a menu, it could just represent a single item of a menu. (Perhaps `MenuElement` would have been a more descriptive name.) Representing menus and menu items with the same base type seems a little strange at first, but it makes sense when you consider that menus can be hierarchical. A menu item might well be a nested menu, in which case, it makes sense for that menu item to be represented by an object whose class derives from `Menu`.

The main job of the `Menu` class is to represent the structure of a menu. You can find out whether a particular `Menu` object is a leaf item or an item with children by examining its `IsParent` property. If `IsParent` is `true`, its child items will be in a collection on the object's `MenuItems` property.

You will never use the `Menu` class directly. Its constructor is protected, which means that to obtain a reference to a `Menu`, you must instead create one of its derivatives: `MainMenu`, `ContextMenu`, or `MenuItem`.

The `MainMenu` class represents a form's main menu, and `ContextMenu` represents a pop-up context menu. Every menu structure has one or the other of these at its root, and you'll see more about how to use them later on. But everything else in the menu is represented by `MenuItem` objects. Every line that the user sees in a menu (and every top-level menu in a form's main menu) is represented by a `MenuItem`. A leaf item (i.e., a menu item that does not lead to a submenu) is indicated by the fact that it has no children. If the item leads to a submenu, the same object represents both the item and the submenu.

Figure 4-1 shows an example application with a main menu. As you can see, a single `MenuItem` object represents both the Edit caption and the menu associated with it. Each entry in the menu (Undo, Redo, etc.) has its own `MenuItem` object. The object that corresponds to the Find and Replace item also represents the submenu (although the entries in that submenu all have their own `MenuItem` objects).

We'll now look at how to go about building such hierarchies of objects to add menus to an application.

Building menus

The easiest way to create a menu is to use the Visual Studio .NET Forms Designer. It provides two menu-related controls in the tool box: `MainMenu` and `ContextMenu`. Each of these provides a visual interface for editing the contents of a menu. Somewhat confusingly, Visual Studio uses the same interface for both. This is a little strange, because it means that the editor makes context menus look like

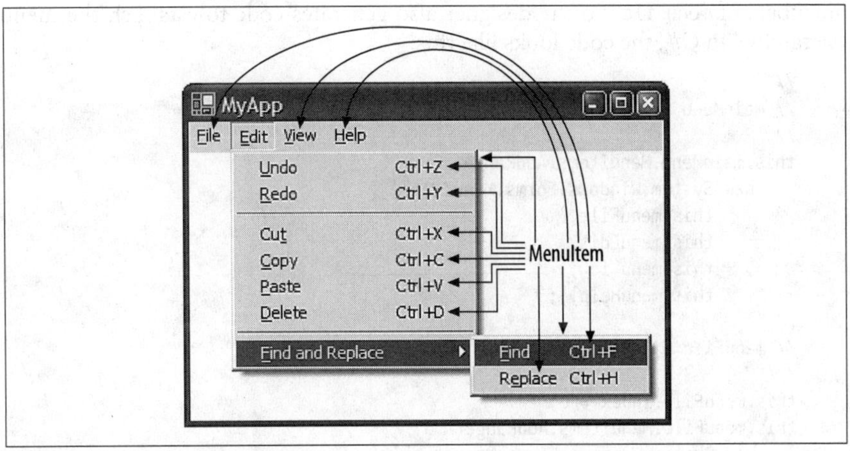
MyApp
File
Edit
View
Help
Undo
Ctrl+Z
Redo
Ctrl+Y
Cut
Ctrl+X
Copy
Ctrl+C
Paste
Ctrl+V
Delete
Ctrl+D
Find and Replace
Find
Ctrl+F
Replace
Ctrl+H
MenuItem

Figure 4-1. Menus and their objects

the form's main menu. But this is just a design-time anomaly—context menus are displayed correctly at runtime.

As we have seen in previous chapters, anything done in the Forms Designer simply ends up generating code. Menus are no exception, and regardless of which kind of menu you create, the Forms Designer generates the same kind of code. It will create a top-level menu (either a `MainMenu` or a `ContextMenu`), and then one `MenuItem` for each element of each menu. The C# code appears as follows:

```
this.mainMenu = new System.Windows.Forms.MainMenu( );
this.menuFile = new System.Windows.Forms.MenuItem( );
this.menuFileNew = new System.Windows.Forms.MenuItem();
this.menuFileOpen = new System.Windows.Forms.MenuItem( );
this.menuFileClose = new System.Windows.Forms.MenuItem( );
this.menuFileExit = new System.Windows.Forms.MenuItem( );
```

The corresponding VB code is:

```
Me.mainMenu = New System.Windows.Forms.MainMenu( )
Me.menuFile = New System.Windows.Forms.MenuItem( )
Me.menuFileNew = New System.Windows.Forms.MenuItem()
Me.menuFileOpen = New System.Windows.Forms.MenuItem( )
Me.menuFileClose = New System.Windows.Forms.MenuItem( )
Me.menuFileExit = New System.Windows.Forms.MenuItem( )
```

> By default, the Designer will choose unhelpful names for the menu items, such as `menuItem1`, `menuItem2`, etc. If you want your code to be readable, it is a good idea to change each menu item's `Name` property to something more meaningful in the Designer, as has been done in this example. (The `Name` property is in the Design category of the Properties window.)

Of course, creating a few menu items is not enough to describe the menu fully—with the code as it stands, Windows Forms will have no idea that `menuFile` is an item of `mainMenu`, or that `menuFileNew`, `menuFileOpen`, and `menuFileClose` are members of menuFile. So the designer also generates code to establish the menu hierarchy.* In C#, the code looks like this:

```
//
// mainMenu
//
this.mainMenu.MenuItems.AddRange(
    new System.Windows.Forms.MenuItem[] {
        this.menuFile,
        this.menuEdit,
        this.menuView,
        this.menuHelp});
//
// menuFile
//
this.menuFile.Index = 0;
this.menuFile.MenuItems.AddRange(
    new System.Windows.Forms.MenuItem[] {
        this.menuFileNew,
        this.menuFileOpen,
        this.menuFileClose,
        this.menuFileExit});
```

In VB:

```
'mainMenu
'
Me.mainMenu.MenuItems.AddRange( _
    New System.Windows.Forms.MenuItem( ) _
        {Me.menuFile, _
         Me.menuEdit, _
         Me.menuView,
         Me.menuHelp})
'
'menuFile
'
Me.menuFile.Index = 0
Me.menuFile.MenuItems.AddRange( _
    New System.Windows.Forms.MenuItem( ) _
        {Me.menuFileNew, _
         Me.menuFileOpen, _
         Me.menuFileClose, _
         Me.menuFileExit})
```

Note that the designer uses the same code for adding items to the main menu as for adding items to the File submenu. This illustrates why all the various menu classes derive from the Menu base class—Menu supplies the functionality common to all menu elements, such as the ability to contain menu items.

A menu's items are stored in the MenuItems property, whose type is the special-purpose collection class Menu.MenuItemCollection. The code uses this collection's AddRange method to add a list of MenuItem objects. Of course, because each

* The other top level menus referenced here (menuEdit, menuView, and menuHelp) would be built in the same way as the File menu. The relevant code has been omitted for conciseness.

MenuItem inherits from Menu, it has a MenuItems property too, and can have further subitems added—this is how nested menu structures are built.

The order in which you add menu items to a parent menu has no bearing on the order in which they appear on screen. Their order is controlled by the Index property. This property is an int or Integer, and it is used to number child items sequentially starting from 0. (The Designer does this automatically, and adjusts the Index properties when you reorder items visually.)

The framework will also need to know what text should be displayed for each menu item, and whether it has any keyboard shortcut associated with it. So for each item, the Designer generates code like this in C#:

```
this.menuFileNew.Index = 0;
this.menuFileNew.Shortcut = System.Windows.Forms.Shortcut.CtrlN;
this.menuFileNew.Text = "&New...";
```

And code like this in VB:

```
Me.menuFileNew.Index = 0
Me.menuFileNew.Shortcut = System.Windows.Forms.Shortcut.CtrlN
Me.menuFileNew.Text = "&New..."
```

As we have already seen, the Index property determines the order in which menu items appear. The Text property determines what text should be displayed. (If you set this to a hyphen, the menu item will appear as a separator—a dividing line between menu items.) The ampersand denotes something called an accelerator; both this and the Shortcut property allow experienced users to use menus much more quickly than would otherwise be possible.

Accelerators and shortcut keys

Most Windows applications can be controlled from the keyboard as well as with the mouse. In fact, this is a requirement for earning the Designed for Windows logo. Accelerator keys and shortcut keys are two long-established mechanisms for making menus easier to use from the keyboard.

Menus can be navigated with the arrow keys, but with large menu structures, this rapidly becomes tiresome, so *accelerator keys* are also supported. These are keys that can be pressed to select a particular menu item without having to use the mouse or arrow keys. Each item in a menu can have a letter associated with it, and if the user presses that key while the menu is visible, the effect is the same as clicking on the item.

The previous code fragments illustrate how to choose an accelerator key: in the Text property, we simply place an ampersand in front of the relevant letter. So in this example, if the user presses the N key while the File menu is open, the New menu item will be selected. The user can find out what accelerator keys are available by pressing the Alt key while the menu is open: the accelerators will be underlined, as shown in Figure 4-2. (Older versions of Windows show the accelerators at all times, even when Alt has not been pressed.)

Menu accelerators can make it easy for experienced users to use menus quickly without taking their hands off the keyboard. However, for very frequently used operations, keyboard shortcuts provide a more direct form of access.

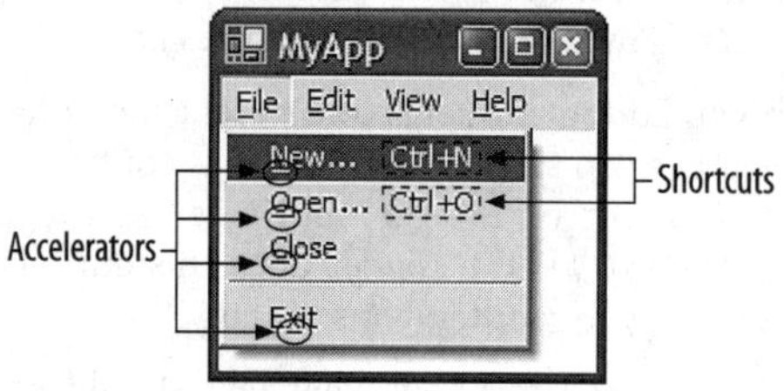
MyApp
File Edit View Help
New... Ctrl+N
Open... Ctrl+O
Close
Exit
Accelerators
Shortcuts

Figure 4-2. Menu with accelerators and shortcuts

Unlike menu accelerators, which can only be used while the relevant menu is visible, a shortcut key can be used at any time. In this example, the New menu item's shortcut key is Ctrl-N. The user can press Ctrl-N without a menu visible, and it will be as if he had selected the New item from the File menu.

Shortcuts are assigned with the `Shortcut` property on the `MenuItem` class, and its value must be one of the key combinations enumerated in the `Shortcut` enumeration. This is a subset of all possible key presses; it includes the function keys, with various combinations of modifier keys (e.g., `F12` or `CtrlShiftF3`), and the alphanumeric keys with Ctrl or Ctrl and Shift, (e.g., `CtrlA`, `CtrlShiftQ`, `Ctrl3`). By default, the shortcut will be displayed in the menu, as shown in Figure 4-2, although this can be disabled by setting the `ShowShortcut` property to `false`.

Shortcut keys only work because the `Form` class knows about menus—when handling key presses, a form will offer keys to the both the main menu and the context menu for that form. This means that shortcuts only work properly for menus that have been attached to a form (as described later on). You would usually not use them on context menus that have been attached to specific controls.

So we know how to create hierarchical menu structures, and how to assign text, accelerators, and shortcut keys to menu items. But for all this to be of any use, we need to know when the user clicks on one of our menu items. So we will now look at the events raised by menus.

Event Handling

The entire point of adding menus to an application is so that users can ask the application to do something, such as save a file or perform a search. So as developers, we want our code to be notified whenever the user chooses an item from a menu. Menus therefore provide events to inform us of user input.

The most important menu event is `Click`. This is very similar to the `Control` class's `Click` event*—a `MenuItem` raises this event when the user clicks on the menu item or performs an equivalent key press (using either an accelerator or a shortcut key). It even has the same signature as `Control.Click`: `EventHandler`. If you double-click on

* It is not the same event, despite looking identical. This is because the `Menu` class is something of an anomaly—despite being a visual class, it does not in fact inherit from `Control`. It derives directly from `System.ComponentModel.Component` (as does `Control`). This seems to be because menus don't behave quite like other controls.

a menu item in the Designer, Visual Studio .NET will add a new method and attach it to the menu item's Click event, as shown in C# in Example 4-1 and in VB in Example 4-2.

Example 4-1. Menu Click handler in C#

```
private void InitializeComponent()
{
    . . .
    this.menuFileNew.Click +=
        new System.EventHandler(this.menuFileNew_Click);
    . . .
}

private void menuFileNew_Click(object sender, System.EventArgs e)
{
    . . . handle click here
}
```

Example 4-2. Menu click handler in VB

```
Friend WithEvents menuFileNew As System.Windows.Forms.MenuItem

Private Sub menuFileNew_Click(ByVal sender As System.Object, _
            ByVal e As System.EventArgs) Handles menuFileNew.Click
    . . . handle click here
End Sub
```

The handler method's first parameter is, as always, the source of the event (the MenuItem object, in this case). The second parameter is the usual placeholder and will normally be EventArgs.Empty.

The MenuItem class also provides a Popup event, which is fired whenever a menu is about to be displayed. This provides a useful opportunity to make sure that the state of all the items is up to date (e.g., you can place ticks by certain menu items, as described in the next section). The event occurs on the MenuItem that represents the menu that is about to appear. Its parent is not notified, and neither are the individual items that make up the menu. For example, when the File menu in the preceding examples is about to be displayed, the Popup event would occur on the menuFile object, not on the main menu, and not on any of the File menu's items.

You can also be notified when an item has been highlighted (i.e., when the mouse moves over it). That item's Select event is raised when this happens. This event also occurs when the item is selected with the arrow keys. The name Select is slightly misleading. Selecting a menu item sounds like a fairly positive operation by the user, but it typically indicates that the mouse has simply moved over the item. The Click event is the one raised when a user actively chooses an item.

If you are familiar with the old C++ MFC Library, you might be expecting to see events for handling menu item state. In that library, every time a menu item was displayed, an event was raised asking whether the item should be enabled and whether it should have a tick by it. In .NET, things are a little different—Windows Forms exposes these features as properties on the MenuItem object.

Menu Item State

You will often want a menu item's appearance to change according to the application's state. For example, a menu item that turns something on or off (such as a status bar) can have a tick beside it to indicate that the feature is currently on. Some menu items may sometimes be unavailable and should be grayed out or even hidden. We will now see how to modify the appearance and behavior of menus at runtime to achieve this.

Each `MenuItem` has an `Enabled` property. By default, it is set to `true`, but when it is `false`, the item will be grayed out and will not be clickable. More drastically, you can set the `Visible` property to `false`, which will prevent the item from appearing at all. The `MenuItem` class also provides a `Checked` property. When this is set, a tick will be displayed next to the menu item.

> If you preferred the old MFC approach, in which you decided which items should be ticked or disabled at the last minute, you can still do this. Simply supply a `Popup` handler for the menu and set the flags for each menu item in it. This approach can be useful, because it guarantees that menu items are always up to date, but an event-driven approach is no longer mandatory, so you can use whichever is simpler for your particular application. Remember that the `Popup` event is raised for the menu, not for each of its items, so your code will not look quite the same as it did with MFC—you will have a single handler setting the state of all necessary items, rather than one handler per item.

So, we now know how to create menus, how to handle the events they generate, and how to modify the appearance of individual items. All that remains is to make sure these menus appear when and where we want them, which is the subject of the next section.

Attaching Menus

There are two ways in which a menu can appear. It can either be permanently visible at the top of a form, or it can be a so-called Context Menu that pops up when the user clicks the right (or alternate) mouse button. In either case, we simply associate a hierarchy of menu items with a form or a control.

The menu that appears at the top of a window is determined by the `Form` class's Menu property. You can set this property to a `MainMenu` object representing the root of a hierarchy of `MenuItem` objects. The Forms Designer does this automatically when you add a main menu to a form.

Setting a context menu is very similar, except context menus may be assigned to any control, not just a form. This means that you can provide different context menus for each control in a window. This is done by setting the `ContextMenu` property of the control or form.

Remember that the `Form` class derives from `Control`, so it is possible to set a context menu for the whole form. Be aware though that when you add a context menu to a form with the designer, Visual Studio .NET does not presume that the menu should be attached to the form—for all it knows, you might be planning to associate it with a control, so it leaves it unattached. You must explicitly attach the menu either to the form or to a control by setting the relevant object's `ContextMenu` property.

Be aware that keyboard shortcuts for a context menu will only work if the control that owns the menu is able to process keys. For a context menu attached to a form, this means that the shortcuts will work so long as the form is active, but for menus attached to a particular control on a form, the shortcuts will only work when that control has the focus. So it is not always useful to put shortcut keys on a context menu attached to a control, because the whole point of shortcut keys is that they can be used from any context. (The exception would be if your control can receive the focus and presents a nontrivial interactive user interface. For example, a text box provides clipboard shortcuts such as Ctrl-C for copy. In this case, it makes sense for the shortcuts only to be available when the control has the focus.)

Sometimes it is useful to know if a menu is currently being displayed to avoid distracting or interrupting the user—it can be annoying if an application pops up a notification dialog while you are using a menu, because this causes the menu to be closed. If you want to disable or defer certain operations while a menu is open, you simply need to observe the `Form` class's `MenuStart` and `MenuComplete` events. These are fired just before a menu receives the focus and just after it disappears. These events are fired for the form's context menu as well as for its main menu. Unfortunately, the form does not raise these events for a control-specific context menu, and although you could handle such a menu's `Popup` event, there is unfortunately no corresponding event to tell you when it goes away.

Menus & Toolbars

Menu Merging

Many applications present several forms that all have similar but slightly different menus. This is particularly common when forms inheritance is in use (see Chapter 6). MDI applications often have a related requirement: a form may make subtle changes to its menu structure depending on which child window (if any) is active.

Unfortunately, we cannot exploit inheritance here as we would for building a group of similar forms: whereas the structure and behavior of a form is represented by a class definition, the structure and behavior of a menu is defined by an object graph constructed at runtime. All menus are made from a collection of objects that are always of the same types (several `MenuItem` objects and either one `MainMenu` or one `ContextMenu`), so inheritance cannot help us here.

The good news is that the `Menu` class provides a solution. It provides a method called `MergeMenu` that allows us to take an existing menu structure and extend or modify it to create a new menu. The resulting menu will be the combination of the two menus, as illustrated in Figure 4-3.

Figure 4-3 illustrates the simplest way of using menu merging—two menus are combined, and the result is a menu containing all the items from each. The `MergeMenu` method does a deep copy, so any submenus will also be duplicated.

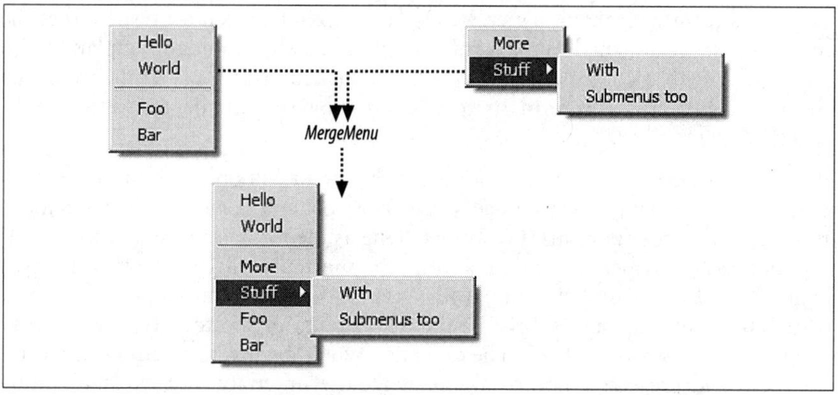
Hello
World
Foo
Bar
More
Stuff
With
Submenus too
MergeMenu
Hello
World
More
Stuff
With
Submenus too
Foo
Bar

Figure 4-3. Merged menus

This merging is easy to do—the following C# code (the VB code is almost identical) shows how to create a new context menu by merging the items from two other menus:

```
ContextMenu mergedMenu = new ContextMenu( );
mergedMenu.MergeMenu(menuFirst);
mergedMenu.MergeMenu(menuSecond);
```

But even this simple example raises an interesting question: how does the framework decide the order in which to place the items in the created menu? While it has not reordered the items from each individual menu in Figure 4-3, it has decided to insert the items from the second menu halfway through those of the first menu. The framework determines how to interleave the menus' contents by looking at the `MergeOrder` property on each `MenuItem`. This property is an `int` or `Integer`, and the framework guarantees that when combining menus, it will merge items in ascending `MergeOrder` order. So the reason the framework decides to insert the second menu's contents halfway down becomes clear when we see the `MergeOrder` property settings on the original menus:*

```
this.menuHello.MergeOrder = 5;
this.menuWorld.MergeOrder = 5;
this.menuSeparator1.MergeOrder = 10;
this.menuFoo.MergeOrder = 100;
this.menuBar.MergeOrder = 100;

this.menuMore.MergeOrder = 20;
this.menuStuff.MergeOrder = 20;
```

The More and Stuff items in the second menu have a merge order of 20, which means that they appear between the separator and the Foo entry, which have orders of 10 and 100, respectively. You can choose whatever values you like for a merge order, but using 0 for the items you want to appear first, 100 for those you want to appear last, and more or less evenly spaced values for those in between is a popular choice. (The default `MergeOrder` is 0.)

* The code is shown in C#. Once again, the VB code is similar, except that the C# `this` keyword is replaced with `Me`, and VB does not use the semicolon to terminate a code statement.

Advanced merging

The merging technique shown above is sufficient for many purposes, but you might need to do something a little more complex. For example, sometimes it is not enough simply to add new items to a menu—you may wish to remove items. Also, if you want to insert new items into a submenu instead of the top level menu, the naïve approach is insufficient: by default you will end up with two identically named submenus.

To support these more subtle merging techniques, the `MenuItem` class provides a `MergeType` property, which controls the way an item is treated when it is merged. By default, its value is `MenuMerge.Add`, meaning that all items in the menu being merged will be added as new items.

You can set `MergeType` to `MenuMerge.Remove`, which causes the corresponding entry not to appear. You would use this value if the menu you are modifying contains an entry you would like to remove.

> You must set the `MergeType` property on both source menus for this technique to work. If the new menu being merged into the original menu attempts to remove an item, that attempt will be ignored unless the original menu's corresponding item (the item with the same `MergeOrder`) is also marked as `MenuMerge.Remove`.
>
> So the `MergeType` property really has two meanings—on the original item it indicates the allowable operations, and on the new item it indicates the operation being requested. Unfortunately, not only is this overloading slightly confusing, it is somewhat restrictive—there is no way to create a menu item that allows both the `MergeItem` and the `Remove` operations. Conflicts are also dealt with a little inconsistently—if the original is `Add` and the new is `Remove`, the new item is ignored; if the original is `Remove` and the new is `MergeItem`, the item is replaced!

Setting `MergeType` to `MenuMerge.Replace` is similar to remove, except it replaces the original item with the one in the menu being merged. Finally, `MergeType` can be set to `MenuMerge.MergeItems`. This value is used when you wish to modify the contents of a submenu. Although you could modify a submenu by replacing it entirely, `MergeItems` is useful when you want to make only minor modifications. You use this by supplying a `MergeItems` item corresponding to the submenu item in the original menu, and then put child items underneath it, using `Add`, `Remove`, `Replace`, or `MergeItems` as appropriate. For example, if you wanted to add an item to a main menu's File menu, you would not replace the entire main menu, or even the entire File menu. The following code (in C#) would suffice:

```
MenuItem mergingFileMenu = new MenuItem( );
mergingFileMenu.MergeType = MenuMerge.MergeItems;
mergingFileMenu.Text = "&File";

MenuItem menuExtraFileItem = new MenuItem( );
menuExtraFileItem.Text = "Ext&ra";
menuExtraFileItem.MergeOrder = 10;
MenuItem menuExtraFileSeparator = new MenuItem( );
```

```
    menuExtraFileSeparator.Text = "-";
    menuExtraFileSeparator.MergeOrder = 10;

    mergingFileMenu.MenuItems.AddRange(new MenuItem[] {
        menuExtraFileItem,
        menuExtraFileSeparator});

    MainMenu mergingMainMenu = new MainMenu(new MenuItem[] {
        mergingFileMenu });
    mainMenu.MergeMenu(mergingMainMenu);
```

This adds an item labeled Extra to the File menu, followed by a separator. So even though we are merging two main menus together, we are able to modify one of its submenus without having to replace that submenu wholesale. And although this may look like a lot of code to add a single item, it is rather less than would be required to reconstruct the whole menu. Furthermore, building a modified File menu from scratch presents code maintenance issues—if you want to change the basic File menu, you would also need to change all the places where you build a modified version. But if you use menu merging, any changes to the basic menu will automatically propagate to the modified versions.

Remember that this will only work if the original main menu's File menu item also has its `MergeType` set to `MenuMerge.MergeItems`; if it were set to the default of `MenuMerge.Add`, you would end up with two File submenus in the main menu.

Merging and MDI applications

If you build an MDI application, the framework can automatically take advantage of menu merging. The menus in such applications typically consist of two types of items: those that are associated with a document window and those that are a part of the main application frame. The set of available menu items is determined by whether a document window is active (and if there is more than one kind of document window, it will depend on which one is active).

The application-level menu items are those that should always be present and that make sense even if there are no open documents, such as items for file opening, document creation, or application configuration. Document-level menu items are those that only make sense in the context of a document, such as items for file closing or saving, editing operations, or view settings. MDI applications usually present just a single menu bar as part of the main application frame, but its contents change between being just the application-level items or the complete set, according to whether a document is active.

This seems like an ideal opportunity to use menu merging—the application-level items could be placed into one `MainMenu`, the document level items into a second `MainMenu`, and these could be merged to create a third. All that would need to be done would be to swap in the appropriate merged or unmerged version according to whether a child window is active. Indeed, this is exactly how MDI applications usually work in .NET, but it turns out that Windows Forms can do the menu merging automatically.

If you use the framework's built-in support for MDI applications (i.e., you establish the parent/child relationship with the `Form` class's `MdiParent` or `MdiChildren` properties), it will assume that the parent form's MainMenu contains the application-level menu items, and that any child form's MainMenu contains document-level items. Whenever an MDI child form is activated, the framework will automatically merge its menu into the parent form's menu. If all MDI child windows are closed, it reverts to the original parent form's menu.

So using menu merging in MDI applications requires almost no effort. The only thing you need to be careful about is setting the correct MergeType—very often a child window will want to add entries (such as for adding a save and a close entry to the File menu) into an existing menu in the parent. Both the parent and the child form's main menus will need to contain File submenus, which must both have the same MergeOrder, and they must both have a MergeType of MenuMerge.MergeItems.

Merging and forms inheritance

It is possible to define a form that derives from another form. We will be looking at the use of inheritance in detail in Chapter 6, but we will quickly examine the inheritance-related aspects of menu merging here.

When building an inherited form, the derived class will automatically acquire the base class's menu. However, if you try to edit the menu in the derived class, the Forms Designer will prevent you, complaining that the menu is defined on the base class. To modify a menu on the derived form, you must use menu merging.

To modify the menu in the derived class, you must add a new MainMenu component to the form. Place whatever modifications you require in this menu. To merge this menu in with the main menu requires a little code. Add the following C# code to your constructor:

```
MainMenu mainMenu = new MainMenu( );
mainMenu.MergeMenu(this.Menu);
mainMenu.MergeMenu(mainMenuDerived);
this.Menu = mainMenu;
```

The equivalent VB code is:

```
Dim mainMenu As New MainMenu( )
mainMenu.MergeMenu(Me.Menu)
mainMenu.MergeMenu(mainMenuDerived)
Me.Menu = mainMenu
```

This builds a new MainMenu object, which takes the original menu and merges in mainMenuDerived (or whatever you choose to call the MainMenu that you added to your derived form). It then sets this merged menu as the new main menu of the form.

Owner-Drawn Menus

The standard appearance provided by the Windows Forms framework for menu items is pretty basic—you get simple text, and you can optionally annotate menu items with a tick (just set the Checked property). If you want to draw your own annotations, or otherwise provide richer visual information, the framework lets you draw your own menu items. The use of GDI+ to perform custom drawing is discussed in detail in Chapter 7, but here we will look at the menu-specific aspects of owner drawing.

You can decide to do your own drawing on a per-item basis by setting the MenuItem object's OwnerDraw property to true. Unfortunately, it is an all or nothing decision: if you ask the framework to let you draw a particular item, you are required to manage the whole drawing process. First, you must tell the framework the size of your menu item by handling the MeasureItem event; otherwise, the item will default to having a height of 0 pixels. And you must also handle the DrawItem event, in which you are responsible for drawing everything, including the text of the menu. (Turning on OwnerDraw will prevent Windows from drawing anything other than the menu background.)

> Because owner drawing is a per-item decision, it is possible to have a single menu with a mixture of owner-drawn and system-drawn items.

You will receive the DrawItem event every time the item needs redrawing. This happens when the menu appears, directly after the MeasureItem event, but it also happens again every time the mouse moves on or off the menu item, so that you can highlight your item like Windows does for normal items. Your event handler will be passed a DrawItemEventArgs object, whose State member indicates how the item should be drawn. This field is of type DrawItemState, which is a bit field, so it may indicate multiple styles simultaneously. The flags that may be set are Selected (indicating that the mouse is currently over the item), NoAccelerator (indicating that accelerator keys should not be displayed; this will normally be set unless the user is operating the menu through the keyboard), and Checked (indicating that a tick should be drawn by the item).

Examples 4-3 and 4-4 show a pair of event handlers for a very simple owner-drawn menu. The item is always the same size because the MeasureItem handler always returns the same width and height. The DrawItem handler simply draws an ellipse as the menu item, but it illustrates an important technique: it checks the item's state to see if it is selected, and if so, it draws the menu background in the normal selected menu item color, and draws the ellipse in the same color as selected text in a menu would be drawn. Note the use of the DrawBackground method of the DrawItemEventArgs object to fill in the menu background—it draws the background in the appropriate color (i.e., SystemColors.Menu, unless the item is selected, in which case it uses SystemColors.Highlight). We call this whether the item is in the selected state or not. You might think that this is unnecessary because, as mentioned above, the framework draws the background for us. Unfortunately it only does that when the menu is first opened, so if we change the background when our item is selected, we are required to put it back again when it is deselected.

Example 4-3. Simple owner-drawn menu item in C#

```
private void menuItem_MeasureItem(object sender,
    System.Windows.Forms.MeasureItemEventArgs e)
{
    e.ItemHeight = 17;
    e.ItemWidth = 100;
}
```

Example 4-3. Simple owner-drawn menu item in C# (continued)

```
private void menuItem_DrawItem(object sender,
    System.Windows.Forms.DrawItemEventArgs e)
{
    Graphics g = e.Graphics;
    bool selected = (e.State & DrawItemState.Selected) != 0;
    Brush b = selected ?
        SystemBrushes.HighlightText : Brushes.Blue;
    e.DrawBackground( );
    g.FillEllipse(b, e.Bounds);
}
```

Example 4-4. Simple owner-drawn menu item in VB

```
Private Sub menuItem_MeasureItem(sender As Object, _
            e As System.Windows.Forms.MeasureItemEventArgs) _
            Handles menuItem.MeasureItem
    e.ItemHeight = 17
    e.ItemWidth = 100
End Sub

Private Sub menuItem_DrawItem(sender As Object, _
            e As System.Windows.Forms.DrawItemEventArgs) _
            Handles menuItem.DrawItem
    Dim g As Graphics = e.Graphics
    Dim selected As Boolean = (e.State & DrawItemState.Selected) <> 0
    Dim b As Brush
    If selected Then
        b = SystemBrushes.HighlightText
    Else
        b = Brushes.Blue
    End If
    e.DrawBackground( )
    g.FillEllipse(b, e.Bounds)
End Sub
```

Now that we have seen how to create menus, let us see how we can provide expert users with more direct access to the most frequently used operations with toolbars.

Toolbars

Toolbars usually provide access to features that are also accessible through menus, but there's a tradeoff. Because a toolbar is always visible, it can be clicked without having to navigate through a menu structure, but toolbars have a slightly higher learning curve, because items are normally represented by buttons with a small bitmap; it is much harder to represent an operation unambiguously with a tiny picture than it is to describe it with some text in a menu.

In Windows Forms, toolbars are represented by the ToolBar class, and individual buttons on it are represented by the ToolBarButton class. Note that these classes provide a fairly basic style of toolbar—Windows Forms provides no support for undocking toolbars or even rearranging them.

The ToolBar Class

ToolBar is a fairly simple class. It inherits from Control and must be docked; most applications dock the toolbar to the top of the window. ToolBar is a simple class to use—it adds only a few properties to its base class.

The class provides an Appearance property, which must be one of the members of the ToolBarAppearance enumeration: either Normal (the default) or Flat. When set to Normal, each toolbar button has a button-like raised edge. However, most applications favor the Flat style these days, where the toolbar appears completely flat, and the buttons have no outline except when the mouse is over them.

The ToolBar also controls where any text associated with a button appears through its TextAlign property. (A toolbar button may optionally have a text label, like the Back button on Internet Explorer.) This property's type is the ToolBarTextAlign enumeration, and it can be either Right or Underneath. The default is Underneath.

The most important property of a toolbar is Buttons, whose type is ToolBarButtonCollection. This contains all the ToolBarButton objects on the toolbar. This is used in a similar way to the other collections we have seen, such as the MenuItems collection. As usual, items are added with the AddRange method, as shown in the following C# code:

```
this.toolBar1.Buttons.AddRange(
    new System.Windows.Forms.ToolBarButton[] {
        this.toolBarFileNew,
        this.toolBarFileOpen,
        this.toolBarFileSave});
```

Most of the interesting features of the buttons are managed through the ToolBarButton class itself, but there is one exception. Most buttons have images on them, and these images must be contained in an ImageList object. This is stored in the ToolBar object's ImageList property. An image list is a collection of images all of equal size, gathered into a single resource for efficiency, and a toolbar has just one ImageList containing all the images required for the whole toolbar; individual buttons just specify indexes into this list. (Image lists are also used by the TreeView and ListView controls.)

Visual Studio .NET provides an editor for building image lists. It merges multiple bitmap files into a single long thin bitmap resource, which is the most efficient way of initializing an image list. The editor allows individual images to be removed or added, and for the list to be reordered. (Unfortunately, it won't find all the places in your code where you referred to an image by its index, so exercise caution when reordering the images.)

Note that the buttons on a toolbar are not proper controls—the only control is the toolbar itself. Because of this, the ToolTip control will not be able to annotate individual toolbar buttons with the ToolTip extender property. Instead, the ToolBar class provides its own support for ToolTips—just set its ShowToolTips property to true. In the following section, we will see how to assign a ToolTip to each button, along with other button-specific properties.

The ToolBarButton Class

For each button contained in a ToolBar control, there is a corresponding object of class ToolBarButton. This turns out not to be a proper control—the class inherits from System.ComponentModel.Component, not Control. This is because in Windows, toolbars have always acted as single controls that provide the illusion of multiple buttons through careful redrawing and event handling to avoid creating too many controls.*

Toolbar buttons can have one of three appearances, determined by the Style property, which has the enumeration type ToolBarButtonStyle. This can be PushButton, which is a normal button. Or it can be ToggleButton, which looks the same as a normal button, except its state alternates between pushed and unpushed each time it is clicked. Or it can be a DropDownButton, in which case it should have a ContextMenu associated with its DropDownMenu property—with this style, the item will have a small downward-pointing arrow next to it, which will cause the context menu to be displayed. For all three styles, the exact appearance is determined by the parent ToolBar object's Appearance property.

The Style property can also be set to Separator, in which case the item doesn't behave like a button at all—it simply separates groups of other buttons.

You can specify which image the button contains with the ImageIndex property—this is an index into the containing ToolBar control's image list. You can also display some text by setting the Text property. Remember that the location of the text (either beside or underneath the image) is controlled by the containing ToolBar, through its TextAlign property. (All buttons on a toolbar have the same text alignment.)

You can also provide ToolTip text for each button, through its ToolTipText property. This is essential if you want users to be able to learn what your buttons do without resorting to trial and error, unless your drawing skills are so good that you can convey any concept in a 15×15 pixel bitmap.

So we can now create toolbars and fill them with buttons. But as with menus, for this to be of any use, we must provide event handlers for when the buttons are clicked. The next section describes how to do this.

Event Handling

Handling events from toolbars is slightly inconvenient, because individual ToolBarButton objects do not raise events. Whenever the user clicks a button on a toolbar, the object that raises the event is the toolbar itself, through its ButtonClick event.

The ButtonClick event handler type is ToolBarButtonClickEventHandler. As usual, the first parameter is the sender of the event (the toolbar). The second is of type

* This is because versions of Windows with strong 16-bit lineage such as Windows 98 and Windows ME have severe limitations on the number of controls that can be displayed at once. Until this code base finally dies out (which will probably not happen until a few years after the average desktop machine ships with a 64-bit processor as standard), these problems will still make their presence felt, through resource-conscious design decisions such as these.

ToolBarButtonClickEventArgs, which contains a single property, Button. This is a reference to the ToolBarButton that was clicked. (There is also a ButtonDropDown event of the same type, which is raised for buttons whose style is DropDownButton.)

There is no direct way to associate a single handler method with a particular button. However, you can call the Buttons.IndexOf method on the toolbar to find the index of the button that was pressed—the buttons are numbered from left to right, starting at index 0. So you could handle these clicks with a switch statement, as shown in the C# code in Example 4-5, or with a Select Case statement, as shown in the VB code in Example 4-6.

Example 4-5. Simple toolbar button click handling in C#

```
private void InitializeComponent( )
{
    . . .
    this.toolBar.ButtonClick +=
      new System.Windows.Forms.ToolBarButtonClickEventHandler(
           this.toolBar_ButtonClick);
    . . .
}

private void toolBar_ButtonClick(object sender,
    System.Windows.Forms.ToolBarButtonClickEventArgs e)
{
    switch(toolBar.Buttons.IndexOf(e.Button))
    {
        case 0:
            MessageBox.Show("New");
            break;

        case 1:
            MessageBox.Show("Open");
            break;
    }
}
```

Example 4-6. Simple toolbar button click handling in VB

```
Private Sub toolBar_ButtonClick(sender As Object, _
        e As System.Windows.Forms.ToolBarButtonClickEventArgs)
   Select Case toolBar.Buttons.IndexOf(e.Button)
      Case 0
         MsgBox("New")
      Case 1:
         MsgBox("Open")
   End Select
End Sub
```

However, because most toolbar buttons are directly equivalent to a menu item, you might find the unified technique described in the next section more convenient.

Unified Event Handling

The majority of toolbar buttons act as shortcuts to menu items, so it makes sense to handle equivalent clicks with a single event handler. Unfortunately, Windows Forms does not provide a direct way of doing this. However, it is fairly easy to arrange such a scheme. We can write an event handler for the toolbar that locates the appropriate menu item and then calls its event handler.

All we need is some way of associating toolbar buttons with menu items. For this, we can use a class provided by the .NET Framework class libraries called `System.Collections.Hashtable`—it is designed to store associations between objects. We can use this to remember which toolbar buttons are equivalent to which menu items. Although the Designer cannot store these associations in a hash table for you automatically, it only requires a small amount of code in your form's constructor. The following is the necessary C# code:

```
// Hashtable to associate buttons with menu items
private Hashtable toolbarButtonToMenu;
public MyForm()
{
    InitializeComponent();

    // Create hash table
    toolbarButtonToMenu = new Hashtable();

    // Associate ToolBarButtons with MenuItems
    toolbarButtonToMenu(toolBarFileNew)    = menuFileNew;
    toolbarButtonToMenu(toolBarFileOpen)   = menuFileOpen;
    toolbarButtonToMenu(toolBarEditCopy)   = menuEditCopy;
    toolbarButtonToMenu(toolBarEditCut)    = menuEditCut;
    toolbarButtonToMenu(toolBarEditPaste)  = menuEditPaste;
    toolbarButtonToMenu(toolBarEditDelete) = menuEditDelete;
}
```

The following is its VB equivalent:

```
' Hashtable to associate buttons with menu items
Private toolbarButtonToMenu As HashTable

Public Sub New()

    InitializeComponent()

    ' Create hash table
    toolbarButtonToMenu = New Hashtable()

    ' Associate ToolBarButtons with MenuItems
    toolbarButtonToMenu(toolBarFileNew)    = menuFileNew
    toolbarButtonToMenu(toolBarFileOpen)   = menuFileOpen
    toolbarButtonToMenu(toolBarEditCopy)   = menuEditCopy
    toolbarButtonToMenu(toolBarEditCut)    = menuEditCut
    toolbarButtonToMenu(toolBarEditPaste)  = menuEditPaste
    toolbarButtonToMenu(toolBarEditDelete) = menuEditDelete
End Sub
```

This creates a hash table called toolbarButtonToMenu, which associates toolbar buttons (toolBarFileNew, toolBarFileOpen, etc.) with their respective menu items (menuFileNew, menuFileOpen, etc.). With this association in place, the following C# code can be placed in the toolbar's ButtonClick handler to direct all clicks on toolbar buttons to the appropriate menu item:

```
private void toolBar_ButtonClick(object sender,
    System.Windows.Forms.ToolBarButtonClickEventArgs e)
{
    MenuItem mi = toolbarButtonToMenu[e.Button] as MenuItem;
    if (mi != null)
        mi.PerformClick( );
}
```

The corresponding VB code is:

```
Private Sub toolBar_ButtonClick(sender As Object, _
      e As System.Windows.Forms.ToolBarButtonClickEventArgs) _
      Handles toolBar.ButtonClick

   Dim mi As MenuItem = toolbarButtonToMenu(e.Button)
   If Not mi Is Nothing Then
      mi.PerformClick( )
   End If
End Sub
```

This simply looks in toolbarButtonToMenu to see if the button that was clicked has an associated menu item. If it does, it uses the MenuItem class's PerformClick method, which generates a Click event on that item. This will then be handled by that menu item's click handler.

So with this code in place, clicking on a toolbar button will cause the associated menu item's Click event to be raised, allowing you to handle these two events with a single event handler.

Office-Style Menus and Toolbars

The Microsoft Office suite provides menus and toolbars that are a little different from the standard ones. Menu items have icons next to them, usually matching the icons used in the toolbar. The latest versions have the new "flat" look. (Menus don't have the raised border, nor do toolbar buttons, even when highlighted.) The menus themselves are on toolbars that can be dragged around, and items can even be dragged between the menu bar and other toolbars.

A commonly asked question is: can I get Office-style menus and toolbars with Windows Forms? Unfortunately, at the time this book went to press, the answer was no. Currently, the only two options are to recreate the behavior of Office menus and toolbars yourself, or to buy a third-party component to supply this behavior. Writing this behavior from scratch is nontrivial—you can get part of the way there by using owner-drawn menus, but you would still need to write a completely new toolbar.

For some reason, the development tools have always provided menu and toolbar support that is at least one generation behind the menu system used by the development environment itself. This is still true with Visual Studio .NET 2003—the IDE has Office-style toolbars, and yet provides no easy way of adding these to your own applications. With luck, this will be addressed in a future version of the tools.

Summary

Almost all Windows applications provide menus, Because they are the easiest way to provide a wide array of functionality without cluttering up the user interface. In Windows Forms, menus are represented as hierarchies of objects, with each menu item represented by an instance of the `MenuItem` class. A simple event model is used to notify the program when the user makes a menu selection. Keyboard accelerators and shortcuts are handled automatically, and integrate into the same event model. Menu structures can be reused and extended through menu merging, and the basic appearance of a menu can be replaced by supplying owner-drawn menu items. Toolbars can provide easy access to frequently used menu items, allowing expert users to work with an application more efficiently. Although toolbar and menu events are handled separately, it is relatively easy to channel events from both into a single set of click handlers.

5

Building Controls

Windows Forms provides a rich array of built-in controls. It allows you to customize their behavior and, to some extent, their appearance. But powerful as these controls are, it is very useful to be able to augment this toolkit of standard user interface elements with controls of your own devising.

There are several ways in which you can define your own controls. The easiest is to create a composite control—a user interface element built out of a collection of other controls. This has the virtue of being simple, but sometimes you will require greater flexibility. You can write a custom control, where you dictate all aspects of its behavior. You can also create classes that inherit from other controls.

All user interface elements derive from the `Control` class, and any that you write are no exception. This means that even when writing a custom control, you can rely on the base class to supply all the required basic functionality; you only need to write code for the behavior unique to your control.

In this chapter, we will look at how to compose a group of controls into a single reusable user interface element with the `UserControl` class. We will then see how to write your own custom control from scratch. Finally we will look at some of the software design issues that user-defined controls must deal with.

Composite Controls

The built-in controls are undeniably very useful—almost every Windows application uses them. Not only does this avoid reinventing the wheel, it also enhances usability: consistency is a desirable property in interactive applications. By using the standard controls, you guarantee consistency, both within your program and also with other Windows applications. Arguably one of Windows' greatest strengths is that most applications have a great deal in common—experienced users are familiar with all the standard control types, such as buttons and comboboxes. Using controls that users know and understand reduces the amount of learning required to use your application.

So it makes sense to use the standard Windows controls wherever possible. But your application may also be able to reap the usability benefits of consistent design on a larger scale—it may be possible to reuse whole chunks of the user interface, not just individual controls. For example, consider an email application. Many email clients allow items to be viewed through a preview pane in the main window as well as in a standalone window. These two views are likely to have a great deal in common—the main area showing the contents of the email will need to do the same thing in both cases. The area showing parts of the email header (fields such as From, To, and Subject) will be either the same or similar. And in a high-quality application, these parts of the UI are likely to be fairly sophisticated. You might want the From and To fields to provide pop-up menus allowing the user to send mail to individual recipients, or add them to an address list.

It would be irritating if the header fields behaved inconsistently, because they are supposed to represent the same things in both locations. If these fields presented a pop-up menu when examining an email in its own window, but failed to do so in the preview pane, it would likely frustrate the user. Not only is it annoying for the user, it is clearly counterproductive for the developer: if a section of the UI that has the same function must appear in two different places, you won't want to write the same code twice—not only do you risk inconsistent behavior, you are wasting your time.

What we want is some way of taking such sections of the user interface and turning them into reusable components. This is exactly what composite controls are all about. In Windows Forms, we build composite controls with the `UserControl` class.

The UserControl Class

The `UserControl` class is the base class for all *composite controls*, which are reusable portions of user interface. Any class based on `UserControl` consists of one or more child controls and some code that manages their behavior. Once you have created such a composite user interface element, any Windows Forms application can use it just like any other control.

The `UserControl` class is surprisingly similar to the `Form` class. Both derive from `ContainerControl`, enabling them to manage the focus as it moves around the child controls. Both can be scrollable, because `ContainerControl` derives from `ScrollableControl`. Both let you assemble child controls into a useful chunk of user interface. Both are even edited in the same way in Visual Studio .NET—the Forms Designer can design a `UserControl` as well as a `Form`.

The main difference between a `Form` and a `UserControl` is that the `UserControl` is designed to be dropped into a container—either a `Form` or another `UserControl`.* Consequently, a `UserControl` has no border or titlebar, and cannot be a top-level window.

Figure 5-1 shows an example of a composite control displayed in the Visual Studio .NET Designer. As with a form, the selection outline and grid points are

* In fact, there is nothing preventing a form from being a child of another window—this is how MDI applications work. It is just that there is no support for this in the designer.

visible, you can drag and drop controls into here from the Toolbox, and you can use any control, including ones you have designed yourself. Any control that works in a form also works in a composite control. (Recursion is not allowed though—it would make no sense for a control to contain a copy of itself.)

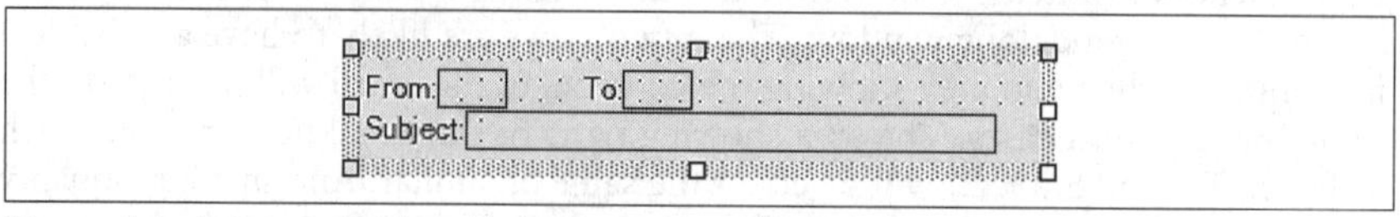

From:
To:
Subject:

Figure 5-1. A UserControl in the Designer

The control in Figure 5-1 consists of several label controls, some of which are empty because their values are determined at runtime, and displays information from an email header. (The empty controls have been indicated with a dotted outline above so that you can see them.) Although it just looks like a few labels on a form, such a control could easily be fairly complex. For example, it would probably have custom layout logic to deal with different lengths of email address. And emails often go to many recipients, so this layout might be nontrivial, maybe even needing scrollbars on the recipient list. The email addresses would most likely have context menus associated with them for the reasons discussed earlier. The control might optionally support displaying other header items. For a professional quality application, this kind of feature list can run on and on.

In other words, a simple-looking part of the user interface can turn out to have a surprising amount of code associated with it. So if that user interface fragment is likely to be used in multiple contexts (e.g., in the standalone and preview views shown in Figures 5-2 and 5-3*), you will want to be able to reuse the code rather than copying it into two different places. By encapsulating this piece of the user interface as a `UserControl`, you make such reuse simple. You also guarantee consistency by making sure that just one component is used in both contexts.

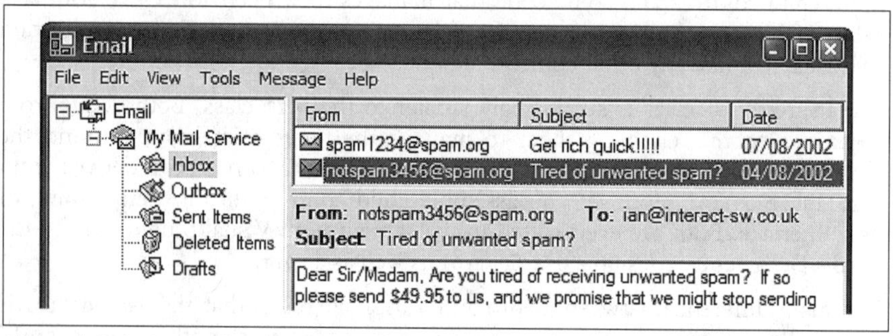

Email
File Edit View Tools Message Help
Email
My Mail Service
Inbox
Outbox
Sent Items
Deleted Items
Drafts
From
Subject
Date
spam1234@spam.org
Get rich quick!!!!!
07/08/2002
notspam3456@spam.org
Tired of unwanted spam?
04/08/2002
From: notspam3456@spam.org
To: ian@interact-sw.co.uk
Subject: Tired of unwanted spam?
Dear Sir/Madam, Are you tired of receiving unwanted spam? If so please send $49.95 to us, and we promise that we might stop sending

Figure 5-2. A composite control in a preview panel

* If you are wondering why some of the labels appear to be in a different font from that in Figure 5-1, this particular control uses an emboldened version of the font for these labels (as specified by the `Font` property). This font selection is done at runtime, which is why it doesn't show in the Designer.

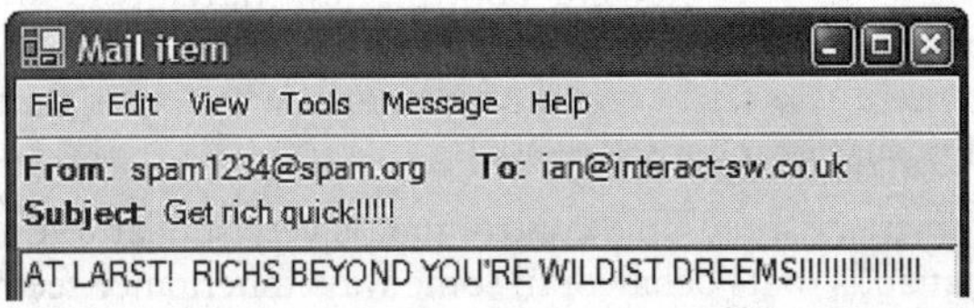
Mail item
File Edit View Tools Message Help
From: spam1234@spam.org To: ian@interact-sw.co.uk
Subject Get rich quick!!!!!
AT LARST! RICHS BEYOND YOU'RE WILDIST DREEMS!!!!!!!!!!!!!

Figure 5-3. A composite control in a standalone window

From the point of view of a form that uses a composite control (such as those in Figure 5-2 and 5-3), the control is no different from any other. It derives (indirectly) from `Control`, and so it supports all the normal properties and behavior. For example, in these two cases, docking has been used to position the controls. Developers using your component would not necessarily be aware that it was based on `UserControl`—as far as they are concerned, it's just another control.

In fact, Visual Studio .NET can even put your class into the Toolbox automatically. If your solution contains a `UserControl`, it will appear in the Toolbox when you edit any other form or user control in the designer. (If you are using Visual Studio .NET 2002, the control will appear at the bottom of the Windows Forms tab in the Toolbox. If you are using Visual Studio .NET 2003, it will appear in the My User Controls tab.) Note that you must do two things for this to work: first, your project must have been built (without errors) for it to appear; second, you may need to close the Designer window and reopen it after building before the control will appear in the Toolbox. (This only works when using a control defined in the same solution. If you want to use a control defined elsewhere, you will need to add the component to the Toolbox manually.)

Because the `UserControl` class is so similar to the `Form` class, it should come as no surprise that creating a composite control is essentially the same as designing a form—you arrange the constituent controls and handle events in the same way for both. The Visual Studio .NET Designer generates almost exactly the same code for forms and composite controls. Apart from the absence of a window border or support for a main menu, the only difference between writing a form and a composite control is that with a control, you are not only designing a user interface, you are also providing a programming interface—your control will be used by other developers, and you must bear their requirements in mind as well as the needs of the end user. The issues here are the same for all user-defined controls, so we will discuss them towards the end of the chapter.

Reusing Without Inheritance

The purpose of composite controls is to enable reuse—a section of user interface can be encapsulated in a control and reused in any number of different contexts. Code that reuses a composite control is not required to inherit from it. This shouldn't be surprising, but it is worth stressing because many people often equate reuse in an object-oriented system with inheritance. The most important form of reuse is containment; for example, a form can contain one or more instances of a composite control. Inheritance is a much more specialized technique.

When designing a new composite control, few developers would make the mistake of attempting to derive from another user control when it would be inappropriate.* But there is a fairly common scenario where it is much easier to fall into the trap of misuse of inheritance.

You may want to create a reusable control that is very similar to one of the built-in controls, but that adds to its behavior in some way. Inheritance seems like an attractive option here—after all, the whole point of inheritance may appear to be that you can take a class and extend it in some way. But while inheritance can be the right way to go in these circumstances (and the next chapter explains how to do this), it is more often the wrong approach. To understand why, we must bear in mind that inheritance always implies an "is a" relationship. If you make your control derive from some other control, you are making a strong statement: you are saying that your control is compatible in every respect with the control from which it derives.

Consider a control whose purpose is to present an XML document through a tree-like view. We already have a built-in control for showing tree-like structures: the `TreeView`. Basing our control on this will be the right thing to do, because there is no sense in writing our own tree control from scratch. However, it would be a mistake to inherit from `TreeView`—our control merely uses a `TreeView` to provide the display we require, it is not accurate to say that our control "is a" `TreeView`.

Suppose we did simply inherit from `TreeView`. Our control's programming interface would be an extension of `TreeView`. Every method and property provided by `TreeView` would also be available on our class—that's what inheritance does. So in the case of our control, what would it mean if a form that uses our hypothetical `XmlTreeView` were to call `Nodes.Add("Another node")`? This is allowable on a normal `TreeView`—it will add a new root node to the tree. And if it is allowable on a `TreeView`, then by definition it is also allowable on anything that derives from `TreeView`. But our `XmlTreeView` is supposed to provide a view of an XML document, and they're not allowed to have more than one root element.

In theory, we could work around this particular semantic mismatch; we could, for instance, override the `Nodes` property and throw an exception for this specific case, or maybe we could make the root of the document implicit, in which case adding a new node would not be invalid (assuming we aren't trying to enforce conformance with a schema or DTD). But the fact is we probably didn't want to go this route at all. Building a visual tree that represents the structure of an existing document is one thing. Trying to apply any changes made to that tree back to the document is something else entirely. It may not even be possible—we might not be able to save the XML document after having modified it, because not all document sources are writable. In any case, by inheriting from `TreeView`, we have committed ourselves to providing its public programming interface while preserving whatever our control's semantics are. In doing so, we have almost certainly bought into much more complexity than we really wanted.

So what is the alternative? Reuse through containment is a much better approach here. You can use the `TreeView` as part of your control's implementation details,

* Inheritance is not always the wrong thing to do—see the next chapter. It is just a less widely applicable mechanism than is commonly supposed.

but you won't be committing yourself to exposing its API. You can present whatever methods and properties you like, providing just the functionality you require, rather than all the functionality implied by inheriting from some control. The part that often trips people up is that although the `TreeView` is then a private implementation detail that is invisible to code that uses your control, it remains visible to the end user. As far as the control's visible behavior at runtime goes, it will look exactly like a normal `TreeView`.

Fortunately, it turns out to be remarkably easy to reuse controls in this way. If you want to create a control that looks and feels to the end user just like one of the built-in controls, but that you wish to wrap in some extra code, `UserControl` provides an easy way of doing this without using inheritance. Simply create a new composite control in the normal way, use the designer to add an instance of the control you wish to reuse, and set the added control's `Dock` property to `Dock.Fill`. This will cause the contained control to be the same size as your composite control (i.e., whatever size the code that uses your control decides to make it). From the end user's point of view, the control will look and behave exactly like the control on which yours is based. But from a software design point of view, the contained control is an internal implementation detail. It will be inaccessible to code that uses your component, which means that you will remain in charge of its behavior.

The `UserControl` class provides a great way to build reusable pieces of user interface out of other controls. But sometimes the functionality you require just isn't supplied by any of the built-in types and cannot easily be created by combining them. For example, if you are writing a vector drawing program, it would be heroically foolhardy to attempt to build an interactive picture editor from a combination of edit boxes and picture box controls. It would be much better to build a control from scratch, so that you can make it behave exactly as you require.

Custom Controls

If your application needs a UI component whose behavior is sufficiently different from any of the built-in controls, it usually makes sense to write a special-purpose control for the job. And although writing a control from scratch is slightly harder work than just reusing existing controls, it is normally more straightforward than trying to bend an unsuitable control to meet your needs.

Custom controls derive directly from `Control`. This means that you're not really starting from scratch at all—your class will automatically have all the functionality that is common to all controls. But there are two areas in which you are on your own: your control's appearance and the way it handles input from the user.

With a custom control, you are given a blank slate. It is your responsibility to determine the control's appearance. In fact, the main reason for creating a custom control is often that none of the built-in ones looks right for the application. So we will now see how your control can draw itself, and we will then look at how to deal with input from the user.

Redrawing

When your control first becomes visible at runtime, Windows Forms will ask it to draw itself. It does this by calling your control's `OnPaint` method. This method is defined by the Control class, but its implementation doesn't draw anything. The built-in control types supply an implementation of OnPaint for you, but with a custom control, it is your job to override this and draw the control as you see fit.

> Visual Studio .NET provides wizards for adding both user controls and custom controls. However, the wizard for custom controls is not available directly from the menus. You must choose the Add New Item... menu item. You can find the custom control wizard in the UI category of the Add New Item dialog.

If you add a custom control to a project using Visual Studio .NET, you will see that it provides you with a skeleton class definition consisting of a constructor and an OnPaint method like that shown for C# in Example 5-1[*] and for VB in Example 5-2. Note that it has added a call to the base class's OnPaint method. You are required to do this whenever you override any of the Control class's methods that begin with On. These methods all correspond to events (so there is an OnClick and an OnLayout method, for example). The framework always raises an event by calling the associated On*Xxx* method, which gives the control class the chance to process that event before any event handlers are called. If you failed to call the base class's method after having overridden it, the event would never be raised—it is the Control.On*Xxx* methods that are responsible for calling any event handlers that clients of this control may have attached. They also very often do other work too, so you must always make sure you call them when you override such a method.

Example 5-1. A skeleton OnPaint function in C#

```
protected override void OnPaint(PaintEventArgs pe)
{
    // TODO: Add custom paint code here

    // Calling the base class OnPaint
    base.OnPaint(pe);
}
```

Example 5-2. A skeleton OnPaint function in VB

```
Protected Overrides Sub OnPaint( _
            ByVal pe As System.Windows.Forms.PaintEventArgs)
   MyBase.OnPaint(pe)
   'Add your custom paint code here
End Sub
```

The existence of an OnPaint method implies that all controls raise a Paint event. This is indeed the case, and by handling that event, you can actually modify the appearance of other controls by drawing over them. (However, some controls deliberately hide the Paint event in the Forms Designer. This is usually because they are doing something unusual that will cause handling of the Paint method

* First you will have to switch to the code view; when you create a new custom control, Visual Studio .NET inexplicably shows the design view, even though you cannot do anything useful to custom controls in it.

not to have the anticipated effects. For example, if you set the Button control's FlatStyle property to FlatStyle.System, it will let the operating system draw the button. This is not likely to interact well with any drawing done in the button's Paint event handler.)

But in a custom control, there is no need to add an event handler for the Paint event—we simply take the direct route and override OnPaint. Notice that this method is passed an object of type PaintEventArgs, as shown in Examples 5-1 and 5-2. This provides us with two properties: Graphics and ClipRectangle. The ClipRectangle property returns an object of type Rectangle that tells us exactly which part of the control must be redrawn. We may well not be required to draw the entire control—possibly a window that is on top of our control has been moved slightly, causing a small, previously hidden portion to come into view. We would be wasting our time if we attempted to draw parts that didn't need redrawing. There's no actual harm in drawing too much—Windows Forms clips whatever we draw to the part that actually needs redrawing—but if your control's appearance is complex, it will speed things up if you use the ClipRectangle property to work out which parts you don't need to redraw.

> Examples 5-1 and 5-2 both call the OnPaint method in the base class by calling base.OnPaint and MyBase.OnPaint, respectively. Unfortunately, the skeleton class produced by Visual Studio .NET for a Visual Basic custom control suggests that any drawing code should appear after this call to the base class—it places the comment on the following line. This is unhelpful because such drawing should take place *before* calling the base class's OnPaint method. (The C# skeleton has the comment in the correct place.)
>
> A common misconception is that the base class OnPaint method is responsible for drawing the control background and that it should therefore be called first. This is untrue: the background is painted in OnPaintBackground, which is called before OnPaint. All that the base class does in OnPaint is raise the Paint event. It is important to make sure this happens after your control has finished painting itself, because otherwise, clients of your control that handle the Paint event will end up painting underneath your control instead of over it.

The most important feature of the PaintEventArgs object is the Graphics property, whose type is a class also called Graphics. This object is our entry point into GDI+, the part of the .NET Framework class libraries dedicated to drawing. It is the subject of Chapter 7, so we will not go into much detail here. For the purposes of illustrating how to implement the OnPaint method, it is sufficient to know that the Graphics object provides various methods for drawing shapes and text onto the screen.

Example 5-3 shows a simple implementation of OnPaint in C# that draws a basic table. Example 5-4 shows the equivalent code in VB. (Figure 5-4 shows how this control will look in the Designer when it is used on a form.) The core of this method is the loop that prints out each table entry to the screen using the Graphics object's DrawString method. The DrawString method will be discussed in detail in Chapter 7, along with the other GDI+ features.

Example 5-3. Drawing a simple table in C#

```
protected override void OnPaint(PaintEventArgs pe)
{
    const int tableEntries = 10;
    const int entryHeight = 12;

    using (Brush b = new SolidBrush(ForeColor))
    {
        for (int i = 0; i < tableEntries; ++i)
        {
            string s = string.Format("Table entry {0}", i+1);
            Point position = new Point(0, i * entryHeight);
            pe.Graphics.DrawString(s, Font, b, position);
        }
    }

    // Calling the base class OnPaint
    base.OnPaint(pe);
}
```

Example 5-4. Drawing a simple table in VB

```
Protected Overrides Sub OnPaint( _
            ByVal pe As System.Windows.Forms.PaintEventArgs)

   Const tableEntries As Integer = 10
   Const entryHeight As Integer = 12

   Dim b As Brush = New SolidBrush(ForeColor)
   Try
      Dim i As Integer
      Dim s As String
      Dim position As New PointF( )

      For i = 0 To tableEntries - 1
         s = String.Format("Table entry {0}", i + 1)
         position.X = 0
         position.Y = i * entryHeight
         pe.Graphics.DrawString(s, Font, b, position)
      Next
   Finally
      b.Dispose()
   End Try

   ' Calling the base class OnPaint
   MyBase.OnPaint(pe)
End Sub
```

The code in Examples 5-3 and 5-4 also highlights a very important feature common to most `OnPaint` methods—it honors the settings of certain properties on the control. The Control class provides a Font property, and because we are displaying text, we pass the Font object returned by that property to the DrawString method. So if the user modifies our Font object, we will draw with whatever font she has specified; otherwise we will use the ambient font, as determined for us by the Control class. Likewise, we have used the Color object returned by the ForeColor property, also supplied by Control (and also an ambient property) to determine the color in which the text should be drawn. (The use of the Brush class will be discussed in Chapter 7, although you will recognize the using construct from Chapter 3 in the C# code in Example 5-3—this ensures that the Brush object's resources are released as soon as we have finished drawing. Because VB does not provide an equivalent to the using construct, we've had to add a call to the Dispose method ourselves.)

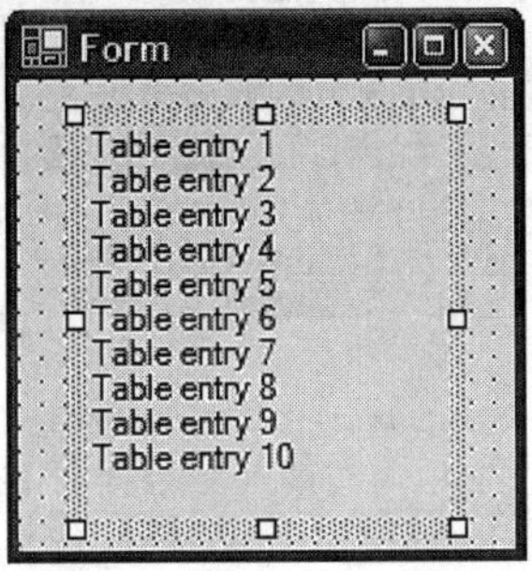
Form
Table entry 1
Table entry 2
Table entry 3
Table entry 4
Table entry 5
Table entry 6
Table entry 7
Table entry 8
Table entry 9
Table entry 10

Figure 5-4. A custom control in use

Figure 5-4 raises a interesting point. We are looking at the Forms Designer here, as the grid points and selection outline make clear. But our control is displayed correctly, which implies that its OnPaint method must have been called—there is no other way that the table could have appeared. This is an important feature to understand about the Designer—it creates instances of your controls' classes at design time, and will call certain methods on them, such as OnPaint. This is why your controls must have been built successfully before they can be used in the Designer—if they haven't been built, they certainly can't be loaded or have their methods run. Even if they have been built without error, certain methods (such as OnPaint) must execute correctly for the control to work properly in the Designer. Chapter 9 will talk about the design-time environment in depth.

If you are trying out code in Visual Studio .NET as you read this book, you may have hit a problem at this point. It is not entirely obvious how you use a custom control from the Forms Designer. Although the development environment is smart enough to detect when you have added a UserControl to your project, and adds it to the Toolbox automatically, it doesn't do this for custom controls. You have to right-click on the Toolbox, select Customize Toolbox..., choose the .NET Framework Components tab, and browse for the DLL containing your control. Once you have added the DLL, the Toolbox will show any custom controls that it contains.

Drawing your components is essentially straightforward: override OnPaint and use GDI+ to paint your control. Because GDI+ is dealt with in Chapter 7, we will now move on to dealing with user input.

Handling Input

The custom control in the previous section is inert—it will always look the same and will not respond to any user input. Some of the built-in controls are like this; for example, `PictureBox` just displays an image. But most of your controls will need to deal with mouse or keyboard input, and they may need to modify their appearance in response to this input.

Mouse input

Your control could simply attach event handlers to itself at runtime—because it derives from `Control`, all the standard events described in Chapter 2 are available. However, there is a much more direct way of receiving events. In the previous section, instead of attaching an event handler to the `Paint` event, we simply overrode the `OnPaint` method. We can do the same thing for input handling. For example, instead of handling the `MouseDown` and `MouseUp` events, we can simply override their counterparts,* as shown in Example 5-5 in C# and Example 5-6 in VB. Overriding these `On`*`Xxx`* methods is the preferred approach when writing your own controls because it is more efficient than attaching event handlers, and lets you determine whether your code runs before or after any attached event handlers.

Example 5-5. Handling mouse events in a custom control in C#

```
private bool pressed = false;
protected override void OnMouseDown(MouseEventArgs e)
{
    if (e.Button == MouseButtons.Left)
    {
        pressed = true;
        Invalidate();
    }
    base.OnMouseDown(e);
}

protected override void OnMouseUp(MouseEventArgs e)
{
    if (e.Button == MouseButtons.Left)
    {
        pressed = false;
```

* If you are using C# in Visual Studio .NET, here is a useful timesaving tip: you can get the IDE to add declarations for such overrides automatically. Having added a new custom control, go to your project's Class View window (hit Ctrl-Shift-C, or simply select it from the View menu), expand the tree item for your control, and drill down through the Bases and Interfaces item and into the Control item. This will list all the methods on the `Control` class. Right-click on the one you require, such as `OnMouseDown`, and under the Add item, select Override from the submenu. This will add an empty function definition with the correct signature. Sadly, it doesn't add the call to the base implementation (e.g., `base.OnMouseDown(e)`) so don't forget to add that yourself. Note that the Add option does not appear on the context menu in projects using Visual Basic. If you are using VS.NET 2003, you do not need to use the Class View—if you simply type the word `override` inside a C# class definition, an IntelliSense pop-up will appear showing a list of overridable methods.

Example 5-5. Handling mouse events in a custom control in C# (continued)

```
        Invalidate();
    }
    base.OnMouseUp(e);
}
```

Example 5-6. Handling mouse events in a custom control in VB

```
Protected Overrides Sub OnMouseDown(ByVal e As MouseEventArgs)
   If e.Button = MouseButtons.Left Then
      pressed = True
      Invalidate()
   End If
   MyBase.OnMouseDown(e)
End Sub

Protected Overrides Sub OnMouseUp(ByVal e As MouseEventArgs)
   If e.Button = MouseButtons.Left Then
      pressed = False
      Invalidate()
   End If
   MyBase.OnMouseUp(e)
End Sub
```

Examples 5-5 and 5-6 illustrate three important techniques. First, notice that the handlers call the base class's `OnMouseUp` and `OnMouseDown` methods—this is mandatory in all such overrides. Second, the control is maintaining some internal state that is modified by the user's input—the pressed field will be `true` whenever the mouse's left button is held down over the control, and `false` when it is not. (Remember that Windows Forms automatically captures the mouse when a button is pressed while over a control. So our `OnMouseUp` method will always be called even if the mouse moves away from our control after `OnMouseDown` was called.)

The final point to note is that the methods call `Invalidate` once they have changed the control's state. This is a method of the `Control` class that tells the framework that what is currently on screen is no longer a valid representation of the state of the object. This will cause the framework to redraw the control. You must do this whenever you change any of the data that the control uses to determine how to draw itself.

Examples 5-7 and 5-8 show a simple `OnPaint` method in C# and VB, respectively, that makes the control's appearance reflect its internal state. Most of the time, this will just draw the text normally, but when the left button is held down (i.e., pressed is `true`), it inverts the color of the control by filling the control's area with a rectangle using the control's foreground color, and then drawing the text over it in the background color.

Example 5-7. Representing internal state through appearance in C#

```
protected override void OnPaint(PaintEventArgs pe)
{
    Graphics g = pe.Graphics;
```

Example 5-7. Representing internal state through appearance in C# (continued)

```
    using (Brush fore = new SolidBrush(ForeColor),
                 back = new SolidBrush(BackColor))
    {

        Brush rbrush = pressed ? fore : back;
        Brush tbrush = pressed ? back : fore;

        g.FillRectangle(rbrush, ClientRectangle);
        g.DrawString(Text, Font, tbrush, ClientRectangle);
    }

    // Calling the base class OnPaint
    base.OnPaint(pe);
}
```

Example 5-8. Representing internal state through appearance in VB

```
Protected Overrides Sub OnPaint(ByVal pe As PaintEventArgs)

    Dim g As Graphics = pe.Graphics
    Dim fore As Brush = New SolidBrush(ForeColor)
    Dim back As Brush = New SolidBrush(BackColor)

    Try
       Dim rBrush, tBrush As Brush
       If pressed Then
          rBrush = fore
          tBrush = back
       Else
          rBrush = back
          tBrush = fore
       End If

       g.FillRectangle(rBrush, ClientRectangle)
       Dim crectf As New RectangleF(ClientRectangle.X, _
                                    ClientRectangle.Y, _
                                    ClientRectangle.Width, _
                                    ClientRectangle.Height)
       g.DrawString(Text, Font, tBrush, crectf)
    Finally
      fore.Dispose( )
      back.Dispose( )
    End Try

    ' Calling the base class OnPaint
    MyBase.OnPaint(pe)
End Sub
```

The `OnPaint` method will be called by the framework whenever a redraw is required, because the mouse event handlers (shown in Examples 5-5 and 5-6) call

Invalidate whenever they change the control's state. It is your responsibility to do this because the framework has no idea whether a change in your object's state will require the control to be redrawn. It only calls OnPaint when you tell it that what is currently on screen is no longer valid.

This is a very simple example, but more complex custom controls work in much the same way. For example, you might write a custom control that displays an editable picture. Its OnPaint method would have a lot more work to do—it would need to iterate through all the items in the drawing and call the appropriate methods on the Graphics object to display them (probably using the ClipRectangle property in the PaintEventArgs object to determine which parts of the drawing don't need to be drawn). But the principle is still the same: OnPaint draws a representation of the control's internal state onto the screen, and whenever that state changes, it is your program's responsibility to notify the framework.

Sometimes you will change the state in such a way that only a small part of the control's display needs redrawing. For example, if your control shows a table, and you change a single cell in that table, you wouldn't want to redraw the entire table. Because of this, the Invalidate method is overloaded, allowing you to be more selective. The version we used in Example 5-5 takes no parameters and invalidates the entire control, but you can pass parameters indicating which part has changed. For example, you can supply a Rectangle, indicating which area you would like to redraw. This can enable your control to update itself much more quickly, which can be particularly important if you are updating the display because of a drag operation—if the user is moving an item around with the mouse, you will want your control to repaint itself as responsively as possible; otherwise, the application will feel sluggish, and it will feel to the user as though the mouse has become bogged down in treacle.

Keyboard input

Of course, the mouse is not the only input device. Most controls that support mouse input will also want to allow themselves to be controlled with the keyboard, for ease of use and accessibility. By and large, this is fairly straightforward—you just override the appropriate methods, such as OnKeyPress. (This corresponds to the KeyPress event described in Chapter 2.)

For controls that allow text to be typed in, there is an obvious interpretation for key presses—each letter that the user types will cause a character to appear on the screen. But for controls that don't need to support text entry, it may still be worth supporting keyboard input for accessibility. For example, most of the standard controls will behave as though you clicked on them if you press the spacebar while they have the focus. If you wish to do this, the way to fake a click event is to call the OnClick method yourself. Overriding this method in your control ensures that your control does the same thing as it would have done if it really had been clicked, and when the base class's OnClick method runs, it will raise the control's Click event.

The Control class can handle certain standard types of input for you. For example, your control can automatically detect double-clicks and raise the DoubleClick event. However, you might not always want this behavior. Fortunately, it can be disabled—it is one of a number of standard control features that can be turned on and off using the SetStyle method.

Control Styles

The Control class provides a great deal of functionality. However, you won't necessarily want all the features switched on for all the controls that you define, so Windows Forms makes certain features optional. You select the features you require by setting *control styles*.

The Control class provides a method called SetStyle that lets you turn styles on and off. You specify the styles that you wish to change with the ControlStyles enumeration. This is a flags-style enumeration, so you can pass any combination to SetStyle, along with a bool or Boolean indicating whether you are enabling or disabling the specified styles. This allows you to modify certain styles while leaving others unchanged. This is particularly useful when deriving from another control type—it means you do not need to determine the full set of styles it uses to change a single style. Examples 5-9 and 5-10 show how to modify a control's styles.

Example 5-9. Modifying a control's styles in C#

```
public MyControl()
{
    SetStyle(ControlStyles.ResizeRedraw |
             ControlStyles.StandardClick,
             true);
    SetStyle(ControlStyles.StandardDoubleClick,
             false);
}
```

Example 5-10. Modifying a control's styles in VB

```
Public Sub New()
   SetStyle(ControlStyles.ResizeRedraw Or _
            ControlStyles.StandardClick,
            True)
   SetStyle(ControlStyles.StandardDoubleClick,
            False)
End Sub
```

Examples 5-9 and 5-10 show the constructor of a control in C# and VB, respectively, that modifies the following features:

- It enables the ResizeRedraw style. This causes Windows Forms to redraw the entire control every time it is resized, which is appropriate if the control adjusts its appearance according to its size.
- It enables the StandardClick behavior, indicating that it wants Windows Forms to call the OnClick method as normal.
- It disables the StandardDoubleClick behavior, indicating that Windows Forms should never call OnDoubleClick.

> If this control is derived directly from `Control`, enabling `StandardClick` would be superfluous because it is on by default. However, it is necessary if you are deriving from some other control class and you are not sure how it sets its styles. In any case, it is good practice to turn on the styles you know that you need even if you think they are on by default. It makes it clear to anyone reading your code that you are relying on that feature.

You can also determine whether the control can receive the focus by using the `Selectable` style. And you can prevent your control from being resized by setting the `FixedHeight` and `FixedWidth` styles. There are also several styles that are used to manage the way the control is redrawn; these are described in Chapter 7.

The `SetStyle` method is protected. You cannot modify another control's styles—you are only allowed to set the styles on a control you have written yourself. This is because it is difficult for a developer to be sure of whether someone else's control is relying on a particular combination of styles.

Scrollable Custom Controls

One of the main reasons for writing a custom control is to provide a visual representation of your application's data. In some applications, the amount of data to be displayed will not necessarily always fit in the space available, in which case it probably makes sense for your control to be scrollable.

Both the `Form` and the `UserControl` classes can automatically provide scrollbars, but the basic `Control` class cannot. Fortunately, there is a simple solution to this: instead of inheriting directly from `Control`, you can inherit from `ScrollableControl` and set the `AutoScrollMinSize` property to the total scrollable size you require. You will not inherit any unwanted extra functionality—`ScrollableControl` itself inherits directly from `Control`. You will still be writing a custom control responsible for its own appearance and behavior; it will simply have the option to be scrollable.

If you do this, it is your responsibility to take into account the current scroll position when redrawing. If you draw a string at position (0, 0) it will always be drawn at the top-left corner of the control, regardless of what the current scroll position is. Worse, when the user moves the scrollbar, the contents of your window are simply moved rather than redrawn with a call to `OnPaint`. Only the newly exposed part at the edge of the control will be redrawn. If you haven't taken the scroll offset into account, this leads to an inconsistent mess in the control.

Fortunately, it is easy to adjust the drawing position according to the current scroll position. We don't have to offset all the coordinates ourselves because the `Graphics` class has a method for doing just this, as illustrated in the following code fragment:

```
// C# code
protected override void OnPaint(PaintEventArgs pe)
{
    pe.Graphics.TranslateTransform(
        AutoScrollPosition.X, AutoScrollPosition.Y);
    . . .
```

```
' VB code
Protected Overrides Sub OnPaint(pe As PaintEventArgs)
    pe.Graphics.TranslateTransform( _
        AutoScrollPosition.X, AutoScrollPosition.Y)
    . . .
```

Having done this, the Graphics object will automatically offset all the coordinates you supply. (AutoScrollPosition is a member of ScrollableControl, and its value describes the current scroll position.) Of course, if your mouse input handlers need to know the exact location that was clicked (e.g., your control displays a table and you need to calculate which row and column was clicked), you will have to apply the reverse transformation. The mouse events ignore the scroll position and supply you with coordinates relative to the top-left corner of the control. It is very easy to perform the reverse translation in C#:

```
protected override void OnMouseDown(MouseEventArgs e)
{
    Point mousePos = new Point(e.X, e.Y) -
        new Size(AutoScrollPosition);
    . . .
}
```

In VB, the code is a little more cumbersome:

```
Protected Overrides Sub OnMouseDown( _
               ByVal e As System.Windows.Forms.MouseEventArgs)

    Dim mousePos As New Point(e.X, e.Y)
    mousePos = Point.op_Subtraction(mousePos, _
               New Size(AutoScrollPosition))

End Sub
```

The Point and Size types are used to represent positions and two-dimensional sizes. (These types are discussed in more detail in Chapter 7.) They use operator overloading to allow a Point to be adjusted by a Size, which is why we are able to use the - sign in the C# code. Overloaded operators are translated by the .NET Common Language Runtime into calls to an op_*operation* method, which is why we are able to call the Point class's shared op_Subtraction method from VB.

Designing for Developers

Regardless of whether we choose the composite approach—constructing a new UI element by assembling together several other controls—or we decide to write a complete control from scratch, there are some design issues that we must consider when designing a new type of control. The problem that faces all controls is that they must be a servant to two masters: the software developer who will reuse the control and the end user who will interact with the control.

Non-visual classes don't suffer from this problem. They have a single interface—their public programming interface. Their internal workings are their own business. Likewise, visual components not designed for reuse, such as most forms, only present one public face—their user interface. The majority of forms have no public programming interface at all, and those that do usually have a very simple one (such as properties for setting or retrieving fields on a form designed to present or collect data).

But a reusable visual component must consider both types of user—it has both a user interface and a programming interface. It is important not to confuse the two when designing your control; we have already seen how tempting it can be to misuse inheritance when we want to implement one control using the user interface of another. As a rule of thumb, the way the user interface does its job is an implementation detail, and should therefore not be visible to client code.

Because your class derives (either directly or indirectly) from the `Control` class, a large amount of its programming interface is already taken care of. It will already have all the standard properties such as `Location` and `Dock`, and ambient properties such as `Font` and `BackColor` will propagate automatically. Most controls add very little to this standard feature set—the unique programmable aspects of a control are usually small in number.

Most of your efforts will go into making the user interface work well. The best design heuristic for the programming interface is this: keep it simple. Before making anything a public feature of your control's API, stop and think whether it wouldn't be better off being private.

Programmers who use your control will almost certainly do so by dropping it onto a form in the Forms Designer. A well-designed control should take certain steps to ensure that it works well in this environment. Fortunately, it is relatively easy to help Visual Studio .NET present your component more effectively.

Designer Integration

Visual Studio .NET can provide visual editing facilities for your controls, but to do this, it expects them to be designed in a particular way. The most important requirement is that your classes must expose all editable features as *properties* (not fields or methods). Doing this will make your properties visible in the designer, but you will normally want to apply certain attributes to those properties to make sure that they are represented correctly at design time.

Examples 5-11 and 5-12 show an excerpt in C# and VB, respectively, from a control that provides a public property called `BorderColor`. Visual Studio .NET will detect this property (it uses the reflection facility provided by the CLR to determine what properties are available) and expose it in the property page for the control.

Example 5-11. Exposing an editable property in C#

```
private Color bcol;
public Color BorderColor
{
    get
    {
        return bcol;
    }
    set
    {
```

Example 5-11. Exposing an editable property in C# (continued)

```
        if (!bcol.Equals(value))
        {
            bcol = value;
            Invalidate( );
        }
    }
}
```

Example 5-12. Exposing an editable property in VB

```
Private bcol As Color

Public Property BorderColor( ) As Color
    Get
        Return bcol
    End Get
    Set(ByVal Value As Color)
        If Not bcol.Equals(Value) Then
            bcol = Value
            Invalidate( )
        End If
    End Set
End Property
```

Figure 5-5 shows how Visual Studio .NET's property window will display this property. Notice that it has recognized the property's type—`Color`—and provided its standard color editing user interface for the property. Visual Studio .NET has built-in editors for all the types used by the built-in controls, such as `Color`, `Font`, `ContentAlignment`, and `Image`, and supports any properties that use the intrinsic types. It will also display a drop-down box of valid values if you use an enumeration type. (It is also possible to allow editing of properties that use custom types, but this requires a lot more work, and is described in Chapters 8 and 9.)

Misc
BorderColor
OrangeRed

Figure 5-5. A property shown in Visual Studio .NET

There is just one problem with this—the property appears in the Misc category, when it really belongs in the Appearance section. Fortunately, it is possible to tell the Forms Designer which category our control belongs to. We do this by annotating the property with an attribute. In fact, this is just one example of the many attributes defined by Windows Forms to manage the design-time behavior of a component.

The development environment will present all your component's public properties in the property window when using the component in the Forms Designer. It is reasonably intelligent about working out when to use special-purpose editors for certain property types such as colors and fonts. But there are limits to what it can deduce, and it will not always guess correctly, so it relies on the use of attributes to control its behavior.

We might want to provide a property that is only meant to be used at runtime—it makes no sense to allow design-time editing of certain properties. For example, the `ListView` control has a `ListViewItemSorter` property, which allows the order in which items appear to be controlled, but because code needs to be written to set this property usefully, it is inappropriate to provide visual editing. So you won't see this item in a list view's property page in the Designer. We can do the same thing with our own controls' properties—we can make them invisible to the designer by using the `Browsable` attribute. The property shown in Example 5-13 will not appear at design time. (But it will still be accessible to code.)

Example 5-13. Making a property invisible at design time

```
// C# code
[Browsable(false)]
public bool Connected
{
    get
    {
        . . .
' VB code
<Browsable(False)> Public Property Connected( ) As Boolean
   Get
      . . .
```

We can also control in which categories those properties that are visible will appear. By default, they will appear as Misc, but the `Category` attribute lets us select something more appropriate. If we modify the property shown in Example 5-11 by adding a `Category` attribute, as shown in Example 5-14, the property will now appear in the appropriate category in the Designer.

Example 5-14. Setting the category for a property

```
// C# code
[Category("Appearance")]
public Color BorderColor
{
    . . . as before

' VB code
<Category("Appearance")> Public Property BorderColor( ) As Color
    . . . as before
```

Although you can use any category name you like, it is best to use one of the standard categories recognized by the designer such as Appearance or Behavior (see the reference section for a complete list). This is partly because it means your control's properties will appear in categories with which the user is already familiar. But it also makes internationalizing your class easier. If you use a standard category, the string will automatically be localized (i.e., the category name will be translated into the local language.) But if you use a category of your own devising, the only way to arrange for it to be translated for different locales is to use your own attribute derived from `CategoryAttribute`.

Building Controls

You can also annotate your property with a Description attribute. This controls the text that will be displayed in the area at the bottom of the Properties window—most properties provide a short (one sentence) description of the property's purpose. Because the Description attribute is always used to define a new property (i.e., you don't need to supply a description for properties defined by the Control class), there are no standard description strings. This means that localization of the description cannot be automated. The only way to supply localizable descriptions is to derive your own attribute class from DescriptionAttribute. (Chapter 8 describes how to create a localizable Description attribute.)

ToolboxBitmap is another interesting attribute. It lets you determine how your control will appear in the Toolbox. Visual Studio .NET supplies its own default bitmap for your controls, but if you provide your own, it will use that instead. Use it by applying the ToolboxBitmap attribute to your control class. To use this attribute, you must build a bitmap into your component as an embedded resource. You can add a bitmap to the project as a New Item (see Visual Studio .NET's Project menu), and you should set its Build Action in the properties window to Embedded Resource. You should give the file the same root filename as your control but with a *.bmp* extension. Having done this, you can then simply add an attribute to your control class as follows:

```
// C# code
[ToolboxBitmap(typeof(MyControl))]
public class MyControl : Control
{
. . .

' VB code
<ToolboxBitmap(GetType(CustomControl4))> _
Public Class CustomControl4
    Inherits System.Windows.Forms.Control
   . . .
```

When you add your component to Visual Studio .NET's Toolbox, it will detect this attribute and use the name of the specified class to determine the name of the bitmap resource. In this case, it will look for *Namespace.MyControl.bmp*, where *Namespace* is the namespace in which MyControl is defined. Visual Studio .NET adds the project's default namespace to the filename automatically at build time, so the bitmap in your project would be called just *MyControl.bmp*.

Many controls will not need to use anything more than the Category, Description, and ToolboxBitmap attributes to integrate satisfactorily into the Forms Designer. However, if you want to provide properties with nonstandard types, making sure that Visual Studio .NET is able to set your properties correctly is nontrivial. We will look at the techniques involved for supporting custom types and providing your own user interfaces for editing properties in Chapters 8 and 9.

Summary

By writing your own controls, you can encapsulate pieces of user interface in reusable classes. The level of sophistication of these controls can be anywhere from a single label with some added feature to a feature-rich, fully custom control presenting a detailed interactive view of a complex piece of data (e.g., a drawing editor). The `UserControl` class lets you create a component by assembling several other controls into one larger control, arranging them with the same editor that you use when designing a form. For more exotic requirements, you can write a full custom control that inherits directly from `Control` (or `ScrollableControl`) and manages all aspects of your control's appearance and behavior. Regardless of how you build your control, you must bear in mind the needs of two kinds of user—the end user and the software developer. Confusing the requirements of these two groups of people can lead to poor software design choices.

Most of the time, if you choose to base your control on another control, you should prefer reuse by containment over reuse by inheritance. However, there are situations in which inheritance is the right style of reuse, so we will look at this in the next chapter.

6
Inheritance and Reuse

Inheritance is at the heart of the Windows Forms architecture—all visual classes inherit from the `Control` class. Not only does this ensure that there is a single programming interface for common user interface functionality, it also guarantees consistent behavior because all controls inherit the same implementation. Control authors need only write code for the features unique to their components, and developers that use these controls will not be troubled by subtle differences in behavior. This is a welcome improvement over ActiveX controls, the previous visual component technology in Windows, where each control had to provide a complete implementation of the standard functionality, with not entirely consistent results.

Inheritance can offer further benefits when we write our own UI components. Not only can we take advantage of the `Control` class's features, we can also derive from other controls such as `Button` or `TextBox`. We can extend the behavior of almost any control, not just those built into the framework—third-party controls can also be used as base classes. The Forms Designer provides support for two special cases of inheritance: forms that inherit from other forms, and controls that derive from other composite controls. It allows us to edit such inherited components visually.

As mentioned in the previous chapter, inheritance must be used with care—deriving from a class makes a strong statement about your own class: you are declaring that your class is everything that the base class is; inheritance defines an "is a" relationship. This makes sense when deriving from `Control`—if you are building a visual component, then by definition, it is a control. But for less generic base classes such as `TextBox`, it is important to be clear whether your control really is a `TextBox`, or whether it simply uses one in its implementation.

We will therefore start by looking at the situations in which inheritance is an appropriate technique. Then, we will see how to inherit from classes based on `Form` and `UserControl`, both of which have special support from the IDE. Next we will look at inheriting directly from other controls. Finally, some of the pitfalls of inheritance will be examined.

When to Inherit

As mentioned in the previous chapter, inheritance is not always the most appropriate form of reuse. There are two ways to create a control class that, from the end user's point of view, looks and behaves just like an existing control. You could either inherit from the control, or simply create a `UserControl` that contains it. Both approaches are equally easy. The decision must be based on which is better software design for your control.

There are two important points to understand to make this choice. The first is that the decision to inherit is something that affects your control's programming interface, not its user interface. (Recall that in the last chapter we saw that all controls have two sets of users: programmers and end users.) The second point is that inheritance defines an "is a" relationship—if your control inherits from, say, `ListView`, any instance of your control is by definition also an instance of the `ListView` class.

Sometimes this will be what you require. For example, you might decide to write a text box that automatically filters its input to certain characters, For instance, you could create a `TelephoneTextBox` that only allows digits, hyphens, spaces, and the + symbol. In this case, it would be reasonable to use inheritance, because your control is just like a `TextBox` from the developer's point of view; it just has some special modified behavior from the end user's perspective. There is no problem with letting the developer do anything to a `TelephoneTextBox` that they might also do to a normal `TextBox`, in which case we may safely declare that our `TelephoneTextBox` is a `TextBox`, as in Example 6-1 (which contains the C# version) and Example 6-2 (which contains the VB version).

Example 6-1. A derived control in C#

```
public class TelephoneTextBox : System.Windows.Forms.TextBox
{
    private string accept = "0123456789 +-";
    protected override void OnKeyPress(
                System.Windows.Forms.KeyPressEventArgs e)
    {
        if (accept.IndexOf(e.KeyChar) < 0)
        {
            // Not a valid character, prevent
            // default handling.
            e.Handled = true;
        }
        base.OnKeyPress(e);
    }
}
```

Example 6-2. A derived control in VB

```
Public Class TelephoneTextBox
       Inherits System.Windows.Forms.TextBox

    Private accept As String = "0123456789 +-"

    Protected Overrides Sub OnKeyPress( _
              ByVal e As System.Windows.Forms.KeyPressEventArgs)
```

Inheritance & Reuse

Example 6-2. A derived control in VB (continued)

```
        If accept.IndexOf(e.KeyChar) < 0 Then
            ' Not a valid character, prevent
            ' default handling.
            e.Handled = True
        End If

        MyBase.OnKeyPress(e)
    End Sub

End Class
```

The general rule is that if you want the public API of the control you are reusing to be accessible to developers using your control, inheritance is likely to be the right solution. Programmers will view your control as being an extended version of the base control. But if you want the control you are reusing to be visible only to the user, and not to the developer, reuse through containment is the best answer.

A very common case in which inheritance is not appropriate is if the purpose of your class is to provide a visual representation of something, such as a list of items in an email folder. Such a control might well be based on a `ListView`, but it would not want to expose the `ListView` API. That would permit all sorts of operations that would most likely not make sense, such as the ability to add new column headings or change the view type; those are normal operations for a `ListView`, but they do not have any obvious meaning for a view of a mail folder's contents—what exactly would it mean to add a new column, for example?

Sometimes, there will be gray areas. To see why, let us look again at the `TelephoneTextBox`. It is not necessarily true to say that it can be used in exactly the same way as a `TextBox`: its `Text` property presents a problem. The control is only supposed to be able to hold a telephone number, and it enforces this by filtering the user's input. But what if some code that uses this control attempts to set the `Text` property to a value such as "Hello," which is not a valid phone number? The code in Example 6-1 or 6-2 does not deal with this, so the control's text will be set just like it would be with a normal text box. This breaks the intent of our control—it is only supposed to hold phone numbers. We could fix this by overriding the `Text` property and throwing an exception if it is set to an invalid value, but that would then break the "is a" relationship—there would then be things that you could do with a `TextBox` that you couldn't do with a `TelephoneTextBox`.

Purists would argue that you should always stick to the Lyskov Substitution Principle: you should only use inheritance if your class can do absolutely everything that the base class can. However, this can often be unduly restrictive. There are plenty of examples in the Windows Forms libraries where derived classes remove functionality that is present in the base classes. For example, the `Control` class supplies `Click` and `DoubleClick` events, but derived controls can disable these if they want to (e.g., the `TreeView` doesn't raise `Click` events). So in practice, it is often not a problem to bend the rules slightly.* But if you find yourself creating a

* With sufficiently careful documentation, it is even possible to do this and conform to the Lyskov Substitution Principle—your base class must simply document all the variations in behavior that derived classes are allowed to introduce.

control that is programmatically incompatible with its base type in many ways, inheritance is almost certainly the wrong choice.

Visual Studio .NET has special support for inherited forms. Forms are controls like any other visual element (i.e., they inherit indirectly from `Control`), and the rules mentioned so far apply just as well to forms as to any other class. However, the way that forms are normally used means that inheritance is more likely to be the right choice for forms than it is for most other control types.

When to Inherit from a Form

Forms inheritance is very useful if your application needs to present several similar dialogs. You can define a base form that contains the features common to all your windows, and then create specialized classes for each variation.

If you derive from a form, your derived class will represent a window that has all the same controls on it as the base class, and you may optionally add more controls of your own. You will only be able to modify the controls on the base class if they have the appropriate protection level. (The relevant levels are `protected` or `public`, or for forms in the same assembly as yours, `internal` in C# or `Friend` in VB.) The Forms Designer in Visual Studio .NET supports visual editing of inherited forms. It displays controls from both the base class and the derived class, but only allows you to edit the properties of controls to which your class has access—i.e., to those specific to your derived form, and those on the base form with an appropriate protection level.

Forms are more often a suitable candidate for inheritance than other controls, because forms often add little or nothing by way of programming interface to the `Form` class. They usually stand alone as top-level windows, rather than being contained within another control, and this self-contained nature means that they have no need for much of an API. The only interface they have that matters is the user interface. Because most of the problems associated with derivation revolve around the implications of inheriting the programming interface, this means that forms are usually a safe bet for inheritance.

There is another reason you might use inheritance with forms more often than with controls. Chapter 5 discussed a reuse technique that provides an alternative to inheritance—wrapping the control to be reused in a `UserControl`. This technique is not available to forms—you cannot contain a whole form inside a `UserControl`. If you want to base one form on another, inheritance is your only choice (not counting everybody's favorite code reuse mechanism: the clipboard).

Note that Visual Studio .NET also has special support for inheriting from controls based on `UserControl`. The main reason for this is that `Form` and `UserControl` are very similar—they are both composite user interface elements (i.e., they consist of a collection of child controls). The development environment uses the same editor for forms and user controls, so it is not surprising that it supports visual inheritance for both. However, controls based on `UserControl` are used very differently from forms—controls are designed to be contained by other UI components, but forms normally stand alone. This means that for a `UserControl`, the programming interface is usually much more significant than it is for a `Form`. So although visual editing of inherited components is supported for both forms and composite controls, it is usually more useful for forms.

Inheriting from Forms and User Controls

Visual Studio .NET allows you to add an inherited form or control as a new item to a project. When you add such an item, it will display the Inheritance Picker dialog, which lists appropriate classes from the solutions in your project (this includes all the forms you have defined, or all the user controls, if you are creating an inherited control). Inheriting from a form or a user control requires the relevant projects in your solution to have been built. If classes you expect to see are missing from the list, check that your solution builds without errors. The Inheritance Picker also provides a Browse button, so that you can derive from classes defined in components outside your solution.

Once you have selected your base class, the usual Forms Designer will be shown, just as it would be for a normal form or composite control. But rather than displaying a blank canvas, the editor will show the contents of the base class—your new user interface element will initially look exactly like its base class. Not surprising, as inherited classes always have all their base class's members.

Of course, inheritance allows us to extend the functionality of the base class, not just to replicate it, so the editor lets us add new controls to the derived class. The editor annotates base class controls with a small icon, as shown on the text box and button in Figure 6-1, to enable you to tell the difference between controls from the base class and controls added in the derived class.

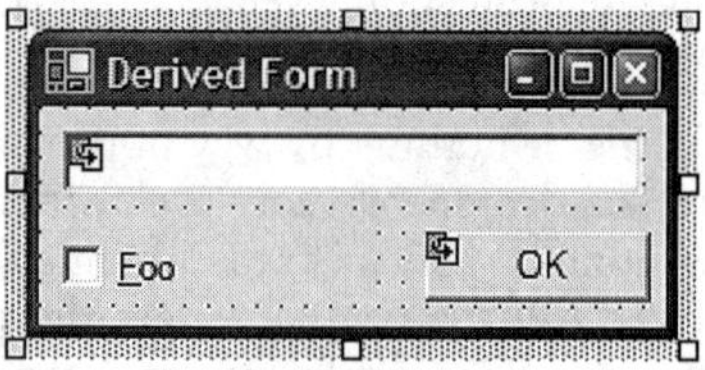
Derived Form
Foo
OK

Figure 6-1. Showing controls from the base form

The code generated for derived forms and controls is straightforward. As Examples 6-3 and 6-4 show, it is almost identical to the code generated for a normal form. So there is the usual constructor, which calls the `InitializeComponent` method where the form's controls are created and initialized. There is also the normal `Dispose` function, where resources are cleaned up. As usual, you can add your own initialization code at the end of the constructor and your own cleanup code in the `Dispose` method. The only obvious difference between this and a normal form is that the class no longer derives directly from `Form`; it inherits from your chosen base class (as the bold line shows).

Example 6-3. A derived form's basic structure in C#

```
public class DerivedForm : BaseForm
{
    private System.ComponentModel.IContainer components = null;

    public DerivedForm()
    {
        InitializeComponent();
    }
```

Example 6-3. A derived form's basic structure in C# (continued)

```
    protected override void Dispose( bool disposing )
    {
        if( disposing )
        {
            if (components != null)
            {
                components.Dispose( );
            }
        }
        base.Dispose( disposing );
    }

    private void InitializeComponent( )
    {
        . . .
        Usual designer-generated code
        . . .
    }
}
```

Example 6-4. A derived form's basic structure in VB

```
Public Class DerivedForm
    Inherits BaseForm

    Public Sub New( )
        MyBase.New( )

        InitializeComponent( )
    End Sub

    Protected Overloads Overrides Sub Dispose(ByVal disposing As Boolean)
        If disposing Then
            If Not (components Is Nothing) Then
                components.Dispose( )
            End If
        End If
        MyBase.Dispose(disposing)
    End Sub

    Private components As System.ComponentModel.IContainer

    Private Sub InitializeComponent( )
        . . .
        Usual designer-generated code
        . . .
    End Sub

End Class
```

This similarity of structure means that both the base and the derived classes will have `InitializeComponent` and `Dispose` methods. If the class is going to initialize new instances correctly, both `InitializeComponent` methods need to run. Likewise, both `Dispose` methods need to execute when the form is destroyed. This will

Inheritance & Reuse

indeed happen, although it works differently for initialization and disposal—there is a subtle distinction between the ways the `InitializeComponent` and `Dispose` methods interact with their counterparts in the base class.

Because `InitializeComponent` is always declared as `private`, the base and derived implementations are considered by the CLR to be two completely different methods—the `IntializeComponent` method in the derived class does not override the one in the base class, because you cannot override a private method. Both of these will run because of the way the CLR constructs objects: first the base class's constructor will run, calling the base class's `InitializeComponent` method, and then the derived class's constructor will run, calling the derived class's `InitializeComponent` method. In the VB version shown in Example 6-4, the base class's constructor is called explicitly in any case by the `MyBase.New` statement.

Conversely, the `Dispose` method is always marked as `protected override` in C# and as `Protected Overloads Overrides` in VB. This means that the method replaces the base class's implementation. However, there is a call to `base.Dispose` or `MyBase.Dispose` at the end of this method (just as there would be in the implementation of `Dispose` in the base class). This is the standard pattern—derived classes always override `Dispose` and then call the base class's `Dispose` at the end, ensuring that all the classes in the hierarchy get a chance to clean up properly. This means that, unlike the `InitializeComponent` methods, the first `Dispose` method to run will be that of the most derived class, and the calls then work their way up the inheritance hierarchy* (until they get to `System.ComponentModel.Component`, the base class of `Control`, which is the place in the hierarchy where the `Dispose` method is introduced). This model supports any depth of inheritance—it is entirely possible to derive from an inherited form or control. Each class can add its own collection of controls to the set supplied by the base class.

If you build an inherited UI component in C#, you will notice that by default the Designer restricts what you can do to a base class's controls. We will now examine how the interaction between a derived class and its base's controls works, and how to grant a derived class access to the controls in a base class.

Interacting with Controls in the Base Class

In the last chapter, we saw how the controls you write have two faces: the API seen by the developer and the user interface seen by the end user. Inheritance complicates the picture a little—there are two different ways a developer can use your control: one is simply to instantiate it and use it, but the other is to derive from it. Developers who write derived classes will get to see the programming interface. But most forms are written without much of an API, which can cause problems for a deriving class. As we will see, a base form often needs to be written with deriving classes in mind for inheritance to be successful.

Unlike C#, VB.NET makes the protection level `Friend` by default. (This is equivalent to `internal` in C#.) This means that controls will be accessible to any code in the same component. So if you derive from a VB.NET form or user control, the

* Although the mechanisms involved are very different, this echoes C++, where construction starts with the base class, but destruction starts with the most derived class.

behavior you see will depend on whether your derived class is in the same project as the base class. If it is in the same project, all the controls will be accessible, but if it is not, the behavior will be the same as you would see in C#—the controls in the base class will be inaccessible.

The most obvious difference between a control's API and its UI is that features visible to the end user are usually inaccessible to the developer. On screen, it might be clear that a composite control consists of some labels, text boxes, and buttons, but the child controls that represent these are usually private implementation details of the form's class. So although any deriving class that you write will have all the same child controls, they will not be directly accessible to your code because they will be private members of your base class.

Figure 6-2 shows a base form and a class derived from that form in the editor. In both cases, the OK button has been selected, but notice how the selection outline is different. With the base class, which is where the OK button is defined, we see the normal outline with resize handles. But on the derived class, we get a solid outline with no handles. This is how the form editor shows us that a control cannot be modified. Any attempt to move, resize, or otherwise change the control will be unsuccessful. Indeed, the control will be completely invisible to any code in the derived form even though it will be present on screen, so for controls with readable properties, such as a text box, the deriving class will not even be able to read those properties.

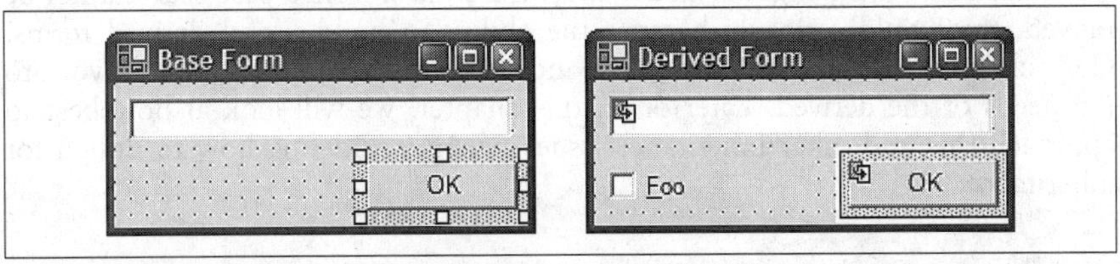
Base Form
OK
Derived Form
Foo
OK

Figure 6-2. A base form and a derived form

This is the default behavior for C# base classes—if you do not take steps in your base class to make your controls accessible to derived classes, they will be present but untouchable, like the OK button above. However, it is easy enough to change this—control accessibility is based entirely around the member protection provided by the CLR. The OK button is inaccessible to the derived class because its associated member will have been defined as `private` in the base class, as shown in Example 6-5. (Note, if the base class was written in VB.NET, it would be marked `Friend`, as shown in Example 6-6. This would mean that if the derived form were in the same project as the base class, the button would be inaccessible.)

Example 6-5. A control accessible only to the base class

```
// C#
private System.Windows.Forms.Button buttonOK;
```

Example 6-6. A control accessible only to other classes in the same project

```
// VB
Friend WithEvents Button1 As System.Windows.Forms.Button
```

If you change this to `protected`, the control will become visible to all derived classes. The Designer provides a way of doing this: in the properties page for a control there is a property called Modifiers under the Design section. By default, this is `private` (in C# projects) or `Friend` (in VB projects), but you can choose any protection level offered by the CLR. If you make this accessible to derived classes (i.e., `protected`), they will be able to retrieve and modify your control's properties. The Forms Editor indicates this by showing a normal outline with resize handles when you select the control, as shown in Figure 6-3.

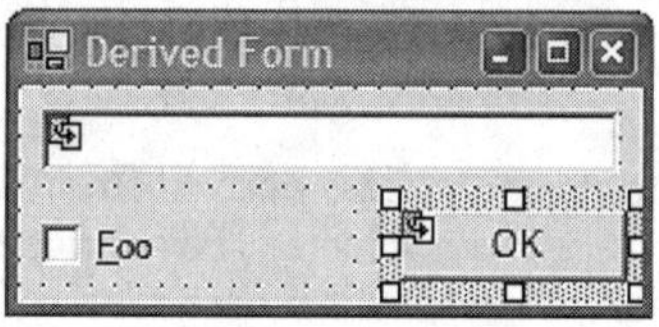

Derived Form
Foo
OK

Figure 6-3. A base's control accessible in a derived form

Once a control from the base class is no longer private, your derived class can modify any of its properties except its name. This means that you can, for example, move it, resize it, change its caption, enable or disable it, or make it invisible.

Deciding which controls should be accessible to derived classes is an important consideration when designing a base class. If a control from a base class cannot be moved, this could seriously hamper the ability to build useful derived forms. Controls marked as `private` cannot be moved or resized to adapt their layout to the needs of the derived. Later on in this chapter, we will look at how best to approach this and other inheritance issues when considering how to design for inheritance.

> For the truly determined, gaining access to `private` controls is not an insurmountable problem. Although the member field in the base class is `private`, that merely prevents you from using the control through that particular field. If you can obtain a reference to it by other means, you can still modify all its properties. It is always possible to do this because all the controls on a form can be accessed through its `Controls` property. This collection is enumerable, so you can just search for the control with a `foreach` loop. This is not recommended though. It might help you as a last resort, but it's a bit of a hack—the base class will not expect you to surreptitiously modify its `private` controls like this. Furthermore, there is no support for it in the Designer—you must write code to do this.

Event Handling

If the base class provides a non-private control, not only can you modify its properties, you can also add event handlers. So in the example above, we could add our own `Click` handler for the OK button. However, there is a subtle difference between the way events work and the way most properties work, which means this will not always have the effect you anticipate.

The crucial thing to remember when handling events in a derived class is that event sources can support multiple handlers. This makes events different from properties such as Location—if the derived class sets that property, it will replace any value that the base class gave it. With an event, if the derived class adds an event handler, that handler will be called in addition to any that were specified by the base class. So in the example above, if the base class has already attached a Click handler to the OK button, and we then add another of our own, it will run after the base class's handler.

So when it comes to handling events from child controls, we cannot replace the base class's behavior, we can only add to it. Again, this illustrates that unless the base class is designed with inheritance in mind, we could run into trouble.

Beyond certain pitfalls with poorly designed base classes, inheriting from forms or composite controls is mostly straightforward, thanks to the support provided by the Forms Designer. However, it is possible to derive from other types of controls, albeit with less help from the development environment, as we will now see.

Inheriting from Other Controls

Because inheritance is central to the way controls work in the Windows Forms framework, we are not limited to deriving from forms or composite controls. In principle, we can use any control as a base class (unless it has marked itself as sealed in C# or NonInheritable in VB, but very few controls do this). We must live without the convenience of visual editing when deriving from other control types, but of course that is also the case when we write custom controls.

The usual reason for inheriting from some non-composite control (e.g., one of the built-in controls) is to provide a version of that control with some useful extra feature. For example, we will see later how to add an autocompletion facility to the TextBox control. As always, it is crucially important only to use inheritance where it makes sense—developers must be able to use our derived control just as they would use the base control.

Visual Studio .NET does not provide a direct way of creating a new derived control with a non-composite base class. However, it is reasonably easy to get started: simply add a new Custom Control to the project, delete the OnPaint method it supplies, and change the base class from Control to whichever control class you want to derive from. Alternatively, just create a new normal class definition from scratch that inherits from the base class of your choice. (These two techniques are exactly equivalent. Although it is more straightforward just to create a normal class, using the Custom Control template with C# provides you with a useful set of using declarations at the top of the file.)

Thanks to the wonders of inheritance, your derived control will now be capable of doing everything that the base control can do. All that remains is to add whatever extra functionality you require. There are two ways in which controls are typically extended. The first involves modifying its programming interface by adding or overriding methods or properties. The second involves modifying the behavior of the control itself. A deriving control can use either or both of these modes of extension. We will now look at each in turn.

Extending the Programming Interface

Sometimes we will want to use a built-in control, but to make some change to its programming interface. We can do this without changing its visual behavior—as far as the user is concerned, the control will appear to be just another `ListView` or `Label`. We are modifying the control purely to make things more convenient for the developer. This might be as simple as adding some helper methods to populate a `ListView` with a collection of some application-specific data type. Such methods are straightforward: the code usually looks exactly the same as it would in a non-inheritance situation; it just happens to have been bolted onto an existing class using inheritance. The more challenging and interesting changes are those that extend the behavior of existing methods.

Modifying the behavior of existing methods can be particularly useful in a multithreaded program. Remember the golden rule for threads in Windows Forms introduced in Chapter 3: you should only use a control from the thread on which it was created; the only exception is you can use the `Invoke`, `BeginInvoke`, and `EndInvoke` methods, and the `InvokeRequired` property. While this is a simple rule, it is often tedious to comply with—marshaling all calls through `Invoke` or `BeginInvoke` adds unwanted complexity, and introduces scope for programming errors.

So if you have a worker thread that needs to update the user interface on a regular basis (e.g., updating a text field to keep the user informed of the thread's progress), it might be worth creating a control that has slightly more relaxed threading constraints. So we will now look at how to build a control derived from `Label` that allows its `Text` property to be accessed safely from any thread.

Remember that the correct way to use a control from a worker thread is to direct all calls through either `Invoke` or `BeginInvoke`. These will arrange for the call to occur on the correct thread. They both need to know which method you would like to invoke, so they take a delegate as a parameter. None of the delegates defined by the framework quite meet our needs, so our multithreaded* label class starts with a couple of private delegate type definitions. In C#, the code is as follows:

```
public class LabelMT : System.Windows.Forms.Label
{
    private delegate string GetTextDelegate( );
    private delegate void SetTextDelegate(string s);
```

The equivalent VB code is:

```
Public Class LabelMT
    Inherits System.Windows.Forms.Label

    Private Delegate Function GetTextDelegate( ) As String
    Private Delegate Sub SetTextDelegate(ByVal s As String)
```

The first delegate will be used when setting the text, and the second will be used when retrieving it. Next, we override the `Text` property itself to make it safe for use in a multithreaded environment. The C# code that does this is:

* Strictly speaking, it's not fully thread-safe—we are only enabling the `Text` property for multithreaded use to keep things simple.

```
public override string Text
{
    get
    {
        if (DesignMode || !InvokeRequired)
        {
            return base.Text;
        }
        else
        {
            return (string) Invoke(new GetTextDelegate(DoGetText));
        }
    }
    set
    {
        if (DesignMode || !InvokeRequired)
        {
            base.Text = value;
        }
        else
        {
            object[] args = { value };
            BeginInvoke(new SetTextDelegate(DoSetText),
                args);
        }
    }
}
```

The VB code to override the Text property is:

```
Public Overrides Property Text( ) As String
   Get
      If DesignMode OrElse Not InvokeRequired Then
         Return MyBase.Text
      Else
         Return DirectCast(Invoke(New GetTextDelegate( _
                           AddressOf DoGetText)), String)
      End If
   End Get
   Set(ByVal Value As String)
      If DesignMode OrElse Not InvokeRequired Then
         MyBase.Text = Value
      Else
         Dim args( ) As Object = {Value}
         BeginInvoke(New SetTextDelegate(AddressOf DoSetText), _
                     args)
      End If
   End Set
End Property
```

Note that both of these start by checking to see if they actually need to marshal the call to another thread. If the property is being used from the correct thread, we just defer directly to the base class's implementation, avoiding the overhead of a call through Invoke. (And in the case of the property set method, we use BeginInvoke—this doesn't wait for the UI thread to complete the call, and just returns immediately. If you don't need to wait for a return value, it is usually

Inheritance & Reuse

better to use BeginInvoke instead of Invoke—it returns more quickly, and it can reduce the chance of accidentally freezing your application by causing a deadlock.)

The InvokeRequired property tells us whether we are already on the UI thread. You may be wondering why this code also tests the DesignMode flag. The reason is that when our control is in design mode (i.e., it is being displayed in the Forms Editor in Visual Studio .NET), certain things don't work in quite the same way as they do at runtime. Controls are initialized differently in design mode, so some features are unavailable. One of these is the Invoke mechanism—any attempt to use it will cause an error. Unfortunately, InvokeRequired is always true in design mode, despite the fact that it is not actually possible to use Invoke. So if we are in design mode, we just ignore the InvokeRequired property and always call the base class's implementation. (It is safe to assume that the Forms Designer will never access our controls on the wrong thread, so it will always be safe to ignore InvokeRequired here.)

If we are not in design mode (i.e., the control is running normally, not inside the Designer) but InvokeRequired indicates that we are on the wrong thread, we use the Invoke method to marshal the call to the correct thread. We pass it a delegate wrapped around either the DoGetText or the DoSetText method, which will then be called by the framework on the UI thread. These methods simply call the base class implementation. Their C# code is:

```
private string DoGetText( )
{
    Debug.Assert(!InvokeRequired);
    return base.Text;
}

private void DoSetText(string s)
{
    Debug.Assert(!InvokeRequired);
    base.Text = s;
}
```

Their equivalent VB code is:

```
Private Function DoGetText( ) As String
    Debug.Assert(Not InvokeRequired)
    Return MyBase.Text
End Function

Private Sub DoSetText(ByVal s As String)
    Debug.Assert(Not InvokeRequired)
    MyBase.Text = s
End Sub
```

These methods are only ever called via the Invoke or BeginInvoke method, which means that they will always run on the UI thread.* This means that they can simply access the property directly using the base class's implementation.

* In this example, this assumption has been encoded in a Debug.Assert call—these assertions will fail on debug builds if any developer later modifies this control and tries to call these methods on the wrong thread. As with most assertion mechanisms, these aren't compiled into release builds.

> If you are used to writing multithreaded code, you might be surprised at the absence of locks or critical sections. Most thread-safe code protects itself by synchronizing access to shared data using locking primitives supplied by the system (such as critical sections in Win32). The CLR provides these kinds of facilities, and both VB and C# have intrinsic support for them with their `lock` and `SyncLock` keywords, but they turn out to be unnecessary here. Concurrency is never an issue because we make sure that all work is done on the UI thread, and a thread can only do one piece of work at a time.

Threading issues aside, this is an example of a common pattern: overriding a feature of the base class but calling back to the base class's original implementation to do the bulk of the work. The code in the derived class simply adds some value on top of the original code (correct operation in a multithreaded environment in this case). But we will now look at the other way of extending a control—modifying the behavior seen by the user.

Extending Behavior

The second way of extending a control is to modify the behavior that the end user sees. This typically means changing the way the control reacts to user input, or altering its appearance. It always involves overriding the internal event handling methods (i.e., the `On`*`Xxx`* methods, such as `OnPaint` or `OnMouseDown`) to change the way the control behaves.

Examples 6-7 and 6-8 show a class, `AutoTextBox`, that derives from the built-in `TextBox` control. It augments the basic `TextBox` by adding a simple autocomplete functionality. This is a common feature of many text fields in Windows applications—the control has some list of potential values for the field, and if the text that the user has typed in so far matches any of those values, it prompts the user with them. This is a very useful enhancement. It can save a lot of typing and is becoming increasingly widely adopted. In Windows XP, most text fields that accept filenames will autocomplete, using the filesystem as the source of potential values. Internet Explorer uses a list of recently visited pages when you type into the address bar. So it could be good to provide this functionality in our own applications.

The example shown here is pretty simple—it has a very low-tech API for setting the list of known strings,* and it will only provide one suggestion at a time, as shown in Figure 6-4. (Internet Explorer will show you all possible matches in a drop-down list.) It is left as an exercise to the reader to add advanced features such as supporting data binding for the known string list, and an Internet Explorer–style drop-down suggestions list. But even this minimal implementation is surprisingly useful.

To use this control, a developer would simply add it to a form as she would a normal `TextBox`. It will behave in exactly the same way thanks to inheritance. The only difference is that at some point during initialization (probably in the form's

* So this control actually illustrates both types of extension—it augments the original control's user interface as well as its API. The API extensions are trivial, though.

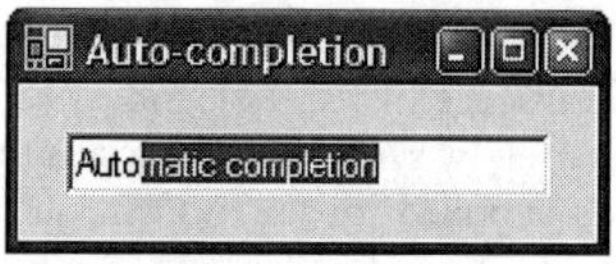
Auto-completion
Automatic completion

Figure 6-4. Automatic completion in action

constructor) there would be a series of calls to the AutoTextBox object's AddAutoCompleteString method to provide the control with its suggestion list.

At runtime, the main autocompletion work is done in the overridden OnTextChanged method. This method will be called by the base TextBox class every time the control's text changes. (It corresponds to the TextChanged event.) We simply examine the text that has been typed in so far (by looking at the Text property) and see if it matches the start of any of our suggestion strings. If it does, we put the full suggested text into the control. We also select the part of the text that we added (i.e., everything after what the user had already typed). This means that if our suggestion is wrong and the user continues typing, the text we added will be wiped out—text boxes automatically delete the selection if you type over it. (This is the standard behavior for automatic text completion.)

Example 6-7. An autocompleting TextBox in C#

```
using System.Collections.Specialized;
using System.Windows.Forms;

public class AutoTextBox : System.Windows.Forms.TextBox
{
    private StringCollection suggestions = new StringCollection( );
    public void AddAutoCompleteString(string s)
    {
        suggestions.Add(s);
    }

    private bool ignoreNextChange = false;
    protected override void OnTextChanged(EventArgs e)
    {
        if (!ignoreNextChange)
        {
            foreach (string str in suggestions)
            {
                if (str.StartsWith(Text))
                {
                    if (str.Length == Text.Length)
                        return;
                    int origLength = Text.Length;
                    Text = str;
                    Select(origLength, str.Length - origLength);
                }
        }
        base.OnTextChanged(e);
    }
```

Example 6-7. An autocompleting TextBox in C# (continued)

```
    protected override void OnKeyDown(KeyEventArgs e)
    {
        switch (e.KeyCode)
        {
            case Keys.Back:
            case Keys.Delete:
                ignoreNextChange = true;
                break;
            default:
                ignoreNextChange = false;
                break;
        }
        base.OnKeyDown(e);
    }
}
```

Example 6-8. An autocompleting TextBox in VB

```
Imports System.Collections.Specialized
Imports System.Windows.Forms

Public Class AutoTextBox
   Inherits System.Windows.Forms.TextBox

   Private ignoreNextChange As Boolean = False
   Private suggestions As New StringCollection( )

   Public Sub AddAutoCompleteString(ByVal s As String)
      suggestions.Add(s)
   End Sub

   Protected Overrides Sub OnTextChanged(ByVal e As EventArgs)
      If Not ignoreNextChange Then
         Dim str As String
         Dim origLength As Integer
         For Each str In suggestions
            If str.StartsWith(Text) Then
               If str.Length = Text.Length Then Return
               origLength = Text.Length
               Text = str
               [Select](origLength, str.Length - origLength)
            End If
         Next
      End If
      MyBase.OnTextChanged(e)
   End Sub

   Protected Overrides Sub OnKeyDown(ByVal e As KeyEventArgs)
      Select Case e.KeyCode
         Case Keys.Back
            ignoreNextChange = True
         Case Keys.Delete
            ignoreNextChange = True
```

Inheritance & Reuse

Example 6-8. An autocompleting TextBox in VB (continued)

```
            Case Else
                ignoreNextChange = False
        End Select
        MyBase.OnKeyDown(e)
    End Sub

End Class
```

There is one minor complication that requires a little more code than just the text change handler. Notice that `AutoTextBox` also overrides the `OnKeyDown` method. This is because we need to handle deletion differently. With nothing more than an `OnTextChanged` method, when the user hits the Backspace key, the control will delete the selection if one is active. For this control, the selection will most likely be the tail end of the last suggestion. This deletion will cause the `OnTextChanged` method to be called, which will promptly put the same suggestion straight back again!

This will make it seem as though the Backspace key isn't working. So we need to detect when the user has just deleted something and not attempt to autocomplete. So we override the `OnKeyDown` method, and if either Backspace or Delete is pressed, we set the `ignoreNextChange` flag to indicate to the `OnTextChanged` method that it shouldn't try to suggest anything this time round. The `default` or `else` case is important—if the key is not performing a deletion, we do want to provide a suggestion if there is a matching one.

Although this code is fairly simple (it overrides just two methods, using only a handful of lines of code), it illustrates an important point: the derived class's implementation is dependent upon the base class's behavior. This is partly evident in the complication surrounding deletion—the derived class has to understand the input model of the base class and work around it. It's less obvious is whether the code in Examples 6-7 and 6-8 is necessarily the right way to achieve this—why present the suggestions in `OnTextChanged` and not `OnKeyDown`, `OnKeyPress`, `ProcessKeyMessage`, or any of the other methods that sound like they might be relevant? To find the answer involves examining the documentation for every likely looking method, and then using trial and error on the ones that look as though they might work.*

Even if we identify the right method or methods to override, we can never be completely sure that we have anticipated all the issues, such as special handling for deletion. As it happens, we haven't in this case—the `TextBox` control has a context menu with a Delete entry. This doesn't work properly with the code as it stands (because of the same deletion issue that required `OnKeyPress` to be overridden), and as there is no direct way to detect that this Delete menu item was selected, this is not a simple issue to solve.†

* To save you the effort in this particular case, `ProcessKeyMessage` is far too low-level, `OnKeyDown` and `OnKeyPress` look as though they should work but turn out not to due to a subtlety in the order in which events percolate through the system, so `OnTextChanged` wins the day.

† If you would like to fix this problem as an exercise, a better approach is to make `OnTextChanged` remember what text had been typed in (excluding any suggestion) last time round. If it sees the same text twice running, it should not attempt to supply a suggestion the second time. You will then need to deal with the fact that setting the `Text` property causes a second reentrant call to `OnTextChanged`. With this solution you will no longer need to override `OnKeyDown`.

Even more insidiously, we cannot be completely sure that this will continue to work in the future. The standard controls in Windows have evolved over the years, and will almost certainly continue to do so. We cannot reasonably expect to anticipate every new feature that might emerge for every control.

So even for a fairly undemanding extension to a simple control, there are numerous hazards to negotiate, many of which are not obvious. So we will now consider the general nature of the problems you will encounter when deriving from controls, so that you can have a fighting chance of avoiding problems.

Pitfalls of Inheritance

Inheritance is a troublesome facility; although it is undoubtedly powerful, it can cause a great many problems. To steer clear of these, it is important to understand what it is about inheritance that makes it so easy to go wrong. We have already discussed simple misuse, caused by the failure to understand that inheritance defines an "is a" relationship—if your derived class cannot be substituted for its base class, you will run into difficulties. But even when this design rule has not been broken, inheritance is still potentially dangerous. The fundamental problem with inheritance is that it tends to require the derived class to have an exceptionally close relationship with the base class.

In the autocompletion example above, we needed to know more than is healthy about the way that the `TextBox` class works. First of all, we needed a pretty detailed understanding simply to determine which methods to override. To implement these overrides correctly, we also needed considerable lateral knowledge of the inner workings of the control, to anticipate issues such as the deletion problem. Inheritance requires knowledge of how the base class works both in breadth and in depth.

This tight coupling between the derived and base classes introduces another problem. If the base class evolves over time, it could easily break classes that derive from it. In the `AutoTextBox` class, we elected to autocomplete the control's text in our override of `OnTextChanged` and not in `OnKeyPress`, because we observed that the former appears to work where the latter appears not to work in this particular case. But this is not a clearly documented feature of the `TextBox` class; what if the next version behaves slightly differently?

There is a reasonable argument that says authors of base classes simply shouldn't make changes like this—after all, if they made such changes to the public API, it would break all client code, not just deriving classes.* But there are two reasons why derived classes are more vulnerable to changes in the base class than normal clients. First, derived classes get to see a larger API—they can access all the `protected` members, where normal clients only see the `public` ones. Second, and more importantly, derived classes usually modify the behavior of the base class in

* In this particular case, the `OnTextChanged` and `OnKeyPress` methods are directly associated with the public `TextChanged` and `KeyPress` events. Changes to the nature of these protected methods would imply a corresponding change in public behavior, which is one reason we can be reasonably confident that this particular feature of `TextBox` won't change in future versions of the framework.

some way; modifications are likely to be much more sensitive to implementation details than straightforward usage will be.

This problem is often described as the "fragile base class" issue: you can't touch the base class without breaking something. The main technology offered by .NET to mitigate this is its support for side-by-side deployment—multiple versions of a component can be installed on one machine, so that each application can use the exact version of the component it was built against. But even that can go wrong: the base class author might sneakily issue an update without changing the component's version number, or he might ship a publisher policy with an update, declaring the new version to be fully backwards compatible with the old one—either of these could potentially upset derived classes. And even if this doesn't happen, you might run into trouble when you next rebuild your application—if you have updated the components on your system, you will probably be building against the newer versions.

Given the tight coupling between the base and the derived class, it should come as no surprise to discover that inheritance is often at its most successful when both the base and derived class are written by the same author or team. When derived classes start to do things that the base class author didn't originally anticipate, there are far fewer problems if the same developer wrote both. That developer can then modify the base class to meet the derived class's needs.

The classes you should be most suspicious of are those that have never been used as a base class before. It is extremely difficult to anticipate what requirements derived classes will place on your code. When the base and derived classes are under common ownership, most base classes evolve considerably the first few times they are derived from. One reason the `Control` class makes such successful use of inheritance is that the Windows Forms team wrote such a large number of classes that derive from it before it was released. You can be sure that `Control` changed considerably as these derived classes were developed. This work hardening of its design means that it is now pretty mature, and tends to work well as a base class most of the time.

There is a classic observation that despite the best design intentions in the world, no code is reusable until it has been used in at least two different scenarios, preferably many more. This is especially true for as tricky a relationship as inheritance. Despite this, there are some steps you can take to reduce the likelihood of running into certain kinds of problems.

Design Heuristics for Inheritance

The most important fact to bear in mind when considering the use of inheritance is that it never works by accident. There is a widely held but ultimately misguided belief that the support for inheritance built into the CLR means that we will be able to inherit from any control and expect everything to work perfectly. The reality is that inheritance only works when the designer of the base class considered possible inheritance scenarios. It only works really well when the base class has been revised to incorporate the lessons learned from attempts to use inheritance. Deriving from a control that was designed without inheritance in mind will at best lead to a severe case of fragile base class syndrome, but will more likely lead to slightly flaky control syndrome.

So how should you go about designing your classes if you want them to be suitable as base classes? The obvious answer is to try creating a few derived classes to see how it goes. But even without doing this there are several issues you should consider when designing your class.

Protection levels

The most obvious inheritance-related aspect of your class is the protection level of its members—which should be `public`, which should be `protected`, and which should be `private`? First, remember that `protected` members are a part of your class's programming interface even though they are only accessible to derived classes. This means that you should not make all your class's internal workings `protected` just in case some derived class needs access to them—defining a `protected` member should be something you think through just as carefully as you would when defining a `public` member.

It is instructive to look at how the Windows Forms libraries use access specifiers. The framework uses `protected` for two distinct reasons. One is for methods designed to be overridden. This includes all the `On`*`Xxx`* methods—these are `protected` to allow you to modify the control's behavior when certain things happen; they are deliberately not `public`, because only the control itself should be able to decide when to raise an event. The other is for members that are not meant to be overridden, and that only need to be accessible if you are changing the operation of the control. For example, the `SetStyle` method is `protected` (but not `virtual`). Changing any of the control's style flags typically involves providing some corresponding code to deal with the change, so it makes sense only to let derived classes change them.

If a member doesn't fall into one (or both) of these two categories, it should be either `private` or `public`. If `protected` does seem like the right option, you should always ask yourself if you are exposing an implementation detail you might want to change. In an ideal world, the internal workings of a class would be completely invisible to the outside world, and both the `public` and `protected` members would present a perfectly encapsulated view. In practice, expediency tends to demand that the `protected` parts of the interface provide a certain amount of insight into the class's construction. It is hard to come up with any hard and fast rules as to how much information is too much, but you should at least consider how difficult it would be to change the implementation given the existence of each `protected` member. If it looks as though you might be painting yourself into a corner, you should reconsider your design.

> VB.NET defaults to `Friend` protection level for controls on forms and user controls. (`Friend` is the equivalent of `internal` in C#.) This is superficially convenient—it means that you don't need to change the protection level of a control on a form to use it in a derived form, yet it makes the controls inaccessible to external components. However, it is better to make controls `private` unless you have a good reason not to—you don't wat to restrict your code's scope for change any more than you have to. And if you need to make controls available to a derived class, `protected` is usually a better choice than `Friend`.

Virtual methods

In .NET, methods and properties can only be overridden if the base class chooses to allow it by marking them as `virtual` (in C#) or `Overridable` (in VB). There is a school of thought that says everything should be `virtual`, the argument being that this is the most flexible approach possible. But the argument is misguided.

All non-private methods represent a kind of contract between the object and its clients. Some methods are designed just to be called (all public non-virtual methods). Here the contract is apparently straightforward—if the client calls the method, the object will do whatever the method is documented to do. When examined in detail, the contract can turn out to be quite subtle—the precise semantics of the method and the full consequences of calling it can be surprisingly extensive once any side effects have been taken into account. This often goes well beyond the documented behavior—it is very common for client code to be dependent on undocumented subtleties in the behavior of a class's programming interface. (For example, the `AutoTextBox` shown earlier relies on events being processed in a particular order.)

Conversely, some methods are designed just to be overridden. There is no way of enforcing this—such methods are usually defined as `protected virtual`, but nothing stops a deriving class from calling them as well as deriving them. Most of the `On`*`Xxx`* methods (e.g., `OnHandleCreated`) fall into this category. Here, the contract is typically fairly straightforward—the framework guarantees to call such method under certain circumstances to allow you to modify the control's behavior, often in a fairly narrowly scoped way.

So what about `public virtual` methods? These are tricky because they are subject to both sets of issues described above. Moreover, if the derived class overrides a `public virtual` method, it becomes responsible for preserving the semantics of the original method. It is tempting to think that if you are using your derived class in a controlled environment, it won't matter if you change the way the method behaves. However for controls, you often have much less leeway than you expect, for two reasons. First, at design time, the Forms Designer makes certain assumptions about how the control will behave. (For example, our partially thread-safe `TextBox` had to take special action because the Designer presumes that the `Text` property can be used in an environment where the `Invoke` method is unusable. This constraint is not immediately obvious from the documentation.) Second, the framework may also make use of certain methods or properties when you are not anticipating it, and it may expect behavior you have not supplied. For example, it is not uncommon for controls that manage their own size or layout to interact badly with the `ScrollableControl`, because it makes certain assumptions about how controls determine their own size.

This is not to say that you should never make `public` members `virtual`. But if you do, be prepared to document the full set of requirements that the derived class will be taking on if it overrides the method. It is usually safest to mandate that the derived class calls back into your class's implementation. (The majority of the `virtual` methods defined by the framework require this.)

Event handling

In Windows Forms, every public event will have an associated protected virtual `On`*`Xxx`* method. Overriding such methods is the preferred way for derived classes to handle these events. If you are designing a class with inheritance in mind, you should define similar methods for any public events you add to your class.

So if you add a new event called, say, `Highlighted` to your class, you should also add an `OnHighlighted` method. Its signature should be the same as the event delegate signature but without the first `object sender` or `sender As Object` parameter—derived classes can just use the `this` or `Me` keyword if they need a reference to the object from which the event originates. The `OnHighlighted` method would be responsible for raising the event through the delegate. You should also make clear in your documentation that deriving classes must call the base class implementation of the `On`*`Xxx`* method for the event to be raised. You should also document whether it is OK for deriving classes to "swallow" the event (i.e., prevent it from being raised) by not calling the base implementation.

Be aware that derived classes may decide to call the `On`*`Xxx`* method directly to raise the event artificially. If for some reason it is difficult for you to accommodate this, document the fact.

Summary

Inheritance is crucially important to the .NET Framework in general and to Windows Forms in particular. All visual classes must inherit from the `Control` class either directly or indirectly. Inheritance is a powerful technique that lets us incorporate the full implementation of a base class into our own controls, but it is a double-edged sword.

It is helpful that all controls and all containers are based on a single implementation provided by the `Control` class. This greatly increases the chances of successful interoperation between controls. But inheritance is a complex relationship, and it is very difficult to define a good base class. Most base classes only become truly reusable as a result of multiple design iterations based on experience gained by attempts to derive from them. If the base and derived classes are under common ownership, this is less of a problem. The base class can be modified on demand as shortcomings in its design are identified, and the author of the derived class is less likely to make false assumptions about how the base class works when deriving from it. But it is wise to be wary of inheriting from a class you do not control unless that class has been work-hardened through refactoring driven by experience.

7

Redrawing and GDI+

Windows Forms applications are nothing if not visual—the display of information is central to most programs with a user interface. And although the framework ships with a useful range of built-in controls, some applications have presentation requirements that cannot be met by the standard controls or even by third-party components. Fortunately, controls can customize their appearance using GDI+, .NET's powerful and feature-rich drawing library.

All custom controls must manage their own appearance, because the `Control` class does no drawing at all. So we will start off by looking at the model Windows Forms uses for letting controls draw themselves. Then we will look at the GDI+ library itself, examining the classes it defines and the drawing facilities it supplies.

Drawing and Controls

Every control owns an area of the screen, and it is responsible for drawing its visual representation onto that part of the display. So far we have not had to deal with this—we have relied on the fact that the built-in controls all draw themselves. But to customize the appearance of our applications, we must first understand the mechanism by which user interface elements are displayed.

The approach used by Windows Forms (and indeed by Windows itself) is that every time any part of a control becomes visible, it is asked to redraw itself. This usually happens for one of two reasons: either the control is being displayed for the first time (e.g., it is on a window that has just appeared), or it was behind some other window that has just been moved out of its way.

In either case, the framework will call the control's `OnPaint` method. All custom controls will need to override this to draw themselves. This is why Visual Studio .NET automatically supplies an override of the `OnPaint` method when you add a new custom control to your project. Its signature looks like this:

```
// C#
protected override void OnPaint(PaintEventArgs pe)

' VB
Protected Overrides Sub OnPaint(ByVal pe As PaintEventArgs)
```

Your `OnPaint` method must always call the base class's `OnPaint` method as the last thing it does, so Visual Studio .NET adds this call for you. But you must supply the code to draw your control, using the facilities supplied in the `PaintEventArgs` parameter. The `PaintEventArgs` object contains two properties. The first, `ClipRectangle`, tells you which part of your control needs redrawing. If your control is partially obscured by a window, when that window closes or moves, only the parts of your control that were hidden need to be redrawn; the `ClipRectangle` property provides a `Rectangle` that indicates which part that is. The other property is `Graphics`, which returns an object that allows us to draw things—this is our entry point into GDI+. The use of `Graphics` objects is the subject of the majority of this chapter.

Forcing a Redraw

It is possible to get the framework to call `OnPaint` even when a control is already visible. This is useful because you might want to change your control's appearance due to some change in status. (For example, if your control displays any text, it will need to make sure that it is redrawn whenever the `Text` or `Font` properties are changed.) The `Control` class provides a method to do this: `Invalidate`. The `Invalidate` method is overloaded—if you pass no parameters, the entire control will be redrawn, but you can also specify smaller areas to be updated.

`Invalidate` does not call `OnPaint` directly—it simply tells the framework that all or part of the control is invalid (i.e., it should be redrawn at some point). If the area in question happens not to be visible, it won't be redrawn until it becomes visible, so you might not see a call to `OnPaint` for every call to `Invalidate`. The framework may also aggregate multiple calls to `Invalidate` into a single `OnPaint`. If you call `Invalidate` inside some event handler, the framework will typically not bother to call `OnPaint` until you have returned from that handler, so if you call it more than once, these calls will be summarized into a single call to `OnPaint` after your handler returns. (If you need the framework to update the control before you return, calling the `Control` class's `Update` method will cause any invalidated areas to be painted immediately. You can also call the `Refresh` method, which has the same effect as calling `Invalidate` followed by `Update`. However, it does not let you specify the area to be invalidated, so if you need to be selective, use `Invalidate` instead.)

Painting Other Controls

Methods whose names begin with *On* are usually associated with an event, and `OnPaint` is no exception—the `Control` class provides a corresponding `Paint` event. Its delegate type is `PaintEventHandler`, and as you would expect, handlers of this type are provided with the same `PaintEventArgs` object as the `OnPaint` method. Client code that handles a control's `Paint` event gets to draw whatever it likes into the control on top of what the control itself paints.

> You might have only limited success using the `Paint` event with certain built-in controls, because some rely on the underlying Windows operating system to do some of their drawing instead of the `OnPaint` method.

Flicker-Free Drawing

Whenever a control is redrawn, either as a result of normal window activity, or an explicit call to `Invalidate`, the `OnPaint` method is effectively starting from a blank canvas. This is because the control always clears its background before calling `OnPaint`. (If it didn't, then unless `OnPaint` happened to paint the entire control area itself, whatever was on the screen before the control appeared would still be visible, leading to a mangled display.)

> The control background is painted in the `Control` class's `OnPaintBackground` method, which is called directly before `OnPaint`. If you want something other than the default control colored background, you can override `OnPaintBackground`. Note that `OnPaintBackground` is unusual in that there is no corresponding public `PaintBackground` event.

Although it is useful that the control's background is automatically cleared, it does cause one problem. The `OnPaint` method takes a certain amount of time to run. This means that there is a short period when the control will be blank, rather than showing its contents. The `OnPaint` method usually runs quickly enough for this to be unobtrusive most of the time. However, if you redraw a control frequently (e.g., you update it regularly to indicate the status of your program), this two-stage redrawing will cause the control to flicker occasionally. This can range from barely noticeable to highly intrusive—it depends on various factors such as the frequency of updates, the complexity of the `OnPaint` method, and the speed of the computer.

Ideally, we would like to prevent this flickering. But there is only one way to achieve this: the redrawing process must paint the control in one fell swoop. The flickering is caused by the fact that the drawing process does not happen instantaneously—it is the result of catching a glimpse of the control in a partially drawn state. So we must draw the control atomically to avoid flicker.*

There is a well-known technique for achieving a single-step redraw, known as *double buffering*. It involves drawing everything into an off-screen bitmap and only transferring the results onto the screen once drawing is complete. When you invalidate a control that uses such a technique, the screen never contains any intermediate contents—the very first change to hit the screen will be the fully drawn end result as it is copied from the off-screen buffer. At no time does the screen

* Game authors and television engineers will point out that there is another way—synchronizing your redraw code with the refresh of the monitor. Unfortunately, Windows has only ever exposed such support through DirectX, which is not yet directly supported by .NET. Even then, it is difficult to guarantee the absence of flicker, because this is a real-time technique, and Windows is not a real-time operating system. So in practice, we must aim for an atomic redraw.

contain the initial background color, nor does it ever contain half-drawn results. It either contains the previous version or the new version, thus avoiding flicker.*

With classic Win32 programming, the only way to use this technique was to write code to do it yourself. Fortunately, Windows Forms can do all the work for you. All you need to do is tell it that you would like double buffering switched on for your control, and the framework will take care of it. You don't need to make any changes to the way your `OnPaint` method works; just add the following code to your constructor:

```
// C#
SetStyle(ControlStyles.DoubleBuffer |
    ControlStyles.AllPaintingInWmPaint |
    ControlStyles.UserPaint,
    true);

' VB
SetStyle(ControlStyles.DoubleBuffer Or
    ControlStyles.AllPaintingInWmPaint Or
    ControlStyles.UserPaint,
    true);
```

The first style, `DoubleBuffer`, is self-explanatory. The other two must be set for double buffering to work. If you're curious as to what they actually do, `AllPaintingInWmPaint` makes sure that when the control erases the background before calling `OnPaint`, it does that erasing in the off-screen buffer, not on the screen. `UserPaint` indicates that this control manages its own painting, which discourages the operating system from trying to help with the drawing; this is important because the whole point is to try to do the drawing in a single step.

Because double buffering is so simple to use in .NET, you might be wondering why it isn't always on. The main reason is that it's not free—memory must be allocated for the off-screen buffer. The cost of this depends on the size of the control. For something the size of a button, the control occupies about 1500 pixels. Most modern PCs have a 32-bit color display, which means that 1500 pixels occupy about 6 KB of memory. On a current PC, 6 KB is as close to nothing as makes no difference, so the double buffering cost here is very low. But some controls are larger—a control representing a document may even be the size of the screen if the user maximizes the application's windows. For a 1600 × 1200 32-bit color display, the screen occupies over 7 MB of memory. Memory may be cheap, but even with current technology, 7 MB is large enough to make you think twice.

> The memory is only allocated temporarily. This means that a large control does not require memory for the whole time that it is visible, only while it is being redrawn. So the working set implications are not as bad as they could be, but double buffering does make the garbage collector work a lot harder.

* Pedants will observe that you might catch the occasional glimpse in which half of the control shows the old image and half contains the new image. This won't cause flicker, but if you are animating the control, it can cause a different artifact known as tearing. To fix this, you will need to use some rather more exotic techniques involving DirectX. GDI+ is not designed to display broadcast-quality moving pictures.

So double buffering should only be used on controls for which the difference it makes is worth the memory it requires. This is not always an easy judgment to make. For controls that are never updated, it is probably not worth using double buffering—its purpose is to avoid flicker, which is something that only afflicts controls that change their appearance from time to time. If your control never calls `Invalidate`, it probably doesn't need double buffering.* For large controls, the frequency of update is probably the single most significant factor. Drawing programs almost certainly want double buffering turned on because they can update the display tens of times a second when items are being dragged around with the mouse. But for a large control that only updates its display a few times a day, it would be hard to justify the overhead.

It may also be possible to get a flicker-free display without needing to turn on double buffering. This happens in the fairly unusual case when your `OnPaint` method only needs to draw one thing that covers the entire control. In this case, you already have an atomic redraw, so there is no need for double buffering. This usually only happens when your control just shows a bitmap or draws a filled rectangle the size of the control. (As we will see later, you can get some interesting visual effects by drawing a single rectangle with some exotic GDI+ options turned on, so this is not as pointless as it sounds.) If your control fits into this category, you can tell Windows Forms by putting the following code into your constructor:

```
SetStyle(ControlStyles.Opaque, true);
```

This tells the framework that your control completely covers its whole area when it redraws itself. This causes the framework not to bother filling the control with the default background before calling your `OnPaint` method, thus eliminating flicker without the overhead of double buffering. But your control *must* fill its entire area if you set this flag. If it doesn't, the control will look rather strange, with garbage appearing in the parts that you leave blank.

GDI+

GDI+ is the name of the drawing API in .NET. It is exposed through classes defined in the `System.Drawing` namespace and its descendants, `System.Drawing.Drawing2D`, `System.Drawing.Imaging`, and `System.Drawing.Text`. It provides a simple but powerful set of tools for drawing text, bitmaps, and vector graphics.

There is a small group of classes that are crucial for drawing anything—some represent fundamental concepts such as colors, coordinates, and drawing styles, others represent entities that can be drawn into, such as bitmaps or windows. We will start by seeing what each of these classes is for, and how they relate to each other. Then, we will look at the various drawing facilities supplied by GDI+ and how to use them. Finally, we will look at some of the advanced support for changing the coordinate system used for drawing.

* The exception here is if you have set the `ResizeRedraw` control style—this will cause the control to be redrawn every time the control is resized.

> **GDI+ Naming**
>
> None of the GDI+ classes have the name "GDI+" in them anywhere. The API is named after its predecessor, GDI (the Graphics Device Interface), which was the Win32 drawing API. GDI+ is not in fact a part of .NET—all the same facilities are available to Win32 programs on Windows XP (or older versions of Windows if GDI+ has been installed; GDI+ is put in automatically on these platforms when the .NET Framework is installed). The `System.Drawing` namespaces are the managed interface to GDI+.

Essential GDI+ Classes

There are certain classes defined in the `System.Drawing` namespace that are used in almost all drawing code. This is because they represent concepts fundamental to all drawing operations such as coordinates or colors. We will examine this toolkit of drawing objects, looking at the purpose of each class and how it fits into the GDI+ framework.

Before we start though, there is an issue that concerns almost all the GDI+ classes. Because these classes are a wrapper on top of the underlying GDI+ facilities, they all represent unmanaged resources. When you create a GDI+ object, it consumes some OS resources, so it is vitally important that you free the object when you are done, because otherwise you could exhaust the system's resources, preventing your application (and maybe others) from running. Most classes in `System.Drawing` therefore implement `IDisposable`, the interface implemented by all classes that need to be freed in a timely fashion.

Drawing code therefore usually makes extensive use of the C# `using` keyword to free resources automatically. So most GDI+ code will look like this:

```
using (Brush foreBrush = new SolidBrush (ForeColor))
{
    g.FillRectangle (foreBrush, 0, 0, 100, 100);
}
```

VB lacks the convenience of the C# `using` construct, which the C# compiler translates into a call to the `Dispose` method within a `finally` block. As a result, you'll have to call `Dispose` yourself. The previous C# code fragment would be implemented as follows in VB:

```
Dim foreBrush As Brush = New SolidBrush(ForeColor)
Try
    g.FillRectangle(foreBrush, 0, 0, 100, 100)
Finally
    foreBrush.Dispose( )
End Try
```

This creates a new `Brush` object (described below), uses it to draw a rectangle, and then frees it. You should use this approach whenever you create a GDI+ object. Of course, this only applies to classes. Value types are not allocated on the heap, so their lifetime is defined by their containing scope. Values therefore do not use this pattern. (The value types will be pointed out as we come to them, although if in doubt, try adding a `using` statement—the compiler will complain if you use one on the wrong kind of type. Likewise, in VB, if you try to call the `Dispose` method on an object that does not require disposal, it will not compile.)

You should only use this pattern if you created the object—for certain types of object (especially the `Graphics` class) the system will supply the object rather than requiring you to create it. In an `OnPaint` handler, for example, a `Graphics` object is supplied as a property of the `PaintEventArgs` parameter. In these cases, it is not your responsibility to dispose of the object—the framework will free it for you. But if you cause an object to be created, it becomes your job to call `Dispose` on it.

Occasionally, it is not possible to determine when an object has fallen out of use: if a control's `Font` property is changed, should that control dispose of the `Font` object that it was previously using? It should not, because it has no way of knowing whether any other controls are still using the same `Font` object. Discovering when there are no more controls using the `Font` object is a hard problem, and in this case we usually have to rely on the garbage collector. This strategy, which is effectively an admission of defeat, is not as bad as it would be for a resource such as a database connection, because most GDI+ objects are not all that expensive. If a few are leaked on a very occasional basis, it is not the end of the world if they don't release their resources until the garbage collector finally notices them. But you should not take this as a license not to bother disposing of your objects: if you fail to call `Dispose` on any of the objects you create in your `OnPaint` method, you can run into problems. `OnPaint` can be called frequently enough that you could exhaust your GDI+ resources before the garbage collector runs.

You should get into the habit of writing a `using` statement in C# or of calling `IDisposable.Dispose` from your code in VB whenever you use a GDI+ object. All the examples in this chapter will do this, and you should make sure that this practice becomes second nature. So let us now examine the objects we will be using to draw our controls.

Graphics

The `Graphics` class is the single most important type in GDI+. Without a `Graphics` object, we cannot draw anything because it is this class that provides the methods that perform drawing operations. A `Graphics` object represents something that can be drawn onto, usually either a window or a bitmap.

We do not normally need to create a `Graphics` object ourselves. This is because the most common place for drawing code is the `OnPaint` method, in which one is supplied for us as the `Graphics` property of the `PaintEventArgs` parameter, as shown in Example 7-1 for C# and Example 7-2 for VB. This `Graphics` object lets us draw things onto the control's window.

Example 7-1. Using a Graphics object in OnPaint with C#

```
protected override void OnPaint(PaintEventArgs pe)
{
    Graphics g = pe.Graphics;
    using (Brush b = new SolidBrush(ForeColor))
    {
        g.DrawString(text, Font, b, 0, 0);
        g.FillRectangle(b, 20, 20, 30, 30);
```

Example 7-1. Using a Graphics object in OnPaint with C# (continued)

```
    }
    base.OnPaint(pe);
}
```

Example 7-2. Using a Graphics object in OnPaint with VB

```
Protected Overrides Sub OnPaint(ByVal pe As PaintEventArgs)
  Dim g As Graphics = pe.Graphics
  Dim b As Brush = New SolidBrush(ForeColor)
  Try
     g.DrawString(Text, Font, b, 0, 0)
     g.FillRectangle(b, 20, 20, 30, 30)
  Finally
     brush.Dispose()
  End Try
  MyBase.OnPaint(pe)
End Sub
```

Examples 7-1 and 7-2 illustrate a common technique used for conciseness: because the `Graphics` property of the `PaintEventArgs` object needs to be used for every single drawing operation, a reference is typically held in a local variable with a short name (usually *g*). This avoids the rather verbose alternative of writing `pe.Graphics` in front of every single drawing method.

Example 7-1 also illustrates a couple of other important techniques. It has created a `Brush` object to control the appearance of the items that it draws (see below), but it has done so inside a `using` statement to make sure that the object is freed when it is no longer being used. It has also called the base class's `OnPaint` method—as mentioned above, you are required to do this whenever you override `OnPaint`.

The majority of methods supplied by the `Graphics` class begin with either `Draw...` or `Fill...`. The `Draw...` methods are typically used for drawing shape outlines; for example, `DrawRectangle`, `DrawEllipse`, and `DrawPolygon` will draw the outline of a rectangle, an ellipse, and a polygon, respectively. The corresponding `Fill...` methods draw the same shape, but they fill in the shape's interior rather than just drawing an outline. (There are exceptions to this. For example, `DrawString` draws a normal text string—it doesn't draw character outlines. `DrawImage` draws an image such as a bitmap; there isn't even a sensible interpretation of drawing an outline for a bitmap. But for shapes that support both filled and outline versions, there will be both `Draw...` and `Fill...` methods.)

To draw shapes, the `Graphics` object needs to know things like what color should be used, and what style should be used for an outline. These requirements are fulfilled by the `Brush` and `Pen` classes, described later. But GDI+ also needs to know where it should draw things, and how large they should be, so there are some types relating to size and position.

Redrawing & GDI+

Point, Size, and Rectangle

Coordinates are fundamentally important to any drawing system, so GDI+ defines a few types to deal with location and size. The `Point` type represents a single two-dimensional point. The `Size` type represents something's dimensions (i.e., width and height). Rectangle is a combination of the two—it has both a location and a size. These are all value types, so you don't need to bother with using statements in C# or with calls to IDisposable.Dispose in VB.

GDI+ uses a two-dimensional Cartesian coordinate system. By default, increasing values of the x coordinate will move to the right, and increasing values of the y coordinate will move down. This is consistent with the Win32 GDI, although not with traditional graph orientation in mathematics, where increasing values of y move up, not down. The default units for the coordinate system are screen pixels for most Graphics objects. These are only the defaults—it is possible to change the orientation and units of the coordinate system, as we will see later.

The Point type has two properties, X and Y. Similarly, Size has Width and Height properties. These are all of type int or Integer. Both Point and Size define an IsEmpty property, which returns true if both dimensions' values are zero. Both define explicit conversion operators to convert from one to the other, so you can convert a Point to a Size and vice versa in C#, as shown in Example 7-3. These conversions map X onto Width and Y onto Height.

Example 7-3. Converting between Point and Size in C#

```
Point p = new Point (10, 10);
Size s = (Size) p;     // same as s = new Size (p.X, p.Y);
s.Width += 5;
Point p2 = (Point) s; // same as p2 =
                      //   new Point(s.Width, s.Height);
```

Because VB doesn't directly support conversion operators, you have to take advantage of the fact that the conversion operators are translated into op_Explicit method calls, as shown in Example 7-4. (Alternatively, you could simply construct new Point or Size values directly.)

Example 7-4. Converting between Point and Size in VB

```
Dim p As New Point(10, 10)
Dim s As Size = p.op_Explicit(p)
s.Width += 5
Dim p2 As Point = s.op_Explicit(s)
```

The Point and Size types also overload the addition and subtraction operators. For Size this is straightforward—adding one Size to another creates a new Size whose Width and Height are the sum of the Width and Height properties of the originals. For the Point type, it is a little more complex—the only thing you can add to or subtract from a Point is a Size. (This is because conceptually a Point doesn't have a magnitude, so it's not clear what addition or subtraction of two Point values would mean.) Addition and subtraction move the position of the Point by the amount specified in the Size. Example 7-5 creates a Point and then moves it 5 pixels down and 2 pixels along by adding a Size, leaving the Point p at (12, 15).

Example 7-5. Moving a Point by adding a Size in C#

```
Point p = new Point (10, 10);
Size s = new Size (2, 5);
p = p + s;
```

Again, because VB doesn't support operator overloading, you can call the `op_Addition` method, the method that the overloaded addition operator is actually translated into at runtime. The VB that is equivalent to the C# code in Example 7-5 is shown in Example 7-6.

Example 7-6. Moving a Point by adding a Size in VB

```
Dim p As New Point(10, 10)
Dim s As New Size (2, 5)
p = Point.op_Addition(p, s)
```

The `Rectangle` class has both position and size. It can be constructed either from a `Point` and a `Size`, or with four integers, as shown in Example 7-7. Note that, except for slight syntactical differences, the C# and VB code are nearly identical.

Example 7-7. Creating a Rectangle

```
// C# code
Point p = new Point (10, 10);
Size s = new Size (20, 20);
Rectangle r = new Rectangle(p, s);
Rectangle r2 = new Rectangle(10, 10, 20, 20);

' VB code
Dim p As New Point(10, 10)
Dim s As New Size(20, 20)
Dim r As New Rectangle(p, s)
Dim r2 As New Rectangle(10, 10, 20, 20)
```

`Rectangle` provides a `Location` property of type `Point`, and a `Size` property of type `Size`. `Rectangle` also makes the same location and size information accessible through the `X`, `Y`, `Width`, and `Height` properties; this is just for convenience—these represent the same information as the `Location` and `Size` properties. This may seem pointless, but there is a subtle issue that means the following code will not compile:

```
myRectangle.Size.Width = 10;  // Won't compile
```

The compiler will complain that the `Width` property of a `Size` object can only be set if that `Size` is a variable, not a property. This is because the `Size` type is a value type, and `Rectangle.Size` is a property, not a field; this has the effect that the `Size` property can only be used to change the rectangle's size in its entirety, i.e., setting both the width and height in one operation. So the `Width` and `Size` properties supplied by the `Rectangle` are convenient because they make it possible to adjust the two dimensions independently, as shown in Example 7-8. The `X` and `Y` properties do the same job for the location, because `Point` is also a value type.

Redrawing & GDI+

Example 7-8. The correct way to adjust a rectangle's width

```
myRectangle.Width = 10;
```

`Rectangle` also provides `Top`, `Bottom`, `Left`, and `Right` properties. These are read-only, because it is not obvious whether changing one of them should move or resize the rectangle. The rectangle's `Location` refers to its top left corner. So the `Left` property is synonymous with `X`, and `Top` with `Y`. These names presume a coordinate system where increasing values of x and y move to the right and down, respectively.

Rectangle does not overload the addition and subtraction operators, because it is ambiguous: should they move or resize the rectangle? Moving it is simple enough—just adding a Size to its Location property works:

```
myRectangle.Location += new Size (10, 20);
```

Here again, because VB does not support operator overloading (in this case, as we have seen earlier, the overloading of the Point type returned by the Location property), we have to call the Point type's op_Addition property, as follows:

```
myRectangle.Location = Point.op_Addition(myRectangle.Location, _
                       New Size(10, 20))
```

To change the size, you can add a Size to the Size property in much the same way. Alternatively, you can call the Inflate method. This also adjusts the size, but in a slightly different way—inflating a rectangle by, say, (10, 10) actually moves all four edges of the rectangle out by 10. This makes each edge 20 units longer, and also adjusts the position so that the rectangle's center remains in the same place.

All these are value types, not reference types. This is partly because coordinates are used and modified extensively when using GDI+, so the overhead of putting them on the heap would be high. Also, coordinates are value-like entities—it doesn't really make any sense for a coordinate object to have its own identity. That would lead to the potential for bugs in which a programmer could set the Size of two rectangles to be the same, and then fail to realize that (because they are reference types) modifying the Size of one would also implicitly modify the other. This doesn't happen with value types, although they are not without their own complications, such as the issue with independent adjustment of width and height of a Rectangle, discussed above.

The three types discussed here all represent coordinates using int or Integer. GDI+ also supports the use of float or Single for all coordinates. This can allow applications much greater flexibility for their internal coordinate systems, and also makes it easier to apply certain kinds of transformations correctly. And because modern processors can manage floating-point arithmetic extremely quickly, there are no performance reasons not to use floating-point values. So each type discussed so far has a floating-point counterpart—the PointF, SizeF, and RectangleF types are similar to Point, Size, and Rectangle, respectively, except they use float or Single instead of int or Integer.

You may be wondering what a coordinate represented by a Point means in terms of position on the screen. By default, the units used by the coordinate system correspond to pixels—the Point whose value is (10, 20) represents a position 10 pixels to the right and 20 pixels down from the origin. The origin is usually the top lefthand corner of whatever is being drawn into (e.g., the window or a bitmap). But as you will see towards the end of this chapter, GDI+ lets you use different coordinate systems if you want to—it can automatically apply a transform to all coordinates to map them onto pixel positions.

Of course, position and size aren't everything. In order to draw something, GDI+ will need to know what color it should use, so we will now look at how colors are represented in this programming model.

Color

All drawing needs to be done in some color or other.* In GDI+ the Color type represents a color. It is used anywhere that a color needs to be specified. Color is a value type.

Color can represent any color that can be expressed as a combination of red, green, and blue components, using 8-bit values for each. (This is the usual way of specifying colors in computing, because of how color displays work.) It can also support transparency with an *alpha* channel, another 8-bit value that indicates whether the color should be displayed as opaque, and if not, how transparent it should be—this is used when drawing one color on top of another. (The transparent drop shadows that Windows XP draws around menus use alpha blending, for example.)

Example 7-9 shows how to build a color value from its red, green, and blue components. This particular color will be orange (which is approximately two parts red to one part green when using additive primary colors).

Example 7-9. Building a color from RGB components

```
// C#
Color orange = Color.FromArgb(255, 128, 0);

' VB
Dim orange As Color = Color.FromArgb(255, 128, 0)
```

The Argb part of the method stands for "alpha, red, green, and blue." This is a little confusing because there are several overloads, not all of which take all the components. Example 7-9 just passes RGB but not A, for example. It is equivalent to this code:

```
// C#
Color orange = Color.FromArgb(255, 255, 128, 0);

' VB
Dim orange As Color = Color.FromArgb(255, 255, 128, 0)
```

This specifies an alpha value of 255, i.e., a completely non-transparent color. The three-component version shown in Example 7-9 always builds a non-transparent color. (It would have been less confusing if the RGB-only method was just called FromRgb, rather than being an overload of FromArgb.)

As well as building colors from their component parts, you can also use named colors. The Color type has static properties for each standard named web colors, so you can just specify colors such as Color.Teal or Color.AliceBlue. Alternatively you can use the SystemColors class, which provides static properties for each user-configurable system color, such as those used for window titles, menu items, etc. So to draw something in the color currently defined for control backgrounds, simply use SystemColors.Control.

* For the purposes of this discussion, black and white are considered to be colors too.

If you are overriding the OnPaint method in a control, you should use the built-in ForeColor and BackColor properties where appropriate, rather than hard-wiring colors in. And if you need more colors in your control than a foreground and background color, consider adding extra properties to allow the user to edit these.

It is useful to be aware of the ControlPaint utility class. One of the facilities it provides is the ability to create a modified version of a color for drawing things such as shadows and highlights. For example, if you want to draw a bezel or similar 3D effect, you should always choose colors that are based on the background color; for example, use ControlPaint.Dark to get the "in shadow" version of a color, and ControlPaint.Light to get the pale version. Examples 7-10 and 7-11 draw a 3D dividing line at the top of the control, using whatever the control's background color is. (And because BackColor is an ambient property, by default, this will be whatever the background color of the containing form is.)

Example 7-10. Sensitivity to background color in C#

```
protected override void OnPaint(PaintEventArgs pe)
{
    Graphics g = pe.Graphics;

    using (Pen light = new Pen(ControlPaint.Light(BackColor)),
               dark = new Pen(ControlPaint.Dark(BackColor)))
    {
        g.DrawLine(dark, 0, 0, Width, 0);
        g.DrawLine(light, 0, 1, Width, 1);
    }
    base.OnPaint(pe)
}
```

Example 7-11. Sensitivity to background color in VB

```
Protected Overrides Sub OnPaint(pe As PaintEventArgs)
   Dim g As  Graphics = pe.Graphics
   Dim light As New Pen(ControlPaint.Light(BackColor))
   Dim dark As New Pen(ControlPaint.Dark(BackColor))

   Try
      g.DrawLine(dark, 0, 0, Width, 0)
      g.DrawLine(light, 0, 1, Width, 1)
   Finally
      light.Dispose( )
      dark.Dispose( )
   End Try
   MyBase.OnPaint(pe)
End Sub
```

Note that Color is a value type, not a class, for much the same reasons as the Point, Size, and Rectangle types—because colors are used extensively, and they make more sense as values than as objects. So Color values do not need to be freed with a using statement in C# or a call to Dispose in VB. (The using block in Example 7-10 frees the Pen objects, not the Color values.)

The Color type cannot be used in isolation when drawing. There is more to the way that GDI+ draws things than mere color, so GDI+ requires that all filled shapes be drawn with a Brush object, and outlines be drawn with a Pen object. So we will now look at these.

Brushes

GDI+ uses the Brush class to determine how it should paint areas of the screen. So you must pass a Brush of some kind to all the Fill*Xxx* methods of the Graphics class, and also to the DrawString method.

Brush is an abstract class. This is because there are several different ways GDI+ can fill in an area: it can use a single color, a pattern, a bitmap, or even a range of colors using so-called gradient fills. For each of these fill styles, there is a corresponding concrete class deriving from Brush.

The simplest type of brush is SolidBrush. When painting an area with this kind of brush, GDI+ will paint with a single color. This is the most common type of brush, particularly for text, where more complex textured or patterned brushes would be likely to make the text illegible. Examples 7-12 and 7-13 use two solid brushes. The first is based on the control's ForeColor property and is used to draw some text. The second is a pale shade of green used to draw a rectangle.

Example 7-12. Using SolidBrush in C#

```
protected override void OnPaint(PaintEventArgs pe)
{
    Graphics g = pe.Graphics;

    Color transparentGreen = Color.FromArgb(128, Color.PaleGreen);
    using (Brush fb = new SolidBrush(ForeColor),
                 gb = new SolidBrush(transparentGreen))
    {
        g.DrawString("Hello!", Font, fb, 0, 5);
        g.FillRectangle(gb, 10, 0, 15, 25);
    }
     base.OnPaint(pe);
}
```

Example 7-13. Using SolidBrush in VB

```
Protected Overrides Sub OnPaint(ByVal pe As PaintEventArgs)

   Dim g As Graphics = pe.Graphics
   Dim transparentGreen As Color = Color.FromArgb(128, _
                                   Color.PaleGreen)
   Dim fb As Brush = New SolidBrush(ForeColor)
   Dim gb As Brush = New SolidBrush(transparentGreen)

   Try
      g.DrawString("Hello!", Font, fb, 0, 5)
      g.FillRectangle(gb, 10, 0, 15, 25)
   Finally
      fb.Dispose()
      fb.Dispose()
```

Redrawing & GDI+

Example 7-13. Using SolidBrush in VB (continued)

```
    End Try

    MyBase.OnPaint(pe)

End Sub
```

The output of this code, shown in Figure 7-1, illustrates that the `SolidBrush` class has a slightly misleading name. The `transparentGreen` color is see-through—even though the rectangle is drawn on top of the text, the "Hello!" string remains visible through the rectangle. If you try this code, you will see that the text is also tinted green underneath the rectangle. This is because the color has a partially transparent alpha value—it was built using the version of `Color.FromArgb` that takes an alpha value and a color as parameters and returns a transparent version of the color. So it turns out that the `SolidBrush` can be used to draw transparent colors. This is because the "Solid" name simply indicates that the same color (transparent or not) is used across the entire area of the fill.

Hello!

Figure 7-1. A transparent SolidBrush

It is not always necessary to construct your own `SolidBrush`. If you require a brush that represents a system color (such as the control background or menu text color) GDI+ can provide ready-built brushes. There are two classes that supply `Brush` objects as static properties: `Brushes` and `SystemBrushes`. These provide solid brushes whose colors are those provided by the static members in `Color` and `SystemColors`. Because these are globally available brushes, it is not your responsibility to free them after using them—you are only required to call `Dispose` on objects that you created or caused to be created. In fact, you are not allowed to dispose of such brushes—doing so will cause an exception to be thrown. (Disposing of a brush obtained from the `Brushes` class does not currently throw an exception immediately. You will get an exception the next time you try to use a brush of the same color from the `Brushes` class.) As Example 7-14 shows, we can just use such a brush directly, and we don't need the `using` syntax in C#, nor do we need to call `Dispose` directly in VB. (In this case, we are painting the control with the background color of a ToolTip. `ClientRectangle` is a property of the `Control` class that returns a `Rectangle` indicating the area of the control that can be drawn on; for most controls, this is the control's size, but for a form, it is just the client area, without the borders or titlebar.)

Example 7-14. Using SystemBrushes

```
// C# code
protected override void OnPaint(PaintEventArgs pe)
{
    Graphics g = pe.Graphics;
    g.FillRectangle(SystemBrushes.Info, ClientRectangle);
    base.OnPaint(pe);
}
```

Example 7-14. Using SystemBrushes (continued)

```
' VB code
Protected Overrides Sub OnPaint(ByVal pe As PaintEventArgs)
    Dim g As Graphics = pe.Graphics
    g.FillRectangle(SystemBrushes.Info, ClientRectangle)
    MyBase.OnPaint(pe)
End Sub
```

Annoyingly, there are certain omissions from `SystemBrushes`. It only supplies the colors considered to be background colors. This mostly makes sense when you realize that there is a corresponding `SystemPens` class for the foreground colors, but it is unhelpful, because you sometimes need a brush for a foreground color, such as when displaying text. (So the absence of `SystemBrushes.MenuText` is particularly unhelpful for owner-drawn menus.) Fortunately, you can still get the system to supply you with an appropriate brush by calling the static `SystemBrushes.FromSystemColor` method. As with brushes returned by the static properties, you should not dispose of these brushes—they are cached by GDI+.

If you don't want to paint the entire fill area uniformly with one color, you might find the `HatchBrush` class to be more appropriate. (This class is defined in the `System.Drawing.Drawing2D` namespace, so you may need to add an extra `using` (in C#) or `Imports` (in VB) declaration at the top of your source file to use this brush.) This allows a repeating pattern to be drawn with two colors. The pattern must be one of those listed in the `HatchStyle` enumeration, which contains a list of patterns that will be familiar to long-term Windows developers, such as `Trellis` or `Plaid`. Although this requirement is fairly limiting—you can't define your own hatch styles—it can be useful for certain effects if a system style happens to suit your needs. Examples 7-15 and 7-16 show a `HatchBrush` being used to draw a half-transparent blue hatch pattern over a control. The result will look like Figure 7-2—Internet Explorer uses a similar effect to highlight bitmaps when you select parts of a web page by dragging the mouse.

Example 7-15. Using a HatchBrush in C#

```
protected override void OnPaint(PaintEventArgs pe)
{
    Graphics g = pe.Graphics;

    using (Brush tb = new SolidBrush (ForeColor),
                 rb = new HatchBrush (HatchStyle.Percent50,
                                      SystemColors.Highlight,
                                      Color.Transparent))
    {
        g.DrawString ("Hello", Font, tb, 0, 0);
        g.FillRectangle(rb, ClientRectangle);
    }
    base.OnPaint(pe);
}
```

Example 7-16. Using a HatchBrush in VB

```
Protected Overrides Sub OnPaint(ByVal pe As PaintEventArgs)
   Dim g As Graphics = pe.Graphics
```

Redrawing & GDI+

Example 7-16. Using a HatchBrush in VB (continued)

```
    Dim tb As Brush = New SolidBrush(ForeColor)
    Dim rb As Brush = New HatchBrush(HatchStyle.Percent50, _
                                     SystemColors.Highlight, _
                                     Color.Transparent)
    Try
       g.DrawString("Hello", Font, tb, 0, 0)
       g.FillRectangle(rb, ClientRectangle)
    Finally
       tb.Dispose( )
       rb.Dispose( )
    End Try
    MyBase.OnPaint(pe)
End Sub
```

Figure 7-2. A HatchBrush in action

The HatchBrush draws in two colors, one for the foreground parts of the hatch pattern, and one for the background parts. This example has used Color.Transparent (a completely transparent color) for the background, which is why the text is visible through the hatched rectangle, even though the rectangle was drawn over it.

The HatchBrush class is very convenient to use because it comes with a set of built-in patterns. But this is also its weak point—it is not customizable. Fortunately, there is another type of brush that lets you use any fill pattern you like: TextureBrush. You construct a TextureBrush by supplying an Image object. The Image class represents pictures, typically bitmaps, and we will look at it shortly, but for now, we will just expose a property whose type is Image, which will enable users to supply a bitmap using the Forms Designer.

Examples 7-17 and 7-18 show how to create a TextureBrush based on an Image, and also how to pass the responsibility for creating the Image on to the user by making her supply one in the Forms Designer. The results can be seen in Figure 7-3—the text has been painted with a bitmap filling. TextureBrush also supports transparency, including bitmaps whose transparency is determined per-pixel.

Example 7-17. Creating and using a TextureBrush in C#

```
private Image fill;

[Category("Appearance")]
public Image FillImage
{
    get
    {
        return fill;
    }
    set
    {
```

Example 7-17. Creating and using a TextureBrush in C# (continued)

```
        if (value != fill)
        {
            fill = value;
            Invalidate( );
        }
    }
}

protected override void OnPaint(PaintEventArgs pe)
{
    Graphics g = pe.Graphics;

    if (fill != null)
    {
        using (Brush b = new TextureBrush(fill))
        {
            g.DrawString ("Hello", Font, b, 0, 0);
        }
    }
    base.OnPaint(pe);
}
```

Example 7-18. Creating and using a TextureBrush in VB

```
Private fill As Image

<Category("Appearance")> Public Property FillImage( ) As Image
    Get
        Return fill
    End Get
    Set(ByVal Value As Image)
        If Not fill Is Value Then
            fill = Value
            Invalidate( )
        End If
    End Set
End Property

Protected Overrides Sub OnPaint(ByVal pe As PaintEventArgs)

    Dim g As Graphics = pe.Graphics

    If Not fill Is Nothing Then
        Dim b As Brush = New TextureBrush(fill)
        Try
            g.DrawString("Hello", Font, b, 0, 0)
        Finally
            b.Dispose( )
        End Try
    End If
    MyBase.OnPaint(pe)
End Sub
```

Hello

Figure 7-3. A TextureBrush in action

There is also a style of brush to support gradient fills. A gradient fill changes color from one place to another. These are used extensively in Windows XP to provide a less flat appearance to the UI. Examples 7-19 and 7-20 show how to paint the control's background with a gradient fill ranging from the foreground color at the top to the background color at the bottom. (Recall that Windows Forms will call `OnPaintBackground` to clear your control's background before calling `OnPaint`.) The results can be seen in Figure 7-4. (In a real application, you would normally want to pick a pair of colors that were more similar to get a less dramatic spread of colors for the background. Most of Windows XP's gradient background fills use only a very subtle change in color.)

Example 7-19. Using a LinearGradientBrush in C#

```
protected override void OnPaintBackground(PaintEventArgs pe)
{
    Graphics g = pe.Graphics;

    using (Brush bg = new LinearGradientBrush(ClientRectangle,
                          ForeColor, BackColor,
                          LinearGradientMode.Vertical))
    {
        g.FillRectangle(bg, ClientRectangle);
    }
    // No need to call base for OnPaintBackground
}
```

Example 7-20. Using a LinearGradientBrush in VB

```
Protected Overrides Sub OnPaintBackground(ByVal pe As PaintEventArgs)
    Dim g As Graphics = pe.Graphics

    Dim bg As Brush = New LinearGradientBrush(ClientRectangle, _
                      ForeColor, BackColor, _
                      LinearGradientMode.Vertical)
    Try
        g.FillRectangle(bg, ClientRectangle)
    Finally
        bg.Dispose( )
    End Try
    ' No need to call base for OnPaintBackground
End Sub
```

In Examples 7-19 and 7-20, we have used a `LinearGradientBrush`. Its constructor is overloaded, allowing the fill to be set up in various ways. The constructors all take a start color and an end color; what differs is the way the start and end coordinates of the fill can be set. In this case, we have passed a rectangle to specify the bounds of the fill and used the LinearGradientMode enumeration to indicate how the gradient should fill the rectangle. The options are self-explanatory—Horizontal, Vertical, ForwardDiagonal, and BackwardDiagonal. If you want more control over the angle of the fill, there is another constructor that takes a float or Single in place of a LinearGradientMode, specifying the fill angle in degrees. There is also a constructor that takes a pair of points, indicating the start and end points of the fill. It is even possible to specify multi-stage fills that use several different colors, using the InterpolationColors property—see the ColorBlend class in the reference section for details.

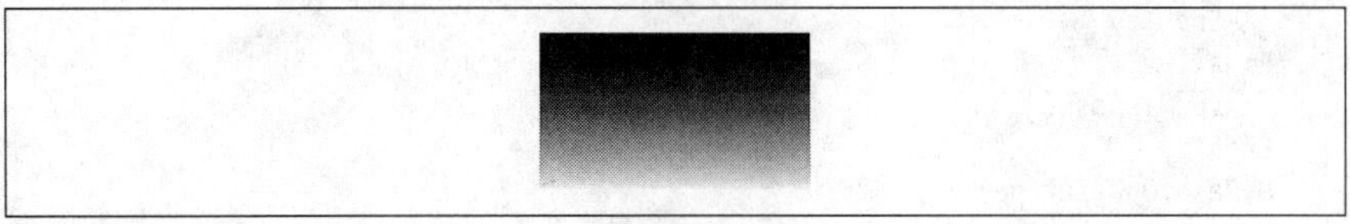

Figure 7-4. A linear gradient fill

GDI+ supports two different kinds of gradient fill brushes. As well as the simple linear gradient, there is the PathGradientBrush class. While the LinearGradientBrush can only draw gradients going in a single direction, the PathGradientBrush can handle any shape. Examples 7-21 and 7-22 show how to create and use a PathGradientBrush to draw an ellipse-shaped gradient fill. (The GraphicsPath class in the System.Drawing.Drawing2D namespace will be described later on in this chapter. For now it is enough to know that it can describe arbitrary shapes; in this case, we are using it to describe an ellipse.)

Example 7-21. Using a PathGradientBrush in C#

```
protected override void OnPaint(PaintEventArgs pe)
{
    Graphics g = pe.Graphics;
    using (GraphicsPath gp = new GraphicsPath( ))
    {
        gp.AddEllipse(ClientRectangle);
        using (PathGradientBrush b = new PathGradientBrush(gp))
        {
            b.CenterColor = Color.Cyan;
            Color[] outerColor = {Color.Navy};
            b.SurroundColors = outerColor;
            g.FillEllipse(b, ClientRectangle);
        }
    }
    base.OnPaint(pe)
}
```

Example 7-22. Using a PathGradientBrush in VB

```
Protected Overrides Sub OnPaint(ByVal pe As PaintEventArgs)

    Dim g As Graphics = pe.Graphics
    Dim gp As New GraphicsPath( )

    Try
```

Example 7-22. Using a PathGradientBrush in VB (continued)

```
        gp.AddEllipse(ClientRectangle)
        Dim b As PathGradientBrush = New PathGradientBrush(gp)
        Try
            b.CenterColor = Color.Cyan
            Dim outerColor( ) As Color = {Color.Navy}
            b.SurroundColors = outerColor
            g.FillEllipse(b, ClientRectangle)
        Finally
            b.Dispose( )
        End Try
    Finally
        gp.Dispose( )
    End Try
    MyBase.OnPaint(pe)
End Sub
```

The result of this is shown in Figure 7-5. As you can see, the shading changes from the center in accordance with the shape of the path. In this case, we have drawn the object to be the same shape as the fill path, but this is not mandatory—we could equally have drawn some text with such a fill.

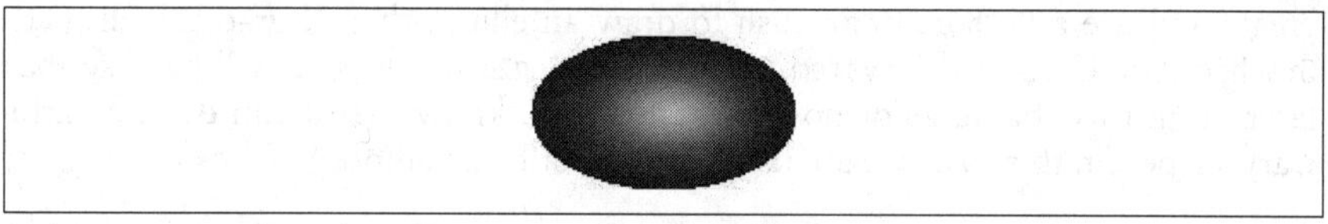

Figure 7-5. A path gradient fill

So we have seen how to control the way in which GDI+ fills in an area when painting to the screen. We can use a simple single color, a predefined hatch pattern, a bitmap, or a gradient fill. But many of the drawing operations provided by the `Graphics` class do not fill areas of the screen—they draw outlines instead. The options available for an outline's appearance are quite different from those for a filled area, so GDI+ defines a separate type to deal with this: `Pen`.

Pens

Just as the `Brush` class defines the way in which GDI+ will fill in areas of the screen, the `Pen` class determines how it draws outlines. However, `Pen` is not *abstract*; on the contrary, it is `sealed` or `NonInheritable`, which means that unlike the `Brush` family of classes, there is only one type of `Pen`. However, a `Pen` can use a `Brush` to control how it paints, so it supports all the same drawing techniques.

The `Pen` class provides features unique to outline drawing. For example, it allows a line thickness to be specified. Examples 7-23 and 7-24 draw 10 lines of varying thickness. Note that in this case, each `Pen` object is created based on a `Color`. We could also have supplied a `SolidBrush` of the appropriate color, but in this case it is easier to use the `Pen` constructor that takes a `Color` and a thickness (as a `float` or `Single`). Examples 7-23 and 7-24 also show the use of the `StartCap` and `EndCap` properties to set the style of the starts and ends of the lines.

Example 7-23. Selecting the line thickness in C#

```
protected override void OnPaint(PaintEventArgs pe)
{
    Graphics g = pe.Graphics;

    for (int i = 0; i < 10; ++i)
    {
        using (Pen p = new Pen(ForeColor, i))
        {
            p.StartCap = LineCap.Square;
            p.EndCap = LineCap.ArrowAnchor;
            g.DrawLine(p, i*15 + 10, 10, i*15 + 50, 50);
        }
    }

    base.OnPaint(pe);
}
```

Example 7-24. Selecting the line thickness in VB

```
Protected Overrides Sub OnPaint(ByVal pe As PaintEventArgs)

    Dim g As Graphics = pe.Graphics
    Dim i As Integer

    For i = 0 to 9
        Dim p As New Pen(ForeColor, i)
        Try
            p.StartCap = LineCap.Square
            p.EndCap = LineCap.ArrowAnchor
            g.DrawLine(p, i*15 + 10, 10, i*15 + 50, 50)
        Finally
            p.Dispose( )
        End Try
    Next
    MyBase.OnPaint(pe)
End Sub
```

The results are shown in Figure 7-6. Note that the first two lines appear to be the same width. This is because their widths are 0.0 and 1.0 respectively, and a line will always be drawn at least 1 pixel thick. (The default coordinate system when painting to the screen uses pixels as units, so the line whose width is 1.0 is also one pixel thick.)

Figure 7-6. Line thickness and caps

Drawing a thick line has the side effect that its bounding box on screen might be larger than the bounding box containing its endpoints. Figure 7-7 shows the same lines with their centers overlaid. This illustrates that both the width and the cap style can influence whether painting happens outside the bounds of the endpoints. This is a particularly important issue if your implementation of `OnPaint` uses the `ClipRectangle` property on the `PaintEventArgs` object to determine what does and doesn't need to be drawn. If your drawing test works on line coordinates alone you might decide not to draw a line that is in fact partially visible. You must always add sufficient leeway to take the width into account.

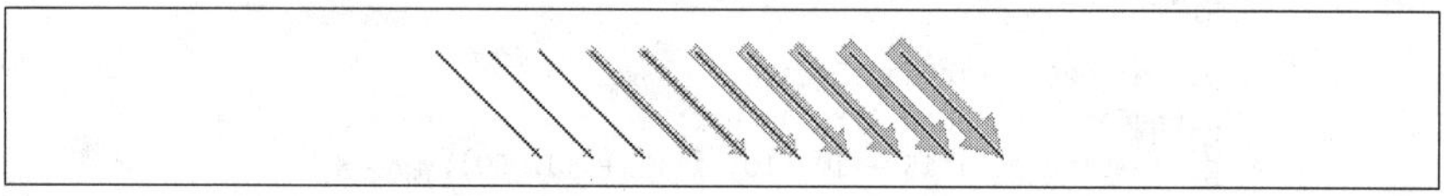

Figure 7-7. Line centers

By default, a `Pen` object will draw a solid line with no breaks. However, if you set the `DashStyle` property, you can draw dashed lines. This property's type is the `DashStyle` enumeration, which provides eponymous `Dash`, `DashDot`, `DashDotDot`, and `Dot` patterns. If these do not suit your needs, you can use the `Custom` style to define your own dash pattern. In this case, you must set the `DashPattern` property of the `Pen` to an array specifying the pattern. Each `float` or `Single` in this array alternately defines the length of a dash or a gap between two dashes.

Examples 7-25 and 7-26 draw a line with a custom dash pattern with alternating medium and long dashes, interspersed with short breaks, as defined by the `pattern` array.

Example 7-25. Creating a custom dash pattern in C#

```
protected override void OnPaint(PaintEventArgs pe)
{
    Graphics g = pe.Graphics;

    using (Pen p = new Pen(Color.Black))
    {
        p.DashStyle = DashStyle.Custom;
        float[] pattern = { 10, 2, 20, 2 };
        p.DashPattern = pattern;
        g.DrawLine(p, 2, 2, 100, 2);
    }

    base.OnPaint(pe);
}
```

Example 7-26. Creating a custom dash pattern in VB

```
Protected Overrides Sub OnPaint(ByVal pe As PaintEventArgs)

    Dim g As Graphics = pe.Graphics

    Dim p AS New Pen(Color.Black)
    Try
        p.DashStyle = DashStyle.Custom
        Dim pattern() As Single = { 10, 2, 20, 2 }
        p.DashPattern = pattern
```

Example 7-26. Creating a custom dash pattern in VB (continued)

```
        g.DrawLine(p, 22, 22, 100, 22)
    Finally
        p.Dispose( )
    End Try
    MyBase.OnPaint(pe)
End Sub
```

Figure 7-8 shows the result.

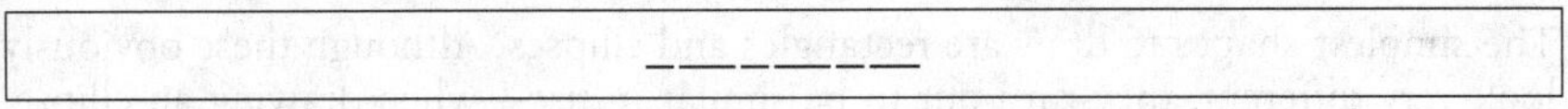

Figure 7-8. A custom dash pattern

When drawing a shape with corners (such as a rectangle), there are several different ways the corners can be displayed. You can set the Pen class's LineJoin property to be rounded off (LineJoin.Round), beveled (LineJoin.Bevel), or mitered (LineJoin.Miter), as shown in Figure 7-9.

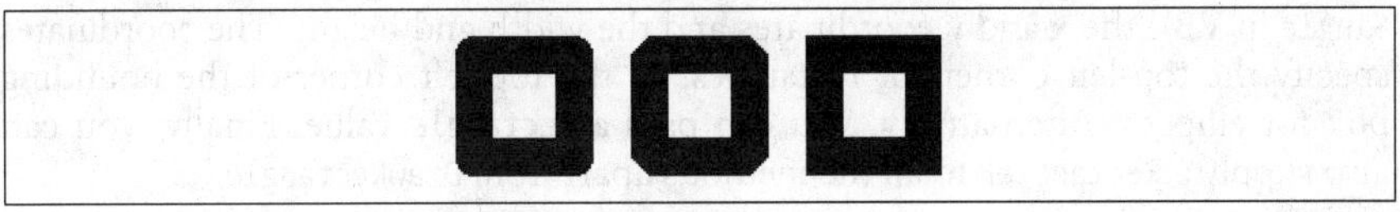

Figure 7-9. Round, beveled, and mitered corners

A Pen can be constructed using either a Color or a Brush. But as with brushes, if you just need a simple pen to draw in either a well-known color or a system color, you can use the static properties in the Pens and SystemPens classes, respectively. Just as SystemBrushes only supplies brushes for the background-like colors, SystemPens only provides foreground-like colors, but again you can obtain a Pen for any of the missing system colors with the static FromSystemColor method. As with brushes, you must not call Dispose on pens obtained from the Pens or SystemPens classes, because they are cached, and are therefore considered to be owned by GDI+, not by you. Attempting to dispose of them will cause an exception to be thrown.

We have now seen the basic toolkit of objects used for drawing. Graphics represents a surface that we can draw onto, typically a window or a bitmap. Coordinates and sizes are represented by Point, Size, and Rectangle, and their floating-point equivalents, PointF, SizeF, and RectangleF. We tell the Graphics object how we would like it to paint areas and outlines using the Brush and Pen classes, and we use Color to specify the colors with which we would like to draw. So let us now look at how to use these to perform some specific drawing operations.

Shapes

The purpose of GDI+ is to allow us to draw images. GDI+ therefore provides us with a set of building blocks—primitive shapes from which we can construct drawings. We have already seen simple examples of this when looking at the brushes and pens, but we will now take a more detailed look at the available facilities.

We draw shapes by calling methods on a `Graphics` object, which represents the surface we are drawing on, be it a window or a bitmap or something else. These methods fall into two categories: those that paint filled areas, and those that draw outlines. With certain exceptions, the former all begin with `Fill...` and the latter begin with `Draw...`. In most cases, the same kinds of shapes can be drawn either filled or in outline; i.e., for any given shape, there is normally a `Fill...` and a `Draw...` method.

Rectangles and ellipses

The simplest shapes to draw are rectangles and ellipses. Although these obviously look very different, they turn out to be similar in use—when drawing an ellipse, you specify its size and position in exactly the same way as for a rectangle.

The `Graphics` class provides four methods for drawing these shapes. `DrawRectangle` and `DrawEllipse` draw the shapes in outline using a `Pen`, and `FillRectangle` and `FillEllipse` fill the shapes using a `Brush`. These methods are all overloaded, allowing you to specify the size and position in a variety of different ways. You can supply four numbers (either as `int`/`Integer` in VB—or `float`/`Single` in VB): the x and y coordinates and the width and height. The coordinates specify the top-left corner for rectangles, or the top-left corner of the bounding box for ellipses. Alternatively, you can pass a `Rectangle` value. Finally, you can also supply a `RectangleF` to all the methods apart from `DrawRectangle`.*

Sometimes you will want to draw several rectangles. For example, a control that draws a bar graph is likely to need to draw many. Instead of calling `DrawRectangle` or `FillRectangle` for each, it might be faster to pass an array of `Rectangle` or `RectangleF` values to the `DrawRectangles` and `FillRectangles` methods. (Despite the fact that you cannot pass a `RectangleF` to `DrawRectangle`, you can pass an array of them to `DrawRectangles`.)

These methods do not provide a direct way of rotating the shapes—their axes are always aligned with the horizontal and vertical drawing axis. However, it is still possible to draw a rotated ellipse or rectangle if necessary by using a transform—see the "Coordinate Systems and Transformations" section later on for details.

Lines and polygons

If you need to draw shapes that are more complex than rectangles and ellipses, you might be able to construct the picture you require out of straight lines. The `Graphics` class provides methods for drawing individual lines and groups of lines.

To draw a single line, use the `DrawLine` method, passing an appropriate `Pen`. You can specify the end points either by passing a pair of `Point` (or `PointF`) values, or you can pass the two coordinates as four numbers of type `int` (`Integer` in VB) or `float` (`Single` in VB), as shown previously in Example 7-23.

If you want to draw a series of connected lines, you can either call `DrawLines` or `DrawPolygon`. The difference between these is that the latter automatically draws a closed shape (i.e., it will draw an extra line connecting the final point back to the

* This appears to be an accidental omission. Future versions of the framework may rectify this.

first one). Because a polygon is a closed shape, you can also draw a filled one with the FillPolygon method. Each of these methods takes an array of Point or PointF values.

When drawing a polygon, it is possible to specify points in such a way that some of its edges intersect each other. This presents FillPolygon with a problem—what should it do for areas that are enclosed by multiple edges? Figure 7-10 illustrates such a shape—the edge cuts in on itself, creating two squares in the middle of the shape. GDI+ can use two different rules to determine whether such regions should be filled. You can choose which rule is used by passing a value from the FillMode enumeration to FillPolygon.

The default is FillMode.Alternate, which means that each time a boundary is crossed, GDI+ will alternate between filling and not filling. For the first shape shown in Figure 7-10, this means that neither interior square is filled.

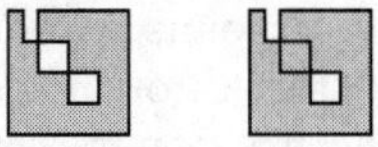

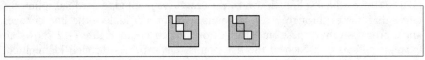

Figure 7-10. The Alternate and Winding fill modes

The other mode, FillMode.Winding, is a little more complex—it takes the direction that edges are pointing into account,* which means that interior regions may or may not be filled. This mode is rarely used—certain graphics systems have supported it historically, but unless you need compatibility with these, you will probably not use it.

Shapes made out of straight lines are all very well, but sometimes you will want to draw curved lines instead. GDI+ has full support for these too.

Curves

There are several different ways of drawing curved shapes. GDI+ lets you draw elliptical arcs, Bézier curves, and cardinal splines.

There are two ways of drawing sections of an ellipse: arcs and pies. An arc is a subsection of the perimeter of an ellipse, and as such can only be drawn in outline. So there is a DrawArc method, but no corresponding Fill... method. A pie is similar to an arc, but it defines a closed area by adding two lines joining the ends of the arc to the center of the ellipse—it is called a "pie" because you would use these to draw a segment of a pie chart. Because a pie is a closed area, there are both DrawPie and FillPie methods. Example output of each method is shown in Figure 7-11.†

Because all three methods describe a segment of an ellipse, they all take similar sets of parameters. There are methods that take six numbers (either as int/Integer or

* More precisely, when working across the shape, it maintains a count that is incremented every time an upward-facing edge is crossed and decremented every time a downward facing edge is encountered. It will fill the shape in any regions for which this count is nonzero. For this reason, this mode is also sometimes known as the nonzero winding rule.

† There is no direct support for drawing a chord, but this is easy enough to recreate using paths, which are described in the next section.

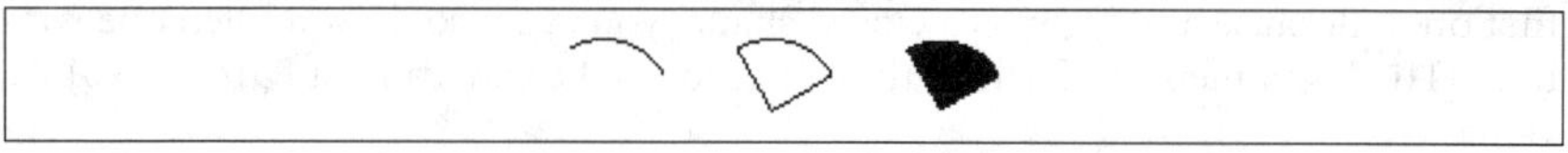

Figure 7-11. Output from DrawArc, DrawPie and FillPie

`float`/`Single`), four of which describe the ellipse's x and y position and its width and height, and the other two of which describe the starting angle of the segment (in degrees, clockwise from the x axis) and the sweep angle. Alternatively, there are methods that use a `Rectangle` to describe the ellipse, with two `float`/`Single` parameters to describe the start and sweep angles. Finally, there are versions that take a `RectangleF` and two `float`/`Single` angles, although in another curious omission, `FillPie` only has three of these overloads and does not accept a `RectangleF`.*

Elliptical segments are useful for certain applications, but you will often need a more flexible way of drawing curves. One of the other curve types offered by GDI+ is the cardinal spline, drawn by the `DrawCurve` method. A cardinal spline is a curve that passes through a set of points without any kinks—the line changes angle progressively to pass smoothly through each point. Figure 7-12 shows an example spline, with each of the five points that it passes through highlighted. (The points have been added for illustrative purposes. The `DrawCurve` method does not highlight the points like this.) There is also a `DrawClosedCurve` method, which draws a loop by joining the last point back to the starting point. Because this defines a closed shape, there is also a corresponding `FillClosedCurve` method.

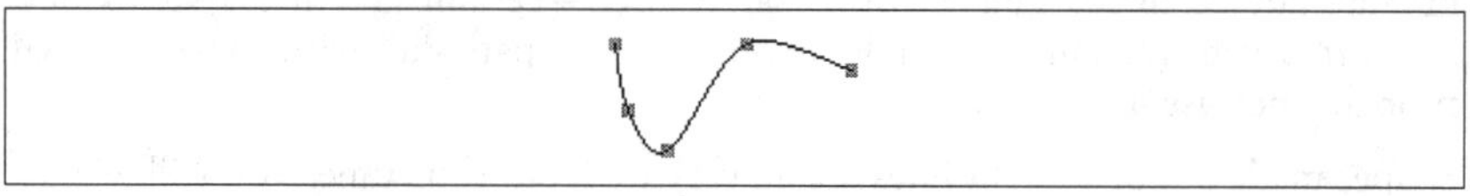

Figure 7-12. A cardinal spline

Each of these methods can take an array of either `Point` or `PointF` values. They also take an optional `float`/`Single` representing the "tension" in the curve—this controls how close the curvature comes to the points. As the tension approaches zero, the curvature becomes tighter and happens closer to the points, with the lines becoming entirely straight at zero tension. As the tension increases, the lines become flatter around the control points, with the curvature being pushed out to the middle of the segments. The default tension is 0.5.

Another popular type of spline is a Bézier curve. With Bézier curves, each line segment is controlled by four points. As well as the start and end points, there are two other *control points* that determine the tangent and the rate of curvature at each end of the segment. This allows much more precise control of the shape than is possible with a cardinal spline's tension parameter, as the curvature can be adjusted on a per-segment basis.

Bézier curves are widely used in font design and for many graphic design applications because they offer such a high level of control. They do, however, require a

* There is another more subtle anomaly: in the all-numbers versions, where the rectangle is specified in integer units, the angles are too, but in the methods that take a `Rectangle`, which uses integer units, the angles are specified as `float`/`Single`.

> **Tension in Cardinal Splines**
>
> This tension parameter exists because cardinal splines are meant to model the behavior of the wooden splines that were used for drafting in the days before CAD. Curves were drawn using flexible pieces of wood called splines; the bendiness of the wood influenced the shape of the curve, so several different thicknesses of spline were usually available to provide different effects. The tension parameter is designed to model this level of flexibility.

little more effort to use than cardinal splines, on account of needing two control points to be defined for each segment, not just its endpoints. Because the control points define the tangent of the curve, you are also responsible for making sure that adjacent segments are cotangential if you want to avoid discontinuities in the curve, as Figure 7-13 shows. (The control points and the tangents that they form have been shown on this diagram. As you can see, the tangents on the point shared by the two segments at the top do not line up, so the curve has a kink.)

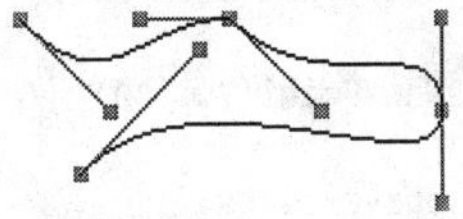

Figure 7-13. Bézier curves with discontinuity

Bézier curves are always drawn as open curves, so there are no `Fill...` methods for them on the `Graphics` class. (They can still be used to paint filled areas by building them into a path as described in the next section.) The `DrawBezier` method can be passed the four control points as `Point` or `PointF` values, or eight `float` values (but not `int` values for some reason). There is also `DrawBeziers`, which draws a connected series of curves. It takes an array of `Point` or `PointF` values. `DrawBeziers` presumes that each segment's endpoint will be the following segment's starting point, so although four points are required for the first segment, each subsequent segment only requires three more points. This is illustrated in Examples 7-27 and 7-28, which draw the curve shown previously in Figure 7-13.

Example 7-27. Using DrawBeziers in C#

```
protected override void OnPaint(PaintEventArgs pe)
{
    Graphics g = pe.Graphics;

    Point[] curvePoints =
        {
            // First segment
            new Point(10, 10), new Point (40, 40),
            new Point(50, 10), new Point (80, 10),

            // Second segment
```

Redrawing & GDI+

Example 7-27. Using DrawBeziers in C# (continued)

```
            new Point(110, 40), new Point(150, 10),
            new Point(150, 40),

            // Third segment
            new Point(150, 70), new Point(70, 20),
            new Point(30, 60)
        };
    g.DrawBeziers(Pens.Black, curvePoints);

    base.OnPaint(pe);
}
```

Example 7-28. Using DrawBeziers in VB

```
Protected Overrides Sub OnPaint(ByVal pe As PaintEventArgs)

    Dim g As Graphics = pe.Graphics
    Dim curvePoints() As Point = _
        { New Point(10, 10), New Point (40, 40), _
          New Point(50, 10), New Point (80, 10), _
          New Point(110, 40), New Point(150, 10), _
          New Point(150, 40), _
          New Point(150, 70), New Point(70, 20), _
          New Point(30, 60) }
    g.DrawBeziers(Pens.Black, curvePoints)

    MyBase.OnPaint(pe)
End Sub
```

The `DrawBeziers` method requires the points to be specified in a certain order. It starts with the first point on the line, but the next two points are control points. So in Examples 7-27 and 7-28, the curve starts at `(10, 10)`, with the tangent heading towards the first control point `(40, 40)`. The next coordinate is also a control point—the tangent for the other end of the first segment heads towards `(50, 10)`. The next coordinate specifies the next point on the line, i.e., the end of the first segment. It also doubles as the starting point of the next segment. For each following segment, the three points are the two control points (specifying the tangent at the start and end of the segment, respectively) and the end point of the segment. In each case, the end point of a segment doubles as the start point of the following segment, except for the very last segment.

So we have a powerful selection of different curve types at our disposal. But there are certain restrictions—what if we want to fill an area defined with Bézier curves rather than merely drawing an outline? Or what if we would like to draw or fill a shape that uses more than one of these curve styles, or even a mixture of curves and straight lines? We can do all these things by using graphics paths, which are described next.

Paths

GDI+ provides the `System.Drawing.Drawing2D.GraphicsPath` class, which allows any combination of the shapes defined so far to be combined into a single object.

You can then get the Graphics object to draw this composite shape either filled or in outline, just as it would draw any of the built-in shapes. This allows you to paint areas using shapes that don't have their own Fill... method. You can also add text to a path, and paths may even be combined.

Using a GraphicsPath is a two-step process. First you must create the shape, then draw the shape that you have created. Creating a shape with the GraphicsPath class is very similar to drawing with the Graphics class—it provides a method for each of the primitive shapes described so far. But rather than calling, say, FillRectangle or DrawEllipse, you call methods beginning with Add.... Because a path defines a shape rather than a drawing operation, it does not distinguish between fills and outlines; you get to make that decision when you actually draw the path—the Graphics class has both DrawPath and FillPath methods. For example, there are AddRectangle, AddEllipse, AddBezier methods, and each is used in exactly the same way as the corresponding method on Graphics. None of these methods takes a Pen or a Brush, again because you get to specify that when you draw the shape, not when you create it.

Examples 7-29 and 7-30 show how to create and draw a closed path using both Bézier curves and straight line segments. It starts by adding three Bézier curves (using the same point data as in Examples 7-27 and 7-28) and then a straight line. Finally, it calls the CloseFigure method, which converts the path from open to closed, allowing us to use it for fills as well as outlines.

Example 7-29. Building a closed path in C#

```
protected override void OnPaint(PaintEventArgs pe)
{
    Graphics g = pe.Graphics;

    Point[] curvePoints =
        {
            new Point(10, 10), new Point (40, 40),
            new Point(50, 10), new Point (80, 10),
            new Point(110, 40), new Point(150, 10),
            new Point(150, 40), new Point(150, 70),
            new Point(70, 20), new Point(30, 60)
        };

    using (GraphicsPath gp = new GraphicsPath())
    using (Brush b = new HatchBrush(HatchStyle.Trellis,
              Color.Aqua, Color.Navy))
    using (Pen p = new Pen(Color.Black, 5))
    {
        gp.AddBeziers(curvePoints);
        gp.AddLine(30, 60, 10, 60);
        gp.CloseFigure();
        g.FillPath(b, gp);
        g.DrawPath(p, gp);
    }

    base.OnPaint(pe);
}
```

Redrawing & GDI+

Example 7-30. Building a closed path in VB

```
Protected Overrides Sub OnPaint(ByVal pe As PaintEventArgs)

    Dim g AS Graphics = pe.Graphics
    Dim gp As New GraphicsPath( )
    Dim b As Brush = New HatchBrush(HatchStyle.Trellis, _
                    Color.Aqua, Color.Navy)
    Dim p As New Pen(Color.Black, 5)
    Dim curvePoints As Point( ) = _
        { New Point(10, 10), New Point (40, 40), _
          New Point(50, 10), New Point (80, 10), _
          New Point(110, 40), New Point(150, 10), _
          New Point(150, 40), New Point(150, 70), _
          New Point(70, 20), New Point(30, 60) }

    Try
        gp.AddBeziers(curvePoints)
        gp.AddLine(30, 60, 10, 60)
        gp.CloseFigure( )
        g.FillPath(b, gp)
        g.DrawPath(p, gp)
    Finally
        gp.Dispose( )
        b.Dispose( )
        p.Dispose( )
    End Try
    MyBase.OnPaint(pe)
End Sub
```

As you can see from Figure 7-14, `GraphicsPath` has enabled us to use Bézier curves to paint both an outline and a fill despite the fact that the `Graphics` class has no `FillBeziers` method. Also note that although we only added one straight line to the path, this shape actually has two straight lines in it at the bottom left corner. The horizontal one is the line we added by calling `AddLine`. The vertical one was created as a result of calling `ClosePath`—GDI+ detected that our shape's first and last points were in different positions, so it added an extra line segment to close the loop.

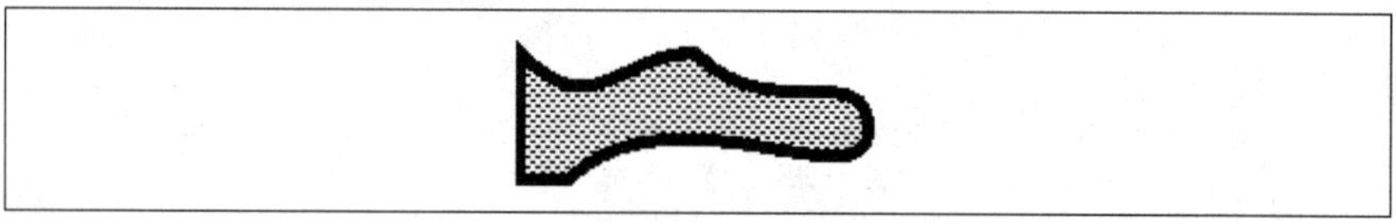

Figure 7-14. A GraphicsPath in use

A path may contain multiple closed areas—once you have called `CloseFigure`, you can carry on adding more elements to the shape. Each closed area in a path is referred to as a *figure*. The ability to contain multiple figures is particularly useful when their areas overlap—this allows shapes with holes to be created. For example, if you wanted to create a path in the shape of the capital letter R, you can use one figure to define the letter's outline, and a second to define the shape of the hole in the loop of the R, as shown in Figure 7-15.

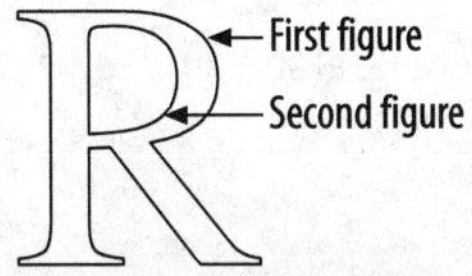
First figure
Second figure

Figure 7-15. Creating holes with a multi-figure shape

These two figures can be combined into a single `GraphicsPath`. The exact behavior of a path when two figures overlap is determined by its `FillMode` property. This works in the same way as for `DrawPolygon`—the default is `FillMode.Alternate`, which for this example will have the expected behavior: the body of the R will be filled, but the hole in the loop will not be painted at all.

Paths with holes allow you to draw things in a way that would otherwise not be possible. If you could not create such paths, the only way to draw shapes like the letter R would be to fill the outline, and then to paint the hole in a different color. The problem with that is it obscures whatever was behind the letter in the first place. But as Figure 7-16 shows, when you paint a path with holes in it, the background shows through those holes.

Figure 7-16. A path with holes

The code that draws Figure 7-16 is shown in Examples 7-31 and 7-32. It illustrates another interesting point. Whenever you add a primitive shape that is intrinsically closed to a path, there is no need to call `CloseFigure`. This particular example builds an ellipse and then knocks a rectangular hole in it. Because ellipses and rectangles are always closed, we did not need to call `CloseFigure` at any point. `CloseFigure` is provided to enable you to construct closed shapes using primitives that are normally open, such as lines and curves.

Example 7-31. Drawing a shape with a hole in C#

```
protected override void OnPaint(PaintEventArgs pe)
{
    Graphics g = pe.Graphics;

    using (GraphicsPath gp = new GraphicsPath( ))
    using (Brush background = new HatchBrush(HatchStyle.Trellis,
            Color.AntiqueWhite, Color.DarkBlue))
    using (Brush foreground = new HatchBrush(HatchStyle.Weave,
            Color.Black, Color.Green))
    {
        g.FillRectangle(background, ClientRectangle);

        gp.AddEllipse(new Rectangle(10, 10, 60, 60));
```

Redrawing & GDI+

Example 7-31. Drawing a shape with a hole in C# (continued)

```
        gp.AddRectangle(new Rectangle(30, 30, 20, 20));
        g.FillPath(foreground, gp);
    }

    base.OnPaint(pe);
}
```

Example 7-32. Drawing a shape with a hole in VB

```
Protected Overrides Sub OnPaint(ByVal pe As PaintEventArgs)

    Dim g As Graphics = pe.Graphics
    Dim gp As New GraphicsPath( )
    Dim background As Brush = New HatchBrush(HatchStyle.Trellis, _
            Color.AntiqueWhite, Color.DarkBlue)
    Dim foreground As Brush = New HatchBrush(HatchStyle.Weave, _
            Color.Black, Color.Green)

    Try
        g.FillRectangle(background, ClientRectangle)

        gp.AddEllipse(new Rectangle(10, 10, 60, 60))
        gp.AddRectangle(new Rectangle(30, 30, 20, 20))
        g.FillPath(foreground, gp)
    Finally
        gp.Dispose( )
        background.Dispose( )
        foreground.Dispose( )
    End Try
    MyBase.OnPaint(pe)
End Sub
```

`GraphicsPath` also provides a solution to a problem mentioned earlier: when drawing an outline with a pen thickness greater than 1 pixel, the bounding box of the drawn line is usually slightly larger than the bounding box of all its points. (And in the case of splines, the bounding box can be considerably larger even with single-pixel–thick lines.) `GraphicsPath` has a `Widen` method that takes a `Pen` and converts the path to the shape its outline would have if it were drawn using that `Pen`. For example, calling `Widen` on a straight line with a thick pen converts it to a rectangle; calling `Widen` on an ellipse with a thick pen converts it into a pair of concentric ellipses. In general, calling `Widen` and then drawing the result with `FillPath` gives exactly the same results as drawing with `DrawPath`.

The `Widen` method is useful because it enables you to find out exactly what shape will be drawn on screen when you draw an outline. Calling `GetBounds` on a widened `GraphicsPath` will give you the true bounding box, taking things like line width and end cap styles into account. (Note that it is not necessary to use this for hit testing—`GraphicsPath` supplies two hit test functions, `IsVisible` and `IsOutlineVisible`. These will tell you whether a particular point lies under the shape when drawn filled and when drawn as an outline with a particular pen.)

Another interesting feature of GraphicsPath is that you can use it to clip other drawing operations. If you create a path and then pass it to the Graphics class's SetClip method, the path will be used as a stencil through which all further drawing is done. Examples 7-33 and 7-34 show how to do this in C# and VB, respectively—the code creates a GraphicsPath containing the text "Stencil" and then draws a series of concentric circles through it.

Example 7-33. Using a GraphicsPath as a stencil in C#

```
protected override void OnPaint(PaintEventArgs pe)
{
    Graphics g = pe.Graphics;

    using (GraphicsPath gp = new GraphicsPath())
    using (Pen p = new Pen(ForeColor, 3))
    {
        gp.AddString("Stencil",
            FontFamily.GenericSerif, (int) FontStyle.Bold, 48,
            new Point(10, 10), new StringFormat());
        g.SetClip(gp);

        Rectangle rect = new Rectangle(93, 35, 10, 10);
        for (int i = 0; i < 30; ++i)
        {
            g.DrawEllipse(p, rect);
            rect.Inflate(4, 4);
        }
    }

    base.OnPaint(pe);
}
```

Example 7-34. Using a GraphicsPath as a stencil in VB

```
Protected Overrides Sub OnPaint(ByVal pe As PaintEventArgs)

    Dim g As Graphics = pe.Graphics
    Dim gp As New GraphicsPath()
    Dim p As New Pen(ForeColor, 3)

    Try
        Dim i As Integer

        gp.AddString("Stencil", _
            FontFamily.GenericSerif, FontStyle.Bold, 48, _
            New Point(10, 10), New StringFormat())
        g.SetClip(gp)

        Dim rect As New Rectangle(93, 35, 10, 10)
        For i = 0 to 29
            g.DrawEllipse(p, rect)
            rect.Inflate(4, 4)
        Next
    Finally
```

Example 7-34. Using a GraphicsPath as a stencil in VB (continued)

```
        gp.Dispose()
        p.Dispose()
    End Try
    MyBase.OnPaint(pe)
End Sub
```

The results are shown in Figure 7-17. It is possible to combine stencils—the `SetClip` method is overloaded. You can pass a member of the `CombineMode` enumeration as an optional second parameter. This supports various set operations, which will be described in the next section. The default is `CombineMode.Replace`, which just replaces the previous clip region with the new one.

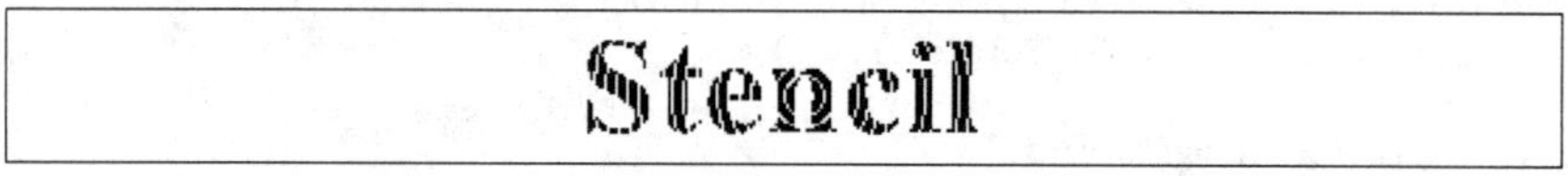
Stencil

Figure 7-17. Drawing through a GraphicsPath

The `Graphics` object allows the clip region to be specified in other ways—as well as passing a `GraphicsPath`, you can also provide a `Rectangle` or a `Region`. It turns out that the `Graphics` class uses `Region` as its fundamental clipping primitive, and it just converts other shapes into regions, so we will now look at the `Region` class.

Regions

A `Region` is similar to a `GraphicsPath` in that it can be used to define arbitrary shapes. But they are designed to be used in different contexts—paths are used for defining shapes that will normally be drawn, whereas regions tend to be used for pixel-related operations such as clipping or hit testing. For example, there is no way to draw a region. Likewise, a path must be converted to a region before it can be used for clipping (although passing a path to a `Graphic` object's `SetClip` method does this automatically).

A `Region` can be created from a `Rectangle`, a `RectangleF`, or a `GraphicsPath`. Regions can also be combined, and one of the differences between regions and paths is the way in which combination works. You can add as many graphics paths as you like together, but the result is always the sum of its parts, and the only control you have over the way that overlapping paths combine is with the `FillMode` you specify when drawing the path. Regions offer a little more flexibility—they can be combined using various set operations.

The simplest way of combining two regions is to use the `Region` class's `Union` method. This results in a region that contains all the areas from both regions. Alternatively you can use `Intersect`, which creates a region containing only those areas that were covered by both regions. Slightly more subtle is the `Exclude` method, which creates a region that contains only those parts of the original region that were not also in the second region. (In other words, it calculates the intersection, and then subtracts that from the original. This lets you use one region to take bites out of another.) `Complement` does much the same thing only in reverse—it calculates the intersection and subtracts that from the second region instead of the original region. Finally, there is the `Xor` method, which performs an exclusive or operation; it creates a region containing all areas that were either in the first or the second region, but not in both. (Xor is effectively equivalent to FillMode.Alternate. There is no equivalent to FillMode.Winding because the winding rule depends on path direction, but regions are only concerned with area.)

The CombineMode enumeration has entries representing each combination type. This can be passed to the Graphics class's SetClip method (described earlier) to describe exactly how the new clip region should be combined with the old one. The enumeration also defines a Replace value, allowing the new clip region to replace the old one instead of being combined with it.

Regions also allow for flexible hit testing. Although GraphicsPath supplies simple hit testing with its IsVisible and IsOutlineVisible methods, these are of limited use. If you wish to test whether the mouse pointer is over a particular object, it is usually necessary to give the user a few pixels of leeway. (Many users have their mouse configured to move so quickly that they cannot actually hit certain pixels at all.) The hit testing supported by GraphicsPath is unfortunately all single pixel. However, the Region class has an overloaded IsVisible method that allows a Rectangle to be passed, and it will test whether any part of the Rectangle intersects with any part of the region. This makes it straightforward to perform hit testing with support for an arbitrary degree of sloppiness—the larger the rectangle, the greater the margin you allow for user inaccuracy.

Regions can also be used to set the shape of a control. The Control class has a property called Region, which can be used to define a nonrectangular shape for a control. This works both for forms and normal controls. Examples 7-35 and 7-36 show how to create an elliptical window. (For this to be useful, more work would be required in practice—the titlebar is mostly obscured, as are the corners of the window, so such a form would need to provide alternate mechanisms for moving and resizing the window.)

Example 7-35. Creating an elliptical window in C#

```
public MyForm()
{
    InitializeComponent();

    using (GraphicsPath gp = new GraphicsPath())
    {
        gp.AddEllipse(ClientRectangle);
        Region = new Region(gp);
    }
}
```

Example 7-36. Creating an elliptical window in VB

```
Public Sub New()

    InitializeComponent()

    Dim gp As New GraphicsPath()
```

Example 7-36. Creating an elliptical window in VB (continued)

```
    Try
        gp.AddEllipse(ClientRectangle)
        Region = new Region(gp)
    Finally
        gp.Dispose( )
    End Try
End Sub
```

So we have seen that GDI+ has extensive and flexible support for shapes. This ranges from simple constructs such as rectangles and ellipses, through lines and curves, to composite shapes represented either as paths or regions. But we have not yet looked at text. Although text could be considered as just another kind of shape, it has many unique features that require special consideration. So we will now look at the support for text in GDI+.

Text

Almost all applications need to display text. In many cases, this can be dealt with by using built-in controls. Even when parts of the display are custom-drawn, you can often get away with using the `Label` class to display text. But for some controls, you will need display text from within the `OnPaint` method.

To represent text strings, GDI+ simply uses the .NET runtime's intrinsic `System.String` type (or `string`, as it is usually abbreviated in C#, and `String`, as it is usually abbreviated in VB). The only types that GDI+ defines are for modifying the text's appearance. These types fall roughly into two categories: those used to choose the typeface in which the text will be drawn, and those used to control the formatting of the text. We will start by looking at the classes used to select a typeface and associated attributes.

Fonts

The `Font` class determines the style in which text will be drawn. It specifies the typeface (e.g., Times Roman, Univers, or Palatino), but it also controls details such as whether bold or italic are in use, and the size of the text.

If you are writing a control, the easiest way to obtain a `Font` object is to use the `Control` class's `Font` property. This will pick up the ambient font (which is usually the default font—8.25pt Microsoft Sans Serif) unless the property has been set explicitly by the user. The advantages of this are that your text will be in harmony with all other text on the form by default, and you don't need to create the `Font` object yourself. Drawing text can be as simple as this:

```
// C# code
protected override void OnPaint(PaintEventArgs pe)
{
    Graphics g = pe.Graphics;

    using (Brush b = new SolidBrush(ForeColor))
    {
        g.DrawString("Hello", Font, b, 0, 0);
    }
```

```
        base.OnPaint(pe);
    }

    ' VB code
    Protected Overrides Sub OnPaint(ByVal pe As PaintEventArgs)

        Dim g As Graphics = pe.Graphics
        Dim b As Brush = New SolidBrush(ForeColor)
        Try
            g.DrawString("Hello", Font, b, 0, 0)
        Finally
            b.Dispose( )
        End Try
        MyBase.OnPaint(pe)
    End Sub
```

Here, we have simply provided a text string to be displayed, and we are painting it using the font and color specified by the control's Font and ForeColor properties. The last two parameters to DrawString specify the position at which to draw the text, so this text will appear at the top-left corner of the control.

You will not always be able to rely on the Control class's Font property to supply you with a Font object. Your control might need to use more than one font, in which case you will need to build your own Font objects. The first thing to be aware of is that Font objects are immutable—having created a font, you cannot modify properties such as size or boldness. If you want an emboldened version of a font, you must create a new one. Fortunately, the Font class provides constructors that make it easy to build a font that is a slight variation on an existing one.

To build a font by modifying the use of styles such as italic or bold, you can use the Font constructor, which takes a Font and a FontStyle. FontStyle is an enumeration containing Bold, Italic, Strikeout, and Underline members to determine the style in which the text will be drawn. You can use these in any combination; for example:

```
FontStyle.Bold|FontStyle.Italic
```

or:

```
FontStyle.Bold Or FontStyle.Italic
```

or you can specify FontStyle.Regular to indicate that you require a plain version of the font. Be aware that not all typefaces support all styles—for example, some typefaces are only available in bold, and attempting to create a regular version will cause an error—later on we will see how to anticipate and avoid such problems by using the FontFamily class.

There is also a constructor that takes an existing Font and a new size. The size is an *em size*, which is to say it specifies the width of the letter M in the typeface. (This is the standard way of defining typeface sizes.) This will be in units of points (i.e., 1/72 of an inch; for historical reasons typeface sizes are almost always measured in points), although there is another constructor that also takes a value from the GraphicsUnit enumeration, allowing you to specify other units such as pixels or millimeters.

But if you want to create a new font from scratch, rather than basing it on an existing font, you need to tell GDI+ which font family you would like it to use. You can do this either by specifying a family name as a string (e.g., "Arial") or a FontFamily object. Using a string, such as new Font("Arial", 12) is the most straightforward, but there are certain advantages to using the FontFamily class.

Certain typeface names are a fairly safe bet—Arial, for instance, is ubiquitous because it ships with Windows. But in general there is always the risk that the typeface name you specify will not always be available. To avoid the errors that this will cause, it is usually better to use a FontFamily object. FontFamily lets you enumerate all the available typefaces, which is helpful if you want to let the user pick a font from a list. Examples 7-37 and 7-38 show how to display a list of font family names in a listbox. The code first obtains an array of FontFamily objects by calling FontFamily.GetFamilies; this must be provided with a Graphics object because the selection of fonts available may sometimes be dictated by where the drawing is taking place. So in this case, we are using the Control class's CreateGraphics method to obtain a Graphics object for our control. We then pass the FontFamily array to the listbox (listFonts) as a data source, and tell it to display the font names as list entries.

Example 7-37. Showing font families in a listbox using C#

```
using (Graphics g = CreateGraphics( ))
{
    FontFamily[] families = FontFamily.GetFamilies(g);
    listFonts.DataSource = families;
    listFonts.DisplayMember = "Name";
}
```

Example 7-38. Showing font families in a listbox using VB

```
Dim g As Graphics = CreateGraphics( )
Dim families( ) As FontFamily = FontFamily.GetFamilies(g)
listFonts.DataSource = families
listFonts.DisplayMember = "Name"
g.Dispose( )
```

This technique guarantees that you are only using font families that you know are present. It also enables you to find out whether a particular style of font is available. As mentioned above, not all fonts support all styles—it is quite common for a typeface to be bold only. The FontFamily class lets you find out whether a particular style is available by passing the FontStyle you would like to its IsAvailable method. This returns a bool/Boolean to indicate whether the style is supported.

Having established that the typeface you require is available in the appropriate style, you can use the Font class constructor that takes a FontFamily, a size (float/Single) and a FontStyle. This will create a brand new Font object built to your specifications.

Sometimes you will simply require a font that looks approximately right—it might be sufficient to use any old sans-serif font without caring whether it's Arial or Linotype Helvetica. The FontFamily class therefore provides some static properties that return non-specific FontFamily objects with certain broad visual characteristics. It provides a GenericSansSerif property that will return a family such as Microsoft Sans Serif or Arial. There is a GenericSerif property, which will return something like Times New Roman. Finally there is GenericMonospace, which will return a monospaced font such as Courier New.

Having chosen a typeface, we need to be able to control how it is displayed, so we will now consider how to manage features such as alignment and cropping.

Formatting

The Graphics class provides several overloads of the DrawString method. The simplest just takes a string, a Font, a Brush, and a position, and will draw the text from left to right starting exactly at the position specified. For many applications this is sufficient, but sometimes a little more control is required to get the text to appear in exactly the right position.

The most obvious example of where the simple approach falls down is if you need to right-align your text—e.g., you need some text to appear up against the far right edge of your control. It is difficult to do this by specifying the position of the top-left corner of the string—you would need to find out how long the string will be and adjust the start position accordingly. And although you can do this, there is a much simpler way.

One of the overloads of the DrawString method lets you specify the position by supplying a rectangle rather than a point. You can then pass a parameter of type StringFormat, which controls, among other things, how the string is positioned within this rectangle. The StringFormat class has properties that control horizontal and vertical positioning: Alignment and LineAlignment. These both use the StringAlignment enumeration type, and can be one of Center, Far, or Near. Near means left or top for horizontal or vertical positioning, respectively, while Far means right or bottom.* So it is now simple to position text without measuring it. Examples 7-39 and 7-40 draw text that is vertically centered and aligned to the righthand side of the control.

Example 7-39. Aligning text using C#

```
protected override void OnPaint(PaintEventArgs pe)
{
    Graphics g = pe.Graphics;

    using (Brush b = new SolidBrush(ForeColor))
    using (StringFormat sf = new StringFormat( ))
    {
        sf.Alignment = StringAlignment.Far;
        sf.LineAlignment = StringAlignment.Center;

        g.DrawString("Hello", Font, b, ClientRectangle, sf);
    }
    base.OnPaint(pe);
}
```

* These can be inverted—the StringFormat class can be configured for right-to-left text for languages where this appropriate. In this case, Near would be the right and Far would be the left.

Example 7-40. Aligning text using VB

```
Protected Overrides Sub OnPaint(ByVal pe As PaintEventArgs)

    Dim g As Graphics = pe.Graphics
    Dim b As Brush = New SolidBrush(ForeColor)
    Dim sf As New StringFormat( )

    Try
        sf.Alignment = StringAlignment.Far
        sf.LineAlignment = StringAlignment.Center

        g.DrawString("Hello", Font, b, _
              RectangleF.op_Implicit(ClientRectangle), sf)
    Finally
        b.Dispose( )
        sf.Dispose( )
    End Try
    MyBase.OnPaint(pe)

End Sub
```

Note that we have used the `Control` class's `ClientRectangle` property, which defines the bounds of the control. This means that the text will automatically be aligned to the control's righthand edge. When using `DrawString` in this way, it will also break text over multiple lines if necessary. (It will do this when the rectangle is too narrow to hold the whole string, but tall enough to hold multiple lines. If the string is too long to fit even when split, it is simply truncated.)

Many controls choose to expose an alignment property of type `ContentAlignment` (e.g., the `Button` class's `TextAlign` property). This allows the horizontal and vertical alignment to be set through a single property. Because there are three possible positions for each dimension (`Near`, `Center`, and `Far`), the `ContentAlignment` enumeration has nine values. Unfortunately, the framework does not currently supply a way of creating a `StringFormat` object whose `Alignment` and `LineAlignment` properties match the positions specified in a `ContentAlignment` value. The only solution, presented in Examples 7-41 and 7-42, is somewhat ugly.

Example 7-41. Converting from ContentAlignment to StringFormat in C#

```
private StringFormat FormatFromContentAlignment(ContentAlignment align)
{
    StringFormat sf = new StringFormat( );
    switch (align)
    {
        case ContentAlignment.BottomCenter:
        case ContentAlignment.MiddleCenter:
        case ContentAlignment.TopCenter:
            sf.Alignment = StringAlignment.Center;
            break;
        case ContentAlignment.BottomRight:
        case ContentAlignment.MiddleRight:
```

Example 7-41. Converting from ContentAlignment to StringFormat in C# (continued)

```
        case ContentAlignment.TopRight:
            sf.Alignment = StringAlignment.Far;
            break;
        default:
            sf.Alignment = StringAlignment.Near;
            break;
    }
    switch (align)
    {
        case ContentAlignment.BottomCenter:
        case ContentAlignment.BottomLeft:
        case ContentAlignment.BottomRight:
            sf.LineAlignment = StringAlignment.Far;
            break;
        case ContentAlignment.TopCenter:
        case ContentAlignment.TopLeft:
        case ContentAlignment.TopRight:
            sf.LineAlignment = StringAlignment.Near;
            break;
        default:
            sf.LineAlignment = StringAlignment.Center;
            break;
    }
    return sf;
}
```

Example 7-42. Converting from ContentAlignment to StringFormat in VB

```
Option Strict On

Imports System
Imports System.ComponentModel
Imports System.Drawing
Imports System.Drawing.Drawing2D
Imports System.Windows.Forms

Public Class FormatLib

Private Function FormatFromContentAlignment(align As ContentAlignment) As
StringFormat

    Dim sf As New StringFormat()

    Select Case align
        Case ContentAlignment.BottomCenter, _
             ContentAlignment.MiddleCenter, _
             ContentAlignment.TopCenter
            sf.Alignment = StringAlignment.Center
        Case ContentAlignment.BottomRight, _
             ContentAlignment.MiddleRight, _
             ContentAlignment.TopRight
            sf.Alignment = StringAlignment.Far
```

Example 7-42. Converting from ContentAlignment to StringFormat in VB (continued)

```
        Case Else
            sf.Alignment = StringAlignment.Near
    End Select
    Select Case align
        Case ContentAlignment.BottomCenter, _
             ContentAlignment.BottomLeft, _
             ContentAlignment.BottomRight
            sf.LineAlignment = StringAlignment.Far
        Case ContentAlignment.TopCenter, _
             ContentAlignment.TopLeft, _
             ContentAlignment.TopRight
            sf.LineAlignment = StringAlignment.Near
        Case Else
            sf.LineAlignment = StringAlignment.Center
    End Select

    Return sf

End Function

End Class
```

The `StringFormat` class also allows us to control other aspects of the text's appearance. For example, we can draw the text vertically by setting the `StringFormatFlags.DirectionVertical` flag on its `FormatFlags` property. The `FormatFlags` property can be set at construction time by passing in a `StringFormatFlags` value. See the reference section for other `FormatFlags` options.

> There is a much more flexible way of rotating than using FormatFlags. See the "Coordinate Systems and Transformations" section later in this chapter.

The `StringFormat` class also supports drawing hot key underlines on your controls, such as those that appear on buttons and menu items if the Alt key is held down. This is particularly useful if you are drawing your own menu items. Simply set the `StringFormat` class's `HotkeyPrefix` member to `HotkeyPrefix.Show`, and GDI+ will add an underline on strings containing ampersands. For example, the string `E&xit` would be drawn with the `x` underlined. (The ampersand itself is just a marker and will not be displayed.) GDI+ will also strip the ampersands out without displaying the underlines if you specify `HotkeyPrefix.Hide`. You would use this in an owner-drawn menu when you are asked to draw a menu without accelerators (i.e., when the `DrawItemEventArgs` object's `State` member has the `NoAccelerator` flag set). The default is `HotkeyPrefix.None`, which means that ampersands don't get any special treatment—they are just displayed as normal characters.

Sometimes it will be necessary to measure a string before drawing it. This is particularly important if you are drawing anything that manages its layout dynamically. For example, owner-drawn menus need to calculate the size of their text to handle the `MeasureItem` event correctly. The `Graphics` class therefore provides the `MeasureString` method.

MeasureString is overloaded. At its simplest, it just takes a string and a Font, and returns the size of that string (i.e., how much space the string would take up if drawn with that font using DrawString). However, the DrawString methods that take a rectangle can change the size of the drawn string, due to issues such as cropping. So you can pass a SizeF value to MeasureString to indicate the size of the rectangle you will be using. Because a StringFormat object can also influence the size of the output, there are overloads that accept a StringFormat as well. All these methods return a SizeF indicating how much space the string will take up when displayed.

Examples 7-43 and 7-44 illustrate the use of MeasureString in the context of an owner-drawn menu. When drawing your own menu items, Windows Forms will raise the MeasureItem event to find out how wide your owner-drawn items are. It needs to know this to determine how large the menu should be. Menu width is normally determined by the text in the menu, so we use MeasureString to find this out. Note that we don't use the height as calculated by MeasureString; we use the nominal height given by the Font object's Height property. This is to make sure that all menu items come out the same height. (We also add in the size of the menu check—system-drawn menus always leave space for this on the left. It also doesn't look right unless you make the menu item 3 pixels higher and 8 pixels wider than necessary to hold the string—the system appears to add this much padding when drawing its own menus.)

Example 7-43. Using MeasureString for an owner-drawn menu item in C#

```
private void Menu_MeasureItem(object sender,
    MeasureItemEventArgs e)
{
    MenuItem item = (MenuItem) sender;

    Font menuFont = SystemInformation.MenuFont;
    e.ItemHeight = menuFont.Height + 3;

    StringFormat sf = new StringFormat(
            StringFormatFlags.DisplayFormatControl);
    sf.HotkeyPrefix = System.Drawing.Text.HotkeyPrefix.Hide;

    int textWidth = (int) e.Graphics.MeasureString(item.Text,
        menuFont, new PointF(0,0), sf).Width;

    Size checkSize = SystemInformation.MenuCheckSize;
    e.ItemWidth = textWidth + checkSize.Width + 8;
}
```

Example 7-44. Using MeasureString for an owner-drawn menu item in VB

```
Private Sub Menu_MeasureItem(sender As Object, _
    e As MeasureItemEventArgs) Handles menuFile.MeasureItem

    Dim item As MenuItem = DirectCast(sender, MenuItem)

    Dim  menuFont As Font = SystemInformation.MenuFont
    e.ItemHeight = menuFont.Height + 3
```

Redrawing & GDI+

Example 7-44. Using MeasureString for an owner-drawn menu item in VB (continued)

```
    Dim sf As New StringFormat( _
            StringFormatFlags.DisplayFormatControl)
    sf.HotkeyPrefix = System.Drawing.Text.HotkeyPrefix.Hide

    Dim textWidth As Integer = CInt(e.Graphics.MeasureString( _
            item.Text, menuFont, new PointF(0,0), sf).Width)

    Dim checkSize As Size = SystemInformation.MenuCheckSize
    e.ItemWidth = textWidth + checkSize.Width + 8
End Sub
```

So we have now seen how to draw images using either text or shapes. But sometimes we will not wish to construct pictures using these primitives—we might already have an image stored on disk that we wish to display as is. So we will now look at the GDI+ facilities for dealing with images.

Images

Pictures do not necessarily have to be drawn on the fly—it is possible to store a prebuilt image in a number of formats. GDI+ defines the `Image` class as an abstract representation of any such image.

GDI+ supports two different types of image, bitmaps and metafiles, and there is a class deriving from `Image` for each: `Bitmap` and `Metafile`. Bitmaps store information as raw pixel data—a bitmap image's size is always a fixed number of pixels, and displaying them at any other size requires a certain amount of image processing and can have mixed results. Conversely, metafiles store information as a series of primitive drawing operations. This means that they can be resized and rotated more easily than bitmaps, although they are usually slower to draw than bitmaps drawn at their natural size and orientation.

Regardless of their type, images are displayed by using the `Graphics` class's `DrawImage` method. There are several overloads of this method, but they all take an `Image`. Some just take the position at which to draw the image, while others take a position and a size, allowing the image to be scaled. Some also take a rectangle indicating which part of the image should be displayed, so that you can draw a subsection of the image.

Images can be created as well as displayed—it is possible to use GDI+ to build a new bitmap or metafile. This is made possible by the `Graphics` class's static `FromImage` method, which creates a `Graphics` object that lets you draw into an image.

Bitmaps

The `Bitmap` class represents an image stored as pixel data. You can create `Bitmap` objects from files. Several formats are supported, including BMP, JPEG, PNG, TIFF, and GIF. You can also create new images from scratch.

Be aware that there are licensing issues with GIF. It uses a data compression system that is subject to a patent owned by Unisys. If your application supports GIF files, you may need to obtain a license. Contact Unisys for further information.

The Bitmap class is often used to draw bitmaps that are stored in files. To create a new Bitmap object based on a file, simply pass the filename as a string to the constructor. (Or you can pass a Stream if that is more convenient; this can be useful if your bitmap file is stored as an embedded resource.) Examples 7-45 and 7-46 create and display a Bitmap object based on one of the standard Windows background bitmaps. (You would not use a hardcoded path like this in practice of course—this is just to keep the sample code simple.)

Example 7-45. Creating and drawing a Bitmap object in C#

```
private Image myImage;

public MyControl()
{
    myImage = new Bitmap("c:\\windows\\Prairie Wind.bmp");
}

protected override void OnPaint(PaintEventArgs pe)
{
    Graphics g = pe.Graphics;
    g.DrawImage(myImage, 0, 0);
    base.OnPaint(pe);
}
```

Example 7-46. Creating and drawing a Bitmap object in VB

```
Private myImage As Image

Public Sub New()
    myImage = New Bitmap("c:\\windows\\Prairie Wind.bmp")
End Sub

Protected Overrides Sub OnPaint(ByVal pe As PaintEventArgs)
    Dim g As Graphics = pe.Graphics
    g.DrawImage(myImage, 0, 0)
    MyBase.OnPaint(pe)
End Sub
```

This code displays the whole image at full size. But we can easily change this by passing an extra two parameters to specify the size:

```
g.DrawImage(myImage, 0, 0, 50, 50);
```

This will reduce the image to a 50×50 pixel square. Scaling images is intrinsically tricky, and there is always a tradeoff between time taken to draw the image and the resulting image quality. The Graphics object lets you specify whether you want to favor quality or speed through its InterpolationMode property. This can be set to values from the InterpolationMode enumeration, which from fastest to slowest are NearestNeighbor, Bilinear (the default value), HighQualityBilinear, Bicubic, and HighQualityBicubic. While the ones at the front of that list are faster, they will produce lower-quality results. It is beyond the scope of this book to describe the image processing algorithms implied by each of these settings, which makes it hard to offer more specific advice than that you should pick the fastest value that produces results that are good enough for your application. However, NearestNeighbor is unlikely to provide satisfactory results unless you are either scaling pictures by integer factors, or scaling things up to be so large that individual pixels will be clearly visible.

Another way of using the Bitmap class is to build a new bitmap. There are two reasons you might want to do this. One is that your application requires a particularly complex piece of drawing to be done, and you want to draw it just once into a bitmap to make subsequent redraws work more quickly. The other reason is that you want to save a picture to disk as a bitmap.

To create a brand new Bitmap from scratch, you can simply specify the width and height you require as construction parameters. However, it is usually a good idea to pass in a reference to a Graphics object as well. This guarantees that the new bitmap has characteristics that are compatible with the Graphics object (such as color depth and resolution). Examples 7-47 and 7-48 create a new bitmap with the text "Hello" drawn into it.

> If you want to create a bitmap that has attributes that are different from any available Graphics object (e.g., you want to create an image with a low color depth to conserve space), there is a constructor that takes a PixelFormat value, allowing you to specify the exact color format you require. You would normally only do this if you planned to save the bitmap to a file.

Example 7-47. Creating a Bitmap from scratch using C#

```
using (Graphics gOrig = CreateGraphics( ))
{
    myBitmap = new Bitmap(50, 50, gOrig);
    using (Graphics g = Graphics.FromImage(myBitmap))
    {
        g.FillRectangle(Brushes.White, 0, 0,
            myBitmap.Width, myBitmap.Height);
        g.DrawString("Hello",
            new Font (FontFamily.GenericSerif, 14),
            Brushes.Blue, 0, 0);
    }
}
```

Example 7-48. Creating a Bitmap from scratch using VB

```
Dim gOrig As Graphics = CreateGraphics( )
Try
    myBitmap = new Bitmap(50, 50, gOrig)
    Dim g As Graphics = Graphics.FromImage(myBitmap)
    Try
```

Example 7-48. Creating a Bitmap from scratch using VB (continued)

```
        g.FillRectangle(Brushes.White, 0, 0, _
            myBitmap.Width, myBitmap.Height)
        g.DrawString("Hello", _
            new Font (FontFamily.GenericSerif, 14), _
            Brushes.Blue, 0, 0)
    Finally
        g.Dispose( )
    End Try
Finally
    gOrig.Dispose( )
End Try
```

Note how this code fills the entire bitmap with a white background before starting. This is important because by default bitmaps start out completely transparent. This can have some surprising effects if you paint text onto them with `ClearType` or font smoothing enabled.

Examples 7-47 and 7-48 are unusual in that they have a couple of `using` statements disposing of `Graphics` objects in the C# code and of calls to `Graphics` objects' `Dispose` methods in the VB code. Normally we do not need to call `Dispose` on a `Graphics` object. But remember, the rule is that you are responsible for disposing of any object that you create. Generally speaking, we don't create `Graphics` objects—we just use the ones supplied by the system. But here we are creating two, one to obtain a set of properties with which to initialize the `Bitmap` object, and another to let us draw on the bitmap. Because we created them, we must also call `Dispose` on them, which will be done automatically at the end of the `using` blocks in C#. (The `CreateGraphics` method being called on the first line is a method supplied by the `Control` class—as we saw in Examples 7-37 and 7-38, it lets you obtain a `Graphics` object for the control in contexts where you wouldn't otherwise have one, such as in its constructor.)

The bitmap created in Examples 7-47 and 7-48 could then be drawn using the same `OnPaint` method as in Examples 7-45 and 7-46. Alternatively it can be saved to disk. The `Image` class provides a `Save` method, allowing a filename and file format to be specified. Example 7-49 saves the bitmap in PNG format.

Example 7-49. Saving a Bitmap

```
myBitmap.Save("c:\\MyPic.png", ImageFormat.Png);
```

The `Graphics` class provides overloads of the `DrawImage` method that allow you to draw rotated and sheared bitmaps. These all work the same way—you can tell the method where to draw the bitmap by specifying three points. These are used as positions for three of the four corners of the bitmap, and the position of the fourth is inferred by forming a parallelogram. However, it is easier to achieve rotation by drawing with a transformation, which will be described later in this chapter.

The `Bitmap` class is great when you want to display a picture stored as a bitmap file, or when you wish to cache a fixed-size image for fast redraw. But if you require a little more flexibility when redrawing, a metafile might be a more appropriate choice, so we will now look at the support in GDI+ for these.

Metafiles

As with bitmaps, metafiles can be used in two ways. A metafile can be loaded from disk and displayed. Alternatively, a new metafile can be created, either for later display or to be saved to disk.

Creating a `Metafile` object based on a file works in exactly the same way as for bitmaps—you simply pass the filename as a constructor parameter (or a `Stream` if that is more convenient). Building a new `Metafile` from scratch turns out to be slightly more involved, because the `Metafile` object insists on having an `HDC`* (that is, a handle to a Win32 device context) to determine the characteristics of the metafile. (These characteristics include factors such as the resolution; although metafiles do not store raw pixel data, they are aware of the resolution of the device for which they were originally created.) This is easy enough to deal with because we can obtain an `HDC` from the `Graphics` class, but it means that the creation process is a little more long-winded than for a bitmap, as Examples 7-50 and 7-51 show.

Example 7-50. Creating a metafile from scratch in C#

```
using (Graphics og = CreateGraphics( ))
{
    IntPtr hdc = og.GetHdc( );
    try
    {
        myImage = new Metafile(hdc, EmfType.EmfPlusOnly);
        using (Graphics g = Graphics.FromImage(myImage))
        {
            g.DrawString("Hello",
                new Font (FontFamily.GenericSerif, 14),
                Brushes.Blue, 0, 0);
        }
    }
    finally
    {
        og.ReleaseHdc(hdc);
    }
}
```

Example 7-51. Creating a metafile from scratch in VB

```
Dim og As Graphics = CreateGraphics( )
Try
    Dim hdc As IntPtr = og.GetHdc( )
    Try
        myImage = New Metafile(hdc, EmfType.EmfPlusOnly)
        Dim g As Graphics = Graphics.FromImage(myImage)
        Try
            g.DrawString("Hello", _
                New Font (FontFamily.GenericSerif, 14), _
```

* This is a curious anachronism. An `HDC` is Win32's nearest equivalent to a `Graphics` object. It is somewhat strange that the `Metafile` class insists on having one of these to create a new `Metafile` from scratch instead of just using a `Graphics` object.

Example 7-51. Creating a metafile from scratch in VB (continued)

```
                Brushes.Blue, 0, 0)
        Finally
            g.Dispose( )
        End Try
    Finally
        og.ReleaseHdc(hdc)
    End Try
Finally
    og.Dispose( )
End Try
```

Both examples use a `try...finally` block to make absolutely sure that the `HDC` is released. Because an `HDC` is an unmanaged type (i.e., a classic Win32 type, not a .NET type), we are responsible for making sure it is freed under all circumstances. If we forget, the garbage collector will not help us—an `HDC` is just an `IntPtr`, which is a value type large enough to hold either a pointer or an `int`/`Integer`; on 32-bit systems, this is a 32-bit value. Value types are not garbage collected, so if we forget to clean up this resource, it will be leaked. (This is much worse than forgetting to clean up GDI+ resources—with those, the garbage collector will eventually come to our aid.) The use of a `try...finally` block means that the call to `ReleaseHdc` will always occur even if an exception is thrown in the `try` block.

The metafile created in Examples 7-50 and 7-51 can be drawn using the same `OnPaint` method shown in Examples 7-45 and 7-46—`DrawImage` works in exactly the same way for metafiles as for bitmaps. Note that when creating a metafile, we did not need to fill the background color to white before starting. This is because metafiles work differently—bitmaps work as a drawing surface that must be wiped clean before starting; metafiles simply list drawing operations to be applied, so the results are independent of background color. This means that it is much easier to create a transparent metafile than a transparent bitmap if you wish to use antialiasing.

Color transformations

When displaying either metafiles or bitmaps, it is possible to perform a limited amount of color processing on the images as they are drawn. Several of the overloads of the `DrawImage` method take an `ImageAttributes` parameter, which allows color transformations to be specified.

The `ImageAttributes` class is particularly useful for applying simple effects such as building a grayscale version of a color image or making a solid image partially transparent. The mechanism by which it achieves this is a color matrix. This is a matrix that can be applied to every color in the source image to transform it to a new image.

A description of the details of matrix multiplication is beyond the scope of this book, but if you are familiar with this branch of mathematics, here is how color matrixes are used. A color matrix is a 5×5 matrix. Each pixel in the source image (or each color, if the source image is a metafile) is represented as a 1×5 vector. The first four numbers represent red, green, blue, and alpha values with the `float`/`Single` type, where the values range from 0.0 to 1.0. The fifth value is a dummy column that is always 1.0—this is provided to allow the color matrix to perform translations as well as scaling operations. Each color is then multiplied by the color matrix, with the resulting 5×1 matrix used as the new color (with the fifth column ignored).

So what does this mean in practice? You can use a color matrix to perform global changes to color and transparency on an image. Examples 7-52 and 7-53 draw any image with a 40% alpha channel (i.e., see-through), regardless of whether that image has intrinsic transparency. It uses a `DrawImage` overload that takes an `ImageAttributes` object. (As it happens this particular overload can also scale the image; unfortunately, there aren't any overloads that use `ImageAttributes` that don't also do other operations like scaling or rotation, so there is a certain amount of unwanted complexity just to draw the image at its original size.)

Example 7-52. Drawing an image with transparency in C#

```
protected override void OnPaint(PaintEventArgs pe)
{
    Graphics g = pe.Graphics;

    g.DrawString("Behind image", Font, Brushes.LightGreen, 0, 0);
    using (ImageAttributes ia = new ImageAttributes())
    {
        ColorMatrix cm = BuildTransparencyMatrix(0.4f);
        ia.SetColorMatrix(cm);
        int w = myImage.Width;
        int h = myImage.Height;
        Rectangle dest = new Rectangle(0, 0, w, h);
        g.DrawImage(myImage, dest, 0, 0, w, h, GraphicsUnit.Pixel, ia);
    }
    base.OnPaint(pe);
}

private ColorMatrix BuildTransparencyMatrix(float alpha)
{
    ColorMatrix cm = new ColorMatrix();
    cm.Matrix33 = 0;
    cm.Matrix43 = alpha;
    return cm;
}
```

Example 7-53. Drawing an image with transparency in VB

```
Protected Overrides Sub OnPaint(ByVal pe As PaintEventArgs)

    Dim g As Graphics = pe.Graphics

    g.DrawString("Behind image", Font, Brushes.LightGreen, _
                 0, 0)
    Dim ia As New ImageAttributes()
    Try
        Dim cm As ColorMatrix = BuildTransparencyMatrix(0.4f)
        ia.SetColorMatrix(cm)
        Dim w As Integer = myImage.Width
```

Example 7-53. Drawing an image with transparency in VB (continued)

```
        Dim h As Integer = myImage.Height
        Dim dest As New Rectangle(0, 0, w, h)
        g.DrawImage(myImage, dest, 0, 0, w, h, _
                    GraphicsUnit.Pixel, ia)
    Finally
       ia.Dispose()
    End Try

    MyBase.OnPaint(pe)
End Sub

Private Function BuildTransparencyMatrix(alpha As Single) _
                 As ColorMatrix
    Dim cm As New ColorMatrix()
    cm.Matrix33 = 0
    cm.Matrix43 = alpha
    Return cm
End Function
```

The results of this code can be seen in Figure 7-18. Observe that in Example 7-52 and Example 7-53, the bitmap is drawn after the text—i.e., it is drawn right over it. The text is only visible because the image was drawn transparently.

Behind image

Figure 7-18. A bitmap drawn transparently with a ColorMatrix

The BuildTransparencyMatrix method in Examples 7-52 and 7-53 is just one example. It is easy enough to create other simple transforms. For instance, Examples 7-54 and 7-55 build a color matrix that will convert color images into grayscale (black and white) images.

Example 7-54. A color matrix to build grayscale images using C#

```
private ColorMatrix BuildGrayscaleMatrix()
{
    float[][] matrixValues =
        {
            new float[] { 0.3f, 0.3f, 0.3f, 0, 0 },
            new float[] { 0.5f, 0.5f, 0.5f, 0, 0 },
            new float[] { 0.2f, 0.2f, 0.2f, 0, 0 },
            new float[] { 0,       0,    0, 1, 0 },
            new float[] { 0,       0,    0, 0, 1 }
    };
    return new ColorMatrix(matrixValues);
}
```

Example 7-55. A color matrix to build grayscale images using VB

```
Private Function BuildGrayscaleMatrix() As ColorMatrix
    Dim matrixValues()() As Single = _
```

Example 7-55. A color matrix to build grayscale images using VB (continued)

```
    { New Single( ) { 0.3f, 0.3f, 0.3f, 0, 0 }, _
      New Single( ) { 0.5f, 0.5f, 0.5f, 0, 0 }, _
      New Single( ) { 0.2f, 0.2f, 0.2f, 0, 0 }, _
      New Single( ) { 0,    0,    0,    1, 0 }, _
      New Single( ) { 0,    0,    0,    0, 1 }  _
    }
    MsgBox(matrixValues(3)(2))
    Return New ColorMatrix(matrixValues)
End Function
```

If you want grayed out versions of images for your user interface, the `ControlPaint` class provides a `DrawImageDisabled` method that will do this for you. It performs a slightly different color transformation from the one shown in Examples 7-54 and 7-55—it reduces the contrast so you will never see anything as dark as black, or as pale as white. (You could easily do this with a `ColorMatrix` by reducing the scale factors and adding in offsets on the fourth row of the matrix. But because the `ControlPaint` class can do this for you, there is usually no need.)

So we have seen how to draw images with or without various color transformations, text, and a wide variety of shapes. Finally, we will look at the facilities supplied by GDI+ for applying geometrical transformations to our output.

Coordinate Systems and Transformations

Whenever we draw something with GDI+, we specify its position and any relevant size information. For these numbers to mean anything, there must be some coordinate system in place. By default, coordinates are in terms of screen pixels, but we can actually modify the coordinate system to transform our output, allowing translations, rotations, and shearing to be applied automatically to everything we draw.

There are many reasons why this could be useful. For example, there are certain drawing primitives for which the relevant methods on the `Graphics` class do not provide a means of rotating or shearing the output. The only way to draw rotated or sheared versions of such objects is to draw with an appropriate transformation in place. Also, if you are writing a control that provides a view of a large area, transforms can make it simple to implement facilities such as scrolling and zooming. Likewise, if you have a piece of code that paints a particular drawing, a transformation is likely to be the easiest way to allow rotated views of that picture.

Example 7-56 shows a very common way of modifying the *world transform* (the transform applied by a `Graphics` object to every drawing operation). This is the `OnPaint` method inside a `ScrollableControl`. Any control deriving from `ScrollableControl` should make sure that it offsets everything it draws by the current scroll position. (The `ScrollableControl` class provides a property called `AutoScrollPosition`, which is a `Point` indicating the scroll position.) This example simply adjusts the world transform by adding in a translation based on the current scroll position. The rest of the drawing code could be written without needing to build in any awareness of the scroll position, because GDI+ is automatically offsetting everything we draw.

Example 7-56. Translating the transform for scrolling

```
// C#
protected override void OnPaint(PaintEventArgs pe)
{
    Graphics g = pe.Graphics;
    g.TranslateTransform(AutoScrollPosition.X,
        AutoScrollPosition.Y);
    . . .
}

' VB
Protected Overrides Sub OnPaint(ByVal pe As PaintEventArgs)
    Dim g As Graphics = pe.Graphics
    g.TranslateTransform(AutoScrollPosition.X, _
                         AutoScrollPosition.Y)
    . . .
End Sub
```

Example 7-57 shows how to rotate the transform to draw some text rotated by 45 degrees. This illustrates an important point. Sometimes you will want to apply a temporary transformation just to alter how one item is drawn; in this example, only the text string is to be drawn rotated. In such cases, you will want to take the transform back off again before continuing to draw. The `Graphics` class supplies a `ResetTransform` method, which removes any transform currently in place. This method will often be appropriate, but it does not work if the transform is also being used for other purposes such as scrolling because of the way that transforms are combined.

The nature of transformation matrixes is that you can apply as many different transformations as you like—a single matrix can be used to represent the combined effect of any number of individual matrixes. So it is definitely allowable to translate the transform for scrolling purposes and to then rotate it. The problem is that calling `ResetTransform` removes all current transforms, which would include the translation applied for scrolling purposes. Example 7-57 is sensitive to this: it retrieves the current transform, applies a rotation for its own drawing, and then puts the original transform back when it has finished. (The `Transform` property always returns a copy of the current `Transform`, so the `Matrix` it returns will not be modified when we call `RotateTransform`.) This means that any code that follows will not be affected by the rotation, but will still benefit from the translation that was applied for scrolling.

Example 7-57. Rotating the transform

```
// C#
Matrix origTx = g.Transform;
g.RotateTransform(45);
g.DrawString("Rotated", Font, Brushes.LightGreen, 20, 20);
g.Transform = origTx;
```

Example 7-57. Rotating the transform (continued)

```
' VB
Dim origTx As Matrix = g.Transform
g.RotateTransform(45)
g.DrawString("Rotated", Font, Brushes.LightGreen, 20, 20)
g.Transform = origTx
```

The `Graphics` transform can be used to apply any affine transformation*—it just uses a 3×3 matrix, where the third row is used to apply translations. (Just as a dummy fifth column was added to colors for color matrixes, a dummy third column is added to each two-dimensional coordinate for transformation, to allow translations.) As well as being able to translate and rotate the transform, there is a `ScaleTransform` method, which can be useful for implementing a zoom feature.

There is no method for explicitly shearing the transformation. To do this, you will need to use the `Matrix` class directly. `Matrix` represents a 3×3 matrix used for two-dimensional transforms, and enables you to set each individual element if you need that level of control. (The `Graphics.Transform` property is of type `Matrix`.) You can also apply a `Matrix` object to a `GraphicsPath` using the `Warp` method to transform all the elements of a path without needing to go through a `Graphics` object.

Summary

GDI+ provides a very powerful set of drawing tools. Access to drawing surfaces, whether they are windows, bitmaps, or metafiles, is provided through the `Graphics` class. This supplies methods for drawing primitive shapes whose visual attributes are specified with `Brush` and `Pen` objects. We can augment the set of primitives by building our own composite shapes using the `GraphicsPath` class. There is special support for text, both for specifying the appearance with the `Font` class, and for controlling formatting with the `StringFormat` class. There is also support for creating and displaying predrawn images using either the `Bitmap` or `Metafile` classes. Such images can be loaded from disk or created on the fly. Finally, we saw how the `Graphics` object can automatically apply a transformation to every drawing operation, making it easy to implement features such as scrolling and zooming, and allowing us to draw sheared and rotated elements even with primitives that provide no direct support for this.

All these facilities enable us to exert a very fine level of control over our components' behavior. In the next two chapters we will see how to further enhance our controls by building in awareness of the development environment, and adding so-called design-time features.

* An *affine transformation* is any transformation that can be applied with a 2×2 matrix, optionally combined with a translation. This allows rotation, scaling, shearing, and translation.

8
Property Grids

Many applications need to present sets of information that can be edited. The data could be patient details in a healthcare system, shape attributes in a drawing program, control properties in a form designer, or any number of other kinds of information. Windows Forms provides a control that makes presenting and editing such data easy, while allowing great flexibility in the way in which information is presented—the `PropertyGrid` control.

Visual Studio .NET itself uses the `PropertyGrid` control to present properties for all controls and other components in the Forms Designer. This means that even if you don't plan to use a `PropertyGrid` directly in your own applications, it is helpful to have a good understanding of how it works so you may control the way your components' properties are presented. Visual Studio .NET lets you customize the appearance of the property pages for your components using the techniques described here.

In this chapter, we will start by looking at how to display the properties of a simple object in a `PropertyGrid`. Then, we will see how to enable editing of custom types by using type converters. Finally, we will see how to add our own custom property editing user interfaces for when a text-based representation is insufficient.

Displaying Simple Objects

The `PropertyGrid` makes it remarkably easy to provide an interface for editing the properties of an object. It uses the CLR's reflection facility to discover what properties are available and presents them automatically. This means that it can be used on simple classes such as those shown in Examples 8-1 and 8-2.

Example 8-1. A simple class using C#

```
public class CustomerDetails
{
    private string firstName, lastName, address;
    private DateTime dob;
```

Example 8-1. A simple class using C# (continued)

```
    public string FirstName
    {
        get { return firstName; }
        set { firstName = value; }
    }

    public string LastName
    {
        get { return lastName; }
        set { lastName = value; }
    }

    public DateTime DateOfBirth
    {
        get { return dob; }
        set { dob = value; }
    }

    public string Address
    {
        get { return address; }
        set { address = value; }
    }
}
```

Example 8-2. A simple class using VB

```
Public Class CustomerDetails

    Private sFirstName, sLastName, sAddress As String
    Private dob As Date

    Public Property FirstName As String
        Get
           Return sFirstName
        End Get
        Set
            sFirstName = Value
        End Set
    End Property

    Public Property LastName As String
        Get
            Return sLastName
        End Get
        Set
            sLastName = value
        End Set
    End Property

    Public Property DateOfBirth As Date
        Get
            Return dob
```

Example 8-2. A simple class using VB (continued)

```
        End Get
        Set
            dob = Value
        End Set
    End Property

    Public Property Address As String
        Get
            Return sAddress
        End Get
        Set
            sAddress = Value
        End Set
    End Property

End Class
```

Displaying an instance of this class in a `PropertyGrid` is trivial. Simply drag a `PropertyGrid` control onto a form, and then in that form's constructor, create an instance of the object you wish to display, and pass it to the grid by setting its `SelectedObject` property, as shown in Example 8-3.

> The `PropertyGrid` control may not appear on your toolbox. To add this control to the toolbox, right-click on the toolbox and select Customize Toolbox.... Select the .NET Framework Components tab and make sure that the checkbox for the Property Grid control is checked.

Example 8-3. Displaying an object in a PropertyGrid

```
// C# code
CustomerDetails cd = new CustomerDetails();
cd.FirstName = "John";
cd.LastName = "D'Oh";
cd.Address = "742, Evergreen Terrace, Springfield";
cd.DateOfBirth = new DateTime(1956, 5, 12);

propertyGrid.SelectedObject = cd;

' VB code
Dim cd As New CustomerDetails()
cd.FirstName = "John"
cd.LastName = "D'Oh"
cd.Address = "742, Evergreen Terrace, Springfield"
cd.DateOfBirth = #5/12/1956#

PropertyGrid1.SelectedObject = cd
```


The property grid will then examine the object and discover that it has four public properties, which it will present for editing as shown in Figure 8-1.

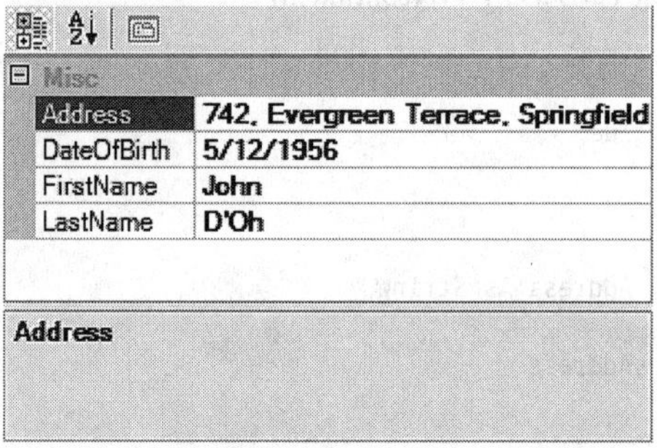
Misc
Address
742, Evergreen Terrace, Springfield
DateOfBirth
5/12/1956
FirstName
John
LastName
D'Oh
Address

Figure 8-1. A simple object in a PropertyGrid

The grid is shown here with its default settings—the toolbar is present along the top, the properties are sorted by category, and the description pane is visible. For the object being displayed, none of this is particularly useful, because the properties are not categorized (which is why everything appears under Misc), and they do not have descriptions. These unused features are easy enough to switch off—setting the `ToolbarVisible` and `HelpVisible` properties to `false` will remove the toolbar and description pane, while setting the `PropertySort` property to `PropertySort.Alphabetical` will prevent the grid from trying to display category names. However, descriptions and categorizations can be very useful, so it would be better to modify our `CustomerDetails` class to make use of them.

The way we supply the `PropertyGrid` with category and description information is to annotate our properties with custom attributes. In fact, we use the same `Category` and `Description` attributes that we would when annotating a control's properties for Visual Studio .NET's benefit, as described in Chapter 5. This should come as no surprise, because the Forms Designer uses a `PropertyGrid` to display a control's properties. So if we add relevant attributes, as shown in Example 8-4, the `PropertyGrid` will use them to display the appropriate categories and descriptions for our object.

Example 8-4. Annotating a property

```
// C# code
[Category("Name")]
[Description("The customer's first name")]
public string FirstName
{
    . . . As before

' VB code
<Category("Name"), _
 Description("The customer's first name")> _
Public Property FirstName As String
    . . . As before
```

These attributes are all defined in the `System.ComponentModel` namespace, so make sure you have a `using` (in C#) or `Imports` (in VB) statement at the top of your file to bring that namespace into scope. Figure 8-2 shows how the PropertyGrid uses these attributes when presenting our object's properties.

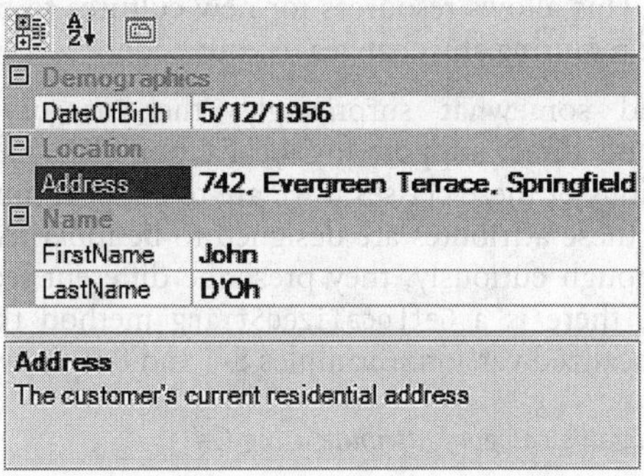
Demographics
DateOfBirth
5/12/1956
Location
Address
742, Evergreen Terrace, Springfield
Name
FirstName
John
LastName
D'Oh
Address
The customer's current residential address

Figure 8-2. Properties shown with categories and descriptions

As with components displayed in Visual Studio .NET, any properties marked with the [Browsable(false)] attribute will not be displayed by default. But this is not the only way of filtering which properties the grid will display—the PropertyGrid control provides a property called BrowsableAttributes. This can be set to an AttributeCollection containing a list of attributes that must be present on a property for it to be displayed. The code shown in Example 8-5 will cause only those properties belonging to the Name category to be shown. (Note that the grid will only show those properties that have *all* the attributes specified. So if you were to build a list with two different category attributes in it, you would end up with nothing in the grid.) You don't have to use category attributes in this list—any kind of attribute can be specified, so if you want to filter properties on some other criteria, you could define your own custom attribute class.

Example 8-5. Filtering on category

```
// C# code
propertyGrid.BrowsableAttributes = new AttributeCollection(
    new Attribute[] { new CategoryAttribute("Name") });

' VB code
PropertyGrid1.BrowsableAttributes = New AttributeCollection( _
    New Attribute( ) {New CategoryAttribute("Name")})
```

The ability to supply category names and descriptions is a powerful usability enhancement. However, the problem with the examples we have seen so far is that they hardcode strings into the source code. This is bad practice because it makes it difficult to display localized versions of the strings when your software runs in other locales. You can avoid this by making localizable versions of these attributes.

Localizable Descriptions and Categories

The strings used for the Category and Description attributes are intended to be read by end users. Unfortunately, they require you to hardcode such strings into your source code, which makes it very awkward to create localized versions of your application. As we saw in Chapter 3, you should retrieve all culture-specific properties from a ResourceManager to allow the appropriate values to be determined at runtime. This allows resources for new cultures to be added as satellite assemblies without requiring any changes to your code.

Unfortunately, and somewhat surprisingly, the Category and Description attributes provide no direct support for localization. We must derive our own culture-aware versions of these classes if we are to support multiple cultures. The classes that define these attributes are designed to be inherited from for localization purposes, although curiously, they prescribe different techniques. With the Category attribute, there is a GetLocalizedString method that we overload in order to supply a localized version. Examples 8-6 and 8-7 show how to do this.

Example 8-6. A localizable category attribute using C#

```
[AttributeUsage(AttributeTargets.All)]
public class LocalizableCategoryAttribute : CategoryAttribute
{
    private Type t;

    public LocalizableCategoryAttribute(string n, Type resBase)
        : base (n)
    {
        t = resBase;
    }

    protected override string GetLocalizedString(string value)
    {
        ResourceManager rm = new ResourceManager(t);
        string tx = rm.GetString(value);
        if (tx != null)
            return tx;

        return base.GetLocalizedString(value);
    }
}
```

Example 8-7. A localizable category attribute using VB

```
<AttributeUsage(AttributeTargets.All)> _
Public Class LocalizableCategoryAttribute
   Inherits CategoryAttribute

   Private t As Type

    Public Sub New(n As String, resBase As Type)
       MyBase.New(n)
       t = resBase
    End Sub

    Protected Overrides Function GetLocalizedString(value As String) As String
```

Example 8-7. A localizable category attribute using VB (continued)

```
        Dim rm As New ResourceManager(t)
        Dim tx As String = rm.GetString(value)
        If tx <> Nothing Then Return tx

        Return MyBase.GetLocalizedString(value)
    End Function
End Class
```

Note that when deriving from an existing attribute, you must redeclare the valid target types, hence, the `AttributeUsage` attribute. (The `Category` attribute declares itself to be valid for all target types, so we follow suit.) The overridden `GetLocalizedString` method just uses a `ResourceManager` to look up the localized version of the string. If this fails, it defers to the base class (which will just return the original string).

To create a `ResourceManager`, we need to supply enough information for the framework to locate the appropriate resource file. The standard way of doing this is to use a `Type` object—resources are typically associated with a type. In Visual Studio .NET the way you manage this is to name the resource file after the class it is to be associated with. So to use localizable resources on our `CustomerDetails` class, we would add a new Assembly Resource File called *CustomerDetails.resx*. Having done this, we can then use the localizable form of this attribute on our class's properties:

```
// C# code
[LocalizableCategory("Name", typeof (CustomerDetails))]
public string FirstName
{
    get { return firstName; }
    set { firstName = value; }
}

' VB code
<LocalizableCategory("Name", GetType(CustomerDetails))> _
Public Property FirstName As String
   Get
      Return sFirstName
   End Get
   Set
      sFirstName = Value
   End Set
End Property
```

So when the `PropertyGrid` control attempts to use our modified `CustomerDetails` object, it will look for the `Category` attribute as usual, but it will actually get our `LocalizableCategory` instead. When the grid asks the attribute for the category name, our `GetLocalizedString` method will be called. This will ask the `ResourceManager` to find a definition for the string that is appropriate to the current locale. If the `ResourceManager` cannot find one, our attribute will just return the unlocalized string. To see this in action, let us add a culture-specific resource file to our project, as shown in Figure 8-3.

	name	value	comment	type	mimetype
▶	Name	Nom	(null)	(null)	(null)
	Demographics	Démographiques	(null)	(null)	(null)
	Location	Location	(null)	(null)	(null)
*					

Figure 8-3. A culture-specific resource file

Figure 8-3 shows a *.resx* file as presented by Visual Studio .NET. This particular file is called *CustomerDetails.fr-FR.resx*. The *fr-FR* part indicates that this file contains French resources. This will cause Visual Studio .NET to compile it into a so-called satellite assembly (a culture-specific resource-only assembly) and place it in the *fr-FR* subdirectory.

> The first *fr* in the resource filename indicates the language: French. The second *FR* indicates the region: France. Region and language are specified independently, because either on its own is not enough—French is spoken in many countries, many of which also speak other languages. For example, Canada (*fr-CA*) or Belgium (*fr-BE*).

If we run our application in a French locale, when the property grid asks our `LocalizableCategory` for the category name, our `GetLocalizedString` method will pass the hardcoded name (e.g., Demographics) to the `GetString` method of the `ResourceManager`. The resource manager will look for a satellite assembly in the *fr-FR* subdirectory because the current culture is French. It will find the satellite assembly containing the resource file shown in Figure 8-3, and will look up the entry whose name is Demographics, and return its value, Démographiques. Consequently, when the property grid appears, the category names appear in French, not in English, as shown in Figure 8-4.

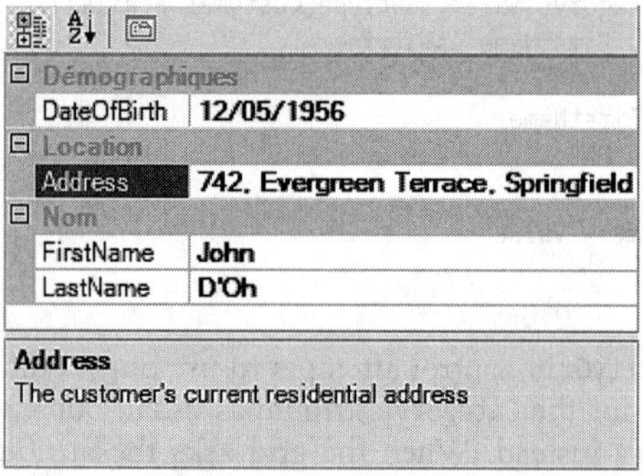
Démographiques
DateOfBirth
12/05/1956
Location
Address
742, Evergreen Terrace, Springfield
Nom
FirstName
John
LastName
D'Oh
Address
The customer's current residential address

Figure 8-4. Translated category names

We are not done yet—the description and property names are still in English. The description can be fixed in much the same way that categories were—we define our own custom attribute that derives from the `Description` attribute. As before, the `Description` attribute was designed to be derived from, so this is relatively straightforward, although for some reason the prescribed way of supporting localization is somewhat different—we are expected to translate the string just once, and store it in a protected property called DescriptionValue. Examples 8-8 and 8-9 show an implementation of this.

Example 8-8. A localizable description attribute using C#

```
[AttributeUsage(AttributeTargets.All)]
public class LocalizableDescriptionAttribute : DescriptionAttribute
{
    private Type t;
    public LocalizableDescriptionAttribute(string name, Type resBase)
      : base(name)
    {
        t = resBase;
    }

    private bool localized = false;
    public override string Description
    {
        get
        {
            if (!localized)
            {
                localized = true;
                ResourceManager rm = new ResourceManager(t);
                string tx = rm.GetString(DescriptionValue);
                if (tx != null)
                    DescriptionValue = tx;
            }
            return base.Description;
        }
    }
}
```

Example 8-9. A localizable description attribute using VB

```
<AttributeUsage(AttributeTargets.All)> _
Public Class LocalizableDescriptionAttribute
   Inherits DescriptionAttribute

   Private t As Type
   Private localized As Boolean = False

   Public Sub New(ByVal name As String, _
                  ByVal resBase As Type)
     MyBase.New(name)
      t = resBase
   End Sub

   Public Overrides ReadOnly Property Description( ) As String
      Get
         If Not localized Then
            localized = True
```

Property Grids

Example 8-9. A localizable description attribute using VB (continued)

```
            Dim rm As New ResourceManager(t)
            Dim tx As String = rm.GetString(DescriptionValue)
            If Not tx Is Nothing Then DescriptionValue = tx
         End If
         Return MyBase.Description
      End Get
   End Property
End Class
```

This conforms to the idiom required by the `Description` attribute, and it works in a slightly curious fashion. In our override of the `Description` property's get method, we are required to read the `DescriptionValue` property, translate it, and then write back the translated value. We must then defer to the base class's get implementation, which just returns the value of `DescriptionValue`. This is a somewhat roundabout way of doing things, but it is what the documentation for `DescriptionAttribute` instructs us to do.

Apart from the slightly peculiar way in which the overridden `Description` property works, this class uses the same technique as we used for our localizable category—it relies on a `ResourceManager` to find the appropriate string for the current culture. However, you will probably want to use this attribute slightly differently, as Example 8-10 shows.

Example 8-10. Using a localizable description attribute

```
// C#
[LocalizableDescription("LastName.Description",
                        typeof(CustomerDetails))]
public string LastName
{
    . . . as before

' VB
<LocalizableDescription("LastName.Description", _
                        GetType(CustomerDetails))> _
Public Property LastName( ) As String
    . . . as before
```

Example 8-10 shows the `LocalizableDescription` attribute in use. Notice that the string being supplied to the attribute (`LastName.Description`) is not the full description. This is because, for non-English cultures, this string will be used to look up the translated string. Using a full English sentence as a key to look up information is error prone (not to mention inefficient). There is nothing stopping you from using the full sentence in the attribute, it is just that you are more likely to run into problems. (However, it does have the advantage that you don't need to supply an entry for the string in the default resources.) If you use the technique shown in Example 8-10 you will obviously need to supply entries for these strings in your neutral resources (i.e., the resources compiled into the main executable, not a satellite assembly) so that the correct strings appear for your default culture.

As Figure 8-5 shows, both the category names and the descriptions are now localized. However, we are still not quite done. The property names are still displayed in English. To change this, we will need to use something called a `TypeConverter`, which enables us to modify the way in which a `PropertyGrid` presents properties. In fact, we can do far more with a `TypeConverter` than just changing the displayed name of the property.

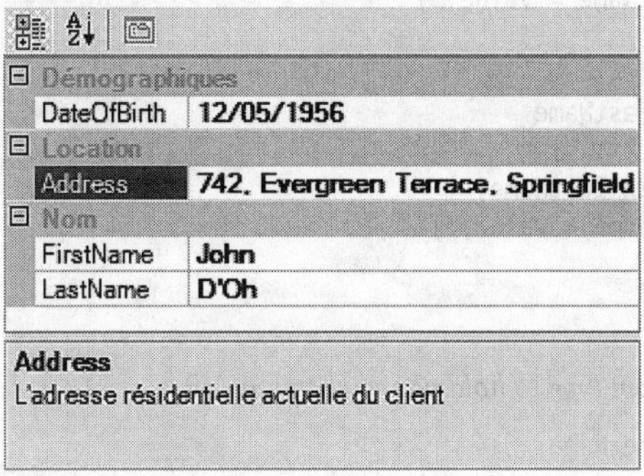

Démographiques
DateOfBirth
12/05/1956
Location
Address
742, Evergreen Terrace, Springfield
Nom
FirstName
John
LastName
D'Oh
Address
L'adresse résidentielle actuelle du client

Figure 8-5. Translated categories and descriptions

Type Conversion

The `PropertyGrid` is able to edit many different kinds of data, and can provide special-purpose user interfaces for certain types. For example, the `CustomerDetails` class shown earlier has a `DateTime` or `Date` field, and the `PropertyGrid` can display a date picker control when you edit this control. It supports all the built-in types, and all the types used on common properties on controls. It is also possible to extend its capabilities so that it can edit new types.

The `PropertyGrid` turns out not to have a long list of types that it knows how to display and edit. The control itself knows nothing about, say, the `DateTime` or `Color` types, and yet it is still able to present them for editing. This is because it has a very flexible open architecture that allows any type to make itself editable.

A type can provide various levels of support for the `PropertyGrid`, even going as far as supplying a special-purpose user interface for editing that type (like the pickers that appear for `Color` and `ContentAlignment`). We will see how to do that later, but for many types, simple text editing will suffice. So at the bare minimum, our type must support conversion to and from text—its value will be converted to text when it is first displayed in the grid. If the user changes that text, the new `string` must be converted back to an instance of our type for the edit to take effect.

We will now introduce a custom type to the `CustomerDetails` example and then add support for basic type conversion to and from a string. Rather than storing the customer name as first and last name strings, we will define a separate `CustomerName` type, as shown in Examples 8-11 and 8-12. The `CustomerDetails` class defined in Examples 8-1 and 8-2 will be modified to expose a single property `Name` of type `CustomerName` instead of the original `FirstName` and `LastName` properties. This `CustomerName` class is shown in Examples 8-11 and 8-12.

Example 8-11. Custom type to hold name written in C#

```
public class CustomerName
{
    private string firstName, lastName;
    public string FirstName
    {
        get { return firstName; }
        set { firstName = value; }
    }

    public string LastName
    {
        get { return lastName; }
        set { lastName = value; }
    }
}
```

Example 8-12. Custom type to hold name written in VB

```
Public Class CustomerName
   Private sFirstName, sLastName As String

   Public Property FirstName( ) As String
      Get
         Return sFirstName
      End Get
      Set
         sFirstName = Value
      End Set
   End Property

   Public Property LastName( ) As STring
      Get
         Return sLastName
      End Get
      Set
         sLastName = Value
      End Set
   End Property
End Class
```

So far we have not provided any support for the benefit of `PropertyGrid`. Consequently, when we display the modified `CustomerDetails` in the grid, its Name field is not especially helpful. Figure 8-6 shows how the property will be displayed.

Name
CustomerName

Figure 8-6. An unsupported type in a PropertyGrid

The field is displayed, but not with any useful information—just the name of the field's type. The reason that the type name has appeared is that `PropertyGrid` just calls the `ToString` method on types it doesn't know how to deal with, and the default implementation of ToString is to return the type name. We can override this in the CustomerName class easily enough to provide some more useful information:

```
// C# code
public override string ToString( )
{
    return string.Format("{0}, {1}", LastName, FirstName);
}

' VB code
Public Overrides Function ToString( ) As String
   Return String.Format("{0}, {1}", LastName, FirstName)
End Function
```

This improves matters slightly—as you can see in Figure 8-7, the grid now shows a meaningful representation of the property's value. But it is grayed out, and the PropertyGrid will not let the user edit the text. This is because although the PropertyGrid was able to convert our type to a string by calling ToString, it does not know how to convert a string back to an instance of our type. It cannot allow the value to be edited because it has no way of writing the edited value back into our object.

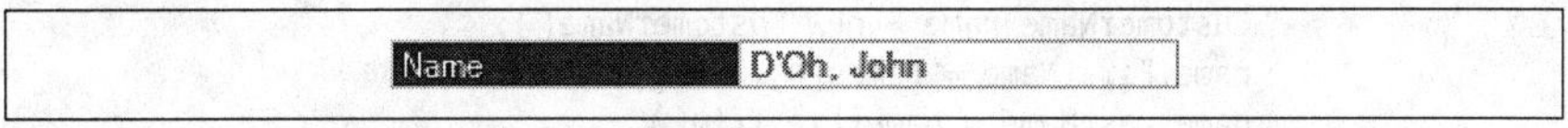
Name
D'Oh, John

Figure 8-7. Using ToString in a PropertyGrid

To allow our CustomerName type to be edited in a PropertyGrid, we will need to provide a conversion facility allowing the property to be set using a string. We do this by writing a class that derives from TypeConverter. Examples 8-13 and 8-14 show how to do this for our type. It overrides two methods. First, it overrides CanConvertFrom—this method can be called to find out whether a particular source type can be converted into our CustomerName type. The PropertyGrid control will call this method to find out whether it will be able to convert from a string to a CustomerName—values are typically edited as text on a property grid. So we test the *sourceType* parameter and return true if it we are being asked to convert to a string.

Example 8-13. A custom TypeConverter using C#

```
public class CustomerNameConverter : TypeConverter
{
    public override bool CanConvertFrom(
        ITypeDescriptorContext context, Type sourceType)
    {
        return sourceType == typeof(string);
    }

    public override object ConvertFrom(
        ITypeDescriptorContext context, CultureInfo culture,
        object value)
    {
        if (value == null)
            return null;
```

Example 8-13. A custom TypeConverter using C# (continued)

```
        // Make sure this is a string
        string sval = value as string;
        if (sval == null)
            throw new NotSupportedException("Unsupported type");

        // If comma is present, treat this as "Last, First"
        string[] names = sval.Split(',');
        if (names.Length == 2)
        {
            CustomerName name = new CustomerName( );
            name.LastName = names[0].Trim( );
            name.FirstName = names[1].Trim( );
            return name;
        }
        else if (names.Length == 1)
        {
            // No comma, must be "First Last"
            names = sval.Split(' ');
            if (names.Length == 2)
            {
                CustomerName name = new CustomerName( );
                name.FirstName = names[0].Trim( );
                name.LastName = names[1].Trim( );
                return name;
            }
        }
        // Unable to make sense of the string
        throw new NotSupportedException("Invalid format");

    }
}
```

Example 8-14. A custom TypeConverter using VB

```
Public Class CustomerNameConverter
    Inherits TypeConverter

    Public Overloads Overrides Function CanConvertFrom( _
            context As ITypeDescriptorContext, _
            sourceType As Type) _
            As Boolean
        Return sourceType Is GetType(String)
    End Function

    Public Overloads Overrides Function ConvertFrom( _
            context As ITypeDescriptorContext, _
            culture As CultureInfo, _
            value As Object) _
            As Object

        If value Is Nothing Then Return Nothing
```

Example 8-14. A custom TypeConverter using VB (continued)

```
        ' Make sure this is a string
        Dim sVal As String
        If TypeName(value) <> "String" Then
            Throw New NotSupportedException("Unsupported type")
        Else
            sVal = DirectCast(value, String)
        End If

        ' If comma is present, treat this as "Last, First"
        Dim names( ) As String = sval.Split(","c)
        If names.Length = 2 Then
            Dim name As New CustomerName( )
            name.LastName = names(0).Trim( )
            name.FirstName = names(1).Trim( )
            Return name
        Else If names.Length = 1 Then
            ' No comma, must be "First Last"
            names = sval.Split(" "c)
            If names.Length = 2 Then
                Dim name As New CustomerName( )
                name.FirstName = names(0).Trim( )
                name.LastName = names(1).Trim( )
                Return name
            End If
        End If
        ' Unable to make sense of the string
        Throw New NotSupportedException("Invalid format")
    End Function
End Class
```

The second method that we override is the `ConvertFrom` method. This is where we do the conversion, parsing the string to create a `CustomerName`. (This particular example allows the name to be passed in two formats: "First Last" and "Last, First." It uses the presence or absence of a comma to work out which format is being used.)

There are two other methods we might consider overriding here: `CanConvertTo` and `ConvertTo`. These perform the reverse transformation; for `CustomerNameConverter`, this means converting from a `CustomerName` to a `string`. In this case, there is no need to override these—the implementation supplied by the base class, `TypeConverter`, already handles conversion to a `string` by calling `ToString`. Because we provided a suitable `ToString` method on `CustomerName`, we don't need to add anything here. But if you wanted to support editing of a type whose `ToString` method returned an inappropriate value, you could bypass it by overriding `ConvertTo` in the `TypeConverter`. (Because the default `CanConvertTo` method always returns `true` for `string`, you do not need to override it when providing custom string conversion in `ConvertTo`. You would only need to override `CanConvertTo` if you decide to support other conversions.)

This `TypeConverter` now provides the conversion facilities required by the `PropertyGrid`. The only remaining question is this: how does the `PropertyGrid` know that it should use this `CustomerNameConverter` when editing a `CustomerName`?

It won't just guess from the class names—it needs a more positive hint than that. The answer is that when the PropertyGrid encounters a data type that it doesn't intrinsically know how to deal with, it will look to see if that type has the TypeConverter attribute. So we can use this to annotate our CustomerName class, as shown in Example 8-15.

Example 8-15. Associating a type with its TypeConverter

```
// C# code
[TypeConverter(typeof(CustomerNameConverter))]
public class CustomerName
{
    . . . as before

' VB code
<TypeConverter(GetType(CustomerNameConverter))> _
Public Class CustomerName
    . . . as before
```

If the TypeConverter attribute is present, the PropertyGrid will use the converter that it specifies to do all conversion to and from strings. With this attribute in place, our Name field becomes editable. When we make a change to the Name field, the PropertyGrid will pass the edited text to the ConvertFrom method of the CustomerNameConverter, which will parse the string and build a new CustomerName based on its contents. In other words, our property can now be edited like any other.

The PropertyGrid control will search for the TypeConverter attribute both on the definition of the type being edited, and also on the property. This can be useful for two reasons. If your class has a property of a type whose definition you don't control, that type may well not have an associated converter. This is not a problem, because you can write your own converter and just specify it on the property where you use the type in question, as Example 8-16 shows. Similarly, you might be using a type you didn't write that does have an associated converter, but for some reason you need to use a different one (e.g., to deal with localization issues). The PropertyGrid will check for the TypeConverter attribute on the property first, so you can replace a type's default converter with your own.

Example 8-16. Specifying a converter on a property

```
// C# code
public class CustomerDetails
{
    private CustomerName name;
    private string address;
    private DateTime dob;

    [TypeConverter(typeof(CustomerNameConverter))]
    public CustomerName Name
    {
        get { return name; }
        set { name = value; }
    }
```

Example 8-16. Specifying a converter on a property (continued)

```
    . . . as before
}

' VB code
Public Class CustomerDetails

    Private oName As New CustomerName()
    Private sAddress As String
    Private dob As Date

    <TypeConverter(GetType(CustomerNameConverter))> _
    Public Property Name() As CustomerName
        Get
            Return oName
        End Get
        Set(ByVal Value As CustomerName)
            oName = Value
        End Set
    End Property

    . . . . as before
```

Being able to edit a `CustomerName` is good, but we can do better. Windows Forms often uses similar properties—just as `CustomerName` has its `FirstName` and `LastName` properties, the `Size` property of a form also has some subproperties, `Width` and `Height`. And while you can edit a control's size by typing in the width and height as a single string, it also allows the `Size` property to be expanded, with the `Width` and `Height` properties displayed as children. We can do exactly the same thing—`PropertyGrid` lets any property display such nested properties. All we need to do is supply an appropriate `TypeConverter`.

Nested Properties

A *nested property* is any property of an object that itself is a property of some other object. For example, the `Name` property on our `CustomerDetails` type has two nested properties, `FirstName` and `LastName`. The property grid is able to make properties such as `Name` expandable—a plus sign can be added, and when clicked, it will show the nested properties in the grid.

This facility is enabled by using an appropriate `TypeConverter`. The simplest approach is to use the converter supplied by the system for this purpose—`ExpandableObjectConverter`:

```
[TypeConverter(typeof(ExpandableObjectConverter))]
public class CustomerName
{
    . . . as before
```

This will use reflection to discover what properties are available, and supply these to the `PropertyGrid`, enabling it to display them as shown in Figure 8-8.

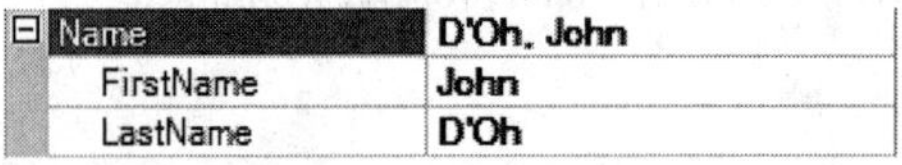
Name
D'Oh, John
FirstName
John
LastName
D'Oh

Figure 8-8. Nested properties in a PropertyGrid

There are two problems with this. First, because we are no longer using the purpose-built `CustomerNameConverter` (we replaced that with `ExpandableObjectConverter`) the `PropertyGrid` no longer has any way of converting text back to a `CustomerName`—the `ExpandableObjectConverter` has no knowledge of the parsing rules we are using for the conversion. This means that the text against the `Name` field in the grid is no longer editable; the `Name` property can only be changed by editing its nested properties. Second, the `PropertyGrid` will not update the text next to the `Name` field when you edit either the `FirstName` or `LastName` fields because it doesn't know that the fields are related.

The simple way to solve both of these problems is to change the `CustomerName` class's `ToString` method to return an empty string. This makes the fact that the `Name` field cannot be edited less obtrusive, because there will be nothing there to edit. And if the field is always empty, it no longer matters that it isn't updated when the nested properties change.

However, we can do better than this. Properties of type `Size` and `Position` allow their values to be edited either as a whole or through their nested properties. We can provide the same flexibility with our own types. To make sure that the main property value is refreshed every time one of its nested properties changes, simply mark all nested properties with the `RefreshProperties` attribute:

```
[RefreshProperties(RefreshProperties.Repaint)]
public string FirstName
{
    . . . as before
```

This will cause the `PropertyGrid` to check the parent property's value after the nested property changes, and update the display if necessary. But having done this, we still need to arrange for the parent property (`Name` in this case) to be editable directly. What we really want is a type converter that has the nested object facility of the `ExpandableObjectConverter`, but that also has the parsing logic of our `CustomerNameConverter`. This is easy to achieve—simply modify the `CustomerNameConverter` so that it inherits from `ExpandableObjectConverter`, and change the `TypeConverter` attribute on the `CustomerName` class back to refer to `CustomerNameConverter`, as in Example 8-15.

Although our nested properties now appear to be behaving in the same way as `Size` and similar standard properties, there is a more subtle difference: the framework tends to use value types for such properties, but our `CustomerName` is a class. Unfortunately, if you try to change `CustomerName` to be a value type, you will find that this example stops working. This is because value types require special treatment when used in a `PropertyGrid`.

Value types

Some properties use value types—there are several examples in the Control class alone (Location, Size, and Bounds, for example; their respective types are Point, Size, and Rectangle, which are all value types). But these are slightly trickier for the PropertyGrid to use—nested properties don't work without special treatment. This is mainly because to change a value type property, you must update the whole property. (If you retrieve the Size property, and then change the Width, you will simply be changing the Width in your local copy of the Size. You must then write this modified Size back to update the property.)

Suppose that CustomerName were a value type, and that we wished to display its nested properties in a PropertyGrid as before. If the user modifies the FirstName nested property of the Name, the grid somehow has to apply that change back to the property. It cannot modify the FirstName in situ*—its only option is to build a CustomerName with the correct value and assign that to the Name. But how is it supposed to know how to create a CustomerName? Again, the TypeConverter comes to the rescue—it has two methods we can override to provide the PropertyGrid with the facility that it requires. Examples 8-17 and 8-18 illustrate this.

Example 8-17. Supporting value types in a TypeConverter using C#

```
public override bool GetCreateInstanceSupported(
    ITypeDescriptorContext context)
{
    return true;
}

public override object CreateInstance(
    ITypeDescriptorContext context,
    System.Collections.IDictionary propertyValues)
{
    CustomerName n = new CustomerName( );
    n.FirstName = (string) propertyValues["FirstName"];
    n.LastName = (string) propertyValues["LastName"];
    return n;
}
```

Example 8-18. Supporting value types in a TypeConverter using VB

```
Public Overrides Overloads Function GetCreateInstanceSupported( _
       context As ITypeDescriptorContext) _
       As Boolean
    Return True
End Function

Public Overrides Overloads Function CreateInstance( _
       context As ITypeDescriptorContext, _
       propertyValues As System.Collections.IDictionary) _
```

* This is for exactly the same reason that you can't do it in code. If you tried to write customer.Name.FirstName = "Fred"; the compiler would complain that this is not possible because the Name property uses a value type.

Property Grids

Example 8-18. Supporting value types in a TypeConverter using VB (continued)

```
        As Object
    Dim n As New CustomerName()
    n.FirstName = CStr(propertyValues("FirstName"))
    n.LastName = CStr(propertyValues("LastName"))
    Return n
End Function
```

Examples 8-17 and 8-18 illustrate how to provide support for a value type in a `TypeConverter`. The `PropertyGrid` will call the `GetCreateInstanceSupported` method to find out whether our converter provides a value creation facility. We simply return `true` to indicate that we do. We then supply the `CreateInstance` method, which it will call when it needs us to create a new value. For example, if the user edits the `FirstName` nested property, the `PropertyGrid` will call `CreateInstance`. It will pass in an `IDictionary`* containing the modified `FirstName` value and the original `LastName` value as strings. We convert these strings back into a complete `CustomerName` that the `PropertyGrid` can then use to set the `Name` property on the `CustomerDetails` object.

You do not need to use the `RefreshProperties` attribute on the properties of value types. This is because the parent property is always updated in its entirety whenever any of the nested properties change, so the grid always refreshes it.

The `ExpandableObjectConverter` type provides a convenient way of allowing nested properties to be edited, but there is nothing magic about it—it just overrides a couple of methods of the `TypeConverter` class that are there to support nested properties. It can be useful to do this yourself if you need more control over the way in which properties are presented. For example, this is the only way to make your property names localizable. So we will now look in a little more detail at the mechanism on which nested properties are based.

Property Descriptors

The `PropertyGrid` control always uses the objects that it presents through a level of indirection. Instead of accessing properties directly (or as directly as is possible using reflection), it always goes through a `PropertyDescriptor`. You can control exactly what descriptors the `PropertyGrid` gets to see, or even create your own descriptors, simply by overriding the appropriate methods of your class's `TypeConverter`. This allows you to customize how the `PropertyGrid` sees your type, and therefore to control how it appears in the grid.

Whenever it displays any object (whether it is the main object or an object supplying nested properties), the `PropertyGrid` first obtains a set of `PropertyDescriptor` objects to determine what needs to be shown in the grid. It will attempt to get this list from the object's associated `TypeConverter` (if it has one). First, it will call the converter's `GetPropertiesSupported` method to find out whether this particular `TypeConverter` is able to supply property descriptors. If the `GetPropertiesSupported` method returns `true`, it will then call `GetProperties` to retrieve a list of `PropertyDescriptor` objects. The grid will display whatever

* This is just a collection of (name, value) pairs.

properties are in this list, regardless of what properties the object might really have. (If it is unable to get these descriptors from a converter, it falls back to calling the TypeDescriptor class's GetProperties method for the main object in the grid, which builds the list using reflection; for nested objects, it falls back to not displaying any properties at all.)

This means that by supplying a type converter and overriding these two methods, we have complete control over what properties the grid will display. We can filter the properties, modify how they will appear, or even fake them up entirely. If we create a PropertyDescriptor for which there is no real underlying property, the grid will never know, because it never interacts with properties directly—it always goes through a PropertyDescriptor.

> Building fake descriptors is somewhat harder than filtering because this requires you to write your own class that inherits from PropertyDescriptor. This is not completely trivial, because PropertyDescriptor has many abstract methods. However, TypeConverter provides a nested class, SimplePropertyDescriptor, that makes it much easier. It derives from PropertyDescriptor for you and provides implementations for most of the methods. If you plan to create your own property descriptors, it is usually easiest to use SimplePropertyDescriptor as a base class.
>
> Unfortunately, Visual Basic .NET currently has a limitation that prevents it from using this class. SimplePropertyDescriptor is a defined as a *protected* nested class. According to the .NET type system rules, this means that the only way to define a class derived from SimplePropertyDescriptor is to make that derived class a nested class inside a class that derives from TypeConverter. This works fine in C#, but Visual Basic unfortunately does not support this, due to a bug in the compiler. Until this bug is fixed, there is no way of using the SimplePropertyDescriptor class in Visual Basic .NET. Consequently, the examples in this section will be in C# only.

The ExpandableObjectConverter just builds a list of property descriptors for whichever object it is being asked to represent. This is trivial, because the TypeDescriptor class will do this for you. Example 8-19 shows a custom TypeConverter that is exactly equivalent to the ExpandableObjectConverter.

Example 8-19. Do-it-yourself ExpandableObjectConverter

```
public class MyExpandableObjectConverter : TypeConverter
{
    public override bool GetPropertiesSupported(
        ITypeDescriptorContext context)
    {
        return true;
    }

    public override PropertyDescriptorCollection GetProperties(
        ITypeDescriptorContext context, object value,
        Attribute[] attributes)
```

Example 8-19. Do-it-yourself ExpandableObjectConverter (continued)

```
    {
        return TypeDescriptor.GetProperties(value, attributes, true);
    }
}
```

This is not especially useful as it stands—you might as well use the built-in `ExpandableObjectConverter` class. However, not only is it interesting to see how easy it is to provide property descriptors, it can also act as a useful starting point. It is fairly easy to modify this class to build a `TypeConverter` that provides filtered views by removing items from the collection returned by the `TypeDescriptor` class. For example, we can use this facility to complete what we started earlier: we can write a `TypeConverter` that makes property names localizable.

Localization with property descriptors

Earlier in this chapter, we saw how to create localizable versions of the `Category` and `Description` attributes. This enabled the category names and property descriptions to be shown in the appropriate language for the current culture. We will now finish the job by writing a `TypeConverter` that can localize the property names displayed in the grid.

This seems as though it might be a hard problem—after all, the names of a class's properties are part of the source code and are not easily modifiable through the normal localization techniques. Fortunately, as we have just seen, the `PropertyGrid` does not access properties directly—it always goes through a level of indirection in the form of a `PropertyDescriptor`. All we need to do is provide a `TypeConverter` that supplies `PropertyDescriptor` objects with the names we want.

The `PropertyDescriptor` class was designed with this kind of thing in mind, because it supports two different names for any property. The descriptor's `Name` property is the real name, i.e., the name in the source code. But is also has a `DisplayName` property, which is the name that is to be displayed in the user interface whenever this property is shown. The `PropertyGrid` always uses the `DisplayName`, so all we need to do is make sure that it contains the localized version of the property name.

Although the framework supplies some classes that derive from `PropertyDescriptor`, none of the concrete ones allows the `DisplayName` to be different from the `Name`. This means we will have to write our own. Fortunately, we are writing one as part of a `TypeConverter`—this is good because `TypeConverter` provides a useful abstract base class for writing your own `PropertyDescriptor`, called `TypeConverter.SimplePropertyDescriptor`. This does most of the work we require, so we only need to write a small amount of code to build a concrete class derived from `PropertyDescriptor` that meets our needs.

> `TypeConverter.SimplePropertyDescriptor` is a nested class of `TypeConverter`, and it is marked as `protected`. This means that a class that derives from `TypeConverter.SimplePropertyDescriptor` must be a nested classes defined inside a class derived from `TypeConverter`.

Before we look at the code, we will consider how our localizing TypeConverter will be used in practice. We want it to be simple, having as little impact as possible on code that uses it. This complicates the implementation a little, but this converter only has to be written once, whereas the client code will be written everywhere that our converter is used, so it makes sense to complicate the converter to simplify its use. If we call our custom converter LocalizableTypeConverter, client code will look like this:

```
[TypeConverter(typeof(LocalizableTypeConverter))]
public class CustomerDetails
{
    public CustomerName Name { . . . }
    public DateTime DateOfBirth { . . . }
    . . .
}
```

In other words, the impact is no worse than supporting any other TypeConverter. There is one snag with this—because our TypeConverter will be localizing strings, it will need to create a ResourceManager. In order to create a resource manager, we need access to a Type object (or at least an Assembly). Fortunately, our TypeConverter will be able to discover the type of the class it has been attached to, and it can use that as its resource source. So in this case, it would use CustomerDetails. While this makes for a minimum of code, it does rather increase the number of *.resx* files you will need in your project—it will require a resource file for every class that uses this converter. So we will therefore define an optional custom attribute that allows a different type to be specified as the basis for resources. Example 8-20 shows a type that uses this attribute to share a resource file with the CustomerDetails class.

Example 8-20. Specifying a type for resource location

```
[TypeConverter(typeof(LocalizableTypeConverter))]
[LocalizationResourceType(typeof(CustomerDetails))]
public class CustomerName
{
    . . . as before
```

These attributes are all that we will require the client code to use. Our localizing type converter will use the real names of the properties to look up the localized names in the resource manager. So simply adding entries in the culture-specific resource file mapping, say, Name to Nom, will be all that is required to localize the property names.

Let us look at the code for the LocalizableTypeConverter and associated classes. Rather than presenting all the code in one go, we will look at it one piece at a time. Don't worry—there are no missing pieces. First is the LocalizationResourceType attribute, which is shown in Example 8-21.

Example 8-21. The LocalizationResourceType attribute

```
[AttributeUsage(AttributeTargets.All)]
public class LocalizationResourceTypeAttribute : Attribute
{
    private Type t;

    public LocalizationResourceTypeAttribute(Type resBase)
    {
        t = resBase;
    }

    public Type ResBase { get { return t; } }
}
```

This is a straightforward custom attribute that holds a `Type` object for the benefit of the `TypeConverter`. Example 8-20 shows how this attribute will be used. This is just a perfectly normal and not very exciting custom attribute class, so we will move on to the converter's class declaration and its one field:

```
public class LocalizableTypeConverter : TypeConverter
{
    private Type resBase = null;
```

Our class inherits from `TypeConverter`, because it is a type converter. The `resBase` field is used to hold the `Type` object for the class that will be used to initialize a `ResourceManager`. This will determine the name of the resource file that will contain the localized versions of the names. Next is the first override:

```
public override bool GetPropertiesSupported(
    ITypeDescriptorContext context)
{
    return true;
}
```

Here we are simply indicating that our `TypeConverter` will supply `PropertyDescriptor` objects. The whole purpose of this class is to supply the `PropertyGrid` with appropriately tweaked descriptors, but it will only ask us for descriptors if we return true from this method, as we did in Example 8-19. Next is the `GetProperties` method, where we create our descriptors:

```
public override PropertyDescriptorCollection GetProperties(
    ITypeDescriptorContext context, object value,
    Attribute[] attributes)
{
    EnsureAttrsRead(value);
    PropertyDescriptorCollection pdc;
    pdc = TypeDescriptor.GetProperties(value, attributes, true);
    PropertyDescriptor[] props = new PropertyDescriptor[pdc.Count];
    for (int i = 0; i < pdc.Count; ++i)
    {
        Attribute[] attrs = new Attribute[pdc[i].Attributes.Count];
        pdc[i].Attributes.CopyTo(attrs, 0);
```

```
            props[i] = new LocalizablePropertyDescriptor(resBase,
                pdc[i], attrs);
        }
        PropertyDescriptorCollection pdcOut =
            new PropertyDescriptorCollection(props);

        return pdcOut;
    }
```

The EnsureAttrsRead method, shown below, makes sure that we have checked for the presence of the LocalizationResourceType attribute before proceeding. We use the TypeDescriptor class to provide us with a complete set of nonlocalized PropertyDescriptor objects. We will rely on these to do most of the work, because we only want to change one aspect of their behavior; most of this function is concerned with building a copy of the information associated with these descriptors. So we build a new list of descriptors, using our LocalizablePropertyDescriptor class (shown later). This is the class that will provide the localized name in its DisplayName property.

Next, the EnsureAttrsRead method checks for the LocalizationResourceType attribute:

```
    private void EnsureAttrsRead(object o)
    {
        if (resBase == null)
        {
            object[] attr = o.GetType( ).GetCustomAttributes(
                typeof(LocalizationResourceTypeAttribute), true);
            if (attr != null && attr.Length != 0)
            {
                resBase = ((LocalizationResourceTypeAttribute)
                                attr[0]).ResBase;
            }
            if (resBase == null)
                resBase = o.GetType( );
        }
    }
```

This method is passed a single parameter: the object whose property names we are translating. It checks to see if that object's type definition has the LocalizationResourceType attribute. If it does, we store the Type object that it specifies in the resBase field. If the attribute is not present, we fall back to using the Type of the object itself.

Next is the descriptor class itself. Rather than deriving directly from PropertyDescriptor, we use the helper base class provided by TypeConverter:

```
    private class LocalizablePropertyDescriptor :
                TypeConverter.SimplePropertyDescriptor
    {
        private Type resBase;
        private string localizedName = null;
        private PropertyDescriptor realProp;
```

```
        public LocalizablePropertyDescriptor(Type resBase,
            PropertyDescriptor prop, Attribute[] attributes)
          : base (prop.ComponentType, prop.Name,
                prop.PropertyType, attributes)
        {
            this.resBase = resBase;
            realProp = prop;
        }
```

As before, the resBase property holds the Type object that will be used to initialize the ResourceManager. The localizedName field will hold the localized name once it has been looked up—we cache it here to avoid doing the lookup more than once. The realProp class holds a reference to the original PropertyDescriptor returned by TypeDescriptor.GetProperties—we rely on this because our class does nothing more than localizing the display name. It defers to the real descriptor for everything else.

The TypeConverter.SimplePropertyDescriptor class provides implementations for most of the abstract methods of PropertyDescriptor, but not GetValue or SetValue. This is because it doesn't presume that your descriptor will necessarily represent a real property, so it lets you implement them however you like. We just defer to the original PropertyDescriptor, which will just read and write the property respectively:

```
    public override object GetValue(object component)
    {
        return realProp.GetValue(component);
    }
    public override void SetValue(object component, object value)
    {
        realProp.SetValue(component, value);
    }
```

Finally, we come to the part that this has all been building up to—the DisplayName property where we substitute the localized version of the name:

```
    public override string DisplayName
    {
        get
        {
            if (localizedName == null)
            {
                ResourceManager rm = new ResourceManager(resBase);
                string tx = rm.GetString(base.DisplayName);
                if (tx != null)
                    localizedName = tx;
                else
                    localizedName = base.DisplayName;
            }
            return localizedName;
        }
    }
```

This looks almost identical to the core of the localizable category and description attributes. This is because they do much the same thing—we obtain a resource manager and use it to look up the localized string. This descriptor makes sure that it only does this lookup once, by caching the result in the `localizedName` property.

So with this code in place, and the relevant attributes in use, all that is required are some suitable entries in the culture-specific resource file as shown in Figure 8-9. Our `PropertyGrid` is now fully localized, as Figure 8-10 shows. (The property values still look remarkably un-French, but because values are usually supplied by the user, it is not our job to localize them.)

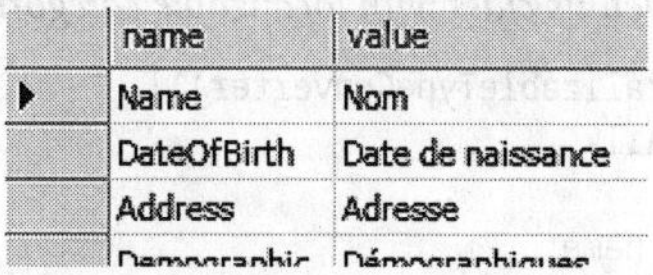
name
value
Name
Nom
DateOfBirth
Date de naissance
Address
Adresse

Figure 8-9. Localized strings for property names

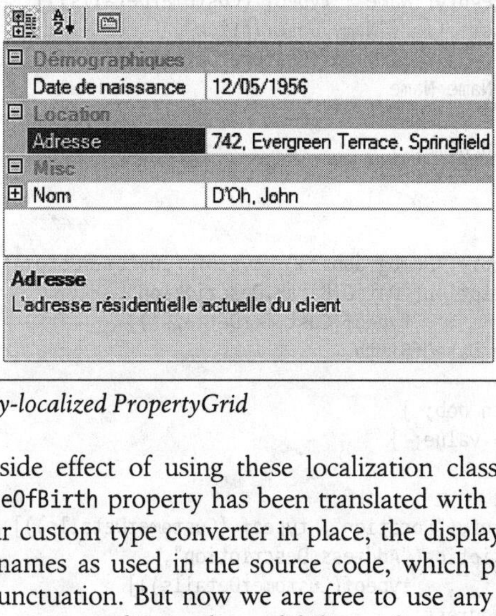
Démographiques
Date de naissance
12/05/1956
Location
Adresse
742, Evergreen Terrace, Springfield
Misc
Nom
D'Oh, John
Adresse
L'adresse résidentielle actuelle du client

Figure 8-10. The fully-localized PropertyGrid

There is a useful side effect of using these localization classes. Notice how in Figure 8-10 the `DateOfBirth` property has been translated with spaces between the words. Without our custom type converter in place, the displayed property names were just the real names as used in the source code, which precludes the use of spaces and most punctuation. But now we are free to use any text we like as the display name. You can employ such readability enhancements in your native language—the `ResourceManager` is quite happy to look up resources even in the default culture, so long as you provide an appropriate *.resx* file. So if you supply a culture-neutral resource file, you can create entries mapping "DateOfBirth" onto "Date of Birth." So the fact that these classes allow you to decouple the display name from the real name is useful even when not translating text to another language.

> A culture-neutral resource file is one without a culture in the file name, such as *CustomerDetails.resx*. Such resources are built into the main assembly, not satellite assemblies.

There is one limitation with these classes. If you use the LocalizableTypeConverter, you can no longer use other converters, such as the ExpandableObject or converters of your own devising. For the latter this is fairly easy to fix—simply modify your own converters to inherit from LocalizableTypeConverter instead of TypeConverter. Of course, you can't do this with ExpandableObject—only Microsoft gets to decide what that derives from. Fortunately, LocalizableTypeConverter already does everything that ExpandableObject does, so in practice it doesn't matter.

Our CustomerDetails class has evolved since the version shown in Example 8-1, so Example 8-22 shows the modified class with all the relevant attributes in place.

Example 8-22. CustomerDetails class with localizable categories and descriptions

```
[TypeConverter(typeof(LocalizableTypeConverter))]
public class CustomerDetails
{
    private CustomerName name;
    private string address;
    private DateTime dob;

    [LocalizableCategory("Name", typeof (CustomerDetails))]
    [LocalizableDescription("Name.Description",
                            typeof(CustomerDetails))]
    public CustomerName Name
    {
        get { return name; }
        set { name = value; }
    }

    [LocalizedCategory("Demographics", typeof (CustomerDetails))]
    [LocalizedDescription("DateOfBirth.Description",
                          typeof(CustomerDetails))]
    public DateTime DateOfBirth
    {
        get { return dob; }
        set { dob = value; }
    }

    [LocalizedCategory("Location", typeof (CustomerDetails))]
    [LocalizedDescription("Address.Description",
                          typeof(CustomerDetails))]
    public string Address
    {
        get { return address; }
        set { address = value; }
    }

}
```

So, we have seen how to control which properties appear in the grid, what they are called, and how type conversions occur when moving data to and from the grid. But so far, the user interface for each individual property has consisted of nothing more exciting than an editable text field. We will now see how to add our own editing user interfaces to items on a PropertyGrid.

Custom Type Editors

The PropertyGrid allows us to replace the built-in text-based editing. We can assign a custom editor that supplies its own user interface. The framework calls such editors UI Type Editors. Not only can these provide a special-purpose editing user interface, they can change how the property's value is displayed even when we are not editing its value.

Supplying a UI Type Editor is simple. We simply write a class that derives from System.Drawing.Design.UITypeEditor and associate it with the property or type in question using the Editor attribute. We only need to override two methods in our editor class. The first, GetEditStyle, is called to determine what style of editing UI we support; we can open a standalone modal dialog, drop down a UI in the PropertyGrid itself, or supply no editing UI. The second method, EditValue, is called when we are required to show our editing interface.

Let us add a new property to our CustomerDetails class (as shown in Example 8-22) so that we can supply a custom editing user interface for it. The new property is Happiness, and it indicates the level of customer satisfaction, on a range of 0 to 100%. It is shown in Examples 8-23 and 8-24. The editor has been specified with the Editor attribute. (The second parameter is always required to be UITypeEditor in the current version of the framework.) The property's type here is int or Integer, but we can provide custom UI editors for any type, whether it is a custom type or a built-in type.

Example 8-23. Happiness property with editor using C#

```
private int happy;

[Editor(typeof(HappinessEditor), typeof(UITypeEditor))]
public int Happiness
{
    get { return happy; }
    set { happy = value; }
}
```

Example 8-24. Happiness property with editor using VB

```
Private happy As Integer

<Editor(GetType( HappinessEditor), GetType(UITypeEditor))> _
Public Property Happiness As Integer
    Get
        Return happy
    End Get
    Set
        happy = Value
    End Set
End Property
```

The simplest editing user interface that we can show is a modal dialog. Creating an editor class to provide this is very straightforward. Examples 8-25 and 8-26 show a custom type editor that simply presents a message box as its user interface. It asks

Property Grids

the user if they are happy (yes or no), and sets their happiness as either 100% or 0% accordingly. (If the user hits cancel, the happiness is left unaltered.)

Example 8-25. Modal dialog custom type editor using C#

```
public class HappinessEditor : UITypeEditor
{
    public override UITypeEditorEditStyle GetEditStyle(
        ITypeDescriptorContext context)
    {
        return UITypeEditorEditStyle.Modal;
    }

    public override object EditValue(ITypeDescriptorContext context,
        IServiceProvider provider, object value)
    {
        DialogResult rc = MessageBox.Show("Are you happy?",
            "Happiness", MessageBoxButtons.YesNoCancel);
        if (rc == DialogResult.Yes)
            return 100;
        if (rc == DialogResult.No)
            return 0;
        return value;
    }
}
```

Example 8-26. Modal dialog custom type editor using VB

```
Public Class HappinessEditor
    Inherits UITypeEditor

    Public Overloads Overrides Function GetEditStyle( _
                     context As ITypeDescriptorContext) _
                     As UITypeEditorEditStyle
        Return UITypeEditorEditStyle.Modal
    End Function

    Public Overloads Overrides Function EditValue( _
                     context As ITypeDescriptorContext, _
                     provider As IServiceProvider, _
                     value As Object) As Object
        Dim rc As MsgBoxResult = MsgBox("Are you happy?", _
            MsgBoxStyle.YesNoCancel, "Happiness")
        If rc = MsgBoxResult.Yes Then
            Return 100
        ElseIf rc = MsgBoxResult.No Then
            Return 0
        End If
        Return value
    End Function
End Class
```

The PropertyGrid will indicate the availability of this editor by placing a small button with an ellipsis in the property's value field when it is given the focus, as shown in Figure 8-11. The `PropertyGrid` knows to show the button because of the value returned by our editor class's `GetEditStyle` method.

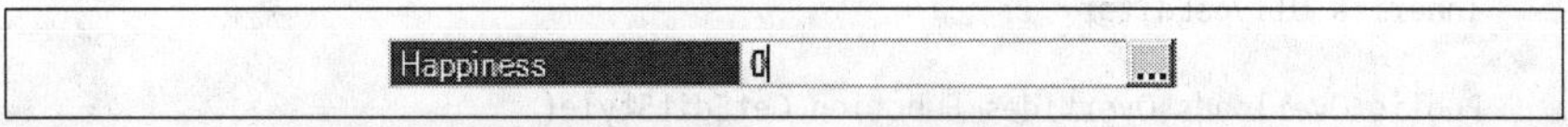
Happiness
0
...

Figure 8-11. A modal editing UI offered in a PropertyGrid

Modal dialog editors are easy to write, but they are usually not the most convenient kind of editor to use. Most of the system-supplied editors use the drop-down style, because it is less disruptive to the use of the program and makes it feel as if the property is an integrated part of the `PropertyGrid`.

Showing a drop-down editor is almost as easy as showing a modal dialog. The main difference is that we have to supply a control rather than a form. A `UserControl` is likely to be the easiest option, although you can use a custom control. (In fact, you could even use one of the built-in controls.)

Examples 8-27 and 8-28 show a type editor that displays a control called `HappinessControl`. The most interesting part of this is the way in which it displays the control as a drop-down editor in the `PropertyGrid`. To do this, we must ask the grid for a service object. We do this through the `IServiceProvider` passed as the *provider* argument—this is a generic interface that allows hosted components to ask their environment for certain facilities. In this case, we are asking the grid control for the service that lets us display drop-down editors, which is provided through the `IWindowsFormsEditorService` interface.

Example 8-27. A drop-down type editor using C#

```
public class HappinessEditor : UITypeEditor
{
    public override UITypeEditorEditStyle GetEditStyle(
        ITypeDescriptorContext context)
    {
        return UITypeEditorEditStyle.DropDown;
    }

    public override object EditValue(ITypeDescriptorContext context,
        IServiceProvider provider, object value)
    {
        IWindowsFormsEditorService wfes = provider.GetService(
            typeof(IWindowsFormsEditorService)) as
            IWindowsFormsEditorService;
        if (wfes != null)
        {
            HappinessControl hc = new HappinessControl( );
            hc.Value = (int) value;
            wfes.DropDownControl(hc);
            value = hc.Value;
        }
        return value;
    }
}
```

Example 8-28. A drop-down type editor using VB

```
Public Class HappinessEditor
    Inherits UITypeEditor

    Public Overloads Overrides Function GetEditStyle( _
                     context As ITypeDescriptorContext) _
                     As UITypeEditorEditStyle
        Return UITypeEditorEditStyle.DropDown
    End Function

    Public Overloads Overrides Function EditValue( _
                     context As ITypeDescriptorContext, _
                     provider As IServiceProvider, _
                     value As Object) As Object

        Dim wfes As IWindowsFormsEditorService = _
                    CType(provider.GetService( _
                    GetType(IWindowsFormsEditorService)), _
                    IWindowsFormsEditorService)
        If Not wfes Is Nothing Then
            Dim hc As New HappinessControl( )
            hc.Value = CInt(value)
            wfes.DropDownControl(hc)
            value = hc.Value
        End If
        Return value
    End Function

End Class
```

When we call the DropDownControl method on the service object, it displays our control in the appropriate position on the PropertyGrid. It adjusts its size so that it is the same width as the value field, as shown in Figure 8-12. (The HappinessControl is just a UserControl. The most interesting code is the part that draws the face, which we will see shortly.)

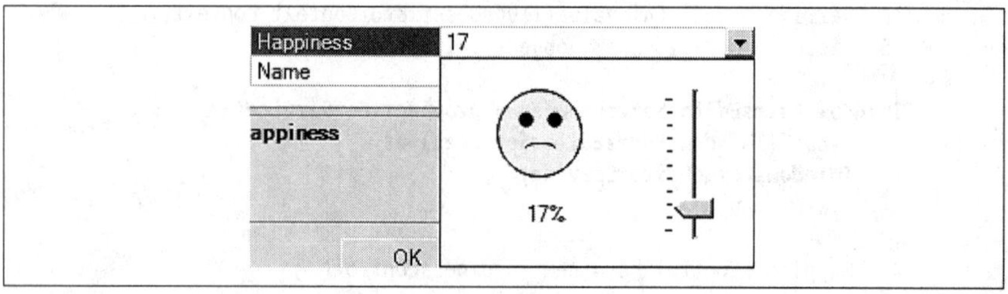
Happiness
17
Name
appiness
17%
OK

Figure 8-12. A drop-down editor in action

As you can see, in contrast to the rather dry yes/no interface provided by the MessageBox class or the VB MsgBox function, here we have gone for a slightly more emotive interface—the customer satisfaction level is indicated by how happy or sad the face looks. The code from the Happiness control that draws this is shown in Examples 8-29 and 8-30.

Example 8-29. Putting a happy face on the control using C#

```
public static void PaintFace(Graphics g, Rectangle r, int happiness)
{
    r.Width -= 1; r.Height -= 1;
    float w = r.Width;
    float h = r.Height;

    // Draw face
    g.FillEllipse(Brushes.Yellow, r);
    g.DrawEllipse(Pens.Black, r);

    // Draw eyes
    float eyeLevel =  h / 4;
    float eyeOffset = w / 4;
    float eyeSize =   w / 6;
    g.FillEllipse(Brushes.Black, w/2 - eyeOffset, eyeLevel,
        eyeSize, eyeSize);
    g.FillEllipse(Brushes.Black, w/2 + eyeOffset - eyeSize + 1, eyeLevel,
        eyeSize, eyeSize);

    // Draw smile
    float smileWidth = w/3;
    float smileLevel = (h*7)/10;
    float offs = ((happiness - 50) * h/4)/100;
    PointF[] points =
        {
            new PointF ((w - smileWidth)/2, smileLevel),
            new PointF ((w - smileWidth)/2, smileLevel + offs),
            new PointF ((w + smileWidth)/2+1, smileLevel + offs),
            new PointF ((w + smileWidth)/2+1, smileLevel)
    };
    g.DrawBeziers(Pens.Black, points);
}
```

Example 8-30. Putting a happy face on the control using VB

```
Public Shared Sub PaintFace(g As Graphics, r As Rectangle, _
                            happiness As Integer)
   r.Width -= 1
   r.Height -= 1
   Dim w As Single = r.Width
   Dim h As Single = r.Height

   ' Draw face
   g.FillEllipse(Brushes.Yellow, r)
   g.DrawEllipse(Pens.Black, r)

   ' Draw eyes
   Dim eyeLevel As Single =  h / 4
   Dim eyeOffset As Single = w / 4
   Dim eyeSize As Single = w / 6
   g.FillEllipse(Brushes.Black, w/2 - eyeOffset, eyeLevel, _
              eyeSize, eyeSize)
```

Property Grids

Example 8-30. Putting a happy face on the control using VB (continued)

```
    g.FillEllipse(Brushes.Black, w/2 + eyeOffset - eyeSize + 1, _
                  eyeLevel, eyeSize, eyeSize)

    ' Draw smile
    Dim smileWidth As Single = w/3
    Dim smileLevel As Single = (h*7)/10
    Dim offs As Single = ((happiness - 50) * h/4)/100
    Dim points( ) As PointF = _
      {   new PointF ((w - smileWidth)/2, smileLevel), _
          new PointF ((w - smileWidth)/2, smileLevel + offs), _
          new PointF ((w + smileWidth)/2+1, smileLevel + offs), _
          new PointF ((w + smileWidth)/2+1, smileLevel) }
    g.DrawBeziers(Pens.Black, points)
End Sub
```

The PropertyGrid control also lets us draw into the value field even when our editor is not running. Because the PaintFace method shown in Examples 8-29 and 8-30 has been written to scale its drawing to whatever space is available, we can call the same code from our HappinessEditor class to draw a small version of the face into the PropertyGrid, as shown in Examples 8-31 and 8-32.

Example 8-31. Custom value painting using C#

```
public override bool GetPaintValueSupported(
    ITypeDescriptorContext context)
{
    return true;
}

public override void PaintValue(PaintValueEventArgs e)
{
    System.Drawing.Drawing2D.SmoothingMode sm = e.Graphics.SmoothingMode;
    e.Graphics.SmoothingMode =
        System.Drawing.Drawing2D.SmoothingMode.HighQuality;
    HappinessControl.PaintFace(e.Graphics, e.Bounds, (int) e.Value);
    e.Graphics.SmoothingMode = sm;
}
```

Example 8-32. Custom value painting using VB

```
Public Overloads Overrides Function GetPaintValueSupported( _
                 context As ITypeDescriptorContext) As Boolean
    Return True
End Function

Public Overloads Overrides Sub PaintValue(e As PaintValueEventArgs)

    Dim sm As SmoothingMode = e.Graphics.SmoothingMode
    e.Graphics.SmoothingMode = SmoothingMode.HighQuality
    HappinessControl.PaintFace(e.Graphics, e.Bounds, CInt(e.Value))
    e.Graphics.SmoothingMode = sm

End Sub
```

To get our drawing into the value field, we are required to override the `GetPaintValueSupported` method and return `true`. Having done this, the `PropertyGrid` will call our `PaintValue` method whenever it repaints the value field. We just call the static `PaintFace` method supplied by the `HappinessControl`. Notice how we turn on the high-quality smoothing mode on the `Graphics` object first—this enables antialiasing, which is particularly important on small drawings. Without switching this on, the drawing would look rather ragged. Having changed the smoothing mode, it is important to restore it to its original value before the method terminates, because we are drawing with the same `Graphics` object that the `PropertyGrid` uses to draw itself. The results of this painting can be seen in Figure 8-13.

Happiness
98

Figure 8-13. Drawing in the value field

Summary

The `PropertyGrid` provides a simple but effective way of presenting data for editing. It uses reflection to discover which properties are available for editing. It allows every aspect of the property editing process to be controlled by using a `TypeConverter`. We can manage conversions between the text displayed and edited onscreen, and the types stored in the object. We can control which properties are displayed, and how they are presented. We can even supply our own editor user interfaces for when simple text editing is insufficient.

The `PropertyGrid` is also central to the Windows Forms Designer, so an understanding of how it works is crucial to integrating your controls with the development environment successfully. In the next chapter, we will look in detail at Visual Studio .NET's other design-time integration features.

9

Controls and the IDE

In Visual Studio .NET, the Windows Forms Designer is central to building Windows applications. Although it is possible to build Windows Forms programs with non-visual coding alone, it is much easier to use the Designer, not only because it makes laying out the contents of forms much simpler, but also because it provides a very rich user interface for specifying controls' properties. The IDE provides the same quality of user interface for user-designed controls as it does for the built-in controls. Although this design-time support is mostly automated, a little extra effort can greatly enhance the way in which your control is presented in the Designer.

In this chapter, we will look at how to extend our controls so that they integrate fully with the Forms Designer, either by modifying their behavior at design time, or by writing a custom designer class. We will examine the way in which controls and designers interact with Visual Studio .NET. Finally, we will see how to write an extender provider, a component that can augment the capabilities of any control on a form.

Design Time Versus Runtime

There are two contexts in which controls have to operate: design time and runtime. *Design time* refers to when the control is being displayed in the Forms Designer. *Runtime* simply means normal execution of a program that uses the control.

Controls do not need to provide any explicit support to allow the Forms Designer to host them. As we saw in Chapter 5, even a very simple custom control derived directly from `System.Windows.Forms.Control` with nothing more than an override of the `OnPaint` method added can be dropped onto a form in the Designer. Visual Studio .NET just creates an instance of the control to render it in the Designer. It uses the normal control painting mechanisms to do this, so controls do not need any special code to make this work. Selection outlines and resize handles are added by the Forms Designer after the control has drawn itself.

The Forms Designer intercepts all mouse and keyboard input. This means that all controls automatically get the standard editing facilities, such as drag-and-drop resizing and positioning and double-clicking to add a default event handler. So again, no special code is required to make a control behave properly at design time.

Detecting Design Time

Many controls will not need special code to be useful at design time. However, certain controls may need to change their behavior in order to work correctly in the Forms Designer. They will therefore need to detect whether they are operating in a runtime or a design-time environment and behave accordingly.

For example, suppose you wrote a control that connected to a web service and provided live information from that service. (For example, your control might be a stock price monitor.) You might not want the component to connect to the real service at design time if that service is slow or only sporadically available during the development phase of your project. It would be irritating to have to wait for the control to try to connect to the service every time you use it in the Forms Designer. At design time, you typically won't care about the correctness of the displayed data; you merely want to make sure the layout of your form is correct. (Data-bound controls usually behave differently at design time and runtime for this reason.) Fortunately, it is trivial to determine whether your control is being hosted in the designer or is running for real—simply test the `Control` class's `DesignMode` property, as shown in Example 9-1.

> The `Control` class inherits `DesignMode` from its base class, `Component`, so all components can detect when they are being used at design time, not just controls.

Example 9-1. Modifying a control's design-time appearance with DesignMode

```
// C# code
protected override void OnPaint(PaintEventArgs pe)
{
    pe.Graphics.DrawString(DesignMode ? "Design" : "Runtime",
        Font, Brushes.Black, ClientRectangle);

    base.OnPaint(pe);
}
' VB Code
Protected Overrides Sub OnPaint(pe As PaintEventArgs)
    pe.Graphics.DrawString(IIf(DesignMode, "Design", "Runtime"),
        Font, Brushes.Black, ClientRectangle)

    MyBase.OnPaint(pe)
End Sub
```

There is one caveat with the `DesignMode` property: you should not use it in a constructor. The control's `DesignMode` property is simply a shortcut for the `ISite.DesignMode` property of the component's `Site` property, and `Site` will always be `null` or `Nothing` during construction. The `Site` property is used to provide components with a means of communicating with their containing environment, enabling us to integrate our controls with certain Visual Studio .NET design-time features. The Forms Designer sets all components' `Site` properties at design time. (Visual Studio .NET 2003 supplies an object of type `Microsoft.VisualStudio.Designer.Host.DesignSite` for the `Site`. This object's `ISite.DesignMode` property always returns `true`.)

The reason `DesignMode` cannot be used during construction is that the Forms Designer must create an instance of our control before it can set the `Site` property. This means that the `Site` property will not be set until after the constructor completes. Consequently, the control's `DesignMode` property will not be able to ask the `Site` for its `ISite.DesignMode` property, and so it always returns its default value of `false` during construction.

> There is a way to obtain a `Site` during construction, but it turns out not to solve this particular problem. The Forms Designer recognizes an alternate constructor that takes an `IContainer` as a parameter. If the constructor calls `Add(this)` or `Add(Me)` on the supplied container, the container will set the `Site` property, making it available for the rest of the constructor:
>
> ```
> public MyControl(IContainer c)
> {
>     c.Add(this);
>     // Site property now valid...
> }
> ```
>
> Unfortunately, although the Forms Designer will generate code that uses this constructor at runtime in the `InitializeComponent` method, at design time it insists on using the parameterless constructor. So there is no way of accessing the `Site` during the constructor at design time, even if you supply this extra constructor.
>
> This alternate constructor is only used to provide the component with a reference to the containing form's `components` member. This ensures that the component's `Dispose` method will be called automatically by the form's `Dispose` method, as described in Chapter 3.

Fortunately, Windows Forms provides a two-phase initialization style for controls. If your control implements the `ISupportInitialize` interface defined in the `System.ComponentModel` namespace, it will get an opportunity to run initialization code after the `Site` property has been set. In fact, it gets two opportunities—`ISupportInitialize` defines two methods, `BeginInit` and `EndInit`. Examples 9-2 and 9-3 illustrate the use of these methods.

Example 9-2. Detecting design-time initialization with ISupportInitialize using C#

```
public class MyControl :
  System.Windows.Forms.Control,
  System.ComponentModel.ISupportInitialize
{
    public void BeginInit( )
    {
        Debug.WriteLine(DesignMode);
    }
```

Example 9-2. Detecting design-time initialization with ISupportInitialize using C#

```
    public void EndInit( )
    {
        Debug.WriteLine(DesignMode);
    }
    . . .
}
```

Example 9-3. Detecting design-time initialization with ISupportInitialize using VB

```
Public Class MyControl
  Inherits System.Windows.Forms.Control
  Implements System.ComponentModel.ISupportInitialize

  Public Sub BeginInit( ) Implements ISupportInitialize.BeginInit
    Debug.WriteLine(DesignMode)
  End Sub

  Public Sub EndInit( ) Implements ISupportInitialize.EndInit
    Debug.WriteLine(DesignMode)
  End Sub
  . . .
End Class
```

The Forms Designer will set the `Site` property before calling either `BeginInit` or `EndInit`, so in Example 9-2, the `DesignMode` property will be `true` in both methods at design time. The difference between these two methods is that `BeginInit` will be called before any of the component's properties are set, and `EndInit` will be called after all properties have been set.

Armed with the knowledge of which kind of environment they are running in, many components can integrate successfully with the development environment by simply adjusting their behavior and appearance suitably at design time. They can also modify certain aspects of the way they are presented using the attributes discussed in Chapters 5 and 8. However, some controls will want to go further than this—they may want to modify the behavior of the Forms Designer as well as their own behavior. So we will now look at how to write a control that customizes Visual Studio .NET's behavior.

Custom Component Designers

Visual Studio .NET enables controls to customize the Forms Designer. New commands can be added in the property grid. Resize and move drag operations can be altered, and mouse handling within the control can be customized. Design-time adornments may be added (adornments are editing features such as resize handles). Hit testing can be provided for nonrectangular controls. Controls may elect to act as containers of child controls. Controls may even modify the way that properties are presented in the property panel. All these facilities revolve around supplying a custom component designer.

A component designer is a class associated with the control class, whose job is to handle design-time interaction with the development environment. It must derive from the ControlDesigner class, which is defined in the System.Windows.Forms.Design namespace. (In fact, any component may have a designer, not just a control. A non-visual component's designer derives from the ComponentDesigner class, which is defined in the System.ComponentModel.Design namespace.)

> The terminology is unfortunate—there are three designers involved at design time:
>
> - The Forms Designer (the visual editing environment provided by Visual Studio .NET for building Windows Forms applications)
> - The control's custom designer class
> - The developer who is designing the form
>
> To avoid ambiguity, in this book, the Forms Designer is always referred to with a capital D. A designer with a lower case D refers to the custom designer class. We avoid using the term designer to refer to the developer.

All controls are required to have an associated designer. If you do not specify one, your control will just use the default, ControlDesigner. But you can choose a custom designer by applying the DesignerAttribute custom attribute to your class as Example 9-4 shows. (DesignerAttribute is defined in the System.ComponentModel namespace. It is not entirely clear what it is doing in there when the System.ComponentModel.Design namespace would have been the more obvious choice.)

Example 9-4. Specifying a custom designer for a class

```
// C# code
[DesignerAttribute(typeof(MyControlDesigner))]
public class MyControl :
   System.Windows.Forms.Control
{
   . . .
}

public class MyControlDesigner :
  System.Windows.Forms.Design.ControlDesigner
{
   . . .
}

' VB code
<Designer(GetType(MyControlDesigner))> _
Public Class MyControl
   Inherits System.Windows.Forms.Control
   . . .
End Class

Public Class MyControlDesigner
   Inherits System.Windows.Forms.Design.ControlDesigner
   . . .
End Class
```

Design-time behavior is customized by overriding various methods or properties of the ControlDesigner class. We will now examine each customizable aspect in turn.

Designer Verbs

Visual Studio .NET provides extensive support for modifying control properties of all kinds. It has built-in editors for a wide range of standard property types, and because it uses the PropertyGrid, it is easy to provide custom editors for new types—all the techniques discussed in Chapter 8 for customizing the PropertyGrid work just fine for properties of a control. However, for certain kinds of properties, it can still be cumbersome to use the PropertyGrid to perform frequently used operations. So the Forms Editor allows a component designer to add *verbs*—custom operations available through a single click in the editor.

Consider the built-in TabControl class, which allows several user interface panels to be contained inside a standard tabbed view, such as that used by Windows Explorer's file properties windows. The first thing that a developer is likely to want to do with a newly created TabControl is to add some new panels. This can be done by adding new TabPage objects to the control's TabPages property. TabPages is a collection property, so editing this property displays the standard collection editor dialog, which can be used to add new TabPage objects.

The TabControl component's requirements are met by the PropertyGrid. However, it is all rather cumbersome—the developer must first locate the TabPages property in the property grid, then two clicks are required to bring up the collection editor, which is a modal dialog and hence must be dismissed once the new pages have been added. This is somewhat inconvenient, given that developers will almost always need to add new pages whenever they use the TabControl.

To make life easier for developers, the TabControl therefore defines two designer verbs, one for adding new panels and one for removing existing panels. Figure 9-1 shows how the property grid displays the verbs for a TabControl.

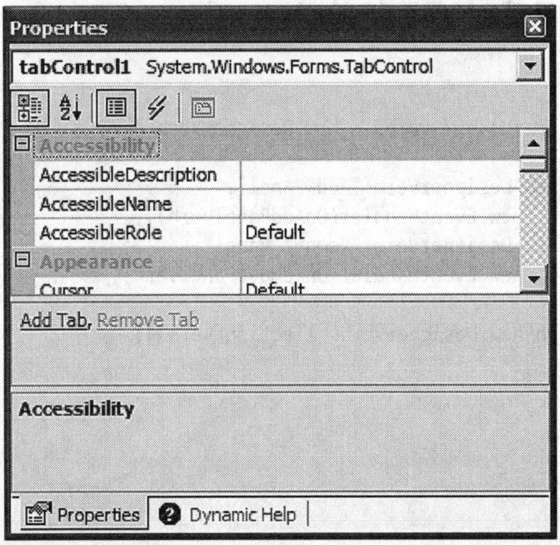
Properties
tabControl1 System.Windows.Forms.TabControl
Accessibility
AccessibleDescription
AccessibleName
AccessibleRole
Default
Appearance
Cursor
Default
Add Tab, Remove Tab
Accessibility
Properties
Dynamic Help

Figure 9-1. A property grid with a verbs panel

The Add Tab and Remove Tab verbs in the central panel in Figure 9-1 are also available through the context menu, as shown in Figure 9-2.

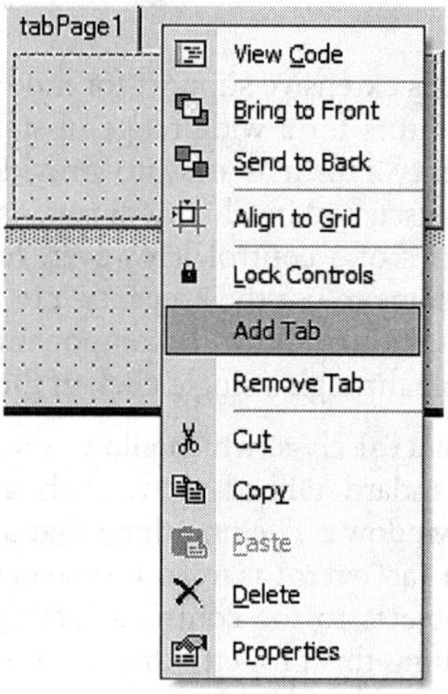
tabPage1
View Code
Bring to Front
Send to Back
Align to Grid
Lock Controls
Add Tab
Remove Tab
Cut
Copy
Paste
Delete
Properties

Figure 9-2. A context menu with verbs

If your custom control could benefit from a similar one-click interface for common but cumbersome operations, it is easy to add designer verbs. Simply override the `Verbs` property in your custom designer class, as shown in Examples 9-5 and 9-6. (Note that this property's type, `DesignerVerbCollection`, is defined in the `System.ComponentModel.Designer` namespace.)

Example 9-5. Adding designer verbs using C#

```
public class MyControlDesigner : ControlDesigner
{
    public override DesignerVerbCollection Verbs
    {
        get
        {
            DesignerVerb[] verbs = new DesignerVerb[]
            {
                new DesignerVerb("Add Panel",
                   new EventHandler(OnAddPanelVerb)),
                new DesignerVerb("Remove Panel",
                   new EventHandler(OnRemovePanelVerb))
            };
            return new DesignerVerbCollection(verbs);

        }
    }
```

Example 9-5. Adding designer verbs using C# (continued)

```
    private void OnAddPanelVerb(object sender, EventArgs e)
    {
        MyControl ctl = (MyControl) this.Control;
        . . .
    }

    private void OnRemovePanelVerb(object sender, EventArgs e)
    {
        MyControl ctl = (MyControl) this.Control;
        . . .
    }
}
```

Example 9-6. Adding designer verbs using VB

```
Public Class MyControlDesigner
   Inherits System.Windows.Forms.Design.ControlDesigner

   Public Overrides ReadOnly Property Verbs( ) As DesignerVerbCollection
      Get
         Dim vrbs(1) As DesignerVerb
         vrbs(0) = New DesignerVerb("Add Panel", _
                   AddressOf OnAddPanelVerb)
         vrbs(1) = New DesignerVerb("Remove Panel", _
                   AddressOf OnRemovePanelVerb)
         Return New DesignerVerbCollection(vrbs)
      End Get
   End Property

   Private Sub OnAddPanelVerb(sender As Object, e As EventArgs)
      Dim ctl As MyControl = DirectCast(Me.Control, MyControl)
      . . .
   End Sub

   Private Sub OnRemovePanelVerb(sender As Object, e As EventArgs)
      Dim ctl As MyControl = DirectCast(Me.Control, MyControl)
      . . .
   End Sub

End Class
```

The Verbs property must return a collection of DesignerVerb objects, one for each verb that is to appear on the property page. (The easiest way to create a DesignerVerbCollection is to use the constructor that takes a DesignerVerb[] array, as shown here.) Each DesignerVerb object contains two pieces of information: the name of the verb (as it will appear on the property panel and in the context menu) and the method of the component designer that should be called if the verb is invoked. The method to be invoked must be referred to with an EventHandler delegate.

Controls and the IDE

> When the Forms Designer calls the method for your verb (i.e., when the user clicks on the verb), the object passed as the `sender` parameter is *not* the control, as you might have expected. It is a reference to the `DesignerVerb` object in the collection that you returned in the `Verbs` property. This is not usually particularly useful.
>
> To access the control that your custom designer is editing, simply use the `Control` property defined by the `ControlDesigner` class (i.e., your designer's base class), as illustrated in Examples 9-5 and 9-6.

DesignerVerb properties

The `DesignerVerb` object has properties that allow you to modify the appearance of your verbs. For example, if you set the `Enabled` property to `false`, the verb will be grayed out. Setting the `Checked` property to `true` will cause a tick to appear beside the verb on the context menu. (It has no effect on its appearance in the property grid.)

You can set these properties when you create the verbs in your `Verbs` property. You can also modify the properties later on, and the Forms Designer will track these changes. For example, if you change the `Enabled` property of a verb while your control is selected, the verb's appearance will change appropriately in the property panel. However, every time your control is deselected and reselected, the Designer will read your `Verbs` property again—it does not cache verbs between selections. This means that any changes you make to your verbs' properties will be lost when the selection changes unless you make your `Verbs` property return the same objects every time.

Although it is possible to write a `Verbs` property that returns the same set of verbs every time, you should not rely on this technique. The Forms Designer reserves the right to destroy your component designer object at any time and create a new one as needed. For example, if the user closes the Designer window for the form that contains your control and then reopens it, a new instance of your designer class will be created. You should therefore make sure that your `Verbs` property always creates `DesignerVerb` objects that are appropriately initialized to be consistent with the control's state. And in general, your designer should be written to assume that it might be destroyed and recreated at any time, and should therefore not rely on being able to store state between operations.

Selection and Resizing

When writing a custom component designer for a control, your class will normally derive from the `ControlDesigner` class. This class provides the standard support for selecting, moving, and resizing controls with the mouse. You can influence the way in which these operations work by overriding certain properties and methods.

Hit testing

By default, a control can be selected by clicking anywhere inside its bounding rectangle. Because most controls are rectangular, this is reasonable behavior, but for controls with a more unusual shape, it can be confusing. So the Designer lets you modify this behavior by overriding the GetHitTest method in your control designer class.

The Designer will call the GetHitTest method repeatedly whenever the mouse pointer is over your control. It uses the return value to decide what kind of mouse cursor to display—if the method returns true, the Designer will display the four-way cursor to indicate that the control can be selected and moved. If the method returns false, the default mouse cursor will be displayed to indicate that the pointer is not considered to be over any control right now. GetHitTest will also be called when the mouse is clicked on your control to determine whether to select the control or not. Examples 9-7 and 9-8 show a simple custom control that draws an ellipse in its client area, and a corresponding designer with a GetHitTest method that only returns true when the mouse pointer is over the ellipse.

Example 9-7. A control designer with hit testing using C#

```
[Designer(typeof(EllipseDesigner))]
public class EllipseControl : System.Windows.Forms.Control
{
    public EllipseControl( )
    {
        SetStyle(ControlStyles.ResizeRedraw, true);
    }

    protected override void OnPaint(PaintEventArgs pe)
    {
        using (Brush b = new SolidBrush(ForeColor))
        {
            pe.Graphics.FillEllipse(b, ClientRectangle);
        }
        base.OnPaint(pe);
    }
}

public class EllipseDesigner : ControlDesigner
{
    protected override bool GetHitTest(System.Drawing.Point point)
    {
        // Avoid divide-by-zero problems with zero-sized controls

        if (this.Control.Width == 0 || this.Control.Height == 0)
            return true;


        // Map point from screen to client coordinates.

        PointF p = this.Control.PointToClient(point);


        // Test for containment by ellipse.

        double w = this.Control.Width;
```

Controls and the IDE

Example 9-7. A control designer with hit testing using C# (continued)

```
        double h = this.Control.Height;

        double ratio = w / h;

        double sx = p.X - w/2;
        double sy = (p.Y - h/2)*ratio;

        return (sx*sx + sy*sy) >= w*w/4.0;
    }
}
```

Example 9-8. A control designer with hit testing using VB

```
Imports System
Imports System.ComponentModel
Imports System.Drawing
Imports System.Windows.Forms
Imports System.Windows.Forms.Design

<Designer(GetType(EllipseDesigner))> _
Public Class EllipseControl
       Inherits System.Windows.Forms.Control

    Public Sub New( )
        SetStyle(ControlStyles.ResizeRedraw, True)
    End Sub

    Protected Overrides Sub OnPaint(pe As PaintEventArgs)
        Dim b As Brush = New SolidBrush(ForeColor)
        Try
            pe.Graphics.FillEllipse(b, ClientRectangle)
        Finally
            Dim disp As IDisposable
            If TypeOf b Is IDisposable Then
               disp =  b
               disp.Dispose( )
            End If
        End Try
        MyBase.OnPaint(pe)
    End Sub
End Class

Public class EllipseDesigner : Inherits ControlDesigner

    Protected Overrides Function GetHitTest( _
              point As System.Drawing.Point) As Boolean

        ' Avoid divide-by-zero problems with 0-sized controls
        If Me.Control.Width = 0 Or Me.Control.Height = 0 Then
            Return True
        End If
```

Example 9-8. A control designer with hit testing using VB (continued)

```
        ' Map point from screen to client coordinates.
        Dim p As PointF = _
            Point.op_Implicit(Me.Control.PointToClient(point))

        ' Test for containment by ellipse.
        Dim w As Double = Me.Control.Width
        Dim h As Double = Me.Control.Height

        Dim ratio As Double = w / h

        Dim sx As Double = p.X - w/2
        Dim sy As Double = (p.Y - h/2)*ratio

        Return (sx*sx + sy*sy) >= w*w/4.0
    End Function
End Class
```

Examples 9-7 and 9-8 illustrate a curious feature of `GetHitTest`. The `Point` that is passed as a parameter is relative to the top-left corner of the screen. (This is at odds with what the documentation claims at the time this book went to press—it says that the `Point` will be relative to the top-left corner of the control.) This means that the first thing we must do is convert the `Point` from screen coordinates to control coordinates. Fortunately, the `Control` class has a built-in method for doing this: `PointToClient`. The remainder of the method simply calculates whether the point is contained within the ellipse.

> If your control sets its shape by modifying its `Region` property, you do not need to supply your own `GetHitTest` implementation. The default `ControlDesigner` class automatically manages hit testing for such shaped controls.

Resizing and moving

The `ControlDesigner` class provides automatic support for resizing and moving controls. You can control this facility by overriding the `SelectionRules` property in your own designer class. You must return some combination of the values defined in the `SelectionRules` enumeration, which is defined in the `System.Windows.Forms.Design` namespace.

There is no way to take complete control of the resizing and moving process unless you are prepared to disable the built-in support completely and draw your own adornments. (Returning `SelectionRules.None` from the `SelectionRules` property will turn off the standard support, and the next section describes how to add your own adornments. But even then, you will be restricted to drawing adornments that lie within the control's client rectangle.) However, you will normally be able to achieve what you require just by choosing a more restrictive set of selection rules than the default of `SelectionRules.AllSizeable | SelectionRules.Moveable` (`SelectionRules.AllSizeable Or SelectionRules.Moveable` in VB), which allows the control to be moved and to be resized in all directions.

If you want the designer to draw a border on your control, then no matter what other values you choose from the SelectionRules enumeration, you must include SelectionRules.Visible. If you just specify this in conjunction with SelectionRules.Moveable, your control will have a fixed size, but will be able to be moved around the form. You can also selectively enable sizing of individual edges using the TopSizeable, BottomSizeable, LeftSizeable, and RightSizeable enumeration members. Example 9-9 shows an example SelectionRules property implementation that does not allow the control to be moved, and only allows its left edge to be resized.

Example 9-9. Modifying support for moving and resizing

```
// C# code
public override SelectionRules SelectionRules
{
    get
    {
        return SelectionRules.Visible |
            SelectionRules.LeftSizeable;
    }
}

' VB code
Public Overrides ReadOnly Property SelectionRules() _
                As SelectionRules
    Get
        Return SelectionRules.Visible Or _
               SelectionRules.LeftSizable
    End Get
End Property
```

Figure 9-3 shows the result of Example 9-9. This is how the Forms Designer displays such a control when it is selected. The visual cue is not especially obvious. In case you missed it, the Designer indicates the resizable edge by coloring its center handle white, while coloring the handles that cannot be dragged pale gray. (It is slightly more obvious when using the control in the Designer, because the mouse cursor only changes into a resize cursor when it is over that handle.)

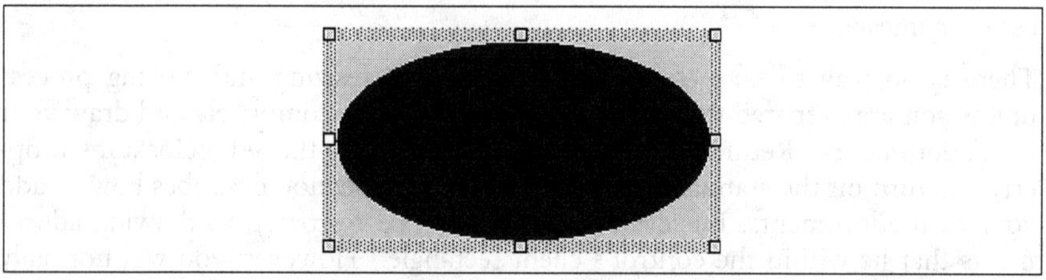

Figure 9-3. A control with one resizable edge

Adornments

An adornment is a user interface feature that is only painted on a control at design time. (Selection outlines and resize handles are examples of built-in adornments.) Adornments are not drawn by the control—they are supplied by the control designer class, enabling you to add extra design-time handles appropriate to your class.

To show how to display adornments, we need a control that can make use of extra resize handles beyond the standard ones. We will use a control that displays a box with rounded edges. Examples 9-10 and 9-11 show the complete source for such a control, and it is shown in action in Figure 9-4.

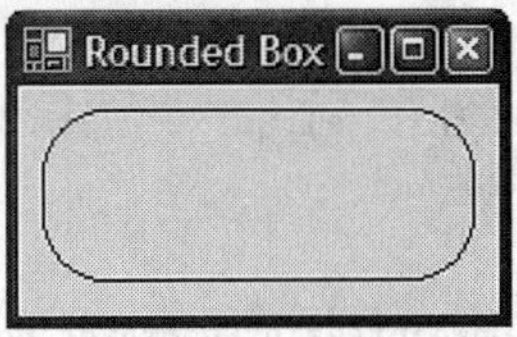
Rounded Box

Figure 9-4. A rounded box control

There is nothing unusual about this control—it uses standard techniques already discussed in previous chapters. It provides a single property called `CornerSize` (along with the usual associated change notification event and overridable `OnCornerSizeChanged` method). This property determines how large the curved corners are. This property can be edited using the property grid in the normal way, but we will provide a custom designer that draws a drag handle adornment to allow the corner size to be modified by dragging with the mouse.

Example 9-10. A rounded box control using C#

```
[Designer(typeof(RoundedBoxDesigner))]
public class RoundedBoxControl : System.Windows.Forms.Control
{
    public RoundedBoxControl( )
    {
        SetStyle(ControlStyles.ResizeRedraw, true);
    }

    [Category("Appearance")]
    [DefaultValue(10)]
    public int CornerSize
    {
        get
        {
            return cornerSizeVal;
        }
        set
        {
            if (cornerSizeVal != value)
            {
```

Example 9-10. A rounded box control using C# (continued)

```
                cornerSizeVal = value;
                OnCornerSizeChanged(EventArgs.Empty);
                Refresh( );
            }
        }
    }
    private int cornerSizeVal = 10;

    [Category("Property Changed")]
    public event EventHandler CornerSizeChanged;

    protected virtual void OnCornerSizeChanged(EventArgs e)
    {
        if (CornerSizeChanged != null)
            CornerSizeChanged(this, e);
    }


    protected override void OnPaint(PaintEventArgs pe)
    {
        // Truncate rounded corner sizes so that the
        // corners aren't larger than the box.
        int cwidth = cornerSizeVal*2 > Width ? Width : cornerSizeVal*2;
        int cheight = cornerSizeVal*2 > Height ? Height : cornerSizeVal*2;
        Rectangle corner = new Rectangle(0, 0, cwidth, cheight);

        using (GraphicsPath gp = new GraphicsPath( ))
        {
            // GraphicsPath.AddArc complains about
            // zero-sized arcs, so just use a
            // standard Rectangle in that case.
            if (cwidth == 0 || cheight == 0)
            {
                Rectangle cr = ClientRectangle;
                if (cr.Width != 0) cr.Width -= 1;
                if (cr.Height != 0) cr.Height -= 1;
                gp.AddRectangle(cr);
            }
            else
            {
                gp.AddArc(corner, 180, 90);
                corner.X = Width - 1 - cwidth;
                gp.AddArc(corner, 270, 90);
                corner.Y = Height - 1 - cheight;
                gp.AddArc(corner, 0, 90);
                corner.X = 0;
                gp.AddArc(corner, 90, 90);
                gp.CloseFigure( );
            }

            using (Pen p = new Pen(ForeColor, 1))
            {
```

Example 9-10. A rounded box control using C# (continued)

```
                pe.Graphics.DrawPath(p, gp);
            }
        }

        // Calling the base class OnPaint
        base.OnPaint(pe);
    }
}
```

Example 9-11. A rounded box control using VB

```
<Designer(GetType(RoundedBoxDesigner))> _
Public Class RoundedBoxControl
     Inherits System.Windows.Forms.Control

    Private cornerSizeVal As Integer = 10

    Public Sub New( )
        SetStyle(ControlStyles.ResizeRedraw, True)
    End Sub

    <Category("Appearance"), _
     DefaultValue(10)> _
    Public Property CornerSize( ) As Integer
        Get
            Return cornerSizeVal
        End Get
        Set
            If cornerSizeVal <> Value Then
                cornerSizeVal = Value
                OnCornerSizeChanged(EventArgs.Empty)
                Refresh( )
            End If
        End Set
    End Property

    <Category("Property Changed")> _
    Public Event CornerSizeChanged(sender As Object, _
                                   e As EventArgs)

    Protected Overridable Sub OnCornerSizeChanged( _
              e As EventArgs)
        RaiseEvent CornerSizeChanged(Me, e)
    End Sub

    Protected Overrides Sub OnPaint(pe As PaintEventArgs)
        ' Truncate rounded corner sizes so that the
        ' corners aren't larger than the box.
        Dim cwidth As Integer
        If cornerSizeVal*2 > Width Then
           cwidth = Width
        Else
           cwidth = cornerSizeVal*2
```

Example 9-11. A rounded box control using VB (continued)

```
        End If
        Dim cheight As Integer
        If cornerSizeVal*2 > Height Then
            cheight = Height
        Else
            cheight = cornerSizeVal*2
        End If
        Dim corner As New Rectangle(0, 0, cwidth, cheight)

        Dim gp As New GraphicsPath( )
        Try
            ' GraphicsPath.AddArc complains about
            ' zero-sized arcs, so just use a
            ' standard Rectangle in that case.
            If cwidth = 0 Or cheight = 0 Then
                Dim cr As Rectangle = ClientRectangle
                If cr.Width <> 0 Then cr.Width -= 1
                If cr.Height <> 0 Then cr.Height -= 1
                gp.AddRectangle(cr)
            Else
                gp.AddArc(corner, 180, 90)
                corner.X = Width - 1 - cwidth
                gp.AddArc(corner, 270, 90)
                corner.Y = Height - 1 - cheight
                gp.AddArc(corner, 0, 90)
                corner.X = 0
                gp.AddArc(corner, 90, 90)
                gp.CloseFigure( )
            End If

            Dim p As New Pen(ForeColor, 1)
            Try
                pe.Graphics.DrawPath(p, gp)
            Finally
                Dim disp As IDisposable
                If TypeOf p Is IDisposable Then
                    disp = p
                    disp.Dispose( )
                End If
            End Try
        Finally
            Dim disp As IDisposable
            If TypeOf disp Is IDisposable Then
                disp = gp
                disp.Dispose( )
            End If
        End Try

        ' Calling the base class OnPaint
        MyBase.OnPaint(pe)
    End Sub
End Class
```

To draw a drag handle, we simply provide an appropriate designer that overrides the `OnPaintAdornments` method. This designer class is shown in Examples 9-12 and 9-13. (Note that the class definition in Examples 9-10 and 9-11 is marked with the `Designer` custom attribute. This is how Visual Studio .NET knows to use our `RoundedBoxDesigner` class.)

Example 9-12. Drawing grab handle adornments using C#

```
public class RoundedBoxDesigner : ControlDesigner
{
    private const int grabSize = 7;

    protected override void OnPaintAdornments(PaintEventArgs pe)
    {
        Rectangle grabRect = GetGrabRectangle( );
        ControlPaint.DrawGrabHandle(pe.Graphics, grabRect,
                                    true, true);
    }

    private Rectangle GetGrabRectangle( )
    {
        RoundedBoxControl ctl = (RoundedBoxControl) Control;
        return new Rectangle(ctl.CornerSize - grabSize/2, 0,
                             grabSize, grabSize);
    }

    . . .
}
```

Example 9-13. Drawing grab handle adornments using VB

```
Public Class RoundedBoxDesigner : Inherits ControlDesigner

    Private Const grabSize As Integer = 7

    Protected Overrides Sub OnPaintAdornments( _
                         pe As PaintEventArgs)
        Dim grabRect As Rectangle = GetGrabRectangle( )
        ControlPaint.DrawGrabHandle(pe.Graphics, grabRect, _
                                    True, True)
    End Sub

    Private Function GetGrabRectangle( ) As Rectangle
        Dim ctl As RoundedBoxControl = DirectCast(Control, RoundedBoxControl)
        Return New Rectangle(CInt(ctl.CornerSize - grabSize/2), _
                             0, grabSize, grabSize)
    End Function

    . . .
End Class
```

With this designer in place, the control will now have an extra grab handle at design time, as shown in Figure 9-5.

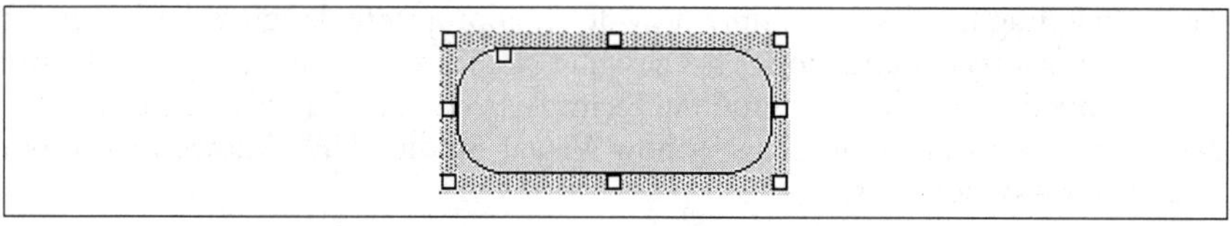

Figure 9-5. The RoundedBoxControl at design time

The designer class in Examples 9-12 and 9-13 is not complete. As it stands, it only draws the grab handle. It does nothing to manage clicks or drags on the handle. To make the handle useful, we must override more methods. First we will want to provide feedback with the mouse cursor—we should display the left-right resize cursor when the mouse is over our drag handle to indicate how it can be moved. This is done by overriding the designer class's `OnSetCursor` method, as shown in Examples 9-14 and 9-15.

Example 9-14. Modifying the mouse cursor at design time using C#

```
protected override void OnSetCursor( )
{
    Point cp = Control.PointToClient(Cursor.Position);
    if (GrabHitTest(cp))
    {
        Cursor.Current = Cursors.SizeWE;
    }
    else
        base.OnSetCursor( );
}

private bool GrabHitTest(Point p)
{
    Rectangle grabRect = GetGrabRectangle( );
    return grabRect.Contains(p);
}
```

Example 9-15. Modifying the mouse cursor at design time using VB

```
Protected Overrides Sub OnSetCursor( )
    Dim cp As Point = Control.PointToClient(Cursor.Position)
    If GrabHitTest(cp) Then
        Cursor.Current = Cursors.SizeWE
    Else
        MyBase.OnSetCursor( )
    End If
End Sub

Private Function GrabHitTest(p As Point) As Boolean
    Dim grabRect As Rectangle = GetGrabRectangle( )
    Return grabRect.Contains(p)
End Function
```

Note that `OnSetCursor` does not pass the mouse cursor's position. We must therefore retrieve it from the `Cursor` class directly. The `Cursor` class's `Position` property returns the mouse position in screen coordinates, so we need to translate these into control coordinates using the PointToClient method. Then we test to see if the mouse is over the handle. (The hit test logic has been factored out into a separate method, GrabHitTest, because we will also need to perform hit testing in another method shortly. This in turn uses the GetGrabRectangle method we defined earlier, which is also used to determine where the grab handle is drawn.)

Our control will now provide feedback at design time when the user moves the mouse over our drag handle. But we still need to handle the drag operation itself. To do this, we must override three methods: OnMouseDragBegin, OnMouseDragMove, and OnMouseDragEnd. The code is fairly straightforward, with only two minor complications. First, we need to be able to reset the property to its original value if the drag is cancelled. Second, it is good practice to make sure that if the user doesn't click dead in the center of the drag handle, we don't end up making the handle leap to the clicked location. (Naïve handling of the OnMouseDragMove event would cause this to happen—we are using the offset field to avoid this.) Examples 9-16 and 9-17 show the drag handling code.

Example 9-16. Handling adornment mouse events using C#

```
private int oldCornerSize;  // Used for handling cancellation
private int offset;
private bool dragging;

protected override void OnMouseDragBegin(int x, int y)
{
    Point dp = Control.PointToClient(new Point(x, y));
    if (GrabHitTest(dp))
    {
        RoundedBoxControl ctl = (RoundedBoxControl) Control;
        oldCornerSize = ctl.CornerSize;
        offset = oldCornerSize - dp.X;
        dragging = true;
    }
    else
        base.OnMouseDragBegin(x, y);
}

protected override void OnMouseDragMove(int x, int y)
{
    if (dragging)
    {
        Point dp = Control.PointToClient(new Point(x, y));

        int newCornerSize = dp.X - offset;
        if (newCornerSize < 0) newCornerSize = 0;

        RoundedBoxControl ctl = (RoundedBoxControl) Control;
        ctl.CornerSize = newCornerSize;
    }
    else
        base.OnMouseDragMove(x, y);

}
```

Example 9-16. Handling adornment mouse events using C# (continued)

```
protected override void OnMouseDragEnd(bool cancel)
{
    if (dragging)
    {
        RoundedBoxControl ctl = (RoundedBoxControl) Control;
        if (cancel)
        {
            ctl.CornerSize = oldCornerSize;
        }
        else
        {
            // Update property in property grid
            PropertyDescriptor pd =
                TypeDescriptor.GetProperties(typeof(RoundedBoxControl))
                  ["CornerSize"];
            pd.SetValue(ctl, ctl.CornerSize);
        }

    }

    dragging = false;


    // Always call base class.
    base.OnMouseDragEnd(cancel);
}
```

Example 9-17. Handling adornment mouse events using VB

```
Private oldCornerSize As Integer  ' Used for handling cancellation
Private offset As  Integer
Private dragging As Boolean

Protected Overrides Sub OnMouseDragBegin(x As Integer, y As Integer)
    Dim dp As Point = Control.PointToClient(New Point(x, y))
    If GrabHitTest(dp) Then
        Dim ctl As RoundedBoxControl = DirectCast(Control, RoundedBoxControl)
        oldCornerSize = ctl.CornerSize
        offset = oldCornerSize - dp.X
        dragging = True
    Else
        MyBase.OnMouseDragBegin(x, y)
    End If
End Sub

Protected Overrides Sub OnMouseDragMove(x As Integer, y As Integer)
    If dragging Then
        Dim dp As Point = Control.PointToClient(New Point(x, y))

        Dim newCornerSize As Integer = dp.X - offset
        If newCornerSize < 0 Then newCornerSize = 0

        Dim ctl As RoundedBoxControl = DirectCast(Control, RoundedBoxControl)
```

Example 9-17. Handling adornment mouse events using VB (continued)

```
        ctl.CornerSize = newCornerSize
    Else
        MyBase.OnMouseDragMove(x, y)
    End If
End Sub

Protected Overrides Sub OnMouseDragEnd(cancel As Boolean)
    If dragging Then
        Dim ctl As RoundedBoxControl = DirectCast(Control, _
                                        RoundedBoxControl)
        If cancel Then
            ctl.CornerSize = oldCornerSize
        Else
            ' Update property in property grid
            Dim pd As PropertyDescriptor = _
                TypeDescriptor.GetProperties( _
                GetType(RoundedBoxControl))("CornerSize")
            pd.SetValue(ctl, ctl.CornerSize)
        End If
    End If

    dragging = False

    ' Always call base class.
    MyBase.OnMouseDragEnd(cancel)
End Sub
```

Note that all three methods defer to the base class implementation when they are not handling the drag operation (i.e., when the user clicks somewhere other than on the drag handle). This is necessary to make sure that the control can still be moved in the Designer using normal drag and drop. Also note that the `OnMouseDragEnd` method always calls the base class method, regardless of whether the handle was being dragged or not. This is necessary because otherwise the drag operation will not be completed correctly, and the Forms Designer will start to malfunction.

The `OnMouseDragEnd` method has some slightly strange-looking code that runs when the drag is not cancelled. It obtains a `PropertyDescriptor` object for the `RoundedBoxControl` class's `CornerSize` property, and then uses this to set that property to the value it is already set to. On the face of it, this may seem pointless. However, despite the fact that the `CornerSize` property raises property change notifications, the property grid appears not to detect the change. Pushing the update through the `PropertyDescriptor` causes the property grid to refresh its display of the `CornerSize` property correctly.

Containment

As we saw in Chapter 3, all controls are able to contain child controls. But it doesn't always make sense for a control to act as a parent. For example, although you can write code that puts child controls inside a `Button`, the results are not helpful. Fortunately, the Forms Designer prevents you from placing child controls inside controls that are not designed to act as parents. It only allows children to be added to controls for which it is appropriate, such as `Panel` or `GroupBox`.

By default, any controls we write will not be treated as containers by the Forms Designer. If you try to drop a control inside one of your custom controls, the new control's parent will be the form, not your control. However, it is easy to make your control behave like a `Panel`: simply give it a designer that derives from the `ParentControlDesigner` class. `ParentControlDesigner` derives from `ControlDesigner` and provides all the same functionality, and it also signals to the Forms Designer that the control can act as a container.

If you do not require any special design-time behavior other than the ability to act as a parent, it is sufficient to choose the `ParentControlDesigner` class itself as your designer. As Example 9-18 illustrates, there is no need to derive your own designer class.

Example 9-18. A simple parent control

```
// C# code
[Designer(typeof(ParentControlDesigner))]
public class MyParentControl : Control
{
    . . .
}

' VB code
<Designer(GetType(ParentControlDesigner))> _
Public Class MyParentControl : Inherits Control
   . . .
End Class
```

If you need to supply a designer class for other design-time features, such as painting adornments, you can simply change its base class to be `ParentControlDesigner`. Example 9-19 shows a modified version of the designer class for our `RoundedBoxControl`, previously shown in Examples 9-12 and 9-13. We have changed it to inherit from `ParentControlDesigner`, which will cause the Forms Designer to allow child controls to be added to it.

Example 9-19. A parent control designer

```
// C# code
public class RoundedBoxDesigner : ParentControlDesigner
{
    As before
    . . .
}

' VB code
Public Class RoundedBoxDesigner
       Inherits ParentControlDesigner
   . . . As before
End Class
```

You can be selective about which controls you contain. Your designer class can override the `CanParent` method. The Forms Designer will call this when the user drags a control over your control. If this method returns `false`, the Designer will display the no entry mouse cursor to indicate that the control being dragged cannot be dropped into your control.

`CanParent` is an overloaded method. You must override the overload that takes a `Control` as a parameter. This will be called when a control that is already on the form is being dragged around. (It is not clear when the other overload, which takes a `ControlDesigner`, is called. You might expect it to be called when a new instance is dragged from the Toolbox. But this is not the case; there appears to be no way of controlling which types of new instances can be added to your control.)

Metadata Filtering

In the previous chapter, we saw how the `PropertyGrid` control provides a virtual view of an object's properties: although it relies on reflection to determine what properties are present, it has extensibility hooks that allow us to modify what the user sees. We exploited this by writing a type converter to support localization of property names. Because Visual Studio .NET uses the `PropertyGrid` to edit control properties, we have the same flexibility for the way our controls are presented at design time. On top of this, the Forms Designer provides us with some extra support for common ways of modifying and filtering properties without having to go to the trouble of writing a type converter.

If your control already has a designer class associated with it, you can use this to perform many of the tricks that would otherwise require a type converter. In particular, you can hide certain properties, rename them, intercept reads and writes, and even add new properties.

> Because there is some overlap in what can be achieved by writing a custom type converter and by writing a custom designer, you will sometimes have requirements that could be met by writing either. It doesn't matter which you choose. The main restriction to be aware of is that designer classes can only be used in Visual Studio .NET, and only at design time. So if you need metadata filtering at runtime (usually because you are using the `PropertyGrid` control) a type converter will be the right solution.

At the center of this mechanism are six methods. Three of these are intended to let you add new properties, events and attributes, and they are, respectively, `PreFilterProperties`, `PreFilterEvents`, and `PreFilterAttributes`. Each is passed a dictionary into which it can add descriptors. (The descriptors you add should be of type `PropertyDescriptor`, `EventDescriptor`, and `AttributeDescriptor`, respectively. These are all defined in the `System.ComponentModel` namespace.) This dictionary will already contain entries for all the component's real properties, events, or attributes. (Or if the component has an associated type converter, the dictionary will contain whatever that returned.) But the designer class has the option to add to these.

The remaining three methods are PostFilterProperties, PostFilterEvents, and PostFilterAttributes. These are passed the same dictionary as before, but this time the method is allowed to remove or modify entries. (In practice, there is currently not much difference between the Pre... and Post... methods—the Post... methods are called directly after the Pre... methods, and you can do whatever you like to the dictionary in either. But you should stick to the rule of only adding entries in the Pre... methods, and performing any modifications or removals in the Post... methods, just in case a future version of the Forms Designer decides to enforce this.)

Examples 9-20 and 9-21 show an implementation of PreFilterProperties that adds an extra property, Fooness, to the control at design time. Although the underlying control will not have such a property, it will still appear in the property panel for the control because the designer class has added it to the dictionary of property descriptors. Note that the designer class itself has provided the implementation of the Fooness property to which the descriptor refers. (The designer class might then use this property to modify its design-time behavior.)

Example 9-20. Adding a design-time property using C#

```
protected override void PreFilterProperties(IDictionary properties)
{
    base.PreFilterProperties(properties);

    properties["Fooness"] = TypeDescriptor.CreateProperty(
        typeof(MyDesigner),
        "Fooness",
        typeof(bool),
        CategoryAttribute.Design,
        DesignOnlyAttribute.Yes);
}

public bool Fooness
{
    get { return fooVal; }
    set { fooVal = value; }
}
private bool fooVal;
```

Example 9-21. Adding a design-time property using VB

```
Protected Overrides Sub PreFilterProperties(properties As IDictionary)
   MyBase.PreFilterProperties(properties)

   properties("Fooness") = TypeDescriptor.CreateProperty( _
       GetType(MyDesigner), _
       "Fooness", _
       GetType(Boolean), _
       CategoryAttribute.Design, _
       DesignOnlyAttribute.Yes)
End Sub

Public Property Fooness As Boolean
```

Example 9-21. Adding a design-time property using VB (continued)

```
    Get
        Return fooVal
    End Get
    Set
        fooVal = Value
    End Set
End Property
```

The PropertyDescriptor is created using the CreateProperty factory method supplied by the TypeDescriptor class. As well as specifying the type that really implements the property (the designer class, in this case) along with the name and type of the property, we can also optionally specify a list of custom attributes. (CreateProperty takes a variable length argument list, so you can supply as many attributes as you like.) In this case, we have specified a CategoryAttribute (this will determine which category the property appears under in the PropertyGrid) and the DesignOnlyAttribute, which informs the development environment that this is a design-time property, which it should not attempt to set at runtime. All properties added this way should specify DesignOnlyAttribute.Yes, because otherwise, the Forms Designer will generate code that attempts to set these properties at runtime. Such code will not compile, because these design-time properties are not available at runtime.

> This technique of adding extra properties at design time is used by Visual Studio .NET itself. It adds a Locked property to every control, which can be used to prevent accidental editing. The Control class does not define a Locked property—this is a design-time property automatically added by the ControlDesigner class's PreFilterProperties method.

Shadow properties

A common design-time requirement is to prevent certain properties from being set at design time. The most obvious example is the Visible property. If the user sets a control's Visible property to false, we don't really want to make the control invisible in the Designer, because this would make it hard to edit. We want the control to remain visible in the Designer, but for the Visible property to be honored at runtime. One solution would be for controls to ignore their Visible property at design time. However, the ControlDesigner class provides a more elegant solution than this, known as *shadow properties*, that doesn't require special design-time behavior from the control class.

The technique for making sure that the underlying property is only set to the specified value at runtime is to replace its PropertyDescriptor in the PostFilterProperties method with one that refers to a property supplied by the designer class. (So it is very similar to the technique of adding a design-time property shown in Examples 9-20 and 9-21.) This allows the designer class to remember the user's intended setting for the property without having to set that property on the control itself. The property will be set to the intended value at runtime, but not at design time.

To save you from having to declare fields for each of the properties you wish to shadow in your designer class, the base ControlDesigner class provides a protected property called ShadowProperties. This is a collection class that holds name/value pairs. As a convenience, if you try to retrieve a value for a name that is not in the collection, it will retrieve the property of the same name from the control itself, which means you don't need to initialize any of your shadow properties either. This makes the code for adding a shadow property relatively simple, as Examples 9-22 and 9-23 show.

Example 9-22. Shadowing the Anchor property using C#

```
protected override void PostFilterProperties(
    System.Collections.IDictionary properties)
{
    base.PostFilterProperties(properties);
    properties["Anchor"] = TypeDescriptor.CreateProperty(
        typeof(RoundedBoxDesigner),
        (PropertyDescriptor) properties["Anchor"]);
}

public AnchorStyles Anchor
{
    get { return (AnchorStyles) ShadowProperties["Anchor"]; }
    set { ShadowProperties["Anchor"] = value; }
}
```

Example 9-23. Shadowing the Anchor property using VB

```
Protected Overrides Sub PostFilterProperties( _
    properties As System.Collections.IDictionary)

    MyBase.PostFilterProperties(properties)
    properties("Anchor") = TypeDescriptor.CreateProperty( _
        GetType(RoundedBoxDesigner), _
        CType(properties("Anchor"), PropertyDescriptor))
End Sub

Public Property Anchor( ) As AnchorStyles
    Get
        Return CType(ShadowProperties("Anchor"), AnchorStyles)
    End Get
    Set
        ShadowProperties("Anchor") = Value
    End Set
End Property
```

This will have the effect of disabling anchoring behavior at design time, but leaving it enabled at runtime. Note that we are using a different version of the CreateProperty factory function. This one takes an existing PropertyDescriptor (the one already in the properties dictionary) and builds a new one based on that. This preserves all the attributes of the original, and merely has the effect of redirecting to our designer class's property.

The ControlDesigner automatically shadows certain standard properties for you. Visible and Enabled are shadowed because it would difficult to edit invisible or disabled controls. Controls are therefore always visible and enabled at design time, but will honor their settings at runtime. ContextMenu and AllowDrop are also shadowed because the Forms Designer provides its own context menus and uses drag and drop for editing the contents of the form.

Designer Host Interfaces

The custom designer classes we have seen so far have been essentially passive. They rely on the Forms Designer to create designer instances when needed, and to call their methods only when particular services are required. But sometimes your designer class will need to be a bit more proactive, explicitly requesting certain services from the Forms Designer. There is a generic mechanism to enable any container to provide arbitrary services on demand to the contained component.

A component can request a service from its container by calling the GetService method. (This method is available in both the Component class and the ComponentDesigner class, so both controls and their designer classes can request services.) GetService takes a single parameter, a Type object. This should be the type of an interface, indicating which service is required. If the container does not provide the requested service (or if there is no container, which is typically the case at runtime) GetService will return null or Nothing. But if the service is available, it will return an object that implements the requested service.

One of the standard services provided by Visual Studio .NET is ISelectionService. This allows designer classes and controls to find out which items have been selected by the user. Examples 9-24 and 9-25 illustrate how to use this service to modify the design-time appearance of a control according to whether it is selected or not. The example shows modifications to the RoundedBoxDesigner class we first saw in the C# code in Examples 9-12, 9-14, and 9-16, and in the VB code in Examples 9-13, 9-15, and 9-17. Here we override the Initialize method (which will be called when the designer class is instantiated), and ask the container for the ISelectionService interface. If this service is present (it always will be in Visual Studio .NET), our designer class attaches a handler to the SelectionChanged event. Our designer can now track the selection status of the control, causing the control to be redrawn each time it is selected or deselected. The OnPaintAdornments method has been modified so that it only paints the grab handle when the control is selected. (This is more consistent with the behavior of the standard resize handles and selection outline, which are only drawn when the control is selected.)

Example 9-24. Drawing adornments only when selected using C#

```
private ISelectionService iss;

public override void Initialize(IComponent component)
{
```

Example 9-24. Drawing adornments only when selected using C# (continued)

```
    // Call base class so that it can initialize itself

    base.Initialize(component);


    iss = GetService(typeof(ISelectionService)) as ISelectionService;
    if (iss != null)
    {
        iss.SelectionChanged += new EventHandler(OnSelectionChanged);
    }
    else
    {
        // ISelectionService is always available in VS.NET, but
        // if we're being hosted somewhere odd that doesn't have
        // it, just display adornments at all times.
    }
}

protected override void Dispose(bool disposing)
{
    if (disposing && iss != null)
    {
        iss.SelectionChanged -= new EventHandler(OnSelectionChanged);
    }

    base.Dispose(disposing);
}


private bool selected = false;

private void OnSelectionChanged(object sender, EventArgs e)
{
    bool previouslySelected = selected;
    selected = iss.GetComponentSelected(this.Control);
    if (selected != previouslySelected)
        this.Control.Invalidate( );
}

protected override void OnPaintAdornments(PaintEventArgs pe)
{
    if (selected)
    {
        Rectangle grabRect = GetGrabRectangle( );
        ControlPaint.DrawGrabHandle(pe.Graphics, grabRect, true, true);
    }
}
```

Example 9-25. Drawing adornments only when selected using VB

```
Private iss As ISelectionService
Private selected As Boolean = False
```

Example 9-25. Drawing adornments only when selected using VB (continued)

```
Public Overrides Sub Initialize(component As IComponent)

    ' Call base class so that it can initialize itself
    MyBase.Initialize(component)

    iss = CType(GetService(GetType(ISelectionService)), _
            ISelectionService)
    If Not iss Is Nothing Then
        AddHandler iss.SelectionChanged, _
                AddressOf OnSelectionChanged
    Else
        ' ISelectionService is always available in VS.NET, but
        ' if we're being hosted somewhere odd that doesn't have
        ' it, just display adornments at all times.
    End If
End Sub

Protected Overrides Overloads Sub Dispose(disposing As Boolean)
    If disposing And Not iss Is Nothing Then
        RemoveHandler iss.SelectionChanged, _
                    AddressOf OnSelectionChanged
    End If

    MyBase.Dispose(disposing)
End Sub

Private Sub OnSelectionChanged(sender As Object, e As EventArgs)
    Dim previouslySelected As Boolean = selected
    selected = iss.GetComponentSelected(Me.Control)
    If selected <> previouslySelected Then
        Me.Control.Invalidate()
    End If
End Sub

Protected Overrides Sub OnPaintAdornments(pe As PaintEventArgs)
    If selected Then
        Dim grabRect As Rectangle = GetGrabRectangle()
        ControlPaint.DrawGrabHandle(pe.Graphics, grabRect, _
                                    True, True)
    End If
End Sub
```

`ISelectionService` is just one of the many different services available to components and designer classes running in the Forms Designer. Table 9-1 lists the available services and provides a brief description of each service's purpose. These interfaces, which are all defined in the `System.ComponentModel.Design` namespace, are described in more detail in the reference section.

Table 9-1. Designer services

Service type	Purpose
`IComponentChangeService`	Provides notifications when components are added to and removed from the form, and when existing components are modified.
`IDesignerEventService`	Provides access to all the designers active on the form, and provides notifications when designers come and go.
`IDesignerHost`	Provides notification as modifications to a form progress through their various phases. (It supports a lightweight transaction model for these modifications.) Also provides access to the *root component*—i.e., the `Form` or the `UserControl` that contains the control.
`IDesignerOptionService`	Provides access to the designer options chosen by the user. (Currently only used for grid settings such as snap-to-grid.)
`IDictionaryService`	A generic name/value store, allowing the designer class to store arbitrary data.
`IEventBindingService`	Used to make events appear in the property grid.
`IExtenderListService`	Allows a list of extender providers present on the form to be retrieved.
`IExtenderProviderService`	Allows extender providers to be added to or removed from the form.
`IHelpService`	Allows extra hints to be passed to the IDE to improve the suggestions offered by the context-sensitive help system.
`IInheritanceService`	Allows components that inherit from particular base classes to be located.
`IMenuCommandService`	Allows extra menu commands to be added to the development environment.
`IReferenceService`	Provides a way of locating references to a particular component within a project.
`IResourceService`	Allows access to culture-specific resources at design time.
`IRootDesigner`	Retrieves the root designer in environments that support nested designers.
`ISelectionService`	Provides notifications when the selection changes, and allows the list of selected controls to be retrieved.
`ITypeDescriptorFilterService`	Allows metadata filtering.
`ITypeResolutionService`	Allows specified assemblies or types to be found and loaded.

Extender Providers

As we saw in the previous section, it is possible to extend the set of properties that a control presents at design time by writing a custom designer class and implementing one or more of the metadata filtering methods. But what if you want to extend the property set of more than one control? You could write a designer class that is used as the base class for several controls' designers, but what if you would like to be able to extend the property sets of controls you did not write?

The Forms Designer supports a special kind of component called an extender provider, which is able to extend the property set of any control. For example, the built-in `ToolTip` component is an extender provider—if you add a `ToolTip` component to a form, every control on the form gets an extra `ToolTip` property. (Such properties are known as *extender properties*.) We already saw how to use extender providers in Chapter 3, but we will now see how to implement such a component.

Extender providers are not controls, because they do not participate directly in the user interface. In the Forms Designer, they appear in the component tray rather than on the form itself, as shown in Figure 9-6. So instead of inheriting from the `Control` class, an extender provider must derive directly from the `Component` class, which is defined in the `System.ComponentModel` namespace.

toolTip1

Figure 9-6. An extender provider in the component tray

As the `ToolTip` component illustrates, extender providers can augment a control's runtime behavior. Recall from Chapter 3 how an extender property is set at runtime: the Forms Designer generates code that calls a method on the extender provider itself. In this call, it passes in a reference to the object on which the property is notionally being set. Example 9-26 shows the `ToolTip` extender property being set on a control called `button1`.

Example 9-26. Setting an extender property

```
// C# code
this.toolTip1.SetToolTip(this.button1, "This is a button!");

' VB code
Me.toolTip1.SetToolTip(Me.button1, "This is a button!")
```

In general, anything that augments the behavior of a control is often best implemented as an extender provider, if possible. This gives users of the component much greater flexibility than the alternative and more obvious design choice, inheritance. For example, suppose you want a reusable facility that automatically validates the contents of a text box against a regular expression. You might create a `RegExTextBox` control that derives from the built-in `TextBox` control. But what if the user of your control also wants the autocomplete functionality we implemented in the `AutoTextBox` in Chapter 6? The .NET runtime only supports single inheritance, which means this will be an either/or decision. But if we implement regular expression validation as an extender property, we are free to add it to any derivative of `TextBox`. (Arguably, autocompletion would also have been better implemented through an extender provider.)

To create an extender provider, we simply write a component that implements the `IExtenderProvider` interface. This only requires us to implement a single method, `CanExtend`. The Forms Designer will call this at design time, passing in each component on the form in turn to find out whether our provider wants to extend that component's property set. Our validating extender will just check that the component derives from `Control`—otherwise, it might end up trying to add validation support to non-visual components. The only other requirement for our provider class is that it must indicate with `ProvidePropertyAttribute` what properties it will add and provide accessor functions for those properties. Examples 9-27 and 9-28 show our regular expression validation provider.

Example 9-27. An extender provider written in C#

```
using System;
using System.Collections;
using System.Windows.Forms;
using System.ComponentModel;
using System.Text.RegularExpressions;

[ProvideProperty("RegexValidate", typeof(Control))]
public class RegexValidator : Component, IExtenderProvider
{
    private Hashtable ht = new Hashtable( );

    public bool CanExtend(object extendee)
    {
        return extendee is Control;
    }

    public void SetRegexValidate(Control ctl, string expr)
    {
        if (!DesignMode)
        {
            Validator v = new Validator(expr, ctl);
            ctl.Validating += new CancelEventHandler(v.OnValidating);
        }
        ht[ctl] = expr;
    }

    public string GetRegexValidate(Control ctl)
    {
        return (string) ht[ctl];
    }

    private class Validator
    {
        public Validator(string expr, Control ctl)
        {
            reExpr = expr;
            target = ctl;
        }

        private string reExpr;
        private Control target;
        private Regex re;

        public void OnValidating(object sender, CancelEventArgs e)
        {
            if (re == null)
            {
                re = new Regex (reExpr);
            }
            if (!re.IsMatch(target.Text))
            {
```

Example 9-27. An extender provider written in C# (continued)

```
                e.Cancel = true;
            }
        }
    }

}
```

Example 9-28. An extender provider written in VB

```
Option Strict On

Imports System
Imports System.Collections
Imports System.Windows.Forms
Imports System.ComponentModel
Imports System.Text.RegularExpressions

<ProvideProperty("RegexValidate", GetType(Control))> _
Public Class RegexValidator
    Inherits Component
    Implements IExtenderProvider

    Private ht As New Hashtable( )

    Public Function CanExtend(extendee As Object) As Boolean _
            Implements IExtenderProvider.CanExtend
        Return TypeOf extendee Is Control
    End Function

    Public Sub SetRegexValidate(ctl As Control, expr As String)
        If Not DesignMode Then
            Dim v As New Validator(expr, ctl)
            AddHandler ctl.Validating, AddressOf v.OnValidating
        End If
        ht(ctl) = expr
    End Sub

    Public Function GetRegexValidate(ctl As Control) As String
        Return CStr(ht(ctl))
    End Function

    Private Class Validator

        Private reExpr As String
        Private target As Control
        Private re As RegEx

        Public Sub New(expr As String, ctl As Control)
            reExpr = expr
            target = ctl
        End Sub
```

Example 9-28. An extender provider written in VB (continued)

```
        Public Sub OnValidating(sender As Object, e As CancelEventArgs)
            If re Is Nothing Then
                re = New Regex(reExpr)
            End If
            If Not re.IsMatch(target.Text) Then
                e.Cancel = true
            End If
        End Sub
    End Class
End Class
```

The accessors must be functions named Get*Xxx* and Set*Xxx* where *Xxx* is the name of the extender property. You must provide both a get and a set accessor, or Visual Studio .NET will refuse to use your extender provider. This means we are responsible for remembering what the values have been set to for each control. For this, we just use a `Hashtable` (from the `System.Collections` namespace).

When the `SetRegexValidate` method is called, we check to see if we are in design mode or runtime mode. If this is runtime, we build an instance of the private `Validator` class. This is a nested class that does the work of validating the control, using the `Regex` class from the `System.Text.RegularExpressions` namespace. We just attach the `Validator` class's `OnValidating` method to the target control's `Validating` event. When the focus leaves the relevant control, its `Validating` event will fire as usual, and our extender provider will use the regular expression to validate the control.

Figure 9-7 shows how this extender property looks in Visual Studio .NET's property panel. (The regular expression here is a somewhat naïve test for a valid-looking email address.) Example 9-29 shows the code that is generated for this property.

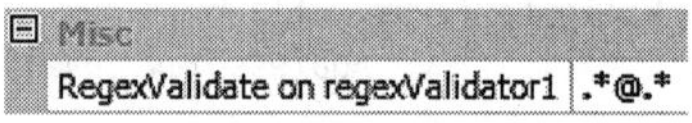

Misc
RegexValidate on regexValidator1
.*@.*

Figure 9-7. An extender property in use

Example 9-29. Code generated for an extender property

```
// C#
this.regexValidator1.SetRegexValidate(this.textBox1, ".*@.*");

' VB
Me.regexValidator1.SetRegexValidate(Me.textBox1, ".*@.*")
```

For this extender provider to be of much use, you would want to add support for error reporting. This would be easy enough to do—you would simply add a second extender property to hold the error text. You could either display a message box to show the message, or you might use the `ErrorProvider` class to show the error. (To do this, you would provide a normal property on the extender provider component itself to tell it which `ErrorProvider` to use.)

Summary

Visual Studio .NET provides visual editing for all controls and property editing for any kind of component without requiring any special effort from the developers of those components. It also provides those developers with many ways of enhancing the design-time behavior of their components. This usually involves writing a special designer class that is associated with the component and manages most design-time aspects of that component's behavior. A designer class can add extra commands to the Forms Designer user interface, it can modify the drag-and-drop editing behavior, it can add its own adornments for visual editing, and it can extend and modify the set of properties seen at design time. It is also possible to write an extender provider, a component that extends the properties available on other components.

10
Data Binding

Windows Forms lets us create rich user interfaces for viewing and editing information. But these applications are often just frontends to a larger system—the information they present typically resides elsewhere. You would not want to entrust your mission-critical data to the `Text` property of a `TextBox` control, and so a great many Windows Forms applications don't own the information they present—the master copy of the data will typically be inside a database. Even applications that do not warrant the use of a full-blown database will usually still maintain a distinction between their internal representation of the data and the presentation of that data.

To help us build applications that have cleanly separated data and presentation layers, the .NET Framework provides a facility called data binding. This is a remarkably flexible architecture for managing the connection between information sources and user interface elements. It provides full support for .NET's data-access architecture, ADO.NET, but it is also extensible—it is simple to write your own data sources, and any control, including any user controls or custom controls that you write, can participate in the presentation of data.

In this chapter, we will start by examining simple data binding, which allows any source of information to be connected to any property of a control. We will then look at complex binding, which is the specialized support for more complex data sources offered by certain controls. We will then look at some of the classes in ADO.NET that are designed to be used for data binding. Finally, we will look at the `DataGrid` control, which makes it easy to present large amounts of structured data to the user.

Data Sources and Bindings

A data source is any object that provides information. The object could be of any type—it could be an ADO.NET `DataSet`, but it could also be a class that you have defined or a standard .NET array. All data sources provide one or more pieces of information. We can arrange for these pieces of information to be displayed by *binding* them to controls.

Consider the simple class shown in C# in Example 10-1 and in VB in Example 10-2. It has just two properties, and as you can see, there is nothing unusual about the code. But despite its simplicity, it is able to act as a data source thanks to the very flexible nature of the Windows Forms binding architecture.

Example 10-1. A simple class with two properties, written in C#

```
public class MySource
{
    public string Name
    {
        get { return nameVal; }
        set { nameVal = value; }
    }
    private string nameVal;

    public int Age
    {
        get { return ageVal; }
        set { ageVal = value; }
    }
    private int ageVal;
}
```

Example 10-2. A simple class with two properties, written in VB

```
Public Class MySource

    Private nameVal As String
    Private ageVal As Integer

    Public Property Name() As String
        Get
           Return nameVal
        End Get
        Set
           nameVal = Value
        End Set
    End Property

    Public Property Age() As Integer
        Get
            Return ageVal
        End Get
        Set
            ageVal = Value
        End Set
    End Property
End Class
```

Example 10-3 shows some C# code from a simple form containing two TextBox controls. (The standard InitializeComponent and Dispose methods have been omitted because they contain nothing unusual in this example.) Notice that the form also has a private field containing an instance of the MySource class we defined in Example 10-1. This object will act as a data source. The form's constructor binds the Text properties of the two TextBox controls to the Name and Age properties of the data source by adding appropriate entries to ControlBindingsCollection exposed by the control's DataBinding property.

Example 10-3. Binding controls to a simple data source

```
public class MyForm : System.Windows.Forms.Form
{
    private System.Windows.Forms.TextBox txtName;
    private System.Windows.Forms.TextBox txtAge;

    private MySource myDataSource = new MySource( );

    public MyForm( )
    {
        InitializeComponent( );

        myDataSource.Name = "Foo";
        myDataSource.Age = 42;
        txtName.DataBindings.Add("Text", myDataSource, "Name");
        txtAge.DataBindings.Add("Text", myDataSource, "Age");
    }

    . . .
}
```

The ControlBindingsCollection class's Add method is overloaded. Here we are using the form that takes the name of the control property to be bound, the data source, and the name of the property on the data source. The Add method creates an instance of the Binding class (passing the three parameters directly in to its constructor) and places it in the collection. The other overload of the Add method takes a Binding object as a parameter. So the call to Add in Example 10-3 is equivalent to calling:

```
txtAge.DataBindings.Add(new Binding(("Text", myDataSource, "Age"))
```

The result of this is that whenever the user edits the text in one of the TextBox controls, the relevant property of the object will be updated to reflect the change. This connection between a control property and a data source property is called a *binding*.

Any property of any control can be bound to any property of any data source, although the Text property is the most common binding target because it will display the relevant data on screen. But because any property is a valid target, including any properties you define for your own controls, a single control could have many bindings associated with it. (In theory, it could have one for each property, although for certain properties such as BorderStyle or TabIndex, binding would only make sense if you were using it to store form layout information in a database to support user-customization.) However, any single control property cannot be bound to more than one data source.

Although a given control property can be bound to at most one data source property, the converse is not true: a single data source property can be bound to any number of control properties. For example, we could modify the example above to have two text boxes, each of which has its Text property bound to the Name property of the same MySource object. If the user edits one of these text boxes, the change will automatically be propagated to the other—Windows Forms tracks all the active data bindings for a given object, so it makes sure that when one control's property values change, any other control properties bound to the same source property are updated to reflect the change.

This raises an interesting question: what if you want to change the data source's value yourself? If you write some code that modifies the value of a property of a data source, it is useful to be able to make sure that any bound control properties will reflect the update. If you are using the ADO.NET DataSet as your data source, it will automatically notify Windows Forms of these updates. But a simple class such as that in Examples 10-1 and 10-2 will not do this.

It is possible to modify our class so that it raises special events known as property change notifications. This will ensure that whenever we change a property from our code, that change will be reflected in any bound controls. The data-binding architecture defines a standard idiom for doing this: whenever it binds to a property, it looks for an associated event whose name will be the property's name with Changed appended. So if binding to the Name property, it will look for a NameChanged event. If such an event exists, it will register an event handler, and every time the event is raised, it will refresh any controls that are bound to this property. Examples 10-4 and 10-5 show an appropriately modified version of the MySource class from Examples 10-1 and 10-2.

Example 10-4. A data source with property change notifications in C#

```
public class MySource
{
    public event EventHandler NameChanged;

    protected virtual void OnNameChanged( )
    {
        if (NameChanged != null)
            NameChanged(this, EventArgs.Empty);
    }

    public string Name
    {
        get { return nameVal; }
        set
        {
            if (nameVal != value)
            {
                nameVal = value;
                OnNameChanged( );
            }
```

Example 10-4. A data source with property change notifications in C# (continued)

```
        }
    }

    private string nameVal;


    public event EventHandler AgeChanged;

    protected virtual void OnAgeChanged( )
    {
        if (AgeChanged != null)
            AgeChanged(this, EventArgs.Empty);
    }

    public int Age
    {
        get { return ageVal; }
        set
        {
            if (ageVal != value)
            {
                ageVal = value;
                OnAgeChanged( );
            }
        }
    }

    private int ageVal;

}
```

Example 10-5. A data source with property change notifications in VB

```
Imports System

Public Class MySource

    Private ageVal As Integer
    Private nameVal As String

    Public Event NameChanged(sender As Object, e As EventArgs)
    Public Event AgeChanged(sender As Object, e As EventArgs)

    Public Property Name( ) As String
        Get
            Return nameVal
        End Get
        Set
            If nameVal <> Value Then
                nameVal = Value
                OnNameChanged( )
            End If
        End Set
```

Example 10-5. A data source with property change notifications in VB (continued)

```
    End Property

    Public Property Age( ) As Integer
        Get
            Return ageVal
        End Get
        Set
            If ageVal <> Value Then
                ageVal = Value
                OnAgeChanged( )
            End If
        End Set
    End Property

    Protected Sub OnNameChanged( )
        RaiseEvent NameChanged(Me, EventArgs.Empty)
    End Sub

    Protected Sub OnAgeChanged( )
        RaiseEvent AgeChanged(Me, EventArgs.Empty)
    End Sub

End Class
```

Property change notification events always use the standard `EventHandler` delegate type; that is, the event handler takes two parameters. The first is an `Object` instance representing the event's sender. The second is an `EventArgs` instance containing information about the event. Here we have also used the standard event handling idiom, where for each public event there is an associated protected method that raises the event. So the `NameChanged` event is always raised by calling the `OnNameChanged` method and `AgeChanged` is raised by calling `OnAgeChanged`. These methods are not mandatory—the data binding architecture doesn't care how we raise the events—but this style, which we also use for events raised by controls, provides derived classes with a hook into the event handling.

With the code for raising property change notifications in place, our data source in Example 10-4 will always be displayed correctly, even when it is modified directly by code such as that in Example 10-6.

Example 10-6. Modifying a data source

```
private void GetOlder( )
{
    myDataSource.Age += 1;
}
```

But what if we are unable to change the data source's implementation? We might want to bind to a class that we did not write, and that does not provide property change notifications. One of the aims of the data-binding architecture is to be able to use any object as a data source, so it is possible to force the display to be updated even if the object in question does not raise property change notifications.

To achieve this, a little more work is required, but first we must understand how Windows Forms tracks bound data sources.

Binding Managers

For every distinct data source in use on a form, Windows Forms creates a binding manager.* This is an object that acts as a kind of clearing house for all changes to the data source. It knows about all the data bindings for the source, which is what enables changes made by one control to be propagated to any other controls bound to the same source. If we want updates to be pushed out this way when the data source does not provide property change notifications, we too must use the binding manager.

It is easy to get hold of the binding manager for a particular data source. The `Form` class has a property called `BindingContext`, which is a collection containing all the binding managers for the whole form. (So far we have only got one data source, but it is possible to have several distinct data sources on a single form, each of which would have its own binding manager.) It is an indexed collection, so to acquire the binding manager for the source, we just pass in the source itself as an index, as shown in Example 10-7.

Example 10-7. Acquiring a binding manager

```
// C#
BindingManagerBase bindMgr = BindingContext[myDataSource];

' VB
Dim bindMgr As BindingManagerBase = BindingContext(myDataSource)
```

`BindingManagerBase` is the base class from which all binding managers derive. The exact type of manager returned will depend on the nature of the data being bound to. (In this case, it will be a `PropertyManager`, which is the manager for binding directly to properties of a single object.) Having got a reference to the binding manager for our data source, we need to make it refresh all the control properties that are bound to it. Unfortunately, there is no method designed to do this, but there is one that has this side effect: `CancelCurrentEdit`. As with Example 10-6, the method in Example 10-8 modifies a property on the data source.

Example 10-8. Using CancelCurrentEdit to make property changes visible

```
private void GetOlder( )
{
    myDataSource.Age += 1;
    BindingContext[myDataSource].CancelCurrentEdit( );
}
```

Because Example 10-8 assumes that the data source does not provide property change notifications, it explicitly forces that change to be propagated to all bound

* Strictly speaking, it does this per binding context, not per form. But by default, each form just has one binding context. We will discuss multiple binding contexts shortly.

controls. The use of CancelCurrentEdit might be regarded as a hack—this method is intended for when the user has started to modify some data in a text field, but then has a change of heart. Calling CancelCurrentEdit pushes the value stored in the source out to any bound control properties, overwriting any edits that the user might have made. We are not quite using this method as intended—we have modified the data source directly and want that change to be pushed out. But it has the effect that we require.

If at all possible you should use data sources that provide change notifications. This will mean that you don't have to remember to force an update every time you change a property.

List Sources

So far we have just used a single object as a data source. However, many data sources return lists of information, database tables being a particularly important example. The data-binding architecture therefore has support for binding to lists of data as well as to individual items.

As with single data sources, Windows Forms is extremely flexible about what kinds of list-like sources it will bind to—it can bind to lists of data contained in any object that implements the IList interface. Because all arrays implement this interface, we can bind to an array of the simple class defined earlier, as shown in the C# code in Example 10-9 and in the VB code in Example 10-10.

Example 10-9. Binding to an array of simple objects using C#

```
public class MyForm : System.Windows.Forms.Form
{
    private System.Windows.Forms.TextBox txtName;
    private System.Windows.Forms.TextBox txtAge;

    private MySource[] myDataListSource;

    public MyForm( )
    {
        InitializeComponent( );

        myDataListSource = new MySource[10];
        for (int i = 0; i < myDataListSource.Length; ++i)
        {
            myDataListSource[i] = new MySource( );
            myDataListSource[i].Name = "Foo" + i;
            myDataListSource[i].Age = 20 + i;
        }

        txtName.DataBindings.Add("Text", myDataListSource, "Name");
        txtAge.DataBindings.Add("Text", myDataListSource, "Age");
    }

    . . .
}
```

Example 10-10. Binding to an array of simple objects using VB

```
Public Class MyForm : Inherits Form

    Private WithEvents txtName As TextBox
    Private WithEvents txtAge As  TextBox

    Dim myDataListSource(10) As MySource

    Public Sub New( )
        MyBase.New( )

        InitializeComponent( )

        ReDim myDataListSource(10)
        Dim i As Integer

        For i = 0 to myDataListSource.Length - 1
            myDataListSource(i) = new MySource( )
            myDataListSource(i).Name = "Foo" + CStr(i)
            myDataListSource(i).Age = 20 + i
        Next

        txtName.DataBindings.Add("Text", myDataListSource, "Name")
        txtAge.DataBindings.Add("Text", myDataListSource, "Age")
    End Sub

    . . .
End Class
```

The code in Examples 10-9 and 10-10 is almost identical to that in Example 10-3, the only difference being that we have replaced a single `MySource` object with an array of `MySource` objects. As it stands, it is not very interesting, because it will only allow the first object in the array to be edited. However, the binding manager for our data source provides us with ways of iterating through the list. We might expose this by adding Previous and Next buttons to the form.

Examples 10-11 and 10-12 show `Click` event handlers for Previous and Next buttons, which allow the user to move back and forth through the list. They work by acquiring the binding manager for the data source and adjusting its `Position` property. The `Position` property determines which list item's properties are currently displayed in the bound controls. (The binding manager ignores this property when binding to a single object as in Example 10-3.)

Example 10-11. Scrolling through items in a bound list using C#

```
private void btnPrevious_Click(object sender, EventArgs e)
{
    BindingManagerBase bm = BindingContext[myDataListSource];
    if (bm.Position == 0)
        return;

    bm.Position -= 1;

}
```

Example 10-11. Scrolling through items in a bound list using C# (continued)

```
private void btnNext_Click(object sender, EventArgs e)
{
    BindingManagerBase bm = BindingContext[myDataListSource];
    if (bm.Position == bm.Count - 1)
        return;

    bm.Position += 1;
}
```

Example 10-12. Scrolling through items in a bound list using VB

```
Public Sub btnPrevious_Click(sender As Object, e As EventArgs) _
        Handles btnPrevious.Click
    Dim bm As BindingManagerBase = BindingContext(myDataListSource)

    If bm.Position = 0 Then Return

    bm.Position -= 1
End Sub

Public Sub btnNext_Click(sender As Object, e As EventArgs) _
        Handles btnNext.Click
    Dim bm As BindingManagerBase = BindingContext(myDataListSource)

    If bm.Position = bm.Count - 1 Then Return

    bm.Position += 1
End Sub
```

Because the `Position` is a property of the binding manager, and each data source has exactly one binding manager, all controls bound to a particular data source will reflect the property values for the same list entry at any given time. So adjusting the position on our example will cause the two bound `TextBox` controls to be updated. If you examine the binding manager returned for lists of data, you will see that it is of type `CurrencyManager`. This is because it is responsible for keeping track of the *current* position. (It doesn't have anything to do with money.)

Remember that in Example 10-6, we wrote a method that modified one of the data source's properties. This example now needs to be modified to work in the context of a list. It must determine which particular item in the list it should modify. This is easy to do because the `BindingManagerBase` class provides a `Current` property that returns the current item from the list. We can also use the `Position` property as an index into the array. We will use the latter here because otherwise we would need to cast the `object` returned by `Current` back to `MySource`.

As with a single data source, if a list entry's class provides property change notification events, the modification that Example 10-13 makes to the `Age` property will automatically be propagated to any bound controls. But if you are working with a data source that does not supply such events, once again you will need to provide manual notification of the updates. Although the `CancelCurrentEdit` technique shown in Example 10-8 will work, a slightly more elegant solution is available when binding to a list; it is shown in Example 10-14.

Example 10-13. Modifying the current item in a list

```
private void GetOlder( )
{
    int pos = BindingContext[myDataListSource].Position;
    MySource src = myDataListSource[pos];
    src.Age += 1;
}
```

Example 10-14. Modifying a list item that does not provide property change notifications

```
private void GetOlder( )
{
    CurrencyManager cm = (CurrencyManager)
                BindingContext[myDataListSource];
    MySource src = myDataListSource[cm.Position];
    src.Age += 1;
    cm.Refresh( );
}
```

In Example 10-14, we are exploiting the fact that the binding manager will always be an instance of the `CurrencyManager` class when dealing with a list-like source. And unlike `PropertyManager`, `CurrencyManager` provides a `Refresh` method to push modifications out to any bound controls.

The `Refresh` method can also be useful even if your data source class provides property change notifications. If you want to add or remove items from the list, the fact that the objects in the list raise notifications when individual properties are changed will not be sufficient to notify the binding architecture that the list now has new entries. This is particularly important if you are using controls that can display information from all the entries in the list at once and not just the current one. (We will see how to do this shortly.) Certain data sources (notably the `DataSet`) can raise automatic notifications when the contents of the list change as well as when individual entries' values change, but simple arrays will not do this, nor will the `ArrayList` class. So when adding, removing, or replacing objects from such data sources, you should always call the `Refresh` method to inform the `CurrencyManager` that the list's contents have changed.

It is not clear why the `Refresh` method is defined by `CurrencyManager` instead of its base class, `BindingManagerBase`—it would be useful in all binding scenarios, not just list-based binding. (This is precisely the method we wanted earlier when we had to resort to the less satisfactory `CancelCurrentEdit`.)

Simple and Complex Binding

The examples we have seen so far all use the technique known as *simple binding*. Simple binding has two defining characteristics:

- Bindings deal with single pieces of information, both in the sense that single source properties are bound to single control properties, and also in the sense that only a single item from a list can be shown at any one time.
- Simple binding requires no special support from the control—the data-binding architecture is able to bind to any control property, including any new properties you introduce in your custom controls.

Complex binding overcomes the restrictions of simple binding—it can allow a single control to display multiple entries from a list, and multiple properties from any single item. However, it requires special support from the control—most of the built-in controls do not support complex binding, and if you want your own controls to support it, you will need to do most of the work yourself. But don't be put off by the name—complex binding is only complex for the developer who creates the control; it can actually make things much simpler for developers who use the control.

The built-in controls that support complex binding are `ListBox`, `ComboBox`, and `DataGrid`. The first two work the same and we will start by looking at those. The `DataGrid` control's data-binding support is rather more extensive, and we will examine it later.

List Control Binding

The `ListBox` and `ComboBox` controls have a great deal in common. They share the same base class, `ListControl`, and this common base supplies their complex data-binding support. Both of these controls are able to bind to a list data source (such as an array) and display the entire contents of the list rather than just a single item.

Figure 10-1 shows a simple Windows Forms program.

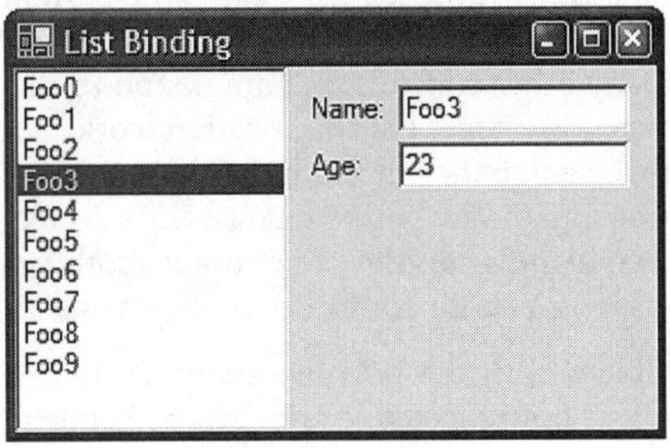
List Binding
Foo0
Foo1
Foo2
Foo3
Foo4
Foo5
Foo6
Foo7
Foo8
Foo9
Name:
Foo3
Age:
23

Figure 10-1. Binding a ListBox to an array

The program in Figure 10-1 has three controls all bound to the same data source, which is an array of the `MySource` class defined earlier in C# in Example 10-4 and in VB in Example 10-5. The two `TextBox` controls on the right have been bound to this data source using simple binding, using exactly the same code as Example 10-9. This program has simply added one more control to Example 10-9, a `ListBox`. It is bound to the data source with the C# code shown in Example 10-15; the VB code is identical, except that it lacks the closing semicolon.

Example 10-15. Binding a ListBox to an array with complex binding

```
listBox.DataSource = myDataListSource;
listBox.DisplayMember = "Name";
```

Notice that we are no longer using the DataBindings property to bind the control to the data source, because DataBindings only supports simple binding. Instead, we are using the DataSource property, which is only present on controls that support complex binding. By setting this property to refer to the array, we are telling the ListBox that we would like it to display the whole array and not just the current entry of the array.

The ListBox control needs to know how it should display the items. By default, it will simply call the ToString method on every item in the list to which it is bound. This would not be helpful in this example because our MySource class does not override ToString, the default behavior of which is to return the name of the class. A ListBox in which every entry was the class name would not be very useful, so here we have instructed the ListBox to extract each item's Name property and display that. We achieved this by setting the ListBox control's DisplayMember property.

Notice that in Figure 10-1 the text fields are displaying the properties for the selected item in the listbox. This happens automatically because all three controls are bound to the same data source. Remember that the data-binding framework creates one binding manager for each data source in use on a form, and any control that is bound to that source is associated with that binding manager, whether it is using simple or complex binding. In this case, the data source is an array, so the binding manager will be a CurrencyManager. This CurrencyManager is responsible for keeping track of which list item is the current one. Whenever the listbox's current selection is changed, it notifies the CurrencyManager for the data source, thus causing any other controls that are bound to the same data source to reflect the newly selected list item. This notification works in both directions, so if something else were to change the current item, the CurrencyManager would notify all bound controls, causing the listbox to change the selected item. (For example, if you were to bind two listboxes to the same source, both would always show the same selected item, as long as both controls share the same BindingContext.)

There is a slight problem with the previous example. If you edit the text in the name field, the change is not reflected in the listbox. While the change is made to the underlying data, it is simply not noticed by the listbox, despite the fact that our MySource class now raises property change notifications. The problem arises because all controls that support complex data binding expect data sources that change their contents to implement a special interface derived from IList called IBindingList. The array class does not implement this interface, and it is not trivial to implement. However, there are some specialized data source classes that we will now look at that support IBindingList. Using these instead of a simple array can solve this problem.

DataTable, DataSet, and Friends

Although the data-binding architecture is flexible enough to bind to any property of any object, the .NET Framework provides a group of classes (part of ADO.NET) that have much more extensive data-binding support. At the center of this family are the `DataSet` and `DataTable` classes in the `System.Data` namespace. These form the basis for the disconnected use of data from a database, and they are designed to allow flexible presentation of data while making efficient use of server resources.

All presentation of data from a database in Windows Forms is based around a disconnected model—clients connect to a database and retrieve all the data they require in a single step. They do not hold onto any server-side resources (such as cursors) after this data has been retrieved, and can therefore release their connection to the database. (In practice, the connection will normally be returned to a pool rather than being freed completely.) This is a departure from previous data-binding models, where disconnected operation was strictly optional. This new model reduces the workload on the server, because at any given instant it has to deal with fewer clients, thus improving the scalability of the system.

The `DataTable` class allows a snapshot of part (or all) of a database table to be held on the client. The `DataSet` class can hold any number of `DataTable` objects, and can also contain information about relations between these tables. (Relations are represented as `DataRelation` objects.)

This rich client-side data representation allows us to present an extensive amount of data while only requiring a single round trip to the database. For example, we can build a user interface that shows lists of data and can then present detailed information for each item as it is selected without needing to make a further trip to the database.

Obviously, you will need to exercise a little restraint here—although it is theoretically possible to build a complete snapshot of the entire database on the client, this will usually not be a sensible approach. But the ability to have client-side relational snapshots of small subsections of the database is very useful.

Although the `DataSet` and `DataTable` classes are typically used to store data that has been retrieved from a database, they can be used to store any kind of data. For example, you can also use XML as a data source with the `DataSet` class's `ReadXml` method, or you can build up tables from scratch in code.

We will now see how to use these classes and how to bind controls to them. We will start with a single table. Then we will add this to a `DataSet` along with some related tables to illustrate the use of relations in data binding.

Using the DataTable Class

The `DataTable` class represents tabular data such as would be returned from a SQL `SELECT` statement. A `DataTable` contains information about the names and types of each column in the table and a collection of rows. We usually fill `DataTable` objects with data from a database or an XML document, but it is also possible to build one from scratch in code, as shown in Examples 10-16 and 10-17.

Example 10-16. Building a DataTable from scratch using C#

```
DataTable customers = new DataTable("Customers");

customers.Columns.Add("CustomerID", typeof(int));
customers.Columns.Add("FirstName", typeof(string));
customers.Columns.Add("LastName", typeof(string));

customers.PrimaryKey = new DataColumn[]
              { customers.Columns["CustomerID"] };

customers.Rows.Add(new object[] { 1, "Homer", "Simpson" });
customers.Rows.Add(new object[] { 2, "Arthur", "Pewty" });
```

Example 10-17. Building a DataTable from scratch using VB

```
Dim customers As New DataTable("Customers")

customers.Columns.Add("CustomerID", GetType(Integer))
customers.Columns.Add("FirstName", GetType(String))
customers.Columns.Add("LastName", GetType(String))

customers.PrimaryKey = new DataColumn() _
                       { customers.Columns("CustomerID") }

customers.Rows.Add(new object() { 1, "Homer", "Simpson" })
customers.Rows.Add(new object() { 2, "Arthur", "Pewty" })
```

This code creates a new table called `Customers`. Passing the name to the constructor is optional, but will be useful later on when we will be using multiple related tables. Next, we tell the `DataTable` what columns it will have, supplying a name and a `Type` object representing the data type for each column. We also tell the `DataTable` which of these columns acts as a primary key. (The `DataTable` supports compound keys, so its `PrimaryKey` property expects to be passed an array. Here we are just using our `CustomerID` column as the key, so we pass an array containing just one element.) The `DataTable` enforces the uniqueness of the primary key—if you attempt to add a row with a duplicate key to a `DataTable`, it will throw an exception.

Having supplied this metadata, we are now free to add the real data to the table by calling the `Add` method on the table's `Rows` property, as shown at the end of Examples 10-16 and 10-17. Note that because the table knows what columns it expects to see, it will check any new rows that are added. If the row data does not match the expected column types, the `Add` method will throw a `System.ArgumentException` exception.

We can now read the data back out from the table. The `Rows` property provides two ways of extracting rows. One is an indexer property, allowing individual rows to be accessed by number. (This is just an offset into the list of rows; it bears no relation to the primary key.) It also supports enumeration, allowing the C# `foreach` construct or the VB `For Each...Next` construct to be used. Examples 10-18 and 10-19 illustrate both techniques. In either case, each row is represented by a `DataRow` object. The `DataRow` object also supplies indexer properties allowing columns in the row to be accessed either by index or by name.

Example 10-18. Retrieving data from a DataTable using C#

```
DataRow firstRow = customers.Rows[0];
Console.WriteLine("First CustomerID is {0}",
    firstRow["CustomerID"]);

foreach (DataRow row in customers.Rows)
{
    Console.WriteLine("Customer {0} is called {1} {2}",
        row["CustomerID"], row["FirstName"], row["LastName"]);
}
```

Example 10-19. Retrieving data from a DataTable using VB

```
Dim row As DataRow
Dim firstRow As DataRow = customers.Rows(0)
Console.WriteLine("First CustomerID is {0}", _
    firstRow("CustomerID"))

For Each row in customers.Rows
    Console.WriteLine("Customer {0} is called {1} {2}", _
        row("CustomerID"), row("FirstName"), row("LastName"))
Next
```

More usefully, we can bind control properties to this table. This works in exactly the same way as it did for binding to a simple class, both for simple and complex binding. Example 10-20 shows the C# code that uses simple binding to bind the three column values to a `Label` control and two `TextBox` controls, using exactly the same technique shown in Example 10-3 for binding to a class property. (The VB code is identical, without the semicolons that terminate each statement.) Example 10-20 also uses complex binding to bind the entire table to a `ListBox` control, and again the technique is identical to that shown in Example 10-15—we specify the data source and also the member that we would like to use for the list item text.

Example 10-20. Binding to a DataTable

```
labelCustomerID.DataBindings.Add("Text", customers, "CustomerID");
textBoxFirstName.DataBindings.Add("Text", customers, "FirstName");
textBoxLastName.DataBindings.Add("Text", customers, "LastName");

listBoxCustomers.DataSource = customers;
listBoxCustomers.DisplayMember = "LastName";
```

Figure 10-2 shows the form containing these controls in action. As before, the simple-bound controls (the `Label` and `TextBox` controls) always show the values for whichever item is currently selected in the `ListBox` control. This is because when a `DataTable` is used as a data source, the Windows Forms data-binding architecture creates a `CurrencyManager` as the associated binding manager, just as it did for the array source. As before, this keeps track of the currently selected item, and makes sure that all controls bound to that data source show values from that same current item.

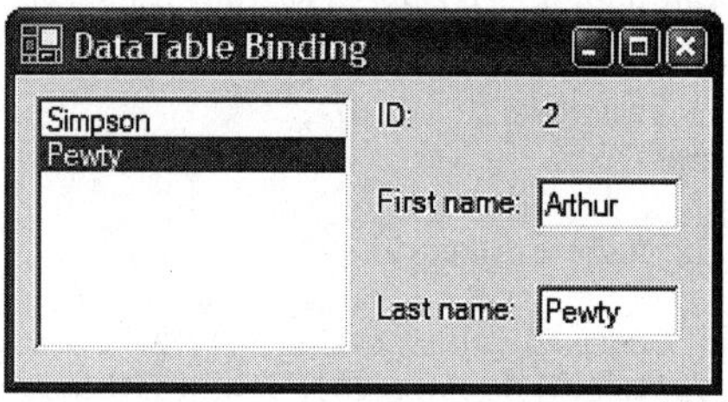
DataTable Binding
Simpson
Pewty
ID:
2
First name:
Arthur
Last name:
Pewty

Figure 10-2. A form with controls bound to a DataTable

Because the `DataTable` class is designed to be used for data binding, it automatically generates update notifications. So you do not need to take any steps to ensure that changes made to a table's contents will be reflected in any controls that are bound to that table. It even supplies an implementation of `IBindingList`. As mentioned earlier, this means that if rows are added to or removed from the list, or if an item in the table other than the currently selected one is modified, these changes will be reflected by any complex-bound controls.

Using the DataSet Class

Databases rarely consist of a single table. Applications that use a relational database will usually deal with multiple related tables. So when it comes to presenting data from the database in a client application, it follows that we will often want to present data from more than one table. The relations between tables are also likely to be important to the client application. The `DataSet` class can contain multiple `DataTable` objects, and can also contain `DataRelation` objects that describe the relations that exist between the tables.

In the previous section, our examples had just a single table, `Customers`. Let us now add a second table called `Orders`. This will hold a simple list of orders made by customers, as shown in Examples 10-21 and 10-22.

Example 10-21. Creating a second DataTable using C#

```
orders = new DataTable("Orders");
orders.Columns.Add("OrderID", typeof(int));
orders.Columns.Add("CustomerID", typeof(int));
orders.Columns.Add("Product", typeof(string));
orders.Columns.Add("Quantity", typeof(int));
orders.PrimaryKey = new DataColumn[] { orders.Columns["OrderID"] };

orders.Rows.Add(new Object[] { 1, 1, "Donuts", 500 } );
orders.Rows.Add(new Object[] { 2, 1, "Cans of beer", 200 } );
orders.Rows.Add(new Object[] { 3, 2, "Pencils", 20 } );
```

Example 10-22. Creating a second DataTable using VB

```
Dim orders As New DataTable("Orders")
orders.Columns.Add("OrderID", GetType(Integer))
orders.Columns.Add("CustomerID", GetType(Integer))
orders.Columns.Add("Product", GetType(String))
```

Example 10-22. Creating a second DataTable using VB (continued)

```
orders.Columns.Add("Quantity", GetType(Integer))
orders.PrimaryKey = New DataColumn( ) { orders.Columns("OrderID") }

orders.Rows.Add(new Object( ) { 1, 1, "Donuts", 500 } )
orders.Rows.Add(new Object( ) { 2, 1, "Cans of beer", 200 } )
orders.Rows.Add(new Object( ) { 3, 2, "Pencils", 20 } )
```

This table has its own primary key, `OrderID`. The `Product` and `Quantity` columns represent the item being ordered and the quantity required, respectively. But notice that there is also a `CustomerID` column. This will be used as a foreign key that relates rows in this table to rows in the `Customers` table. We establish this association by placing both tables into a `DataSet` object and creating a relation between them, as shown in Examples 10-23 and 10-24.

Example 10-23. Adding related tables to a DataSet using C#

```
DataSet ds = new DataSet( );
ds.Tables.Add(customers);
ds.Tables.Add(orders);

ds.Relations.Add("OrdersRelation",
    customers.Columns["CustomerID"],
    orders.Columns["CustomerID"]);
```

Example 10-24. Adding related tables to a DataSet using VB

```
Dim ds As New DataSet( )
ds.Tables.Add(customers)
ds.Tables.Add(orders)

ds.Relations.Add("OrdersRelation", _
    customers.Columns("CustomerID"), _
    orders.Columns("CustomerID"))
```

This adds a named relation called `OrdersRelation` that defines the relationship between these two tables. Relations are directional, and by default, they will be traversed from the parent to the child. The first column passed to the `Add` method is considered to be the parent and the second column the child. So in this case, it will be possible to use the relation to find the orders that correspond to a customer row by calling the `DataRow` class's `GetChildRows` method. It is also possible to traverse the relation in the opposite direction using the `GetParentRows` method of the child row. In this particular case, it is not possible to set up the relation in the opposite direction, because the parent column is required to be unique. (In other words, the `DataSet` supports one-to-many relations, but not many-to-one relations.)

> The name of a relation is not significant. It simply needs to be unique within the scope of the `DataSet` to which it applies. Although it is common for the relation to have the same name as the child table, as Example 10-23 shows, this is not a requirement.

Adding a relation to a DataSet sets up a constraint—with this relation in place, any row added to the Orders table will be checked, and if its CustomerID value does not have a corresponding entry in the Customers table with the same CustomerID, a System.Data.InvalidConstraintException will be thrown. (Be aware that the DataSet has no way of checking that the relations you create correspond to the relations in the database's underlying schema. It is up to you to make sure that you create the correct relations.)

While enforcing foreign key constraints is useful, there is a more interesting side effect of defining relations when data binding is being used. If a relation exists between two tables, it is possible to use this in conjunction with complex binding to show only those items from a child list that are related to the currently selected items in the parent list. So as Figure 10-3 shows, we could add a second list control to show all the orders for the currently selected customer.

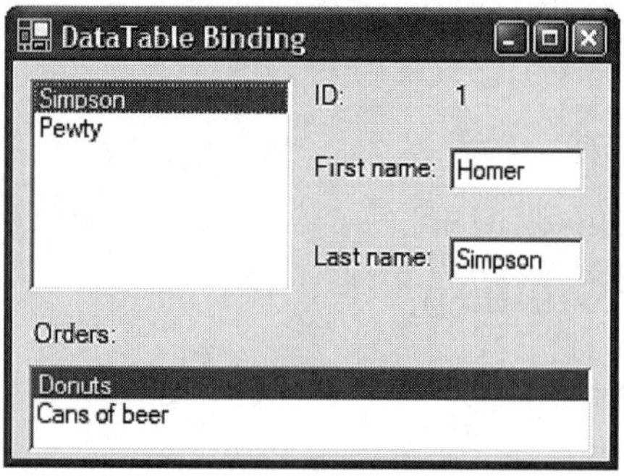
DataTable Binding
Simpson
Pewty
ID:
1
First name:
Homer
Last name:
Simpson
Orders:
Donuts
Cans of beer

Figure 10-3. Master/details binding

The Orders DataTable itself has three rows (see Examples 10-21 and 10-22), but only two are shown here. This is because the orders ListBox only shows items that correspond to the currently selected customer (i.e., orders whose CustomerID is equal to 1). The code to achieve this is very simple and is shown in C# in Example 10-25. (Once again, the VB code is identical except for the absence of the closing semicolons.)

Example 10-25. Complex binding through a relation

```
listBoxOrders.DataSource = customers;
listBoxOrders.DisplayMember = "OrdersRelation.Product";
```

Notice that although the DataSource property has been set to the Customers table, the ListBox is showing items from the Orders table. This is because the DisplayMember property has been set to OrdersRelation.Product. Setting DisplayMember to a string with a period in it indicates that relations are in use. Here we are indicating that we wish to bind through the OrdersRelation relation that we set up in Examples 10-23 and 10-24, and that we wish to show the Product column from the child table (Orders).

The complete code for creating these tables, establishing the relations, and binding the controls is shown in Examples 10-26 and 10-27.

Example 10-26. Display a master/details view using C#

```
// Create the Customers table

DataTable customers = new DataTable("Customers");

customers.Columns.Add("CustomerID", typeof(int));
customers.Columns.Add("FirstName", typeof(string));
customers.Columns.Add("LastName", typeof(string));
customers.PrimaryKey = new DataColumn[]
    { customers.Columns["CustomerID"] };

customers.Rows.Add(new object[] { 1, "Homer", "Simpson" });
customers.Rows.Add(new object[] { 2, "Arthur", "Pewty" });


// Create the Orders table

DataTable orders = new DataTable("Orders");
orders.Columns.Add("OrderID", typeof(int));
orders.Columns.Add("CustomerID", typeof(int));
orders.Columns.Add("Product", typeof(string));
orders.Columns.Add("Quantity", typeof(int));
orders.PrimaryKey = new DataColumn[]
    { orders.Columns["OrderID"] };

orders.Rows.Add(new Object[] { 1, 1, "Donuts", 500 } );
orders.Rows.Add(new Object[] { 2, 1, "Cans of beer", 200 } );
orders.Rows.Add(new Object[] { 3, 2, "Pencils", 20 } );


// Add both tables to a DataSet and establish
// the relation between their CustomerID columns

DataSet ds = new DataSet( );
ds.Tables.Add(customers);
ds.Tables.Add(orders);
ds.Relations.Add("OrdersRelation", customers.Columns["CustomerID"],
    orders.Columns["CustomerID"]);


// Bind the controls

labelCustomerID.DataBindings.Add("Text", customers, "CustomerID");
textBoxFirstName.DataBindings.Add("Text", customers, "FirstName");
textBoxLastName.DataBindings.Add("Text", customers, "LastName");

listBoxCustomers.DataSource = customers;
listBoxCustomers.DisplayMember = "LastName";

listBoxOrders.DataSource = customers;
listBoxOrders.DisplayMember = "OrdersRelation.Product";
```

Example 10-27. Display a master/details view using VB

```
' Create the Customers table

Dim customers As New DataTable("Customers")

customers.Columns.Add("CustomerID", GetType(Integer))
customers.Columns.Add("FirstName", GetType(String))
customers.Columns.Add("LastName", GetType(String))

customers.PrimaryKey = new DataColumn( ) _
         { customers.Columns("CustomerID") }

customers.Rows.Add(new object( ) { 1, "Homer", "Simpson" })
customers.Rows.Add(new object( ) { 2, "Arthur", "Pewty" })

' Create the Orders table

Dim orders As New DataTable("Orders")
orders.Columns.Add("OrderID", GetType(Integer))
orders.Columns.Add("CustomerID", GetType(Integer))
orders.Columns.Add("Product", GetType(String))
orders.Columns.Add("Quantity", GetType(Integer))
orders.PrimaryKey = New DataColumn( ) { orders.Columns("OrderID") }

orders.Rows.Add(new Object( ) { 1, 1, "Donuts", 500 } )
orders.Rows.Add(new Object( ) { 2, 1, "Cans of beer", 200 } )
orders.Rows.Add(new Object( ) { 3, 2, "Pencils", 20 } )

' Add both tables to a DataSet and establish
' the relation between their CustomerID columns
Dim ds As New DataSet( )
ds.Tables.Add(customers)
ds.Tables.Add(orders)

ds.Relations.Add("OrdersRelation", _
             customers.Columns("CustomerID"), _
             orders.Columns("CustomerID"))

' Bind the controls

labelCustomerID.DataBindings.Add("Text", customers, "CustomerID")
textBoxFirstName.DataBindings.Add("Text", customers, "FirstName")
textBoxLastName.DataBindings.Add("Text", customers, "LastName")

listBoxCustomers.DataSource = customers
listBoxCustomers.DisplayMember = "LastName"

listBoxOrders.DataSource = customers
listBoxOrders.DisplayMember = "OrdersRelation.Product"
```

Populating a DataSet from a Database

The previous example builds DataSet and DataTable objects from scratch. However, most applications will fill these objects with data from a database. There is a class that automates this process, called the DataAdapter class, which is defined in the System.Data.Common namespace. It connects to a database, retrieves one or more tables of data, adds them to a DataSet, and then disconnects from the database. (Unfortunately, it cannot automatically retrieve relations from the database schema, so you must write code to set these up yourself.)

DataAdapter is an abstract base class, so you must use one of the concrete classes derived from it. The class you use will depend on what kind of database you are using. If you are using SQL Server, you will use the SqlDataAdapter class in the System.Data.SqlClient namespace. If you are using an OLE DB data source, you will use the OleDbDataAdapter class in the System.Data.OleDb namespace. But regardless of what database you use, the adapter classes all work in much the same way. Example 10-28 shows an example written in C#.

Example 10-28. Filling a DataSet with a DataAdapter

```
string command = "SELECT * FROM Products";
string connect = "data source=.;initial catalog=Northwind;" +
    "integrated security=SSPI";

SqlDataAdapter adapter = new SqlDataAdapter(command, connect);
adapter.TableMappings.Add("Table", "Products");

DataSet ds = new DataSet( );
adapter.Fill(ds);
```

Here we are using the SQL Server data adapter, SqlDataAdapter, but the code would look almost identical for any other database—we would just use, say, the OleDbDataAdapter class, or some vendor-specific adapter class. To create a data adapter, we simply need a connection string indicating which database will supply the data and a command to execute to retrieve the data. Here we are connecting to the Northwind database, a sample database shipped with SQL Server, and we are retrieving the entire contents of the Products table.

Calling the Fill method causes the data adapter to connect to the database, execute the command, copy the results into the DataSet supplied, and disconnect. This means that the database connection is in use for the smallest amount of time possible, which reduces the load on the server. We can then use the results at our leisure. In this case, the DataSet will only contain a single table because that is all the SQL command returned. (Data adapters can add multiple tables to a DataSet if executing an appropriate batch statement or stored procedure.) The adapter will use the metadata that comes back with the results to add all the appropriate columns to the table it creates, but by default it will call that table Table. So here we have added an entry to the adapter's TableMappings property indicating that instead of calling the table Table, it should call it Products. Note that if a table of the specified name already exists in the DataSet, the data adapter will attempt to add rows to it instead of creating a new table.

Remember that a DataSet can contain as many tables as you like. There are two ways of using data adapters to put multiple tables into a DataSet. One is to use more than one adapter—you can create a single data set and then pass it as the parameter to the Fill method on any number of different data adapters. As long as their TableMappings are set up so as not to collide, each will add its own table to the DataSet. However, if all the tables are coming from a single database, it is more efficient to merge all these into a single batch SQL statement, as shown in C# in Example 10-29.

Example 10-29. Reading multiple tables with a data adapter

```
string connect = "data source=.;initial catalog=Northwind;" +
    "integrated security=SSPI";
string command = "SELECT * FROM Customers; " +
    "SELECT * FROM Orders; SELECT * FROM [Order Details]";

SqlDataAdapter adapter = new SqlDataAdapter(command, connect);
adapter.TableMappings.Add("Table", "Customers");
adapter.TableMappings.Add("Table1", "Orders");
adapter.TableMappings.Add("Table2", "Order Details");

DataSet ds = new DataSet( );
adapter.Fill(ds);
```

This code is almost identical to Example 10-28. The only differences are that the command is now a batch of three SELECT statements, and there are now three table mappings. Note that when the SqlDataAdapter returns multiple tables, by default, it just names them sequentially as Table, Table1, Table2, etc.

The sample Northwind database has a similar structure to our previous example in that we have a table of customers and a related table of orders. (It is a little more complex because an order can consist of several items, contained in the Order Details table, and there is also a Products table to represent the kinds of items that can be ordered. But complexity aside, the same principles apply.) We will therefore want to represent the relations in the DataSet as before. Example 10-30 establishes the relations appropriate to these tables.

Example 10-30. Establishing relations

```
ds.Relations.Add("CustomerOrdersRelation",
    ds.Tables["Customers"].Columns["CustomerID"],
    ds.Tables["Orders"].Columns["CustomerID"]);
ds.Relations.Add("OrderDetailsRelation",
    ds.Tables["Orders"].Columns["OrderID"],
    ds.Tables["Order Details"].Columns["OrderID"]);
```

Having done this, we can bind controls to this data in much the same way that we did when building our own DataTable objects from scratch. This is shown in Example 10-31. There are some minor differences from the original code shown in Examples 10-26 and 10-27 because the structure of information in the Northwind database is not quite the same as that in the earlier example. (Names are not separated into first and last names here. And because in Northwind, orders can consist of multiple items, we just show the order date in the orders ListBox instead of the product name.)

Example 10-31. Binding to data from a database

```
labelCustomerID.DataBindings.Add("Text", ds, "Customers.CustomerID");
textBoxCompanyName.DataBindings.Add("Text", ds, "Customers.CompanyName");
textBoxContactName.DataBindings.Add("Text", ds, "Customers.ContactName");

listBoxCustomers.DataSource = ds;
listBoxCustomers.DisplayMember = "Customers.CompanyName";

listBoxOrders.DataSource = ds;
listBoxOrders.DisplayMember =
    "Customers.CustomerOrdersRelation.OrderDate";
```

Also note that here we are using the DataSet itself as the data source and naming the table in the data member. Before, we were using the table itself as the data source. It doesn't matter which you use although you must be consistent, because otherwise you may cause the data-binding system to create two CurrencyManager objects, which could cause your controls to get out of sync. In this case, we are using the DataSet because it is more convenient—the data adapter created the tables for us automatically, so we don't have any references to them handy.

Figure 10-4 shows the modified user interface, displaying the data as retrieved from the database. As before, the orders ListBox will only show those orders for the item currently selected in the customer ListBox.

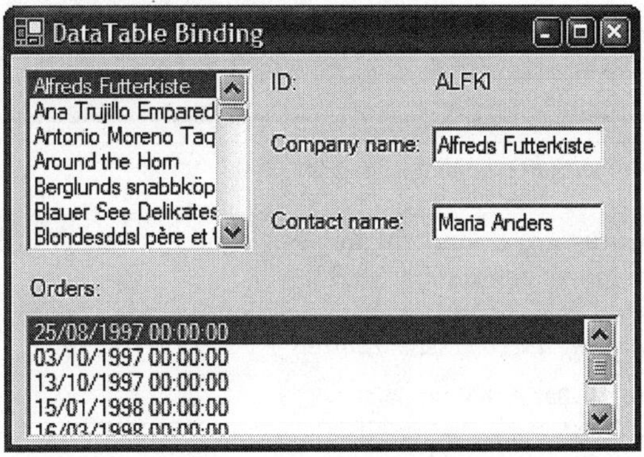
DataTable Binding
Alfreds Futterkiste
Ana Trujillo Empared
Antonio Moreno Taq
Around the Horn
Berglunds snabbköp
Blauer See Delikates
Blondesddsl père et f
ID:
ALFKI
Company name:
Alfreds Futterkiste
Contact name:
Maria Anders
Orders:
25/08/1997 00:00:00
03/10/1997 00:00:00
13/10/1997 00:00:00
15/01/1998 00:00:00

Figure 10-4. A form showing a master/details view from a database

Multiple Binding Contexts

By default, all controls that are bound to a single source share a binding manager. This is useful because it keeps those controls synchronized, and is the basis for the master/details views shown above. But what if you don't want this automatic synchronization? Sometimes it is useful to have two controls showing the same list. If these controls share a binding manager, they will always show the same item as being selected—changing the current selection in one will automatically change the current selection in the other. To get around this, you must use multiple binding contexts.

A binding context is essentially a collection of binding managers. All controls are associated with a binding context, and it is through this context that they find the binding managers for any data sources they are bound to. By default, a control will simply use its parent's binding context, which means that controls will usually use their containing form's context. But this is easily changed—you can change a control's binding context by setting its `BindingContext` property.

Figure 10-5 shows a form with two binding contexts. It is similar to the form shown in Figure 10-4, except that it has an extra `GroupBox` control, which contains an extra set of controls bound to the same data source and properties as those on the top left. Notice that these are clearly using a different currency manager, because the currently selected item on the right is different from that on the left.

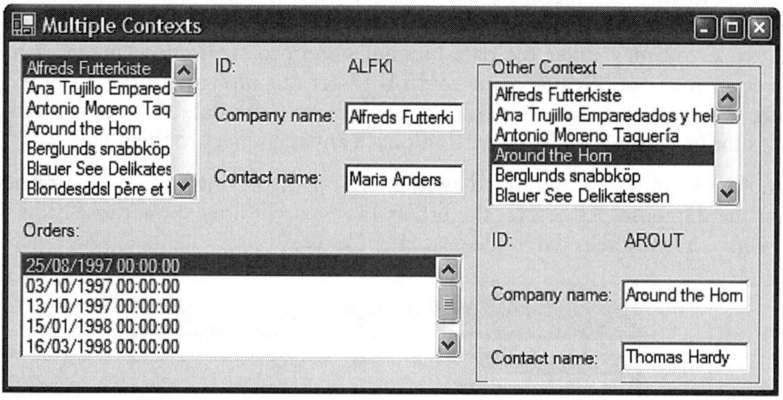
Multiple Contexts
Alfreds Futterkiste
Ana Trujillo Empared
Antonio Moreno Taq
Around the Horn
Berglunds snabbköp
Blauer See Delikates
Blondesddsl père et f
ID:
ALFKI
Company name:
Alfreds Futterki
Contact name:
Maria Anders
Orders:
25/08/1997 00:00:00
03/10/1997 00:00:00
13/10/1997 00:00:00
15/01/1998 00:00:00
16/03/1998 00:00:00
Other Context
Alfreds Futterkiste
Ana Trujillo Emparedados y hel
Antonio Moreno Taquería
Around the Horn
Berglunds snabbköp
Blauer See Delikatessen
ID:
AROUT
Company name:
Around the Horn
Contact name:
Thomas Hardy

Figure 10-5. A form with two binding contexts

These extra controls are bound to the data source in exactly the same way as before, as shown in C# in Example 10-32.

Example 10-32. Binding a second set of controls

```
labelOtherCustomerID.DataBindings.Add
    ("Text", ds, "Customers.CustomerID");
textBoxOtherCompanyName.DataBindings.Add
    ("Text", ds, "Customers.CompanyName");
textBoxOtherContactName.DataBindings.Add
    ("Text", ds, "Customers.ContactName");

listBoxOtherCustomers.DataSource = ds;
listBoxOtherCustomers.DisplayMember = "Customers.CompanyName";
```

To enable these controls to maintain their own position in the data source, independent of the other set, they will need their own currency manager. We must make sure that they have their own binding context. We could set the `BindingContext` property on each control, but it is simpler to exploit the fact that controls will use their parent's binding context by default. All these controls are children of the GroupBox, so we only have to set the binding on that, as shown in Example 10-33.

Example 10-33. Specifying a binding context

```
groupBoxOther.BindingContext = new BindingContext();
```

This will cause the GroupBox and any of its children to use this newly created context for data binding. They will therefore all get their own binding manager (and hence their own notion of the current position) rather than using the one for the form's binding context.

The DataGrid Control

So far, we have only looked at complex binding to the ListBox control. However, both this control and its close relative the ComboBox can only show a single property for each item they display. This can be somewhat limiting—in the previous example, it would have been useful to be able to display more information about the orders. (The Northwind database contains information about the due date, the actual fulfillment date, the date on which the order was placed, and the current status of the order, to name a few properties.) Fortunately, Windows Forms supplies a control that supports complex binding and that does not suffer from these limitations: the DataGrid control.

Like the ListBox and ComboBox controls, the DataGrid control supports complex binding. But unlike those controls, it is able to display all the properties of each list item instead of a single property. Example 10-34 shows the C# code used to bind a DataGrid control to the Orders table via the relation with the Customers table.

Example 10-34. DataGrid binding

```
dataGridOrders.DataSource = ds;
dataGridOrders.DataMember = "Customers.CustomerOrdersRelation";
```

This is very similar to Example 10-31. The main difference is that where the ListBox control's DisplayMember property was set to a string that specified both the table to be bound to and the property to be displayed, the DataGrid control's DataMember property just describes which table to use—the control will display all the properties. (Remember that if you set the ListBox control's DisplayMember to be the name of the table, it simply calls the data source's ToString method, which is not normally useful.) The DataGrid control is shown in Figure 10-6.

We now have considerably more information than we really wanted. By default, the DataGrid will display every available property. In this case, that includes the CustomerID property, which is extraneous because it will always be the ID of whichever customer is currently selected. We will see how to filter the columns shortly.

Another interesting feature of the DataGrid in Figure 10-6 is that each entry has a + symbol by it. The DataGrid adds this whenever it displays a table that is related to another table. In this case, it has detected the relation that we set up between the Orders table and the Order Details table in Example 10-30. Clicking on the

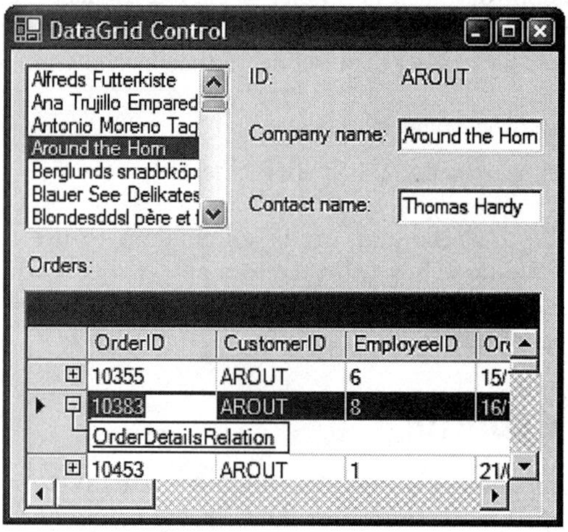
DataGrid Control
Alfreds Futterkiste
Ana Trujillo Empared
Antonio Moreno Taq
Around the Horn
Berglunds snabbköp
Blauer See Delikates
Blondesddsl père et f
ID:
AROUT
Company name:
Around the Horn
Contact name:
Thomas Hardy
Orders:
OrderID
CustomerID
EmployeeID
10355
AROUT
6
10383
AROUT
8
OrderDetailsRelation
10453
AROUT
1

Figure 10-6. The DataGrid control in action

plus symbol expands the row to show all related tables, as shown on the second row. We have only added one related table to the `DataSet` here, so the grid just shows `Order Details.` It is drawn to look like a hyperlink because clicking on it drills down into the table, as shown in Figure 10-7.

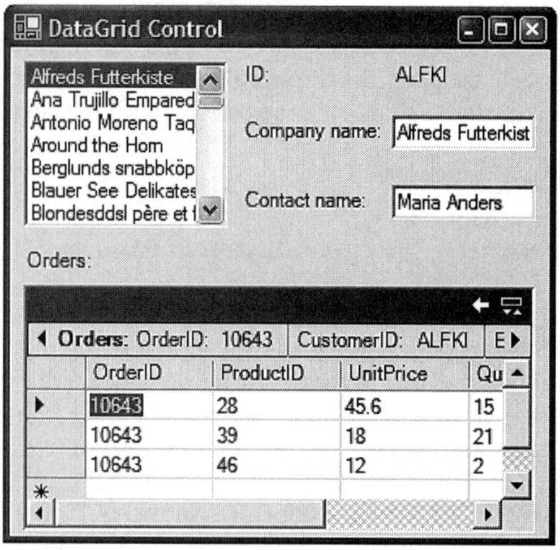
DataGrid Control
Alfreds Futterkiste
Ana Trujillo Empared
Antonio Moreno Taq
Around the Horn
Berglunds snabbköp
Blauer See Delikates
Blondesddsl père et f
ID:
ALFKI
Company name:
Alfreds Futterkist
Contact name:
Maria Anders
Orders:
Orders: OrderID: 10643
CustomerID: ALFKI
OrderID
ProductID
UnitPrice
Qu
10643
28
45.6
15
10643
39
18
21
10643
46
12
2

Figure 10-7. DataGrid showing a related table

The `DataGrid` is now showing us all rows from the `Order Details` table that have the same `OrderID` as the row we selected from the `Orders` table. Notice that this original row from the `Orders` table is still visible at the top of the control.

The DataGrid allows relations to be explored to any depth. We no longer strictly need the ListBox control showing the customer—we could just bind the DataGrid to the Customers table, and it would then allow each customer's orders to be explored in the grid. In this example, our DataSet does not have any tables related to the Order Details table, so the rows do not have a + symbol, but if we had included further related tables from the database (such as the Products table), we would be able to drill down further.

So the DataGrid provides a very easy way of allowing users to browse through all the data in a DataSet. The one problem, as has already been observed, is that it sometimes shows too much, so we will now see how to filter what it shows.

Filtering the DataGrid Display

By default, the DataGrid control will display every available property from the data source. Because this is not always appropriate, it also provides a mechanism for controlling which columns are shown and how they are presented.

The DataGrid control has a property called TableStyles. This is a collection of DataGridTableStyle objects that control how the grid will display a particular table. We can add an entry for each table we plan to display to override the grid's default behavior of showing everything

The DataGridTableStyle object itself has a GridColumnStyles property, which is a collection of DataGridColumnStyle objects. The DataGrid will display one column for each DataGridColumnStyle object. So to control which columns appear, we must simply build a DataGridTableStyle object whose GridColumnStyles property only contains DataGridColumnStyle objects for the columns we wish to display.

Building all these objects from scratch is hard work. If all you want to do is prevent certain columns from appearing, it is much easier to let the framework build a complete DataGridTableStyle object for you, and then remove the columns you don't want, as shown in Examples 10-35 and 10-36.

Example 10-35. Removing unwanted columns from a DataGrid using C#

```
CurrencyManager cm = BindingContext[ds, "Orders"] as CurrencyManager;
DataGridTableStyle ordersStyle = new DataGridTableStyle(cm);

ordersStyle.GridColumnStyles.Remove(
    ordersStyle.GridColumnStyles["CustomerID"]);
ordersStyle.GridColumnStyles.Remove(
    ordersStyle.GridColumnStyles["OrderID"]);
ordersStyle.GridColumnStyles.Remove(
    ordersStyle.GridColumnStyles["EmployeeID"]);

dataGridOrders.TableStyles.Add(ordersStyle);


cm = BindingContext[ds, "Order Details"] as CurrencyManager;
DataGridTableStyle detailsStyle = new DataGridTableStyle(cm);
```

Example 10-35. Removing unwanted columns from a DataGrid using C# (continued)

```
detailsStyle.GridColumnStyles.Remove(
    detailsStyle.GridColumnStyles["OrderID"]);

dataGridOrders.TableStyles.Add(detailsStyle);
```

Example 10-36. Removing unwanted columns from a DataGrid using VB

```
Dim cm As CurrencyManager = DirectCast(BindingContext(ds, "Orders"), _
                                       CurrencyManager)
Dim ordersStyle As New DataGridTableStyle(cm)

ordersStyle.GridColumnStyles.Remove( _
    ordersStyle.GridColumnStyles("CustomerID"))
ordersStyle.GridColumnStyles.Remove( _
    ordersStyle.GridColumnStyles("OrderID"))
ordersStyle.GridColumnStyles.Remove( _
    ordersStyle.GridColumnStyles("EmployeeID"))

dataGridOrders.TableStyles.Add(ordersStyle)


cm = DirectCast(BindingContext(ds, "Order Details"), _
                CurrencyManager)
Dim detailsStyle As New DataGridTableStyle(cm)

detailsStyle.GridColumnStyles.Remove( _
    detailsStyle.GridColumnStyles("OrderID"))

dataGridOrders.TableStyles.Add(detailsStyle)
```

The easiest way to get the framework to create a fully populated `DataGridTableStyle` object is to pass the `CurrencyManager` for the table in question as a constructor parameter. We then remove the columns we don't wish to see. (In this case, we are removing all the key columns because they don't contain information that is meaningful to the end user.) We then add the object to the `DataGrid` control's `TableStyles` property, so that the `DataGrid` knows which columns to display when showing the `Orders` table. Because the `DataGrid` is able to follow relations, it can also show the `Order Details` table, so we repeat the process for that table, removing the `OrderID` column. The result is shown in Figure 10-8.

> In general, it is more efficient to filter out unwanted columns at the SQL level—if you do not need data, you should not ask the database to send it to you because you will be wasting time, CPU cycles, and network bandwidth. However, in this particular example, we do not have this luxury. We need the ID columns because we are using them to enable the relational master/details view, so filtering in the `DataGrid` is still the correct technique.

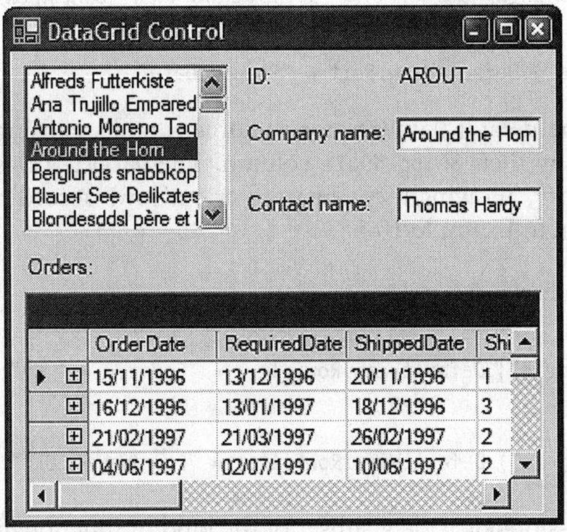
DataGrid Control
Alfreds Futterkiste
Ana Trujillo Empared
Antonio Moreno Taq
Around the Horn
Berglunds snabbköp
Blauer See Delikates
Blondesddsl père et f
ID:
AROUT
Company name:
Around the Horn
Contact name:
Thomas Hardy
Orders:
OrderDate
RequiredDate
ShippedDate
Shi
15/11/1996
13/12/1996
20/11/1996
1
16/12/1996
13/01/1997
18/12/1996
3
21/02/1997
21/03/1997
26/02/1997
2
04/06/1997
02/07/1997
10/06/1997
2

Figure 10-8. A DataGrid with filtered columns

The DataGrid control's table and column style support is not limited to filtering columns. It can also be used to control certain aspects of the way in which data is displayed. For example, the DataGridColumnStyle class has a Width property allowing the column width to be changed, and its HeaderText property allows different text to be shown in the column header. See the reference section for further details.

The DataView Class

The master/details views shown earlier illustrate that the data-binding architecture is capable of showing a filtered view of the contents of a table—if you bind a DataGrid or a ListBox to a child of a relation in a data source, you will just see the related items in the child table instead of all of them. This relational view is just one of the ways in which we can filter the underlying data. The data-binding architecture also provides the DataView class, whose purpose is to provide modified views of tables.

We have already been using the DataView class implicitly. The DataSet class itself does not implement all the binding interfaces discussed earlier—it defers to the DataView. If you call the GetType method on the List property of a CurrencyManager for a DataSet, you will see that its type is not DataSet or DataTable; it is DataView.

The DataSet provides a default view for each of its tables, and this is the view to which controls will normally bind. We can modify the default view's properties, as Example 10-37 shows.

Example 10-37. Changing the sort order of the default view

```
// C# code
ds.Tables["Orders"].DefaultView.Sort = "ShippedDate";
```

Example 10-37. Changing the sort order of the default view (continued)

```
' VB code
ds.Tables("Orders").DefaultView.Sort = "ShippedDate"
```

This modifies the default DataView for the Orders table, causing it to display the contents sorted by their ShippedDate column. The DataView class also provides a RowFilter property, allowing the view to filter out rows according to the specified criteria, as shown in Example 10-38.

Example 10-38. Filtering a DataView

```
// C# code
ds.Tables["Customers"].DefaultView.RowFilter = "Country = 'UK'";

' VB code
ds.Tables("Customers").DefaultView.RowFilter = "Country = 'UK'"
```

Row filter expressions provide a subset of the kind of functionality typically available with SQL WHERE clauses. They use the ADO.NET data expression language, a powerful language whose full capabilities are beyond the scope of this discussion. But to give a brief flavor of what is available, comparison operators are supported (for comparisons with constants, or with other column values), a LIKE operator is provided for wildcard filtering, and you can even navigate relations. For example, the row filter expression "Parent(MyRelation).Name LIKE 'Q*'" requires that the table being filtered is the child in a relation called MyRelation. A DataView with this filter will only show those rows for which the related row in the parent table's Name column begins with Q.

Controls usually use the default view for the data source to which they are bound, but you can specify a different view. Example 10-39 shows how to do this.

Example 10-39. Binding directly to a DataView

```
// C# code
DataView dv = new DataView(ds.Tables["Customers"]);
dv.RowFilter = "Count(Child(CustomerOrdersRelation).OrderID) > 20";

listBoxCustomers.DataSource = dv;
listBoxCustomers.DisplayMember = "CompanyName";

' VB code
Dim dv As New DataView(ds.Tables("Customers"))
dv.RowFilter = "Count(Child(CustomerOrdersRelation).OrderID) > 20"

listBoxCustomers.DataSource = dv
listBoxCustomers.DisplayMember = "CompanyName"
```

This creates a new DataView for the Customers table, and specifies this DataView as the DataSource for the ListBox control. It also illustrates the use of an aggregate function from the data expression language, Count. This filter will only show rows from the Customers table with more than 20 related entries in the Orders table.

Summary

Windows Forms provides a very flexible architecture for binding data sources to control properties. Any property of any object can act as a data source, and any control can participate. Lists of objects can also act as data sources, and for these the system will provide a `CurrencyManager` object to track the current position in the list. Certain controls support complex binding, which means that they are able to display entire lists at a time. There are also specialized data sources—the `DataTable` and `DataSet` classes allow multiple tables of data to be held in memory along with information about relations between those tables. Using these, programs can let the user browse through substantial sets of data, and selectively display related details with a minimal number of round trips to the database. Controls bound to a `DataSet` or `DataTable` always present data as filtered by a `DataView`. By default, this will either show the whole table or will just display rows related to a selected item in a parent table, but it is possible to build custom views with arbitrary filtering criteria. The `DataGrid` control provides highly specialized support for data binding, allowing all properties of all items in a table to be displayed, and it can even traverse relations between multiple tables.

II

API Quick Reference

Part II devotes separate chapters to documenting each of the following eight namespaces, which are the most commonly used in Windows Forms programming:

```
System.ComponentModel
System.Drawing
System.Drawing.Drawing2d
System.Drawing.Imaging
System.Drawing.Printing
System.Drawing.Text
System.Windows.Forms
System.Windows.Forms.Design
```

The chapters are organized alphabetically by namespace name. Information on all types and their members is shown using C# syntax.

In addition, the initial chapter of Part II explains how to use the documentation, while the second chapter shows Visual Basic programmers how to convert the C# syntax used in this book to Visual Basic syntax.

11
How to Use This Quick Reference

The quick-reference section that follows packs a lot of information into a small space. This introduction explains how to get the most out of that information. It describes how the quick reference is organized and how to read the individual reference entries.

Finding a Quick-Reference Entry

The quick reference is organized into chapters, one per namespace. Each chapter begins with an overview of the namespace and includes a hierarchy diagram for the types (classes, interfaces, enumerations, delegates, and structs) in the namespace. Following the overview are quick-reference entries for all the types in the namespace.

All quick-reference entries are expressed using C# syntax. If you're a VB developer, Chapter 12 explains how to convert from C# to VB syntax.

Figure 11-1 is a sample diagram showing the notation used in this book. This notation is similar to that used in *Java in a Nutshell*, but borrows some features from UML.

Abstract classes (or MustInherit classes in Visual Basic) are shown as slanted rectangles, and sealed classes (NonInheritable in Visual Basic) as octagonal rectangles. Inheritance is shown as a solid line from the subtype, ending with a hollow triangle that points to the supertype.

There are two notations that indicate interface implementation. The lollipop notation is used most of the time, because it is easier to read. In some cases, especially where many types implement a given interface, the shaded box notation with the dashed line is used.

Important relationships between types (associations) are shown with a dashed line ending with an arrow. The figures don't show every possible association. Some types have strong containing relationships with one another. For example, a System.Net.WebException includes a System.Net.WebResponse that represents the HTTP response containing the error details (HTTP status code and error message). To show a relationship such as this, a filled diamond is attached to the containing type with a solid line that points to the contained type.

Entries are organized alphabetically by type *and* namespace, so that related types are grouped near each other. Thus, to look up a quick reference entry for a particular type, you must also know the name of the namespace that contains that type. Usually, the namespace is obvious from the context, and you should have no trouble looking up the quick-reference entry you want. Use the tabs on the outside edge of the book and the dictionary-style headers on the upper outside corner of each page to help you find the namespace and type you are looking for.

Occasionally, you may need to look up a type whose namespace you do not already know. In this case, refer to Appendix B. This index allows you to look up a type by its name and find out what namespace it is part of.

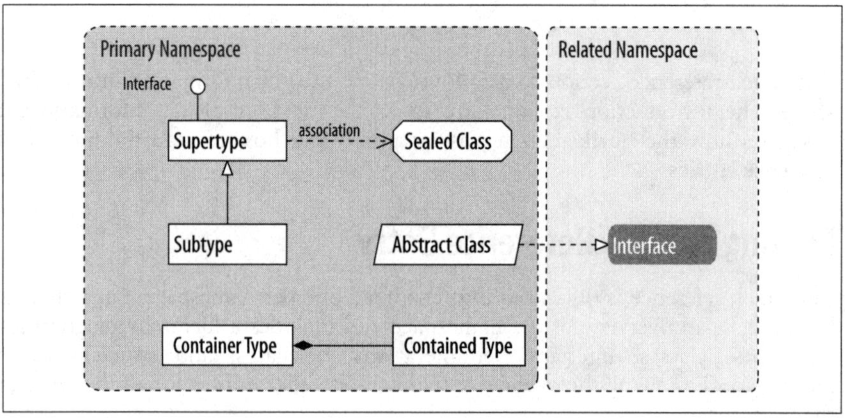

Primary Namespace
Interface
Supertype
association
Sealed Class
Subtype
Abstract Class
Container Type
Contained Type
Related Namespace
Interface

Figure 11-1. Class hierarchy notation

Reading a Quick-Reference Entry

Each quick-reference entry contains quite a bit of information. The sections that follow describe the structure of a quick-reference entry, explaining what information is available, where it is found, and what it means. While reading the descriptions that follow, you will find it helpful to flip through the reference section itself to find examples of the features being described.

Type Name, Namespace, Assembly, Type Category, and Flags

Each quick-reference entry begins with a four-part title that specifies the name, namespace (followed by the assembly in parentheses), and type category of the type, and may also specify various additional flags that describe the type. The type name appears in bold at the upper left of the title. The namespace and assembly appear, in smaller print, in the lower left, below the type name.

The lower-right portion of the title indicates the type category of the type (class, delegate, enum, interface, or struct). The class category may include modifiers such as sealed or abstract.

In the upper-right corner of the title you may find a list of flags that describe the type. The possible flags and their meanings are as follows:

ECMA
: The type is part of the ECMA CLI specification.

serializable
: The type, or a supertype, implements **System.Runtime.Serialization.ISerializable** or has been flagged with the **System.Serializable** attribute.

marshal by reference
: This class, or a superclass, derives from **System.MarshalByRefObject**.

context bound
: This class, or a superclass, derives from **System.ContextBoundObject**.

disposable
: The type implements the **System.IDisposable** interface.

flag
: The enumeration is marked with the **System.FlagsAttribute** attribute.

Reference Guide

Description

The title of each quick-reference entry is followed by a short description of the most important features of the type. This description may be anywhere from a couple of sentences to several paragraphs long.

Synopsis

The most important part of every quick-reference entry is the synopsis, which follows the title and description. The synopsis for a type looks a lot like its source code, except that the member bodies are omitted and some additional annotations are added. If you know C# syntax, you know how to read the type synopsis. If you know VB syntax, refer to Chapter 12.

The first line of the synopsis contains information about the type itself. It begins with a list of type modifiers, such as **abstract** and **sealed**. These modifiers are followed by the **class**, **delegate**, **enum**, **interface**, or **struct** keyword and then by the name of the type. The type name may be followed by a colon (:) and a supertype or interfaces that the type implements.

The type definition line is followed by a list of the members that the type defines. This list includes only those members that are explicitly declared in the type, are overridden from a base class, or are implementations of an interface member. Members that are simply inherited from a base class are not shown; you will need to look up the base class definition to find those members. Once again, if you understand basic C# syntax, you should have no trouble making sense of these lines. The listing for each member includes the modifiers, type, and name of the member. For methods, the synopsis also includes the type and name of each method parameter. The member names are in boldface, so it is easy to scan the list of members looking for the one you want. The names of method parameters are in italics to indicate that they are not to be used literally. The member listings are printed on alternating gray and white backgrounds to keep them visually separate.

Member availability and flags

Each member listing is a single line that defines the API for that member. These listings use C# syntax, so their meaning is immediately clear to any C# programmer. There is some auxiliary information associated with each member synopsis, however, that requires explanation.

The area to the right of the member synopsis is used to display a variety of flags that provide additional information about the member. Some of these flags indicate additional specification details that do not appear in the member API itself.

The following flags may be displayed as comments to the right of a member synopsis:

overrides
: Indicates that a method overrides a method in one of its supertypes. The flag is followed by the name of the supertype that the method overrides.

implements
: Indicates that a method implements a method in an interface. The flag is followed by the name of the interface that is implemented.

=
: For enumeration fields and constant fields, this flag is followed by the constant value of the field. Only constants of primitive and `String` types and constants with the value `null` are displayed. Some constant values are specification details, while others are implementation details. Some constants are platform dependent, such as `System.BitConverter.IsLittleEndian`. Platform-dependent values shown in this book conform to the `System.PlatformID.Win32NT` platform (32-bit Windows NT, 2000, or XP). The reason that symbolic constants are defined, however, is so you can write code that does not rely directly upon the constant value. Use this flag to help you understand the type, but do not rely upon the constant values in your own programs.

Functional grouping of members

Within a type synopsis, the members are not listed in strict alphabetical order. Instead, they are broken down into functional groups and listed alphabetically within each group. Constructors, events, fields, methods, and properties are all listed separately. Instance methods are kept separate from static (class) methods. Public members are listed separately from protected members. Grouping members by category breaks a type down into smaller, more comprehensible segments, making the type easier to understand. This grouping also makes it easier for you to find a desired member.

Functional groups are separated from each other in a type synopsis with C# comments, such as `// Public Constructors`, `// Protected Instance Properties`, and `// Events`. The various functional categories are as follows (in the order in which they appear in a type synopsis):

Constructors
: Displays the constructors for the type. Public constructors and protected constructors are displayed separately in subgroupings. If a type defines no constructor at all, the C# compiler adds a default no-argument constructor that is displayed here. If a type defines only private constructors, it cannot be instantiated, so no constructor appears. Constructors are listed first because the first thing you do with most types is instantiate them by calling a constructor.

Fields
: Displays all the fields defined by the type, including constants. Public and protected fields are displayed in separate subgroups. Fields are listed here, near the top of the synopsis, because constant values are often used throughout the type as legal values for method parameters and return values.

Properties
: Lists all the properties of the type, breaking them down into subgroups for public and protected static properties and public and protected instance properties. After the property name, its accessors (get and/or set) are shown.

Static Methods
: Lists the static methods (class methods) of the type, broken down into subgroups for public static methods and protected static methods.

Public Instance Methods
: Contains all the public instance methods.

Protected Instance Methods
: Contains all the protected instance methods.

Class Hierarchy

For any type that has a nontrivial inheritance hierarchy, the synopsis is followed by a "Hierarchy" section. This section lists all the supertypes of the type, as well as any interfaces implemented by those supertypes. It will also list any interfaces implemented by an interface. In the hierarchy listing, arrows indicate supertype to subtype relationships, while the interfaces implemented by a type follow the type name in parentheses. For example, the following hierarchy indicates that **System.IO.Stream** implements **IDisposable** and extends **MarshalByRefObject**, which itself extends **Object**:

```
System.Object→System.MarshalByRefObject→System.IO.Stream(System.
IDisposable)
```

If a type has subtypes, the "Hierarchy" section is followed by a "Subtypes" section that lists those subtypes. If an interface has implementations, the "Hierarchy" section is followed by an "Implementations" section that lists those implementations. While the "Hierarchy" section shows ancestors of the type, the "Subtypes" or "Implementations" section shows descendants.

Cross-References

The hierarchy section of a quick-reference entry is followed by a number of optional cross-reference sections that indicate other, related types and methods that may be of interest. These sections are the following:

Passed To
: This section lists all the members (from other types) that are passed an object of this type as an argument, including properties whose values can be set to this type. This is useful when you have an object of a given type and want to know where it can be used.

Returned By
: This section lists all the members that return an object of this type, including properties whose values can take on this type. This is useful when you know that you want to work with an existing instance of this type, but don't know how to obtain one.

Valid On
: For attributes, this lists the attribute targets that the attribute can be applied to.

Associated Events
: For delegates, lists the events it can handle.

A Note About Type Names

Throughout the quick reference, you'll notice that types are sometimes referred to by type name alone and at other times referred to by type name and namespace. If namespaces were always used, the type synopses would become long and hard to read. On the other hand, if namespaces were never used, it would sometimes be difficult to know what type was being referred to. The rules for including or omitting the namespace name are complex. They can be summarized approximately as follows, however:

- If the type name alone is ambiguous, the namespace name is always used.
- In the case of a very commonly used type like `System.Collection.ICollection`, the namespace is omitted.
- If the type being referred to is part of the current namespace (and has a quick-reference entry in the current chapter), the namespace is omitted. The namespace is also omitted if the type being referred to is part of a namespace that contains the current namespace.

12
Converting from C# to VB Syntax

Although information on all types and their members is shown using C# syntax, it is easy to mentally convert to Visual Basic syntax. This chapter will provide the information you need to convert the documentation for each type into the syntax used by Visual Basic.

> This chapter does not aim at providing complete coverage of the syntax for each language element it discusses. Instead, it focuses on direct translation of the syntax of the types used in Windows Forms programming from C# to VB.

General Considerations

The most evident difference between C# and VB syntax is that C# uses the semicolon (;) as a statement terminator, whereas VB uses a line break. Hence, while a statement in C# can occupy multiple lines as long as it is terminated with a semicolon, a VB statement must occupy a single line. Multiline statements in VB must appear with the VB line continuation character (a space followed by an underscore) on all but the last line.

A second, and not quite so evident, difference is that C# is case sensitive, whereas VB is not. (Uniform casing for VB code is enforced by the Visual Studio environment, but it is by no means required.)

Finally, all types and their members have access modifiers that determine the type or member's accessibility. The keywords for these access modifiers are nearly identical in VB and C#, as Table 12-1 shows.

Table 12-1. Access modifiers in C# and VB

C# keyword	VB keyword
public	Public
private	Private
protected	Protected
internal	Friend
protected internal	Protected Friend

Classes

C# uses the class statement along with opening and closing braces to indicate the beginning and end of a class definition. For example:

```
public class Form : ContainerControl {
   // member definitions
}
```

In VB, a class definition is indicated by the Class... End Class construct:

```
Public Class Form
   ' member definitions
End Class
```

In addition, C# classes can be marked as abstract or sealed; these correspond to the VB MustInherit and NonInheritable keywords, as shown in Table 12-2.

Table 12-2. C# and equivalent VB class modifiers

C# keyword	VB keyword
abstract	MustInherit
sealed	NonInheritable

C# uses the colon to indicate either inheritance or interface implementation. Both the base class and the implemented interfaces are part of the class statement. For example:

```
public class Control : Component, ISynchronizeInvoke, IWin32Window
```

In VB, a base class and any implemented interfaces are specified on separate lines immediately following the Class statement. A class's base class is indicated by preceding its name with the Inherits keyword; any implemented interfaces are indicated by the Implements keyword. Hence, the previous definition of the Control class in C# would appear as follows in VB:

```
Public Class Control
   Inherits Component
   Implements ISynchronizeInvoke, IWin32Window
```

Structures

C# uses the **struct** statement along with opening and closing braces to indicate the beginning and end of a structure definition. For example:

```
public struct DataGridCell {
   // member definitions
}
```

In VB, a structure definition is indicated by the **Structure... End Structure** construct:

```
Public Structure DataGridCell
   ' member definitions
End Structure
```

C# uses the colon with structures to indicate interface implementation. Any implemented interfaces are part of the **class** statement. In VB, any implemented interfaces are specified by an **Implements** statement on the line immediately following the **Structure** statement. However, none of the structures documented in the reference section of this book use interface inheritance.

Interfaces

C# uses the **interface** statement along with opening and closing braces to indicate the beginning and end of an interface definition. For example:

```
public interface IUIService {
   // member definitions
}
```

In VB, an interface definition is indicated by the **Interface... End Structure** construct:

```
Public Interface IUIService
   ' member definitions
End Interface
```

C# uses the colon with interfaces to specify any implemented interfaces. For example:

```
public interface ISite : IServiceProvider
```

In VB, any implemented interfaces are specified by an **Implements** statement on the line immediately following the **Interface** statement. Hence, the previous definition of **ISite** in C# would appear as follows in VB:

```
Public Interface ISite
   Implements IServiceProvider
```

Class, Structure, and Interface Members

Classes, structures, and interfaces can contain one or more fields, methods, properties, and events. This section will discuss converting the C# syntax for each of these constructs to VB.

Note that .NET supports both static (or shared) members (which apply to the type as a whole, and typically do not require that an object of that type be instantiated) and instance members (which apply only to an instance of that type). Shared or static members are indicated by using the **static** keyword in C#. For example:

```
public static bool IsMnemonic(char charCode, string text);
```

The corresponding VB keyword is **Shared**. Hence, the **FromResource** method, when converted to VB, has the following syntax:

```
Public Shared Function IsMnemonic(charCode As Char, text As String) _
   As Boolean
```

Fields

A field is simply a constant or a variable that is exposed as a publicly accessible member of a type. In C#, for example, the **Nowhere** field of the **DataGrid.HitTestInfo** class has the syntax:

```
public static readonly DataGrid.HitTestInfo Nowhere;
```

Note that C# indicates the data type of a field before the name of the field. (For C# data types and their VB equivalents, see Table 12-3.) Also note that fields are most often read-only. Constant fields, in fact, are always read-only. As a result, the use of the C# **readonly** keyword and the VB **ReadOnly** keyword with fields is quite common.

The syntax for the **Nowhere** field in Visual Basic then becomes:

```
Public Shared ReadOnly Nowhere As DataGrid.HitTestInfo
```

Methods

In C#, all methods have a return value, which appears before the name of the function; in contrast, VB differentiates between function and subprocedures. C# functions without an explicit return value return **void**. For example, one of the overloads of the Bitmap class's **MakeTransparent** method has the following syntax in C#:

```
public void MakeTransparent( );
```

C# methods that return **void** are expressed as subprocedures in VB. So the corresponding syntax of the **MakeTransparent** method is:

```
Public Sub MakeTransparent( )
```

All C# methods other than those returning **void** are functions in VB. The function's return value follows appears in an **As** clause at the end of the function declaration. C# data types and their VB equivalents are shown in Table 12-3. Methods that return arrays are indicated by adding braces ([]) to the return data type in C# and parentheses (( ))to the return data type in VB.

For example, the **Focus** method of the **Control** class has the C# syntax:

```
public bool Focus( );
```

The VB equivalent is:

```
Public Function Focus( ) As Boolean
```

Table 12-3. C# data types and their VB equivalents

C# data type	VB data type
bool	Boolean
byte	Byte
char	Char
decimal	Decimal
double	Double
float	Single
int	Integer
long	Long
object	Object
sbyte	System.SByte
short	Short
string	String
System.Currency	Currency
System.DateTime	Date
uint	System.UInt32
ulong	System.UInt64
ushort	System.UInt16
<class_name>	*<class_name>*
<delegate_name>	*<delegate_name>*
<interface_name>	*<interface_name>*
<structure_name>	*<structure_name>*

Method parameters in C# take the general form:

```
<data_type> <parameter_name>
```

In VB, method parameters take the form:

```
<parameter_name> As <data_type>
```

where *<data_type>* is any of the data types listed in Table 12-3. If a parameter is an array, its data type is followed by braces in C# (e.g., string[] Name), while the parameter name is followed by parentheses in VB (e.g., Name() As String).

For example, one of the versions of the Color class's FromArgb method has the following syntax in C#:

```
public static Color FromArgb(int red, int green, int blue);
```

Its VB equivalent is:

```
Public Shared Function FromArgb(red As Integer, _
                                green As Integer, _
                                blue As Integer) As Color
```

VB allows methods to be called using either named or positional parameters. If named parameters are used, the parameter name must correspond to that shown in the documentation. For instance, Color.FromArgb can be called as follows using named parameters:

```
NewColor = Color.FromArgb(blue:=125, _
                          red:=125,
                          green:=125)
```

C# also uses a number of object-oriented qualifiers with methods. These, and their VB equivalents, are shown in Table 12-4.

Table 12-4. C# keywords used with methods and their VB equivalents

C# keyword	VB keyword
abstract	MustOverride
override	Overrides
sealed	NotOverridable
virtual	Overridable

In both C# and VB, constructors have a special syntax. In C#, constructors have the same name as the classes whose objects they instantiate and do not indicate a return value. For example, the constructor for the Button class is:

```
public Button( );
```

In VB, the constructor is represented by a call to a class's New subprocedure. The equivalent call to the Button class constructor in VB is:

```
Public Sub New( )
```

Properties

The FileDialog.Title property provides a more or less typical example of a property definition using C# syntax:

```
public string Title {get; set;}
```

Like all C# type definitions, the property's data type precedes the property name. The get; and set; property accessors indicate that this is a read-write property. Read-only properties are indicated with a get; only, while write-only properties are indicated with a set; only.

The equivalent VB property definition is:

```
Public Property Title As String
```

Note that read-write properties are not decorated with additional keywords in VB. Read-only properties, on the other hand, are indicated with the ReadOnly keyword in front of the Property keyword, while write-only properties have the WriteOnly keyword before the Property keyword.

The shared **ProductName** property of the **Application** class is read-only. Its C# syntax appears as follows:

```
public static string ProductName {get;}
```

The corresponding VB syntax is:

```
Public Shared ReadOnly Property ProductName As String
```

Note that properties, like methods, can use the object-oriented modifiers listed in Table 12-4.

Events

Events are declared in C# using the **event** keyword, which is followed by the delegate type returned by the event and the name of the event. For example, the **Parse** event of the **Binding** class has the following syntax:

```
public event ConvertEventHandler Parse;
```

The equivalent VB syntax is:

```
Public Event Parse As ConvertEventHandler
```

In addition, the C# **event** and the VB **Event** keywords can be preceded by the object modifiers listed in Table 12-4.

Delegates

The syntax for a delegate in C# closely follows the syntax for a method. The **delegate** statement is followed by the delegate's return type (or **void**, if there is none) and the delegate name. This in turn is followed by the delegate's parameter list, in which each parameter takes the form:

```
<parameter_type> <parameter_name>
```

For example:

```
public delegate void DragEventHandler(
   object sender,
   DragEventArgs e);
```

In a VB **Delegate** statement, the **Delegate** keyword is followed by the **Sub** keyword (if the delegate returns a **void** in C#) or the **Function** keyword (if the delegate returns some other value). For example, in VB, the **DragEventHandler** delegate has the following syntax:

```
Public Delegate Sub DragEventHandler( _
   sender As Object, _
   e As DragEventArgs)
```

Enumerations

C# uses the **enum** statement along with opening and closing braces to indicate the beginning and end of an enumeration definition. For example:

```
public enum CheckedState {
   // enumeration members
}
```

In VB, an enumeration is defined by the **Enum... End Enum** construct. For example, the VB version of the **CheckedState** enum declaration is:

```
Public Enum CheckedState
   ' enumeration members
End Enum
```

In both C# and VB, the member listing consists of the name of the enumerated member and its value. These are identical in C# and VB, except that C# adds a comma to separate one member of the enumeration from another, whereas VB requires that they be on separate lines. For example, the full declaration of the **CheckedState** enumeration in C# is:

```
public enum CheckedState {
   Unchecked = 0,
   Checked = 1,
   Indeterminate = 2
}
```

The VB equivalent is:

```
Public Enum CheckedState
   Unchecked = 0
   Checked = 1
   Indeterminate = 2
End Enum
```

13
The System.ComponentModel Namespace

The System.ComponentModel namespace provides many of the classes that support the design-time features of the framework. The key class is Component, which provides a means of encapsulating a class for design-time hosting. IContainer and ISite provide a means to host Component objects and bind them to the design-time environment. Support for custom designers is provided by the System.ComponentModel.Design.IDesigner interface, System.Drawing.Design.UITypeEditor, and custom TypeConverter classes. Figure 13-1 shows many types from this namespace.

There are also a number of classes related to license management.

The designer environment is largely controlled through metadata provided by custom attributes. Classes and properties are adorned with these attributes to indicate how they should appear in the designer host, which custom designers to use, and how they should be serialized. Figure 13-2 shows the attributes in this namespace.

Note that several of the essential classes for the design-time environment can be found in System.ComponentModel.Design, System.Windows.Forms.Design, and System.Drawing.Design.

In addition to the design-time component support, this namespace has become a dumping ground for classes (such as IListSource) that support the data-binding framework, but are not specifically UI related (and hence, are not to be found in the System.Windows.Forms namespace). There are also a couple of refugees from System.Configuration relating to the System.Configuration.Install.Installer framework.

Figure 13-3 shows the delegates and event arguments from this namespace, and Figure 13-4 shows type converters and miscellaneous types.

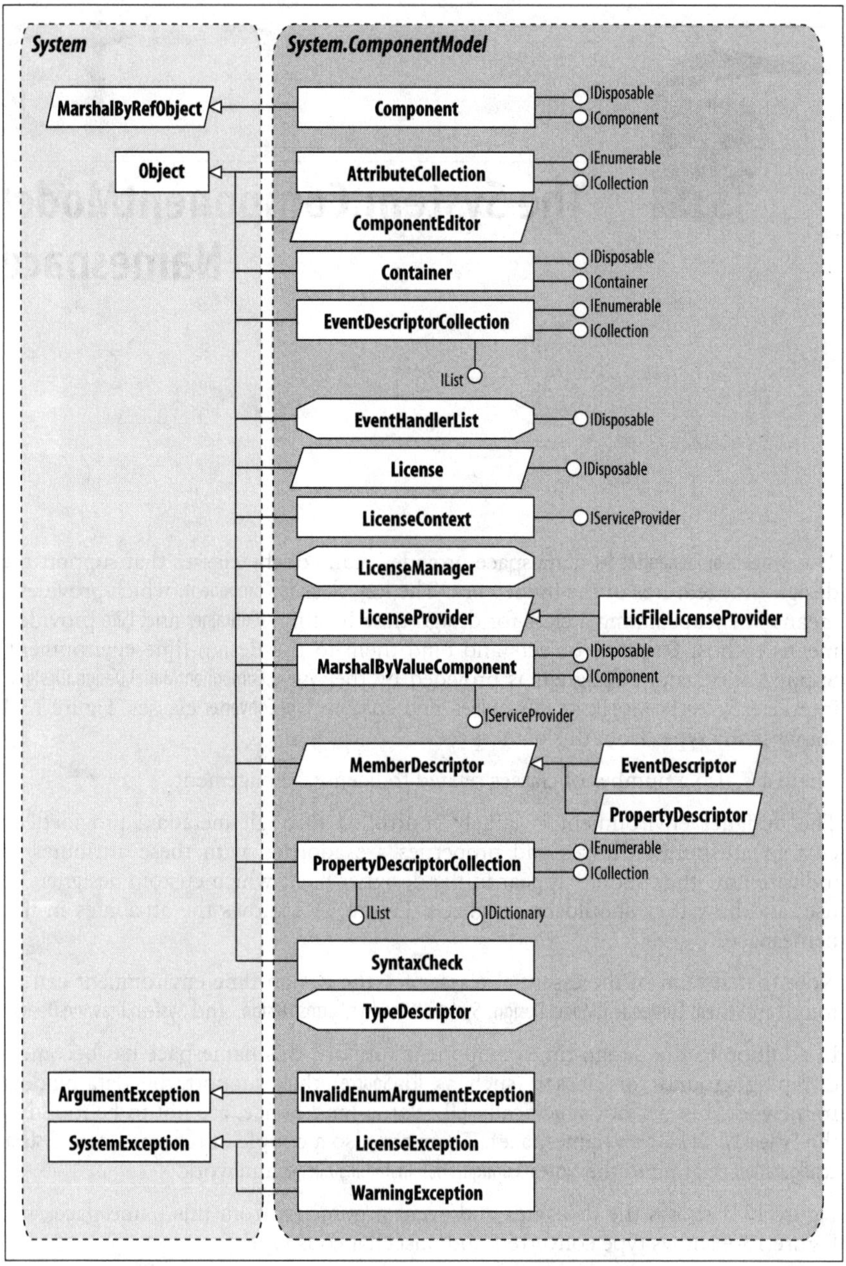

System
System.ComponentModel
MarshalByRefObject
Component
IDisposable
IComponent
Object
AttributeCollection
IEnumerable
ICollection
ComponentEditor
Container
IDisposable
IContainer
EventDescriptorCollection
IEnumerable
ICollection
IList
EventHandlerList
IDisposable
License
IDisposable
LicenseContext
IServiceProvider
LicenseManager
LicenseProvider
LicFileLicenseProvider
MarshalByValueComponent
IDisposable
IComponent
IServiceProvider
MemberDescriptor
EventDescriptor
PropertyDescriptor
PropertyDescriptorCollection
IEnumerable
ICollection
IList
IDictionary
SyntaxCheck
TypeDescriptor
ArgumentException
InvalidEnumArgumentException
SystemException
LicenseException
WarningException

Figure 13-1. Many types from the System.ComponentModel namespace

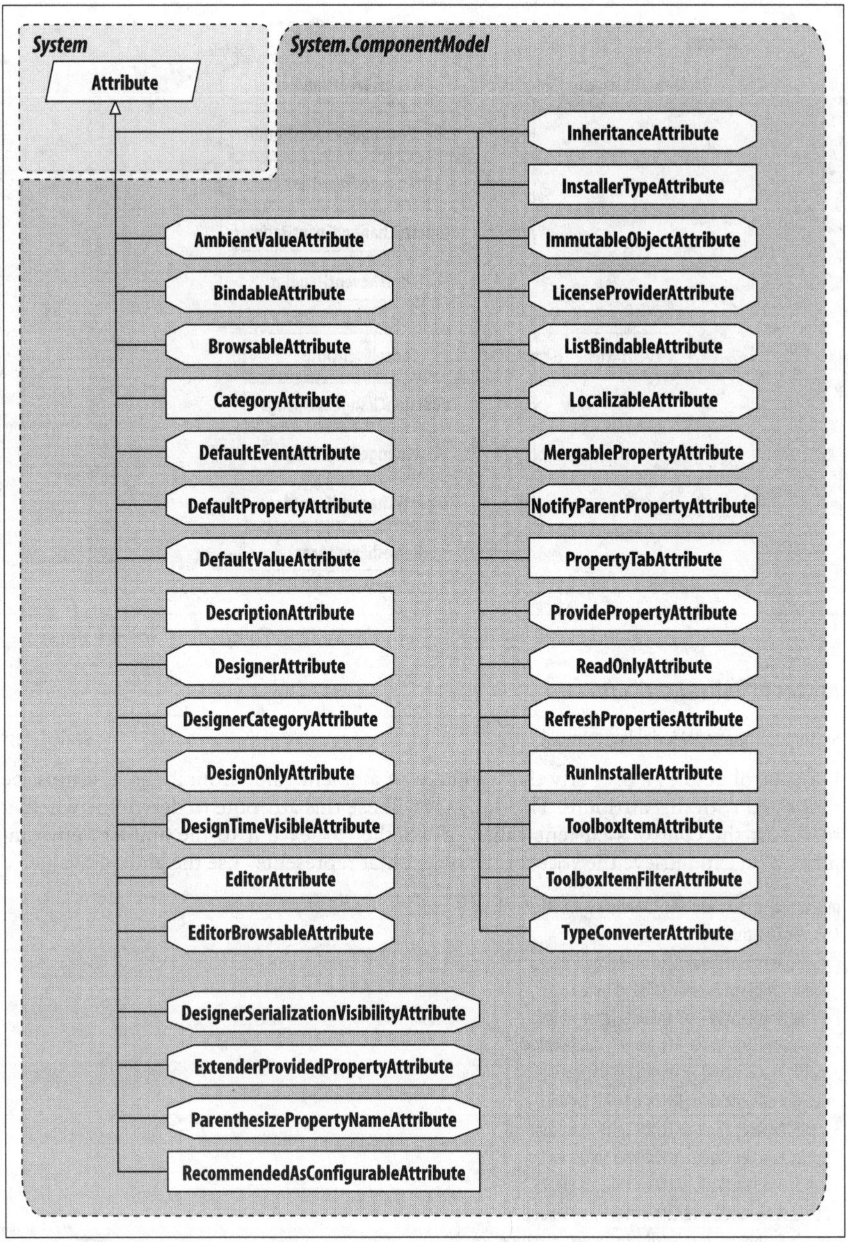
System
Attribute
System.ComponentModel
InheritanceAttribute
InstallerTypeAttribute
ImmutableObjectAttribute
LicenseProviderAttribute
ListBindableAttribute
LocalizableAttribute
MergablePropertyAttribute
NotifyParentPropertyAttribute
PropertyTabAttribute
ProvidePropertyAttribute
ReadOnlyAttribute
RefreshPropertiesAttribute
RunInstallerAttribute
ToolboxItemAttribute
ToolboxItemFilterAttribute
TypeConverterAttribute
AmbientValueAttribute
BindableAttribute
BrowsableAttribute
CategoryAttribute
DefaultEventAttribute
DefaultPropertyAttribute
DefaultValueAttribute
DescriptionAttribute
DesignerAttribute
DesignerCategoryAttribute
DesignOnlyAttribute
DesignTimeVisibleAttribute
EditorAttribute
EditorBrowsableAttribute
DesignerSerializationVisibilityAttribute
ExtenderProvidedPropertyAttribute
ParenthesizePropertyNameAttribute
RecommendedAsConfigurableAttribute

Figure 13-2. Attributes from this namespace

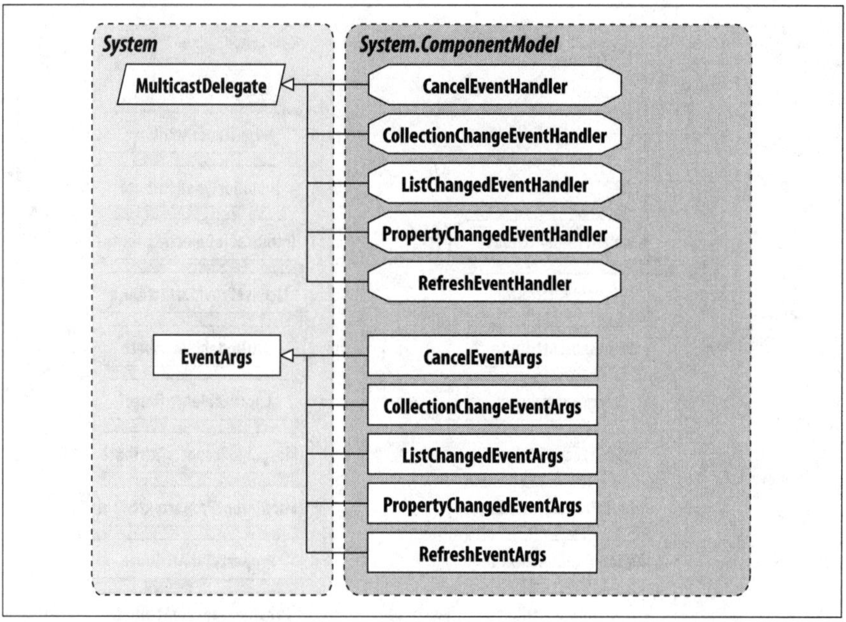
System
System.ComponentModel
MulticastDelegate
CancelEventHandler
CollectionChangeEventHandler
ListChangedEventHandler
PropertyChangedEventHandler
RefreshEventHandler
EventArgs
CancelEventArgs
CollectionChangeEventArgs
ListChangedEventArgs
PropertyChangedEventArgs
RefreshEventArgs

Figure 13-3. Delegates and event arguments from the System.ComponentModel namespace

AmbientValueAttribute

System.ComponentModel (system.dll) sealed class

If a control defines a property that can take an ambient value from its host, it must be decorated with this attribute. The designer will use this attribute to determine whether to persist the control's current value, or whether to leave it to the ambient environment. You can retrieve the **Value** for the object that represents "use the ambient value."

```
public sealed class AmbientValueAttribute : Attribute {
// Public Constructors
   public AmbientValueAttribute(bool value);
   public AmbientValueAttribute(byte value);
   public AmbientValueAttribute(char value);
   public AmbientValueAttribute(double value);
   public AmbientValueAttribute(short value);
   public AmbientValueAttribute(int value);
   public AmbientValueAttribute(long value);
   public AmbientValueAttribute(object value);
   public AmbientValueAttribute(float value);
   public AmbientValueAttribute(string value);
   public AmbientValueAttribute(Type type, string value);
// Public Instance Properties
   public object Value{get; }
// Public Instance Methods
   public override bool Equals(object obj);                // overrides Attribute
   public override int GetHashCode( );                     // overrides Attribute
}
```

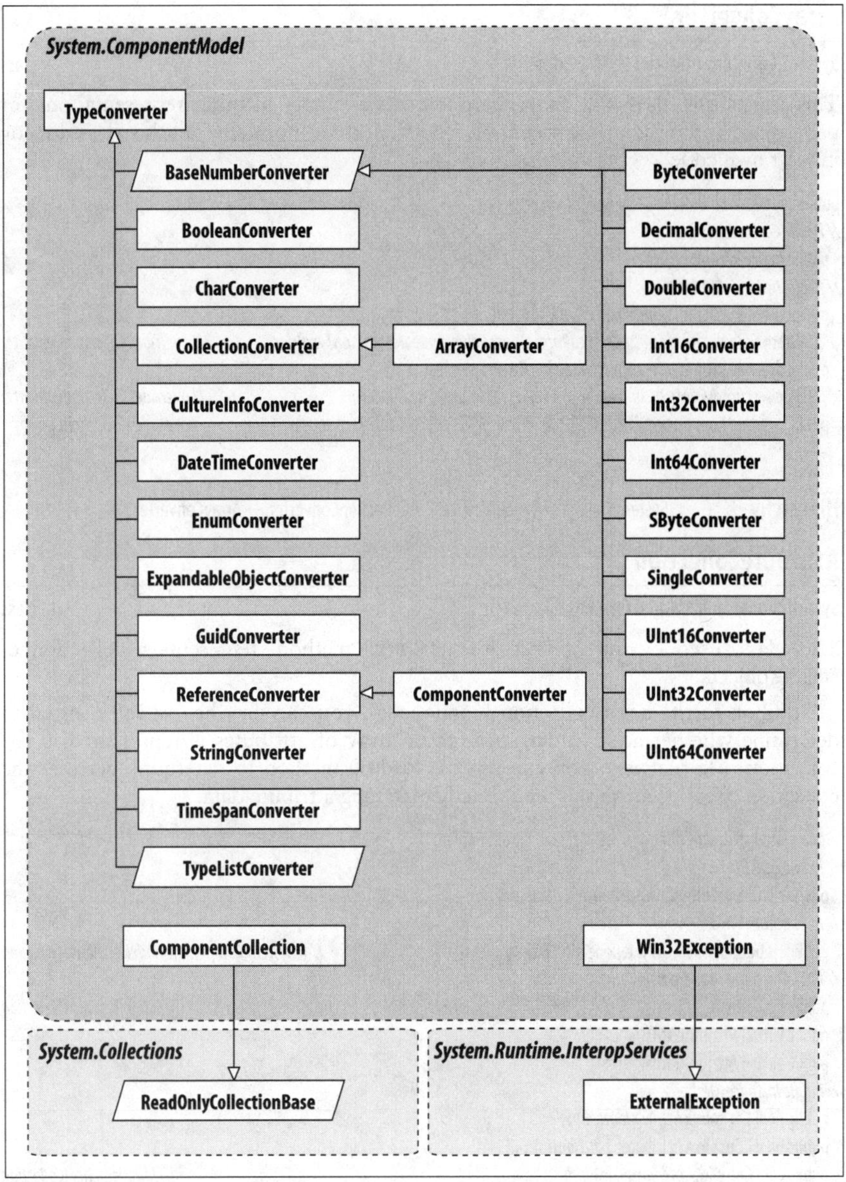
System.ComponentModel
TypeConverter
BaseNumberConverter
ByteConverter
BooleanConverter
DecimalConverter
CharConverter
DoubleConverter
CollectionConverter
ArrayConverter
Int16Converter
CultureInfoConverter
Int32Converter
DateTimeConverter
Int64Converter
EnumConverter
SByteConverter
ExpandableObjectConverter
SingleConverter
GuidConverter
UInt16Converter
ReferenceConverter
ComponentConverter
UInt32Converter
StringConverter
UInt64Converter
TimeSpanConverter
TypeListConverter
ComponentCollection
Win32Exception
System.Collections
ReadOnlyCollectionBase
System.Runtime.InteropServices
ExternalException

Figure 13-4. Type converters and miscellaneous types from this namespace

Hierarchy System.Object → System.Attribute → AmbientValueAttribute

Valid On All

ArrayConverter

System.ComponentModel (system.dll) class

This TypeConverter class will convert an array to a variety of other representations for persistence and design-time scenarios. You should not normally call this class directly in your own code.

```
public class ArrayConverter : CollectionConverter {
// Public Constructors
   public ArrayConverter( );
// Public Instance Methods
   public override object ConvertTo(ITypeDescriptorContext context,
      System.Globalization.CultureInfo culture, object value, Type destinationType);      // overrides CollectionConverter
   public override PropertyDescriptorCollection GetProperties(
      ITypeDescriptorContext context, object value, Attribute[ ] attributes);      // overrides CollectionConverter
   public override bool GetPropertiesSupported(ITypeDescriptorContext context);      // overrides CollectionConverter
}
```

Hierarchy System.Object → TypeConverter → CollectionConverter → ArrayConverter

AttributeCollection

System.ComponentModel (system.dll) class

This class, used by the TypeDescriptor.GetAttributes( ) method, represents a collection of Attribute objects.

In addition to the basic collection functionality, you can use the Contains() method to determine whether a particular attribute or array of attributes is represented in the collection. Alternatively, you can use the Matches() method to determine whether the collection contains attributes with exactly matching attribute data.

```
public class AttributeCollection : ICollection, IEnumerable {
// Public Constructors
   public AttributeCollection(Attribute[ ] attributes);
// Public Static Fields
   public static readonly AttributeCollection Empty;      // =System.ComponentModel.AttributeCollection
// Public Instance Properties
   public int Count{get; }      // implements ICollection
   public virtual Attribute this{get; }
   public virtual Attribute this{get; }
// Public Instance Methods
   public bool Contains(Attribute attribute);
   public bool Contains(Attribute[ ] attributes);
   public void CopyTo(Array array, int index);      // implements ICollection
   public IEnumerator GetEnumerator( );      // implements IEnumerable
   public bool Matches(Attribute attribute);
   public bool Matches(Attribute[ ] attributes);
// Protected Instance Methods
   protected Attribute GetDefaultAttribute(Type attributeType);
}
```

Returned By IComNativeDescriptorHandler.GetAttributes( ), ICustomTypeDescriptor.GetAttributes( ), MemberDescriptor.{Attributes, CreateAttributeCollection( )}, TypeDescriptor.GetAttributes( ), System.Windows.Forms.PropertyGrid.BrowsableAttributes

Passed To System.Windows.Forms.PropertyGrid.BrowsableAttributes

BaseNumberConverter

System.ComponentModel (system.dll) abstract class

This abstract class provides a base for TypeConverter implementations that translates integer numeric types (such as int).

It also provides an implementation that converts string objects, including those with hexadecimal representations.

```
public abstract class BaseNumberConverter : TypeConverter {
// Protected Constructors
   protected BaseNumberConverter( );
// Public Instance Methods
   public override bool CanConvertFrom(ITypeDescriptorContext context, Type sourceType);    // overrides TypeConverter
   public override bool CanConvertTo(ITypeDescriptorContext context, Type t);               // overrides TypeConverter
   public override object ConvertFrom(ITypeDescriptorContext context,
      System.Globalization.CultureInfo culture, object value);                              // overrides TypeConverter
   public override object ConvertTo(ITypeDescriptorContext context,
      System.Globalization.CultureInfo culture, object value, Type destinationType);        // overrides TypeConverter
}
```

Hierarchy System.Object → TypeConverter → BaseNumberConverter

Subclasses ByteConverter, DecimalConverter, DoubleConverter, Int16Converter, Int32Converter, Int64Converter, SByteConverter, SingleConverter, UInt16Converter, UInt32Converter, UInt64Converter

BindableAttribute

System.ComponentModel (system.dll) sealed class

This attribute class is applied to properties to indicate to the designer that you would normally expect to use them in a data-binding scenario.

While you can use the data-binding framework to bind to any property, this attribute allows you to hint to the designer that this property should be listed in any preferred set of bound properties.

You can use the Bindable property to determine the state of the attribute, but you must compare to the static BindableSupport.Yes or BindableSupport.No values for equality.

```
public sealed class BindableAttribute : Attribute {
// Public Constructors
   public BindableAttribute(BindableSupport flags);
   public BindableAttribute(bool bindable);
// Public Static Fields
   public static readonly BindableAttribute Default;    // =System.ComponentModel.BindableAttribute
   public static readonly BindableAttribute No;         // =System.ComponentModel.BindableAttribute
   public static readonly BindableAttribute Yes;        // =System.ComponentModel.BindableAttribute
```

Component-Model

```
// Public Instance Properties
  public bool Bindable{get; }
// Public Instance Methods
  public override bool Equals(object obj);                              // overrides Attribute
  public override int GetHashCode( );                                   // overrides Attribute
  public override bool IsDefaultAttribute( );                           // overrides Attribute
}
```

Hierarchy System.Object → System.Attribute → BindableAttribute

Valid On All

BindableSupport **serializable**

System.ComponentModel (system.dll) **enum**

This enumeration specifies the possible settings for **BindableAttribute**.

```
public enum BindableSupport {
  No = 0,
  Yes = 1,
  Default = 2
}
```

Hierarchy System.Object → System.ValueType → System.Enum(System.IComparable, System.IFormattable, System.IConvertible) → BindableSupport

Passed To BindableAttribute.BindableAttribute( ), ListBindableAttribute.ListBindableAttribute( )

BooleanConverter

System.ComponentModel (system.dll) **class**

This TypeConverter translates a Boolean into other representations for serialization and design-time scenarios. You should not call this directly from your own code.

```
public class BooleanConverter : TypeConverter {
// Public Constructors
  public BooleanConverter( );
// Public Instance Methods
  public override bool CanConvertFrom(ITypeDescriptorContext context, Type sourceType);   // overrides TypeConverter
  public override object ConvertFrom(ITypeDescriptorContext context,
    System.Globalization.CultureInfo culture, object value);                              // overrides TypeConverter
  public override StandardValuesCollection GetStandardValues(ITypeDescriptorContext context); // overrides TypeConverter
  public override bool GetStandardValuesExclusive(ITypeDescriptorContext context);        // overrides TypeConverter
  public override bool GetStandardValuesSupported(ITypeDescriptorContext context);        // overrides TypeConverter
}
```

Hierarchy System.Object → TypeConverter → BooleanConverter

BrowsableAttribute

System.ComponentModel (system.dll) sealed class

This attribute class is applied to properties to indicate whether they should be shown in a designer. Note that unattributed properties are visible by default.

Use the Browsable property to determine the state of the attribute. Note that the constructor takes a Boolean value, but you can compare instances against the Yes or No values for equality.

```
public sealed class BrowsableAttribute : Attribute {
// Public Constructors
   public BrowsableAttribute(bool browsable);
// Public Static Fields
   public static readonly BrowsableAttribute Default;        // =System.ComponentModel.BrowsableAttribute
   public static readonly BrowsableAttribute No;             // =System.ComponentModel.BrowsableAttribute
   public static readonly BrowsableAttribute Yes;            // =System.ComponentModel.BrowsableAttribute
// Public Instance Properties
   public bool Browsable{get; }
// Public Instance Methods
   public override bool Equals(object obj);                  // overrides Attribute
   public override int GetHashCode( );                       // overrides Attribute
   public override bool IsDefaultAttribute( );               // overrides Attribute
}
```

Hierarchy System.Object → System.Attribute → BrowsableAttribute

Valid On All

ByteConverter

System.ComponentModel (system.dll) class

This TypeConverter translates a Byte into other representations for serialization and design-time scenarios. You should not call this directly from your own code.

```
public class ByteConverter : BaseNumberConverter {
// Public Constructors
   public ByteConverter( );
}
```

Hierarchy System.Object → TypeConverter → BaseNumberConverter → ByteConverter

CancelEventArgs

System.ComponentModel (system.dll) class

This class should be used as the base for classes that encapsulate the data for events that can be canceled.

It provides a Cancel property that can be set by the client of the event to indicate that the action that raised the event should be aborted.

```
public class CancelEventArgs : EventArgs {
// Public Constructors
   public CancelEventArgs( );
   public CancelEventArgs(bool cancel);
// Public Instance Properties
   public bool Cancel{set; get; }
}
```

Hierarchy System.Object → System.EventArgs → CancelEventArgs

Subclasses System.Drawing.Printing.PrintEventArgs, System.Windows.Forms.{InputLanguageChangingEventArgs, TreeViewCancelEventArgs}

Passed To CancelEventHandler.{BeginInvoke( ), Invoke( )}, System.Windows.Forms.Control.OnValidating( ), System.Windows.Forms.FileDialog.OnFileOk( ), System.Windows.Forms.Form.OnClosing( )

CancelEventHandler

serializable

System.ComponentModel (system.dll) **delegate**

This is a delegate for events that use the CancelEventArgs class.

```
public delegate void CancelEventHandler(object sender, CancelEventArgs e);
```

Associated Events Multiple types

CategoryAttribute

System.ComponentModel (system.dll) **class**

This attribute class should be applied to properties to indicate to the design-time environment how they should be visually grouped within a designer.

You can retrieve the Category, which may be one of several standard values (such as Appearance and Behavior) that are defined through static properties.

Note that if you choose one of these standard values, they will be localized for you automatically. If you choose a custom value, you are responsible for localization yourself.

```
public class CategoryAttribute : Attribute {
// Public Constructors
   public CategoryAttribute( );
   public CategoryAttribute(string category);
// Public Static Properties
   public static CategoryAttribute Action{get; }
   public static CategoryAttribute Appearance{get; }
   public static CategoryAttribute Behavior{get; }
   public static CategoryAttribute Data{get; }
   public static CategoryAttribute Default{get; }
   public static CategoryAttribute Design{get; }
   public static CategoryAttribute DragDrop{get; }
   public static CategoryAttribute Focus{get; }
   public static CategoryAttribute Format{get; }
   public static CategoryAttribute Key{get; }
```

```
public static CategoryAttribute Layout{get; }
public static CategoryAttribute Mouse{get; }
public static CategoryAttribute WindowStyle{get; }
// Public Instance Properties
public string Category{get; }
// Public Instance Methods
public override bool Equals(object obj);                                    // overrides Attribute
public override int GetHashCode( );                                         // overrides Attribute
public override bool IsDefaultAttribute( );                                 // overrides Attribute
// Protected Instance Methods
protected virtual string GetLocalizedString(string value);
}
```

Hierarchy System.Object → System.Attribute → CategoryAttribute

Valid On All

CharConverter

System.ComponentModel (system.dll) class

This TypeConverter transforms to and from a char representation for serialization and design-time scenarios. You should not normally call this class directly from your own code.

```
public class CharConverter : TypeConverter {
// Public Constructors
public CharConverter( );
// Public Instance Methods
public override object ConvertFrom(ITypeDescriptorContext context,
   System.Globalization.CultureInfo culture, object value);                 // overrides TypeConverter
public override object ConvertTo(ITypeDescriptorContext context,
   System.Globalization.CultureInfo culture, object value, Type destinationType);  // overrides TypeConverter
}
```

Hierarchy System.Object → TypeConverter → CharConverter

CollectionChangeAction serializable

System.ComponentModel (system.dll) enum

This enumeration defines how a collection has changed for the CollectionChangeEventArgs. This is used in data-binding applications to notify interested parties that a data source has been modified in some way (e.g., the System.Data.DataColumnCollection.CollectionChanged event).

```
public enum CollectionChangeAction {
  Add = 1,
  Remove = 2,
  Refresh = 3
}
```

Hierarchy System.Object → System.ValueType → System.Enum(System.IComparable, System.IFormattable, System.IConvertible) → CollectionChangeAction

Returned By CollectionChangeEventArgs.Action

Passed To CollectionChangeEventArgs.CollectionChangeEventArgs( )

CollectionChangeEventArgs

System.ComponentModel (system.dll) class

This class encapsulates the data for the various CollectionChanged events raised by the collection classes in the System.Data namespace, such as the System.Data.DataTableCollection and System.Data.DataColumnCollection.

You can determine how the collection changed using the Action property, and which value actually changed with Element.

Although this class is present to support the data-binding framework, there is no reason you cannot use it in your own notifying collection classes.

```
public class CollectionChangeEventArgs : EventArgs {
// Public Constructors
  public CollectionChangeEventArgs(CollectionChangeAction action, object element);
// Public Instance Properties
  public virtual CollectionChangeAction Action{get; }
  public virtual object Element{get; }
}
```

Hierarchy System.Object → System.EventArgs → CollectionChangeEventArgs

Passed To CollectionChangeEventHandler.{BeginInvoke( ), Invoke( )}, System.Windows.Forms.BindingContext.OnCollectionChanged( ), System.Windows.Forms.BindingsCollection.OnCollectionChanged( ), System.Windows.Forms.GridColumnStylesCollection.OnCollectionChanged( ), System.Windows.Forms.GridTableStylesCollection.OnCollectionChanged( )

CollectionChangeEventHandler serializable

System.ComponentModel (system.dll) delegate

This is the delegate for events that use the CollectionChangeEventArgs class to encapsulate their data.

```
public delegate void CollectionChangeEventHandler(object sender, CollectionChangeEventArgs e);
```

Associated Events System.Windows.Forms.BindingContext.CollectionChanged( ), System.Windows.Forms.BindingsCollection.CollectionChanged( ), System.Windows.Forms.ControlBindingsCollection.CollectionChanged( ), System.Windows.Forms.GridColumnStylesCollection.CollectionChanged( ), System.Windows.Forms.GridTableStylesCollection.CollectionChanged( )

CollectionConverter

System.ComponentModel (system.dll) class

This TypeConverter translates classes that implement System.Collections.ICollection to and from other types. This is used in serialization and design-time scenarios, and you would not normally class this class directly from your own code.

```
public class CollectionConverter : TypeConverter {
// Public Constructors
   public CollectionConverter( );
// Public Instance Methods
   public override object ConvertTo(ITypeDescriptorContext context,
      System.Globalization.CultureInfo culture, object value, Type destinationType);     // overrides TypeConverter
   public override PropertyDescriptorCollection GetProperties(
      ITypeDescriptorContext context, object value, Attribute[ ] attributes);            // overrides TypeConverter
   public override bool GetPropertiesSupported(ITypeDescriptorContext context);         // overrides TypeConverter
}
```

Hierarchy System.Object → TypeConverter → CollectionConverter

Subclasses ArrayConverter

Component marshal by reference, disposable

System.ComponentModel (system.dll) class

This is the base for classes that can be hosted in a container such as those provided by the design-time environment. Note that it is a marshal-by-reference object. If you need marshal-by-value semantics, use MarshalByValueComponent.

You can obtain the Container that hosts the component and the Site that binds the component to the container. Derived classes also can use the protected DesignMode property to determine whether the class is hosted in a designer.

Note that the class implements the IDisposable interface. The Container ensures that the object is disposed correctly (if you have a Container, but you should ensure that your resource release code is added to the Dispose( ) method.

There are actually two dispose methods, and you would normally override the protected member that takes a Boolean. This is to support different cleanup behavior when Dispose( ) is called by the Container, and when it is called by the Component object's finalizer.

Typically, Component-derived classes are those non-windowed classes that you wish to present in the designer environment. They can use the GetService( ) method of the Site to make use of facilities provided by the designer host.

Classes that display a window should derive instead from System.Windows.Forms.Control, which itself derives from Component.

```
public class Component : MarshalByRefObject : IComponent, IDisposable {
// Public Constructors
   public Component( );
// Public Instance Properties
   public IContainer Container{get; }
   public virtual ISite Site{set; get; }                                 // implements IComponent
// Protected Instance Properties
   protected bool DesignMode{get; }
   protected EventHandlerList Events{get; }
// Public Instance Methods
   public void Dispose( );                                               // implements IDisposable
   public override string ToString( );                                   // overrides object
// Protected Instance Methods
   protected virtual void Dispose(bool disposing);
```

```
  protected override void Finalize( );                                    // overrides object
  protected virtual object GetService(Type service);
// Events
  public event EventHandler Disposed;                                     // implements IComponent
}
```

Hierarchy System.Object → System.MarshalByRefObject → Component(IComponent, System.IDisposable)

Subclasses Multiple types

ComponentCollection

System.ComponentModel (system.dll) class

This class encapsulates the collection of Component objects owned by the Container. Note that while this collection is read-only, you add components to the Container using the IContainer.Add( ) method.

```
public class ComponentCollection : ReadOnlyCollectionBase {
// Public Constructors
  public ComponentCollection(IComponent[ ] components);
// Public Instance Properties
  public virtual IComponent this{get; }
  public virtual IComponent this{get; }
// Public Instance Methods
  public void CopyTo(IComponent[ ] array, int index);
}
```

Hierarchy System.Object → System.Collections.ReadOnlyCollectionBase(System.Collections.ICollection, System.Collections.IEnumerable) → ComponentCollection

Returned By Container.Components, IContainer.Components

ComponentConverter

System.ComponentModel (system.dll) class

This TypeConverter is used to transform to and from Component-derived classes in serialization and design-time scenarios. You would not normally call this class directly from your own code.

```
public class ComponentConverter : ReferenceConverter {
// Public Constructors
  public ComponentConverter(Type type);
// Public Instance Methods
  public override PropertyDescriptorCollection GetProperties(
     ITypeDescriptorContext context, object value, Attribute[ ] attributes);    // overrides TypeConverter
  public override bool GetPropertiesSupported(ITypeDescriptorContext context);  // overrides TypeConverter
}
```

Hierarchy System.Object → TypeConverter → ReferenceConverter → ComponentConverter

ComponentEditor

System.ComponentModel (system.dll) abstract class

This is the abstract base class for a custom editor for a Component. You should override the EditComponent( ) method to display a modal user interface, which the designer can use to configure the object.

System.Windows.Forms.Design.WindowsFormsComponentEditor provides a base for a property sheet–like implementation of this class.

```
public abstract class ComponentEditor {
// Protected Constructors
   protected ComponentEditor( );
// Public Instance Methods
   public abstract bool EditComponent(ITypeDescriptorContext context, object component);
   public bool EditComponent(object component);
}
```

Subclasses System.Windows.Forms.Design.WindowsFormsComponentEditor

Container disposable

System.ComponentModel (system.dll) class

This class provides an implementation of the IContainer interface to encapsulate a queue of Component objects.

You can Add( ) and Remove( ) components from the queue, and get a collection of all the Components it contains.

When an instance is disposed, it will call Dispose( ) on all the Component objects it owns.

```
public class Container : IContainer, IDisposable {
// Public Constructors
   public Container( );
// Public Instance Properties
   public virtual ComponentCollection Components{get; }              // implements IContainer
// Public Instance Methods
   public virtual void Add(IComponent component);                    // implements IContainer
   public virtual void Add(IComponent component, string name);       // implements IContainer
   public void Dispose( );                                           // implements IDisposable
   public virtual void Remove(IComponent component);                 // implements IContainer
// Protected Instance Methods
   protected virtual ISite CreateSite(IComponent component, string name);
   protected virtual void Dispose(bool disposing);
   protected override void Finalize( );                              // overrides object
   protected virtual object GetService(Type service);
}
```

CultureInfoConverter

System.ComponentModel (system.dll) class

This TypeConverter transforms a System.Globalization.CultureInfo object to and from other types in serialization and design-time scenarios. You would not normally call this class directly from your own code.

```
public class CultureInfoConverter : TypeConverter {
// Public Constructors
   public CultureInfoConverter( );
// Public Instance Methods
   public override bool CanConvertFrom(ITypeDescriptorContext context, Type sourceType);        // overrides TypeConverter
   public override bool CanConvertTo(ITypeDescriptorContext context, Type destinationType);     // overrides TypeConverter
   public override object ConvertFrom(ITypeDescriptorContext context,
      System.Globalization.CultureInfo culture, object value);                                   // overrides TypeConverter
   public override object ConvertTo(ITypeDescriptorContext context,
      System.Globalization.CultureInfo culture, object value, Type destinationType);             // overrides TypeConverter
   public override StandardValuesCollection GetStandardValues(ITypeDescriptorContext context);  // overrides TypeConverter
   public override bool GetStandardValuesExclusive(ITypeDescriptorContext context);             // overrides TypeConverter
   public override bool GetStandardValuesSupported(ITypeDescriptorContext context);             // overrides TypeConverter
}
```

Hierarchy System.Object → TypeConverter → CultureInfoConverter

DateTimeConverter

System.ComponentModel (system.dll) class

As a TypeConverter class, this transforms to and from the System.DateTime type in serialization and design-time scenarios. You would not normally call this class from your own code.

```
public class DateTimeConverter : TypeConverter {
// Public Constructors
   public DateTimeConverter( );
// Public Instance Methods
   public override bool CanConvertFrom(ITypeDescriptorContext context, Type sourceType);        // overrides TypeConverter
   public override bool CanConvertTo(ITypeDescriptorContext context, Type destinationType);     // overrides TypeConverter
   public override object ConvertFrom(ITypeDescriptorContext context,
      System.Globalization.CultureInfo culture, object value);                                   // overrides TypeConverter
   public override object ConvertTo(ITypeDescriptorContext context,
      System.Globalization.CultureInfo culture, object value, Type destinationType);             // overrides TypeConverter
}
```

Hierarchy System.Object → TypeConverter → DateTimeConverter

DecimalConverter

System.ComponentModel (system.dll) class

This class, derived from TypeConverter, transforms between Decimal and other types, for serialization and design-time applications. You would not normally call this class from your own code.

```
public class DecimalConverter : BaseNumberConverter {
// Public Constructors
   public DecimalConverter( );
// Public Instance Methods
   public override bool CanConvertTo(ITypeDescriptorContext context,
      Type destinationType);                                                          // overrides BaseNumberConverter
   public override object ConvertTo(ITypeDescriptorContext context,
      System.Globalization.CultureInfo culture, object value, Type destinationType);  // overrides BaseNumberConverter
}
```

Hierarchy System.Object → TypeConverter → BaseNumberConverter → DecimalConverter

DefaultEventAttribute

System.ComponentModel (system.dll) sealed class

This attribute decorates a class to indicate which of the events should be the default. The VS.NET designers will add code to handle the default event when the component is double-clicked.

You can retrieve the Name of the default Attribute.

```
public sealed class DefaultEventAttribute : Attribute {
// Public Constructors
   public DefaultEventAttribute(string name);
// Public Static Fields
   public static readonly DefaultEventAttribute Default;       // =System.ComponentModel.DefaultEventAttribute
// Public Instance Properties
   public string Name{get; }
// Public Instance Methods
   public override bool Equals(object obj);                    // overrides Attribute
   public override int GetHashCode( );                         // overrides Attribute
}
```

Hierarchy System.Object → System.Attribute → DefaultEventAttribute

Valid On Class

DefaultPropertyAttribute

System.ComponentModel (system.dll) sealed class

Decorate a class with this attribute to indicate which of the properties should be treated as the default.

You can retrieve the Name of the default property from the attribute.

```
public sealed class DefaultPropertyAttribute : Attribute {
// Public Constructors
   public DefaultPropertyAttribute(string name);
// Public Static Fields
   public static readonly DefaultPropertyAttribute Default;    // =System.ComponentModel.DefaultPropertyAttribute
// Public Instance Properties
   public string Name{get; }
// Public Instance Methods
   public override bool Equals(object obj);                    // overrides Attribute
   public override int GetHashCode( );                         // overrides Attribute
}
```

Hierarchy System.Object → System.Attribute → DefaultPropertyAttribute

Valid On Class

DefaultValueAttribute

System.ComponentModel (system.dll) **sealed class**

This attribute decorates a property to indicate its default value. The VS.NET designer will display a property that is set to its default value using a plain style, whereas non-default values will be displayed in bold.

You should ensure that the Value of the attribute matches the initial value assigned to the property, as code generators may choose not to persist default properties.

```
public sealed class DefaultValueAttribute : Attribute {
// Public Constructors
   public DefaultValueAttribute(bool value);
   public DefaultValueAttribute(byte value);
   public DefaultValueAttribute(char value);
   public DefaultValueAttribute(double value);
   public DefaultValueAttribute(short value);
   public DefaultValueAttribute(int value);
   public DefaultValueAttribute(long value);
   public DefaultValueAttribute(object value);
   public DefaultValueAttribute(float value);
   public DefaultValueAttribute(string value);
   public DefaultValueAttribute(Type type, string value);
// Public Instance Properties
   public object Value{get; }
// Public Instance Methods
   public override bool Equals(object obj);                    // overrides Attribute
   public override int GetHashCode( );                         // overrides Attribute
}
```

Hierarchy System.Object → System.Attribute → DefaultValueAttribute

Valid On All

DescriptionAttribute

System.ComponentModel (system.dll) **class**

You can decorate a property with this attribute to provide some descriptive help text (the Description).

```
public class DescriptionAttribute : Attribute {
// Public Constructors
   public DescriptionAttribute( );
   public DescriptionAttribute(string description);
// Public Static Fields
   public static readonly DescriptionAttribute Default;    // =System.ComponentModel.DescriptionAttribute
// Public Instance Properties
   public virtual string Description{get; }
// Protected Instance Properties
   protected string DescriptionValue{set; get; }
// Public Instance Methods
   public override bool Equals(object obj);                    // overrides Attribute
```

```
public override int GetHashCode( );                    // overrides Attribute
}
```

Hierarchy System.Object → System.Attribute → DescriptionAttribute

Subclasses System.Diagnostics.MonitoringDescriptionAttribute, System.IO.IODescriptionAttribute, System.Timers.TimersDescriptionAttribute

Valid On All

DesignerAttribute

System.ComponentModel (system.dll) sealed class

To provide a custom designer for a Component or System.Windows.Forms.Control, you should decorate the class with this attribute. (See EditorAttribute for information on custom type editors for a specific property within a component).

You can specify the DesignerTypeName: the name of the type that implements the System.ComponentModel.Design.IDesigner interface on behalf of our designable class. You can also specify the base type of the designer with DesignerBaseTypeName. While this would default to System.ComponentModel.Design.IDesigner, you can specify a different System.ComponentModel.Design.IDesigner-derived interface such as System.ComponentModel.Design.IRootDesigner

```
public sealed class DesignerAttribute : Attribute {
// Public Constructors
   public DesignerAttribute(string designerTypeName);
   public DesignerAttribute(string designerTypeName, string designerBaseTypeName);
   public DesignerAttribute(string designerTypeName, Type designerBaseType);
   public DesignerAttribute(Type designerType);
   public DesignerAttribute(Type designerType, Type designerBaseType);
// Public Instance Properties
   public string DesignerBaseTypeName{get; }
   public string DesignerTypeName{get; }
   public override object TypeId{get; }                // overrides Attribute
// Public Instance Methods
   public override bool Equals(object obj);            // overrides Attribute
   public override int GetHashCode( );                 // overrides Attribute
}
```

Hierarchy System.Object → System.Attribute → DesignerAttribute

Valid On Class, Interface

DesignerCategoryAttribute

System.ComponentModel (system.dll) sealed class

You should apply this attribute to a class with a custom designer to indicate the nature of that designer. The design-time environment is entitled to refuse to use your designer if you do not supply this attribute.

The Category should be chosen from one of the standard options (Component, Form, or Generic) if you wish to integrate with the VS.NET designers. You could extend this with your own custom categories if you are providing your own design-time host.

```
public sealed class DesignerCategoryAttribute : Attribute {
// Public Constructors
   public DesignerCategoryAttribute( );
   public DesignerCategoryAttribute(string category);
// Public Static Fields
   public static readonly DesignerCategoryAttribute Component;    // =System.ComponentModel.DesignerCategoryAttribute
   public static readonly DesignerCategoryAttribute Default;      // =System.ComponentModel.DesignerCategoryAttribute
   public static readonly DesignerCategoryAttribute Form;         // =System.ComponentModel.DesignerCategoryAttribute
   public static readonly DesignerCategoryAttribute Generic;      // =System.ComponentModel.DesignerCategoryAttribute
// Public Instance Properties
   public string Category{get; }
   public override object TypeId{get; }                           // overrides Attribute
// Public Instance Methods
   public override bool Equals(object obj);                       // overrides Attribute
   public override int GetHashCode( );                            // overrides Attribute
   public override bool IsDefaultAttribute( );                    // overrides Attribute
}
```

Hierarchy System.Object → System.Attribute → DesignerCategoryAttribute

Valid On Class

DesignerSerializationVisibility **serializable**

System.ComponentModel (system.dll) **enum**

This enumeration lists the options for DesignerSerializationVisibilityAttribute.

```
public enum DesignerSerializationVisibility {
   Hidden = 0,
   Visible = 1,
   Content = 2
}
```

Hierarchy System.Object → System.ValueType → System.Enum(System.IComparable, System.IFormattable, System.IConvertible) → DesignerSerializationVisibility

Returned By DesignerSerializationVisibilityAttribute.Visibility, PropertyDescriptor.SerializationVisibility

Passed To DesignerSerializationVisibilityAttribute.DesignerSerializationVisibilityAttribute( )

DesignerSerializationVisibilityAttribute

System.ComponentModel (system.dll) **sealed class**

Some properties may be visible in the designer, but should not be serialized. Alternatively, you may need to serialize the Content of the property rather than its value (as might be the case with a collection class). In these circumstances, you should adorn the property with this attribute.

The standard visibility options are presented through the static Content, Hidden, and Visible members. The default is Visible. You can also determine the Visibility encapsulated in the attribute.

```
public sealed class DesignerSerializationVisibilityAttribute : Attribute {
// Public Constructors
   public DesignerSerializationVisibilityAttribute(DesignerSerializationVisibility visibility);
// Public Static Fields
   public static readonly DesignerSerializationVisibilityAttribute Content;
                                  // =System.ComponentModel.DesignerSerializationVisibilityAttribute
   public static readonly DesignerSerializationVisibilityAttribute Default;
                                  // =System.ComponentModel.DesignerSerializationVisibilityAttribute
   public static readonly DesignerSerializationVisibilityAttribute Hidden;
                                  // =System.ComponentModel.DesignerSerializationVisibilityAttribute
   public static readonly DesignerSerializationVisibilityAttribute Visible;
                                  // =System.ComponentModel.DesignerSerializationVisibilityAttribute
// Public Instance Properties
   public DesignerSerializationVisibility Visibility{get; }
// Public Instance Methods
   public override bool Equals(object obj);                       // overrides Attribute
   public override int GetHashCode( );                            // overrides Attribute
   public override bool IsDefaultAttribute( );                    // overrides Attribute
}
```

Hierarchy System.Object → System.Attribute → DesignerSerializationVisibilityAttribute

Valid On Method, Property

DesignOnlyAttribute

System.ComponentModel (system.dll) sealed class

You can mark a property with this attribute to indicate that its value can be modified only at design time. This indicates that no code will be generated when the user changes the property in the designer.

Compare this with the ReadOnlyAttribute, which will prevent the designer from modifying the value.

```
public sealed class DesignOnlyAttribute : Attribute {
// Public Constructors
   public DesignOnlyAttribute(bool isDesignOnly);
// Public Static Fields
   public static readonly DesignOnlyAttribute Default;   // =System.ComponentModel.DesignOnlyAttribute
   public static readonly DesignOnlyAttribute No;        // =System.ComponentModel.DesignOnlyAttribute
   public static readonly DesignOnlyAttribute Yes;       // =System.ComponentModel.DesignOnlyAttribute
// Public Instance Properties
   public bool IsDesignOnly{get; }
// Public Instance Methods
   public override bool Equals(object obj);                       // overrides Attribute
   public override int GetHashCode( );                            // overrides Attribute
   public override bool IsDefaultAttribute( );                    // overrides Attribute
}
```

Hierarchy System.Object → System.Attribute → DesignOnlyAttribute

Valid On All

DesignTimeVisibleAttribute

System.ComponentModel (system.dll) **sealed class**

This is internal to framework and should not be used in your own applications.

```
public sealed class DesignTimeVisibleAttribute : Attribute {
// Public Constructors
   public DesignTimeVisibleAttribute( );
   public DesignTimeVisibleAttribute(bool visible);
// Public Static Fields
   public static readonly DesignTimeVisibleAttribute Default;      // =System.ComponentModel.DesignTimeVisibleAttribute
   public static readonly DesignTimeVisibleAttribute No;           // =System.ComponentModel.DesignTimeVisibleAttribute
   public static readonly DesignTimeVisibleAttribute Yes;          // =System.ComponentModel.DesignTimeVisibleAttribute
// Public Instance Properties
   public bool Visible{get; }
// Public Instance Methods
   public override bool Equals(object obj);                        // overrides Attribute
   public override int GetHashCode( );                             // overrides Attribute
   public override bool IsDefaultAttribute( );                     // overrides Attribute
}
```

Hierarchy System.Object → System.Attribute → DesignTimeVisibleAttribute

Valid On Class, Interface

DoubleConverter

System.ComponentModel (system.dll) **class**

This TypeConverter is used to transform a double to and from other types in serialization and design-time scenarios. You would not normally use this class directly in your own code.

```
public class DoubleConverter : BaseNumberConverter {
// Public Constructors
   public DoubleConverter( );
}
```

Hierarchy System.Object → TypeConverter → BaseNumberConverter → DoubleConverter

EditorAttribute

System.ComponentModel (system.dll) **sealed class**

You can decorate a specific property, or an entire, class with this attribute to indicate a custom editor that should be used to modify the type. Similar to DesignerAttribute, you can specify EditorTypeName, and EditorBaseTypeName. Note that this must be System.Drawing.Design.UITypeEditor.

See System.Drawing.Design.UITypeEditor for more details.

```
public sealed class EditorAttribute : Attribute {
// Public Constructors
   public EditorAttribute( );
   public EditorAttribute(string typeName, string baseTypeName);
```

```
  public EditorAttribute(string typeName, Type baseType);
  public EditorAttribute(Type type, Type baseType);
// Public Instance Properties
  public string EditorBaseTypeName{get; }
  public string EditorTypeName{get; }
  public override object TypeId{get; }                    // overrides Attribute
// Public Instance Methods
  public override bool Equals(object obj);                 // overrides Attribute
  public override int GetHashCode( );                      // overrides Attribute
}
```

Hierarchy System.Object → System.Attribute → EditorAttribute

Valid On All

EditorBrowsableAttribute

System.ComponentModel (system.dll) — sealed class

This attribute is used to adorn classes, structs, and members to indicate whether they should appear in an editor. You can retrieve EditorBrowsableState for the attribute using the State property. It determines which fields appear in the IntelliSense pop-up menus in the editor.

```
public sealed class EditorBrowsableAttribute : Attribute {
// Public Constructors
  public EditorBrowsableAttribute( );
  public EditorBrowsableAttribute(EditorBrowsableState state);
// Public Instance Properties
  public EditorBrowsableState State{get; }
// Public Instance Methods
  public override bool Equals(object obj);                 // overrides Attribute
  public override int GetHashCode( );                      // overrides Attribute
}
```

Hierarchy System.Object → System.Attribute → EditorBrowsableAttribute

Valid On Class, Struct, Enum, Constructor, Method, Property, Field, Event, Interface, Delegate

EditorBrowsableState — serializable

System.ComponentModel (system.dll) — enum

This enumeration determines whether a class or member should be visible in an editor. It is used by EditorBrowsableAttribute to determine whether the element should be shown Never, Always, or only shown when Advanced elements are visible.

```
public enum EditorBrowsableState {
  Always = 0,
  Never = 1,
  Advanced = 2
}
```

Hierarchy System.Object → System.ValueType → System.Enum(System.IComparable, System.IFormattable, System.IConvertible) → EditorBrowsableState

Returned By EditorBrowsableAttribute.State

Passed To EditorBrowsableAttribute.EditorBrowsableAttribute( )

EnumConverter

System.ComponentModel (system.dll) class

This TypeConverter class is used to transform to and from enumerations. It is used in design-time and serialization scenarios, and should not normally be called from your own code.

```
public class EnumConverter : TypeConverter {
// Public Constructors
   public EnumConverter(Type type);
// Protected Instance Properties
   protected virtual IComparer Comparer{get; }
   protected Type EnumType{get; }
   protected StandardValuesCollection Values{set; get; }
// Public Instance Methods
   public override bool CanConvertFrom(ITypeDescriptorContext context, Type sourceType);          // overrides TypeConverter
   public override bool CanConvertTo(ITypeDescriptorContext context, Type destinationType);       // overrides TypeConverter
   public override object ConvertFrom(ITypeDescriptorContext context,
      System.Globalization.CultureInfo culture, object value);                                     // overrides TypeConverter
   public override object ConvertTo(ITypeDescriptorContext context,
      System.Globalization.CultureInfo culture, object value, Type destinationType);              // overrides TypeConverter
   public override StandardValuesCollection GetStandardValues(ITypeDescriptorContext context);   // overrides TypeConverter
   public override bool GetStandardValuesExclusive(ITypeDescriptorContext context);               // overrides TypeConverter
   public override bool GetStandardValuesSupported(ITypeDescriptorContext context);               // overrides TypeConverter
   public override bool IsValid(ITypeDescriptorContext context, object value);                    // overrides TypeConverter
}
```

Hierarchy System.Object → TypeConverter → EnumConverter

Subclasses System.Drawing.FontUnitConverter

EventDescriptor

System.ComponentModel (system.dll) abstract class

This class, derived from MemberDescriptor, encapsulates the information about an event. In addition to the base functionality, you can discover the ComponentType that declares the event, and the EventType that describes the delegate for the event. You can also determine whether the delegate IsMulticast.

AddEventHandler( ) and RemoveEventHandler( ) allow you to control the binding to the encapsulated event.

```
public abstract class EventDescriptor : MemberDescriptor {
// Protected Constructors
   protected EventDescriptor(MemberDescriptor descr);
   protected EventDescriptor(MemberDescriptor descr, Attribute[ ] attrs);
```

```
protected EventDescriptor(string name, Attribute[ ] attrs);
// Public Instance Properties
public abstract Type ComponentType{get; }
public abstract Type EventType{get; }
public abstract bool IsMulticast{get; }
// Public Instance Methods
public abstract void AddEventHandler(object component, Delegate value);
public abstract void RemoveEventHandler(object component, Delegate value);
}
```

Hierarchy System.Object → MemberDescriptor → EventDescriptor

Returned By EventDescriptorCollection.{Find( ), this}, IComNativeDescriptorHandler.GetDefaultEvent( ), ICustomTypeDescriptor.GetDefaultEvent( ), TypeDescriptor.{CreateEvent( ), GetDefaultEvent( )}

Passed To EventDescriptorCollection.{Add( ), Contains( ), EventDescriptorCollection( ), IndexOf( ), Insert( ), Remove( )}, TypeDescriptor.CreateEvent( )

EventDescriptorCollection

System.ComponentModel (system.dll) class

This class implements a collection of EventDescriptor objects and is returned by the TypeDescriptor.GetEvents( ) method.

```
public class EventDescriptorCollection : IList, ICollection, IEnumerable {
// Public Constructors
public EventDescriptorCollection(EventDescriptor[ ] events);
// Public Static Fields
public static readonly EventDescriptorCollection Empty;      // =System.ComponentModel.EventDescriptorCollection
// Public Instance Properties
public int Count{get; }                                      // implements ICollection
public virtual EventDescriptor this{get; }
public virtual EventDescriptor this{get; }
// Public Instance Methods
public int Add(EventDescriptor value);
public void Clear( );                                        // implements IList
public bool Contains(EventDescriptor value);
public virtual EventDescriptor Find(string name, bool ignoreCase);
public IEnumerator GetEnumerator( );                         // implements IEnumerable
public int IndexOf(EventDescriptor value);
public void Insert(int index, EventDescriptor value);
public void Remove(EventDescriptor value);
public void RemoveAt(int index);                             // implements IList
public virtual EventDescriptorCollection Sort( );
public virtual EventDescriptorCollection Sort(System.Collections.IComparer comparer);
public virtual EventDescriptorCollection Sort(string[ ] names);
public virtual EventDescriptorCollection Sort(string[ ] names, System.Collections.IComparer comparer);
// Protected Instance Methods
protected void InternalSort(System.Collections.IComparer sorter);
```

```
  protected void InternalSort(string[ ] names);
}
```

Returned By IComNativeDescriptorHandler.GetEvents( ), ICustomTypeDescriptor.GetEvents( ), TypeDescriptor.GetEvents( )

EventHandlerList **disposable**

System.ComponentModel (system.dll) **sealed class**

This class encapsulates a set of event handlers. You can use AddHandler( ) and RemoveHandler( ) to manipulate the list of delegates bound to particular objects, and you can retrieve the delegate bound to a particular object by using the Item property (this is the indexer for the class).

Note that this class does not implement any of the standard collection interfaces.

```
public sealed class EventHandlerList : IDisposable {
// Public Constructors
  public EventHandlerList( );
// Public Instance Properties
  public Delegate this{set; get; }
// Public Instance Methods
  public void AddHandler(object key, Delegate value);
  public void Dispose( );                                    // implements IDisposable
  public void RemoveHandler(object key, Delegate value);
}
```

Returned By Component.Events, MarshalByValueComponent.Events

ExpandableObjectConverter

System.ComponentModel (system.dll) **class**

This class represent a TypeConverter for expandable objects. While you would not normally call on this class from your own code, you can select it as your class's TypeConverter to display contained types in the designer.

```
public class ExpandableObjectConverter : TypeConverter {
// Public Constructors
  public ExpandableObjectConverter( );
// Public Instance Methods
  public override PropertyDescriptorCollection GetProperties(ITypeDescriptorContext context,
    object value, Attribute[ ] attributes);                  // overrides TypeConverter
  public override bool GetPropertiesSupported(ITypeDescriptorContext context);   // overrides TypeConverter
}
```

Hierarchy System.Object → TypeConverter → ExpandableObjectConverter

Subclasses System.Drawing.IconConverter, System.Drawing.Printing.MarginsConverter, System.Windows.Forms.ListViewItemConverter

ExtenderProvidedPropertyAttribute

System.ComponentModel (system.dll) sealed class

This is an internal class and should not be used in your own code.

```
public sealed class ExtenderProvidedPropertyAttribute : Attribute {
// Public Constructors
   public ExtenderProvidedPropertyAttribute( );
// Public Instance Properties
   public PropertyDescriptor ExtenderProperty{get; }
   public IExtenderProvider Provider{get; }
   public Type ReceiverType{get; }
// Public Instance Methods
   public override bool Equals(object obj);                    // overrides Attribute
   public override int GetHashCode( );                         // overrides Attribute
   public override bool IsDefaultAttribute( );                 // overrides Attribute
}
```

Hierarchy System.Object → System.Attribute → ExtenderProvidedPropertyAttribute

Valid On All

GuidConverter

System.ComponentModel (system.dll) class

This TypeConverter is used to convert a Guid to and from other types in serialization and design-time scenarios, and should not normally be used in your own code.

```
public class GuidConverter : TypeConverter {
// Public Constructors
   public GuidConverter( );
// Public Instance Methods
   public override bool CanConvertFrom(ITypeDescriptorContext context, Type sourceType);      // overrides TypeConverter
   public override bool CanConvertTo(ITypeDescriptorContext context, Type destinationType);   // overrides TypeConverter
   public override object ConvertFrom(ITypeDescriptorContext context,
      System.Globalization.CultureInfo culture, object value);                                // overrides TypeConverter
   public override object ConvertTo(ITypeDescriptorContext context,
      System.Globalization.CultureInfo culture, object value, Type destinationType);          // overrides TypeConverter
}
```

Hierarchy System.Object → TypeConverter → GuidConverter

IBindingList

System.ComponentModel (system.dll) interface

This interface is implemented by classes such as System.Data.DataView that wish to support list-like data binding. It is derived from the standard collection interfaces to present basic collection facilities such as Add( ) and Remove( ).

In addition to this, it has properties that determine whether the class will AllowEdit or AllowNew items to be added. AllowRemove determines whether you can remove items from the list, and IsSorted determines whether the list items have been sorted. Note that this does not imply any kind of auto-sorting behavior—it just determines whether the list has been sorted. SupportsSorting determines whether the list can be sorted. For sorted lists, you can specify the SortDirection and the SortProperty (the property of the elements in the list that provides the sort data). To apply the sort, use the ApplySort() and RemoveSort() methods.

Methods are provided to AddNew() items to the list and Find() a row with a particular PropertyDescriptor.

You can also use AddIndex() and RemoveIndex() to manage indexes to improve the search capabilities of your list. Your particular class doesn't actually have to do anything in the implementation of these methods if it doesn't support indexes.

```
public interface IBindingList : IList, ICollection, IEnumerable {
// Public Instance Properties
   public bool AllowEdit{get; }
   public bool AllowNew{get; }
   public bool AllowRemove{get; }
   public bool IsSorted{get; }
   public ListSortDirection SortDirection{get; }
   public PropertyDescriptor SortProperty{get; }
   public bool SupportsChangeNotification{get; }
   public bool SupportsSearching{get; }
   public bool SupportsSorting{get; }
// Public Instance Methods
   public void AddIndex(PropertyDescriptor property);
   public object AddNew( );
   public void ApplySort(PropertyDescriptor property, ListSortDirection direction);
   public int Find(PropertyDescriptor property, object key);
   public void RemoveIndex(PropertyDescriptor property);
   public void RemoveSort( );
// Events
   public event ListChangedEventHandler ListChanged;
}
```

IComNativeDescriptorHandler

System.ComponentModel (system.dll) **interface**

This is a class private to the framework, which should not be used in your own code.

```
public interface IComNativeDescriptorHandler {
// Public Instance Methods
   public AttributeCollection GetAttributes(
      object component);
   public string GetClassName(object component);
   public TypeConverter GetConverter(object component);
   public EventDescriptor GetDefaultEvent(object component);
   public PropertyDescriptor GetDefaultProperty(object component);
   public object GetEditor(object component, Type baseEditorType);
   public EventDescriptorCollection GetEvents(object component);
   public EventDescriptorCollection GetEvents(object component, Attribute[ ] attributes);
   public string GetName(object component);
   public PropertyDescriptorCollection GetProperties(object component, Attribute[ ] attributes);
```

```
public object GetPropertyValue(object component, int dispid, ref bool success);
public object GetPropertyValue(object component, string propertyName, ref bool success);
}
```

Returned By TypeDescriptor.ComNativeDescriptorHandler

Passed To TypeDescriptor.ComNativeDescriptorHandler

IComponent

disposable

System.ComponentModel (system.dll) **interface**

This interface, implemented by Component and MarshalByValueComponent provides the basic functionality required by components in the framework. Specifically, this means providing a way of setting the Site for the component (through which the component can discover the services provided by its hosting environment), and a Disposed event, to inform the host when it has been cleaned up.

In your own applications, you would normally derive from one of the classes that implement this interface, such as Component or System.Windows.Forms.Control.

```
public interface IComponent : IDisposable {
// Public Instance Properties
   public ISite Site{set; get; }
// Events
   public event EventHandler Disposed;
}
```

Implemented By Component, MarshalByValueComponent

Returned By ComponentCollection.this, ISite.Component, System.Drawing.Design.ToolboxComponentsCreatedEventArgs.Components, System.Drawing.Design.ToolboxItem.{CreateComponents( ), CreateComponentsCore( )}, System.Windows.Forms.Design.ComponentEditorPage.{Component, GetSelectedComponent( )}, System.Windows.Forms.Design.ParentControlDesigner.CreateToolCore( )

Passed To Multiple types

IContainer

disposable

System.ComponentModel (system.dll) **interface**

This interface is implemented by classes (such as Container) that hold and manage a set of Component objects. Contrast this with ISite, which binds a component to a host and provides the host's services to that component. It provides members to Add( ) and Remove( ) a Component, and also get the set of Components in the container.

```
public interface IContainer : IDisposable {
// Public Instance Properties
   public ComponentCollection Components{get; }
// Public Instance Methods
   public void Add(IComponent component);
   public void Add(IComponent component, string name);
   public void Remove(IComponent component);
}
```

Implemented By Container

Returned By Component.Container, ISite.Container, ITypeDescriptorContext.Container, MarshalByValueComponent.Container

Passed To System.Windows.Forms.ImageList.ImageList( ), System.Windows.Forms.NotifyIcon.NotifyIcon( ), System.Windows.Forms.Timer.Timer( ), System.Windows.Forms.ToolTip.ToolTip( )

ICustomTypeDescriptor

System.ComponentModel (system.dll) interface

Classes implement this interface to provide dynamic type information about themselves. Contrast this with the TypeDescriptor, which provides static type information.

It provides an interface very similar to the TypeDescriptor signature, with members to access attributes, properties, events, and the GetConverter( ) method to get a custom TypeConverter for the class.

```
public interface ICustomTypeDescriptor {
// Public Instance Methods
   public AttributeCollection GetAttributes( );
   public string GetClassName( );
   public string GetComponentName( );
   public TypeConverter GetConverter( );
   public EventDescriptor GetDefaultEvent( );
   public PropertyDescriptor GetDefaultProperty( );
   public object GetEditor(Type editorBaseType);
   public EventDescriptorCollection GetEvents( );
   public EventDescriptorCollection GetEvents(Attribute[ ] attributes);
   public PropertyDescriptorCollection GetProperties( );
   public PropertyDescriptorCollection GetProperties(Attribute[ ] attributes);
   public object GetPropertyOwner(PropertyDescriptor pd);
}
```

Implemented By System.Windows.Forms.AxHost

IDataErrorInfo

System.ComponentModel (system.dll) interface

This interface is implemented by classes that wish to provide additional error information to the user interface in data-binding scenarios. The Error property gives an error message that indicates what is wrong with the object. The Item property (which is the indexer in C#) allows the UI to find the specific error message for the property with a given name.

As an example, it is implemented by System.Data.DataView and the System.Windows.Forms.DataGrid uses it to display error information.

```
public interface IDataErrorInfo {
// Public Instance Properties
   public string Error{get; }
   public string this{get; }
}
```

IEditableObject

System.ComponentModel (system.dll) interface

This interface should be implemented by classes that provide edit-rollback/commit semantics in data-binding scenarios (such as System.Data.DataRowView).

BeginEdit( ) should initiate an editing session, CancelEdit( ) should perform a rollback, discarding any changes that have been made, and EndEdit( ) should commit any such changes.

```
public interface IEditableObject {
// Public Instance Methods
  public void BeginEdit( );
  public void CancelEdit( );
  public void EndEdit( );
}
```

IExtenderProvider

System.ComponentModel (system.dll) interface

This interface is implemented by classes that wish to offer additional properties for particular objects in the designer. For example, the System.Windows.Forms.ToolTip component adds a ToolTip property to other System.Windows.Forms.Control objects owned by its host. This is done by implementing the CanExtend( ) method to determine whether the class can extend a particular object (implementations usually filter by the type of the object) and adding a series of property-like methods called GetMyProperty( ) and SetMyProperty( ), which take an additional parameter for the object they are extending (e.g., a System.Windows.Forms.Control, in the case of the ToolTip. Finally, you decorate the class with a ProvidePropertyAttribute for each of these extended properties.

You would typically derive a class that implements this interface from Component, to add it to a designer surface.

```
public interface IExtenderProvider {
// Public Instance Methods
  public bool CanExtend(object extendee);
}
```

Implemented By System.Windows.Forms.{ErrorProvider, HelpProvider, ToolTip}, System.Windows.Forms.Design.{ComponentTray, PropertyTab}

Returned By ExtenderProvidedPropertyAttribute.Provider

IListSource

System.ComponentModel (system.dll) interface

This interface is implemented by classes (such as System.Data.DataSet and System.Data.DataTable) that can provide one or more lists for a data-binding scenario but are not actually bindable lists in and of themselves.

The ContainsListCollection property determines whether the list is actually a collection of lists itself (as in the System.Data.DataSet-System.Data.DataTable relationship), and the GetList( ) method returns the System.Collections.IList for the binding scenario.

```
public interface IListSource {
// Public Instance Properties
   public bool ContainsListCollection{get; }
// Public Instance Methods
   public IList GetList( );
}
```

ImmutableObjectAttribute

System.ComponentModel (system.dll) sealed class

This attribute is applied to classes that have no editable properties, and can therefore be displayed as read-only in the designer.

Commonly, this is applied to expandable objects (see ExpandableObjectConverter) whose properties should be displayed as read-only in a System.Windows.Forms.PropertyGrid.

```
public sealed class ImmutableObjectAttribute : Attribute {
// Public Constructors
   public ImmutableObjectAttribute(bool immutable);
// Public Static Fields
   public static readonly ImmutableObjectAttribute Default;      // =System.ComponentModel.ImmutableObjectAttribute
   public static readonly ImmutableObjectAttribute No;           // =System.ComponentModel.ImmutableObjectAttribute
   public static readonly ImmutableObjectAttribute Yes;          // =System.ComponentModel.ImmutableObjectAttribute
// Public Instance Properties
   public bool Immutable{get; }
// Public Instance Methods
   public override bool Equals(object obj);                                              // overrides Attribute
   public override int GetHashCode( );                                                   // overrides Attribute
   public override bool IsDefaultAttribute( );                                           // overrides Attribute
}
```

Hierarchy System.Object → System.Attribute → ImmutableObjectAttribute

Valid On All

InheritanceAttribute

System.ComponentModel (system.dll) sealed class

The System.ComponentModel.Design.IInheritanceService uses this attribute to follow the hierarchy of components in the designer.

You can use this attribute to specify the InheritanceLevel of the property that it adorns. Note that this inheritance does not mean class-level inheritance, but rather that one Component exposes another Component through a public property.

```
public sealed class InheritanceAttribute : Attribute {
// Public Constructors
   public InheritanceAttribute( );
   public InheritanceAttribute(InheritanceLevel inheritanceLevel);
// Public Static Fields
   public static readonly InheritanceAttribute Default;                                   // =NotInherited
   public static readonly InheritanceAttribute Inherited;                                 // =Inherited
                                                                                          // =InheritedReadOnly
```

```
  public static readonly InheritanceAttribute InheritedReadOnly;
  public static readonly InheritanceAttribute NotInherited;                // =NotInherited
// Public Instance Properties
  public InheritanceLevel InheritanceLevel{get; }
// Public Instance Methods
  public override bool Equals(object value);                               // overrides Attribute
  public override int GetHashCode( );                                      // overrides Attribute
  public override bool IsDefaultAttribute( );                              // overrides Attribute
  public override string ToString( );                                      // overrides object
}
```

Hierarchy System.Object → System.Attribute → InheritanceAttribute

Valid On Property, Field, Event

InheritanceLevel serializable

System.ComponentModel (system.dll) enum

This enumeration determines whether a component is Inherited from another; InheritedReadOnly, which implies that the component is derived from another but only has read only access to the inherited properties; or NotInherited, which implies that the component is at the root.

```
public enum InheritanceLevel {
  Inherited = 1,
  InheritedReadOnly = 2,
  NotInherited = 3
}
```

Hierarchy System.Object → System.ValueType → System.Enum(System.IComparable, System.IFormattable, System.IConvertible) → InheritanceLevel

Returned By InheritanceAttribute.InheritanceLevel

Passed To InheritanceAttribute.InheritanceAttribute( )

InstallerTypeAttribute

System.ComponentModel (system.dll) class

This attribute is used to adorn components to indicate the type of the object that should be used to install them (the InstallerType). See System.Configuration for more information on installers.

```
public class InstallerTypeAttribute : Attribute {
// Public Constructors
  public InstallerTypeAttribute(string typeName);
  public InstallerTypeAttribute(Type installerType);
// Public Instance Properties
  public virtual Type InstallerType{get; }
// Public Instance Methods
  public override bool Equals(object obj);                                 // overrides Attribute
```

Component-Model

```
public override int GetHashCode( );                                    // overrides Attribute
}
```

Hierarchy System.Object → System.Attribute → InstallerTypeAttribute

Valid On Class

Int16Converter

System.ComponentModel (system.dll) class

This is a TypeConverter for an Int16, for use in serialization and design-time scenarios. You would not normally call it from your own code.

```
public class Int16Converter : BaseNumberConverter {
// Public Constructors
   public Int16Converter( );
}
```

Hierarchy System.Object → TypeConverter → BaseNumberConverter → Int16Converter

Int32Converter

System.ComponentModel (system.dll) class

This TypeConverter is used to transform an Int32 to and from other types in design-time and serialization scenarios. You should not normally use it in your own code.

```
public class Int32Converter : BaseNumberConverter {
// Public Constructors
   public Int32Converter( );
}
```

Hierarchy System.Object → TypeConverter → BaseNumberConverter → Int32Converter

Subclasses System.Windows.Forms.ImageIndexConverter

Int64Converter

System.ComponentModel (system.dll) class

This is a TypeConverter that is used to convert to and from an Int64 in design-time and serialization scenarios. You should not normally call it from your own code.

```
public class Int64Converter : BaseNumberConverter {
// Public Constructors
   public Int64Converter( );
}
```

Hierarchy System.Object → TypeConverter → BaseNumberConverter → Int64Converter

InvalidEnumArgumentException

System.ComponentModel (system.dll) class

This exception class is thrown when an invalid enumeration is passed to a method or property.

```
public class InvalidEnumArgumentException : ArgumentException {
// Public Constructors
   public InvalidEnumArgumentException( );
   public InvalidEnumArgumentException(string message);
   public InvalidEnumArgumentException(string argumentName, int invalidValue, Type enumClass);
}
```

Hierarchy System.Object → System.Exception(System.Runtime.Serialization.ISerializable) → System.SystemException → System.ArgumentException → InvalidEnumArgumentException

ISite

System.ComponentModel (system.dll) interface

This interface, derived from IServiceProvider is used to connect a Component to its Container.

In addition to providing accessors for the host services, you can find the Name of the component and whether the component is currently being used in DesignMode.

```
public interface ISite : IServiceProvider {
// Public Instance Properties
   public IComponent Component{get; }
   public IContainer Container{get; }
   public bool DesignMode{get; }
   public string Name{set; get; }
}
```

Returned By Component.Site, Container.CreateSite( ), IComponent.Site, MarshalByValueComponent.Site, MemberDescriptor.GetSite( )

Passed To Component.Site, IComponent.Site, MarshalByValueComponent.Site

ISupportInitialize

System.ComponentModel (system.dll) interface

Classes should implement this interface if they support the batched initialization of their properties. You would also implement it if you need to know that you are in the designer in your constructor, as DesignMode is not yet valid (because your Site will not have been set).

BeginInit( ) is called to start batching updates, and EndInit( ) ends batching and normally causes any update events to be raised.

```
public interface ISupportInitialize {
// Public Instance Methods
   public void BeginInit( );
   public void EndInit( );
}
```

Implemented By System.Diagnostics.{EventLog, PerformanceCounter}, System.IO.FileSystemWatcher, System.Timers.Timer, System.Windows.Forms.{AxHost, DataGrid, NumericUpDown, StatusBarPanel, TrackBar}

ISynchronizeInvoke

System.ComponentModel (system.dll) interface

This interface is implemented by components (specifically System.Windows.Forms.Control) that support the synchronous (through Invoke( )) or asynchronous (through BeginInvoke( ) and EndInvoke( )) execution of delegates, allowing the components to marshal the delegates into a particular context.

The implementation in System.Windows.Forms.Control is used to ensure that the execution of the delegate is marshaled onto the thread on which the System.Windows.Forms.Control was created.

```
public interface ISynchronizeInvoke {
// Public Instance Properties
  public bool InvokeRequired{get; }
// Public Instance Methods
  public IAsyncResult BeginInvoke(Delegate method, object[ ] args);
  public object EndInvoke(IAsyncResult result);
  public object Invoke(Delegate method, object[ ] args);
}
```

Implemented By System.Windows.Forms.Control

Returned By System.Diagnostics.EventLog.SynchronizingObject, System.Diagnostics.Process.SynchronizingObject, System.IO.FileSystemWatcher.SynchronizingObject, System.Timers.Timer.SynchronizingObject

Passed To System.Diagnostics.EventLog.SynchronizingObject, System.Diagnostics.Process.SynchronizingObject, System.IO.FileSystemWatcher.SynchronizingObject, System.Timers.Timer.SynchronizingObject

ITypeDescriptorContext

System.ComponentModel (system.dll) interface

This interface is implemented by classes to allow clients to discover information about the context in which the component is in use.

You can find the Container that owns the component, the Instance of the object that aggregates the component, and the PropertyDescriptor that describes the component.

This might typically be used by a custom TypeConverter that wishes to make a contextual decision about how to deal with the conversion process.

```
public interface ITypeDescriptorContext : IServiceProvider {
// Public Instance Properties
  public IContainer Container{get; }
  public object Instance{get; }
  public PropertyDescriptor PropertyDescriptor{get; }
// Public Instance Methods
```

```
 public void OnComponentChanged( );
 public bool OnComponentChanging( );
}
```

Returned By System.Drawing.Design.PaintValueEventArgs.Context

Passed To Multiple types

ITypedList

System.ComponentModel (system.dll) interface

This interface is implemented by classes that expose a typed list for data-binding scenarios. It provides a GetItemProperties( ) method to discover the properties of the list elements, rather than the properties of the container itself.

```
public interface ITypedList {
// Public Instance Methods
 public PropertyDescriptorCollection GetItemProperties(PropertyDescriptor[ ] listAccessors);
 public string GetListName(PropertyDescriptor[ ] listAccessors);
}
```


License disposable

System.ComponentModel (system.dll) abstract class

This is the abstract base class for licenses that can be granted to a component. It provides a LicenseKey property, which returns a string representing the license for the component. You must also implement the Dispose( ) member.

A License is returned by the LicenseProvider.GetLicense( ) method when a valid license is available for a particular object in the current LicenseContext.

See LicenseManager for more information on licensing.

```
public abstract class License : IDisposable {
// Protected Constructors
 protected License( );
// Public Instance Properties
 public abstract string LicenseKey{get; }
// Public Instance Methods
 public abstract void Dispose( );                                    // implements IDisposable
}
```

Returned By LicenseProvider.GetLicense( )

Passed To LicenseManager.IsValid( )

LicenseContext

System.ComponentModel (system.dll) class

This class provides a means of discovering licensing information about the types in an application domain. The UsageMode determines whether this is a Designtime or Runtime context (the default is a Runtime context; see System.ComponentModel.Design.DesigntimeLicenseContext for an example of a design-time context).

You can use GetSavedLicenseKey( ) and SetSavedLicenseKey( ) to get or set the license key for a specified type.

The active context can be retrieved using the LicenseManager.CurrentContext property.

By supporting different contexts, the license management environment allows you to support separate licensing models for design-time, runtime, or even custom-user contexts.

```
public class LicenseContext : IServiceProvider {
// Public Constructors
   public LicenseContext( );
// Public Instance Properties
   public virtual LicenseUsageMode UsageMode{get; }
// Public Instance Methods
   public virtual string GetSavedLicenseKey(Type type, System.Reflection.Assembly resourceAssembly);
   public virtual object GetService(Type type);                          // implements IServiceProvider
   public virtual void SetSavedLicenseKey(Type type, string key);
}
```

Returned By LicenseManager.CurrentContext

Passed To LicenseManager.{CreateWithContext( ), CurrentContext}, LicenseProvider.GetLicense( )

LicenseException

System.ComponentModel (system.dll) class

This exception is thrown by LicenseManager.Validate( ) if a component cannot be granted a license.

You can get the type of the component that failed the license validation with the LicensedType property.

```
public class LicenseException : SystemException {
// Public Constructors
   public LicenseException(Type type);
   public LicenseException(Type type, object instance);
   public LicenseException(Type type, object instance, string message);
   public LicenseException(Type type, object instance, string message, Exception innerException);
// Public Instance Properties
   public Type LicensedType{get; }
}
```

Hierarchy System.Object → System.Exception(System.Runtime.Serialization.ISerializable) → System.SystemException → LicenseException

LicenseManager

System.ComponentModel (system.dll) sealed class

This class offers a set of static utility functions to support the licensing of components.

You can retrieve the CurrentContext and the UsageMode (to determine whether this is a runtime or design-time context). You can lock and unlock the context for a particular object, effectively disabling the ability to get license information for that object, using the LockContext( ) and UnlockContext( ) methods.

To determine whether a particular object is licensed, you can use the IsLicensed() method. IsValid() and Validate() determine whether a valid license for an object can be granted. These methods use the LicenseProvider for the class to obtain a validated license.

Typically, a licensable class is adorned with the LicenseProviderAttribute which indicates the type of LicenseProvider to use. It then makes a call to Validate() in its constructor, to ensure that a suitable license is present for the current context.

```
public sealed class LicenseManager {
// Public Static Properties
   public static LicenseContext CurrentContext{set; get; }
   public static LicenseUsageMode UsageMode{get; }
// Public Static Methods
   public static object CreateWithContext(Type type, LicenseContext creationContext);
   public static object CreateWithContext(Type type, LicenseContext creationContext, object[ ] args);
   public static bool IsLicensed(Type type);
   public static bool IsValid(Type type);
   public static bool IsValid(Type type, object instance, out License license);
   public static void LockContext(object contextUser);
   public static void UnlockContext(object contextUser);
   public static License Validate(Type type, object instance);
   public static void Validate(Type type);
}
```

Component-Model

LicenseProvider

System.ComponentModel (system.dll) abstract class

This abstract base class provides the basis for the implementation of a license provider. You should override the GetLicense() method to return a suitable license for the object, given the current LicenseContext and the type of the object requesting the license. If no valid license is available, you should throw a LicenseException.

For a standard implementation of LicenseProvider, see LicFileLicenseProvider.

```
public abstract class LicenseProvider {
// Protected Constructors
   protected LicenseProvider( );
// Public Instance Methods
   public abstract License GetLicense(LicenseContext context, Type type, object instance, bool allowExceptions);
}
```

Subclasses LicFileLicenseProvider

LicenseProviderAttribute

System.ComponentModel (system.dll) sealed class

This attribute is used to adorn a class with information about the LicenseProvider that will provide a suitable License for that class.

See LicenseManager for more information on license management.

```
public sealed class LicenseProviderAttribute : Attribute {
// Public Constructors
   public LicenseProviderAttribute( );
```

```
  public LicenseProviderAttribute(string typeName);
  public LicenseProviderAttribute(Type type);
// Public Static Fields
  public static readonly LicenseProviderAttribute Default;    // =System.ComponentModel.LicenseProviderAttribute
// Public Instance Properties
  public Type LicenseProvider{get; }
  public override object TypeId{get; }                        // overrides Attribute
// Public Instance Methods
  public override bool Equals(object value);                  // overrides Attribute
  public override int GetHashCode( );                         // overrides Attribute
}
```

Hierarchy System.Object → System.Attribute → LicenseProviderAttribute

Valid On Class

LicenseUsageMode serializable

System.ComponentModel (system.dll) enum

This enumeration specifies whether the current LicenseContext is a Designtime or Runtime context.

```
public enum LicenseUsageMode {
  Runtime = 0,
  Designtime = 1
}
```

Hierarchy System.Object → System.ValueType → System.Enum(System.IComparable, System.IFormattable, System.IConvertible) → LicenseUsageMode

Returned By LicenseContext.UsageMode, LicenseManager.UsageMode

LicFileLicenseProvider

System.ComponentModel (system.dll) class

In this implementation of LicenseProvider, the GetLicense( ) member looks for a file called ClassName.LIC in the same directory as the *.dll* containing the component. It then uses the IsKeyValid( ) method to see if the file contains the key string provided by the GetKey( ) method. By default, the string is: "ClassName is a licensed component." You could derive a class that overrides one or both of these methods to provide a more complex *.LIC* file licensing scheme.

```
public class LicFileLicenseProvider : LicenseProvider {
// Public Constructors
  public LicFileLicenseProvider( );
// Public Instance Methods
  public override License GetLicense(LicenseContext context, Type type, object instance,
     bool allowExceptions);                                   // overrides LicenseProvider
// Protected Instance Methods
  protected virtual string GetKey(Type type);
  protected virtual bool IsKeyValid(string key, Type type);
}
```

Hierarchy System.Object → LicenseProvider → LicFileLicenseProvider

ListBindableAttribute

System.ComponentModel (system.dll) sealed class

This attribute is used to adorn a component to indicate that it can be used as a list in a data-binding scenario.

The ListBindable property determines whether the property is bindable. Note that while this is a Boolean, the attribute can be compared with the static Yes or No values for equality.

```
public sealed class ListBindableAttribute : Attribute {
// Public Constructors
   public ListBindableAttribute(BindableSupport flags);
   public ListBindableAttribute(bool listBindable);
// Public Static Fields
   public static readonly ListBindableAttribute Default;     // =System.ComponentModel.ListBindableAttribute
   public static readonly ListBindableAttribute No;          // =System.ComponentModel.ListBindableAttribute
   public static readonly ListBindableAttribute Yes;         // =System.ComponentModel.ListBindableAttribute
// Public Instance Properties
   public bool ListBindable{get; }
// Public Instance Methods
   public override bool Equals(object obj);                  // overrides Attribute
   public override int GetHashCode( );                       // overrides Attribute
   public override bool IsDefaultAttribute( );               // overrides Attribute
}
```

Hierarchy System.Object → System.Attribute → ListBindableAttribute

Valid On All

ListChangedEventArgs

System.ComponentModel (system.dll) class

This class encapsulates the data for the IBindingList.ListChanged event. You can determine the OldIndex and NewIndex of the item that was changed. The ListChangedType determines what kind of change raised the event.

```
public class ListChangedEventArgs : EventArgs {
// Public Constructors
   public ListChangedEventArgs(
      ListChangedType listChangedType, int newIndex);
   public ListChangedEventArgs(
      ListChangedType listChangedType, int newIndex,
      int oldIndex);
   public ListChangedEventArgs(
      ListChangedType listChangedType,
      PropertyDescriptor propDesc);
// Public Instance Properties
   public ListChangedType ListChangedType{get; }
   public int NewIndex{get; }
```

```
  public int OldIndex{get; }
}
```

Hierarchy System.Object → System.EventArgs → ListChangedEventArgs

Passed To ListChangedEventHandler.{BeginInvoke( ), Invoke( )}

ListChangedEventHandler

serializable

System.ComponentModel (system.dll)

delegate

This is a delegate for the IBindingList.ListChanged event.

```
public delegate void ListChangedEventHandler(object sender,
    ListChangedEventArgs e);
```

Associated Events IBindingList.ListChanged( )

ListChangedType

serializable

System.ComponentModel (system.dll)

enum

This enumeration is used by the ListChangedEventArgs class to specify the kind of change that caused the event to be raised. The possible change types relate to either items being added, removed or changed, or to the schema of the list changing. The Reset option indicates that substantial changes have been made to the list, and that the observer should refresh its entire display.

```
public enum ListChangedType {
  Reset = 0,
  ItemAdded = 1,
  ItemDeleted = 2,
  ItemMoved = 3,
  ItemChanged = 4,
  PropertyDescriptorAdded = 5,
  PropertyDescriptorDeleted = 6,
  PropertyDescriptorChanged = 7
}
```

Hierarchy System.Object → System.ValueType → System.Enum(System.IComparable, System.IFormattable, System.IConvertible) → ListChangedType

Returned By ListChangedEventArgs.ListChangedType

Passed To ListChangedEventArgs.ListChangedEventArgs( )

ListSortDirection

serializable

System.ComponentModel (system.dll)

enum

This enumeration determines whether an IBindingList should be sorted in Ascending or Descending order.

```
public enum ListSortDirection {
  Ascending = 0,
  Descending = 1
}
```

Hierarchy System.Object → System.ValueType → System.Enum(System.IComparable, System.IFormattable, System.IConvertible) → ListSortDirection

Returned By IBindingList.SortDirection

Passed To IBindingList.ApplySort( )

LocalizableAttribute

System.ComponentModel (system.dll) sealed class

This attribute adorns properties to specify how their values should be serialized by the designer. If the class is unadorned, or marked with an attribute for which IsLocalizable is false, the designer will attempt to serialize the value in code. If IsLocalizable is true, it will serialize to a resource file and inject code to retrieve the value from there instead.


```
public sealed class LocalizableAttribute : Attribute {
// Public Constructors
  public LocalizableAttribute(bool isLocalizable);
// Public Static Fields
  public static readonly LocalizableAttribute Default;    // =System.ComponentModel.LocalizableAttribute
  public static readonly LocalizableAttribute No;         // =System.ComponentModel.LocalizableAttribute
  public static readonly LocalizableAttribute Yes;        // =System.ComponentModel.LocalizableAttribute
// Public Instance Properties
  public bool IsLocalizable{get; }
// Public Instance Methods
  public override bool Equals(object obj);                // overrides Attribute
  public override int GetHashCode( );                     // overrides Attribute
  public override bool IsDefaultAttribute( );             // overrides Attribute
}
```

Hierarchy System.Object → System.Attribute → LocalizableAttribute

Valid On All

MarshalByValueComponent disposable

System.ComponentModel (system.dll) class

This implementation of the IComponent interface uses marshal-by-value semantics rather than the marshal-by-reference semantics employed by its cousin Component.

```
public class MarshalByValueComponent : IComponent, IDisposable, IServiceProvider {
// Public Constructors
  public MarshalByValueComponent( );
// Public Instance Properties
  public virtual IContainer Container{get; }
  public virtual bool DesignMode{get; }
```

```
  public virtual ISite Site{set; get; }                                    // implements IComponent
// Protected Instance Properties
  protected EventHandlerList Events{get; }
// Public Instance Methods
  public void Dispose( );                                                  // implements IDisposable
  public virtual object GetService(Type service);                          // implements IServiceProvider
  public override string ToString( );                                      // overrides object
// Protected Instance Methods
  protected virtual void Dispose(bool disposing);
  protected override void Finalize( );                                     // overrides object
// Events
  public event EventHandler Disposed;                                      // implements IComponent
}
```

MemberDescriptor

System.ComponentModel (system.dll) abstract class

This is the abstract base for classes that represent the member of class, such as properties and events (e.g., PropertyDescriptor and EventDescriptor). You can get the Name and DisplayName of the member.

In addition, you can get the collection of Attributes adorning the member. It also provides a set of utility accessors that indicate the values of particular attribute types: the Category, Description, DesignTimeOnly, and IsBrowsable members.

```
public abstract class MemberDescriptor {
// Protected Constructors
  protected MemberDescriptor(MemberDescriptor descr);
  protected MemberDescriptor(MemberDescriptor oldMemberDescriptor, Attribute[ ] newAttributes);
  protected MemberDescriptor(string name);
  protected MemberDescriptor(string name, Attribute[ ] attributes);
// Public Instance Properties
  public virtual AttributeCollection Attributes{get; }
  public virtual string Category{get; }
  public virtual string Description{get; }
  public virtual bool DesignTimeOnly{get; }
  public virtual string DisplayName{get; }
  public virtual bool IsBrowsable{get; }
  public virtual string Name{get; }
// Protected Instance Properties
  protected virtual Attribute[ ] AttributeArray{set; get; }
  protected virtual int NameHashCode{get; }
// Protected Static Methods
  protected static MethodInfo FindMethod(Type componentClass, string name, Type[ ] args, Type returnType);
  protected static MethodInfo FindMethod(Type componentClass, string name, Type[ ] args, Type returnType,
      bool publicOnly);
  protected static object GetInvokee(Type componentClass, object component);
  protected static ISite GetSite(object component);
// Public Instance Methods
  public override bool Equals(object obj);                                 // overrides object
  public override int GetHashCode( );                                      // overrides object
// Protected Instance Methods
```

```
  protected virtual AttributeCollection CreateAttributeCollection( );
  protected virtual void FillAttributes(System.Collections.IList attributeList);
}
```

Subclasses EventDescriptor, PropertyDescriptor

Passed To EventDescriptor.EventDescriptor( ), PropertyDescriptor.PropertyDescriptor( )

MergablePropertyAttribute

System.ComponentModel (system.dll) sealed class

This attribute adorns a property to indicate whether it can be merged with the properties owned by other classes in a designer that supports a set of objects. The AllowMerge property returns this state.

For example, the System.Windows.Forms.PropertyGrid can bind to several objects to display the common properties. If any one of these properties is marked with a MergableProperty(false) attribute, that property will not appear in the grid, even if all objects provide a property of that name and signature.

```
public sealed class MergablePropertyAttribute : Attribute {
// Public Constructors
  public MergablePropertyAttribute(bool allowMerge);
// Public Static Fields
  public static readonly MergablePropertyAttribute Default;   // =System.ComponentModel.MergablePropertyAttribute
  public static readonly MergablePropertyAttribute No;        // =System.ComponentModel.MergablePropertyAttribute
  public static readonly MergablePropertyAttribute Yes;       // =System.ComponentModel.MergablePropertyAttribute
// Public Instance Properties
  public bool AllowMerge{get; }
// Public Instance Methods
  public override bool Equals(object obj);                    // overrides Attribute
  public override int GetHashCode( );                         // overrides Attribute
  public override bool IsDefaultAttribute( );                 // overrides Attribute
}
```

Hierarchy System.Object → System.Attribute → MergablePropertyAttribute

Valid On All

NotifyParentPropertyAttribute

System.ComponentModel (system.dll) sealed class

You can mark a property with this attribute if it should cause its parent property to be updated when updated itself. The NotifyParent property determines whether the parent should be notified.

For example, the System.Drawing.Size type has two child properties, Width and Height. If either of these properties is updated, the parent should be updated.

```
public sealed class NotifyParentPropertyAttribute : Attribute {
// Public Constructors
  public NotifyParentPropertyAttribute(bool notifyParent);
// Public Static Fields
```

Component-Model

```
  public static readonly NotifyParentPropertyAttribute Default;  // =System.ComponentModel.NotifyParentPropertyAttribute
  public static readonly NotifyParentPropertyAttribute No;       // =System.ComponentModel.NotifyParentPropertyAttribute
  public static readonly NotifyParentPropertyAttribute Yes;      // =System.ComponentModel.NotifyParentPropertyAttribute
// Public Instance Properties
  public bool NotifyParent{get; }
// Public Instance Methods
  public override bool Equals(object obj);                       // overrides Attribute
  public override int GetHashCode( );                            // overrides Attribute
  public override bool IsDefaultAttribute( );                    // overrides Attribute
}
```

Hierarchy System.Object → System.Attribute → NotifyParentPropertyAttribute

Valid On Property

ParenthesizePropertyNameAttribute

System.ComponentModel (system.dll) sealed class

You can mark a property with this attribute if its name should be placed in parentheses when displayed in a designer. Note that this has the side effect of bumping it near to the top of its category or list. Typically, it is used to indicate derived properties.

```
public sealed class ParenthesizePropertyNameAttribute : Attribute {
// Public Constructors
  public ParenthesizePropertyNameAttribute( );
  public ParenthesizePropertyNameAttribute(bool needParenthesis);
// Public Static Fields
  public static readonly ParenthesizePropertyNameAttribute Default;
                                        // =System.ComponentModel.ParenthesizePropertyNameAttribute
// Public Instance Properties
  public bool NeedParenthesis{get; }
// Public Instance Methods
  public override bool Equals(object o);                         // overrides Attribute
  public override int GetHashCode( );                            // overrides Attribute
  public override bool IsDefaultAttribute( );                    // overrides Attribute
}
```

Hierarchy System.Object → System.Attribute → ParenthesizePropertyNameAttribute

Valid On All

PropertyChangedEventArgs

System.ComponentModel (system.dll) class

This class encapsulates the data for the OnPropertyChanging( ) event raised by the System.Data.DataSet, System.Data.DataTable, and System.Data.DataColumn classes.

You can determine the PropertyName of the property that changed.

```
public class PropertyChangedEventArgs : EventArgs {
// Public Constructors
  public PropertyChangedEventArgs(string propertyName);
```

```
// Public Instance Properties
   public virtual string PropertyName{get; }
}
```

Hierarchy System.Object → System.EventArgs → PropertyChangedEventArgs

Passed To PropertyChangedEventHandler.{BeginInvoke( ), Invoke( )}

PropertyChangedEventHandler

serializable

System.ComponentModel (system.dll) **delegate**

This is a delegate for the OnPropertyChanging( ) event.

```
public delegate void PropertyChangedEventHandler(object sender, PropertyChangedEventArgs e);
```

PropertyDescriptor

System.ComponentModel (system.dll) **abstract class**

This is an abstract base class derived from MemberDescriptor for objects that encapsulate information about a property.

In addition to the base attribute utilities, you can determine whether the property IsLocalizable or IsReadOnly. You can also check the SerializationVisibility. ShouldSerializeValue( ) can be used to determine whether the property of a particular component should be serialized. The default implementation of this method uses DefaultValueAttribute or a ShouldSerialize[PropertyName] method to determine whether it is necessary to serialize the property. See DefaultValueAttribute for more information on this.

You can also use ComponentType to determine the type of the component to which this property belongs. Converter retrieves a TypeConverter and GetEditor( ) gets a custom editor of the specified base type (in case several types of editor are defined for the property).

AddValueChanged( ) and RemoveValueChanged( ) allow you to bind an event handler, to be notified when the property changes. You can use GetValue( ), SetValue( ), and ResetValue( ) to access and modify that value. PropertyType indicates the type of that value.

If this is a parent property, you can retrieve the PropertyDescriptor objects for the children with the GetChildProperties( ) member.

```
public abstract class PropertyDescriptor : MemberDescriptor {
// Protected Constructors
   protected PropertyDescriptor(MemberDescriptor descr);
   protected PropertyDescriptor(MemberDescriptor descr, Attribute[ ] attrs);
   protected PropertyDescriptor(string name, Attribute[ ] attrs);
// Public Instance Properties
   public abstract Type ComponentType{get; }
   public virtual TypeConverter Converter{get; }
   public virtual bool IsLocalizable{get; }
   public abstract bool IsReadOnly{get; }
   public abstract Type PropertyType{get; }
   public DesignerSerializationVisibility SerializationVisibility{get; }
// Public Instance Methods
   public virtual void AddValueChanged(object component, EventHandler handler);
   public abstract bool CanResetValue(object component);
```

Component-Model

```
public override bool Equals(object obj);                    // overrides MemberDescriptor
public PropertyDescriptorCollection GetChildProperties( );
public PropertyDescriptorCollection GetChildProperties(Attribute[ ] filter);
public PropertyDescriptorCollection GetChildProperties(object instance);
public virtual PropertyDescriptorCollection GetChildProperties(object instance, Attribute[ ] filter);
public virtual object GetEditor(Type editorBaseType);
public override int GetHashCode( );                         // overrides MemberDescriptor
public abstract object GetValue(object component);
public virtual void RemoveValueChanged(object component, EventHandler handler);
public abstract void ResetValue(object component);
public abstract void SetValue(object component, object value);
public abstract bool ShouldSerializeValue(object component);
// Protected Instance Methods
protected object CreateInstance(Type type);
protected Type GetTypeFromName(string typeName);
protected virtual void OnValueChanged(object component, EventArgs e);
}
```

Hierarchy System.Object → MemberDescriptor → PropertyDescriptor

Returned By ExtenderProvidedPropertyAttribute.ExtenderProperty, IBindingList.SortProperty, IComNativeDescriptorHandler.GetDefaultProperty( ), ICustomTypeDescriptor.GetDefaultProperty( ), ITypeDescriptorContext.PropertyDescriptor, PropertyDescriptorCollection.{Find( ), this}, TypeDescriptor.{CreateProperty( ), GetDefaultProperty( )}, System.Windows.Forms.DataGridColumnStyle.PropertyDescriptor, System.Windows.Forms.Design.PropertyTab.GetDefaultProperty( ), System.Windows.Forms.GridItem.PropertyDescriptor

Passed To Multiple types

PropertyDescriptorCollection

System.ComponentModel (system.dll) class

This class encapsulates a standard collection of PropertyDescriptor objects, for use with members such as TypeDescriptor.GetProperties( ) and PropertyDescriptor.GetChildProperties( ).

```
public class PropertyDescriptorCollection : IList, ICollection, IEnumerable, IDictionary {
// Public Constructors
public PropertyDescriptorCollection(PropertyDescriptor[ ] properties);
// Public Static Fields
public static readonly PropertyDescriptorCollection Empty;  // =System.ComponentModel.PropertyDescriptorCollection
// Public Instance Properties
public int Count{get; }                                     // implements ICollection
public virtual PropertyDescriptor this{get; }
public virtual PropertyDescriptor this{get; }
// Public Instance Methods
public int Add(PropertyDescriptor value);
public void Clear( );                                       // implements System.Collections.IDictionary
public bool Contains(PropertyDescriptor value);
public void CopyTo(Array array, int index);                 // implements ICollection
public virtual PropertyDescriptor Find(string name, bool ignoreCase);
```

```
  public virtual IEnumerator GetEnumerator( );                              // implements IEnumerable
  public int IndexOf(PropertyDescriptor value);
  public void Insert(int index, PropertyDescriptor value);
  public void Remove(PropertyDescriptor value);
  public void RemoveAt(int index);                                          // implements IList
  public virtual PropertyDescriptorCollection Sort( );
  public virtual PropertyDescriptorCollection Sort(System.Collections.IComparer comparer);
  public virtual PropertyDescriptorCollection Sort(string[ ] names);
  public virtual PropertyDescriptorCollection Sort(string[ ] names, System.Collections.IComparer comparer);
// Protected Instance Methods
  protected void InternalSort(System.Collections.IComparer sorter);
  protected void InternalSort(string[ ] names);
}
```

Returned By IComNativeDescriptorHandler.GetProperties( ), ICustomTypeDescriptor.GetProperties( ), ITypedList.GetItemProperties( ), PropertyDescriptor.GetChildProperties( ), TypeConverter.{GetProperties( ), SortProperties( )}, TypeDescriptor.GetProperties( ), System.Windows.Forms.BindingManagerBase.GetItemProperties( ), System.Windows.Forms.Design.PropertyTab.GetProperties( )

Passed To TypeConverter.SortProperties( )

Component-Model

PropertyTabAttribute

System.ComponentModel (system.dll) class

You apply this attribute to a class or property to indicate that a particular class of property tab should be added into a designer (such as one derived from a System.Windows.Forms.PropertyGrid) when an instance of the attributed class is selected.

You can get an array of types indicating the TabClasses that the attribute represents, along with the PropertyTabScope for the tabs. The tab scope indicates how and when the tabs should be shown (e.g., whenever the current component is selected, when the document containing the component is selected, etc.).

See System.Windows.Forms.Design.PropertyTab for an implementation of a property tab.

```
public class PropertyTabAttribute : Attribute {
// Public Constructors
  public PropertyTabAttribute( );
  public PropertyTabAttribute(string tabClassName);
  public PropertyTabAttribute(string tabClassName, PropertyTabScope tabScope);
  public PropertyTabAttribute(Type tabClass);
  public PropertyTabAttribute(Type tabClass, PropertyTabScope tabScope);
// Public Instance Properties
  public Type[ ] TabClasses{get; }
  public PropertyTabScope[ ] TabScopes{get; }
// Protected Instance Properties
  protected string[ ] TabClassNames{get; }
// Public Instance Methods
  public override bool Equals(object other);                                // overrides Attribute
  public bool Equals(PropertyTabAttribute other);
  public override int GetHashCode( );                                       // overrides Attribute
// Protected Instance Methods
```

```
    protected void InitializeArrays(string[ ] tabClassNames, PropertyTabScope[ ] tabScopes);
    protected void InitializeArrays(Type[ ] tabClasses, PropertyTabScope[ ] tabScopes);
}
```

Hierarchy System.Object → System.Attribute → PropertyTabAttribute

Valid On All

PropertyTabScope **serializable**

System.ComponentModel (system.dll) **enum**

This enumeration is used by PropertyTabAttribute to indicate how and when a particular tab should be shown in a designer.

```
public enum PropertyTabScope {
    Static = 0,
    Global = 1,
    Document = 2,
    Component = 3
}
```

Hierarchy System.Object → System.ValueType → System.Enum(System.IComparable, System.IFormattable, System.IConvertible) → PropertyTabScope

Returned By PropertyTabAttribute.TabScopes

Passed To PropertyTabAttribute.{InitializeArrays( ), PropertyTabAttribute( )}, System.Windows.Forms.PropertyGrid.RefreshTabs( ), System.Windows.Forms.PropertyTabCollection.{AddTabType( ), Clear( )}

ProvidePropertyAttribute

System.ComponentModel (system.dll) **sealed class**

This attribute adorns classes that implement IExtenderProvider in order to indicate the properties it will provide for the components that it extends. Multiple instances can be added to support multiple extender properties.

You can retrieve the PropertyName of the extender property. The ReceiverTypeName is the name of the root data type that this class can extend.

See IExtenderProvider for more information on extended properties.

```
public sealed class ProvidePropertyAttribute : Attribute {
// Public Constructors
    public ProvidePropertyAttribute(string propertyName, string receiverTypeName);
    public ProvidePropertyAttribute(string propertyName, Type receiverType);
// Public Instance Properties
    public string PropertyName{get; }
    public string ReceiverTypeName{get; }
    public override object TypeId{get; }                        // overrides Attribute
// Public Instance Methods
    public override bool Equals(object obj);                    // overrides Attribute
    public override int GetHashCode( );                         // overrides Attribute
}
```

Hierarchy System.Object → System.Attribute → ProvidePropertyAttribute

Valid On Class

ReadOnlyAttribute

System.ComponentModel (system.dll) sealed class

If you mark a property with this attribute, you can indicate whether it is read-only or read- write in the designer. Compare this with the DesignOnlyAttribute.

You can use the IsReadOnly property to determine the state of the attribute, but an instance of the attribute can also be compared against the Yes and No values for equality.

```
public sealed class ReadOnlyAttribute : Attribute {
// Public Constructors
   public ReadOnlyAttribute(bool isReadOnly);
// Public Static Fields
   public static readonly ReadOnlyAttribute Default;        // =System.ComponentModel.ReadOnlyAttribute
   public static readonly ReadOnlyAttribute No;             // =System.ComponentModel.ReadOnlyAttribute
   public static readonly ReadOnlyAttribute Yes;            // =System.ComponentModel.ReadOnlyAttribute
// Public Instance Properties
   public bool IsReadOnly{get; }
// Public Instance Methods
   public override bool Equals(object value);               // overrides Attribute
   public override int GetHashCode( );                      // overrides Attribute
   public override bool IsDefaultAttribute( );              // overrides Attribute
}
```

Hierarchy System.Object → System.Attribute → ReadOnlyAttribute

Valid On All

RecommendedAsConfigurableAttribute

System.ComponentModel (system.dll) class

This attribute is added to a class to mark it as an application setting. A property decorated with this attribute will appear in the Configurations section of the designer and will allow you to map its value to a particular key in a configuration file.

The RecommendedAsConfigurable property determines the state of the attribute, but you should compare against the static Yes and No values for equality.

```
public class RecommendedAsConfigurableAttribute : Attribute {
// Public Constructors
   public RecommendedAsConfigurableAttribute(bool recommendedAsConfigurable);
// Public Static Fields
   public static readonly RecommendedAsConfigurableAttribute Default;
                              // =System.ComponentModel.RecommendedAsConfigurableAttribute
   public static readonly RecommendedAsConfigurableAttribute No;
                              // =System.ComponentModel.RecommendedAsConfigurableAttribute
   public static readonly RecommendedAsConfigurableAttribute Yes;
                              // =System.ComponentModel.RecommendedAsConfigurableAttribute
// Public Instance Properties
```

```
  public bool RecommendedAsConfigurable{get; }
// Public Instance Methods
  public override bool Equals(object obj);                                    // overrides Attribute
  public override int GetHashCode( );                                         // overrides Attribute
  public override bool IsDefaultAttribute( );                                 // overrides Attribute
}
```

Hierarchy System.Object → System.Attribute → RecommendedAsConfigurableAttribute

Valid On Property

ReferenceConverter

System.ComponentModel (system.dll) class

This TypeConverter is used in serialization and design-time scenarios to translate to and from reference types. You should not normally call it directly from your own code.

```
public class ReferenceConverter : TypeConverter {
// Public Constructors
  public ReferenceConverter(Type type);
// Public Instance Methods
  public override bool CanConvertFrom( ITypeDescriptorContext context, Type sourceType);     // overrides TypeConverter
  public override object ConvertFrom(ITypeDescriptorContext context,
     System.Globalization.CultureInfo culture, object value);                               // overrides TypeConverter
  public override object ConvertTo(ITypeDescriptorContext context,
     System.Globalization.CultureInfo culture, object value, Type destinationType);         // overrides TypeConverter
  public override StandardValuesCollection GetStandardValues(ITypeDescriptorContext context); // overrides TypeConverter
  public override bool GetStandardValuesExclusive(ITypeDescriptorContext context);           // overrides TypeConverter
  public override bool GetStandardValuesSupported(ITypeDescriptorContext context);           // overrides TypeConverter
// Protected Instance Methods
  protected virtual bool IsValueAllowed(ITypeDescriptorContext context, object value);
}
```

Hierarchy System.Object → TypeConverter → ReferenceConverter

Subclasses ComponentConverter

RefreshEventArgs

System.ComponentModel (system.dll) class

This class encapsulates the data for the TypeDescriptor.Refreshed event, which is raised (at design time) when a component's properties or events are updated. You can retrieve the identity of the component that was modified with the ComponentChanged property, and the type of that component is given by TypeChanged.

```
public class RefreshEventArgs : EventArgs {
// Public Constructors
  public RefreshEventArgs(object componentChanged);
  public RefreshEventArgs(Type typeChanged);
// Public Instance Properties
  public object ComponentChanged{get; }
```

```
    public Type TypeChanged{get; }
}
```

Hierarchy System.Object → System.EventArgs → RefreshEventArgs

Passed To RefreshEventHandler.{BeginInvoke( ), Invoke( )}

RefreshEventHandler — serializable

System.ComponentModel (system.dll) — delegate

This is a delegate for the TypeDescriptor.Refreshed event.

```
public delegate void RefreshEventHandler(RefreshEventArgs e);
```

Associated Events TypeDescriptor.Refreshed( )

RefreshProperties — serializable

System.ComponentModel (system.dll) — enum

This enumeration is used by RefreshPropertiesAttribute to determine how a properties window should be updated when a particular property is changed.

```
public enum RefreshProperties {
    None = 0,
    All = 1,
    Repaint = 2
}
```

Hierarchy System.Object → System.ValueType → System.Enum(System.IComparable, System.IFormattable, System.IConvertible) → RefreshProperties

Returned By RefreshPropertiesAttribute.RefreshProperties

Passed To RefreshPropertiesAttribute.RefreshPropertiesAttribute( )

RefreshPropertiesAttribute

System.ComponentModel (system.dll) — sealed class

You can adorn a property with this attribute to indicate how a designer properties window should be updated when its values changes. The RefreshProperties member can be set to Default if only the modified property should be updated, Repaint if all the properties (including this one) should be repainted, and All if all the properties should be queried afresh, and then repainted.

```
public sealed class RefreshPropertiesAttribute : Attribute {
// Public Constructors
    public RefreshPropertiesAttribute(RefreshProperties refresh);
// Public Static Fields
    public static readonly RefreshPropertiesAttribute All;         // =System.ComponentModel.RefreshPropertiesAttribute
    public static readonly RefreshPropertiesAttribute Default;     // =System.ComponentModel.RefreshPropertiesAttribute
    public static readonly RefreshPropertiesAttribute Repaint;     // =System.ComponentModel.RefreshPropertiesAttribute
```

```
// Public Instance Properties
   public RefreshProperties RefreshProperties{get; }
// Public Instance Methods
   public override bool Equals(object value);                    // overrides Attribute
   public override int GetHashCode( );                           // overrides Attribute
   public override bool IsDefaultAttribute( );                   // overrides Attribute
}
```

Hierarchy System.Object → System.Attribute → RefreshPropertiesAttribute

Valid On All

RunInstallerAttribute

System.ComponentModel (system.dll) class

You mark a class derived from System.Configuration.Install.Installer with this attribute to indicate that it should be invoked as a custom action when the assembly is installed. See the documentation for that namespace, and see InstallUtil.exe for more information on installers and custom actions.

You can retrieve the state of the attribute with the RunInstaller property, but note that you must compare the object against the static Yes and No values for equality.

```
public class RunInstallerAttribute : Attribute {
// Public Constructors
   public RunInstallerAttribute(bool runInstaller);
// Public Static Fields
   public static readonly RunInstallerAttribute Default;   // =System.ComponentModel.RunInstallerAttribute
   public static readonly RunInstallerAttribute No;        // =System.ComponentModel.RunInstallerAttribute
   public static readonly RunInstallerAttribute Yes;       // =System.ComponentModel.RunInstallerAttribute
// Public Instance Properties
   public bool RunInstaller{get; }
// Public Instance Methods
   public override bool Equals(object obj);                      // overrides Attribute
   public override int GetHashCode( );                           // overrides Attribute
   public override bool IsDefaultAttribute( );                   // overrides Attribute
}
```

Hierarchy System.Object → System.Attribute → RunInstallerAttribute

Valid On Class

SByteConverter

System.ComponentModel (system.dll) class

This class provides a TypeConverter for the SByte type in serialization and design-time scenarios. You would not normally call this class from your own code.

```
public class SByteConverter : BaseNumberConverter {
// Public Constructors
   public SByteConverter( );
}
```

Hierarchy System.Object → TypeConverter → BaseNumberConverter → SByteConverter

SingleConverter

System.ComponentModel (system.dll) class

This TypeConverter for the single-precision floating-point type is used in serialization and design-time scenarios, and would not normally be called from your own code.

```
public class SingleConverter : BaseNumberConverter {
// Public Constructors
   public SingleConverter( );
}
```

Hierarchy System.Object → TypeConverter → BaseNumberConverter → SingleConverter

StringConverter

System.ComponentModel (system.dll) class

This class implements a TypeConverter to transform to and from the string type in serialization and design-time scenarios. You should not normally call it from your own code.

```
public class StringConverter : TypeConverter {
// Public Constructors
   public StringConverter( );
// Public Instance Methods
   public override bool CanConvertFrom( ITypeDescriptorContext context, Type sourceType);    // overrides TypeConverter
   public override object ConvertFrom(ITypeDescriptorContext context,
      System.Globalization.CultureInfo culture, object value);                               // overrides TypeConverter
}
```

Hierarchy System.Object → TypeConverter → StringConverter

SyntaxCheck

System.ComponentModel (system.dll) class

This is a class private to the framework, which should not be used in your own code.

```
public class SyntaxCheck {
// Public Static Methods
   public static bool CheckMachineName(string value);
   public static bool CheckPath(string value);
   public static bool CheckRootedPath(string value);
}
```

TimeSpanConverter

System.ComponentModel (system.dll) class

This class provides a TypeConverter for the TimeSpan type. It is used in design-time and serialization scenarios, and would not normally be called from your own code.

```
public class TimeSpanConverter : TypeConverter {
// Public Constructors
   public TimeSpanConverter( );
// Public Instance Methods
   public override bool CanConvertFrom(ITypeDescriptorContext context, Type sourceType);        // overrides TypeConverter
   public override bool CanConvertTo(ITypeDescriptorContext context, Type destinationType);     // overrides TypeConverter
   public override object ConvertFrom(ITypeDescriptorContext context,
      System.Globalization.CultureInfo culture, object value);                                   // overrides TypeConverter
   public override object ConvertTo(ITypeDescriptorContext context,
      System.Globalization.CultureInfo culture, object value, Type destinationType);             // overrides TypeConverter
}
```

Hierarchy System.Object → TypeConverter → TimeSpanConverter

ToolboxItemAttribute

System.ComponentModel (system.dll) class

You can decorate an item with this attribute to indicate that it should provide a particular System.Drawing.Design.ToolboxItem. You can determine the type of the ToolboxItem with the ToolboxItemType property, and its name with ToolboxItemTypeName. You can compare against the Default and None values for equality.

```
public class ToolboxItemAttribute : Attribute {
// Public Constructors
   public ToolboxItemAttribute(bool defaultType);
   public ToolboxItemAttribute(string toolboxItemTypeName);
   public ToolboxItemAttribute(Type toolboxItemType);
// Public Static Fields
   public static readonly ToolboxItemAttribute Default;          // =System.ComponentModel.ToolboxItemAttribute
   public static readonly ToolboxItemAttribute None;             // =System.ComponentModel.ToolboxItemAttribute
// Public Instance Properties
   public Type ToolboxItemType{get; }
   public string ToolboxItemTypeName{get; }
// Public Instance Methods
   public override bool Equals(object obj);                      // overrides Attribute
   public override int GetHashCode( );                           // overrides Attribute
   public override bool IsDefaultAttribute( );                   // overrides Attribute
}
```

Hierarchy System.Object → System.Attribute → ToolboxItemAttribute

Valid On All

ToolboxItemFilterAttribute serializable

System.ComponentModel (system.dll) sealed class

This attribute adorns a class to allow the framework to filter its availability conditionally on the presence of a similar attribute on the designer, or using a custom filter provided by the designer by implementing the System.Drawing.Design.IToolboxUser.GetToolSupported( ) method.

You can retrieve the FilterString and FilterType for the attribute.

```
public sealed class ToolboxItemFilterAttribute : Attribute {
// Public Constructors
   public ToolboxItemFilterAttribute(string filterString);
   public ToolboxItemFilterAttribute(string filterString, ToolboxItemFilterType filterType);
// Public Instance Properties
   public string FilterString{get; }
   public ToolboxItemFilterType FilterType{get; }
   public override object TypeId{get; }                                    // overrides Attribute
// Public Instance Methods
   public override bool Equals(object obj);                                // overrides Attribute
   public override int GetHashCode( );                                     // overrides Attribute
   public override bool Match(object obj);                                 // overrides Attribute
}
```

Hierarchy System.Object → System.Attribute → ToolboxItemFilterAttribute

Valid On Class

ToolboxItemFilterType serializable

System.ComponentModel (system.dll) enum

This enumeration lists the various options for the method of filtering to be used when applying the ToolboxItemFilterAttribute.

```
public enum ToolboxItemFilterType {
   Allow = 0,
   Custom = 1,
   Prevent = 2,
   Require = 3
}
```

Hierarchy System.Object → System.ValueType → System.Enum(System.IComparable, System.IFormattable, System.IConvertible) → ToolboxItemFilterType

Returned By ToolboxItemFilterAttribute.FilterType

Passed To ToolboxItemFilterAttribute.ToolboxItemFilterAttribute( )

TypeConverter

System.ComponentModel (system.dll) class

This class provides a means to translate between one type and other representations of that type—typically a string representation. The designer environment uses type converters to translate between types it does not understand (for example, a System.Drawing.Size) and one it can represent in a System.Windows.Forms.PropertyGrid (for example, a string).

One of the quickest and simplest ways to make your custom type available in a designer is to implement a TypeConverter for it and adorn it with a TypeConverterAttribute to bind the appropriate converter. For finer control, you can add the attribute to a particular property to change the type converter for that particular instance of the type.

To implement a TypeConverter you should override the CanConvertFrom( ), CanConvertTo( ), ConvertFrom( ) and ConvertTo( ) methods. At a minimum, you should implement conversion to and from a string, and you may also want to support InstanceDescriptor to support more complex initialization scenarios in design-time serialization.

If your object is immutable and requires recreation to modify it, you need to override CreateInstance( ) and GetCreateInstanceSupported( ). This will be passed a System.Collections.IDictionary of property name/value pairs and optionally an ITypeDescriptorContext, which you may need to use in the conversion process.

If the type contains properties or you wish to extend it to appear to support properties of its own, you can override the GetProperties( ) and GetPropertiesSupported( ) methods. If you want add your own properties, derive them from SimplePropertyDescriptor (overriding the GetValue( ) and SetValue( ) methods.

A type can also support standard values (well-known values that can be assigned to the type). Implement GetStandardValues( ) and GetStandardValuesSupported( ) to provide standard values. If you also override GetStandardValuesExclusive( ), you can indicate that the type will only accept one of the standard values.

```
public class TypeConverter {
// Public Constructors
   public TypeConverter( );
// Public Instance Methods
   public virtual bool CanConvertFrom(ITypeDescriptorContext context, Type sourceType);
   public bool CanConvertFrom(Type sourceType);
   public virtual bool CanConvertTo(ITypeDescriptorContext context, Type destinationType);
   public bool CanConvertTo(Type destinationType);
   public virtual object ConvertFrom(ITypeDescriptorContext context, System.Globalization.CultureInfo culture, object value);
   public object ConvertFrom(object value);
   public object ConvertFromInvariantString(ITypeDescriptorContext context, string text);
   public object ConvertFromInvariantString(string text);
   public object ConvertFromString(ITypeDescriptorContext context, System.Globalization.CultureInfo culture, string text);
   public object ConvertFromString(ITypeDescriptorContext context, string text);
   public object ConvertFromString(string text);
   public virtual object ConvertTo(ITypeDescriptorContext context, System.Globalization.CultureInfo culture,
      object value, Type destinationType);
   public object ConvertTo(object value, Type destinationType);
   public string ConvertToInvariantString(ITypeDescriptorContext context, object value);
   public string ConvertToInvariantString(object value);
   public string ConvertToString(ITypeDescriptorContext context, System.Globalization.CultureInfo culture, object value);
   public string ConvertToString(ITypeDescriptorContext context, object value);
   public string ConvertToString(object value);
   public object CreateInstance(System.Collections.IDictionary propertyValues);
   public virtual object CreateInstance(ITypeDescriptorContext context, System.Collections.IDictionary propertyValues);
   public bool GetCreateInstanceSupported( );
   public virtual bool GetCreateInstanceSupported(ITypeDescriptorContext context);
   public PropertyDescriptorCollection GetProperties(ITypeDescriptorContext context, object value);
   public virtual PropertyDescriptorCollection GetProperties(ITypeDescriptorContext context, object value,
      Attribute[ ] attributes);
   public PropertyDescriptorCollection GetProperties(ITypeDescriptorContext context, object value, object value);
   public bool GetPropertiesSupported( );
   public virtual bool GetPropertiesSupported(ITypeDescriptorContext context);
   public ICollection GetStandardValues( );
```

```
public virtual StandardValuesCollection GetStandardValues(ITypeDescriptorContext context);
public bool GetStandardValuesExclusive( );
public virtual bool GetStandardValuesExclusive(ITypeDescriptorContext context);
public bool GetStandardValuesSupported( );
public virtual bool GetStandardValuesSupported(ITypeDescriptorContext context);
public virtual bool IsValid(ITypeDescriptorContext context, object value);
public bool IsValid(object value);
// Protected Instance Methods
protected Exception GetConvertFromException(object value);
protected Exception GetConvertToException(object value, Type destinationType);
protected PropertyDescriptorCollection SortProperties(PropertyDescriptorCollection props, string[ ] names);
}
```

Subclasses Multiple types

Returned By IComNativeDescriptorHandler.GetConverter( ), ICustomTypeDescriptor.GetConverter( ), PropertyDescriptor.Converter, TypeDescriptor.GetConverter( )

TypeConverter.StandardValuesCollection

System.ComponentModel (system.dll) class

This class implements a collection of standard values for the TypeConverter.GetStandardValues( ) method.

```
public class TypeConverter.StandardValuesCollection : ICollection, IEnumerable {
// Public Constructors
public TypeConverter.StandardValuesCollection(System.Collections.ICollection values);
// Public Instance Properties
public int Count{get; }                                    // implements ICollection
public object this{get; }
// Public Instance Methods
public void CopyTo(Array array, int index);                // implements ICollection
public IEnumerator GetEnumerator( );                       // implements IEnumerable
}
```

TypeConverterAttribute

System.ComponentModel (system.dll) sealed class

You can adorn a class or property with this attribute to bind it to a particular TypeConverter class. The framework then uses this converter to attempt to translate a user-defined type that it doesn't understand into one that it does.

You can get the type name of the converter with the ConverterTypeName property.

```
public sealed class TypeConverterAttribute : Attribute {
// Public Constructors
public TypeConverterAttribute( );
public TypeConverterAttribute(string typeName);
public TypeConverterAttribute(Type type);
// Public Static Fields
public static readonly TypeConverterAttribute Default;   // =System.ComponentModel.TypeConverterAttribute
// Public Instance Properties
```

```
    public string ConverterTypeName{get; }
// Public Instance Methods
    public override bool Equals(object obj);                                    // overrides Attribute
    public override int GetHashCode( );                                         // overrides Attribute
}
```

Hierarchy System.Object → System.Attribute → TypeConverterAttribute

Valid On All

TypeDescriptor

System.ComponentModel (system.dll) sealed class

This class encapsulates the information about a component. It provides a set of static utility methods to get details of the attributes, properties, and events. You can also get the default property or event.

While this appears to provide exactly the same information as System.Type, it adds an extra level of indirection, allowing you to provide virtual types that would not be represented by the standard type infrastructure.

GetClassName( ) gets the name of the class, while GetComponentName( ) gets the name of the component. You can retrieve the TypeConverter for the class with the GetConverter( ) method, and you can create the designer associated with the type with the CreateDesigner( ) method.

There are two versions of each method: one takes a Type that can be used if you do not have an actual instance of the type and the other takes an object if you do have a suitable instance.

```
public sealed class TypeDescriptor {
// Public Static Properties
    public static IComNativeDescriptorHandler ComNativeDescriptorHandler{set; get; }
// Public Static Methods
    public static void AddEditorTable(Type editorBaseType, System.Collections.Hashtable table);
    public static IDesigner CreateDesigner(IComponent component, Type designerBaseType);
    public static EventDescriptor CreateEvent(Type componentType, EventDescriptor oldEventDescriptor,
        params Attribute[ ] attributes);
    public static EventDescriptor CreateEvent(Type componentType, string name, Type type, params Attribute[ ] attributes);
    public static PropertyDescriptor CreateProperty(Type componentType, PropertyDescriptor oldPropertyDescriptor,
        params Attribute[ ] attributes);
    public static PropertyDescriptor CreateProperty(Type componentType, string name, Type type,
        params Attribute[ ] attributes);
    public static AttributeCollection GetAttributes(object component);
    public static AttributeCollection GetAttributes(object component, bool noCustomTypeDesc);
    public static AttributeCollection GetAttributes(Type componentType);
    public static string GetClassName(object component);
    public static string GetClassName(object component, bool noCustomTypeDesc);
    public static string GetComponentName(object component);
    public static string GetComponentName(object component, bool noCustomTypeDesc);
    public static TypeConverter GetConverter(object component);
    public static TypeConverter GetConverter(object component, bool noCustomTypeDesc);
    public static TypeConverter GetConverter(Type type);
    public static EventDescriptor GetDefaultEvent(object component);
    public static EventDescriptor GetDefaultEvent(object component, bool noCustomTypeDesc);
```

```
  public static EventDescriptor GetDefaultEvent(Type componentType);
  public static PropertyDescriptor GetDefaultProperty(object component);
  public static PropertyDescriptor GetDefaultProperty(object component, bool noCustomTypeDesc);
  public static PropertyDescriptor GetDefaultProperty(Type componentType);
  public static object GetEditor(object component, Type editorBaseType);
  public static object GetEditor(object component, Type editorBaseType, bool noCustomTypeDesc);
  public static object GetEditor(Type type, Type editorBaseType);
  public static EventDescriptorCollection GetEvents(object component);
  public static EventDescriptorCollection GetEvents(object component, Attribute[ ] attributes);
  public static EventDescriptorCollection GetEvents(object component, Attribute[ ] attributes, bool noCustomTypeDesc);
  public static EventDescriptorCollection GetEvents(object component, bool noCustomTypeDesc);
  public static EventDescriptorCollection GetEvents(Type componentType);
  public static EventDescriptorCollection GetEvents(Type componentType, Attribute[ ] attributes);
  public static PropertyDescriptorCollection GetProperties(object component);
  public static PropertyDescriptorCollection GetProperties(object component, Attribute[ ] attributes);
  public static PropertyDescriptorCollection GetProperties(object component, Attribute[ ] attributes,
    bool noCustomTypeDesc);
  public static PropertyDescriptorCollection GetProperties(object component, bool noCustomTypeDesc);
  public static PropertyDescriptorCollection GetProperties(Type componentType);
  public static PropertyDescriptorCollection GetProperties(Type componentType, Attribute[ ] attributes);
  public static void Refresh(System.Reflection.Assembly assembly);
  public static void Refresh(System.Reflection.Module module);
  public static void Refresh(object component);
  public static void Refresh(Type type);
  public static void SortDescriptorArray(System.Collections.IList infos);
// Events
  public event RefreshEventHandler Refreshed;
}
```

TypeListConverter

System.ComponentModel (system.dll) abstract class

This class implements a TypeConverter for a list of types. It can be used in serialization and design-time scenarios, and would not normally be called from your own code.

```
public abstract class TypeListConverter : TypeConverter {
// Protected Constructors
  protected TypeListConverter(Type[ ] types);
// Public Instance Methods
  public override bool CanConvertFrom(ITypeDescriptorContext context, Type sourceType);         // overrides TypeConverter
  public override bool CanConvertTo(ITypeDescriptorContext context, Type destinationType);      // overrides TypeConverter
  public override object ConvertFrom( ITypeDescriptorContext context,
    System.Globalization.CultureInfo culture, object value);                                    // overrides TypeConverter
  public override object ConvertTo(ITypeDescriptorContext context,
    System.Globalization.CultureInfo culture, object value, Type destinationType);              // overrides TypeConverter
  public override StandardValuesCollection GetStandardValues(ITypeDescriptorContext context);   // overrides TypeConverter
  public override bool GetStandardValuesExclusive(ITypeDescriptorContext context);              // overrides TypeConverter
  public override bool GetStandardValuesSupported(ITypeDescriptorContext context);              // overrides TypeConverter
}
```

Hierarchy System.Object → TypeConverter → TypeListConverter

UInt16Converter

System.ComponentModel (system.dll) **class**

This TypeConverter converts between a UInt16 and other types for serialization and design-time scenarios. You would not normally call it from your own code.

```
public class UInt16Converter : BaseNumberConverter {
// Public Constructors
   public UInt16Converter( );
}
```

Hierarchy System.Object → TypeConverter → BaseNumberConverter → UInt16Converter

UInt32Converter

System.ComponentModel (system.dll) **class**

This class provides a TypeConverter for a UInt32. It is used in serialization and design-time scenarios, and should not normally be called from your own code.

```
public class UInt32Converter : BaseNumberConverter {
// Public Constructors
   public UInt32Converter( );
}
```

Hierarchy System.Object → TypeConverter → BaseNumberConverter → UInt32Converter

UInt64Converter

System.ComponentModel (system.dll) **class**

This class implements a TypeConverter for a UInt64 in serialization and design-time scenarios. It should not normally be called from your own code.

```
public class UInt64Converter : BaseNumberConverter {
// Public Constructors
   public UInt64Converter( );
}
```

Hierarchy System.Object → TypeConverter → BaseNumberConverter → UInt64Converter

WarningException

System.ComponentModel (system.dll) **class**

This implements an exception that should be treated as a warning rather than an error. You can specify a HelpTopic and HelpUrl (the URI of the help file associated with the problem).

```
public class WarningException : SystemException {
// Public Constructors
   public WarningException(string message);
   public WarningException(string message, string helpUrl);
   public WarningException(string message, string helpUrl, string helpTopic);
```

```
// Public Instance Properties
   public string HelpTopic{get; }
   public string HelpUrl{get; }
}
```

Hierarchy System.Object → System.Exception(System.Runtime.Serialization.ISerializable) → System.SystemException → WarningException

Win32Exception

serializable

System.ComponentModel (system.dll) class

This class encapsulates an exception that is thrown to wrap the failure of a Win32 native method call. The NativeErrorCode property can retrieve the underlying Win32 error code that caused the exception to be thrown.

```
public class Win32Exception : System.Runtime.InteropServices.ExternalException {
// Public Constructors
   public Win32Exception( );
   public Win32Exception(int error);
   public Win32Exception(int error, string message);
// Protected Constructors
   protected Win32Exception(System.Runtime.Serialization.SerializationInfo info,
      System.Runtime.Serialization.StreamingContext context);
// Public Instance Properties
   public int NativeErrorCode{get; }
// Public Instance Methods
   public override void GetObjectData(System.Runtime.Serialization.SerializationInfo info,
      System.Runtime.Serialization.StreamingContext context);              // overrides Exception
}
```

Hierarchy System.Object → System.Exception(System.Runtime.Serialization.ISerializable) → System.SystemException → System.Runtime.InteropServices.ExternalException → Win32Exception

Subclasses System.Net.Sockets.SocketException

14

The System.Drawing Namespace

The System.Drawing namespace contains the classes that make up the .NET implementation of GDI+—Microsoft's next-generation graphics architecture. If you are familiar with the C++ implementation shipped with Microsoft's Platform SDK, then you will recognize most of the classes found here. However, System.Drawing is not a wrapper around the C++ code; both are implemented in terms of a common, low-level graphics architecture, which at the time of writing has an unpublished API.

All drawing is carried out on a Graphics surface, using various kinds of Pen, Brush, and Image objects. You can control the Color (including transparency), Font, line style, and fill patterns of these objects, but the Graphics surface itself is responsible for the actual painting, providing methods such as DrawString( ), DrawRectangle( ), and FillClosedCurve( ) for this purpose. You can set up clipping Regions, control rendering styles such as antialiasing and compositing, or use a *transform matrix* (see System.Drawing.Drawing2D.Matrix) to rotate, scale, shear, and translate the drawing.

Usually, you will be supplied a Graphics surface on which to draw in the PaintEventArgs passed to your Control object's paint handler. However, you can also create surfaces from Control objects, Image objects (such as Bitmap and Metafile), or native GDI device contexts (through interop).

Because there are no objects that represent the drawing operations themselves, you cannot simply persist an object graph to store your drawing. .NET offers two other options, both of which have their limitations. First, you can save a Bitmap to a stream or file using the standard raster graphics encoders (e.g., BMP, PNG, JPG) by calling one of the Save( ) methods. Alternatively, you can use the Metafile support in System.Drawing.Imaging to store and restore a scalable, vectorized version of your drawing operations. At the present time, it is not possible to write your own encoders, but this may be possible in future versions of the platform.

The System.Drawing.Drawing2D contains classes that offer enhanced vector graphics support (such as the Matrix transforms), and System.Drawing.Imaging provides classes that offer enhanced imaging facilities (such as color transforms and direct pixel data access). Printing support can be found in **System.Drawing.Printing**.

Figure 14-1 shows many of the types in this namespace, and Figure 14-2 shows various converters.

Bitmap **serializable, marshal by reference, disposable**

System.Drawing (system.drawing.dll) **sealed class**

This subclass of **Image** encapsulates a picture represented by a 2D array of pixel data. It supports a range of **PixelFormats**, including both true-color and palette-color bitmaps, and those with an alpha channel for transparency.

A **Bitmap** conceptually represents a system bitmap and is ultimately implemented through a native GDI+ bitmap handle. As with most drawing classes that wrap limited resources (**Pen** and **Brush** being other examples), you should have a well-defined lifetime management plan, calling **Dispose( )** when you are finished to release the resources back to the system (the **using** idiom in C# is useful here: see the main body of the text for details). If you rely on the garbage collector to do this, the **Bitmap** object will be collected but its pixel data will be leaked until the garbage collector happens to run, which may be too late.

There are several ways to construct a **Bitmap** object. One of the most is common is to provide the filename of the picture that you want to load. The framework will use the installed CODECs (BMP, PNG, JPG, and GIF) to attempt to load the image. Note that the file itself will remain locked until the **Bitmap** that loaded it is disposed. However, you can **Clone( )** the bitmap and **Dispose( )** the original to release the file.

Alternatively, you can construct bitmaps of a specific size and **PixelFormat**, or bitmaps compatible with a particular **Graphics** surface. You can also construct from another **Image** (optionally rescaling the original in the process), or from a block of pixel data referenced via an **IntPtr**. The latter is most useful in interop scenarios, as are the static methods **FromHicon( )** and **FromResource( )**, which return a **Bitmap** wrapper for Win32 icons and bitmap resources. (By preference, you would use the **Icon** class instead, for a fully managed solution.)

You can also **Clone( )** a specific **Rectangle** from a **Bitmap**, optionally changing its **PixelFormat** in the process, or use the override of **GetThumbnailImage( )** to retrieve a smaller version of the original. This method does expose its unmanaged origins somewhat, inconveniently requiring you to pass an **Abort** delegate that is required to do nothing, and a null pointer (**IntPtr.Zero**). It is recommended that you use the rescaling constructor instead.

You can manipulate the image using the **GetPixel( )** and **SetPixel( )** methods, but this is not especially efficient! A better approach for image processing is to use the **LockBits( )** method to retrieve a **BitmapData** object, which allows direct access to the underlying pixel data. **LockBits( )** actually ensures that the pixel data is fixed into system memory, and will not move while you are using it. For heavy duty processing, you would typically hand this off through interop to an unmanaged routine, but managed code will often perform adequately if care is taken with the selection of the processing algorithm, and you are prepared to support unsafe code in your assembly. When you have finished, you can use **UnlockBits( )** to unlock the pixel data again.

There are a couple of built-in manipulation functions, including **RotateFlip( )** to let you perform fixed rotations and flipping, and **MakeTransparent( )**, which lets you make a selected color transparent when drawing the image. Classes providing more advanced manipulation of the bitmap can be found in the **System.Drawing.Imaging** namespace.

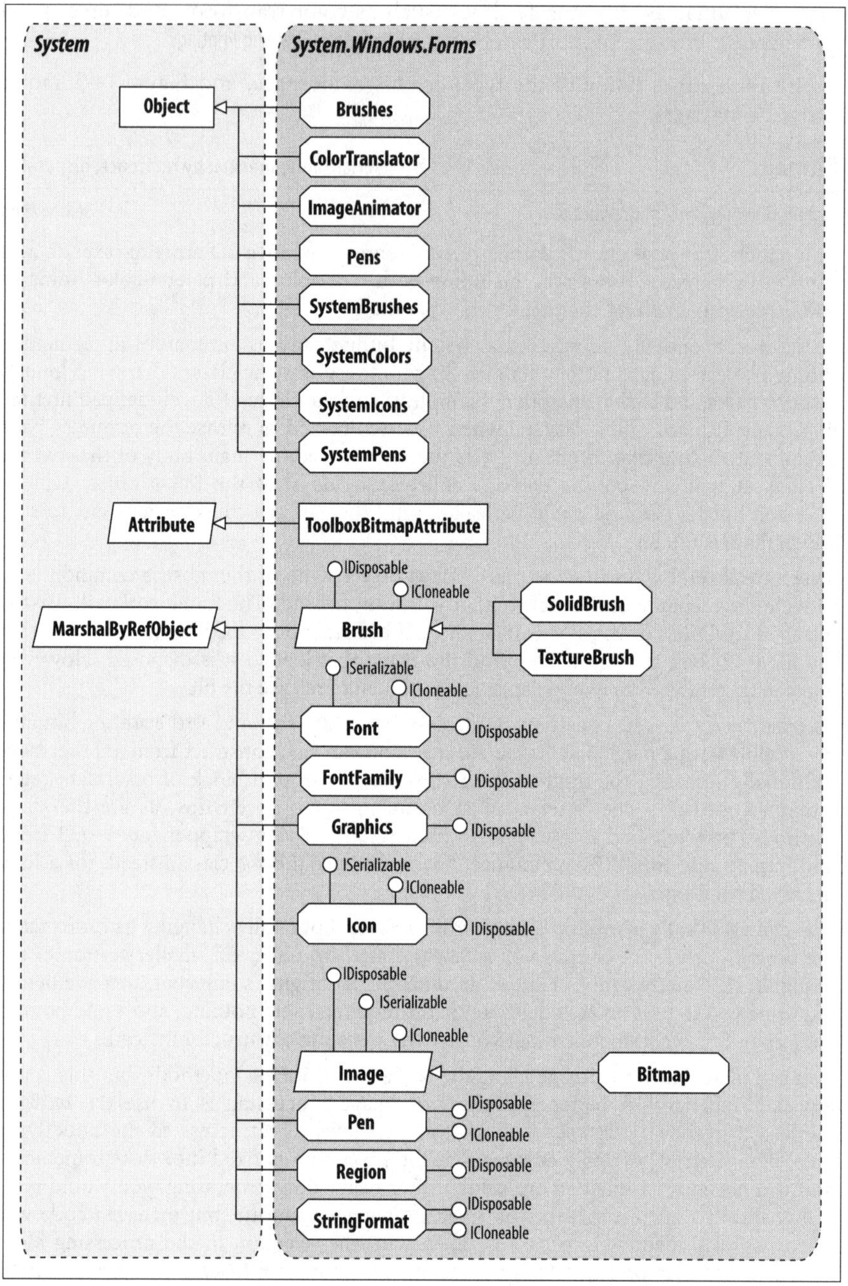
System
System.Windows.Forms
Object
Brushes
ColorTranslator
ImageAnimator
Pens
SystemBrushes
SystemColors
SystemIcons
SystemPens
Attribute
ToolboxBitmapAttribute
IDisposable
ICloneable
MarshalByRefObject
Brush
SolidBrush
TextureBrush
ISerializable
ICloneable
Font
IDisposable
FontFamily
IDisposable
Graphics
IDisposable
ISerializable
ICloneable
Icon
IDisposable
IDisposable
ISerializable
ICloneable
Image
Bitmap
Pen
IDisposable
ICloneable
Region
IDisposable
StringFormat
IDisposable
ICloneable

Figure 14-1. Many types from the System.Drawing namespace

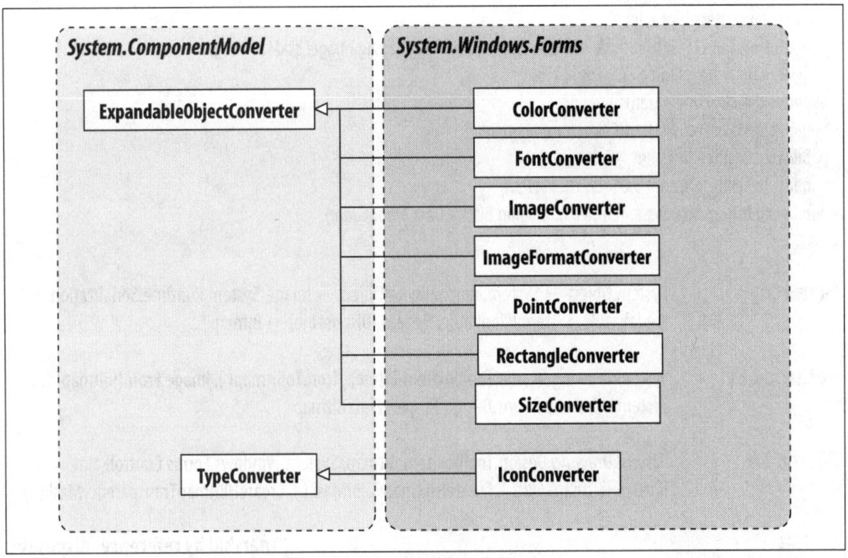
System.ComponentModel
System.Windows.Forms
ExpandableObjectConverter
ColorConverter
FontConverter
ImageConverter
ImageFormatConverter
PointConverter
RectangleConverter
SizeConverter
TypeConverter
IconConverter

Figure 14-2. Converters in the System.Drawing namespace

To draw an image on a Graphics surface, use Graphics.DrawImage( ) and Graphics.DrawImageUnscaled( ). The Graphics.CompositingMode, Graphics.CompositingQuality, and Graphics.InterpolationMode determine how the pixel data will be drawn onto the surface.

If you want to paint onto the Bitmap itself, you can use Graphics.FromImage( ) to create a Graphics surface bound to the bitmap object. Any painting on that surface will be reflected on the Bitmap.

```
public sealed class Bitmap : Image {
// Public Constructors
   public Bitmap(Image original);
   public Bitmap(Image original, int width, int height);
   public Bitmap(Image original, Size newSize);
   public Bitmap(int width, int height);
   public Bitmap(int width, int height, Graphics g);
   public Bitmap(int width, int height, int stride, System.Drawing.Imaging.PixelFormat format, IntPtr scan0);
   public Bitmap(int width, int height, System.Drawing.Imaging.PixelFormat format);
   public Bitmap(System.IO.Stream stream);
   public Bitmap(System.IO.Stream stream, bool useIcm);
   public Bitmap(string filename);
   public Bitmap(string filename, bool useIcm);
   public Bitmap(Type type, string resource);
// Public Static Methods
   public static Bitmap FromHicon(IntPtr hicon);
   public static Bitmap FromResource(IntPtr hinstance, string bitmapName);
// Public Instance Methods
   public Bitmap Clone(RectangleF rect, System.Drawing.Imaging.PixelFormat format);
   public Bitmap Clone(Rectangle rect, System.Drawing.Imaging.PixelFormat format);
   public IntPtr GetHbitmap( );
   public IntPtr GetHbitmap(Color background);
   public IntPtr GetHicon( );
```

Drawing

```
  public Color GetPixel(int x, int y);
  public BitmapData LockBits(Rectangle rect, System.Drawing.Imaging.ImageLockMode flags,
     System.Drawing.Imaging.PixelFormat format);
  public void MakeTransparent( );
  public void MakeTransparent(Color transparentColor);
  public void SetPixel(int x, int y, Color color);
  public void SetResolution(float xDpi, float yDpi);
  public void UnlockBits(System.Drawing.Imaging.BitmapData bitmapdata);
}
```

Hierarchy System.Object → System.MarshalByRefObject → Image(System.Runtime.Serialization.ISerializable, System.ICloneable, System.IDisposable) → Bitmap

Returned By System.Drawing.Design.ToolboxItem.Bitmap, Icon.ToBitmap( ), Image.FromHbitmap( ), System.Windows.Forms.Design.PropertyTab.Bitmap

Passed To System.Drawing.Design.ToolboxItem.Bitmap, System.Windows.Forms.ControlPaint.{CreateHBitmap16Bit( ), CreateHBitmapColorMask( ), CreateHBitmapTransparencyMask( )}

Brush — marshal by reference, disposable

System.Drawing (system.drawing.dll) — abstract class

This abstract base represents the class of objects that determine how shapes will be filled. Concrete subclasses such as SolidBrush and System.Drawing.Drawing2D.LinearGradientBrush can be instantiated to achieve a variety of different fill styles and techniques.

If you just need a basic SolidBrush of a well-known color, you can use the Brushes or SystemBrushes class to retrieve one.

As all brushes are resource-based entities, you should manage their lifetime appropriately, calling Dispose( ) when you are finished to avoid leaking system resources. (See Brushes and SystemBrushes for exceptions to this rule.)

```
public abstract class Brush : MarshalByRefObject : ICloneable, IDisposable {
// Public Instance Methods
  public abstract object Clone( );                              // implements ICloneable
  public void Dispose( );                                       // implements IDisposable
// Protected Instance Methods
  protected virtual void Dispose(bool disposing);
  protected override void Finalize( );                          // overrides object
}
```

Hierarchy System.Object → System.MarshalByRefObject → Brush(System.ICloneable, System.IDisposable)

Subclasses SolidBrush, TextureBrush, System.Drawing.Drawing2D.{HatchBrush, LinearGradientBrush, PathGradientBrush}

Returned By Multiple types

Passed To Graphics.{DrawString( ), FillClosedCurve( ), FillEllipse( ), FillPath( ), FillPie( ), FillPolygon( ), FillRectangle( ), FillRectangles( ), FillRegion( )}, Pen.{Brush, Pen( )}, System.Windows.Forms.DataGridTextBoxColumn.PaintText( )

Brushes

System.Drawing (system.drawing.dll) **sealed class**

This class provides a set of static properties that return Brushes for all the standard web colors.

Unlike most brushes, you must not Dispose() the ones returned from this class, as they are returned from a system cache and you will leave a nasty hole behind for the next person to try to use.

To retrieve a Brush for one of the basic system colors, see SystemBrushes.

```
public sealed class Brushes {
// Public Static Properties
   public static Brush AliceBlue{get; }
   public static Brush AntiqueWhite{get; }
   public static Brush Aqua{get; }
   public static Brush Aquamarine{get; }
   public static Brush Azure{get; }
   public static Brush Beige{get; }
   public static Brush Bisque{get; }
   public static Brush Black{get; }
   public static Brush BlanchedAlmond{get; }
   public static Brush Blue{get; }
   public static Brush BlueViolet{get; }
   public static Brush Brown{get; }
   public static Brush BurlyWood{get; }
   public static Brush CadetBlue{get; }
   public static Brush Chartreuse{get; }
   public static Brush Chocolate{get; }
   public static Brush Coral{get; }
   public static Brush CornflowerBlue{get; }
   public static Brush Cornsilk{get; }
   public static Brush Crimson{get; }
   public static Brush Cyan{get; }
   public static Brush DarkBlue{get; }
   public static Brush DarkCyan{get; }
   public static Brush DarkGoldenrod{get; }
   public static Brush DarkGray{get; }
   public static Brush DarkGreen{get; }
   public static Brush DarkKhaki{get; }
   public static Brush DarkMagenta{get; }
   public static Brush DarkOliveGreen{get; }
   public static Brush DarkOrange{get; }
   public static Brush DarkOrchid{get; }
   public static Brush DarkRed{get; }
   public static Brush DarkSalmon{get; }
   public static Brush DarkSeaGreen{get; }
   public static Brush DarkSlateBlue{get; }
   public static Brush DarkSlateGray{get; }
   public static Brush DarkTurquoise{get; }
   public static Brush DarkViolet{get; }
   public static Brush DeepPink{get; }
```

```
public static Brush DeepSkyBlue{get; }
public static Brush DimGray{get; }
public static Brush DodgerBlue{get; }
public static Brush Firebrick{get; }
public static Brush FloralWhite{get; }
public static Brush ForestGreen{get; }
public static Brush Fuchsia{get; }
public static Brush Gainsboro{get; }
public static Brush GhostWhite{get; }
public static Brush Gold{get; }
public static Brush Goldenrod{get; }
public static Brush Gray{get; }
public static Brush Green{get; }
public static Brush GreenYellow{get; }
public static Brush Honeydew{get; }
public static Brush HotPink{get; }
public static Brush IndianRed{get; }
public static Brush Indigo{get; }
public static Brush Ivory{get; }
public static Brush Khaki{get; }
public static Brush Lavender{get; }
public static Brush LavenderBlush{get; }
public static Brush LawnGreen{get; }
public static Brush LemonChiffon{get; }
public static Brush LightBlue{get; }
public static Brush LightCoral{get; }
public static Brush LightCyan{get; }
public static Brush LightGoldenrodYellow{get; }
public static Brush LightGray{get; }
public static Brush LightGreen{get; }
public static Brush LightPink{get; }
public static Brush LightSalmon{get; }
public static Brush LightSeaGreen{get; }
public static Brush LightSkyBlue{get; }
public static Brush LightSlateGray{get; }
public static Brush LightSteelBlue{get; }
public static Brush LightYellow{get; }
public static Brush Lime{get; }
public static Brush LimeGreen{get; }
public static Brush Linen{get; }
public static Brush Magenta{get; }
public static Brush Maroon{get; }
public static Brush MediumAquamarine{get; }
public static Brush MediumBlue{get; }
public static Brush MediumOrchid{get; }
public static Brush MediumPurple{get; }
public static Brush MediumSeaGreen{get; }
public static Brush MediumSlateBlue{get; }
public static Brush MediumSpringGreen{get; }
public static Brush MediumTurquoise{get; }
public static Brush MediumVioletRed{get; }
public static Brush MidnightBlue{get; }
```

```
public static Brush MintCream{get; }
public static Brush MistyRose{get; }
public static Brush Moccasin{get; }
public static Brush NavajoWhite{get; }
public static Brush Navy{get; }
public static Brush OldLace{get; }
public static Brush Olive{get; }
public static Brush OliveDrab{get; }
public static Brush Orange{get; }
public static Brush OrangeRed{get; }
public static Brush Orchid{get; }
public static Brush PaleGoldenrod{get; }
public static Brush PaleGreen{get; }
public static Brush PaleTurquoise{get; }
public static Brush PaleVioletRed{get; }
public static Brush PapayaWhip{get; }
public static Brush PeachPuff{get; }
public static Brush Peru{get; }
public static Brush Pink{get; }
public static Brush Plum{get; }
public static Brush PowderBlue{get; }
public static Brush Purple{get; }
public static Brush Red{get; }
public static Brush RosyBrown{get; }
public static Brush RoyalBlue{get; }
public static Brush SaddleBrown{get; }
public static Brush Salmon{get; }
public static Brush SandyBrown{get; }
public static Brush SeaGreen{get; }
public static Brush SeaShell{get; }
public static Brush Sienna{get; }
public static Brush Silver{get; }
public static Brush SkyBlue{get; }
public static Brush SlateBlue{get; }
public static Brush SlateGray{get; }
public static Brush Snow{get; }
public static Brush SpringGreen{get; }
public static Brush SteelBlue{get; }
public static Brush Tan{get; }
public static Brush Teal{get; }
public static Brush Thistle{get; }
public static Brush Tomato{get; }
public static Brush Transparent{get; }
public static Brush Turquoise{get; }
public static Brush Violet{get; }
public static Brush Wheat{get; }
public static Brush White{get; }
public static Brush WhiteSmoke{get; }
public static Brush Yellow{get; }
public static Brush YellowGreen{get; }
}
```

Drawing

CharacterRange

System.Drawing (system.drawing.dll) struct

This value type is used to define a range of characters within a string, by specifying the starting character and the length of the substring.

```
public struct CharacterRange {
// Public Constructors
   public CharacterRange(int First, int Length);
// Public Instance Properties
   public int First{set; get; }
   public int Length{set; get; }
}
```

Hierarchy System.Object → System.ValueType → CharacterRange

Passed To StringFormat.SetMeasurableCharacterRanges( )

Color serializable

System.Drawing (system.drawing.dll) struct

The Color structure is a value type that represents a point in the RGB color space, with optional support for a transparency alpha channel.

You can obtain the value of a particular Color by using one of the static properties that return a well-known web color. Alternatively, FromArgb( ) allows you to define a specific color from its red, green, blue, and alpha components. FromKnownColor( ) allows you to create a Color from an entry in KnownColor enumeration, and FromName( ) takes a string containing the name of well-known color.

There is also a special field, Empty, which represents a null color. This is necessary because Color is a value type, and therefore nullness cannot be represented by a null reference. It is usually used when a class can optionally inherit its color from an ambient property (e.g., the ForeColor of a Control is inherited from its Parent if set to Empty). The IsEmpty property allows you to check for nullness.

There are properties that allow you to retrieve the A, R, G, and B values of the color, and the color's Name (either the well-known name or a string description of the ARGB values as appropriate). In addition, there are methods—GetHue( ), GetSaturation( ), and GetBrightness( )—to transform the values to the HSB color space.

If you need to know whether a color is well-known, you can use the IsKnownColor, IsNamedColor, and IsSystemColor properties.

The Color structure is used pervasively throughout the framework wherever color is needed.

```
public struct Color {
// Public Static Fields
   public static readonly Color Empty;                    // =Color [Empty]
// Public Static Properties
   public static Color AliceBlue{get; }
   public static Color AntiqueWhite{get; }
   public static Color Aqua{get; }
   public static Color Aquamarine{get; }
   public static Color Azure{get; }
```

public static Color **Beige**{get; }
public static Color **Bisque**{get; }
public static Color **Black**{get; }
public static Color **BlanchedAlmond**{get; }
public static Color **Blue**{get; }
public static Color **BlueViolet**{get; }
public static Color **Brown**{get; }
public static Color **BurlyWood**{get; }
public static Color **CadetBlue**{get; }
public static Color **Chartreuse**{get; }
public static Color **Chocolate**{get; }
public static Color **Coral**{get; }
public static Color **CornflowerBlue**{get; }
public static Color **Cornsilk**{get; }
public static Color **Crimson**{get; }
public static Color **Cyan**{get; }
public static Color **DarkBlue**{get; }
public static Color **DarkCyan**{get; }
public static Color **DarkGoldenrod**{get; }
public static Color **DarkGray**{get; }
public static Color **DarkGreen**{get; }
public static Color **DarkKhaki**{get; }
public static Color **DarkMagenta**{get; }
public static Color **DarkOliveGreen**{get; }
public static Color **DarkOrange**{get; }
public static Color **DarkOrchid**{get; }
public static Color **DarkRed**{get; }
public static Color **DarkSalmon**{get; }
public static Color **DarkSeaGreen**{get; }
public static Color **DarkSlateBlue**{get; }
public static Color **DarkSlateGray**{get; }
public static Color **DarkTurquoise**{get; }
public static Color **DarkViolet**{get; }
public static Color **DeepPink**{get; }
public static Color **DeepSkyBlue**{get; }
public static Color **DimGray**{get; }
public static Color **DodgerBlue**{get; }
public static Color **Firebrick**{get; }
public static Color **FloralWhite**{get; }
public static Color **ForestGreen**{get; }
public static Color **Fuchsia**{get; }
public static Color **Gainsboro**{get; }
public static Color **GhostWhite**{get; }
public static Color **Gold**{get; }
public static Color **Goldenrod**{get; }
public static Color **Gray**{get; }
public static Color **Green**{get; }
public static Color **GreenYellow**{get; }
public static Color **Honeydew**{get; }
public static Color **HotPink**{get; }
public static Color **IndianRed**{get; }
public static Color **Indigo**{get; }

```
public static Color Ivory{get; }
public static Color Khaki{get; }
public static Color Lavender{get; }
public static Color LavenderBlush{get; }
public static Color LawnGreen{get; }
public static Color LemonChiffon{get; }
public static Color LightBlue{get; }
public static Color LightCoral{get; }
public static Color LightCyan{get; }
public static Color LightGoldenrodYellow{get; }
public static Color LightGray{get; }
public static Color LightGreen{get; }
public static Color LightPink{get; }
public static Color LightSalmon{get; }
public static Color LightSeaGreen{get; }
public static Color LightSkyBlue{get; }
public static Color LightSlateGray{get; }
public static Color LightSteelBlue{get; }
public static Color LightYellow{get; }
public static Color Lime{get; }
public static Color LimeGreen{get; }
public static Color Linen{get; }
public static Color Magenta{get; }
public static Color Maroon{get; }
public static Color MediumAquamarine{get; }
public static Color MediumBlue{get; }
public static Color MediumOrchid{get; }
public static Color MediumPurple{get; }
public static Color MediumSeaGreen{get; }
public static Color MediumSlateBlue{get; }
public static Color MediumSpringGreen{get; }
public static Color MediumTurquoise{get; }
public static Color MediumVioletRed{get; }
public static Color MidnightBlue{get; }
public static Color MintCream{get; }
public static Color MistyRose{get; }
public static Color Moccasin{get; }
public static Color NavajoWhite{get; }
public static Color Navy{get; }
public static Color OldLace{get; }
public static Color Olive{get; }
public static Color OliveDrab{get; }
public static Color Orange{get; }
public static Color OrangeRed{get; }
public static Color Orchid{get; }
public static Color PaleGoldenrod{get; }
public static Color PaleGreen{get; }
public static Color PaleTurquoise{get; }
public static Color PaleVioletRed{get; }
public static Color PapayaWhip{get; }
public static Color PeachPuff{get; }
public static Color Peru{get; }
```

```
public static Color Pink{get; }
public static Color Plum{get; }
public static Color PowderBlue{get; }
public static Color Purple{get; }
public static Color Red{get; }
public static Color RosyBrown{get; }
public static Color RoyalBlue{get; }
public static Color SaddleBrown{get; }
public static Color Salmon{get; }
public static Color SandyBrown{get; }
public static Color SeaGreen{get; }
public static Color SeaShell{get; }
public static Color Sienna{get; }
public static Color Silver{get; }
public static Color SkyBlue{get; }
public static Color SlateBlue{get; }
public static Color SlateGray{get; }
public static Color Snow{get; }
public static Color SpringGreen{get; }
public static Color SteelBlue{get; }
public static Color Tan{get; }
public static Color Teal{get; }
public static Color Thistle{get; }
public static Color Tomato{get; }
public static Color Transparent{get; }
public static Color Turquoise{get; }
public static Color Violet{get; }
public static Color Wheat{get; }
public static Color White{get; }
public static Color WhiteSmoke{get; }
public static Color Yellow{get; }
public static Color YellowGreen{get; }
// Public Instance Properties
public byte A{get; }
public byte B{get; }
public byte G{get; }
public bool IsEmpty{get; }
public bool IsKnownColor{get; }
public bool IsNamedColor{get; }
public bool IsSystemColor{get; }
public string Name{get; }
public byte R{get; }
// Public Static Methods
public static Color FromArgb(int argb);
public static Color FromArgb(int alpha, Color baseColor);
public static Color FromArgb(int red, int green, int blue);
public static Color FromArgb(int alpha, int red, int green, int blue);
public static Color FromKnownColor(KnownColor color);
public static Color FromName(string name);
public static bool operator !=(Color left, Color right);
public static bool operator ==(Color left, Color right);
// Public Instance Methods
```

Drawing

```
    public override bool Equals(object obj);                                    // overrides ValueType
    public float GetBrightness( );
    public override int GetHashCode( );                                         // overrides ValueType
    public float GetHue( );
    public float GetSaturation( );
    public int ToArgb( );
    public KnownColor ToKnownColor( );
    public override string ToString( );                                         // overrides ValueType
}
```

Hierarchy System.Object → System.ValueType → Color

Returned By Multiple types

Passed To Multiple types

ColorConverter

System.Drawing (system.drawing.dll) class

This subclass of TypeConverter is used to transform Color objects to other types. Specifically, it can convert to and from a string representation used in persistence and design-time scenarios. Normally, you would use Color.ToString( ) and Color.Name to do this conversion yourself.

```
public class ColorConverter : System.ComponentModel.TypeConverter {
// Public Constructors
    public ColorConverter( );
// Public Instance Methods
    public override bool CanConvertFrom(System.ComponentModel.ITypeDescriptorContext context,
        Type sourceType);                                  // overrides System.ComponentModel.TypeConverter
    public override bool CanConvertTo(System.ComponentModel.ITypeDescriptorContext context,
        Type destinationType);                             // overrides System.ComponentModel.TypeConverter
    public override object ConvertFrom(System.ComponentModel.ITypeDescriptorContext context,
        System.Globalization.CultureInfo culture, object value);  // overrides System.ComponentModel.TypeConverter
    public override object ConvertTo(System.ComponentModel.ITypeDescriptorContext context,
        System.Globalization.CultureInfo culture,
        object value, Type destinationType);               // overrides System.ComponentModel.TypeConverter
    public override StandardValuesCollection GetStandardValues(
        System.ComponentModel.ITypeDescriptorContext context);    // overrides System.ComponentModel.TypeConverter
    public override bool GetStandardValuesSupported(
        System.ComponentModel.ITypeDescriptorContext context);    // overrides System.ComponentModel.TypeConverter
}
```

Hierarchy System.Object → System.ComponentModel.TypeConverter → ColorConverter

ColorTranslator

System.Drawing (system.drawing.dll) sealed class

This class is used to translate a Color to and from various interop color representations, including an HTML color string, Win32 GDI, and Win32 OLE colors.

```
public sealed class ColorTranslator {
// Public Static Methods
   public static Color FromHtml(string htmlColor);
   public static Color FromOle(int oleColor);
   public static Color FromWin32(int win32Color);
   public static string ToHtml(Color c);
   public static int ToOle(Color c);
   public static int ToWin32(Color c);
}
```

ContentAlignment **serializable**

System.Drawing (system.drawing.dll) **enum**

This enumeration provides a set of values that represent a variety of different alignment styles. It is not used by any other classes in the drawing namespaces, but many Control classes use it to define the way their text labels and other visual content should be aligned when rendered.

```
public enum ContentAlignment {
   TopLeft = 1,
   TopCenter = 2,
   TopRight = 4,
   MiddleLeft = 16,
   MiddleCenter = 32,
   MiddleRight = 64,
   BottomLeft = 256,
   BottomCenter = 512,
   BottomRight = 1024
}
```

Hierarchy System.Object → System.ValueType → System.Enum(System.IComparable, System.IFormattable, System.IConvertible) → ContentAlignment

Returned By System.Windows.Forms.ButtonBase.{ImageAlign, TextAlign}, System.Windows.Forms.CheckBox.CheckAlign, System.Windows.Forms.Control.RtlTranslateContent( ), System.Windows.Forms.Label.{ImageAlign, TextAlign}, System.Windows.Forms.RadioButton.CheckAlign

Passed To System.Windows.Forms.ButtonBase.{ImageAlign, TextAlign}, System.Windows.Forms.CheckBox.CheckAlign, System.Windows.Forms.Control.{RtlTranslateAlignment( ), RtlTranslateContent( )}, System.Windows.Forms.Label.{CalcImageRenderBounds( ), DrawImage( ), ImageAlign, TextAlign}, System.Windows.Forms.RadioButton.CheckAlign

Font **serializable, marshal by reference, disposable**

System.Drawing (system.drawing.dll) **sealed class**

This class encapsulates a particular visual representation of a textual character set.

A Font is a resource-based object, and its lifetime therefore needs careful management. As with other such objects, you should Dispose( ) the object when you are finished with it to release the resources back to the system.

There are a number of constructors that allow you to create a **Font** from a particular **FontFamily**, or with a particular face **Name** (represented as a string) and of a particular **Size**. From the **GraphicsUnit** enumeration, you can choose which **Unit** is used to measure the size. Typically, this might be **GraphicsUnit.Point** or **GraphicsUnit.Pixel**. In addition, you can specify a variety of **Style** attributes, including **Bold**, **Italic**, **Strikeout**, and **Underline**. The style elements can be queried individually using the Boolean properties provided, or by examining the **FontStyle** object returned from the **Style** property.

However, it is not possible to set any of these values and change the Font. If you wish to create a new object based on an existing **Font** but with a different style, you should use the constructor that takes a prototype **Font** and a new **FontStyle** (perhaps then calling **Dispose( )** on the original to release it if it is no longer needed). Similarly, to create an object sharing a **FontFamily**, you can use the constructor that takes a **FontFamily** and a size.

There are also a number of static members that allow you to create a **Font** from various entities in interop scenarios, including **FromHdc( )**, **FromHfont( )**, and **FromLogFont( )**. There are comparable methods to convert **ToHfont( )** and **ToLogFont( )**.

To draw a string in a particular **Font**, you can use the **Graphics.DrawString( )** method. You can also call the **GetHeight( )** method to determine the height a particular font would be if it were rendered on a specific **Graphics** surface. However, there is no method to retrieve the average character width as there is in the Win32 API. Instead, you should use the **Graphics.MeasureString( )** method to determine the bounding rectangle of a particular string as it would be rendered on that surface.

Font objects are also used pervasively throughout the frameworks wherever text is rendered.

```
public sealed class Font : MarshalByRefObject : ICloneable, System.Runtime.Serialization.ISerializable, IDisposable {
// Public Constructors
   public Font(FontFamily family, float emSize);
   public Font(FontFamily family, float emSize, FontStyle style);
   public Font(FontFamily family, float emSize, FontStyle style, GraphicsUnit unit);
   public Font(FontFamily family, float emSize, FontStyle style, GraphicsUnit unit, byte gdiCharSet);
   public Font(FontFamily family, float emSize, FontStyle style, GraphicsUnit unit, byte gdiCharSet, bool gdiVerticalFont);
   public Font(FontFamily family, float emSize, GraphicsUnit unit);
   public Font(Font prototype, FontStyle newStyle);
   public Font(string familyName, float emSize);
   public Font(string familyName, float emSize, FontStyle style);
   public Font(string familyName, float emSize, FontStyle style, GraphicsUnit unit);
   public Font(string familyName, float emSize, FontStyle style, GraphicsUnit unit, byte gdiCharSet);
   public Font(string familyName, float emSize, FontStyle style, GraphicsUnit unit, byte gdiCharSet, bool gdiVerticalFont);
   public Font(string familyName, float emSize, GraphicsUnit unit);
// Public Instance Properties
   public bool Bold{get; }
   public FontFamily FontFamily{get; }
   public byte GdiCharSet{get; }
   public bool GdiVerticalFont{get; }
   public int Height{get; }
   public bool Italic{get; }
   public string Name{get; }
   public float Size{get; }
   public float SizeInPoints{get; }
   public bool Strikeout{get; }
   public FontStyle Style{get; }
```

```
 public bool Underline{get; }
 public GraphicsUnit Unit{get; }
// Public Static Methods
 public static Font FromHdc(IntPtr hdc);
 public static Font FromHfont(IntPtr hfont);
 public static Font FromLogFont(object lf);
 public static Font FromLogFont(object lf, IntPtr hdc);
// Public Instance Methods
 public object Clone( );                                        // implements ICloneable
 public void Dispose( );                                        // implements IDisposable
 public override bool Equals(object obj);                       // overrides object
 public override int GetHashCode( );                            // overrides object
 public float GetHeight( );
 public float GetHeight(Graphics graphics);
 public float GetHeight(float dpi);
 public IntPtr ToHfont( );
 public void ToLogFont(object logFont);
 public void ToLogFont(object logFont, Graphics graphics);
 public override string ToString( );                            // overrides object
// Protected Instance Methods
 protected override void Finalize( );                           // overrides object
}
```

Hierarchy System.Object → System.MarshalByRefObject → Font(System.ICloneable, System.Runtime.Serialization.ISerializable, System.IDisposable)

Returned By Multiple types

Passed To Multiple types

FontConverter

System.Drawing (system.drawing.dll) class

Derived from TypeConverter, this class converts Font objects to and from other types, specifically a string representation used in persistence and design-time scenarios.

```
public class FontConverter : System.ComponentModel.TypeConverter {
// Public Constructors
 public FontConverter( );
// Public Instance Methods
 public override bool CanConvertFrom(System.ComponentModel.ITypeDescriptorContext context,
    Type sourceType);                          // overrides System.ComponentModel.TypeConverter
 public override bool CanConvertTo(System.ComponentModel.ITypeDescriptorContext context,
    Type destinationType);                     // overrides System.ComponentModel.TypeConverter
 public override object ConvertFrom(System.ComponentModel.ITypeDescriptorContext context,
    System.Globalization.CultureInfo culture, object value);   // overrides System.ComponentModel.TypeConverter
 public override object ConvertTo(System.ComponentModel.ITypeDescriptorContext context,
    System.Globalization.CultureInfo culture, object value,
    Type destinationType);                     // overrides System.ComponentModel.TypeConverter
 public override object CreateInstance(System.ComponentModel.ITypeDescriptorContext context,
    System.Collections.IDictionary propertyValues);   // overrides System.ComponentModel.TypeConverter
 public override bool GetCreateInstanceSupported(
    System.ComponentModel.ITypeDescriptorContext context);   // overrides System.ComponentModel.TypeConverter
```

```
  public override PropertyDescriptorCollection GetProperties(System.ComponentModel.ITypeDescriptorContext context,
    object value, Attribute[ ] attributes);                    // overrides System.ComponentModel.TypeConverter
  public override bool GetPropertiesSupported(
    System.ComponentModel.ITypeDescriptorContext context);     // overrides System.ComponentModel.TypeConverter
}
```

Hierarchy System.Object → System.ComponentModel.TypeConverter → FontConverter

FontConverter.FontNameConverter

System.Drawing (system.drawing.dll) **sealed class**

This class, derived from TypeConverter, is specifically documented as being for internal use only, despite being in the public interface—you should therefore not use this class. It is present to support the designers that deal with font properties.

```
public sealed class FontConverter.FontNameConverter : System.ComponentModel.TypeConverter {
// Public Constructors
  public FontConverter.FontNameConverter( );
// Public Instance Methods
  public override bool CanConvertFrom(System.ComponentModel.ITypeDescriptorContext context,
    Type sourceType);                                          // overrides System.ComponentModel.TypeConverter
  public override object ConvertFrom(System.ComponentModel.ITypeDescriptorContext context,
    System.Globalization.CultureInfo culture, object value);   // overrides System.ComponentModel.TypeConverter
  public override StandardValuesCollection GetStandardValues(
    System.ComponentModel.ITypeDescriptorContext context);     // overrides System.ComponentModel.TypeConverter
  public override bool GetStandardValuesExclusive(             // overrides System.ComponentModel.TypeConverter
    System.ComponentModel.ITypeDescriptorContext context);
  public override bool GetStandardValuesSupported(             // overrides System.ComponentModel.TypeConverter
    System.ComponentModel.ITypeDescriptorContext context);
// Protected Instance Methods
  protected override void Finalize( );                         // overrides object
}
```

Hierarchy System.Object → System.ComponentModel.TypeConverter → FontNameConverter

FontConverter.FontUnitConverter

System.Drawing (system.drawing.dll) **class**

This class, derived from TypeConverter, is specifically documented as being for internal use only, despite being in the public interface—you should therefore not use this class. It is present to support the designers that deal with font properties.

```
public class FontConverter.FontUnitConverter : System.ComponentModel.EnumConverter {
// Public Constructors
  public FontConverter.FontUnitConverter( );
// Public Instance Methods
  public override StandardValuesCollection GetStandardValues(
    System.ComponentModel.ITypeDescriptorContext context);     // overrides System.ComponentModel.EnumConverter
}
```

Hierarchy System.Object → System.ComponentModel.TypeConverter → System.ComponentModel.EnumConverter → FontUnitConverter

FontFamily — marshal by reference, disposable

System.Drawing (system.drawing.dll) — sealed class

A FontFamily represents a set of typefaces that share a common design, varying in particular stylistic ways. The fonts Arial, Arial Bold, and Arial Italic might make up a font family called Arial, for example.

A FontFamily is a resource-based object, and therefore its lifetime should be carefully managed, calling Dispose( ) to release the resources when they are no longer needed.

It can be constructed from a string containing the family name, from an entry in the System.Drawing.Text.GenericFontFamilies enumeration, or by providing a name to associate with a specific System.Drawing.Text.FontCollection, if you want to create your own family. In addition, there are static properties to get a GenericMonospace, GenericSansSerif, or GenericSerifFontFamily.

You can use a FontFamily to help manage font selection in your application—often where font selection is being determined through a user interface. To do this, there are Font constructors that enable you to select and instantiate a specific Font from a FontFamily.

```
public sealed class FontFamily : MarshalByRefObject : IDisposable {
// Public Constructors
   public FontFamily(System.Drawing.Text.GenericFontFamilies genericFamily);
   public FontFamily(string name);
   public FontFamily(string name, System.Drawing.Text.FontCollection fontCollection);
// Public Static Properties
   public static FontFamily[ ] Families{get; }
   public static FontFamily GenericMonospace{get; }
   public static FontFamily GenericSansSerif{get; }
   public static FontFamily GenericSerif{get; }
// Public Instance Properties
   public string Name{get; }
// Public Static Methods
   public static FontFamily[ ] GetFamilies(Graphics graphics);
// Public Instance Methods
   public void Dispose( );                                    // implements IDisposable
   public override bool Equals(object obj);                   // overrides object
   public int GetCellAscent(FontStyle style);
   public int GetCellDescent(FontStyle style);
   public int GetEmHeight(FontStyle style);
   public override int GetHashCode( );                        // overrides object
   public int GetLineSpacing(FontStyle style);
   public string GetName(int language);
   public bool IsStyleAvailable(FontStyle style);
   public override string ToString( );                        // overrides object
// Protected Instance Methods
   protected override void Finalize( );                       // overrides object
}
```

Hierarchy System.Object → System.MarshalByRefObject → FontFamily(System.IDisposable)

Returned By Font.FontFamily, System.Drawing.Text.FontCollection.Families

Passed To System.Drawing.Drawing2D.GraphicsPath.AddString( ), Font.Font( )

FontStyle

serializable, flag

System.Drawing (system.drawing.dll) **enum**

This enumeration provides a set of style modifiers that can be used on a Font. Because it is marked with the FlagsAttribute, you can combine several values using the bitwise operator (e.g., |) to generate compound styles such as (Bold | Italic).

```
public enum FontStyle {
  Regular = 0x00000000,
  Bold = 0x00000001,
  Italic = 0x00000002,
  Underline = 0x00000004,
  Strikeout = 0x00000008
}
```

Hierarchy System.Object → System.ValueType → System.Enum(System.IComparable, System.IFormattable, System.IConvertible) → FontStyle

Returned By Font.Style

Passed To Font.Font( ), FontFamily.{GetCellAscent( ), GetCellDescent( ), GetEmHeight( ), GetLineSpacing( ), IsStyleAvailable( )}

Graphics

marshal by reference, disposable

System.Drawing (system.drawing.dll) **sealed class**

This class is at the heart of the drawing architecture. It encapsulates a surface on which drawing is performed.

Typically, you are passed a Graphics object in the Paint handler of a Control.

Additionally, you can use the static FromImage( ) method to get a Graphics surface for one of the classes derived from Image (such as Bitmap or Metafile). Any painting on that surface will be reflected in the image itself.

For interop scenarios, there are static FromHdc( ) and FromHwnd( ) methods to construct a Graphics object for a DC or Win32 window, and the corresponding GetHdc( ) member to retrieve a Win32 device context for the managed surface.

There are a large number of methods that allow you to paint onto the surface. They fall into four broad categories:

- Outline drawing
- Surface filling
- Image compositing
- Drawing text strings

The outline drawing methods all begin with Draw. The first parameter is a Pen object, which determines the weight, color, and style of the line itself. The remaining parameters vary with the kind of line to be drawn and define the geometric shape in question.

The surface filling methods all begin with Fill. The first parameter is a Brush object, which specifies the color and pattern that will be used to fill the surface. The remaining parameters again vary with the kind of line to be drawn and define the geometric surface to fill.

Most draw and fill methods offer both integer and floating-point versions of the parameters that allow you to define the shapes concerned—**Point** and **PointF**, **Rectangle** and **RectangleF** for example. The integer methods do not offer any performance advantage in the first release, as they are all implemented in terms of the floating-point version.

There are outline drawing methods for both open and closed geometric shapes. The surface filling methods support closed shapes only.

There are methods for Arcs (portions of an ellipse), Beziers (defined by two anchor points through which the curve passes and two control points towards which it tends but through which it does not pass—like a chain nailed at both ends, with magnets nearby), Curves (cardinal splines defined by a set of points through which the line passes and a tension parameter—like a nailed-down rubber tube), Ellipses, Straight Lines, Pies (portions of an ellipse with radial lines drawn to the center), Polygons (straight-sided geometric shapes), and Rectangles. There is also a method to paint a **System.Drawing.Drawing2D.GraphicsPath** object—a connected or disconnected set of these elements.

For image compositing, there are **DrawIcon()** and **DrawImage()** methods. Both also offer what are theoretically optimized unscaled versions. The **Icon** method is called **DrawIconUnstretched()**, whereas the **Image** method is **DrawImageUnscaled()**. In practice, the optimized version is actually implemented in terms of the non-optimized method, so there is no benefit to be gained in this version of the framework.

There are several overloads of the **DrawImage()** method, offering control over various aspects of the rendering process. In addition to allowing you to specify the source rectangle within the original image and the destination rectangle on the **Graphics** surface (including the **GraphicsUnit** of measurement for those rectangles), you can provide a **System.Drawing.Imaging.ImageAttributes** object to control the way the individual pixel colors are rendered for this image.

There is also an optional **DrawImageAbort** delegate and an **IntPtr** for the user data that is passed to that delegate. The underlying GDI+ rendering mechanism calls on the delegate to determine whether the long painting operation should be aborted (for example, the user has scrolled the window and you need to start painting again). The delegate returns true if the painting should be aborted, and false otherwise. If the operation aborts, a **System.Runtime.InteropServices.ExternalException** with the exception text "Function aborted" is thrown, so you need to put your rendering code in a try/catch block. This is a very thin wrapper over the unmanaged implementation, and should be used with caution, particularly when passing data in the **IntPtr**.

Text strings are drawn using the **DrawString()** family of methods. These typically take the string to paint, a **Font** with which to render the string, and a **Brush** that determines how the characters will be filled. Note that if you wish to paint the outline of a string rather than fill the characters, you will need to use a **System.Drawing.Drawing2D.GraphicsPath** and its **AddString()** method. You can also specify either the top-left corner of the string or its bounding **Rectangle**.

You can determine what the minimum containing rectangle for the string on the surface might be by calling the **MeasureString()** method, or **MeasureCharacterRanges()** to determine the bounding rectangles of various substrings within the string itself, given a particular overall layout scheme and bounding rectangle. (You might do this to calculate areas to highlight selected portions of a string, for example.)

Various aspects of the text rendering can be controlled using the **StringFormat** object, including line spacing, wrapping, alignment, and clipping characteristics.

There are several properties of the Graphics surface that let you control the rendering techniques used by all these methods. In each case, there is a trade-off between rendering time and image quality.

You can set the CompositingMode, which determines how source and destination pixels are combined (see System.Drawing.Drawing2D.CompositingMode for details). You can also modify the CompositingQuality, which determines the algorithm chosen to combine pixels into the surface for a particular mode (see System.Drawing.Drawing2D.CompositingQuality).

The InterpolationMode determines how pixel values are calculated during scaling and gradient operations (see System.Drawing.Drawing2D.InterpolationMode), and the PixelOffsetMode determines how pixels are translated from a sub-pixel accurate geometric world to the whole-pixel reality of the device underlying the Graphics surface.

The SmoothingMode (System.Drawing.Drawing2D.SmoothingMode) determines the antialiasing technique used for the line and curve drawing (but not text and images). Text quality is determined by the TextRenderingHint (System.Drawing.Text.TextRenderingHint). You can also set the gamma correction value for ClearType and Antialiased text rendering with the TextContrast property (an integer between 0 and 12, with 4 being the default); however, at present this does not appear to make any difference to the appearance of the rendered text.

There are three coordinate spaces in operation on a graphics surface. The World coordinate space, the Page coordinate space, and the Device coordinate space. The transform from the World coordinate space to the Page space is called the World Transform, and is stored as a System.Drawing.Drawing2D.Matrix in the Transform property. The getter for this property actually returns a copy of the Transform, rather than a reference to the transform itself, so to modify it, you need to go through a three-phase get, modify, set procedure. As this is rather inefficient, there are the MultiplyTransform(), TranslateTransform(), RotateTransform(), and ScaleTransform() methods as well.

To transform from the Page space to the Device space, you can set a GraphicsUnit in the PageUnit property, and the calibration for that unit in the PageScale property. (You can retrieve the PageScale using the DpiX and DpiY properties.)

You can also define a clipping region for the surface. The Clip property allows you to specify a Region to which the drawing is clipped. This can be a simple, complex, hollow or disconnected shape. You can also query the ClipBounds—the minimum containing rectangle of the clip region—the VisibleClipBounds, which is the intersection of the ClipBounds for the Graphics surface, and the current clip rectangle for the window to which the Graphics object is bound (if appropriate).

```
public sealed class Graphics : MarshalByRefObject : IDisposable {
// Public Instance Properties
   public Region Clip{set; get; }
   public RectangleF ClipBounds{get; }
   public CompositingMode CompositingMode{set; get; }
   public CompositingQuality CompositingQuality{set; get; }
   public float DpiX{get; }
   public float DpiY{get; }
   public InterpolationMode InterpolationMode{set; get; }
   public bool IsClipEmpty{get; }
   public bool IsVisibleClipEmpty{get; }
   public float PageScale{set; get; }
   public GraphicsUnit PageUnit{set; get; }
   public PixelOffsetMode PixelOffsetMode{set; get; }
   public Point RenderingOrigin{set; get; }
   public SmoothingMode SmoothingMode{set; get; }
```

```
  public int TextContrast{set; get; }
  public TextRenderingHint TextRenderingHint{set; get; }
  public Matrix Transform{set; get; }
  public RectangleF VisibleClipBounds{get; }
// Public Static Methods
  public static Graphics FromHdc(IntPtr hdc);
  public static Graphics FromHdc(IntPtr hdc, IntPtr hdevice);
  public static Graphics FromHdcInternal(IntPtr hdc);
  public static Graphics FromHwnd(IntPtr hwnd);
  public static Graphics FromHwndInternal(IntPtr hwnd);
  public static Graphics FromImage(Image image);
  public static IntPtr GetHalftonePalette( );
// Public Instance Methods
  public void AddMetafileComment(byte[ ] data);
  public GraphicsContainer BeginContainer( );
  public GraphicsContainer BeginContainer(RectangleF dstrect, RectangleF srcrect, GraphicsUnit unit);
  public GraphicsContainer BeginContainer(Rectangle dstrect, Rectangle srcrect, GraphicsUnit unit);
  public void Clear(Color color);
  public void Dispose( );                                          // implements IDisposable
  public void DrawArc(Pen pen, int x, int y, int width, int height, int startAngle, int sweepAngle);
  public void DrawArc(Pen pen, RectangleF rect, float startAngle, float sweepAngle);
  public void DrawArc(Pen pen, Rectangle rect, float startAngle, float sweepAngle);
  public void DrawArc(Pen pen, float x, float y, float width, float height, float startAngle, float sweepAngle);
  public void DrawBezier(Pen pen, PointF pt1, PointF pt2, PointF pt3, PointF pt4);
  public void DrawBezier(Pen pen, Point pt1, Point pt2, Point pt3, Point pt4);
  public void DrawBezier(Pen pen, float x1, float y1, float x2, float y2, float x3, float y3, float x4, float y4);
  public void DrawBeziers(Pen pen, Point[ ] points);
  public void DrawBeziers(Pen pen, PointF[ ] points);
  public void DrawClosedCurve(Pen pen, Point[ ] points);
  public void DrawClosedCurve(Pen pen, Point[ ] points, float tension, System.Drawing.Drawing2D.FillMode fillmode);
  public void DrawClosedCurve(Pen pen, PointF[ ] points);
  public void DrawClosedCurve(Pen pen, PointF[ ] points, float tension, System.Drawing.Drawing2D.FillMode fillmode);
  public void DrawCurve(Pen pen, Point[ ] points);
  public void DrawCurve(Pen pen, Point[ ] points, int offset, int numberOfSegments, float tension);
  public void DrawCurve(Pen pen, Point[ ] points, float tension);
  public void DrawCurve(Pen pen, PointF[ ] points);
  public void DrawCurve(Pen pen, PointF[ ] points, int offset, int numberOfSegments);
  public void DrawCurve(Pen pen, PointF[ ] points, int offset, int numberOfSegments, float tension);
  public void DrawCurve(Pen pen, PointF[ ] points, float tension);
  public void DrawEllipse(Pen pen, int x, int y, int width, int height);
  public void DrawEllipse(Pen pen, Rectangle rect);
  public void DrawEllipse(Pen pen, RectangleF rect);
  public void DrawEllipse(Pen pen, float x, float y, float width, float height);
  public void DrawIcon(Icon icon, int x, int y);
  public void DrawIcon(Icon icon, Rectangle targetRect);
  public void DrawIconUnstretched(Icon icon, Rectangle targetRect);
  public void DrawImage(Image image, int x, int y);
  public void DrawImage(Image image, int x, int y, int width, int height);
  public void DrawImage(Image image, int x, int y, Rectangle srcRect, GraphicsUnit srcUnit);
  public void DrawImage(Image image, Point point);
  public void DrawImage(Image image, Point[ ] destPoints);
  public void DrawImage(Image image, Point[ ] destPoints, Rectangle srcRect, GraphicsUnit srcUnit);
```

```
public void DrawImage(Image image, Point[ ] destPoints, Rectangle srcRect, GraphicsUnit srcUnit,
    System.Drawing.Imaging.ImageAttributes imageAttr);
public void DrawImage(Image image, Point[ ] destPoints, Rectangle srcRect, GraphicsUnit srcUnit,
    System.Drawing.Imaging.ImageAttributes imageAttr, DrawImageAbort callback);
public void DrawImage(Image image, Point[ ] destPoints, Rectangle srcRect, GraphicsUnit srcUnit,
    System.Drawing.Imaging.ImageAttributes imageAttr, DrawImageAbort callback, int callbackData);
public void DrawImage(Image image, PointF point);
public void DrawImage(Image image, PointF[ ] destPoints);
public void DrawImage(Image image, PointF[ ] destPoints, RectangleF srcRect, GraphicsUnit srcUnit);
public void DrawImage(Image image, PointF[ ] destPoints, RectangleF srcRect, GraphicsUnit srcUnit,
    System.Drawing.Imaging.ImageAttributes imageAttr);
public void DrawImage(Image image, PointF[ ] destPoints, RectangleF srcRect, GraphicsUnit srcUnit,
    System.Drawing.Imaging.ImageAttributes imageAttr, DrawImageAbort callback);
public void DrawImage(Image image, PointF[ ] destPoints, RectangleF srcRect, GraphicsUnit srcUnit,
    System.Drawing.Imaging.ImageAttributes imageAttr, DrawImageAbort callback, int callbackData);
public void DrawImage(Image image, Rectangle rect);
public void DrawImage(Image image, RectangleF rect);
public void DrawImage(Image image, RectangleF destRect, RectangleF srcRect, GraphicsUnit srcUnit);
public void DrawImage(Image image, Rectangle destRect, int srcX, int srcY, int srcWidth, int srcHeight,
    GraphicsUnit srcUnit);
public void DrawImage(Image image, Rectangle destRect, int srcX, int srcY, int srcWidth, int srcHeight,
    GraphicsUnit srcUnit, System.Drawing.Imaging.ImageAttributes imageAttr);
public void DrawImage(Image image, Rectangle destRect, int srcX, int srcY, int srcWidth, int srcHeight,
    GraphicsUnit srcUnit, System.Drawing.Imaging.ImageAttributes imageAttr, DrawImageAbort callback);
public void DrawImage(Image image, Rectangle destRect, int srcX, int srcY, int srcWidth, int srcHeight,
    GraphicsUnit srcUnit, System.Drawing.Imaging.ImageAttributes imageAttrs, DrawImageAbort callback,
    IntPtr callbackData);
public void DrawImage(Image image, Rectangle destRect, Rectangle srcRect, GraphicsUnit srcUnit);
public void DrawImage(Image image, Rectangle destRect, float srcX, float srcY, float srcWidth, float srcHeight,
    GraphicsUnit srcUnit);
public void DrawImage(Image image, Rectangle destRect, float srcX, float srcY, float srcWidth, float srcHeight,
    GraphicsUnit srcUnit, System.Drawing.Imaging.ImageAttributes imageAttrs);
public void DrawImage(Image image, Rectangle destRect, float srcX, float srcY, float srcWidth, float srcHeight,
    GraphicsUnit srcUnit, System.Drawing.Imaging.ImageAttributes imageAttrs, DrawImageAbort callback);
public void DrawImage(Image image, Rectangle destRect, float srcX, float srcY, float srcWidth, float srcHeight,
    GraphicsUnit srcUnit, System.Drawing.Imaging.ImageAttributes imageAttrs, DrawImageAbort callback,
    IntPtr callbackData);
public void DrawImage(Image image, float x, float y);
public void DrawImage(Image image, float x, float y, RectangleF srcRect, GraphicsUnit srcUnit);
public void DrawImage(Image image, float x, float y, float width, float height);
public void DrawImageUnscaled(Image image, int x, int y);
public void DrawImageUnscaled(Image image, int x, int y, int width, int height);
public void DrawImageUnscaled(Image image, Point point);
public void DrawImageUnscaled(Image image, Rectangle rect);
public void DrawLine(Pen pen, int x1, int y1, int x2, int y2);
public void DrawLine(Pen pen, PointF pt1, PointF pt2);
public void DrawLine(Pen pen, Point pt1, Point pt2);
public void DrawLine(Pen pen, float x1, float y1, float x2, float y2);
public void DrawLines(Pen pen, Point[ ] points);
public void DrawLines(Pen pen, PointF[ ] points);
public void DrawPath(Pen pen, System.Drawing.Drawing2D.GraphicsPath path);
public void DrawPie(Pen pen, int x, int y, int width, int height, int startAngle, int sweepAngle);
public void DrawPie(Pen pen, RectangleF rect, float startAngle, float sweepAngle);
```

```
public void DrawPie(Pen pen, Rectangle rect, float startAngle, float sweepAngle);
public void DrawPie(Pen pen, float x, float y, float width, float height, float startAngle, float sweepAngle);
public void DrawPolygon(Pen pen, Point[ ] points);
public void DrawPolygon(Pen pen, PointF[ ] points);
public void DrawRectangle(Pen pen, int x, int y, int width, int height);
public void DrawRectangle(Pen pen, Rectangle rect);
public void DrawRectangle(Pen pen, float x, float y, float width, float height);
public void DrawRectangles(Pen pen, Rectangle[ ] rects);
public void DrawRectangles(Pen pen, RectangleF[ ] rects);
public void DrawString(string s, Font font, Brush brush, PointF point);
public void DrawString(string s, Font font, Brush brush, PointF point, StringFormat format);
public void DrawString(string s, Font font, Brush brush, RectangleF layoutRectangle);
public void DrawString(string s, Font font, Brush brush, RectangleF layoutRectangle, StringFormat format);
public void DrawString(string s, Font font, Brush brush, float x, float y);
public void DrawString(string s, Font font, Brush brush, float x, float y, StringFormat format);
public void EndContainer(System.Drawing.Drawing2D.GraphicsContainer container);
public void EnumerateMetafile(System.Drawing.Imaging.Metafile metafile, Point[ ] destPoints,
  EnumerateMetafileProc callback);
public void EnumerateMetafile(System.Drawing.Imaging.Metafile metafile, Point[ ] destPoints,
  EnumerateMetafileProc callback, IntPtr callbackData);
public void EnumerateMetafile(System.Drawing.Imaging.Metafile metafile, Point[ ] destPoints,
  EnumerateMetafileProc callback, IntPtr callbackData, System.Drawing.Imaging.ImageAttributes imageAttr);
public void EnumerateMetafile(System.Drawing.Imaging.Metafile metafile, Point[ ] destPoints,
  Rectangle srcRect, GraphicsUnit srcUnit, EnumerateMetafileProc callback);
public void EnumerateMetafile(System.Drawing.Imaging.Metafile metafile, Point[ ] destPoints,
  Rectangle srcRect, GraphicsUnit srcUnit, EnumerateMetafileProc callback, IntPtr callbackData);
public void EnumerateMetafile(System.Drawing.Imaging.Metafile metafile, Point[ ] destPoints,
  Rectangle srcRect, GraphicsUnit srcUnit, EnumerateMetafileProc callback, IntPtr callbackData,
  System.Drawing.Imaging.ImageAttributes imageAttr);
public void EnumerateMetafile(System.Drawing.Imaging.Metafile metafile, Point destPoint,
  EnumerateMetafileProc callback);
public void EnumerateMetafile(System.Drawing.Imaging.Metafile metafile, Point destPoint,
  EnumerateMetafileProc callback, IntPtr callbackData);
public void EnumerateMetafile(System.Drawing.Imaging.Metafile metafile, Point destPoint,
  EnumerateMetafileProc callback, IntPtr callbackData, System.Drawing.Imaging.ImageAttributes imageAttr);
public void EnumerateMetafile(System.Drawing.Imaging.Metafile metafile, PointF[ ] destPoints,
  EnumerateMetafileProc callback);
public void EnumerateMetafile(System.Drawing.Imaging.Metafile metafile, PointF[ ] destPoints,
  EnumerateMetafileProc callback, IntPtr callbackData);
public void EnumerateMetafile(System.Drawing.Imaging.Metafile metafile, PointF[ ] destPoints,
  EnumerateMetafileProc callback, IntPtr callbackData, System.Drawing.Imaging.ImageAttributes imageAttr);
public void EnumerateMetafile(System.Drawing.Imaging.Metafile metafile, PointF[ ] destPoints, RectangleF srcRect,
  GraphicsUnit srcUnit, EnumerateMetafileProc callback);
public void EnumerateMetafile(System.Drawing.Imaging.Metafile metafile, PointF[ ] destPoints, RectangleF srcRect,
  GraphicsUnit srcUnit, EnumerateMetafileProc callback, IntPtr callbackData);
public void EnumerateMetafile(System.Drawing.Imaging.Metafile metafile, PointF[ ] destPoints, RectangleF srcRect,
  GraphicsUnit unit, EnumerateMetafileProc callback, IntPtr callbackData,
  System.Drawing.Imaging.ImageAttributes imageAttr);
public void EnumerateMetafile(System.Drawing.Imaging.Metafile metafile, PointF destPoint,
  EnumerateMetafileProc callback);
public void EnumerateMetafile(System.Drawing.Imaging.Metafile metafile, PointF destPoint,
  EnumerateMetafileProc callback, IntPtr callbackData);
```

```
public void EnumerateMetafile(System.Drawing.Imaging.Metafile metafile, PointF destPoint,
    EnumerateMetafileProc callback, IntPtr callbackData, System.Drawing.Imaging.ImageAttributes imageAttr);
public void EnumerateMetafile(System.Drawing.Imaging.Metafile metafile, PointF destPoint, RectangleF srcRect,
    GraphicsUnit srcUnit, EnumerateMetafileProc callback);
public void EnumerateMetafile(System.Drawing.Imaging.Metafile metafile, PointF destPoint, RectangleF srcRect,
    GraphicsUnit srcUnit, EnumerateMetafileProc callback, IntPtr callbackData);
public void EnumerateMetafile(System.Drawing.Imaging.Metafile metafile, PointF destPoint, RectangleF srcRect,
    GraphicsUnit unit, EnumerateMetafileProc callback, IntPtr callbackData,
    System.Drawing.Imaging.ImageAttributes imageAttr);
public void EnumerateMetafile(System.Drawing.Imaging.Metafile metafile, Point destPoint, Rectangle srcRect,
    GraphicsUnit srcUnit, EnumerateMetafileProc callback);
public void EnumerateMetafile(System.Drawing.Imaging.Metafile metafile, Point destPoint, Rectangle srcRect,
    GraphicsUnit srcUnit, EnumerateMetafileProc callback, IntPtr callbackData);
public void EnumerateMetafile(System.Drawing.Imaging.Metafile metafile, Point destPoint, Rectangle srcRect,
    GraphicsUnit unit, EnumerateMetafileProc callback, IntPtr callbackData,
    System.Drawing.Imaging.ImageAttributes imageAttr);
public void EnumerateMetafile(System.Drawing.Imaging.Metafile metafile, Rectangle destRect,
    EnumerateMetafileProc callback);
public void EnumerateMetafile(System.Drawing.Imaging.Metafile metafile, Rectangle destRect,
    EnumerateMetafileProc callback, IntPtr callbackData);
public void EnumerateMetafile(System.Drawing.Imaging.Metafile metafile, Rectangle destRect,
    EnumerateMetafileProc callback, IntPtr callbackData, System.Drawing.Imaging.ImageAttributes imageAttr);
public void EnumerateMetafile(System.Drawing.Imaging.Metafile metafile, RectangleF destRect,
    EnumerateMetafileProc callback);
public void EnumerateMetafile(System.Drawing.Imaging.Metafile metafile, RectangleF destRect,
    EnumerateMetafileProc callback, IntPtr callbackData);
public void EnumerateMetafile(System.Drawing.Imaging.Metafile metafile, RectangleF destRect,
    EnumerateMetafileProc callback, IntPtr callbackData, System.Drawing.Imaging.ImageAttributes imageAttr);
public void EnumerateMetafile(System.Drawing.Imaging.Metafile metafile, RectangleF destRect, RectangleF srcRect,
    GraphicsUnit srcUnit, EnumerateMetafileProc callback);
public void EnumerateMetafile(System.Drawing.Imaging.Metafile metafile, RectangleF destRect, RectangleF srcRect,
    GraphicsUnit srcUnit, EnumerateMetafileProc callback, IntPtr callbackData);
public void EnumerateMetafile(System.Drawing.Imaging.Metafile metafile, RectangleF destRect, RectangleF srcRect,
    GraphicsUnit unit, EnumerateMetafileProc callback, IntPtr callbackData,
    System.Drawing.Imaging.ImageAttributes imageAttr);
public void EnumerateMetafile(System.Drawing.Imaging.Metafile metafile, Rectangle destRect, Rectangle srcRect,
    GraphicsUnit srcUnit, EnumerateMetafileProc callback);
public void EnumerateMetafile(System.Drawing.Imaging.Metafile metafile, Rectangle destRect, Rectangle srcRect,
    GraphicsUnit srcUnit, EnumerateMetafileProc callback, IntPtr callbackData);
public void EnumerateMetafile(System.Drawing.Imaging.Metafile metafile, Rectangle destRect, Rectangle srcRect,
    GraphicsUnit unit, EnumerateMetafileProc callback, IntPtr callbackData,
    System.Drawing.Imaging.ImageAttributes imageAttr);
public void ExcludeClip(Rectangle rect);
public void ExcludeClip(Region region);
public void FillClosedCurve(Brush brush, Point[ ] points);
public void FillClosedCurve(Brush brush, Point[ ] points, System.Drawing.Drawing2D.FillMode fillmode);
public void FillClosedCurve(Brush brush, Point[ ] points, System.Drawing.Drawing2D.FillMode fillmode, float tension);
public void FillClosedCurve(Brush brush, PointF[ ] points);
public void FillClosedCurve(Brush brush, PointF[ ] points, System.Drawing.Drawing2D.FillMode fillmode);
public void FillClosedCurve(Brush brush, PointF[ ] points, System.Drawing.Drawing2D.FillMode fillmode, float tension);
public void FillEllipse(Brush brush, int x, int y, int width, int height);
public void FillEllipse(Brush brush, Rectangle rect);
public void FillEllipse(Brush brush, RectangleF rect);
```

```
public void FillEllipse(Brush brush, float x, float y, float width, float height);
public void FillPath(Brush brush, System.Drawing.Drawing2D.GraphicsPath path);
public void FillPie(Brush brush, int x, int y, int width, int height, int startAngle, int sweepAngle);
public void FillPie(Brush brush, Rectangle rect, float startAngle, float sweepAngle);
public void FillPie(Brush brush, float x, float y, float width, float height, float startAngle, float sweepAngle);
public void FillPolygon(Brush brush, Point[ ] points);
public void FillPolygon(Brush brush, Point[ ] points, System.Drawing.Drawing2D.FillMode fillMode);
public void FillPolygon(Brush brush, PointF[ ] points);
public void FillPolygon(Brush brush, PointF[ ] points, System.Drawing.Drawing2D.FillMode fillMode);
public void FillRectangle(Brush brush, int x, int y, int width, int height);
public void FillRectangle(Brush brush, Rectangle rect);
public void FillRectangle(Brush brush, RectangleF rect);
public void FillRectangle(Brush brush, float x, float y, float width, float height);
public void FillRectangles(Brush brush, Rectangle[ ] rects);
public void FillRectangles(Brush brush, RectangleF[ ] rects);
public void FillRegion(Brush brush, Region region);
public void Flush( );
public void Flush(System.Drawing.Drawing2D.FlushIntention intention);
public IntPtr GetHdc( );
public Color GetNearestColor(Color color);
public void IntersectClip(Rectangle rect);
public void IntersectClip(RectangleF rect);
public void IntersectClip(Region region);
public bool IsVisible(int x, int y);
public bool IsVisible(int x, int y, int width, int height);
public bool IsVisible(Point point);
public bool IsVisible(PointF point);
public bool IsVisible(Rectangle rect);
public bool IsVisible(RectangleF rect);
public bool IsVisible(float x, float y);
public bool IsVisible(float x, float y, float width, float height);
public Region[ ] MeasureCharacterRanges(string text, Font font, RectangleF layoutRect, StringFormat stringFormat);
public SizeF MeasureString(string text, Font font);
public SizeF MeasureString(string text, Font font, int width);
public SizeF MeasureString(string text, Font font, int width, StringFormat format);
public SizeF MeasureString(string text, Font font, PointF origin, StringFormat stringFormat);
public SizeF MeasureString(string text, Font font, SizeF layoutArea);
public SizeF MeasureString(string text, Font font, SizeF layoutArea, StringFormat stringFormat);
public SizeF MeasureString(string text, Font font, SizeF layoutArea, StringFormat stringFormat, out int charactersFitted,
    out int linesFilled);
public void MultiplyTransform(System.Drawing.Drawing2D.Matrix matrix);
public void MultiplyTransform(System.Drawing.Drawing2D.Matrix matrix,
    System.Drawing.Drawing2D.MatrixOrder order);
public void ReleaseHdc(IntPtr hdc);
public void ReleaseHdcInternal(IntPtr hdc);
public void ResetClip( );
public void ResetTransform( );
public void Restore(System.Drawing.Drawing2D.GraphicsState gstate);
public void RotateTransform(float angle);
public void RotateTransform(float angle, System.Drawing.Drawing2D.MatrixOrder order);
public GraphicsState Save( );
public void ScaleTransform(float sx, float sy);
```

Drawing

```
  public void ScaleTransform(float sx, float sy, System.Drawing.Drawing2D.MatrixOrder order);
  public void SetClip(Graphics g);
  public void SetClip(Graphics g, System.Drawing.Drawing2D.CombineMode combineMode);
  public void SetClip(System.Drawing.Drawing2D.GraphicsPath path);
  public void SetClip(System.Drawing.Drawing2D.GraphicsPath path,
    System.Drawing.Drawing2D.CombineMode combineMode);
  public void SetClip(Rectangle rect);
  public void SetClip(Rectangle rect, System.Drawing.Drawing2D.CombineMode combineMode);
  public void SetClip(RectangleF rect);
  public void SetClip(RectangleF rect, System.Drawing.Drawing2D.CombineMode combineMode);
  public void SetClip(Region region, System.Drawing.Drawing2D.CombineMode combineMode);
  public void TransformPoints(System.Drawing.Drawing2D.CoordinateSpace destSpace,
    System.Drawing.Drawing2D.CoordinateSpace srcSpace, Point[ ] pts);
  public void TransformPoints(System.Drawing.Drawing2D.CoordinateSpace destSpace,
    System.Drawing.Drawing2D.CoordinateSpace srcSpace, PointF[ ] pts);
  public void TranslateClip(int dx, int dy);
  public void TranslateClip(float dx, float dy);
  public void TranslateTransform(float dx, float dy);
  public void TranslateTransform(float dx, float dy, System.Drawing.Drawing2D.MatrixOrder order);
// Protected Instance Methods
  protected override void Finalize( );                                          // overrides object
}
```

Hierarchy System.Object → System.MarshalByRefObject → Graphics(System.IDisposable)

Returned By System.Drawing.Design.PaintValueEventArgs.Graphics, System.Drawing.Printing.PrintController.OnStartPage( ), System.Drawing.Printing.PrinterSettings.CreateMeasurementGraphics( ), System.Drawing.Printing.PrintPageEventArgs.Graphics, System.Windows.Forms.Control.CreateGraphics( ), System.Windows.Forms.DrawItemEventArgs.Graphics, System.Windows.Forms.MeasureItemEventArgs.Graphics, System.Windows.Forms.PaintEventArgs.Graphics

Passed To Multiple types

Graphics.DrawImageAbort **serializable**

System.Drawing (system.drawing.dll) **delegate**

This is the delegate for the callback used when your DrawImage method should abort. (See Graphics for more information.)

```
public delegate bool Graphics.DrawImageAbort(IntPtr callbackdata);
```

Graphics.EnumerateMetafileProc **serializable**

System.Drawing (system.drawing.dll) **delegate**

This delegate defines the callback used in the Graphics.EnumerateMetafile( ) method.

```
public delegate bool Graphics.EnumerateMetafileProc(System.Drawing.Imaging.EmfPlusRecordType recordType,
    int flags, int dataSize, IntPtr data, System.Drawing.Imaging.PlayRecordCallback callbackData);
```

GraphicsUnit **serializable**

System.Drawing (system.drawing.dll) enum

This enumeration determines the units used for a graphic measurement. The framework automatically provides translation between units to allow you to use the most convenient scheme for your particular application.

```
public enum GraphicsUnit {
  World = 0,
  Display = 1,
  Pixel = 2,
  Point = 3,
  Inch = 4,
  Document = 5,
  Millimeter = 6
}
```

Hierarchy System.Object → System.ValueType → System.Enum(System.IComparable, System.IFormattable, System.IConvertible) → GraphicsUnit

Returned By Font.Unit, Graphics.PageUnit

Passed To Font.Font( ), Graphics.{BeginContainer( ), DrawImage( ), EnumerateMetafile( ), PageUnit}, Image.GetBounds( )

Icon **serializable, marshal by reference, disposable**

System.Drawing (system.drawing.dll) sealed class

This class, which is not derived from the Image class (whatever may be implied by parts of the documentation shipped with VS.NET 2002!), represents a small, transparent bitmap—a Win32 icon, in fact. As such, it intrinsically supports a variety of different resolutions and bit-depths.

As with Bitmap, this is a resource-based class, and therefore you should carefully manage its lifetime, calling Dispose( ) when it is no longer needed, to avoid leaking system resources.

You can construct an Icon from a file, or from another Icon optionally looking for the image that best matches a particular resolution.

The FromHandle( ) static method, and the Handle property allow you translate to and from native icon handles in interop scenarios. (Note that you must not delete the handle retrieved from this property as it is the original, not a copy)

Finally, you can translate the Icon to a Bitmap with the ToBitmap( ) method.

Note that you have very little control over the particular image, resolution, and bit-depth that is ultimately rendered by the Graphics.DrawIcon( ) method. If you need that degree of control, then a Bitmap and its Bitmap.MakeTransparent( ) method might be a better choice. The icon is something of a hang-over from the days when bitmaps didn't have alpha channels.

```
public sealed class Icon : MarshalByRefObject : System.Runtime.Serialization.ISerializable, ICloneable, IDisposable {
// Public Constructors
   public Icon(Icon original, int width, int height);
   public Icon(Icon original, Size size);
   public Icon(System.IO.Stream stream);
   public Icon(System.IO.Stream stream, int width, int height);
   public Icon(string fileName);
   public Icon(Type type, string resource);
// Public Instance Properties
   public IntPtr Handle{get; }
   public int Height{get; }
   public Size Size{get; }
   public int Width{get; }
// Public Static Methods
   public static Icon FromHandle(IntPtr handle);
// Public Instance Methods
   public object Clone( );                                          // implements ICloneable
   public void Dispose( );                                          // implements IDisposable
   public void Save(System.IO.Stream outputStream);
   public Bitmap ToBitmap( );
   public override string ToString( );                              // overrides object
// Protected Instance Methods
   protected override void Finalize( );                             // overrides object
}
```

Hierarchy System.Object → System.MarshalByRefObject → Icon(System.Runtime.Serialization.ISerializable, System.ICloneable, System.IDisposable)

Returned By Multiple types

Passed To Graphics.{DrawIcon( ), DrawIconUnstretched( )}, System.Windows.Forms.Design.ComponentEditorPage.Icon, System.Windows.Forms.ErrorProvider.Icon, System.Windows.Forms.Form.Icon, System.Windows.Forms.ImageCollection.Add( ), System.Windows.Forms.NotifyIcon.Icon, System.Windows.Forms.PrintPreviewDialog.Icon, System.Windows.Forms.StatusBarPanel.Icon

IconConverter

System.Drawing (system.drawing.dll) class

This class, derived from System.ComponentModel.ExpandableObjectConverter (a kind of TypeConverter), is used to convert icons to and from other types—specifically, it can convert to strings and byte arrays, for persistence and design-time scenarios.

```
public class IconConverter : System.ComponentModel.ExpandableObjectConverter {
// Public Constructors
   public IconConverter( );
// Public Instance Methods
   public override bool CanConvertFrom(System.ComponentModel.ITypeDescriptorContext context,
      Type sourceType);                        // overrides System.ComponentModel.TypeConverter
   public override bool CanConvertTo(System.ComponentModel.ITypeDescriptorContext context,
      Type destinationType);                   // overrides System.ComponentModel.TypeConverter
```

```
public override object ConvertFrom(System.ComponentModel.ITypeDescriptorContext context,
    System.Globalization.CultureInfo culture, object value);          // overrides System.ComponentModel.TypeConverter
public override object ConvertTo(System.ComponentModel.ITypeDescriptorContext context,
    System.Globalization.CultureInfo culture, object value,
    Type destinationType);                                              // overrides System.ComponentModel.TypeConverter
}
```

Hierarchy System.Object → System.ComponentModel.TypeConverter → System.ComponentModel.ExpandableObjectConverter → IconConverter

Image **serializable, marshal by reference, disposable**

System.Drawing (system.drawing.dll) abstract class

This abstract class is the base for Bitmap and System.Drawing.Imaging.Metafile. Microsoft's documentation claims that it is also the base for Icon, but this is not in fact the case in the first release of the framework.

It serves to define a drawing that has its own Page coordinate space, including a Size, HorizontalResolution, and VerticalResolution. It also supports multiframe images, in a variety of different dimensions such as time and resolution, as defined in the System.Drawing.Imaging.FrameDimension class.

Images can be drawn using the Graphics.DrawImage( ) method.

```
public abstract class Image : MarshalByRefObject : System.Runtime.Serialization.ISerializable, ICloneable, IDisposable {
// Public Instance Properties
   public int Flags{get; }
   public Guid[ ] FrameDimensionsList{get; }
   public int Height{get; }
   public float HorizontalResolution{get; }
   public ColorPalette Palette{set; get; }
   public SizeF PhysicalDimension{get; }
   public PixelFormat PixelFormat{get; }
   public int[ ] PropertyIdList{get; }
   public PropertyItem[ ] PropertyItems{get; }
   public ImageFormat RawFormat{get; }
   public Size Size{get; }
   public float VerticalResolution{get; }
   public int Width{get; }
// Public Static Methods
   public static Image FromFile(string filename);
   public static Image FromFile(string filename, bool useEmbeddedColorManagement);
   public static Bitmap FromHbitmap(IntPtr hbitmap);
   public static Bitmap FromHbitmap(IntPtr hbitmap, IntPtr hpalette);
   public static Image FromStream(System.IO.Stream stream);
   public static Image FromStream(System.IO.Stream stream, bool useEmbeddedColorManagement);
   public static int GetPixelFormatSize(System.Drawing.Imaging.PixelFormat pixfmt);
   public static bool IsAlphaPixelFormat(System.Drawing.Imaging.PixelFormat pixfmt);
   public static bool IsCanonicalPixelFormat(System.Drawing.Imaging.PixelFormat pixfmt);
   public static bool IsExtendedPixelFormat(System.Drawing.Imaging.PixelFormat pixfmt);
// Public Instance Methods
   public object Clone( );                                            // implements ICloneable
   public void Dispose( );                                            // implements IDisposable
```

```
    public RectangleF GetBounds(ref GraphicsUnit pageUnit);
    public EncoderParameters GetEncoderParameterList(Guid encoder);
    public int GetFrameCount(System.Drawing.Imaging.FrameDimension dimension);
    public PropertyItem GetPropertyItem(int propid);
    public Image GetThumbnailImage(int thumbWidth, int thumbHeight, GetThumbnailImageAbort callback,
       IntPtr callbackData);
    public void RemovePropertyItem(int propid);
    public void RotateFlip(RotateFlipType rotateFlipType);
    public void Save(System.IO.Stream stream, System.Drawing.Imaging.ImageCodecInfo encoder,
       System.Drawing.Imaging.EncoderParameters encoderParams);
    public void Save(System.IO.Stream stream, System.Drawing.Imaging.ImageFormat format);
    public void Save(string filename);
    public void Save(string filename, System.Drawing.Imaging.ImageCodecInfo encoder,
       System.Drawing.Imaging.EncoderParameters encoderParams);
    public void Save(string filename, System.Drawing.Imaging.ImageFormat format);
    public void SaveAdd(System.Drawing.Imaging.EncoderParameters encoderParams);
    public void SaveAdd(Image image, System.Drawing.Imaging.EncoderParameters encoderParams);
    public int SelectActiveFrame(System.Drawing.Imaging.FrameDimension dimension, int frameIndex);
    public void SetPropertyItem(System.Drawing.Imaging.PropertyItem propitem);
// Protected Instance Methods
    protected virtual void Dispose(bool disposing);
    protected override void Finalize();                                          // overrides object
}
```

Hierarchy System.Object → System.MarshalByRefObject → Image(System.Runtime.Serialization.ISerializable, System.ICloneable, System.IDisposable)

Subclasses Bitmap, System.Drawing.Imaging.Metafile

Returned By Multiple types

Passed To Multiple types

Image.GetThumbnailImageAbort serializable

System.Drawing (system.drawing.dll) delegate

This is a delegate for the callback that is used to abort the Image.GetThumbnailImage() method.

```
public delegate bool Image.GetThumbnailImageAbort();
```

ImageAnimator

System.Drawing (system.drawing.dll) sealed class

This class provides static methods to support the animation of an Image class that contains multiple frames in the System.Drawing.Imaging.FrameDimension.Time dimension: a complex way of saying a time-based image sequence.

The Animate() method takes an image and a callback delegate, which is called whenever a new frame is needed. You can then paint the image on the appropriate Graphics surface at that time. StopAnimate() brings the animation to a halt.

There is a CanAnimate() method that tells you whether a particular Image has multiple frames in the time dimension, and an UpdateFrames() function that advances to the next frame immediately.

This may seem like a complex way of allowing you to render an animated GIF (not forgetting your UniSys licensing, of course), but it means the image framework can provide much more complex animation schemes than that—key frame–based vector graphics animation for a cartoon, say, or on-the-fly interpolation of bitmap frames. And if you do just want basic drop-in-and-go animation control, the System.Windows.Forms.PictureBox component will do the job.

```
public sealed class ImageAnimator {
// Public Static Methods
   public static void Animate(Image image, EventHandler onFrameChangedHandler);
   public static bool CanAnimate(Image image);
   public static void StopAnimate(Image image, EventHandler onFrameChangedHandler);
   public static void UpdateFrames( );
   public static void UpdateFrames(Image image);
}
```

ImageConverter

System.Drawing (system.drawing.dll) class

This class, derived from System.ComponentModel.TypeConverter, is used to transform Image classes to and from other types, specifically strings, and byte arrays in persistence and design-time scenarios.

```
public class ImageConverter : System.ComponentModel.TypeConverter {
// Public Constructors
   public ImageConverter( );
// Public Instance Methods
   public override bool CanConvertFrom(System.ComponentModel.ITypeDescriptorContext context,
      Type sourceType);                         // overrides System.ComponentModel.TypeConverter
   public override bool CanConvertTo(System.ComponentModel.ITypeDescriptorContext context,
      Type destinationType);                    // overrides System.ComponentModel.TypeConverter
   public override object ConvertFrom(System.ComponentModel.ITypeDescriptorContext context,
      System.Globalization.CultureInfo culture, object value);  // overrides System.ComponentModel.TypeConverter
   public override object ConvertTo(System.ComponentModel.ITypeDescriptorContext context,
     System.Globalization.CultureInfo culture, object value,
      Type destinationType);                    // overrides System.ComponentModel.TypeConverter
   public override PropertyDescriptorCollection GetProperties(System.ComponentModel.ITypeDescriptorContext context,
      object value, Attribute[ ] attributes);   // overrides System.ComponentModel.TypeConverter
   public override bool GetPropertiesSupported(
      System.ComponentModel.ITypeDescriptorContext context);  // overrides System.ComponentModel.TypeConverter
}
```

Hierarchy System.Object → System.ComponentModel.TypeConverter → ImageConverter

Drawing

ImageFormatConverter

System.Drawing (system.drawing.dll) **class**

This class, derived from System.ComponentModel.TypeConverter is used to transform System.Drawing.Imaging.ImageFormat objects to and from other types, specifically strings, for persistence and design-time scenarios.

```
public class ImageFormatConverter : System.ComponentModel.TypeConverter {
// Public Constructors
   public ImageFormatConverter( );
// Public Instance Methods
   public override bool CanConvertFrom( System.ComponentModel.ITypeDescriptorContext context,
      Type sourceType);                       // overrides System.ComponentModel.TypeConverter
   public override bool CanConvertTo(System.ComponentModel.ITypeDescriptorContext context,
      Type destinationType);                  // overrides System.ComponentModel.TypeConverter
   public override object ConvertFrom(System.ComponentModel.ITypeDescriptorContext context,
      System.Globalization.CultureInfo culture, object value);  // overrides System.ComponentModel.TypeConverter
   public override object ConvertTo(System.ComponentModel.ITypeDescriptorContext context,
      System.Globalization.CultureInfo culture, object value,
      Type destinationType);                  // overrides System.ComponentModel.TypeConverter
   public override StandardValuesCollection GetStandardValues(
      System.ComponentModel.ITypeDescriptorContext context);  // overrides System.ComponentModel.TypeConverter
   public override bool GetStandardValuesSupported(
      System.ComponentModel.ITypeDescriptorContext context);  // overrides System.ComponentModel.TypeConverter
}
```

Hierarchy System.Object → System.ComponentModel.TypeConverter → ImageFormatConverter

KnownColor **serializable**

System.Drawing (system.drawing.dll) **enum**

This enumeration contains a list of all the well-known colors. This includes both the web colors (such as Aqua and LightSteelBlue) and the system colors (such as ControlText). It is used by such methods as Color.FromKnownColor( ) to refer to a particular Color. Note that the entries in this enumeration are, by their nature, just integers and not the actual Color values themselves.

```
public enum KnownColor {
   ActiveBorder = 1,
   ActiveCaption = 2,
   ActiveCaptionText = 3,
   AppWorkspace = 4,
   Control = 5,
   ControlDark = 6,
   ControlDarkDark = 7,
   ControlLight = 8,
   ControlLightLight = 9,
   ControlText = 10,
   Desktop = 11,
   GrayText = 12,
   Highlight = 13,
   HighlightText = 14,
   HotTrack = 15,
```

```
InactiveBorder = 16,
InactiveCaption = 17,
InactiveCaptionText = 18,
Info = 19,
InfoText = 20,
Menu = 21,
MenuText = 22,
ScrollBar = 23,
Window = 24,
WindowFrame = 25,
WindowText = 26,
Transparent = 27,
AliceBlue = 28,
AntiqueWhite = 29,
Aqua = 30,
Aquamarine = 31,
Azure = 32,
Beige = 33,
Bisque = 34,
Black = 35,
BlanchedAlmond = 36,
Blue = 37,
BlueViolet = 38,
Brown = 39,
BurlyWood = 40,
CadetBlue = 41,
Chartreuse = 42,
Chocolate = 43,
Coral = 44,
CornflowerBlue = 45,
Cornsilk = 46,
Crimson = 47,
Cyan = 48,
DarkBlue = 49,
DarkCyan = 50,
DarkGoldenrod = 51,
DarkGray = 52,
DarkGreen = 53,
DarkKhaki = 54,
DarkMagenta = 55,
DarkOliveGreen = 56,
DarkOrange = 57,
DarkOrchid = 58,
DarkRed = 59,
DarkSalmon = 60,
DarkSeaGreen = 61,
DarkSlateBlue = 62,
DarkSlateGray = 63,
DarkTurquoise = 64,
DarkViolet = 65,
DeepPink = 66,
DeepSkyBlue = 67,
```

```
DimGray = 68,
DodgerBlue = 69,
Firebrick = 70,
FloralWhite = 71,
ForestGreen = 72,
Fuchsia = 73,
Gainsboro = 74,
GhostWhite = 75,
Gold = 76,
Goldenrod = 77,
Gray = 78,
Green = 79,
GreenYellow = 80,
Honeydew = 81,
HotPink = 82,
IndianRed = 83,
Indigo = 84,
Ivory = 85,
Khaki = 86,
Lavender = 87,
LavenderBlush = 88,
LawnGreen = 89,
LemonChiffon = 90,
LightBlue = 91,
LightCoral = 92,
LightCyan = 93,
LightGoldenrodYellow = 94,
LightGray = 95,
LightGreen = 96,
LightPink = 97,
LightSalmon = 98,
LightSeaGreen = 99,
LightSkyBlue = 100,
LightSlateGray = 101,
LightSteelBlue = 102,
LightYellow = 103,
Lime = 104,
LimeGreen = 105,
Linen = 106,
Magenta = 107,
Maroon = 108,
MediumAquamarine = 109,
MediumBlue = 110,
MediumOrchid = 111,
MediumPurple = 112,
MediumSeaGreen = 113,
MediumSlateBlue = 114,
MediumSpringGreen = 115,
MediumTurquoise = 116,
MediumVioletRed = 117,
MidnightBlue = 118,
MintCream = 119,
```

```
MistyRose = 120,
Moccasin = 121,
NavajoWhite = 122,
Navy = 123,
OldLace = 124,
Olive = 125,
OliveDrab = 126,
Orange = 127,
OrangeRed = 128,
Orchid = 129,
PaleGoldenrod = 130,
PaleGreen = 131,
PaleTurquoise = 132,
PaleVioletRed = 133,
PapayaWhip = 134,
PeachPuff = 135,
Peru = 136,
Pink = 137,
Plum = 138,
PowderBlue = 139,
Purple = 140,
Red = 141,
RosyBrown = 142,
RoyalBlue = 143,
SaddleBrown = 144,
Salmon = 145,
SandyBrown = 146,
SeaGreen = 147,
SeaShell = 148,
Sienna = 149,
Silver = 150,
SkyBlue = 151,
SlateBlue = 152,
SlateGray = 153,
Snow = 154,
SpringGreen = 155,
SteelBlue = 156,
Tan = 157,
Teal = 158,
Thistle = 159,
Tomato = 160,
Turquoise = 161,
Violet = 162,
Wheat = 163,
White = 164,
WhiteSmoke = 165,
Yellow = 166,
YellowGreen = 167
}
```

Hierarchy System.Object → System.ValueType → System.Enum(System.IComparable, System.IFormattable, System.IConvertible) → KnownColor

Returned By Color.ToKnownColor( )

Passed To Color.FromKnownColor( )

Pen marshal by reference, disposable

System.Drawing (system.drawing.dll) sealed class

This class describes the kind of line that is drawn when using the Graphics.DrawXXX( ) members.

Pens are resource-based entities, and it is therefore important to manage their lifetime carefully, calling Dispose( ) when you are finished with them, to release the resource to the system.

You can construct a Pen from a Color, Brush, or (optionally) a Width. If you use a Color, the line will be a solid, uniform color. If you use a Brush, you can take advantage of specific properties to render the line with a gradient or image texture. If you do not specify a width, the default value of 1 is used.

The width of the Pen is measured in pixels and is modified by any transforms that apply during the rendering process. As a geometric line has no intrinsic width, you can also specify an Alignment property, which determines where the pixels are rendered relative to the geometric line (see System.Drawing.Drawing2D.PenAlignment for more information on this). The default is to center the pixels across this theoretical line.

You can choose how to render the beginning and end of the line by specifying the StartCap and EndCap properties. You can choose one of several different styles from the System.Drawing.Drawing2D.LineCap enumeration, including butt-ends, round-ends, and simple arrows. If the predefined styles are not suitable, you can specify a CustomStartCap or CustomEndCap with an instance of the System.Drawing.Drawing2D.CustomLineCap class. This allows you to render more complex arrows or markers. The endcap size is scaled by the line width, in addition to any transforms that may be applicable.

The Pen does not necessarily have to consist of a single, continuous stroke. You can specify one of a number of predefined dash styles, found in the System.Drawing.Drawing2D.DashStyle enumeration, or define a custom DashPattern by specifying an array of real numbers that represent the lengths of each dash segment. Note that these values are multiplied by the line width and scaled by any applicable transforms before they are used. If you wish, you can provide a DashOffset value, which determines how far along the line the dash pattern begins. You can also specify the style of the endcaps on the dash line segments using the DashCap property. This is similar to the LineCap properties for the line itself, but the System.Drawing.Drawing2D.DashCap enumeration offers a smaller set of cap styles.

In addition to the DashStyle, which determines a dash pattern along the length of the line, you can specify a CompoundArray, which specifies a pattern of parallel lines. Alternate elements in the array specify a gap-width, then a line-width, as a proportion of the whole line width. That is, a value of 0.2 in the array represents a line or gap that is 20% of the total width. Note that you are precluded from using a compound line if the Alignment property is set to PenAlignment.Inset.

Finally, if the pen is being used to render multiple line segments, you can specify the LineJoin style with one of the elements in the System.Drawing.Drawing2D.LineJoin enumeration. If you pick a mitered style, the MiterLimit property determines the point at which the join is clipped.

```
public sealed class Pen : MarshalByRefObject : System.Drawing.Internal.ISystemColorTracker, ICloneable, IDisposable {
// Public Constructors
   public Pen(Brush brush);
   public Pen(Brush brush, float width);
   public Pen(Color color);
   public Pen(Color color, float width);
// Public Instance Properties
   public PenAlignment Alignment{set; get; }
   public Brush Brush{set; get; }
   public Color Color{set; get; }
   public float[ ] CompoundArray{set; get; }
   public CustomLineCap CustomEndCap{set; get; }
   public CustomLineCap CustomStartCap{set; get; }
   public DashCap DashCap{set; get; }
   public float DashOffset{set; get; }
   public float[ ] DashPattern{set; get; }
   public DashStyle DashStyle{set; get; }
   public LineCap EndCap{set; get; }
   public LineJoin LineJoin{set; get; }
   public float MiterLimit{set; get; }
   public PenType PenType{get; }
   public LineCap StartCap{set; get; }
   public Matrix Transform{set; get; }
   public float Width{set; get; }
// Public Instance Methods
   public object Clone( );                                    // implements ICloneable
   public void Dispose( );                                    // implements IDisposable
   public void MultiplyTransform(System.Drawing.Drawing2D.Matrix matrix);
   public void MultiplyTransform(System.Drawing.Drawing2D.Matrix matrix,
      System.Drawing.Drawing2D.MatrixOrder order);
   public void ResetTransform( );
   public void RotateTransform(float angle);
   public void RotateTransform(float angle, System.Drawing.Drawing2D.MatrixOrder order);
   public void ScaleTransform(float sx, float sy);
   public void ScaleTransform(float sx, float sy, System.Drawing.Drawing2D.MatrixOrder order);
   public void SetLineCap(System.Drawing.Drawing2D.LineCap startCap, System.Drawing.Drawing2D.LineCap endCap,
      System.Drawing.Drawing2D.DashCap dashCap);
   public void TranslateTransform(float dx, float dy);
   public void TranslateTransform(float dx, float dy, System.Drawing.Drawing2D.MatrixOrder order);
// Protected Instance Methods
   protected override void Finalize( );                       // overrides object
}
```

Hierarchy System.Object → System.MarshalByRefObject → Pen(System.Drawing.Internal.ISystemColorTracker, System.ICloneable, System.IDisposable)

Returned By Multiple types

Passed To Multiple types

Pens

System.Drawing (system.drawing.dll) sealed class

This class provides a set of static properties, each of which returns a Pen with the default width (1) of the specified well-known color.

Unlike other pens, you must not Dispose() the returned object to avoid leaving a disposed object in the underlying system pens table.

```
public sealed class Pens {
// Public Static Properties
   public static Pen AliceBlue{get; }
   public static Pen AntiqueWhite{get; }
   public static Pen Aqua{get; }
   public static Pen Aquamarine{get; }
   public static Pen Azure{get; }
   public static Pen Beige{get; }
   public static Pen Bisque{get; }
   public static Pen Black{get; }
   public static Pen BlanchedAlmond{get; }
   public static Pen Blue{get; }
   public static Pen BlueViolet{get; }
   public static Pen Brown{get; }
   public static Pen BurlyWood{get; }
   public static Pen CadetBlue{get; }
   public static Pen Chartreuse{get; }
   public static Pen Chocolate{get; }
   public static Pen Coral{get; }
   public static Pen CornflowerBlue{get; }
   public static Pen Cornsilk{get; }
   public static Pen Crimson{get; }
   public static Pen Cyan{get; }
   public static Pen DarkBlue{get; }
   public static Pen DarkCyan{get; }
   public static Pen DarkGoldenrod{get; }
   public static Pen DarkGray{get; }
   public static Pen DarkGreen{get; }
   public static Pen DarkKhaki{get; }
   public static Pen DarkMagenta{get; }
   public static Pen DarkOliveGreen{get; }
   public static Pen DarkOrange{get; }
   public static Pen DarkOrchid{get; }
   public static Pen DarkRed{get; }
   public static Pen DarkSalmon{get; }
   public static Pen DarkSeaGreen{get; }
   public static Pen DarkSlateBlue{get; }
   public static Pen DarkSlateGray{get; }
   public static Pen DarkTurquoise{get; }
   public static Pen DarkViolet{get; }
   public static Pen DeepPink{get; }
   public static Pen DeepSkyBlue{get; }
   public static Pen DimGray{get; }
```

public static Pen **DodgerBlue**{get; }
public static Pen **Firebrick**{get; }
public static Pen **FloralWhite**{get; }
public static Pen **ForestGreen**{get; }
public static Pen **Fuchsia**{get; }
public static Pen **Gainsboro**{get; }
public static Pen **GhostWhite**{get; }
public static Pen **Gold**{get; }
public static Pen **Goldenrod**{get; }
public static Pen **Gray**{get; }
public static Pen **Green**{get; }
public static Pen **GreenYellow**{get; }
public static Pen **Honeydew**{get; }
public static Pen **HotPink**{get; }
public static Pen **IndianRed**{get; }
public static Pen **Indigo**{get; }
public static Pen **Ivory**{get; }
public static Pen **Khaki**{get; }
public static Pen **Lavender**{get; }
public static Pen **LavenderBlush**{get; }
public static Pen **LawnGreen**{get; }
public static Pen **LemonChiffon**{get; }
public static Pen **LightBlue**{get; }
public static Pen **LightCoral**{get; }
public static Pen **LightCyan**{get; }
public static Pen **LightGoldenrodYellow**{get; }
public static Pen **LightGray**{get; }
public static Pen **LightGreen**{get; }
public static Pen **LightPink**{get; }
public static Pen **LightSalmon**{get; }
public static Pen **LightSeaGreen**{get; }
public static Pen **LightSkyBlue**{get; }
public static Pen **LightSlateGray**{get; }
public static Pen **LightSteelBlue**{get; }
public static Pen **LightYellow**{get; }
public static Pen **Lime**{get; }
public static Pen **LimeGreen**{get; }
public static Pen **Linen**{get; }
public static Pen **Magenta**{get; }
public static Pen **Maroon**{get; }
public static Pen **MediumAquamarine**{get; }
public static Pen **MediumBlue**{get; }
public static Pen **MediumOrchid**{get; }
public static Pen **MediumPurple**{get; }
public static Pen **MediumSeaGreen**{get; }
public static Pen **MediumSlateBlue**{get; }
public static Pen **MediumSpringGreen**{get; }
public static Pen **MediumTurquoise**{get; }
public static Pen **MediumVioletRed**{get; }
public static Pen **MidnightBlue**{get; }
public static Pen **MintCream**{get; }
public static Pen **MistyRose**{get; }

```
public static Pen Moccasin{get; }
public static Pen NavajoWhite{get; }
public static Pen Navy{get; }
public static Pen OldLace{get; }
public static Pen Olive{get; }
public static Pen OliveDrab{get; }
public static Pen Orange{get; }
public static Pen OrangeRed{get; }
public static Pen Orchid{get; }
public static Pen PaleGoldenrod{get; }
public static Pen PaleGreen{get; }
public static Pen PaleTurquoise{get; }
public static Pen PaleVioletRed{get; }
public static Pen PapayaWhip{get; }
public static Pen PeachPuff{get; }
public static Pen Peru{get; }
public static Pen Pink{get; }
public static Pen Plum{get; }
public static Pen PowderBlue{get; }
public static Pen Purple{get; }
public static Pen Red{get; }
public static Pen RosyBrown{get; }
public static Pen RoyalBlue{get; }
public static Pen SaddleBrown{get; }
public static Pen Salmon{get; }
public static Pen SandyBrown{get; }
public static Pen SeaGreen{get; }
public static Pen SeaShell{get; }
public static Pen Sienna{get; }
public static Pen Silver{get; }
public static Pen SkyBlue{get; }
public static Pen SlateBlue{get; }
public static Pen SlateGray{get; }
public static Pen Snow{get; }
public static Pen SpringGreen{get; }
public static Pen SteelBlue{get; }
public static Pen Tan{get; }
public static Pen Teal{get; }
public static Pen Thistle{get; }
public static Pen Tomato{get; }
public static Pen Transparent{get; }
public static Pen Turquoise{get; }
public static Pen Violet{get; }
public static Pen Wheat{get; }
public static Pen White{get; }
public static Pen WhiteSmoke{get; }
public static Pen Yellow{get; }
public static Pen YellowGreen{get; }
}
```

Point

serializable

System.Drawing (system.drawing.dll) **struct**

This value type represents a point in a 2D coordinate system. It uses integers to define the X and Y coordinates of that point.

A point has no size in and of itself, but on a pixel-based device context, the pixels are of finite size. The point {0,0} is therefore located at the center of the pixel (0,0).

You can compare a point to another point using the standard equality operator, and add or subtract Size quantities from it. There is a conversion operator from Point to Size if required.

The PointF class is equivalent to Point but uses real values instead of integers. You can convert from PointF to Point using the Round( ), Truncate( ), and Ceiling( ) members to control the loss of precision. To go the other way, there is a conversion operator from Point to PointF.

It also provides an Empty property to represent a null point.

```
public struct Point {
// Public Constructors
   public Point(int dw);
   public Point(int x, int y);
   public Point(Size sz);
// Public Static Fields
   public static readonly Point Empty;                                    // ={X=0,Y=0}
// Public Instance Properties
   public bool IsEmpty{get; }
   public int X{set; get; }
   public int Y{set; get; }
// Public Static Methods
   public static Point Ceiling(PointF value);
   public static Point Round(PointF value);
   public static Point Truncate(PointF value);
   public static Point operator -(Point pt, Size sz);
   public static Point operator +(Point pt, Size sz);
   public static bool operator !=(Point left, Point right);
   public static bool operator ==(Point left, Point right);
   public static explicit operator Size(Point p);
   public static implicit operator PointF(Point p);
// Public Instance Methods
   public override bool Equals(object obj);                               // overrides ValueType
   public override int GetHashCode( );                                    // overrides ValueType
   public void Offset(int dx, int dy);
   public override string ToString( );                                    // overrides ValueType
}
```

Hierarchy System.Object → System.ValueType → Point

Returned By Multiple types

Passed To Multiple types

PointConverter

System.Drawing (system.drawing.dll) class

This class, derived from System.ComponentModel.TypeConverter, is used to convert between a Point and other types for persistence and design-time scenarios.

```
public class PointConverter : System.ComponentModel.TypeConverter {
// Public Constructors
   public PointConverter( );
// Public Instance Methods
   public override bool CanConvertFrom(System.ComponentModel.ITypeDescriptorContext context,
      Type sourceType);                                    // overrides System.ComponentModel.TypeConverter
   public override bool CanConvertTo(System.ComponentModel.ITypeDescriptorContext context,
      Type destinationType);                               // overrides System.ComponentModel.TypeConverter
   public override object ConvertFrom(System.ComponentModel.ITypeDescriptorContext context,
      System.Globalization.CultureInfo culture, object value);   // overrides System.ComponentModel.TypeConverter
   public override object ConvertTo(System.ComponentModel.ITypeDescriptorContext context,
      System.Globalization.CultureInfo culture, object value,
      Type destinationType);                               // overrides System.ComponentModel.TypeConverter
   public override object CreateInstance(System.ComponentModel.ITypeDescriptorContext context,
      System.Collections.IDictionary propertyValues);      // overrides System.ComponentModel.TypeConverter
   public override bool GetCreateInstanceSupported(
      System.ComponentModel.ITypeDescriptorContext context);   // overrides System.ComponentModel.TypeConverter
   public override PropertyDescriptorCollection GetProperties(System.ComponentModel.ITypeDescriptorContext context,
      object value, Attribute[ ] attributes);              // overrides System.ComponentModel.TypeConverter
   public override bool GetPropertiesSupported(
      System.ComponentModel.ITypeDescriptorContext context);   // overrides System.ComponentModel.TypeConverter
}
```

Hierarchy System.Object → System.ComponentModel.TypeConverter → PointConverter

PointF **serializable**

System.Drawing (system.drawing.dll) struct

This is a value type that represents a point in a 2D coordinate system. It uses reals to define the X and Y coordinates of that point (c.f. Point).

As with Point, a PointF {0.0, 0.0} is located at the center of the pixel (0,0). However, if you specify a point at {0.5, 0.5} and draw a single pixel at that location, the rendering engine must resolve that into something it can draw on the device's pixel array, as it will impact at least 4 adjacent pixels in that grid. The method it uses to resolve that issue is determined by various properties of the Graphics object, including PixelOffsetMode, CompositingMode, and SmoothingMode.

There are comparison operators between PointF objects, and addition and subtraction operators for Size objects (but not SizeF objects, curiously).

Conversions between PointF and Point are handled through methods and operators on the Point class.

```
public struct PointF {
// Public Constructors
   public PointF(float x, float y);
// Public Static Fields
```

```
public static readonly PointF Empty;                                    // ={X=0, Y=0}
// Public Instance Properties
  public bool IsEmpty{get; }
  public float X{set; get; }
  public float Y{set; get; }
// Public Static Methods
  public static PointF operator -(PointF pt, Size sz);
  public static PointF operator +(PointF pt, Size sz);
  public static bool operator !=(PointF left, PointF right);
  public static bool operator ==(PointF left, PointF right);
// Public Instance Methods
  public override bool Equals(object obj);                              // overrides ValueType
  public override int GetHashCode( );                                   // overrides ValueType
  public override string ToString( );                                   // overrides ValueType
}
```

Hierarchy System.Object → System.ValueType → PointF

Returned By System.Drawing.Drawing2D.GraphicsPath.{GetLastPoint( ), PathPoints}, System.Drawing.Drawing2D.PathData.Points, System.Drawing.Drawing2D.PathGradientBrush.{CenterPoint, FocusScales}, RectangleF.Location, SizeF.ToPointF( )

Passed To Multiple types

Rectangle

serializable

System.Drawing (system.drawing.dll) struct

Drawing

This value type defines a rectangular region on a 2D surface using integers. Unlike the Win32 RECT structure, the Rectangle is defined in terms of the X and Y coordinate of its top-left point (also referred to as its Location), and its Width and Height (also referred to as its Size). These properties can be both read and modified. In addition, you can read values for the Left, Top, Right, and Bottom independently, and there is a static method, FromLTRB( ), to allow you to construct a Rectangle from these values in interop/legacy situations.

As with Point, there is an equivalent RectangleF structure for real coordinates, and a set of members—Round( ), Truncate( ), and Ceiling( )—to convert from the real to the integer representation. Comparison operators are also provided, along with an Empty field to allow you to represent a null rectangle. There is no intrinsic performance advantage in using the integer version, as the drawing methods are mostly implemented in terms of the floating point structure anyway (c.f. Point/PointF)

Methods are provided to test whether a rectangle Contains( ) a Point, and whether one rectangle IntersectsWith( ) another for hit testing.

You can also manipulate the rectangle itself in various ways. There is a static member, Union( ), which returns the minimum containing rectangle of two rectangles. Then there is the member function, Intersect( ), which modifies a Rectangle such that it represents the area of intersection between itself and the rectangle supplied as its parameter.

Finally, there are methods to Offset( ) the rectangle by a fixed amount, or Inflate( ) the rectangle. There are both static and non-static versions of Inflate( ) to return a new rectangle or modify the original, respectively. You can independently control the inflation in each dimension, and the value in question is subtracted from the Location and added to the Size, leading to an overall increase of twice the supplied value in each dimension.

```
public struct Rectangle {
// Public Constructors
   public Rectangle(int x, int y, int width, int height);
   public Rectangle(Point location, Size size);
// Public Static Fields
   public static readonly Rectangle Empty;                      // ={X=0,Y=0,Width=0,Height=0}
// Public Instance Properties
   public int Bottom{get; }
   public int Height{set; get; }
   public bool IsEmpty{get; }
   public int Left{get; }
   public Point Location{set; get; }
   public int Right{get; }
   public Size Size{set; get; }
   public int Top{get; }
   public int Width{set; get; }
   public int X{set; get; }
   public int Y{set; get; }
// Public Static Methods
   public static Rectangle Ceiling(RectangleF value);
   public static Rectangle FromLTRB(int left, int top, int right, int bottom);
   public static Rectangle Inflate(Rectangle rect, int x, int y);
   public static Rectangle Intersect(Rectangle a, Rectangle b);
   public static Rectangle Round(RectangleF value);
   public static Rectangle Truncate(RectangleF value);
   public static Rectangle Union(Rectangle a, Rectangle b);
   public static bool operator !=(Rectangle left, Rectangle right);
   public static bool operator ==(Rectangle left, Rectangle right);
// Public Instance Methods
   public bool Contains(int x, int y);
   public bool Contains(Point pt);
   public bool Contains(Rectangle rect);
   public override bool Equals(object obj);                     // overrides ValueType
   public override int GetHashCode( );                          // overrides ValueType
   public void Inflate(int width, int height);
   public void Inflate(Size size);
   public void Intersect(Rectangle rect);
   public bool IntersectsWith(Rectangle rect);
   public void Offset(int x, int y);
   public void Offset(Point pos);
   public override string ToString( );                          // overrides ValueType
}
```

Hierarchy System.Object → System.ValueType → Rectangle

Returned By Multiple types

Passed To Multiple types

RectangleConverter

System.Drawing (system.drawing.dll) class

This class, derived from System.ComponentModel.TypeConverter, converts between Rectangle values and other types, specifically strings, in persistence and design-time scenarios.

```
public class RectangleConverter : System.ComponentModel.TypeConverter {
// Public Constructors
   public RectangleConverter( );
// Public Instance Methods
   public override bool CanConvertFrom(System.ComponentModel.ITypeDescriptorContext context,
      Type sourceType);                                   // overrides System.ComponentModel.TypeConverter
   public override bool CanConvertTo(System.ComponentModel.ITypeDescriptorContext context,
      Type destinationType);                              // overrides System.ComponentModel.TypeConverter
   public override object ConvertFrom(System.ComponentModel.ITypeDescriptorContext context,
      System.Globalization.CultureInfo culture, object value);  // overrides System.ComponentModel.TypeConverter
   public override object ConvertTo(System.ComponentModel.ITypeDescriptorContext context,
      System.Globalization.CultureInfo culture, object value,
      Type destinationType);                              // overrides System.ComponentModel.TypeConverter
   public override object CreateInstance(System.ComponentModel.ITypeDescriptorContext context,
      System.Collections.IDictionary propertyValues);     // overrides System.ComponentModel.TypeConverter
   public override bool GetCreateInstanceSupported(
      System.ComponentModel.ITypeDescriptorContext context);  // overrides System.ComponentModel.TypeConverter
   public override PropertyDescriptorCollection GetProperties(System.ComponentModel.ITypeDescriptorContext context,
      object value, Attribute[ ] attributes);             // overrides System.ComponentModel.TypeConverter
   public override bool GetPropertiesSupported(
      System.ComponentModel.ITypeDescriptorContext context);  // overrides System.ComponentModel.TypeConverter
}
```

Hierarchy System.Object → System.ComponentModel.TypeConverter → RectangleConverter

RectangleF serializable

System.Drawing (system.drawing.dll) struct

This value type is the real equivalent of the integer-based Rectangle. Again, it defines a rectangular region of a 2D surface. It offers all the basic facilities of the Rectangle structure, and a conversion operator to convert from a Rectangle.

As with the Point/PointF pair, there is no intrinsic performance advantage in using the integer Rectangle, as all the Graphics painting methods are implemented in terms of the real version anyway (in the first release of the framework).

The same rendering issues also apply as for Rectangle-based shapes if you are not aligned to the pixel boundaries of the target device.

```
public struct RectangleF {
// Public Constructors
   public RectangleF(PointF location, SizeF size);
   public RectangleF(float x, float y, float width, float height);
// Public Static Fields
   public static readonly RectangleF Empty;               // ={X=0,Y=0,Width=0,Height=0}
// Public Instance Properties
   public float Bottom{get; }
   public float Height{set; get; }
```

Drawing

```
  public bool IsEmpty{get; }
  public float Left{get; }
  public PointF Location{set; get; }
  public float Right{get; }
  public SizeF Size{set; get; }
  public float Top{get; }
  public float Width{set; get; }
  public float X{set; get; }
  public float Y{set; get; }
// Public Static Methods
  public static RectangleF FromLTRB(float left, float top, float right, float bottom);
  public static RectangleF Inflate(RectangleF rect, float x, float y);
  public static RectangleF Intersect(RectangleF a, RectangleF b);
  public static RectangleF Union(RectangleF a, RectangleF b);
  public static bool operator !=(RectangleF left, RectangleF right);
  public static bool operator ==(RectangleF left, RectangleF right);
  public static implicit operator RectangleF(Rectangle r);
// Public Instance Methods
  public bool Contains(PointF pt);
  public bool Contains(RectangleF rect);
  public bool Contains(float x, float y);
  public override bool Equals(object obj);                    // overrides ValueType
  public override int GetHashCode( );                         // overrides ValueType
  public void Inflate(float x, float y);
  public void Inflate(SizeF size);
  public void Intersect(RectangleF rect);
  public bool IntersectsWith(RectangleF rect);
  public void Offset(PointF pos);
  public void Offset(float x, float y);
  public override string ToString( );                         // overrides ValueType
}
```

Hierarchy System.Object → System.ValueType → RectangleF

Returned By System.Drawing.Drawing2D.GraphicsPath.GetBounds( ), System.Drawing.Drawing2D.LinearGradientBrush.Rectangle, System.Drawing.Drawing2D.PathGradientBrush.Rectangle, Graphics.{ClipBounds, VisibleClipBounds}, Image.GetBounds( ), Region.{GetBounds( ), GetRegionScans( )}

Passed To Multiple types

Region — marshal by reference, disposable

System.Drawing (system.drawing.dll) — sealed class

This class is used to define an arbitrary region on a 2D surface.

This is a resource-based entity (unlike the Rectangle and Point value types), and therefore requires careful lifetime management. You should Dispose( ) the object when you are finished with it to release the resources back to the system.

At its simplest, you can construct a Region from a Rectangle or RectangleF. More complex regions can be constructed from a System.Drawing.Drawing2D.GraphicsPath. For interop with the Win32 HRGN, you can use GetHrgn( ) and FromHrgn( ).

You can then manipulate the region in a variety of ways, including logical operations with another Region, System.Drawing.Drawing2D.GraphicsPath, or Rectangle/RectangleF. It can also be made to represent no area at all with the MakeEmpty() method, or the whole of the infinite plane with MakeInfinite(). You can create the Complement() (the area of the supplied object that does not intersect with the Region), Intersect() two regions, create Union() of two regions (the combined areas of both), and Xor() two regions (which is equivalent to the Union()—Intersect()).

You can also provide a Matrix and Transform() the region, or simply Translate() it. This is not an ambient transformation like the ones provided for a Pen or Graphics surface—it actually manipulates the underlying System.Drawing.Drawing2D.RegionData.

There is an Equals() method, which determines whether two Region objects would be equivalent on a given Graphics surface, and you can determine whether a Point or any portion of a Rectangle (expressed in a variety of ways) will intersect with the region on a particular Graphics surface.

```
public sealed class Region : MarshalByRefObject : IDisposable {
// Public Constructors
   public Region();
   public Region(System.Drawing.Drawing2D.GraphicsPath path);
   public Region(Rectangle rect);
   public Region(RectangleF rect);
   public Region(System.Drawing.Drawing2D.RegionData rgnData);
// Public Static Methods
   public static Region FromHrgn(IntPtr hrgn);
// Public Instance Methods
   public Region Clone();
   public void Complement(System.Drawing.Drawing2D.GraphicsPath path);
   public void Complement(Rectangle rect);
   public void Complement(RectangleF rect);
   public void Complement(Region region);
   public void Dispose();                                             // implements IDisposable
   public bool Equals(Region region, Graphics g);
   public void Exclude(System.Drawing.Drawing2D.GraphicsPath path);
   public void Exclude(Rectangle rect);
   public void Exclude(RectangleF rect);
   public void Exclude(Region region);
   public RectangleF GetBounds(Graphics g);
   public IntPtr GetHrgn(Graphics g);
   public RegionData GetRegionData();
   public RectangleF[] GetRegionScans(System.Drawing.Drawing2D.Matrix matrix);
   public void Intersect(System.Drawing.Drawing2D.GraphicsPath path);
   public void Intersect(Rectangle rect);
   public void Intersect(RectangleF rect);
   public void Intersect(Region region);
   public bool IsEmpty(Graphics g);
   public bool IsInfinite(Graphics g);
   public bool IsVisible(int x, int y, Graphics g);
   public bool IsVisible(int x, int y, int width, int height);
   public bool IsVisible(int x, int y, int width, int height, Graphics g);
   public bool IsVisible(Point point);
   public bool IsVisible(PointF point);
   public bool IsVisible(PointF point, Graphics g);
```

```
  public bool IsVisible(Point point, Graphics g);
  public bool IsVisible(Rectangle rect);
  public bool IsVisible(RectangleF rect);
  public bool IsVisible(RectangleF rect, Graphics g);
  public bool IsVisible(Rectangle rect, Graphics g);
  public bool IsVisible(float x, float y);
  public bool IsVisible(float x, float y, Graphics g);
  public bool IsVisible(float x, float y, float width, float height);
  public bool IsVisible(float x, float y, float width, float height, Graphics g);
  public void MakeEmpty( );
  public void MakeInfinite( );
  public void Transform(System.Drawing.Drawing2D.Matrix matrix);
  public void Translate(int dx, int dy);
  public void Translate(float dx, float dy);
  public void Union(System.Drawing.Drawing2D.GraphicsPath path);
  public void Union(Rectangle rect);
  public void Union(RectangleF rect);
  public void Union(Region region);
  public void Xor(System.Drawing.Drawing2D.GraphicsPath path);
  public void Xor(Rectangle rect);
  public void Xor(RectangleF rect);
  public void Xor(Region region);
// Protected Instance Methods
  protected override void Finalize( );                                    // overrides object
}
```

Hierarchy System.Object → System.MarshalByRefObject → Region(System.IDisposable)

Returned By Graphics.{Clip, MeasureCharacterRanges( )}, System.Windows.Forms.Control.Region

Passed To Graphics.{Clip, ExcludeClip( ), FillRegion( ), IntersectClip( ), SetClip( )}, System.Windows.Forms.Control.{Invalidate( ), Region}

RotateFlipType — serializable

System.Drawing (system.drawing.dll) — enum

This enumeration is used by the Image.RotateFlip( ) member to determine the nature of the flipping/rotation operation to be formed.

```
public enum RotateFlipType {
  Rotate180FlipXY = 0,
  RotateNoneFlipNone = 0,
  Rotate90FlipNone = 1,
  Rotate270FlipXY = 1,
  Rotate180FlipNone = 2,
  RotateNoneFlipXY = 2,
  Rotate270FlipNone = 3,
  Rotate90FlipXY = 3,
  RotateNoneFlipX = 4,
  Rotate180FlipY = 4,
  Rotate90FlipX = 5,
  Rotate270FlipY = 5,
```

```
  Rotate180FlipX = 6,
  RotateNoneFlipY = 6,
  Rotate270FlipX = 7,
  Rotate90FlipY = 7
}
```

Hierarchy System.Object → System.ValueType → System.Enum(System.IComparable, System.IFormattable, System.IConvertible) → RotateFlipType

Passed To Image.RotateFlip( )

Size serializable

System.Drawing (system.drawing.dll) struct

Size is part of the set of value types, including Point and Rectangle, that are used to define basic drawing geometry. It uses integers to represent horizontal and vertical extent (such as the width and height of a Rectangle).

In addition to being able to retrieve the Width and Height, you can determine whether the Size value is Empty (which means both the Width and Height are equal to 0).

As with the other fundamental value types in the framework, there is an equivalent floating-point structure called SizeF. Three conversion functions (Round( ), Truncate( ), and Ceiling( )) are provided to allow you to convert from the float representation to the integer, and there is an operator that allows you to cast the other way. You can also convert to a Point.

You are also provided with addition, subtraction, and comparison operators.

Note that there is no intrinsic performance advantage in using the integer version of this type over the floating-point equivalent. As of v1.0 of the .NET Framework, most drawing functions are implemented in terms of the floating-point version anyway.

```
public struct Size {
// Public Constructors
  public Size(int width, int height);
  public Size(Point pt);
// Public Static Fields
  public static readonly Size Empty;                           // ={Width=0, Height=0}
// Public Instance Properties
  public int Height{set; get; }
  public bool IsEmpty{get; }
  public int Width{set; get; }
// Public Static Methods
  public static Size Ceiling(SizeF value);
  public static Size Round(SizeF value);
  public static Size Truncate(SizeF value);
  public static Size operator Ói(Size sz1, Size sz2);      ***NOTE TO PROD: CHARACTERS DIDN'T TRANSLATE***
  public static Size operator +(Size sz1, Size sz2);
  public static bool operator !=(Size sz1, Size sz2);
  public static bool operator ==(Size sz1, Size sz2);
  public static explicit operator Point(Size size);
  public static implicit operator SizeF(Size p);
// Public Instance Methods
```

Drawing

```
    public override bool Equals(object obj);                                        // overrides ValueType
    public override int GetHashCode( );                                             // overrides ValueType
    public override string ToString( );                                            // overrides ValueType
}
```

Hierarchy System.Object → System.ValueType → Size

Returned By Multiple types

Passed To Multiple types

SizeConverter

System.Drawing (system.drawing.dll) class

This class, derived from System.ComponentModel.TypeConverter, converts between Size values and other types, specifically strings, in persistence and design-time scenarios.

```
public class SizeConverter : System.ComponentModel.TypeConverter {
// Public Constructors
    public SizeConverter( );
// Public Instance Methods
    public override bool CanConvertFrom( System.ComponentModel.ITypeDescriptorContext context,
        Type sourceType);                                    // overrides System.ComponentModel.TypeConverter
    public override bool CanConvertTo(System.ComponentModel.ITypeDescriptorContext context,
        Type destinationType);                               // overrides System.ComponentModel.TypeConverter
    public override object ConvertFrom(System.ComponentModel.ITypeDescriptorContext context,
        System.Globalization.CultureInfo culture, object value);  // overrides System.ComponentModel.TypeConverter
    public override object ConvertTo(System.ComponentModel.ITypeDescriptorContext context,
        System.Globalization.CultureInfo culture, object value,
        Type destinationType);                               // overrides System.ComponentModel.TypeConverter
    public override object CreateInstance(System.ComponentModel.ITypeDescriptorContext context,
        System.Collections.IDictionary propertyValues);      // overrides System.ComponentModel.TypeConverter
    public override bool GetCreateInstanceSupported(
        System.ComponentModel.ITypeDescriptorContext context);  // overrides System.ComponentModel.TypeConverter
    public override PropertyDescriptorCollection GetProperties(System.ComponentModel.ITypeDescriptorContext context,
        object value, Attribute[ ] attributes);              // overrides System.ComponentModel.TypeConverter
    public override bool GetPropertiesSupported(
        System.ComponentModel.ITypeDescriptorContext context);  // overrides System.ComponentModel.TypeConverter
}
```

Hierarchy System.Object → System.ComponentModel.TypeConverter → SizeConverter

SizeF serializable

System.Drawing (system.drawing.dll) struct

A member of the family of basic geometry types, this value is the floating-point equivalent of the integer-based Size structure.

It provides all the functionality of the integer version, plus a ToSize( ) member, which uses truncation to perform the conversion.

```
public struct SizeF {
// Public Constructors
   public SizeF(PointF pt);
   public SizeF(float width, float height);
   public SizeF(SizeF size);
// Public Static Fields
   public static readonly SizeF Empty;                    // ={Width=0, Height=0}
// Public Instance Properties
   public float Height{set; get; }
   public bool IsEmpty{get; }
   public float Width{set; get; }
// Public Static Methods
   public static SizeF operator -(SizeF sz1, SizeF sz2);
   public static SizeF operator +(SizeF sz1, SizeF sz2);
   public static bool operator !=(SizeF sz1, SizeF sz2);
   public static bool operator ==(SizeF sz1, SizeF sz2);
   public static explicit operator PointF(SizeF size);
// Public Instance Methods
   public override bool Equals(object obj);               // overrides ValueType
   public override int GetHashCode( );                    // overrides ValueType
   public PointF ToPointF( );
   public Size ToSize( );
   public override string ToString( );                    // overrides ValueType
}
```

Hierarchy System.Object → System.ValueType → SizeF

Returned By Graphics.MeasureString( ), Image.PhysicalDimension, RectangleF.Size, System.Windows.Forms.Form.GetAutoScaleSize( )

Passed To Graphics.MeasureString( ), RectangleF.{Inflate( ), RectangleF( ), Size}, Size.{Ceiling( ), Round( ), Truncate( )}

SolidBrush — marshal by reference, disposable

System.Drawing (system.drawing.dll) — sealed class

This class is the day-to-day workhorse of the GDI+ world. If you cannot find the brush you need in SystemBrushes or Brushes, and you don't need the fancy effects of the options found in System.Drawing.Drawing2D, you will be using instances of this class (derived from Brush) to fill solid areas of color in your shapes, including the font stroke color when painting text. You can construct an instance from a Color value, and can also set and retrieve the Color through a property of that name over the lifetime of the object.

As with most GDI+ resources, this implements IDisposable and must therefore have its lifetime managed carefully, calling Dispose( ) when you are finished with it. As with other examples, the C# using idiom is useful here.

```
public sealed class SolidBrush : Brush : System.Drawing.Internal.ISystemColorTracker {
// Public Constructors
   public SolidBrush(Color color);
// Public Instance Properties
   public Color Color{set; get; }
```

```
// Public Instance Methods
   public override object Clone( );                                    // overrides Brush
// Protected Instance Methods
   protected override void Dispose(bool disposing);                    // overrides Brush
}
```

Hierarchy System.Object → System.MarshalByRefObject → Brush(System.ICloneable, System.IDisposable) → SolidBrush(System.Drawing.Internal.ISystemColorTracker)

StringAlignment **serializable**

System.Drawing (system.drawing.dll) **enum**

This enumeration is used in several places throughout the framework to specify the positioning of a text string within its clip box. For example, the StringFormat class uses it for both horizontal text alignment and vertical line alignment.

The Center/Near/Far notation (rather than left/right or top/bottom, for example) enables you to specify both horizontal and vertical alignments and to support locales where right-to-left reading is appropriate. For example, a string drawn with a horizontal alignment, Far, will be drawn at the right of the rectangle in a left-to-right locale, but would be rendered at the left side of a rectangle with a right-to-left locale.

```
public enum StringAlignment {
   Near = 0,
   Center = 1,
   Far = 2
}
```

Hierarchy System.Object → System.ValueType → System.Enum(System.IComparable, System.IFormattable, System.IConvertible) → StringAlignment

Returned By StringFormat.{Alignment, LineAlignment}

Passed To StringFormat.{Alignment, LineAlignment}

StringDigitSubstitute **serializable**

System.Drawing (system.drawing.dll) **enum**

This enumeration is used by the StringFormat class when you need to render digits in a font that doesn't provide those digits (typically non-Western language fonts). You can choose between official National standards, Traditional methods, or no substitution. There is also the option of a User substitution scheme, but the framework does not expose the same detailed degree of control over font substitution as is available in the Platform SDK internationalization services (e.g., UniScribe).

```
public enum StringDigitSubstitute {
   User = 0,
   None = 1,
   National = 2,
   Traditional = 3
}
```

Hierarchy System.Object → System.ValueType → System.Enum(System.IComparable, System.IFormattable, System.IConvertible) → StringDigitSubstitute

Returned By StringFormat.DigitSubstitutionMethod

Passed To StringFormat.SetDigitSubstitution( )

StringFormat — marshal by reference, disposable

System.Drawing (system.drawing.dll) — sealed class

This class provides an encapsulation of all the information needed to specify how a text string should be formatted when rendered to a **Graphics** surface (e.g., through the **Graphics.DrawString( )** method). Correspondingly, the string measurement methods (e.g., **Graphics.MeasureString( )**) also require a **StringFormat** object.

You can specify basic formatting and alignment features (e.g., horizontal **Alignment**, vertical **LineAlignment**, and the **StringFormatFlags** familiar to anybody who has rendered text in GDI/GDI+ before, specifying wrapping and layout rules). You can also set display parameters such as the method for dealing with truncated strings (**Trimming**), whether to underline **HotkeyPrefix**, and the Unicode digit substitution method (see **StringDigitSubstitute**). There is also basic control of the tab ruler with **SetTabStops( )** and **GetTabStops( )**, and the **SetMeasurableCharacterRanges( )** method allows you to package up the text string into a series of ranges of characters whose individual regions can be measured. This might be useful if you needed to highlight selected portions of the text, for example.

In case all this seems a little overwhelming just to render a text string, there are two static properties, **GenericDefault** and **GenericTypographic**, that provide **StringFormat** objects appropriate for general UI rendering and formal text display (e.g., in a word processing control), respectively.

```
public sealed class StringFormat : MarshalByRefObject : ICloneable, IDisposable {
// Public Constructors
   public StringFormat( );
   public StringFormat(StringFormat format);
   public StringFormat(StringFormatFlags options);
   public StringFormat(StringFormatFlags options, int language);
// Public Static Properties
   public static StringFormat GenericDefault{get; }
   public static StringFormat GenericTypographic{get; }
// Public Instance Properties
   public StringAlignment Alignment{set; get; }
   public int DigitSubstitutionLanguage{get; }
   public StringDigitSubstitute DigitSubstitutionMethod{get; }
   public StringFormatFlags FormatFlags{set; get; }
   public HotkeyPrefix HotkeyPrefix{set; get; }
   public StringAlignment LineAlignment{set; get; }
   public StringTrimming Trimming{set; get; }
// Public Instance Methods
   public object Clone( );                                  // implements ICloneable
   public void Dispose( );                                  // implements IDisposable
   public float[ ] GetTabStops(out float firstTabOffset);
   public void SetDigitSubstitution(int language, StringDigitSubstitute substitute);
   public void SetMeasurableCharacterRanges(CharacterRange[ ] ranges);
```

Drawing

```
  public void SetTabStops(float firstTabOffset, float[ ] tabStops);
  public override string ToString( );                                    // overrides object
// Protected Instance Methods
  protected override void Finalize( );                                   // overrides object
}
```

Hierarchy System.Object → System.MarshalByRefObject → StringFormat(System.ICloneable, System.IDisposable)

Passed To System.Drawing.Drawing2D.GraphicsPath.AddString( ), Graphics.{DrawString( ), MeasureCharacterRanges( ), MeasureString( )}, System.Windows.Forms.ControlPaint.DrawStringDisabled( )

StringFormatFlags serializable, flag

System.Drawing (system.drawing.dll) enum

This enumeration provides a variety of flags that control the way a text string is formatted during rendering and measurement. Most of the flags relate to the relationship between the string and its bounding rectangle, but there are also flags that enable you to specify the text direction (e.g., left-to-right or right-to-left) and whether font-substitution is to be used when a character found in the string does not have a corresponding glyph in the font of choice. These flags should be familiar to people who have previously used the Win32 GDI text-rendering methods.

```
public enum StringFormatFlags {
  DirectionRightToLeft = 0x00000001,
  DirectionVertical = 0x00000002,
  FitBlackBox = 0x00000004,
  DisplayFormatControl = 0x00000020,
  NoFontFallback = 0x00000400,
  MeasureTrailingSpaces = 0x00000800,
  NoWrap = 0x00001000,
  LineLimit = 0x00002000,
  NoClip = 0x00004000
}
```

Hierarchy System.Object → System.ValueType → System.Enum(System.IComparable, System.IFormattable, System.IConvertible) → StringFormatFlags

Returned By StringFormat.FormatFlags

Passed To StringFormat.{FormatFlags, StringFormat( )}

StringTrimming serializable

System.Drawing (system.drawing.dll) enum

This enumeration contains the options for the StringFormat.Trimming property, which determines what happens to a string that is too large for its bounding box. You can choose not to crop at all (None) or to crop at Character or Word boundaries. On top of that, you can choose to add an ellipsis (...) where the cropping occurs, which may of course trim even more text to fit it in (there are EllipsisCharacter and EllipsisWord elements to choose this option). There is also the special case of EllipsisPath which treats the string as a file path and crops in the middle of the string, between \ characters, adding an appropriate ellipsis.

```
public enum StringTrimming {
  None = 0,
  Character = 1,
  Word = 2,
  EllipsisCharacter = 3,
  EllipsisWord = 4,
  EllipsisPath = 5
}
```

Hierarchy System.Object → System.ValueType → System.Enum(System.IComparable, System.IFormattable, System.IConvertible) → StringTrimming

Returned By StringFormat.Trimming

Passed To StringFormat.Trimming

StringUnit serializable

System.Drawing (system.drawing.dll) enum

This enumeration allegedly specifies the units of measurement for a string. But as all the string measurement functions actually use the (remarkably similar!) GraphicsUnit enumeration instead, we will pretend that we never saw it, and move along quietly....

```
public enum StringUnit {
  World = 0,
  Display = 1,
  Pixel = 2,
  Point = 3,
  Inch = 4,
  Document = 5,
  Millimeter = 6,
  Em = 32
}
```

Hierarchy System.Object → System.ValueType → System.Enum(System.IComparable, System.IFormattable, System.IConvertible) → StringUnit

SystemBrushes

System.Drawing (system.drawing.dll) sealed class

This class provides a set of static properties that return Brush objects for (almost) all the standard system colors. Unfortunately, some of the system colors were deemed to be "not for filling surfaces"—InactiveCaptionText for instance—so you'll have to fall back on SystemColors and SolidBrush if you want to use them.

Unlike most brushes, you do not need to Dispose( ) the ones returned from this class. In fact, you mustn't dispose of it, or you will leave an unpleasant hole in the thread-local system brush table.

To retrieve a Brush for one of the web colors, see Brushes.

```
public sealed class SystemBrushes {
// Public Static Properties
  public static Brush ActiveBorder{get; }
  public static Brush ActiveCaption{get; }
  public static Brush ActiveCaptionText{get; }
  public static Brush AppWorkspace{get; }
  public static Brush Control{get; }
  public static Brush ControlDark{get; }
  public static Brush ControlDarkDark{get; }
  public static Brush ControlLight{get; }
  public static Brush ControlLightLight{get; }
  public static Brush ControlText{get; }
  public static Brush Desktop{get; }
  public static Brush Highlight{get; }
  public static Brush HighlightText{get; }
  public static Brush HotTrack{get; }
  public static Brush InactiveBorder{get; }
  public static Brush InactiveCaption{get; }
  public static Brush Info{get; }
  public static Brush Menu{get; }
  public static Brush ScrollBar{get; }
  public static Brush Window{get; }
  public static Brush WindowText{get; }
// Public Static Methods
  public static Brush FromSystemColor(Color c);
}
```

SystemColors

System.Drawing (system.drawing.dll) sealed class

This class contains a set of static properties that return appropriate Color values for current the system theme.

If you are retrieving the color just to create a SolidBrush or Pen, you should use the SystemBrushes or SystemPens class instead.

```
public sealed class SystemColors {
// Public Static Properties
  public static Color ActiveBorder{get; }
  public static Color ActiveCaption{get; }
  public static Color ActiveCaptionText{get; }
  public static Color AppWorkspace{get; }
  public static Color Control{get; }
  public static Color ControlDark{get; }
  public static Color ControlDarkDark{get; }
  public static Color ControlLight{get; }
  public static Color ControlLightLight{get; }
  public static Color ControlText{get; }
  public static Color Desktop{get; }
  public static Color GrayText{get; }
  public static Color Highlight{get; }
```

```
public static Color HighlightText{get; }
public static Color HotTrack{get; }
public static Color InactiveBorder{get; }
public static Color InactiveCaption{get; }
public static Color InactiveCaptionText{get; }
public static Color Info{get; }
public static Color InfoText{get; }
public static Color Menu{get; }
public static Color MenuText{get; }
public static Color ScrollBar{get; }
public static Color Window{get; }
public static Color WindowFrame{get; }
public static Color WindowText{get; }
}
```

SystemIcons

System.Drawing (system.drawing.dll) **sealed class**

This class provides you with properties to retrieve those handy system icons, such as the Error and Information symbols. As an added bonus, you've also got a Hand and the WinLogo.

While these icons implement IDisposable, don't release the resources yourself or you will leave the disposed remains of an icon in the internal system icons table for the next poor client to use. Unfortunately, the implementation only tests for nullness before recreating the Icon rather than checking IsDisposed.

```
public sealed class SystemIcons {
// Public Static Properties
   public static Icon Application{get; }
   public static Icon Asterisk{get; }
   public static Icon Error{get; }
   public static Icon Exclamation{get; }
   public static Icon Hand{get; }
   public static Icon Information{get; }
   public static Icon Question{get; }
   public static Icon Warning{get; }
   public static Icon WinLogo{get; }
}
```

SystemPens

System.Drawing (system.drawing.dll) **sealed class**

This class provides a set of static properties that return Pen objects for (almost) all the standard system colors. Sadly, as some of the system colors were deemed to be "not for drawing lines"—InactiveCaption for instance—you'll have to fall back on SystemColors and Pen if you want to use them in some kind of inverse colors cheme.

Like most of these SystemXXX classes, although IDisposable is implemented, you must not dispose of the object yourself. The internal implementation caches the pens in a system table, but only tests for nullness and not whether the object has been disposed, so you will leave an unpleasant surprise for the next person to use that pen!

To retrieve a Pen for one of the web colors, see Pens.

```
public sealed class SystemPens {
// Public Static Properties
   public static Pen ActiveCaptionText{get; }
   public static Pen Control{get; }
   public static Pen ControlDark{get; }
   public static Pen ControlDarkDark{get; }
   public static Pen ControlLight{get; }
   public static Pen ControlLightLight{get; }
   public static Pen ControlText{get; }
   public static Pen GrayText{get; }
   public static Pen Highlight{get; }
   public static Pen HighlightText{get; }
   public static Pen InactiveCaptionText{get; }
   public static Pen InfoText{get; }
   public static Pen MenuText{get; }
   public static Pen WindowFrame{get; }
   public static Pen WindowText{get; }
// Public Static Methods
   public static Pen FromSystemColor(Color c);
}
```

TextureBrush — marshal by reference, disposable

System.Drawing (system.drawing.dll) — sealed class

This class provides a means of filling a surface with an image. You can specify how the image is to be tiled with the WrapMode, and you can also apply a Transform matrix to the brush so that the image appears appropriately in your particular coordinate space.

```
public sealed class TextureBrush : Brush {
// Public Constructors
   public TextureBrush(Image bitmap);
   public TextureBrush(Image image, Rectangle dstRect);
   public TextureBrush(Image image, RectangleF dstRect);
   public TextureBrush(Image image, RectangleF dstRect, System.Drawing.Imaging.ImageAttributes imageAttr);
   public TextureBrush(Image image, Rectangle dstRect, System.Drawing.Imaging.ImageAttributes imageAttr);
   public TextureBrush(Image image, System.Drawing.Drawing2D.WrapMode wrapMode);
   public TextureBrush(Image image, System.Drawing.Drawing2D.WrapMode wrapMode, Rectangle dstRect);
   public TextureBrush(Image image, System.Drawing.Drawing2D.WrapMode wrapMode, RectangleF dstRect);
// Public Instance Properties
   public Image Image{get; }
   public Matrix Transform{set; get; }
   public WrapMode WrapMode{set; get; }
// Public Instance Methods
   public override object Clone( );                                        // overrides Brush
   public void MultiplyTransform(System.Drawing.Drawing2D.Matrix matrix);
   public void MultiplyTransform(System.Drawing.Drawing2D.Matrix matrix,
      System.Drawing.Drawing2D.MatrixOrder order);
   public void ResetTransform( );
   public void RotateTransform(float angle);
   public void RotateTransform(float angle, System.Drawing.Drawing2D.MatrixOrder order);
   public void ScaleTransform(float sx, float sy);
   public void ScaleTransform(float sx, float sy, System.Drawing.Drawing2D.MatrixOrder order);
```

```
  public void TranslateTransform(float dx, float dy);
  public void TranslateTransform(float dx, float dy, System.Drawing.Drawing2D.MatrixOrder order);
}
```

Hierarchy System.Object → System.MarshalByRefObject → Brush(System.ICloneable, System.IDisposable) → TextureBrush

ToolboxBitmapAttribute

System.Drawing (system.drawing.dll) class

This Attribute class is something of a refugee from the System.Drawing.Design namespace. If you apply the attribute to a component and specify either the filename of a 16 × 16 bitmap, or a component type (e.g., typeof(SomeOtherComponent)), the appropriate image (either your bitmap or the image specified for the other type) will be displayed in the designer toolbox next to your component's name.

You can also specify both, and it will fallback on the type imagery if the bitmap file doesn't exist.

This is, of course, extremely useful; but what it is doing in this namespace is a mystery.

```
public class ToolboxBitmapAttribute : Attribute {
// Public Constructors
  public ToolboxBitmapAttribute(string imageFile);
  public ToolboxBitmapAttribute(Type t);
  public ToolboxBitmapAttribute(Type t, string name);
// Public Static Fields
  public static readonly ToolboxBitmapAttribute Default;      // =System.Drawing.ToolboxBitmapAttribute
// Public Static Methods
  public static Image GetImageFromResource(Type t, string imageName, bool large);
// Public Instance Methods
  public override bool Equals(object value);                  // overrides Attribute
  public override int GetHashCode();                          // overrides Attribute
  public Image GetImage(object component);
  public Image GetImage(object component, bool large);
  public Image GetImage(Type type);
  public Image GetImage(Type type, bool large);
  public Image GetImage(Type type, string imgName, bool large);
}
```

Hierarchy System.Object → System.Attribute → ToolboxBitmapAttribute

Valid On Class

15

The System.Drawing. Drawing2D Namespace

The System.Drawing.Drawing2D namespace provides a number of classes that support more advanced features of the vector drawing facilities in GDI+, including custom fill types, paths, and regions.

Most GDI+ applications make extensive use of the classes in this namespace. Figure 15-1 shows the types in this namespace.

AdjustableArrowCap — marshal by reference, disposable

System.Drawing.Drawing2D (system.drawing.dll) — sealed class

This class, derived from CustomLineCap, provides an arrow-like start- or endcap for a path or line. Unlike the default endcaps, you have control over the shape and size of the arrow.

In addition to functionality of the base class, you can specify whether the arrow is Filled or Hollow, along with the Width and Height of the arrow head itself. In addition, the MiddleInset property allows you to adjust the "barbs" of the arrow.

```
public sealed class AdjustableArrowCap : CustomLineCap {
// Public Constructors
  public AdjustableArrowCap(float width, float height);
  public AdjustableArrowCap(float width, float height, bool isFilled);
// Public Instance Properties
  public bool Filled{set; get; }
  public float Height{set; get; }
  public float MiddleInset{set; get; }
  public float Width{set; get; }
}
```

Hierarchy System.Object → System.MarshalByRefObject → CustomLineCap(System.ICloneable, System.IDisposable) → AdjustableArrowCap

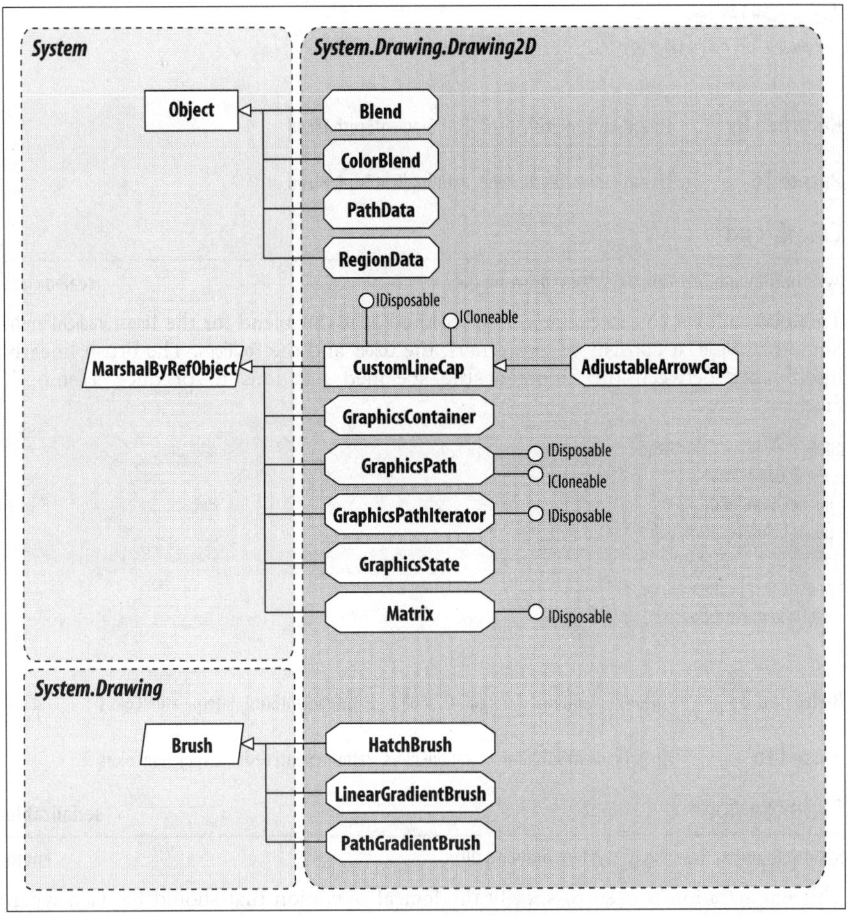
System
System.Drawing.Drawing2D
Object
Blend
ColorBlend
PathData
RegionData
IDisposable
ICloneable
MarshalByRefObject
CustomLineCap
AdjustableArrowCap
GraphicsContainer
GraphicsPath
IDisposable
ICloneable
GraphicsPathIterator
IDisposable
GraphicsState
Matrix
IDisposable
System.Drawing
Brush
HatchBrush
LinearGradientBrush
PathGradientBrush

Figure 15-1. Types from the System.Drawing.Drawing2D namespace

Blend

System.Drawing.Drawing2D (system.drawing.dll) sealed class

This allows you to define a gradient scheme for the LinearGradientBrush. It consists of two arrays: the Factors and the Positions. The Factors indicate the relative proportions of the two colors at the corresponding Positions. The system linearly interpolates between the specified positions to produce a smooth gradient.

Note that the values in the Factors array must be between 0.0 and 1.0 (from 100% color 2, to 100% color 1).

See ColorBlend for a multicolored blend.

```
public sealed class Blend {
// Public Constructors
   public Blend( );
   public Blend(int count);
// Public Instance Properties
```

```
  public float[ ] Factors{set; get; }
  public float[ ] Positions{set; get; }
}
```

Returned By LinearGradientBrush.Blend, PathGradientBrush.Blend

Passed To LinearGradientBrush.Blend, PathGradientBrush.Blend

ColorBlend

System.Drawing.Drawing2D (system.drawing.dll) sealed class

This class allows you to define a multicolored gradient blend for the LinearGradientBrush. Similar to Blend, it consists of two arrays: the Colors and the Positions. The brush linearly interpolates between the colors at the specified positions to produce a smooth gradient.

```
public sealed class ColorBlend {
// Public Constructors
  public ColorBlend( );
  public ColorBlend(int count);
// Public Instance Properties
  public Color[ ] Colors{set; get; }
  public float[ ] Positions{set; get; }
}
```

Returned By LinearGradientBrush.InterpolationColors, PathGradientBrush.InterpolationColors

Passed To LinearGradientBrush.InterpolationColors, PathGradientBrush.InterpolationColors

CombineMode serializable

System.Drawing.Drawing2D (system.drawing.dll) enum

This enumeration is used to specify the logical operation that should be used when combining clipping System.Drawing.Region objects.

```
public enum CombineMode {
  Replace = 0,
  Intersect = 1,
  Union = 2,
  Xor = 3,
  Exclude = 4,
  Complement = 5
}
```

Hierarchy System.Object → System.ValueType → System.Enum(System.IComparable, System.IFormattable, System.IConvertible) → CombineMode

Passed To System.Drawing.Graphics.SetClip( )

CompositingMode serializable

System.Drawing.Drawing2D (system.drawing.dll) enum

This enumeration is used with the System.Drawing.Graphics.CompositingMode property to determine how alpha-blended colors are merged while drawing. SourceCopy effectively disables alpha blending while drawing into the bitmap, writing whatever color is specified (including its alpha value) directly into the bitmap. SourceOver reenables alpha blending, causing colors to be merged as they are drawn.

```
public enum CompositingMode {
 SourceOver = 0,
 SourceCopy = 1
}
```

Hierarchy System.Object → System.ValueType → System.Enum(System.IComparable, System.IFormattable, System.IConvertible) → CompositingMode

Returned By System.Drawing.Graphics.CompositingMode

Passed To System.Drawing.Graphics.CompositingMode

CompositingQuality serializable

System.Drawing.Drawing2D (system.drawing.dll) enum

This enumeration is used with the System.Drawing.Graphics.CompositingQuality member to specify how pixels will be rendered. Each step up in rendering quality causes a corresponding decrease in rendering speed. This is because the better rendering quality is achieved by examining a number of pixels around the target pixel and blending values using one of several sub-pixel interpolation algorithms.

```
public enum CompositingQuality {
 Default = 0,
 HighSpeed = 1,
 HighQuality = 2,
 GammaCorrected = 3,
 AssumeLinear = 4,
 Invalid = -1
}
```

Hierarchy System.Object → System.ValueType → System.Enum(System.IComparable, System.IFormattable, System.IConvertible) → CompositingQuality

Returned By System.Drawing.Graphics.CompositingQuality

Passed To System.Drawing.Graphics.CompositingQuality

CoordinateSpace serializable

System.Drawing.Drawing2D (system.drawing.dll) enum

This enumeration specifies the three possible coordinate spaces to use with the System.Drawing.Graphics.TransformPoints( ) method. The Device coordinate space is the physical coordinate space of the target output device (the monitor or printer, for example). The Page coordinate space is the logical coordinate space of the graphics surface, and the World coordinate space is the surface coordinate space with the current Graphics.Transform applied. That transform is commonly referred to as the "World Transform."

```
public enum CoordinateSpace {
  World = 0,
  Page = 1,
  Device = 2
}
```

Hierarchy System.Object → System.ValueType → System.Enum(System.IComparable, System.IFormattable, System.IConvertible) → CoordinateSpace

Passed To System.Drawing.Graphics.TransformPoints( )

CustomLineCap

marshal by reference, disposable

System.Drawing.Drawing2D (system.drawing.dll) class

This class is used to create your own custom imagery for a linecap. It is also a base class for the AdjustableArrowCap.

You can specify the BaseCap on which the custom cap is based. You should pick the cap most similar to the one you are about to draw. The BaseInset allows you to move the relative position of the end of the line and the endcap. The StrokeJoin is used to specify the join-style of the line segments in the cap, and the WidthScale is used to specify how the cap should be scaled as the line width changes.

The actual shape of the cap is specified at construction time, by specifying two GraphicsPath objects: one to make the outline (the stroke path) and the other to make the fill (the fill path).

Note that a defect in the current version of the GDI+ rendering engine means that the framework does not correctly calculate the bounds of a path using a custom endcap, if that endcap has radically different proportions to its BaseCap.

```
public class CustomLineCap : MarshalByRefObject : ICloneable, IDisposable {
// Public Constructors
  public CustomLineCap(GraphicsPath fillPath, GraphicsPath strokePath);
  public CustomLineCap(GraphicsPath fillPath, GraphicsPath strokePath, LineCap baseCap);
  public CustomLineCap(GraphicsPath fillPath, GraphicsPath strokePath, LineCap baseCap, float baseInset);
// Public Instance Properties
  public LineCap BaseCap{set; get; }
  public float BaseInset{set; get; }
  public LineJoin StrokeJoin{set; get; }
  public float WidthScale{set; get; }
// Public Instance Methods
  public object Clone( );                                              // implements ICloneable
  public void Dispose( );                                              // implements IDisposable
  public void GetStrokeCaps(out LineCap startCap, out LineCap endCap);
  public void SetStrokeCaps(LineCap startCap, LineCap endCap);
// Protected Instance Methods
  protected virtual void Dispose(bool disposing);
  protected override void Finalize( );                                 // overrides object
}
```

Hierarchy System.Object → System.MarshalByRefObject → CustomLineCap(System.ICloneable, System.IDisposable)

Subclasses AdjustableArrowCap

Returned By System.Drawing.Pen.{CustomEndCap, CustomStartCap}

Passed To System.Drawing.Pen.{CustomEndCap, CustomStartCap}

DashCap serializable

System.Drawing.Drawing2D (system.drawing.dll) enum

This enumeration is used by the System.Drawing.Pen.DashCap property to specify the cap to use on each end of each individual dash segment.

```
public enum DashCap {
  Flat = 0,
  Round = 2,
  Triangle = 3
}
```

Hierarchy System.Object → System.ValueType → System.Enum(System.IComparable, System.IFormattable, System.IConvertible) → DashCap

Returned By System.Drawing.Pen.DashCap

Passed To System.Drawing.Pen.{DashCap, SetLineCap( )}

DashStyle serializable

System.Drawing.Drawing2D (system.drawing.dll) enum

This enumeration specifies the dash pattern of a line. You can set a dash pattern using the System.Drawing.Pen.DashStyle property.

```
public enum DashStyle {
  Solid = 0,
  Dash = 1,
  Dot = 2,
  DashDot = 3,
  DashDotDot = 4,
  Custom = 5
}
```

Hierarchy System.Object → System.ValueType → System.Enum(System.IComparable, System.IFormattable, System.IConvertible) → DashStyle

Returned By System.Drawing.Pen.DashStyle

Passed To System.Drawing.Pen.DashStyle

FillMode

serializable

System.Drawing.Drawing2D (system.drawing.dll) — enum

This enumeration is used to specify the mode to be used to fill a closed path. It is used by the GraphicsPath and System.Drawing.Graphics members that fill closed shapes.

```
public enum FillMode {
  Alternate = 0,
  Winding = 1
}
```

Hierarchy System.Object → System.ValueType → System.Enum(System.IComparable, System.IFormattable, System.IConvertible) → FillMode

Returned By GraphicsPath.FillMode

Passed To GraphicsPath.{FillMode, GraphicsPath( )}, System.Drawing.Graphics.{DrawClosedCurve( ), FillClosedCurve( ), FillPolygon( )}

FlushIntention

serializable

System.Drawing.Drawing2D (system.drawing.dll) — enum

This enumeration is used by the System.Drawing.Graphics.Flush( ) method to determine whether the system should wait for rendering to be completed (Sync) or whether the graphics operations should be flushed asynchronously (Flush).

```
public enum FlushIntention {
  Flush = 0,
  Sync = 1
}
```

Hierarchy System.Object → System.ValueType → System.Enum(System.IComparable, System.IFormattable, System.IConvertible) → FlushIntention

Passed To System.Drawing.Graphics.Flush( )

GraphicsContainer

marshal by reference

System.Drawing.Drawing2D (system.drawing.dll) — sealed class

This class encapsulates the state of a Graphics object. It is returned from System.Drawing.Graphics.BeginContainer( ) and can be used to restore the graphics state with System.Drawing.Graphics.EndContainer( ). It is an opaque type and offers no additional methods.

```
public sealed class GraphicsContainer : MarshalByRefObject {
// No public or protected members
}
```

Hierarchy System.Object → System.MarshalByRefObject → GraphicsContainer

Returned By System.Drawing.Graphics.BeginContainer( )

Passed To System.Drawing.Graphics.EndContainer( )

System.Drawing.Drawing2D (system.drawing.dll) sealed class

This class implements a complex graphics path that can be used to encapsulate a number of different drawing elements in a single container. It can be used in conjunction with the System.Drawing.Graphics.DrawPath( ) and System.Drawing.Graphics.FillPath( ) members to render outlines or filled shapes. The FillMode specifies the winding mode for filled shapes. If the path is an open shape, the system automatically adds a straight line to close the path if it is to be filled; this does not affect outline drawing.

The path can also be used for hit-testing. The IsOutlineVisible( ) method will widen the path with the specified pen, and then return a value indicating whether a particular point is to be found under that path. Note that this is non-destructive, whereas the Widen( ) method followed by IsVisible( ), while logically similar, will irreversibly flatten the path first. (See below for information on flattened paths.) In a similar vein, GetBounds( ) will give you the minimum containing rectangle for the path.

A path consists of one or more figures. A figure is a connected set of drawing objects. A figure is automatically started when the path is created, and you can then use the various AddXXX( ) methods to insert shapes into the path. Those shapes are not actually inserted as-is, but approximated with a set of straight line or Bezier spline segments.

You then call CloseFigure( ) if you wish to create a closed shape and start a new figure, or alternatively call StartFigure( ) to leave the previous figure open, and start a new one. CloseAllFigures( ) can subsequently be used to close any remaining open figures, if required.

To modify the path, you can apply a Transform( ), or alternatively, you can Warp( ) the actual path, as defined by a rectangle and a parallelogram. This method actually flattens the path into a series of straight line segments and moves those points. As a result, you cannot undo this operation. (See below for information on flattening paths).

You can retrieve the underlying PathData, which consists of a set of Point and PathPointType objects. Alternatively, you can retrieve the PathPoints and PathTypes independently. You can also retrieve the PointCount, the number of elements in those arrays.

One feature that can be particularly useful if you need an efficient means of approximating your complex path for geometric purposes (such as length or area calculations) is the Flatten( ) method. This returns a set of points representing the straight line segments approximating the line. You can specify how accurate this approximation should be, and the default of 0.25 is sufficient to give you an approximation that is visually difficult to distinguish from the "real thing." Note that you can apply a transform as part of the flattening process so that the approximation can be made in page or device coordinates for best accuracy.

```
public sealed class GraphicsPath : MarshalByRefObject : ICloneable, IDisposable {
// Public Constructors
   public GraphicsPath( );
   public GraphicsPath(FillMode fillMode);
   public GraphicsPath(System.Drawing.Point[ ] pts, byte[ ] types);
   public GraphicsPath(System.Drawing.Point[ ] pts, byte[ ] types, FillMode fillMode);
   public GraphicsPath(System.Drawing.PointF[ ] pts, byte[ ] types);
   public GraphicsPath(System.Drawing.PointF[ ] pts, byte[ ] types, FillMode fillMode);
// Public Instance Properties
   public FillMode FillMode{set; get; }
   public PathData PathData{get; }
   public PointF[ ] PathPoints{get; }
```

```
public byte[ ] PathTypes{get; }
public int PointCount{get; }
// Public Instance Methods
public void AddArc(int x, int y, int width, int height, float startAngle, float sweepAngle);
public void AddArc(System.Drawing.RectangleF rect,
   float startAngle, float sweepAngle);
public void AddArc(System.Drawing.Rectangle rect,
   float startAngle, float sweepAngle);
public void AddArc(float x, float y, float width,
   float height, float startAngle, float sweepAngle);
public void AddBezier(int x1, int y1, int x2, int y2,
   int x3, int y3, int x4, int y4);
public void AddBezier(System.Drawing.PointF pt1,
   System.Drawing.PointF pt2,
   System.Drawing.PointF pt3,
   System.Drawing.PointF pt4);
public void AddBezier(System.Drawing.Point pt1,
   System.Drawing.Point pt2, System.Drawing.Point pt3,
   System.Drawing.Point pt4);
public void AddBezier(float x1, float y1, float x2,
   float y2, float x3, float y3, float x4, float y4);
public void AddBeziers(System.Drawing.Point[ ] points);
public void AddBeziers(System.Drawing.PointF[ ] points);
public void AddClosedCurve(System.Drawing.Point[ ] points);
public void AddClosedCurve(System.Drawing.Point[ ] points, float tension);
public void AddClosedCurve(System.Drawing.PointF[ ] points);
public void AddClosedCurve(System.Drawing.PointF[ ] points, float tension);
public void AddCurve(System.Drawing.Point[ ] points);
public void AddCurve(System.Drawing.Point[ ] points, int offset, int numberOfSegments, float tension);
public void AddCurve(System.Drawing.Point[ ] points, float tension);
public void AddCurve(System.Drawing.PointF[ ] points);
public void AddCurve(System.Drawing.PointF[ ] points, int offset, int numberOfSegments, float tension);
public void AddCurve(System.Drawing.PointF[ ] points, float tension);
public void AddEllipse(int x, int y, int width, int height);
public void AddEllipse(System.Drawing.Rectangle rect);
public void AddEllipse(System.Drawing.RectangleF rect);
public void AddEllipse(float x, float y, float width, float height);
public void AddLine(int x1, int y1, int x2, int y2);
public void AddLine(System.Drawing.PointF pt1, System.Drawing.PointF pt2);
public void AddLine(System.Drawing.Point pt1, System.Drawing.Point pt2);
public void AddLine(float x1, float y1, float x2, float y2);
public void AddLines(System.Drawing.Point[ ] points);
public void AddLines(System.Drawing.PointF[ ] points);
public void AddPath(GraphicsPath addingPath, bool connect);
public void AddPie(int x, int y, int width, int height, float startAngle, float sweepAngle);
public void AddPie(System.Drawing.Rectangle rect, float startAngle, float sweepAngle);
public void AddPie(float x, float y, float width, float height, float startAngle, float sweepAngle);
public void AddPolygon(System.Drawing.Point[ ] points);
public void AddPolygon(System.Drawing.PointF[ ] points);
public void AddRectangle(System.Drawing.Rectangle rect);
public void AddRectangle(System.Drawing.RectangleF rect);
```

```
public void AddRectangles(System.Drawing.Rectangle[ ] rects);
public void AddRectangles(System.Drawing.RectangleF[ ] rects);
public void AddString(string s, System.Drawing.FontFamily family, int style, float emSize,
    System.Drawing.PointF origin, System.Drawing.StringFormat format);
public void AddString(string s, System.Drawing.FontFamily family, int style, float emSize,
    System.Drawing.Point origin, System.Drawing.StringFormat format);
public void AddString(string s, System.Drawing.FontFamily family, int style, float emSize,
    System.Drawing.RectangleF layoutRect, System.Drawing.StringFormat format);
public void AddString(string s, System.Drawing.FontFamily family, int style, float emSize,
    System.Drawing.Rectangle layoutRect, System.Drawing.StringFormat format);
public void ClearMarkers( );
public object Clone( );                                                    // implements ICloneable
public void CloseAllFigures( );
public void CloseFigure( );
public void Dispose( );                                                    // implements IDisposable
public void Flatten( );
public void Flatten(Matrix matrix);
public void Flatten(Matrix matrix, float flatness);
public RectangleF GetBounds( );
public RectangleF GetBounds(Matrix matrix);
public RectangleF GetBounds(Matrix matrix, System.Drawing.Pen pen);
public PointF GetLastPoint( );
public bool IsOutlineVisible(int x, int y, System.Drawing.Pen pen);
public bool IsOutlineVisible(int x, int y, System.Drawing.Pen pen, System.Drawing.Graphics graphics);
public bool IsOutlineVisible(System.Drawing.PointF point, System.Drawing.Pen pen);
public bool IsOutlineVisible(System.Drawing.PointF pt, System.Drawing.Pen pen, System.Drawing.Graphics graphics);
public bool IsOutlineVisible(System.Drawing.Point point, System.Drawing.Pen pen);
public bool IsOutlineVisible(System.Drawing.Point pt, System.Drawing.Pen pen, System.Drawing.Graphics graphics);
public bool IsOutlineVisible(float x, float y, System.Drawing.Pen pen);
public bool IsOutlineVisible(float x, float y, System.Drawing.Pen pen, System.Drawing.Graphics graphics);
public bool IsVisible(int x, int y);
public bool IsVisible(int x, int y, System.Drawing.Graphics graphics);
public bool IsVisible(System.Drawing.Point point);
public bool IsVisible(System.Drawing.PointF point);
public bool IsVisible(System.Drawing.PointF pt, System.Drawing.Graphics graphics);
public bool IsVisible(System.Drawing.Point pt, System.Drawing.Graphics graphics);
public bool IsVisible(float x, float y);
public bool IsVisible(float x, float y, System.Drawing.Graphics graphics);
public void Reset( );
public void Reverse( );
public void SetMarkers( );
public void StartFigure( );
public void Transform(Matrix matrix);
public void Warp(System.Drawing.PointF[ ] destPoints, System.Drawing.RectangleF srcRect);
public void Warp(System.Drawing.PointF[ ] destPoints, System.Drawing.RectangleF srcRect, Matrix matrix);
public void Warp(System.Drawing.PointF[ ] destPoints, System.Drawing.RectangleF srcRect, Matrix matrix,
    WarpMode warpMode);
public void Warp(System.Drawing.PointF[ ] destPoints, System.Drawing.RectangleF srcRect, Matrix matrix,
    WarpMode warpMode, float flatness);
public void Widen(System.Drawing.Pen pen);
public void Widen(System.Drawing.Pen pen, Matrix matrix);
```

```
 public void Widen(System.Drawing.Pen pen, Matrix matrix, float flatness);
// Protected Instance Methods
 protected override void Finalize( );                                    // overrides object
}
```

Hierarchy System.Object → System.MarshalByRefObject → GraphicsPath(System.ICloneable, System.IDisposable)

Passed To Multiple types

GraphicsPathIterator — marshal by reference, disposable

System.Drawing.Drawing2D (system.drawing.dll) — sealed class

This class is used to iterate the subpaths in a GraphicsPath object.

It can be constructed from a GraphicsPath object, and you can then step through the markers, subpaths, or connected line segments of the same type using the NextMarker( ), NextSubpath( ), and NextPathType( ) methods.

The Enumerate( ) function copies the path data into the specified arrays, and the CopyData( ) method allows you to copy just the path segments in a particular range (as retrieved from the enumeration methods mentioned above).

```
public sealed class GraphicsPathIterator : MarshalByRefObject : IDisposable {
// Public Constructors
 public GraphicsPathIterator(GraphicsPath path);
// Public Instance Properties
 public int Count{get; }
 public int SubpathCount{get; }
// Public Instance Methods
 public int CopyData(ref System.Drawing.PointF[ ] points, ref byte[ ] types, int startIndex, int endIndex);
 public void Dispose( );                                    // implements IDisposable
 public int Enumerate(ref System.Drawing.PointF[ ] points, ref byte[ ] types);
 public bool HasCurve( );
 public int NextMarker(GraphicsPath path);
 public int NextMarker(out int startIndex, out int endIndex);
 public int NextPathType(out byte pathType, out int startIndex, out int endIndex);
 public int NextSubpath(GraphicsPath path, out bool isClosed);
 public int NextSubpath(out int startIndex, out int endIndex, out bool isClosed);
 public void Rewind( );
// Protected Instance Methods
 protected override void Finalize( );                                    // overrides object
}
```

Hierarchy System.Object → System.MarshalByRefObject → GraphicsPathIterator(System.IDisposable)

GraphicsState — marshal by reference

System.Drawing.Drawing2D (system.drawing.dll) — sealed class

This opaque type represents the state of a System.Drawing.Graphics object as saved using the Graphics.Save( ) method. You can restore the state using the Graphics.Restore( ) method. Compare this with the GraphicsContainer class, which offers equivalent functionality.

```
public sealed class GraphicsState : MarshalByRefObject {
// No public or protected members
}
```

Hierarchy System.Object → System.MarshalByRefObject → GraphicsState

Returned By System.Drawing.Graphics.Save( )

Passed To System.Drawing.Graphics.Restore( )

HatchBrush — marshal by reference, disposable

System.Drawing.Drawing2D (system.drawing.dll) — sealed class

This defines a brush that can be used to fill shapes with a specific HatchStyle. You can also specify the BackgroundColor and ForegroundColor for the hatch.

```
public sealed class HatchBrush : System.Drawing.Brush {
// Public Constructors
   public HatchBrush(HatchStyle hatchstyle, System.Drawing.Color foreColor);
   public HatchBrush(HatchStyle hatchstyle, System.Drawing.Color foreColor, System.Drawing.Color backColor);
// Public Instance Properties
   public Color BackgroundColor{get; }
   public Color ForegroundColor{get; }
   public HatchStyle HatchStyle{get; }
// Public Instance Methods
   public override object Clone( );                         // overrides System.Drawing.Brush
}
```

Hierarchy System.Object → System.MarshalByRefObject → System.Drawing.Brush(System.ICloneable, System.IDisposable) → HatchBrush

HatchStyle — serializable

System.Drawing.Drawing2D (system.drawing.dll) — enum

This enumeration specifies the various different types of hatch grid that can be used with a HatchBrush.

```
public enum HatchStyle {
   Horizontal = 0,
   Min = 0,
   Vertical = 1,
   ForwardDiagonal = 2,
   BackwardDiagonal = 3,
   Cross = 4,
   LargeGrid = 4,
   Max = 4,
   DiagonalCross = 5,
   Percent05 = 6,
   Percent10 = 7,
   Percent20 = 8,
   Percent25 = 9,
   Percent30 = 10,
```

```
Percent40 = 11,
Percent50 = 12,
Percent60 = 13,
Percent70 = 14,
Percent75 = 15,
Percent80 = 16,
Percent90 = 17,
LightDownwardDiagonal = 18,
LightUpwardDiagonal = 19,
DarkDownwardDiagonal = 20,
DarkUpwardDiagonal = 21,
WideDownwardDiagonal = 22,
WideUpwardDiagonal = 23,
LightVertical = 24,
LightHorizontal = 25,
NarrowVertical = 26,
NarrowHorizontal = 27,
DarkVertical = 28,
DarkHorizontal = 29,
DashedDownwardDiagonal = 30,
DashedUpwardDiagonal = 31,
DashedHorizontal = 32,
DashedVertical = 33,
SmallConfetti = 34,
LargeConfetti = 35,
ZigZag = 36,
Wave = 37,
DiagonalBrick = 38,
HorizontalBrick = 39,
Weave = 40,
Plaid = 41,
Divot = 42,
DottedGrid = 43,
DottedDiamond = 44,
Shingle = 45,
Trellis = 46,
Sphere = 47,
SmallGrid = 48,
SmallCheckerBoard = 49,
LargeCheckerBoard = 50,
OutlinedDiamond = 51,
SolidDiamond = 52
}
```

Hierarchy System.Object → System.ValueType → System.Enum(System.IComparable, System.IFormattable, System.IConvertible) → HatchStyle

Returned By HatchBrush.HatchStyle

Passed To HatchBrush.HatchBrush( )

InterpolationMode serializable

System.Drawing.Drawing2D (system.drawing.dll) enum

This enumeration is used by System.Drawing.Graphics.InterpolationMode to determine how pixel colors are merged when scaling images. The higher the quality of the interpolation, the slower the rendering will be.

```
public enum InterpolationMode {
  Default = 0,
  Low = 1,
  High = 2,
  Bilinear = 3,
  Bicubic = 4,
  NearestNeighbor = 5,
  HighQualityBilinear = 6,
  HighQualityBicubic = 7,
  Invalid = -1
}
```

Hierarchy System.Object → System.ValueType → System.Enum(System.IComparable, System.IFormattable, System.IConvertible) → InterpolationMode

Returned By System.Drawing.Graphics.InterpolationMode

Passed To System.Drawing.Graphics.InterpolationMode

LinearGradientBrush marshal by reference, disposable

System.Drawing.Drawing2D (system.drawing.dll) sealed class

This brush class can be used to draw both two color and multicolor gradient fills.

For a two-color gradient, you set the LinearColors and the Blend properties. For a multicolor gradient, you instead set a ColorBlend object into the InterpolationColors member. In either case, you can enable GammaCorrection when rendering the gradient.

You can specify the logical Rectangle that defines the gradient, either in the constructor or, thereafter, through the Rectangle property. If the fill extends beyond this rectangle, the WrapMode determines how the areas outside the rectangle will be filled. When constructing the brush, but not thereafter, you can specify the LinearGradientMode or, alternatively, the angle (in degrees) at which the gradient should run across that rectangle.

You can also apply a Transform to the brush. There are the usual helper utilities MultiplyTransform( ), ResetTransform( ), RotateTransform( ), TranslateTransform( ), and ScaleTransform( ) to save you the trouble of the get/modify/set required to modify the Transform itself.

There are two other helper utilities: SetBlendTriangularShape( ) and SetSigmaBellShape( ) set up two common gradient shapes for you.

For non-rectangular fills, see PathGradientBrush.

```
public sealed class LinearGradientBrush : System.Drawing.Brush {
// Public Constructors
  public LinearGradientBrush(System.Drawing.PointF point1, System.Drawing.PointF point2,
     System.Drawing.Color color1, System.Drawing.Color color2);
  public LinearGradientBrush(System.Drawing.Point point1, System.Drawing.Point point2,
     System.Drawing.Color color1, System.Drawing.Color color2);
```


Drawing2D

```
  public LinearGradientBrush(System.Drawing.Rectangle rect, System.Drawing.Color color1,
     System.Drawing.Color color2, LinearGradientMode linearGradientMode);
  public LinearGradientBrush(System.Drawing.Rectangle rect, System.Drawing.Color color1,
     System.Drawing.Color color2, float angle);
  public LinearGradientBrush(System.Drawing.Rectangle rect, System.Drawing.Color color1,
     System.Drawing.Color color2, float angle, bool isAngleScaleable);
  public LinearGradientBrush(System.Drawing.RectangleF rect, System.Drawing.Color color1,
     System.Drawing.Color color2, LinearGradientMode linearGradientMode);
  public LinearGradientBrush(System.Drawing.RectangleF rect, System.Drawing.Color color1,
     System.Drawing.Color color2, float angle);
  public LinearGradientBrush(System.Drawing.RectangleF rect, System.Drawing.Color color1,
     System.Drawing.Color color2, float angle, bool isAngleScaleable);
// Public Instance Properties
  public Blend Blend{set; get; }
  public bool GammaCorrection{set; get; }
  public ColorBlend InterpolationColors{set; get; }
  public Color[ ] LinearColors{set; get; }
  public RectangleF Rectangle{get; }
  public Matrix Transform{set; get; }
  public WrapMode WrapMode{set; get; }
// Public Instance Methods
  public override object Clone( );                          // overrides System.Drawing.Brush
  public void MultiplyTransform(Matrix matrix);
  public void MultiplyTransform(Matrix matrix, MatrixOrder order);
  public void ResetTransform( );
  public void RotateTransform(float angle);
  public void RotateTransform(float angle, MatrixOrder order);
  public void ScaleTransform(float sx, float sy);
  public void ScaleTransform(float sx, float sy, MatrixOrder order);
  public void SetBlendTriangularShape(float focus);
  public void SetBlendTriangularShape(float focus, float scale);
  public void SetSigmaBellShape(float focus);
  public void SetSigmaBellShape(float focus, float scale);
  public void TranslateTransform(float dx, float dy);
  public void TranslateTransform(float dx, float dy, MatrixOrder order);
}
```

Hierarchy System.Object → System.MarshalByRefObject → System.Drawing.Brush(System.ICloneable, System.IDisposable) → LinearGradientBrush

LinearGradientMode **serializable**

System.Drawing.Drawing2D (system.drawing.dll) **enum**

This enumeration lists the predefined angles that can be applied to a LinearGradientBrush.

```
public enum LinearGradientMode {
  Horizontal = 0,
  Vertical = 1,
  ForwardDiagonal = 2,
  BackwardDiagonal = 3
}
```

Hierarchy System.Object → System.ValueType → System.Enum(System.IComparable, System.IFormattable, System.IConvertible) → LinearGradientMode

Passed To LinearGradientBrush.LinearGradientBrush( )

LineCap serializable

System.Drawing.Drawing2D (system.drawing.dll) enum

This enumeration lists the various kinds of linecap that be applied to the line drawn by a System.Drawing.Pen.

They come into two categories: the *caps*, which provide endcaps the same width as the line, and the *anchors*, which provide marker shapes at the end of the line. If you wish to use a CustomLineCap, you need to specify the Custom value here.

```
public enum LineCap {
  Flat = 0,
  Square = 1,
  Round = 2,
  Triangle = 3,
  NoAnchor = 16,
  SquareAnchor = 17,
  RoundAnchor = 18,
  DiamondAnchor = 19,
  ArrowAnchor = 20,
  AnchorMask = 240,
  Custom = 255
}
```

Hierarchy System.Object → System.ValueType → System.Enum(System.IComparable, System.IFormattable, System.IConvertible) → LineCap

Returned By CustomLineCap.BaseCap, System.Drawing.Pen.{EndCap, StartCap}

Passed To CustomLineCap.{BaseCap, CustomLineCap( ), GetStrokeCaps( ), SetStrokeCaps( )}, System.Drawing.Pen.{EndCap, SetLineCap( ), StartCap}

Drawing2D

LineJoin serializable

System.Drawing.Drawing2D (system.drawing.dll) enum

Where two line segments join, you can specify the join style using this enumeration. It is used by the System.Drawing.Pen.LineJoin property.

```
public enum LineJoin {
  Miter = 0,
  Bevel = 1,
  Round = 2,
  MiterClipped = 3
}
```

Hierarchy System.Object → System.ValueType → System.Enum(System.IComparable, System.IFormattable, System.IConvertible) → LineJoin

Returned By CustomLineCap.StrokeJoin, System.Drawing.Pen.LineJoin

Passed To CustomLineCap.StrokeJoin, System.Drawing.Pen.LineJoin

Matrix

marshal by reference, disposable

System.Drawing.Drawing2D (system.drawing.dll) sealed class

This class encapsulates a 3x3 transformation matrix for use with most of the graphics elements in the System.Drawing and nested namespaces.

You can get an array of the Elements in the array (ordered {1,1},{1,2},{2,1},{2,2},{3,1},{3,2}). {1,3}, {2,3}, {3,3} are wired to {0,0,1} and hence do not appear in the array. {3,1} and {3,2} apply a translation and can be retrieved independently through the OffsetX and OffsetY properties. You can also determine if the matrix IsInvertible (you invert it with the aptly named Invert( ) method). If the matrix is the identity matrix {1,0,0},{0,1,0},{0,0,1}, IsIdentity will be true.

There are then a host of methods that allow you to transform the matrix. You can Rotate( ), Translate( ), Scale( ), and Shear( ) the object. You can also Reset( ) the matrix back to the identity or Multiply( ) by another matrix. Each method can be performed either prepending or appending the transform: matrix arithmetic is not commutative.

In addition to being able to apply the matrix to a variety of different graphics structures, you can use the TransformPoints( ) and TransformVectors( ) methods to transform a set of points. The latter does not apply the offset with the transform.

```
public sealed class Matrix : MarshalByRefObject : IDisposable {
// Public Constructors
   public Matrix( );
   public Matrix(System.Drawing.RectangleF rect, System.Drawing.PointF[ ] plgpts);
   public Matrix(System.Drawing.Rectangle rect, System.Drawing.Point[ ] plgpts);
   public Matrix(float m11, float m12, float m21, float m22, float dx, float dy);
// Public Instance Properties
   public float[ ] Elements{get; }
   public bool IsIdentity{get; }
   public bool IsInvertible{get; }
   public float OffsetX{get; }
   public float OffsetY{get; }
// Public Instance Methods
   public Matrix Clone( );
   public void Dispose( );                                    // implements IDisposable
   public override bool Equals(object obj);                   // overrides object
   public override int GetHashCode( );                        // overrides object
   public void Invert( );
   public void Multiply(Matrix matrix);
   public void Multiply(Matrix matrix, MatrixOrder order);
   public void Reset( );
   public void Rotate(float angle);
   public void Rotate(float angle, MatrixOrder order);
   public void RotateAt(float angle, System.Drawing.PointF point);
   public void RotateAt(float angle, System.Drawing.PointF point, MatrixOrder order);
   public void Scale(float scaleX, float scaleY);
   public void Scale(float scaleX, float scaleY, MatrixOrder order);
```

```
  public void Shear(float shearX, float shearY);
  public void Shear(float shearX, float shearY, MatrixOrder order);
  public void TransformPoints(System.Drawing.Point[ ] pts);
  public void TransformPoints(System.Drawing.PointF[ ] pts);
  public void TransformVectors(System.Drawing.Point[ ] pts);
  public void TransformVectors(System.Drawing.PointF[ ] pts);
  public void Translate(float offsetX, float offsetY);
  public void Translate(float offsetX, float offsetY, MatrixOrder order);
  public void VectorTransformPoints(System.Drawing.Point[ ] pts);
// Protected Instance Methods
  protected override void Finalize( );                              // overrides object
}
```

Hierarchy System.Object → System.MarshalByRefObject → Matrix(System.IDisposable)

Returned By LinearGradientBrush.Transform, PathGradientBrush.Transform, System.Drawing.Graphics.Transform, System.Drawing.Pen.Transform, System.Drawing.TextureBrush.Transform

Passed To Multiple types

MatrixOrder serializable

System.Drawing.Drawing2D (system.drawing.dll) enum

This enumeration is used by the various classes and methods that apply a transform to a matrix or graphics object to determine whether the matrix is pre- or post-multiplied. (Remember: matrixes are non-commutative, so the multiplication order is important).

```
public enum MatrixOrder {
  Prepend = 0,
  Append = 1
}
```

Hierarchy System.Object → System.ValueType → System.Enum(System.IComparable, System.IFormattable, System.IConvertible) → MatrixOrder

Passed To Multiple types

PathData

System.Drawing.Drawing2D (system.drawing.dll) sealed class

This class encapsulates the Points and Types (PathPointType values) that define a GraphicsPath.

```
public sealed class PathData {
// Public Constructors
  public PathData( );
// Public Instance Properties
  public PointF[ ] Points{set; get; }
  public byte[ ] Types{set; get; }
}
```

Returned By GraphicsPath.PathData

Drawing2D

PathGradientBrush **marshal by reference, disposable**

System.Drawing.Drawing2D (system.drawing.dll) **sealed class**

This class defines a gradient brush that shades from one color at the center of a **GraphicsPath** to another at each edge of the path. The **CenterPoint** can be set arbitrarily.

You can define a basic fade by setting the **CenterColor**, populating the **SurroundColors** array with one **Color** value for each of the points defining the path, and setting the **Blend** object.

Alternatively, you can go for a more complex fade, by setting a **ColorBlend** object into the **InterpolationColors** property.

You can also set the bounding **Rectangle** for the path, and the **WrapMode** defining how points outside that rectangle should be filled.

The path itself is set in the constructor of the object and cannot be modified subsequently, but you can apply a **Transform** with the usual array of helper methods, such as RotateTransform( ) and MultiplyTransform( ).

```
public sealed class PathGradientBrush : System.Drawing.Brush {
// Public Constructors
   public PathGradientBrush(GraphicsPath path);
   public PathGradientBrush(System.Drawing.Point[ ] points);
   public PathGradientBrush(System.Drawing.Point[ ] points, WrapMode wrapMode);
   public PathGradientBrush(System.Drawing.PointF[ ] points);
   public PathGradientBrush(System.Drawing.PointF[ ] points, WrapMode wrapMode);
// Public Instance Properties
   public Blend Blend{set; get; }
   public Color CenterColor{set; get; }
   public PointF CenterPoint{set; get; }
   public PointF FocusScales{set; get; }
   public ColorBlend InterpolationColors{set; get; }
   public RectangleF Rectangle{get; }
   public Color[ ] SurroundColors{set; get; }
   public Matrix Transform{set; get; }
   public WrapMode WrapMode{set; get; }
// Public Instance Methods
   public override object Clone( );                              // overrides System.Drawing.Brush
   public void MultiplyTransform(Matrix matrix);
   public void MultiplyTransform(Matrix matrix, MatrixOrder order);
   public void ResetTransform( );
   public void RotateTransform(float angle);
   public void RotateTransform(float angle, MatrixOrder order);
   public void ScaleTransform(float sx, float sy);
   public void ScaleTransform(float sx, float sy, MatrixOrder order);
   public void SetBlendTriangularShape(float focus);
   public void SetBlendTriangularShape(float focus, float scale);
   public void SetSigmaBellShape(float focus);
   public void SetSigmaBellShape(float focus, float scale);
   public void TranslateTransform(float dx, float dy);
   public void TranslateTransform(float dx, float dy, MatrixOrder order);
}
```

Hierarchy System.Object → System.MarshalByRefObject → System.Drawing.Brush(System.ICloneable, System.IDisposable) → PathGradientBrush

PathPointType serializable

System.Drawing.Drawing2D (system.drawing.dll) enum

This enumeration is used to specify the type of a point in a GraphicsPath. You can OR the line types with the DashMode and CloseSubpath values to close the figure, or to apply a dash style to the line.

```
public enum PathPointType {
  Start = 0,
  Line = 1,
  Bezier = 3,
  Bezier3 = 3,
  PathTypeMask = 7,
  DashMode = 16,
  PathMarker = 32,
  CloseSubpath = 128
}
```

Hierarchy System.Object → System.ValueType → System.Enum(System.IComparable, System.IFormattable, System.IConvertible) → PathPointType

PenAlignment serializable

System.Drawing.Drawing2D (system.drawing.dll) enum

This enumeration is used to specify how a System.Drawing.Pen (which has certain width) is to be painted over the theoretical line of width 0 that defines a path. In v1.0 of GDI+, only the Center option appears to work correctly.

```
public enum PenAlignment {
  Center = 0,
  Inset = 1,
  Outset = 2,
  Left = 3,
  Right = 4
}
```

Hierarchy System.Object → System.ValueType → System.Enum(System.IComparable, System.IFormattable, System.IConvertible) → PenAlignment

Returned By System.Drawing.Pen.Alignment

Passed To System.Drawing.Pen.Alignment

PenType serializable

System.Drawing.Drawing2D (system.drawing.dll) enum

A System.Drawing.Pen can have a System.Drawing.Brush assigned to fill the stroke (as opposed to fill the shape). The type of brush that has been assigned can be determined via the System.Drawing.Pen.PenType property. The value returned is chosen from this enumeration.

```
public enum PenType {
  SolidColor = 0,
```

```
  HatchFill = 1,
  TextureFill = 2,
  PathGradient = 3,
  LinearGradient = 4
}
```

Hierarchy System.Object → System.ValueType → System.Enum(System.IComparable, System.IFormattable, System.IConvertible) → PenType

Returned By System.Drawing.Pen.PenType

PixelOffsetMode serializable

System.Drawing.Drawing2D (system.drawing.dll) enum

This enumeration is used to define the options for the System.Drawing.Graphics.PixelOffsetMode property. This is another parameter that affects rendering quality at the expense of rendering speed.

```
public enum PixelOffsetMode {
  Default = 0,
  HighSpeed = 1,
  HighQuality = 2,
  None = 3,
  Half = 4,
  Invalid = -1
}
```

Hierarchy System.Object → System.ValueType → System.Enum(System.IComparable, System.IFormattable, System.IConvertible) → PixelOffsetMode

Returned By System.Drawing.Graphics.PixelOffsetMode

Passed To System.Drawing.Graphics.PixelOffsetMode

QualityMode serializable

System.Drawing.Drawing2D (system.drawing.dll) enum

This enumeration is not actually used in the framework but represents the basic rendering quality options available. You can see its equivalent in the InterpolationMode and TextRenderingHint enumerations.

```
public enum QualityMode {
  Default = 0,
  Low = 1,
  High = 2,
  Invalid = -1
}
```

Hierarchy System.Object → System.ValueType → System.Enum(System.IComparable, System.IFormattable, System.IConvertible) → QualityMode

RegionData

System.Drawing.Drawing2D (system.drawing.dll) sealed class

This class encapsulates the data that makes up a System.Drawing.Region object. You can get at the byte array that defines the region through the Data property.

You could use this data to serialize a Region, for example.

```
public sealed class RegionData {
// Public Instance Properties
   public byte[ ] Data{set; get; }
}
```

Returned By System.Drawing.Region.GetRegionData( )

Passed To System.Drawing.Region.Region( )

SmoothingMode serializable

System.Drawing.Drawing2D (system.drawing.dll) enum

This enumeration determines the antialiasing mode used when rendering graphics objects. As with all the rendering hints, this is a trade-off between rendering quality and rendering time.

```
public enum SmoothingMode {
   Default = 0,
   HighSpeed = 1,
   HighQuality = 2,
   None = 3,
   AntiAlias = 4,
   Invalid = -1
}
```

Hierarchy System.Object → System.ValueType → System.Enum(System.IComparable, System.IFormattable, System.IConvertible) → SmoothingMode

Returned By System.Drawing.Graphics.SmoothingMode

Passed To System.Drawing.Graphics.SmoothingMode

WarpMode serializable

System.Drawing.Drawing2D (system.drawing.dll) enum

When using the GraphicsPath.Warp( ) method, this enumeration defines how the warp is applied. A bilinear warp preserves horizontal and vertical lines and distorts other lines into curves, whereas a perspective warp preserves straight lines but foreshortens the image, distorting parallel lines.

```
public enum WarpMode {
   Perspective = 0,
   Bilinear = 1
}
```

Hierarchy System.Object → System.ValueType → System.Enum(System.IComparable, System.IFormattable, System.IConvertible) → WarpMode

Passed To GraphicsPath.Warp( )

WrapMode

serializable

System.Drawing.Drawing2D (system.drawing.dll) **enum**

This enumeration is used by the various gradient brushes to determine how the pixels outside a brush's Rectangle are to be filled.

```
public enum WrapMode {
  Tile = 0,
  TileFlipX = 1,
  TileFlipY = 2,
  TileFlipXY = 3,
  Clamp = 4
}
```

Hierarchy System.Object → System.ValueType → System.Enum(System.IComparable, System.IFormattable, System.IConvertible) → WrapMode

Returned By LinearGradientBrush.WrapMode, PathGradientBrush.WrapMode, System.Drawing.TextureBrush.WrapMode

Passed To LinearGradientBrush.WrapMode, PathGradientBrush.{PathGradientBrush( ), WrapMode}, System.Drawing.Imaging.ImageAttributes.SetWrapMode( ), System.Drawing.TextureBrush.{TextureBrush( ), WrapMode}

16

The System.Drawing.Imaging Namespace

This namespace contains a variety of classes and enumerations that are used in imaging applications (as opposed to the vector drawing facilities found in System.Drawing.Drawing2D). Figure 16-1 shows the types in this namespace.

BitmapData

System.Drawing.Imaging (system.drawing.dll) sealed class

This class encapsulates the raw data of a System.Drawing.Bitmap. It is returned by LockBits( ), and the Bitmap.UnlockBits( ) method releases the data.

You can retrieve the Width, Height, PixelFormat, and Stride (the number of bytes per line including padding, as opposed to the number of pixels). The sign of the Stride can also be used to determine whether this is a top-down or bottom-up bitmap.

The pixel data itself can be retrieved through the Scan0 member, which returns an IntPtr to the start of the image. This can be handed off to either managed or (more commonly) unmanaged image processing code.

```
public sealed class BitmapData {
// Public Constructors
 public BitmapData( );
// Public Instance Properties
 public int Height{set; get; }
 public PixelFormat PixelFormat{set; get; }
 public int Reserved{set; get; }
 public IntPtr Scan0{set; get; }
 public int Stride{set; get; }
 public int Width{set; get; }
}
```

Returned By System.Drawing.Bitmap.LockBits( )

Passed To System.Drawing.Bitmap.UnlockBits( )

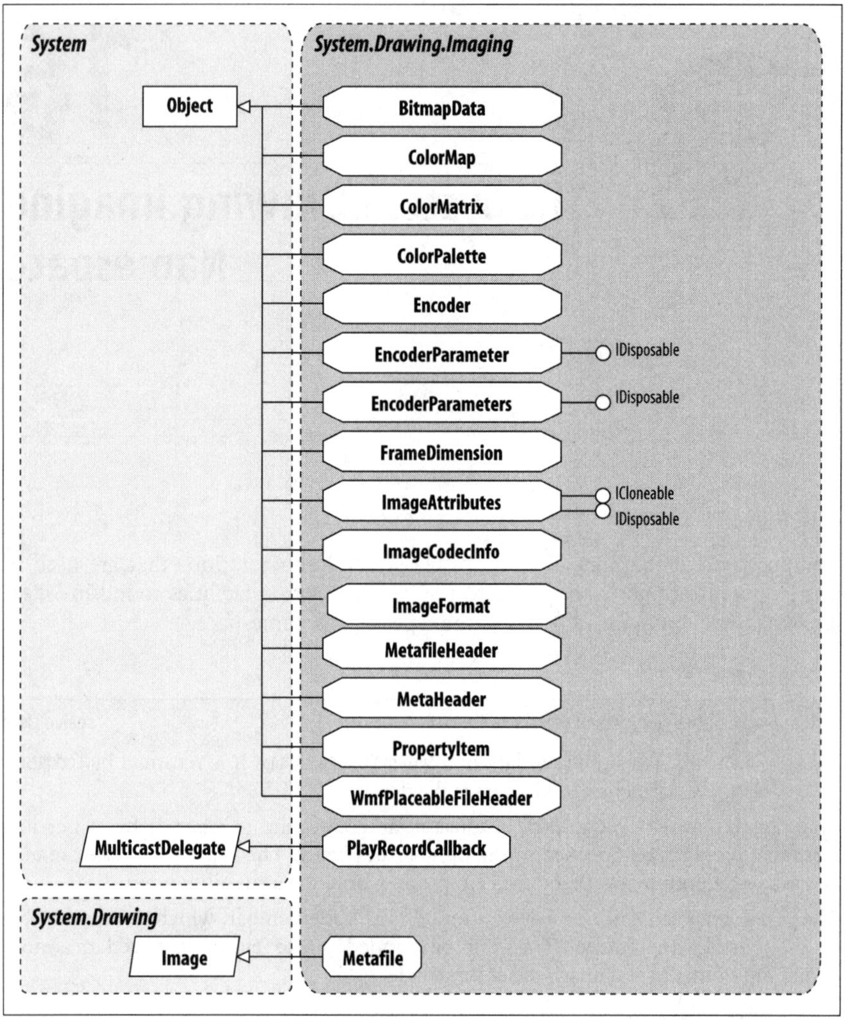
System
System.Drawing.Imaging
Object
BitmapData
ColorMap
ColorMatrix
ColorPalette
Encoder
EncoderParameter
IDisposable
EncoderParameters
IDisposable
FrameDimension
ImageAttributes
ICloneable
IDisposable
ImageCodecInfo
ImageFormat
MetafileHeader
MetaHeader
PropertyItem
WmfPlaceableFileHeader
MulticastDelegate
PlayRecordCallback
System.Drawing
Image
Metafile

Figure 16-1. Types from the System.Drawing.Imaging namespace

ColorAdjustType **serializable**

System.Drawing.Imaging (system.drawing.dll) **enum**

This enumeration is used by various methods in the ImageAttributes class to determine which types of GDI+ object will be affected by the color transform it defines.

```
public enum ColorAdjustType {
  Default = 0,
  Bitmap = 1,
  Brush = 2,
  Pen = 3,
  Text = 4,
  Count = 5,
```

```
  Any = 6
}
```

Hierarchy System.Object → System.ValueType → System.Enum(System.IComparable, System.IFormattable, System.IConvertible) → ColorAdjustType

Passed To Multiple types

ColorChannelFlag serializable

System.Drawing.Imaging (system.drawing.dll) enum

This enumeration is used by the ImageAttributes.SetOutputChannel( ) to determine which of the CMYK channels should be output when the image is drawn. This can be used for color-space conversion.

```
public enum ColorChannelFlag {
  ColorChannelC = 0,
  ColorChannelM = 1,
  ColorChannelY = 2,
  ColorChannelK = 3,
  ColorChannelLast = 4
}
```

Hierarchy System.Object → System.ValueType → System.Enum(System.IComparable, System.Formattable, System.IConvertible) → ColorChannelFlag

Passed To ImageAttributes.SetOutputChannel( )

ColorMap

System.Drawing.Imaging (system.drawing.dll) sealed class

This class defines a mapping of one color to another: the NewColor and the OldColor. Several of the ImageAttributes methods (such as ImageAttributes.SetRemapTable( )) use an array of these objects to define a color mapping table.

```
public sealed class ColorMap {
// Public Constructors
  public ColorMap( );
// Public Instance Properties
  public Color NewColor{set; get; }
  public Color OldColor{set; get; }
}
```

Passed To ImageAttributes.{SetBrushRemapTable( ), SetRemapTable( )}

ColorMapType serializable

System.Drawing.Imaging (system.drawing.dll) enum

This enumeration distinguishes between a Brush and the Default types of color map. It is not used in the public interface of the framework. The ColorAdjustType enumeration is used where you might expect this to be needed.

```
public enum ColorMapType {
  Default = 0,
  Brush = 1
}
```

Hierarchy System.Object → System.ValueType → System.Enum(System.IComparable, System.IFormattable, System.IConvertible) → ColorMapType

ColorMatrix

System.Drawing.Imaging (system.drawing.dll) **sealed class**

A color matrix (also commonly called a "color twist matrix") is used to transform one color into another, by considering the color definition to be a 3D vector into a color cube. Only because we now have an alpha channel, it is actually a 4D vector into a color hypercube!

It is a 5x5 matrix and is used to transform an {R,G,B,A,1} color. Note that the color vector is considered to be "wide" rather than "tall" (compare this to the System.Drawing.Drawing2D.Matrix class and a Point, which is considered to be tall, rather than wide).

You can retrieve any Item from the matrix (this is the indexer property), or you can use one of the 25 properties prefixed with "Matrix" to get or set the values.

The matrix is applied with the ImageAttributes.SetColorMatrix( ) method.

```
public sealed class ColorMatrix {
// Public Constructors
  public ColorMatrix( );
  public ColorMatrix(float[ ][ ] newColorMatrix);
// Public Instance Properties
  public float Matrix00{set; get; }
  public float Matrix01{set; get; }
  public float Matrix02{set; get; }
  public float Matrix03{set; get; }
  public float Matrix04{set; get; }
  public float Matrix10{set; get; }
  public float Matrix11{set; get; }
  public float Matrix12{set; get; }
  public float Matrix13{set; get; }
  public float Matrix14{set; get; }
  public float Matrix20{set; get; }
  public float Matrix21{set; get; }
  public float Matrix22{set; get; }
  public float Matrix23{set; get; }
  public float Matrix24{set; get; }
  public float Matrix30{set; get; }
  public float Matrix31{set; get; }
  public float Matrix32{set; get; }
  public float Matrix33{set; get; }
  public float Matrix34{set; get; }
  public float Matrix40{set; get; }
  public float Matrix41{set; get; }
  public float Matrix42{set; get; }
```

```
 public float Matrix43{set; get; }
 public float Matrix44{set; get; }
 public float this{set; get; }
}
```

Passed To ImageAttributes.{SetColorMatrices( ), SetColorMatrix( )}

ColorMatrixFlag

serializable

System.Drawing.Imaging (system.drawing.dll) **enum**

This enumeration is used to specify how a ColorMatrix should be applied to a GDI+ object. You can use the Default mode, or SkipGrays will ensure that gray values (those with identical red, green, and blue components) will not be affected.

```
public enum ColorMatrixFlag {
 Default = 0,
 SkipGrays = 1,
 AltGrays = 2
}
```

Hierarchy System.Object → System.ValueType → System.Enum(System.IComparable, System.IFormattable, System.IConvertible) → ColorMatrixFlag

Passed To ImageAttributes.{SetColorMatrices( ), SetColorMatrix( )}

ColorMode

serializable

System.Drawing.Imaging (system.drawing.dll) **enum**

This enumeration is used to specify whether color components are 32-bit or 64-bit values. It is not used in the public interface of the framework.

```
public enum ColorMode {
 Argb32Mode = 0,
 Argb64Mode = 1
}
```

Hierarchy System.Object → System.ValueType → System.Enum(System.IComparable, System.IFormattable, System.IConvertible) → ColorMode

ColorPalette

System.Drawing.Imaging (system.drawing.dll) **sealed class**

This class encapsulates an array of related colors that make up a color palette.

You can retrieve an array of the Entries in the palette (each is a System.Drawing.Color value).

You can also get a Flags integer that rather unpleasantly depends on the magic cookies 0x01 to indicate that the colors contain alpha information, 0x02 to indicate that the colors represent grayscales, and 0x04 to indicate that the array contains halftone values. Those values are listed in the PaletteFlags enumeration, but you have to cast them to an integer before they can be used.

```
public sealed class ColorPalette {
// Public Instance Properties
  public Color[ ] Entries{get; }
  public int Flags{get; }
}
```

Returned By System.Drawing.Image.Palette

Passed To System.Drawing.Image.Palette, ImageAttributes.GetAdjustedPalette( )

EmfPlusRecordType **serializable**

System.Drawing.Imaging (system.drawing.dll) **enum**

This enumeration lists the types of record that can be defined in a GDI+-format enhanced metafile (EMF). Note that GDI+ extends the standard EMF format with several new record types. You can play records from a metafile using the Metafile.PlayRecord( ) method.

```
public enum EmfPlusRecordType {
  EmfMin = 1,
  EmfHeader = 1,
  EmfPolyBezier = 2,
  EmfPolygon = 3,
  EmfPolyline = 4,
  EmfPolyBezierTo = 5,
  EmfPolyLineTo = 6,
  EmfPolyPolyline = 7,
  EmfPolyPolygon = 8,
  EmfSetWindowExtEx = 9,
  EmfSetWindowOrgEx = 10,
  EmfSetViewportExtEx = 11,
  EmfSetViewportOrgEx = 12,
  EmfSetBrushOrgEx = 13,
  EmfEof = 14,
  EmfSetPixelV = 15,
  EmfSetMapperFlags = 16,
  EmfSetMapMode = 17,
  EmfSetBkMode = 18,
  EmfSetPolyFillMode = 19,
  EmfSetROP2 = 20,
  EmfSetStretchBltMode = 21,
  EmfSetTextAlign = 22,
  EmfSetColorAdjustment = 23,
  EmfSetTextColor = 24,
  EmfSetBkColor = 25,
  EmfOffsetClipRgn = 26,
  EmfMoveToEx = 27,
  EmfSetMetaRgn = 28,
  EmfExcludeClipRect = 29,
  EmfIntersectClipRect = 30,
  EmfScaleViewportExtEx = 31,
  EmfScaleWindowExtEx = 32,
```

```
EmfSaveDC = 33,
EmfRestoreDC = 34,
EmfSetWorldTransform = 35,
EmfModifyWorldTransform = 36,
EmfSelectObject = 37,
EmfCreatePen = 38,
EmfCreateBrushIndirect = 39,
EmfDeleteObject = 40,
EmfAngleArc = 41,
EmfEllipse = 42,
EmfRectangle = 43,
EmfRoundRect = 44,
EmfRoundArc = 45,
EmfChord = 46,
EmfPie = 47,
EmfSelectPalette = 48,
EmfCreatePalette = 49,
EmfSetPaletteEntries = 50,
EmfResizePalette = 51,
EmfRealizePalette = 52,
EmfExtFloodFill = 53,
EmfLineTo = 54,
EmfArcTo = 55,
EmfPolyDraw = 56,
EmfSetArcDirection = 57,
EmfSetMiterLimit = 58,
EmfBeginPath = 59,
EmfEndPath = 60,
EmfCloseFigure = 61,
EmfFillPath = 62,
EmfStrokeAndFillPath = 63,
EmfStrokePath = 64,
EmfFlattenPath = 65,
EmfWidenPath = 66,
EmfSelectClipPath = 67,
EmfAbortPath = 68,
EmfReserved069 = 69,
EmfGdiComment = 70,
EmfFillRgn = 71,
EmfFrameRgn = 72,
EmfInvertRgn = 73,
EmfPaintRgn = 74,
EmfExtSelectClipRgn = 75,
EmfBitBlt = 76,
EmfStretchBlt = 77,
EmfMaskBlt = 78,
EmfPlgBlt = 79,
EmfSetDIBitsToDevice = 80,
EmfStretchDIBits = 81,
EmfExtCreateFontIndirect = 82,
EmfExtTextOutA = 83,
EmfExtTextOutW = 84,
```

Imaging

```
EmfPolyBezier16 = 85,
EmfPolygon16 = 86,
EmfPolyline16 = 87,
EmfPolyBezierTo16 = 88,
EmfPolylineTo16 = 89,
EmfPolyPolyline16 = 90,
EmfPolyPolygon16 = 91,
EmfPolyDraw16 = 92,
EmfCreateMonoBrush = 93,
EmfCreateDibPatternBrushPt = 94,
EmfExtCreatePen = 95,
EmfPolyTextOutA = 96,
EmfPolyTextOutW = 97,
EmfSetIcmMode = 98,
EmfCreateColorSpace = 99,
EmfSetColorSpace = 100,
EmfDeleteColorSpace = 101,
EmfGlsRecord = 102,
EmfGlsBoundedRecord = 103,
EmfPixelFormat = 104,
EmfDrawEscape = 105,
EmfExtEscape = 106,
EmfStartDoc = 107,
EmfSmallTextOut = 108,
EmfForceUfiMapping = 109,
EmfNamedEscpae = 110,
EmfColorCorrectPalette = 111,
EmfSetIcmProfileA = 112,
EmfSetIcmProfileW = 113,
EmfAlphaBlend = 114,
EmfSetLayout = 115,
EmfTransparentBlt = 116,
EmfReserved117 = 117,
EmfGradientFill = 118,
EmfSetLinkedUfis = 119,
EmfSetTextJustification = 120,
EmfColorMatchToTargetW = 121,
EmfCreateColorSpaceW = 122,
EmfMax = 122,
Invalid = 16384,
EmfPlusRecordBase = 16384,
Header = 16385,
Min = 16385,
EndOfFile = 16386,
Comment = 16387,
GetDC = 16388,
MultiFormatStart = 16389,
MultiFormatSection = 16390,
MultiFormatEnd = 16391,
Object = 16392,
Clear = 16393,
FillRects = 16394,
```

```
DrawRects = 16395,
FillPolygon = 16396,
DrawLines = 16397,
FillEllipse = 16398,
DrawEllipse = 16399,
FillPie = 16400,
DrawPie = 16401,
DrawArc = 16402,
FillRegion = 16403,
FillPath = 16404,
DrawPath = 16405,
FillClosedCurve = 16406,
DrawClosedCurve = 16407,
DrawCurve = 16408,
DrawBeziers = 16409,
DrawImage = 16410,
DrawImagePoints = 16411,
DrawString = 16412,
SetRenderingOrigin = 16413,
SetAntiAliasMode = 16414,
SetTextRenderingHint = 16415,
SetTextContrast = 16416,
SetInterpolationMode = 16417,
SetPixelOffsetMode = 16418,
SetCompositingMode = 16419,
SetCompositingQuality = 16420,
Save = 16421,
Restore = 16422,
BeginContainer = 16423,
BeginContainerNoParams = 16424,
EndContainer = 16425,
SetWorldTransform = 16426,
ResetWorldTransform = 16427,
MultiplyWorldTransform = 16428,
TranslateWorldTransform = 16429,
ScaleWorldTransform = 16430,
RotateWorldTransform = 16431,
SetPageTransform = 16432,
ResetClip = 16433,
SetClipRect = 16434,
SetClipPath = 16435,
SetClipRegion = 16436,
OffsetClip = 16437,
Max = 16438,
DrawDriverString = 16438,
Total = 16439,
WmfRecordBase = 65536,
WmfSaveDC = 65566,
WmfRealizePalette = 65589,
WmfSetPalEntries = 65591,
WmfCreatePalette = 65783,
WmfSetBkMode = 65794,
```

```
WmfSetMapMode = 65795,
WmfSetROP2 = 65796,
WmfSetRelAbs = 65797,
WmfSetPolyFillMode = 65798,
WmfSetStretchBltMode = 65799,
WmfSetTextCharExtra = 65800,
WmfRestoreDC = 65831,
WmfInvertRegion = 65834,
WmfPaintRegion = 65835,
WmfSelectClipRegion = 65836,
WmfSelectObject = 65837,
WmfSetTextAlign = 65838,
WmfResizePalette = 65849,
WmfDibCreatePatternBrush = 65858,
WmfSetLayout = 65865,
WmfDeleteObject = 66032,
WmfCreatePatternBrush = 66041,
WmfSetBkColor = 66049,
WmfSetTextColor = 66057,
WmfSetTextJustification = 66058,
WmfSetWindowOrg = 66059,
WmfSetWindowExt = 66060,
WmfSetViewportOrg = 66061,
WmfSetViewportExt = 66062,
WmfOffsetWindowOrg = 66063,
WmfOffsetViewportOrg = 66065,
WmfLineTo = 66067,
WmfMoveTo = 66068,
WmfOffsetCilpRgn = 66080,
WmfFillRegion = 66088,
WmfSetMapperFlags = 66097,
WmfSelectPalette = 66100,
WmfCreatePenIndirect = 66298,
WmfCreateFontIndirect = 66299,
WmfCreateBrushIndirect = 66300,
WmfPolygon = 66340,
WmfPolyline = 66341,
WmfScaleWindowExt = 66576,
WmfScaleViewportExt = 66578,
WmfExcludeClipRect = 66581,
WmfIntersectClipRect = 66582,
WmfEllipse = 66584,
WmfFloodFill = 66585,
WmfRectangle = 66587,
WmfSetPixel = 66591,
WmfFrameRegion = 66601,
WmfAnimatePalette = 66614,
WmfTextOut = 66849,
WmfPolyPolygon = 66872,
WmfExtFloodFill = 66888,
WmfRoundRect = 67100,
WmfPatBlt = 67101,
```

```
  WmfEscape = 67110,
  WmfCreateRegion = 67327,
  WmfArc = 67607,
  WmfPie = 67610,
  WmfChord = 67632,
  WmfBitBlt = 67874,
  WmfDibBitBlt = 67904,
  WmfExtTextOut = 68146,
  WmfStretchBlt = 68387,
  WmfDibStretchBlt = 68417,
  WmfSetDibToDev = 68915,
  WmfStretchDib = 69443
}
```

Hierarchy System.Object → System.ValueType → System.Enum(System.IComparable, System.IFormattable, System.IConvertible) → EmfPlusRecordType

Passed To System.Drawing.EnumerateMetafileProc.{BeginInvoke( ), Invoke( )}, Metafile.PlayRecord( ), PlayRecordCallback.{BeginInvoke( ), Invoke( )}

EmfType serializable

System.Drawing.Imaging (system.drawing.dll) enum

This enumeration is used to specify whether an enhanced metafile should support the pre-GDI+ EMF format only (EmfOnly), both pre-GDI+ and new GDI+ renderers (EmfPlusDual), or GDI+ renderers only (EmfPlusOnly). This issue comes about because GDI+ extends the EMF format with some new record types of its own.

It is used in several of the Metafile constructors.

```
public enum EmfType {
  EmfOnly = 3,
  EmfPlusOnly = 4,
  EmfPlusDual = 5
}
```

Hierarchy System.Object → System.ValueType → System.Enum(System.IComparable, System.IFormattable, System.IConvertible) → EmfType

Passed To Metafile.Metafile( )

Encoder

System.Drawing.Imaging (system.drawing.dll) sealed class

The EncoderParameter class is used to pass parameters to a GDI+ image-storage codec when saving images. This class wraps a Guid identifying a particular encoder category for that parameter.

For example, the parameter might relate to the Compression mode, the RenderMethod or the Quality of the image that will be output by the codec.

```
public sealed class Encoder {
// Public Constructors
```

Imaging

```
  public Encoder(Guid guid);
// Public Static Fields
  public static readonly Encoder ChrominanceTable;              // =System.Drawing.Imaging.Encoder
  public static readonly Encoder ColorDepth;                    // =System.Drawing.Imaging.Encoder
  public static readonly Encoder Compression;                   // =System.Drawing.Imaging.Encoder
  public static readonly Encoder LuminanceTable;                // =System.Drawing.Imaging.Encoder
  public static readonly Encoder Quality;                       // =System.Drawing.Imaging.Encoder
  public static readonly Encoder RenderMethod;                  // =System.Drawing.Imaging.Encoder
  public static readonly Encoder SaveFlag;                      // =System.Drawing.Imaging.Encoder
  public static readonly Encoder ScanMethod;                    // =System.Drawing.Imaging.Encoder
  public static readonly Encoder Transformation;                // =System.Drawing.Imaging.Encoder
  public static readonly Encoder Version;                       // =System.Drawing.Imaging.Encoder
// Public Instance Properties
  public Guid Guid{get; }
}
```

Returned By EncoderParameter.Encoder

Passed To EncoderParameter.{Encoder, EncoderParameter( )}

EncoderParameter **disposable**

System.Drawing.Imaging (system.drawing.dll) **sealed class**

This class encapsulates a parameter to pass to a GDI+ image-storage codec when saving an image using the Image.Save( ) method. This can give you control over a number of different aspects of the image storage process, as enumerated in the Encoder class.

You can determine the Encoder category defining the property that the parameter affects (such as the Quality of the stored image). The Type and ValueType properties curiously both get the same information: the type of the data stored in the parameter (as listed in the EncoderParameterValueType enumeration).

You can also determine the count of the data values in the parameter using the NumberOfValues property.

The values themselves can only be set in the constructor of the parameter. Some of these common values are listed in the EncoderValue enumeration.

```
public sealed class EncoderParameter : IDisposable {
// Public Constructors
  public EncoderParameter(Encoder encoder, byte value);
  public EncoderParameter(Encoder encoder, byte[ ] value);
  public EncoderParameter(Encoder encoder, byte[ ] value, bool undefined);
  public EncoderParameter(Encoder encoder, byte value, bool undefined);
  public EncoderParameter(Encoder encoder, short value);
  public EncoderParameter(Encoder encoder, short[ ] value);
  public EncoderParameter(Encoder encoder, int[ ] numerator, int[ ] denominator);
  public EncoderParameter(Encoder encoder, int[ ] numerator1, int[ ] denominator1,
    int[ ] numerator2, int[ ] denominator2);
  public EncoderParameter(Encoder encoder, int numerator, int demoninator);
  public EncoderParameter(Encoder encoder, int NumberOfValues, int Type, int Value);
  public EncoderParameter(Encoder encoder, int numerator1, int demoninator1,
    int numerator2, int demoninator2);
  public EncoderParameter(Encoder encoder, long value);
```

```
  public EncoderParameter(Encoder encoder, long[ ] value);
  public EncoderParameter(Encoder encoder, long[ ] rangebegin, long[ ] rangeend);
  public EncoderParameter(Encoder encoder, long rangebegin, long rangeend);
  public EncoderParameter(Encoder encoder, string value);
// Public Instance Properties
  public Encoder Encoder{set; get; }
  public int NumberOfValues{get; }
  public EncoderParameterValueType Type{get; }
  public EncoderParameterValueType ValueType{get; }
// Public Instance Methods
  public void Dispose( );                                    // implements IDisposable
// Protected Instance Methods
  protected override void Finalize( );                       // overrides object
}
```

Returned By EncoderParameters.Param

Passed To EncoderParameters.Param

EncoderParameters **disposable**

System.Drawing.Imaging (system.drawing.dll) sealed class

This class implements a collection of EncoderParameter objects. It is used to pass a set of parameters to the Image.Save( ) method.

Unlike regular collection classes, you can only get or set the contents through the Param property.

```
public sealed class EncoderParameters : IDisposable {
// Public Constructors
  public EncoderParameters( );
  public EncoderParameters(int count);
// Public Instance Properties
  public EncoderParameter[ ] Param{set; get; }
// Public Instance Methods
  public void Dispose( );                                    // implements IDisposable
}
```

Returned By System.Drawing.Image.GetEncoderParameterList( )

Passed To System.Drawing.Image.{Save( ), SaveAdd( )}

EncoderParameterValueType **serializable**

System.Drawing.Imaging (system.drawing.dll) enum

This enumeration lists the various data types that can be used to provide parameter values for a GDI+ image encoder. See EncoderParameters for more information.

```
public enum EncoderParameterValueType {
  ValueTypeByte = 1,
  ValueTypeAscii = 2,
  ValueTypeShort = 3,
  ValueTypeLong = 4,
```

```
  ValueTypeRational = 5,
  ValueTypeLongRange = 6,
  ValueTypeUndefined = 7,
  ValueTypeRationalRange = 8
}
```

Hierarchy System.Object → System.ValueType → System.Enum(System.IComparable, System.IFormattable, System.IConvertible) → EncoderParameterValueType

Returned By EncoderParameter.{Type, ValueType}

EncoderValue

serializable

System.Drawing.Imaging (system.drawing.dll) **enum**

This enumeration lists some common parameter values that can be passed to the JPEG, TIFF, and PNG encoders.

Note that ColorTypeCMYK, ColorTypeYCCK, FrameDimensionResolution, FrameDimensionTime, RenderNonProgressive, RenderProgressive, ScanMethodInterlaced, ScanMethodNonInterlaced, VersionGif87, and VersionGif89 are not supported in the current version of GDI+.

See EncoderParameter for more information on parameter values.

```
public enum EncoderValue {
  ColorTypeCMYK = 0,
  ColorTypeYCCK = 1,
  CompressionLZW = 2,
  CompressionCCITT3 = 3,
  CompressionCCITT4 = 4,
  CompressionRle = 5,
  CompressionNone = 6,
  ScanMethodInterlaced = 7,
  ScanMethodNonInterlaced = 8,
  VersionGif87 = 9,
  VersionGif89 = 10,
  RenderProgressive = 11,
  RenderNonProgressive = 12,
  TransformRotate90 = 13,
  TransformRotate180 = 14,
  TransformRotate270 = 15,
  TransformFlipHorizontal = 16,
  TransformFlipVertical = 17,
  MultiFrame = 18,
  LastFrame = 19,
  Flush = 20,
  FrameDimensionTime = 21,
  FrameDimensionResolution = 22,
  FrameDimensionPage = 23
}
```

Hierarchy System.Object → System.ValueType → System.Enum(System.IComparable, System.IFormattable, System.IConvertible) → EncoderValue

FrameDimension

System.Drawing.Imaging (system.drawing.dll) **sealed class**

An **Image** is capable of supporting several different frames in a single image. This class encapsulates three different types of frame. You can get an instance of the class representing a **Time**-based frame (an animation), a **Resolution**-based frame (which allows you to extract multi-resolution versions of the image data), and a **Page**-based frame (to extract several pages from the image), using the static properties of those names.

The class actually wraps a **Guid** identifying the particular frame dimension.

You use this class in the **Image.GetFrameCount( )** and **Image.SelectActiveFrame( )** methods.

```
public sealed class FrameDimension {
// Public Constructors
   public FrameDimension(Guid guid);
// Public Static Properties
   public static FrameDimension Page{get; }
   public static FrameDimension Resolution{get; }
   public static FrameDimension Time{get; }
// Public Instance Properties
   public Guid Guid{get; }
// Public Instance Methods
   public override bool Equals(object o);                  // overrides object
   public override int GetHashCode( );                     // overrides object
   public override string ToString( );                     // overrides object
}
```

Passed To System.Drawing.Image.{GetFrameCount( ), SelectActiveFrame( )}

ImageAttributes **disposable**

System.Drawing.Imaging (system.drawing.dll) **sealed class**

This class is used to set various color-manipulation effects when rendering on a graphics surface. You can pass an **ImageAttributes** object to the **System.Drawing.Graphics.DrawImage( )** and **System.Drawing.Graphics.EnumerateMetafile( )**

There are two methods to remap colors using a **ColorMap**: **SetBrushRemapTable( )** and **SetRemapTable( )**. You can apply a **ColorMatrix** using the **SetColorMatrix( )** method. If you want to set separate matrixes for the color and grayscale parts of an image, you can use the **SetColorMatrices( )** variant. **SetThreshold( )** applies a bi-level threshold to the image (everything below the threshold is clamped to 0, and everything above is clamped to the maximum representable value). You can control the gamma with **SetGamma( )**.

You can enable basic color keying with **SetColorKey( )**. This allows you to set a range of colors that will be rendered as transparent, allowing the background to show through.

The **SetOutputChannel( )** allows you to limit the image rendered to one or more of the CMYK channels (as listed in the **ColorChannelFlag** enumeration). This allows you to perform basic color separations for printing. **SetOutputChannelColorProfile( )** allows you to choose a color-match profile file for the CMYK conversion, to better match the characteristics of the target output device. Installed color profiles are found in the **%SystemRoot%\System32\Spool\Drivers\Color** directory, and the system will look in here for the filename you specify. If the profile file is not installed in that directory, you have to specify a fully qualified filename.

Each of these methods prefixed by "Set" can be made to apply to any and all the GDI+ object types specified in the ColorAdjustType enumeration. There is also an equivalent Clear... method to remove the specified color transform. You can also use the SetNoOp() method to disable all color transforms for a particular ColorAdjustType.

```
public sealed class ImageAttributes : ICloneable, IDisposable {
// Public Constructors
   public ImageAttributes( );
// Public Instance Methods
   public void ClearBrushRemapTable( );
   public void ClearColorKey( );
   public void ClearColorKey(ColorAdjustType type);
   public void ClearColorMatrix( );
   public void ClearColorMatrix(ColorAdjustType type);
   public void ClearGamma( );
   public void ClearGamma(ColorAdjustType type);
   public void ClearNoOp( );
   public void ClearNoOp(ColorAdjustType type);
   public void ClearOutputChannel( );
   public void ClearOutputChannel(ColorAdjustType type);
   public void ClearOutputChannelColorProfile( );
   public void ClearOutputChannelColorProfile(ColorAdjustType type);
   public void ClearRemapTable( );
   public void ClearRemapTable(ColorAdjustType type);
   public void ClearThreshold( );
   public void ClearThreshold(ColorAdjustType type);
   public object Clone( );                                    // implements ICloneable
   public void Dispose( );                                    // implements IDisposable
   public void GetAdjustedPalette(ColorPalette palette, ColorAdjustType type);
   public void SetBrushRemapTable(ColorMap[ ] map);
   public void SetColorKey(System.Drawing.Color colorLow, System.Drawing.Color colorHigh);
   public void SetColorKey(System.Drawing.Color colorLow, System.Drawing.Color colorHigh, ColorAdjustType type);
   public void SetColorMatrices(ColorMatrix newColorMatrix, ColorMatrix grayMatrix);
   public void SetColorMatrices(ColorMatrix newColorMatrix, ColorMatrix grayMatrix, ColorMatrixFlag flags);
   public void SetColorMatrices(ColorMatrix newColorMatrix, ColorMatrix grayMatrix, ColorMatrixFlag mode,
      ColorAdjustType type);
   public void SetColorMatrix(ColorMatrix newColorMatrix);
   public void SetColorMatrix(ColorMatrix newColorMatrix, ColorMatrixFlag flags);
   public void SetColorMatrix(ColorMatrix newColorMatrix, ColorMatrixFlag mode, ColorAdjustType type);
   public void SetGamma(float gamma);
   public void SetGamma(float gamma, ColorAdjustType type);
   public void SetNoOp( );
   public void SetNoOp(ColorAdjustType type);
   public void SetOutputChannel(ColorChannelFlag flags);
   public void SetOutputChannel(ColorChannelFlag flags, ColorAdjustType type);
   public void SetOutputChannelColorProfile(string colorProfileFilename);
   public void SetOutputChannelColorProfile(string colorProfileFilename, ColorAdjustType type);
   public void SetRemapTable(ColorMap[ ] map);
   public void SetRemapTable(ColorMap[ ] map, ColorAdjustType type);
   public void SetThreshold(float threshold);
   public void SetThreshold(float threshold, ColorAdjustType type);
   public void SetWrapMode(System.Drawing.Drawing2D.WrapMode mode);
```

```
public void SetWrapMode(System.Drawing.Drawing2D.WrapMode mode, System.Drawing.Color color);
public void SetWrapMode(System.Drawing.Drawing2D.WrapMode mode, System.Drawing.Color color, bool clamp);
// Protected Instance Methods
protected override void Finalize( );                                        // overrides object
}
```

Passed To System.Drawing.Graphics.{DrawImage( ), EnumerateMetafile( )}, System.Drawing.TextureBrush.TextureBrush( )

ImageCodecFlags

serializable, flag

System.Drawing.Imaging (system.drawing.dll) — enum

This enumeration lists a set of flags that apply to an image storage codec. You can get/set these flags with the ImageCodecInfo.Flags property.

```
public enum ImageCodecFlags {
  Encoder = 0x00000001,
  Decoder = 0x00000002,
  SupportBitmap = 0x00000004,
  SupportVector = 0x00000008,
  SeekableEncode = 0x00000010,
  BlockingDecode = 0x00000020,
  Builtin = 0x00010000,
  System = 0x00020000,
  User = 0x00040000
}
```

Hierarchy System.Object → System.ValueType → System.Enum(System.IComparable, System.IFormattable, System.IConvertible) → ImageCodecFlags

Returned By ImageCodecInfo.Flags

Passed To ImageCodecInfo.Flags

ImageCodecInfo

System.Drawing.Imaging (system.drawing.dll) — sealed class

This class encapsulates information about the installed image codecs (components that can encode and decode images for storage).

Typically, you will use the static GetImageDecoders( ) and GetImageEncoders( ) methods to retrieve the installed encoders or decoders. You can then enumerate those lists to look for a codec that matches your requirements. You might compare against the MimeType of the codec, the CodecName, or the FormatDescription (a textual description of the file format).

```
public sealed class ImageCodecInfo {
// Public Instance Properties
  public Guid Clsid{set; get; }
  public string CodecName{set; get; }
  public string DllName{set; get; }
  public string FilenameExtension{set; get; }
  public ImageCodecFlags Flags{set; get; }
  public string FormatDescription{set; get; }
```

Imaging

```
  public Guid FormatID{set; get; }
  public string MimeType{set; get; }
  public byte[ ][ ] SignatureMasks{set; get; }
  public byte[ ][ ] SignaturePatterns{set; get; }
  public int Version{set; get; }
// Public Static Methods
  public static ImageCodecInfo[ ] GetImageDecoders( );
  public static ImageCodecInfo[ ] GetImageEncoders( );
}
```

Passed To System.Drawing.Image.Save( )

ImageFlags

serializable, flag

System.Drawing.Imaging (system.drawing.dll) **enum**

This enumeration lists various attributes of the underlying pixel data stored in a System.Drawing.Image object. It can be retrieved using the System.Drawing.Image.Flags property.

```
public enum ImageFlags {
  None = 0x00000000,
  Scalable = 0x00000001,
  HasAlpha = 0x00000002,
  HasTranslucent = 0x00000004,
  PartiallyScalable = 0x00000008,
  ColorSpaceRgb = 0x00000010,
  ColorSpaceCmyk = 0x00000020,
  ColorSpaceGray = 0x00000040,
  ColorSpaceYcbcr = 0x00000080,
  ColorSpaceYcck = 0x00000100,
  HasRealDpi = 0x00001000,
  HasRealPixelSize = 0x00002000,
  ReadOnly = 0x00010000,
  Caching = 0x00020000
}
```

Hierarchy System.Object → System.ValueType → System.Enum(System.IComparable, System.IFormattable, System.IConvertible) → ImageFlags

ImageFormat

System.Drawing.Imaging (system.drawing.dll) sealed class

This class represents the native format of a System.Drawing.Image object. It encapsulates a Guid uniquely identifying the format. There are a set of static properties that return a format object for the well-known image format types (e.g., Bmp, Jpeg, and MemoryBmp).

You can get the internal format of an image by using the RawFormat property.

```
public sealed class ImageFormat {
// Public Constructors
  public ImageFormat(Guid guid);
// Public Static Properties
  public static ImageFormat Bmp{get; }
  public static ImageFormat Emf{get; }
```

```
  public static ImageFormat Exif{get; }
  public static ImageFormat Gif{get; }
  public static ImageFormat Icon{get; }
  public static ImageFormat Jpeg{get; }
  public static ImageFormat MemoryBmp{get; }
  public static ImageFormat Png{get; }
  public static ImageFormat Tiff{get; }
  public static ImageFormat Wmf{get; }
// Public Instance Properties
  public Guid Guid{get; }
// Public Instance Methods
  public override bool Equals(object o);                    // overrides object
  public override int GetHashCode( );                       // overrides object
  public override string ToString( );                       // overrides object
}
```

Returned By System.Drawing.Image.RawFormat

Passed To System.Drawing.Image.Save( )

ImageLockMode serializable

System.Drawing.Imaging (system.drawing.dll) enum

This enumeration lists the various ways in which you can lock a bitmap with the Bitmap.LockBits( ) method. You should pick the option that most closely matches your requirements, as the framework can optimize the marshaling of the pixel data.

```
public enum ImageLockMode {
  ReadOnly = 1,
  WriteOnly = 2,
  ReadWrite = 3,
  UserInputBuffer = 4
}
```

Hierarchy System.Object → System.ValueType → System.Enum(System.IComparable, System.IFormattable, System.IConvertible) → ImageLockMode

Passed To System.Drawing.Bitmap.LockBits( )

Imaging

Metafile serializable, marshal by reference, disposable

System.Drawing.Imaging (system.drawing.dll) sealed class

A metafile represents a set of records, each of which encapsulates a graphics operation.

There are a large number of different constructors, which allow you to construct a metafile from a file or stream (in Windows Enhanced Metafile File format), a system HDC (which can be obtained from a Graphics surface if necessary), or a Windows EMF handle. You can subsequently retrieve the EMF handle (for interop) with the GetHenhmetafile( ) method. Many of the methods also allow you to specify a rectangle that positions the metafile on the page, along with the units that define that rectangle (see MetafileFrameUnit).

You can retrieve the MetafileHeader with the GetMetafileHeader( ) method.

While you can use the System.Drawing.Graphics.DrawImage( ) method to paint the metafile, you can play an individual record with the PlayRecord( ) method. See EmfPlusRecordType for information about EMF records.

To record a metafile, you should create a reference System.Drawing.Graphics surface, and then use the System.Drawing.Graphics.GetHdc( ) to lock its Win32 HDC. You can then pass this as the reference HDC in an appropriate constructor for your Metafile object. You can then use the System.Drawing.Graphics.FromImage( ) method to get a graphics surface for the metafile. Everything you then draw on the surface will be recorded on the metafile. If you specified a filename or stream in the Metafile constructor, the image will automatically be stored, or you can call the Save( ) method. You should then Dispose( ) the System.Drawing.Graphics object, the Metafile, and call System.Drawing.Graphics.ReleaseHdc( ).

```
public sealed class Metafile : System.Drawing.Image {
// Public Constructors
   public Metafile(IntPtr henhmetafile, bool deleteEmf);
   public Metafile(IntPtr referenceHdc, EmfType emfType);
   public Metafile(IntPtr referenceHdc, EmfType emfType, string description);
   public Metafile(IntPtr referenceHdc, System.Drawing.Rectangle frameRect);
   public Metafile(IntPtr referenceHdc, System.Drawing.RectangleF frameRect);
   public Metafile(IntPtr referenceHdc, System.Drawing.RectangleF frameRect, MetafileFrameUnit frameUnit);
   public Metafile(IntPtr referenceHdc, System.Drawing.RectangleF frameRect, MetafileFrameUnit frameUnit, EmfType type);
   public Metafile(IntPtr referenceHdc, System.Drawing.RectangleF frameRect, MetafileFrameUnit frameUnit, EmfType type,
      string description);
   public Metafile(IntPtr referenceHdc, System.Drawing.Rectangle frameRect, MetafileFrameUnit frameUnit);
   public Metafile(IntPtr referenceHdc, System.Drawing.Rectangle frameRect, MetafileFrameUnit frameUnit, EmfType type);
   public Metafile(IntPtr referenceHdc, System.Drawing.Rectangle frameRect, MetafileFrameUnit frameUnit, EmfType type,
      string desc);
   public Metafile(IntPtr hmetafile, WmfPlaceableFileHeader wmfHeader);
   public Metafile(IntPtr hmetafile, WmfPlaceableFileHeader wmfHeader, bool deleteWmf);
   public Metafile(System.IO.Stream stream);
   public Metafile(System.IO.Stream stream, IntPtr referenceHdc);
   public Metafile(System.IO.Stream stream, IntPtr referenceHdc, EmfType type);
   public Metafile(System.IO.Stream stream, IntPtr referenceHdc, EmfType type, string description);
   public Metafile(System.IO.Stream stream, IntPtr referenceHdc, System.Drawing.Rectangle frameRect);
   public Metafile(System.IO.Stream stream, IntPtr referenceHdc, System.Drawing.RectangleF frameRect);
   public Metafile(System.IO.Stream stream, IntPtr referenceHdc, System.Drawing.RectangleF frameRect,
      MetafileFrameUnit frameUnit);
   public Metafile(System.IO.Stream stream, IntPtr referenceHdc, System.Drawing.RectangleF frameRect,
      MetafileFrameUnit frameUnit, EmfType type);
   public Metafile(System.IO.Stream stream, IntPtr referenceHdc, System.Drawing.RectangleF frameRect,
      MetafileFrameUnit frameUnit, EmfType type, string description);
   public Metafile(System.IO.Stream stream, IntPtr referenceHdc, System.Drawing.Rectangle frameRect,
      MetafileFrameUnit frameUnit);
   public Metafile(System.IO.Stream stream, IntPtr referenceHdc, System.Drawing.Rectangle frameRect,
      MetafileFrameUnit frameUnit, EmfType type);
   public Metafile(System.IO.Stream stream, IntPtr referenceHdc, System.Drawing.Rectangle frameRect,
      MetafileFrameUnit frameUnit, EmfType type, string description);
   public Metafile(string filename);
   public Metafile(string fileName, IntPtr referenceHdc);
   public Metafile(string fileName, IntPtr referenceHdc, EmfType type);
   public Metafile(string fileName, IntPtr referenceHdc, EmfType type, string description);
   public Metafile(string fileName, IntPtr referenceHdc, System.Drawing.Rectangle frameRect);
```

```
public Metafile(string fileName, IntPtr referenceHdc, System.Drawing.RectangleF frameRect);
public Metafile(string fileName, IntPtr referenceHdc, System.Drawing.RectangleF frameRect,
   MetafileFrameUnit frameUnit);
public Metafile(string fileName, IntPtr referenceHdc, System.Drawing.RectangleF frameRect,
   MetafileFrameUnit frameUnit, EmfType type);
public Metafile(string fileName, IntPtr referenceHdc, System.Drawing.RectangleF frameRect,
   MetafileFrameUnit frameUnit, EmfType type, string description);
public Metafile(string fileName, IntPtr referenceHdc, System.Drawing.RectangleF frameRect,
   MetafileFrameUnit frameUnit, string desc);
public Metafile(string fileName, IntPtr referenceHdc, System.Drawing.Rectangle frameRect,
   MetafileFrameUnit frameUnit);
public Metafile(string fileName, IntPtr referenceHdc, System.Drawing.Rectangle frameRect,
   MetafileFrameUnit frameUnit, EmfType type);
public Metafile(string fileName, IntPtr referenceHdc, System.Drawing.Rectangle frameRect,
   MetafileFrameUnit frameUnit, EmfType type, string description);
public Metafile(string fileName, IntPtr referenceHdc, System.Drawing.Rectangle frameRect,
   MetafileFrameUnit frameUnit, string description);
// Public Static Methods
public static MetafileHeader GetMetafileHeader(IntPtr henhmetafile);
public static MetafileHeader GetMetafileHeader(IntPtr hmetafile, WmfPlaceableFileHeader wmfHeader);
public static MetafileHeader GetMetafileHeader(System.IO.Stream stream);
public static MetafileHeader GetMetafileHeader(string fileName);
// Public Instance Methods
public IntPtr GetHenhmetafile( );
public MetafileHeader GetMetafileHeader( );
public void PlayRecord(EmfPlusRecordType recordType, int flags, int dataSize, byte[ ] data);
}
```

Hierarchy System.Object → System.MarshalByRefObject → System.Drawing.Image(System.Runtime.Serialization.ISerializable, System.ICloneable, System.IDisposable) → Metafile

Passed To System.Drawing.Graphics.EnumerateMetafile( )

MetafileFrameUnit — serializable

System.Drawing.Imaging (system.drawing.dll) — enum

This enumeration is used to determine the unit of measurement used to define the Rectangle that positions and sizes the metafile on the page. It used in several of the Metafile constructor overloads.

```
public enum MetafileFrameUnit {
  Pixel = 2,
  Point = 3,
  Inch = 4,
  Document = 5,
  Millimeter = 6,
  GdiCompatible = 7
}
```

Hierarchy System.Object → System.ValueType → System.Enum(System.IComparable, System.IFormattable, System.IConvertible) → MetafileFrameUnit

Passed To Metafile.Metafile( )

MetafileHeader

System.Drawing.Imaging (system.drawing.dll) sealed class

This class encapsulates various attributes of a Metafile. It can be retrieved using the Metafile.GetMetafileHeader( ) method.

You can find the resolution of the metafile with the DpiX, DpiY, LogicalDpiX, and LogicalDpiY properties. The Bounds of the metafile on the page can also be obtained.

The header also contains a lot of information about the file itself. You can discover the EmfPlusHeaderSize and MetafileSize in bytes. The Type (from the MetafileType enumeration) and Version are also accessible. There is also a set of utility accessor methods to determine the type of metafile (e.g., IsEmfPlus( )). As with all this grungy metafile support, these are something of a hangover from the unmanaged GDI+ interface.

```
public sealed class MetafileHeader {
// Public Instance Properties
   public Rectangle Bounds{get; }
   public float DpiX{get; }
   public float DpiY{get; }
   public int EmfPlusHeaderSize{get; }
   public int LogicalDpiX{get; }
   public int LogicalDpiY{get; }
   public int MetafileSize{get; }
   public MetafileType Type{get; }
   public int Version{get; }
   public MetaHeader WmfHeader{get; }
// Public Instance Methods
   public bool IsDisplay( );
   public bool IsEmf( );
   public bool IsEmfOrEmfPlus( );
   public bool IsEmfPlus( );
   public bool IsEmfPlusDual( );
   public bool IsEmfPlusOnly( );
   public bool IsWmf( );
   public bool IsWmfPlaceable( );
}
```

Returned By Metafile.GetMetafileHeader( )

MetafileType serializable

System.Drawing.Imaging (system.drawing.dll) enum

This enumeration lists the various types of metafile supported by the framework, including the new GDI+ EMF+ types. It is used by the MetafileHeader.Type property.

```
public enum MetafileType {
   Invalid = 0,
   Wmf = 1,
   WmfPlaceable = 2,
   Emf = 3,
   EmfPlusOnly = 4,
   EmfPlusDual = 5
}
```

Hierarchy System.Object → System.ValueType → System.Enum(System.IComparable, System.IFormattable, System.IConvertible) → MetafileType

Returned By MetafileHeader.Type

MetaHeader

System.Drawing.Imaging (system.drawing.dll) sealed class

This class represents a traditional Windows Metafile Header. It can be obtained from the MetafileHeader.WmfHeader property.

You can determine the HeaderSize in bytes, the number of objects (NoObjects) in the metafile, the size of the largest record in the file (MaxRecord), the Size of the metafile, the Type of the metafile, and the Version of the header.

```
public sealed class MetaHeader {
// Public Constructors
   public MetaHeader( );
// Public Instance Properties
   public short HeaderSize{set; get; }
   public int MaxRecord{set; get; }
   public short NoObjects{set; get; }
   public short NoParameters{set; get; }
   public int Size{set; get; }
   public short Type{set; get; }
   public short Version{set; get; }
}
```

Returned By MetafileHeader.WmfHeader

PaletteFlags serializable

System.Drawing.Imaging (system.drawing.dll) enum

This enumeration lists the various types of color information that can be stored in a palette. See the ColorPalette.Flags property for more information.

```
public enum PaletteFlags {
   HasAlpha = 1,
   GrayScale = 2,
   Halftone = 4
}
```

Hierarchy System.Object → System.ValueType → System.Enum(System.IComparable, System.IFormattable, System.IConvertible) → PaletteFlags

Imaging

PixelFormat serializable

System.Drawing.Imaging (system.drawing.dll) enum

This enumeration lists the various formats that can be used for pixel image data. It is most commonly used when constructing a System.Drawing.Bitmap object and when locking the bitmap data with the System.Drawing.Bitmap.LockBits( ) method.

```
public enum PixelFormat {
  DontCare = 0,
  Undefined = 0,
  Max = 15,
  Indexed = 65536,
  Gdi = 131072,
  Format16bppRgb555 = 135173,
  Format16bppRgb565 = 135174,
  Format24bppRgb = 137224,
  Format32bppRgb = 139273,
  Format1bppIndexed = 196865,
  Format4bppIndexed = 197634,
  Format8bppIndexed = 198659,
  Alpha = 262144,
  Format16bppArgb1555 = 397319,
  PAlpha = 524288,
  Format32bppPArgb = 925707,
  Extended = 1048576,
  Format16bppGrayScale = 1052676,
  Format48bppRgb = 1060876,
  Format64bppPArgb = 1851406,
  Canonical = 2097152,
  Format32bppArgb = 2498570,
  Format64bppArgb = 3424269
}
```

Hierarchy System.Object → System.ValueType → System.Enum(System.IComparable, System.IFormattable, System.IConvertible) → PixelFormat

Returned By System.Drawing.Image.PixelFormat, BitmapData.PixelFormat

Passed To System.Drawing.Bitmap.{Bitmap( ), Clone( ), LockBits( )}, System.Drawing.Image.{GetPixelFormatSize( ), IsAlphaPixelFormat( ), IsCanonicalPixelFormat( ), IsExtendedPixelFormat( )}, BitmapData.PixelFormat

PlayRecordCallback

serializable

System.Drawing.Imaging (system.drawing.dll) delegate

This delegate is used by the System.Drawing.Graphics.EnumerateMetafileProc method to provide a callback to deal with each record in the Metafile as it is enumerated.

```
public delegate void PlayRecordCallback(EmfPlusRecordType recordType, int flags, int dataSize, IntPtr recordData);
```

Passed To System.Drawing.EnumerateMetafileProc.{BeginInvoke( ), Invoke( )}

PropertyItem

System.Drawing.Imaging (system.drawing.dll) sealed class

A System.Drawing.Image object supports the addition of arbitrary metadata through the System.Drawing.Image.SetPropertyItem( ) and System.Drawing.Image.RemovePropertyItem( ) methods. This class encapsulates that property.

You can specify an integer Id for the property, along with its length (Len) in bytes and its type (a short). The value itself is an array of bytes, the length of which is determined by the Len property mentioned earlier.

As with much of the more advanced parts of the GDI+ framework, this byte-oriented arbitrary data storage hints rather heavily at the fact that it is a thin wrapper over an unmanaged (but undocumented) API.

```
public sealed class PropertyItem {
// Public Instance Properties
   public int Id{set; get; }
   public int Len{set; get; }
   public short Type{set; get; }
   public byte[ ] Value{set; get; }
}
```

Returned By System.Drawing.Image.{GetPropertyItem( ), PropertyItems}

Passed To System.Drawing.Image.SetPropertyItem( )

WmfPlaceableFileHeader

System.Drawing.Imaging (system.drawing.dll) sealed class

This class encapsulates the file header of a placeable metafile.

You can specify a bounding box for the metafile on the output device using the BboxBottom, BboxLeft, BboxRight, and BboxTop properties. You can also specify the scaling for the metafile using the Inch property. This indicates the number of twips per inch. A twip is a twentieth of a point, so there should be 1440 twips/inch.

The Hmf can get or set a Win32 handle to the metafile, and the Key is a magic number (0x9AC6CDD7) indicating that this is a placeable metafile header.

There is a also a Checksum that is calculated by XOR-ing the Key, Hmf, bounding box (in the order Left, Top, Right, Bottom), and Inch values.

As you may have noticed, this is a very thin and nasty veneer over the unmanaged implementation methods. Fortunately, you should rarely need this class in your own code, as it is not exposed anywhere else in the framework.

```
public sealed class WmfPlaceableFileHeader {
// Public Constructors
   public WmfPlaceableFileHeader( );
// Public Instance Properties
   public short BboxBottom{set; get; }
   public short BboxLeft{set; get; }
   public short BboxRight{set; get; }
   public short BboxTop{set; get; }
   public short Checksum{set; get; }
   public short Hmf{set; get; }
   public short Inch{set; get; }
   public int Key{set; get; }
   public int Reserved{set; get; }
}
```

Passed To Metafile.{GetMetafileHeader( ), Metafile( )}

Imaging

17

The System.Drawing.Printing Namespace

This namespace contains the non-visual classes that support printing.

The PrintDocument encapsulates the pages to be printed, while the PrintController manages the printing process. PrinterSettings represent the printer device and its settings, while the PageSettings encapsulate the format of the output page.

Look at System.Windows.Forms.PrintDialog and System.Windows.Forms.PrintPreviewDialog for handy prebuilt controls to support typical printing scenarios. Figure 17-1 shows the types in this namespace.

Duplex **serializable**

System.Drawing.Printing (system.drawing.dll) **enum**

This enumeration is used by the PrinterSettings.Duplex property to define the double-sided printing mode.

```
public enum Duplex {
  Simplex = 1,
  Vertical = 2,
  Horizontal = 3,
  Default = -1
}
```

Hierarchy System.Object → System.ValueType → System.Enum(System.IComparable, System.IFormattable, System.IConvertible) → Duplex

Returned By PrinterSettings.Duplex

Passed To PrinterSettings.Duplex

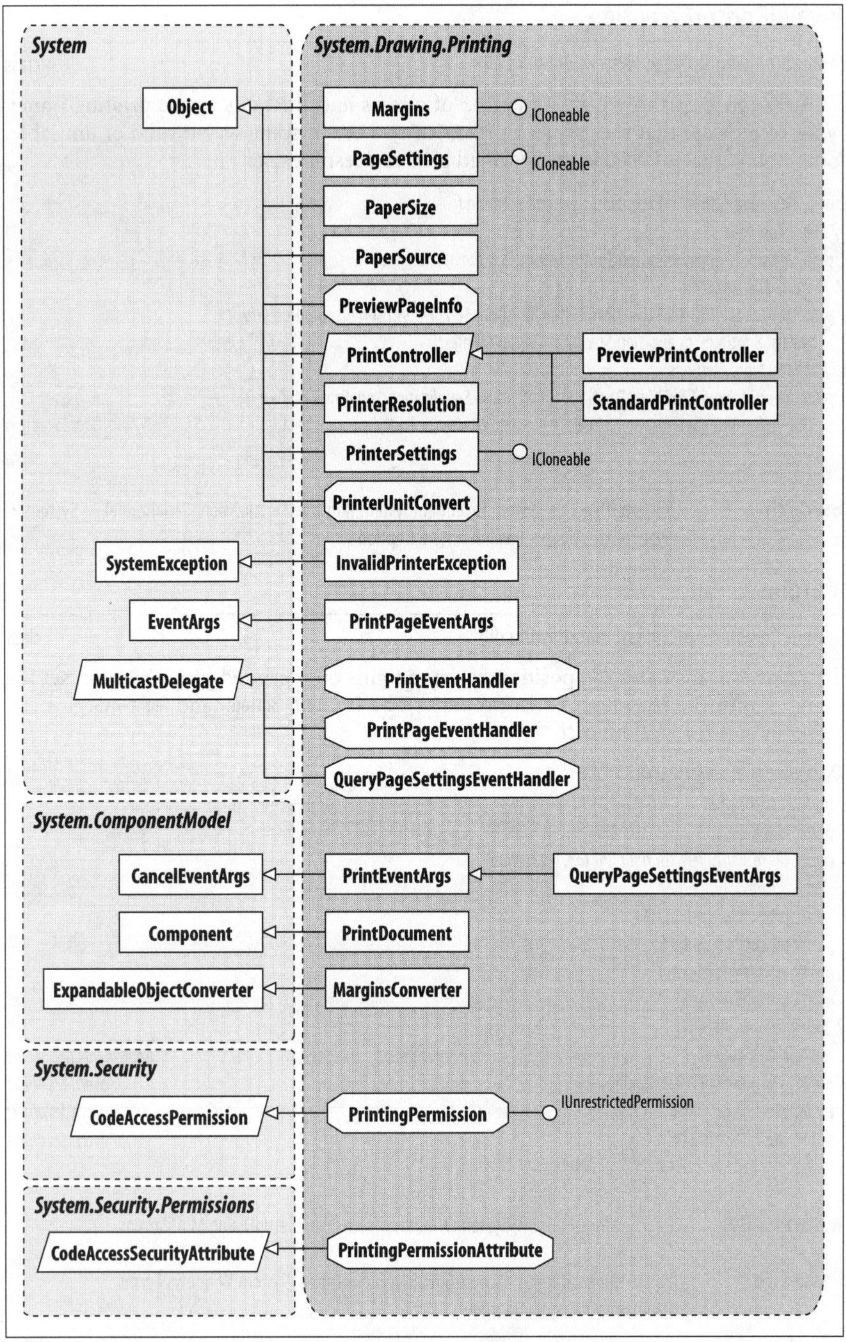
System
System.Drawing.Printing
Object
Margins
ICloneable
PageSettings
ICloneable
PaperSize
PaperSource
PreviewPageInfo
PrintController
PreviewPrintController
StandardPrintController
PrinterResolution
PrinterSettings
ICloneable
PrinterUnitConvert
SystemException
InvalidPrinterException
EventArgs
PrintPageEventArgs
MulticastDelegate
PrintEventHandler
PrintPageEventHandler
QueryPageSettingsEventHandler
System.ComponentModel
CancelEventArgs
PrintEventArgs
QueryPageSettingsEventArgs
Component
PrintDocument
ExpandableObjectConverter
MarginsConverter
System.Security
CodeAccessPermission
PrintingPermission
IUnrestrictedPermission
System.Security.Permissions
CodeAccessSecurityAttribute
PrintingPermissionAttribute

Figure 17-1. Types from the System.Drawing.Printing namespace

InvalidPrinterException

System.Drawing.Printing (system.drawing.dll) class

This exception is thrown by a number of classes and methods in the printing framework to indicate that the printer or PrinterSettings were in some way invalid or unusable. Commonly, this is because the specified printer doesn't exist.

```
public class InvalidPrinterException : SystemException {
// Public Constructors
   public InvalidPrinterException(PrinterSettings settings);
// Protected Constructors
   protected InvalidPrinterException(System.Runtime.Serialization.SerializationInfo info,
      System.Runtime.Serialization.StreamingContext context);
// Public Instance Methods
   public override void GetObjectData(System.Runtime.Serialization.SerializationInfo info,
      System.Runtime.Serialization.StreamingContext context);                // overrides Exception
}
```

Hierarchy System.Object → System.Exception(System.Runtime.Serialization.ISerializable) → System. SystemException → InvalidPrinterException

Margins

System.Drawing.Printing (system.drawing.dll) class

This class encapsulates the position of the margins on a printed page. You can set the margins with the PageSettings.Margins property. The Top, Left, Bottom, and Right margins can be set in units of 1/100th inch.

```
public class Margins : ICloneable {
// Public Constructors
   public Margins( );
   public Margins(int left, int right, int top, int bottom);
// Public Instance Properties
   public int Bottom{set; get; }
   public int Left{set; get; }
   public int Right{set; get; }
   public int Top{set; get; }
// Public Instance Methods
   public object Clone( );                                 // implements ICloneable
   public override bool Equals(object obj);                // overrides object
   public override int GetHashCode( );                     // overrides object
   public override string ToString( );                     // overrides object
}
```

Returned By PageSettings.Margins, System.Windows.Forms.PageSetupDialog.MinMargins

Passed To PageSettings.Margins, PrinterUnitConvert.Convert( ), System.Windows.Forms. PageSetupDialog.MinMargins

MarginsConverter

System.Drawing.Printing (system.drawing.dll) class

This is the TypeConverter for a Margins object, transforming it to and from other types in serialization and design-time scenarios. You should not call this class directly from your own code.

```
public class MarginsConverter : System.ComponentModel.ExpandableObjectConverter {
// Public Constructors
   public MarginsConverter( );
// Public Instance Methods
   public override bool CanConvertFrom( System.ComponentModel.ITypeDescriptorContext context,
      Type sourceType);                              // overrides System.ComponentModel.TypeConverter
   public override bool CanConvertTo(System.ComponentModel.ITypeDescriptorContext context,
      Type destinationType);                         // overrides System.ComponentModel.TypeConverter
   public override object ConvertFrom(System.ComponentModel.ITypeDescriptorContext context,
      System.Globalization.CultureInfo culture, object value);   // overrides System.ComponentModel.TypeConverter
   public override object ConvertTo(System.ComponentModel.ITypeDescriptorContext context,
      System.Globalization.CultureInfo culture, object value,
      Type destinationType);                         // overrides System.ComponentModel.TypeConverter
   public override object CreateInstance(System.ComponentModel.ITypeDescriptorContext context,
      System.Collections.IDictionary propertyValues);  // overrides System.ComponentModel.TypeConverter
   public override bool GetCreateInstanceSupported(
      System.ComponentModel.ITypeDescriptorContext context);   // overrides System.ComponentModel.TypeConverter
}
```

Hierarchy System.Object → System.ComponentModel.TypeConverter → System.ComponentModel.ExpandableObjectConverter → MarginsConverter

PageSettings

System.Drawing.Printing (system.drawing.dll) class

This class encapsulates information that defines how a single page will be printed. The default page settings for a document are specified using the PrintDocument.DefaultPageSettings property, but you can modify them on a page-by-page basis by handling the PrintDocument.QueryPageSettings event. Note that the PrintDocument.PrintPage event also allows you to change the page settings, so you do not necessarily need both.

You can get the Bounds of the page, taking into account the Landscape property, which can be used to set the orientation of the output. This includes the printable area of the page, excluding the Margins that have been defined. You can also retrieve the actual PaperSize for the selected PaperSource.

You can also find some information about the printer, including the PrinterResolution (see the PrinterResolution class for more information) and the PrinterSettings.

```
public class PageSettings : ICloneable {
// Public Constructors
   public PageSettings( );
   public PageSettings(PrinterSettings printerSettings);
// Public Instance Properties
   public Rectangle Bounds{get; }
   public bool Color{set; get; }
   public bool Landscape{set; get; }
```

Printing

```
  public Margins Margins{set; get; }
  public PaperSize PaperSize{set; get; }
  public PaperSource PaperSource{set; get; }
  public PrinterResolution PrinterResolution{set; get; }
  public PrinterSettings PrinterSettings{set; get; }
// Public Instance Methods
  public object Clone( );                                    // implements ICloneable
  public void CopyToHdevmode(IntPtr hdevmode);
  public void SetHdevmode(IntPtr hdevmode);
  public override string ToString( );                        // overrides object
}
```

Returned By PrintDocument.DefaultPageSettings, PrinterSettings.DefaultPageSettings, PrintPageEventArgs.PageSettings, QueryPageSettingsEventArgs.PageSettings, System.Windows.Forms.PageSetupDialog.PageSettings

Passed To PrintDocument.DefaultPageSettings, PrinterSettings.GetHdevmode( ), PrintPageEventArgs.PrintPageEventArgs( ), QueryPageSettingsEventArgs.{PageSettings, QueryPageSettingsEventArgs( )}, System.Windows.Forms.PageSetupDialog.PageSettings

PaperKind **serializable**

System.Drawing.Printing (system.drawing.dll) enum

This enumeration lists the various standard paper sizes supported by the framework.

```
public enum PaperKind {
  Custom = 0,
  Letter = 1,
  LetterSmall = 2,
  Tabloid = 3,
  Ledger = 4,
  Legal = 5,
  Statement = 6,
  Executive = 7,
  A3 = 8,
  A4 = 9,
  A4Small = 10,
  A5 = 11,
  B4 = 12,
  B5 = 13,
  Folio = 14,
  Quarto = 15,
  Standard10x14 = 16,
  Standard11x17 = 17,
  Note = 18,
  Number9Envelope = 19,
  Number10Envelope = 20,
  Number11Envelope = 21,
  Number12Envelope = 22,
  Number14Envelope = 23,
  CSheet = 24,
  DSheet = 25,
```

```
ESheet = 26,
DLEnvelope = 27,
C5Envelope = 28,
C3Envelope = 29,
C4Envelope = 30,
C6Envelope = 31,
C65Envelope = 32,
B4Envelope = 33,
B5Envelope = 34,
B6Envelope = 35,
ItalyEnvelope = 36,
MonarchEnvelope = 37,
PersonalEnvelope = 38,
USStandardFanfold = 39,
GermanStandardFanfold = 40,
GermanLegalFanfold = 41,
IsoB4 = 42,
JapanesePostcard = 43,
Standard9x11 = 44,
Standard10x11 = 45,
Standard15x11 = 46,
InviteEnvelope = 47,
LetterExtra = 50,
LegalExtra = 51,
TabloidExtra = 52,
A4Extra = 53,
LetterTransverse = 54,
A4Transverse = 55,
LetterExtraTransverse = 56,
APlus = 57,
BPlus = 58,
LetterPlus = 59,
A4Plus = 60,
A5Transverse = 61,
B5Transverse = 62,
A3Extra = 63,
A5Extra = 64,
B5Extra = 65,
A2 = 66,
A3Transverse = 67,
A3ExtraTransverse = 68,
JapaneseDoublePostcard = 69,
A6 = 70,
JapaneseEnvelopeKakuNumber2 = 71,
JapaneseEnvelopeKakuNumber3 = 72,
JapaneseEnvelopeChouNumber3 = 73,
JapaneseEnvelopeChouNumber4 = 74,
LetterRotated = 75,
A3Rotated = 76,
A4Rotated = 77,
A5Rotated = 78,
B4JisRotated = 79,
```

Printing

```
    B5JisRotated = 80,
    JapanesePostcardRotated = 81,
    JapaneseDoublePostcardRotated = 82,
    A6Rotated = 83,
    JapaneseEnvelopeKakuNumber2Rotated = 84,
    JapaneseEnvelopeKakuNumber3Rotated = 85,
    JapaneseEnvelopeChouNumber3Rotated = 86,
    JapaneseEnvelopeChouNumber4Rotated = 87,
    B6Jis = 88,
    B6JisRotated = 89,
    Standard12x11 = 90,
    JapaneseEnvelopeYouNumber4 = 91,
    JapaneseEnvelopeYouNumber4Rotated = 92,
    Prc16K = 93,
    Prc32K = 94,
    Prc32KBig = 95,
    PrcEnvelopeNumber1 = 96,
    PrcEnvelopeNumber2 = 97,
    PrcEnvelopeNumber3 = 98,
    PrcEnvelopeNumber4 = 99,
    PrcEnvelopeNumber5 = 100,
    PrcEnvelopeNumber6 = 101,
    PrcEnvelopeNumber7 = 102,
    PrcEnvelopeNumber8 = 103,
    PrcEnvelopeNumber9 = 104,
    PrcEnvelopeNumber10 = 105,
    Prc16KRotated = 106,
    Prc32KRotated = 107,
    Prc32KBigRotated = 108,
    PrcEnvelopeNumber1Rotated = 109,
    PrcEnvelopeNumber2Rotated = 110,
    PrcEnvelopeNumber3Rotated = 111,
    PrcEnvelopeNumber4Rotated = 112,
    PrcEnvelopeNumber5Rotated = 113,
    PrcEnvelopeNumber6Rotated = 114,
    PrcEnvelopeNumber7Rotated = 115,
    PrcEnvelopeNumber8Rotated = 116,
    PrcEnvelopeNumber9Rotated = 117,
    PrcEnvelopeNumber10Rotated = 118
}
```

Hierarchy System.Object → System.ValueType → System.Enum(System.IComparable, System.IFormattable, System.IConvertible) → PaperKind

Returned By PaperSize.Kind

PaperSize

System.Drawing.Printing (system.drawing.dll) class

This class defines the dimensions of a sheet of paper. You can retrieve the Width and Height of the paper (in units of 1/100th inch), the Kind of the paper (see PaperKind), and a string representing the name of the particular sheet size (PaperName).

```
public class PaperSize {
// Public Constructors
   public PaperSize(string name, int width, int height);
// Public Instance Properties
   public int Height{set; get; }
   public PaperKind Kind{get; }
   public string PaperName{set; get; }
   public int Width{set; get; }
// Public Instance Methods
   public override string ToString( );                                  // overrides object
}
```

Returned By PageSettings.PaperSize, PaperSizeCollection.this

Passed To PageSettings.PaperSize, PaperSizeCollection.PaperSizeCollection( )

PaperSource

System.Drawing.Printing (system.drawing.dll) class

This class encapsulates the selection of a paper tray.

You can retrieve the Kind of paper source (see PaperSourceKind) and a string representing the name of the paper source (SourceName).

```
public class PaperSource {
// Public Instance Properties
   public PaperSourceKind Kind{get; }
   public string SourceName{get; }
// Public Instance Methods
   public override string ToString( );                                  // overrides object
}
```

Returned By PageSettings.PaperSource, PaperSourceCollection.this

Passed To PageSettings.PaperSource, PaperSourceCollection.PaperSourceCollection( )

PaperSourceKind serializable

System.Drawing.Printing (system.drawing.dll) enum

This enumeration lists the various types of paper tray that can be offered by a printer. See PaperSource for more information.

```
public enum PaperSourceKind {
   Upper = 1,
   Lower = 2,
   Middle = 3,
   Manual = 4,
   Envelope = 5,
   ManualFeed = 6,
   AutomaticFeed = 7,
   TractorFeed = 8,
   SmallFormat = 9,
   LargeFormat = 10,
```

Printing

```
  LargeCapacity = 11,
  Cassette = 14,
  FormSource = 15,
  Custom = 257
}
```

Hierarchy System.Object → System.ValueType → System.Enum(System.IComparable, System.IFormattable, System.IConvertible) → PaperSourceKind

Returned By PaperSource.Kind

PreviewPageInfo

System.Drawing.Printing (system.drawing.dll) sealed class

This class encapsulates the information required for the print preview of a single page. You can retrieve an Image representing the page to be printed and the PhysicalSize of that page (in units of 1/100th inch).

```
public sealed class PreviewPageInfo {
// Public Constructors
  public PreviewPageInfo(System.Drawing.Image image, System.Drawing.Size physicalSize);
// Public Instance Properties
  public Image Image{get; }
  public Size PhysicalSize{get; }
}
```

Returned By PreviewPrintController.GetPreviewPageInfo( )

PreviewPrintController

System.Drawing.Printing (system.drawing.dll) class

This class, derived from PrintController, manages the printing of a document to a series of Image objects, which can then be displayed to the user as a preview of the final printed output.

You would typically use a System.Windows.Forms.PrintPreviewDialog or System.Windows.Forms.PrintPreviewControl, which then uses this class in its implementation to display a series of page images to the user.

You can enable antialiasing to improve display quality, with the UseAntiAlias property. GetPreviewPageInfo( ) returns an array of PreviewPageInfo objects, which encapsulate the images representing each page to be printed.

To use a PreviewPrintController independently of the aforementioned controls, you can construct an instance and assign it to the PrintDocument.PrintController. If you then call PrintDocument.Print( ), the controller will be populated with the images, which you can then retrieve with the GetPreviewPageInfo( ) method.

```
public class PreviewPrintController : PrintController {
// Public Constructors
  public PreviewPrintController( );
// Public Instance Properties
  public virtual bool UseAntiAlias{set; get; }
// Public Instance Methods
```

```
public PreviewPageInfo[ ] GetPreviewPageInfo( );
public override void OnEndPage(PrintDocument document, PrintPageEventArgs e);          // overrides PrintController
public override void OnEndPrint(PrintDocument document, PrintEventArgs e);             // overrides PrintController
public override Graphics OnStartPage(PrintDocument document, PrintPageEventArgs e);    // overrides PrintController
public override void OnStartPrint(PrintDocument document, PrintEventArgs e);           // overrides PrintController
}
```

Hierarchy System.Object → PrintController → PreviewPrintController

PrintController

System.Drawing.Printing (system.drawing.dll) abstract class

This is the abstract base for classes that manage the printing of a PrintDocument.

You set a PrintController instance into the PrintDocument.PrintController property. Then, when you call PrintDocument.Print( ), it invokes the OnStartPrint( ), then OnStartPage( ), OnEndPage( ), and finally OnEndPrint( ) methods.

The start and end print methods receive the PrintDocument and a PrintEventArgs instance, while the start and end page methods receive the PrintDocument and a PrintPageEventArgs property. These methods control the sending of the document and its pages to the print device. This is the actual printer, in the case of the StandardPrintController or PrintControllerWithStatusDialog, but is a set of images, in the case of the PreviewPrintController.

```
public abstract class PrintController {
// Public Constructors
   public PrintController( );
// Public Instance Methods
   public virtual void OnEndPage(PrintDocument document, PrintPageEventArgs e);
   public virtual void OnEndPrint(PrintDocument document, PrintEventArgs e);
   public virtual Graphics OnStartPage(PrintDocument document, PrintPageEventArgs e);
   public virtual void OnStartPrint(PrintDocument document, PrintEventArgs e);
}
```

Subclasses PreviewPrintController, StandardPrintController, System.Windows.Forms.PrintControllerWithStatusDialog

Returned By PrintDocument.PrintController

Passed To PrintDocument.PrintController, System.Windows.Forms.PrintControllerWithStatusDialog.PrintControllerWithStatusDialog( )

PrintDocument marshal by reference, disposable

System.Drawing.Printing (system.drawing.dll) class

This class encapsulates a document to be printed.

On construction, the DefaultPageSettings and PrinterSettings represent the default system printer, but you could create a set of PageSettings and assign them to the DefaultPageSettings property, and/or a set of PrinterSettings, which you assign to the PrinterSettings property if you want to customize the printer output. You can also modify individual properties in the existing settings (such as the PrinterSettings.Copies to change the number of copies to print). You can also set the DocumentName to a display name for the print job. You'd see this in the printer queue or a status dialog.

Once the settings are to your satisfaction, you can set a **PrintController**. The default is a **PrintControllerWithStatusDialog**, but you can choose a **StandardPrintController** or a **PreviewPrintController**. Call **Print( )** to send the document to the printer.

You're not done yet. To determine what to print, you have to handle several events raised by the document. **BeginPrint** is raised when printing is started for the document. Then, the **PrintPage** event provides the **System.Drawing.Graphics** object on which to draw your page, along with a bunch of other settings that allow you to format the output for the page dimensions and page settings (see the **PrintPageEventArgs** for details). If you have more pages to print, you can set the **HasMorePages** property to true; otherwise, set it to false and the document printing can come to an end. When this happens, **EndPrint** is raised and you can clean up. All these events support the **Cancel** property to abandon printing.

Immediately before the **PrintPage** event, the framework raises the **QueryPageSettings** event. You can use this to modify the settings on a page-by-page basis (by modifying the **QueryPageSettingsEventArgs.PageSettings** property), without having to inject code into your existing **PrintPage** handler.

```
public class PrintDocument : System.ComponentModel.Component {
// Public Constructors
   public PrintDocument( );
// Public Instance Properties
   public PageSettings DefaultPageSettings{set; get; }
   public string DocumentName{set; get; }
   public PrintController PrintController{set; get; }
   public PrinterSettings PrinterSettings{set; get; }
// Public Instance Methods
   public void Print( );
   public override string ToString( );                    // overrides System.ComponentModel.Component
// Protected Instance Methods
   protected virtual void OnBeginPrint(PrintEventArgs e);
   protected virtual void OnEndPrint(PrintEventArgs e);
   protected virtual void OnPrintPage(PrintPageEventArgs e);
   protected virtual void OnQueryPageSettings(QueryPageSettingsEventArgs e);
// Events
   public event PrintEventHandler BeginPrint;
   public event PrintEventHandler EndPrint;
   public event PrintPageEventHandler PrintPage;
   public event QueryPageSettingsEventHandler QueryPageSettings;
}
```

Hierarchy System.Object → System.MarshalByRefObject → System.ComponentModel.Component(System.ComponentModel.IComponent, System.IDisposable) → PrintDocument

Returned By System.Windows.Forms.PageSetupDialog.Document, System.Windows.Forms.PrintDialog.Document, System.Windows.Forms.PrintPreviewControl.Document, System.Windows.Forms.PrintPreviewDialog.Document

Passed To PrintController.{OnEndPage( ), OnEndPrint( ), OnStartPage( ), OnStartPrint( )}, System.Windows.Forms.PageSetupDialog.Document, System.Windows.Forms.PrintDialog.Document, System.Windows.Forms.PrintPreviewControl.Document, System.Windows.Forms.PrintPreviewDialog.Document

PrinterResolution

System.Drawing.Printing (system.drawing.dll) class

This class encapsulates the horizontal X and vertical Y resolution (in dots per inch) of the printer device, and the resolution Kind this represents. The Kind is chosen from the PrinterResolutionKind enumeration and indicates a print quality (e.g., Draft or High quality).

```
public class PrinterResolution {
// Public Instance Properties
   public PrinterResolutionKind Kind{get; }
   public int X{get; }
   public int Y{get; }
// Public Instance Methods
   public override string ToString( );                                    // overrides object
}
```

Returned By PageSettings.PrinterResolution, PrinterResolutionCollection.this

Passed To PageSettings.PrinterResolution, PrinterResolutionCollection.PrinterResolutionCollection( )

PrinterResolutionKind serializable

System.Drawing.Printing (system.drawing.dll) enum

This enumeration is used to specify the print quality of a particular resolution for the PrinterResolution.Kind property.

```
public enum PrinterResolutionKind {
   Custom = 0,
   High = -4,
   Medium = -3,
   Low = -2,
   Draft = -1
}
```

Hierarchy System.Object → System.ValueType → System.Enum(System.IComparable, System.IFormattable, System.IConvertible) → PrinterResolutionKind

Returned By PrinterResolution.Kind

PrinterSettings serializable

System.Drawing.Printing (system.drawing.dll) class

This class encapsulates a printer device, and its associated settings.

First, it offers a static property to retrieve the list of the names of the InstalledPrinters. When you construct a printer settings object, you set the PrinterName property to one of these values to indicate which printer to use. The default is the system default printer. Whether you set the name or leave the default, all the properties will be correctly set to the defaults for that printer. You can determine if it is currently using the default printer by checking the IsDefaultPrinter property.

You can then override any of those values. This might include the Duplex setting, the number of Copies to print, whether to Collate the output, and the PrintRange. If you set the range to PrintRange.SomePages, a simple range can be set with the FromPage and ToPage properties. (Note that the System.Windows.Forms.PrintDialog handles the page printing for you.

The default PageSettings for the printer can be retrieved, and you can also use properties such as PaperSizes, PaperSources, and PrinterResolutions to determine the options for overriding some of those default PageSettings.

There are also three properties that tell you about the capabilities of the printer: CanDuplex, SupportsColor, and IsPlotter.

To help determine how a document will be printed, you can use the CreateMeasurementGraphics( ) method to create a reference System.Drawing.Graphics surface. This can be used to determine the layout for your pages but is not the actual printer device surface.

See PrintDocument for more information on how to use the PrinterSettings to print a document.

```
public class PrinterSettings : ICloneable {
// Public Constructors
   public PrinterSettings( );
// Public Static Properties
   public static StringCollection InstalledPrinters{get; }
// Public Instance Properties
   public bool CanDuplex{get; }
   public bool Collate{set; get; }
   public short Copies{set; get; }
   public PageSettings DefaultPageSettings{get; }
   public Duplex Duplex{set; get; }
   public int FromPage{set; get; }
   public bool IsDefaultPrinter{get; }
   public bool IsPlotter{get; }
   public bool IsValid{get; }
   public int LandscapeAngle{get; }
   public int MaximumCopies{get; }
   public int MaximumPage{set; get; }
   public int MinimumPage{set; get; }
   public PaperSizeCollection PaperSizes{get; }
   public PaperSourceCollection PaperSources{get; }
   public string PrinterName{set; get; }
   public PrinterResolutionCollection PrinterResolutions{get; }
   public PrintRange PrintRange{set; get; }
   public bool PrintToFile{set; get; }
   public bool SupportsColor{get; }
   public int ToPage{set; get; }
// Public Instance Methods
   public object Clone( );                                     // implements ICloneable
   public Graphics CreateMeasurementGraphics( );
   public IntPtr GetHdevmode( );
   public IntPtr GetHdevmode(PageSettings pageSettings);
   public IntPtr GetHdevnames( );
   public void SetHdevmode(IntPtr hdevmode);
   public void SetHdevnames(IntPtr hdevnames);
   public override string ToString( );                         // overrides object
}
```

Returned By PageSettings.PrinterSettings, PrintDocument.PrinterSettings, System.Windows.Forms.PageSetupDialog.PrinterSettings, System.Windows.Forms.PrintDialog.PrinterSettings

Passed To InvalidPrinterException.InvalidPrinterException( ), PageSettings.{PageSettings( ), PrinterSettings}, PrintDocument.PrinterSettings, System.Windows.Forms.PageSetupDialog.PrinterSettings, System.Windows.Forms.PrintDialog.PrinterSettings

PrinterSettings.PaperSizeCollection

System.Drawing.Printing (system.drawing.dll) class

This represents a collection of PaperSize objects and is returned by the PrinterSettings.PaperSizes property.

```
public class PrinterSettings.PaperSizeCollection : ICollection, IEnumerable {
// Public Constructors
   public PrinterSettings.PaperSizeCollection(PaperSize[ ] array);
// Public Instance Properties
   public int Count{get; }                                    // implements ICollection
   public virtual PaperSize this{get; }
// Public Instance Methods
   public IEnumerator GetEnumerator( );                       // implements IEnumerable
}
```

PrinterSettings.PaperSourceCollection

System.Drawing.Printing (system.drawing.dll) class

This represents a collection of PaperSource objects and is returned by the PrinterSettings.PaperSources property.

```
public class PrinterSettings.PaperSourceCollection : ICollection, IEnumerable {
// Public Constructors
   public PrinterSettings.PaperSourceCollection(PaperSource[ ] array);
// Public Instance Properties
   public int Count{get; }                                    // implements ICollection
   public virtual PaperSource this{get; }
// Public Instance Methods
   public IEnumerator GetEnumerator( );                       // implements IEnumerable
}
```

PrinterSettings.PrinterResolutionCollection

System.Drawing.Printing (system.drawing.dll) class

This class encapsulates a collection PrinterResolution objects and is returned by the PrinterSettings.PrinterResolutions property.

```
public class PrinterSettings.PrinterResolutionCollection : ICollection, IEnumerable {
// Public Constructors
   public PrinterSettings.PrinterResolutionCollection(PrinterResolution[ ] array);
// Public Instance Properties
   public int Count{get; }                                    // implements ICollection
   public virtual PrinterResolution this{get; }
// Public Instance Methods
```

Printing

```
  public IEnumerator GetEnumerator( );                                    // implements IEnumerable
}
```

PrinterSettings.StringCollection

System.Drawing.Printing (system.drawing.dll) class

This class represents an array of strings and is returned by the PrinterSettings.InstalledPrinters property. Contrary to the information in the MSDN documentation, this is not for internal use only, as you are quite entitled to access this collection to determine the set of printers installed on the machine.

```
public class PrinterSettings.StringCollection : ICollection, IEnumerable {
// Public Constructors
  public PrinterSettings.StringCollection(string[ ] array);
// Public Instance Properties
  public int Count{get; }                                                 // implements ICollection
  public virtual string this{get; }
// Public Instance Methods
  public IEnumerator GetEnumerator( );                                    // implements IEnumerable
}
```

PrinterUnit serializable

System.Drawing.Printing (system.drawing.dll) enum

This enumeration lists the device resolution units permissible in Win32 print device contexts. See PrinterUnitConvert.Convert( ) for information on how to convert a type from one set of units to another.

```
public enum PrinterUnit {
  Display = 0,
  ThousandthsOfAnInch = 1,
  HundredthsOfAMillimeter = 2,
  TenthsOfAMillimeter = 3
}
```

Hierarchy System.Object → System.ValueType → System.Enum(System.IComparable, System.IFormattable, System.IConvertible) → PrinterUnit

Passed To PrinterUnitConvert.Convert( )

PrinterUnitConvert

System.Drawing.Printing (system.drawing.dll) sealed class

This class provides one static utility method, Convert( ), to convert a value (such as an integer, a System.Drawing.Rectangle, etc.) from one PrinterUnit to another.

```
public sealed class PrinterUnitConvert {
// Public Static Methods
  public static double Convert(double value, PrinterUnit fromUnit, PrinterUnit toUnit);
  public static int Convert(int value, PrinterUnit fromUnit, PrinterUnit toUnit);
  public static Margins Convert(Margins value, PrinterUnit fromUnit, PrinterUnit toUnit);
  public static Point Convert(System.Drawing.Point value, PrinterUnit fromUnit, PrinterUnit toUnit);
```

```
public static Rectangle Convert(System.Drawing.Rectangle value, PrinterUnit fromUnit, PrinterUnit toUnit);
public static Size Convert(System.Drawing.Size value, PrinterUnit fromUnit, PrinterUnit toUnit);
}
```

PrintEventArgs

System.Drawing.Printing (system.drawing.dll) class

This class encapsulates the data for the PrintDocument.BeginPrint and PrintDocument.EndPrint events.

If you handle this event, you can cancel the print job by setting the Cancel property in this object.

```
public class PrintEventArgs : System.ComponentModel.CancelEventArgs {
// Public Constructors
public PrintEventArgs( );
}
```

Hierarchy System.Object → System.EventArgs → System.ComponentModel.CancelEventArgs → PrintEventArgs

Subclasses QueryPageSettingsEventArgs

Passed To PrintController.{OnEndPrint( ), OnStartPrint( )}, PrintDocument.{OnBeginPrint( ), OnEndPrint( )}, PrintEventHandler.{BeginInvoke( ), Invoke( )}

PrintEventHandler serializable

System.Drawing.Printing (system.drawing.dll) delegate

This is a delegate for the PrintDocument.BeginPrint and PrintDocument.EndPrint events.

```
public delegate void PrintEventHandler(object sender,
    PrintEventArgs e);
```

Associated Events PrintDocument.{BeginPrint( ), EndPrint( )}

PrintingPermission serializable

System.Drawing.Printing (system.drawing.dll) sealed class

This class encapsulates the permissions the executing code might have to use a printer.

You can determine the access Level that the currently executing code has to printing services (see PrintingPermissionLevel).

You can also set declarative permissions by using the PrintingPermissionAttribute.

```
public sealed class PrintingPermission : System.Security.CodeAccessPermission : System.Security.Permissions.
IUnrestrictedPermission {
// Public Constructors
public PrintingPermission(System.Security.Permissions.PermissionState state);
public PrintingPermission(PrintingPermissionLevel printingLevel);
// Public Instance Properties
public PrintingPermissionLevel Level{set; get; }
// Public Instance Methods
```

```
  public override IPermission Copy( );                                                     // overrides CodeAccessPermission
  public override void FromXml(System.Security.SecurityElement esd);                       // overrides CodeAccessPermission
  public override IPermission Intersect(System.Security.IPermission target);               // overrides CodeAccessPermission
  public override bool IsSubsetOf(System.Security.IPermission target);                     // overrides CodeAccessPermission
  public bool IsUnrestricted( );                                                           // implements IUnrestrictedPermission
  public override SecurityElement ToXml( );                                                // overrides CodeAccessPermission
  public override IPermission Union(System.Security.IPermission target);                   // overrides CodeAccessPermission
}
```

Hierarchy System.Object → System.Security.CodeAccessPermission(System.Security.IPermission, System.Security.ISecurityEncodable, System.Security.IStackWalk) → PrintingPermission(System.Security.Permissions.IUnrestrictedPermission)

PrintingPermissionAttribute

System.Drawing.Printing (system.drawing.dll) sealed class

This attribute can be used to adorn a class or member to require a certain Level of printer-access permissions to be available before the code can execute. See PrintingPermissionLevel for valid access levels.

```
public sealed class PrintingPermissionAttribute : System.Security.Permissions.CodeAccessSecurityAttribute {
// Public Constructors
  public PrintingPermissionAttribute(System.Security.Permissions.SecurityAction action);
// Public Instance Properties
  public PrintingPermissionLevel Level{set; get; }
// Public Instance Methods
  public override IPermission CreatePermission( );          // overrides System.Security.Permissions.SecurityAttribute
}
```

Hierarchy System.Object → System.Attribute → System.Security.Permissions.SecurityAttribute → System.Security.Permissions.CodeAccessSecurityAttribute → PrintingPermissionAttribute

Valid On All

PrintingPermissionLevel serializable

System.Drawing.Printing (system.drawing.dll) enum

This enumeration allows you to determine how access to the printing services can be restricted. You can allow full access with AllPrinting, no access with NoPrinting, or one of two restricted settings: SafePrinting, which only allows printing through a (restricted) dialog box, and DefaultPrinting, which extends these permissions to allow full access to the default printer.

```
public enum PrintingPermissionLevel {
  NoPrinting = 0,
  SafePrinting = 1,
  DefaultPrinting = 2,
  AllPrinting = 3
}
```

Hierarchy System.Object → System.ValueType → System.Enum(System.IComparable, System.IFormattable, System.IConvertible) → PrintingPermissionLevel

Returned By PrintingPermission.Level, PrintingPermissionAttribute.Level

Passed To PrintingPermission.{Level, PrintingPermission( )}, PrintingPermissionAttribute.Level

PrintPageEventArgs

System.Drawing.Printing (system.drawing.dll) class

This class encapsulates the data for the PrintDocument.PrintPage event.

You should handle this event and paint the page's imagery on the supplied Graphics surface. To determine how the page should be printed, you can use the MarginBounds, PageBounds, and PageSettings.

If the document contains more pages that need printing, you should set the HasMorePages property to true, but if not, set it to false and the print job will be completed.

To abandon the print job, you can set the Cancel property.

```
public class PrintPageEventArgs : EventArgs {
// Public Constructors
   public PrintPageEventArgs(System.Drawing.Graphics graphics, System.Drawing.Rectangle marginBounds,
      System.Drawing.Rectangle pageBounds, PageSettings pageSettings);
// Public Instance Properties
   public bool Cancel{set; get; }
   public Graphics Graphics{get; }
   public bool HasMorePages{set; get; }
   public Rectangle MarginBounds{get; }
   public Rectangle PageBounds{get; }
   public PageSettings PageSettings{get; }
}
```

Hierarchy System.Object → System.EventArgs → PrintPageEventArgs

Passed To PrintController.{OnEndPage( ), OnStartPage( )}, PrintDocument.OnPrintPage( ), PrintPageEventHandler.{BeginInvoke( ), Invoke( )}

PrintPageEventHandler serializable

System.Drawing.Printing (system.drawing.dll) delegate

This is a delegate for the PrintDocument.PrintPage event.

```
public delegate void PrintPageEventHandler(object sender, PrintPageEventArgs e);
```

Associated Events PrintDocument.PrintPage( )

PrintRange serializable

System.Drawing.Printing (system.drawing.dll) enum

This enumeration determines the type of range of pages to be printed, from AllPages to just a Selection. See PrinterSettings for more information.

```
public enum PrintRange {
  AllPages = 0,
  Selection = 1,
  SomePages = 2
}
```

Hierarchy System.Object → System.ValueType → System.Enum(System.IComparable, System.IFormattable, System.IConvertible) → PrintRange

Returned By PrinterSettings.PrintRange

Passed To PrinterSettings.PrintRange

QueryPageSettingsEventArgs

System.Drawing.Printing (system.drawing.dll) class

This class contains the data for the PrintDocument.QueryPageSettings event. It extends the PrintPageEventArgs with the PageSettings property. You can modify these settings to control the page setup on a page-by-page basis.

```
public class QueryPageSettingsEventArgs : PrintEventArgs {
// Public Constructors
  public QueryPageSettingsEventArgs(PageSettings pageSettings);
// Public Instance Properties
  public PageSettings PageSettings{set; get; }
}
```

Hierarchy System.Object → System.EventArgs → System.ComponentModel.CancelEventArgs → PrintEventArgs → QueryPageSettingsEventArgs

Passed To PrintDocument.OnQueryPageSettings( ), QueryPageSettingsEventHandler.{BeginInvoke( ), Invoke( )}

QueryPageSettingsEventHandler **serializable**

System.Drawing.Printing (system.drawing.dll) delegate

This is a delegate for the PrintDocument.QueryPageSettings event.

```
public delegate void QueryPageSettingsEventHandler(object sender, QueryPageSettingsEventArgs e);
```

Associated Events PrintDocument.QueryPageSettings( )

StandardPrintController

System.Drawing.Printing (system.drawing.dll) class

This class implements PrintController to send the print information to a standard printer. You typically set an instance of this class into the PrintDocument.PrintController property to determine how a document will be printed. See PrintDocument for more information on the printing process.

```
public class StandardPrintController : PrintController {
// Public Constructors
   public StandardPrintController( );
// Public Instance Methods
   public override void OnEndPage(PrintDocument document, PrintPageEventArgs e);          // overrides PrintController
   public override void OnEndPrint(PrintDocument document, PrintEventArgs e);             // overrides PrintController
   public override Graphics OnStartPage(PrintDocument document, PrintPageEventArgs e);    // overrides PrintController
   public override void OnStartPrint(PrintDocument document, PrintEventArgs e);           // overrides PrintController
}
```

Hierarchy System.Object → PrintController → StandardPrintController

18

The System.Drawing.Text Namespace

The System.Drawing.Text namespace contains various classes related to text and font management in the framework. Figure 18-1 shows the types in this namespace.

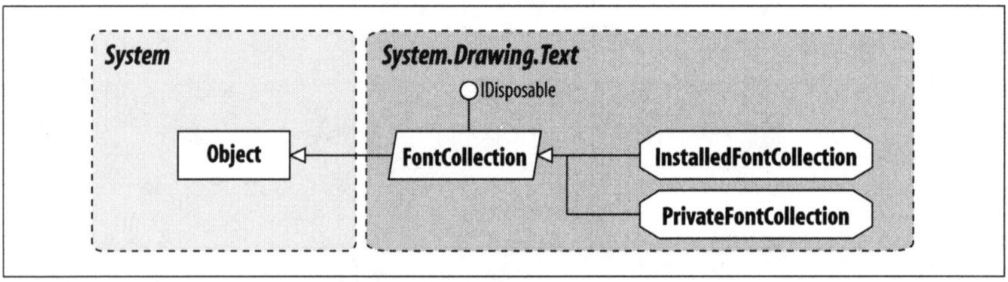
System
System.Drawing.Text
IDisposable
Object
FontCollection
InstalledFontCollection
PrivateFontCollection

Figure 18-1. Types from the System.Drawing.Text namespace

FontCollection **disposable**

System.Drawing.Text (system.drawing.dll) abstract class

This class is the abstract base for a collection of fonts.

You can use the Families property to retrieve an array of System.Drawing.FontFamily objects representing the fonts in the collection.

See InstalledFontCollection and PrivateFontCollection for more information.

```
public abstract class FontCollection : IDisposable {
// Public Instance Properties
   public FontFamily[ ] Families{get; }
// Public Instance Methods
   public void Dispose( );                                    // implements IDisposable
// Protected Instance Methods
   protected virtual void Dispose(bool disposing);
   protected override void Finalize( );                       // overrides object
}
```

Subclasses InstalledFontCollection, PrivateFontCollection

Passed To System.Drawing.FontFamily.FontFamily( )

GenericFontFamilies serializable

System.Drawing.Text (system.drawing.dll) enum

This enumeration lists the three generic font families.

Systems can have wildly different sets of fonts installed (particularly in cross-platform environments). By specifying one of the generic families, you can retrieve a Monospace, SansSerif, or Serif font appropriate to the current platform, regardless of what might actually be present. For example, the SansSerif font could be Arial on one machine and Helvetica on another.

```
public enum GenericFontFamilies {
  Serif = 0,
  SansSerif = 1,
  Monospace = 2
}
```

Hierarchy System.Object → System.ValueType → System.Enum(System.IComparable, System.IFormattable, System.IConvertible) → GenericFontFamilies

Passed To System.Drawing.FontFamily.FontFamily( )

HotkeyPrefix serializable

System.Drawing.Text (system.drawing.dll) enum

This enumeration is used by the System.Drawing.StringFormat.HotkeyPrefix property to determine how shortcut keys (as designated by an & character) are displayed in a string.

```
public enum HotkeyPrefix {
  None = 0,
  Show = 1,
  Hide = 2
}
```

Hierarchy System.Object → System.ValueType → System.Enum(System.IComparable, System.IFormattable, System.IConvertible) → HotkeyPrefix

Returned By System.Drawing.StringFormat.HotkeyPrefix

Passed To System.Drawing.StringFormat.HotkeyPrefix

InstalledFontCollection disposable

System.Drawing.Text (system.drawing.dll) sealed class

This class, derived from FontCollection, represents all the font families that have been installed on the system. You can enumerate the Families property to find a font suitable for your purposes.

```
public sealed class InstalledFontCollection : FontCollection {
// Public Constructors
```

```
  public InstalledFontCollection( );
}
```

Hierarchy System.Object → FontCollection(System.IDisposable) → InstalledFontCollection

PrivateFontCollection

disposable

System.Drawing.Text (system.drawing.dll) sealed class

This class, derived from FontCollection, represents a set of fonts that have not been installed on the system.

You can add a font to the collection using the AddFontFile( ) and AddMemoryFont( ) methods. The second of these is a thin wrapper over the unmanaged implementation code, and you should be careful to ensure that the memory you pass in will not be garbage collected before you are done with the collection.

You can then enumerate the Families in the collection in the normal way.

```
public sealed class PrivateFontCollection : FontCollection {
// Public Constructors
  public PrivateFontCollection( );
// Public Instance Methods
  public void AddFontFile(string filename);
  public void AddMemoryFont(IntPtr memory, int length);
// Protected Instance Methods
  protected override void Dispose(bool disposing);          // overrides FontCollection
}
```

Hierarchy System.Object → FontCollection(System.IDisposable) → PrivateFontCollection

TextRenderingHint

serializable

System.Drawing.Text (system.drawing.dll) enum

This enumeration is used by the System.Drawing.Graphics.TextRenderingHint to determine the quality with which text is rendered on the graphics surface. As will all the GDI+ rendering hints, there is a trade-off between rendering quality and speed, from SingleBitPerPixel to ClearTypeGridFit.

```
public enum TextRenderingHint {
  SystemDefault = 0,
  SingleBitPerPixelGridFit = 1,
  SingleBitPerPixel = 2,
  AntiAliasGridFit = 3,
  AntiAlias = 4,
  ClearTypeGridFit = 5
}
```

Hierarchy System.Object → System.ValueType → System.Enum(System.IComparable, System.IFormattable, System.IConvertible) → TextRenderingHint

Returned By System.Drawing.Graphics.TextRenderingHint

Passed To System.Drawing.Graphics.TextRenderingHint

19
The System.Windows.Forms Namespace

The System.Windows.Forms namespace contains the classes that you use to build rich client applications—the windows, buttons, drop-down lists, and labels that make up the UIs with which you are familiar. At the center of this universe is the Control class. Any window that appears on the screen, from dialogs to checkboxes, is derived from Control, and this class provides almost all the basic behavior a window needs. All the common windows controls provide relatively minor modifications or extensions to Control to add their own behaviors (painting, click handling, etc.), so a good understanding of the Control class goes a long, long way.

Figures 19-1 and 19-2 show many of the types in this namespace. Figure 19-3 shows many of this namespace's event arguments, and Figure 19-4 shows the delegates. The components are shown in Figure 19-5 and the controls are shown in Figures 19-6 and 19-7.

Unlike the Win32 world, all UI construction is done by writing code. The Designer environment actually generates source code, rather than generating the dialog resource files that have existed since Windows was first introduced. It also attempts to round-trip any changes you make to that code, incorporating them back into the visual editor. Admittedly, this round-tripping comes with do-not-touch warnings in Version 1.0, but with all due care and attention, you can modify the generated code and have the designers reflect those changes for you.

The other advantage gained by making code the first-class way of generating a UI is that it becomes simple to build plug-in architectures. You can leverage the reflection APIs to find appropriate controls to instantiate. The Control.Dock and Control.Anchor architecture make it easy to ensure that the generated UI looks consistent and attractive. Compare this with the old Win32 hacking of dialog templates, and you'll see a whole new world of UI design opportunities.

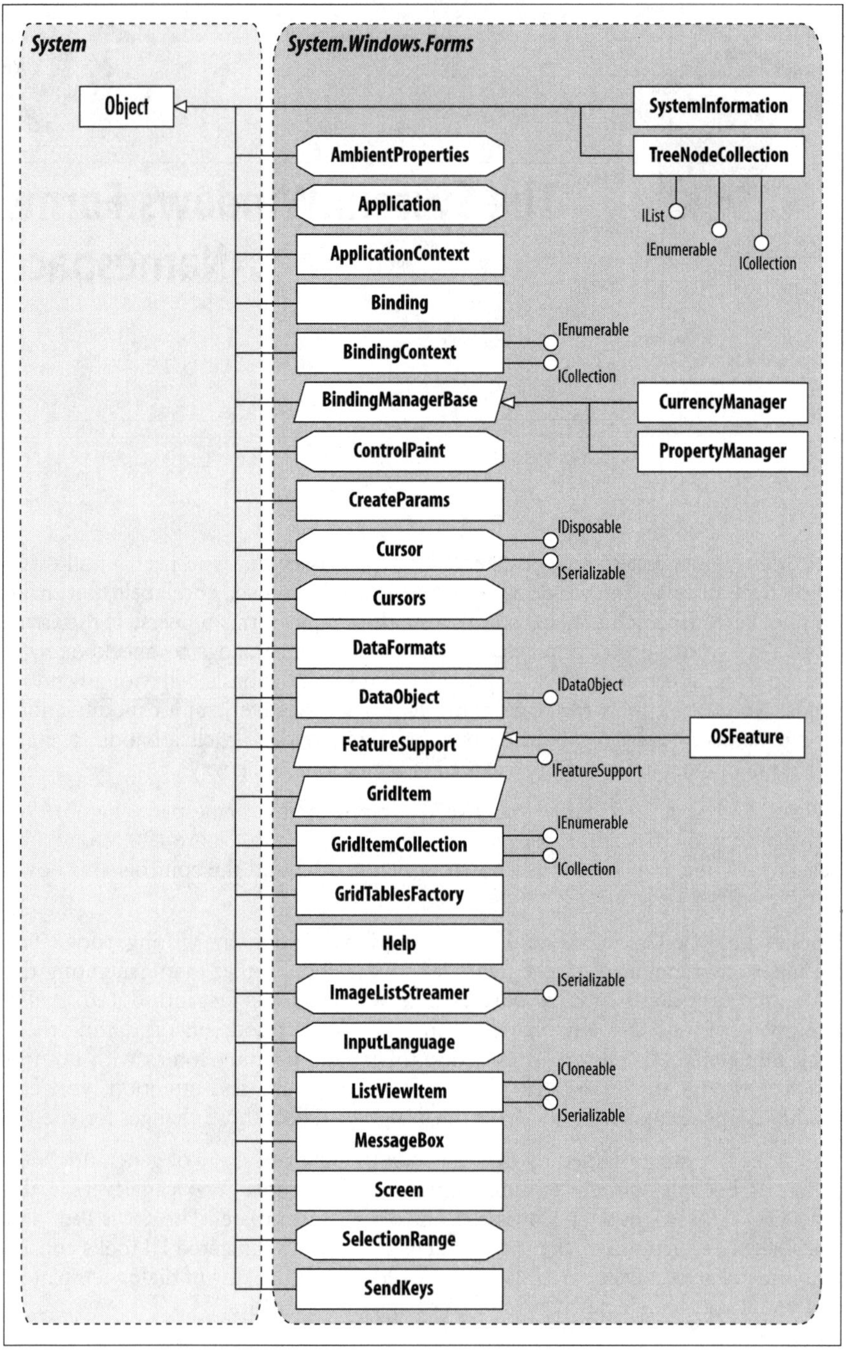
System
System.Windows.Forms
Object
SystemInformation
TreeNodeCollection
IList
IEnumerable
ICollection
AmbientProperties
Application
ApplicationContext
Binding
BindingContext
IEnumerable
ICollection
BindingManagerBase
CurrencyManager
PropertyManager
ControlPaint
CreateParams
Cursor
IDisposable
ISerializable
Cursors
DataFormats
DataObject
IDataObject
FeatureSupport
OSFeature
IFeatureSupport
GridItem
GridItemCollection
IEnumerable
ICollection
GridTablesFactory
Help
ImageListStreamer
ISerializable
InputLanguage
ListViewItem
ICloneable
ISerializable
MessageBox
Screen
SelectionRange
SendKeys

Figure 19-1. Many types from the System.Windows.Forms namespace

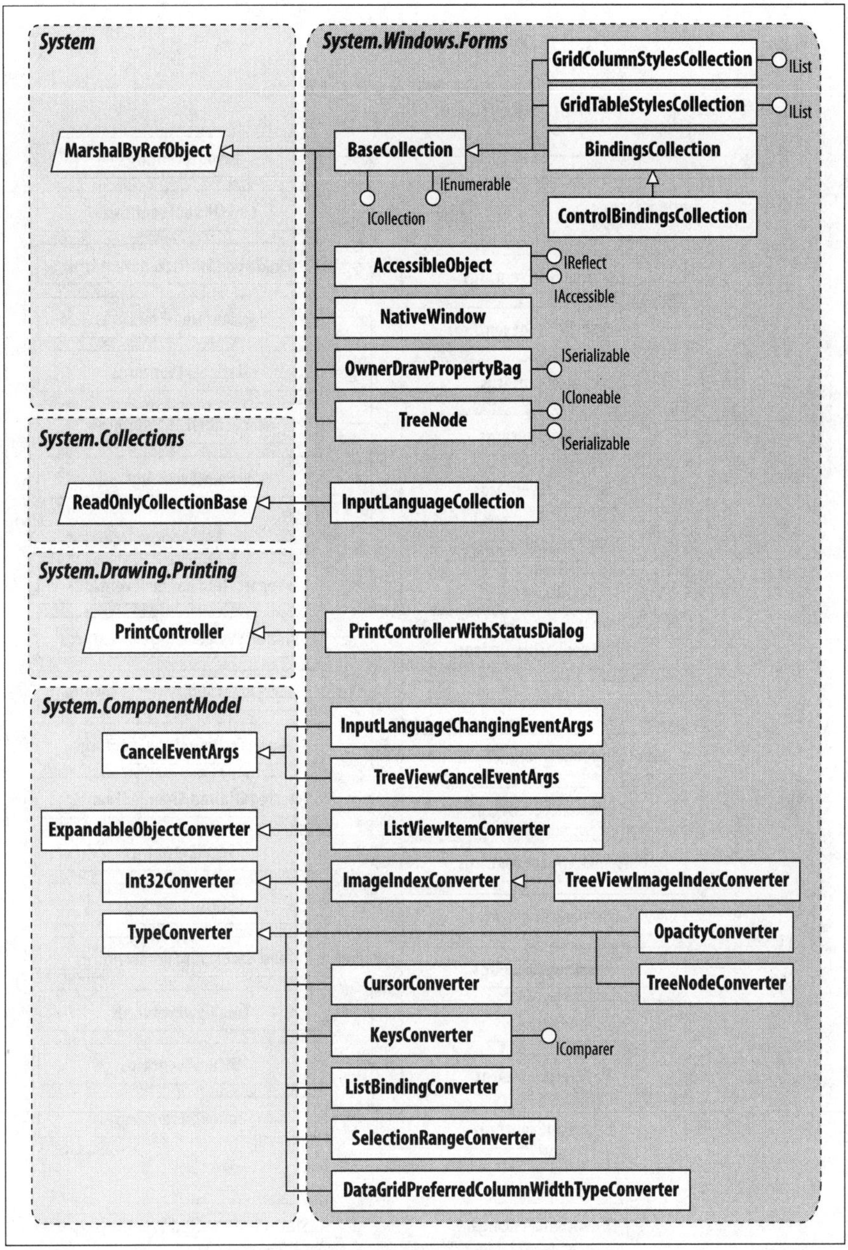
System
System.Windows.Forms
MarshalByRefObject
BaseCollection
IEnumerable
ICollection
GridColumnStylesCollection
IList
GridTableStylesCollection
IList
BindingsCollection
ControlBindingsCollection
AccessibleObject
IReflect
IAccessible
NativeWindow
OwnerDrawPropertyBag
ISerializable
TreeNode
ICloneable
ISerializable
System.Collections
ReadOnlyCollectionBase
InputLanguageCollection
System.Drawing.Printing
PrintController
PrintControllerWithStatusDialog
System.ComponentModel
CancelEventArgs
InputLanguageChangingEventArgs
TreeViewCancelEventArgs
ExpandableObjectConverter
ListViewItemConverter
Int32Converter
ImageIndexConverter
TreeViewImageIndexConverter
TypeConverter
OpacityConverter
TreeNodeConverter
CursorConverter
KeysConverter
IComparer
ListBindingConverter
SelectionRangeConverter
DataGridPreferredColumnWidthTypeConverter

Figure 19-2. More types from the System.Windows.Forms namespace

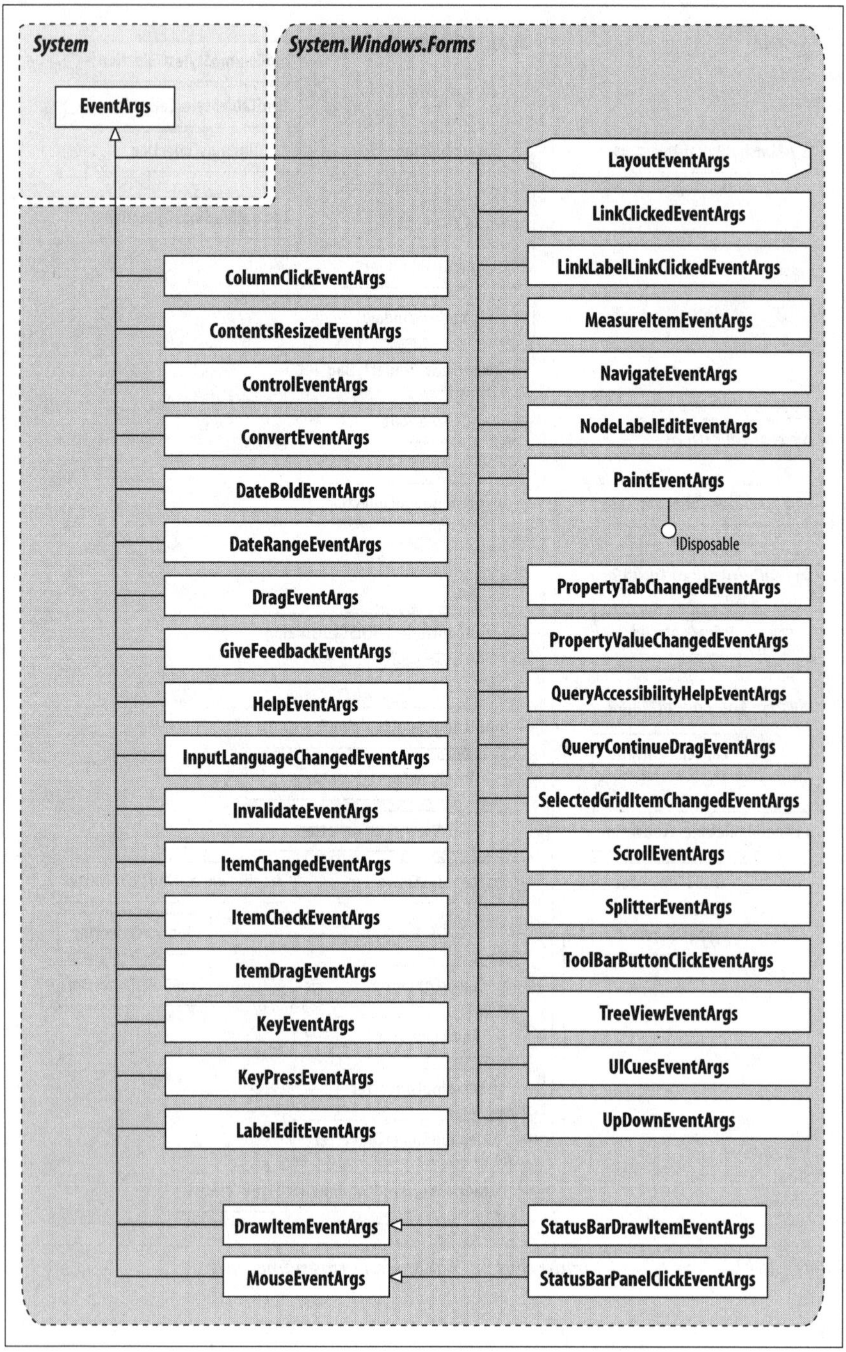
System
System.Windows.Forms
EventArgs
LayoutEventArgs
LinkClickedEventArgs
LinkLabelLinkClickedEventArgs
MeasureItemEventArgs
NavigateEventArgs
NodeLabelEditEventArgs
PaintEventArgs
IDisposable
PropertyTabChangedEventArgs
PropertyValueChangedEventArgs
QueryAccessibilityHelpEventArgs
QueryContinueDragEventArgs
SelectedGridItemChangedEventArgs
ScrollEventArgs
SplitterEventArgs
ToolBarButtonClickEventArgs
TreeViewEventArgs
UICuesEventArgs
UpDownEventArgs
ColumnClickEventArgs
ContentsResizedEventArgs
ControlEventArgs
ConvertEventArgs
DateBoldEventArgs
DateRangeEventArgs
DragEventArgs
GiveFeedbackEventArgs
HelpEventArgs
InputLanguageChangedEventArgs
InvalidateEventArgs
ItemChangedEventArgs
ItemCheckEventArgs
ItemDragEventArgs
KeyEventArgs
KeyPressEventArgs
LabelEditEventArgs
DrawItemEventArgs
StatusBarDrawItemEventArgs
MouseEventArgs
StatusBarPanelClickEventArgs

Figure 19-3. Event arguments in the System.Windows.Forms namespace

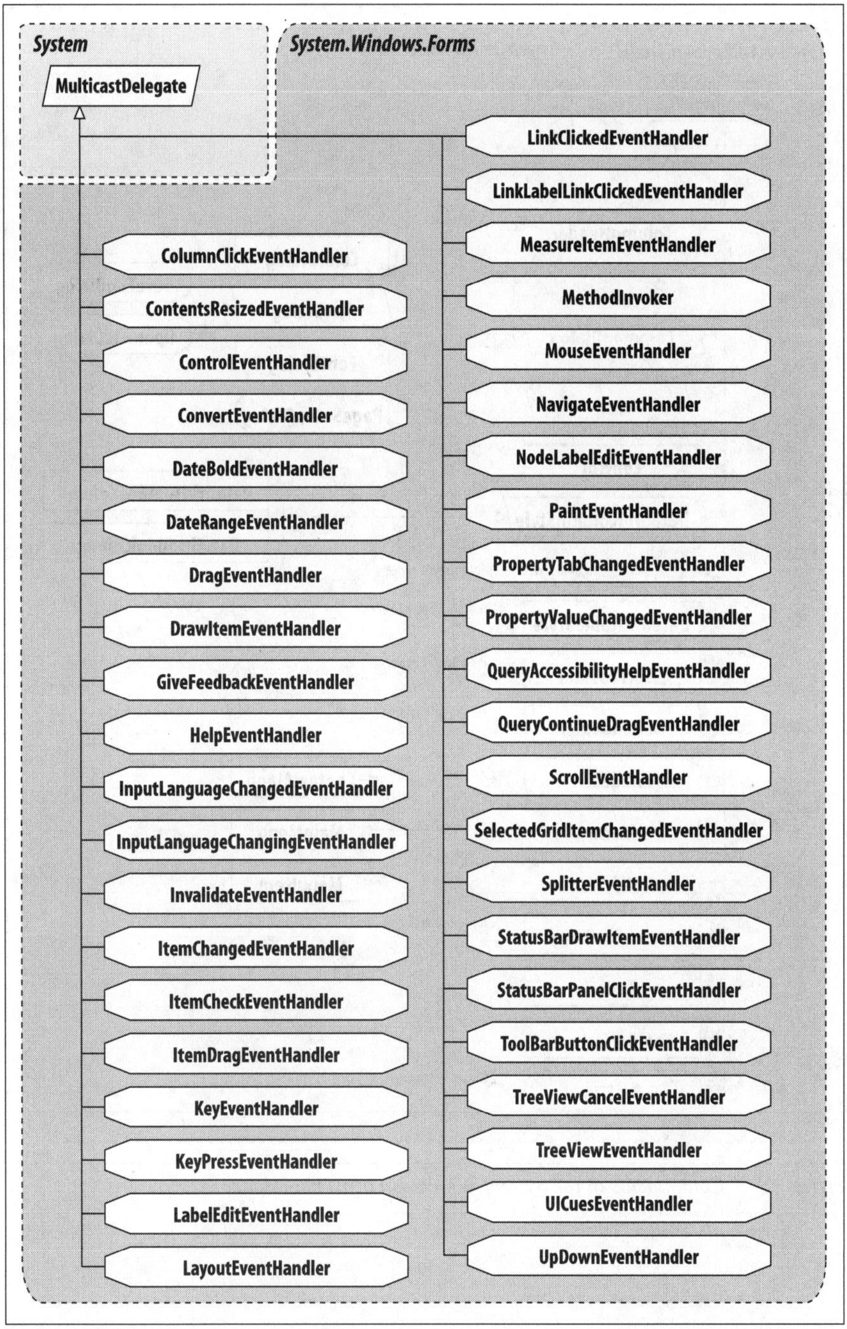
System
MulticastDelegate
System.Windows.Forms
ColumnClickEventHandler
ContentsResizedEventHandler
ControlEventHandler
ConvertEventHandler
DateBoldEventHandler
DateRangeEventHandler
DragEventHandler
DrawItemEventHandler
GiveFeedbackEventHandler
HelpEventHandler
InputLanguageChangedEventHandler
InputLanguageChangingEventHandler
InvalidateEventHandler
ItemChangedEventHandler
ItemCheckEventHandler
ItemDragEventHandler
KeyEventHandler
KeyPressEventHandler
LabelEditEventHandler
LayoutEventHandler
LinkClickedEventHandler
LinkLabelLinkClickedEventHandler
MeasureItemEventHandler
MethodInvoker
MouseEventHandler
NavigateEventHandler
NodeLabelEditEventHandler
PaintEventHandler
PropertyTabChangedEventHandler
PropertyValueChangedEventHandler
QueryAccessibilityHelpEventHandler
QueryContinueDragEventHandler
ScrollEventHandler
SelectedGridItemChangedEventHandler
SplitterEventHandler
StatusBarDrawItemEventHandler
StatusBarPanelClickEventHandler
ToolBarButtonClickEventHandler
TreeViewCancelEventHandler
TreeViewEventHandler
UICuesEventHandler
UpDownEventHandler

Figure 19-4. Delegates from System.Windows.Forms

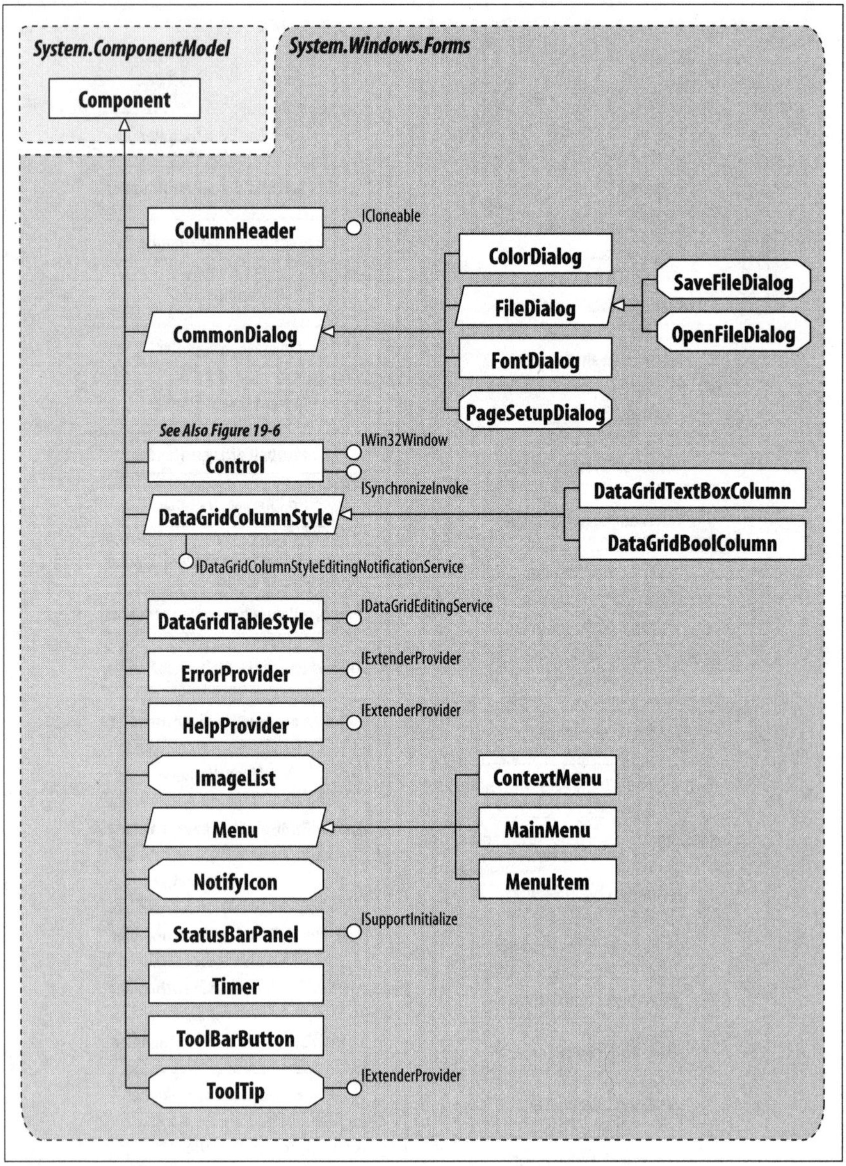

System.ComponentModel
Component
System.Windows.Forms
ColumnHeader
ICloneable
ColorDialog
SaveFileDialog
FileDialog
OpenFileDialog
CommonDialog
FontDialog
PageSetupDialog
See Also Figure 19-6
IWin32Window
Control
ISynchronizeInvoke
DataGridTextBoxColumn
DataGridColumnStyle
DataGridBoolColumn
IDataGridColumnStyleEditingNotificationService
DataGridTableStyle
IDataGridEditingService
ErrorProvider
IExtenderProvider
HelpProvider
IExtenderProvider
ImageList
ContextMenu
Menu
MainMenu
NotifyIcon
MenuItem
StatusBarPanel
ISupportInitialize
Timer
ToolBarButton
ToolTip
IExtenderProvider

Figure 19-5. Components in the System.Windows.Forms namespace

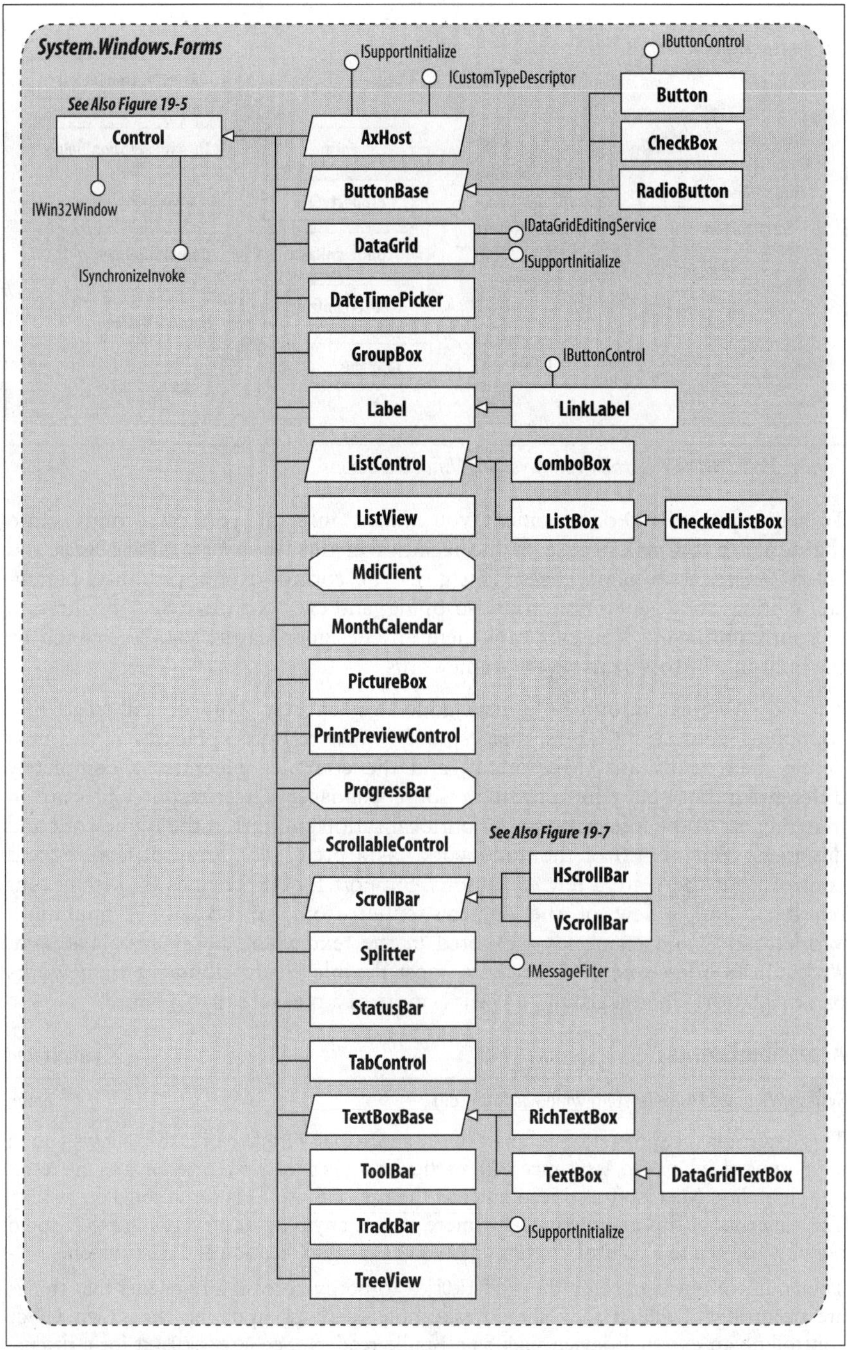
System.Windows.Forms
See Also Figure 19-5
Control
IWin32Window
ISynchronizeInvoke
ISupportInitialize
ICustomTypeDescriptor
AxHost
ButtonBase
IButtonControl
Button
CheckBox
RadioButton
DataGrid
IDataGridEditingService
ISupportInitialize
DateTimePicker
GroupBox
Label
IButtonControl
LinkLabel
ListControl
ComboBox
ListBox
CheckedListBox
ListView
MdiClient
MonthCalendar
PictureBox
PrintPreviewControl
ProgressBar
ScrollableControl
See Also Figure 19-7
ScrollBar
HScrollBar
VScrollBar
Splitter
IMessageFilter
StatusBar
TabControl
TextBoxBase
RichTextBox
TextBox
DataGridTextBox
ToolBar
TrackBar
ISupportInitialize
TreeView

Figure 19-6. Controls from System.Windows.Forms

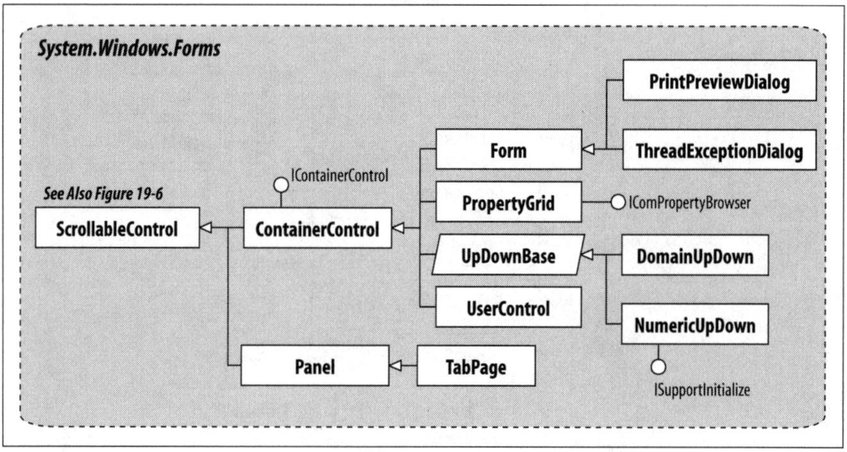
System.Windows.Forms
PrintPreviewDialog
Form
ThreadExceptionDialog
IContainerControl
See Also Figure 19-6
PropertyGrid
IComPropertyBrowser
ScrollableControl
ContainerControl
UpDownBase
DomainUpDown
UserControl
NumericUpDown
Panel
TabPage
ISupportInitialize

Figure 19-7. More controls from System.Windows.Forms

To help support RAD development, you can also integrate your own controls into the designer, by making use of the facilities in the System.Windows.Forms.Design and System.ComponentModel namespaces. This gives you control over appearance, parameter editing, code generation, round-tripping, and even wizard-style configuration of your component. You can implement any designer feature you see offered by the built-in controls by using the frameworks.

This doesn't mean resource files have gone away entirely. You can still create files containing your string tables, images, and similar resources. However, you now define them using an XML format, and the compiler generates a completely different kind of binary from the old resource manager. These resource files are an integral part of the internationalization/localization support in the framework and designers. Version 1.0 of the framework has a pretty rich array of features and controls, but there are a few exceptions. Support for XP Themes is sketchy (but possible), and a few of the controls suffer from an occasional limitation. Workarounds and examples are noted in the text where necessary. That said, Windows.Forms offers one of the richest, most flexible UI development frameworks on any platform, and learning to use it is more of a pleasure than a chore!

AccessibleEvents — serializable

System.Windows.Forms (system.windows.forms.dll) — enum

This (enormous) enumeration is a part of the accessibility framework, that allows you to support users who need assistance with particular aspects of the UI, perhaps as the result of a disability. Microsoft also recommends the use of these APIs for automated testing. The elements of this enumeration list more or less anything and everything that could possibly happen to a control, from properties changing to creation and destruction.

The enumeration is used by the AccessibleObject to notify accessibility clients that things are occurring of which they should take note (perhaps updating their own UI or controlling an external device such as a Braille reader). See AccessibleObject for a discussion of the accessibility framework.

```
public enum AccessibleEvents {
  SystemSound = 1,
  SystemAlert = 2,
  SystemForeground = 3,
  SystemMenuStart = 4,
  SystemMenuEnd = 5,
  SystemMenuPopupStart = 6,
  SystemMenuPopupEnd = 7,
  SystemCaptureStart = 8,
  SystemCaptureEnd = 9,
  SystemMoveSizeStart = 10,
  SystemMoveSizeEnd = 11,
  SystemContextHelpStart = 12,
  SystemContextHelpEnd = 13,
  SystemDragDropStart = 14,
  SystemDragDropEnd = 15,
  SystemDialogStart = 16,
  SystemDialogEnd = 17,
  SystemScrollingStart = 18,
  SystemScrollingEnd = 19,
  SystemSwitchStart = 20,
  SystemSwitchEnd = 21,
  SystemMinimizeStart = 22,
  SystemMinimizeEnd = 23,
  Create = 32768,
  Destroy = 32769,
  Show = 32770,
  Hide = 32771,
  Reorder = 32772,
  Focus = 32773,
  Selection = 32774,
  SelectionAdd = 32775,
  SelectionRemove = 32776,
  SelectionWithin = 32777,
  StateChange = 32778,
  LocationChange = 32779,
  NameChange = 32780,
  DescriptionChange = 32781,
  ValueChange = 32782,
  ParentChange = 32783,
  HelpChange = 32784,
  DefaultActionChange = 32785,
  AcceleratorChange = 32786
}
```

Hierarchy System.Object → System.ValueType → System.Enum(System.IComparable, System.IFormattable, System.IConvertible) → AccessibleEvents

Passed To Control.AccessibilityNotifyClients( ), ControlAccessibleObject.NotifyClients( )

AccessibleNavigation

serializable

System.Windows.Forms (system.windows.forms.dll) — enum

Another part of the accessibility framework, this enumeration is used when notifying clients that the focus is changing.

```
public enum AccessibleNavigation {
   Up = 1,
   Down = 2,
   Left = 3,
   Right = 4,
   Next = 5,
   Previous = 6,
   FirstChild = 7,
   LastChild = 8
}
```

Hierarchy System.Object → System.ValueType → System.Enum(System.IComparable, System.IFormattable, System.IConvertible) → AccessibleNavigation

Passed To AccessibleObject.Navigate( )

AccessibleObject

marshal by reference

System.Windows.Forms (system.windows.forms.dll) — class

This class encapsulates the information needed by applications that support users who need assistance with a UI. This might include magnifiers, Braille readers, specialized pointing devices, etc.

Developers may derive from this class to provide their own accessibility information, to announce navigation, property, and state changes to these accessibility clients. To make life easier, Microsoft already provides a class called Control.AccessibilityObject. Unless you create your own custom controls, this provides all the accessibility information required for your own applications, and you never really need to worry about this stuff—you get it all for free. If you do create a custom control that adds its own special state or navigation handling, you may need to derive your own accessibility object and override the appropriate members to notify clients when your state changes.

```
public class AccessibleObject : MarshalByRefObject : System.Reflection.IReflect, Accessibility.IAccessible, IEnumVariant {
// Public Constructors
   public AccessibleObject( );
// Public Instance Properties
   public virtual Rectangle Bounds{get; }
   public virtual string DefaultAction{get; }
   public virtual string Description{get; }
   public virtual string Help{get; }
   public virtual string KeyboardShortcut{get; }
   public virtual string Name{set; get; }
   public virtual AccessibleObject Parent{get; }
   public virtual AccessibleRole Role{get; }
   public virtual AccessibleStates State{get; }
   public virtual string Value{set; get; }
// Public Instance Methods
```

```
public virtual void DoDefaultAction( );
public virtual AccessibleObject GetChild(int index);
public virtual int GetChildCount( );
public virtual AccessibleObject GetFocused( );
public virtual int GetHelpTopic(out string fileName);
public virtual AccessibleObject GetSelected( );
public virtual AccessibleObject HitTest(int x, int y);
public virtual AccessibleObject Navigate(AccessibleNavigation navdir);
public virtual void Select(AccessibleSelection flags);
// Protected Instance Methods
protected void UseStdAccessibleObjects(IntPtr handle);
protected void UseStdAccessibleObjects(IntPtr handle, int objid);
}
```

Hierarchy System.Object → System.MarshalByRefObject → AccessibleObject(System.Reflection.IReflect, Accessibility.IAccessible, IEnumVariant)

Subclasses ChildAccessibleObject, ControlAccessibleObject, DomainItemAccessibleObject, System.Windows.Forms.Design.ControlDesignerAccessibleObject

Returned By Control.{AccessibilityObject, CreateAccessibilityInstance( )}, DataGridColumnStyle.{CreateHeaderAccessibleObject( ), HeaderAccessibleObject}, System.Windows.Forms.Design.ControlDesigner.AccessibilityObject, System.Windows.Forms.Design.ControlDesignerAccessibleObject.{GetChild( ), GetFocused( ), GetSelected( ), HitTest( ), Parent}

Passed To DomainItemAccessibleObject.DomainItemAccessibleObject( )

AccessibleRole **serializable**

System.Windows.Forms (system.windows.forms.dll) **enum**

This enumeration defines the various well-defined roles that your object plays within an application environment. Accessibility clients can then use the fact that they know your object is a Diagram or a Clock or whatever, to offer customized assistance to the end user.

```
public enum AccessibleRole {
  None = 0,
  TitleBar = 1,
  MenuBar = 2,
  ScrollBar = 3,
  Grip = 4,
  Sound = 5,
  Cursor = 6,
  Caret = 7,
  Alert = 8,
  Window = 9,
  Client = 10,
  MenuPopup = 11,
  MenuItem = 12,
  ToolTip = 13,
  Application = 14,
  Document = 15,
```

```
    Pane = 16,
    Chart = 17,
    Dialog = 18,
    Border = 19,
    Grouping = 20,
    Separator = 21,
    ToolBar = 22,
    StatusBar = 23,
    Table = 24,
    ColumnHeader = 25,
    RowHeader = 26,
    Column = 27,
    Row = 28,
    Cell = 29,
    Link = 30,
    HelpBalloon = 31,
    Character = 32,
    List = 33,
    ListItem = 34,
    Outline = 35,
    OutlineItem = 36,
    PageTab = 37,
    PropertyPage = 38,
    Indicator = 39,
    Graphic = 40,
    StaticText = 41,
    Text = 42,
    PushButton = 43,
    CheckButton = 44,
    RadioButton = 45,
    ComboBox = 46,
    DropList = 47,
    ProgressBar = 48,
    Dial = 49,
    HotkeyField = 50,
    Slider = 51,
    SpinButton = 52,
    Diagram = 53,
    Animation = 54,
    Equation = 55,
    ButtonDropDown = 56,
    ButtonMenu = 57,
    ButtonDropDownGrid = 58,
    WhiteSpace = 59,
    PageTabList = 60,
    Clock = 61,
    Default = -1
}
```

Hierarchy System.Object → System.ValueType → System.Enum(System.IComparable, System.IFormattable, System.IConvertible) → AccessibleRole

Returned By Control.AccessibleRole, System.Windows.Forms.Design.ControlDesignerAccessibleObject.Role, PrintPreviewDialog.AccessibleRole

Passed To Control.AccessibleRole, PrintPreviewDialog.AccessibleRole

AccessibleSelection

serializable, flag

System.Windows.Forms (system.windows.forms.dll) **enum**

Users can select items in various ways. This enumeration lists the predefined selection methods understood by the accessibility framework. It is used to notify accessibility clients that selections are taking place.

```
public enum AccessibleSelection {
  None = 0x00000000,
  TakeFocus = 0x00000001,
  TakeSelection = 0x00000002,
  ExtendSelection = 0x00000004,
  AddSelection = 0x00000008,
  RemoveSelection = 0x00000010
}
```

Hierarchy System.Object → System.ValueType → System.Enum(System.IComparable, System.IFormattable, System.IConvertible) → AccessibleSelection

Passed To AccessibleObject.Select( )

AccessibleStates

serializable, flag

System.Windows.Forms (system.windows.forms.dll) **enum**

This enumeration lists a variety of states that a UI object can take for interactions with accessibility clients.

```
public enum AccessibleStates {
  None = 0x00000000,
  Unavailable = 0x00000001,
  Selected = 0x00000002,
  Focused = 0x00000004,
  Pressed = 0x00000008,
  Checked = 0x00000010,
  Mixed = 0x00000020,
  Indeterminate = 0x00000020,
  ReadOnly = 0x00000040,
  HotTracked = 0x00000080,
  Default = 0x00000100,
  Expanded = 0x00000200,
  Collapsed = 0x00000400,
  Busy = 0x00000800,
  Floating = 0x00001000,
  Marqueed = 0x00002000,
  Animated = 0x00004000,
  Invisible = 0x00008000,
  Offscreen = 0x00010000,
```

```
    Sizeable = 0x00020000,
    Moveable = 0x00040000,
    SelfVoicing = 0x00080000,
    Focusable = 0x00100000,
    Selectable = 0x00200000,
    Linked = 0x00400000,
    Traversed = 0x00800000,
    MultiSelectable = 0x01000000,
    ExtSelectable = 0x02000000,
    AlertLow = 0x04000000,
    AlertMedium = 0x08000000,
    AlertHigh = 0x10000000,
    Protected = 0x20000000,
    Valid = 0x3FFFFFFF
}
```

Hierarchy System.Object → System.ValueType → System.Enum(System.IComparable, System.IFormattable, System.IConvertible) → AccessibleStates

Returned By System.Windows.Forms.Design.ControlDesignerAccessibleObject.State

AmbientProperties

System.Windows.Forms (system.windows.forms.dll) sealed class

The Site is the object that hosts a Control. Control objects can inherit certain properties from their Site, and these are called ambient properties. At present, the ambient properties are ForeColor, BackColor, Cursor, and Font. If you haven't specified a particular value for any of these properties, the control will retrieve an AmbientProperties object from the site by using the GetService( ) method. The service required is typeof(AmbientProperties). The control can pull the ambient value from it. If the control is not hosted in a site, or if the site doesn't support ambient properties, the Control.DefaultXXX member will be used to provide the value instead.

```
public sealed class AmbientProperties {
// Public Constructors
    public AmbientProperties( );
// Public Instance Properties
    public Color BackColor{set; get; }
    public Cursor Cursor{set; get; }
    public Font Font{set; get; }
    public Color ForeColor{set; get; }
}
```

AnchorStyles serializable, flag

System.Windows.Forms (system.windows.forms.dll) enum

This is used by Control objects to suggest to layout managers how they should be treated. The default layout manager first looks at Control.Dock on each contained object to see if it should be locked to one edge or another (see DockStyle). If it is not docked, it then examines the Control.Anchor property.

If a Control is anchored to a particular edge, it means that the side nearest to that edge will be maintained at a fixed distance from it. You can anchor to more than one edge, allowing you to create controls that move or resize as their container is resized.

You can replace the default layout management by overriding the OnLayout() method. You might do this in conjunction with a System.ComponentModel.IExtenderProvider that adds additional properties to the contained Control objects to help manage the new layout mechanism.

```
public enum AnchorStyles {
  None = 0x00000000,
  Top = 0x00000001,
  Bottom = 0x00000002,
  Left = 0x00000004,
  Right = 0x00000008
}
```

Hierarchy System.Object → System.ValueType → System.Enum(System.IComparable, System.IFormattable, System.IConvertible) → AnchorStyles

Returned By Control.Anchor

Passed To Control.Anchor

Appearance

serializable

System.Windows.Forms (system.windows.forms.dll) enum

This enumeration is used by CheckBox and RadioButton objects to determine whether they should be rendered in the Normal way or like a Button.

```
public enum Appearance {
  Normal = 0,
  Button = 1
}
```

Hierarchy System.Object → System.ValueType → System.Enum(System.IComparable, System.IFormattable, System.IConvertible) → Appearance

Returned By CheckBox.Appearance, RadioButton.Appearance

Passed To CheckBox.Appearance, RadioButton.Appearance

Application

System.Windows.Forms (system.windows.forms.dll) sealed class

This class provides a variety of static methods to start message processing for a Windows Forms application, and to retrieve information about the execution environment of the current application, including such useful details as the shared and user data paths, registry keys, locale/culture settings, and others.

You can also get notifications of and some control over application startup and shutdown, although the exit notification is not signaled if you use the parameterless version of Run().

Finally, there is a facility to install and remove message filters for your application with AddMessageFilter( ) and RemoveMessageFilter( ). See IMessageFilter for information on this feature.

```
public sealed class Application {
// Public Static Properties
   public static bool AllowQuit{get; }
   public static string CommonAppDataPath{get; }
   public static RegistryKey CommonAppDataRegistry{get; }
   public static string CompanyName{get; }
   public static CultureInfo CurrentCulture{set; get; }
   public static InputLanguage CurrentInputLanguage{set; get; }
   public static string ExecutablePath{get; }
   public static string LocalUserAppDataPath{get; }
   public static bool MessageLoop{get; }
   public static string ProductName{get; }
   public static string ProductVersion{get; }
   public static string SafeTopLevelCaptionFormat{set; get; }
   public static string StartupPath{get; }
   public static string UserAppDataPath{get; }
   public static RegistryKey UserAppDataRegistry{get; }
// Public Static Methods
   public static void AddMessageFilter(IMessageFilter value);
   public static void DoEvents( );
   public static void Exit( );
   public static void ExitThread( );
   public static ApartmentState OleRequired( );
   public static void OnThreadException(Exception t);
   public static void RemoveMessageFilter(IMessageFilter value);
   public static void Run( );
   public static void Run(ApplicationContext context);
   public static void Run(Form mainForm);
// Events
   public event EventHandler ApplicationExit;
   public event EventHandler Idle;
   public event ThreadExceptionEventHandler ThreadException;
   public event EventHandler ThreadExit;
}
```

ApplicationContext

System.Windows.Forms (system.windows.forms.dll) class

Normally, you call Application.Run( ), passing in the Form you wish to use as the MainForm of the application. An alternative is to use this class, which then allows you to control several features, including starting the message loop (again, optionally with a MainForm), stopping the message loop, and handling ThreadExit events related to the application terminating. You can also override the OnMainFormClosed( ) method to determine whether the message pump is terminated when the main form is closed.

```
public class ApplicationContext {
// Public Constructors
   public ApplicationContext( );
   public ApplicationContext(Form mainForm);
```

```
// Public Instance Properties
   public Form MainForm{set; get; }
// Public Instance Methods
   public void Dispose( );
   public void ExitThread( );
// Protected Instance Methods
   protected virtual void Dispose(bool disposing);
   protected virtual void ExitThreadCore( );
   protected override void Finalize( );                                    // overrides object
   protected virtual void OnMainFormClosed(object sender, EventArgs e);
// Events
   public event EventHandler ThreadExit;
}
```

Passed To Application.Run( )

ArrangeDirection

serializable

System.Windows.Forms (system.windows.forms.dll) **enum**

This enumeration is used by the SystemInformation class in its ArrangeDirection property, to determine how minimized windows are arranged.

```
public enum ArrangeDirection {
   Left = 0,
   Right = 0,
   Down = 4,
   Up = 4
}
```

Hierarchy System.Object → System.ValueType → System.Enum(System.IComparable, System.IFormattable, System.IConvertible) → ArrangeDirection

Returned By SystemInformation.ArrangeDirection

ArrangeStartingPosition

serializable

System.Windows.Forms (system.windows.forms.dll) **enum**

This enumeration is used by the ArrangeStartingPosition property of the SystemInformation class to determine how minimized windows are arranged (see ArrangeDirection).

```
public enum ArrangeStartingPosition {
   BottomLeft = 0,
   BottomRight = 1,
   TopLeft = 2,
   TopRight = 3,
   Hide = 8
}
```

Hierarchy System.Object → System.ValueType → System.Enum(System.IComparable, System.IFormattable, System.IConvertible) → ArrangeStartingPosition

Returned By SystemInformation.ArrangeStartingPosition

AxHost

System.Windows.Forms (system.windows.forms.dll) abstract class

This Control class wraps ActiveX controls that have been imported into the managed environment (either by use of the *Aximp.exe* tool or, more commonly, by adding them to the designer by customizing the toolbox). It extends the base services to provide methods to get the underlying OCX control (GetOcx( )) and show property pages (ShowPropertyPages( )), if they are present (HasPropertyPages( )).

Note that several of the events you would normally expect from a Control are not supported (e.g., color and font property changes), and attempting to bind to them will cause a NotSupportedException. The Liskov substitution principle states that you should be able to use any instance of a derived class in place of an instance of the base class. Throwing that exception means that this class violates that principle. Therefore, you have to take care if you are using Control objects polymorphically in your application (e.g., in your own custom host), in case someone drops an ActiveX control into the equation.

```
public abstract class AxHost : Control : System.ComponentModel.ISupportInitialize, System.ComponentModel.
ICustomTypeDescriptor {
// Protected Constructors
   protected AxHost(string clsid);
   protected AxHost(string clsid, int flags);
// Public Instance Properties
   public override Color BackColor{set; get; }                          // overrides Control
   public override Image BackgroundImage{set; get; }                    // overrides Control
   public ContainerControl ContainingControl{set; get; }
   public override ContextMenu ContextMenu{set; get; }                  // overrides Control
   public override Cursor Cursor{set; get; }                            // overrides Control
   public bool EditMode{get; }
   public virtual bool Enabled{set; get; }                              // overrides Control
   public override Font Font{set; get; }                                // overrides Control
   public override Color ForeColor{set; get; }                          // overrides Control
   public bool HasAboutBox{get; }
   public State OcxState{set; get; }
   public virtual bool RightToLeft{set; get; }
   public override ISite Site{set; }                                    // overrides Control
   public override string Text{set; get; }                              // overrides Control
// Protected Instance Properties
   protected override CreateParams CreateParams{get; }                  // overrides Control
   protected override Size DefaultSize{get; }                           // overrides Control
// Protected Static Methods
   protected static Color GetColorFromOleColor(uint color);
   protected static Font GetFontFromIFont(object font);
   protected static Font GetFontFromIFontDisp(object font);
   protected static object GetIFontDispFromFont(System.Drawing.Font font);
   protected static object GetIFontFromFont(System.Drawing.Font font);
   protected static object GetIPictureDispFromPicture(System.Drawing.Image image);
   protected static object GetIPictureFromCursor(Cursor cursor);
   protected static object GetIPictureFromPicture(System.Drawing.Image image);
   protected static double GetOADateFromTime(DateTime time);
   protected static uint GetOleColorFromColor(System.Drawing.Color color);
   protected static Image GetPictureFromIPicture(object picture);
   protected static Image GetPictureFromIPictureDisp(object picture);
```

```
   protected static DateTime GetTimeFromOADate(double date);
// Public Instance Methods
   public void BeginInit( );                              // implements System.ComponentModel.ISupportInitialize
   public void DoVerb(int verb);
   public void EndInit( );                                // implements System.ComponentModel.ISupportInitialize
   public object GetOcx( );
   public bool HasPropertyPages( );
   public void InvokeEditMode( );
   public void MakeDirty( );
   public override bool PreProcessMessage(ref Message msg);                              // overrides Control
   public void ShowAboutBox( );
   public void ShowPropertyPages( );
   public void ShowPropertyPages(Control control);
// Protected Instance Methods
   protected virtual void AttachInterfaces( );
   protected override void CreateHandle( );                                              // overrides Control
   protected virtual void CreateSink( );
   protected override void DestroyHandle( );                                             // overrides Control
   protected virtual void DetachSink( );
   protected override void Dispose(bool disposing);                                      // overrides Control
   protected override bool IsInputChar(char charCode);                                   // overrides Control
   protected override void OnBackColorChanged(EventArgs e);                              // overrides Control
   protected override void OnFontChanged(EventArgs e);                                   // overrides Control
   protected override void OnForeColorChanged(EventArgs e);                              // overrides Control
   protected override void OnHandleCreated(EventArgs e);                                 // overrides Control
   protected virtual void OnInPlaceActive( );
   protected override void OnLostFocus(EventArgs e);                                     // overrides Control
   protected override bool ProcessMnemonic(char charCode);                               // overrides Control
   protected bool PropsValid( );
   protected void RaiseOnMouseDown(short button, short shift, int x, int y);
   protected void RaiseOnMouseDown(short button, short shift, float x, float y);
   protected void RaiseOnMouseDown(object o1, object o2, object o3, object o4);
   protected void RaiseOnMouseMove(short button, short shift, int x, int y);
   protected void RaiseOnMouseMove(short button, short shift, float x, float y);
   protected void RaiseOnMouseMove(object o1, object o2, object o3, object o4);
   protected void RaiseOnMouseUp(short button, short shift, int x, int y);
   protected void RaiseOnMouseUp(short button, short shift, float x, float y);
   protected void RaiseOnMouseUp(object o1, object o2, object o3, object o4);
   protected void SetAboutBoxDelegate(AboutBoxDelegate d);
   protected override void SetBoundsCore(int x, int y, int width, int height, BoundsSpecified specified);   // overrides Control
   protected override void SetVisibleCore(bool value);                                   // overrides Control
   protected override void WndProc(ref Message m);                                       // overrides Control
// Events
   public event EventHandler BackColorChanged;                                           // overrides Control
   public event EventHandler BackgroundImageChanged;                                     // overrides Control
   public event EventHandler BindingContextChanged;                                      // overrides Control
   public event UICuesEventHandler ChangeUICues;                                         // overrides Control
   public event EventHandler Click;                                                      // overrides Control
   public event EventHandler ContextMenuChanged;                                         // overrides Control
   public event EventHandler CursorChanged;                                              // overrides Control
   public event EventHandler DoubleClick;                                                // overrides Control
   public event DragEventHandler DragDrop;                                               // overrides Control
```

```
    public event DragEventHandler DragEnter;                                    // overrides Control
    public event EventHandler DragLeave;                                        // overrides Control
    public event DragEventHandler DragOver;                                     // overrides Control
    public event EventHandler EnabledChanged;                                   // overrides Control
    public event EventHandler FontChanged;                                      // overrides Control
    public event EventHandler ForeColorChanged;                                 // overrides Control
    public event GiveFeedbackEventHandler GiveFeedback;                         // overrides Control
    public event HelpEventHandler HelpRequested;                                // overrides Control
    public event EventHandler ImeModeChanged;                                   // overrides Control
    public event KeyEventHandler KeyDown;                                       // overrides Control
    public event KeyPressEventHandler KeyPress;                                  // overrides Control
    public event KeyEventHandler KeyUp;                                         // overrides Control
    public event LayoutEventHandler Layout;                                     // overrides Control
    public event MouseEventHandler MouseDown;                                   // overrides Control
    public event EventHandler MouseEnter;                                       // overrides Control
    public event EventHandler MouseHover;                                       // overrides Control
    public event EventHandler MouseLeave;                                       // overrides Control
    public event MouseEventHandler MouseMove;                                   // overrides Control
    public event MouseEventHandler MouseUp;                                     // overrides Control
    public event MouseEventHandler MouseWheel;                                  // overrides Control
    public event PaintEventHandler Paint;                                       // overrides Control
    public event QueryAccessibilityHelpEventHandler QueryAccessibilityHelp;     // overrides Control
    public event QueryContinueDragEventHandler QueryContinueDrag;               // overrides Control
    public event EventHandler RightToLeftChanged;                               // overrides Control
    public event EventHandler StyleChanged;                                     // overrides Control
    public event EventHandler TabIndexChanged;                                  // overrides Control
    public event EventHandler TabStopChanged;                                   // overrides Control
    public event EventHandler TextChanged;                                      // overrides Control
}
```

Hierarchy

System.Object → System.MarshalByRefObject → System.ComponentModel.Component(System.ComponentModel.IComponent, System.IDisposable) → Control(IOleControl, IOleObject, IOleInPlaceObject, IOleInPlaceActiveObject, IOleWindow, IViewObject, IViewObject2, IPersist, IPersistStreamInit, IPersistPropertyBag, IPersistStorage, IQuickActivate, System.ComponentModel.ISynchronizeInvoke, IWin32Window) → AxHost(System.ComponentModel.ISupportInitialize, System.ComponentModel.ICustomTypeDescriptor)

AxHost.ActiveXInvokeKind

serializable

System.Windows.Forms (system.windows.forms.dll) — enum

This enumeration is used by the InvalidActiveXStateException constructor to specify the kind of access that was attempted while the control was in an invalid state.

```
public enum AxHost.ActiveXInvokeKind {
    MethodInvoke = 0,
    PropertyGet = 1,
    PropertySet = 2
}
```

Hierarchy

System.Object → System.ValueType → System.Enum(System.IComparable, System.IFormattable, System.IConvertible) → ActiveXInvokeKind

AxHost.AxComponentEditor

System.Windows.Forms (system.windows.forms.dll) class

This class is for internal use only and should not be called from your own code.

```
public class AxHost.AxComponentEditor : System.Windows.Forms.Design.WindowsFormsComponentEditor {
// Public Constructors
   public AxHost.AxComponentEditor( );
// Public Instance Methods
   public override bool EditComponent(System.ComponentModel.ITypeDescriptorContext context,
      object obj, IWin32Window parent);          // overrides System.Windows.Forms.Design.WindowsFormsComponentEditor
}
```

Hierarchy System.Object → System.ComponentModel.ComponentEditor → System.Windows.Forms.Design.WindowsFormsComponentEditor → AxComponentEditor

AxHost.ClsidAttribute

System.Windows.Forms (system.windows.forms.dll) sealed class

This attribute class is for internal use only and should not be used to decorate your own code.

```
public sealed class AxHost.ClsidAttribute : Attribute {
// Public Constructors
   public AxHost.ClsidAttribute(string clsid);
// Public Instance Properties
   public string Value{get; }
}
```

Hierarchy System.Object → System.Attribute → ClsidAttribute

Valid On Class

AxHost.ConnectionPointCookie

System.Windows.Forms (system.windows.forms.dll) class

This class is for internal use only and should not be used in your own code.

```
public class AxHost.ConnectionPointCookie {
// Public Constructors
   public AxHost.ConnectionPointCookie(object source, object sink, Type eventInterface);
// Public Instance Methods
   public void Disconnect( );
// Protected Instance Methods
   protected override void Finalize( );                                    // overrides object
}
```

AxHost.InvalidActiveXStateException

System.Windows.Forms (system.windows.forms.dll) class

This class represents the exception that is thrown when an ActiveX control is used while it is in an invalid state.

```
public class AxHost.InvalidActiveXStateException : Exception {
// Public Constructors
   public AxHost.InvalidActiveXStateException(string name, ActiveXInvokeKind kind);
// Public Instance Methods
   public override string ToString( );                                     // overrides Exception
}
```

Hierarchy System.Object → System.Exception(System.Runtime.Serialization.ISerializable) → InvalidActiveXStateException

AxHost.State serializable

System.Windows.Forms (system.windows.forms.dll) class

This opaque class encapsulates the state of an ActiveX control in persistence scenarios. You can retrieve the state using the AxHost.OcxState property, although more normally it would be read from or written to a stream.

```
public class AxHost.State : System.Runtime.Serialization.ISerializable {
// Public Constructors
   public AxHost.State(System.IO.Stream ms, int storageType, bool manualUpdate, string licKey);
}
```

AxHost.StateConverter

System.Windows.Forms (system.windows.forms.dll) class

This System.ComponentModel.TypeConverter is used in design-time and serialization scenarios to transform a State object to and from other types. You would not normally call this class from your own code.

```
public class AxHost.StateConverter : System.ComponentModel.TypeConverter {
// Public Constructors
   public AxHost.StateConverter( );
// Public Instance Methods
   public override bool CanConvertFrom(System.ComponentModel.ITypeDescriptorContext context,
      Type sourceType);                               // overrides System.ComponentModel.TypeConverter
   public override bool CanConvertTo(System.ComponentModel.ITypeDescriptorContext context,
      Type destinationType);                          // overrides System.ComponentModel.TypeConverter
   public override object ConvertFrom(System.ComponentModel.ITypeDescriptorContext context,
      System.Globalization.CultureInfo culture, object value);   // overrides System.ComponentModel.TypeConverter
   public override object ConvertTo(System.ComponentModel.ITypeDescriptorContext context,
      System.Globalization.CultureInfo culture, object value,
      Type destinationType);                          // overrides System.ComponentModel.TypeConverter
}
```

Hierarchy System.Object → System.ComponentModel.TypeConverter → StateConverter

AxHost.TypeLibraryTimeStampAttribute

System.Windows.Forms (system.windows.forms.dll) sealed class

This attribute class is for internal use only and should not be used in your own code.

```
public sealed class AxHost.TypeLibraryTimeStampAttribute : Attribute {
// Public Constructors
   public AxHost.TypeLibraryTimeStampAttribute(string timestamp);
// Public Instance Properties
   public DateTime Value{get; }
}
```

Hierarchy System.Object → System.Attribute → TypeLibraryTimeStampAttribute

Valid On Assembly

BaseCollection

marshal by reference

System.Windows.Forms (system.windows.forms.dll) class

This class is for internal use only and should not be used in your own code.

```
public class BaseCollection : MarshalByRefObject : ICollection, IEnumerable {
// Public Constructors
   public BaseCollection( );
// Public Instance Properties
   public virtual int Count{get; }                          // implements ICollection
   public bool IsReadOnly{get; }
   public bool IsSynchronized{get; }                        // implements ICollection
   public object SyncRoot{get; }                            // implements ICollection
// Protected Instance Properties
   protected virtual ArrayList List{get; }
// Public Instance Methods
   public void CopyTo(Array ar, int index);                 // implements ICollection
   public IEnumerator GetEnumerator( );                     // implements IEnumerable
}
```

Hierarchy System.Object → System.MarshalByRefObject → BaseCollection(System.Collections.ICollection, System.Collections.IEnumerable)

Subclasses BindingsCollection, GridColumnStylesCollection, GridTableStylesCollection

Binding

System.Windows.Forms (system.windows.forms.dll) class

This class is used in the data-binding framework to bind a property on an object to a property on a Control (e.g., the Name property of a business object to the Text property on a Control). This process is called simple binding.

A bag of these bindings are held by a BindingManagerBase that manages a set of related bindings. The binding manager makes sure the current value in the data source is reflected in each Binding it contains.

Finally, a bag of binding managers is called a BindingContext. The BindingContext is associated with a particular control and contains all the binding managers for all the controls owned by that container.

The Binding is created by specifying the name of the Control property to which you are binding (e.g., "Text"), the object that is going to provide the data (e.g., a hypothetical Employee business object), and a string that determines the property to be used on the data source (e.g., the **Employee** object **Name**). This final parameter can be an empty string to bind to the value of the object itself, the name of a property on the object, or a dot-separated path navigating to the appropriate property (e.g., through the tables and relations of a **System.Data.DataSet**). These are subsequently obtained through the **Control**, **DataSource**, and **PropertyName** properties of the **Binding** class.

When the **Binding** is created, it automatically finds a binding manager for the data source in the **Control** objects **BindingContext** and adds itself. You can find this binding manager with the **Item** property (the index for the class).

The **Binding** object also provides two events that allow you to control the data-binding process more closely.

The **Format** event is raised whenever data is transferred into the **Control**. You can use it to modify the information as it is transferred, converting from one data type to another to get over those awkward impedance problems when there is no default data type converter.

The other half of this partnership is the **Parse** event. It allows you to perform the conversion back the other way when the **Control** data is transferred back to the bound object. The **Parse** event is raised if the **Control** objects **Validated** event occurs, if **EndCurrentEdit( )** is called on the **BindingManagerBase**, or if the **Position** changes on the **BindingManagerBase** (i.e., the **Current** object in the data binding changes). For the standard **Control** objects (such as **ListBox** and **DataGrid**), these events occur automatically and the binding proceeds normally without your intervention.

```
public class Binding {
// Public Constructors
   public Binding(string propertyName, object dataSource, string dataMember);
// Public Instance Properties
   public BindingManagerBase BindingManagerBase{get; }
   public BindingMemberInfo BindingMemberInfo{get; }
   public Control Control{get; }
   public object DataSource{get; }
   public bool IsBinding{get; }
   public string PropertyName{get; }
// Protected Instance Methods
   protected virtual void OnFormat(ConvertEventArgs cevent);
   protected virtual void OnParse(ConvertEventArgs cevent);
// Events
   public event ConvertEventHandler Format;
   public event ConvertEventHandler Parse;
}
```

Returned By BindingsCollection.this, ControlBindingsCollection.this

Passed To BindingsCollection.{AddCore( ), RemoveCore( )}, ControlBindingsCollection.{Add( ), Remove( )}

BindingContext

System.Windows.Forms (system.windows.forms.dll) class

This class represents a bag of **BindingManagerBase** objects for a set of data bound controls. You can retrieve the **BindingContext** for a **Control** using the **Control.BindingContext** member. You can retrieve the binding manager for a particular child control using Item (this is the indexer property).

The BindingContext class Add() and Remove() methods, which allow you to add (or remove) a new binding manager for a data source, are actually protected. To create additional binding managers for a container BindingContext, you create a new BindingContext object and assign it to the Control.BindingContext of your child control(s). This has the effect of creating a new binding manager in the parent's BindingContext.

See Binding for more information about the data-binding hierarchy.

```
public class BindingContext : ICollection, IEnumerable {
// Public Constructors
   public BindingContext( );
// Public Instance Properties
   public bool IsReadOnly{get; }
   public BindingManagerBase this{get; }
   public BindingManagerBase this{get; }
// Public Instance Methods
   public bool Contains(object dataSource);
   public bool Contains(object dataSource, string dataMember);
// Protected Instance Methods
   protected internal void Add(object dataSource, BindingManagerBase listManager);
   protected virtual void AddCore(object dataSource, BindingManagerBase listManager);
   protected internal void Clear( );
   protected virtual void ClearCore( );
   protected virtual void OnCollectionChanged(System.ComponentModel.CollectionChangeEventArgs ccevent);
   protected internal void Remove(object dataSource);
   protected virtual void RemoveCore(object dataSource);
// Events
   public event CollectionChangeEventHandler CollectionChanged;
}
```

Returned By Control.BindingContext

Passed To Control.BindingContext, GridTablesFactory.CreateGridTables( )

BindingManagerBase

System.Windows.Forms (system.windows.forms.dll) abstract class

This class represents a mapping of a property (or column) in a data source to a property on a Control. In the case of simple binding, it uses a bag of Binding objects to handle those mappings. For complex data binding, you can derive a class that handles the data-binding process.

Each binding manager maintains a current Position in the data source, to allow multiple bound controls to remain in sync, each control displaying a different column in the same selected row.

For example, a ListBox and a TextBox can be bound to a data source with same binding manager (simple binding for the TextBox providing a Binding object, complex binding for the ListBox without an explicit binding object). The two will remain synchronized as the ListBox selection changes. Another ListBox and TextBox bound to the same data source but through a second binding manager will also remain synchronized with one another, but will not be synchronized with the first pair. (See BindingContext to find out how to create an independent binding manager for your second pair of controls.)

If the current row in the data source changes, the binding manager raises PositionChanged. If the value of the bound object changes, the CurrentChanged event is raised. See CurrencyManager for information about how this works in practice, and Binding for more information about the data-binding hierarchy.

```
public abstract class BindingManagerBase {
// Public Constructors
   public BindingManagerBase( );
// Protected Instance Fields
   protected EventHandler onCurrentChangedHandler;
   protected EventHandler onPositionChangedHandler;
// Public Instance Properties
   public BindingsCollection Bindings{get; }
   public abstract int Count{get; }
   public abstract object Current{get; }
   public abstract int Position{set; get; }
// Public Instance Methods
   public abstract void AddNew( );
   public abstract void CancelCurrentEdit( );
   public abstract void EndCurrentEdit( );
   public abstract PropertyDescriptorCollection GetItemProperties();
   public abstract void RemoveAt(int index);
   public abstract void ResumeBinding( );
   public abstract void SuspendBinding( );
// Protected Instance Methods
   protected internal virtual PropertyDescriptorCollection GetItemProperties(System.Collections.ArrayList dataSources,
      System.Collections.ArrayList listAccessors);
   protected virtual PropertyDescriptorCollection GetItemProperties(Type listType, int offset,
      System.Collections.ArrayList dataSources, System.Collections.ArrayList listAccessors);
   protected internal abstract string GetListName(System.Collections.ArrayList listAccessors);
   protected internal abstract void OnCurrentChanged(EventArgs e);
   protected void PullData( );
   protected void PushData( );
   protected abstract void UpdateIsBinding( );
// Events
   public event EventHandler CurrentChanged;
   public event EventHandler PositionChanged;
}
```

Subclasses CurrencyManager, PropertyManager

Returned By Binding.BindingManagerBase, BindingContext.this

Passed To BindingContext.AddCore( )

BindingMemberInfo

System.Windows.Forms (system.windows.forms.dll) struct

This value is returned by the Binding.BindingMemberInfo property and represents the property that was passed in the constructor of a Binding object.

```
public struct BindingMemberInfo {
// Public Constructors
   public BindingMemberInfo(string dataMember);
// Public Instance Properties
   public string BindingField{get; }
   public string BindingMember{get; }
   public string BindingPath{get; }
// Public Instance Methods
   public override bool Equals(object otherObject);                    // overrides ValueType
   public override int GetHashCode( );                                  // overrides ValueType
}
```

Hierarchy System.Object → System.ValueType → BindingMemberInfo

Returned By Binding.BindingMemberInfo

BindingsCollection marshal by reference

System.Windows.Forms (system.windows.forms.dll) class

This class represents the collection of Binding objects for a Control, accessed through the Bindings property.

```
public class BindingsCollection : BaseCollection {
// Public Instance Properties
   public override int Count{get; }                                     // overrides BaseCollection
   public Binding this{get; }
// Protected Instance Properties
   protected override ArrayList List{get; }                             // overrides BaseCollection
// Protected Instance Methods
   protected internal void Add(Binding binding);
   protected virtual void AddCore(Binding dataBinding);
   protected internal void Clear( );
   protected virtual void ClearCore( );
   protected virtual void OnCollectionChanged(System.ComponentModel.CollectionChangeEventArgs ccevent);
   protected internal void Remove(Binding binding);
   protected internal void RemoveAt(int index);
   protected virtual void RemoveCore(Binding dataBinding);
   protected internal bool ShouldSerializeMyAll( );
// Events
   public event CollectionChangeEventHandler CollectionChanged;
}
```

Hierarchy System.Object → System.MarshalByRefObject → BaseCollection(System.Collections.ICollection, System.Collections.IEnumerable) → BindingsCollection

Subclasses ControlBindingsCollection

Returned By BindingManagerBase.Bindings

BootMode

serializable

System.Windows.Forms (system.windows.forms.dll) **enum**

This enumeration represents the different modes in which a system can have been started. It is returned by the BootMode property of the SystemInformation class.

```
public enum BootMode {
  Normal = 0,
  FailSafe = 1,
  FailSafeWithNetwork = 2
}
```

Hierarchy System.Object → System.ValueType → System.Enum(System.IComparable, System.IFormattable, System.IConvertible) → BootMode

Returned By SystemInformation.BootMode

Border3DSide

serializable, flag

System.Windows.Forms (system.windows.forms.dll) **enum**

This enumeration is used by the ControlPaint.DrawBorder3D( ) method to determine which sides of the border should be drawn.

```
public enum Border3DSide {
  Left = 0x00000001,
  Top = 0x00000002,
  Right = 0x00000004,
  Bottom = 0x00000008,
  Middle = 0x00000800,
  All = 0x0000080F
}
```

Hierarchy System.Object → System.ValueType → System.Enum(System.IComparable, System.IFormattable, System.IConvertible) → Border3DSide

Passed To ControlPaint.DrawBorder3D( )

Border3DStyle

serializable

System.Windows.Forms (system.windows.forms.dll) **enum**

Used by the ControlPaint.DrawBorder3D( ) method, this enumeration determines how the 3D border should appear (e.g., Etched, Flat, Raised, etc.)

```
public enum Border3DStyle {
  RaisedOuter = 1,
  SunkenOuter = 2,
  RaisedInner = 4,
  Raised = 5,
  Etched = 6,
  SunkenInner = 8,
  Bump = 9,
  Sunken = 10,
```

```
  Adjust = 8192,
  Flat = 16394
}
```

Hierarchy System.Object → System.ValueType → System.Enum(System.IComparable, System.IFormattable, System.IConvertible) → Border3DStyle

Passed To ControlPaint.DrawBorder3D( )

BorderStyle

serializable

System.Windows.Forms (system.windows.forms.dll) **enum**

This enumeration is used by many Control classes in the framework to determine how their edges should appear.

```
public enum BorderStyle {
  None = 0,
  FixedSingle = 1,
  Fixed3D = 2
}
```

Hierarchy System.Object → System.ValueType → System.Enum(System.IComparable, System.IFormattable, System.IConvertible) → BorderStyle

Returned By DataGrid.BorderStyle, Label.BorderStyle, ListBox.BorderStyle, ListView.BorderStyle, Panel.BorderStyle, PictureBox.BorderStyle, Splitter.BorderStyle, TextBoxBase.BorderStyle, ToolBar.BorderStyle, TreeView.BorderStyle, UpDownBase.BorderStyle

Passed To DataGrid.BorderStyle, Label.BorderStyle, ListBox.BorderStyle, ListView.BorderStyle, Panel.BorderStyle, PictureBox.BorderStyle, Splitter.BorderStyle, TextBoxBase.BorderStyle, ToolBar.BorderStyle, TreeView.BorderStyle, UpDownBase.BorderStyle

BoundsSpecified

serializable, flag

System.Windows.Forms (system.windows.forms.dll) **enum**

You use this enumeration to specify to the Control.SetBounds( ) method which aspects of the Control object's bounds you are setting. It is akin to the size and location related flags in the Win32 SetWindowPos( ) method.

```
public enum BoundsSpecified {
  None = 0x00000000,
  X = 0x00000001,
  Y = 0x00000002,
  Location = 0x00000003,
  Width = 0x00000004,
  Height = 0x00000008,
  Size = 0x0000000C,
  All = 0x0000000F
}
```

Hierarchy System.Object → System.ValueType → System.Enum(System.IComparable, System.IFormattable, System.IConvertible) → BoundsSpecified

Passed To Control.{SetBounds( ), SetBoundsCore( )}

Button

marshal by reference, disposable

System.Windows.Forms (system.windows.forms.dll) class

This Control represents the standard windows pushbutton. Derived from ButtonBase, it adds the ability to specify a DialogResult that will be returned from the Form.ShowDialog( ) method if this button is clicked to dismiss it.

```
public class Button : ButtonBase : IButtonControl {
// Public Constructors
   public Button( );
// Public Instance Properties
   public virtual DialogResult DialogResult{set; get; }                    // implements IButtonControl
// Protected Instance Properties
   protected override CreateParams CreateParams{get; }                     // overrides ButtonBase
// Public Instance Methods
   public virtual void NotifyDefault(bool value);                          // implements IButtonControl
   public void PerformClick( );                                            // implements IButtonControl
   public override string ToString( );             // overrides System.ComponentModel.Component
// Protected Instance Methods
   protected override void OnClick(EventArgs e);                           // overrides Control
   protected override void OnMouseUp(MouseEventArgs mevent);               // overrides ButtonBase
   protected override bool ProcessMnemonic(char charCode);                 // overrides Control
   protected override void WndProc(ref Message m);                         // overrides ButtonBase
// Events
   public event EventHandler DoubleClick;                                  // overrides Control
}
```

Hierarchy System.Object → System.MarshalByRefObject → System.ComponentModel.Component(System.ComponentModel.IComponent, System.IDisposable) → Control(IOleControl, IOleObject, IOleInPlaceObject, IOleInPlaceActiveObject, IOleWindow, IViewObject, IViewObject2, IPersist, IPersistStreamInit, IPersistPropertyBag, IPersistStorage, IQuickActivate, System.ComponentModel.ISynchronizeInvoke, IWin32Window) → ButtonBase → Button(IButtonControl)

ButtonBase

marshal by reference, disposable

System.Windows.Forms (system.windows.forms.dll) abstract class

This Control is the base class for the various button-like controls supported by the .NET Framework, including Button (a pushbutton), CheckBox, and RadioButton.

In addition to the standard control features, it provides support for an Image (which can then be positioned in the control using the ImageAlign property) and for alignment of the text (using the TextAlign property).

Note that the default FlatStyle for this class supports .NET features such as images, font, and color changes, but does not support Windows XP themes. You must set the FlatStyle to System in this case, but you will lose the .NET features.

```
public abstract class ButtonBase : Control {
// Protected Constructors
   protected ButtonBase( );
```

```
// Public Instance Properties
   public FlatStyle FlatStyle{set; get; }
   public Image Image{set; get; }
   public ContentAlignment ImageAlign{set; get; }
   public int ImageIndex{set; get; }
   public ImageList ImageList{set; get; }
   public ImeMode ImeMode{set; get; }                                    // overrides Control
   public virtual ContentAlignment TextAlign{set; get; }
// Protected Instance Properties
   protected override CreateParams CreateParams{get; }                  // overrides Control
   protected override ImeMode DefaultImeMode{get; }                     // overrides Control
   protected override Size DefaultSize{get; }                           // overrides Control
   protected bool IsDefault{set; get; }
// Protected Instance Methods
   protected override AccessibleObject CreateAccessibilityInstance();   // overrides Control
   protected override void Dispose(bool disposing);                     // overrides Control
   protected override void OnEnabledChanged(EventArgs e);               // overrides Control
   protected override void OnGotFocus(EventArgs e);                     // overrides Control
   protected override void OnKeyDown(KeyEventArgs kevent);              // overrides Control
   protected override void OnKeyUp(KeyEventArgs kevent);                // overrides Control
   protected override void OnLostFocus(EventArgs e);                    // overrides Control
   protected override void OnMouseDown(MouseEventArgs mevent);          // overrides Control
   protected override void OnMouseEnter(EventArgs eventargs);           // overrides Control
   protected override void OnMouseLeave(EventArgs eventargs);           // overrides Control
   protected override void OnMouseMove(MouseEventArgs mevent);          // overrides Control
   protected override void OnMouseUp(MouseEventArgs mevent);            // overrides Control
   protected override void OnPaint(PaintEventArgs pevent);              // overrides Control
   protected override void OnParentChanged(EventArgs e);                // overrides Control
   protected override void OnTextChanged(EventArgs e);                  // overrides Control
   protected override void OnVisibleChanged(EventArgs e);               // overrides Control
   protected void ResetFlagsandPaint( );
   protected override void WndProc(ref Message m);                      // overrides Control
}
```

Hierarchy System.Object → System.MarshalByRefObject → System.ComponentModel.Component(System.ComponentModel.IComponent, System.IDisposable) → Control(IOleControl, IOleObject, IOleInPlaceObject, IOleInPlaceActiveObject, IOleWindow, IViewObject, IViewObject2, IPersist, IPersistStreamInit, IPersistPropertyBag, IPersistStorage, IQuickActivate, System.ComponentModel.ISynchronizeInvoke, IWin32Window) → ButtonBase

Subclasses Button, CheckBox, RadioButton

ButtonBase.ButtonBaseAccessibleObject — marshal by reference

System.Windows.Forms (system.windows.forms.dll) — class

This class is for internal use only and should not be used by your own classes.

```
public class ButtonBase.ButtonBaseAccessibleObject : ControlAccessibleObject {
// Public Constructors
   public ButtonBase.ButtonBaseAccessibleObject(Control owner);
```

```
// Public Instance Methods
  public override void DoDefaultAction( );                          // overrides AccessibleObject
}
```

Hierarchy System.Object → System.MarshalByRefObject → AccessibleObject(System.Reflection.IReflect, Accessibility.IAccessible, IEnumVariant) → ControlAccessibleObject → ButtonBaseAccessibleObject

ButtonBorderStyle

serializable

System.Windows.Forms (system.windows.forms.dll) **enum**

To draw a button-like border, you can use the ControlPaint.DrawBorder( ) method and pass in a value from this enumeration to determine the type of border to draw.

```
public enum ButtonBorderStyle {
  None = 0,
  Dotted = 1,
  Dashed = 2,
  Solid = 3,
  Inset = 4,
  Outset = 5
}
```

Hierarchy System.Object → System.ValueType → System.Enum(System.IComparable, System.IFormattable, System.IConvertible) → ButtonBorderStyle

Passed To ControlPaint.DrawBorder( )

ButtonState

serializable, flag

System.Windows.Forms (system.windows.forms.dll) **enum**

This enumeration is used by various ControlPaint methods that deal with drawing buttons, to specify the state in which the button imagery should be drawn.

```
public enum ButtonState {
  Normal = 0x00000000,
  Inactive = 0x00000100,
  Pushed = 0x00000200,
  Checked = 0x00000400,
  Flat = 0x00004000,
  All = 0x00004700
}
```

Hierarchy System.Object → System.ValueType → System.Enum(System.IComparable, System.IFormattable, System.IConvertible) → ButtonState

Passed To ControlPaint.{DrawButton( ), DrawCaptionButton( ), DrawCheckBox( ), DrawComboButton( ), DrawMixedCheckBox( ), DrawRadioButton( ), DrawScrollButton( )}

CaptionButton

serializable

System.Windows.Forms (system.windows.forms.dll) — enum

This enumeration lists the various types of window caption button that the system knows how to render (e.g., the close button). It is used by the ControlPaint.DrawCaptionButton( ) method to specify the imagery to be drawn.

```
public enum CaptionButton {
  Close = 0,
  Minimize = 1,
  Maximize = 2,
  Restore = 3,
  Help = 4
}
```

Hierarchy System.Object → System.ValueType → System.Enum(System.IComparable, System.IFormattable, System.IConvertible) → CaptionButton

Passed To ControlPaint.DrawCaptionButton( )

CharacterCasing

serializable

System.Windows.Forms (system.windows.forms.dll) — enum

This enumeration allows you to specify that a TextBox control should force the case of characters typed into it, through the TextBox.CharacterCasing property.

```
public enum CharacterCasing {
  Normal = 0,
  Upper = 1,
  Lower = 2
}
```

Hierarchy System.Object → System.ValueType → System.Enum(System.IComparable, System.IFormattable, System.IConvertible) → CharacterCasing

Returned By TextBox.CharacterCasing

Passed To TextBox.CharacterCasing

CheckBox

marshal by reference, disposable

System.Windows.Forms (system.windows.forms.dll) — class

This Control, derived from ButtonBase, represents a checkable option box. It can represent a two- or ThreeState checkbox. There are two accessors to get the checked state: Checked (a Boolean for a two-state box) and CheckState (Checked, Unchecked, and Indeterminate for a three-state box). You can handle the CheckedChanged and CheckStateChanged events that are raised when these properties are modified.

In addition, you can specify whether the box should AutoCheck when it is clicked (the alternative being to handle the Click event and set the state yourself), and whether the check should appear to the left or the right of the descriptive text (using the CheckAlign property).

Compare this to RadioButton for the selection of one option from several.

```
public class CheckBox : ButtonBase {
// Public Constructors
   public CheckBox( );
// Public Instance Properties
   public Appearance Appearance{set; get; }
   public bool AutoCheck{set; get; }
   public ContentAlignment CheckAlign{set; get; }
   public bool Checked{set; get; }
   public CheckState CheckState{set; get; }
   public override ContentAlignment TextAlign{set; get; }                    // overrides ButtonBase
   public bool ThreeState{set; get; }
// Protected Instance Properties
   protected override CreateParams CreateParams{get; }                       // overrides ButtonBase
   protected override Size DefaultSize{get; }                                // overrides ButtonBase
// Public Instance Methods
   public override string ToString( );                 // overrides System.ComponentModel.Component
// Protected Instance Methods
   protected override AccessibleObject CreateAccessibilityInstance( );       // overrides ButtonBase
   protected virtual void OnAppearanceChanged(EventArgs e);
   protected virtual void OnCheckedChanged(EventArgs e);
   protected virtual void OnCheckStateChanged(EventArgs e);
   protected override void OnClick(EventArgs e);                             // overrides Control
   protected override void OnHandleCreated(EventArgs e);                     // overrides Control
   protected override void OnMouseUp(MouseEventArgs mevent);                 // overrides ButtonBase
   protected override bool ProcessMnemonic(char charCode);                   // overrides Control
// Events
   public event EventHandler AppearanceChanged;
   public event EventHandler CheckedChanged;
   public event EventHandler CheckStateChanged;
}
```

Hierarchy System.Object → System.MarshalByRefObject → System.ComponentModel.Component(System.ComponentModel.IComponent, System.IDisposable) → Control(IOleControl, IOleObject, IOleInPlaceObject, IOleInPlaceActiveObject, IOleWindow, IViewObject, IViewObject2, IPersist, IPersistStreamInit, IPersistPropertyBag, IPersistStorage, IQuickActivate, System.ComponentModel.ISynchronizeInvoke, IWin32Window) → ButtonBase → CheckBox

CheckBox.CheckBoxAccessibleObject **marshal by reference**

System.Windows.Forms (system.windows.forms.dll) class

This class is for internal use and should not be called from your own code.

```
public class CheckBox.CheckBoxAccessibleObject : ButtonBaseAccessibleObject {
// Public Constructors
   public CheckBox.CheckBoxAccessibleObject(Control owner);
// Public Instance Properties
   public override string DefaultAction{get; }           // overrides Control.ControlAccessibleObject
   public override AccessibleRole Role{get; }            // overrides Control.ControlAccessibleObject
```

```
  public override AccessibleStates State{get; }                    // overrides AccessibleObject
}
```


Hierarchy System.Object → System.MarshalByRefObject → AccessibleObject(System.Reflection.IReflect, Accessibility.IAccessible, IEnumVariant) → ControlAccessibleObject → ButtonBaseAccessibleObject → CheckBoxAccessibleObject

CheckedListBox

marshal by reference, disposable

System.Windows.Forms (system.windows.forms.dll) class

This control, derived from ListBox, provides a list of items with a check beside each one, providing an alternative selection mechanism. It extends the base listbox by providing you with two collection accessors: CheckedItemCollection, which returns the set of all the checked items in the list, and CheckedIndexCollection, which returns a set containing the index of each checked item in the list. You can then use the GetItemChecked( ) and GetItemCheckState( ) methods to determine the actual check state for the item.

You can support either two- or three-state checkboxes, and ThreeDCheckBoxes, or flat ones. You can also choose whether the item is checked when it is selected, or whether the checkbox itself must be clicked.

```
public class CheckedListBox : ListBox {
// Public Constructors
  public CheckedListBox( );
// Public Instance Properties
  public CheckedIndexCollection CheckedIndices{get; }
  public CheckedItemCollection CheckedItems{get; }
  public bool CheckOnClick{set; get; }
  public override DrawMode DrawMode{set; get; }                    // overrides ListBox
  public override int ItemHeight{set; get; }                       // overrides ListBox
  public ObjectCollection Items{get; }                             // overrides ListBox
  public override SelectionMode SelectionMode{set; get; }          // overrides ListBox
  public bool ThreeDCheckBoxes{set; get; }
// Protected Instance Properties
  protected override CreateParams CreateParams{get; }              // overrides ListBox
// Public Instance Methods
  public bool GetItemChecked(int index);
  public CheckState GetItemCheckState(int index);
  public void SetItemChecked(int index, bool value);
  public void SetItemCheckState(int index, CheckState value);
// Protected Instance Methods
  protected override AccessibleObject CreateAccessibilityInstance( );   // overrides Control
  protected override ObjectCollection CreateItemCollection( );          // overrides ListBox
  protected override void OnBackColorChanged(EventArgs e);              // overrides Control
  protected override void OnClick(EventArgs e);                         // overrides Control
  protected override void OnDrawItem(DrawItemEventArgs e);              // overrides ListBox
  protected override void OnFontChanged(EventArgs e);                   // overrides ListBox
  protected override void OnHandleCreated(EventArgs e);                 // overrides ListBox
  protected virtual void OnItemCheck(ItemCheckEventArgs ice);
  protected override void OnKeyPress(KeyPressEventArgs e);              // overrides Control
  protected override void OnMeasureItem(MeasureItemEventArgs e);        // overrides ListBox
  protected override void OnSelectedIndexChanged(EventArgs e);          // overrides ListBox
```

```
 protected override void WmReflectCommand(ref Message m);                    // overrides ListBox
 protected override void WndProc(ref Message m);                             // overrides ListBox
// Events
 public event EventHandler Click;                                            // overrides ListBox
 public event DrawItemEventHandler DrawItem;                                 // overrides ListBox
 public event ItemCheckEventHandler ItemCheck;
 public event MeasureItemEventHandler MeasureItem;                           // overrides ListBox
}
```

Hierarchy

System.Object → System.MarshalByRefObject → System.ComponentModel.Component(System.ComponentModel.IComponent, System.IDisposable) → Control(IOleControl, IOleObject, IOleInPlaceObject, IOleInPlaceActiveObject, IOleWindow, IViewObject, IViewObject2, IPersist, IPersistStreamInit, IPersistPropertyBag, IPersistStorage, IQuickActivate, System.ComponentModel.ISynchronizeInvoke, IWin32Window) → ListControl → ListBox → CheckedListBox

Passed To

ObjectCollection.ObjectCollection( )

CheckedListBox.CheckedIndexCollection

System.Windows.Forms (system.windows.forms.dll) class

This collection class is used to specify the list of checked indexes in the CheckedListBox control.

```
public class CheckedListBox.CheckedIndexCollection : IList, ICollection, IEnumerable {
// Public Instance Properties
 public int Count{get; }                                                     // implements ICollection
 public bool IsReadOnly{get; }                                               // implements IList
 public int this{get; }
// Public Instance Methods
 public bool Contains(int index);
 public void CopyTo(Array dest, int index);                                  // implements ICollection
 public IEnumerator GetEnumerator( );                                        // implements IEnumerable
 public int IndexOf(int index);
}
```

CheckedListBox.CheckedItemCollection

System.Windows.Forms (system.windows.forms.dll) class

This collection class is used to specify the list of checked items in the CheckedListBox control.

```
public class CheckedListBox.CheckedItemCollection : IList, ICollection, IEnumerable {
// Public Instance Properties
 public int Count{get; }                                                     // implements ICollection
 public bool IsReadOnly{get; }                                               // implements IList
 public object this{set; get; }                                              // implements IList
// Public Instance Methods
 public bool Contains(object item);                                          // implements IList
 public void CopyTo(Array dest, int index);                                  // implements ICollection
 public IEnumerator GetEnumerator( );                                        // implements IEnumerable
```

```
  public int IndexOf(object item);                                    // implements IList
}
```

CheckedListBox.ObjectCollection

System.Windows.Forms (system.windows.forms.dll) class

This class represents the collection of items in a CheckedListBox.

```
public class CheckedListBox.ObjectCollection : ObjectCollection {
// Public Constructors
  public CheckedListBox.ObjectCollection(CheckedListBox owner);
// Public Instance Methods
  public int Add(object item, bool isChecked);
  public int Add(object item, CheckState check);
}
```

Hierarchy System.Object → ObjectCollection(System.Collections.IList, System.Collections.ICollection, System.Collections.IEnumerable) → ObjectCollection

CheckState serializable

System.Windows.Forms (system.windows.forms.dll) enum

Used by CheckBox and CheckedListBox, this enumeration determines whether an item is Checked, Unchecked, or Indeterminate.

```
public enum CheckState {
  Unchecked = 0,
  Checked = 1,
  Indeterminate = 2
}
```

Hierarchy System.Object → System.ValueType → System.Enum(System.IComparable, System.IFormattable, System.IConvertible) → CheckState

Returned By CheckBox.CheckState, CheckedListBox.GetItemCheckState( ), ItemCheckEventArgs.{CurrentValue, NewValue}

Passed To CheckBox.CheckState, CheckedListBox.SetItemCheckState( ), ObjectCollection.Add( ), ItemCheckEventArgs.{ItemCheckEventArgs( ), NewValue}

Clipboard

System.Windows.Forms (system.windows.forms.dll) sealed class

This class allows you to put data onto (SetDataObject( )) and get data from (GetDataObject( )) the clipboard. See IDataObject and DataObject for information on how to encapsulate data for the clipboard and drag-and-drop operations.

```
public sealed class Clipboard {
// Public Static Methods
  public static IDataObject GetDataObject( );
  public static void SetDataObject(object data);
```

```
public static void SetDataObject(object data, bool copy);
}
```

ColorDepth **serializable**

System.Windows.Forms (system.windows.forms.dll) **enum**

This enumeration specifies the number of colors in an image in an ImageList control (through the ImageList.ColorDepth property).

```
public enum ColorDepth {
 Depth4Bit = 4,
 Depth8Bit = 8,
 Depth16Bit = 16,
 Depth24Bit = 24,
 Depth32Bit = 32
}
```

Hierarchy System.Object → System.ValueType → System.Enum(System.IComparable, System.IFormattable, System.IConvertible) → ColorDepth

Returned By ImageList.ColorDepth

Passed To ImageList.ColorDepth

ColorDialog **marshal by reference, disposable**

System.Windows.Forms (system.windows.forms.dll) **class**

This common dialog allows you to present a standard interface to allow the user to select and define a color. You can programmatically show or hide the custom color definition part of the dialog by default by specifying the FullOpen property, and you can predefine the set of custom colors by using the CustomColors property. Unfortunately, this betrays its interop origins, because the colors have to be specified as Int32 values encapsulating the ARGB color, rather than as an array of System.Drawing.Color values.

You can retrieve the user's selection through the System.Drawing.Color property.

```
public class ColorDialog : CommonDialog {
// Public Constructors
 public ColorDialog( );
// Public Instance Properties
 public virtual bool AllowFullOpen{set; get; }
 public virtual bool AnyColor{set; get; }
 public Color Color{set; get; }
 public int[ ] CustomColors{set; get; }
 public virtual bool FullOpen{set; get; }
 public virtual bool ShowHelp{set; get; }
 public virtual bool SolidColorOnly{set; get; }
// Protected Instance Properties
 protected virtual IntPtr Instance{get; }
 protected virtual int Options{get; }
// Public Instance Methods
 public override void Reset( );                    // overrides CommonDialog
 public override string ToString( );               // overrides System.ComponentModel.Component
```

```
// Protected Instance Methods
   protected override bool RunDialog(IntPtr hwndOwner);                // overrides CommonDialog
}
```

Hierarchy System.Object → System.MarshalByRefObject → System.ComponentModel.Component(System.ComponentModel.IComponent, System.IDisposable) → CommonDialog → ColorDialog

ColumnClickEventArgs

System.Windows.Forms (system.windows.forms.dll) class

This System.EventArgs class is sent as the data with the ColumnClick event from the ListView control, when one of the header items is clicked. It contains the Column index of the clicked header in the ListView object's Columns collection.

```
public class ColumnClickEventArgs : EventArgs {
// Public Constructors
   public ColumnClickEventArgs(int column);
// Public Instance Properties
   public int Column{get; }
}
```

Hierarchy System.Object → System.EventArgs → ColumnClickEventArgs

Passed To ColumnClickEventHandler.{BeginInvoke( ), Invoke( )}, ListView.OnColumnClick( )

ColumnClickEventHandler serializable

System.Windows.Forms (system.windows.forms.dll) delegate

This is the delegate used for the ListView.ColumnClick event.

```
public delegate void ColumnClickEventHandler(object sender, ColumnClickEventArgs e);
```

Associated Events ListView.ColumnClick( )

ColumnHeader marshal by reference, disposable

System.Windows.Forms (system.windows.forms.dll) class

This class represents the heading of a column in a ListView control. Headers are added to a ListView through its Columns property, using the Add( ) method.

You can specify the Text to use to label the column, and how it is to be aligned horizontally within the column (TextAlign). You do not receive events directly from the header; instead, you should monitor the ListView class for appropriate notifications (e.g., the ColumnClick event).

```
public class ColumnHeader : System.ComponentModel.Component : ICloneable {
// Public Constructors
   public ColumnHeader( );
// Public Instance Properties
   public int Index{get; }
   public ListView ListView{get; }
   public string Text{set; get; }
```

```
  public HorizontalAlignment TextAlign{set; get; }
  public int Width{set; get; }
// Public Instance Methods
  public object Clone( );                                    // implements ICloneable
  public override string ToString( );       // overrides System.ComponentModel.Component
// Protected Instance Methods
  protected override void Dispose(bool disposing);  // overrides System.ComponentModel.Component
}
```

Hierarchy System.Object → System.MarshalByRefObject → System.ComponentModel.Component(System.ComponentModel.IComponent, System.IDisposable) → ColumnHeader(System.ICloneable)

Returned By ColumnHeaderCollection.this

Passed To ColumnHeaderCollection.{Add( ), AddRange( ), Contains( ), IndexOf( ), Insert( ), Remove( )}

ColumnHeaderStyle **serializable**

System.Windows.Forms (system.windows.forms.dll) **enum**

Used by ListView.HeaderStyle to determine whether the headers are clickable.

```
public enum ColumnHeaderStyle {
  None = 0,
  Nonclickable = 1,
  Clickable = 2
}
```

Hierarchy System.Object → System.ValueType → System.Enum(System.IComparable, System.IFormattable, System.IConvertible) → ColumnHeaderStyle

Returned By ListView.HeaderStyle

Passed To ListView.HeaderStyle

ComboBox **marshal by reference, disposable**

System.Windows.Forms (system.windows.forms.dll) **class**

This control represents an edit box with a drop-down list—a standard Win32 combobox. It extends the base ListControl that supports a variety of list-like controls. In addition to the standard control facilities, you can set the DropDownStyle property, which determines whether the edit box allows you to type into it and whether the list view is always visible, and set the DropDownWidth property of the drop-down list. You can set the IntegralHeight property, which can automatically adjust the height of the control to ensure that only whole items are displayed. The MaxDropDownItems property sets the maximum number of items that will be displayed in the drop-down list (without scrolling), and the MaxLength property sets the number of characters allowed in the edit field.

The selected item can be retrieved through the SelectedItem and SelectedIndex properties, which should not be confused with the SelectedText property, which gets the selected text in the edit field.

You can add and remove objects from the **Items** collection to alter the contents of the listbox, and the very useful members **FindString( )** and **FindStringExact( )** can help you locate a particular item in the list. Finally, you can select the text in the edit field using **Select( )** or **SelectAll( )**.

Unfortunately, the implementation of **ComboBox** in Version 1.0 of the framework is something of a minor fiasco. The edit control doesn't support the standard pop-up menus, and the selection and edit behavior is idiosyncratic to say the least (especially when hosted on a **TabPage**). Microsoft has indicated that this will almost certainly be improved in the next release.

```
public class ComboBox : ListControl {
// Public Constructors
   public ComboBox( );
// Public Instance Properties
   public override Color BackColor{set; get; }                          // overrides Control
   public override Image BackgroundImage{set; get; }                    // overrides Control
   public DrawMode DrawMode{set; get; }
   public ComboBoxStyle DropDownStyle{set; get; }
   public int DropDownWidth{set; get; }
   public bool DroppedDown{set; get; }
   public override bool Focused{get; }                                  // overrides Control
   public override Color ForeColor{set; get; }                          // overrides Control
   public bool IntegralHeight{set; get; }
   public int ItemHeight{set; get; }
   public ObjectCollection Items{get; }
   public int MaxDropDownItems{set; get; }
   public int MaxLength{set; get; }
   public int PreferredHeight{get; }
   public override int SelectedIndex{set; get; }                        // overrides ListControl
   public object SelectedItem{set; get; }
   public string SelectedText{set; get; }
   public int SelectionLength{set; get; }
   public int SelectionStart{set; get; }
   public bool Sorted{set; get; }
   public override string Text{set; get; }                              // overrides Control
// Protected Instance Properties
   protected override CreateParams CreateParams{get; }                  // overrides Control
   protected override Size DefaultSize{get; }                           // overrides Control
// Public Instance Methods
   public void BeginUpdate( );
   public void EndUpdate( );
   public int FindString(string s);
   public int FindString(string s, int startIndex);
   public int FindStringExact(string s);
   public int FindStringExact(string s, int startIndex);
   public int GetItemHeight(int index);
   public void Select(int start, int length);
   public void SelectAll( );
   public override string ToString( );             // overrides System.ComponentModel.Component
// Protected Instance Methods
   protected virtual void AddItemsCore(object[ ] value);
   protected override void Dispose(bool disposing);                     // overrides Control
```

```
 protected override bool IsInputKey(Keys keyData);                                          // overrides ListControl
 protected override void OnBackColorChanged(EventArgs e);                                   // overrides Control
 protected override void OnDataSourceChanged(EventArgs e);                                  // overrides ListControl
 protected override void OnDisplayMemberChanged(EventArgs e);                               // overrides ListControl
 protected virtual void OnDrawItem(DrawItemEventArgs e);
 protected virtual void OnDropDown(EventArgs e);
 protected virtual void OnDropDownStyleChanged(EventArgs e);
 protected override void OnFontChanged(EventArgs e);                                        // overrides Control
 protected override void OnForeColorChanged(EventArgs e);                                   // overrides Control
 protected override void OnHandleCreated(EventArgs e);                                      // overrides Control
 protected override void OnHandleDestroyed(EventArgs e);                                    // overrides Control
 protected override void OnKeyPress(KeyPressEventArgs e);                                   // overrides Control
 protected virtual void OnMeasureItem(MeasureItemEventArgs e);
 protected override void OnParentBackColorChanged(EventArgs e);                             // overrides Control
 protected override void OnResize(EventArgs e);                                             // overrides Control
 protected override void OnSelectedIndexChanged(EventArgs e);                               // overrides ListControl
 protected virtual void OnSelectedItemChanged(EventArgs e);
 protected virtual void OnSelectionChangeCommitted(EventArgs e);
 protected override void RefreshItem(int index);                                            // overrides ListControl
 protected override void SetBoundsCore(int x, int y, int width, int height, BoundsSpecified specified);   // overrides Control
 protected override void SetItemCore(int index, object value);                              // overrides ListControl
 protected override void SetItemsCore(System.Collections.IList value);                      // overrides ListControl
 protected override void WndProc(ref Message m);                                            // overrides Control
// Events
 public event DrawItemEventHandler DrawItem;
 public event EventHandler DropDown;
 public event EventHandler DropDownStyleChanged;
 public event MeasureItemEventHandler MeasureItem;
 public event PaintEventHandler Paint;                                                      // overrides Control
 public event EventHandler SelectedIndexChanged;
 public event EventHandler SelectionChangeCommitted;
}
```

Hierarchy System.Object → System.MarshalByRefObject → System.ComponentModel.Component(System.ComponentModel.IComponent, System.IDisposable) → Control(IOleControl, IOleObject, IOleInPlaceObject, IOleInPlaceActiveObject, IOleWindow, IViewObject, IViewObject2, IPersist, IPersistStreamInit, IPersistPropertyBag, IPersistStorage, IQuickActivate, System.ComponentModel.ISynchronizeInvoke, IWin32Window) → ListControl → ComboBox

Passed To ChildAccessibleObject.ChildAccessibleObject( ), ObjectCollection.ObjectCollection( )

ComboBox.ChildAccessibleObject — marshal by reference

System.Windows.Forms (system.windows.forms.dll) — class

This class is for internal use only and should not be called from your own code.

```
public class ComboBox.ChildAccessibleObject : AccessibleObject {
// Public Constructors
 public ComboBox.ChildAccessibleObject(ComboBox owner, IntPtr handle);
// Public Instance Properties
```

```
    public override string Name{get; }                                    // overrides AccessibleObject
}
```

Hierarchy System.Object → System.MarshalByRefObject → AccessibleObject(System.Reflection.IReflect, Accessibility.IAccessible, IEnumVariant) → ChildAccessibleObject

ComboBox.ObjectCollection

System.Windows.Forms (system.windows.forms.dll) class

This class represents the collection of items in a ComboBox.

```
public class ComboBox.ObjectCollection : IList, ICollection, IEnumerable {
// Public Constructors
    public ComboBox.ObjectCollection(ComboBox owner);
// Public Instance Properties
    public int Count{get; }                                               // implements ICollection
    public bool IsReadOnly{get; }                                         // implements IList
    public virtual object this{set; get; }                                // implements IList
// Public Instance Methods
    public int Add(object item);                                          // implements IList
    public void AddRange(object[ ] items);
    public void Clear( );                                                 // implements IList
    public bool Contains(object value);                                   // implements IList
    public void CopyTo(object[ ] dest, int arrayIndex);
    public IEnumerator GetEnumerator( );                                  // implements IEnumerable
    public int IndexOf(object value);                                     // implements IList
    public void Insert(int index, object item);                           // implements IList
    public void Remove(object value);                                     // implements IList
    public void RemoveAt(int index);                                      // implements IList
}
```

ComboBoxStyle serializable

System.Windows.Forms (system.windows.forms.dll) enum

This enumeration is used by ComboBox.DropDownStyle to determine the appearance of the combobox.

```
public enum ComboBoxStyle {
    Simple = 0,
    DropDown = 1,
    DropDownList = 2
}
```

Hierarchy System.Object → System.ValueType → System.Enum(System.IComparable, System.IFormattable, System.IConvertible) → ComboBoxStyle

Returned By ComboBox.DropDownStyle

Passed To ComboBox.DropDownStyle

CommonDialog

marshal by reference, disposable

System.Windows.Forms (system.windows.forms.dll) — abstract class

This is the base class for the set of common system dialogs, such as the File and Print dialogs. You should not use this class directly.

```
public abstract class CommonDialog : System.ComponentModel.Component {
// Public Constructors
   public CommonDialog( );
// Public Instance Methods
   public abstract void Reset( );
   public DialogResult ShowDialog( );
   public DialogResult ShowDialog(IWin32Window owner);
// Protected Instance Methods
   protected virtual IntPtr HookProc(IntPtr hWnd, int msg, IntPtr wparam, IntPtr lparam);
   protected virtual void OnHelpRequest(EventArgs e);
   protected virtual IntPtr OwnerWndProc(IntPtr hWnd, int msg, IntPtr wparam, IntPtr lparam);
   protected abstract bool RunDialog(IntPtr hwndOwner);
// Events
   public event EventHandler HelpRequest;
}
```

Hierarchy System.Object → System.MarshalByRefObject → System.ComponentModel.Component(System.ComponentModel.IComponent, System.IDisposable) → CommonDialog

Subclasses ColorDialog, FileDialog, FontDialog, PageSetupDialog, PrintDialog

ContainerControl

marshal by reference, disposable

System.Windows.Forms (system.windows.forms.dll) — class

This control extends ScrollableControl and also implements the IContainerControl interface. It provides the base functionality required to manage the focus control and tab ordering for the controls that it hosts. It also adds support for a ParentForm member, which provides the root containing form for the control, and the ActiveControl (implementing the IContainerControl interface), which determines which of the hosted controls has the focus.

Note that the ContainerControl never takes the focus itself. It always passes it through to one of the contained controls.

You would not normally derive your own containers from this class. Instead, you should look at UserControl or Form.

```
public class ContainerControl : ScrollableControl : IContainerControl {
// Public Constructors
   public ContainerControl( );
// Public Instance Properties
   public Control ActiveControl{set; get; }                          // implements IContainerControl
   public override BindingContext BindingContext{set; get; }         // overrides Control
   public Form ParentForm{get; }
// Protected Instance Properties
   protected override CreateParams CreateParams{get; }               // overrides ScrollableControl
// Public Instance Methods
   public bool Validate( );
```

```
// Protected Instance Methods
   protected override void AdjustFormScrollbars(bool displayScrollbars);        // overrides ScrollableControl
   protected override void Dispose(bool disposing);                              // overrides Control
   protected override void OnControlRemoved(ControlEventArgs e);                 // overrides Control
   protected override void OnCreateControl( );                                   // overrides Control
   protected override bool ProcessDialogChar(char charCode);                     // overrides Control
   protected override bool ProcessDialogKey(Keys keyData);                       // overrides Control
   protected override bool ProcessMnemonic(char charCode);                       // overrides Control
   protected virtual bool ProcessTabKey(bool forward);
   protected override void Select(bool directed, bool forward);                  // overrides Control
   protected virtual void UpdateDefaultButton( );
   protected override void WndProc(ref Message m);                               // overrides ScrollableControl
}
```

Hierarchy System.Object → System.MarshalByRefObject → System.ComponentModel.Component(System.ComponentModel.IComponent, System.IDisposable) → Control(IOleControl, IOleObject, IOleInPlaceObject, IOleInPlaceActiveObject, IOleWindow, IViewObject, IViewObject2, IPersist, IPersistStreamInit, IPersistPropertyBag, IPersistStorage, IQuickActivate, System.ComponentModel.ISynchronizeInvoke, IWin32Window) → ScrollableControl → ContainerControl(IContainerControl)

Subclasses Form, PropertyGrid, UpDownBase, UserControl

Returned By AxHost.ContainingControl, ErrorProvider.ContainerControl

Passed To AxHost.ContainingControl, ErrorProvider.{ContainerControl, ErrorProvider( )}

ContentsResizedEventArgs

System.Windows.Forms (system.windows.forms.dll) class

These are the EventArgs for the ContentsResized event, raised by the RichTextBox class when a contained element is resized. It allows you to retrieve the NewRectangle for the contents.

```
public class ContentsResizedEventArgs : EventArgs {
// Public Constructors
   public ContentsResizedEventArgs(System.Drawing.Rectangle newRectangle);
// Public Instance Properties
   public Rectangle NewRectangle{get; }
}
```

Hierarchy System.Object → System.EventArgs → ContentsResizedEventArgs

Passed To ContentsResizedEventHandler.{BeginInvoke( ), Invoke( )}, RichTextBox.OnContentsResized( )

ContentsResizedEventHandler serializable

System.Windows.Forms (system.windows.forms.dll) delegate

This is the delegate for RichTextBox.ContentsResized.

```
public delegate void ContentsResizedEventHandler(object sender, ContentsResizedEventArgs e);
```

Associated Events RichTextBox.ContentsResized( )

ContextMenu

marshal by reference, disposable

System.Windows.Forms (system.windows.forms.dll) class

Derived from Menu, this represents a pop-up menu. Extending the base functionality, you can Show() the menu at a particular System.Drawing.Point, and you can set the owner Control, which you can retrieve through the SourceControl property.

```
public class ContextMenu : Menu {
// Public Constructors
  public ContextMenu( );
  public ContextMenu(MenuItem[ ] menuItems);
// Public Instance Properties
  public virtual RightToLeft RightToLeft{set; get; }
  public Control SourceControl{get; }
// Public Instance Methods
  public void Show(Control control, System.Drawing.Point pos);
// Protected Instance Methods
  protected internal virtual void OnPopup(EventArgs e);
// Events
  public event EventHandler Popup;
}
```

Hierarchy System.Object → System.MarshalByRefObject → System.ComponentModel.Component(System.ComponentModel.IComponent, System.IDisposable) → Menu → ContextMenu

Returned By Control.ContextMenu, Menu.GetContextMenu( ), NotifyIcon.ContextMenu

Passed To Control.ContextMenu, NotifyIcon.ContextMenu

Control

marshal by reference, disposable

System.Windows.Forms (system.windows.forms.dll) class

This is the fundamental base class for all the controls and forms in the framework.

After constructing a Control, you can add it to the Controls collection of a parent control and Show( ) it. (You can subsequently Hide( ) it again or change the Visible property.) You can also toggle whether it is Enabled.

Adding it to the Controls collection causes its Parent property to be set appropriately. HasChildren determines whether this control contains any children itself. Its index in the parent collection also determines its position in the z-order. You can use BringToFront( ) and SendToBack( ) for gross control of this feature.

TopLevelControl returns the top-level container—this is (usually) the outermost Form in which you will find the control. Note that if the control is contained in a TabPage that is not currently showing in the TabControl, the TopLevelControl property will return null.

You can set a ForeColor, BackColor, and Font with which to paint the control imagery (in particular, the Text). If you do not set these explicitly, it will inherit the AmbientProperties from its container. If all else fails, it will use the DefaultForeColor, DefaultBackColor, or DefaultFont. You can also specify a BackgroundImage that will be tiled across the control. Should the system theme or colors change, you can bind to the SystemColorsChanged event to update the controls appearance.

The general shape of the control can be specified with the Bounds property and SetBounds( ) method. To support nonrectangular controls you can assign a custom Region. Anything outside that region will be truly transparent.

You can query the ClientRectangle and the DisplayRectangle. In the base implementation, these are equivalent, but derived classes may return a smaller DisplayRectangle to account for some additional imagery when laying out children (a GroupBox-like control might do this, for example).

The Anchor and Dock properties are used by the default layout manager to determine how the control is moved and resized within it parent container. (See AnchorStyles and DockStyle for more details).

SuspendLayout( ) and ResumeLayout( ) temporarily disable (or reenable) layout management, and you can bind to the Layout event to provide your own layout handling. PerformLayout( ) forces the control to refresh the layout. You can also handle the Resize, Move, SizeChanged, and LocationChanged events if you are only interested in the controls bounding box, rather than full layout support. You can also Scale( ) the control and all its children by some factor. This is used by Form.AutoScale to manage the resizing of a form to allow for different sizes of default font.

Several members deal with the translation of coordinates from one system to another: RectangleToClient( ), PointToClient( ), RectangleToScreen( ), and PointToScreen( ).

To support non-western scripts, you can also change the RightToLeft mode, and the ImeMode. Note that not all derived classes deal with these properties very well, but you should be aware of the need to support them when rendering your own custom controls.

Some controls can be selected or focused in their own right, whereas others (typically container controls) always pass their selection/focus on to another (such as a child). CanSelect and CanFocus determine whether this is the case. You can determine if the control or one of its children has the focus with the ContainsFocus property. If the control itself has the focus, the Focused property is true. You can set the Focus( ) to the control or Select( ) it. If you want to pass the activation on, call SelectNextControl( ) to give it up to the control with the next TabIndex. The TabIndex property controls the standard tab order, in conjunction with the TabStop flag. To track the selection/focus, bind to the Enter and Leave, or LostFocus and GotFocus events. The next item in the tab order is returned from the GetNextControl( ) method.

A right-click can be used to show a particular ContextMenu. Alternatively, you can handle the MouseDown, MouseUp, MouseWheel, MouseMove, MouseLeave, MouseEnter, and MouseHover events to deal with mouse activity. Note that you will only ever get one MouseHover event for each MouseEnter/MouseLeave pair. See MouseEventArgs for more information.

Similarly, keyboard support is provided via the KeyDown, KeyPress, and KeyUp events. See the KeyEventArgs and KeyPressEventArgs for more on this.

The user input can be validated by binding to the Validating and Validated events. If CausesValidation is true, any controls that require it will be validated when this control receives the focus. This slightly roundabout route to validation means your control must necessarily lose the focus to validate.

To support drag and drop, you can set the AllowDrop property to accept data dragged into the control. Handle the DragEnter, DragLeave, QueryContinueDrag, and DragDrop events to manage the drag-drop process. To initiate a drag from the control, simply call DoDragDrop( ). The framework will pump messages for you until the drag is completed. See DataObject and DragEventArgs for more information on drag and drop.

It is important to know that Control objects have a strong thread affinity. While you can create controls on any thread, you cannot call any members from a thread other than that on which it was created. Even if you think you're getting away with it, don't do it! InvokeRequired determines whether you must use the Invoke( ) (or BeginInvoke( )/EndInvoke( )) methods first to marshal the call back onto the correct thread, or whether it can be called directly.

To handle custom painting for your control, you can override the protected OnPaint( ) and OnPaintBackground( ) members or bind to the Paint event. (Note that there is no PaintBackground event.) See PaintEventArgs for more information on this. At any time, you can use the CreateGraphics( ) method to create a graphics surface on which to paint (or measure) your imagery. You can Invalidate( ) portions of the control for repainting and force an immediate repaint with the Update( ) method, although updating can swiftly become inefficient, as the operating system already attempts to optimize the process.

```
public class Control : System.ComponentModel.Component : IOleControl, IOleObject, IOleInPlaceObject,
    IOleInPlaceActiveObject, IOleWindow, IViewObject, IViewObject2, IPersist, IPersistStreamInit, IPersistPropertyBag,
    IPersistStorage, IQuickActivate, System.ComponentModel.ISynchronizeInvoke, IWin32Window {
// Public Constructors
  public Control( );
  public Control(Control parent, string text);
  public Control(Control parent, string text, int left, int top, int width, int height);
  public Control(string text);
  public Control(string text, int left, int top, int width, int height);
// Public Static Properties
  public static Color DefaultBackColor{get; }
  public static Font DefaultFont{get; }
  public static Color DefaultForeColor{get; }
  public static Keys ModifierKeys{get; }
  public static MouseButtons MouseButtons{get; }
  public static Point MousePosition{get; }
// Public Instance Properties
  public AccessibleObject AccessibilityObject{get; }
  public string AccessibleDefaultActionDescription{set; get; }
  public string AccessibleDescription{set; get; }
  public string AccessibleName{set; get; }
  public AccessibleRole AccessibleRole{set; get; }
  public virtual bool AllowDrop{set; get; }
  public virtual AnchorStyles Anchor{set; get; }
  public virtual Color BackColor{set; get; }
  public virtual Image BackgroundImage{set; get; }
  public virtual BindingContext BindingContext{set; get; }
  public int Bottom{get; }
  public Rectangle Bounds{set; get; }
  public bool CanFocus{get; }
  public bool CanSelect{get; }
  public bool Capture{set; get; }
  public bool CausesValidation{set; get; }
  public Rectangle ClientRectangle{get; }
  public Size ClientSize{set; get; }
  public string CompanyName{get; }
  public bool ContainsFocus{get; }
  public virtual ContextMenu ContextMenu{set; get; }
  public ControlCollection Controls{get; }
  public bool Created{get; }
```

```
public virtual Cursor Cursor{set; get; }
public ControlBindingsCollection DataBindings{get; }
public virtual Rectangle DisplayRectangle{get; }
public bool Disposing{get; }
public virtual DockStyle Dock{set; get; }
public bool Enabled{set; get; }
public virtual bool Focused{get; }
public virtual Font Font{set; get; }
public virtual Color ForeColor{set; get; }
public IntPtr Handle{get; }                                    // implements IWin32Window
public bool HasChildren{get; }
public int Height{set; get; }
public ImeMode ImeMode{set; get; }
public bool InvokeRequired{get; }          // implements System.ComponentModel.ISynchronizeInvoke
public bool IsAccessible{set; get; }
public bool IsDisposed{get; }
public bool IsHandleCreated{get; }
public int Left{set; get; }
public Point Location{set; get; }
public string Name{set; get; }
public Control Parent{set; get; }
public string ProductName{get; }
public string ProductVersion{get; }
public bool RecreatingHandle{get; }
public Region Region{set; get; }
public int Right{get; }
public virtual RightToLeft RightToLeft{set; get; }
public override ISite Site{set; get; }           // overrides System.ComponentModel.Component
public Size Size{set; get; }
public int TabIndex{set; get; }
public bool TabStop{set; get; }
public object Tag{set; get; }
public virtual string Text{set; get; }
public int Top{set; get; }
public Control TopLevelControl{get; }
public bool Visible{set; get; }
public int Width{set; get; }
public IWindowTarget WindowTarget{set; get; }
// Protected Instance Properties
protected virtual CreateParams CreateParams{get; }
protected virtual ImeMode DefaultImeMode{get; }
protected virtual Size DefaultSize{get; }
protected int FontHeight{set; get; }
protected bool RenderRightToLeft{get; }
protected bool ResizeRedraw{set; get; }
protected virtual bool ShowFocusCues{get; }
protected bool ShowKeyboardCues{get; }
// Public Static Methods
public static Control FromChildHandle(IntPtr handle);
public static Control FromHandle(IntPtr handle);
public static bool IsMnemonic(char charCode, string text);
```

```
// Protected Static Methods
   protected static bool ReflectMessage(IntPtr hWnd, ref Message m);
// Public Instance Methods
   public IAsyncResult BeginInvoke(Delegate method);
   public IAsyncResult BeginInvoke(Delegate method,
      object[ ] args);                                   // implements System.ComponentModel.ISynchronizeInvoke
   public void BringToFront( );
   public bool Contains(Control ctl);
   public void CreateControl( );
   public Graphics CreateGraphics( );
   public DragDropEffects DoDragDrop(object data, DragDropEffects allowedEffects);
   public object EndInvoke(IAsyncResult asyncResult);    // implements System.ComponentModel.ISynchronizeInvoke
   public Form FindForm( );
   public bool Focus( );
   public Control GetChildAtPoint(System.Drawing.Point pt);
   public IContainerControl GetContainerControl( );
   public Control GetNextControl(Control ctl, bool forward);
   public void Hide( );
   public void Invalidate( );
   public void Invalidate(bool invalidateChildren);
   public void Invalidate(System.Drawing.Rectangle rc);
   public void Invalidate(System.Drawing.Rectangle rc, bool invalidateChildren);
   public void Invalidate(System.Drawing.Region region);
   public void Invalidate(System.Drawing.Region region, bool invalidateChildren);
   public object Invoke(Delegate method);
   public object Invoke(Delegate method, object[ ] args);  // implements System.ComponentModel.ISynchronizeInvoke
   public void PerformLayout( );
   public void PerformLayout(Control affectedControl, string affectedProperty);
   public Point PointToClient(System.Drawing.Point p);
   public Point PointToScreen(System.Drawing.Point p);
   public virtual bool PreProcessMessage(ref Message msg);
   public Rectangle RectangleToClient(System.Drawing.Rectangle r);
   public Rectangle RectangleToScreen(System.Drawing.Rectangle r);
   public virtual void Refresh( );
   public virtual void ResetBackColor( );
   public void ResetBindings( );
   public virtual void ResetCursor( );
   public virtual void ResetFont( );
   public virtual void ResetForeColor( );
   public void ResetImeMode( );
   public virtual void ResetRightToLeft( );
   public virtual void ResetText( );
   public void ResumeLayout( );
   public void ResumeLayout(bool performLayout);
   public void Scale(float ratio);
   public void Scale(float dx, float dy);
   public void Select( );
   public bool SelectNextControl(Control ctl, bool forward, bool tabStopOnly, bool nested, bool wrap);
   public void SendToBack( );
   public void SetBounds(int x, int y, int width, int height);
   public void SetBounds(int x, int y, int width, int height, BoundsSpecified specified);
   public void Show( );
```

```
public void SuspendLayout( );
public void Update( );
// Protected Instance Methods
protected void AccessibilityNotifyClients(AccessibleEvents accEvent, int childID);
protected virtual AccessibleObject CreateAccessibilityInstance();
protected virtual ControlCollection CreateControlsInstance( );
protected virtual void CreateHandle( );
protected virtual void DefWndProc(ref Message m);
protected virtual void DestroyHandle( );
protected override void Dispose(bool disposing);                    // overrides System.ComponentModel.Component
protected bool GetStyle(ControlStyles flag);
protected bool GetTopLevel( );
protected virtual void InitLayout( );
protected void InvokeGotFocus(Control toInvoke, EventArgs e);
protected void InvokeLostFocus(Control toInvoke, EventArgs e);
protected void InvokeOnClick(Control toInvoke, EventArgs e);
protected void InvokePaint(Control c, PaintEventArgs e);
protected void InvokePaintBackground(Control c, PaintEventArgs e);
protected virtual bool IsInputChar(char charCode);
protected virtual bool IsInputKey(Keys keyData);
protected virtual void NotifyInvalidate(System.Drawing.Rectangle invalidatedArea);
protected virtual void OnBackColorChanged(EventArgs e);
protected virtual void OnBackgroundImageChanged(EventArgs e);
protected virtual void OnBindingContextChanged(EventArgs e);
protected virtual void OnCausesValidationChanged(EventArgs e);
protected virtual void OnChangeUICues(UICuesEventArgs e);
protected virtual void OnClick(EventArgs e);
protected virtual void OnContextMenuChanged(EventArgs e);
protected virtual void OnControlAdded(ControlEventArgs e);
protected virtual void OnControlRemoved(ControlEventArgs e);
protected virtual void OnCreateControl( );
protected virtual void OnCursorChanged(EventArgs e);
protected virtual void OnDockChanged(EventArgs e);
protected virtual void OnDoubleClick(EventArgs e);
protected virtual void OnDragDrop(DragEventArgs drgevent);
protected virtual void OnDragEnter(DragEventArgs drgevent);
protected virtual void OnDragLeave(EventArgs e);
protected virtual void OnDragOver(DragEventArgs drgevent);
protected virtual void OnEnabledChanged(EventArgs e);
protected virtual void OnEnter(EventArgs e);
protected virtual void OnFontChanged(EventArgs e);
protected virtual void OnForeColorChanged(EventArgs e);
protected virtual void OnGiveFeedback(GiveFeedbackEventArgs gfbevent);
protected virtual void OnGotFocus(EventArgs e);
protected virtual void OnHandleCreated(EventArgs e);
protected virtual void OnHandleDestroyed(EventArgs e);
protected virtual void OnHelpRequested(HelpEventArgs hevent);
protected virtual void OnImeModeChanged(EventArgs e);
protected virtual void OnInvalidated(InvalidateEventArgs e);
protected virtual void OnKeyDown(KeyEventArgs e);
protected virtual void OnKeyPress(KeyPressEventArgs e);
protected virtual void OnKeyUp(KeyEventArgs e);
```

```
protected virtual void OnLayout(LayoutEventArgs levent);
protected virtual void OnLeave(EventArgs e);
protected virtual void OnLocationChanged(EventArgs e);
protected virtual void OnLostFocus(EventArgs e);
protected virtual void OnMouseDown(MouseEventArgs e);
protected virtual void OnMouseEnter(EventArgs e);
protected virtual void OnMouseHover(EventArgs e);
protected virtual void OnMouseLeave(EventArgs e);
protected virtual void OnMouseMove(MouseEventArgs e);
protected virtual void OnMouseUp(MouseEventArgs e);
protected virtual void OnMouseWheel(MouseEventArgs e);
protected virtual void OnMove(EventArgs e);
protected virtual void OnNotifyMessage(Message m);
protected virtual void OnPaint(PaintEventArgs e);
protected virtual void OnPaintBackground(PaintEventArgs pevent);
protected virtual void OnParentBackColorChanged(EventArgs e);
protected virtual void OnParentBackgroundImageChanged(EventArgs e);
protected virtual void OnParentBindingContextChanged(EventArgs e);
protected virtual void OnParentChanged(EventArgs e);
protected virtual void OnParentEnabledChanged(EventArgs e);
protected virtual void OnParentFontChanged(EventArgs e);
protected virtual void OnParentForeColorChanged(EventArgs e);
protected virtual void OnParentRightToLeftChanged(EventArgs e);
protected virtual void OnParentVisibleChanged(EventArgs e);
protected virtual void OnQueryContinueDrag(QueryContinueDragEventArgs qcdevent);
protected virtual void OnResize(EventArgs e);
protected virtual void OnRightToLeftChanged(EventArgs e);
protected virtual void OnSizeChanged(EventArgs e);
protected virtual void OnStyleChanged(EventArgs e);
protected virtual void OnSystemColorsChanged(EventArgs e);
protected virtual void OnTabIndexChanged(EventArgs e);
protected virtual void OnTabStopChanged(EventArgs e);
protected virtual void OnTextChanged(EventArgs e);
protected virtual void OnValidated(EventArgs e);
protected virtual void OnValidating(System.ComponentModel.CancelEventArgs e);
protected virtual void OnVisibleChanged(EventArgs e);
protected virtual bool ProcessCmdKey(ref Message msg, Keys keyData);
protected virtual bool ProcessDialogChar(char charCode);
protected virtual bool ProcessDialogKey(Keys keyData);
protected virtual bool ProcessKeyEventArgs(ref Message m);
protected internal virtual bool ProcessKeyMessage(ref Message m);
protected virtual bool ProcessKeyPreview(ref Message m);
protected virtual bool ProcessMnemonic(char charCode);
protected void RaiseDragEvent(object key, DragEventArgs e);
protected void RaiseKeyEvent(object key, KeyEventArgs e);
protected void RaiseMouseEvent(object key, MouseEventArgs e);
protected void RaisePaintEvent(object key, PaintEventArgs e);
protected void RecreateHandle( );
protected void ResetMouseEventArgs( );
protected ContentAlignment RtlTranslateAlignment(System.Drawing.ContentAlignment align);
protected HorizontalAlignment RtlTranslateAlignment(HorizontalAlignment align);
protected LeftRightAlignment RtlTranslateAlignment(LeftRightAlignment align);
```

```
protected ContentAlignment RtlTranslateContent(System.Drawing.ContentAlignment align);
protected HorizontalAlignment RtlTranslateHorizontal(HorizontalAlignment align);
protected LeftRightAlignment RtlTranslateLeftRight(LeftRightAlignment align);
protected virtual void ScaleCore(float dx, float dy);
protected virtual void Select(bool directed, bool forward);
protected virtual void SetBoundsCore(int x, int y, int width, int height, BoundsSpecified specified);
protected virtual void SetClientSizeCore(int x, int y);
protected void SetStyle(ControlStyles flag, bool value);
protected void SetTopLevel(bool value);
protected virtual void SetVisibleCore(bool value);
protected void UpdateBounds( );
protected void UpdateBounds(int x, int y, int width, int height);
protected void UpdateBounds(int x, int y, int width, int height, int clientWidth, int clientHeight);
protected void UpdateStyles( );
protected void UpdateZOrder( );
protected virtual void WndProc(ref Message m);
// Events
public event EventHandler BackColorChanged;
public event EventHandler BackgroundImageChanged;
public event EventHandler BindingContextChanged;
public event EventHandler CausesValidationChanged;
public event UICuesEventHandler ChangeUICues;
public event EventHandler Click;
public event EventHandler ContextMenuChanged;
public event ControlEventHandler ControlAdded;
public event ControlEventHandler ControlRemoved;
public event EventHandler CursorChanged;
public event EventHandler DockChanged;
public event EventHandler DoubleClick;
public event DragEventHandler DragDrop;
public event DragEventHandler DragEnter;
public event EventHandler DragLeave;
public event DragEventHandler DragOver;
public event EventHandler EnabledChanged;
public event EventHandler Enter;
public event EventHandler FontChanged;
public event EventHandler ForeColorChanged;
public event GiveFeedbackEventHandler GiveFeedback;
public event EventHandler GotFocus;
public event EventHandler HandleCreated;
public event EventHandler HandleDestroyed;
public event HelpEventHandler HelpRequested;
public event EventHandler ImeModeChanged;
public event InvalidateEventHandler Invalidated;
public event KeyEventHandler KeyDown;
public event KeyPressEventHandler KeyPress;
public event KeyEventHandler KeyUp;
public event LayoutEventHandler Layout;
public event EventHandler Leave;
public event EventHandler LocationChanged;
public event EventHandler LostFocus;
public event MouseEventHandler MouseDown;
```

```
  public event EventHandler MouseEnter;
  public event EventHandler MouseHover;
  public event EventHandler MouseLeave;
  public event MouseEventHandler MouseMove;
  public event MouseEventHandler MouseUp;
  public event MouseEventHandler MouseWheel;
  public event EventHandler Move;
  public event PaintEventHandler Paint;
  public event EventHandler ParentChanged;
  public event QueryAccessibilityHelpEventHandler QueryAccessibilityHelp;
  public event QueryContinueDragEventHandler QueryContinueDrag;
  public event EventHandler Resize;
  public event EventHandler RightToLeftChanged;
  public event EventHandler SizeChanged;
  public event EventHandler StyleChanged;
  public event EventHandler SystemColorsChanged;
  public event EventHandler TabIndexChanged;
  public event EventHandler TabStopChanged;
  public event EventHandler TextChanged;
  public event EventHandler Validated;
  public event CancelEventHandler Validating;
  public event EventHandler VisibleChanged;
}
```

Hierarchy System.Object → System.MarshalByRefObject → System.ComponentModel.Component(System.ComponentModel.IComponent, System.IDisposable) → Control(IOleControl, IOleObject, IOleInPlaceObject, IOleInPlaceActiveObject, IOleWindow, IViewObject, IViewObject2, IPersist, IPersistStreamInit, IPersistPropertyBag, IPersistStorage, IQuickActivate, System.ComponentModel.ISynchronizeInvoke, IWin32Window)

Subclasses Multiple types

Returned By Multiple types

Passed To Multiple types

Control.ControlAccessibleObject

marshal by reference

System.Windows.Forms (system.windows.forms.dll) class

This class is for internal use only and should not be called from your own code.

```
public class Control.ControlAccessibleObject : AccessibleObject {
// Public Constructors
  public Control.ControlAccessibleObject(Control ownerControl);
// Public Instance Properties
  public override string DefaultAction{get; }                    // overrides AccessibleObject
  public override string Description{get; }                      // overrides AccessibleObject
  public IntPtr Handle{set; get; }
  public override string Help{get; }                             // overrides AccessibleObject
  public override string KeyboardShortcut{get; }                 // overrides AccessibleObject
```

```
  public override string Name{set; get; }                              // overrides AccessibleObject
  public Control Owner{get; }
  public override AccessibleRole Role{get; }                           // overrides AccessibleObject
// Public Instance Methods
  public override int GetHelpTopic(out string fileName);              // overrides AccessibleObject
  public void NotifyClients(AccessibleEvents accEvent);
  public void NotifyClients(AccessibleEvents accEvent, int childID);
  public override string ToString( );                                  // overrides object
}
```

Hierarchy System.Object → System.MarshalByRefObject → AccessibleObject(System.Reflection.IReflect, Accessibility.IAccessible, IEnumVariant) → ControlAccessibleObject

Control.ControlCollection

System.Windows.Forms (system.windows.forms.dll) class

This class represents the collection of child Controls in a Control object.

```
public class Control.ControlCollection : IList, ICollection, IEnumerable, ICloneable {
// Public Constructors
  public Control.ControlCollection(Control owner);
// Public Instance Properties
  public int Count{get; }                                              // implements ICollection
  public bool IsReadOnly{get; }                                        // implements IList
  public virtual Control this{get; }
// Public Instance Methods
  public virtual void Add(Control value);
  public virtual void AddRange(Control[ ] controls);
  public virtual void Clear( );                                        // implements IList
  public bool Contains(Control control);
  public void CopyTo(Array dest, int index);                           // implements ICollection
  public override bool Equals(object other);                           // overrides object
  public int GetChildIndex(Control child);
  public int GetChildIndex(Control child, bool throwException);
  public IEnumerator GetEnumerator( );                                 // implements IEnumerable
  public override int GetHashCode( );                                  // overrides object
  public int IndexOf(Control control);
  public virtual void Remove(Control value);
  public void RemoveAt(int index);                                     // implements IList
  public void SetChildIndex(Control child, int newIndex);
}
```

ControlBindingsCollection marshal by reference

System.Windows.Forms (system.windows.forms.dll) class

This class, derived from BindingsCollection, implements a set of data Binding objects for a Control, and is accessed through the Control objects DataBindings property. See Binding and its associated classes for more details on the data-binding framework.

```
public class ControlBindingsCollection : BindingsCollection {
// Public Instance Properties
   public Control Control{get; }
   public Binding this{get; }
// Public Instance Methods
   public Binding Add(string propertyName, object dataSource, string dataMember);
   public void Add(Binding binding);                                  // overrides BindingsCollection
   public void Clear( );                                              // overrides BindingsCollection
   public void Remove(Binding binding);                               // overrides BindingsCollection
   public void RemoveAt(int index);                                   // overrides BindingsCollection
// Protected Instance Methods
   protected override void AddCore(Binding dataBinding);              // overrides BindingsCollection
   protected override void ClearCore( );                              // overrides BindingsCollection
   protected override void RemoveCore(Binding dataBinding);           // overrides BindingsCollection
}
```

Hierarchy System.Object → System.MarshalByRefObject → BaseCollection(System.Collections.ICollection, System.Collections.IEnumerable) → BindingsCollection → ControlBindingsCollection

Returned By Control.DataBindings, PrintPreviewDialog.DataBindings

ControlEventArgs

System.Windows.Forms (system.windows.forms.dll) class

These are the EventArgs for the ControlAdded and ControlRemoved events, raised by a Control when objects are added to, or removed from, its ControlCollection. You can retrieve the identity of the object affected by using the Control property.

```
public class ControlEventArgs : EventArgs {
// Public Constructors
   public ControlEventArgs(Control control);
// Public Instance Properties
   public Control Control{get; }
}
```

Hierarchy System.Object → System.EventArgs → ControlEventArgs

Passed To Control.{OnControlAdded( ), OnControlRemoved( )}, ControlEventHandler.{BeginInvoke( ), Invoke( )}

ControlEventHandler serializable

System.Windows.Forms (system.windows.forms.dll) delegate

This is the delegate for the ControlAdded and ControlRemoved events raised by a Control. (See ControlEventArgs for more details).

```
public delegate void ControlEventHandler(object sender, ControlEventArgs e);
```

Associated Events Multiple types

ControlPaint

System.Windows.Forms (system.windows.forms.dll) sealed class

This class encapsulates a variety of static methods to help you paint your own custom controls and maintain consistency with the appearance of the rest of the UI. Unfortunately, none of these methods support Windows XP themes.

Most common UI elements are supported, including caption buttons, resizing grips, buttons, edit fields, comboboxes, various kinds of flat and 3D borders and frames, focus rectangles, and grids.

In addition, there is a class of methods that will automatically generate the **Light( )**, **LightLight( )**, **Dark( )**, and **DarkDark( )** versions of a specific **System.Drawing.Color**. If your control is, say, **Red** instead of **Control**, you don't want to use **System.Drawing.SystemColors.ControlDark** to paint a dark edge. Instead, use **Dark( )** to retrieve a dark version of **Red** instead.

Probably the most frequently asked question in Windows.Forms development is "How do I draw a rubberband box/line?" **ControlPaint** offers **DrawReversibleLine( )**, **DrawReversibleFrame( )**, and **FillReversibleRectangle( )**. Again, it is worth noting that Windows XP doesn't use XOR-ed rectangles any more, because of their limitations when painting over a mid-level color, so you should consider an alternative drawing strategy. One possible approach is to paint a semitransparent rectangle to represent your selection instead, calling **Control.Invalidate( )** to restore the previous background between updates. This works best (and flicker free!) if your selection rectangle is painted as part of your **Control.OnPaint( )** override, and your control has **ControlStyles.DoubleBuffer** set.

```
public sealed class ControlPaint {
// Public Static Properties
   public static Color ContrastControlDark{get; }
// Public Static Methods
   public static IntPtr CreateHBitmap16Bit(System.Drawing.Bitmap bitmap, System.Drawing.Color background);
   public static IntPtr CreateHBitmapColorMask(System.Drawing.Bitmap bitmap, IntPtr monochromeMask);
   public static IntPtr CreateHBitmapTransparencyMask(System.Drawing.Bitmap bitmap);
   public static Color Dark(System.Drawing.Color baseColor);
   public static Color Dark(System.Drawing.Color baseColor, float percOfDarkDark);
   public static Color DarkDark(System.Drawing.Color baseColor);
   public static void DrawBorder(System.Drawing.Graphics graphics, System.Drawing.Rectangle bounds,
      System.Drawing.Color color, ButtonBorderStyle style);
   public static void DrawBorder(System.Drawing.Graphics graphics, System.Drawing.Rectangle bounds,
      System.Drawing.Color leftColor, int leftWidth, ButtonBorderStyle leftStyle, System.Drawing.Color topColor, int topWidth,
      ButtonBorderStyle topStyle, System.Drawing.Color rightColor, int rightWidth, ButtonBorderStyle rightStyle,
      System.Drawing.Color bottomColor, int bottomWidth, ButtonBorderStyle bottomStyle);
   public static void DrawBorder3D(System.Drawing.Graphics graphics, int x, int y, int width, int height);
   public static void DrawBorder3D(System.Drawing.Graphics graphics, int x, int y, int width, int height, Border3DStyle style);
   public static void DrawBorder3D(System.Drawing.Graphics graphics, int x, int y, int width, int height, Border3DStyle style,
      Border3DSide sides);
   public static void DrawBorder3D(System.Drawing.Graphics graphics, System.Drawing.Rectangle rectangle);
   public static void DrawBorder3D(System.Drawing.Graphics graphics, System.Drawing.Rectangle rectangle,
      Border3DStyle style);
   public static void DrawBorder3D(System.Drawing.Graphics graphics, System.Drawing.Rectangle rectangle,
      Border3DStyle style, Border3DSide sides);
   public static void DrawButton(System.Drawing.Graphics graphics, int x, int y, int width, int height, ButtonState state);
   public static void DrawButton(System.Drawing.Graphics graphics, System.Drawing.Rectangle rectangle,
      ButtonState state);
```

public static void **DrawCaptionButton**(System.Drawing.Graphics *graphics*, int *x*, int *y*, int *width*, int *height*, CaptionButton *button*, ButtonState *state*);
public static void **DrawCaptionButton**(System.Drawing.Graphics *graphics*, System.Drawing.Rectangle *rectangle*, CaptionButton *button*, ButtonState *state*);
public static void **DrawCheckBox**(System.Drawing.Graphics *graphics*, int *x*, int *y*, int *width*, int *height*, ButtonState *state*);
public static void **DrawCheckBox**(System.Drawing.Graphics *graphics*, System.Drawing.Rectangle *rectangle*, ButtonState *state*);
public static void **DrawComboButton**(System.Drawing.Graphics *graphics*, int *x*, int *y*, int *width*, int *height*, ButtonState *state*);
public static void **DrawComboButton**(System.Drawing.Graphics *graphics*, System.Drawing.Rectangle *rectangle*, ButtonState *state*);
public static void **DrawContainerGrabHandle**(System.Drawing.Graphics *graphics*, System.Drawing.Rectangle *bounds*);
public static void **DrawFocusRectangle**(System.Drawing.Graphics *graphics*, System.Drawing.Rectangle *rectangle*);
public static void **DrawFocusRectangle**(System.Drawing.Graphics *graphics*, System.Drawing.Rectangle *rectangle*, System.Drawing.Color *foreColor*, System.Drawing.Color *backColor*);
public static void **DrawGrabHandle**(System.Drawing.Graphics *graphics*, System.Drawing.Rectangle *rectangle*, bool *primary*, bool *enabled*);
public static void **DrawGrid**(System.Drawing.Graphics *graphics*, System.Drawing.Rectangle *area*, System.Drawing.Size *pixelsBetweenDots*, System.Drawing.Color *backColor*);
public static void **DrawImageDisabled**(System.Drawing.Graphics *graphics*, System.Drawing.Image *image*, int *x*, int *y*, System.Drawing.Color *background*);
public static void **DrawLockedFrame**(System.Drawing.Graphics *graphics*, System.Drawing.Rectangle *rectangle*, bool *primary*);
public static void **DrawMenuGlyph**(System.Drawing.Graphics *graphics*, int *x*, int *y*, int *width*, int *height*, MenuGlyph *glyph*);
public static void **DrawMenuGlyph**(System.Drawing.Graphics *graphics*, System.Drawing.Rectangle *rectangle*, MenuGlyph *glyph*);
public static void **DrawMixedCheckBox**(System.Drawing.Graphics *graphics*, int *x*, int *y*, int *width*, int *height*, ButtonState *state*);
public static void **DrawMixedCheckBox**(System.Drawing.Graphics *graphics*, System.Drawing.Rectangle *rectangle*, ButtonState *state*);
public static void **DrawRadioButton**(System.Drawing.Graphics *graphics*, int *x*, int *y*, int *width*, int *height*, | ButtonState *state*);
public static void **DrawRadioButton**(System.Drawing.Graphics *graphics*, System.Drawing.Rectangle *rectangle*, ButtonState *state*);
public static void **DrawReversibleFrame**(System.Drawing.Rectangle *rectangle*, System.Drawing.Color *backColor*, FrameStyle *style*);
public static void **DrawReversibleLine**(System.Drawing.Point *start*, System.Drawing.Point *end*, System.Drawing.Color *backColor*);
public static void **DrawScrollButton**(System.Drawing.Graphics *graphics*, int *x*, int *y*, int *width*, int *height*, ScrollButton *button*, ButtonState *state*);
public static void **DrawScrollButton**(System.Drawing.Graphics *graphics*, System.Drawing.Rectangle *rectangle*, ScrollButton *button*, ButtonState *state*);
public static void **DrawSelectionFrame**(System.Drawing.Graphics *graphics*, bool *active*, System.Drawing.Rectangle *outsideRect*, System.Drawing.Rectangle *insideRect*, System.Drawing.Color *backColor*);
public static void **DrawSizeGrip**(System.Drawing.Graphics *graphics*, System.Drawing.Color *backColor*, int *x*, int *y*, int *width*, int *height*);
public static void **DrawSizeGrip**(System.Drawing.Graphics *graphics*, System.Drawing.Color *backColor*, System.Drawing.Rectangle *bounds*);
public static void **DrawStringDisabled**(System.Drawing.Graphics *graphics*, string *s*, System.Drawing.Font *font*, System.Drawing.Color *color*, System.Drawing.RectangleF *layoutRectangle*, System.Drawing.StringFormat *format*);

```
public static void FillReversibleRectangle(System.Drawing.Rectangle rectangle, System.Drawing.Color backColor);
public static Color Light(System.Drawing.Color baseColor);
public static Color Light(System.Drawing.Color baseColor, float percOfLightLight);
public static Color LightLight(System.Drawing.Color baseColor);
}
```

ControlStyles serializable, flag

System.Windows.Forms (system.windows.forms.dll) enum

This enumeration is used by Control.SetStyle() to enable or disable a variety of different features in a custom control.

Several features relate to the painting of the control. AllPaintingInWmPaint causes both the OnPaint() and OnPaintBackground() methods to be called during WM_PAINT handling, rather than WM_PAINT and WM_ERASEBACKGROUND as normal.

UserPaint indicates to the platform that you will be painting the control yourself, rather than relying on the operating system to do it for you (i.e., your control does not wrap a Win32 control and you therefore expect to handle WM_PAINT yourself).

DoubleBuffer enables automatic double buffering for your control. A back buffer is created before OnPaint() is called, and the System.Drawing.Graphics surface for that buffer is passed to your paint handler. When you complete your painting, the buffer is blitted to the window surface, dramatically reducing the amount of flicker that occurs when you paint, at the cost of one extra blit into the window, and potentially an awful lot of extra committed memory for the back buffer. To get double buffering to work properly, you should also set AllPaintingInWmPaint (to prevent two separate blits for the background and the foreground, which will induce flicker) and UserPaint.

SupportsTransparentBackColor allows you to set a back System.Drawing.Color with an Alpha value less than 255. Because standard Win32 controls do not really support true transparency, the default OnPaintBackground() fakes the painting of the background for you by getting the parent to paint itself into your object's System.Drawing.Graphics surface. While this is OK in simple scenarios, it starts to work badly when you have nested or overlapping transparent controls. Note that the technique used is different from (and less effective than) the XP API DrawThemeParentBackground(), so interop may offer some additional benefit if you can rely on XP deployment. The system requires that you also set UserPaint for transparency.

ResizeRedraw causes the entire control to be repainted each time it is resized. Note that while this used to be the default behavior in MFC applications, for .NET, it is turned off unless you explicitly enable it. This is a good thing, because it allows your repaint to be much more efficient, only invalidating the newly exposed rectangles as the control expands. However, if your painted content is scaled to fit, you should re-enable the feature to allow you to repaint the whole thing every time.

Finally, there is Opaque. If you enable this, it implies that you are going to cover every visible pixel in your control in the OnPaint() function, and that there is therefore no need to paint the background at all. Be prepared for a total mess if you fail to cover every pixel!

The second class of styles apply to the input behavior of the object.

If you enable StandardClick, the framework will automatically handle mouse button clicks, and raise the Control.Click event for you. If you set StandardDoubleClick as well, it will raise Control.DoubleClick too.

Similar to UserPaint, enabling UserMouse lets the framework know you will be dealing with the mouse handling, rather than wrapping a Win32 control that does that work for you.

The remaining styles are a mixed bag of other bits and pieces.

The Selectable style can be enabled to indicate that the control can receive the focus, and ContainerControl indicates the object may act as the parent to other controls (like a GroupBox, for example). Two styles, FixedWidth and FixedHeight, indicate that you cannot resize the control in one or both of these directions.

Finally, there is the EnableNotifyMessage style. This causes OnNotifyMessage( ) to be called for every WM_XXX message passed to your control. This allows you to handle the message, but not to change it. Compare this with the Control.WndProc( ) method that requires the System.Security.Permissions.SecurityPermissionFlag.UnmanagedCode permission to override it, but gives you considerably greater opportunity to mess with the messages as they pass through.

```
public enum ControlStyles {
  ContainerControl = 0x00000001,
  UserPaint = 0x00000002,
  Opaque = 0x00000004,
  ResizeRedraw = 0x00000010,
  FixedWidth = 0x00000020,
  FixedHeight = 0x00000040,
  StandardClick = 0x00000100,
  Selectable = 0x00000200,
  UserMouse = 0x00000400,
  SupportsTransparentBackColor = 0x00000800,
  StandardDoubleClick = 0x00001000,
  AllPaintingInWmPaint = 0x00002000,
  CacheText = 0x00004000,
  EnableNotifyMessage = 0x00008000,
  DoubleBuffer = 0x00010000
}
```

Hierarchy System.Object → System.ValueType → System.Enum(System.IComparable, System.IFormattable, System.IConvertible) → ControlStyles

Passed To Control.{GetStyle( ), SetStyle( )}

ConvertEventArgs

System.Windows.Forms (system.windows.forms.dll) class

Part of the data-binding framework, this EventArgs class is used when the Binding.Format event is raised. You can find out what the DesiredType is to which the Value object should be converted. See Binding for more information.

```
public class ConvertEventArgs : EventArgs {
// Public Constructors
  public ConvertEventArgs(object value, Type desiredType);
// Public Instance Properties
  public Type DesiredType{get; }
  public object Value{set; get; }
}
```

Hierarchy System.Object → System.EventArgs → ConvertEventArgs

Passed To Binding.{OnFormat( ), OnParse( )}, ConvertEventHandler.{BeginInvoke( ), Invoke( )}

ConvertEventHandler — serializable

System.Windows.Forms (system.windows.forms.dll) — delegate

This is the delegate for the Binding.Format event. See ConvertEventArgs and Binding for more information.

```
public delegate void ConvertEventHandler(object sender, ConvertEventArgs e);
```

Associated Events Binding.{Format( ), Parse( )}

CreateParams

System.Windows.Forms (system.windows.forms.dll) — class

This class wraps the set of parameters passed to a Win32 window in its CreateWindow( ) or CreateWindowEx( ) function. If you are wrapping a Win32 control with your own managed Control, you can override the Control.CreateParams member to return a modified set of creation attributes. You should not use this class under any other circumstances.

```
public class CreateParams {
// Public Constructors
   public CreateParams( );
// Public Instance Properties
   public string Caption{set; get; }
   public string ClassName{set; get; }
   public int ClassStyle{set; get; }
   public int ExStyle{set; get; }
   public int Height{set; get; }
   public object Param{set; get; }
   public IntPtr Parent{set; get; }
   public int Style{set; get; }
   public int Width{set; get; }
   public int X{set; get; }
   public int Y{set; get; }
// Public Instance Methods
   public override string ToString( );                                    // overrides object
}
```

Returned By Control.CreateParams

Passed To NativeWindow.CreateHandle( )

CurrencyManager

System.Windows.Forms (system.windows.forms.dll) — class

This class represents a bag of Binding objects for a list-like data source. List-like objects (such as arrays, collections, and System.Data.DataTable objects) implement IList, System.ComponentModel.IListSource, or System.ComponentModel.IBindingList. Compare this with PropertyManager that deals with simple properties.

It maintains the concept of the Current item in the list. When the current item is changed (by setting the Position property, or because the System.ComponentModel.IBindingList.ListChanged event was raised), all the objects bound to the data source through the Binding objects are updated with the new value. (See Binding for details on how this update can be controlled through the Parse and Format events).

Note that the standard controls such as ListBox and DataGrid will update the Position automatically as the UI selection changes.

See Binding for more information on the data-binding hierarchy.

```
public class CurrencyManager : BindingManagerBase {
// Protected Instance Fields
   protected Type finalType;
   protected int listposition;
// Public Instance Properties
   public override int Count{get; }                                  // overrides BindingManagerBase
   public override object Current{get; }                             // overrides BindingManagerBase
   public IList List{get; }
   public override int Position{set; get; }                          // overrides BindingManagerBase
// Public Instance Methods
   public override void AddNew( );                                   // overrides BindingManagerBase
   public override void CancelCurrentEdit( );                        // overrides BindingManagerBase
   public override void EndCurrentEdit( );                           // overrides BindingManagerBase
   public override PropertyDescriptorCollection GetItemProperties( ); // overrides BindingManagerBase
   public void Refresh( );
   public override void RemoveAt(int index);                         // overrides BindingManagerBase
   public override void ResumeBinding( );                            // overrides BindingManagerBase
   public override void SuspendBinding( );                           // overrides BindingManagerBase
// Protected Instance Methods
   protected void CheckEmpty( );
   protected internal override string GetListName(
      System.Collections.ArrayList listAccessors);                  // overrides BindingManagerBase
   protected internal override void OnCurrentChanged(EventArgs e);  // overrides BindingManagerBase
   protected virtual void OnItemChanged(ItemChangedEventArgs e);
   protected virtual void OnPositionChanged(EventArgs e);
   protected override void UpdateIsBinding( );                       // overrides BindingManagerBase
// Events
   public event ItemChangedEventHandler ItemChanged;
}
```

Hierarchy System.Object → BindingManagerBase → CurrencyManager

Returned By ListControl.DataManager

Passed To DataGridColumnStyle.CheckValidDataSource( ), DataGridTableStyle.DataGridTableStyle( )

Cursor

serializable, disposable

System.Windows.Forms (system.windows.forms.dll) sealed class

This class wraps a Win32 cursor—the image that represents the mouse pointer. Cursor is a slightly curious class in that it wraps up both GDI-like functionality and global system cursor/pointer behavior.

Unlike Win32, .NET cursors are static images—you cannot create them from animations. You can, however, create cursors from COM IPicture objects, files and streams, and Win32 cursor handles. You can also retrieve a Win32 handle using the Handle property, or get a copy of the underlying Win32 object with the CopyHandle( ) method. Predefined cursors are available as static properties on the Cursors class.

Similar to most of the System.Drawing objects, Cursor objects are a scarce system resource, and therefore you should manage their lifetimes carefully, calling Dispose( ) when you are finished to release the resources back to the OS. Also in keeping with the drawing objects, you can paint the cursor imagery on a System.Drawing.Graphics surface using the Draw( ) and DrawStretched( ) methods. The object's dimensions can be obtained from the Size property.

Each Control object has a Cursor property, which you can use to the set the default cursor shown while the mouse is over the control. You can also temporarily set the cursor to something else (such as the Cursors.WaitCursor) by using the static Current property. This overrides any other settings until you either set the Current value back to Cursors.Default or call the DoEvents( ) method.

You can find the screen coordinates at which the cursor is currently being rendered by using the static Position property, and the expected dimensions of the system cursor from the static Clip.

You can also Show( ) and Hide( ) the cursor through static methods of those names. If the cursor is hidden, Current will return null.

```
public sealed class Cursor : IDisposable, System.Runtime.Serialization.ISerializable {
// Public Constructors
   public Cursor(IntPtr handle);
   public Cursor(System.IO.Stream stream);
   public Cursor(string fileName);
   public Cursor(Type type, string resource);
// Public Static Properties
   public static Rectangle Clip{set; get; }
   public static Cursor Current{set; get; }
   public static Point Position{set; get; }
// Public Instance Properties
   public IntPtr Handle{get; }
   public Size Size{get; }
// Public Static Methods
   public static void Hide( );
   public static void Show( );
   public static bool operator !=(Cursor left, Cursor right);
   public static bool operator ==(Cursor left, Cursor right);
// Public Instance Methods
   public IntPtr CopyHandle( );
   public void Dispose( );                                                    // implements IDisposable
   public void Draw(System.Drawing.Graphics g, System.Drawing.Rectangle targetRect);
   public void DrawStretched(System.Drawing.Graphics g, System.Drawing.Rectangle targetRect);
   public override bool Equals(object obj);                                  // overrides object
   public override int GetHashCode( );                                       // overrides object
   public override string ToString( );                                       // overrides object
// Protected Instance Methods
   protected override void Finalize( );                                      // overrides object
}
```

Returned By Multiple types

Passed To AmbientProperties.Cursor, AxHost.GetIPictureFromCursor( ), Control.Cursor, LinkLabel.OverrideCursor

CursorConverter

System.Windows.Forms (system.windows.forms.dll) class

This class converts between Cursor objects and String objects or Byte arrays, for various serialization scenarios. This should not be used directly in your own applications.

```
public class CursorConverter : System.ComponentModel.TypeConverter {
// Public Constructors
   public CursorConverter( );
// Public Instance Methods
   public override bool CanConvertFrom(System.ComponentModel.ITypeDescriptorContext context,
      Type sourceType);                                  // overrides System.ComponentModel.TypeConverter
   public override bool CanConvertTo(System.ComponentModel.ITypeDescriptorContext context,
      Type destinationType);                             // overrides System.ComponentModel.TypeConverter
   public override object ConvertFrom(System.ComponentModel.ITypeDescriptorContext context,
      System.Globalization.CultureInfo culture, object value);   // overrides System.ComponentModel.TypeConverter
   public override object ConvertTo(System.ComponentModel.ITypeDescriptorContext context,
      System.Globalization.CultureInfo culture, object value,
      Type destinationType);                             // overrides System.ComponentModel.TypeConverter
   public override StandardValuesCollection GetStandardValues(
      System.ComponentModel.ITypeDescriptorContext context);     // overrides System.ComponentModel.TypeConverter
   public override bool GetStandardValuesSupported(
      System.ComponentModel.ITypeDescriptorContext context);     // overrides System.ComponentModel.TypeConverter
}
```

Hierarchy System.Object → System.ComponentModel.TypeConverter → CursorConverter

Cursors

System.Windows.Forms (system.windows.forms.dll) sealed class

This class provides a set of standard cursors, such as the Hand, WaitCursor, and IBeam for you to use. In addition, there is the special Default cursor that allows you to restore the default appearance after you have set a custom Cursor for a Control, or changed the Cursor.Current value.

```
public sealed class Cursors {
// Public Static Properties
   public static Cursor AppStarting{get; }
   public static Cursor Arrow{get; }
   public static Cursor Cross{get; }
   public static Cursor Default{get; }
   public static Cursor Hand{get; }
   public static Cursor Help{get; }
   public static Cursor HSplit{get; }
   public static Cursor IBeam{get; }
   public static Cursor No{get; }
   public static Cursor NoMove2D{get; }
```

```
public static Cursor NoMoveHoriz{get; }
public static Cursor NoMoveVert{get; }
public static Cursor PanEast{get; }
public static Cursor PanNE{get; }
public static Cursor PanNorth{get; }
public static Cursor PanNW{get; }
public static Cursor PanSE{get; }
public static Cursor PanSouth{get; }
public static Cursor PanSW{get; }
public static Cursor PanWest{get; }
public static Cursor SizeAll{get; }
public static Cursor SizeNESW{get; }
public static Cursor SizeNS{get; }
public static Cursor SizeNWSE{get; }
public static Cursor SizeWE{get; }
public static Cursor UpArrow{get; }
public static Cursor VSplit{get; }
public static Cursor WaitCursor{get; }
}
```

DataFormats

System.Windows.Forms (system.windows.forms.dll) class

The Clipboard and drag-and-drop operations require you to encapsulate data into an IDataObject derived class. In part, this demands that you specify the Format of the data encapsulated, represented as string. There are several standard formats that the system understands, such as Dib (device-independent bitmap) and UnicodeText, and static properties are provided that return an appropriate format string to identify them. For more complex situations, there are also two static GetFormat() methods. Both return a Format object, mapping a format identification string to a clipboard format ID (an integer). The string version also registers the specified clipboard format with the OS if it hasn't been registered previously.

```
public class DataFormats {
// Public Static Fields
   public static readonly string Bitmap;                          // =Bitmap
   public static readonly string CommaSeparatedValue;             // =Csv
   public static readonly string Dib;                             // =DeviceIndependentBitmap
   public static readonly string Dif;                             // =DataInterchangeFormat
   public static readonly string EnhancedMetafile;                // =EnhancedMetafile
   public static readonly string FileDrop;                        // =FileDrop
   public static readonly string Html;                            // =HTML Format
   public static readonly string Locale;                          // =Locale
   public static readonly string MetafilePict;                    // =MetaFilePict
   public static readonly string OemText;                         // =OEMText
   public static readonly string Palette;                         // =Palette
   public static readonly string PenData;                         // =PenData
   public static readonly string Riff;                            // =RiffAudio
   public static readonly string Rtf;                             // =Rich Text Format
   public static readonly string Serializable;                    // =WindowsForms10PersistentObject
   public static readonly string StringFormat;                    // =System.String
```

```
  public static readonly string SymbolicLink;                          // =SymbolicLink
  public static readonly string Text;                                          // =Text
  public static readonly string Tiff;                          // =TaggedImageFileFormat
  public static readonly string UnicodeText;                            // =UnicodeText
  public static readonly string WaveAudio;                                // =WaveAudio
// Public Static Methods
  public static Format GetFormat(int ID);
  public static Format GetFormat(string format);
}
```

DataFormats.Format

System.Windows.Forms (system.windows.forms.dll) class

This class encapsulates the Id and Name of a Clipboard data format.

```
public class DataFormats.Format {
// Public Constructors
  public DataFormats.Format(string name, int ID);
// Public Instance Properties
  public int Id{get; }
  public string Name{get; }
}
```

DataGrid marshal by reference, disposable

System.Windows.Forms (system.windows.forms.dll) class

This class is the successor to the old unmanaged FlexGrid control, and has considerably more power, fully supporting complex data-binding scenarios.

A grid offers a two dimensional view of the rows and columns on a data source. The data source itself may consist of several related tables, each with different rows and columns, so the grid offers support for drilling down through these relations, updating the display to reflect the current view on the data.

There are a variety of basic areas in the grid whose appearance you can change. You can show and hide a caption (title) area with the CaptionVisible property. You can set the CaptionFont, CaptionForeColor, and CaptionBackColor, as well as the CaptionText.

If a particular row in the data source has been defined to have relations to another table, the grid displays a hyperlink for you to click on to follow that relation. You can set its LinkColor and LinkHoverColor. This drill-down behavior is enabled and disabled with the AllowNavigation property. When you have drilled down into a table, a line is added to display the parent rows through which you have navigated. You can set the ParentRowsBackColor, ParentRowsForeColor, and visibility (ParentRowsVisible). In addition, you can set the ParentRowsLabelStyle to display either the parent ColumnName, TableName, or both. You can also NavigateTo() a particular row and relation, or NavigateBack() to the parent of the current view.

Then, there are the column headers (which run across the top of the grid) and the row headers (which run down the side of the grid). You can make the ColumnHeadersVisible and the RowHeadersVisible, and also set the RowHeaderWidth. Their appearance can be modified with the HeaderBackColor, HeaderForeColor, and HeaderFont. (Note that this means the row and column headers must have the same basic appearance).

Finally, there are the data rows themselves. You can optionally display gridlines between the rows and/or columns by setting **GridLineStyle** and **GridLineColor**. You can set a **PreferredRowHeight** property that acts as a hint for the default row height, and find out the number of displayed rows using the **VisibleRowCount** property.

Rows can be selected, either with the mouse or programmatically through the **Select( )** and **UnSelect( )** methods (note the capital "S"), and you can set the **SelectionForeColor** and **SelectionBackColor**. The **IsSelected( )** method determines the selection state of a particular row, and the **CurrentRowIndex** property tells you which row is currently selected. You can also set an **AlternatingBackColor** property to enable a ledger-like appearance for unselected rows.

The columns divide each row up into a series of cells. You can get the identity of the **CurrentCell**. Alternatively, you can get or set the value of a particular cell using the **Item** property (which is the indexer property). The display bounds of a particular cell can be retrieved using the **GetCellBounds( )** method, or **GetCurrentCellBounds( )** for the cell with the focus. You can choose whether the columns should be sorted by clicking on their headers by setting the **AllowSorting** property.

By default, the system automatically generates all the columns needed for each of the tables in the data source, generating textual, numeric, and Boolean columns as appropriate. However, you can also take control over the entire grid through the **TableStyles** property. This allows you to set up custom columns for each table. (See **DataGridTableStyle** and **DataGridColumnStyle** for more information on this feature of data grids.) Note that you must add your **DataGridColumnStyle** objects to your **DataGridTableStyle** objects before you add the table styles to the **DataGrid**, or the framework will handily create a default set of columns for you.

```
public class DataGrid : Control : System.ComponentModel.ISupportInitialize, IDataGridEditingService {
// Public Constructors
   public DataGrid( );
// Public Instance Properties
   public bool AllowNavigation{set; get; }
   public bool AllowSorting{set; get; }
   public Color AlternatingBackColor{set; get; }
   public override Color BackColor{set; get; }                          // overrides Control
   public Color BackgroundColor{set; get; }
   public override Image BackgroundImage{set; get; }                    // overrides Control
   public BorderStyle BorderStyle{set; get; }
   public Color CaptionBackColor{set; get; }
   public Font CaptionFont{set; get; }
   public Color CaptionForeColor{set; get; }
   public string CaptionText{set; get; }
   public bool CaptionVisible{set; get; }
   public bool ColumnHeadersVisible{set; get; }
   public DataGridCell CurrentCell{set; get; }
   public int CurrentRowIndex{set; get; }
   public override Cursor Cursor{set; get; }                            // overrides Control
   public string DataMember{set; get; }
   public object DataSource{set; get; }
   public int FirstVisibleColumn{get; }
   public bool FlatMode{set; get; }
   public override Color ForeColor{set; get; }                          // overrides Control
   public Color GridLineColor{set; get; }
   public DataGridLineStyle GridLineStyle{set; get; }
```

```
public Color HeaderBackColor{set; get; }
public Font HeaderFont{set; get; }
public Color HeaderForeColor{set; get; }
public Color LinkColor{set; get; }
public Color LinkHoverColor{set; get; }
public Color ParentRowsBackColor{set; get; }
public Color ParentRowsForeColor{set; get; }
public DataGridParentRowsLabelStyle ParentRowsLabelStyle{set; get; }
public bool ParentRowsVisible{set; get; }
public int PreferredColumnWidth{set; get; }
public int PreferredRowHeight{set; get; }
public bool ReadOnly{set; get; }
public bool RowHeadersVisible{set; get; }
public int RowHeaderWidth{set; get; }
public Color SelectionBackColor{set; get; }
public Color SelectionForeColor{set; get; }
public override ISite Site{set; get; }                                    // overrides Control
public GridTableStylesCollection TableStyles{get; }
public override string Text{set; get; }                                   // overrides Control
public object this{set; get; }
public object this{set; get; }
public int VisibleColumnCount{get; }
public int VisibleRowCount{get; }
// Protected Instance Properties
protected override Size DefaultSize{get; }                                // overrides Control
protected ScrollBar HorizScrollBar{get; }
protected internal CurrencyManager ListManager{set; get; }
protected ScrollBar VertScrollBar{get; }
// Public Instance Methods
public bool BeginEdit(DataGridColumnStyle gridColumn, int rowNumber);    // implements IDataGridEditingService
public void BeginInit( );                              // implements System.ComponentModel.ISupportInitialize
public void Collapse(int row);
public bool EndEdit(DataGridColumnStyle gridColumn, int rowNumber,
    bool shouldAbort);                                                    // implements IDataGridEditingService
public void EndInit( );                                // implements System.ComponentModel.ISupportInitialize
public void Expand(int row);
public Rectangle GetCellBounds(DataGridCell dgc);
public Rectangle GetCellBounds(int row, int col);
public Rectangle GetCurrentCellBounds( );
public HitTestInfo HitTest(int x, int y);
public HitTestInfo HitTest(System.Drawing.Point position);
public bool IsExpanded(int rowNumber);
public bool IsSelected(int row);
public void NavigateBack( );
public void NavigateTo(int rowNumber, string relationName);
public void ResetAlternatingBackColor( );
public override void ResetBackColor( );                                   // overrides Control
public override void ResetForeColor( );                                   // overrides Control
public void ResetGridLineColor( );
public void ResetHeaderBackColor( );
public void ResetHeaderFont( );
```

```
public void ResetHeaderForeColor( );
public void ResetLinkColor( );
public void ResetLinkHoverColor( );
public void ResetSelectionBackColor( );
public void ResetSelectionForeColor( );
public void Select(int row);
public void SetDataBinding(object dataSource, string dataMember);
public void SubObjectsSiteChange(bool site);
public void UnSelect(int row);
// Protected Instance Methods
protected virtual void CancelEditing( );
protected internal virtual void ColumnStartedEditing(Control editingControl);
protected internal virtual void ColumnStartedEditing(System.Drawing.Rectangle bounds);
protected override AccessibleObject CreateAccessibilityInstance( );                 // overrides Control
protected virtual DataGridColumnStyle CreateGridColumn(System.ComponentModel.PropertyDescriptor prop);
protected virtual DataGridColumnStyle CreateGridColumn(System.ComponentModel.PropertyDescriptor prop,
    bool isDefault);
protected override void Dispose(bool disposing);                                    // overrides Control
protected virtual string GetOutputTextDelimiter( );
protected virtual void GridHScrolled(object sender, ScrollEventArgs se);
protected virtual void GridVScrolled(object sender, ScrollEventArgs se);
protected virtual void OnAllowNavigationChanged(EventArgs e);
protected void OnBackButtonClicked(object sender, EventArgs e);
protected override void OnBackColorChanged(EventArgs e);                            // overrides Control
protected virtual void OnBackgroundColorChanged(EventArgs e);
protected override void OnBindingContextChanged(EventArgs e);                       // overrides Control
protected virtual void OnBorderStyleChanged(EventArgs e);
protected virtual void OnCaptionVisibleChanged(EventArgs e);
protected virtual void OnCurrentCellChanged(EventArgs e);
protected virtual void OnDataSourceChanged(EventArgs e);
protected override void OnEnter(EventArgs e);                                       // overrides Control
protected virtual void OnFlatModeChanged(EventArgs e);
protected override void OnFontChanged(EventArgs e);                                 // overrides Control
protected override void OnForeColorChanged(EventArgs e);                            // overrides Control
protected override void OnHandleCreated(EventArgs e);                               // overrides Control
protected override void OnHandleDestroyed(EventArgs e);                             // overrides Control
protected override void OnKeyDown(KeyEventArgs ke);                                 // overrides Control
protected override void OnKeyPress(KeyPressEventArgs kpe);                          // overrides Control
protected override void OnLayout(LayoutEventArgs levent);                           // overrides Control
protected override void OnLeave(EventArgs e);                                       // overrides Control
protected override void OnMouseDown(MouseEventArgs e);                              // overrides Control
protected override void OnMouseLeave(EventArgs e);                                  // overrides Control
protected override void OnMouseMove(MouseEventArgs e);                              // overrides Control
protected override void OnMouseUp(MouseEventArgs e);                                // overrides Control
protected override void OnMouseWheel(MouseEventArgs e);                             // overrides Control
protected void OnNavigate(NavigateEventArgs e);
protected override void OnPaint(PaintEventArgs pe);                                 // overrides Control
protected override void OnPaintBackground(PaintEventArgs ebe);                      // overrides Control
protected virtual void OnParentRowsLabelStyleChanged(EventArgs e);
protected virtual void OnParentRowsVisibleChanged(EventArgs e);
protected virtual void OnReadOnlyChanged(EventArgs e);
```

```
  protected override void OnResize(EventArgs e);                                    // overrides Control
  protected void OnRowHeaderClick(EventArgs e);
  protected void OnScroll(EventArgs e);
  protected void OnShowParentDetailsButtonClicked(object sender, EventArgs e);
  protected override bool ProcessDialogKey(Keys keyData);                           // overrides Control
  protected bool ProcessGridKey(KeyEventArgs ke);
  protected override bool ProcessKeyPreview(ref Message m);                         // overrides Control
  protected bool ProcessTabKey(Keys keyData);
  protected void ResetSelection( );
  protected virtual bool ShouldSerializeAlternatingBackColor( );
  protected virtual bool ShouldSerializeBackgroundColor( );
  protected virtual bool ShouldSerializeCaptionBackColor( );
  protected virtual bool ShouldSerializeCaptionForeColor( );
  protected virtual bool ShouldSerializeGridLineColor( );
  protected virtual bool ShouldSerializeHeaderBackColor( );
  protected bool ShouldSerializeHeaderFont( );
  protected virtual bool ShouldSerializeHeaderForeColor( );
  protected virtual bool ShouldSerializeLinkHoverColor( );
  protected virtual bool ShouldSerializeParentRowsBackColor( );
  protected virtual bool ShouldSerializeParentRowsForeColor( );
  protected bool ShouldSerializePreferredRowHeight( );
  protected bool ShouldSerializeSelectionBackColor( );
  protected virtual bool ShouldSerializeSelectionForeColor( );
// Events
  public event EventHandler AllowNavigationChanged;
  public event EventHandler BackButtonClick;
  public event EventHandler BackgroundColorChanged;
  public event EventHandler BorderStyleChanged;
  public event EventHandler CaptionVisibleChanged;
  public event EventHandler CurrentCellChanged;
  public event EventHandler DataSourceChanged;
  public event EventHandler FlatModeChanged;
  public event NavigateEventHandler Navigate;
  public event EventHandler ParentRowsLabelStyleChanged;
  public event EventHandler ParentRowsVisibleChanged;
  public event EventHandler ReadOnlyChanged;
  public event EventHandler Scroll;
  public event EventHandler ShowParentDetailsButtonClick;
}
```

Hierarchy System.Object → System.MarshalByRefObject → System.ComponentModel.Component(System.ComponentModel.IComponent, System.IDisposable) → Control(IOleControl, IOleObject, IOleInPlaceObject, IOleInPlaceActiveObject, IOleWindow, IViewObject, IViewObject2, IPersist, IPersistStreamInit, IPersistPropertyBag, IPersistStorage, IQuickActivate, System.ComponentModel.ISynchronizeInvoke, IWin32Window) → DataGrid(System.ComponentModel.ISupportInitialize, IDataGridEditingService)

Returned By DataGridTableStyle.DataGrid

Passed To DataGridColumnStyle.{SetDataGrid( ), SetDataGridInColumn( )}, DataGridTableStyle.DataGrid, DataGridTextBox.SetDataGrid( )

DataGrid.HitTestInfo

System.Windows.Forms (system.windows.forms.dll) **sealed class**

This class is used by the DataGrid.HitTest( ) method to determine where a particular point is with respect to the grid. You can get the DataGrid.HitTestType from the Type property, as well as the index of the Column and Row that were hit.

The static Nowhere property returns an instance that represents a point entirely outside the grid.

```
public sealed class DataGrid.HitTestInfo {
// Public Static Fields
   public static readonly HitTestInfo Nowhere;                    // ={ None,-1,-1}
// Public Instance Properties
   public int Column{get; }
   public int Row{get; }
   public HitTestType Type{get; }
// Public Instance Methods
   public override bool Equals(object value);                     // overrides object
   public override int GetHashCode( );                            // overrides object
   public override string ToString( );                            // overrides object
}
```

DataGrid.HitTestType **serializable, flag**

System.Windows.Forms (system.windows.forms.dll) **enum**

This enumeration indicates the area of the grid that was hit. It is used by the DataGrid.HitTestInfo class.

```
public enum DataGrid.HitTestType {
   None = 0x00000000,
   Cell = 0x00000001,
   ColumnHeader = 0x00000002,
   RowHeader = 0x00000004,
   ColumnResize = 0x00000008,
   RowResize = 0x00000010,
   Caption = 0x00000020,
   ParentRows = 0x00000040
}
```

Hierarchy System.Object → System.ValueType → System.Enum(System.IComparable, System.IFormattable, System.IConvertible) → HitTestType

DataGridBoolColumn **marshal by reference, disposable**

System.Windows.Forms (system.windows.forms.dll) **class**

This DataGridColumnStyle class supports true/false values, representing them as a checkbox. If you set the AllowNull property, you can extend this to true/false/null support, with a tristate checkbox.

In addition to the base behavior, you can set the TrueValue, FalseValue, and NullValue properties (the object values that represent true, false, and null), in the particular data type of the bound column.

```
public class DataGridBoolColumn : DataGridColumnStyle {
// Public Constructors
   public DataGridBoolColumn( );
   public DataGridBoolColumn(System.ComponentModel.PropertyDescriptor prop);
   public DataGridBoolColumn(System.ComponentModel.PropertyDescriptor prop, bool isDefault);
// Public Instance Properties
   public bool AllowNull{set; get; }
   public object FalseValue{set; get; }
   public object NullValue{set; get; }
   public object TrueValue{set; get; }
// Protected Instance Methods
   protected internal override void Abort(int rowNum);                               // overrides DataGridColumnStyle
   protected internal override bool Commit(CurrencyManager dataSource, int rowNum);  // overrides DataGridColumnStyle
   protected internal override void ConcedeFocus( );                                 // overrides DataGridColumnStyle
   protected internal override void Edit(CurrencyManager source, int rowNum,
      System.Drawing.Rectangle bounds, bool readOnly, string instantText,
      bool cellIsVisible);                                                           // overrides DataGridColumnStyle
   protected internal override void EnterNullValue( );                               // overrides DataGridColumnStyle
   protected internal override object GetColumnValueAtRow(CurrencyManager lm,
      int row);                                                                      // overrides DataGridColumnStyle
   protected internal override int GetMinimumHeight( );                              // overrides DataGridColumnStyle
   protected internal override int GetPreferredHeight(System.Drawing.Graphics g,
      object value);                                                                 // overrides DataGridColumnStyle
   protected internal override Size GetPreferredSize(System.Drawing.Graphics g,
      object value);                                                                 // overrides DataGridColumnStyle
   protected internal override void Paint(System.Drawing.Graphics g,
      System.Drawing.Rectangle bounds, CurrencyManager source, int rowNum);          // overrides DataGridColumnStyle
   protected internal override void Paint(System.Drawing.Graphics g, System.Drawing.Rectangle bounds,
      CurrencyManager source, int rowNum, bool alignToRight);                        // overrides DataGridColumnStyle
   protected internal override void Paint(System.Drawing.Graphics g, System.Drawing.Rectangle bounds,
      CurrencyManager source, int rowNum, System.Drawing.Brush backBrush,
      System.Drawing.Brush foreBrush, bool alignToRight);                            // overrides DataGridColumnStyle
   protected internal override void SetColumnValueAtRow(
      CurrencyManager lm, int row, object value);                                    // overrides DataGridColumnStyle
// Events
   public event EventHandler AllowNullChanged;
   public event EventHandler FalseValueChanged;
   public event EventHandler TrueValueChanged;
}
```

Hierarchy System.Object → System.MarshalByRefObject → System.ComponentModel.Component(System.ComponentModel.IComponent, System.IDisposable) → DataGridColumnStyle(IDataGridColumnStyleEditingNotificationService) → DataGridBoolColumn

DataGridCell

System.Windows.Forms (system.windows.forms.dll) struct

This value type represents a particular RowNumber and ColumnNumber in a data grid.

```
public struct DataGridCell {
// Public Constructors
```

```
public DataGridCell(int r, int c);
// Public Instance Properties
public int ColumnNumber{set; get; }
public int RowNumber{set; get; }
// Public Instance Methods
public override bool Equals(object o);                    // overrides ValueType
public override int GetHashCode( );                       // overrides ValueType
public override string ToString( );                       // overrides ValueType
}
```

Hierarchy System.Object → System.ValueType → DataGridCell

Returned By DataGrid.CurrentCell

Passed To DataGrid.{CurrentCell, GetCellBounds( ), this, this}

DataGridColumnStyle — marshal by reference, disposable

System.Windows.Forms (system.windows.forms.dll) — abstract class

DataGridColumnStyle objects tell the data grid how to manage and display a particular column of data. First, you can specify the name of the data member to which this particular column is bound using the MappingName property. Note that you can only have one column per unique mapping. Then, specify the column HeaderText, the Alignment of the column text, and the Width of the column.

While various column style objects are provided by the system (such as DataGridBoolColumn and DataGridTextBoxColumn), you can derive your own to provide custom display and/or editing facilities.

You can override the Paint( ) method to provide custom rendering. Editing is initiated with the Edit( ) method, giving you the opportunity to show your own editing control, and Abort( ) is called if the grid wants you to attempt to abandon editing. If you need control over the row height, you can override GetMinimumHeight( ), GetPreferredHeight( ), and GetPreferredSize( ) to indicate to the system the requirements for this particular column.

```
public abstract class DataGridColumnStyle : System.ComponentModel.Component :
IDataGridColumnStyleEditingNotificationService {
// Public Constructors
public DataGridColumnStyle( );
public DataGridColumnStyle(System.ComponentModel.PropertyDescriptor prop);
// Public Instance Properties
public virtual HorizontalAlignment Alignment{set; get; }
public virtual DataGridTableStyle DataGridTableStyle{get; }
public AccessibleObject HeaderAccessibleObject{get; }
public virtual string HeaderText{set; get; }
public string MappingName{set; get; }
public virtual string NullText{set; get; }
public virtual PropertyDescriptor PropertyDescriptor{set; get; }
public virtual bool ReadOnly{set; get; }
public virtual int Width{set; get; }
// Protected Instance Properties
protected int FontHeight{get; }
// Public Instance Methods
```

```
    public void ResetHeaderText( );
// Protected Instance Methods
    protected internal abstract void Abort(int rowNum);
    protected void BeginUpdate( );
    protected void CheckValidDataSource(CurrencyManager value);
    protected internal virtual void ColumnStartedEditing(
        Control editingControl);                    // implements IDataGridColumnStyleEditingNotificationService
    protected internal abstract bool Commit(CurrencyManager dataSource, int rowNum);
    protected internal virtual void ConcedeFocus( );
    protected virtual AccessibleObject CreateHeaderAccessibleObject( );
    protected internal virtual void Edit(CurrencyManager source, int rowNum, System.Drawing.Rectangle bounds,
        bool readOnly);
    protected internal virtual void Edit(CurrencyManager source, int rowNum, System.Drawing.Rectangle bounds,
        bool readOnly, string instantText);
    protected internal abstract void Edit(CurrencyManager source, int rowNum, System.Drawing.Rectangle bounds,
        bool readOnly, string instantText, bool cellIsVisible);
    protected void EndUpdate( );
    protected internal virtual void EnterNullValue( );
    protected internal virtual object GetColumnValueAtRow(CurrencyManager source, int rowNum);
    protected internal abstract int GetMinimumHeight( );
    protected internal abstract int GetPreferredHeight(System.Drawing.Graphics g, object value);
    protected internal abstract Size GetPreferredSize(System.Drawing.Graphics g, object value);
    protected virtual void Invalidate( );
    protected internal abstract void Paint(System.Drawing.Graphics g, System.Drawing.Rectangle bounds,
        CurrencyManager source, int rowNum);
    protected internal abstract void Paint(System.Drawing.Graphics g, System.Drawing.Rectangle bounds,
        CurrencyManager source, int rowNum, bool alignToRight);
    protected internal virtual void Paint(System.Drawing.Graphics g, System.Drawing.Rectangle bounds,
        CurrencyManager source, int rowNum, System.Drawing.Brush backBrush, System.Drawing.Brush foreBrush,
        bool alignToRight);
    protected internal virtual void SetColumnValueAtRow(CurrencyManager source, int rowNum, object value);
    protected virtual void SetDataGrid(DataGrid value);
    protected virtual void SetDataGridInColumn(DataGrid value);
    protected internal virtual void UpdateUI(CurrencyManager source, int rowNum, string instantText);
// Events
    public event EventHandler AlignmentChanged;
    public event EventHandler FontChanged;
    public event EventHandler HeaderTextChanged;
    public event EventHandler MappingNameChanged;
    public event EventHandler NullTextChanged;
    public event EventHandler PropertyDescriptorChanged;
    public event EventHandler ReadOnlyChanged;
    public event EventHandler WidthChanged;
}
```

Hierarchy System.Object → System.MarshalByRefObject → System.ComponentModel.Component(System.ComponentModel.IComponent, System.IDisposable) → DataGridColumnStyle(IDataGridColumnStyleEditingNotificationService)

Subclasses DataGridBoolColumn, DataGridTextBoxColumn

Returned By DataGrid.CreateGridColumn( ), GridColumnStylesCollection.this

Passed To DataGrid.{BeginEdit( ), EndEdit( )}, DataGridTableStyle.{BeginEdit( ), EndEdit( )}, GridColumnStylesCollection.{Add( ), AddRange( ), Contains( ), IndexOf( ), Remove( )}, IDataGridEditingService.{BeginEdit( ), EndEdit( )}

DataGridLineStyle serializable

System.Windows.Forms (system.windows.forms.dll) enum

This enumeration specifies whether the data grid has Solid grid lines or None at all.

```
public enum DataGridLineStyle {
  None = 0,
  Solid = 1
}
```

Hierarchy System.Object → System.ValueType → System.Enum(System.IComparable, System.IFormattable, System.IConvertible) → DataGridLineStyle

Returned By DataGrid.GridLineStyle, DataGridTableStyle.GridLineStyle

Passed To DataGrid.GridLineStyle, DataGridTableStyle.GridLineStyle

DataGridParentRowsLabelStyle serializable

System.Windows.Forms (system.windows.forms.dll) enum

This enumeration is used to specify how parent rows are labeled in a grid control. See DataGrid for more information.

```
public enum DataGridParentRowsLabelStyle {
  None = 0,
  TableName = 1,
  ColumnName = 2,
  Both = 3
}
```

Hierarchy System.Object → System.ValueType → System.Enum(System.IComparable, System.IFormattable, System.IConvertible) → DataGridParentRowsLabelStyle

Returned By DataGrid.ParentRowsLabelStyle

Passed To DataGrid.ParentRowsLabelStyle

DataGridPreferredColumnWidthTypeConverter

System.Windows.Forms (system.windows.forms.dll) class

This System.ComponentModel.TypeConverter is used to transform to and from the integer DataGrid.PreferredColumnWidth value, in serialization and design-time scenarios.

```
public class DataGridPreferredColumnWidthTypeConverter : System.ComponentModel.TypeConverter {
// Public Constructors
```

```
    public DataGridPreferredColumnWidthTypeConverter( );
// Public Instance Methods
    public override bool CanConvertFrom(System.ComponentModel.ITypeDescriptorContext context,
       Type sourceType);                       // overrides System.ComponentModel.TypeConverter
    public override object ConvertFrom(System.ComponentModel.ITypeDescriptorContext context,
       System.Globalization.CultureInfo culture, object value);    // overrides System.ComponentModel.TypeConverter
    public override object ConvertTo(System.ComponentModel.ITypeDescriptorContext context,
       System.Globalization.CultureInfo culture, object value,
       Type destinationType);                  // overrides System.ComponentModel.TypeConverter
}
```

Hierarchy System.Object → System.ComponentModel.TypeConverter → DataGridPreferredColumnWidthTypeConverter

DataGridTableStyle — marshal by reference, disposable

System.Windows.Forms (system.windows.forms.dll) — class

This class is used to customize the binding and appearance of a DataGrid. While the default implementation will automatically create appropriate tables and columns for your data source, you can take more control by adding this information by hand.

You do this through the DataGrid.TableStyles property. For each table in your data source that you want to display in the grid, you create a DataGridTableStyle object. First, you can set the data table to which this object is bound through the MappingName property. You can then independently control the colors, grid lines, widths, and heights for which you set defaults in the parent grid, before adding DataGridColumnStyle objects to the GridColumnStyles collection that represent each column in that table.

```
public class DataGridTableStyle : System.ComponentModel.Component : IDataGridEditingService {
// Public Constructors
    public DataGridTableStyle( );
    public DataGridTableStyle(bool isDefaultTableStyle);
    public DataGridTableStyle(CurrencyManager listManager);
// Public Static Fields
    public static DataGridTableStyle DefaultTableStyle;    // =System.Windows.Forms.DataGridTableStyle
// Public Instance Properties
    public bool AllowSorting{set; get; }
    public Color AlternatingBackColor{set; get; }
    public Color BackColor{set; get; }
    public bool ColumnHeadersVisible{set; get; }
    public virtual DataGrid DataGrid{set; get; }
    public Color ForeColor{set; get; }
    public virtual GridColumnStylesCollection GridColumnStyles{get; }
    public Color GridLineColor{set; get; }
    public DataGridLineStyle GridLineStyle{set; get; }
    public Color HeaderBackColor{set; get; }
    public Font HeaderFont{set; get; }
    public Color HeaderForeColor{set; get; }
    public Color LinkColor{set; get; }
    public Color LinkHoverColor{set; get; }
    public string MappingName{set; get; }
    public int PreferredColumnWidth{set; get; }
```

```
public int PreferredRowHeight{set; get; }
public virtual bool ReadOnly{set; get; }
public bool RowHeadersVisible{set; get; }
public int RowHeaderWidth{set; get; }
public Color SelectionBackColor{set; get; }
public Color SelectionForeColor{set; get; }
// Public Instance Methods
public bool BeginEdit(DataGridColumnStyle gridColumn, int rowNumber);         // implements IDataGridEditingService
public bool EndEdit(DataGridColumnStyle gridColumn, int rowNumber,
   bool shouldAbort);                                                           // implements IDataGridEditingService
public void ResetAlternatingBackColor( );
public void ResetBackColor( );
public void ResetForeColor( );
public void ResetGridLineColor( );
public void ResetHeaderBackColor( );
public void ResetHeaderFont( );
public void ResetHeaderForeColor( );
public void ResetLinkColor( );
public void ResetLinkHoverColor( );
public void ResetSelectionBackColor( );
public void ResetSelectionForeColor( );
// Protected Instance Methods
protected internal virtual DataGridColumnStyle CreateGridColumn(System.ComponentModel.PropertyDescriptor prop);
protected internal virtual DataGridColumnStyle CreateGridColumn(System.ComponentModel.PropertyDescriptor prop,
   bool isDefault);
protected override void Dispose(bool disposing);                            // overrides System.ComponentModel.Component
protected virtual void OnAllowSortingChanged(EventArgs e);
protected virtual void OnAlternatingBackColorChanged(EventArgs e);
protected virtual void OnBackColorChanged(EventArgs e);
protected virtual void OnColumnHeadersVisibleChanged(EventArgs e);
protected virtual void OnForeColorChanged(EventArgs e);
protected virtual void OnGridLineColorChanged(EventArgs e);
protected virtual void OnGridLineStyleChanged(EventArgs e);
protected virtual void OnHeaderBackColorChanged(EventArgs e);
protected virtual void OnHeaderFontChanged(EventArgs e);
protected virtual void OnHeaderForeColorChanged(EventArgs e);
protected virtual void OnLinkColorChanged(EventArgs e);
protected virtual void OnLinkHoverColorChanged(EventArgs e);
protected virtual void OnMappingNameChanged(EventArgs e);
protected virtual void OnPreferredColumnWidthChanged(EventArgs e);
protected virtual void OnPreferredRowHeightChanged(EventArgs e);
protected virtual void OnReadOnlyChanged(EventArgs e);
protected virtual void OnRowHeadersVisibleChanged(EventArgs e);
protected virtual void OnRowHeaderWidthChanged(EventArgs e);
protected virtual void OnSelectionBackColorChanged(EventArgs e);
protected virtual void OnSelectionForeColorChanged(EventArgs e);
protected virtual bool ShouldSerializeAlternatingBackColor( );
protected bool ShouldSerializeBackColor( );
protected bool ShouldSerializeForeColor( );
protected virtual bool ShouldSerializeGridLineColor( );
protected virtual bool ShouldSerializeHeaderBackColor( );
```

```
  protected virtual bool ShouldSerializeHeaderForeColor( );
  protected virtual bool ShouldSerializeLinkColor( );
  protected virtual bool ShouldSerializeLinkHoverColor( );
  protected bool ShouldSerializePreferredRowHeight( );
  protected bool ShouldSerializeSelectionBackColor( );
  protected virtual bool ShouldSerializeSelectionForeColor( );
// Events
  public event EventHandler AllowSortingChanged;
  public event EventHandler AlternatingBackColorChanged;
  public event EventHandler BackColorChanged;
  public event EventHandler ColumnHeadersVisibleChanged;
  public event EventHandler ForeColorChanged;
  public event EventHandler GridLineColorChanged;
  public event EventHandler GridLineStyleChanged;
  public event EventHandler HeaderBackColorChanged;
  public event EventHandler HeaderFontChanged;
  public event EventHandler HeaderForeColorChanged;
  public event EventHandler LinkColorChanged;
  public event EventHandler LinkHoverColorChanged;
  public event EventHandler MappingNameChanged;
  public event EventHandler PreferredColumnWidthChanged;
  public event EventHandler PreferredRowHeightChanged;
  public event EventHandler ReadOnlyChanged;
  public event EventHandler RowHeadersVisibleChanged;
  public event EventHandler RowHeaderWidthChanged;
  public event EventHandler SelectionBackColorChanged;
  public event EventHandler SelectionForeColorChanged;
}
```

Hierarchy System.Object → System.MarshalByRefObject → System.ComponentModel.Component(System.ComponentModel.IComponent, System.IDisposable) → DataGridTableStyle(IDataGridEditingService)

Returned By DataGridColumnStyle.DataGridTableStyle, GridTablesFactory.CreateGridTables( ), GridTableStylesCollection.this

Passed To GridTablesFactory.CreateGridTables( ), GridTableStylesCollection.{Add( ), AddRange( ), Contains( ), Remove( )}

DataGridTextBox — marshal by reference, disposable

System.Windows.Forms (system.windows.forms.dll) — class

This class, derived from the standard TextBox control, is used by the DataGridTextBoxColumn to support the editing of column text. You can access the DataGridTextBox for a specific column by using the DataGridTextBoxColumn.TextBox property. You could then hook the text box for validation, for example.

```
public class DataGridTextBox : TextBox {
// Public Constructors
  public DataGridTextBox( );
// Public Instance Properties
```

```
  public bool IsInEditOrNavigateMode{set; get; }
// Public Instance Methods
  public void SetDataGrid(DataGrid parentGrid);
// Protected Instance Methods
  protected override void OnKeyPress(KeyPressEventArgs e);                       // overrides Control
  protected override void OnMouseWheel(MouseEventArgs e);                        // overrides Control
  protected internal override bool ProcessKeyMessage(ref Message m);             // overrides Control
}
```

Hierarchy System.Object → System.MarshalByRefObject → System.ComponentModel. Component(System.ComponentModel.IComponent, System.IDisposable) → Control(IOleControl, IOleObject, IOleInPlaceObject, IOleInPlaceActiveObject, IOleWindow, IViewObject, IViewObject2, IPersist, IPersistStreamInit, IPersistPropertyBag, IPersistStorage, IQuickActivate, System.ComponentModel.ISynchronizeInvoke, IWin32Window) → TextBoxBase → TextBox → DataGridTextBox

DataGridTextBoxColumn — marshal by reference, disposable

System.Windows.Forms (system.windows.forms.dll) — class

This DataGridColumnStyle-derived class supports columns that display strings and are editable using a standard text box.

In addition to the base-class features, you can set optional Format and FormatInfo, to format numeric or DateTime values using the standard .NET formatting strings. This enables the column style to support Byte, DateTime, Decimal, Double, Int16, Int64, UInt16, UInt64, and Single types, in addition to string itself.

```
public class DataGridTextBoxColumn : DataGridColumnStyle {
// Public Constructors
  public DataGridTextBoxColumn( );
  public DataGridTextBoxColumn(System.ComponentModel.PropertyDescriptor prop);
  public DataGridTextBoxColumn(System.ComponentModel.PropertyDescriptor prop, bool isDefault);
  public DataGridTextBoxColumn(System.ComponentModel.PropertyDescriptor prop, string format);
  public DataGridTextBoxColumn(System.ComponentModel.PropertyDescriptor prop, string format, bool isDefault);
// Public Instance Properties
  public string Format{set; get; }
  public IFormatProvider FormatInfo{set; get; }
  public override PropertyDescriptor PropertyDescriptor{set; }        // overrides DataGridColumnStyle
  public override bool ReadOnly{set; get; }                           // overrides DataGridColumnStyle
  public virtual TextBox TextBox{get; }
// Protected Instance Methods
  protected internal override void Abort(int rowNum);                 // overrides DataGridColumnStyle
  protected internal override bool Commit(CurrencyManager dataSource, int rowNum);  // overrides DataGridColumnStyle
  protected internal override void ConcedeFocus( );                   // overrides DataGridColumnStyle
  protected internal override void Edit(CurrencyManager source, int rowNum,
     System.Drawing.Rectangle bounds, bool readOnly, string instantText,
     bool cellIsVisible);                                             // overrides DataGridColumnStyle
  protected void EndEdit( );
  protected internal override void EnterNullValue( );                 // overrides DataGridColumnStyle
  protected internal override int GetMinimumHeight( );                // overrides DataGridColumnStyle
  protected internal override int GetPreferredHeight(System.Drawing.Graphics g,
     object value);                                                   // overrides DataGridColumnStyle
```

```
    protected internal override Size GetPreferredSize(System.Drawing.Graphics g,
        object value);                                          // overrides DataGridColumnStyle
    protected void HideEditBox( );
    protected internal override void Paint(System.Drawing.Graphics g, System.Drawing.Rectangle bounds,
        CurrencyManager source, int rowNum);                    // overrides DataGridColumnStyle
    protected internal override void Paint(System.Drawing.Graphics g, System.Drawing.Rectangle bounds,
        CurrencyManager source, int rowNum, bool alignToRight); // overrides DataGridColumnStyle
    protected internal override void Paint(System.Drawing.Graphics g, System.Drawing.Rectangle bounds,
        CurrencyManager source, int rowNum, System.Drawing.Brush backBrush,
        System.Drawing.Brush foreBrush, bool alignToRight);     // overrides DataGridColumnStyle
    protected void PaintText(System.Drawing.Graphics g, System.Drawing.Rectangle bounds, string text,
        bool alignToRight);
    protected void PaintText(System.Drawing.Graphics g, System.Drawing.Rectangle textBounds, string text,
        System.Drawing.Brush backBrush, System.Drawing.Brush foreBrush, bool alignToRight);
    protected override void SetDataGridInColumn(DataGrid value);           // overrides DataGridColumnStyle
    protected internal override void UpdateUI(CurrencyManager source, int rowNum,
        string instantText);                                    // overrides DataGridColumnStyle
}
```

Hierarchy System.Object → System.MarshalByRefObject → System.ComponentModel.Component(System.ComponentModel.IComponent, System.IDisposable) → DataGridColumnStyle(IDataGridColumnStyleEditingNotificationService) → DataGridTextBoxColumn

DataObject

System.Windows.Forms (system.windows.forms.dll) class

This class provides a basic implementation of the **IDataObject** interface that supports data transfer in **Clipboard** and drag-and-drop scenarios.

You can add the data you wish to encapsulate in one or more different formats using the SetData( ) method. There are three overloads that allow you to add the data either specifying a string indicating the format (perhaps from the **DataFormats** class), using a **Type** name as the format ID, or with no extra information, which defaults to using the class name as the ID.

When you are on the receiving end of one of these objects, you can use the **GetData( )** method to retrieve the data for a particular format ID, perhaps using the **GetDataPresent( )** method to determine whether there is any data stored in a particular format. You can also call **GetFormats( )** to get a list of all the formats for which data is stored in the object.

```
public class DataObject : IDataObject, IOleDataObject {
// Public Constructors
    public DataObject( );
    public DataObject(object data);
    public DataObject(string format, object data);
// Public Instance Methods
    public virtual object GetData(string format);                       // implements IDataObject
    public virtual object GetData(string format, bool autoConvert);     // implements IDataObject
    public virtual object GetData(Type format);                         // implements IDataObject
    public virtual bool GetDataPresent(string format);                  // implements IDataObject
    public virtual bool GetDataPresent(string format, bool autoConvert); // implements IDataObject
    public virtual bool GetDataPresent(Type format);                    // implements IDataObject
```

```
  public virtual string[ ] GetFormats( );                                    // implements IDataObject
  public virtual string[ ] GetFormats(bool autoConvert);                     // implements IDataObject
  public virtual void SetData(object data);                                  // implements IDataObject
  public virtual void SetData(string format, bool autoConvert, object data); // implements IDataObject
  public virtual void SetData(string format, object data);                   // implements IDataObject
  public virtual void SetData(Type format, object data);                     // implements IDataObject
}
```

DateBoldEventArgs

System.Windows.Forms (system.windows.forms.dll) class

This class is for internal use only and should not be called from your own code.

```
public class DateBoldEventArgs : EventArgs {
// Public Instance Properties
  public int[ ] DaysToBold{set; get; }
  public int Size{get; }
  public DateTime StartDate{get; }
}
```

Hierarchy System.Object → System.EventArgs → DateBoldEventArgs

Passed To DateBoldEventHandler.{BeginInvoke( ), Invoke( )}

DateBoldEventHandler serializable

System.Windows.Forms (system.windows.forms.dll) delegate

This delegate is for internal use only and should not be used in your own code.

```
public delegate void DateBoldEventHandler(object sender, DateBoldEventArgs e);
```

DateRangeEventArgs

System.Windows.Forms (system.windows.forms.dll) class

This class encapsulates the event arguments for the MonthCalendar.DateChanged and DateSelected events. You can retrieve the Start and End date of the new selection from this object.

```
public class DateRangeEventArgs : EventArgs {
// Public Constructors
  public DateRangeEventArgs(DateTime start, DateTime end);
// Public Instance Properties
  public DateTime End{get; }
  public DateTime Start{get; }
}
```

Hierarchy System.Object → System.EventArgs → DateRangeEventArgs

Passed To DateRangeEventHandler.{BeginInvoke( ), Invoke( )}, MonthCalendar.{OnDateChanged( ), OnDateSelected( )}

DateRangeEventHandler **serializable**

System.Windows.Forms (system.windows.forms.dll) **delegate**

This is the delegate for the MonthCalendar.DateChanged and MonthCalendar.DateSelected events.

```
public delegate void DateRangeEventHandler(object sender, DateRangeEventArgs e);
```

Associated Events MonthCalendar.{DateChanged( ), DateSelected( )}

DateTimePicker **marshal by reference, disposable**

System.Windows.Forms (system.windows.forms.dll) **class**

This Control class wraps the Win32 date/time selection common control. This is perhaps the least used of all the common controls—most commercial applications seem to roll their own Outlook-style date and time pickers (or use one of several third-party controls available).

First, you can set the Format of the control. This can cause considerable changes in behavior from a Long or Short date (in which case you are provided with a drop-down calendar date picker and a formatted date edit field) to a Time (in which case you lose the calendar and gain a formatted time edit field). There is also Custom, which requires you to set the CustomFormat property and use your own date-time format string. The standard formats are derived from the system locale settings.

As well as the standard Control appearance properties, you can independently set the CalendarFont, CalendarForeColor, CalendarMonthBackground, CalendarTitleBackColor, CalendarTitleForeColor, and CalendarTrailingForeColor (that's the color of the days from last and next month that are shown on this months calendar grid). You can choose how the calendar drop-down menu is aligned (to the LeftRightAlignment.Left or Right edge of the control), by using the DropDownAlign property.

The control can display a checkbox using the ShowCheckBox property. It indicates whether a value is actually selected (Checked)—this lets you support null dates. You can also add a spin button with ShowUpDown that gives you another way to adjust the date.

The date range available can be set with MaxDate and MinDate (and there are static MaxDateTime and MinDateTime properties, which get the theoretical maximum and minimum values, that can be displayed by the control). However, you can only select a single Value in the control, which defaults to DateTime.Now. Compare this to the MonthCalendar control which allows you to select a range of dates, embolden certain dates, etc.

```
public class DateTimePicker : Control {
// Public Constructors
   public DateTimePicker( );
// Public Static Fields
   public static readonly DateTime MaxDateTime;                    // =12/31/9998 12:00:00 AM
   public static readonly DateTime MinDateTime;                    // =1/1/1753 12:00:00 AM
// Protected Static Fields
   protected static readonly Color DefaultMonthBackColor;          // =Color [Window]
   protected static readonly Color DefaultTitleBackColor;          // =Color [ActiveCaption]
   protected static readonly Color DefaultTitleForeColor;          // =Color [ActiveCaptionText]
   protected static readonly Color DefaultTrailingForeColor;       // =Color [GrayText]
// Public Instance Properties
   public override Color BackColor{set; get; }                     // overrides Control
```

```
public override Image BackgroundImage{set; get; }                    // overrides Control
public Font CalendarFont{set; get; }
public Color CalendarForeColor{set; get; }
public Color CalendarMonthBackground{set; get; }
public Color CalendarTitleBackColor{set; get; }
public Color CalendarTitleForeColor{set; get; }
public Color CalendarTrailingForeColor{set; get; }
public bool Checked{set; get; }
public string CustomFormat{set; get; }
public LeftRightAlignment DropDownAlign{set; get; }
public override Color ForeColor{set; get; }                          // overrides Control
public DateTimePickerFormat Format{set; get; }
public DateTime MaxDate{set; get; }
public DateTime MinDate{set; get; }
public int PreferredHeight{get; }
public bool ShowCheckBox{set; get; }
public bool ShowUpDown{set; get; }
public override string Text{set; get; }                              // overrides Control
public DateTime Value{set; get; }
// Protected Instance Properties
protected override CreateParams CreateParams{get; }                  // overrides Control
protected override Size DefaultSize{get; }                           // overrides Control
// Public Instance Methods
public override string ToString( );           // overrides System.ComponentModel.Component
// Protected Instance Methods
protected override AccessibleObject CreateAccessibilityInstance( );  // overrides Control
protected override void CreateHandle( );                             // overrides Control
protected override void DestroyHandle( );                            // overrides Control
protected override bool IsInputKey(Keys keyData);                    // overrides Control
protected virtual void OnCloseUp(EventArgs eventargs);
protected virtual void OnDropDown(EventArgs eventargs);
protected override void OnFontChanged(EventArgs e);                  // overrides Control
protected virtual void OnFormatChanged(EventArgs e);
protected override void OnSystemColorsChanged(EventArgs e);          // overrides Control
protected virtual void OnValueChanged(EventArgs eventargs);
protected override void SetBoundsCore(int x, int y, int width, int height, BoundsSpecified specified);   // overrides Control
protected override void WndProc(ref Message m);                      // overrides Control
// Events
public event EventHandler CloseUp;
public event EventHandler DropDown;
public event EventHandler FormatChanged;
public event PaintEventHandler Paint;                                // overrides Control
public event EventHandler ValueChanged;
}
```

Hierarchy System.Object → System.MarshalByRefObject → System.ComponentModel.Component(System.ComponentModel.IComponent, System.IDisposable) → Control(IOleControl, IOleObject, IOleInPlaceObject, IOleInPlaceActiveObject, IOleWindow, IViewObject, IViewObject2, IPersist, IPersistStreamInit, IPersistPropertyBag, IPersistStorage, IQuickActivate, System.ComponentModel.ISynchronizeInvoke, IWin32Window) → DateTimePicker

Passed To DateTimePickerAccessibleObject.DateTimePickerAccessibleObject( )

DateTimePicker.DateTimePickerAccessibleObject — marshal by reference

System.Windows.Forms (system.windows.forms.dll) — class

This class is for internal use only and should not be called from your own code.

```
public class DateTimePicker.DateTimePickerAccessibleObject : ControlAccessibleObject {
// Public Constructors
   public DateTimePicker.DateTimePickerAccessibleObject(DateTimePicker owner);
// Public Instance Properties
   public override AccessibleStates State{get; }                    // overrides AccessibleObject
   public override string Value{get; }                              // overrides AccessibleObject
}
```

Hierarchy System.Object → System.MarshalByRefObject → AccessibleObject(System.Reflection.IReflect, Accessibility.IAccessible, IEnumVariant) → ControlAccessibleObject → DateTimePickerAccessibleObject

DateTimePickerFormat — serializable

System.Windows.Forms (system.windows.forms.dll) — enum

This enumeration allows you to specify the format for a DateTimePicker control.

```
public enum DateTimePickerFormat {
   Long = 1,
   Short = 2,
   Time = 4,
   Custom = 8
}
```

Hierarchy System.Object → System.ValueType → System.Enum(System.IComparable, System.IFormattable, System.IConvertible) → DateTimePickerFormat

Returned By DateTimePicker.Format

Passed To DateTimePicker.Format

Day — serializable

System.Windows.Forms (system.windows.forms.dll) — enum

This enumeration is used by the MonthCalendar control to set the FirstDayOfWeek property.

```
public enum Day {
   Monday = 0,
   Tuesday = 1,
   Wednesday = 2,
   Thursday = 3,
   Friday = 4,
   Saturday = 5,
   Sunday = 6,
```

```
Default = 7
}
```

Hierarchy System.Object → System.ValueType → System.Enum(System.IComparable, System.IFormattable, System.IConvertible) → Day

Returned By MonthCalendar.FirstDayOfWeek

Passed To MonthCalendar.FirstDayOfWeek

DialogResult

serializable

System.Windows.Forms (system.windows.forms.dll) enum

This enumeration defines the standard user responses from a dialog. A value from this enumeration is returned from the Form.ShowDialog( ) method once the (modal) form has been closed. You can also specify a Button object's DialogResult property to determine which value is returned when that particular button is used to close the dialog.

```
public enum DialogResult {
  None = 0,
  OK = 1,
  Cancel = 2,
  Abort = 3,
  Retry = 4,
  Ignore = 5,
  Yes = 6,
  No = 7
}
```

Hierarchy System.Object → System.ValueType → System.Enum(System.IComparable, System.IFormattable, System.IConvertible) → DialogResult

Returned By Button.DialogResult, CommonDialog.ShowDialog( ), System.Windows.Forms.Design.ComponentEditorForm.ShowForm( ), System.Windows.Forms.Design.IUIService.{ShowDialog( ), ShowMessage( )}, System.Windows.Forms.Design.IWindowsFormsEditorService.ShowDialog( ), Form.{DialogResult, ShowDialog( )}, IButtonControl.DialogResult, MessageBox.Show( )

Passed To Button.DialogResult, Form.DialogResult, IButtonControl.DialogResult

DockStyle

serializable

System.Windows.Forms (system.windows.forms.dll) enum

This enumeration is used to specify how the default layout manager should treat a particular control. You can set the Control.Dock property to one of these values, to ensure that the control is attached to the specified edge of the parent, expanded to the full width and/or height, or resized as the parent changes its layout.

```
public enum DockStyle {
  None = 0,
  Top = 1,
```

```
    Bottom = 2,
    Left = 3,
    Right = 4,
    Fill = 5
}
```

Hierarchy System.Object → System.ValueType → System.Enum(System.IComparable, System.IFormattable, System.IConvertible) → DockStyle

Returned By Control.Dock

Passed To Control.Dock

DomainUpDown marshal by reference, disposable

System.Windows.Forms (system.windows.forms.dll) class

This Control allows you to specify a list of Items from which you can select—similar to a ListBox or ComboBox, except only a single item is displayed at any one time, and there are up-down spin buttons to enable selection from that list. You can retrieve the SelectedIndex or SelectedItem.

This control is extremely difficult to use, and you should always consider using a ComboBox instead, unless there is really no room on your display for the drop list (e.g., you have a 320 × 100 LCD) .

```
public class DomainUpDown : UpDownBase {
// Public Constructors
    public DomainUpDown( );
// Public Instance Properties
    public DomainUpDownItemCollection Items{get; }
    public int SelectedIndex{set; get; }
    public object SelectedItem{set; get; }
    public bool Sorted{set; get; }
    public bool Wrap{set; get; }
// Public Instance Methods
    public override void DownButton( );                                    // overrides UpDownBase
    public override string ToString( );           // overrides System.ComponentModel.Component
    public override void UpButton( );                                      // overrides UpDownBase
// Protected Instance Methods
    protected override AccessibleObject CreateAccessibilityInstance( );       // overrides Control
    protected override void OnChanged(object source, EventArgs e);           // overrides UpDownBase
    protected void OnSelectedItemChanged(object source, EventArgs e);
    protected override void OnTextBoxKeyDown(object source, KeyEventArgs e); // overrides UpDownBase
    protected override void UpdateEditText( );                              // overrides UpDownBase
    protected override void WndProc(ref Message m);                    // overrides ContainerControl
// Events
    public event EventHandler SelectedItemChanged;
}
```

Hierarchy System.Object → System.MarshalByRefObject → System.ComponentModel.Component(System.ComponentModel.IComponent, System.IDisposable) → Control(IOleControl, IOleObject, IOleInPlaceObject, IOleInPlaceActiveObject, IOleWindow, IViewObject, IViewObject2, IPersist, IPersistStreamInit, IPersistPropertyBag, IPersistStorage, IQuickActivate, System.ComponentModel.ISynchronizeInvoke, IWin32Window) → ScrollableControl → ContainerControl(IContainerControl) → UpDownBase → DomainUpDown

DomainUpDown.DomainItemAccessibleObject — marshal by reference

System.Windows.Forms (system.windows.forms.dll) — class

This class is for internal use and should not be called from your own code.

```
public class DomainUpDown.DomainItemAccessibleObject : AccessibleObject {
// Public Constructors
   public DomainUpDown.DomainItemAccessibleObject(string name, AccessibleObject parent);
// Public Instance Properties
   public override string Name{set; get; }                    // overrides AccessibleObject
   public override AccessibleObject Parent{get; }             // overrides AccessibleObject
   public override AccessibleRole Role{get; }                 // overrides AccessibleObject
   public override AccessibleStates State{get; }              // overrides AccessibleObject
   public override string Value{get; }                        // overrides AccessibleObject
}
```

Hierarchy System.Object → System.MarshalByRefObject → AccessibleObject(System.Reflection.IReflect, Accessibility.IAccessible, IEnumVariant) → DomainItemAccessibleObject

DomainUpDown.DomainUpDownAccessibleObject — marshal by reference

System.Windows.Forms (system.windows.forms.dll) — class

This class is for internal use and should not be called from your own code.

```
public class DomainUpDown.DomainUpDownAccessibleObject : ControlAccessibleObject {
// Public Constructors
   public DomainUpDown.DomainUpDownAccessibleObject(Control owner);
// Public Instance Properties
   public override AccessibleRole Role{get; }         // overrides Control.ControlAccessibleObject
// Public Instance Methods
   public override AccessibleObject GetChild(int index);      // overrides AccessibleObject
   public override int GetChildCount( );                      // overrides AccessibleObject
}
```

Hierarchy System.Object → System.MarshalByRefObject → AccessibleObject(System.Reflection.IReflect, Accessibility.IAccessible, IEnumVariant) → ControlAccessibleObject → DomainUpDownAccessibleObject

DomainUpDown.DomainUpDownItemCollection

System.Windows.Forms (system.windows.forms.dll) — class

This class represents the set of objects in the DomainUpDown.Items collection.

```
public class DomainUpDown.DomainUpDownItemCollection : ArrayList {
// Public Instance Properties
  public override object this{set; get; }                          // overrides System.Collections.ArrayList
// Public Instance Methods
  public override int Add(object item);                            // overrides System.Collections.ArrayList
  public override void Insert(int index, object item);             // overrides System.Collections.ArrayList
  public override void Remove(object item);                        // overrides System.Collections.ArrayList
  public override void RemoveAt(int item);                         // overrides System.Collections.ArrayList
}
```

Hierarchy System.Object → System.Collections.ArrayList(System.Collections.IList, System.Collections.ICollection, System.Collections.IEnumerable, System.ICloneable) → DomainUpDownItemCollection

DragAction

serializable

System.Windows.Forms (system.windows.forms.dll) enum

You should set a value selected from this enumeration in the QueryContinueDragEventArgs.Action property to specify whether the framework should Cancel, Continue, or Drop the drag operation in your QueryContinueDragEventHandler.

```
public enum DragAction {
  Continue = 0,
  Drop = 1,
  Cancel = 2
}
```

Hierarchy System.Object → System.ValueType → System.Enum(System.IComparable, System.IFormattable, System.IConvertible) → DragAction

Returned By QueryContinueDragEventArgs.Action

Passed To QueryContinueDragEventArgs.{Action, QueryContinueDragEventArgs( )}

DragDropEffects

serializable, flag

System.Windows.Forms (system.windows.forms.dll) enum

This bitfield enumeration is used to specify how a drop operation might be concluded by a drop target. See DragEventArgs for more information.

```
public enum DragDropEffects {
  None = 0x00000000,
  Copy = 0x00000001,
  Move = 0x00000002,
  Link = 0x00000004,
  Scroll = 0x80000000,
  All = 0x80000003
}
```

Hierarchy System.Object → System.ValueType → System.Enum(System.IComparable, System.IFormattable, System.IConvertible) → DragDropEffects

Returned By Control.DoDragDrop( ), DragEventArgs.{AllowedEffect, Effect}, GiveFeedbackEventArgs.Effect

Passed To Control.DoDragDrop( ), DragEventArgs.{DragEventArgs( ), Effect}, GiveFeedbackEventArgs.GiveFeedbackEventArgs( )

DragEventArgs

System.Windows.Forms (system.windows.forms.dll) class

This class encapsulates the event arguments for the Control.DragEnter, Control.DragDrop, and Control.DragOver events.

When you start a drag-drop operation using Control.DoDragDrop( ), you can specify the DragDropEffects that the drag source can support.

Then, as the drag-drop action proceeds, controls receive DragEnter, DragDrop, and DragOver events, which have DragEventArgs. You can retrieve the AllowedEffect property to determine what the source will permit, and then set the Effect property to specify which you can support as a target. It will also raise GiveFeedback events, which allow you to determine the current Effect, perhaps changing the Control object's appearance or cursors. You might base this on the KeyState. Sadly, the KeyState has not been well encapsulated, and you have to mess around with magic numbers in a bitfield:

1 The left mouse button

2 The right mouse button

4 The Shift key

8 The Control key

16 The middle mouse button

32 The Alt key

You can also retrieve the actual Data that is being dragged, through the IDataObject that encapsulates it.

```
public class DragEventArgs : EventArgs {
// Public Constructors
   public DragEventArgs(IDataObject data, int keyState, int x, int y, DragDropEffects allowedEffect,
      DragDropEffects effect);
// Public Instance Properties
   public DragDropEffects AllowedEffect{get; }
   public IDataObject Data{get; }
   public DragDropEffects Effect{set; get; }
   public int KeyState{get; }
   public int X{get; }
   public int Y{get; }
}
```

Hierarchy System.Object → System.EventArgs → DragEventArgs

Passed To Control.RaiseDragEvent( ), System.Windows.Forms.Design.ComponentTray.{OnDragDrop( ), OnDragEnter( ), OnDragOver( )}, System.Windows.Forms.Design.ControlDesigner.{OnDragDrop( ), OnDragEnter( ), OnDragOver( )}, DragEventHandler.{BeginInvoke( ), Invoke( )}

DragEventHandler **serializable**

System.Windows.Forms (system.windows.forms.dll) **delegate**

This is the delegate for the Control.DragEnter, Control.DragDrop and Control.DragOver events.

```
public delegate void DragEventHandler(object sender, DragEventArgs e);
```

Associated Events Multiple types

DrawItemEventArgs

System.Windows.Forms (system.windows.forms.dll) **class**

This class encapsulates the event arguments for owner-draw events. CheckedListBox, ComboBox, ListBox, MenuItem, StatusBar, and TabControl controls all support owner draw features, if you set their DrawMode property appropriately.

When you handle an item's DrawItem event, you can retrieve information about the BackColor, ForeColor, and Font of the item to be painted. You can also get the System.Drawing.Graphics surface on which to paint the item, and the Bounds of the item to draw on that surface.

Other properties specify the Index of the item to paint, and the State of the item from the DrawItemState enumeration.

Two utility methods will DrawBackground( ) or DrawFocusRectangle( ) imagery.

```
public class DrawItemEventArgs : EventArgs {
// Public Constructors
   public DrawItemEventArgs(System.Drawing.Graphics graphics, System.Drawing.Font font,
      System.Drawing.Rectangle rect, int index, DrawItemState state);
   public DrawItemEventArgs(System.Drawing.Graphics graphics, System.Drawing.Font font,
      System.Drawing.Rectangle rect, int index, DrawItemState state, System.Drawing.Color foreColor,
      System.Drawing.Color backColor);
// Public Instance Properties
   public Color BackColor{get; }
   public Rectangle Bounds{get; }
   public Font Font{get; }
   public Color ForeColor{get; }
   public Graphics Graphics{get; }
   public int Index{get; }
   public DrawItemState State{get; }
// Public Instance Methods
   public virtual void DrawBackground( );
   public virtual void DrawFocusRectangle( );
}
```

Hierarchy System.Object → System.EventArgs → DrawItemEventArgs

Subclasses StatusBarDrawItemEventArgs

Passed To ComboBox.OnDrawItem( ), DrawItemEventHandler.{BeginInvoke( ), Invoke( )}, ListBox.OnDrawItem( ), MenuItem.OnDrawItem( ), TabControl.OnDrawItem( )

DrawItemEventHandler serializable

System.Windows.Forms (system.windows.forms.dll) delegate

This is the delegate for the various DrawItem events that are raised to permit owner drawing of items in a Control. See DrawItemEventArgs for more information on owner draw.

```
public delegate void DrawItemEventHandler(object sender, DrawItemEventArgs e);
```

Associated Events CheckedListBox.DrawItem( ), ComboBox.DrawItem( ), ListBox.DrawItem( ), MenuItem.DrawItem( ), TabControl.DrawItem( )

DrawItemState serializable, flag

System.Windows.Forms (system.windows.forms.dll) enum

This bitfield enumeration can specify the various styles with which you should paint an item in an owner draw operation (e.g., with or without Focus, Checked, etc.) See DrawItemEventArgs for more information on owner draw.

```
public enum DrawItemState {
  None = 0x00000000,
  Selected = 0x00000001,
  Grayed = 0x00000002,
  Disabled = 0x00000004,
  Checked = 0x00000008,
  Focus = 0x00000010,
  Default = 0x00000020,
  HotLight = 0x00000040,
  Inactive = 0x00000080,
  NoAccelerator = 0x00000100,
  NoFocusRect = 0x00000200,
  ComboBoxEdit = 0x00001000
}
```

Hierarchy System.Object → System.ValueType → System.Enum(System.IComparable, System.IFormattable, System.IConvertible) → DrawItemState

Returned By DrawItemEventArgs.State

Passed To DrawItemEventArgs.DrawItemEventArgs( ), StatusBarDrawItemEventArgs.StatusBarDrawItemEventArgs( )

DrawMode serializable

System.Windows.Forms (system.windows.forms.dll) enum

This enumeration is used by Control objects that support owner drawing. If you set their DrawMode properties to OwnerDrawFixed, you will raise DrawItem events to paint each item in the Control. The height of each item is fixed to the value in the ItemHeight property. On the other hand, if you set it to OwnerDrawVariable, the framework will also raise MeasureItem events that allow you to individually specify the height of each item in the list. See DrawItemEventArgs for more information on the owner draw painting process.

```
public enum DrawMode {
  Normal = 0,
  OwnerDrawFixed = 1,
  OwnerDrawVariable = 2
}
```

Hierarchy System.Object → System.ValueType → System.Enum(System.IComparable, System.IFormattable, System.IConvertible) → DrawMode

Returned By ComboBox.DrawMode, ListBox.DrawMode

Passed To ComboBox.DrawMode, ListBox.DrawMode

ErrorBlinkStyle serializable

System.Windows.Forms (system.windows.forms.dll) enum

This enumeration allows you to set the ErrorProvider.BlinkStyle. It controls whether the error icon will NeverBlink, AlwaysBlink, or only blink when an icon is already displayed, and the error changes (BlinkIfDifferentError). If the ErrorProvider.BlinkRate is set to zero, these are all equivalent to NeverBlink.

```
public enum ErrorBlinkStyle {
  BlinkIfDifferentError = 0,
  AlwaysBlink = 1,
  NeverBlink = 2
}
```

Hierarchy System.Object → System.ValueType → System.Enum(System.IComparable, System.IFormattable, System.IConvertible) → ErrorBlinkStyle

Returned By ErrorProvider.BlinkStyle

Passed To ErrorProvider.BlinkStyle

ErrorIconAlignment serializable

System.Windows.Forms (system.windows.forms.dll) enum

The enumeration specifies the locations at which you can place an ErrorProvider icon, relative to a particular Control.

```
public enum ErrorIconAlignment {
  TopLeft = 0,
  TopRight = 1,
  MiddleLeft = 2,
  MiddleRight = 3,
  BottomLeft = 4,
  BottomRight = 5
}
```

Hierarchy System.Object → System.ValueType → System.Enum(System.IComparable, System.IFormattable, System.IConvertible) → ErrorIconAlignment

Returned By ErrorProvider.GetIconAlignment( )

Passed To ErrorProvider.SetIconAlignment( )

ErrorProvider **marshal by reference, disposable**

System.Windows.Forms (system.windows.forms.dll) class

This component allows you to display a small Icon next to a Control to indicate that there is something wrong with the user input. When the user hovers the mouse over the icon, a ToolTip appears containing some text descriptive of the error.

First, you must set the ContainerControl property to the container for the controls that need validation. This happens automatically if the ErrorProvider is dropped onto a designer surface. You can also set a specific Icon if the default red circle with a white exclamation is not to your taste or culture. The position at which an icon should appear is set using the Get/SetIconAlignment( ) and Get/SetIconPadding( ) methods. The icon can also be made to blink using the BlinkRate and BlinkStyle properties. (See ErrorBlinkStyle for more information about this).

There are two principle modes of operation. The simplest is to set the DataSource property to refer to a System.Data.DataSet, and you will automatically get errors displayed for any rows that have a column error (either set by the framework, or with the System.Data.DataRow.SetColumnError( ) method).

The alternative is to use the SetError( ) method, which allows you to set specific error text for any control. To clear the error condition, call SetError( ) for the control with an empty string ("").

```
public class ErrorProvider : System.ComponentModel.Component : System.ComponentModel.IExtenderProvider {
// Public Constructors
   public ErrorProvider( );
   public ErrorProvider(ContainerControl parentControl);
// Public Instance Properties
   public int BlinkRate{set; get; }
   public ErrorBlinkStyle BlinkStyle{set; get; }
   public ContainerControl ContainerControl{set; get; }
   public string DataMember{set; get; }
   public object DataSource{set; get; }
   public Icon Icon{set; get; }
   public override ISite Site{set; }                    // overrides System.ComponentModel.Component
// Public Instance Methods
   public void BindToDataAndErrors(object newDataSource, string newDataMember);
   public bool CanExtend(object extendee);              // implements System.ComponentModel.IExtenderProvider
   public string GetError(Control control);
   public ErrorIconAlignment GetIconAlignment(Control control);
   public int GetIconPadding(Control control);
   public void SetError(Control control, string value);
   public void SetIconAlignment(Control control, ErrorIconAlignment value);
   public void SetIconPadding(Control control, int padding);
   public void UpdateBinding( );
// Protected Instance Methods
   protected override void Dispose(bool disposing);     // overrides System.ComponentModel.Component
}
```

Hierarchy System.Object → System.MarshalByRefObject → System.ComponentModel.Component(System.ComponentModel.IComponent, System.IDisposable) → ErrorProvider(System.ComponentModel.IExtenderProvider)

FeatureSupport

System.Windows.Forms (system.windows.forms.dll) **abstract class**

This abstract base class provides a mechanism to determine whether particular features are supported by a particular class or object.

There methods to find out whether a particular feature or version of a feature IsPresent( ), and another method to determine exactly which version of particular feature is available: GetVersionPresent( ).

The OSFeature class, derived from FeatureSupport, allows you to determine whether particular operating system features are present.

You can also derive your own classes from FeatureSupport (or the IFeatureSupport interface it implements) to give an indication of the features in your own frameworks. You have two design choices: you can either implement the IFeatureSupport interface on each of your objects that support feature presentation, in which case you can use the static versions of IsPresent( ) and GetVersionPresent( ), or you can inherit from FeatureSupport and override the GetVersionPresent( ) and/or IsPresent( ) members that handle the feature information for arbitrary named classes.

```
public abstract class FeatureSupport : IFeatureSupport {
// Protected Constructors
   protected FeatureSupport( );
// Public Static Methods
   public static Version GetVersionPresent(string featureClassName, string featureConstName);
   public static bool IsPresent(string featureClassName, string featureConstName);
   public static bool IsPresent(string featureClassName, string featureConstName, Version minimumVersion);
// Public Instance Methods
   public abstract Version GetVersionPresent(object feature);                          // implements IFeatureSupport
   public virtual bool IsPresent(object feature);                                      // implements IFeatureSupport
   public virtual bool IsPresent(object feature, Version minimumVersion);              // implements IFeatureSupport
}
```

Subclasses OSFeature

FileDialog

marshal by reference, disposable

System.Windows.Forms (system.windows.forms.dll) **abstract class**

This CommonDialog class is the abstract base for OpenFileDialog and SaveFileDialog objects.

The AddExtension property determines whether the DefaultExt (file extension) is automatically added to the end of the filename if no extension is present.

There are two properties, CheckFileExists and CheckPathExists, which when true, cause the dialog to test whether a path or file exists and display a warning if not.

The DereferenceLinks property tells the dialog whether it should display shortcuts as the underlying *.lnk* file (false) or link to the referenced file.

The standard file dialogs can filter the displayed list of files. The Filter string can be set, and the FilterIndex determines which filter from that string is currently selected. For some reason, no one I know can ever remember the exact format of a filter string, so here is an example in case you suffer from the same affliction. "Text files (*.txt)|*.TXT|Image Files (*.BMP;*.JPG;*.GIF)|*.BMP;*.JPG;*.GIF|All files (*.*)|*.*"

The InitialDirectory can be specified, and you can also set a property called RestoreDirectory to determine whether the system will reset the current directory back to where it was initially, if the dialog is closed.

Finally, to retrieve the selected file or files, you can use the FileName and FileNames properties.

```
public abstract class FileDialog : CommonDialog {
// Protected Static Fields
   protected static readonly object EventFileOk;                          // =System.Object
// Public Instance Properties
   public bool AddExtension{set; get; }
   public virtual bool CheckFileExists{set; get; }
   public bool CheckPathExists{set; get; }
   public string DefaultExt{set; get; }
   public bool DereferenceLinks{set; get; }
   public string FileName{set; get; }
   public string[ ] FileNames{get; }
   public string Filter{set; get; }
   public int FilterIndex{set; get; }
   public string InitialDirectory{set; get; }
   public bool RestoreDirectory{set; get; }
   public bool ShowHelp{set; get; }
   public string Title{set; get; }
   public bool ValidateNames{set; get; }
// Protected Instance Properties
   protected virtual IntPtr Instance{get; }
   protected int Options{get; }
// Public Instance Methods
   public override void Reset( );                                         // overrides CommonDialog
   public override string ToString( );            // overrides System.ComponentModel.Component
// Protected Instance Methods
   protected override IntPtr HookProc(IntPtr hWnd, int msg, IntPtr wparam, IntPtr lparam);     // overrides CommonDialog
   protected void OnFileOk(System.ComponentModel.CancelEventArgs e);
   protected override bool RunDialog(IntPtr hWndOwner);                  // overrides CommonDialog
// Events
   public event CancelEventHandler FileOk;
}
```

Hierarchy System.Object → System.MarshalByRefObject → System.ComponentModel.Component(System.ComponentModel.IComponent, System.IDisposable) → CommonDialog → FileDialog

Subclasses OpenFileDialog, SaveFileDialog

FlatStyle

serializable

System.Windows.Forms (system.windows.forms.dll) — enum

This enumeration specifies the drawing style for button-like classes, including group boxes, checkboxes, etc.

The Flat, Popup, and Standard styles are fairly self-explanatory. The System style causes the repaint to be handled by the OS rather than the framework. You should set the System style if you wish to support Windows XP Themes on these objects, but bear in mind that you will then lose the framework features such as font and image support.

```
public enum FlatStyle {
  Flat = 0,
  Popup = 1,
  Standard = 2,
  System = 3
}
```

Hierarchy System.Object → System.ValueType → System.Enum(System.IComparable, System.IFormattable, System.IConvertible) → FlatStyle

Returned By ButtonBase.FlatStyle, GroupBox.FlatStyle, Label.FlatStyle

Passed To ButtonBase.FlatStyle, GroupBox.FlatStyle, Label.FlatStyle

FontDialog

marshal by reference, disposable

System.Windows.Forms (system.windows.forms.dll) — class

This CommonDialog allows users to select a particular Font and System.Drawing.Color.

There are various properties that can permit or deny particular types of font such as AllowSimulations, AllowVectorFonts, AllowVerticalFonts, ScriptsOnly (which eliminates nontext fonts such as Wingdings) and FixedPitchOnly (which limits the list to monospaced fonts such as Courier).

In addition, there are a variety of properties to control the appearance and function of the dialog. The ShowApply property determines whether the dialog has an apply button. ShowColor enables or disables the System.Drawing.Color selector, interacting with the ShowEffects property, which determines whether the group of controls that allow you to set effects such as bold, underline, and the System.Drawing.Color, is shown.

```
public class FontDialog : CommonDialog {
// Public Constructors
  public FontDialog( );
// Protected Static Fields
  protected static readonly object EventApply;                    // =System.Object
// Public Instance Properties
  public bool AllowScriptChange{set; get; }
  public bool AllowSimulations{set; get; }
  public bool AllowVectorFonts{set; get; }
  public bool AllowVerticalFonts{set; get; }
  public Color Color{set; get; }
  public bool FixedPitchOnly{set; get; }
  public Font Font{set; get; }
```

```
public bool FontMustExist{set; get; }
public int MaxSize{set; get; }
public int MinSize{set; get; }
public bool ScriptsOnly{set; get; }
public bool ShowApply{set; get; }
public bool ShowColor{set; get; }
public bool ShowEffects{set; get; }
public bool ShowHelp{set; get; }
// Protected Instance Properties
protected int Options{get; }
// Public Instance Methods
public override void Reset( );                                          // overrides CommonDialog
public override string ToString( );                       // overrides System.ComponentModel.Component
// Protected Instance Methods
protected override IntPtr HookProc(IntPtr hWnd, int msg, IntPtr wparam, IntPtr lparam);  // overrides CommonDialog
protected virtual void OnApply(EventArgs e);
protected override bool RunDialog(IntPtr hWndOwner);                    // overrides CommonDialog
// Events
public event EventHandler Apply;
}
```

Hierarchy System.Object → System.MarshalByRefObject → System.ComponentModel.Component(System.ComponentModel.IComponent, System.IDisposable) → CommonDialog → FontDialog

Form — marshal by reference, disposable

System.Windows.Forms (system.windows.forms.dll) — class

A Form is a specialization of Control that supports top-level windows such as tool windows, frame windows, application pop-ups, and MDI child windows.

The appearance of the form's non-client imagery can be set using the FormBorderStyle to determine the basic appearance, along with the SizeGripStyle to determine whether to show the resizing grippy. The non-client controls are enabled and disabled with the ControlBox (which enables the system menu and close button), MaximizeBox, MinimizeBox, and HelpButton properties. You can also set the Icon to use for the ControlBox.

The Form can also show a Menu, and a MergedMenu can be retrieved for the current context if you are using the MDI idiom.

You can create and Show( ) a form modelessly as with any other control, or use the ShowDialog( ) method to create and show a modal window. The Modal property can be used to determine which method is used to display the form. How the Form is initially positioned is determined by the StartPosition property. You can subsequently minimize or maximize the form by setting the WindowState. It will float above all other windows if you set TopMost to true. While it is showing, it can be made to appear in the taskbar by setting the ShowInTaskbar property.

When the Form is closed, the ShowDialog( ) method returns the DialogResult.

Default button processing is handled through the AcceptButton and CancelButton properties. You can assign any IButtonControl-derived class to this property (which includes Button and LinkLabel, for example). When the button is clicked, it will close the window, setting the DialogResult property appropriately.

Normally, a Form cannot be contained by another control. There are two exceptions to this rule. MDI support is provided through the MdiParent property. If you host a Form in another by setting its MdiParent, it will appear in the containing Form objects MdiChildren array, and the ActiveMdiChild can also be retrieved. Alternatively, you can set the TopLevel property to false to allow you to embed the form in another ContainerControl. Note that if the control has MdiChildren, TopLevel must remain set to true. You can tile or stack the MdiChildren by calling the LayoutMdi( ) method.

Unlike Win32, there are two separate, well-defined Form hierarchies: the Parent, which determines containment relationships of non-toplevel objects (as with all Control objects), and the Owner, which determines the message routing and ownership hierarchy of toplevel windows. For example, a Form object should be the Owner of its pop-up tool windows, dialogs, etc.

The Form has the ability to intercept keyboard messages destined for its child controls. You can set the KeyPreview property to true, and then receive KeyPress, KeyUp, and KeyDown events that would normally (and will eventually) be sent to a child.

A Form can automatically resize itself and scale its contained controls when the Font size changes—the same kind of behavior as Win32 dialogs, only without the horrible complexities of dialog units to pixel mapping. This is enabled using the AutoScale property. Before you show the Form, you can set the AutoScaleBaseSize to specify the size of the default Font. The designer environment will set this property for you, but if you need to do it yourself, you should set it to the font's em-height and average character width. While on the subject of sizing, you can specify a MinimumSize and a MaximumSize, and you can get the DesktopBounds and DesktopLocation, in addition to the standard Location and Bounds.

Finally, you can support transparent forms in two ways. You can set the overall Opacity of the form (1.00 is completely opaque, and 0.00 is completely transparent, with 0.50 partially transparent). Note that this is different to the 0–255 range for the alpha value of System.Drawing.Color objects. Alternatively, you can set a TransparencyKey for a simple chroma-key effect. Any pixel painted in that System.Drawing.Color will become transparent. Note that the transparency features are supported only on Windows 2000 and above, and there is absolutely no per-pixel alpha transparency support.

```
public class Form : ContainerControl {
// Public Constructors
   public Form( );
// Public Static Properties
   public static Form ActiveForm{get; }
// Public Instance Properties
   public IButtonControl AcceptButton{set; get; }
   public Form ActiveMdiChild{get; }
   public bool AllowTransparency{set; get; }
   public bool AutoScale{set; get; }
   public virtual Size AutoScaleBaseSize{set; get; }
   public override bool AutoScroll{set; get; }                    // overrides ScrollableControl
   public override Color BackColor{set; get; }                    // overrides Control
   public IButtonControl CancelButton{set; get; }
   public Size ClientSize{set; get; }                             // overrides Control
   public bool ControlBox{set; get; }
   public Rectangle DesktopBounds{set; get; }
   public Point DesktopLocation{set; get; }
   public DialogResult DialogResult{set; get; }
```

```
public FormBorderStyle FormBorderStyle{set; get; }
public bool HelpButton{set; get; }
public Icon Icon{set; get; }
public bool IsMdiChild{get; }
public bool IsMdiContainer{set; get; }
public bool IsRestrictedWindow{get; }
public bool KeyPreview{set; get; }
public bool MaximizeBox{set; get; }
public Size MaximumSize{set; get; }
public Form[ ] MdiChildren{get; }
public Form MdiParent{set; get; }
public MainMenu Menu{set; get; }
public MainMenu MergedMenu{get; }
public bool MinimizeBox{set; get; }
public Size MinimumSize{set; get; }
public bool Modal{get; }
public double Opacity{set; get; }
public Form[ ] OwnedForms{get; }
public Form Owner{set; get; }
public bool ShowInTaskbar{set; get; }
public Size Size{set; get; }                                        // overrides Control
public SizeGripStyle SizeGripStyle{set; get; }
public FormStartPosition StartPosition{set; get; }
public int TabIndex{set; get; }                                     // overrides Control
public bool TopLevel{set; get; }
public bool TopMost{set; get; }
public Color TransparencyKey{set; get; }
public FormWindowState WindowState{set; get; }
// Protected Instance Properties
protected override CreateParams CreateParams{get; }                 // overrides ContainerControl
protected override ImeMode DefaultImeMode{get; }                    // overrides Control
protected override Size DefaultSize{get; }                          // overrides Control
protected Rectangle MaximizedBounds{set; get; }
// Public Static Methods
public static SizeF GetAutoScaleSize(System.Drawing.Font font);
// Public Instance Methods
public void Activate( );
public void AddOwnedForm(Form ownedForm);
public void Close( );
public void LayoutMdi(MdiLayout value);
public void RemoveOwnedForm(Form ownedForm);
public void SetDesktopBounds(int x, int y, int width, int height);
public void SetDesktopLocation(int x, int y);
public DialogResult ShowDialog( );
public DialogResult ShowDialog(IWin32Window owner);
public override string ToString( );                  // overrides System.ComponentModel.Component
// Protected Instance Methods
protected void ActivateMdiChild(Form form);
protected override void AdjustFormScrollbars(bool displayScrollbars);  // overrides ContainerControl
protected void ApplyAutoScaling( );
protected void CenterToParent( );
```

```
protected void CenterToScreen( );
protected override ControlCollection CreateControlsInstance( );                    // overrides Control
protected override void CreateHandle( );                                           // overrides Control
protected override void DefWndProc(ref Message m);                                 // overrides Control
protected override void Dispose(bool disposing);                          // overrides ContainerControl
protected virtual void OnActivated(EventArgs e);
protected virtual void OnClosed(EventArgs e);
protected virtual void OnClosing(System.ComponentModel.CancelEventArgs e);
protected override void OnCreateControl( );                               // overrides ContainerControl
protected virtual void OnDeactivate(EventArgs e);
protected override void OnFontChanged(EventArgs e);                                // overrides Control
protected override void OnHandleCreated(EventArgs e);                              // overrides Control
protected override void OnHandleDestroyed(EventArgs e);                            // overrides Control
protected virtual void OnInputLanguageChanged(InputLanguageChangedEventArgs e);
protected virtual void OnInputLanguageChanging(InputLanguageChangingEventArgs e);
protected virtual void OnLoad(EventArgs e);
protected virtual void OnMaximizedBoundsChanged(EventArgs e);
protected virtual void OnMaximumSizeChanged(EventArgs e);
protected virtual void OnMdiChildActivate(EventArgs e);
protected virtual void OnMenuComplete(EventArgs e);
protected virtual void OnMenuStart(EventArgs e);
protected virtual void OnMinimumSizeChanged(EventArgs e);
protected override void OnPaint(PaintEventArgs e);                                 // overrides Control
protected override void OnResize(EventArgs e);                                     // overrides Control
protected override void OnStyleChanged(EventArgs e);                               // overrides Control
protected override void OnTextChanged(EventArgs e);                                // overrides Control
protected override void OnVisibleChanged(EventArgs e);                   // overrides ScrollableControl
protected override bool ProcessCmdKey(ref Message msg, Keys keyData);              // overrides Control
protected override bool ProcessDialogKey(Keys keyData);                   // overrides ContainerControl
protected override bool ProcessKeyPreview(ref Message m);                          // overrides Control
protected override bool ProcessTabKey(bool forward);                      // overrides ContainerControl
protected override void ScaleCore(float x, float y);                     // overrides ScrollableControl
protected override void Select(bool directed, bool forward);              // overrides ContainerControl
protected override void SetBoundsCore(int x, int y, int width, int height, BoundsSpecified specified);  // overrides Control
protected override void SetClientSizeCore(int x, int y);                           // overrides Control
protected override void SetVisibleCore(bool value);                                // overrides Control
protected override void UpdateDefaultButton( );                           // overrides ContainerControl
protected override void WndProc(ref Message m);                           // overrides ContainerControl
// Events
public event EventHandler Activated;
public event EventHandler Closed;
public event CancelEventHandler Closing;
public event EventHandler Deactivate;
public event InputLanguageChangedEventHandler InputLanguageChanged;
public event InputLanguageChangingEventHandler InputLanguageChanging;
public event EventHandler Load;
public event EventHandler MaximizedBoundsChanged;
public event EventHandler MaximumSizeChanged;
public event EventHandler MdiChildActivate;
public event EventHandler MenuComplete;
public event EventHandler MenuStart;
```

```
  public event EventHandler MinimumSizeChanged;
}
```

Hierarchy System.Object → System.MarshalByRefObject → System.ComponentModel.Component(System.ComponentModel.IComponent, System.IDisposable) → Control(IOleControl, IOleObject, IOleInPlaceObject, IOleInPlaceActiveObject, IOleWindow, IViewObject, IViewObject2, IPersist, IPersistStreamInit, IPersistPropertyBag, IPersistStorage, IQuickActivate, System.ComponentModel.ISynchronizeInvoke, IWin32Window) → ScrollableControl → ContainerControl(IContainerControl) → Form

Subclasses PrintPreviewDialog, ThreadExceptionDialog, System.Windows.Forms.Design.ComponentEditorForm

Returned By ApplicationContext.MainForm, ContainerControl.ParentForm, Control.FindForm( ), MainMenu.GetForm( ), MdiClient.MdiChildren

Passed To Application.Run( ), ApplicationContext.{ApplicationContext( ), MainForm}, System.Windows.Forms.Design.IUIService.ShowDialog( ), System.Windows.Forms.Design.IWindowsFormsEditorService.ShowDialog( ), ControlCollection.ControlCollection( )

Form.ControlCollection

System.Windows.Forms (system.windows.forms.dll) class

This collection class represents the set of objects contained by a Form.

```
public class Form.ControlCollection : ControlCollection {
// Public Constructors
  public Form.ControlCollection(Form owner);
// Public Instance Methods
  public override void Add(Control value);                  // overrides Control.ControlCollection
  public override void Remove(Control value);               // overrides Control.ControlCollection
}
```

Hierarchy System.Object → ControlCollection(System.Collections.IList, System.Collections.ICollection, System.Collections.IEnumerable, System.ICloneable) → ControlCollection

FormBorderStyle serializable

System.Windows.Forms (system.windows.forms.dll) enum

This enumeration allows you to set the appearance of the non-client area of a Form.

```
public enum FormBorderStyle {
  None = 0,
  FixedSingle = 1,
  Fixed3D = 2,
  FixedDialog = 3,
  Sizable = 4,
  FixedToolWindow = 5,
  SizableToolWindow = 6
}
```

Hierarchy System.Object → System.ValueType → System.Enum(System.IComparable, System.IFormattable, System.IConvertible) → FormBorderStyle

Returned By Form.FormBorderStyle, PrintPreviewDialog.FormBorderStyle

Passed To Form.FormBorderStyle, PrintPreviewDialog.FormBorderStyle

FormStartPosition serializable

System.Windows.Forms (system.windows.forms.dll) enum

The position at which a Form appears when it is first shown can be defined by a value from this enumeration. Note that you must set StartPosition before a Form is shown for it to have any effect.

```
public enum FormStartPosition {
  Manual = 0,
  CenterScreen = 1,
  WindowsDefaultLocation = 2,
  WindowsDefaultBounds = 3,
  CenterParent = 4
}
```

Hierarchy System.Object → System.ValueType → System.Enum(System.IComparable, System.IFormattable, System.IConvertible) → FormStartPosition

Returned By Form.StartPosition, PrintPreviewDialog.StartPosition

Passed To Form.StartPosition, PrintPreviewDialog.StartPosition

FormWindowState serializable

System.Windows.Forms (system.windows.forms.dll) enum

Specifies whether a Form is Minimized, Maximized, or Normal. Note that a Form is Normal before it has been shown, regardless of the Form.StartPosition.

```
public enum FormWindowState {
  Normal = 0,
  Minimized = 1,
  Maximized = 2
}
```

Hierarchy System.Object → System.ValueType → System.Enum(System.IComparable, System.IFormattable, System.IConvertible) → FormWindowState

Returned By Form.WindowState, PrintPreviewDialog.WindowState

Passed To Form.WindowState, PrintPreviewDialog.WindowState

FrameStyle **serializable**

System.Windows.Forms (system.windows.forms.dll) **enum**

This enumeration is used by ControlPaint.DrawReversibleFrame( ) and ControlPaint.DrawReversibleLine( ) to determine the appearance of the line drawn.

```
public enum FrameStyle {
  Dashed = 0,
  Thick = 1
}
```

Hierarchy System.Object → System.ValueType → System.Enum(System.IComparable, System.IFormattable, System.IConvertible) → FrameStyle

Passed To ControlPaint.DrawReversibleFrame( )

GiveFeedbackEventArgs

System.Windows.Forms (system.windows.forms.dll) **class**

This class encapsulates the event arguments for the Control.GiveFeedback event, which is raised during drag-and-drop operations. When you handle this event, you can use the Effect property to determine what sort of drag-and-drop operation is in progress, and then either UseDefaultCursors or set your own custom cursor.

```
public class GiveFeedbackEventArgs : EventArgs {
// Public Constructors
  public GiveFeedbackEventArgs(DragDropEffects effect, bool useDefaultCursors);
// Public Instance Properties
  public DragDropEffects Effect{get; }
  public bool UseDefaultCursors{set; get; }
}
```

Hierarchy System.Object → System.EventArgs → GiveFeedbackEventArgs

Passed To System.Windows.Forms.Design.ComponentTray.OnGiveFeedback( ), System.Windows.Forms.Design.ControlDesigner.OnGiveFeedback( ), GiveFeedbackEventHandler.{BeginInvoke( ), Invoke( )}

GiveFeedbackEventHandler **serializable**

System.Windows.Forms (system.windows.forms.dll) **delegate**

This is the delegate for the Control.GiveFeedback event.

```
public delegate void GiveFeedbackEventHandler(
    object sender, GiveFeedbackEventArgs e);
```

Associated Events Multiple types

GridColumnStylesCollection

marshal by reference

System.Windows.Forms (system.windows.forms.dll) class

This typed collection class represents the list of GridColumnStyles in a GridTableStylesCollection object. As you might expect from a collection, you can Add( ) and Remove( ) objects, find the IndexOf( ) a particular object, or the Item at a particular index (this is the indexer property).

See DataGrid for more information about columns, tables, and grids.

```
public class GridColumnStylesCollection : BaseCollection : IList {
// Public Instance Properties
   public DataGridColumnStyle this{get; }
   public DataGridColumnStyle this{get; }
   public DataGridColumnStyle this{get; }
// Protected Instance Properties
   protected override ArrayList List{get; }                          // overrides BaseCollection
// Public Instance Methods
   public virtual int Add(DataGridColumnStyle column);
   public void AddRange(DataGridColumnStyle[ ] columns);
   public void Clear( );                                              // implements IList
   public bool Contains(DataGridColumnStyle column);
   public bool Contains(System.ComponentModel.PropertyDescriptor propDesc);
   public bool Contains(string name);
   public int IndexOf(DataGridColumnStyle element);
   public void Remove(DataGridColumnStyle column);
   public void RemoveAt(int index);                                   // implements IList
   public void ResetPropertyDescriptors( );
// Protected Instance Methods
   protected void OnCollectionChanged(System.ComponentModel.CollectionChangeEventArgs ccevent);
// Events
   public event CollectionChangeEventHandler CollectionChanged;
}
```

Hierarchy System.Object → System.MarshalByRefObject → BaseCollection(System.Collections.ICollection, System.Collections.IEnumerable) → GridColumnStylesCollection(System.Collections.IList)

Returned By DataGridTableStyle.GridColumnStyles

GridItem

System.Windows.Forms (system.windows.forms.dll) abstract class

This class represents a particular row in a PropertyGrid and is used in the PropertyGrid.SelectedGridItem and PropertyGrid.SelectedGridItemChanged members.

You can discover whether the row is Expandable (and whether it is Expanded), which GridItems are children of this one, and which is its Parent.

The Label and Value can be retrieved (but not set) through those properties, and you can also retrieve the PropertyDescriptor for the item, to discover what type the item Value might be and which System.ComponentModel.TypeConverter is available for it.

The Select() method causes the row represented by this object to be selected in the PropertyGrid.

The GridItemType property is used to determine whether this row in the grid represents an ArrayValue, a Category line (e.g., the Behavior, Layout labels), a simple Property, or a Root item for an expandable row.

```
public abstract class GridItem {
// Protected Constructors
  protected GridItem( );
// Public Instance Properties
  public virtual bool Expandable{get; }
  public virtual bool Expanded{set; get; }
  public abstract GridItemCollection GridItems{get; }
  public abstract GridItemType GridItemType{get; }
  public abstract string Label{get; }
  public abstract GridItem Parent{get; }
  public abstract PropertyDescriptor PropertyDescriptor{get; }
  public abstract object Value{get; }
// Public Instance Methods
  public abstract bool Select( );
}
```

Returned By GridItemCollection.this, PropertyGrid.SelectedGridItem, PropertyValueChangedEventArgs.ChangedItem, SelectedGridItemChangedEventArgs.{NewSelection, OldSelection}

Passed To PropertyGrid.SelectedGridItem, PropertyValueChangedEventArgs.PropertyValueChangedEventArgs( ), SelectedGridItemChangedEventArgs.SelectedGridItemChangedEventArgs( )

GridItemCollection

System.Windows.Forms (system.windows.forms.dll) class

This class is a typed collection of GridItems, and is used to contain the list of child items for a particular GridItem.

As you might expect from a collection, you can Add() and Remove() objects, find the IndexOf() a particular object, or the Item at a particular index (this is the indexer property).

```
public class GridItemCollection : ICollection, IEnumerable {
// Public Static Fields
  public static GridItemCollection Empty;              // =System.Windows.Forms.GridItemCollection
// Public Instance Properties
  public int Count{get; }                                           // implements ICollection
  public GridItem this{get; }
  public GridItem this{get; }
// Public Instance Methods
  public IEnumerator GetEnumerator( );                              // implements IEnumerable
}
```

Returned By GridItem.GridItems

GridItemType

serializable

System.Windows.Forms (system.windows.forms.dll) — enum

An enumeration specifying the various kinds of row in a PropertyGrid. See GridItem and PropertyGrid for more information.

```
public enum GridItemType {
  Property = 0,
  Category = 1,
  ArrayValue = 2,
  Root = 3
}
```

Hierarchy System.Object → System.ValueType → System.Enum(System.IComparable, System.IFormattable, System.IConvertible) → GridItemType

Returned By GridItem.GridItemType

GridTablesFactory

System.Windows.Forms (system.windows.forms.dll) — class

This class is for internal use only and should not be called from your own code.

```
public class GridTablesFactory {
// Public Static Methods
  public static DataGridTableStyle[ ] CreateGridTables(DataGridTableStyle gridTable, object dataSource,
    string dataMember, BindingContext bindingManager);
}
```

GridTableStylesCollection

marshal by reference

System.Windows.Forms (system.windows.forms.dll) — class

This typed collection class represents the list of DataGridTableStyle objects in a DataGrid object. As you might expect from a collection, you can Add( ) and Remove( ) objects, find the IndexOf( ) a particular object, or the Item at a particular index (this is the indexer property).

See DataGrid for more information about columns, tables, and grids.

```
public class GridTableStylesCollection : BaseCollection : IList {
// Public Instance Properties
  public DataGridTableStyle this{get; }
  public DataGridTableStyle this{get; }
// Protected Instance Properties
  protected override ArrayList List{get; }                                // overrides BaseCollection
// Public Instance Methods
  public virtual int Add(DataGridTableStyle table);
  public virtual void AddRange(DataGridTableStyle[ ] tables);
  public void Clear( );                                                   // implements IList
  public bool Contains(DataGridTableStyle table);
  public bool Contains(string name);
  public void Remove(DataGridTableStyle table);
```

```
  public void RemoveAt(int index);                                    // implements IList
// Protected Instance Methods
  protected void OnCollectionChanged(System.ComponentModel.CollectionChangeEventArgs ccevent);
// Events
  public event CollectionChangeEventHandler CollectionChanged;
}
```

Hierarchy System.Object → System.MarshalByRefObject → BaseCollection(System.Collections.ICollection, System.Collections.IEnumerable) → GridTableStylesCollection(System.Collections.IList)

Returned By DataGrid.TableStyles

GroupBox — marshal by reference, disposable

System.Windows.Forms (system.windows.forms.dll) — class

This Control class can contain other controls (like a ContainerControl), but it does not provide scrolling support, instead rendering a label and border around its children, which have been added to the Controls collection.

You can set the FlatStyle for a group box to determine how it will be rendered. Note that you should set the FlatStyle to System if you wish your GroupBox to support Windows XP theming.

```
public class GroupBox : Control {
// Public Constructors
  public GroupBox( );
// Public Instance Properties
  public override bool AllowDrop{set; get; }                          // overrides Control
  public override Rectangle DisplayRectangle{get; }                   // overrides Control
  public FlatStyle FlatStyle{set; get; }
  public bool TabStop{set; get; }                                     // overrides Control
  public override string Text{set; get; }                             // overrides Control
// Protected Instance Properties
  protected override CreateParams CreateParams{get; }                 // overrides Control
  protected override Size DefaultSize{get; }                          // overrides Control
// Public Instance Methods
  public override string ToString( );           // overrides System.ComponentModel.Component
// Protected Instance Methods
  protected override void OnFontChanged(EventArgs e);                 // overrides Control
  protected override void OnPaint(PaintEventArgs e);                  // overrides Control
  protected override bool ProcessMnemonic(char charCode);             // overrides Control
  protected override void WndProc(ref Message m);                     // overrides Control
// Events
  public event EventHandler Click;                                    // overrides Control
  public event EventHandler DoubleClick;                              // overrides Control
  public event KeyEventHandler KeyDown;                               // overrides Control
  public event KeyPressEventHandler KeyPress;                         // overrides Control
  public event KeyEventHandler KeyUp;                                 // overrides Control
  public event MouseEventHandler MouseDown;                           // overrides Control
  public event EventHandler MouseEnter;                               // overrides Control
  public event EventHandler MouseLeave;                               // overrides Control
```

```
public event MouseEventHandler MouseMove;                                    // overrides Control
public event MouseEventHandler MouseUp;                                      // overrides Control
}
```

Hierarchy System.Object → System.MarshalByRefObject → System.ComponentModel.Component(System.ComponentModel.IComponent, System.IDisposable) → Control(IOleControl, IOleObject, IOleInPlaceObject, IOleInPlaceActiveObject, IOleWindow, IViewObject, IViewObject2, IPersist, IPersistStreamInit, IPersistPropertyBag, IPersistStorage, IQuickActivate, System.ComponentModel.ISynchronizeInvoke, IWin32Window) → GroupBox

Help

System.Windows.Forms (system.windows.forms.dll) **class**

This utility class provides two members, ShowHelp( ) and ShowHelpIndex( ), which allow you to display HTML help files in your application.

There are several overrides of the ShowHelp( ) method. One allows you to show specific pages. Others show the index or contents page in a specified *.chm*, *.col*, or *.htm* help file.

For most simple help applications, you should consider using the HelpProvider component instead, which deals with Control.HelpRequested events, automatically showing the appropriate help for a Control.

```
public class Help {
// Public Static Methods
   public static void ShowHelp(Control parent, string url);
   public static void ShowHelp(Control parent, string url, HelpNavigator navigator);
   public static void ShowHelp(Control parent, string url, HelpNavigator command, object param);
   public static void ShowHelp(Control parent, string url, string keyword);
   public static void ShowHelpIndex(Control parent, string url);
   public static void ShowPopup(Control parent, string caption, System.Drawing.Point location);
}
```

HelpEventArgs

System.Windows.Forms (system.windows.forms.dll) **class**

This class encapsulates the event arguments for the Control.HelpRequested event. It includes a Handled property, which you should set to true if you do handle the event, or the framework will pass the event on for further processing.

You can also retrieve the current MousePos if you need to use this to resolve the help item.

You can display help using the Help class, or use the HelpProvider component to provide automated help support.

```
public class HelpEventArgs : EventArgs {
// Public Constructors
   public HelpEventArgs(System.Drawing.Point mousePos);
// Public Instance Properties
   public bool Handled{set; get; }
   public Point MousePos{get; }
}
```

Hierarchy System.Object → System.EventArgs → HelpEventArgs

Passed To Control.OnHelpRequested( ), HelpEventHandler.{BeginInvoke( ), Invoke( )}

HelpEventHandler **serializable**

System.Windows.Forms (system.windows.forms.dll) **delegate**

This is the delegate for the Control.HelpRequested and HelpRequested events.

```
public delegate void HelpEventHandler(object sender, HelpEventArgs hlpevent);
```

Associated Events Multiple types

HelpNavigator **serializable**

System.Windows.Forms (system.windows.forms.dll) **enum**

This enumeration specifies the different types of page that might be shown in an HTML help file by either the Help or HelpProvider classes.

```
public enum HelpNavigator {
   Topic = -2147483647,
   TableOfContents = -2147483646,
   Index = -2147483645,
   Find = -2147483644,
   AssociateIndex = -2147483643,
   KeywordIndex = -2147483642
}
```

Hierarchy System.Object → System.ValueType → System.Enum(System.IComparable, System.IFormattable, System.IConvertible) → HelpNavigator

Returned By HelpProvider.GetHelpNavigator( )

Passed To Help.ShowHelp( ), HelpProvider.SetHelpNavigator( )

HelpProvider **marshal by reference, disposable**

System.Windows.Forms (system.windows.forms.dll) **class**

This System.ComponentModel.Component can be dropped onto a Form design surface to provide help support.

Unfortunately, the naming conventions are not remotely consistent between the HelpProvider and the Help classes, despite the fact that they carry out exactly the same task with different levels of automation. HelpProvider offers extender properties for the HelpKeyword (the Topic ID) and HelpNavigator, and handles help requests (through the Control.HelpRequested event) to show the selected page of the HelpNamespace (the curiously named property that allows you to specify the URI of the help file). See Help for more information on these parameters. Help can be individually switched on and off for a particular Control through another extender property: ShowHelp.

Finally, there is a HelpString extender property, which lets you set a string for What's This? help (the little pop-up ToolTip–like help boxes). Again, the class automatically deals with this for you.

Programmatically, you can access all extender properties through the Get and Set member functions of the same name.

```
public class HelpProvider : System.ComponentModel.Component : System.ComponentModel.IExtenderProvider {
// Public Constructors
   public HelpProvider( );
// Public Instance Properties
   public virtual string HelpNamespace{set; get; }
// Public Instance Methods
   public virtual bool CanExtend(object target);              // implements System.ComponentModel.IExtenderProvider
   public virtual string GetHelpKeyword(Control ctl);
   public virtual HelpNavigator GetHelpNavigator(Control ctl);
   public virtual string GetHelpString(Control ctl);
   public virtual bool GetShowHelp(Control ctl);
   public virtual void ResetShowHelp(Control ctl);
   public virtual void SetHelpKeyword(Control ctl, string keyword);
   public virtual void SetHelpNavigator(Control ctl, HelpNavigator navigator);
   public virtual void SetHelpString(Control ctl, string helpString);
   public virtual void SetShowHelp(Control ctl, bool value);
   public override string ToString( );                        // overrides System.ComponentModel.Component
}
```

Hierarchy System.Object → System.MarshalByRefObject → System.ComponentModel.Component(System.ComponentModel.IComponent, System.IDisposable) → HelpProvider(System.ComponentModel.IExtenderProvider)

HorizontalAlignment

serializable

System.Windows.Forms (system.windows.forms.dll) **enum**

This enumeration is used by most of the Control classes to specify how particular parts of their imagery should be positioned (e.g., the TextBox.TextAlign property).

Note that this enumeration uses Left, Center, and Right rather than the usual Near, Center, and Far, but the Control objects still honor the setting for Control.RightToLeft. So, if you set Left, but also RightToLeft.Yes, the element will actually be aligned to the right.

```
public enum HorizontalAlignment {
   Left = 0,
   Right = 1,
   Center = 2
}
```

Hierarchy System.Object → System.ValueType → System.Enum(System.IComparable, System.IFormattable, System.IConvertible) → HorizontalAlignment

Returned By ColumnHeader.TextAlign, Control.{RtlTranslateAlignment( ), RtlTranslateHorizontal( )}, DataGridColumnStyle.Alignment, RichTextBox.SelectionAlignment, StatusBarPanel.Alignment, TextBox.TextAlign, UpDownBase.TextAlign

Passed To ColumnHeader.TextAlign, Control.{RtlTranslateAlignment( ), RtlTranslateHorizontal( )}, DataGridColumnStyle.Alignment, ColumnHeaderCollection.{Add( ), Insert( )}, RichTextBox.SelectionAlignment, StatusBarPanel.Alignment, TextBox.TextAlign, UpDownBase.TextAlign

HScrollBar

marshal by reference, disposable

System.Windows.Forms (system.windows.forms.dll) class

While most controls provide their own scrollbars—including Form and UserControl objects—sometimes the default behavior of these objects is inadequate. In those cases, you may wish to manage your own scrollbars (the shortened scrollbars at the bottom of an Excel tab-sheet for example).

This class, derived from the base ScrollBar, provides a horizontal bar. See the VScrollBar class for its vertical partner.

```
public class HScrollBar : ScrollBar {
// Public Constructors
   public HScrollBar( );
// Protected Instance Properties
   protected override CreateParams CreateParams{get; }          // overrides ScrollBar
   protected override Size DefaultSize{get; }                   // overrides Control
}
```

Hierarchy System.Object → System.MarshalByRefObject → System.ComponentModel.Component(System.ComponentModel.IComponent, System.IDisposable) → Control(IOleControl, IOleObject, IOleInPlaceObject, IOleInPlaceActiveObject, IOleWindow, IViewObject, IViewObject2, IPersist, IPersistStreamInit, IPersistPropertyBag, IPersistStorage, IQuickActivate, System.ComponentModel.ISynchronizeInvoke, IWin32Window) → ScrollBar → HScrollBar

IButtonControl

System.Windows.Forms (system.windows.forms.dll) interface

This interface is implemented by Control objects such as Button and LinkLabel, which provide button-like behavior.

The framework requires the PerformClick( ) method to provide a way of programmatically clicking the button.

NotifyDefault( ) is called by the framework when the button becomes the default (i.e., when it is set as the active Form object's AcceptButton).

Finally, DialogResult is the property you should implement to maintain the result code that will be set if the button is clicked to terminate a Form that has been shown modally with the ShowDialog( ) method.

```
public interface IButtonControl {
// Public Instance Properties
   public DialogResult DialogResult{set; get; }
// Public Instance Methods
   public void NotifyDefault(bool value);
   public void PerformClick( );
}
```

Implemented By Button, LinkLabel

Returned By Form.{AcceptButton, CancelButton}, PrintPreviewDialog.{AcceptButton, CancelButton}

Passed To Form.{AcceptButton, CancelButton}, PrintPreviewDialog.{AcceptButton, CancelButton}

ICommandExecutor

System.Windows.Forms (system.windows.forms.dll) **interface**

This interface is for internal use only and should not be used from your own code.

```
public interface ICommandExecutor {
// Public Instance Methods
  public void Execute( );
}
```

IComponentEditorPageSite

System.Windows.Forms (system.windows.forms.dll) **interface**

This interface is for internal use only and should not be used from your own code.

```
public interface IComponentEditorPageSite {
// Public Instance Methods
  public Control GetControl( );
  public void SetDirty( );
}
```

Returned By System.Windows.Forms.Design.ComponentEditorPage.PageSite

Passed To System.Windows.Forms.Design.ComponentEditorPage.{PageSite, SetSite( )}

IContainerControl

System.Windows.Forms (system.windows.forms.dll) **interface**

Any derived Control object can be made to contain other controls. In addition to setting the ControlStyles.ContainerControl, you should implement this interface to support the management and activation of child controls.

The current ActiveControl can be set or retrieved, and you should implement ActivateControl( ) to allow the framework to activate a particular child.

```
public interface IContainerControl {
// Public Instance Properties
  public Control ActiveControl{set; get; }
// Public Instance Methods
  public bool ActivateControl(Control active);
}
```

Implemented By ContainerControl

Returned By Control.GetContainerControl( )

IDataGridColumnStyleEditingNotificationService

System.Windows.Forms (system.windows.forms.dll) **interface**

This interface is implemented by the DataGridColumnStyle to manage the start and end of the editing process. The default implementation notifies the containing DataGrid that the column is being edited by calling that object's ColumnStartedEditing( ) method.

```
public interface IDataGridColumnStyleEditingNotificationService {
// Public Instance Methods
   public void ColumnStartedEditing(Control editingControl);
}
```

Implemented By DataGridColumnStyle

IDataGridEditingService

System.Windows.Forms (system.windows.forms.dll) **interface**

This interface is defined for internal purposes and should not be used from your own code.

```
public interface IDataGridEditingService {
// Public Instance Methods
   public bool BeginEdit(DataGridColumnStyle gridColumn, int rowNumber);
   public bool EndEdit(DataGridColumnStyle gridColumn, int rowNumber, bool shouldAbort);
}
```

Implemented By DataGrid, DataGridTableStyle

IDataObject

System.Windows.Forms (system.windows.forms.dll) **interface**

This interface is used by Clipboard and drag-and-drop operations to encapsulate the data that is being moved around. See DataObject for a description of a typical implementation.

You could provide more complex IDataObject implementations than the simple in-memory version offered by DataObject, perhaps using persistent storage for robustness, but DataObject will do fine for most applications.

```
public interface IDataObject {
// Public Instance Methods
   public object GetData(string format);
   public object GetData(string format, bool autoConvert);
   public object GetData(Type format);
   public bool GetDataPresent(string format);
   public bool GetDataPresent(string format, bool autoConvert);
   public bool GetDataPresent(Type format);
   public string[ ] GetFormats( );
   public string[ ] GetFormats(bool autoConvert);
   public void SetData(object data);
   public void SetData(string format, bool autoConvert, object data);
   public void SetData(string format, object data);
   public void SetData(Type format, object data);
}
```

Implemented By DataObject

Returned By Clipboard.GetDataObject( ), DragEventArgs.Data

Passed To DragEventArgs.DragEventArgs( )

IFeatureSupport

System.Windows.Forms (system.windows.forms.dll) **interface**

This interface is implemented by the FeatureSupport and OSFeature classes to allow you to determine whether a specific feature IsPresent( ), and if so which version, using the GetVersionPresent( ) method.

See FeatureSupport for a discussion of these techniques.

```
public interface IFeatureSupport {
// Public Instance Methods
   public Version GetVersionPresent(object feature);
   public bool IsPresent(object feature);
   public bool IsPresent(object feature, Version minimumVersion);
}
```

Implemented By FeatureSupport

IFileReaderService

System.Windows.Forms (system.windows.forms.dll) **interface**

This interface is defined internally by the framework and should not be used in your own code.

```
public interface IFileReaderService {
// Public Instance Methods
   public Stream OpenFileFromSource(string relativePath);
}
```

ImageIndexConverter

System.Windows.Forms (system.windows.forms.dll) **class**

This class is a type converter for image index values. You need a special type converter for these despite the fact that they are just integers, because it needs to be able to support a None value. Typically these are used in Control classes that need to specify the index into an image list for a part of their imagery.

You would not normally need to use this class yourself, as it is to support serialization and design-time scenarios.

```
public class ImageIndexConverter : System.ComponentModel.Int32Converter {
// Public Constructors
   public ImageIndexConverter( );
// Protected Instance Properties
   protected virtual bool IncludeNoneAsStandardValue{get; }
// Public Instance Methods
   public override object ConvertFrom(System.ComponentModel.ITypeDescriptorContext context,
      System.Globalization.CultureInfo culture, object value);     // overrides System.ComponentModel.BaseNumberConverter
   public override object ConvertTo(System.ComponentModel.ITypeDescriptorContext context,
      System.Globalization.CultureInfo culture, object value,
      Type destinationType);                                       // overrides System.ComponentModel.BaseNumberConverter
   public override StandardValuesCollection GetStandardValues(
      System.ComponentModel.ITypeDescriptorContext context);       // overrides System.ComponentModel.TypeConverter
```

```
  public override bool GetStandardValuesExclusive(
    System.ComponentModel.ITypeDescriptorContext context);      // overrides System.ComponentModel.TypeConverter
  public override bool GetStandardValuesSupported(
    System.ComponentModel.ITypeDescriptorContext context);      // overrides System.ComponentModel.TypeConverter
}
```

Hierarchy System.Object → System.ComponentModel.TypeConverter → System.ComponentModel.BaseNumberConverter → System.ComponentModel.Int32Converter → ImageIndexConverter

Subclasses TreeViewImageIndexConverter

ImageList

marshal by reference, disposable

System.Windows.Forms (system.windows.forms.dll) sealed class

This System.ComponentModel.Component wraps a Win32 ImageList control. In theory, this is the best way to manage sets of images for the UI; in practice, there are a few complications, because it tends to reflect the fact that it is a thin wrapper over the Win32 common control, rather than a native part of the .NET Framework.

It offers functions to Draw( ) a specific image from the list onto a System.Drawing.Graphics surface. Unlike the standard GDI+ image classes, support for alpha channel is limited, unless you are using Windows XP and Common Controls v6. You can, however, set a TransparentColor for basic transparency support.

For interop scenarios, you can retrieve the underlying Handle and determine whether the native list has actually been created yet with the HandleCreated property. (The image resources are lazy-allocated the first time they are needed).

The format of the images can be set and retrieved using the ImageSize and ColorDepth properties. The image data itself can be serialized and deserialized using the ImageStream. Typically, you would be deserializing the data from system resources, and this is all handled for you by the design-time environment.

Finally, the actual images in the list can be accessed through the Images property.

The ImageList control is present because several of the Control classes that wrap Win32 objects are a thin veneer over the raw control, and therefore expose the unmanaged image list functionality. If you want to deal with your own sets of images, a managed collection class would probably be the way to go, rather than trying to shoehorn this component into a role for which it is not designed.

```
public sealed class ImageList : System.ComponentModel.Component {
// Public Constructors
  public ImageList( );
  public ImageList(System.ComponentModel.IContainer container);
// Public Instance Properties
  public ColorDepth ColorDepth{set; get; }
  public IntPtr Handle{get; }
  public bool HandleCreated{get; }
  public ImageCollection Images{get; }
  public Size ImageSize{set; get; }
  public ImageListStreamer ImageStream{set; get; }
  public Color TransparentColor{set; get; }
// Public Instance Methods
  public void Draw(System.Drawing.Graphics g, int x, int y, int index);
```

```
 public void Draw(System.Drawing.Graphics g, int x, int y, int width, int height, int index);
 public void Draw(System.Drawing.Graphics g, System.Drawing.Point pt, int index);
 public override string ToString( );                  // overrides System.ComponentModel.Component
// Protected Instance Methods
 protected override void Dispose(bool disposing);     // overrides System.ComponentModel.Component
// Events
 public event EventHandler RecreateHandle;
}
```

Hierarchy System.Object → System.MarshalByRefObject → System.ComponentModel.Component(System.ComponentModel.IComponent, System.IDisposable) → ImageList

Returned By ButtonBase.ImageList, Label.ImageList, ListView.{LargeImageList, SmallImageList, StateImageList}, ListViewItem.ImageList, TabControl.ImageList, ToolBar.ImageList, TreeView.ImageList

Passed To ButtonBase.ImageList, Label.ImageList, ListView.{LargeImageList, SmallImageList, StateImageList}, TabControl.ImageList, ToolBar.ImageList, TreeView.ImageList

ImageList.ImageCollection

System.Windows.Forms (system.windows.forms.dll) sealed class

This collection class represents the set of images in an ImageList control.

```
public sealed class ImageList.ImageCollection : IList, ICollection, IEnumerable {
// Public Instance Properties
 public int Count{get; }                               // implements ICollection
 public bool Empty{get; }
 public bool IsReadOnly{get; }                         // implements IList
 public Image this{set; get; }
// Public Instance Methods
 public int Add(System.Drawing.Image value, System.Drawing.Color transparentColor);
 public void Add(System.Drawing.Icon value);
 public void Add(System.Drawing.Image value);
 public int AddStrip(System.Drawing.Image value);
 public void Clear( );                                 // implements IList
 public bool Contains(System.Drawing.Image image);
 public IEnumerator GetEnumerator( );                  // implements IEnumerable
 public int IndexOf(System.Drawing.Image image);
 public void Remove(System.Drawing.Image image);
 public void RemoveAt(int index);                      // implements IList
}
```

ImageListStreamer serializable

System.Windows.Forms (system.windows.forms.dll) sealed class

This class implements ISerializable and is used to serialize and deserialize ImageList data. Normally, you would be serializing from resources, and this will be handled by the designer for you. If not, this is the type of object you should retrieve from the System.Resources.ResourceManager for ImageList data.

```
public sealed class ImageListStreamer : System.Runtime.Serialization.ISerializable {
// Public Instance Methods
   public void GetObjectData(System.Runtime.Serialization.SerializationInfo si,
      System.Runtime.Serialization.StreamingContext context);          // implements ISerializable
}
```

Returned By ImageList.ImageStream

Passed To ImageList.ImageStream

ImeMode serializable

System.Windows.Forms (system.windows.forms.dll) enum

This enumeration specifies the kind of Input Method Editor to use for a Control. An IME is a utility that allows you to enter characters in complex non-western scripts, such as the far eastern characters.

```
public enum ImeMode {
   NoControl = 0,
   On = 1,
   Off = 2,
   Disable = 3,
   Hiragana = 4,
   Katakana = 5,
   KatakanaHalf = 6,
   AlphaFull = 7,
   Alpha = 8,
   HangulFull = 9,
   Hangul = 10,
   Inherit = -1
}
```

Hierarchy System.Object → System.ValueType → System.Enum(System.IComparable, System.IFormattable, System.IConvertible) → ImeMode

Returned By Multiple types

Passed To ButtonBase.ImeMode, Control.ImeMode, Label.ImeMode, MonthCalendar.ImeMode, PictureBox.ImeMode, PrintPreviewDialog.ImeMode, ProgressBar.ImeMode, ScrollBar.ImeMode, Splitter.ImeMode, StatusBar.ImeMode, ToolBar.ImeMode, TrackBar.ImeMode

IMessageFilter

System.Windows.Forms (system.windows.forms.dll) interface

This interface is implemented by classes that want to filter messages before they are dispatched to your application. You should implement the PreFilterMessage( ) method, to intercept messages, carry out any additional processing you require, and then either pass them on to the rest of the system (by returning false) or cancel the dispatch by returning true.

To install a message filter, you can use the **Application.AddMessageFilter( )** method. Note that the installation of message filters can impede the performance of your application, as it requires a small block of extra code and a method call for every message dispatched.

```
public interface IMessageFilter {
// Public Instance Methods
   public bool PreFilterMessage(ref Message m);
}
```

Implemented By Splitter

Passed To Application.{AddMessageFilter( ), RemoveMessageFilter( )}

InputLanguage

System.Windows.Forms (system.windows.forms.dll) sealed class

This class encapsulates a **Culture** and a keyboard **LayoutName**, which determine how input is handled in the current thread or process.

There are static members, which allow you to retrieve the **CurrentInputLanguage** and the **DefaultInputLanguage**, as well as a list of all the **InstalledInputLanguages** on a system.

You could use this class to provide custom input handling for different environments, perhaps modifying the **Control.RightToLeft** status or changing the IME (see **ImeMode**).

```
public sealed class InputLanguage {
// Public Static Properties
   public static InputLanguage CurrentInputLanguage{set; get; }
   public static InputLanguage DefaultInputLanguage{get; }
   public static InputLanguageCollection InstalledInputLanguages{get; }
// Public Instance Properties
   public CultureInfo Culture{get; }
   public IntPtr Handle{get; }
   public string LayoutName{get; }
// Public Static Methods
   public static InputLanguage FromCulture(System.Globalization.CultureInfo culture);
// Public Instance Methods
   public override bool Equals(object value);                    // overrides object
   public override int GetHashCode( );                           // overrides object
}
```

Returned By Application.CurrentInputLanguage, InputLanguageChangedEventArgs.InputLanguage, InputLanguageChangingEventArgs.InputLanguage, InputLanguageCollection.this

Passed To Application.CurrentInputLanguage, InputLanguageChangedEventArgs. InputLanguageChangedEventArgs( ), InputLanguageChangingEventArgs. InputLanguageChangingEventArgs( ), InputLanguageCollection.{Contains( ), CopyTo( ), IndexOf( )}

InputLanguageChangedEventArgs

System.Windows.Forms (system.windows.forms.dll) class

This encapsulates the event arguments for the Form.InputLanguageChanged event, which is raised when the system regional settings are changed. You can retrieve the CharSet associated with the new input language, the Culture, and the InputLanguage.

```
public class InputLanguageChangedEventArgs : EventArgs {
// Public Constructors
   public InputLanguageChangedEventArgs(System.Globalization.CultureInfo culture, byte charSet);
   public InputLanguageChangedEventArgs(InputLanguage inputLanguage, byte charSet);
// Public Instance Properties
   public byte CharSet{get; }
   public CultureInfo Culture{get; }
   public InputLanguage InputLanguage{get; }
}
```

Hierarchy System.Object → System.EventArgs → InputLanguageChangedEventArgs

Passed To Form.OnInputLanguageChanged( ), InputLanguageChangedEventHandler.{BeginInvoke( ), Invoke( )}

InputLanguageChangedEventHandler

serializable

System.Windows.Forms (system.windows.forms.dll) delegate

This is the delegate for the Form.InputLanguageChanged event.

```
public delegate void InputLanguageChangedEventHandler(object sender, InputLanguageChangedEventArgs e);
```

Associated Events System.Windows.Forms.Design.ComponentEditorForm.InputLanguageChanged( ), Form.InputLanguageChanged( ), PrintPreviewDialog.InputLanguageChanged( ), ThreadExceptionDialog.InputLanguageChanged( )

InputLanguageChangingEventArgs

System.Windows.Forms (system.windows.forms.dll) class

Similar to the InputLanguageChangedEventArgs, this encapsulates the same information but for the InputLanguageChanging event, which is raised before the input language is changed, giving you an opportunity to Cancel it.

```
public class InputLanguageChangingEventArgs : System.ComponentModel.CancelEventArgs {
// Public Constructors
   public InputLanguageChangingEventArgs(System.Globalization.CultureInfo culture, bool sysCharSet);
   public InputLanguageChangingEventArgs(InputLanguage inputLanguage, bool sysCharSet);
// Public Instance Properties
   public CultureInfo Culture{get; }
   public InputLanguage InputLanguage{get; }
   public bool SysCharSet{get; }
}
```

Hierarchy System.Object → System.EventArgs → System.ComponentModel.CancelEventArgs → InputLanguageChangingEventArgs

Passed To Form.OnInputLanguageChanging( ), InputLanguageChangingEventHandler.{BeginInvoke( ), Invoke( )}

InputLanguageChangingEventHandler serializable

System.Windows.Forms (system.windows.forms.dll) delegate

This is the delegate for the Form.InputLanguageChanging event.

```
public delegate void InputLanguageChangingEventHandler(object sender, InputLanguageChangingEventArgs e);
```

Associated Events System.Windows.Forms.Design.ComponentEditorForm.InputLanguageChanging( ), Form.InputLanguageChanging( ), PrintPreviewDialog.InputLanguageChanging( ), ThreadExceptionDialog.InputLanguageChanging( )

InputLanguageCollection

System.Windows.Forms (system.windows.forms.dll) class

This is a read-only collection of InputLanguage objects, obtained from the InputLanguage.InstalledInputLanguages method.

```
public class InputLanguageCollection : ReadOnlyCollectionBase {
// Public Instance Properties
  public InputLanguage this{get; }
// Public Instance Methods
  public bool Contains(InputLanguage value);
  public void CopyTo(InputLanguage[ ] array, int index);
  public int IndexOf(InputLanguage value);
}
```

Hierarchy System.Object → System.Collections.ReadOnlyCollectionBase(System.Collections.ICollection, System.Collections.IEnumerable) → InputLanguageCollection

Returned By InputLanguage.InstalledInputLanguages

InvalidateEventArgs

System.Windows.Forms (system.windows.forms.dll) class

This class encapsulates the InvalidRect of a Control for the Invalidated event, which is raised when an area of the window is dirty and needs repainting.

```
public class InvalidateEventArgs : EventArgs {
// Public Constructors
  public InvalidateEventArgs(System.Drawing.Rectangle invalidRect);
// Public Instance Properties
  public Rectangle InvalidRect{get; }
}
```

Hierarchy System.Object → System.EventArgs → InvalidateEventArgs

Passed To Control.OnInvalidated( ), InvalidateEventHandler.{BeginInvoke( ), Invoke( )}

InvalidateEventHandler

serializable

System.Windows.Forms (system.windows.forms.dll) delegate

This is the delegate for the Control.Invalidated event.

```
public delegate void InvalidateEventHandler(object sender, InvalidateEventArgs e);
```

Associated Events Multiple types

ItemActivation

serializable

System.Windows.Forms (system.windows.forms.dll) enum

This enumeration is used by the ListView control to determine what click behavior it will express: the old-style Standard double-click, the new explorer-style OneClick with link-style highlighting on mouse over, or a TwoClick mode, which couples the link-like highlighting with a double-click.

```
public enum ItemActivation {
  Standard = 0,
  OneClick = 1,
  TwoClick = 2
}
```

Hierarchy System.Object → System.ValueType → System.Enum(System.IComparable, System.IFormattable, System.IConvertible) → ItemActivation

Returned By ListView.Activation

Passed To ListView.Activation

ItemBoundsPortion

serializable

System.Windows.Forms (system.windows.forms.dll) enum

This enumeration specifies the different parts of an item in a ListView and is used in the ListView.GetItemRect( ) and ListViewItem.GetBounds( ) methods.

```
public enum ItemBoundsPortion {
  Entire = 0,
  Icon = 1,
  Label = 2,
  ItemOnly = 3
}
```

Hierarchy System.Object → System.ValueType → System.Enum(System.IComparable, System.IFormattable, System.IConvertible) → ItemBoundsPortion

Passed To ListView.GetItemRect( ), ListViewItem.GetBounds( )

ItemChangedEventArgs

System.Windows.Forms (system.windows.forms.dll) **class**

Encapsulating the data for the CurrencyManager.ItemChanged event, this class allows you to retrieve the Index of the item that changed.

However, it is recommend that you do not handle this event if you are building your own data-aware control. As with the DataGrid, it is recommended that you instead depend on the data source implementing the System.ComponentModel.IBindingList interface and that you bind to the ListChanged event.

```
public class ItemChangedEventArgs : EventArgs {
// Public Instance Properties
   public int Index{get; }
}
```

Hierarchy System.Object → System.EventArgs → ItemChangedEventArgs

Passed To CurrencyManager.OnItemChanged( ), ItemChangedEventHandler.{BeginInvoke( ), Invoke( )}

ItemChangedEventHandler **serializable**

System.Windows.Forms (system.windows.forms.dll) **delegate**

This is the delegate for the CurrencyManager.ItemChanged event.

```
public delegate void ItemChangedEventHandler(object sender, ItemChangedEventArgs e);
```

Associated Events CurrencyManager.ItemChanged( )

ItemCheckEventArgs

System.Windows.Forms (system.windows.forms.dll) **class**

This class is used by the ListView and the CheckedListBox to encapsulate the data for the ItemCheck event, which is raised when one of the items is about to be checked or unchecked.

Note that it occurs before the item is checked. You can retrieve the Index of the item to be changed, and the CurrentValue. You can also get or set the NewValue to which it will be changed, perhaps changing it if the circumstances demand.

```
public class ItemCheckEventArgs : EventArgs {
// Public Constructors
   public ItemCheckEventArgs(int index, CheckState newCheckValue, CheckState currentValue);
// Public Instance Properties
   public CheckState CurrentValue{get; }
   public int Index{get; }
   public CheckState NewValue{set; get; }
}
```

Hierarchy System.Object → System.EventArgs → ItemCheckEventArgs

Passed To CheckedListBox.OnItemCheck( ), ItemCheckEventHandler.{BeginInvoke( ), Invoke( )}, ListView.OnItemCheck( )

ItemCheckEventHandler serializable

System.Windows.Forms (system.windows.forms.dll) delegate

This is the delegate for the ListView and CheckedListBoxItemCheck events.

```
public delegate void ItemCheckEventHandler(object sender, ItemCheckEventArgs e);
```

Associated Events CheckedListBox.ItemCheck( ), ListView.ItemCheck( )

ItemDragEventArgs

System.Windows.Forms (system.windows.forms.dll) class

When the user begins to drag an item from the ListView or TreeView controls, they raise an ItemDrag event. This class encapsulates the Item that is being dragged and the Button that initiated the drag.

```
public class ItemDragEventArgs : EventArgs {
// Public Constructors
   public ItemDragEventArgs(MouseButtons button);
   public ItemDragEventArgs(MouseButtons button, object item);
// Public Instance Properties
   public MouseButtons Button{get; }
   public object Item{get; }
}
```

Hierarchy System.Object → System.EventArgs → ItemDragEventArgs

Passed To ItemDragEventHandler.{BeginInvoke( ), Invoke( )}, ListView.OnItemDrag( ), TreeView.OnItemDrag( )

ItemDragEventHandler serializable

System.Windows.Forms (system.windows.forms.dll) delegate

This is the delegate for the ItemDrag event of the ListView and TreeView controls.

```
public delegate void ItemDragEventHandler(object sender, ItemDragEventArgs e);
```

Associated Events ListView.ItemDrag( ), TreeView.ItemDrag( )

IWin32Window

System.Windows.Forms (system.windows.forms.dll) interface

This interface is implemented by classes that wrap a system window. Most visual classes in the Windows Forms framework ultimately wrap a Win32 window, and this interface is implemented by Control to support that. It provides the Handle property to retrieve the underlying HWND for the window.

Note that not everything that is apparently a window is actually a window. For example, all the components of the Win32 ExplorerBar are actually rendered into a single Win32 window.

```
public interface IWin32Window {
// Public Instance Properties
   public IntPtr Handle{get; }
}
```

Implemented By Control

Returned By System.Windows.Forms.Design.IUIService.GetDialogOwnerWindow( )

Passed To CommonDialog.ShowDialog( ), System.Windows.Forms.Design.ComponentEditorForm.ShowForm( ), System.Windows.Forms.Design.IUIService.ShowComponentEditor( ), System.Windows.Forms.Design.WindowsFormsComponentEditor.EditComponent( ), Form.ShowDialog( ), MessageBox.Show( )

IWindowTarget

System.Windows.Forms (system.windows.forms.dll) interface

This interface is for internal use and should not be called from your own code.

```
public interface IWindowTarget {
// Public Instance Methods
   public void OnHandleChange(IntPtr newHandle);
   public void OnMessage(ref Message m);
}
```

Returned By Control.WindowTarget

Passed To Control.WindowTarget

KeyEventArgs

System.Windows.Forms (system.windows.forms.dll) class

This encapsulates the data for Control.KeyDown and Control.KeyUp events. Unlike the Control.KeyPress event, you can retrieve raw, unprocessed key data for the event.

You can retrieve the state of the modifier keys through the Alt, Control, and Shift properties. The actual KeyCode can be retrieved, which can be directly compared for equality with an entry in the Keys enumeration. The KeyData is similar, but also includes the modifier key status in the upper 4 bits, so you should compare using the & operator. You can also retrieve the KeyValue, which is an integer representation of the KeyData (i.e., the raw value that came from the OS). Finally, you can retrieve the Modifiers only.

If you do not wish to process the event further, you can set the Handled property to true.

```
public class KeyEventArgs : EventArgs {
// Public Constructors
   public KeyEventArgs(Keys keyData);
// Public Instance Properties
   public virtual bool Alt{get; }
   public bool Control{get; }
   public bool Handled{set; get; }
   public Keys KeyCode{get; }
   public Keys KeyData{get; }
```

```
  public int KeyValue{get; }
  public Keys Modifiers{get; }
  public virtual bool Shift{get; }
}
```

Hierarchy System.Object → System.EventArgs → KeyEventArgs

Passed To Control.{OnKeyDown( ), OnKeyUp( ), RaiseKeyEvent( )}, DataGrid.ProcessGridKey( ), KeyEventHandler.{BeginInvoke( ), Invoke( )}, UpDownBase.OnTextBoxKeyDown( )

KeyEventHandler serializable

System.Windows.Forms (system.windows.forms.dll) delegate

This is the delegate for the Control.KeyDown and Control.KeyUp events.

```
public delegate void KeyEventHandler(object sender, KeyEventArgs e);
```

Associated Events Multiple types

KeyPressEventArgs

System.Windows.Forms (system.windows.forms.dll) class

Similar to the KeyEventArgs, this class encapsulates the data for the Control.KeyPress event.

You can simply retrieve the KeyChar corresponding to the key that was pressed. For example, pressing Shift-H would provide H, whereas pressing H would return h (of course, the Caps Lock key would change this).

```
public class KeyPressEventArgs : EventArgs {
// Public Constructors
  public KeyPressEventArgs(char keyChar);
// Public Instance Properties
  public bool Handled{set; get; }
  public char KeyChar{get; }
}
```

Hierarchy System.Object → System.EventArgs → KeyPressEventArgs

Passed To Control.OnKeyPress( ), KeyPressEventHandler.{BeginInvoke( ), Invoke( )}, UpDownBase.OnTextBoxKeyPress( )

KeyPressEventHandler serializable

System.Windows.Forms (system.windows.forms.dll) delegate

This is the delegate for the Control.KeyPress event.

```
public delegate void KeyPressEventHandler(object sender, KeyPressEventArgs e);
```

Associated Events Multiple types

Keys **serializable, flag**

System.Windows.Forms (system.windows.forms.dll) **enum**

This enumeration lists all the raw key values. The enumeration sports the FlagsAttribute, and you can therefore combine the key codes in a bitwise manner to indicate multiple keys pressed simultaneously. In particular, this supports modifier keys such as CTRL, SHIFT, and ALT.

```
public enum Keys {
   None = 0x00000000,
   LButton = 0x00000001,
   RButton = 0x00000002,
   Cancel = 0x00000003,
   MButton = 0x00000004,
   XButton1 = 0x00000005,
   XButton2 = 0x00000006,
   Back = 0x00000008,
   Tab = 0x00000009,
   LineFeed = 0x0000000A,
   Clear = 0x0000000C,
   Return = 0x0000000D,
   Enter = 0x0000000D,
   ShiftKey = 0x00000010,
   ControlKey = 0x00000011,
   Menu = 0x00000012,
   Pause = 0x00000013,
   CapsLock = 0x00000014,
   Capital = 0x00000014,
   KanaMode = 0x00000015,
   HanguelMode = 0x00000015,
   HangulMode = 0x00000015,
   JunjaMode = 0x00000017,
   FinalMode = 0x00000018,
   KanjiMode = 0x00000019,
   HanjaMode = 0x00000019,
   Escape = 0x0000001B,
   IMEConvert = 0x0000001C,
   IMENonconvert = 0x0000001D,
   IMEAceept = 0x0000001E,
   IMEModeChange = 0x0000001F,
   Space = 0x00000020,
   PageUp = 0x00000021,
   Prior = 0x00000021,
   PageDown = 0x00000022,
   Next = 0x00000022,
   End = 0x00000023,
   Home = 0x00000024,
   Left = 0x00000025,
   Up = 0x00000026,
   Right = 0x00000027,
   Down = 0x00000028,
```

```
Select = 0x00000029,
Print = 0x0000002A,
Execute = 0x0000002B,
PrintScreen = 0x0000002C,
Snapshot = 0x0000002C,
Insert = 0x0000002D,
Delete = 0x0000002E,
Help = 0x0000002F,
D0 = 0x00000030,
D1 = 0x00000031,
D2 = 0x00000032,
D3 = 0x00000033,
D4 = 0x00000034,
D5 = 0x00000035,
D6 = 0x00000036,
D7 = 0x00000037,
D8 = 0x00000038,
D9 = 0x00000039,
A = 0x00000041,
B = 0x00000042,
C = 0x00000043,
D = 0x00000044,
E = 0x00000045,
F = 0x00000046,
G = 0x00000047,
H = 0x00000048,
I = 0x00000049,
J = 0x0000004A,
K = 0x0000004B,
L = 0x0000004C,
M = 0x0000004D,
N = 0x0000004E,
O = 0x0000004F,
P = 0x00000050,
Q = 0x00000051,
R = 0x00000052,
S = 0x00000053,
T = 0x00000054,
U = 0x00000055,
V = 0x00000056,
W = 0x00000057,
X = 0x00000058,
Y = 0x00000059,
Z = 0x0000005A,
LWin = 0x0000005B,
RWin = 0x0000005C,
Apps = 0x0000005D,
NumPad0 = 0x00000060,
NumPad1 = 0x00000061,
NumPad2 = 0x00000062,
NumPad3 = 0x00000063,
```

```
NumPad4 = 0x00000064,
NumPad5 = 0x00000065,
NumPad6 = 0x00000066,
NumPad7 = 0x00000067,
NumPad8 = 0x00000068,
NumPad9 = 0x00000069,
Multiply = 0x0000006A,
Add = 0x0000006B,
Separator = 0x0000006C,
Subtract = 0x0000006D,
Decimal = 0x0000006E,
Divide = 0x0000006F,
F1 = 0x00000070,
F2 = 0x00000071,
F3 = 0x00000072,
F4 = 0x00000073,
F5 = 0x00000074,
F6 = 0x00000075,
F7 = 0x00000076,
F8 = 0x00000077,
F9 = 0x00000078,
F10 = 0x00000079,
F11 = 0x0000007A,
F12 = 0x0000007B,
F13 = 0x0000007C,
F14 = 0x0000007D,
F15 = 0x0000007E,
F16 = 0x0000007F,
F17 = 0x00000080,
F18 = 0x00000081,
F19 = 0x00000082,
F20 = 0x00000083,
F21 = 0x00000084,
F22 = 0x00000085,
F23 = 0x00000086,
F24 = 0x00000087,
NumLock = 0x00000090,
Scroll = 0x00000091,
LShiftKey = 0x000000A0,
RShiftKey = 0x000000A1,
LControlKey = 0x000000A2,
RControlKey = 0x000000A3,
LMenu = 0x000000A4,
RMenu = 0x000000A5,
BrowserBack = 0x000000A6,
BrowserForward = 0x000000A7,
BrowserRefresh = 0x000000A8,
BrowserStop = 0x000000A9,
BrowserSearch = 0x000000AA,
BrowserFavorites = 0x000000AB,
BrowserHome = 0x000000AC,
```

```
VolumeMute = 0x000000AD,
VolumeDown = 0x000000AE,
VolumeUp = 0x000000AF,
MediaNextTrack = 0x000000B0,
MediaPreviousTrack = 0x000000B1,
MediaStop = 0x000000B2,
MediaPlayPause = 0x000000B3,
LaunchMail = 0x000000B4,
SelectMedia = 0x000000B5,
LaunchApplication1 = 0x000000B6,
LaunchApplication2 = 0x000000B7,
OemSemicolon = 0x000000BA,
Oemplus = 0x000000BB,
Oemcomma = 0x000000BC,
OemMinus = 0x000000BD,
OemPeriod = 0x000000BE,
OemQuestion = 0x000000BF,
Oemtilde = 0x000000C0,
OemOpenBrackets = 0x000000DB,
OemPipe = 0x000000DC,
OemCloseBrackets = 0x000000DD,
OemQuotes = 0x000000DE,
Oem8 = 0x000000DF,
OemBackslash = 0x000000E2,
ProcessKey = 0x000000E5,
Attn = 0x000000F6,
Crsel = 0x000000F7,
Exsel = 0x000000F8,
EraseEof = 0x000000F9,
Play = 0x000000FA,
Zoom = 0x000000FB,
NoName = 0x000000FC,
Pa1 = 0x000000FD,
OemClear = 0x000000FE,
KeyCode = 0x0000FFFF,
Shift = 0x00010000,
Control = 0x00020000,
Alt = 0x00040000,
Modifiers = 0xFFFF0000
}
```

Hierarchy System.Object → System.ValueType → System.Enum(System.IComparable, System.IFormattable, System.IConvertible) → Keys

Returned By Control.ModifierKeys, KeyEventArgs.{KeyCode, KeyData, Modifiers}

Passed To Control.{IsInputKey( ), ProcessCmdKey( ), ProcessDialogKey( )}, DataGrid.ProcessTabKey( ), KeyEventArgs.KeyEventArgs( )

KeysConverter

System.Windows.Forms (system.windows.forms.dll) class

This System.ComponentModel.TypeConverter object converts between the Keys enumeration and a String. It is used in serialization and design-time scenarios and should not normally be called directly from your code.

```
public class KeysConverter : System.ComponentModel.TypeConverter : IComparer {
// Public Constructors
   public KeysConverter( );
// Public Instance Methods
   public override bool CanConvertFrom(System.ComponentModel.ITypeDescriptorContext context,
      Type sourceType);                                   // overrides System.ComponentModel.TypeConverter
   public int Compare(object a, object b);                // implements System.Collections.IComparer
   public override object ConvertFrom(System.ComponentModel.ITypeDescriptorContext context,
      System.Globalization.CultureInfo culture, object value);   // overrides System.ComponentModel.TypeConverter
   public override object ConvertTo(System.ComponentModel.ITypeDescriptorContext context,
      System.Globalization.CultureInfo culture, object value,
      Type destinationType);                              // overrides System.ComponentModel.TypeConverter
   public override StandardValuesCollection GetStandardValues(
      System.ComponentModel.ITypeDescriptorContext context);   // overrides System.ComponentModel.TypeConverter
   public override bool GetStandardValuesExclusive(
      System.ComponentModel.ITypeDescriptorContext context);   // overrides System.ComponentModel.TypeConverter
   public override bool GetStandardValuesSupported(
      System.ComponentModel.ITypeDescriptorContext context);   // overrides System.ComponentModel.TypeConverter
}
```

Hierarchy System.Object → System.ComponentModel.TypeConverter → KeysConverter(System.Collections.IComparer)

Label **marshal by reference, disposable**

System.Windows.Forms (system.windows.forms.dll) class

This Control provides a simple, non-editable text label.

The control has the ability to AutoSize to the content, although care should be taken to ensure that the layout engine can cope with this neatly. If you set the UseMnemonic property to true, you can use Alt key shortcuts. The control strips out the first &, underlines the subsequent character, and ensures that the focus is set to the next element in the tab order when the Alt key combination is pressed. The label itself cannot receive the focus.

In addition to the Text, you can add an Image or an item from an ImageList (the one at a particular ImageIndex).

Alternatively, you can set the FlatStyle to System, and fall back on the standard OS rendering, perhaps for XP theme support. You lose the image support, however.

```
public class Label : Control {
// Public Constructors
   public Label( );
// Public Instance Properties
   public virtual bool AutoSize{set; get; }
   public override Image BackgroundImage{set; get; }      // overrides Control
   public virtual BorderStyle BorderStyle{set; get; }
```

```
public FlatStyle FlatStyle{set; get; }
public Image Image{set; get; }
public ContentAlignment ImageAlign{set; get; }
public int ImageIndex{set; get; }
public ImageList ImageList{set; get; }
public ImeMode ImeMode{set; get; }                                          // overrides Control
public virtual int PreferredHeight{get; }
public virtual int PreferredWidth{get; }
public bool TabStop{set; get; }                                             // overrides Control
public virtual ContentAlignment TextAlign{set; get; }
public bool UseMnemonic{set; get; }
// Protected Instance Properties
protected override CreateParams CreateParams{get; }                         // overrides Control
protected override ImeMode DefaultImeMode{get; }                            // overrides Control
protected override Size DefaultSize{get; }                                  // overrides Control
protected virtual bool RenderTransparent{set; get; }                        // overrides Control
// Public Instance Methods
public override string ToString( );             // overrides System.ComponentModel.Component
// Protected Instance Methods
protected Rectangle CalcImageRenderBounds(System.Drawing.Image image, System.Drawing.Rectangle r,
   System.Drawing.ContentAlignment align);
protected override AccessibleObject CreateAccessibilityInstance( );         // overrides Control
protected override void Dispose(bool disposing);                            // overrides Control
protected void DrawImage(System.Drawing.Graphics g, System.Drawing.Image image,
   System.Drawing.Rectangle r, System.Drawing.ContentAlignment align);
protected virtual void OnAutoSizeChanged(EventArgs e);
protected override void OnEnabledChanged(EventArgs e);                      // overrides Control
protected override void OnFontChanged(EventArgs e);                         // overrides Control
protected override void OnPaint(PaintEventArgs e);                          // overrides Control
protected override void OnParentChanged(EventArgs e);                       // overrides Control
protected virtual void OnTextAlignChanged(EventArgs e);
protected override void OnTextChanged(EventArgs e);                         // overrides Control
protected override void OnVisibleChanged(EventArgs e);                      // overrides Control
protected override bool ProcessMnemonic(char charCode);                     // overrides Control
protected override void SetBoundsCore(int x, int y, int width, int height, BoundsSpecified specified);   // overrides Control
protected override void WndProc(ref Message m);                             // overrides Control
// Events
public event EventHandler AutoSizeChanged;
public event KeyEventHandler KeyDown;                                       // overrides Control
public event KeyPressEventHandler KeyPress;                                 // overrides Control
public event KeyEventHandler KeyUp;                                         // overrides Control
public event EventHandler TextAlignChanged;
}
```

Hierarchy System.Object → System.MarshalByRefObject → System.ComponentModel.Component(System.ComponentModel.IComponent, System.IDisposable) → Control(IOleControl, IOleObject, IOleInPlaceObject, IOleInPlaceActiveObject, IOleWindow, IViewObject, IViewObject2, IPersist, IPersistStreamInit, IPersistPropertyBag, IPersistStorage, IQuickActivate, System.ComponentModel.ISynchronizeInvoke, IWin32Window) → Label

Subclasses LinkLabel

LabelEditEventArgs

System.Windows.Forms (system.windows.forms.dll) class

The data for the ListView.BeforeLabelEdit and AfterLabelEdit events is encapsulated in this class. BeforeLabelEdit occurs just before the editing begins, and AfterLabelEdit occurs when the user attempts to commit (or abort) an edit. The Item being edited can be retrieved, and the current (or new) Label text can also be obtained. If you wish to abort the operation, you can set the CancelEdit property.

```
public class LabelEditEventArgs : EventArgs {
// Public Constructors
   public LabelEditEventArgs(int item);
   public LabelEditEventArgs(int item, string label);
// Public Instance Properties
   public bool CancelEdit{set; get; }
   public int Item{get; }
   public string Label{get; }
}
```

Hierarchy System.Object → System.EventArgs → LabelEditEventArgs

Passed To LabelEditEventHandler.{BeginInvoke( ), Invoke( )}, ListView.{OnAfterLabelEdit( ), OnBeforeLabelEdit( )}

LabelEditEventHandler serializable

System.Windows.Forms (system.windows.forms.dll) delegate

This is the delegate for the ListView.BeforeLabelEdit and ListView.AfterLabelEdit events.

```
public delegate void LabelEditEventHandler(object sender, LabelEditEventArgs e);
```

Associated Events ListView.{AfterLabelEdit( ), BeforeLabelEdit( )}

LayoutEventArgs

System.Windows.Forms (system.windows.forms.dll) sealed class

This encapsulates the data for the Control.Layout event.

In Win32 applications, you would tend to hook the WM_SIZE event if you were developing a layout manager. However, handling the Control.Resize event is no longer the preferred way of doing this.

The Layout event is raised not just when the window is resized, but also when controls are added, removed, and modified, giving you a single point to hook all the activities that might cause you to reformat the layout of a form. You can also raise a Layout event with the Control.PerformLayout( ) method, which allows you to specify the control that caused the event, and a string indicating the property that changed. These event arguments encapsulate those two pieces of information, although more often than not you will find that they are null when you are dealing with events raised by the framework. The layout event will not be raised if Control.SuspendLayout( ) is called, until the corresponding Control.ResumeLayout( ).

```
public sealed class LayoutEventArgs : EventArgs {
// Public Constructors
  public LayoutEventArgs(Control affectedControl, string affectedProperty);
// Public Instance Properties
  public Control AffectedControl{get; }
  public string AffectedProperty{get; }
}
```

Hierarchy System.Object → System.EventArgs → LayoutEventArgs

Passed To System.Windows.Forms.Design.ComponentTray.OnLayout( ), LayoutEventHandler.{BeginInvoke( ), Invoke( )}

LayoutEventHandler

serializable

System.Windows.Forms (system.windows.forms.dll) delegate

This is the delegate for the Control.Layout event.

```
public delegate void LayoutEventHandler(object sender, LayoutEventArgs e);
```

Associated Events Multiple types

LeftRightAlignment

serializable

System.Windows.Forms (system.windows.forms.dll) enum

This enumeration is used by various controls to align visual components either to the left or the right of the main body of the control (e.g., the DateTimePicker, or the ComboBox). Note that while the values of the enumeration are Left and Right, the RightToLeft status of the control comes into play, so Left would actually appear on the right if RightToLeft is set to Yes.

```
public enum LeftRightAlignment {
  Left = 0,
  Right = 1
}
```

Hierarchy System.Object → System.ValueType → System.Enum(System.IComparable, System.IFormattable, System.IConvertible) → LeftRightAlignment

Returned By Control.RtlTranslateLeftRight( ), DateTimePicker.DropDownAlign, UpDownBase.UpDownAlign

Passed To Control.{RtlTranslateAlignment( ), RtlTranslateLeftRight( )}, DateTimePicker.DropDownAlign, UpDownBase.UpDownAlign

LinkArea

serializable

System.Windows.Forms (system.windows.forms.dll) struct

A LinkLabel class by default contains only one hyperlink attached to the entire text in the control. However, it is actually capable of supporting several links within the text.

A LinkArea value defines the index into the text string at which the hyperlink will Start, and the Length of the link. You can also determine whether the link is Empty.

If you only want one link, but one that does not encompass the entire text, you can assign to the LinkLabel.LinkArea. To add multiple areas, you need to use the LinkLabel.Links property.

```
public struct LinkArea {
// Public Constructors
   public LinkArea(int start, int length);
// Public Instance Properties
   public bool IsEmpty{get; }
   public int Length{set; get; }
   public int Start{set; get; }
// Public Instance Methods
   public override bool Equals(object o);                          // overrides ValueType
   public override int GetHashCode( );                             // overrides ValueType
}
```

Hierarchy System.Object → System.ValueType → LinkArea

Returned By LinkLabel.LinkArea

Passed To LinkLabel.LinkArea

LinkArea.LinkAreaConverter

System.Windows.Forms (system.windows.forms.dll) class

This System.ComponentModel.TypeConverter is used to convert a LinkArea to and from other types in serialization and design-time scenarios. You should not use it from your own code.

```
public class LinkArea.LinkAreaConverter : System.ComponentModel.TypeConverter {
// Public Constructors
   public LinkArea.LinkAreaConverter( );
// Public Instance Methods
   public override bool CanConvertFrom(System.ComponentModel.ITypeDescriptorContext context,
      Type sourceType);                         // overrides System.ComponentModel.TypeConverter
   public override bool CanConvertTo(System.ComponentModel.ITypeDescriptorContext context,
      Type destinationType);                    // overrides System.ComponentModel.TypeConverter
   public override object ConvertFrom(System.ComponentModel.ITypeDescriptorContext context,
      System.Globalization.CultureInfo culture, object value); // overrides System.ComponentModel.TypeConverter
   public override object ConvertTo(System.ComponentModel.ITypeDescriptorContext context,
      System.Globalization.CultureInfo culture, object value,
      Type destinationType);                    // overrides System.ComponentModel.TypeConverter
   public override object CreateInstance(System.ComponentModel.ITypeDescriptorContext context,
      System.Collections.IDictionary propertyValues); // overrides System.ComponentModel.TypeConverter
   public override bool GetCreateInstanceSupported(
      System.ComponentModel.ITypeDescriptorContext context); // overrides System.ComponentModel.TypeConverter
   public override PropertyDescriptorCollection GetProperties(System.ComponentModel.ITypeDescriptorContext context,
      object value, Attribute[ ] attributes);   // overrides System.ComponentModel.TypeConverter
   public override bool GetPropertiesSupported(
      System.ComponentModel.ITypeDescriptorContext context); // overrides System.ComponentModel.TypeConverter
}
```

Hierarchy System.Object → System.ComponentModel.TypeConverter → LinkAreaConverter

LinkBehavior serializable

System.Windows.Forms (system.windows.forms.dll) enum

As with the ListView control, a LinkLabel can display its hyperlinks in a variety of ways. This enumeration defines those modes. You can set a LinkLabel object's link display mode using the LinkLabel.LinkBehavior property.

```
public enum LinkBehavior {
  SystemDefault = 0,
  AlwaysUnderline = 1,
  HoverUnderline = 2,
  NeverUnderline = 3
}
```

Hierarchy System.Object → System.ValueType → System.Enum(System.IComparable, System.IFormattable, System.IConvertible) → LinkBehavior

Returned By LinkLabel.LinkBehavior

Passed To LinkLabel.LinkBehavior

LinkClickedEventArgs

System.Windows.Forms (system.windows.forms.dll) class

This class encapsulates the event arguments for the RichTextBox.LinkClicked event. It allows you to retrieve the LinkText for the particular link that was clicked. See LinkLabelLinkClickedEventArgs for the equivalent for the LinkLabel.

```
public class LinkClickedEventArgs : EventArgs {
// Public Constructors
  public LinkClickedEventArgs(string linkText);
// Public Instance Properties
  public string LinkText{get; }
}
```

Hierarchy System.Object → System.EventArgs → LinkClickedEventArgs

Passed To LinkClickedEventHandler.{BeginInvoke( ), Invoke( )}, RichTextBox.OnLinkClicked( )

LinkClickedEventHandler serializable

System.Windows.Forms (system.windows.forms.dll) delegate

This is the delegate for the LinkLabel.LinkClicked and RichTextBox.LinkClicked events.

```
public delegate void LinkClickedEventHandler(object sender, LinkClickedEventArgs e);
```

Associated Events RichTextBox.LinkClicked( )

LinkLabel

marshal by reference, disposable

System.Windows.Forms (system.windows.forms.dll) class

This Control, derived from Label, adds the ability to insert one or more hyperlinks in the control Text.

By default, the whole text is assigned to a single link. To specify a range of text that constitutes the link (instead of the entire text), you can assign a LinkArea value to the LinkArea property. You can determine whether the link has been clicked through the LinkVisited property.

If you wish to create several links within the text, you can add items to the Links collection. You need to Clear( ) the collection first to get rid of the default link, then create new Link instances to Add( ) to the collection.

See Link for more information on the class.

```
public class LinkLabel : Label : IButtonControl {
// Public Constructors
   public LinkLabel( );
// Public Instance Properties
   public Color ActiveLinkColor{set; get; }
   public Color DisabledLinkColor{set; get; }
   public LinkArea LinkArea{set; get; }
   public LinkBehavior LinkBehavior{set; get; }
   public Color LinkColor{set; get; }
   public LinkCollection Links{get; }
   public bool LinkVisited{set; get; }
   public override string Text{set; get; }                                    // overrides Control
   public Color VisitedLinkColor{set; get; }
// Protected Instance Properties
   protected Cursor OverrideCursor{set; get; }
// Protected Instance Methods
   protected override AccessibleObject CreateAccessibilityInstance( );          // overrides Label
   protected override void CreateHandle( );                                   // overrides Control
   protected override void OnEnabledChanged(EventArgs e);                     // overrides Label
   protected override void OnFontChanged(EventArgs e);                        // overrides Label
   protected override void OnGotFocus(EventArgs e);                           // overrides Control
   protected override void OnKeyDown(KeyEventArgs e);                         // overrides Control
   protected virtual void OnLinkClicked(LinkLabelLinkClickedEventArgs e);
   protected override void OnLostFocus(EventArgs e);                          // overrides Control
   protected override void OnMouseDown(MouseEventArgs e);                     // overrides Control
   protected override void OnMouseLeave(EventArgs e);                         // overrides Control
   protected override void OnMouseMove(MouseEventArgs e);                     // overrides Control
   protected override void OnMouseUp(MouseEventArgs e);                       // overrides Control
   protected override void OnPaint(PaintEventArgs e);                         // overrides Label
   protected override void OnPaintBackground(PaintEventArgs e);               // overrides Control
   protected override void OnTextAlignChanged(EventArgs e);                   // overrides Label
   protected override void OnTextChanged(EventArgs e);                        // overrides Label
   protected Link PointInLink(int x, int y);
   protected override bool ProcessDialogKey(Keys keyData);                    // overrides Control
   protected override void Select(bool directed, bool forward);               // overrides Control
   protected override void SetBoundsCore(int x, int y, int width, int height, BoundsSpecified specified);   // overrides Label
```

```
protected override void WndProc(ref Message msg);                       // overrides Label
// Events
public event LinkLabelLinkClickedEventHandler LinkClicked;
}
```

Hierarchy System.Object → System.MarshalByRefObject → System.ComponentModel.Component(System.ComponentModel.IComponent, System.IDisposable) → Control(IOleControl, IOleObject, IOleInPlaceObject, IOleInPlaceActiveObject, IOleWindow, IViewObject, IViewObject2, IPersist, IPersistStreamInit, IPersistPropertyBag, IPersistStorage, IQuickActivate, System.ComponentModel.ISynchronizeInvoke, IWin32Window) → Label → LinkLabel(IButtonControl)

Passed To LinkCollection.LinkCollection( )

LinkLabel.Link

System.Windows.Forms (system.windows.forms.dll) class

This class encapsulates a section of link text within a LinkLabel control.

It allows you to set the Start and Length of the link, whether it is Enabled or has been Visited, and also the LinkData—an arbitrary object you can associate with the link.

```
public class LinkLabel.Link {
// Public Instance Properties
public bool Enabled{set; get; }
public int Length{set; get; }
public object LinkData{set; get; }
public int Start{set; get; }
public bool Visited{set; get; }
}
```

LinkLabel.LinkCollection

System.Windows.Forms (system.windows.forms.dll) class

This collection class is used to contain the set of LinkLabel.Link objects in a LinkLabel.

```
public class LinkLabel.LinkCollection : IList, ICollection, IEnumerable {
// Public Constructors
public LinkLabel.LinkCollection(LinkLabel owner);
// Public Instance Properties
public int Count{get; }                                                 // implements ICollection
public bool IsReadOnly{get; }                                           // implements IList
public virtual Link this{set; get; }
// Public Instance Methods
public Link Add(int start, int length);
public Link Add(int start, int length, object linkData);
public virtual void Clear( );                                           // implements IList
public bool Contains(Link link);
public IEnumerator GetEnumerator( );                                    // implements IEnumerable
public int IndexOf(Link link);
public void Remove(Link value);
public void RemoveAt(int index);                                        // implements IList
}
```

LinkLabelLinkClickedEventArgs

System.Windows.Forms (system.windows.forms.dll) class

This class encapsulates the event data for the LinkLabel.LinkClicked event. You can retrieve the LinkLabel.Link that has been clicked.

```
public class LinkLabelLinkClickedEventArgs : EventArgs {
// Public Constructors
   public LinkLabelLinkClickedEventArgs(Link link);
// Public Instance Properties
   public Link Link{get; }
}
```

Hierarchy System.Object → System.EventArgs → LinkLabelLinkClickedEventArgs

Passed To LinkLabel.OnLinkClicked( ), LinkLabelLinkClickedEventHandler.{BeginInvoke( ), Invoke( )}

LinkLabelLinkClickedEventHandler serializable

System.Windows.Forms (system.windows.forms.dll) delegate

This is the delegate for the LinkLabel.LinkClicked event.

```
public delegate void LinkLabelLinkClickedEventHandler(object sender, LinkLabelLinkClickedEventArgs e);
```

Associated Events LinkLabel.LinkClicked( )

LinkState serializable

System.Windows.Forms (system.windows.forms.dll) enum

This enumeration is for internal purposes only and should not be called from your own code.

```
public enum LinkState {
   Normal = 0,
   Hover = 1,
   Active = 2,
   Visited = 4
}
```

Hierarchy System.Object → System.ValueType → System.Enum(System.IComparable, System.IFormattable, System.IConvertible) → LinkState

ListBindingConverter

System.Windows.Forms (system.windows.forms.dll) class

This class is a System.ComponentModel.TypeConverter for Binding objects. This is used to support designer and serialization scenarios, and you should not normally create an instance yourself. It is capable of conversion to an System.ComponentModel.Design.Serialization.InstanceDescriptor for serialization.

```
public class ListBindingConverter : System.ComponentModel.TypeConverter {
// Public Constructors
```

```
  public ListBindingConverter( );
// Public Instance Methods
  public override bool CanConvertTo(System.ComponentModel.ITypeDescriptorContext context,
     Type destinationType);                    // overrides System.ComponentModel.TypeConverter
  public override object ConvertTo(System.ComponentModel.ITypeDescriptorContext context,
     System.Globalization.CultureInfo culture, object value,
     Type destinationType);                    // overrides System.ComponentModel.TypeConverter
  public override object CreateInstance(System.ComponentModel.ITypeDescriptorContext context,
     System.Collections.IDictionary propertyValues);   // overrides System.ComponentModel.TypeConverter
  public override bool GetCreateInstanceSupported(
     System.ComponentModel.ITypeDescriptorContext context);   // overrides System.ComponentModel.TypeConverter
}
```

Hierarchy System.Object → System.ComponentModel.TypeConverter → ListBindingConverter

ListBox **marshal by reference, disposable**

System.Windows.Forms (system.windows.forms.dll) class

This Control wraps the Win32 listbox common control, allowing you to display and select one or more items from a list. It derives from the ListControl abstract base class, in common with the ComboBox.

You can add or remove objects in the list by using the Items collection. This could simply be a list of strings, but could equally be any object that can be converted to a string (which, in practice, means pretty much anything through the ToString( ) member).

Alternatively, you can use data binding to bind to a data source. You can independently set a DisplayMember and a ValueMember.

In either case, the selected item can be retrieved through the Text property (which returns the DisplayMember) and SelectedValue (which returns the ValueMember), or you can retrieve its index with the SelectedIndex property.

The SelectionMode allows you to specify the various kinds of single- and multiple-selection modes available. If multiple selection is enabled, you can use the SelectedIndices and SelectedItems collections to enumerate the entire selection. You can select or deselect individual items using the SetSelected( ) method.

If you need to locate a particular item in the list, you can use the FindString( ) and FindStringExact( ) methods. FindString( ) identifies the first item in the list that starts with the string specified, and is therefore extremely useful for those match-as-you-type controls.

If the items added to the control are wider than the control itself, you can enable a HorizontalScrollbar. The HorizontalExtent property is then used to ensure that the scrollbar width is set to the maximum width of an item for the scrollbar to determine the appropriate range across which to scroll.

You can also specify the ItemHeight in owner draw scenarios. (See DrawItemEventArgs for more information on owner draw).

```
public class ListBox : ListControl {
// Public Constructors
  public ListBox( );
// Public Static Fields
  public const int DefaultItemHeight;                              // =13
  public const int NoMatches;                                      // =-1
```

```
// Public Instance Properties
   public override Color BackColor{set; get; }                                   // overrides Control
   public override Image BackgroundImage{set; get; }                             // overrides Control
   public BorderStyle BorderStyle{set; get; }
   public int ColumnWidth{set; get; }
   public virtual DrawMode DrawMode{set; get; }
   public override Color ForeColor{set; get; }                                   // overrides Control
   public int HorizontalExtent{set; get; }
   public bool HorizontalScrollbar{set; get; }
   public bool IntegralHeight{set; get; }
   public virtual int ItemHeight{set; get; }
   public ObjectCollection Items{get; }
   public bool MultiColumn{set; get; }
   public int PreferredHeight{get; }
   public override RightToLeft RightToLeft{set; get; }                           // overrides Control
   public bool ScrollAlwaysVisible{set; get; }
   public override int SelectedIndex{set; get; }                                 // overrides ListControl
   public SelectedIndexCollection SelectedIndices{get; }
   public object SelectedItem{set; get; }
   public SelectedObjectCollection SelectedItems{get; }
   public virtual SelectionMode SelectionMode{set; get; }
   public bool Sorted{set; get; }
   public override string Text{set; get; }                                       // overrides Control
   public int TopIndex{set; get; }
   public bool UseTabStops{set; get; }
// Protected Instance Properties
   protected override CreateParams CreateParams{get; }                           // overrides Control
   protected override Size DefaultSize{get; }                                    // overrides Control
// Public Instance Methods
   public void BeginUpdate( );
   public void ClearSelected( );
   public void EndUpdate( );
   public int FindString(string s);
   public int FindString(string s, int startIndex);
   public int FindStringExact(string s);
   public int FindStringExact(string s, int startIndex);
   public int GetItemHeight(int index);
   public Rectangle GetItemRectangle(int index);
   public bool GetSelected(int index);
   public int IndexFromPoint(int x, int y);
   public int IndexFromPoint(System.Drawing.Point p);
   public void SetSelected(int index, bool value);
   public override string ToString( );                // overrides System.ComponentModel.Component
// Protected Instance Methods
   protected virtual void AddItemsCore(object[ ] value);
   protected virtual ObjectCollection CreateItemCollection( );
   protected override void OnChangeUICues(UICuesEventArgs e);                   // overrides Control
   protected override void OnDataSourceChanged(EventArgs e);                    // overrides ListControl
   protected override void OnDisplayMemberChanged(EventArgs e);                 // overrides ListControl
   protected virtual void OnDrawItem(DrawItemEventArgs e);
   protected override void OnFontChanged(EventArgs e);                          // overrides Control
```

```
  protected override void OnHandleCreated(EventArgs e);                          // overrides Control
  protected override void OnHandleDestroyed(EventArgs e);                        // overrides Control
  protected virtual void OnMeasureItem(MeasureItemEventArgs e);
  protected override void OnParentChanged(EventArgs e);                          // overrides Control
  protected override void OnResize(EventArgs e);                                 // overrides Control
  protected override void OnSelectedIndexChanged(EventArgs e);                   // overrides ListControl
  protected override void RefreshItem(int index);                                // overrides ListControl
  protected override void SetBoundsCore(int x, int y, int width, int height, BoundsSpecified specified);   // overrides Control
  protected override void SetItemCore(int index, object value);                  // overrides ListControl
  protected override void SetItemsCore(System.Collections.IList value);          // overrides ListControl
  protected virtual void Sort( );
  protected virtual void WmReflectCommand(ref Message m);
  protected override void WndProc(ref Message m);                                // overrides Control
// Events
  public event EventHandler Click;                                               // overrides Control
  public event DrawItemEventHandler DrawItem;
  public event MeasureItemEventHandler MeasureItem;
  public event PaintEventHandler Paint;                                          // overrides Control
  public event EventHandler SelectedIndexChanged;
}
```

Hierarchy System.Object → System.MarshalByRefObject → System.ComponentModel.Component(System.ComponentModel.IComponent, System.IDisposable) → Control(IOleControl, IOleObject, IOleInPlaceObject, IOleInPlaceActiveObject, IOleWindow, IViewObject, IViewObject2, IPersist, IPersistStreamInit, IPersistPropertyBag, IPersistStorage, IQuickActivate, System.ComponentModel.ISynchronizeInvoke, IWin32Window) → ListControl → ListBox

Subclasses CheckedListBox

Passed To ObjectCollection.ObjectCollection( ), SelectedIndexCollection.SelectedIndexCollection( ), SelectedObjectCollection.SelectedObjectCollection( )

ListBox.ObjectCollection

System.Windows.Forms (system.windows.forms.dll) class

This collection class represents the set of items in a ListBox.

```
public class ListBox.ObjectCollection : IList, ICollection, IEnumerable {
// Public Constructors
  public ListBox.ObjectCollection(ListBox owner);
  public ListBox.ObjectCollection(ListBox owner, object[ ] value);
  public ListBox.ObjectCollection(ListBox owner, ObjectCollection value);
// Public Instance Properties
  public int Count{get; }                                                        // implements ICollection
  public bool IsReadOnly{get; }                                                  // implements IList
  public virtual object this{set; get; }                                         // implements IList
// Public Instance Methods
  public int Add(object item);                                                   // implements IList
  public void AddRange(object[ ] items);
  public void AddRange(ObjectCollection value);
```

```
public virtual void Clear( );                                          // implements IList
public bool Contains(object value);                                    // implements IList
public void CopyTo(object[ ] dest, int arrayIndex);
public IEnumerator GetEnumerator( );                                   // implements IEnumerable
public int IndexOf(object value);                                      // implements IList
public void Insert(int index, object item);                            // implements IList
public void Remove(object value);                                      // implements IList
public void RemoveAt(int index);                                       // implements IList
}
```

ListBox.SelectedIndexCollection

System.Windows.Forms (system.windows.forms.dll) class

This collection class represents the set of selected indexes in a ListBox.

```
public class ListBox.SelectedIndexCollection : IList, ICollection, IEnumerable {
// Public Constructors
   public ListBox.SelectedIndexCollection(ListBox owner);
// Public Instance Properties
   public int Count{get; }                                             // implements ICollection
   public bool IsReadOnly{get; }                                       // implements IList
   public int this{get; }
// Public Instance Methods
   public bool Contains(int selectedIndex);
   public void CopyTo(Array dest, int index);                          // implements ICollection
   public IEnumerator GetEnumerator( );                                // implements IEnumerable
   public int IndexOf(int selectedIndex);
}
```

ListBox.SelectedObjectCollection

System.Windows.Forms (system.windows.forms.dll) class

This collection class represents the set of selected objects in a ListBox.

```
public class ListBox.SelectedObjectCollection : IList, ICollection, IEnumerable {
// Public Constructors
   public ListBox.SelectedObjectCollection(ListBox owner);
// Public Instance Properties
   public int Count{get; }                                             // implements ICollection
   public bool IsReadOnly{get; }                                       // implements IList
   public object this{set; get; }                                      // implements IList
// Public Instance Methods
   public bool Contains(object selectedObject);                        // implements IList
   public void CopyTo(Array dest, int index);                          // implements ICollection
   public IEnumerator GetEnumerator( );                                // implements IEnumerable
   public int IndexOf(object selectedObject);                          // implements IList
}
```

ListControl

marshal by reference, disposable

System.Windows.Forms (system.windows.forms.dll) — abstract class

This is the abstract base class for list-like Control objects, such as the ListBox, ComboBox, and derived classes.

It provides the basic template for data binding through the DataSource, DisplayMember, and ValueMember properties. Simple selection is accomplished with the SelectedIndex and SelectedValue members.

The concrete derived classes will extend these basic features to offer more specific functionality.

```
public abstract class ListControl : Control {
// Protected Constructors
   protected ListControl( );
// Public Instance Properties
   public object DataSource{set; get; }
   public string DisplayMember{set; get; }
   public abstract int SelectedIndex{set; get; }
   public object SelectedValue{set; get; }
   public string ValueMember{set; get; }
// Protected Instance Properties
   protected CurrencyManager DataManager{get; }
// Public Instance Methods
   public string GetItemText(object item);
// Protected Instance Methods
   protected object FilterItemOnProperty(object item);
   protected object FilterItemOnProperty(object item, string field);
   protected override bool IsInputKey(Keys keyData);                 // overrides Control
   protected override void OnBindingContextChanged(EventArgs e);     // overrides Control
   protected virtual void OnDataSourceChanged(EventArgs e);
   protected virtual void OnDisplayMemberChanged(EventArgs e);
   protected virtual void OnSelectedIndexChanged(EventArgs e);
   protected virtual void OnSelectedValueChanged(EventArgs e);
   protected virtual void OnValueMemberChanged(EventArgs e);
   protected abstract void RefreshItem(int index);
   protected virtual void SetItemCore(int index, object value);
   protected abstract void SetItemsCore(System.Collections.IList items);
// Events
   public event EventHandler DataSourceChanged;
   public event EventHandler DisplayMemberChanged;
   public event EventHandler SelectedValueChanged;
   public event EventHandler ValueMemberChanged;
}
```

Hierarchy System.Object → System.MarshalByRefObject → System.ComponentModel.Component(System.ComponentModel.IComponent, System.IDisposable) → Control(IOleControl, IOleObject, IOleInPlaceObject, IOleInPlaceActiveObject, IOleWindow, IViewObject, IViewObject2, IPersist, IPersistStreamInit, IPersistPropertyBag, IPersistStorage, IQuickActivate, System.ComponentModel.ISynchronizeInvoke, IWin32Window) → ListControl

Subclasses ComboBox, ListBox

ListView marshal by reference, disposable

System.Windows.Forms (system.windows.forms.dll) class

This control wraps the ubiquitous and multifunctional Win32 ListView common control. You will be very familiar with this from the Windows Explorer icon, list, and details views.

To choose the general appearance of the control, you can use the View property, switching between two icon views (View.LargeIcon and View.SmallIcon), the basic View.List and the View.Details report format.

To control what is actually displayed in the list, you can add or remove ListViewItem objects from the Items list. See the ListViewItem class for more information about this.

In all views, you can choose the item Activation style (see ItemActivation for more details).

You can also determine whether CheckBoxes appear next to the items. To find out which items are checked, you can refer to the CheckedIndices or CheckedItems properties. Similarly, the selected items can be retrieved through the SelectedIndices and SelectedItems properties. The item that currently has the focus can be obtained through the FocusedItem property. You can enable or disable multiple selection with the MultiSelect property.

Items can be selected automatically just by hovering over them. The HoverSelection property controls this.

By default, the selection will not be rendered (but still maintained) when the control loses the focus. You can set HideSelection to false if you want the selection to be visible all the time.

Items can be sorted in the list by calling the Sort() method. To specify how the items should be sorted (a lexicographical compare of the labels is the default), you can set a ListViewItemSorter, which is a class derived from the System.Collections.IComparer interface. You can also choose the SortOrder with the Sorting property. The default is None, but you can choose Ascending or Descending.

It is possible to allow the user to edit the label text on items by setting the LabelEdit property. You can handle the BeforeLabelEdit and AfterLabelEdit events to if you want special handling such as validation (see LabelEditEventArgs for more information). Unfortunately, this only allows you to edit the primary label of the item, not any subitem text (such as you would display in a details view). You should consider the DataGrid if you want this more complex behavior.

There are two methods related to the item bounds. You can call GetItemAt() to determine which item is to be found at a particular pixel location. GetItemRect() will return you the bounding rectangle of an item. You can refine this to a particular part of the imagery of an item (see ItemBoundsPortion).

Several features apply only to the icon views. You can set the Alignment of the icons within the container and AutoArrange them. To see how this works, play with the Explorer view "Arrange Icons By..." menu. To programmatically force a rearrangement, you can call ArrangeIcons(). You can also choose whether the LabelWrap feature is enabled, automatically wrapping the icon label text rather than cropping it.

To support the details view, there are a number of additional members. You can Add() (or Remove()) ColumnHeader items to the collection of Columns that will be displayed in the report. The first ColumnHeader corresponds to the root ListViewItem objects in the Items collection. Each subsequent column requires another ListViewItem.ListViewSubItem to be added to each item object's ListViewItem.SubItems collection to build the full row.

The columns can be either fixed in place, or you can AllowColumnReorder, which permits them to be dragged around by the user. You can also change the column HeaderStyle. While the default is ColumnHeaderStyle.Clickable (to support Sorting behavior), you can choose Nonclickable or None, to hide the header altogether.

When you select an item, normally you are only permitted to click on imagery representing the parent item (i.e., the first column in the collection). This can sometimes be awkward, so you can enable FullRowSelect to give users a larger target to stab at with the mouse.

You can also show GridLines between the rows and columns. As with all the common controls wrappers, ListView only supports pre-Windows XP features, so you have to derive your own Control to take advantage of XP supported views such as groups.

```
public class ListView : Control {
// Public Constructors
   public ListView( );
// Public Instance Properties
   public ItemActivation Activation{set; get; }
   public ListViewAlignment Alignment{set; get; }
   public bool AllowColumnReorder{set; get; }
   public bool AutoArrange{set; get; }
   public override Color BackColor{set; get; }                    // overrides Control
   public override Image BackgroundImage{set; get; }              // overrides Control
   public BorderStyle BorderStyle{set; get; }
   public bool CheckBoxes{set; get; }
   public CheckedIndexCollection CheckedIndices{get; }
   public CheckedListViewItemCollection CheckedItems{get; }
   public ColumnHeaderCollection Columns{get; }
   public ListViewItem FocusedItem{get; }
   public override Color ForeColor{set; get; }                    // overrides Control
   public bool FullRowSelect{set; get; }
   public bool GridLines{set; get; }
   public ColumnHeaderStyle HeaderStyle{set; get; }
   public bool HideSelection{set; get; }
   public bool HoverSelection{set; get; }
   public ListViewItemCollection Items{get; }
   public bool LabelEdit{set; get; }
   public bool LabelWrap{set; get; }
   public ImageList LargeImageList{set; get; }
   public IComparer ListViewItemSorter{set; get; }
   public bool MultiSelect{set; get; }
   public bool Scrollable{set; get; }
   public SelectedIndexCollection SelectedIndices{get; }
   public SelectedListViewItemCollection SelectedItems{get; }
   public ImageList SmallImageList{set; get; }
   public SortOrder Sorting{set; get; }
   public ImageList StateImageList{set; get; }
   public override string Text{set; get; }                        // overrides Control
   public ListViewItem TopItem{get; }
   public View View{set; get; }
```

```
// Protected Instance Properties
   protected override CreateParams CreateParams{get; }                    // overrides Control
   protected override Size DefaultSize{get; }                             // overrides Control
// Public Instance Methods
   public void ArrangeIcons( );
   public void ArrangeIcons(ListViewAlignment value);
   public void BeginUpdate( );
   public void Clear( );
   public void EndUpdate( );
   public void EnsureVisible(int index);
   public ListViewItem GetItemAt(int x, int y);
   public Rectangle GetItemRect(int index);
   public Rectangle GetItemRect(int index, ItemBoundsPortion portion);
   public void Sort( );
   public override string ToString( );           // overrides System.ComponentModel.Component
// Protected Instance Methods
   protected override void CreateHandle( );                               // overrides Control
   protected override void Dispose(bool disposing);                       // overrides Control
   protected override bool IsInputKey(Keys keyData);                      // overrides Control
   protected virtual void OnAfterLabelEdit(LabelEditEventArgs e);
   protected virtual void OnBeforeLabelEdit(LabelEditEventArgs e);
   protected virtual void OnColumnClick(ColumnClickEventArgs e);
   protected override void OnEnabledChanged(EventArgs e);                 // overrides Control
   protected override void OnFontChanged(EventArgs e);                    // overrides Control
   protected override void OnHandleCreated(EventArgs e);                  // overrides Control
   protected override void OnHandleDestroyed(EventArgs e);                // overrides Control
   protected virtual void OnItemActivate(EventArgs e);
   protected virtual void OnItemCheck(ItemCheckEventArgs ice);
   protected virtual void OnItemDrag(ItemDragEventArgs e);
   protected virtual void OnSelectedIndexChanged(EventArgs e);
   protected override void OnSystemColorsChanged(EventArgs e);            // overrides Control
   protected void RealizeProperties( );
   protected void UpdateExtendedStyles( );
   protected override void WndProc(ref Message m);                        // overrides Control
// Events
   public event LabelEditEventHandler AfterLabelEdit;
   public event LabelEditEventHandler BeforeLabelEdit;
   public event ColumnClickEventHandler ColumnClick;
   public event EventHandler ItemActivate;
   public event ItemCheckEventHandler ItemCheck;
   public event ItemDragEventHandler ItemDrag;
   public event PaintEventHandler Paint;                                  // overrides Control
   public event EventHandler SelectedIndexChanged;
}
```

Hierarchy

System.Object → System.MarshalByRefObject → System.ComponentModel.Component(System.ComponentModel.IComponent, System.IDisposable) → Control(IOleControl, IOleObject, IOleInPlaceObject, IOleInPlaceActiveObject, IOleWindow, IViewObject, IViewObject2, IPersist, IPersistStreamInit, IPersistPropertyBag, IPersistStorage, IQuickActivate, System.ComponentModel.ISynchronizeInvoke, IWin32Window) → ListView

Returned By ColumnHeader.ListView, ListViewItem.ListView

Passed To CheckedIndexCollection.CheckedIndexCollection( ), CheckedListViewItemCollection.CheckedListViewItemCollection( ), ColumnHeaderCollection.ColumnHeaderCollection( ), ListViewItemCollection.ListViewItemCollection( ), SelectedIndexCollection.SelectedIndexCollection( ), SelectedListViewItemCollection.SelectedListViewItemCollection( )

ListView.CheckedIndexCollection

System.Windows.Forms (system.windows.forms.dll) class

This collection class represents the set of indexes of the checked items in the ListView.

```
public class ListView.CheckedIndexCollection : IList, ICollection, IEnumerable {
// Public Constructors
   public ListView.CheckedIndexCollection(ListView owner);
// Public Instance Properties
   public int Count{get; }                                  // implements ICollection
   public bool IsReadOnly{get; }                            // implements IList
   public int this{get; }
// Public Instance Methods
   public bool Contains(int checkedIndex);
   public IEnumerator GetEnumerator( );                     // implements IEnumerable
   public int IndexOf(int checkedIndex);
}
```

ListView.CheckedListViewItemCollection

System.Windows.Forms (system.windows.forms.dll) class

This collection represents the set of selected items in the ListView.

```
public class ListView.CheckedListViewItemCollection : IList, ICollection, IEnumerable {
// Public Constructors
   public ListView.CheckedListViewItemCollection(ListView owner);
// Public Instance Properties
   public int Count{get; }                                  // implements ICollection
   public bool IsReadOnly{get; }                            // implements IList
   public ListViewItem this{get; }
// Public Instance Methods
   public bool Contains(ListViewItem item);
   public void CopyTo(Array dest, int index);               // implements ICollection
   public IEnumerator GetEnumerator( );                     // implements IEnumerable
   public int IndexOf(ListViewItem item);
}
```

ListView.ColumnHeaderCollection

System.Windows.Forms (system.windows.forms.dll) class

This class represents a collection of column headers in a ListView.

```
public class ListView.ColumnHeaderCollection : IList, ICollection, IEnumerable {
// Public Constructors
```

```
public ListView.ColumnHeaderCollection(ListView owner);
// Public Instance Properties
public int Count{get; }                                                    // implements ICollection
public bool IsReadOnly{get; }                                              // implements IList
public virtual ColumnHeader this{get; }
// Public Instance Methods
public virtual ColumnHeader Add(string str, int width, HorizontalAlignment textAlign);
public virtual int Add(ColumnHeader value);
public virtual void AddRange(ColumnHeader[ ] values);
public virtual void Clear( );                                              // implements IList
public bool Contains(ColumnHeader value);
public IEnumerator GetEnumerator( );                                       // implements IEnumerable
public int IndexOf(ColumnHeader value);
public void Insert(int index, ColumnHeader value);
public void Insert(int index, string str, int width, HorizontalAlignment textAlign);
public virtual void Remove(ColumnHeader column);
public virtual void RemoveAt(int index);                                   // implements IList
}
```

ListView.ListViewItemCollection

System.Windows.Forms (system.windows.forms.dll) class

This class encapsulates a collection of items in a **ListView** control.

```
public class ListView.ListViewItemCollection : IList, ICollection, IEnumerable {
// Public Constructors
public ListView.ListViewItemCollection(ListView owner);
// Public Instance Properties
public int Count{get; }                                                    // implements ICollection
public bool IsReadOnly{get; }                                              // implements IList
public virtual ListViewItem this{set; get; }
// Public Instance Methods
public virtual ListViewItem Add(ListViewItem value);
public virtual ListViewItem Add(string text);
public virtual ListViewItem Add(string text, int imageIndex);
public void AddRange(ListViewItem[ ] values);
public virtual void Clear( );                                              // implements IList
public bool Contains(ListViewItem item);
public void CopyTo(Array dest, int index);                                 // implements ICollection
public IEnumerator GetEnumerator( );                                       // implements IEnumerable
public int IndexOf(ListViewItem item);
public ListViewItem Insert(int index, ListViewItem item);
public ListViewItem Insert(int index, string text);
public ListViewItem Insert(int index, string text, int imageIndex);
public virtual void Remove(ListViewItem item);
public virtual void RemoveAt(int index);                                   // implements IList
}
```

ListView.SelectedIndexCollection

System.Windows.Forms (system.windows.forms.dll) class

This class represents the collection of selected indexes in the **ListView** control.

```
public class ListView.SelectedIndexCollection : IList, ICollection, IEnumerable {
// Public Constructors
   public ListView.SelectedIndexCollection(ListView owner);
// Public Instance Properties
   public int Count{get; }                                          // implements ICollection
   public bool IsReadOnly{get; }                                    // implements IList
   public int this{get; }
// Public Instance Methods
   public bool Contains(int selectedIndex);
   public void CopyTo(Array dest, int index);                       // implements ICollection
   public IEnumerator GetEnumerator( );                             // implements IEnumerable
   public int IndexOf(int selectedIndex);
}
```

ListView.SelectedListViewItemCollection

System.Windows.Forms (system.windows.forms.dll) class

This collection class represents the selected items in the ListView control.

```
public class ListView.SelectedListViewItemCollection : IList, ICollection, IEnumerable {
// Public Constructors
   public ListView.SelectedListViewItemCollection(ListView owner);
// Public Instance Properties
   public int Count{get; }                                          // implements ICollection
   public bool IsReadOnly{get; }                                    // implements IList
   public ListViewItem this{get; }
// Public Instance Methods
   public void Clear( );                                            // implements IList
   public bool Contains(ListViewItem item);
   public void CopyTo(Array dest, int index);                       // implements ICollection
   public IEnumerator GetEnumerator( );                             // implements IEnumerable
   public int IndexOf(ListViewItem item);
}
```

ListViewAlignment serializable

System.Windows.Forms (system.windows.forms.dll) enum

This enumeration is used to specify how icons will be aligned in a ListView control.

```
public enum ListViewAlignment {
   Default = 0,
   Left = 1,
   Top = 2,
   SnapToGrid = 5
}
```

Hierarchy System.Object → System.ValueType → System.Enum(System.IComparable, System.IFormattable, System.IConvertible) → ListViewAlignment

Returned By ListView.Alignment

Passed To ListView.{Alignment, ArrangeIcons( )}

ListViewItem **serializable**

System.Windows.Forms (system.windows.forms.dll) **class**

This class represents an item in a **ListView** control. You can add and remove these objects from the **ListView.Items** collection.

In one of the icon views, the imagery displayed comes from the **Text** and **ImageIndex** properties (inherited from the various **ListView** image lists; the list currently in play can be retrieved from **ImageList**). You can also specify various other aspects of the items appearance such as the **Font**, **ForeColor**, and **BackColor**. You can also discover whether the item is **Selected**, **Focused**, or **Checked**. (See **ListView** for more information on these features.)

In the details view, the **ListView** displays several columns, in addition to the simple text and icon for the item. To support this, you should add additional **ListViewSubItem** objects to the **SubItems** collection.

```
public class ListViewItem : ICloneable, System.Runtime.Serialization.ISerializable {
// Public Constructors
   public ListViewItem( );
   public ListViewItem(ListViewSubItem[ ] subItems, int imageIndex);
   public ListViewItem(string text);
   public ListViewItem(string[ ] items);
   public ListViewItem(string[ ] items, int imageIndex);
   public ListViewItem(string[ ] items, int imageIndex, System.Drawing.Color foreColor, System.Drawing.Color backColor,
      System.Drawing.Font font);
   public ListViewItem(string text, int imageIndex);
// Public Instance Properties
   public Color BackColor{set; get; }
   public Rectangle Bounds{get; }
   public bool Checked{set; get; }
   public bool Focused{set; get; }
   public Font Font{set; get; }
   public Color ForeColor{set; get; }
   public int ImageIndex{set; get; }
   public ImageList ImageList{get; }
   public int Index{get; }
   public ListView ListView{get; }
   public bool Selected{set; get; }
   public int StateImageIndex{set; get; }
   public ListViewSubItemCollection SubItems{get; }
   public object Tag{set; get; }
   public string Text{set; get; }
   public bool UseItemStyleForSubItems{set; get; }
// Public Instance Methods
   public void BeginEdit( );
   public virtual object Clone( );                                    // implements ICloneable
   public virtual void EnsureVisible( );
   public Rectangle GetBounds(ItemBoundsPortion portion);
   public virtual void Remove( );
   public override string ToString( );                                // overrides object
// Protected Instance Methods
   protected virtual void Deserialize(System.Runtime.Serialization.SerializationInfo info,
      System.Runtime.Serialization.StreamingContext context);
```

```
  protected virtual void Serialize(System.Runtime.Serialization.SerializationInfo info,
     System.Runtime.Serialization.StreamingContext context);
}
```

Returned By ListView.{FocusedItem, GetItemAt( ), TopItem}, CheckedListViewItemCollection.this, ListViewItemCollection.{Add( ), Insert( ), this}, SelectedListViewItemCollection.this

Passed To Multiple types

ListViewItem.ListViewSubItem serializable

System.Windows.Forms (system.windows.forms.dll) class

This class represents a subitem in ListView. It is similar to a ListViewItem, but does not support the ListViewItem.SubItems property, and so it represents a leaf item in the collection.

```
public class ListViewItem.ListViewSubItem {
// Public Constructors
  public ListViewItem.ListViewSubItem( );
  public ListViewItem.ListViewSubItem(ListViewItem owner, string text);
  public ListViewItem.ListViewSubItem(ListViewItem owner, string text, System.Drawing.Color foreColor,
     System.Drawing.Color backColor, System.Drawing.Font font);
// Public Instance Properties
  public Color BackColor{set; get; }
  public Font Font{set; get; }
  public Color ForeColor{set; get; }
  public string Text{set; get; }
// Public Instance Methods
  public void ResetStyle( );
  public override string ToString( );                                          // overrides object
}
```

ListViewItem.ListViewSubItemCollection

System.Windows.Forms (system.windows.forms.dll) class

This class represents the collection of subitems of a ListViewItem.

```
public class ListViewItem.ListViewSubItemCollection : IList, ICollection, IEnumerable {
// Public Constructors
  public ListViewItem.ListViewSubItemCollection(ListViewItem owner);
// Public Instance Properties
  public int Count{get; }                                                  // implements ICollection
  public bool IsReadOnly{get; }                                                 // implements IList
  public ListViewSubItem this{set; get; }
// Public Instance Methods
  public ListViewSubItem Add(ListViewSubItem item);
  public ListViewSubItem Add(string text);
  public ListViewSubItem Add(string text, System.Drawing.Color foreColor, System.Drawing.Color backColor,
     System.Drawing.Font font);
  public void AddRange(ListViewSubItem[ ] items);
  public void AddRange(string[ ] items);
```

```
    public void AddRange(string[ ] items, System.Drawing.Color foreColor, System.Drawing.Color backColor,
       System.Drawing.Font font);
    public void Clear( );                                                        // implements IList
    public bool Contains(ListViewSubItem subItem);
    public IEnumerator GetEnumerator( );                                         // implements IEnumerable
    public int IndexOf(ListViewSubItem subItem);
    public void Insert(int index, ListViewSubItem item);
    public void Remove(ListViewSubItem item);
    public void RemoveAt(int index);                                             // implements IList
}
```

ListViewItemConverter

System.Windows.Forms (system.windows.forms.dll) class

This System.ComponentModel.TypeConverter is used in serialization and design-time scenarios for the ListViewItem class. You would not normally use this directly from your own code.

```
public class ListViewItemConverter : System.ComponentModel.ExpandableObjectConverter {
// Public Constructors
    public ListViewItemConverter( );
// Public Instance Methods
    public override bool CanConvertTo(System.ComponentModel.ITypeDescriptorContext context,
       Type destinationType);                   // overrides System.ComponentModel.TypeConverter
    public override object ConvertTo(System.ComponentModel.ITypeDescriptorContext context,
       System.Globalization.CultureInfo culture, object value,
       Type destinationType);                   // overrides System.ComponentModel.TypeConverter
}
```

Hierarchy System.Object → System.ComponentModel.TypeConverter → System.ComponentModel.ExpandableObjectConverter → ListViewItemConverter

MainMenu

marshal by reference, disposable

System.Windows.Forms (system.windows.forms.dll) class

A MainMenu is the Menu strip across the top of a Form. You can bind it to a particular form by using the Form.Menu property.

There is an additional typed CloneMenu( ) method, which allows you to copy the menu structure for reuse elsewhere.

See Menu for more information on menu functionality.

```
public class MainMenu : Menu {
// Public Constructors
    public MainMenu( );
    public MainMenu(MenuItem[ ] items);
// Public Instance Properties
    public virtual RightToLeft RightToLeft{set; get; }
// Public Instance Methods
    public virtual MainMenu CloneMenu( );
    public Form GetForm( );
    public override string ToString( );                                          // overrides Menu
// Protected Instance Methods
```

```
  protected override IntPtr CreateMenuHandle( );                    // overrides Menu
  protected override void Dispose(bool disposing);                  // overrides Menu
}
```

Hierarchy System.Object → System.MarshalByRefObject → System.ComponentModel.Component(System.ComponentModel.IComponent, System.IDisposable) → Menu → MainMenu

Returned By Form.{Menu, MergedMenu}, Menu.GetMainMenu( ), PrintPreviewDialog.Menu

Passed To Form.Menu, PrintPreviewDialog.Menu

MdiClient

marshal by reference, disposable

System.Windows.Forms (system.windows.forms.dll) — sealed class

This class is for internal use and should not be called from your own code.

```
public sealed class MdiClient : Control {
// Public Constructors
  public MdiClient( );
// Public Instance Properties
  public override Image BackgroundImage{set; get; }                 // overrides Control
  public Form[ ] MdiChildren{get; }
// Protected Instance Properties
  protected override CreateParams CreateParams{get; }               // overrides Control
// Public Instance Methods
  public void LayoutMdi(MdiLayout value);
// Protected Instance Methods
  protected override ControlCollection CreateControlsInstance( );   // overrides Control
  protected override void OnResize(EventArgs e);                    // overrides Control
  protected override void ScaleCore(float dx, float dy);            // overrides Control
  protected override void SetBoundsCore(int x, int y, int width, int height, BoundsSpecified specified);  // overrides Control
  protected override void WndProc(ref Message m);                   // overrides Control
}
```

Hierarchy System.Object → System.MarshalByRefObject → System.ComponentModel.Component(System.ComponentModel.IComponent, System.IDisposable) → Control(IOleControl, IOleObject, IOleInPlaceObject, IOleInPlaceActiveObject, IOleWindow, IViewObject, IViewObject2, IPersist, IPersistStreamInit, IPersistPropertyBag, IPersistStorage, IQuickActivate, System.ComponentModel.ISynchronizeInvoke, IWin32Window) → MdiClient

Passed To ControlCollection.ControlCollection( )

MdiClient.ControlCollection

System.Windows.Forms (system.windows.forms.dll) — class

This class is for internal use and should not be called from your own code.

```
public class MdiClient.ControlCollection : ControlCollection {
// Public Constructors
  public MdiClient.ControlCollection(MdiClient owner);
```

```
// Public Instance Methods
  public override void Add(Control value);                    // overrides Control.ControlCollection
  public override void Remove(Control value);                 // overrides Control.ControlCollection
}
```

Hierarchy System.Object → ControlCollection(System.Collections.IList, System.Collections.ICollection, System.Collections.IEnumerable, System.ICloneable) → ControlCollection

MdiLayout **serializable**

System.Windows.Forms (system.windows.forms.dll) enum

This enumeration is used by the Form.LayoutMdi( ) method to determine how the Form.MdiChildren will be arranged.

```
public enum MdiLayout {
  Cascade = 0,
  TileHorizontal = 1,
  TileVertical = 2,
  ArrangeIcons = 3
}
```

Hierarchy System.Object → System.ValueType → System.Enum(System.IComparable, System.IFormattable, System.IConvertible) → MdiLayout

Passed To Form.LayoutMdi( ), MdiClient.LayoutMdi( )

MeasureItemEventArgs

System.Windows.Forms (system.windows.forms.dll) class

This class wraps the data for the MeasureItem event, raised by various controls including ListBox, ComboBox, and MenuItem, which support owner draw modes.

MeasureItem is raised when the DrawMode is set to OwnerDrawVariable, and is used to determine the ItemWidth and ItemHeight of the item at a particular Index in the controls collection, when it is drawn on a particular System.Drawing.Graphics surface.

It is not raised when the DrawMode is OwnerDrawFixed. Instead, you should use the ItemHeight property on the owner drawn control.

```
public class MeasureItemEventArgs : EventArgs {
// Public Constructors
  public MeasureItemEventArgs(System.Drawing.Graphics graphics, int index);
  public MeasureItemEventArgs(System.Drawing.Graphics graphics, int index, int itemHeight);
// Public Instance Properties
  public Graphics Graphics{get; }
  public int Index{get; }
  public int ItemHeight{set; get; }
  public int ItemWidth{set; get; }
}
```

Hierarchy System.Object → System.EventArgs → MeasureItemEventArgs

Passed To ComboBox.OnMeasureItem( ), ListBox.OnMeasureItem( ), MeasureItemEventHandler.{BeginInvoke( ), Invoke( )}, MenuItem.OnMeasureItem( )

MeasureItemEventHandler

serializable

System.Windows.Forms (system.windows.forms.dll) delegate

This is the delegate for the MeasureItem event, raised by ListBox, ComboBox, and MenuItem controls, which support owner draw modes.

```
public delegate void MeasureItemEventHandler(object sender, MeasureItemEventArgs e);
```

Associated Events CheckedListBox.MeasureItem( ), ComboBox.MeasureItem( ), ListBox.MeasureItem( ), MenuItem.MeasureItem( )

Menu

marshal by reference, disposable

System.Windows.Forms (system.windows.forms.dll) abstract class

This System.ComponentModel.Component is the abstract base for ContextMenu, MainMenu, and MenuItem classes. It provides most of the functionality of each of these classes but cannot be instantiated itself.

You can add MenuItem objects to the menu through the MenuItems collection. A MenuItem itself can contain further MenuItem objects, to allow for cascading child menus. You can determine if the menu has any children through the IsParent property.

You can also determine which menu item is a special MdiListItem—an item that will display a list of MDI child forms as a child menu. This is a read-only property—you set it through the MenuItem.MdiList property.

The Menu may be hosted in either a ContextMenu or a MainMenu, and you can determine which through the GetContextMenu( ) and GetMainMenu( ) methods.

Finally, there is a MergeMenu( ) method. This merges two menus together (performed automatically for MDI child menus). There is nothing to stop you from using it for your own menu management, however. It is particularly useful where you have a UI plug-in architecture, where various components provide their own little bit of menu structure that you can merge in to the overall menu hierarchy. To control the merge, specify the MenuItem.MergeOrder and MenuItem.MergeType properties (see MenuItem for more information on this).

```
public abstract class Menu : System.ComponentModel.Component {
// Protected Constructors
   protected Menu(MenuItem[ ] items);
// Public Static Fields
   public const int FindHandle;                                    // =0
   public const int FindShortcut;                                  // =1
// Public Instance Properties
   public IntPtr Handle{get; }
   public virtual bool IsParent{get; }
   public MenuItem MdiListItem{get; }
   public MenuItemCollection MenuItems{get; }
// Public Instance Methods
   public MenuItem FindMenuItem(int type, IntPtr value);
   public ContextMenu GetContextMenu( );
   public MainMenu GetMainMenu( );
   public virtual void MergeMenu(Menu menuSrc);
   public override string ToString( );          // overrides System.ComponentModel.Component
// Protected Instance Methods
```

```
  protected void CloneMenu(Menu menuSrc);
  protected virtual IntPtr CreateMenuHandle( );
  protected override void Dispose(bool disposing);             // overrides System.ComponentModel.Component
  protected int FindMergePosition(int mergeOrder);
  protected internal virtual bool ProcessCmdKey(ref Message msg, Keys keyData);
}
```

Hierarchy System.Object → System.MarshalByRefObject → System.ComponentModel.Component(System.ComponentModel.IComponent, System.IDisposable) → Menu

Subclasses ContextMenu, MainMenu, MenuItem

Returned By System.Windows.Forms.Design.IMenuEditorService.GetMenu( ), MenuItem.Parent, ToolBarButton.DropDownMenu

Passed To System.Windows.Forms.Design.IMenuEditorService.SetMenu( ), MenuItemCollection.MenuItemCollection( ), ToolBarButton.DropDownMenu

Menu.MenuItemCollection

System.Windows.Forms (system.windows.forms.dll) class

This class provides a standard collection of MenuItems for the Menu class.

```
public class Menu.MenuItemCollection : IList, ICollection, IEnumerable {
// Public Constructors
  public Menu.MenuItemCollection(Menu owner);
// Public Instance Properties
  public int Count{get; }                                      // implements ICollection
  public bool IsReadOnly{get; }                                // implements IList
  public virtual MenuItem this{get; }
// Public Instance Methods
  public virtual int Add(int index, MenuItem item);
  public virtual int Add(MenuItem item);
  public virtual MenuItem Add(string caption);
  public virtual MenuItem Add(string caption, EventHandler onClick);
  public virtual MenuItem Add(string caption, MenuItem[ ] items);
  public virtual void AddRange(MenuItem[ ] items);
  public virtual void Clear( );                                // implements IList
  public bool Contains(MenuItem value);
  public void CopyTo(Array dest, int index);                   // implements ICollection
  public IEnumerator GetEnumerator( );                         // implements IEnumerable
  public int IndexOf(MenuItem value);
  public virtual void Remove(MenuItem item);
  public virtual void RemoveAt(int index);                     // implements IList
}
```

MenuGlyph serializable

System.Windows.Forms (system.windows.forms.dll) enum

This enumeration lists the various kinds of Arrow, Bullet, and Checkmark glyphs that can be drawn using the ControlPaint.DrawMenuGlyph( ) method. Note that this will render pre-XP glyphs; you will need to provide your own implementation to draw themed imagery.

```
public enum MenuGlyph {
  Arrow = 0,
  Min = 0,
  Checkmark = 1,
  Bullet = 2,
  Max = 2
}
```

Hierarchy System.Object → System.ValueType → System.Enum(System.IComparable, System.IFormattable, System.IConvertible) → MenuGlyph

Passed To ControlPaint.DrawMenuGlyph( )

MenuItem

marshal by reference, disposable

System.Windows.Forms (system.windows.forms.dll) class

This Menu class represents the submenus of either a MainMenu, ContextMenu, or other MenuItem object. You can add it to the MenuItems property of any of these classes to create such a submenu.

You can control the appearance of the item with a number of different properties. You can set the Text for the menu item, and it can be Enabled, and made Visible. The BarBreak and Break properties cause the menu item to start a new column in the menu, with and without a dividing line, respectively. Checked determines whether a check mark appears next to item text, and RadioCheck determines whether the check mark appears as a radio button instead of a checkmark. Note that you have to handle the mutual exclusion yourself. You can set a Shortcut key to associate with the item, and ShowShortcut determines whether the key is displayed to the right of the text. You can also find out which Mnemonic character is acting as an Alt key shortcut.

To support MDI applications, you can mark an item as the MdiListItem. The system will automatically create and maintain a child menu for this object with a list of the MDI windows owned by the parent Form.

Also for the benefit of MDI and similar applications, Menu objects allow the merging of their items to meld together menus from disparate sources. To control this, you can specify the MergeOrder of a particular item. This is essentially a numeric priority for the item when merging two submenus with the same name. A low number will appear higher in the menu than a higher number. It is best to think of these as numeric groups where the same numbers will be bundled together in the final menu.

In addition to the MergeOrder, you can specify the MergeType. This allows you to specify whether the system will Add( ) the item to the existing collection (this is the default), Remove( ) the item when merging (i.e., it will not appear in the final menu), Replace any existing items at the same position in the merged menu, or MergeItems: interleave the items with the existing items, adding and replacing as appropriate. Note that the settings on both parties in the merge affect the end results. It is best to play with these options until you get a feel for how menu merging works in practice.

To determine when items are being manipulated, you can bind to the Click, Popup (a child menu is about to appear), and Select (the item has been highlighted) events. You can programmatically raise these events with the PerformClick( ) and PerformSelect( ) methods.

Note that MenuItem objects also support OwnerDraw. See MeasureItemEventArgs and DrawItemEventArgs for more information on owner draw facilities.

```
public class MenuItem : Menu {
// Public Constructors
   public MenuItem( );
   public MenuItem(MenuMerge mergeType, int mergeOrder, Shortcut shortcut, string text, EventHandler onClick,
      EventHandler onPopup, EventHandler onSelect, MenuItem[ ] items);
   public MenuItem(string text);
   public MenuItem(string text, EventHandler onClick);
   public MenuItem(string text, EventHandler onClick, Shortcut shortcut);
   public MenuItem(string text, MenuItem[ ] items);
// Public Instance Properties
   public bool BarBreak{set; get; }
   public bool Break{set; get; }
   public bool Checked{set; get; }
   public bool DefaultItem{set; get; }
   public bool Enabled{set; get; }
   public int Index{set; get; }
   public override bool IsParent{get; }                              // overrides Menu
   public bool MdiList{set; get; }
   public int MergeOrder{set; get; }
   public MenuMerge MergeType{set; get; }
   public char Mnemonic{get; }
   public bool OwnerDraw{set; get; }
   public Menu Parent{get; }
   public bool RadioCheck{set; get; }
   public Shortcut Shortcut{set; get; }
   public bool ShowShortcut{set; get; }
   public string Text{set; get; }
   public bool Visible{set; get; }
// Protected Instance Properties
   protected int MenuID{get; }
// Public Instance Methods
   public virtual MenuItem CloneMenu( );
   public virtual MenuItem MergeMenu( );
   public void MergeMenu(MenuItem itemSrc);
   public void PerformClick( );
   public virtual void PerformSelect( );
   public override string ToString( );                               // overrides Menu
// Protected Instance Methods
   protected void CloneMenu(MenuItem itemSrc);
   protected override void Dispose(bool disposing);                  // overrides Menu
   protected virtual void OnClick(EventArgs e);
   protected virtual void OnDrawItem(DrawItemEventArgs e);
   protected virtual void OnInitMenuPopup(EventArgs e);
   protected virtual void OnMeasureItem(MeasureItemEventArgs e);
   protected virtual void OnPopup(EventArgs e);
   protected virtual void OnSelect(EventArgs e);
// Events
   public event EventHandler Click;
   public event DrawItemEventHandler DrawItem;
   public event MeasureItemEventHandler MeasureItem;
   public event EventHandler Popup;
```

```
  public event EventHandler Select;
}
```

Hierarchy System.Object → System.MarshalByRefObject → System.ComponentModel.Component(System.ComponentModel.IComponent, System.IDisposable) → Menu → MenuItem

Returned By Menu.{FindMenuItem( ), MdiListItem}, MenuItemCollection.this

Passed To ContextMenu.ContextMenu( ), System.Windows.Forms.Design.IMenuEditorService.SetSelection( ), MainMenu.MainMenu( ), Menu.Menu( ), MenuItemCollection.{Add( ), AddRange( ), Contains( ), IndexOf( ), Remove( )}, MenuItem.MenuItem( )

MenuMerge serializable

System.Windows.Forms (system.windows.forms.dll) enum

This is the enumeration that is used by the MenuItem.MergeType to determine how menu merging should proceed for this item.

```
public enum MenuMerge {
  Add = 0,
  Replace = 1,
  MergeItems = 2,
  Remove = 3
}
```

Hierarchy System.Object → System.ValueType → System.Enum(System.IComparable, System.IFormattable, System.IConvertible) → MenuMerge

Returned By MenuItem.MergeType

Passed To MenuItem.{MenuItem( ), MergeType}

Message

System.Windows.Forms (system.windows.forms.dll) struct

This value type wraps a Win32 message, and is used in message filtering (through the Application.AddMessageFilter( ) method) and Control.WndProc( ) message processing. Obviously, this is very closely bound to the operating system, and you should only use this sort of message processing in interop applications—typically, when you are wrapping a Win32 control for your own purposes. You can retrieve the HWnd, LParam, WParam, and Msg ID. You can also set the Result to be returned to Windows if you handle the message.

You shouldn't create instances of this class directly, but instead use the static Create( ) factory method, which ensures that the message is properly initialized.

```
public struct Message {
// Public Instance Properties
  public IntPtr HWnd{set; get; }
  public IntPtr LParam{set; get; }
  public int Msg{set; get; }
  public IntPtr Result{set; get; }
```

```
  public IntPtr WParam{set; get; }
// Public Static Methods
  public static Message Create(IntPtr hWnd, int msg, IntPtr wparam, IntPtr lparam);
// Public Instance Methods
  public override bool Equals(object o);                          // overrides ValueType
  public override int GetHashCode( );                             // overrides ValueType
  public object GetLParam(Type cls);
  public override string ToString( );                             // overrides ValueType
}
```

Hierarchy System.Object → System.ValueType → Message

Passed To Multiple types

MessageBox

System.Windows.Forms (system.windows.forms.dll) class

This class provides a simple means to display a modal pop-up box with a title, message, and icon, and obtain some basic Yes/No, OK/Cancel information from the user. It is essentially a wrapper around the Win32 MessageBox( ) method.

You can Show( ) a message, which returns the DialogResult indicating which button the end user clicked. When showing the message, you can specify the title and body text, the MessageBoxButtons to show (and which button is the MessageBoxDefaultButton), the MessageBoxIcon, and some MessageBoxOptions that deal with right-to-left mode, multiple desktop alignment, and alignment.

Don't forget that popping up a message box is highly intrusive, forcibly interrupting a users workflow. You might consider ErrorProvider, or even a ToolTip, as a better way of notifying the user of problems.

```
public class MessageBox {
// Public Static Methods
  public static DialogResult Show(IWin32Window owner, string text);
  public static DialogResult Show(IWin32Window owner, string text, string caption);
  public static DialogResult Show(IWin32Window owner, string text, string caption, MessageBoxButtons buttons);
  public static DialogResult Show(IWin32Window owner, string text, string caption, MessageBoxButtons buttons,
    MessageBoxIcon icon);
  public static DialogResult Show(IWin32Window owner, string text, string caption, MessageBoxButtons buttons,
    MessageBoxIcon icon, MessageBoxDefaultButton defaultButton);
  public static DialogResult Show(IWin32Window owner, string text, string caption, MessageBoxButtons buttons,
    MessageBoxIcon icon, MessageBoxDefaultButton defaultButton, MessageBoxOptions options);
  public static DialogResult Show(string text);
  public static DialogResult Show(string text, string caption);
  public static DialogResult Show(string text, string caption, MessageBoxButtons buttons);
  public static DialogResult Show(string text, string caption, MessageBoxButtons buttons, MessageBoxIcon icon);
  public static DialogResult Show(string text, string caption, MessageBoxButtons buttons, MessageBoxIcon icon,
    MessageBoxDefaultButton defaultButton);
  public static DialogResult Show(string text, string caption, MessageBoxButtons buttons, MessageBoxIcon icon,
    MessageBoxDefaultButton defaultButton, MessageBoxOptions options);
}
```

MessageBoxButtons

serializable

System.Windows.Forms (system.windows.forms.dll) **enum**

This enumeration lists the various button combinations you can request in the MessageBox.Show( ) method.

```
public enum MessageBoxButtons {
  OK = 0,
  OKCancel = 1,
  AbortRetryIgnore = 2,
  YesNoCancel = 3,
  YesNo = 4,
  RetryCancel = 5
}
```

Hierarchy System.Object → System.ValueType → System.Enum(System.IComparable, System.IFormattable, System.IConvertible) → MessageBoxButtons

Passed To System.Windows.Forms.Design.IUIService.ShowMessage( ), MessageBox.Show( )

MessageBoxDefaultButton

serializable

System.Windows.Forms (system.windows.forms.dll) **enum**

This enumeration determines which button should be the default accept button in a MessageBox. The left-most in a left-to-right reading message box is Button1.

```
public enum MessageBoxDefaultButton {
  Button1 = 0,
  Button2 = 256,
  Button3 = 512
}
```

Hierarchy System.Object → System.ValueType → System.Enum(System.IComparable, System.IFormattable, System.IConvertible) → MessageBoxDefaultButton

Passed To MessageBox.Show( )

MessageBoxIcon

serializable

System.Windows.Forms (system.windows.forms.dll) **enum**

This enumeration specifies the icon types that can be displayed in a MessageBox.

```
public enum MessageBoxIcon {
  None = 0,
  Hand = 16,
  Error = 16,
  Stop = 16,
  Question = 32,
  Exclamation = 48,
  Warning = 48,
  Asterisk = 64,
```

```
  Information = 64
}
```

Hierarchy System.Object → System.ValueType → System.Enum(System.IComparable, System.IFormattable, System.IConvertible) → MessageBoxIcon

Passed To MessageBox.Show( )

MessageBoxOptions

serializable, flag

System.Windows.Forms (system.windows.forms.dll) enum

This enumeration provides several additional options to a MessageBox, including the right-to-left status (RtlReading), whether the box should always be shown on the DefaultDesktopOnly, whether it should RightAlign the text, and whether this is a ServiceNotification (i.e., the MessageBox is shown even if no user is logged on to the system).

```
public enum MessageBoxOptions {
  DefaultDesktopOnly = 0x00020000,
  RightAlign = 0x00080000,
  RtlReading = 0x00100000,
  ServiceNotification = 0x00200000
}
```

Hierarchy System.Object → System.ValueType → System.Enum(System.IComparable, System.IFormattable, System.IConvertible) → MessageBoxOptions

Passed To MessageBox.Show( )

MethodInvoker

serializable

System.Windows.Forms (system.windows.forms.dll) delegate

This (extremely useful!) delegate encapsulates a void method with no parameters. This is one of the most common utility delegates, and it saves you from repeatedly having to define your own. As an example, you might use it in conjunction with Control.Invoke( ) to marshal an inter-thread call back onto the UI thread. I only wish I'd found it sooner....

```
public delegate void MethodInvoker( );
```

MonthCalendar

marshal by reference, disposable

System.Windows.Forms (system.windows.forms.dll) class

This Control represents a calendar for selecting a single date or a range of dates. It is more powerful than the DateTimePicker control, but it takes up a lot more real estate.

To alter the appearance of the control, you can set the CalendarDimensions to specify the number of columns and rows of months to display (1x1 would look like a single calendar month, 6x2 would allow you to display an entire year). The minimum size of any individual month can be determined with SingleMonthSize.

The current date can be shown with a circle by specifying ShowTodayCircle, or as some text at the bottom of the control with the ShowToday property. You can also change what the calendar believes to be today's date with the TodayDate property. TodayDateSet will tell you whether this has been explicitly modified. You can also specify the FirstDayOfWeek and, optionally, ShowWeekNumbers.

In addition to the standard Control appearance properties, you can independently set the TitleBackColor, TitleForeColor, and TrailingForeColor (the color of the days from last and next month that are shown on a calendar grid).

You can also set specific dates to be displayed with bold text either individually with BoldedDates, monthly with MonthlyBoldedDates, or annually with AnnuallyBoldedDates. While you can use these properties to get and set the dates concerned, they return copies of the internal date arrays. It is more efficient to use AddBoldedDate( ), AddMonthlyBoldedDate( ), and AddAnnuallyBoldedDate( ), along with the Remove( ) and RemoveAll( ) equivalents.

Date selection can be done by setting the SelectionStart and SelectionEnd, or getting/setting both at once through the SelectionRange. You can bind to DateChanged and SelectionChanged events to be notified of the selection changing.

```
public class MonthCalendar : Control {
// Public Constructors
   public MonthCalendar( );
// Public Instance Properties
   public DateTime[ ] AnnuallyBoldedDates{set; get; }
   public override Color BackColor{set; get; }                    // overrides Control
   public override Image BackgroundImage{set; get; }              // overrides Control
   public DateTime[ ] BoldedDates{set; get; }
   public Size CalendarDimensions{set; get; }
   public Day FirstDayOfWeek{set; get; }
   public override Color ForeColor{set; get; }                    // overrides Control
   public ImeMode ImeMode{set; get; }                             // overrides Control
   public DateTime MaxDate{set; get; }
   public int MaxSelectionCount{set; get; }
   public DateTime MinDate{set; get; }
   public DateTime[ ] MonthlyBoldedDates{set; get; }
   public int ScrollChange{set; get; }
   public DateTime SelectionEnd{set; get; }
   public SelectionRange SelectionRange{set; get; }
   public DateTime SelectionStart{set; get; }
   public bool ShowToday{set; get; }
   public bool ShowTodayCircle{set; get; }
   public bool ShowWeekNumbers{set; get; }
   public Size SingleMonthSize{get; }
   public override string Text{set; get; }                        // overrides Control
   public Color TitleBackColor{set; get; }
   public Color TitleForeColor{set; get; }
   public DateTime TodayDate{set; get; }
   public bool TodayDateSet{get; }
   public Color TrailingForeColor{set; get; }
// Protected Instance Properties
   protected override CreateParams CreateParams{get; }            // overrides Control
   protected override ImeMode DefaultImeMode{get; }               // overrides Control
   protected override Size DefaultSize{get; }                     // overrides Control
// Public Instance Methods
   public void AddAnnuallyBoldedDate(DateTime date);
   public void AddBoldedDate(DateTime date);
```

```
  public void AddMonthlyBoldedDate(DateTime date);
  public SelectionRange GetDisplayRange(bool visible);
  public HitTestInfo HitTest(int x, int y);
  public HitTestInfo HitTest(System.Drawing.Point point);
  public void RemoveAllAnnuallyBoldedDates( );
  public void RemoveAllBoldedDates( );
  public void RemoveAllMonthlyBoldedDates( );
  public void RemoveAnnuallyBoldedDate(DateTime date);
  public void RemoveBoldedDate(DateTime date);
  public void RemoveMonthlyBoldedDate(DateTime date);
  public void SetCalendarDimensions(int x, int y);
  public void SetDate(DateTime date);
  public void SetSelectionRange(DateTime date1, DateTime date2);
  public override string ToString( );                    // overrides System.ComponentModel.Component
  public void UpdateBoldedDates( );
// Protected Instance Methods
  protected override void CreateHandle( );                                     // overrides Control
  protected override void Dispose(bool disposing);                             // overrides Control
  protected override bool IsInputKey(Keys keyData);                            // overrides Control
  protected override void OnBackColorChanged(EventArgs e);                     // overrides Control
  protected virtual void OnDateChanged(DateRangeEventArgs drevent);
  protected virtual void OnDateSelected(DateRangeEventArgs drevent);
  protected override void OnFontChanged(EventArgs e);                          // overrides Control
  protected override void OnForeColorChanged(EventArgs e);                     // overrides Control
  protected override void OnHandleCreated(EventArgs e);                        // overrides Control
  protected override void SetBoundsCore(int x, int y, int width, int height, BoundsSpecified specified);  // overrides Control
  protected override void WndProc(ref Message m);                              // overrides Control
// Events
  public event EventHandler Click;                                             // overrides Control
  public event DateRangeEventHandler DateChanged;
  public event DateRangeEventHandler DateSelected;
  public event EventHandler DoubleClick;                                       // overrides Control
  public event PaintEventHandler Paint;                                        // overrides Control
}
```

Hierarchy System.Object → System.MarshalByRefObject → System.ComponentModel.Component(System.ComponentModel.IComponent, System.IDisposable) → Control(IOleControl, IOleObject, IOleInPlaceObject, IOleInPlaceActiveObject, IOleWindow, IViewObject, IViewObject2, IPersist, IPersistStreamInit, IPersistPropertyBag, IPersistStorage, IQuickActivate, System.ComponentModel.ISynchronizeInvoke, IWin32Window) → MonthCalendar

MonthCalendar.HitArea — serializable

System.Windows.Forms (system.windows.forms.dll) — enum

This enumeration defines the various parts of a MonthCalendar control for use with the HitArea property.

```
public enum MonthCalendar.HitArea {
  Nowhere = 0,
  TitleBackground = 1,
  TitleMonth = 2,
```

```
  TitleYear = 3,
  NextMonthButton = 4,
  PrevMonthButton = 5,
  CalendarBackground = 6,
  Date = 7,
  NextMonthDate = 8,
  PrevMonthDate = 9,
  DayOfWeek = 10,
  WeekNumbers = 11,
  TodayLink = 12
}
```

Hierarchy System.Object → System.ValueType → System.Enum(System.IComparable, System.IFormattable, System.IConvertible) → HitArea

MonthCalendar.HitTestInfo

System.Windows.Forms (system.windows.forms.dll) sealed class

This class is used to encapsulate the results of the MonthCalendar.HitTest( ) method. You can use this method to determine the HitArea of the calendar under a particular Point. You can also get the Time represented by that part of the MonthCalendar, if any.

```
public sealed class MonthCalendar.HitTestInfo {
// Public Instance Properties
  public HitArea HitArea{get; }
  public Point Point{get; }
  public DateTime Time{get; }
}
```

MouseButtons serializable, flag

System.Windows.Forms (system.windows.forms.dll) enum

This enumeration is used throughout the framework to specify which mouse buttons are currently pressed. It is decorated with the FlagsAttribute, so the values may be combined with one of the logical operators (and you should test with the & operator rather than simple equality, as more than one bit may be set).

```
public enum MouseButtons {
  None = 0x00000000,
  Left = 0x00100000,
  Right = 0x00200000,
  Middle = 0x00400000,
  XButton1 = 0x00800000,
  XButton2 = 0x01000000
}
```

Hierarchy System.Object → System.ValueType → System.Enum(System.IComparable, System.IFormattable, System.IConvertible) → MouseButtons

Returned By Control.MouseButtons, ItemDragEventArgs.Button, MouseEventArgs.Button

Passed To ItemDragEventArgs.ItemDragEventArgs( ), MouseEventArgs.MouseEventArgs( ), StatusBarPanelClickEventArgs.StatusBarPanelClickEventArgs( )

MouseEventArgs

System.Windows.Forms (system.windows.forms.dll) class

This class encapsulates the data for the Control.MouseDown, Control.MouseUp, and Control.MouseMove events. You can determine the X and Y coordinates of the mouse (in client coordinates—contrast this with Control.MousePosition), the Button that was pressed (note that this is the button that caused the event, not the total set of buttons currently depressed—you should use Control.MouseButtons for this information).

You can also determine the number of Clicks that have occurred (i.e., single, double, triple, etc.), and the Delta through which the mouse wheel has rotated.

```
public class MouseEventArgs : EventArgs {
// Public Constructors
   public MouseEventArgs(MouseButtons button, int clicks, int x, int y, int delta);
// Public Instance Properties
   public MouseButtons Button{get; }
   public int Clicks{get; }
   public int Delta{get; }
   public int X{get; }
   public int Y{get; }
}
```

Hierarchy System.Object → System.EventArgs → MouseEventArgs

Subclasses StatusBarPanelClickEventArgs

Passed To Control.{OnMouseWheel( ), RaiseMouseEvent( )}, System.Windows.Forms.Design.ComponentTray.{OnMouseDown( ), OnMouseMove( ), OnMouseUp( )}, MouseEventHandler.{BeginInvoke( ), Invoke( )}

MouseEventHandler serializable

System.Windows.Forms (system.windows.forms.dll) delegate

This is the delegate for the Control.MouseDown, Control.MouseUp, and Control.MouseMove events.

```
public delegate void MouseEventHandler(object sender, MouseEventArgs e);
```

Associated Events Multiple types

NativeWindow marshal by reference

System.Windows.Forms (system.windows.forms.dll) class

This class encapsulates a system window but does not implement the IWin32Window interface. It provides CreateHandle( ) and AssignHandle( ) methods to wrap a native HWND, and DestroyHandle( ) to clean it up. You can also retrieve a NativeWindow for a particular handle with the static FromHandle( ) method. The Handle can be retrieved at any time.

You can also invoke the DefWndProc( ) with a particular Message.

You would typically use this control when you are creating a System.ComponentModel.Component (rather than a Control) that uses a native Win32 window. An example of this in the framework is the ToolTip. It uses a NativeWindow derived class in its implementation to manage the pop-up tip window.

```
public class NativeWindow : MarshalByRefObject {
// Public Constructors
   public NativeWindow( );
// Public Instance Properties
   public IntPtr Handle{get; }
// Public Static Methods
   public static NativeWindow FromHandle(IntPtr handle);
// Public Instance Methods
   public void AssignHandle(IntPtr handle);
   public virtual void CreateHandle(CreateParams cp);
   public void DefWndProc(ref Message m);
   public virtual void DestroyHandle( );
   public virtual void ReleaseHandle( );
// Protected Instance Methods
   protected override void Finalize( );                                    // overrides object
   protected virtual void OnHandleChange( );
   protected virtual void OnThreadException(Exception e);
   protected virtual void WndProc(ref Message m);
}
```

Hierarchy System.Object → System.MarshalByRefObject → NativeWindow

NavigateEventArgs

System.Windows.Forms (system.windows.forms.dll) class

This class encapsulates the information for the DataGrid.Navigate event, which is raised when the user navigates through a data relation to a new table. You can determine whether the navigation is occurring Forward through the relation or back to the previous table.

```
public class NavigateEventArgs : EventArgs {
// Public Constructors
   public NavigateEventArgs(bool isForward);
// Public Instance Properties
   public bool Forward{get; }
}
```

Hierarchy System.Object → System.EventArgs → NavigateEventArgs

Passed To DataGrid.OnNavigate( ), NavigateEventHandler.{BeginInvoke( ), Invoke( )}

NavigateEventHandler serializable

System.Windows.Forms (system.windows.forms.dll) delegate

This is the delegate for the DataGrid.Navigate event.

```
public delegate void NavigateEventHandler(object sender, NavigateEventArgs ne);
```

Associated Events DataGrid.Navigate( )

NodeLabelEditEventArgs

System.Windows.Forms (system.windows.forms.dll) class

This class represents the data for the TreeView.BeforeLabelEdit and TreeView.AfterLabelEdit events. You can discover the Node that is being edited and the new Label that will be set into the control.

You can also set CancelEdit to cancel the editing process (or get the value to determine if the event has already been canceled).

```
public class NodeLabelEditEventArgs : EventArgs {
// Public Constructors
   public NodeLabelEditEventArgs(TreeNode node);
   public NodeLabelEditEventArgs(TreeNode node, string label);
// Public Instance Properties
   public bool CancelEdit{set; get; }
   public string Label{get; }
   public TreeNode Node{get; }
}
```

Hierarchy System.Object → System.EventArgs → NodeLabelEditEventArgs

Passed To NodeLabelEditEventHandler.{BeginInvoke( ), Invoke( )}, TreeView.{OnAfterLabelEdit( ), OnBeforeLabelEdit( )}

NodeLabelEditEventHandler serializable

System.Windows.Forms (system.windows.forms.dll) delegate

This is the delegate for the TreeView.BeforeLabelEdit and TreeView.AfterLabelEdit events.

```
public delegate void NodeLabelEditEventHandler(object sender, NodeLabelEditEventArgs e);
```

Associated Events TreeView.{AfterLabelEdit( ), BeforeLabelEdit( )}

NotifyIcon marshal by reference, disposable

System.Windows.Forms (system.windows.forms.dll) sealed class

This class creates an icon in the system tray. You can specify the tooltip Text (which must be fewer than 64 characters), the actual Icon itself, and a ContextMenu. You can also show and hide the icon with the Visible property.

Various events are provided to which you can bind to handle Click, DoubleClick, MouseDown, MouseUp, and MouseMove events while the control is visible.

Note that there is no support for the Windows 2000 and above balloon pop-ups, just the standard tooltips.

```
public sealed class NotifyIcon : System.ComponentModel.Component {
// Public Constructors
   public NotifyIcon( );
   public NotifyIcon(System.ComponentModel.IContainer container);
// Public Instance Properties
```

```
public ContextMenu ContextMenu{set; get; }
public Icon Icon{set; get; }
public string Text{set; get; }
public bool Visible{set; get; }
// Protected Instance Methods
protected override void Dispose(bool disposing);           // overrides System.ComponentModel.Component
// Events
public event EventHandler Click;
public event EventHandler DoubleClick;
public event MouseEventHandler MouseDown;
public event MouseEventHandler MouseMove;
public event MouseEventHandler MouseUp;
}
```

Hierarchy System.Object → System.MarshalByRefObject → System.ComponentModel.Component(System.ComponentModel.IComponent, System.IDisposable) → NotifyIcon

NumericUpDown

marshal by reference, disposable

System.Windows.Forms (system.windows.forms.dll) class

This control combines a TextBox with an up-down button to select a number. If the ReadOnly property is set to true, you can only alter the number with the up-down buttons, but otherwise you can also type into the text box. If the user does type into the box, the ValidateEditText( ) method will be called, and the UserEdit property is set to true. Subsequent typing causes the UpdateEditText( ) method to be called, as for all controls derived from UpDownBase. You can override these methods in a derived class to validate user input.

You can specify the Value displayed in the box, in addition to a Text representation of that number. The number may also be displayed with a ThousandsSeparator (the character for which is determined by the Culture settings currently in operation), and you can select the number of DecimalPlaces to show. Alternatively, you can choose a Hexadecimal representation.

Finally, the range of the control is limited by the Minimum and Maximum properties, and the value that will be added or removed as the buttons are clicked is defined by the Increment property.

```
public class NumericUpDown : UpDownBase : System.ComponentModel.ISupportInitialize {
// Public Constructors
public NumericUpDown( );
// Public Instance Properties
public int DecimalPlaces{set; get; }
public bool Hexadecimal{set; get; }
public decimal Increment{set; get; }
public decimal Maximum{set; get; }
public decimal Minimum{set; get; }
public override string Text{set; get; }                                      // overrides UpDownBase
public bool ThousandsSeparator{set; get; }
public decimal Value{set; get; }
// Public Instance Methods
public void BeginInit( );                        // implements System.ComponentModel.ISupportInitialize
public override void DownButton( );                                          // overrides UpDownBase
```

```
public void EndInit( );                                    // implements System.ComponentModel.ISupportInitialize
public override string ToString( );                        // overrides System.ComponentModel.Component
public override void UpButton( );                          // overrides UpDownBase
// Protected Instance Methods
protected override AccessibleObject CreateAccessibilityInstance( );          // overrides Control
protected override void OnTextBoxKeyPress(object source, KeyPressEventArgs e);  // overrides UpDownBase
protected virtual void OnValueChanged(EventArgs e);
protected void ParseEditText( );
protected override void UpdateEditText( );                 // overrides UpDownBase
protected override void ValidateEditText( );               // overrides UpDownBase
// Events
public event EventHandler ValueChanged;
}
```

Hierarchy System.Object → System.MarshalByRefObject → System.ComponentModel.Component(System.ComponentModel.IComponent, System.IDisposable) → Control(IOleControl, IOleObject, IOleInPlaceObject, IOleInPlaceActiveObject, IOleWindow, IViewObject, IViewObject2, IPersist, IPersistStreamInit, IPersistPropertyBag, IPersistStorage, IQuickActivate, System.ComponentModel.ISynchronizeInvoke, IWin32Window) → ScrollableControl → ContainerControl(IContainerControl) → UpDownBase → NumericUpDown(System.ComponentModel.ISupportInitialize)

OpacityConverter

System.Windows.Forms (system.windows.forms.dll) — class

This System.ComponentModel.TypeConverter can convert from an opacity value to a string. It is used in serialization and design-time scenarios and should not normally be called directly from your code.

```
public class OpacityConverter : System.ComponentModel.TypeConverter {
// Public Constructors
public OpacityConverter( );
// Public Instance Methods
public override bool CanConvertFrom( System.ComponentModel.ITypeDescriptorContext context,
   Type sourceType);                                      // overrides System.ComponentModel.TypeConverter
public override object ConvertFrom(System.ComponentModel.ITypeDescriptorContext context,
   System.Globalization.CultureInfo culture, object value);   // overrides System.ComponentModel.TypeConverter
public override object ConvertTo(System.ComponentModel.ITypeDescriptorContext context,
   System.Globalization.CultureInfo culture, object value,
   Type destinationType);                                 // overrides System.ComponentModel.TypeConverter
}
```

Hierarchy System.Object → System.ComponentModel.TypeConverter → OpacityConverter

OpenFileDialog — marshal by reference, disposable

System.Windows.Forms (system.windows.forms.dll) — sealed class

This FileDialog class provides a means for a user to select a file to open. In addition to the base functionality, it adds an OpenFile( ) method, which will open a file Stream for the first selected file.

```
public sealed class OpenFileDialog : FileDialog {
// Public Constructors
   public OpenFileDialog( );
// Public Instance Properties
   public override bool CheckFileExists{set; get; }                    // overrides FileDialog
   public bool Multiselect{set; get; }
   public bool ReadOnlyChecked{set; get; }
   public bool ShowReadOnly{set; get; }
// Public Instance Methods
   public Stream OpenFile( );
   public override void Reset( );                                      // overrides FileDialog
}
```

Hierarchy System.Object → System.MarshalByRefObject → System.ComponentModel.Component(System.ComponentModel.IComponent, System.IDisposable) → CommonDialog → FileDialog → OpenFileDialog

Passed To System.Windows.Forms.Design.FileNameEditor.InitializeDialog( )

Orientation serializable

System.Windows.Forms (system.windows.forms.dll) enum

This enumeration defines Horizontal and Vertical orientation members for the TrackBar class. It could be used by any of your own custom controls that offer horizontal or vertical alternatives.

```
public enum Orientation {
   Horizontal = 0,
   Vertical = 1
}
```

Hierarchy System.Object → System.ValueType → System.Enum(System.IComparable, System.IFormattable, System.IConvertible) → Orientation

Returned By TrackBar.Orientation

Passed To TrackBar.Orientation

OSFeature

System.Windows.Forms (system.windows.forms.dll) class

This class, derived from the FeatureSupport abstract base, is used to determine whether particular operating system features are present.

In Version 1.0 of the framework, it can be used to determine whether LayeredWindows and Themes are present, through static members of those names.

```
public class OSFeature : FeatureSupport {
// Protected Constructors
   protected OSFeature( );
// Public Static Fields
   public static readonly object LayeredWindows;                       // =System.Object
```

```
    public static readonly object Themes;                                    // =System.Object
// Public Static Properties
    public static OSFeature Feature{get; }
// Public Instance Methods
    public override Version GetVersionPresent(object feature);               // overrides FeatureSupport
}
```

Hierarchy System.Object → FeatureSupport(IFeatureSupport) → OSFeature

OwnerDrawPropertyBag **serializable, marshal by reference**

System.Windows.Forms (system.windows.forms.dll) class

This class is for internal use only and should not be called from your own code.

```
public class OwnerDrawPropertyBag : MarshalByRefObject : System.Runtime.Serialization.ISerializable {
// Public Instance Properties
    public Color BackColor{set; get; }
    public Font Font{set; get; }
    public Color ForeColor{set; get; }
// Public Static Methods
    public static OwnerDrawPropertyBag Copy(OwnerDrawPropertyBag value);
// Public Instance Methods
    public virtual bool IsEmpty( );
}
```

Hierarchy System.Object → System.MarshalByRefObject → OwnerDrawPropertyBag(System.Runtime.Serialization.ISerializable)

Returned By TreeView.GetItemRenderStyles( )

PageSetupDialog **marshal by reference, disposable**

System.Windows.Forms (system.windows.forms.dll) sealed class

This CommonDialog allows a user to set up the PageSettings and PrinterSettings for a System.Drawing.Printing.PrintDocument. Use the Document property to specify the System.Drawing.Printing.PrintDocument that will be manipulated by the dialog. Alternatively, you can specify the PageSettings and PrinterSettings individually.

Various parts of the standard dialog can be enabled or disabled with the AllowMargins, AllowOrientation, AllowPaper, AllowPrinter, and ShowNetwork properties. You can also specify the MinMargins that can be set for this particular dialog.

```
public sealed class PageSetupDialog : CommonDialog {
// Public Constructors
    public PageSetupDialog( );
// Public Instance Properties
    public bool AllowMargins{set; get; }
    public bool AllowOrientation{set; get; }
    public bool AllowPaper{set; get; }
    public bool AllowPrinter{set; get; }
    public PrintDocument Document{set; get; }
    public Margins MinMargins{set; get; }
```

```
  public PageSettings PageSettings{set; get; }
  public PrinterSettings PrinterSettings{set; get; }
  public bool ShowHelp{set; get; }
  public bool ShowNetwork{set; get; }
// Public Instance Methods
  public override void Reset( );                                    // overrides CommonDialog
// Protected Instance Methods
  protected override bool RunDialog(IntPtr hwndOwner);              // overrides CommonDialog
}
```

Hierarchy System.Object → System.MarshalByRefObject → System.ComponentModel.Component(System.ComponentModel.IComponent, System.IDisposable) → CommonDialog → PageSetupDialog

PaintEventArgs **disposable**

System.Windows.Forms (system.windows.forms.dll) class

This class encapsulates the data used by the Control.Paint event, raised when the Control needs repainting.

You can retrieve the System.Drawing.Graphics surface on which to draw and the ClipRectangle that needs repainting (to optimize your paint function).

Information about repaint is also included under Control and ControlStyles.

```
public class PaintEventArgs : EventArgs : IDisposable {
// Public Constructors
  public PaintEventArgs(System.Drawing.Graphics graphics, System.Drawing.Rectangle clipRect);
// Public Instance Properties
  public Rectangle ClipRectangle{get; }
  public Graphics Graphics{get; }
// Public Instance Methods
  public void Dispose( );                                           // implements IDisposable
// Protected Instance Methods
  protected virtual void Dispose(bool disposing);
  protected override void Finalize( );                              // overrides object
}
```

Hierarchy System.Object → System.EventArgs → PaintEventArgs(System.IDisposable)

Passed To Control.{InvokePaint( ), InvokePaintBackground( ), OnPaintBackground( ), RaisePaintEvent( )}, System.Windows.Forms.Design.ComponentTray.OnPaint( ), System.Windows.Forms.Design.ControlDesigner.OnPaintAdornments( ), PaintEventHandler.{BeginInvoke( ), Invoke( )}

PaintEventHandler **serializable**

System.Windows.Forms (system.windows.forms.dll) delegate

This is the delegate for the Control.Paint event.

```
public delegate void PaintEventHandler(object sender, PaintEventArgs e);
```

Associated Events Multiple types

Panel

marshal by reference, disposable

System.Windows.Forms (system.windows.forms.dll) class

This Control acts as a container for other controls. The usual reason for creating a Panel is to support a particular layout scheme. It also supports a BorderStyle.

Note that introducing a Panel starts to play havoc with the pseudotransparency supported by the framework (you will often see the background painted into the panel with (0,0) in client coordinates, rather than parent coordinates, which can cause trouble with panels inside group boxes, for example.

When you are creating your own classes, you should derive from UserControl rather than Panel. While the only superficial difference at this time is that you can set the BorderStyle of a Panel, a UserControl also offers design-time support.

```
public class Panel : ScrollableControl {
// Public Constructors
   public Panel( );
// Public Instance Properties
   public BorderStyle BorderStyle{set; get; }
   public bool TabStop{set; get; }                                    // overrides Control
   public override string Text{set; get; }                            // overrides Control
// Protected Instance Properties
   protected override CreateParams CreateParams{get; }                // overrides ScrollableControl
   protected override Size DefaultSize{get; }                         // overrides Control
// Public Instance Methods
   public override string ToString( );              // overrides System.ComponentModel.Component
// Protected Instance Methods
   protected override void OnResize(EventArgs eventargs);             // overrides Control
// Events
   public event KeyEventHandler KeyDown;                              // overrides Control
   public event KeyPressEventHandler KeyPress;                        // overrides Control
   public event KeyEventHandler KeyUp;                                // overrides Control
}
```

Hierarchy System.Object → System.MarshalByRefObject → System.ComponentModel.Component(System.ComponentModel.IComponent, System.IDisposable) → Control(IOleControl, IOleObject, IOleInPlaceObject, IOleInPlaceActiveObject, IOleWindow, IViewObject, IViewObject2, IPersist, IPersistStreamInit, IPersistPropertyBag, IPersistStorage, IQuickActivate, System.ComponentModel.ISynchronizeInvoke, IWin32Window) → ScrollableControl → Panel

Subclasses TabPage, System.Windows.Forms.Design.ComponentEditorPage

PictureBox

marshal by reference, disposable

System.Windows.Forms (system.windows.forms.dll) class

This Control allows you to display an Image in a control. The control itself can adapt to the size of the image by setting the PictureBoxSizeMode. AutoSize locks the horizontal and vertical dimensions of the control to be the same as those of the Image. CenterImage ensures that the center of the image and the center of the control coincide, StretchImage distorts the image to fit the control dimensions (note that this does not preserve the aspect ratio of the original image), and **Normal** ensures that the top left of the control coincides with the top left of the image, regardless of their relative sizes.

If the **Image** supports animation, this control will play that animation. There is no need for a separate animation control such as the one provided by Win32.


```
public class PictureBox : Control {
// Public Constructors
   public PictureBox( );
// Public Instance Properties
   public override bool AllowDrop{set; get; }                                    // overrides Control
   public BorderStyle BorderStyle{set; get; }
   public bool CausesValidation{set; get; }                                      // overrides Control
   public override Font Font{set; get; }                                         // overrides Control
   public override Color ForeColor{set; get; }                                   // overrides Control
   public Image Image{set; get; }
   public ImeMode ImeMode{set; get; }                                            // overrides Control
   public override RightToLeft RightToLeft{set; get; }                           // overrides Control
   public PictureBoxSizeMode SizeMode{set; get; }
   public int TabIndex{set; get; }                                               // overrides Control
   public bool TabStop{set; get; }                                               // overrides Control
   public override string Text{set; get; }                                       // overrides Control
// Protected Instance Properties
   protected override CreateParams CreateParams{get; }                           // overrides Control
   protected override ImeMode DefaultImeMode{get; }                              // overrides Control
   protected override Size DefaultSize{get; }                                    // overrides Control
// Public Instance Methods
   public override string ToString( );              // overrides System.ComponentModel.Component
// Protected Instance Methods
   protected override void Dispose(bool disposing);                              // overrides Control
   protected override void OnEnabledChanged(EventArgs e);                        // overrides Control
   protected override void OnPaint(PaintEventArgs pe);                           // overrides Control
   protected override void OnParentChanged(EventArgs e);                         // overrides Control
   protected override void OnResize(EventArgs e);                                // overrides Control
   protected virtual void OnSizeModeChanged(EventArgs e);
   protected override void OnVisibleChanged(EventArgs e);                        // overrides Control
   protected override void SetBoundsCore(int x, int y, int width, int height, BoundsSpecified specified);   // overrides Control
// Events
   public event EventHandler Enter;                                              // overrides Control
   public event KeyEventHandler KeyDown;                                         // overrides Control
   public event KeyPressEventHandler KeyPress;                                    // overrides Control
   public event KeyEventHandler KeyUp;                                           // overrides Control
   public event EventHandler Leave;                                              // overrides Control
   public event EventHandler SizeModeChanged;
}
```

Hierarchy System.Object → System.MarshalByRefObject → System.ComponentModel.Component(System.ComponentModel.IComponent, System.IDisposable) → Control(IOleControl, IOleObject, IOleInPlaceObject, IOleInPlaceActiveObject, IOleWindow, IViewObject, IViewObject2, IPersist, IPersistStreamInit, IPersistPropertyBag, IPersistStorage, IQuickActivate, System.ComponentModel.ISynchronizeInvoke, IWin32Window) → PictureBox

PictureBoxSizeMode **serializable**

System.Windows.Forms (system.windows.forms.dll) enum

This enumeration specifies the sizing options for a PictureBox control.

```
public enum PictureBoxSizeMode {
  Normal = 0,
  StretchImage = 1,
  AutoSize = 2,
  CenterImage = 3
}
```

Hierarchy System.Object → System.ValueType → System.Enum(System.IComparable, System.IFormattable, System.IConvertible) → PictureBoxSizeMode

Returned By PictureBox.SizeMode

Passed To PictureBox.SizeMode

PrintControllerWithStatusDialog

System.Windows.Forms (system.windows.forms.dll) class

This class, derived from System.Drawing.Printing.PrintController, provides a status dialog while printing occurs. The dialog is hosted on a separate thread, and it automatically updates the document title and page number as printing continues.

The implementation of this class is interesting, as it illustrates one way of managing a multithreaded progress dialog. A decompilation tool such as Anakrino allows you to examine this for yourself.

```
public class PrintControllerWithStatusDialog : System.Drawing.Printing.PrintController {
// Public Constructors
  public PrintControllerWithStatusDialog(System.Drawing.Printing.PrintController underlyingController);

  public PrintControllerWithStatusDialog(System.Drawing.Printing.PrintController underlyingController,
     string dialogTitle);
// Public Instance Methods
  public override void OnEndPage(System.Drawing.Printing.PrintDocument document,
     System.Drawing.Printing.PrintPageEventArgs e);                 // overrides System.Drawing.Printing.PrintController
  public override void OnEndPrint(System.Drawing.Printing.PrintDocument document,
     System.Drawing.Printing.PrintEventArgs e);                     // overrides System.Drawing.Printing.PrintController
  public override Graphics OnStartPage(System.Drawing.Printing.PrintDocument document,
     System.Drawing.Printing.PrintPageEventArgs e);                 // overrides System.Drawing.Printing.PrintController
  public override void OnStartPrint(System.Drawing.Printing.PrintDocument document,
     System.Drawing.Printing.PrintEventArgs e);                     // overrides System.Drawing.Printing.PrintController
}
```

Hierarchy System.Object → System.Drawing.Printing.PrintController → PrintControllerWithStatusDialog

PrintDialog

marshal by reference, disposable

System.Windows.Forms (system.windows.forms.dll) sealed class

This CommonDialog is used to determine which portions of a document to print, on which printer.

You can enable and disable various bits of functionality with the AllowPrintToFile, AllowSelection, AllowSomePages, and ShowNetwork properties. The PrintToFile member allows you to programmatically switch between file and printer output.

The PrinterSettings to be modified can be specified either through the Document, or alternatively, you can choose a particular PrinterSettings object to manipulate.

Finally, you can restore default settings with the Reset( ) method.

```
public sealed class PrintDialog : CommonDialog {
// Public Constructors
   public PrintDialog( );
// Public Instance Properties
   public bool AllowPrintToFile{set; get; }
   public bool AllowSelection{set; get; }
   public bool AllowSomePages{set; get; }
   public PrintDocument Document{set; get; }
   public PrinterSettings PrinterSettings{set; get; }
   public bool PrintToFile{set; get; }
   public bool ShowHelp{set; get; }
   public bool ShowNetwork{set; get; }
// Public Instance Methods
   public override void Reset( );                                    // overrides CommonDialog
// Protected Instance Methods
   protected override bool RunDialog(IntPtr hwndOwner);              // overrides CommonDialog
}
```

Hierarchy System.Object → System.MarshalByRefObject → System.ComponentModel.Component(System.ComponentModel.IComponent, System.IDisposable) → CommonDialog → PrintDialog

PrintPreviewControl

marshal by reference, disposable

System.Windows.Forms (system.windows.forms.dll) class

This Control provides standardized print preview facilities to your application. It includes only the body of the print preview, rather than all the buttons and other facilities. For standard print preview you should use the PrintPreviewDialog, but if you have specific, custom requirements, you can embed this object instead and provide your own supporting UI.

To use the control, you should provide a Document to be previewed. You can then decide how many Columns and Rows of pages will be displayed and whether to AutoZoom to fit (if not, you can specify your own Zoom factor). You can also enable or disable high-quality antialiasing with the UseAntiAlias property.

```
public class PrintPreviewControl : Control {
// Public Constructors
   public PrintPreviewControl( );
```

```
// Public Instance Properties
   public bool AutoZoom{set; get; }
   public int Columns{set; get; }
   public PrintDocument Document{set; get; }
   public int Rows{set; get; }
   public int StartPage{set; get; }
   public override string Text{set; get; }                          // overrides Control
   public bool UseAntiAlias{set; get; }
   public double Zoom{set; get; }
// Protected Instance Properties
   protected override CreateParams CreateParams{get; }              // overrides Control
// Public Instance Methods
   public void InvalidatePreview( );
   public override void ResetBackColor( );                          // overrides Control
   public override void ResetForeColor( );                          // overrides Control
// Protected Instance Methods
   protected override void OnPaint(PaintEventArgs pevent);          // overrides Control
   protected override void OnResize(EventArgs eventargs);           // overrides Control
   protected virtual void OnStartPageChanged(EventArgs e);
   protected override void WndProc(ref Message m);                  // overrides Control
// Events
   public event EventHandler StartPageChanged;
}
```

Hierarchy System.Object → System.MarshalByRefObject → System.ComponentModel.Component(System.ComponentModel.IComponent, System.IDisposable) → Control(IOleControl, IOleObject, IOleInPlaceObject, IOleInPlaceActiveObject, IOleWindow, IViewObject, IViewObject2, IPersist, IPersistStreamInit, IPersistPropertyBag, IPersistStorage, IQuickActivate, System.ComponentModel.ISynchronizeInvoke, IWin32Window) → PrintPreviewControl

Returned By PrintPreviewDialog.PrintPreviewControl

PrintPreviewDialog **marshal by reference, disposable**

System.Windows.Forms (system.windows.forms.dll) class

This Form hosts the PrintPreviewControl to provide a print preview facility in your application, including the standard control buttons you require to alter the zoom factor, display page layout (including the range of pages to view), and to start a print to the default print device.

It exposes the same programmatic interface as the PrintPreviewControl, through delegation.

```
public class PrintPreviewDialog : Form {
// Public Constructors
   public PrintPreviewDialog( );
// Public Instance Properties
   public IButtonControl AcceptButton{set; get; }                   // overrides Form
   public string AccessibleDescription{set; get; }                  // overrides Control
   public string AccessibleName{set; get; }                         // overrides Control
   public AccessibleRole AccessibleRole{set; get; }                 // overrides Control
   public override bool AllowDrop{set; get; }                       // overrides Control
```

```
  public override AnchorStyles Anchor{set; get; }                      // overrides Control
  public bool AutoScale{set; get; }                                    // overrides Form
  public override Size AutoScaleBaseSize{set; get; }                   // overrides Form
  public override bool AutoScroll{set; get; }                          // overrides Form
  public Size AutoScrollMargin{set; get; }                             // overrides ScrollableControl
  public Size AutoScrollMinSize{set; get; }                            // overrides ScrollableControl
  public override Color BackColor{set; get; }                          // overrides Form
  public override Image BackgroundImage{set; get; }                    // overrides Control
  public IButtonControl CancelButton{set; get; }                       // overrides Form
  public bool CausesValidation{set; get; }                             // overrides Control
  public override ContextMenu ContextMenu{set; get; }                  // overrides Control
  public bool ControlBox{set; get; }                                   // overrides Form
  public override Cursor Cursor{set; get; }                            // overrides Control
  public ControlBindingsCollection DataBindings{get; }                 // overrides Control
  public override DockStyle Dock{set; get; }                           // overrides Control
  public DockPaddingEdges DockPadding{get; }                           // overrides ScrollableControl
  public PrintDocument Document{set; get; }
  public bool Enabled{set; get; }                                      // overrides Control
  public override Font Font{set; get; }                                // overrides Control
  public override Color ForeColor{set; get; }                          // overrides Control
  public FormBorderStyle FormBorderStyle{set; get; }                   // overrides Form
  public bool HelpButton{set; get; }                                   // overrides Form
  public Icon Icon{set; get; }                                         // overrides Form
  public ImeMode ImeMode{set; get; }                                   // overrides Control
  public bool IsMdiContainer{set; get; }                               // overrides Form
  public bool KeyPreview{set; get; }                                   // overrides Form
  public Point Location{set; get; }                                    // overrides Control
  public bool MaximizeBox{set; get; }                                  // overrides Form
  public Size MaximumSize{set; get; }                                  // overrides Form
  public MainMenu Menu{set; get; }                                     // overrides Form
  public bool MinimizeBox{set; get; }                                  // overrides Form
  public Size MinimumSize{set; get; }                                  // overrides Form
  public double Opacity{set; get; }                                    // overrides Form
  public PrintPreviewControl PrintPreviewControl{get; }
  public override RightToLeft RightToLeft{set; get; }                  // overrides Control
  public bool ShowInTaskbar{set; get; }                                // overrides Form
  public Size Size{set; get; }                                         // overrides Form
  public SizeGripStyle SizeGripStyle{set; get; }                       // overrides Form
  public FormStartPosition StartPosition{set; get; }                   // overrides Form
  public bool TabStop{set; get; }                                      // overrides Control
  public object Tag{set; get; }                                        // overrides Control
  public override string Text{set; get; }                              // overrides Control
  public bool TopMost{set; get; }                                      // overrides Form
  public Color TransparencyKey{set; get; }                             // overrides Form
  public bool UseAntiAlias{set; get; }
  public bool Visible{set; get; }                                      // overrides Control
  public FormWindowState WindowState{set; get; }                       // overrides Form
// Protected Instance Methods
  protected override void CreateHandle( );                             // overrides Form
  protected override void OnClosing(System.ComponentModel.CancelEventArgs e);  // overrides Form
}
```

Hierarchy System.Object → System.MarshalByRefObject → System.ComponentModel.Component(System.ComponentModel.IComponent, System.IDisposable) → Control(IOleControl, IOleObject, IOleInPlaceObject, IOleInPlaceActiveObject, IOleWindow, IViewObject, IViewObject2, IPersist, IPersistStreamInit, IPersistPropertyBag, IPersistStorage, IQuickActivate, System.ComponentModel.ISynchronizeInvoke, IWin32Window) → ScrollableControl → ContainerControl(IContainerControl) → Form → PrintPreviewDialog

ProgressBar

marshal by reference, disposable

System.Windows.Forms (system.windows.forms.dll) sealed class

The ProgressBar class wraps the Win32 progress control to graphically represent the completion of a long operation.

You can specify the Minimum and Maximum value that can be represented by the control, along with the current Value. The control fills from the minimum on the left to the maximum on the right. Note that it does not honor right-to-left reading, so left and right really do mean left and right.

You can also specify a Step, which will be added to the current Value each time you call PerformStep( ), or you can Increment( ) the value by a particular amount.

```
public sealed class ProgressBar : Control {
// Public Constructors
   public ProgressBar( );
// Public Instance Properties
   public override bool AllowDrop{set; get; }                                    // overrides Control
   public override Color BackColor{set; get; }                                   // overrides Control
   public override Image BackgroundImage{set; get; }                             // overrides Control
   public bool CausesValidation{set; get; }                                      // overrides Control
   public override Font Font{set; get; }                                         // overrides Control
   public override Color ForeColor{set; get; }                                   // overrides Control
   public ImeMode ImeMode{set; get; }                                            // overrides Control
   public int Maximum{set; get; }
   public int Minimum{set; get; }
   public override RightToLeft RightToLeft{set; get; }                           // overrides Control
   public int Step{set; get; }
   public bool TabStop{set; get; }                                               // overrides Control
   public override string Text{set; get; }                                       // overrides Control
   public int Value{set; get; }
// Protected Instance Properties
   protected override CreateParams CreateParams{get; }                           // overrides Control
   protected override ImeMode DefaultImeMode{get; }                              // overrides Control
   protected override Size DefaultSize{get; }                                    // overrides Control
// Public Instance Methods
   public void Increment(int value);
   public void PerformStep( );
   public override string ToString( );              // overrides System.ComponentModel.Component
// Protected Instance Methods
   protected override void CreateHandle( );                                      // overrides Control
   protected override void OnHandleCreated(EventArgs e);                         // overrides Control
// Events
   public event EventHandler DoubleClick;                                        // overrides Control
   public event EventHandler Enter;                                              // overrides Control
```

```
public event KeyEventHandler KeyDown;                                  // overrides Control
public event KeyPressEventHandler KeyPress;                            // overrides Control
public event KeyEventHandler KeyUp;                                    // overrides Control
public event EventHandler Leave;                                       // overrides Control
public event PaintEventHandler Paint;                                  // overrides Control
}
```

Hierarchy System.Object → System.MarshalByRefObject → System.ComponentModel.Component(System.ComponentModel.IComponent, System.IDisposable) → Control(IOleControl, IOleObject, IOleInPlaceObject, IOleInPlaceActiveObject, IOleWindow, IViewObject, IViewObject2, IPersist, IPersistStreamInit, IPersistPropertyBag, IPersistStorage, IQuickActivate, System.ComponentModel.ISynchronizeInvoke, IWin32Window) → ProgressBar

PropertyGrid **marshal by reference, disposable**

System.Windows.Forms (system.windows.forms.dll) class

This Control will be very familiar to users of the Visual Studio .NET IDE, as it is used to provide the property inspector for objects in the designer. You can use it to provide a similar function in your own applications.

At its simplest, you can assign any object to the SelectedObject property, and it will use reflection to discover the properties and events in your object. You can also set an array of SelectedObjects. The grid will then display only those properties common to the entire array. This should not be confused with the SelectedGridItem property, which returns a GridItem representing the currently selected row in the grid. You can bind to the SelectedGridItemChanged event to receive notification when the selection is modified. As the values in the grid change, the PropertyValueChanged event is raised. If the SelectedObject (or SelectedObjects) changes, the grid will fire SelectedObjectsChanged.

Beyond that, you can use several designer attributes to mark up your target objects for use with the PropertyGrid, including System.ComponentModel.CategoryAttribute, which provides a means of visually grouping properties, and System.ComponentModel.DescriptionAttribute, which displays help text.

A property will appear in the grid unless it is annotated with No. You can customize this behavior by creating a new System.ComponentModel.AttributeCollection (passing an array of Attribute objects in the constructor) and assigning it to the grid's BrowsableAttributes property. The object must then be annotated with every attribute in this collection for it to appear.

To facilitate the editing of properties that are not understood by the default designers, you can provide a custom System.ComponentModel.TypeConverter and/or System.Drawing.Design.UITypeEditor for any and all of the types the target object exposes.

The grid can also display any System.ComponentModel.Design.DesignerVerb (essentially design-time commands) that a System.ComponentModel.Design.IDesigner-derived class exposes for the target object through its Verbs property. All these features are exactly like those facilities provided by the design-time environment.

Aside from the design-time features, there are a number of properties that you can use to control the appearance of the grid itself.

The PropertyGrid has a toolbar that allows the user to customize various aspects of its appearance. If you don't require this toolbar, it can be hidden with the ToolbarVisible property.

A panel for the verbs can be shown or hidden using the CommandsVisible property, but you can determine whether this is permissible at all with the CanShowCommands member. You can also decide not to show the verb panel if there are no verbs defined by using the CommandsVisibleIfAvailable property. The color of this pane can be changed with the CommandsBackColor and CommandsForeColor properties.

Similarly, you can show or hide the help region with the HelpVisible property and set its colors with the HelpForeColor and HelpBackColor. The grid will display the text specified in the System.ComponentModel.DescriptionAttribute with which you adorned a property.

By default, the grid sorts the properties into groups according to their System.ComponentModel.CategoryAttributes (with Misc being the default group for unattributed properties). If you don't want this behavior, it can be modified by changing the PropertySort member (Alphabetical, for instance, would display a single alphabetical list).

You can also change the LineColor of the grid lines and the size of the toolbar buttons (with the LargeButtons member).

```
public class PropertyGrid : ContainerControl : System.Windows.Forms.ComponentModel.Com2Interop.
IComPropertyBrowser, IPropertyNotifySink {
// Public Constructors
   public PropertyGrid( );
// Public Instance Properties
   public override bool AutoScroll{set; get; }                          // overrides ScrollableControl
   public override Color BackColor{set; get; }                                   // overrides Control
   public override Image BackgroundImage{set; get; }                             // overrides Control
   public AttributeCollection BrowsableAttributes{set; get; }
   public virtual bool CanShowCommands{get; }
   public Color CommandsBackColor{set; get; }
   public Color CommandsForeColor{set; get; }
   public virtual bool CommandsVisible{get; }
   public virtual bool CommandsVisibleIfAvailable{set; get; }
   public Point ContextMenuDefaultLocation{get; }
   public ControlCollection Controls{get; }                                      // overrides Control
   public override Color ForeColor{set; get; }                                   // overrides Control
   public Color HelpBackColor{set; get; }
   public Color HelpForeColor{set; get; }
   public virtual bool HelpVisible{set; get; }
   public bool LargeButtons{set; get; }
   public Color LineColor{set; get; }
   public PropertySort PropertySort{set; get; }
   public PropertyTabCollection PropertyTabs{get; }
   public GridItem SelectedGridItem{set; get; }
   public object SelectedObject{set; get; }
   public object[ ] SelectedObjects{set; get; }
   public PropertyTab SelectedTab{get; }
   public override ISite Site{set; get; }                                        // overrides Control
   public virtual bool ToolbarVisible{set; get; }
   public Color ViewBackColor{set; get; }
   public Color ViewForeColor{set; get; }
// Protected Instance Properties
   protected override Size DefaultSize{get; }                                    // overrides Control
   protected virtual Type DefaultTabType{get; }
   protected bool DrawFlatToolbar{set; get; }
```

```
  protected override bool ShowFocusCues{get; }                                    // overrides Control
// Public Instance Methods
  public void CollapseAllGridItems( );
  public void ExpandAllGridItems( );
  public override void Refresh( );                                                // overrides Control
  public void RefreshTabs(System.ComponentModel.PropertyTabScope tabScope);
  public void ResetSelectedProperty( );
// Protected Instance Methods
  protected virtual PropertyTab CreatePropertyTab(Type tabType);
  protected override void Dispose(bool disposing);                       // overrides ContainerControl
  protected void OnComComponentNameChanged(System.ComponentModel.Design.ComponentRenameEventArgs e);
  protected override void OnFontChanged(EventArgs e);                             // overrides Control
  protected override void OnGotFocus(EventArgs e);                                // overrides Control
  protected override void OnHandleCreated(EventArgs e);                           // overrides Control
  protected override void OnHandleDestroyed(EventArgs e);                         // overrides Control
  protected override void OnMouseDown(MouseEventArgs me);                         // overrides Control
  protected override void OnMouseMove(MouseEventArgs me);                         // overrides Control
  protected override void OnMouseUp(MouseEventArgs me);                           // overrides Control
  protected void OnNotifyPropertyValueUIItemsChanged(object sender, EventArgs e);
  protected override void OnPaint(PaintEventArgs pevent);                         // overrides Control
  protected virtual void OnPropertyTabChanged(PropertyTabChangedEventArgs e);
  protected virtual void OnPropertyValueChanged(PropertyValueChangedEventArgs e);
  protected override void OnResize(EventArgs e);                                  // overrides Control
  protected virtual void OnSelectedGridItemChanged(SelectedGridItemChangedEventArgs e);
  protected virtual void OnSelectedObjectsChanged(EventArgs e);
  protected override void OnSystemColorsChanged(EventArgs e);                     // overrides Control
  protected override void OnVisibleChanged(EventArgs e);                 // overrides ScrollableControl
  protected override bool ProcessDialogKey(Keys keyData);                // overrides ContainerControl
  protected override void ScaleCore(float dx, float dy);                 // overrides ScrollableControl
  protected void ShowEventsButton(bool value);
  protected override void WndProc(ref Message m);                        // overrides ContainerControl
// Events
  public event EventHandler PropertySortChanged;
  public event PropertyTabChangedEventHandler PropertyTabChanged;
  public event PropertyValueChangedEventHandler PropertyValueChanged;
  public event SelectedGridItemChangedEventHandler SelectedGridItemChanged;
  public event EventHandler SelectedObjectsChanged;
}
```

Hierarchy System.Object → System.MarshalByRefObject → System.ComponentModel.Component(System.ComponentModel.IComponent, System.IDisposable) → Control(IOleControl, IOleObject, IOleInPlaceObject, IOleInPlaceActiveObject, IOleWindow, IViewObject, IViewObject2, IPersist, IPersistStreamInit, IPersistPropertyBag, IPersistStorage, IQuickActivate, System.ComponentModel.ISynchronizeInvoke, IWin32Window) → ScrollableControl → ContainerControl(IContainerControl) → PropertyGrid(System.Windows.Forms.ComponentModel.Com2Interop.IComPropertyBrowser, IPropertyNotifySink)

PropertyGrid.PropertyTabCollection

System.Windows.Forms (system.windows.forms.dll) class

This class represents the collection of System.Windows.Forms.Design.PropertyTab objects being displayed by the PropertyGrid.

```
public class PropertyGrid.PropertyTabCollection : ICollection, IEnumerable {
// Public Instance Properties
   public int Count{get; }                                                // implements ICollection
   public PropertyTab this{get; }
// Public Instance Methods
   public void AddTabType(Type propertyTabType);
   public void AddTabType(Type propertyTabType, System.ComponentModel.PropertyTabScope tabScope);
   public void Clear(System.ComponentModel.PropertyTabScope tabScope);
   public IEnumerator GetEnumerator( );                                   // implements IEnumerable
   public void RemoveTabType(Type propertyTabType);
}
```

PropertyManager

System.Windows.Forms (system.windows.forms.dll) class

This class, derived from BindingManagerBase represents a bag of Binding objects for a simple property-like data source.

While CurrencyManager deals with lists of objects, the PropertyManager is bound to a single item. Therefore, it is hardwired to look like a list with one entry (at Position zero).

It ensures that all the Binding objects update correctly as the value of this single property changes, by binding to an appropriately named event. For example, a component providing a Text property must also raise a TextChanged event.

See Binding for more information on the data-binding architecture.

```
public class PropertyManager : BindingManagerBase {
// Public Constructors
   public PropertyManager( );
// Public Instance Properties
   public override int Count{get; }                                       // overrides BindingManagerBase
   public override object Current{get; }                                  // overrides BindingManagerBase
   public override int Position{set; get; }                               // overrides BindingManagerBase
// Public Instance Methods
   public override void AddNew( );                                        // overrides BindingManagerBase
   public override void CancelCurrentEdit( );                             // overrides BindingManagerBase
   public override void EndCurrentEdit( );                                // overrides BindingManagerBase
   public override PropertyDescriptorCollection GetItemProperties( );     // overrides BindingManagerBase
   public override void RemoveAt(int index);                              // overrides BindingManagerBase
   public override void ResumeBinding( );                                 // overrides BindingManagerBase
   public override void SuspendBinding( );                                // overrides BindingManagerBase
// Protected Instance Methods
   protected internal override string GetListName(
      System.Collections.ArrayList listAccessors);                        // overrides BindingManagerBase
   protected internal override void OnCurrentChanged(EventArgs ea);       // overrides BindingManagerBase
   protected override void UpdateIsBinding( );                            // overrides BindingManagerBase
}
```

Hierarchy System.Object → BindingManagerBase → PropertyManager

PropertySort serializable

System.Windows.Forms (system.windows.forms.dll) enum

This enumeration is used by the PropertyGrid.PropertySort member to determine how the items in the grid are arranged and grouped.

```
public enum PropertySort {
  NoSort = 0,
  Alphabetical = 1,
  Categorized = 2,
  CategorizedAlphabetical = 3
}
```

Hierarchy System.Object → System.ValueType → System.Enum(System.IComparable, System.IFormattable, System.IConvertible) → PropertySort

Returned By PropertyGrid.PropertySort

Passed To PropertyGrid.PropertySort

PropertyTabChangedEventArgs

System.Windows.Forms (system.windows.forms.dll) class

The PropertyGrid control may display a number of different System.Windows.Forms.Design.PropertyTab panes. When the tab changes, the grid raises PropertyGrid.PropertyTabChanged, and this class encapsulates the data for that event.

You can retrieve the NewTab (to which the grid is about to change) and the OldTab (from which the grid is about to change).

```
public class PropertyTabChangedEventArgs : EventArgs {
// Public Constructors
  public PropertyTabChangedEventArgs(System.Windows.Forms.Design.PropertyTab oldTab,
    System.Windows.Forms.Design.PropertyTab newTab);
// Public Instance Properties
  public PropertyTab NewTab{get; }
  public PropertyTab OldTab{get; }
}
```

Hierarchy System.Object → System.EventArgs → PropertyTabChangedEventArgs

Passed To PropertyGrid.OnPropertyTabChanged( ), PropertyTabChangedEventHandler.{BeginInvoke( ), Invoke( )}

PropertyTabChangedEventHandler serializable

System.Windows.Forms (system.windows.forms.dll) delegate

This is the delegate for the PropertyGrid.PropertyTabChanged event.

```
public delegate void PropertyTabChangedEventHandler(object s, PropertyTabChangedEventArgs e);
```

Associated Events PropertyGrid.PropertyTabChanged( )

PropertyValueChangedEventArgs

System.Windows.Forms (system.windows.forms.dll) class

This class encapsulates the event data for the **PropertyGrid.PropertyValueChanged** event. You can retrieve the **GridItem** that changed (from which you can also determine the new value of the property) and the **OldValue** of the object.

```
public class PropertyValueChangedEventArgs : EventArgs {
// Public Constructors
   public PropertyValueChangedEventArgs(GridItem changedItem, object oldValue);
// Public Instance Properties
   public GridItem ChangedItem{get; }
   public object OldValue{get; }
}
```

Hierarchy System.Object → System.EventArgs → PropertyValueChangedEventArgs

Passed To PropertyGrid.OnPropertyValueChanged( ), PropertyValueChangedEventHandler.{BeginInvoke( ), Invoke( )}

PropertyValueChangedEventHandler serializable

System.Windows.Forms (system.windows.forms.dll) delegate

This is the delegate for the **PropertyGrid.PropertyValueChanged** event.

```
public delegate void PropertyValueChangedEventHandler(object s, PropertyValueChangedEventArgs e);
```

Associated Events PropertyGrid.PropertyValueChanged( )

QueryAccessibilityHelpEventArgs

System.Windows.Forms (system.windows.forms.dll) class

When an accessibility client (such as a screen reader) requires help information from a **Control**, it raises the **QueryAccessibilityHelp** event, to allow you to provide custom help information. This class encapsulates the data for this event.

You should set the **HelpNamespace** (the URI of the help file), the **HelpKeyword** (the topic ID within that file, as a string), and the **HelpString** (the What's This? help information) for the control on which help is requested.

```
public class QueryAccessibilityHelpEventArgs : EventArgs {
// Public Constructors
   public QueryAccessibilityHelpEventArgs( );
   public QueryAccessibilityHelpEventArgs(string helpNamespace, string helpString, string helpKeyword);
// Public Instance Properties
   public string HelpKeyword{set; get; }
   public string HelpNamespace{set; get; }
   public string HelpString{set; get; }
}
```

Hierarchy System.Object → System.EventArgs → QueryAccessibilityHelpEventArgs

Passed To QueryAccessibilityHelpEventHandler.{BeginInvoke( ), Invoke( )}

QueryAccessibilityHelpEventHandler **serializable**

System.Windows.Forms (system.windows.forms.dll) **delegate**

This is the delegate for the Control.QueryAccessibilityHelp event.

```
public delegate void QueryAccessibilityHelpEventHandler(object sender, QueryAccessibilityHelpEventArgs e);
```

Associated Events Multiple types

QueryContinueDragEventArgs

System.Windows.Forms (system.windows.forms.dll) **class**

This class encapsulates the data for the Control.QueryContinueDrag event.

The Control raises this event periodically throughout a drag-and-drop operation initiated by Control.DoDragDrop( ).

If you bind to it, you can use this object to set the expected Action, perhaps forcing the operation to Continue or Cancel.

EscapePressed and KeyState provide information as to whether the user pressed the Esc key, and which other modifier keys (CTRL, SHIFT, ALT) were depressed at the time.

```
public class QueryContinueDragEventArgs : EventArgs {
// Public Constructors
   public QueryContinueDragEventArgs(int keyState, bool escapePressed, DragAction action);
// Public Instance Properties
   public DragAction Action{set; get; }
   public bool EscapePressed{get; }
   public int KeyState{get; }
}
```

Hierarchy System.Object → System.EventArgs → QueryContinueDragEventArgs

Passed To Control.OnQueryContinueDrag( ), QueryContinueDragEventHandler.{BeginInvoke( ), Invoke( )}

QueryContinueDragEventHandler **serializable**

System.Windows.Forms (system.windows.forms.dll) **delegate**

This is the delegate for the Control.QueryContinueDrag event.

```
public delegate void QueryContinueDragEventHandler(object sender, QueryContinueDragEventArgs e);
```

Associated Events Multiple types

RadioButton **marshal by reference, disposable**

System.Windows.Forms (system.windows.forms.dll) **class**

This Control provides a means of selecting one of a set of mutually exclusive options. (Compare this with a set of CheckBox objects that may all be selected simultaneously.) All the RadioButton objects within a single container act as a single exclusion group. Therefore, to have several independent groups on the same parent Control, you must place them in different containers. Panel or GroupBox objects will do the job.

You can change the Appearance of the control from the Normal dot with a label to a Button-like style. In the Normal view, the position of the RadioButton relative to the label can be modified with the CheckAlign property.

As with the CheckBox, you can determine whether the item is Checked (although it does not have an equivalent of the CheckBox.CheckState property, as there is no tristate support). You can also enable AutoCheck to ensure that the system automatically checks the selected button and unchecks the others in the group. You can bind to the CheckedChanged event to be notified when the Checked state changes.

```
public class RadioButton : ButtonBase {
// Public Constructors
   public RadioButton( );
// Public Instance Properties
   public Appearance Appearance{set; get; }
   public bool AutoCheck{set; get; }
   public ContentAlignment CheckAlign{set; get; }
   public bool Checked{set; get; }
   public bool TabStop{set; get; }                                   // overrides Control
   public override ContentAlignment TextAlign{set; get; }            // overrides ButtonBase
// Protected Instance Properties
   protected override CreateParams CreateParams{get; }               // overrides ButtonBase
   protected override Size DefaultSize{get; }                        // overrides ButtonBase
// Public Instance Methods
   public void PerformClick( );
   public override string ToString( );               // overrides System.ComponentModel.Component
// Protected Instance Methods
   protected override AccessibleObject CreateAccessibilityInstance( );    // overrides ButtonBase
   protected virtual void OnCheckedChanged(EventArgs e);
   protected override void OnClick(EventArgs e);                     // overrides Control
   protected override void OnEnter(EventArgs e);                     // overrides Control
   protected override void OnHandleCreated(EventArgs e);             // overrides Control
   protected override void OnMouseUp(MouseEventArgs mevent);         // overrides ButtonBase
   protected override bool ProcessMnemonic(char charCode);           // overrides Control
// Events
   public event EventHandler AppearanceChanged;
   public event EventHandler CheckedChanged;
}
```

Hierarchy System.Object → System.MarshalByRefObject → System.ComponentModel.Component(System.ComponentModel.IComponent, System.IDisposable) → Control(IOleControl, IOleObject, IOleInPlaceObject, IOleInPlaceActiveObject, IOleWindow, IViewObject, IViewObject2, IPersist, IPersistStreamInit, IPersistPropertyBag, IPersistStorage, IQuickActivate, System.ComponentModel.ISynchronizeInvoke, IWin32Window) → ButtonBase → RadioButton

Passed To RadioButtonAccessibleObject.RadioButtonAccessibleObject( )

RadioButton.RadioButtonAccessibleObject — marshal by reference

System.Windows.Forms (system.windows.forms.dll) — class

This class is for internal use and should not be called from your own code.

```
public class RadioButton.RadioButtonAccessibleObject : ControlAccessibleObject {
// Public Constructors
   public RadioButton.RadioButtonAccessibleObject(RadioButton owner);
// Public Instance Properties
   public override string DefaultAction{get; }           // overrides Control.ControlAccessibleObject
   public override AccessibleRole Role{get; }            // overrides Control.ControlAccessibleObject
   public override AccessibleStates State{get; }                    // overrides AccessibleObject
// Public Instance Methods
   public override void DoDefaultAction( );                         // overrides AccessibleObject
}
```

Hierarchy System.Object → System.MarshalByRefObject → AccessibleObject(System.Reflection.IReflect, Accessibility.IAccessible, IEnumVariant) → ControlAccessibleObject → RadioButtonAccessibleObject

RichTextBox

marshal by reference, disposable

System.Windows.Forms (system.windows.forms.dll) class

This Control, derived from TextBoxBase, extends the basic text box functionality to include character and paragraph formatting. It can also display embedded objects such as images, all with an arbitrary ZoomFactor and optional ScrollBars.

Content can be assigned with the standard Text property and AppendText( ) methods. In addition to these TextBoxBase methods, LoadFile( ) will bring plain ASCII text or an RTF file into the control. Alternatively, you can assign formatted Rtf markup directly. If the content contains embedded objects, the string obtained from the Text property will include a placeholder character for each such item. The content can be saved to a file as either ASCII or RTF markup using the SaveFile( ) method.

Once you have some text in the control, you can begin to manipulate it. First, some of this content must be selected, either by the user, or programmatically. To assist the user, you can enable the AutoWordSelection property. This provides the highlight-completion behavior seen in Microsoft WordPad: if you double-click or select a portion of a word, the entire word will be highlighted. You can get and set the SelectionStart and the SelectionLength independently, or set both at once with the Select( ) or SelectAll( ) methods. If the SelectionLength is 0, the SelectionStart represents the position of the caret. ScrollToCaret( ) ensures that the current cursor position is visible on screen.

You can also get the SelectionType. This returns a combination of flags from the RichTextBoxSelectionTypes enumeration. For example, you can determine whether the selection is Empty, Text only, or contains an embedded Object. Bind to the SelectionChanged event to be notified when the selection is modified. You can get or set a string object representing either the SelectedText or SelectedRtf (analogous to Text and Rtf).

You can then set the SelectionAlignment, a SelectionBullet style (and the BulletIndent), SelectionIndent, SelectionHangingIndent, SelectionRightIndent, an array of SelectionTabs, the SelectionColor, and SelectionFont.

Text or objects from the clipboard or drag-and-drop operations can be inserted at the current caret position using the Paste( ) method. To determine whether a particular object's DataFormats.Format is suitable, you should call CanPaste( ). The Cut( ) and Copy( ) methods will place the current selection onto the clipboard (removing the selection or leaving it in place respectively).

You can Find( ) text within the control, optionally specifying one or more of the RichTextBoxFinds flags to determine what the control does when it finds the specified string.

It also supports multilevel undo and redo. There are properties to retrieve the current UndoActionName and RedoActionName. If either of these is the empty string (""), it indicates that no action is available at this time. Undo( ) and Redo( ) methods invoke the current action, while ClearUndo( ) empties the undo list.

One final feature the control offers is the ability to automatically DetectUrls in the body of the text. It reformats the text for you and raises the LinkClicked events when the user clicks them.

```
public class RichTextBox : TextBoxBase {
// Public Constructors
   public RichTextBox( );
// Public Instance Properties
   public override bool AllowDrop{set; get; }                                  // overrides Control
   public override bool AutoSize{set; get; }                                   // overrides TextBoxBase
   public bool AutoWordSelection{set; get; }
   public override Image BackgroundImage{set; get; }                           // overrides TextBoxBase
   public int BulletIndent{set; get; }
   public bool CanRedo{get; }
   public bool DetectUrls{set; get; }
   public override Font Font{set; get; }                                       // overrides Control
   public override Color ForeColor{set; get; }                                 // overrides TextBoxBase
   public override int MaxLength{set; get; }                                   // overrides TextBoxBase
   public override bool Multiline{set; get; }                                  // overrides TextBoxBase
   public string RedoActionName{get; }
   public int RightMargin{set; get; }
   public string Rtf{set; get; }
   public RichTextBoxScrollBars ScrollBars{set; get; }
   public string SelectedRtf{set; get; }
   public override string SelectedText{set; get; }                             // overrides TextBoxBase
   public HorizontalAlignment SelectionAlignment{set; get; }
   public bool SelectionBullet{set; get; }
   public int SelectionCharOffset{set; get; }
   public Color SelectionColor{set; get; }
   public Font SelectionFont{set; get; }
   public int SelectionHangingIndent{set; get; }
   public int SelectionIndent{set; get; }
   public override int SelectionLength{set; get; }                             // overrides TextBoxBase
   public bool SelectionProtected{set; get; }
   public int SelectionRightIndent{set; get; }
   public int[ ] SelectionTabs{set; get; }
   public RichTextBoxSelectionTypes SelectionType{get; }
   public bool ShowSelectionMargin{set; get; }
   public override string Text{set; get; }                                     // overrides TextBoxBase
   public override int TextLength{get; }                                       // overrides TextBoxBase
   public string UndoActionName{get; }
   public float ZoomFactor{set; get; }
// Protected Instance Properties
   protected override CreateParams CreateParams{get; }                         // overrides TextBoxBase
   protected override Size DefaultSize{get; }                                  // overrides TextBoxBase
// Public Instance Methods
   public bool CanPaste(Format clipFormat);
```

```
    public int Find(char[ ] characterSet);
    public int Find(char[ ] characterSet, int start);
    public int Find(char[ ] characterSet, int start, int end);
    public int Find(string str);
    public int Find(string str, int start, int end, RichTextBoxFinds options);
    public int Find(string str, int start, RichTextBoxFinds options);
    public int Find(string str, RichTextBoxFinds options);
    public char GetCharFromPosition(System.Drawing.Point pt);
    public int GetCharIndexFromPosition(System.Drawing.Point pt);
    public int GetLineFromCharIndex(int index);
    public Point GetPositionFromCharIndex(int index);
    public void LoadFile(System.IO.Stream data, RichTextBoxStreamType fileType);
    public void LoadFile(string path);
    public void LoadFile(string path, RichTextBoxStreamType fileType);
    public void Paste(Format clipFormat);
    public void Redo( );
    public void SaveFile(System.IO.Stream data, RichTextBoxStreamType fileType);
    public void SaveFile(string path);
    public void SaveFile(string path, RichTextBoxStreamType fileType);
// Protected Instance Methods
    protected virtual object CreateRichEditOleCallback( );
    protected override void OnBackColorChanged(EventArgs e);                     // overrides Control
    protected virtual void OnContentsResized(ContentsResizedEventArgs e);
    protected override void OnContextMenuChanged(EventArgs e);                   // overrides Control
    protected override void OnHandleCreated(EventArgs e);                        // overrides TextBoxBase
    protected override void OnHandleDestroyed(EventArgs e);                      // overrides TextBoxBase
    protected virtual void OnHScroll(EventArgs e);
    protected virtual void OnImeChange(EventArgs e);
    protected virtual void OnLinkClicked(LinkClickedEventArgs e);
    protected virtual void OnProtected(EventArgs e);
    protected override void OnRightToLeftChanged(EventArgs e);                   // overrides Control
    protected virtual void OnSelectionChanged(EventArgs e);
    protected override void OnSystemColorsChanged(EventArgs e);                  // overrides Control
    protected override void OnTextChanged(EventArgs e);                          // overrides Control
    protected virtual void OnVScroll(EventArgs e);
    protected override void WndProc(ref Message m);                              // overrides TextBoxBase
// Events
    public event ContentsResizedEventHandler ContentsResized;
    public event EventHandler DoubleClick;                                       // overrides Control
    public event DragEventHandler DragDrop;                                      // overrides Control
    public event DragEventHandler DragEnter;                                     // overrides Control
    public event EventHandler DragLeave;                                         // overrides Control
    public event DragEventHandler DragOver;                                      // overrides Control
    public event GiveFeedbackEventHandler GiveFeedback;                          // overrides Control
    public event EventHandler HScroll;
    public event EventHandler ImeChange;
    public event LinkClickedEventHandler LinkClicked;
    public event EventHandler Protected;
    public event QueryContinueDragEventHandler QueryContinueDrag;                // overrides Control
    public event EventHandler SelectionChanged;
    public event EventHandler VScroll;
}
```

Hierarchy System.Object → System.MarshalByRefObject → System.ComponentModel.Component(System.ComponentModel.IComponent, System.IDisposable) → Control(IOleControl, IOleObject, IOleInPlaceObject, IOleInPlaceActiveObject, IOleWindow, IViewObject, IViewObject2, IPersist, IPersistStreamInit, IPersistPropertyBag, IPersistStorage, IQuickActivate, System.ComponentModel.ISynchronizeInvoke, IWin32Window) → TextBoxBase → RichTextBox

RichTextBoxFinds

serializable, flag

System.Windows.Forms (system.windows.forms.dll) enum

This enumeration defines a set of flags to use with the RichTextBox.Find( ) method.

```
public enum RichTextBoxFinds {
  None = 0x00000000,
  WholeWord = 0x00000002,
  MatchCase = 0x00000004,
  NoHighlight = 0x00000008,
  Reverse = 0x00000010
}
```

Hierarchy System.Object → System.ValueType → System.Enum(System.IComparable, System.IFormattable, System.IConvertible) → RichTextBoxFinds

Passed To RichTextBox.Find( )

RichTextBoxScrollBars

serializable

System.Windows.Forms (system.windows.forms.dll) enum

This enumeration is used by the RichTextBox.ScrollBars property to determine how the control manages scrolling.

```
public enum RichTextBoxScrollBars {
  None = 0,
  Horizontal = 1,
  Vertical = 2,
  Both = 3,
  ForcedHorizontal = 17,
  ForcedVertical = 18,
  ForcedBoth = 19
}
```

Hierarchy System.Object → System.ValueType → System.Enum(System.IComparable, System.IFormattable, System.IConvertible) → RichTextBoxScrollBars

Returned By RichTextBox.ScrollBars

Passed To RichTextBox.ScrollBars

RichTextBoxSelectionAttribute

serializable

System.Windows.Forms (system.windows.forms.dll) enum

This attribute class is for internal use only and should not be used to adorn your own code.

```
public enum RichTextBoxSelectionAttribute {
  None = 0,
  All = 1,
  Mixed = -1
}
```

Hierarchy System.Object → System.ValueType → System.Enum(System.IComparable, System.IFormattable, System.IConvertible) → RichTextBoxSelectionAttribute

RichTextBoxSelectionTypes

serializable, flag

System.Windows.Forms (system.windows.forms.dll) enum

This enumeration is used by the RichTextBox.SelectionType property to define the nature of the selection.

```
public enum RichTextBoxSelectionTypes {
  Empty = 0x00000000,
  Text = 0x00000001,
  Object = 0x00000002,
  MultiChar = 0x00000004,
  MultiObject = 0x00000008
}
```

Hierarchy System.Object → System.ValueType → System.Enum(System.IComparable, System.IFormattable, System.IConvertible) → RichTextBoxSelectionTypes

Returned By RichTextBox.SelectionType

RichTextBoxStreamType

serializable

System.Windows.Forms (system.windows.forms.dll) enum

This enumeration is used by the RichTextBox.SaveFile( ) method to specify the format of the file to save (e.g., PlainText will replace any embedded OLE objects with spaces and strip out RTF markup, while RichText will save an RTF stream including all the formatting and embedded objects).

```
public enum RichTextBoxStreamType {
  RichText = 0,
  PlainText = 1,
  RichNoOleObjs = 2,
  TextTextOleObjs = 3,
  UnicodePlainText = 4
}
```

Hierarchy System.Object → System.ValueType → System.Enum(System.IComparable, System.IFormattable, System.IConvertible) → RichTextBoxStreamType

Passed To RichTextBox.{LoadFile( ), SaveFile( )}

RichTextBoxWordPunctuations serializable

System.Windows.Forms (system.windows.forms.dll) enum

This enumeration is for internal use only and should not be used in your own code.

```
public enum RichTextBoxWordPunctuations {
  Level1 = 128,
  Level2 = 256,
  Custom = 512,
  All = 896
}
```

Hierarchy System.Object → System.ValueType → System.Enum(System.IComparable, System.IFormattable, System.IConvertible) → RichTextBoxWordPunctuations

RightToLeft serializable

System.Windows.Forms (system.windows.forms.dll) enum

A Control supporting right-to-left reading cultures will use this enumeration to specify whether the RTL behavior is enabled.

```
public enum RightToLeft {
  No = 0,
  Yes = 1,
  Inherit = 2
}
```

Hierarchy System.Object → System.ValueType → System.Enum(System.IComparable, System.IFormattable, System.IConvertible) → RightToLeft

Returned By ContextMenu.RightToLeft, Control.RightToLeft, MainMenu.RightToLeft

Passed To ContextMenu.RightToLeft, Control.RightToLeft, MainMenu.RightToLeft

SaveFileDialog marshal by reference, disposable

System.Windows.Forms (system.windows.forms.dll) sealed class

This FileDialog class provides a means for a user to select a filename with which to save a file. You can choose to display a prompt if the file does not exist by setting the CreatePrompt property.

OverwritePrompt will do the same if a file with the selected name does exist. The OpenFile( ) method will (create and) open a file Stream for the selected filename.

```
public sealed class SaveFileDialog : FileDialog {
// Public Constructors
  public SaveFileDialog( );
```

```
// Public Instance Properties
  public bool CreatePrompt{set; get; }
  public bool OverwritePrompt{set; get; }
// Public Instance Methods
  public Stream OpenFile( );
  public override void Reset( );                                    // overrides FileDialog
}
```

Hierarchy System.Object → System.MarshalByRefObject → System.ComponentModel.Component(System.ComponentModel.IComponent, System.IDisposable) → CommonDialog → FileDialog → SaveFileDialog

Screen

System.Windows.Forms (system.windows.forms.dll) class

This class allows you to enumerate the various displays attached to a system.

There are a number of static properties and methods. AllScreens returns an array of Screen objects, one for each attached display. PrimaryScreen gets the primary display. FromPoint( ) finds the display that contains a specified point, while FromControl( ) and FromRectangle( ) find the display that contains the majority of the specified object. GetBounds( ) and GetWorkingArea( ) return the total bounds and desktop area (respectively) of the display containing the specified Control.

For a particular Screen object, the Bounds property returns the total area of the display, and the WorkingArea returns the desktop bounds (i.e., excluding such things as taskbars, toolbars, etc.). The Primary property specifies whether it is the primary display, and the DeviceName returns the name associated with the display.

```
public class Screen {
// Public Static Properties
  public static Screen[ ] AllScreens{get; }
  public static Screen PrimaryScreen{get; }
// Public Instance Properties
  public Rectangle Bounds{get; }
  public string DeviceName{get; }
  public bool Primary{get; }
  public Rectangle WorkingArea{get; }
// Public Static Methods
  public static Screen FromControl(Control control);
  public static Screen FromHandle(IntPtr hwnd);
  public static Screen FromPoint(System.Drawing.Point point);
  public static Screen FromRectangle(System.Drawing.Rectangle rect);
  public static Rectangle GetBounds(Control ctl);
  public static Rectangle GetBounds(System.Drawing.Point pt);
  public static Rectangle GetBounds(System.Drawing.Rectangle rect);
  public static Rectangle GetWorkingArea(Control ctl);
  public static Rectangle GetWorkingArea(System.Drawing.Point pt);
  public static Rectangle GetWorkingArea(System.Drawing.Rectangle rect);
// Public Instance Methods
  public override bool Equals(object obj);                          // overrides object
  public override int GetHashCode( );                               // overrides object
  public override string ToString( );                               // overrides object
}
```

ScrollableControl

marshal by reference, disposable

System.Windows.Forms (system.windows.forms.dll) — class

This is the base class for controls that support automatic scrolling. This includes ContainerControl (and its subclasses such as UserControl) and Panel.

To enable scrolling, you set the AutoScroll property. You can then specify the AutoScrollMinSize. If the control is made smaller than the AutoScrollMinSize, scrollbars are displayed. Alternatively, if any child controls are found within AutoScrollMargin pixels of the edge of its visible area, the scrollbars will also be shown.

You can set or retrieve the current AutoScrollPosition. Note that when you retrieve the position, it comes back as {-x,-y}, whereas when you set it, you must specify {x,y}.

As the AutoScrollPosition is changed, the window content is automatically blitted into the new position, child controls are offset by the appropriate amount, and any newly revealed parts of the control are invalidated for repaint. While this is the most efficient repaint scheme, it is not necessarily ideal for all applications. As an alternative, you can create and manage your own ScrollBar controls.

```
public class ScrollableControl : Control {
// Public Constructors
   public ScrollableControl( );
// Protected Static Fields
   protected const int ScrollStateAutoScrolling;                         //=1
   protected const int ScrollStateFullDrag;                              //=16
   protected const int ScrollStateHScrollVisible;                        //=2
   protected const int ScrollStateUserHasScrolled;                       //=8
   protected const int ScrollStateVScrollVisible;                        //=4
// Public Instance Properties
   public virtual bool AutoScroll{set; get; }
   public Size AutoScrollMargin{set; get; }
   public Size AutoScrollMinSize{set; get; }
   public Point AutoScrollPosition{set; get; }
   public override Rectangle DisplayRectangle{get; }                     // overrides Control
   public DockPaddingEdges DockPadding{get; }
// Protected Instance Properties
   protected override CreateParams CreateParams{get; }                   // overrides Control
   protected bool HScroll{set; get; }
   protected bool VScroll{set; get; }
// Public Instance Methods
   public void ScrollControlIntoView(Control activeControl);
   public void SetAutoScrollMargin(int x, int y);
// Protected Instance Methods
   protected virtual void AdjustFormScrollbars(bool displayScrollbars);
   protected bool GetScrollState(int bit);
   protected override void OnLayout(LayoutEventArgs levent);             // overrides Control
   protected override void OnMouseWheel(MouseEventArgs e);               // overrides Control
   protected override void OnVisibleChanged(EventArgs e);                // overrides Control
   protected override void ScaleCore(float dx, float dy);                // overrides Control
   protected void SetDisplayRectLocation(int x, int y);
   protected void SetScrollState(int bit, bool value);
   protected override void WndProc(ref Message m);                       // overrides Control
}
```

Hierarchy System.Object → System.MarshalByRefObject → System.ComponentModel.Component(System.ComponentModel.IComponent, System.IDisposable) → Control(IOleControl, IOleObject, IOleInPlaceObject, IOleInPlaceActiveObject, IOleWindow, IViewObject, IViewObject2, IPersist, IPersistStreamInit, IPersistPropertyBag, IPersistStorage, IQuickActivate, System.ComponentModel.ISynchronizeInvoke, IWin32Window) → ScrollableControl

Subclasses ContainerControl, Panel, System.Windows.Forms.Design.ComponentTray

ScrollableControl.DockPaddingEdges

System.Windows.Forms (system.windows.forms.dll) class

This class encapsulates the margins around the edge of a ScrollableControl.

```
public class ScrollableControl.DockPaddingEdges : ICloneable {
// Public Instance Properties
   public int All{set; get; }
   public int Bottom{set; get; }
   public int Left{set; get; }
   public int Right{set; get; }
   public int Top{set; get; }
// Public Instance Methods
   public override bool Equals(object other);                    // overrides object
   public override int GetHashCode( );                           // overrides object
   public override string ToString( );                           // overrides object
}
```

ScrollableControl.DockPaddingEdgesConverter

System.Windows.Forms (system.windows.forms.dll) class

This System.ComponentModel.TypeConverter is used to translate to and from a DockPaddingEdges class in design-time and serialization scenarios.

```
public class ScrollableControl.DockPaddingEdgesConverter : System.ComponentModel.TypeConverter {
// Public Constructors
   public ScrollableControl.DockPaddingEdgesConverter( );
// Public Instance Methods
   public override PropertyDescriptorCollection GetProperties(
      System.ComponentModel.ITypeDescriptorContext context,
      object value, Attribute[ ] attributes);            // overrides System.ComponentModel.TypeConverter
   public override bool GetPropertiesSupported(
      System.ComponentModel.ITypeDescriptorContext context);   // overrides System.ComponentModel.TypeConverter
}
```

Hierarchy System.Object → System.ComponentModel.TypeConverter → DockPaddingEdgesConverter

ScrollBar

marshal by reference, disposable

System.Windows.Forms (system.windows.forms.dll) abstract class

This is the abstract base class for the HScrollBar and the VScrollBar controls.

It has properties that define the Minimum and Maximum values for the scrollbar, and you can get or set the current Value.

The SmallChange property determines the value to be added or subtracted when the buttons are clicked (or the arrow keys are pressed). Similarly, the LargeChange property determines the value to be added or subtracted when the slider body is clicked (or the page up/down keys are pressed).

As the Value is changed, the control raises the ValueChanged event. When the scrollbox moves, it raises a Scroll event. Note that if you drag the slider knob, you get a Scroll when the mouse button is first depressed (with ScrollEventArgs.NewValue == Value). As the mouse moves, you get a Scroll before the Value has been updated, then a ValueChanged event as the Value is updated. Finally, you get another Scroll as the mouse is released (with ScrollEventArgs.NewValue == Value).

```
public abstract class ScrollBar : Control {
// Public Constructors
   public ScrollBar( );
// Public Instance Properties
   public override Color BackColor{set; get; }                                   // overrides Control
   public override Image BackgroundImage{set; get; }                             // overrides Control
   public override Font Font{set; get; }                                         // overrides Control
   public override Color ForeColor{set; get; }                                   // overrides Control
   public ImeMode ImeMode{set; get; }                                            // overrides Control
   public int LargeChange{set; get; }
   public int Maximum{set; get; }
   public int Minimum{set; get; }
   public int SmallChange{set; get; }
   public bool TabStop{set; get; }                                               // overrides Control
   public override string Text{set; get; }                                       // overrides Control
   public int Value{set; get; }
// Protected Instance Properties
   protected override CreateParams CreateParams{get; }                           // overrides Control
   protected override ImeMode DefaultImeMode{get; }                              // overrides Control
// Public Instance Methods
   public override string ToString( );               // overrides System.ComponentModel.Component
// Protected Instance Methods
   protected override void OnEnabledChanged(EventArgs e);                        // overrides Control
   protected override void OnHandleCreated(EventArgs e);                         // overrides Control
   protected virtual void OnScroll(ScrollEventArgs se);
   protected virtual void OnValueChanged(EventArgs e);
   protected void UpdateScrollInfo( );
   protected override void WndProc(ref Message m);                               // overrides Control
// Events
   public event EventHandler Click;                                              // overrides Control
   public event EventHandler DoubleClick;                                        // overrides Control
   public event MouseEventHandler MouseDown;                                     // overrides Control
   public event MouseEventHandler MouseMove;                                     // overrides Control
   public event MouseEventHandler MouseUp;                                       // overrides Control
   public event PaintEventHandler Paint;                                         // overrides Control
   public event ScrollEventHandler Scroll;
   public event EventHandler ValueChanged;
}
```

Hierarchy System.Object → System.MarshalByRefObject → System.ComponentModel.Component(System.ComponentModel.IComponent, System.IDisposable) → Control(IOleControl, IOleObject, IOleInPlaceObject, IOleInPlaceActiveObject, IOleWindow, IViewObject, IViewObject2, IPersist, IPersistStreamInit, IPersistPropertyBag, IPersistStorage, IQuickActivate, System.ComponentModel.ISynchronizeInvoke, IWin32Window) → ScrollBar

Subclasses HScrollBar, VScrollBar

Returned By DataGrid.{HorizScrollBar, VertScrollBar}

ScrollBars serializable

System.Windows.Forms (system.windows.forms.dll) enum

This enumeration is used by TextBox and RichTextBox to determine whether it will show scrollbars when there is too much text to display within the visible area of the control.

```
public enum ScrollBars {
  None = 0,
  Horizontal = 1,
  Vertical = 2,
  Both = 3
}
```

Hierarchy System.Object → System.ValueType → System.Enum(System.IComparable, System.IFormattable, System.IConvertible) → ScrollBars

Returned By TextBox.ScrollBars

Passed To TextBox.ScrollBars

ScrollButton serializable

System.Windows.Forms (system.windows.forms.dll) enum

ControlPaint.DrawScrollButton( ) uses this enumeration to specify the type of button imagery to paint.

```
public enum ScrollButton {
  Min = 0,
  Up = 0,
  Down = 1,
  Left = 2,
  Right = 3,
  Max = 3
}
```

Hierarchy System.Object → System.ValueType → System.Enum(System.IComparable, System.IFormattable, System.IConvertible) → ScrollButton

Passed To ControlPaint.DrawScrollButton( )

ScrollEventArgs

System.Windows.Forms (system.windows.forms.dll) class

This class encapsulates the data for the ScrollBar.Scroll event. You can determine the NewValue of the scrollbar and the Type of the scroll event (see ScrollEventType for details).

```
public class ScrollEventArgs : EventArgs {
// Public Constructors
   public ScrollEventArgs(ScrollEventType type, int newValue);
// Public Instance Properties
   public int NewValue{set; get; }
   public ScrollEventType Type{get; }
}
```

Hierarchy System.Object → System.EventArgs → ScrollEventArgs

Passed To DataGrid.{GridHScrolled( ), GridVScrolled( )}, ScrollBar.OnScroll( ), ScrollEventHandler.{BeginInvoke( ), Invoke( )}

ScrollEventHandler serializable

System.Windows.Forms (system.windows.forms.dll) delegate

This is a delegate for the ScrollBar.Scroll event.

```
public delegate void ScrollEventHandler(object sender, ScrollEventArgs e);
```

Associated Events HScrollBar.Scroll( ), ScrollBar.Scroll( ), VScrollBar.Scroll( )

ScrollEventType serializable

System.Windows.Forms (system.windows.forms.dll) enum

This enumeration lists the various kinds of ScrollBar.Scroll events that can be raised, depending on how the scrollbar was moved.

```
public enum ScrollEventType {
   SmallDecrement = 0,
   SmallIncrement = 1,
   LargeDecrement = 2,
   LargeIncrement = 3,
   ThumbPosition = 4,
   ThumbTrack = 5,
   First = 6,
   Last = 7,
   EndScroll = 8
}
```

Hierarchy System.Object → System.ValueType → System.Enum(System.IComparable, System.IFormattable, System.IConvertible) → ScrollEventType

Returned By ScrollEventArgs.Type

Passed To ScrollEventArgs.ScrollEventArgs( )

SecurityIDType serializable

System.Windows.Forms (system.windows.forms.dll) enum

This enumeration is for internal use only and should not be referenced directly in your own code.

```
public enum SecurityIDType {
  User = 1,
  Group = 2,
  Domain = 3,
  Alias = 4,
  WellKnownGroup = 5,
  DeletedAccount = 6,
  Invalid = 7,
  Unknown = 8,
  Computer = 9
}
```

Hierarchy System.Object → System.ValueType → System.Enum(System.IComparable, System.IFormattable, System.IConvertible) → SecurityIDType

SelectedGridItemChangedEventArgs

System.Windows.Forms (system.windows.forms.dll) class

This class encapsulates the data for the PropertyGrid.SelectedGridItemChanged event. You can retrieve both the OldSelection and the NewSelection.

```
public class SelectedGridItemChangedEventArgs : EventArgs {
// Public Constructors
  public SelectedGridItemChangedEventArgs(GridItem oldSel, GridItem newSel);
// Public Instance Properties
  public GridItem NewSelection{get; }
  public GridItem OldSelection{get; }
}
```

Hierarchy System.Object → System.EventArgs → SelectedGridItemChangedEventArgs

Passed To PropertyGrid.OnSelectedGridItemChanged( ), SelectedGridItemChangedEventHandler.{BeginInvoke( ), Invoke( )}

SelectedGridItemChangedEventHandler serializable

System.Windows.Forms (system.windows.forms.dll) delegate

This is a delegate for the PropertyGrid.SelectedGridItemChanged event.

```
public delegate void SelectedGridItemChangedEventHandler(object sender, SelectedGridItemChangedEventArgs e);
```

Associated Events PropertyGrid.SelectedGridItemChanged( )

SelectionMode

serializable

System.Windows.Forms (system.windows.forms.dll) enum

This enumeration is used by the ListBox and CheckedListBox controls to determine what kind of selection is supported. None implies that selection is disabled (although the control itself is still enabled), One offers single selection, while MultiSimple and MultiExtended reflect the two Windows multiple-selection modes.

```
public enum SelectionMode {
  None = 0,
  One = 1,
  MultiSimple = 2,
  MultiExtended = 3
}
```

Hierarchy System.Object → System.ValueType → System.Enum(System.IComparable, System.IFormattable, System.IConvertible) → SelectionMode

Returned By ListBox.SelectionMode

Passed To ListBox.SelectionMode

SelectionRange

System.Windows.Forms (system.windows.forms.dll) sealed class

This class represents the Start and End of a range of dates in a MonthCalendar control.

```
public sealed class SelectionRange {
// Public Constructors
  public SelectionRange( );
  public SelectionRange(DateTime lower, DateTime upper);
  public SelectionRange(SelectionRange range);
// Public Instance Properties
  public DateTime End{set; get; }
  public DateTime Start{set; get; }
// Public Instance Methods
  public override string ToString( );                    // overrides object
}
```

Returned By MonthCalendar.{GetDisplayRange( ), SelectionRange}

Passed To MonthCalendar.SelectionRange

SelectionRangeConverter

System.Windows.Forms (system.windows.forms.dll) class

This System.ComponentModel.TypeConverter is used in serialization and design-time scenarios and would not normally be used directly in your own code.

```
public class SelectionRangeConverter : System.ComponentModel.TypeConverter {
// Public Constructors
```

```
  public SelectionRangeConverter( );
// Public Instance Methods
  public override bool CanConvertFrom(System.ComponentModel.ITypeDescriptorContext context,
    Type sourceType);                                    // overrides System.ComponentModel.TypeConverter
  public override bool CanConvertTo(System.ComponentModel.ITypeDescriptorContext context,
    Type destinationType);                               // overrides System.ComponentModel.TypeConverter
  public override object ConvertFrom(System.ComponentModel.ITypeDescriptorContext context,
    System.Globalization.CultureInfo culture, object value);   // overrides System.ComponentModel.TypeConverter
  public override object ConvertTo(System.ComponentModel.ITypeDescriptorContext context,
    System.Globalization.CultureInfo culture, object value,
    Type destinationType);                               // overrides System.ComponentModel.TypeConverter
  public override object CreateInstance(System.ComponentModel.ITypeDescriptorContext context,
    System.Collections.IDictionary propertyValues);      // overrides System.ComponentModel.TypeConverter
  public override bool GetCreateInstanceSupported(
    System.ComponentModel.ITypeDescriptorContext context);   // overrides System.ComponentModel.TypeConverter
  public override PropertyDescriptorCollection GetProperties(System.ComponentModel.ITypeDescriptorContext context,
    object value, Attribute[ ] attributes);              // overrides System.ComponentModel.TypeConverter
  public override bool GetPropertiesSupported(
    System.ComponentModel.ITypeDescriptorContext context);   // overrides System.ComponentModel.TypeConverter
}
```

Hierarchy System.Object → System.ComponentModel.TypeConverter → SelectionRangeConverter

SendKeys

System.Windows.Forms (system.windows.forms.dll) class

This utility class offers three methods to dispatch keypresses to the active application. Send( ) sends a string of keystrokes. Nonprintable keys are represented by a series of special character codes between curly braces (for example Page Down is {PGDN}).

Flush( ) pumps messages until the keys have all been sent. SendWait( ) sends the keystrokes and pumps messages until all the keys have been sent. It is equivalent to Send( ) followed by Flush( ).

```
public class SendKeys {
// Public Static Methods
  public static void Flush( );
  public static void Send(string keys);
  public static void SendWait(string keys);
}
```

Shortcut serializable

System.Windows.Forms (system.windows.forms.dll) enum

This enumeration lists the shortcut keys that can be assigned to a MenuItem.Shortcut.

```
public enum Shortcut {
  None = 0,
  Ins = 45,
  Del = 46,
  F1 = 112,
  F2 = 113,
```

```
F3 = 114,
F4 = 115,
F5 = 116,
F6 = 117,
F7 = 118,
F8 = 119,
F9 = 120,
F10 = 121,
F11 = 122,
F12 = 123,
ShiftIns = 65581,
ShiftDel = 65582,
ShiftF1 = 65648,
ShiftF2 = 65649,
ShiftF3 = 65650,
ShiftF4 = 65651,
ShiftF5 = 65652,
ShiftF6 = 65653,
ShiftF7 = 65654,
ShiftF8 = 65655,
ShiftF9 = 65656,
ShiftF10 = 65657,
ShiftF11 = 65658,
ShiftF12 = 65659,
CtrlIns = 131117,
CtrlDel = 131118,
Ctrl0 = 131120,
Ctrl1 = 131121,
Ctrl2 = 131122,
Ctrl3 = 131123,
Ctrl4 = 131124,
Ctrl5 = 131125,
Ctrl6 = 131126,
Ctrl7 = 131127,
Ctrl8 = 131128,
Ctrl9 = 131129,
CtrlA = 131137,
CtrlB = 131138,
CtrlC = 131139,
CtrlD = 131140,
CtrlE = 131141,
CtrlF = 131142,
CtrlG = 131143,
CtrlH = 131144,
CtrlI = 131145,
CtrlJ = 131146,
CtrlK = 131147,
CtrlL = 131148,
CtrlM = 131149,
CtrlN = 131150,
CtrlO = 131151,
```

```
CtrlP = 131152,
CtrlQ = 131153,
CtrlR = 131154,
CtrlS = 131155,
CtrlT = 131156,
CtrlU = 131157,
CtrlV = 131158,
CtrlW = 131159,
CtrlX = 131160,
CtrlY = 131161,
CtrlZ = 131162,
CtrlF1 = 131184,
CtrlF2 = 131185,
CtrlF3 = 131186,
CtrlF4 = 131187,
CtrlF5 = 131188,
CtrlF6 = 131189,
CtrlF7 = 131190,
CtrlF8 = 131191,
CtrlF9 = 131192,
CtrlF10 = 131193,
CtrlF11 = 131194,
CtrlF12 = 131195,
CtrlShift0 = 196656,
CtrlShift1 = 196657,
CtrlShift2 = 196658,
CtrlShift3 = 196659,
CtrlShift4 = 196660,
CtrlShift5 = 196661,
CtrlShift6 = 196662,
CtrlShift7 = 196663,
CtrlShift8 = 196664,
CtrlShift9 = 196665,
CtrlShiftA = 196673,
CtrlShiftB = 196674,
CtrlShiftC = 196675,
CtrlShiftD = 196676,
CtrlShiftE = 196677,
CtrlShiftF = 196678,
CtrlShiftG = 196679,
CtrlShiftH = 196680,
CtrlShiftI = 196681,
CtrlShiftJ = 196682,
CtrlShiftK = 196683,
CtrlShiftL = 196684,
CtrlShiftM = 196685,
CtrlShiftN = 196686,
CtrlShiftO = 196687,
CtrlShiftP = 196688,
CtrlShiftQ = 196689,
CtrlShiftR = 196690,
```

```
    CtrlShiftS = 196691,
    CtrlShiftT = 196692,
    CtrlShiftU = 196693,
    CtrlShiftV = 196694,
    CtrlShiftW = 196695,
    CtrlShiftX = 196696,
    CtrlShiftY = 196697,
    CtrlShiftZ = 196698,
    CtrlShiftF1 = 196720,
    CtrlShiftF2 = 196721,
    CtrlShiftF3 = 196722,
    CtrlShiftF4 = 196723,
    CtrlShiftF5 = 196724,
    CtrlShiftF6 = 196725,
    CtrlShiftF7 = 196726,
    CtrlShiftF8 = 196727,
    CtrlShiftF9 = 196728,
    CtrlShiftF10 = 196729,
    CtrlShiftF11 = 196730,
    CtrlShiftF12 = 196731,
    AltBksp = 262152,
    Alt0 = 262192,
    Alt1 = 262193,
    Alt2 = 262194,
    Alt3 = 262195,
    Alt4 = 262196,
    Alt5 = 262197,
    Alt6 = 262198,
    Alt7 = 262199,
    Alt8 = 262200,
    Alt9 = 262201,
    AltF1 = 262256,
    AltF2 = 262257,
    AltF3 = 262258,
    AltF4 = 262259,
    AltF5 = 262260,
    AltF6 = 262261,
    AltF7 = 262262,
    AltF8 = 262263,
    AltF9 = 262264,
    AltF10 = 262265,
    AltF11 = 262266,
    AltF12 = 262267
}
```

Hierarchy System.Object → System.ValueType → System.Enum(System.IComparable, System.IFormattable, System.IConvertible) → Shortcut

Returned By MenuItem.Shortcut

Passed To MenuItem.{MenuItem( ), Shortcut}

SizeGripStyle

serializable

System.Windows.Forms (system.windows.forms.dll) enum

This enumeration contains the possible settings for the Form.SizeGripStyle.

```
public enum SizeGripStyle {
  Auto = 0,
  Show = 1,
  Hide = 2
}
```

Hierarchy System.Object → System.ValueType → System.Enum(System.IComparable, System.IFormattable, System.IConvertible) → SizeGripStyle

Returned By Form.SizeGripStyle, PrintPreviewDialog.SizeGripStyle

Passed To Form.SizeGripStyle, PrintPreviewDialog.SizeGripStyle

SortOrder

serializable

System.Windows.Forms (system.windows.forms.dll) enum

This enumeration determines how items are sorted with the ListView.Sorting property.

```
public enum SortOrder {
  None = 0,
  Ascending = 1,
  Descending = 2
}
```

Hierarchy System.Object → System.ValueType → System.Enum(System.IComparable, System.IFormattable, System.IConvertible) → SortOrder

Returned By ListView.Sorting

Passed To ListView.Sorting

Splitter

marshal by reference, disposable

System.Windows.Forms (system.windows.forms.dll) class

This Control is automatically docked to either the Top, Bottom, Left, or Right of a control. It is then used to automatically resize the Control object docked to the same edge immediately preceding it in the Z order, as the user drags it around with the mouse.

You can set the minimum dimension for the Control you are adjusting with the MinSize property. The split bar can be further constrained by specifying MinExtra. This determines the minimum size of the remaining portion of the control (i.e., the area into which a Control with the Dock property set to DockStyle.Fill would be positioned).

The current position of the bar can be controlled with the SplitPosition property.

The split bar raises SplitterMoving and SplitterMoved events as it is dragged around and then released. You can modify the splitter position dynamically by binding to these events and changing the event data.

```
public class Splitter : Control : IMessageFilter {
// Public Constructors
   public Splitter( );
// Public Instance Properties
   public override bool AllowDrop{set; get; }                                    // overrides Control
   public override AnchorStyles Anchor{set; get; }                               // overrides Control
   public override Image BackgroundImage{set; get; }                             // overrides Control
   public BorderStyle BorderStyle{set; get; }
   public override DockStyle Dock{set; get; }                                    // overrides Control
   public override Font Font{set; get; }                                         // overrides Control
   public override Color ForeColor{set; get; }                                   // overrides Control
   public ImeMode ImeMode{set; get; }                                            // overrides Control
   public int MinExtra{set; get; }
   public int MinSize{set; get; }
   public int SplitPosition{set; get; }
   public bool TabStop{set; get; }                                               // overrides Control
   public override string Text{set; get; }                                       // overrides Control
// Protected Instance Properties
   protected override CreateParams CreateParams{get; }                           // overrides Control
   protected override ImeMode DefaultImeMode{get; }                              // overrides Control
   protected override Size DefaultSize{get; }                                    // overrides Control
// Public Instance Methods
   public bool PreFilterMessage(ref Message m);                           // implements IMessageFilter
   public override string ToString( );              // overrides System.ComponentModel.Component
// Protected Instance Methods
   protected override void OnKeyDown(KeyEventArgs e);                            // overrides Control
   protected override void OnMouseDown(MouseEventArgs e);                        // overrides Control
   protected override void OnMouseMove(MouseEventArgs e);                        // overrides Control
   protected override void OnMouseUp(MouseEventArgs e);                          // overrides Control
   protected virtual void OnSplitterMoved(SplitterEventArgs sevent);
   protected virtual void OnSplitterMoving(SplitterEventArgs sevent);
   protected override void SetBoundsCore(int x, int y, int width, int height, BoundsSpecified specified);   // overrides Control
// Events
   public event EventHandler Enter;                                              // overrides Control
   public event KeyEventHandler KeyDown;                                         // overrides Control
   public event KeyPressEventHandler KeyPress;                                   // overrides Control
   public event KeyEventHandler KeyUp;                                           // overrides Control
   public event EventHandler Leave;                                              // overrides Control
   public event SplitterEventHandler SplitterMoved;
   public event SplitterEventHandler SplitterMoving;
}
```

Hierarchy System.Object → System.MarshalByRefObject → System.ComponentModel.Component(System.ComponentModel.IComponent, System.IDisposable) → Control(IOleControl, IOleObject, IOleInPlaceObject, IOleInPlaceActiveObject, IOleWindow, IViewObject, IViewObject2, IPersist, IPersistStreamInit, IPersistPropertyBag, IPersistStorage, IQuickActivate, System.ComponentModel.ISynchronizeInvoke, IWin32Window) → Splitter(IMessageFilter)

SplitterEventArgs

System.Windows.Forms (system.windows.forms.dll) class

The data for the Splitter.SplitterMoving and SplitterMoved events is encapsulated by this class. You can retrieve the location of the top left of the Splitter with the SplitX and SplitY members, and the current mouse position (in the client coordinates of the splitters Parent window) with X and Y.

```
public class SplitterEventArgs : EventArgs {
// Public Constructors
   public SplitterEventArgs(int x, int y, int splitX, int splitY);
// Public Instance Properties
   public int SplitX{set; get; }
   public int SplitY{set; get; }
   public int X{get; }
   public int Y{get; }
}
```

Hierarchy System.Object → System.EventArgs → SplitterEventArgs

Passed To Splitter.{OnSplitterMoved( ), OnSplitterMoving( )}, SplitterEventHandler.{BeginInvoke( ), Invoke( )}

SplitterEventHandler serializable

System.Windows.Forms (system.windows.forms.dll) delegate

This is a delegate for the Splitter.SplitterMoving and Splitter.SplitterMoved events.

```
public delegate void SplitterEventHandler(object sender, SplitterEventArgs e);
```

Associated Events Splitter.{SplitterMoved( ), SplitterMoving( )}

StatusBar marshal by reference, disposable

System.Windows.Forms (system.windows.forms.dll) class

This Control can be docked at the bottom of a form to display either a simple Text string, or a number of StatusBarPanel objects.

Initially, the status bar will not contain any panels, and text will be displayed. You can Add( ) one or more StatusBarPanel objects to the Panels property and enable the ShowPanels property, and it will display the panels instead, aligned from left to right.

For resizable containers, you can optionally display a SizingGrip in addition to the basic imagery.

Note that right-to-left reading forms will continue to display the panels on the left and the grippy on the right, regardless of the setting.

You can customize the rendering of the panels by binding to the DrawItem event. Any StatusBarPanel that is enabled for owner draw will cause the StatusBar to raise this event. See StatusBarDrawItemEventArgs for more information.

```
public class StatusBar : Control {
// Public Constructors
```

```
public StatusBar( );
// Public Instance Properties
public override Color BackColor{set; get; }                              // overrides Control
public override Image BackgroundImage{set; get; }                         // overrides Control
public override DockStyle Dock{set; get; }                                // overrides Control
public override Font Font{set; get; }                                     // overrides Control
public override Color ForeColor{set; get; }                               // overrides Control
public ImeMode ImeMode{set; get; }                                        // overrides Control
public StatusBarPanelCollection Panels{get; }
public bool ShowPanels{set; get; }
public bool SizingGrip{set; get; }
public bool TabStop{set; get; }                                           // overrides Control
public override string Text{set; get; }                                   // overrides Control
// Protected Instance Properties
protected override CreateParams CreateParams{get; }                       // overrides Control
protected override ImeMode DefaultImeMode{get; }                          // overrides Control
protected override Size DefaultSize{get; }                                // overrides Control
// Public Instance Methods
public override string ToString( );              // overrides System.ComponentModel.Component
// Protected Instance Methods
protected override void CreateHandle( );                                  // overrides Control
protected override void Dispose(bool disposing);                          // overrides Control
protected virtual void OnDrawItem(StatusBarDrawItemEventArgs sbdievent);
protected override void OnHandleCreated(EventArgs e);                     // overrides Control
protected override void OnHandleDestroyed(EventArgs e);                   // overrides Control
protected override void OnLayout(LayoutEventArgs levent);                 // overrides Control
protected override void OnMouseDown(MouseEventArgs e);                    // overrides Control
protected virtual void OnPanelClick(StatusBarPanelClickEventArgs e);
protected override void OnResize(EventArgs e);                            // overrides Control
protected override void WndProc(ref Message m);                           // overrides Control
// Events
public event StatusBarDrawItemEventHandler DrawItem;
public event PaintEventHandler Paint;                                     // overrides Control
public event StatusBarPanelClickEventHandler PanelClick;
}
```

Hierarchy System.Object → System.MarshalByRefObject → System.ComponentModel.Component(System.ComponentModel.IComponent, System.IDisposable) → Control(IOleControl, IOleObject, IOleInPlaceObject, IOleInPlaceActiveObject, IOleWindow, IViewObject, IViewObject2, IPersist, IPersistStreamInit, IPersistPropertyBag, IPersistStorage, IQuickActivate, System.ComponentModel.ISynchronizeInvoke, IWin32Window) → StatusBar

Returned By StatusBarPanel.Parent

Passed To StatusBarPanelCollection.StatusBarPanelCollection( )

StatusBar.StatusBarPanelCollection

System.Windows.Forms (system.windows.forms.dll) class

This class encapsulates the collection of panels in the StatusBar.Panels property.

```
public class StatusBar.StatusBarPanelCollection : IList, ICollection, IEnumerable {
// Public Constructors
   public StatusBar.StatusBarPanelCollection(StatusBar owner);
// Public Instance Properties
   public int Count{get; }                                          // implements ICollection
   public bool IsReadOnly{get; }                                    // implements IList
   public virtual StatusBarPanel this{set; get; }
// Public Instance Methods
   public virtual int Add(StatusBarPanel value);
   public virtual StatusBarPanel Add(string text);
   public virtual void AddRange(StatusBarPanel[ ] panels);
   public virtual void Clear( );                                    // implements IList
   public bool Contains(StatusBarPanel panel);
   public IEnumerator GetEnumerator( );                             // implements IEnumerable
   public int IndexOf(StatusBarPanel panel);
   public virtual void Insert(int index, StatusBarPanel value);
   public virtual void Remove(StatusBarPanel value);
   public virtual void RemoveAt(int index);                         // implements IList
}
```

StatusBarDrawItemEventArgs

System.Windows.Forms (system.windows.forms.dll) class

This class encapsulates the data for the StatusBar.DrawItem event. It provides the actual Panel to be drawn and its Index in the StatusBar.Panels collection along with the BackColor, ForeColor, and Font of that object.

You can also get a System.Drawing.Graphics surface on which to paint and the Bounds of the panel on that surface.

```
public class StatusBarDrawItemEventArgs : DrawItemEventArgs {
// Public Constructors
   public StatusBarDrawItemEventArgs(System.Drawing.Graphics g, System.Drawing.Font font,
      System.Drawing.Rectangle r, int itemId, DrawItemState itemState, StatusBarPanel panel);
// Public Instance Properties
   public StatusBarPanel Panel{get; }
}
```

Hierarchy System.Object → System.EventArgs → DrawItemEventArgs → StatusBarDrawItemEventArgs

Passed To StatusBar.OnDrawItem( ), StatusBarDrawItemEventHandler.{BeginInvoke( ), Invoke( )}

StatusBarDrawItemEventHandler serializable

System.Windows.Forms (system.windows.forms.dll) delegate

This is the delegate for the StatusBar.DrawItem event.

```
public delegate void StatusBarDrawItemEventHandler(object sender, StatusBarDrawItemEventArgs sbdevent);
```

Associated Events StatusBar.DrawItem( )

StatusBarPanel — marshal by reference, disposable

System.Windows.Forms (system.windows.forms.dll) — class

This class represents a single panel within a StatusBar. It can display Text and/or an Icon. Unlike other controls in the framework, this Icon really must be an Icon and not a generic Image. You can choose the Alignment of the text and icons within the panel, which honors the right-to-left reading status of the parent control (unlike the general layout of the status bar itself).

You can specify a standard Width for the panel as well as its MinWidth. Alternatively, you can set the AutoSize style to size to the Contents or Spring (which will evenly divide up the remaining space in the StatusBar).

The border around the panel is set with the BorderStyle property, and you can assign a ToolTip with the ToolTipText.

If you want to handle the repaint for the panel yourself (for example, creating a progress indicator panel), you can set the Style property to StatusBarPanelStyle.OwnerDraw.

If the user clicks on a panel, the StatusBar raises a PanelClick event. See StatusBarPanelClickEventArgs for more information.

```
public class StatusBarPanel : System.ComponentModel.Component : System.ComponentModel.ISupportInitialize {
// Public Constructors
   public StatusBarPanel( );
// Public Instance Properties
   public HorizontalAlignment Alignment{set; get; }
   public StatusBarPanelAutoSize AutoSize{set; get; }
   public StatusBarPanelBorderStyle BorderStyle{set; get; }
   public Icon Icon{set; get; }
   public int MinWidth{set; get; }
   public StatusBar Parent{get; }
   public StatusBarPanelStyle Style{set; get; }
   public string Text{set; get; }
   public string ToolTipText{set; get; }
   public int Width{set; get; }
// Public Instance Methods
   public void BeginInit( );                     // implements System.ComponentModel.ISupportInitialize
   public void EndInit( );                       // implements System.ComponentModel.ISupportInitialize
   public override string ToString( );           // overrides System.ComponentModel.Component
// Protected Instance Methods
   protected override void Dispose(bool disposing);   // overrides System.ComponentModel.Component
}
```

Hierarchy

System.Object → System.MarshalByRefObject → System.ComponentModel.Component(System.ComponentModel.IComponent, System.IDisposable) → StatusBarPanel(System.ComponentModel.ISupportInitialize)

Returned By

StatusBarPanelCollection.this, StatusBarDrawItemEventArgs.Panel, StatusBarPanelClickEventArgs.StatusBarPanel

Passed To

StatusBarPanelCollection.{Add( ), AddRange( ), Contains( ), IndexOf( ), Insert( ), Remove( ), this}, StatusBarDrawItemEventArgs.StatusBarDrawItemEventArgs( ), StatusBarPanelClickEventArgs.StatusBarPanelClickEventArgs( )

StatusBarPanelAutoSize serializable

System.Windows.Forms (system.windows.forms.dll) enum

This enumeration lists the options for the AutoSize property.

```
public enum StatusBarPanelAutoSize {
  None = 1,
  Spring = 2,
  Contents = 3
}
```

Hierarchy System.Object → System.ValueType → System.Enum(System.IComparable, System.IFormattable, System.IConvertible) → StatusBarPanelAutoSize

Returned By StatusBarPanel.AutoSize

Passed To StatusBarPanel.AutoSize

StatusBarPanelBorderStyle serializable

System.Windows.Forms (system.windows.forms.dll) enum

This enumeration contains the options for the BorderStyle property.

```
public enum StatusBarPanelBorderStyle {
  None = 1,
  Raised = 2,
  Sunken = 3
}
```

Hierarchy System.Object → System.ValueType → System.Enum(System.IComparable, System.IFormattable, System.IConvertible) → StatusBarPanelBorderStyle

Returned By StatusBarPanel.BorderStyle

Passed To StatusBarPanel.BorderStyle

StatusBarPanelClickEventArgs

System.Windows.Forms (system.windows.forms.dll) class

This class encapsulates the data for the StatusBar.PanelClick event. You can determine which Button was pressed, the number of Clicks (single, double, triple, etc.), the Delta through which the mouse wheel has been rotated, and the X and Y coordinates of the click (in the StatusBar coordinate space). You can also find out which StatusBarPanel was clicked.

```
public class StatusBarPanelClickEventArgs : MouseEventArgs {
// Public Constructors
  public StatusBarPanelClickEventArgs(StatusBarPanel statusBarPanel, MouseButtons button, int clicks, int x, int y);
// Public Instance Properties
  public StatusBarPanel StatusBarPanel{get; }
}
```

Hierarchy System.Object → System.EventArgs → MouseEventArgs → StatusBarPanelClickEventArgs

Passed To StatusBar.OnPanelClick( ), StatusBarPanelClickEventHandler.{BeginInvoke( ), Invoke( )}

StatusBarPanelClickEventHandler serializable

System.Windows.Forms (system.windows.forms.dll) delegate

This is the delegate for the StatusBar.PanelClick event.

```
public delegate void StatusBarPanelClickEventHandler(object sender, StatusBarPanelClickEventArgs e);
```

Associated Events StatusBar.PanelClick( )

StatusBarPanelStyle serializable

System.Windows.Forms (system.windows.forms.dll) enum

This enumeration is used by StatusBarPanel.Style to specify the owner draw style.

```
public enum StatusBarPanelStyle {
  Text = 1,
  OwnerDraw = 2
}
```

Hierarchy System.Object → System.ValueType → System.Enum(System.IComparable, System.IFormattable, System.IConvertible) → StatusBarPanelStyle

Returned By StatusBarPanel.Style

Passed To StatusBarPanel.Style

StructFormat serializable

System.Windows.Forms (system.windows.forms.dll) enum

This enumeration is for internal use only and should not be referenced from your own code.

```
public enum StructFormat {
  Ansi = 1,
  Unicode = 2,
  Auto = 3
}
```

Hierarchy System.Object → System.ValueType → System.Enum(System.IComparable, System.IFormattable, System.IConvertible) → StructFormat

SystemInformation

System.Windows.Forms (system.windows.forms.dll) class

This utility class provides a large number of static properties that can give you information about the current system settings, such as the HorizontalScrollBarHeight and whether this is a DebugOS.

Forms

Note that some of these properties, such as ComputerName and UserName, are retrieved from corresponding environment variables and are therefore susceptible to spoofing, and should not be considered to be secure.

```
public class SystemInformation {
// Public Static Properties
  public static ArrangeDirection ArrangeDirection{get; }
  public static ArrangeStartingPosition ArrangeStartingPosition{get; }
  public static BootMode BootMode{get; }
  public static Size Border3DSize{get; }
  public static Size BorderSize{get; }
  public static Size CaptionButtonSize{get; }
  public static int CaptionHeight{get; }
  public static string ComputerName{get; }
  public static Size CursorSize{get; }
  public static bool DbcsEnabled{get; }
  public static bool DebugOS{get; }
  public static Size DoubleClickSize{get; }
  public static int DoubleClickTime{get; }
  public static bool DragFullWindows{get; }
  public static Size DragSize{get; }
  public static Size FixedFrameBorderSize{get; }
  public static Size FrameBorderSize{get; }
  public static bool HighContrast{get; }
  public static int HorizontalScrollBarArrowWidth{get; }
  public static int HorizontalScrollBarHeight{get; }
  public static int HorizontalScrollBarThumbWidth{get; }
  public static Size IconSize{get; }
  public static Size IconSpacingSize{get; }
  public static int KanjiWindowHeight{get; }
  public static Size MaxWindowTrackSize{get; }
  public static Size MenuButtonSize{get; }
  public static Size MenuCheckSize{get; }
  public static Font MenuFont{get; }
  public static int MenuHeight{get; }
  public static bool MidEastEnabled{get; }
  public static Size MinimizedWindowSize{get; }
  public static Size MinimizedWindowSpacingSize{get; }
  public static Size MinimumWindowSize{get; }
  public static Size MinWindowTrackSize{get; }
  public static int MonitorCount{get; }
  public static bool MonitorsSameDisplayFormat{get; }
  public static int MouseButtons{get; }
  public static bool MouseButtonsSwapped{get; }
  public static bool MousePresent{get; }
  public static bool MouseWheelPresent{get; }
  public static int MouseWheelScrollLines{get; }
  public static bool NativeMouseWheelSupport{get; }
  public static bool Network{get; }
  public static bool PenWindows{get; }
  public static Size PrimaryMonitorMaximizedWindowSize{get; }
  public static Size PrimaryMonitorSize{get; }
```

```
    public static bool RightAlignedMenus{get; }
    public static bool Secure{get; }
    public static bool ShowSounds{get; }
    public static Size SmallIconSize{get; }
    public static Size ToolWindowCaptionButtonSize{get; }
    public static int ToolWindowCaptionHeight{get; }
    public static string UserDomainName{get; }
    public static bool UserInteractive{get; }
    public static string UserName{get; }
    public static int VerticalScrollBarArrowHeight{get; }
    public static int VerticalScrollBarThumbHeight{get; }
    public static int VerticalScrollBarWidth{get; }
    public static Rectangle VirtualScreen{get; }
    public static Rectangle WorkingArea{get; }
}
```

TabAlignment — serializable

System.Windows.Forms (system.windows.forms.dll) — enum

This enumeration is used by the TabControl.Alignment property to determine where the tabs will appear relative to the body of the control.

```
public enum TabAlignment {
    Top = 0,
    Bottom = 1,
    Left = 2,
    Right = 3
}
```

Hierarchy System.Object → System.ValueType → System.Enum(System.IComparable, System.IFormattable, System.IConvertible) → TabAlignment

Returned By TabControl.Alignment

Passed To TabControl.Alignment

TabAppearance — serializable

System.Windows.Forms (system.windows.forms.dll) — enum

The TabControl.Appearance property uses a value from this enumeration to determine how the tabs will be rendered.

```
public enum TabAppearance {
    Normal = 0,
    Buttons = 1,
    FlatButtons = 2
}
```

Hierarchy System.Object → System.ValueType → System.Enum(System.IComparable, System.IFormattable, System.IConvertible) → TabAppearance

Returned By TabControl.Appearance

Passed To TabControl.Appearance

TabControl **marshal by reference, disposable**

System.Windows.Forms (system.windows.forms.dll) class

A TabControl is a multipage container that can be used to display several related forms in a compact manner.

The TabControl maintains a collection of TabPages and renders a set of buttons that can be used to switch between those tabs. The number of tabs in the control can be obtained through the TabCount property. You can also retrieve the SelectedTab (or the SelectedIndex in the TabPages collection).

If there are more tabs than there is room for, you can enable Multiline display to show them in multiple rows, rather than allow the default scrolling behavior. The number of these rows is available in the RowCount property. The position of the tabs relative to the container can be set with the Alignment property.

The Appearance of the tabs can be modified. The SizeMode allows you to determine whether the tabs are of a Fixed width size to their content (Normal) or run the entire width of the control (FillToRight—you must enable Multiline to use this mode). You can also enable HotTrack, which changes the appearance of the tab on mouse over. For maximum control, you can set the DrawMode to TabDrawMode.OwnerDrawFixed and bind to the DrawItem event to paint the tabs yourself. See DrawItemEventArgs for more information about owner draw in general.

If you want to support Windows XP themes, you need to ensure that the controls Appearance is set to Normal, and that you have a manifest reference for the Common Controls v6. This will cause the tabs themselves to appear correctly, but the tab page will not render with the XP-style graduated background. You must use the DrawThemeBackground( ) Win32 API and a custom TabPage to achieve the full themed result.

It is also worth noting that the TabControl does not work correctly with pseudotransparency. There is no known workaround for this issue.

When the current tab page changes, the SelectedIndexChanged event is raised, the old page is hidden, and the new page is made visible. Controls on the new page will raise a VisibleChanged event, but not those on the old page.

```
public class TabControl : Control {
// Public Constructors
   public TabControl( );
// Public Instance Properties
   public TabAlignment Alignment{set; get; }
   public TabAppearance Appearance{set; get; }
   public override Color BackColor{set; get; }                    // overrides Control
   public override Image BackgroundImage{set; get; }              // overrides Control
   public override Rectangle DisplayRectangle{get; }              // overrides Control
   public TabDrawMode DrawMode{set; get; }
   public override Color ForeColor{set; get; }                    // overrides Control
   public bool HotTrack{set; get; }
   public ImageList ImageList{set; get; }
   public Size ItemSize{set; get; }
```

```
    public bool Multiline{set; get; }
    public Point Padding{set; get; }
    public int RowCount{get; }
    public int SelectedIndex{set; get; }
    public TabPage SelectedTab{set; get; }
    public bool ShowToolTips{set; get; }
    public TabSizeMode SizeMode{set; get; }
    public int TabCount{get; }
    public TabPageCollection TabPages{get; }
    public override string Text{set; get; }                                  // overrides Control
// Protected Instance Properties
    protected override CreateParams CreateParams{get; }                      // overrides Control
    protected override Size DefaultSize{get; }                               // overrides Control
// Public Instance Methods
    public Control GetControl(int index);
    public Rectangle GetTabRect(int index);
    public override string ToString( );           // overrides System.ComponentModel.Component
// Protected Instance Methods
    protected override ControlCollection CreateControlsInstance( );          // overrides Control
    protected override void CreateHandle( );                                 // overrides Control
    protected virtual object[ ] GetItems( );
    protected virtual object[ ] GetItems(Type baseType);
    protected string GetToolTipText(object item);
    protected override bool IsInputKey(Keys keyData);                        // overrides Control
    protected virtual void OnDrawItem(DrawItemEventArgs e);
    protected override void OnFontChanged(EventArgs e);                      // overrides Control
    protected override void OnHandleCreated(EventArgs e);                    // overrides Control
    protected override void OnHandleDestroyed(EventArgs e);                  // overrides Control
    protected override void OnKeyDown(KeyEventArgs ke);                      // overrides Control
    protected override void OnResize(EventArgs e);                           // overrides Control
    protected virtual void OnSelectedIndexChanged(EventArgs e);
    protected override void OnStyleChanged(EventArgs e);                     // overrides Control
    protected override bool ProcessKeyPreview(ref Message m);                // overrides Control
    protected void RemoveAll( );
    protected void UpdateTabSelection(bool uiselected);
    protected override void WndProc(ref Message m);                          // overrides Control
// Events
    public event DrawItemEventHandler DrawItem;
    public event PaintEventHandler Paint;                                    // overrides Control
    public event EventHandler SelectedIndexChanged;
}
```

Hierarchy System.Object → System.MarshalByRefObject → System.ComponentModel.Component(System.ComponentModel.IComponent, System.IDisposable) → Control(IOleControl, IOleObject, IOleInPlaceObject, IOleInPlaceActiveObject, IOleWindow, IViewObject, IViewObject2, IPersist, IPersistStreamInit, IPersistPropertyBag, IPersistStorage, IQuickActivate, System.ComponentModel.ISynchronizeInvoke, IWin32Window) → TabControl

Passed To ControlCollection.ControlCollection( ), TabPageCollection.TabPageCollection( )

TabControl.ControlCollection

System.Windows.Forms (system.windows.forms.dll) class

This collection class represents the set of controls contained by the **TabControl** class.

```
public class TabControl.ControlCollection : ControlCollection {
// Public Constructors
   public TabControl.ControlCollection(TabControl owner);
// Public Instance Methods
   public override void Add(Control value);                    // overrides Control.ControlCollection
   public override void Remove(Control value);                 // overrides Control.ControlCollection
}
```

Hierarchy System.Object → ControlCollection(System.Collections.IList, System.Collections.ICollection, System.Collections.IEnumerable, System.ICloneable) → ControlCollection

TabControl.TabPageCollection

System.Windows.Forms (system.windows.forms.dll) class

This collection class encapsulates the set of **TabPage** objects being displayed by the TabControl.

```
public class TabControl.TabPageCollection : IList, ICollection, IEnumerable {
// Public Constructors
   public TabControl.TabPageCollection(TabControl owner);
// Public Instance Properties
   public int Count{get; }                                     // implements ICollection
   public bool IsReadOnly{get; }                               // implements IList
   public virtual TabPage this{set; get; }
// Public Instance Methods
   public void Add(TabPage value);
   public void AddRange(TabPage[ ] pages);
   public virtual void Clear( );                               // implements IList
   public bool Contains(TabPage page);
   public IEnumerator GetEnumerator( );                        // implements IEnumerable
   public int IndexOf(TabPage page);
   public void Remove(TabPage value);
   public void RemoveAt(int index);                            // implements IList
}
```

TabDrawMode serializable

System.Windows.Forms (system.windows.forms.dll) enum

This enumeration is used by **TabControl.DrawMode** to determine whether owner draw is to be enabled.

```
public enum TabDrawMode {
   Normal = 0,
   OwnerDrawFixed = 1
}
```

Hierarchy System.Object → System.ValueType → System.Enum(System.IComparable, System.IFormattable, System.IConvertible) → TabDrawMode

Returned By TabControl.DrawMode

Passed To TabControl.DrawMode

TabPage

marshal by reference, disposable

System.Windows.Forms (system.windows.forms.dll) class

This Panel control is used as a container for a page of Control objects to be displayed in a TabControl.

See TabControl for more information.

```
public class TabPage : Panel {
// Public Constructors
   public TabPage( );
   public TabPage(string text);
// Public Instance Properties
   public override AnchorStyles Anchor{set; get; }                  // overrides Control
   public override DockStyle Dock{set; get; }                       // overrides Control
   public bool Enabled{set; get; }                                  // overrides Control
   public int ImageIndex{set; get; }
   public int TabIndex{set; get; }                                  // overrides Control
   public bool TabStop{set; get; }                                  // overrides Panel
   public override string Text{set; get; }                          // overrides Panel
   public string ToolTipText{set; get; }
   public bool Visible{set; get; }                                  // overrides Control
// Public Static Methods
   public static TabPage GetTabPageOfComponent(object comp);
// Public Instance Methods
   public override string ToString( );                              // overrides Panel
// Protected Instance Methods
   protected override ControlCollection CreateControlsInstance( );  // overrides Control
   protected override void SetBoundsCore(int x, int y, int width, int height, BoundsSpecified specified);  // overrides Control
}
```

Hierarchy System.Object → System.MarshalByRefObject → System.ComponentModel.Component(System.ComponentModel.IComponent, System.IDisposable) → Control(IOleControl, IOleObject, IOleInPlaceObject, IOleInPlaceActiveObject, IOleWindow, IViewObject, IViewObject2, IPersist, IPersistStreamInit, IPersistPropertyBag, IPersistStorage, IQuickActivate, System.ComponentModel.ISynchronizeInvoke, IWin32Window) → ScrollableControl → Panel → TabPage

Returned By TabControl.SelectedTab, TabPageCollection.this

Passed To TabControl.SelectedTab, TabPageCollection.{Add( ), AddRange( ), Contains( ), IndexOf( ), Remove( ), this}, TabPageControlCollection.TabPageControlCollection( )

TabPage.TabPageControlCollection

System.Windows.Forms (system.windows.forms.dll) class

This class encapsulates a collection of Control objects contained by a TabPage.

```
public class TabPage.TabPageControlCollection : ControlCollection {
// Public Constructors
  public TabPage.TabPageControlCollection(TabPage owner);
// Public Instance Methods
  public override void Add(Control value);                    // overrides Control.ControlCollection
}
```

Hierarchy System.Object → ControlCollection(System.Collections.IList, System.Collections.ICollection, System.Collections.IEnumerable, System.ICloneable) → TabPageControlCollection

TabSizeMode serializable

System.Windows.Forms (system.windows.forms.dll) enum

This enumeration lists the possible TabControl.SizeMode options.

```
public enum TabSizeMode {
  Normal = 0,
  FillToRight = 1,
  Fixed = 2
}
```

Hierarchy System.Object → System.ValueType → System.Enum(System.IComparable, System.IFormattable, System.IConvertible) → TabSizeMode

Returned By TabControl.SizeMode

Passed To TabControl.SizeMode

TextBox marshal by reference, disposable

System.Windows.Forms (system.windows.forms.dll) class

This Control, derived from TextBoxBase, allows a user to enter and edit simple text strings.

In addition to the base functionality, it allows you to specify the alignment of the text within the control. This TextAlign property respects the right-to-left reading status of the parent. You can also force the CharacterCasing to CharacterCasing.Lower or CharacterCasing.Upper.

The base class provides an AcceptsTab property, which allows the control to receive tab keypresses from the user (and insert them into the text).

TextBox enhances this with an AcceptsReturn property to do the same for the Enter and Return keys.

A PasswordChar can obscure the text displayed for added security. Prior to Windows XP, this was typically *. On Windows XP it is \u25CF (a small round dot).

```
public class TextBox : TextBoxBase {
// Public Constructors
  public TextBox( );
// Public Instance Properties
```

```
  public bool AcceptsReturn{set; get; }
  public CharacterCasing CharacterCasing{set; get; }
  public char PasswordChar{set; get; }
  public ScrollBars ScrollBars{set; get; }
  public override string Text{set; get; }                                    // overrides TextBoxBase
  public HorizontalAlignment TextAlign{set; get; }
// Protected Instance Properties
  protected override CreateParams CreateParams{get; }                        // overrides TextBoxBase
  protected override ImeMode DefaultImeMode{get; }                           // overrides Control
// Protected Instance Methods
  protected override bool IsInputKey(Keys keyData);                          // overrides TextBoxBase
  protected override void OnGotFocus(EventArgs e);                           // overrides Control
  protected override void OnHandleCreated(EventArgs e);                      // overrides TextBoxBase
  protected override void OnMouseUp(MouseEventArgs mevent);                  // overrides Control
  protected virtual void OnTextAlignChanged(EventArgs e);
  protected override void WndProc(ref Message m);                            // overrides TextBoxBase
// Events
  public event EventHandler TextAlignChanged;
}
```

Hierarchy System.Object → System.MarshalByRefObject → System.ComponentModel.Component(System.ComponentModel.IComponent, System.IDisposable) → Control(IOleControl, IOleObject, IOleInPlaceObject, IOleInPlaceActiveObject, IOleWindow, IViewObject, IViewObject2, IPersist, IPersistStreamInit, IPersistPropertyBag, IPersistStorage, IQuickActivate, System.ComponentModel.ISynchronizeInvoke, IWin32Window) → TextBoxBase → TextBox

Subclasses DataGridTextBox

Returned By DataGridTextBoxColumn.TextBox

TextBoxBase **marshal by reference, disposable**

System.Windows.Forms (system.windows.forms.dll) abstract class

This is the base class for the TextBox and RichTextBox classes. It provides the base functionality for a Control into which the user can type and edit text.

You can set the Text in the control, or AppendText( ). You can also find the TextLength. You can Select( ) text, or manipulate the SelectionStart and SelectionLength. A SelectedText property allows you to retrieve the current selection. If the SelectionLength is 0, the SelectionStart represents the current position of the caret. You can ensure that the caret is visible using ScrollToCaret( ). SelectAll( ) will select the entire content, and Clear( ) will remove it.

You can Cut( ) or Copy( ) the selection to the clipboard, and Paste( ) an IDataObject from the clipboard or a drag-and-drop operation.

The textbox is single line by default, but you can enable Multiline support (and find the number of Lines in the control). If you have a multiline control, you can enable WordWrap.

There is basic Undo( ) support. You can find out if the control CanUndo the previous operation, and you can use ClearUndo( ) to clear the undo buffer.

```
public abstract class TextBoxBase : Control {
// Public Instance Properties
  public bool AcceptsTab{set; get; }
```

```
public virtual bool AutoSize{set; get; }
public override Color BackColor{set; get; }                          // overrides Control
public override Image BackgroundImage{set; get; }                    // overrides Control
public BorderStyle BorderStyle{set; get; }
public bool CanUndo{get; }
public override Color ForeColor{set; get; }                          // overrides Control
public bool HideSelection{set; get; }
public string[ ] Lines{set; get; }
public virtual int MaxLength{set; get; }
public bool Modified{set; get; }
public virtual bool Multiline{set; get; }
public int PreferredHeight{get; }
public bool ReadOnly{set; get; }
public virtual string SelectedText{set; get; }
public virtual int SelectionLength{set; get; }
public int SelectionStart{set; get; }
public override string Text{set; get; }                              // overrides Control
public virtual int TextLength{get; }
public bool WordWrap{set; get; }
// Protected Instance Properties
protected override CreateParams CreateParams{get; }                  // overrides Control
protected override Size DefaultSize{get; }                           // overrides Control
// Public Instance Methods
public void AppendText(string text);
public void Clear( );
public void ClearUndo( );
public void Copy( );
public void Cut( );
public void Paste( );
public void ScrollToCaret( );
public void Select(int start, int length);
public void SelectAll( );
public override string ToString( );             // overrides System.ComponentModel.Component
public void Undo( );
// Protected Instance Methods
protected override void CreateHandle( );                             // overrides Control
protected override bool IsInputKey(Keys keyData);                    // overrides Control
protected virtual void OnAcceptsTabChanged(EventArgs e);
protected virtual void OnAutoSizeChanged(EventArgs e);
protected virtual void OnBorderStyleChanged(EventArgs e);
protected override void OnFontChanged(EventArgs e);                  // overrides Control
protected override void OnHandleCreated(EventArgs e);                // overrides Control
protected override void OnHandleDestroyed(EventArgs e);              // overrides Control
protected virtual void OnHideSelectionChanged(EventArgs e);
protected virtual void OnModifiedChanged(EventArgs e);
protected virtual void OnMultilineChanged(EventArgs e);
protected virtual void OnReadOnlyChanged(EventArgs e);
protected override bool ProcessDialogKey(Keys keyData);              // overrides Control
protected override void SetBoundsCore(int x, int y, int width, int height, BoundsSpecified specified);   // overrides Control
protected override void WndProc(ref Message m);                      // overrides Control
// Events
```

```
public event EventHandler AcceptsTabChanged;
public event EventHandler AutoSizeChanged;
public event EventHandler BorderStyleChanged;
public event EventHandler Click;                    // overrides Control
public event EventHandler HideSelectionChanged;
public event EventHandler ModifiedChanged;
public event EventHandler MultilineChanged;
public event PaintEventHandler Paint;               // overrides Control
public event EventHandler ReadOnlyChanged;
}
```

Hierarchy System.Object → System.MarshalByRefObject → System.ComponentModel.Component(System.ComponentModel.IComponent, System.IDisposable) → Control(IOleControl, IOleObject, IOleInPlaceObject, IOleInPlaceActiveObject, IOleWindow, IViewObject, IViewObject2, IPersist, IPersistStreamInit, IPersistPropertyBag, IPersistStorage, IQuickActivate, System.ComponentModel.ISynchronizeInvoke, IWin32Window) → TextBoxBase

Subclasses RichTextBox, TextBox

ThreadExceptionDialog — marshal by reference, disposable

System.Windows.Forms (system.windows.forms.dll) — class

This class is for internal use and should not be called directly from your own code.

```
public class ThreadExceptionDialog : Form {
// Public Constructors
public ThreadExceptionDialog(Exception t);
}
```

Hierarchy System.Object → System.MarshalByRefObject → System.ComponentModel.Component(System.ComponentModel.IComponent, System.IDisposable) → Control(IOleControl, IOleObject, IOleInPlaceObject, IOleInPlaceActiveObject, IOleWindow, IViewObject, IViewObject2, IPersist, IPersistStreamInit, IPersistPropertyBag, IPersistStorage, IQuickActivate, System.ComponentModel.ISynchronizeInvoke, IWin32Window) → ScrollableControl → ContainerControl(IContainerControl) → Form → ThreadExceptionDialog

TickStyle — serializable

System.Windows.Forms (system.windows.forms.dll) — enum

This enumeration is used by the TrackBar.TickStyle property to place the tickmarks on the TrackBar control.

```
public enum TickStyle {
None = 0,
TopLeft = 1,
BottomRight = 2,
Both = 3
}
```

Hierarchy System.Object → System.ValueType → System.Enum(System.IComparable, System.IFormattable, System.IConvertible) → TickStyle

Returned By TrackBar.TickStyle

Passed To TrackBar.TickStyle

Timer

marshal by reference, disposable

System.Windows.Forms (system.windows.forms.dll) class

This class provides a Component that can be used to trigger a periodic event. It is similar to the System.Threading.Timer class, in that it offers an Interval between events (counted in milliseconds), methods to Start() and Stop() the timer (which are thin wrappers around the Enabled property), and a Tick event, which is raised when the interval is elapsed.

The major difference is that the timer event is guaranteed to occur on the main UI thread, rather than coming in on an arbitrary thread, so you can use it transparently in UI situations.

```
public class Timer : System.ComponentModel.Component {
// Public Constructors
   public Timer( );
   public Timer(System.ComponentModel.IContainer container);
// Public Instance Properties
   public virtual bool Enabled{set; get; }
   public int Interval{set; get; }
// Public Instance Methods
   public void Start( );
   public void Stop( );
   public override string ToString( );                    // overrides System.ComponentModel.Component
// Protected Instance Methods
   protected override void Dispose(bool disposing);       // overrides System.ComponentModel.Component
   protected virtual void OnTick(EventArgs e);
// Events
   public event EventHandler Tick;
}
```

Hierarchy System.Object → System.MarshalByRefObject → System.ComponentModel.Component(System.ComponentModel.IComponent, System.IDisposable) → Timer

ToolBar

marshal by reference, disposable

System.Windows.Forms (system.windows.forms.dll) class

This class can be docked to the top of a container to provide a deck of clickable buttons.

You add ToolBarButton objects to the controls Buttons member, and set the ButtonSize and ImageSize for the bar as a whole. If you don't set the sizes, the control will calculate defaults for you. (See ToolBarButton for details of the different types of button you can add).

You can change the Appearance from Normal to Flat, choose whether DropDownArrows are drawn on drop-down buttons, and elect whether to ShowToolTips. TextAlign determines where the text will appear relative to the imagery. Note that this does not honor the right-to-left reading status of the control.

If the toolbar becomes too short for the buttons, Wrappable determines whether it will create a new deck on another line to accommodate them. Note that you bind to the ToolBar to receive ButtonClick events, not the ToolBarButton objects.

```
public class ToolBar : Control {
// Public Constructors
   public ToolBar( );
// Public Instance Properties
   public ToolBarAppearance Appearance{set; get; }
   public bool AutoSize{set; get; }
   public override Color BackColor{set; get; }                                    // overrides Control
   public override Image BackgroundImage{set; get; }                              // overrides Control
   public BorderStyle BorderStyle{set; get; }
   public ToolBarButtonCollection Buttons{get; }
   public Size ButtonSize{set; get; }
   public bool Divider{set; get; }
   public override DockStyle Dock{set; get; }                                     // overrides Control
   public bool DropDownArrows{set; get; }
   public override Color ForeColor{set; get; }                                    // overrides Control
   public ImageList ImageList{set; get; }
   public Size ImageSize{get; }
   public ImeMode ImeMode{set; get; }                                             // overrides Control
   public override RightToLeft RightToLeft{set; get; }                            // overrides Control
   public bool ShowToolTips{set; get; }
   public bool TabStop{set; get; }                                                // overrides Control
   public override string Text{set; get; }                                        // overrides Control
   public ToolBarTextAlign TextAlign{set; get; }
   public bool Wrappable{set; get; }
// Protected Instance Properties
   protected override CreateParams CreateParams{get; }                            // overrides Control
   protected override ImeMode DefaultImeMode{get; }                               // overrides Control
   protected override Size DefaultSize{get; }                                     // overrides Control
// Public Instance Methods
   public override string ToString( );                        // overrides System.ComponentModel.Component
// Protected Instance Methods
   protected override void CreateHandle( );                                       // overrides Control
   protected override void Dispose(bool disposing);                               // overrides Control
   protected virtual void OnButtonClick(ToolBarButtonClickEventArgs e);
   protected virtual void OnButtonDropDown(ToolBarButtonClickEventArgs e);
   protected override void OnFontChanged(EventArgs e);                            // overrides Control
   protected override void OnHandleCreated(EventArgs e);                          // overrides Control
   protected override void OnResize(EventArgs e);                                 // overrides Control
   protected override void SetBoundsCore(int x, int y, int width, int height, BoundsSpecified specified);  // overrides Control
   protected override void WndProc(ref Message m);                                // overrides Control
// Events
   public event ToolBarButtonClickEventHandler ButtonClick;
   public event ToolBarButtonClickEventHandler ButtonDropDown;
   public event PaintEventHandler Paint;                                          // overrides Control
}
```

Hierarchy System.Object → System.MarshalByRefObject → System.ComponentModel.Component(System.ComponentModel.IComponent, System.IDisposable) → Control(IOleControl, IOleObject, IOleInPlaceObject, IOleInPlaceActiveObject, IOleWindow, IViewObject, IViewObject2, IPersist, IPersistStreamInit, IPersistPropertyBag, IPersistStorage, IQuickActivate, System.ComponentModel.ISynchronizeInvoke, IWin32Window) → ToolBar

Forms

Returned By ToolBarButton.Parent

Passed To ToolBarButtonCollection.ToolBarButtonCollection( )

ToolBar.ToolBarButtonCollection

System.Windows.Forms (system.windows.forms.dll) class

This class represents a collection of buttons in a **ToolBar** control.

```
public class ToolBar.ToolBarButtonCollection : IList, ICollection, IEnumerable {
// Public Constructors
  public ToolBar.ToolBarButtonCollection(ToolBar owner);
// Public Instance Properties
  public int Count{get; }                                        // implements ICollection
  public bool IsReadOnly{get; }                                  // implements IList
  public virtual ToolBarButton this{set; get; }
// Public Instance Methods
  public int Add(string text);
  public int Add(ToolBarButton button);
  public void AddRange(ToolBarButton[ ] buttons);
  public void Clear( );                                          // implements IList
  public bool Contains(ToolBarButton button);
  public IEnumerator GetEnumerator( );                           // implements IEnumerable
  public int IndexOf(ToolBarButton button);
  public void Insert(int index, ToolBarButton button);
  public void Remove(ToolBarButton button);
  public void RemoveAt(int index);                               // implements IList
}
```

ToolBarAppearance serializable

System.Windows.Forms (system.windows.forms.dll) enum

This enumeration specifies whether a **ToolBar** will have the **Flat** or **Normal** appearance.

```
public enum ToolBarAppearance {
  Normal = 0,
  Flat = 1
}
```

Hierarchy System.Object → System.ValueType → System.Enum(System.IComparable, System.IFormattable, System.IConvertible) → ToolBarAppearance

Returned By ToolBar.Appearance

Passed To ToolBar.Appearance

ToolBarButton marshal by reference, disposable

System.Windows.Forms (system.windows.forms.dll) class

This component represents a button on a **ToolBar**.

By default, the Style is a regular ToolBarButtonStyle.PushButton, but you can change this to a ToolBarButtonStyle.DropDownButton (displaying a menu or pop-up window when clicked), ToolBarButtonStyle.ToggleButton, or ToolBarButtonStyle.Separator (dividing line between the controls).

You can define the Text it will display and the ImageIndex of an image in the Parent controls ToolBar.ImageList. Note that the position in which the text will be displayed on the button is determined by the ToolBar, not the ToolBarButton

It can be enabled and disabled with the Enabled property, and you can change the Visible state. Toggle buttons can be set Pushed (or a tristate-like PartialPush). Drop-down buttons can have a DropDownMenu assigned.

You can also find the bounding Rectangle of the button in the parent coordinate space.

```
public class ToolBarButton : System.ComponentModel.Component {
// Public Constructors
   public ToolBarButton( );
   public ToolBarButton(string text);
// Public Instance Properties
   public Menu DropDownMenu{set; get; }
   public bool Enabled{set; get; }
   public int ImageIndex{set; get; }
   public ToolBar Parent{get; }
   public bool PartialPush{set; get; }
   public bool Pushed{set; get; }
   public Rectangle Rectangle{get; }
   public ToolBarButtonStyle Style{set; get; }
   public object Tag{set; get; }
   public string Text{set; get; }
   public string ToolTipText{set; get; }
   public bool Visible{set; get; }
// Public Instance Methods
   public override string ToString( );                  // overrides System.ComponentModel.Component
// Protected Instance Methods
   protected override void Dispose(bool disposing);     // overrides System.ComponentModel.Component
}
```

Hierarchy System.Object → System.MarshalByRefObject → System.ComponentModel.Component(System.ComponentModel.IComponent, System.IDisposable) → ToolBarButton

Returned By ToolBarButtonCollection.this, ToolBarButtonClickEventArgs.Button

Passed To ToolBarButtonCollection.{Add( ), AddRange( ), Contains( ), IndexOf( ), Insert( ), Remove( ), this}, ToolBarButtonClickEventArgs.{Button, ToolBarButtonClickEventArgs( )}

ToolBarButtonClickEventArgs

System.Windows.Forms (system.windows.forms.dll) class

This class encapsulates the data for the ToolBar.ButtonClick event. You can determine which Button caused the event.

```
public class ToolBarButtonClickEventArgs : EventArgs {
// Public Constructors
   public ToolBarButtonClickEventArgs(ToolBarButton button);
// Public Instance Properties
```

```
public ToolBarButton Button{set; get; }
}
```

Hierarchy System.Object → System.EventArgs → ToolBarButtonClickEventArgs

Passed To ToolBar.{OnButtonClick( ), OnButtonDropDown( )}, ToolBarButtonClickEventHandler.{BeginInvoke( ), Invoke( )}

ToolBarButtonClickEventHandler serializable

System.Windows.Forms (system.windows.forms.dll) delegate

This is the delegate for the ToolBar.ButtonClick event.

```
public delegate void ToolBarButtonClickEventHandler(object sender, ToolBarButtonClickEventArgs e);
```

Associated Events ToolBar.{ButtonClick( ), ButtonDropDown( )}

ToolBarButtonStyle serializable

System.Windows.Forms (system.windows.forms.dll) enum

This enumeration lists the options for the ToolBarButton.Style property.

```
public enum ToolBarButtonStyle {
  PushButton = 1,
  ToggleButton = 2,
  Separator = 3,
  DropDownButton = 4
}
```

Hierarchy System.Object → System.ValueType → System.Enum(System.IComparable, System.IFormattable, System.IConvertible) → ToolBarButtonStyle

Returned By ToolBarButton.Style

Passed To ToolBarButton.Style

ToolBarTextAlign serializable

System.Windows.Forms (system.windows.forms.dll) enum

This enumeration is used by the ToolBar.TextAlign property to determine whether the text is found to the Right of the image or Underneath the image.

```
public enum ToolBarTextAlign {
  Underneath = 0,
  Right = 1
}
```

Hierarchy System.Object → System.ValueType → System.Enum(System.IComparable, System.IFormattable, System.IConvertible) → ToolBarTextAlign

Returned By ToolBar.TextAlign

Passed To ToolBar.TextAlign

ToolTip — marshal by reference, disposable

System.Windows.Forms (system.windows.forms.dll) — sealed class

The ToolTip component can provide pop-up tips: the little yellow boxes that offer pithy assistance to the user if they hover their mouse over a Control. It implements System.ComponentModel.IExtenderProvider to provide a ToolTip extender property for Control objects on the design surface.

Programatically, you can use GetToolTip( ) and SetToolTip( ) to specify the tip text for a specific Control, and enable or disable the tips with the Active property. You can clear the tips with the RemoveAll( ) method.

The AutoPopDelay is the amount of time for which the tip will show before it disappears.

The InitialDelay is the period for which the user has to hover the mouse before the tip will appear.

The ReshowDelay is the amount of time that must elapse between the user moving the cursor over another control and the tool tip updating with the new tip text.

Instead of setting all these individual elements, you can set the AutomaticDelay property. This sets each property to a sensible number, based on the value you provide.

```
public sealed class ToolTip : System.ComponentModel.Component : System.ComponentModel.IExtenderProvider {
// Public Constructors
   public ToolTip( );
   public ToolTip(System.ComponentModel.IContainer cont);
// Public Instance Properties
   public bool Active{set; get; }
   public int AutomaticDelay{set; get; }
   public int AutoPopDelay{set; get; }
   public int InitialDelay{set; get; }
   public int ReshowDelay{set; get; }
   public bool ShowAlways{set; get; }
// Public Instance Methods
   public bool CanExtend(object target);                  // implements System.ComponentModel.IExtenderProvider
   public string GetToolTip(Control control);
   public void RemoveAll( );
   public void SetToolTip(Control control, string caption);
   public override string ToString( );                    // overrides System.ComponentModel.Component
// Protected Instance Methods
   protected override void Dispose(bool disposing);       // overrides System.ComponentModel.Component
   protected override void Finalize( );                   // overrides System.ComponentModel.Component
}
```

Hierarchy System.Object → System.MarshalByRefObject → System.ComponentModel.Component(System.ComponentModel.IComponent, System.IDisposable) → ToolTip(System.ComponentModel.IExtenderProvider)

TrackBar

marshal by reference, disposable

System.Windows.Forms (system.windows.forms.dll) class

This Control represents a horizontal or vertical slider control, similar to a ScrollBar in function. The Orientation property determines whether the control will offer the horizontal or vertical imagery. You can also specify whether tickmarks appear with the TickStyle and TickFrequency properties.

It has further properties that define the Minimum and Maximum values for the range (SetRange( ) also allows you to do this), and you can get or set the current Value.

The SmallChange property determines the value to be added or subtracted when the arrow keys are pressed. Similarly, the LargeChange property determines the value to be added or subtracted when the slider body is clicked (or the page up/down keys are pressed).

As the Value is changed, the control raises the ValueChanged event. When the slider moves, it raises a Scroll event (this is much simpler than the ScrollBar equivalent).

```
public class TrackBar : Control : System.ComponentModel.ISupportInitialize {
// Public Constructors
   public TrackBar( );
// Public Instance Properties
   public bool AutoSize{set; get; }
   public override Image BackgroundImage{set; get; }                    // overrides Control
   public override Font Font{set; get; }                                // overrides Control
   public override Color ForeColor{set; get; }                          // overrides Control
   public ImeMode ImeMode{set; get; }                                   // overrides Control
   public int LargeChange{set; get; }
   public int Maximum{set; get; }
   public int Minimum{set; get; }
   public Orientation Orientation{set; get; }
   public int SmallChange{set; get; }
   public override string Text{set; get; }                              // overrides Control
   public int TickFrequency{set; get; }
   public TickStyle TickStyle{set; get; }
   public int Value{set; get; }
// Protected Instance Properties
   protected override CreateParams CreateParams{get; }                  // overrides Control
   protected override ImeMode DefaultImeMode{get; }                     // overrides Control
   protected override Size DefaultSize{get; }                           // overrides Control
// Public Instance Methods
   public void BeginInit( );                     // implements System.ComponentModel.ISupportInitialize
   public void EndInit( );                       // implements System.ComponentModel.ISupportInitialize
   public void SetRange(int minValue, int maxValue);
   public override string ToString( );                // overrides System.ComponentModel.Component
// Protected Instance Methods
   protected override void CreateHandle( );                             // overrides Control
   protected override bool IsInputKey(Keys keyData);                    // overrides Control
   protected override void OnBackColorChanged(EventArgs e);             // overrides Control
   protected override void OnHandleCreated(EventArgs e);                // overrides Control
   protected virtual void OnScroll(EventArgs e);
   protected virtual void OnValueChanged(EventArgs e);
   protected override void SetBoundsCore(int x, int y, int width, int height, BoundsSpecified specified);   // overrides Control
   protected override void WndProc(ref Message m);                      // overrides Control
```

```
// Events
  public event EventHandler Click;                                    // overrides Control
  public event EventHandler DoubleClick;                              // overrides Control
  public event PaintEventHandler Paint;                               // overrides Control
  public event EventHandler Scroll;
  public event EventHandler ValueChanged;
}
```

Hierarchy System.Object → System.MarshalByRefObject → System.ComponentModel.Component(System.ComponentModel.IComponent, System.IDisposable) → Control(IOleControl, IOleObject, IOleInPlaceObject, IOleInPlaceActiveObject, IOleWindow, IViewObject, IViewObject2, IPersist, IPersistStreamInit, IPersistPropertyBag, IPersistStorage, IQuickActivate, System.ComponentModel.ISynchronizeInvoke, IWin32Window) → TrackBar(System.ComponentModel.ISupportInitialize)

TreeNode

serializable, marshal by reference

System.Windows.Forms (system.windows.forms.dll) class

This class represents a single node in a TreeView.

You can set its BackColor, ForeColor, and the Text to display on the label. The ImageIndex and SelectedImageIndex can be chosen from the parent TreeView objects ImageList. The selection state can be queried with IsSelected. The node can also be Checked.

If the node has any children in its Nodes collection (GetNodeCount() can tell you this), you can Expand() and Collapse() those children, Toggle() the expanded state, and determine whether the node IsExpanded().

You can get the FirstNode and LastNode from the child Nodes list. Contrast this with the NextNode and PrevNode—these are sibling nodes in the TreeView rather than children of this node. Because those nodes may actually be collapsed, you can also retrieve the NextVisibleNode and PrevVisibleNode.

You can Remove() the node (and all its children) from the parent TreeView or scroll it into view (perhaps expanding any parent nodes) with EnsureVisible().

You can start to edit the node text (if TreeView.LabelEdit is enabled) with BeginEdit(), and cancel or commit an edit with EndEdit(). To query whether the node is being edited, you may use the IsEditing property.

Note that a TreeNode may appear several times in a TreeView. The FullPath property will tell you exactly where you are in the tree control.

```
public class TreeNode : MarshalByRefObject : ICloneable, System.Runtime.Serialization.ISerializable {
// Public Constructors
  public TreeNode( );
  public TreeNode(string text);
  public TreeNode(string text, int imageIndex, int selectedImageIndex);
  public TreeNode(string text, int imageIndex, int selectedImageIndex, TreeNode[ ] children);
  public TreeNode(string text, TreeNode[ ] children);
// Public Instance Properties
  public Color BackColor{set; get; }
  public Rectangle Bounds{get; }
  public bool Checked{set; get; }
  public TreeNode FirstNode{get; }
  public Color ForeColor{set; get; }
```

```
    public string FullPath{get; }
    public IntPtr Handle{get; }
    public int ImageIndex{set; get; }
    public int Index{get; }
    public bool IsEditing{get; }
    public bool IsExpanded{get; }
    public bool IsSelected{get; }
    public bool IsVisible{get; }
    public TreeNode LastNode{get; }
    public TreeNode NextNode{get; }
    public TreeNode NextVisibleNode{get; }
    public Font NodeFont{set; get; }
    public TreeNodeCollection Nodes{get; }
    public TreeNode Parent{get; }
    public TreeNode PrevNode{get; }
    public TreeNode PrevVisibleNode{get; }
    public int SelectedImageIndex{set; get; }
    public object Tag{set; get; }
    public string Text{set; get; }
    public TreeView TreeView{get; }
// Public Static Methods
    public static TreeNode FromHandle(TreeView tree, IntPtr handle);
// Public Instance Methods
    public void BeginEdit( );
    public virtual object Clone( );                    // implements ICloneable
    public void Collapse( );
    public void EndEdit(bool cancel);
    public void EnsureVisible( );
    public void Expand( );
    public void ExpandAll( );
    public int GetNodeCount(bool includeSubTrees);
    public void Remove( );
    public void Toggle( );
    public override string ToString( );                // overrides object
}
```

Hierarchy System.Object → System.MarshalByRefObject → TreeNode(System.ICloneable, System.Runtime.Serialization.ISerializable)

Returned By NodeLabelEditEventArgs.Node, TreeNodeCollection.this, TreeView.{GetNodeAt( ), SelectedNode, TopNode}, TreeViewCancelEventArgs.Node, TreeViewEventArgs.Node

Passed To Multiple types

TreeNodeCollection

System.Windows.Forms (system.windows.forms.dll) class

This class represents a typed collection of TreeNode objects. It is used by the TreeView.Nodes and TreeNode.Nodes properties.

```
public class TreeNodeCollection : IList, ICollection, IEnumerable {
// Public Instance Properties
```

```
public int Count{get; }                                                    // implements ICollection
public bool IsReadOnly{get; }                                              // implements IList
public virtual TreeNode this{set; get; }
// Public Instance Methods
public virtual int Add(TreeNode node);
public virtual TreeNode Add(string text);
public virtual void AddRange(TreeNode[ ] nodes);
public virtual void Clear( );                                              // implements IList
public bool Contains(TreeNode node);
public void CopyTo(Array dest, int index);                                 // implements ICollection
public IEnumerator GetEnumerator( );                                       // implements IEnumerable
public int IndexOf(TreeNode node);
public virtual void Insert(int index, TreeNode node);
public void Remove(TreeNode node);
public virtual void RemoveAt(int index);                                   // implements IList
}
```

Returned By TreeNode.Nodes, TreeView.Nodes

TreeNodeConverter

System.Windows.Forms (system.windows.forms.dll) class

This System.ComponentModel.TypeConverter for TreeNode objects is used in serialization and design-time scenarios, and would not normally be called from your own code.

```
public class TreeNodeConverter : System.ComponentModel.TypeConverter {
// Public Constructors
   public TreeNodeConverter( );
// Public Instance Methods
   public override bool CanConvertTo(System.ComponentModel.ITypeDescriptorContext context,
      Type destinationType);                          // overrides System.ComponentModel.TypeConverter
   public override object ConvertTo(System.ComponentModel.ITypeDescriptorContext context,
      System.Globalization.CultureInfo culture, object value,
      Type destinationType);                          // overrides System.ComponentModel.TypeConverter
}
```

Hierarchy System.Object → System.ComponentModel.TypeConverter → TreeNodeConverter

TreeView

marshal by reference, disposable

System.Windows.Forms (system.windows.forms.dll) class

This Control represents a hierarchical set of nodes in a tree view (similar to the Windows Explorer Folder View). You can add TreeNode objects to the Nodes collection. These are root nodes. To add further elements to the hierarchy you add additional TreeNode objects to the root TreeNode.Nodes collections. GetNodeCount( ) will return you the count of all nodes in the tree.

You can add CheckBoxes for each node, enable HotTracking (link-like) behavior, ShowLines and ShowRootLines (drawn from node to node), and ShowPlusMinus glyphs (little plus-shaped expansion boxes next to nodes with children). You can also set the distance by which to Indent each level of child nodes.

When you select an item, normally you are only permitted to click on imagery representing the label text. This can sometimes be awkward, so you can enable FullRowSelect to give users a larger target. HideSelection determines whether the selection highlight is displayed even when the control loses the focus. You can get or set the selected node with the SelectedNode property.

The nodes can be Sorted, and you can ExpandAll( ) and CollapseAll( ) nodes. To find the node under a particular point, you can use the GetNodeAt( ) method.

The tree raises events both Before and After select, check, collapse, and expand operations. If the control allows LabelEdit, you will also get BeforeLabelEdit and AfterLabelEdit events. The BeforeXXX events use the TreeViewCancelEventArgs class and can therefore be aborted.

```
public class TreeView : Control {
// Public Constructors
   public TreeView( );
// Public Instance Properties
   public override Color BackColor{set; get; }                               // overrides Control
   public override Image BackgroundImage{set; get; }                         // overrides Control
   public BorderStyle BorderStyle{set; get; }
   public bool CheckBoxes{set; get; }
   public override Color ForeColor{set; get; }                               // overrides Control
   public bool FullRowSelect{set; get; }
   public bool HideSelection{set; get; }
   public bool HotTracking{set; get; }
   public int ImageIndex{set; get; }
   public ImageList ImageList{set; get; }
   public int Indent{set; get; }
   public int ItemHeight{set; get; }
   public bool LabelEdit{set; get; }
   public TreeNodeCollection Nodes{get; }
   public string PathSeparator{set; get; }
   public bool Scrollable{set; get; }
   public int SelectedImageIndex{set; get; }
   public TreeNode SelectedNode{set; get; }
   public bool ShowLines{set; get; }
   public bool ShowPlusMinus{set; get; }
   public bool ShowRootLines{set; get; }
   public bool Sorted{set; get; }
   public override string Text{set; get; }                                   // overrides Control
   public TreeNode TopNode{get; }
   public int VisibleCount{get; }
// Protected Instance Properties
   protected override CreateParams CreateParams{get; }                       // overrides Control
   protected override Size DefaultSize{get; }                                // overrides Control
// Public Instance Methods
   public void BeginUpdate( );
   public void CollapseAll( );
   public void EndUpdate( );
   public void ExpandAll( );
   public TreeNode GetNodeAt(int x, int y);
   public TreeNode GetNodeAt(System.Drawing.Point pt);
   public int GetNodeCount(bool includeSubTrees);
   public override string ToString( );           // overrides System.ComponentModel.Component
```

```
// Protected Instance Methods
   protected override void CreateHandle( );                                          // overrides Control
   protected override void Dispose(bool disposing);                                  // overrides Control
   protected OwnerDrawPropertyBag GetItemRenderStyles(TreeNode node, int state);
   protected override bool IsInputKey(Keys keyData);                                 // overrides Control
   protected virtual void OnAfterCheck(TreeViewEventArgs e);
   protected virtual void OnAfterCollapse(TreeViewEventArgs e);
   protected virtual void OnAfterExpand(TreeViewEventArgs e);
   protected virtual void OnAfterLabelEdit(NodeLabelEditEventArgs e);
   protected virtual void OnAfterSelect(TreeViewEventArgs e);
   protected virtual void OnBeforeCheck(TreeViewCancelEventArgs e);
   protected virtual void OnBeforeCollapse(TreeViewCancelEventArgs e);
   protected virtual void OnBeforeExpand(TreeViewCancelEventArgs e);
   protected virtual void OnBeforeLabelEdit(NodeLabelEditEventArgs e);
   protected virtual void OnBeforeSelect(TreeViewCancelEventArgs e);
   protected override void OnHandleCreated(EventArgs e);                             // overrides Control
   protected override void OnHandleDestroyed(EventArgs e);                           // overrides Control
   protected virtual void OnItemDrag(ItemDragEventArgs e);
   protected override void OnKeyDown(KeyEventArgs e);                                // overrides Control
   protected override void OnKeyPress(KeyPressEventArgs e);                          // overrides Control
   protected override void OnKeyUp(KeyEventArgs e);                                  // overrides Control
   protected override void WndProc(ref Message m);                                   // overrides Control
// Events
   public event TreeViewEventHandler AfterCheck;
   public event TreeViewEventHandler AfterCollapse;
   public event TreeViewEventHandler AfterExpand;
   public event NodeLabelEditEventHandler AfterLabelEdit;
   public event TreeViewEventHandler AfterSelect;
   public event TreeViewCancelEventHandler BeforeCheck;
   public event TreeViewCancelEventHandler BeforeCollapse;
   public event TreeViewCancelEventHandler BeforeExpand;
   public event NodeLabelEditEventHandler BeforeLabelEdit;
   public event TreeViewCancelEventHandler BeforeSelect;
   public event ItemDragEventHandler ItemDrag;
   public event PaintEventHandler Paint;                                             // overrides Control
}
```

Hierarchy System.Object → System.MarshalByRefObject → System.ComponentModel.Component(System.ComponentModel.IComponent, System.IDisposable) → Control(IOleControl, IOleObject, IOleInPlaceObject, IOleInPlaceActiveObject, IOleWindow, IViewObject, IViewObject2, IPersist, IPersistStreamInit, IPersistPropertyBag, IPersistStorage, IQuickActivate, System.ComponentModel.ISynchronizeInvoke, IWin32Window) → TreeView

Returned By TreeNode.TreeView

Passed To TreeNode.FromHandle( )

TreeViewAction serializable

System.Windows.Forms (system.windows.forms.dll) enum

This enumeration is used by the TreeViewEventArgs to determine how the particular event was initiated.

```
public enum TreeViewAction {
  Unknown = 0,
  ByKeyboard = 1,
  ByMouse = 2,
  Collapse = 3,
  Expand = 4
}
```

Hierarchy System.Object → System.ValueType → System.Enum(System.IComparable, System.IFormattable, System.IConvertible) → TreeViewAction

Returned By TreeViewCancelEventArgs.Action, TreeViewEventArgs.Action

Passed To TreeViewCancelEventArgs.TreeViewCancelEventArgs( ), TreeViewEventArgs.TreeViewEventArgs( )

TreeViewCancelEventArgs

System.Windows.Forms (system.windows.forms.dll) class

The class encapsulates the event data for the various TreeView.BeforeXXX events. You can determine the Action that caused the event and the Node that will be modified. If you wish to abort the action, you can set the Cancel property.

```
public class TreeViewCancelEventArgs : System.ComponentModel.CancelEventArgs {
// Public Constructors
  public TreeViewCancelEventArgs(TreeNode node, bool cancel, TreeViewAction action);
// Public Instance Properties
  public TreeViewAction Action{get; }
  public TreeNode Node{get; }
}
```

Hierarchy System.Object → System.EventArgs → System.ComponentModel.CancelEventArgs → TreeViewCancelEventArgs

Passed To TreeView.{OnBeforeCheck( ), OnBeforeCollapse( ), OnBeforeExpand( ), OnBeforeSelect( )}, TreeViewCancelEventHandler.{BeginInvoke( ), Invoke( )}

TreeViewCancelEventHandler serializable

System.Windows.Forms (system.windows.forms.dll) delegate

This is a delegate for the various TreeView.BeforeXXX events.

```
public delegate void TreeViewCancelEventHandler(object sender, TreeViewCancelEventArgs e);
```

Associated Events TreeView.{BeforeCheck( ), BeforeCollapse( ), BeforeExpand( ), BeforeSelect( )}

TreeViewEventArgs

System.Windows.Forms (system.windows.forms.dll) class

This class encapsulates the data for the TreeView.AfterXXX events. You can determine the Action that raised the event and the Node that has been modified.

```
public class TreeViewEventArgs : EventArgs {
// Public Constructors
   public TreeViewEventArgs(TreeNode node);
   public TreeViewEventArgs(TreeNode node, TreeViewAction action);
// Public Instance Properties
   public TreeViewAction Action{get; }
   public TreeNode Node{get; }
}
```

Hierarchy System.Object → System.EventArgs → TreeViewEventArgs

Passed To System.Windows.Forms.Design.ComponentEditorForm.OnSelChangeSelector( ), TreeView.{OnAfterCheck( ), OnAfterCollapse( ), OnAfterExpand( ), OnAfterSelect( )}, TreeViewEventHandler.{BeginInvoke( ), Invoke( )}

TreeViewEventHandler **serializable**

System.Windows.Forms (system.windows.forms.dll) **delegate**

This is a delegate for the various TreeView.AfterXXX events.

```
public delegate void TreeViewEventHandler(object sender, TreeViewEventArgs e);
```

Associated Events TreeView.{AfterCheck( ), AfterCollapse( ), AfterExpand( ), AfterSelect( )}

TreeViewImageIndexConverter

System.Windows.Forms (system.windows.forms.dll) class

This System.ComponentModel.TypeConverter is used in serialization and design-time scenarios and would not normally be called from your own code.

```
public class TreeViewImageIndexConverter : ImageIndexConverter {
// Public Constructors
   public TreeViewImageIndexConverter( );
// Protected Instance Properties
   protected override bool IncludeNoneAsStandardValue{get; }        // overrides ImageIndexConverter
}
```

Hierarchy System.Object → System.ComponentModel.TypeConverter → System.ComponentModel.BaseNumberConverter → System.ComponentModel.Int32Converter → ImageIndexConverter → TreeViewImageIndexConverter

UICues **serializable, flag**

System.Windows.Forms (system.windows.forms.dll) **enum**

This set of flags is used by the UICuesEventArgs class to specify which of the UI cues has changed when the Control.ChangeUICues event is raised. The cues include such things as the focus rectangle, Alt key shortcuts, etc.

```
public enum UICues {
   None = 0x00000000,
   ShowFocus = 0x00000001,
   ShowKeyboard = 0x00000002,
```

```
  Shown = 0x00000003,
  ChangeFocus = 0x00000004,
  ChangeKeyboard = 0x00000008,
  Changed = 0x0000000C
}
```

Hierarchy System.Object → System.ValueType → System.Enum(System.IComparable, System.IFormattable, System.IConvertible) → UICues

Returned By UICuesEventArgs.Changed

Passed To UICuesEventArgs.UICuesEventArgs( )

UICuesEventArgs

System.Windows.Forms (system.windows.forms.dll) class

This class encapsulates the data for the Control.ChangeUICues event. It allows you to determine which of the UICues have Changed.

```
public class UICuesEventArgs : EventArgs {
// Public Constructors
  public UICuesEventArgs(UICues uicues);
// Public Instance Properties
  public UICues Changed{get; }
  public bool ChangeFocus{get; }
  public bool ChangeKeyboard{get; }
  public bool ShowFocus{get; }
  public bool ShowKeyboard{get; }
}
```

Hierarchy System.Object → System.EventArgs → UICuesEventArgs

Passed To Control.OnChangeUICues( ), UICuesEventHandler.{BeginInvoke( ), Invoke( )}

UICuesEventHandler serializable

System.Windows.Forms (system.windows.forms.dll) delegate

This is a delegate for the Control.ChangeUICues event.

```
public delegate void UICuesEventHandler(object sender, UICuesEventArgs e);
```

Associated Events Multiple types

UpDownBase marshal by reference, disposable

System.Windows.Forms (system.windows.forms.dll) abstract class

This class provides the base functionality for the DomainUpDown and NumericUpDown controls. It offers a text box with an attached spin control.

InterceptArrowKeys determines whether you can use the arrow keys to spin the value up and down. UpDownAlign sets the spin buttons to the left or right of the control, respecting the right-to-left setting of the context. UpButton( ) and DownButton( ) programmatically invoke the pressing of the respective spin buttons.

```
public abstract class UpDownBase : ContainerControl {
// Public Constructors
   public UpDownBase( );
// Public Instance Properties
   public override bool AutoScroll{set; get; }                                          // overrides ScrollableControl
   public Size AutoScrollMargin{set; get; }                                             // overrides ScrollableControl
   public Size AutoScrollMinSize{set; get; }                                            // overrides ScrollableControl
   public override Color BackColor{set; get; }                                          // overrides Control
   public override Image BackgroundImage{set; get; }                                    // overrides Control
   public BorderStyle BorderStyle{set; get; }
   public override ContextMenu ContextMenu{set; get; }                                  // overrides Control
   public DockPaddingEdges DockPadding{get; }                                           // overrides ScrollableControl
   public override bool Focused{get; }                                                  // overrides Control
   public override Color ForeColor{set; get; }                                          // overrides Control
   public bool InterceptArrowKeys{set; get; }
   public int PreferredHeight{get; }
   public bool ReadOnly{set; get; }
   public override string Text{set; get; }                                              // overrides Control
   public HorizontalAlignment TextAlign{set; get; }
   public LeftRightAlignment UpDownAlign{set; get; }
// Protected Instance Properties
   protected bool ChangingText{set; get; }
   protected override CreateParams CreateParams{get; }                                  // overrides ContainerControl
   protected override Size DefaultSize{get; }                                           // overrides Control
   protected bool UserEdit{set; get; }
// Public Instance Methods
   public abstract void DownButton( );
   public void Select(int start, int length);
   public abstract void UpButton( );
// Protected Instance Methods
   protected virtual void OnChanged(object source, EventArgs e);
   protected override void OnFontChanged(EventArgs e);                                  // overrides Control
   protected override void OnHandleCreated(EventArgs e);                                // overrides Control
   protected override void OnLayout(LayoutEventArgs e);                                 // overrides ScrollableControl
   protected override void OnMouseWheel(MouseEventArgs e);                              // overrides ScrollableControl
   protected virtual void OnTextBoxKeyDown(object source, KeyEventArgs e);
   protected virtual void OnTextBoxKeyPress(object source, KeyPressEventArgs e);
   protected virtual void OnTextBoxLostFocus(object source, EventArgs e);
   protected virtual void OnTextBoxResize(object source, EventArgs e);
   protected virtual void OnTextBoxTextChanged(object source, EventArgs e);
   protected override void SetBoundsCore(int x, int y, int width, int height, BoundsSpecified specified);   // overrides Control
   protected abstract void UpdateEditText( );
   protected virtual void ValidateEditText( );
}
```

Hierarchy System.Object → System.MarshalByRefObject → System.ComponentModel.Component(System.ComponentModel.IComponent, System.IDisposable) → Control(IOleControl, IOleObject, IOleInPlaceObject, IOleInPlaceActiveObject, IOleWindow, IViewObject, IViewObject2, IPersist, IPersistStreamInit, IPersistPropertyBag, IPersistStorage, IQuickActivate, System.ComponentModel.ISynchronizeInvoke, IWin32Window) → ScrollableControl → ContainerControl(IContainerControl) → UpDownBase

Subclasses DomainUpDown, NumericUpDown

UpDownEventArgs

System.Windows.Forms (system.windows.forms.dll) class

This class is for internal use only and should not be called from your own code.

```
public class UpDownEventArgs : EventArgs {
// Public Constructors
   public UpDownEventArgs(int buttonPushed);
// Public Instance Properties
   public int ButtonID{get; }
}
```

Hierarchy System.Object → System.EventArgs → UpDownEventArgs

Passed To UpDownEventHandler.{BeginInvoke( ), Invoke( )}

UpDownEventHandler serializable

System.Windows.Forms (system.windows.forms.dll) delegate

This delegate is for internal use only and should not be used in your own code.

```
public delegate void UpDownEventHandler(object source, UpDownEventArgs e);
```

UserControl marshal by reference, disposable

System.Windows.Forms (system.windows.forms.dll) class

You should derive your own custom container controls from this base class. It manages focus, tab, and mnemonic (shortcut) behavior for you, and provides designer integration support.

```
public class UserControl : ContainerControl {
// Public Constructors
   public UserControl( );
// Public Instance Properties
   public override string Text{set; get; }                                // overrides Control
// Protected Instance Properties
   protected override Size DefaultSize{get; }                            // overrides Control
// Protected Instance Methods
   protected override void OnCreateControl( );                   // overrides ContainerControl
   protected virtual void OnLoad(EventArgs e);
   protected override void OnMouseDown(MouseEventArgs e);                // overrides Control
   protected override void WndProc(ref Message m);               // overrides ContainerControl
// Events
   public event EventHandler Load;
}
```

Hierarchy System.Object → System.MarshalByRefObject → System.ComponentModel.Component(System.ComponentModel.IComponent, System.IDisposable) → Control(IOleControl, IOleObject, IOleInPlaceObject, IOleInPlaceActiveObject, IOleWindow, IViewObject, IViewObject2, IPersist, IPersistStreamInit, IPersistPropertyBag, IPersistStorage, IQuickActivate, System.ComponentModel.ISynchronizeInvoke, IWin32Window) → ScrollableControl → ContainerControl(IContainerControl) → UserControl

View

serializable

System.Windows.Forms (system.windows.forms.dll) enum

The options for the ListView.View property are provided by this enumeration.

```
public enum View {
  LargeIcon = 0,
  Details = 1,
  SmallIcon = 2,
  List = 3
}
```

Hierarchy System.Object → System.ValueType → System.Enum(System.IComparable, System.IFormattable, System.IConvertible) → View

Returned By ListView.View

Passed To ListView.View

VScrollBar

marshal by reference, disposable

System.Windows.Forms (system.windows.forms.dll) class

While most controls provide their own scrollbars (including Form and UserControl objects) sometimes the default behavior of these objects is inadequate. In these circumstances, you may wish to manage your own scrollbars (the shortened scrollbars at the bottom of an Excel tab-sheet for example). This class, derived from the base ScrollBar, provides a vertical bar. See the HScrollBar class for its horizontal partner.

```
public class VScrollBar : ScrollBar {
// Public Constructors
  public VScrollBar( );
// Public Instance Properties
  public override RightToLeft RightToLeft{set; get; }                // overrides Control
// Protected Instance Properties
  protected override CreateParams CreateParams{get; }                // overrides ScrollBar
  protected override Size DefaultSize{get; }                          // overrides Control
}
```

Hierarchy System.Object → System.MarshalByRefObject → System.ComponentModel.Component(System.ComponentModel.IComponent, System.IDisposable) → Control(IOleControl, IOleObject, IOleInPlaceObject, IOleInPlaceActiveObject, IOleWindow, IViewObject, IViewObject2, IPersist, IPersistStreamInit, IPersistPropertyBag, IPersistStorage, IQuickActivate, System.ComponentModel.ISynchronizeInvoke, IWin32Window) → ScrollBar → VScrollBar

20
The System.Windows.Forms.Design Namespace

The System.Windows.Forms.Design namespace contains various classes that relate to the design-time environment. Figure 20-1 shows the types in this namespace.

AnchorEditor

System.Windows.Forms.Design (system.design.dll) sealed class

This class provides the editor for the Anchor property. You would not normally use it directly in your own code.

```
public sealed class AnchorEditor : System.Drawing.Design.UITypeEditor {
// Public Constructors
   public AnchorEditor( );
// Public Instance Methods
   public override object EditValue(System.ComponentModel.ITypeDescriptorContext context,
      IServiceProvider provider, object value);                  // overrides System.Drawing.Design.UITypeEditor
   public override UITypeEditorEditStyle GetEditStyle(
      System.ComponentModel.ITypeDescriptorContext context);     // overrides System.Drawing.Design.UITypeEditor
}
```

Hierarchy System.Object → System.Drawing.Design.UITypeEditor → AnchorEditor

AxImporter

System.Windows.Forms.Design (system.design.dll) class

This class is used by the design environment to generate wrapper classes for an ActiveX control that has been imported into a project. You would not normally use it directly in your own code.

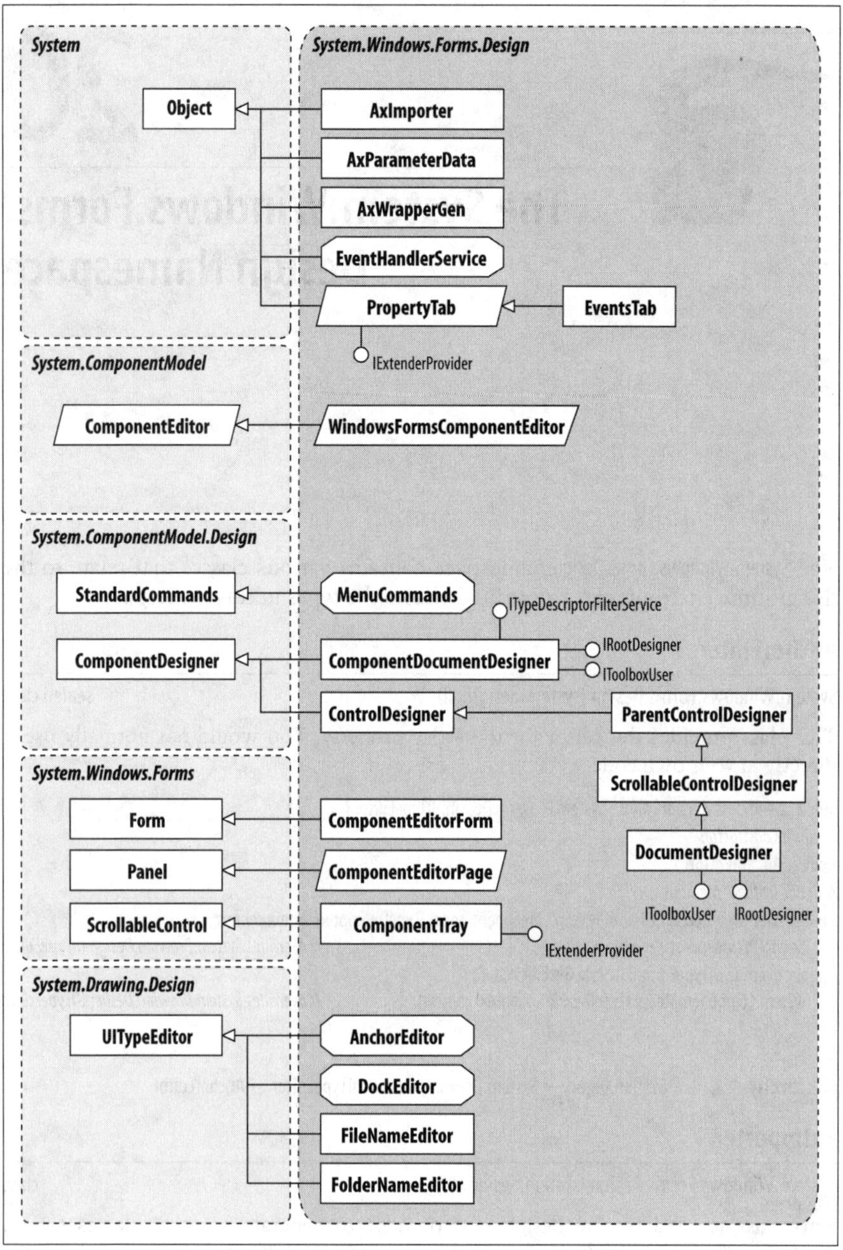

System
System.Windows.Forms.Design
Object
AxImporter
AxParameterData
AxWrapperGen
EventHandlerService
PropertyTab
EventsTab
IExtenderProvider
System.ComponentModel
ComponentEditor
WindowsFormsComponentEditor
System.ComponentModel.Design
StandardCommands
MenuCommands
ITypeDescriptorFilterService
ComponentDesigner
ComponentDocumentDesigner
IRootDesigner
IToolboxUser
ControlDesigner
ParentControlDesigner
ScrollableControlDesigner
DocumentDesigner
IToolboxUser
IRootDesigner
System.Windows.Forms
Form
ComponentEditorForm
Panel
ComponentEditorPage
ScrollableControl
ComponentTray
IExtenderProvider
System.Drawing.Design
UITypeEditor
AnchorEditor
DockEditor
FileNameEditor
FolderNameEditor

Figure 20-1. Types from the System.Windows.Forms.Design namespace

```
public class AxImporter {
// Public Constructors
   public AxImporter(Options options);
// Public Instance Properties
   public string[ ] GeneratedAssemblies{get; }
   public string[ ] GeneratedSources{get; }
   public TYPELIBATTR[ ] GeneratedTypeLibAttributes{get; }
// Public Static Methods
   public static string GetFileOfTypeLib(ref System.Runtime.InteropServices.TYPELIBATTR tlibattr);
// Public Instance Methods
   public string GenerateFromFile(System.IO.FileInfo file);
   public string GenerateFromTypeLibrary(System.Runtime.InteropServices.UCOMITypeLib typeLib);
   public string GenerateFromTypeLibrary(System.Runtime.InteropServices.UCOMITypeLib typeLib, Guid clsid);
}
```

AxImporter.IReferenceResolver

System.Windows.Forms.Design (system.design.dll) — interface

This interface is implemented by wrapper classes generated by the AxImporter class. You would not normally use it directly from your own code.

```
public interface AxImporter.IReferenceResolver {
// Public Instance Methods
   public string ResolveActiveXReference(System.Runtime.InteropServices.UCOMITypeLib typeLib);
   public string ResolveComReference(System.Reflection.AssemblyName name);
   public string ResolveComReference(System.Runtime.InteropServices.UCOMITypeLib typeLib);
   public string ResolveManagedReference(string assemName);
}
```

AxImporter.Options

System.Windows.Forms.Design (system.design.dll) — sealed class

This class is used to specify the options to be used when generating wrapper classes for an ActiveX control, using the AxImporter class. It would not normally be used directly in your own code.

```
public sealed class AxImporter.Options {
// Public Constructors
   public AxImporter.Options( );
// Public Instance Fields
   public bool delaySign;
   public bool genSources;
   public string keyContainer;
   public string keyFile;
   public StrongNameKeyPair keyPair;
   public bool noLogo;
   public string outputDirectory;
   public string outputName;
   public bool overwriteRCW;
```

```
    public byte[ ] publicKey;
    public IReferenceResolver references;
    public bool silentMode;
    public bool verboseMode;
}
```

AxParameterData

System.Windows.Forms.Design (system.design.dll) class

This class is for internal use by the framework and should not be used from your own code.

```
public class AxParameterData {
// Public Constructors
    public AxParameterData(System.Reflection.ParameterInfo info);
    public AxParameterData(System.Reflection.ParameterInfo info, bool ignoreByRefs);
    public AxParameterData(string inname, string typeName);
    public AxParameterData(string inname, Type type);
// Public Instance Properties
    public FieldDirection Direction{get; }
    public bool IsByRef{get; }
    public bool IsIn{get; }
    public bool IsOptional{get; }
    public bool IsOut{get; }
    public string Name{set; get; }
    public Type ParameterType{get; }
    public string TypeName{get; }
// Public Static Methods
    public static AxParameterData[ ] Convert(System.Reflection.ParameterInfo[ ] infos);
    public static AxParameterData[ ] Convert(System.Reflection.ParameterInfo[ ] infos, bool ignoreByRefs);
}
```

AxWrapperGen

System.Windows.Forms.Design (system.design.dll) class

This class is for internal use by the framework and should not be used from your own code.

```
public class AxWrapperGen {
// Public Constructors
    public AxWrapperGen(Type axType);
// Public Static Fields
    public static ArrayList GeneratedSources;                    // =System.Collections.ArrayList
}
```

ComponentDocumentDesigner disposable

System.Windows.Forms.Design (system.design.dll) class

This class is used to provide design-time behavior for a design document that contains one or more System.ComponentModel.Component instances. It provides a component tray extension in which the non-visual components can be rendered.

```
public class ComponentDocumentDesigner : System.ComponentModel.Design.ComponentDesigner : System.
ComponentModel.Design.IRootDesigner, System.Drawing.Design.IToolboxUser, IOleDragClient, System.ComponentModel.
Design.ITypeDescriptorFilterService {
// Public Constructors
   public ComponentDocumentDesigner( );
// Public Instance Properties
   public Control Control{get; }
   public bool TrayAutoArrange{set; get; }
   public bool TrayLargeIcon{set; get; }
// Public Instance Methods
   public override void Initialize(
      System.ComponentModel.IComponent component);      // overrides System.ComponentModel.Design.ComponentDesigner
// Protected Instance Methods
   protected override void Dispose(bool disposing);     // overrides System.ComponentModel.Design.ComponentDesigner
   protected virtual bool GetToolSupported(
      System.Drawing.Design.ToolboxItem tool);                  // implements System.Drawing.Design.IToolboxUser
   protected override void PreFilterProperties(
      System.Collections.IDictionary properties);       // overrides System.ComponentModel.Design.ComponentDesigner
}
```

Hierarchy System.Object → System.ComponentModel.Design.ComponentDesigner(System.ComponentModel.Design.IDesigner, System.IDisposable, System.ComponentModel.Design.IDesignerFilter) → ComponentDocumentDesigner(System.ComponentModel.Design.IRootDesigner, System.Drawing.Design.IToolboxUser, IOleDragClient, System.ComponentModel.Design.ITypeDescriptorFilterService)

ComponentEditorForm — marshal by reference, disposable

System.Windows.Forms.Design (system.windows.forms.dll) — class

This class provides the user interface for a WindowsFormsComponentEditor. It can show a number of ComponentEditorPage objects for a particular component. You specify the source component and the types of the pages to show in the constructor.

It is very similar in conception to the Win32 PropertySheet control, but is used by Visual Studio .NET to display component properties.

```
public class ComponentEditorForm : System.Windows.Forms.Form {
// Public Constructors
   public ComponentEditorForm(object component, Type[ ] pageTypes);
// Public Instance Methods
   public override bool PreProcessMessage(
      ref System.Windows.Forms.Message msg);                      // overrides System.Windows.Forms.Control
   public virtual DialogResult ShowForm( );
   public virtual DialogResult ShowForm(int page);
   public virtual DialogResult ShowForm(System.Windows.Forms.IWin32Window owner);
   public virtual DialogResult ShowForm(System.Windows.Forms.IWin32Window owner, int page);
// Protected Instance Methods
   protected override void OnActivated(EventArgs e);                 // overrides System.Windows.Forms.Form
   protected override void OnHelpRequested(
      System.Windows.Forms.HelpEventArgs e);                      // overrides System.Windows.Forms.Control
   protected virtual void OnSelChangeSelector(object source, System.Windows.Forms.TreeViewEventArgs e);
}
```

Hierarchy System.Object → System.MarshalByRefObject → System.ComponentModel.Component(System.ComponentModel.IComponent, System.IDisposable) → System.Windows.Forms.Control(System.Windows.Forms.IOleControl, System.Windows.Forms.IOleObject, System.Windows.Forms.IOleInPlaceObject, System.Windows.Forms.IOleInPlaceActiveObject, System.Windows.Forms.IOleWindow, System.Windows.Forms.IViewObject, System.Windows.Forms.IViewObject2, System.Windows.Forms.IPersist, System.Windows.Forms.IPersistStreamInit, System.Windows.Forms.IPersistPropertyBag, System.Windows.Forms.IPersistStorage, System.Windows.Forms.IQuickActivate, System.ComponentModel.ISynchronizeInvoke, System.Windows.Forms.IWin32Window) → System.Windows.Forms.ScrollableControl → System.Windows.Forms.ContainerControl(System.Windows.Forms.IContainerControl) → System.Windows.Forms.Form → ComponentEditorForm

ComponentEditorPage

marshal by reference, disposable

System.Windows.Forms.Design (system.windows.forms.dll) — abstract class

This class represents a page of properties for a component that can be displayed in a ComponentEditorForm. The component to edit is determined using the SetComponent( ) method. It is very similar in concept to the Win32 PropertyPage control.

You can set a Title and an Icon for the page. Then, the page can be shown with the Activate( ) method and hidden again with Deactivate( ). You can also use the CommitOnDeactivate property to determine whether the changes made to the component's configuration should be committed before the page is deactivated. Changes are committed using the ApplyChanges( ) method. When all the changes have been committed by all pages in the ComponentEditorForm, the framework calls OnApplyComplete( ).

Help is implemented with the SupportsHelp( ) and ShowHelp( ) methods.

```
public abstract class ComponentEditorPage : System.Windows.Forms.Panel {
// Public Constructors
   public ComponentEditorPage( );
// Public Instance Properties
   public bool CommitOnDeactivate{set; get; }
   public Icon Icon{set; get; }
   public virtual string Title{get; }
// Protected Instance Properties
   protected IComponent Component{set; get; }
   protected override CreateParams CreateParams{get; }            // overrides System.Windows.Forms.Panel
   protected bool FirstActivate{set; get; }
   protected int Loading{set; get; }
   protected bool LoadRequired{set; get; }
   protected IComponentEditorPageSite PageSite{set; get; }
// Public Instance Methods
   public virtual void Activate( );
   public virtual void ApplyChanges( );
   public virtual void Deactivate( );
   public virtual Control GetControl( );
   public virtual bool IsPageMessage(ref System.Windows.Forms.Message msg);
   public virtual void OnApplyComplete( );
   public virtual void SetComponent(System.ComponentModel.IComponent component);
   public virtual void SetSite(System.Windows.Forms.IComponentEditorPageSite site);
   public virtual void ShowHelp( );
```

```
public virtual bool SupportsHelp( );
// Protected Instance Methods
protected void EnterLoadingMode( );
protected void ExitLoadingMode( );
protected IComponent GetSelectedComponent( );
protected bool IsFirstActivate( );
protected bool IsLoading( );
protected abstract void LoadComponent( );
protected virtual void ReloadComponent( );
protected abstract void SaveComponent( );
protected virtual void SetDirty( );
}
```

Hierarchy System.Object → System.MarshalByRefObject → System.ComponentModel.Component(System.ComponentModel.IComponent, System.IDisposable) → System.Windows.Forms.Control(System.Windows.Forms.IOleControl, System.Windows.Forms.IOleObject, System.Windows.Forms.IOleInPlaceObject, System.Windows.Forms.IOleInPlaceActiveObject, System.Windows.Forms.IOleWindow, System.Windows.Forms.IViewObject, System.Windows.Forms.IViewObject2, System.Windows.Forms.IPersist, System.Windows.Forms.IPersistStreamInit, System.Windows.Forms.IPersistPropertyBag, System.Windows.Forms.IPersistStorage, System.Windows.Forms.IQuickActivate, System.ComponentModel.ISynchronizeInvoke, System.Windows.Forms.IWin32Window) → System.Windows.Forms.ScrollableControl → System.Windows.Forms.Panel → ComponentEditorPage

ComponentTray — marshal by reference, disposable

System.Windows.Forms.Design (system.design.dll) — class

This Control implements the component tray portion of the forms designer.

You can retrieve the number of components in the tray using the ComponentCount property. The icons can be automatically lined up using the AutoArrange property, and their appearance can be modified with ShowLargeIcons. The position of an individual icon can be set using SetLocation( ).

The components themselves can be added using CreateComponentFromTool( ) and removed using RemoveComponent( ).

```
public class ComponentTray : System.Windows.Forms.ScrollableControl : System.ComponentModel.IExtenderProvider,
    ISelectionUIHandler, IOleDragClient {
// Public Constructors
public ComponentTray(System.ComponentModel.Design.IDesigner mainDesigner, IServiceProvider serviceProvider);
// Public Instance Properties
public bool AutoArrange{set; get; }
public int ComponentCount{get; }
public bool ShowLargeIcons{set; get; }
// Public Instance Methods
public virtual void AddComponent(System.ComponentModel.IComponent component);
public void CreateComponentFromTool(System.Drawing.Design.ToolboxItem tool);
public Point GetLocation(System.ComponentModel.IComponent receiver);
public virtual void RemoveComponent(System.ComponentModel.IComponent component);
public void SetLocation(System.ComponentModel.IComponent receiver, System.Drawing.Point location);
// Protected Instance Methods
```

```
protected virtual bool CanCreateComponentFromTool(System.Drawing.Design.ToolboxItem tool);
protected virtual bool CanDisplayComponent(System.ComponentModel.IComponent component);
protected void DisplayError(Exception e);
protected override void Dispose(bool disposing);                    // overrides System.Windows.Forms.Control
protected override object GetService(Type serviceType);         // overrides System.ComponentModel.Component
protected override void OnDoubleClick(EventArgs e);                 // overrides System.Windows.Forms.Control
protected override void OnDragDrop(
   System.Windows.Forms.DragEventArgs de);                          // overrides System.Windows.Forms.Control
protected override void OnDragEnter(
   System.Windows.Forms.DragEventArgs de);                          // overrides System.Windows.Forms.Control
protected override void OnDragLeave(EventArgs e);                   // overrides System.Windows.Forms.Control
protected override void OnDragOver(
   System.Windows.Forms.DragEventArgs de);                          // overrides System.Windows.Forms.Control
protected override void OnGiveFeedback(
   System.Windows.Forms.GiveFeedbackEventArgs gfevent);             // overrides System.Windows.Forms.Control
protected override void OnLayout(
    System.Windows.Forms.LayoutEventArgs levent);         // overrides System.Windows.Forms.ScrollableControl
protected virtual void OnLostCapture( );
protected override void OnMouseDown(
   System.Windows.Forms.MouseEventArgs e);                          // overrides System.Windows.Forms.Control
protected override void OnMouseMove(
   System.Windows.Forms.MouseEventArgs e);                          // overrides System.Windows.Forms.Control
protected override void OnMouseUp(
   System.Windows.Forms.MouseEventArgs e);                          // overrides System.Windows.Forms.Control
protected override void OnPaint(
   System.Windows.Forms.PaintEventArgs pe);                         // overrides System.Windows.Forms.Control
protected virtual void OnSetCursor( );
protected override void WndProc(
   ref System.Windows.Forms.Message m);                   // overrides System.Windows.Forms.ScrollableControl
}
```

Hierarchy System.Object → System.MarshalByRefObject → System.ComponentModel.Component(System.ComponentModel.IComponent, System.IDisposable) → System.Windows.Forms.Control(System.Windows.Forms.IOleControl, System.Windows.Forms.IOleObject, System.Windows.Forms.IOleInPlaceObject, System.Windows.Forms.IOleInPlaceActiveObject, System.Windows.Forms.IOleWindow, System.Windows.Forms.IViewObject, System.Windows.Forms.IViewObject2, System.Windows.Forms.IPersist, System.Windows.Forms.IPersistStreamInit, System.Windows.Forms.IPersistPropertyBag, System.Windows.Forms.IPersistStorage, System.Windows.Forms.IQuickActivate, System.ComponentModel.ISynchronizeInvoke, System.Windows.Forms.IWin32Window) → System.Windows.Forms.ScrollableControl → ComponentTray(System.ComponentModel.IExtenderProvider, ISelectionUIHandler, IOleDragClient)

ControlDesigner

disposable

System.Windows.Forms.Design (system.design.dll) class

This class extends System.ComponentModel.Design.ComponentDesigner to provide a designer for Control classes. It provides properties to specify the Control that is being designed, and the SelectionRules that determine how that control can be selected and manipulated.

```
public class ControlDesigner : System.ComponentModel.Design.ComponentDesigner {
// Public Constructors
```

```
public ControlDesigner( );
// Protected Static Fields
   protected static readonly Point InvalidPoint;                  // ={X=-2147483648,Y=-2147483648}
// Protected Instance Fields
   protected AccessibleObject accessibilityObj;
// Public Instance Properties
   public virtual AccessibleObject AccessibilityObject{get; }
   public override ICollection AssociatedComponents{get; } // overrides System.ComponentModel.Design.ComponentDesigner
   public virtual Control Control{get; }
   public virtual SelectionRules SelectionRules{get; }
// Protected Instance Properties
   protected virtual bool EnableDragRect{get; }
// Public Instance Methods
   public virtual bool CanBeParentedTo(System.ComponentModel.Design.IDesigner parentDesigner);
   public override void Initialize(
      System.ComponentModel.IComponent component);      // overrides System.ComponentModel.Design.ComponentDesigner
   public override void InitializeNonDefault( );         // overrides System.ComponentModel.Design.ComponentDesigner
   public override void OnSetComponentDefaults( );       // overrides System.ComponentModel.Design.ComponentDesigner
// Protected Instance Methods
   protected void BaseWndProc(ref System.Windows.Forms.Message m);
   protected void DefWndProc(ref System.Windows.Forms.Message m);
   protected void DisplayError(Exception e);
   protected override void Dispose(bool disposing);      // overrides System.ComponentModel.Design.ComponentDesigner
   protected void EnableDragDrop(bool value);
   protected virtual bool GetHitTest(System.Drawing.Point point);
   protected void HookChildControls(System.Windows.Forms.Control firstChild);
   protected virtual void OnContextMenu(int x, int y);
   protected virtual void OnCreateHandle( );
   protected virtual void OnDragDrop(System.Windows.Forms.DragEventArgs de);
   protected virtual void OnDragEnter(System.Windows.Forms.DragEventArgs de);
   protected virtual void OnDragLeave(EventArgs e);
   protected virtual void OnDragOver(System.Windows.Forms.DragEventArgs de);
   protected virtual void OnGiveFeedback(System.Windows.Forms.GiveFeedbackEventArgs e);
   protected virtual void OnMouseDragBegin(int x, int y);
   protected virtual void OnMouseDragEnd(bool cancel);
   protected virtual void OnMouseDragMove(int x, int y);
   protected virtual void OnMouseEnter( );
   protected virtual void OnMouseHover( );
   protected virtual void OnMouseLeave( );
   protected virtual void OnPaintAdornments(System.Windows.Forms.PaintEventArgs pe);
   protected virtual void OnSetCursor( );
   protected override void PreFilterProperties(
      System.Collections.IDictionary properties);        // overrides System.ComponentModel.Design.ComponentDesigner
   protected void UnhookChildControls(System.Windows.Forms.Control firstChild);
   protected virtual void WndProc(ref System.Windows.Forms.Message m);
}
```

Hierarchy System.Object → System.ComponentModel.Design.ComponentDesigner(System.ComponentModel.Design.IDesigner, System.IDisposable, System.ComponentModel.Design.IDesignerFilter) → ControlDesigner

Subclasses ParentControlDesigner

Passed To ControlDesignerAccessibleObject.ControlDesignerAccessibleObject( ), ParentControlDesigner.CanParent( )

ControlDesigner.ControlDesignerAccessibleObject **marshal by reference**

System.Windows.Forms.Design (system.design.dll) class

This class provides an AccessibleObject for the ControlDesigner. It would not normally be used directly from your own code.

```
public class ControlDesigner.ControlDesignerAccessibleObject : System.Windows.Forms.AccessibleObject {
// Public Constructors
   public ControlDesigner.ControlDesignerAccessibleObject(ControlDesigner designer,
      System.Windows.Forms.Control control);
// Public Instance Properties
   public override Rectangle Bounds{get; }              // overrides System.Windows.Forms.AccessibleObject
   public override string DefaultAction{get; }          // overrides System.Windows.Forms.AccessibleObject
   public override string Description{get; }            // overrides System.Windows.Forms.AccessibleObject
   public override string Name{get; }                   // overrides System.Windows.Forms.AccessibleObject
   public override AccessibleObject Parent{get; }       // overrides System.Windows.Forms.AccessibleObject
   public override AccessibleRole Role{get; }           // overrides System.Windows.Forms.AccessibleObject
   public override AccessibleStates State{get; }        // overrides System.Windows.Forms.AccessibleObject
   public override string Value{get; }                  // overrides System.Windows.Forms.AccessibleObject
// Public Instance Methods
   public override AccessibleObject GetChild(int index);  // overrides System.Windows.Forms.AccessibleObject
   public override int GetChildCount( );                // overrides System.Windows.Forms.AccessibleObject
   public override AccessibleObject GetFocused( );      // overrides System.Windows.Forms.AccessibleObject
   public override AccessibleObject GetSelected( );     // overrides System.Windows.Forms.AccessibleObject
   public override AccessibleObject HitTest(int x, int y);  // overrides System.Windows.Forms.AccessibleObject
}
```

Hierarchy System.Object → System.MarshalByRefObject → System.Windows.Forms.AccessibleObject(System.Reflection.IReflect, Accessibility.IAccessible, System.Windows.Forms.IEnumVariant) → ControlDesignerAccessibleObject

DockEditor

System.Windows.Forms.Design (system.design.dll) sealed class

This class provides an editor for the Dock property.

```
public sealed class DockEditor : System.Drawing.Design.UITypeEditor {
// Public Constructors
   public DockEditor( );
// Public Instance Methods
   public override object EditValue(System.ComponentModel.ITypeDescriptorContext context,
      IServiceProvider provider, object value);         // overrides System.Drawing.Design.UITypeEditor
   public override UITypeEditorEditStyle GetEditStyle(
      System.ComponentModel.ITypeDescriptorContext context);  // overrides System.Drawing.Design.UITypeEditor
}
```

Hierarchy System.Object → System.Drawing.Design.UITypeEditor → DockEditor

DocumentDesigner

disposable

System.Windows.Forms.Design (system.design.dll) class

This class extends ScrollableControlDesigner to provide design-time behavior for forms and user controls. This designer can be extended to include design-time functionality common to a particular class of design documents.

```
public class DocumentDesigner : ScrollableControlDesigner : System.ComponentModel.Design.IRootDesigner,
    System.Drawing.Design.IToolboxUser {
// Public Constructors
  public DocumentDesigner( );
// Protected Instance Fields
  protected IMenuEditorService menuEditorService;
// Public Instance Properties
  public override SelectionRules SelectionRules{get; }                          // overrides ControlDesigner
// Public Instance Methods
  public override void Initialize(System.ComponentModel.IComponent component);  // overrides ParentControlDesigner
// Protected Instance Methods
  protected override void Dispose(bool disposing);                              // overrides ParentControlDesigner
  protected virtual void EnsureMenuEditorService(System.ComponentModel.IComponent c);
  protected virtual bool GetToolSupported(
    System.Drawing.Design.ToolboxItem tool);                      // implements System.Drawing.Design.IToolboxUser
  protected override void OnContextMenu(int x, int y);                          // overrides ControlDesigner
  protected override void OnCreateHandle( );                                    // overrides ControlDesigner
  protected override void PreFilterProperties(System.Collections.IDictionary properties); // overrides ParentControlDesigner
  protected virtual void ToolPicked(
    System.Drawing.Design.ToolboxItem tool);                      // implements System.Drawing.Design.IToolboxUser
  protected override void WndProc(ref System.Windows.Forms.Message m);          // overrides ScrollableControlDesigner
}
```

Hierarchy System.Object → System.ComponentModel.Design.ComponentDesigner(System.ComponentModel.Design.IDesigner, System.IDisposable, System.ComponentModel.Design.IDesignerFilter) → ControlDesigner → ParentControlDesigner(ISelectionUIHandler, IOleDragClient) → ScrollableControlDesigner → DocumentDesigner(System.ComponentModel.Design.IRootDesigner, System.Drawing.Design.IToolboxUser)

EventHandlerService

System.Windows.Forms.Design (system.design.dll) sealed class

This class is for internal use by the framework and should not be used from your own code.

```
public sealed class EventHandlerService : IEventHandlerService {
// Public Constructors
  public EventHandlerService(System.Windows.Forms.Control focusWnd);

// Public Instance Properties
  public Control FocusWindow{get; }                                 // implements IEventHandlerService
// Public Instance Methods
  public object GetHandler(Type handlerType);                       // implements IEventHandlerService
  public void PopHandler(object handler);                           // implements IEventHandlerService
  public void PushHandler(object handler);                          // implements IEventHandlerService
```

```
// Events
  public event EventHandler EventHandlerChanged;                    // implements IEventHandlerService
}
```

EventsTab

System.Windows.Forms.Design (system.windows.forms.dll) class

This class implements a PropertyTab (for a System.Windows.Forms.PropertyGrid) that can be used to list and bind to events. You will be familiar with this control from the Visual Studio .NET designer environment.

```
public class EventsTab : PropertyTab {
// Public Constructors
  public EventsTab(IServiceProvider sp);
// Public Instance Properties
  public override string HelpKeyword{get; }                          // overrides PropertyTab
  public override string TabName{get; }                              // overrides PropertyTab
// Public Instance Methods
  public override bool CanExtend(object extendee);                   // overrides PropertyTab
  public override PropertyDescriptor GetDefaultProperty(object obj); // overrides PropertyTab
  public override PropertyDescriptorCollection GetProperties(System.ComponentModel.ITypeDescriptorContext context,
     object component, Attribute[ ] attributes);                     // overrides PropertyTab
  public override PropertyDescriptorCollection GetProperties(object component,
     Attribute[ ] attributes);                                       // overrides PropertyTab
}
```

Hierarchy System.Object → PropertyTab(System.ComponentModel.IExtenderProvider) → EventsTab

FileNameEditor

System.Windows.Forms.Design (system.design.dll) class

This class provides an editor for the selection of a filename (using the common dialog). You can inherit from this class to provide file and filter extensions, and to set the dialog title.

```
public class FileNameEditor : System.Drawing.Design.UITypeEditor {
// Public Constructors
  public FileNameEditor( );
// Public Instance Methods
  public override object EditValue(System.ComponentModel.ITypeDescriptorContext context,
     IServiceProvider provider, object value);          // overrides System.Drawing.Design.UITypeEditor
  public override UITypeEditorEditStyle GetEditStyle(
     System.ComponentModel.ITypeDescriptorContext context);  // overrides System.Drawing.Design.UITypeEditor
// Protected Instance Methods
  protected virtual void InitializeDialog(System.Windows.Forms.OpenFileDialog openFileDialog);
}
```

Hierarchy System.Object → System.Drawing.Design.UITypeEditor → FileNameEditor

FolderNameEditor

System.Windows.Forms.Design (system.design.dll) class

This class provides an editor for the selection of a folder or path (using the Shell32 common dialog).

```
public class FolderNameEditor : System.Drawing.Design.UITypeEditor {
// Public Constructors
   public FolderNameEditor( );
// Public Instance Methods
   public override object EditValue(System.ComponentModel.ITypeDescriptorContext context,
      IServiceProvider provider, object value);         // overrides System.Drawing.Design.UITypeEditor
   public override UITypeEditorEditStyle GetEditStyle(
      System.ComponentModel.ITypeDescriptorContext context);   // overrides System.Drawing.Design.UITypeEditor
// Protected Instance Methods
   protected virtual void InitializeDialog(FolderBrowser folderBrowser);
}
```

Hierarchy System.Object → System.Drawing.Design.UITypeEditor → FolderNameEditor

IMenuEditorService

System.Windows.Forms.Design (system.design.dll) interface

This interface is implemented by the design-time menu editing service. It provides methods to get the current menu (GetMenu( )) and determine whether the menu IsActive( ). The current menu can be changed with the SetMenu( ) method, and the current menu item can be set with SetSelection( ).

```
public interface IMenuEditorService {
// Public Instance Methods
   public Menu GetMenu( );
   public bool IsActive( );
   public bool MessageFilter(ref System.Windows.Forms.Message m);
   public void SetMenu(System.Windows.Forms.Menu menu);
   public void SetSelection(System.Windows.Forms.MenuItem item);
}
```

IUIService

System.Windows.Forms.Design (system.windows.forms.dll) interface

You can obtain this service from the design-time environment object hosting your designer, which will implement System.IServiceProvider (that's the Site for a Component). It can be used to obtain various functions that you may require to present your designer's UI.

CanShowComponentEditor( ) determines whether the environment supports the display of a ComponentEditorForm for the specified component. You can then use ShowComponentEditor( ) to show the editor. ShowDialog( ) will display the specified Form modally, returning a System.Windows.Forms.DialogResult. ShowMessage( ) and ShowError( ) display a message in a message box, with the appropriate warning icon, and ShowToolWindow( ) displays the tool window with the specified Guid. (Some standard GUIDs can be found in the System.ComponentModel.Design.StandardToolWindows class).

You can also mark the UI as dirty (and therefore needing an update), with SetUIDirty( ), and retrieve a System.Windows.Forms.IWin32Window to use as the owner for your dialogs with the GetDialogOwnerWindow( ) method.

```
public interface IUIService {
// Public Instance Properties
   public IDictionary Styles{get; }
// Public Instance Methods
   public bool CanShowComponentEditor(object component);
   public IWin32Window GetDialogOwnerWindow( );
   public void SetUIDirty( );
   public bool ShowComponentEditor(object component, System.Windows.Forms.IWin32Window parent);
   public DialogResult ShowDialog(System.Windows.Forms.Form form);
   public void ShowError(Exception ex);
   public void ShowError(Exception ex, string message);
   public void ShowError(string message);
   public DialogResult ShowMessage(string message, string caption, System.Windows.Forms.MessageBoxButtons buttons);
   public void ShowMessage(string message);
   public void ShowMessage(string message, string caption);
   public bool ShowToolWindow(Guid toolWindow);
}
```

IWindowsFormsEditorService

System.Windows.Forms.Design (system.windows.forms.dll) interface

This service can be obtained from the local IServiceProvider. Typically, this will be the instance supplied to the EditValue( ) method.

DropDownControl( ) will show a System.Windows.Forms.Control as a drop-down, and CloseDropDown( ) will clear any control currently showing. Alternatively, you can show a System.Windows.Forms.Form using ShowDialog( ).

```
public interface IWindowsFormsEditorService {
// Public Instance Methods
   public void CloseDropDown( );
   public void DropDownControl(System.Windows.Forms.Control control);
   public DialogResult ShowDialog(
      System.Windows.Forms.Form dialog);
}
```

MenuCommands

System.Windows.Forms.Design (system.design.dll) sealed class

This class defines a set of static members that allow you to access the standard menu commands available in the designer host (e.g., KeySelectNext, SelectionMenu), through the System.ComponentModel.Design.IMenuCommandService.

```
public sealed class MenuCommands : System.ComponentModel.Design.StandardCommands {
// Public Constructors
   public MenuCommands( );
// Public Static Fields
   public static readonly CommandID ComponentTrayMenu;        //=74d21312-2aee-11d1-8bfb-00a0c90f26f7 : 1286
```

```
public static readonly CommandID ContainerMenu;          // =74d21312-2aee-11d1-8bfb-00a0c90f26f7 : 1281
public static readonly CommandID DesignerProperties;     // =74d21313-2aee-11d1-8bfb-00a0c90f26f7 : 4097
public static readonly CommandID KeyCancel;              // =1496a755-94de-11d0-8c3f-00c04fc2aae2 : 103
public static readonly CommandID KeyDefaultAction;       // =1496a755-94de-11d0-8c3f-00c04fc2aae2 : 3
public static readonly CommandID KeyMoveDown;            // =1496a755-94de-11d0-8c3f-00c04fc2aae2 : 13
public static readonly CommandID KeyMoveLeft;            // =1496a755-94de-11d0-8c3f-00c04fc2aae2 : 7
public static readonly CommandID KeyMoveRight;           // =1496a755-94de-11d0-8c3f-00c04fc2aae2 : 9
public static readonly CommandID KeyMoveUp;              // =1496a755-94de-11d0-8c3f-00c04fc2aae2 : 11
public static readonly CommandID KeyNudgeDown;           // =1496a755-94de-11d0-8c3f-00c04fc2aae2 : 1225
public static readonly CommandID KeyNudgeHeightDecrease; // =1496a755-94de-11d0-8c3f-00c04fc2aae2 : 1229
public static readonly CommandID KeyNudgeHeightIncrease; // =1496a755-94de-11d0-8c3f-00c04fc2aae2 : 1228
public static readonly CommandID KeyNudgeLeft;           // =1496a755-94de-11d0-8c3f-00c04fc2aae2 : 1224
public static readonly CommandID KeyNudgeRight;          // =1496a755-94de-11d0-8c3f-00c04fc2aae2 : 1226
public static readonly CommandID KeyNudgeUp;             // =1496a755-94de-11d0-8c3f-00c04fc2aae2 : 1227
public static readonly CommandID KeyNudgeWidthDecrease;  // =1496a755-94de-11d0-8c3f-00c04fc2aae2 : 1230
public static readonly CommandID KeyNudgeWidthIncrease;  // =1496a755-94de-11d0-8c3f-00c04fc2aae2 : 1231
public static readonly CommandID KeyReverseCancel;       // =74d21313-2aee-11d1-8bfb-00a0c90f26f7 : 16385
public static readonly CommandID KeySelectNext;          // =1496a755-94de-11d0-8c3f-00c04fc2aae2 : 4
public static readonly CommandID KeySelectPrevious;      // =1496a755-94de-11d0-8c3f-00c04fc2aae2 : 5
public static readonly CommandID KeySizeHeightDecrease;  // =1496a755-94de-11d0-8c3f-00c04fc2aae2 : 14
public static readonly CommandID KeySizeHeightIncrease;  // =1496a755-94de-11d0-8c3f-00c04fc2aae2 : 12
public static readonly CommandID KeySizeWidthDecrease;   // =1496a755-94de-11d0-8c3f-00c04fc2aae2 : 8
public static readonly CommandID KeySizeWidthIncrease;   // =1496a755-94de-11d0-8c3f-00c04fc2aae2 : 10
public static readonly CommandID KeyTabOrderSelect;      // =74d21313-2aee-11d1-8bfb-00a0c90f26f7 : 16405
public static readonly CommandID SelectionMenu;          // =74d21312-2aee-11d1-8bfb-00a0c90f26f7 : 1280
public static readonly CommandID TraySelectionMenu;      // =74d21312-2aee-11d1-8bfb-00a0c90f26f7 : 1283
}
```

Hierarchy System.Object → System.ComponentModel.Design.StandardCommands → MenuCommands

ParentControlDesigner — disposable

System.Windows.Forms.Design (system.design.dll) — class

This designer extends ControlDesigner to support Control objects that can contain child controls.

```
public class ParentControlDesigner : ControlDesigner : ISelectionUIHandler, IOleDragClient {
// Public Constructors
   public ParentControlDesigner( );
// Protected Instance Properties
   protected virtual Point DefaultControlLocation{get; }
   protected virtual bool DrawGrid{set; get; }
   protected override bool EnableDragRect{get; }                    // overrides ControlDesigner
   protected Size GridSize{set; get; }
// Protected Static Methods
   protected static void InvokeCreateTool(ParentControlDesigner toInvoke, System.Drawing.Design.ToolboxItem tool);
// Public Instance Methods
   public virtual bool CanParent(System.Windows.Forms.Control control);
   public virtual bool CanParent(ControlDesigner controlDesigner);
   public override void Initialize(System.ComponentModel.IComponent component);   // overrides ControlDesigner
// Protected Instance Methods
```

```
protected void CreateTool(System.Drawing.Design.ToolboxItem tool);
protected void CreateTool(System.Drawing.Design.ToolboxItem tool, System.Drawing.Point location);
protected void CreateTool(System.Drawing.Design.ToolboxItem tool, System.Drawing.Rectangle bounds);
protected virtual IComponent[ ] CreateToolCore(System.Drawing.Design.ToolboxItem tool, int x,
   int y, int width, int height, bool hasLocation, bool hasSize);
protected override void Dispose(bool disposing);                                        // overrides ControlDesigner
protected Control GetControl(object component);
protected Rectangle GetUpdatedRect(System.Drawing.Rectangle originalRect, System.Drawing.Rectangle dragRect,
   bool updateSize);
protected override void OnDragDrop(System.Windows.Forms.DragEventArgs de);               // overrides ControlDesigner
protected override void OnDragEnter(System.Windows.Forms.DragEventArgs de);              // overrides ControlDesigner
protected override void OnDragLeave(EventArgs e);                                        // overrides ControlDesigner
protected override void OnDragOver(System.Windows.Forms.DragEventArgs de);               // overrides ControlDesigner
protected override void OnGiveFeedback(System.Windows.Forms.GiveFeedbackEventArgs e);   // overrides ControlDesigner
protected override void OnMouseDragBegin(int x, int y);                                  // overrides ControlDesigner
protected override void OnMouseDragEnd(bool cancel);                                     // overrides ControlDesigner
protected override void OnMouseDragMove(int x, int y);                                   // overrides ControlDesigner
protected override void OnMouseEnter( );                                                 // overrides ControlDesigner
protected override void OnMouseHover( );                                                 // overrides ControlDesigner
protected override void OnMouseLeave( );                                                 // overrides ControlDesigner
protected override void OnPaintAdornments(System.Windows.Forms.PaintEventArgs pe);        // overrides ControlDesigner
protected override void OnSetCursor( );                                                  // overrides ControlDesigner
protected override void PreFilterProperties(System.Collections.IDictionary properties);  // overrides ControlDesigner
protected override void WndProc(ref System.Windows.Forms.Message m);                     // overrides ControlDesigner
}
```

Hierarchy System.Object → System.ComponentModel.Design.ComponentDesigner(System.ComponentModel.Design.IDesigner, System.IDisposable, System.ComponentModel.Design.IDesignerFilter) → ControlDesigner → ParentControlDesigner(ISelectionUIHandler, IOleDragClient)

Subclasses ScrollableControlDesigner

PropertyTab

System.Windows.Forms.Design (system.windows.forms.dll) **abstract class**

This class provides an abstract base for the property tabs shown in a System.Windows.Forms.PropertyGrid.

You can specify the TabName and a Bitmap to display in the tab. You can also get or set the array of Components for which the tab will display properties. For help support, you can set the HelpKeyword associated with the tab. The System.Windows.Forms.PropertyGrid will use this to manage help display for the control while it is showing.

To manage the properties of the bound components, GetProperties( ) will return a System.ComponentModel.PropertyDescriptorCollection listing the available properties, and GetDefaultProperty( ) will return the default System.ComponentModel.PropertyDescriptor.

```
public abstract class PropertyTab : System.ComponentModel.IExtenderProvider {
// Protected Constructors
   protected PropertyTab( );
// Public Instance Properties
   public virtual Bitmap Bitmap{get; }
```

```
  public virtual object[ ] Components{set; get; }
  public virtual string HelpKeyword{get; }
  public abstract string TabName{get; }
// Public Instance Methods
  public virtual bool CanExtend(object extendee);          // implements System.ComponentModel.IExtenderProvider
  public virtual void Dispose( );
  public virtual PropertyDescriptor GetDefaultProperty(object component);
  public virtual PropertyDescriptorCollection GetProperties(System.ComponentModel.ITypeDescriptorContext context,
    object component, Attribute[ ] attributes);
  public virtual PropertyDescriptorCollection GetProperties(object component);
  public abstract PropertyDescriptorCollection GetProperties(object component, Attribute[ ] attributes);
// Protected Instance Methods
  protected virtual void Dispose(bool disposing);
  protected override void Finalize( );                                              // overrides object
}
```

Subclasses EventsTab

Returned By System.Windows.Forms.PropertyGrid.{CreatePropertyTab( ), SelectedTab}, System.Windows.Forms.PropertyTabCollection.this, System.Windows.Forms.PropertyTabChangedEventArgs.{NewTab, OldTab}

Passed To System.Windows.Forms.PropertyTabChangedEventArgs.PropertyTabChangedEventArgs( )

ScrollableControlDesigner **disposable**

System.Windows.Forms.Design (system.design.dll) class

This designer extends ParentControlDesigner to provide support for scrollable Control objects.

```
public class ScrollableControlDesigner : ParentControlDesigner {
// Public Constructors
  public ScrollableControlDesigner( );
// Protected Instance Methods
  protected override bool GetHitTest(System.Drawing.Point pt);                    // overrides ControlDesigner
  protected override void WndProc(ref System.Windows.Forms.Message m);      // overrides ParentControlDesigner
}
```

Hierarchy System.Object → System.ComponentModel.Design.ComponentDesigner(System.ComponentModel.Design.IDesigner, System.IDisposable, System.ComponentModel.Design.IDesignerFilter) → ControlDesigner → ParentControlDesigner(ISelectionUIHandler, IOleDragClient) → ScrollableControlDesigner

Subclasses DocumentDesigner

SelectionRules **serializable, flag**

System.Windows.Forms.Design (system.design.dll) enum

This bitfield enumeration is used by the ControlDesigner.SelectionRules property to determine whether the control is selectable, movable, and how it might be resized. The ControlDesigner uses this when rendering selection handles and manipulating the control on the design surface.

```
public enum SelectionRules {
  None = 0x00000000,
  TopSizeable = 0x00000001,
  BottomSizeable = 0x00000002,
  LeftSizeable = 0x00000004,
  RightSizeable = 0x00000008,
  AllSizeable = 0x0000000F,
  Moveable = 0x10000000,
  Visible = 0x40000000,
  Locked = 0x80000000
}
```

Hierarchy System.Object → System.ValueType → System.Enum(System.IComparable, System.IFormattable, System.IConvertible) → SelectionRules

Returned By ControlDesigner.SelectionRules

WindowsFormsComponentEditor

System.Windows.Forms.Design (system.windows.forms.dll) abstract class

This class provides the abstract base for classes that provide a modal dialog that displays tab pages of settings, similar to a Win32 PropertySheet.

The EditComponent( ) method displays an editor window that contains the pages obtained from the protected GetComponentEditorPages( ) method. The protected GetInitialComponentEditorPageIndex( ) retrieves the index of the page in the list that should be displayed by default.

For example, System.Windows.Forms.AxHost.AxComponentEditor derives from this class to display the OLE Property Pages for the hosted ActiveX control.

```
public abstract class WindowsFormsComponentEditor : System.ComponentModel.ComponentEditor {
// Protected Constructors
  protected WindowsFormsComponentEditor( );
// Public Instance Methods
  public override bool EditComponent(System.ComponentModel.ITypeDescriptorContext context,
    object component);                                // overrides System.ComponentModel.ComponentEditor
  public virtual bool EditComponent(System.ComponentModel.ITypeDescriptorContext context,
    object component, System.Windows.Forms.IWin32Window owner);
  public bool EditComponent(object component, System.Windows.Forms.IWin32Window owner);
// Protected Instance Methods
  protected virtual Type[ ] GetComponentEditorPages( );
  protected virtual int GetInitialComponentEditorPageIndex( );
}
```

Hierarchy System.Object → System.ComponentModel.ComponentEditor → WindowsFormsComponentEditor

Subclasses System.Windows.Forms.AxComponentEditor

III

Appendixes

Part III contains two appendixes that supplement the core reference material found in Part II. These include:

Appendix A, *Namespaces and Assemblies*, which lists the namespaces documented in Part II and provides the filenames of the DLLs in which they reside.

Appendix B, *Type, Method, Property, Event, and Field Index*, which lists each type and member documented in Part II and shows either the type or types to which it belongs (in the case of a type member) or the namespace to which it belongs (in the case of a class, structure, or interface).

A
Namespaces and Assemblies

This appendix allows you to look up a namespace and determine which assemblies export it. This information is helpful when constructing the appropriate /reference:<file list> command-line option for the C# and VB.NET compilers.

Namespace	DLLs
System.ComponentModel	*System.dll, System.Windows.Forms.dll*
System.Drawing	*System.Drawing.dll*
System.Drawing.Drawing2d	*System.Drawing.dll*
System.Drawing.Imaging	*System.Drawing.dll*
System.Drawing.Printing	*System.Drawing.dll*
System.Drawing.Text	*System.Drawing.dll*
System.Windows.Forms	*System.Windows.Forms.dll*
System.Windows.Forms.Design	*System.Windows.Forms.dll*

B

Type, Method, Property, Event, and Field Index

Use this index to look up a type or member and see where it is defined. For a type (a class or interface), you can find the enclosing namespace. If you know the name of a member (a method, property, event, or field), you can find all the types that define it.

A

Class Index

B

C

Class Index

Class Index

D

Class Index

Class Index

E

Class Index

F

G

Class Index

Class Index

H

Class Index

I

Class In

Class Index

J

K

L

M

Class Index

N

O

Class Index

P

Q

R

Class Index

Class Index

T

Class Index

U

W

X

Y

Z

Index

We'd like to hear your suggestions for improving our indexes. Send email to *index@oreilly.com*.

B

C

D

E

F

H

I

J

K

L

N

Q

R

S

T

U

V

W

X

Z

About the Authors

Ian Griffiths is a freelance software developer and consultant. He specializes in digital imaging applications, mainly broadcast video and medical imaging systems. He studied computer science at Cambridge University, and then spent several years writing device drivers for data and video networking systems, which has left him with an enduring fondness for low-level details. Since then, he has migrated to the user interface side of software development, and although he still occasionally pines for the logic analyzer, he is now ludicrously enthusiastic about .NET in general and Windows Forms in particular. When not developing software, Ian works as an instructor and course author for DevelopMentor. He also speaks at conferences in both the UK and the USA and writes technical articles for various web sites and paper publications. He lives in London, UK.

Matthew Adams is the director of development at Digital Healthcare, Ltd. The last three years have kept him fully occupied in the development of a C#/.NET–based distributed imaging platform for healthcare applications. Before that, he studied natural sciences at Cambridge University, worked on banking and imaging applications in North America, became a fully paid-up C++ junkie, and was the lead architect on software solutions for drug discovery for a large US corporation. He thinks .NET is a major philosophical stride forward for the computer industry, so much so that he almost doesn't miss his first love—generics—in C#. He has written articles and given papers on the subject to both technical and non-technical audiences, and looks forward to the day when he doesn't have to answer the question "So, what is .NET?" anymore! He lives in Cambridge, UK, where his partner of the last 10 years (Una) studies him and other similar technology geeks, and calls it "sociology."

Colophon

Our look is the result of reader comments, our own experimentation, and feedback from distribution channels. Distinctive covers complement our distinctive approach to technical topics, breathing personality and life into potentially dry subjects.

The animal on the cover of *.NET Windows Forms in a Nutshell* is a darter. The darter, or anhinga, is a slender bird closely related to the cormorant. Darters can be found near inland waters, such as rivers and lakes, in warm climates all over the world. These birds subsist mostly on fish, which they catch by diving into the water and piercing their prey with their dagger-like beaks.

Like cormorants, darters' feathers become heavily saturated with water when they dive, decreasing their buoyancy and enabling them to stay under water for long periods of time. They may also swim around with their entire bodies submerged and only their snake-like necks and heads visible. Because of this, they are sometimes referred to as "snake birds." After swimming, darters perch with their wings spread to dry. Their black skin aids in heat absorption from the sun, helping the birds warm up.

In addition to being strong swimmers, darters are skilled fliers, allowing them to migrate annually. They nest in small colonies, sometimes with herons. Darters feed their young by regurgitating food directly into their beaks.

Linley Dolby was the production editor and copyeditor for *.NET Windows Forms in a Nutshell*. Brian Sawyer and Claire Cloutier provided quality control. Genevieve d'Entremont and Sue Willing provided production assistance. Angela Howard wrote the index.

Ellie Volckhausen designed the cover of this book, based on a series design by Edie Freedman. The cover image is a 19th-century engraving from the Dover Pictorial Archive. Emma Colby produced the cover layout with QuarkXPress 4.1 using Adobe's ITC Garamond font.

David Futato designed the interior layout. He also designed the CD label with QuarkXPress 4.1 using Adobe's ITC Garamond font. This book was converted to FrameMaker 5.5.6 with a format conversion tool created by Erik Ray, Jason McIntosh, Neil Walls, and Mike Sierra that uses Perl and XML technologies. The text font is Linotype Birka; the heading font is Adobe Myriad Condensed; and the code font is LucasFont's TheSans Mono Condensed. The illustrations that appear in the book were produced by Robert Romano and Jessamyn Read using Macromedia FreeHand 9 and Adobe Photoshop 6. The tip and warning icons were drawn by Christopher Bing. This colophon was written by Linley Dolby.

O'REILLY & ASSOCIATES, INC. LICENSE AGREEMENT
.NET Windows Forms in a Nutshell
for Visual Studio .NET

This is a legal agreement between you and O'Reilly & Associates, Inc. ("O'Reilly"). Carefully read all the terms and conditions of this agreement prior to opening the CD envelope. Opening the CD envelope indicates your acceptance of these terms and conditions. If you do not agree to these terms and conditions, return the package and all components of this product to the point of purchase for a refund. If purchased from O'Reilly, upon return of the product within 30 days of purchase, a refund will be given. If purchased from another source, follow their return policy.

LICENSE: This License Agreement permits you to use one copy of the .NET Windows Forms in a Nutshell for Visual Studio .NET CD-ROM ("CD-ROM") you have purchased on any single workstation, provided the CD-ROM is in use on only one workstation at any time. If you have multiple licenses for the CD-ROM, then at any time you may have as many copies of the CD-ROM in use as you have licenses. You may not mount the CD-ROM nor download the contents onto a network or server.

COPYRIGHT: The contents of the CD-ROM are owned by O'Reilly. The CD-ROM is protected by United States and international copyright and other laws. You may not remove, obscure, or alter any notice of patent, copyright, trademark, trade secret, or other proprietary rights. You may not copy the written materials accompanying the CD-ROM, except by prior written permission from the owner of such material, as described above. This license and your right to use the product terminate automatically if you violate any part of this Agreement. In the event of termination, you must immediately destroy all copies of the product or return them to O'Reilly.

LIMITED WARRANTY: O'Reilly warrants the CD-ROM to be free from defects in materials and workmanship for 90 days after delivery. Defective media may be returned for replacement without charge during the 90-day warranty period unless the media has been damaged by acts or actions of the Licensee or while under its control.

O'REILLY MAKES NO OTHER WARRANTIES EXPRESSED OR IMPLIED WITH RESPECT TO THE SOFTWARE (INCLUDING ASSOCIATED WRITTEN MATERIALS), ITS MERCHANTABILITY, OR FITNESS FOR ANY PARTICULAR PURPOSE. IN NO EVENT WILL O'REILLY BE LIABLE FOR INDIRECT OR CONSEQUENTIAL DAMAGES, INCLUDING, WITHOUT LIMITATIONS, LOSS OF INCOME, USE, OR INFORMATION, NOR SHALL THE LIABILITY OF O'REILLY EXCEED THE AMOUNT PAID FOR THE CD-ROM. THIS LIMITED WARRANTY GIVES YOU SPECIFIC LEGAL RIGHTS. YOU MAY HAVE OTHERS, WHICH VARY FROM STATE TO STATE.

Without limitation, O'Reilly does not warrant that the CD-ROM is completely error free, will operate without interruption, or is compatible with any equipment or software configurations. The Licensee expressly assumes all risk for use of the CD-ROM. Repair, replacement, or refund (at the option of O'Reilly) is the exclusive remedy, if there is a defect.

GENERAL: You may not sublicense, assign, or transfer the license or contents, except as expressly provided in this Agreement. This Agreement constitutes the entire agreement between you and O'Reilly and supersedes any prior written or oral agreement concerning the contents of this package. This Agreement is governed by the laws of the State of California as if the parties hereto were both California residents; and you consent to exclusive jurisdiction in the state and federal courts in San Francisco in the event of any dispute.